D1798836

The Modern Law of Trade Marks

The Modern Law of Trade Marks

Christopher Morcom, MA (Cantab)
One of Her Majesty's Counsel
Barrister of the Middle Temple

Ashley Roughton, BSc (Lond) PhD (Cantab)
Barrister of the Inner Temple

James Graham, BEng (Bristol) MSc (Bristol)
Barrister of the Inner Temple

Butterworths
London, Dublin, Edinburgh
1999

United Kingdom	Butterworths, a Division of Reed Elsevier (UK) Ltd, Halsbury House, 35 Chancery Lane, LONDON WC2A 1EL and 4 Hill Street, EDINBURGH EH2 3JZ
Australia	Butterworths, a Division of Reed International Books Australia Pty Ltd, CHATSWOOD, New South Wales
Canada	Butterworths Canada Ltd, MARKHAM, Ontario
Hong Kong	Butterworths Asia (Hong Kong), HONG KONG
India	Butterworths India, NEW DELHI
Ireland	Butterworth (Ireland) Ltd, DUBLIN
Malaysia	Malayan Law Journal Sdn Bhd, KUALA LUMPUR
New Zealand	Butterworths of New Zealand Ltd, WELLINGTON
Singapore	Butterworths Asia, SINGAPORE
South Africa	Butterworths Publishers (Pty) Ltd, DURBAN
USA	Lexis Law Publishing, CHARLOTTESVILLE, Virginia

© Reed Elsevier (UK) Ltd 2000

All rights reserved. No part of this publication may be reproduced in any material form (including photocopying or storing it in any medium by electronic means and whether or not transiently or incidentally to some other use of this publication) without the written permission of the copyright owner except in accordance with the provisions of the Copyright, Designs and Patents Act 1988 or under the terms of a licence issued by the Copyright Licensing Agency Ltd, 90 Tottenham Court Road, London, England W1P 0LP. Applications for the copyright owner's written permission to reproduce any part of this publication should be addressed to the publisher.

Warning: The doing of an unauthorised act in relation to a copyright work may result in both a civil claim for damages and criminal prosecution.

Any Crown copyright material is reproduced with the permission of the Controller of Her Majesty's Stationery Office.

A CIP Catalogue record for this book is available from the British Library.

ISBN 0 406 065519

ISBN 0-406-06551-9

9 780406 065513

Printed and bound in Great Britain by Butler & Tanner Ltd, Frome and London.

Visit us at our website: http://www.butterworths.co.uk

Preface

More than five years have now passed since the Trade Marks Act 1994 received the Royal Assent. The Act, together with many of its implementing rules, came into force on 31 October 1994. An immediate purpose of the Act was to implement the Trade Marks Directive, which aims to harmonise, in part at least, the trade mark laws of the Member States of the European Union. That is still some way from being achieved. During the past five years there have been many decisions of the UK Registry and the courts, a number of them of considerable significance. The number of cases being dealt with under the old law, both by the Registry and the courts, is declining fairly rapidly. Some of the decisions under the new law have adopted approaches which were unexpected, particularly across the English Channel. At the same time the courts of other Member States have handed down their own decisions under their new 'harmonised' laws, and have referred some cases to the European Court of Justice for interpretation of provisions of the Directive. The number of decisions on such references is still quite small, but they provide an important source of guidance for the national courts. The first references to the Court of Justice by English courts, on the interpretation of provisions of the Directive, have only recently been made.

Internationally, there have been several developments of considerable significance in the field of trade marks, some of which were contemplated, and the subject of provisions, in the Act. In particular, the Act paved the way for UK participation in two important developments, namely the international registration of trade marks under the Madrid Protocol of June 1989, and the registration of Community Trade Marks under the Community Trade Mark Regulation adopted on 21 December 1993. The UK ratified the Madrid Protocol on 1 April 1996, and the Community Trade Mark system, administered by OHIM (the Office for the Harmonisation of the Internal Market) came into operation on the same day, as did the secondary legislation under the 1994 Act, which was required for UK participation. These measures provide industry with the means of securing protection of their trade marks internationally, by national registrations in an increasing number of countries obtained through a single filing, and of protecting their marks in the whole of the EU by a single registration having effect in all Member States. Decisions of OHIM and the Boards of Appeal there are being handed down regularly, and the first decision of the Court of First Instance of the European Court of Justice, on appeal from a Board of Appeal, was published in the summer of this year. A further international initiative, more generalised but including some potentially important trade (ma)pro- *mark* visions, is the 'TRIPS' Agreement (Agreement on the Trade-Related Aspects of Intellectual Property Rights), which was annexed to the Marrakech Agreement establishing the World Trade Organisation, concluded on 15 April 1994. The TRIPS Agreement continues the work of international harmonisation of intellectual property laws, begun over a century ago by the Paris Convention, and indeed reaffirms some of the obligations imposed on parties to that Convention.

In attempting to write about the new UK law, the operation of the Madrid Protocol and the Community Trade Mark, the Paris Convention and the TRIPS Agreement, as well as other developments affecting trade mark law and its application in the UK, we are only too conscious of the speed at which the law of trade marks is developing. The Trade Marks Registry and the courts here issuing decisions under the 1994 Act on a regular basis, with guidance from the Court of Justice. In addition, because of the similarity between many provisions of the Directive and corresponding provisions of the CTM Regulation, decisions of OHIM examiners and its Boards of Appeal, and of the Court of Justice on appeal from the latter, may affect the way in which the 1994 Act is interpreted and applied. Also, changes in the law may yet be required for the implementation of the TRIPS Agreement, and even now the World Intellectual Property Organisation ('WIPO') is formulating proposals on a number of topics, including those of well-known trade marks and the Internet. Procedure in the Trade Marks Registry is also still developing. Now that the reforms of Civil Court Procedure are in place, the Registry has been considering how some of those reforms may be reflected in Registry procedure, and new Rules may soon be enacted and come into effect.

My work in writing has been greatly assisted by my colleagues Ashley Roughton and James Graham, who have both made their own substantial contributions to this book. But such is the pace of development, that even as the book is published we shall probably soon be thinking about writing a supplement. In the meantime, I hope that users of this book will find it of some assistance in finding their way through the complexities of, and obtaining the best advantage from, the 1994 Act and, where they need to protect their trade marks in other markets, the Madrid Protocol and the CTM Regulation.

I would like to record our thanks to officials at the Trade Marks Registry for information and assistance on a number of points. Finally, I wish to express my gratitude, and that of my co-authors, to Butterworths for the enormous support and encouragement given by successive members of their staff over a number of years. Without this, and the many aspects of the preparation and presentation of a work of this kind, which can only be undertaken by publishers of the quality of Butterworths, this book could never have been completed.

Every effort has been made to ensure the law is correct as it stands at the date of this Preface.

CM
31 October 1999

Foreword

During my time in practice, the Trade Marks Act 1938 applied. It consolidated the 1905 and 1919 Acts and also the amendments introduced in the Act of 1937. Interpretation and application were approached along traditional lines leading to a comforting feeling for practitioners. Upon joining the EEC, I and other practitioners immersed ourselves in Articles 30, 36 and 85 of the Treaty of Rome, but retained a feeling of security in the knowledge that we were familiar with the general law on trade marks. The position was soon to change. In 1986 service marks became registrable. There followed harmonisation of the trade mark laws of the Member States of the European Union. That resulted in the Trade Marks Act 1994. Knowledge gained over past years appeared to have been destroyed.

As Christopher Morcom, Ashley Roughton and James Graham point out in their book, the 1994 Act adopts the language of the Directive. That prevents conflict, but does not make the Act any easier to interpret, particularly as it is the result of negotiation and compromise. Their book is of particular interest to me as Christopher Morcom has been close to the process that led up to the 1994 Act. He was a member of the Government's Standing Advisory Committee and played an active part in the deliberations relating to Community Trade Mark legislation. His views are therefore particularly interesting and authoritative on the many different issues that arise.

This book is an up-to-date guide to the law and I congratulate the authors on their industry and learning. I urge them to make sure that that remains the position in this fast-moving lane of the law.

LORD JUSTICE ALDOUS
NOVEMBER 1999

Foreword

Contents

Preface   v
Foreword   vii
Table of statutes   xvii
Table of statutory instruments xxix
Table of European legislation xxxvii
Table of International conventions and treaties xlvii
Table of cases li
Acknowledgments lxxv

PART I GENERAL INTRODUCTION
Chapter 1   Subject-matter and history of the law   3
Subject-matter and arrangement of this book   3
Historical development of the law   5
Pre-registration law   5
Legislation   5
The role of trade marks today   7
The Directive and the TMA 1994   8
General comment on the new law   11

PART II REGISTERED MARKS
Chapter 2   The Comptroller-General and the registry   15
The Comptroller-General   15
The registry   16
The register   16
Classification of goods and services   19
The Trade Marks Journal   19
Rules   19
Transaction of business at the registry   21
Costs and the registrar   34
Registrar's costs and liability for costs   34

Chapter 3   Representation at the registry   35
Agents   35
Register of trade mark attorneys   35
Qualification for entry on register of trade mark agents   37
Address for service   37
Professional privilege   40

Contents

Chapter 4   Definition of a trade mark   43
Trade mark   43
'Any sign' – qualification for registration as a trade mark   43
'Capable of being represented graphically'   43
The function of a trade mark   48
'Capable of distinguishing the goods or services of one undertaking from those of other undertakings'   49
The nature of the proprietor's trade or business activity   49

Chapter 5   Registrability   51
Absolute grounds for refusal of registration   51
The basic grounds   57
Colours, sounds and smells   62
The proviso   73
Some decisions under the TMA 1994   81
Overcoming objections under s 3(1)   86
Prior rights   93
Restricting the specification   95
Objections relating to shapes of goods and their packaging   95
Marks contrary to public policy or morality, and deceptive marks   99

Chapter 6   Conflict with earlier rights   51
Meaning of 'relative grounds'   109
Refusal based on an 'earlier trade mark'   110
The grounds   111
Identical marks and identical goods or services   112
The meaning of 'likelihood of confusion'   124
Reputation   135
The requirements of unfair advantage or detriment   136
Refusal on the ground of conflict with a 'well-known' trade mark   139
Refusal based upon other earlier rights   140
Honest concurrent use   143

Chapter 7   Loss of rights and rectification   145
Introduction   145
Revocation   145
Declarations of invalidity   154
Rectification under s 60   157
Rectification or correction of the register   158

Chapter 8   The application for registration   161
The application   161
Registration procedure   164
Ex parte hearings   165
Appeal against refusal   165
Procedure following acceptance   166
Division, merger and registration of a series of marks   167
Applications pending at commencement   168

Chapter 9   Procedures after acceptance and after registration   171
Opposition to registration   171

The grounds   171
Procedure   171
Duration, renewal and alteration   174
Duration   174
Renewal   175
Alteration   176
Surrender   177
Proceedings for revocation, invalidation and rectification or correction of the
    register   178
Proceedings before the registrar   178
Intervention   179
Reference to the court   180
Proceedings before the court   180

Chapter 10 Special categories of trade marks   183
Certification marks   183
The origin of certification trade marks in the UK   183
Differences from ordinary trade marks under the TMA 1994   184
The regulations   184
Existing certification marks and pending applications under the TMA 1938   186
Infringement   186
Revocation and invalidity   186
Collective marks   187
The new provisions for registered collective marks   187
The regulations   188
Infringement   189
Revocation and invalidity   190

Chapter 11 Registered trade marks as property   191
The new provisions   191
Co-ownership   192
Assignment   192
Trusts and equities   194
Licensing of registered trade marks   195
Registration of transactions affecting registered trade marks   199
Other provisions which may be made by rules   202

Chapter 12 Infringement and protection of well-known marks   203
The arrangement of the provisions   203
Rights conferred by a registered trade mark   204
What constitutes infringement?   204
Infringement under s 10(1)-(3)   207
Infringement in relation to labelling or packaging materials   209
What is not infringement   209
Exhaustion of rights   217
Disclaimers   223
Transitional provisions affecting infringement   223
Protection of well known trade marks – s 56   225
Acquiescence   227

Chapter 13 Threats   229
The rationale and objectives   229

Actionable threats 230
Aggrieved person 233
When is a threat not a threat? 234
Defences 235
Remedies 235
Adverse assertions of right 236

PART III PASSING OFF 239
Chapter 14 Passing off 241
Development of the tort of passing off – individual causes of action 241
Ingredients of the tort 242
The 'logical fallacy of the undistributed middle' 244
Passing off – a question of fact 245
Goodwill 246
Misrepresentation 249
Confusion 249
Misrepresentation – the relevant connection 254
Common field of activity 255
Momentary and inconsequential deception 257
Taking advantage of a market developed by another 258
Damage 259
Erosion of goodwill 260
Reverse passing off 260
International exhaustion of rights 262
Instruments of deception 264
Passing off – the class type action – the necessary characteristics 266
Comparison with passing off where traders sue one another (the usual form) 267
Defined class of goods 268
Who may sue? 270
Representative proceedings 270

Chapter 15 Malicious falsehood, trade libel, defamation and emergency 271
Legislation 271
Introduction 271
Malicious falsehood and trade libel v defamation 271

PART IV CIVIL PROCEEDINGS 286
Chapter 16 Procedure 285
Domestic procedure 285
Introduction 285
Prosecution 285
The High Court 297
Appeals to the Court of Appeal and beyond 304
The European Court of Justice 304

Chapter 17 European procedure 313
Introduction 313
OHIM 313
General procedural matters 317
Infringement and related counterclaims 321
Final appeals 323

PART V CUSTOMS AND CRIMINAL OFFENCES   325

Chapter 18   Border controls– the domestic procedure and domestic proceedings   327

The rationale and objectives   327
The means   329
Procedure   330
The High Court   336
The county court   337
The High Court and county courts financial limits   337
The High Court and county courts territorial jurisdiction   339
Condemnation   340
Mode of beginning condemnation proceedings in the High Court and county courts
340

Procedure following issue of originating process   340
The High Court, county courts and costs   341
Procedure in the magistrates' courts – general   342
Civil procedure the magistrates' court   344
Magistrates' courts and costs   349
Procedure – two regimes, the domestic and European comparisons and contrasts
350

Another common feature   352
The domestic regime   352
The notice   354
The prohibition and seizure or detention as liable for forfeiture   356
Defences   363
Further proceedings   365
The court process itself   365

Chapter 19 Border controls – the European procedure   367

The rationale and objectives   367
The means   368
The Community Customs Code   369
First indent of the Basic Regulation, art 1(1)(a) of   372
Second Indent of the Basic regulation, art 1(1)(a) of   373
Goods under customs supervision   374
Goods placed under a suspensive procedure   374
Re-exportation subject to notification or placed in a free zone or free warehouse
375

The Basic Regulation, art 1(1)(a) taken as a whole   376
Are the goods counterfeit?   376
Procedure   378
The retrospective procedure   382
The prospective procedure   385
The AA and the article 3 notice   386
The effects of an article 3 notice   387
The Goods Infringing Intellectual Property Rights (Customs) Regulations 1999
391

The Basic Regulation, arts 6 and 7   396
The Basic Regulation, arts 8–18   404
The Basic Regulation, arts 6 and 7, the (CP)R 1999 and TRIPS   409
The European interpretation route   414

Chapter 20 Criminal Aspects of the law of Trade Marks   413
Introduction   413
Legislative history   421
Criminal aspects of the law of trade marks   425
The TMA 1994   425
Inchoate and auxiliary offences   438
Other Inchoate offences   445
Procedure   462

PART VI INTERNATIONAL TREATIES   479
Chapter 21 International registration under the Madrid Protocol   481
History of the Madrid Protocol   481
Main provisions of the Madrid Agreement   481
The Protocol   483
Provisions under the Act for giving effect to the Protocol   485
International Registrations designating the UK   486
Examination   487
Publication, opposition proceedings and observations   487
Protection   488
Effects of Protected International Trade Mark (UK)   489
Disclaimers and territorial limitations   490
Groundless threats of infringement proceedings   490
International trade mark (UK) as an object of property   490
Revocation and invalidity   492
Effect of acquiescence   492
Importation of infringing goods, materials or articles   493
Offences and forfeiture   493
Falsely representing trade mark as a protected international trade mark (UK)   493
Concurrent registrations   494
Miscellaneous and general provisions   497

Chapter 22 The Paris Convention and the TRIPS Agreement   499
International co-operation in the protection of intellectual property rights   499
The Paris Convention   499
The provisions of the Paris Convention   500
The TRIPS Agreement   508
Conclusions   513

PART V THE COMMUNITY TRADE MARK   515
Chapter 23 The Community Trade Mark Regulation and its implementation in the UK   517
Introduction   517
The scheme of the CTM system and the administration of OHIM   518
Application of the Trade Mark Rules 1994   524

Chapter 24 The CTM Regulation: the law relating to trade marks   527
Definition of a CTM and obtaining a CTM   527
Definition of a CTM   527
Conversion to national procedures under art 108   533

Effects of CTMs   534
Complementary application of national law relating to infringement   537
Restrictions on use of CTMs   537
Use of CTMs   538
Community trade marks as objects of property   540
Transfer of a CTM   541

Chapter 25 Applications for Community trade marks   545
Filing of applications   545
Conditions with which applications must comply   545
Priority   547
Claiming the seniority of a national trade mark   551

Chapter 26 – Registration procedure   553
Registration procedure   553
Examination of applications   553
Search   556
Publication of the application   557
Withdrawal, restriction and amendment of the application   557
Observations by third parties and opposition   558
Opposition   559
Conversion to national procedure   567
Registration   567

**Chapter 27 Maintenance of the Community trade mark and cessation or loss
    of rights   569**
Duration, renewal and alteration of CTMs   569
Surrender, revocation and invalidity   572
Revocation and invalidity   572
Consequences of revocation and invalidity   578
Proceedings in the Office in relation to revocation or invalidity   580

Chapter 28 Procedure before the Office   587
Introduction   587

Chapter 29 Appeals   601
Appeals from decisions in the office   601

Chapter 30 Community collective Marks   607
Community collective marks   607
Definition of a Community collective mark   607

Chapter 31 Proceedings for infringement   611
General   611
The Convention on jurisdiction and enforcement   611

APPENDICES

Table of contents   621

Appendix 1 United Kingdom statutes   625

Appendix 2 Secondary legislation   803

Appendix 3 Rules of Court   879

Appendix 4 International conventions   895
(Reproduced with kind permission of the World Trade Organisation)

Appendix 5 European materials   937

Appendix 6 International registration   1115

Appendix 7 Miscellaneous registry material   1189

INDEX   1267

Table of statutes

*References on the right-hand side are to paragraph numbers. Those paragraph numbers in **bold** indicate where the statute is set out in full or in part.*

Accessories and Abettors Act 1861 . . . 20.47
  s 8 . . . . 20.47, 20.50, 20.51
Administration of Justice (Miscellaneous
  Provisions) Act 1933
  s 7 . . . . 2.43
Anglo-Portuguese Commercial Treaty
  Act 1914 . . . . 5.107
Anglo-Portuguese Commercial Treaty
  Act 1916 . . . . 5.107
Anzac (Restriction on Trade Use of Word)
  Act 1916 . . . . 5.107
Broadcasting Act 1990
  s 166 . . . . 15.3
Civil Evidence Act 1968
  s 15 . . . . 3.12
Civil Evidence Act 1995 . . . . 16.30
Civil Procedure Act 1997
  s 1(1)(a)–(c) 18.51
Companies Act 1985
  s 36B 11.4, 11.9
Companies Act 1989
  s 130(2) 11.9
Copyright, Designs and Patents
  Act 1988 . . . . 20.6; 22.38
  s 84 . . . . 14.25
  275 . . . . 3.6
  276–278 . . . . 3.11
  279 . . . . 3.4
  280 . . . . 3.13, 3.15
  282 . . . . 3.2, 3.3
  283 . . . . 3.3
  283(4) 3.4
  284 . . . . 3.3, 3.13

Copyright, Designs and Patents Act
1988–*contd*
  s 300 . . . . 20.9, 20.10
  303(2) 3.13
  Sch 8 . . . . 3.13
County Courts Act 1984
  s 15 . . . . 16.55
  40–42 . . . . 18.35
Courts and Legal Services Act 1990
  s 1 . . . . 18.30
  1(1)(b) 18.30
Crime and Disorder Act 1998
  s 51 . . . . 20.121
Criminal Attempts Act 1981 . . . 20.69, 20.73
  s 1(1) **20.69**, 20.73, 20.74
  1(1)(2)–(4) **20.69**
  1(3) 20.73
Criminal Justice Act 1967
  s 8 . . . . 20.151
  9 . . . . 20.150, 20.152
Criminal Justice Act 1982 . . . . 20.107
  s 37 . . . . 20.107
Criminal Justice Act 1987 . . . . 20.127
  s 6 . . . . 20.127
Criminal Justice Act 1988
  s 23 . . . . 20.150, 20.152
  23(1)(c)(i), (ii) 20.152
  23(2)(a) 20.152
  23(b)(i), (ii) 20.152
  23(c) 20.152
  23(3)(a), (b) 20.152
  24 . . . . 20.150, 20.152, 20.153, 20.159
  24(1)(c)(i), (ii) 20.153

Criminal Justice Act 1988–*contd*
s 25 . . . . 20.152, 20.153
  25(1), (2) 20.152
Criminal Justice Act 1991
s 1, 2, 6 . . . . 20.109
  17(1). 20.107
  18 . . . . 20.109
  25 . . . . 20.120
Criminal Law Act 1967 . . . . 20.48
s 1 . . . . 20.47
  4, 5 . . . . 20.65
Criminal Law Act 1977 . . . . 20.47
s 1 . . . . 20.68, **20.81**
  1(1)–(4) **20.81**
Criminal Procedure and Investigations
  Act 1996. . . . . . . 20.161, 20.171, 20.180
s 3 . . . . 20.171, 20.172
  3(1)(a), (b) 20.172
  3(6). 20.172
  3(8). 20.172
  3(8)(a)–(e) 20.172
  5(6), (7), (9) 20.174
  7 . . . . 20.171
  7(2)(a), (b) 20.176
  8 . . . . 20.177
  8(1). 20.177
  8(2)(a), (b) 20.177
  9 . . . . 20.177
  10(2), (3) 20.179
  11(3)–(5) 20.179
  12 . . . . 20.172
  13 . . . . 20.172
  13(1). 20.172
  23(1). 20.172
Crown Proceedings Act 1947 . . . . 18.96
s 21 . . . . 18.96, 18.98, 18.100,
                        18.101, 18.102
  21(1) **18.103**, 18.104
  21(1)(a) 18.100
  21(2). 18.104
  38(1). 18.98
Customs and Excise Management
  Act 1979 . . . . 18.6; 19.3
s 1(1). 18.23
  8(1)(b) 18.6
  40 . . . . 18.91
  40(1). 18.7
  40(1)(b) 18.7
  49 . . . . 18.160; 19.143
  49(1)(b). **18.47**, 18.102, 18.127,
                  18.160;19.103, 19.128, 19.143
  50 . . . . 18.157; **19.139**, 19.140
  50(7) 18.157, 19.140

Customs and Excise Management Act
1979–*contd*
s 77 . . . . 18.31
  139 . . . . 18.127, 18.160; 19.95, 19.103,
             19.128, 19.129, 19.143
  139(1). 18.7. 18.174; 19.157
  139(2)(a), (b) 18.7
  139(3), (4) 18.7
  139(5) 18.10, 18.32
  139(6). 18.11
  141(1). 18.8
  142(1). 18.8
  144 . . . . 18.153, 18.120, 18.121;
                     19.103, 19.134
  145 . . . . 18.11; 19.103
  145(1), (2), (6) 18.11
  146 . . . . 18.12; 19.103
  146(1). 18.12
  146(a)–(c). 18.12
  146(2). 18.12
  152 . . . . 18.14, 18.15; 19.103
  153 . . . . 18.20; 19.103
  153(1). 18.19
  153(2). 18.19
  153(2)(a)–(c) 18.19
  153(3). 18.20
  153(4). 18.21
  154 . . . . 18.22; 19.103
  154(1)(a)–(f) 18.22
  154(2). 18.24
  153(2)(b), (c), (f) 18.24
  155 . . . . 19.103
  155(1). 18.26
  155(1)(d) 18.22
  155(2). 18.26
  159(1) 18.20, 18.22; 19.20, 19.22
Sch 3. . . . . 18.11; 19.95, 19.103
para 1(1), (2). 18.11
  2 . . . . 18.11
  3 . . . . 18.12
  4(1), (2) 18.12
  7 . . . . 18.13
  8 . . . . **18.14**
  8(a) 18.30; 19.82
  9. . . . . **18.14**, 18.45
  10(1). 18.16
  10(3). 18.17
  12 . . . . 18.110
  13 . . . . 18.18
Defamation Act 1952. . . . . 15.14
s 2 . . . . 15.3
  3 . . . . 15.3
  3(1) 15.3, 15.15

Defamation Act 1952–*contd*
s 3(1)(a), (b) 18.153; 19.134
4 . . . . 15.6
Documentary Evidence Act 1868 . . . . 18.20
s 1(1), (2) 18.19
2 . . . . 18.20
Emergency Laws (Miscellaneous)
Act 1953 . . . . 15.20
Emergency Powers (Defence)
Act 1939 . . . . 15.20
Emergency Powers (Defence)
Act 1940 . . . . 15.20
s 1 . . . . 15.20
Emergency Powers (Defence)
Act 1945 . . . . 15.20
Evidence Act 1851
s 14 . . . . 20.155
Explosives Substances Act 1883 . . . . . 20.60
European Communities
Act 1972 . . . . 18.93, 18.178; 19.94,
19.161; 22.38
s 1(2) 18.92; 19.93; 22.39
1(2)(o) 18.92; 19.93
2(1) 18.92, 18.160; 19.93, 19.143
2(2) 1.1; 18.3, 18.75, **18.91**;
19.3, **19.92**; 22.39
2(4) 18.75
3 . . . . **16.59**
European Communities (Amendment)
Act 1998 . . . . 19.93
Forgery and Counterfeiting Act 1981
s 20 . . . . 18.156
Geneva Conventions Act 1957 . . . . . . 5.107
Hallmarking Act 1973 . . . . 5.107
Human Rights Act 1998 . . . . 15.5
Insolvency Act 1986
s 126 . . . . 3.10
Interpretation Act 1978
s 5 . . . . 12.25; 18.12
6(c) 18.108
17(2)(b) 8.6
22(1) 8.6
23 . . . . 18.108
Sch 1 . . . . 12.25; 18.12
Sch 2 . . . . 8.6
Legal Aid Act 1988 . . . . 15.4
Limitation Act 1980
s 2, 4A 15.3
Local Government Act 1972
s 112(1) 20.136
Local Government (Wales) Act 1994
s 66(6) 20.129
Sch 16, para 75 . . . . 20.129

Magistrates' Courts Act 1980 . . . . 20.21
Pt II 18.51
Pt IV 18.55
s 5–5F 20.121
6 . . . . 20.121
19(3)(b) 20.120
38 . . . . 20.107, 20.120
51–54 . . . . 18.51
55 . . . . 18.51
55(1) 18.55
56, 57 . . . . 18.51
64 . . . . 18.51, 18.69, **18.69**
64(1)(a) 18.72
65–74 . . . . 18.51
97(3) 18.55
101 . . . . **20.21**, 20 104
123 . . . . **18.56**, 18.57, 18.68
123(2) 18.57
Medicines Act 1968 . . . . 20.112
Merchandise Marks Act 1862 . . . . 1.8
Offences against the Person Act 1861
s 18, 20 . . . . 20.67
Olympic Symbol etc (Protection)
Act 1995 . . . . 1.1; 5.108, 5.116
s 3(1) 5.116
4(5) 5.117
4(5)(a) 5.117
18(1), (2) 5.116
Patents Act 1977 . . . . 3.11, 13.10
s 70(1) 13.13
104, 105 . . . . 3.12, 3.13
121 . . . . 2.1
Patents, Designs and Marks
Act 1986 . . . . 1.1, 1.5; 4.1
Patents, Designs and Trade Marks
Act 1883 . . . . 1.9
Patents, Designs, Copyright and Trade
Marks (Emergency) Act 1939 . . . . 15 20
s 3 . . . . 15 20
6 . . . . 15.21
Police and Criminal Evidence
Act 1984 . . . . 20.132
s 18 . . . . 20.132
Prosecution of Offences Act 1985
s 6(2) 20.116
7(4) 20.116
Registered Designs Act 1949
s 1 . . . . 5.98
Road Traffic Act 1972
s 56(1) 20.50
Sale of Goods Act 1979
s 13 . . . . 20.90
55 . . . . 20.90

Solicitors Act 1974 . . . . 3.11
Supreme Court Act 1981 . . . . 16.36
  s 31 . . . . 18.102
    60(3) 16.19
    61(1) 18.81; 19.82
    69(1) 15.17
  Sch 1
    para 1(i) 18.81; 19.82
Supreme Court of Judicature Act 1873 . . 1.7
Supreme Court of Judicature
  (Consolidation) Act 1925
  s 31 . . . . 16.59
Theft Act 1968
  s 32(1)(a) 20.86
Trade Descriptions Act 1968 . . 5.107; 16.12;
        20.7, 20.12, 20.100; 22.29,
        22.33, 22.49; 23.19; 24.37
  s 1(1) 20.34, 20.35
    1(1)(a) 20.35
    4 . . . . 20.35
    27 . . . . 20.129, 20.130
    28 . . . . 20.129, 20.130, 20.135, 20.137
    28(1) . . **20.131**, 20.133, 20.142, 20.148
    28(1)(a) 20.133, 20.138,
        20.144, 20.145
    28(1)(b) 20.133, 20.139,
        20.144, 20.145
    28(1)(c) 20.133, 20.140,
        20.141, 20.144–145
    28(1)(d) 20.133, 20.141,
        20.144, 20.145
    28(1)(e) 20.133, 20.142,
        20.144, 20.145
    28(2) **20.143**
    28(3) 20.145
    28(3)(a) 20.145
    28(3)(a)(i), (ii) 20.145
    28(3)(a)(b)(i), (ii) 20.146
    28(4) 20.147
    28(5) 20.148
    28(7) 20.141
    29 . . . . 20.129, 20.130
    33 . . . . 20.129, 20.130
Trade Marks Act 1905 . . . . 1.9; 5.29
  s 3 . . . . 4.11
    44 . . . . 5.9
    62 . . . . 10.1
Trade Marks Act 1919 . . . . 1.9
Trade Marks Act 1938 . . 1.1, 1.10–11, 1.14,
    1.23; 2.1, 2.13, 2.20, 2.36; 4.1, 4.3, 4.13;
    5.29, 5.68; 6.10, 6.16, 6.22; 7.2, 7.31;
    8.1, 8.10, 8.21; 9.3, 9.18, 9.21; 16.1,
    16.36; 20.2; 22.24; 24.42; 26.15

Trade Marks Act 1938–*contd*
  s 3 . . . . 4.13; 5.58; 6.81
    4 . . . . 12.51
    4(1) 6.34, 6.37; 12.3, 12.5,
        12.17, 12.51
    4(1)(a), (b) 12.16
    4(3)(a) 12.17
    4(3)(b) 12.29
    4(4) 12.22
    5 . . . . 12.51
    5(2) 12.52
    5(4) 12.51
    7 . . . . 1.23; 6.80; 12.32, 12.51
    8 . . . . 12.24, 12.51
    8(a) 5.120; 12.25
    8(b) 12.27
    9 . . . . 4.1, 4.11, 4.12, 5.50
    9(1) 5.5
    9(1)(c) 5.57
    9(1)(d) 5.53
    9(3)(b) 5.89
    10 . 4.1, 4.11, 4.12; 5.7, 5.45, 5.50, 5.57
    10(2)(b) 5.89
    10(6) 4.14
    11 . . . . 4.13, 5.102, 5.103, 5.104, 5.106,
       5.107; 6.53, 6.76, 6.79; 7.21, 7.22
    12 . . . . 6.16, 6.53
    12(2) 1.23; 6.16, 6.80, 6.81
    12(3) 6.5, 6.6, 6.81
    12(4) 6.81
    15 . . . . 7.18
    16 . . . . 6.10; 11.12; 12.22
    21(1) 8.16
    22 . . . . 11.4; 22.13
    22(2) 11.1
    23 . . . . 8.21
    25 . . . . 8.17; 11.5
    25(3) 11.5
    26 . . . . 2.38; 7.2, 7.3; 7.5, 7.12,
        7.17; 24.43
    26(1)(a) 7.5
    26(2) 7.13
    26(3) 7.10
    27 . . . . 7.17; 8.17
    28 . . . . 11.7, 11.11, 11.17
    28(1), (2) 11.9
    28(3) 11.9, 11.14
    28(4) 11.9
    28(5) 11.14
    28(6) 11.7, 11.14
    28(8)–(10) 11.11
    28(12) 11.9
    30 . . . . 11.11, 11.13, 11.14

Trade Marks Act 1938–*contd*

30(1). 7.7, 7.8, 7.9; 11.13; 12.22
30(2). 7.8; 11.13, 11.14
30(3)–(6) 11.13, 11.14
31. . . . . 11.12, 11.13
31(1) 11.12, 11.14
31(2), (5)–(8) 11.12
32 . . . . 2.38; 7.2, 7.3, 7.29
34 . . . . 7.2, 7.29
34(1)(e) 7.7
35. . . . . 9.12
37. . . . . 10.1
37(1). 10.3
38 . . . . 11.12; 16.5
39A 8.8
46(2). 7.7
48. . . . . 2.43
48(1), (2) 2.43
54. . . . . 7.2
54(a), (b) 2.38
55 . . . . 2.30, 2.32
58A 20.6, **20.9**
58A(1)–(6). **20.9**
63 . . . . 11.2
64 . . . . 11.6
64A 18.2
68(1) 4.3, 4.11; 7.31; 11.1
68(2). 7.6
68(2A). 6.21, 6.23
100 . . . . 7.6
103(1). 7.8; 11.12, 11.14
103(2). 7.6, 7.7, 7.8
Sch 1. . . . . 10.1
Sch 4. . . . . 2.5
Trade Marks Act 1994 . . . . . 1.1, 1.10, 1.14,
1.18, 1.19, 1.23; 2.24; 4.12; 6.1, 6.10,
6.16, 6.22; 15.21; 16.1, 16.63; 18.40,
18.23; 20.2, 20.3; 24.38; 25.3; 27.10
s 1. . . . . . . 4.1, 4.14; 5.6, 5.7, 5.19; 10.2,
10.4, 10.12; 24.2
1(1) 4.1, 4.8, 4.9; 5.7, 5.15,
5.17, 5.23, 5.30, 5.41, 5.45, 5.74,
5.75, 5.78, 5.83; 10.3, 12.11; 24.2
1(2). 4.2
2 . . . . 13.7
2(1) 11.1; **14.56**
2(2). 12.39, 12.58; 24.36
3 . . . 1.23; 4.1; 5.1, 5.5, 5.8, 5.24, 5.41;
7.1, 7.25, 7.30; 16.4
3(1) . . . 5.5, 5.10, 5.13, 5.30, 5.68,5.70,
5.72, 5.73, 5.74, 5.77, 5.85,
5.96, 5.100, 5.104; 6.17;
7.25; 24.11, **24.12**

Trade Marks Act 1994–*contd*

s 3(1)(a) 5.7, 5.15, 5.17, 5.18,
5.19, 5.21, 5.22, 5.23, 5.25, 5.27,
5.28, 5.30, 5.33, 5.35, 5.45, 5.49,
5.51, 5.70, 5.72,5.74, 5.80, 5.100;
7.25; 20.2; 24.12
3(1)(b). 5.5, 5.6, 5.7, 5.15, 5.17,
5.18, 5.19, 5.21, 5.23, 5.24, 5.25,
5.27, 5.28, 5.30, 5.32, 5.33, 5.34,
5.35, 5.38, 5.39, 5.40, 5.41, 5.45,
5.47, 5.48, 5.51, 5.52, 5.64,
3(1)(b). . . . 5.65, 5.70, 5.71, 5.72, 5.73,
5.74, 5.78, 5.87, 5.89, 5.100,
5.104; 7.26; 20.2, 22.17; 24.12
3(1)(c) 5.5, 5.6, 5.7, 5.10, 5.15,
5.17, 5.19, 5.21, 5.23, 5.25, 5.28,
5.38, 5.39, 5.40, 5.51, 5.53,
5.55, 5.56, 5.57, 5.58, 5.63, 5.64,
5.65, 5.66, 5.67, 5.68, 5.69, 5.70,
5.71, 5.72, 5.74, 5.78, 5.86, 5.87,
5.89, 5.94; 7.26; 10.4, 10.12;
12.26;20.2, 22.17; 24.12
3(1)(d). . . . 5.19, 5.21, 5.25, 5.51, 5.69,
5.70, 5.71, 5.72, 5.73, 5.74, 5.78,
5.87, 5.94; 7.26; 22.17; 24.12
3(2) **5.93**, 5.94, 5.95, 5.96, 5.100;
22.19; 24.11
3(2)(a) 5.95, 5.97, 5.101
3(2)(b). 5.72, 5.95, 5.98, 5.101
3(2)(c) 5.95, 5.96, 5.99, 5.101
3(3). 5.15, 5.92, **5.102**, 5.103,
5.105, 5.107, 5.111, 5.119,
6.25; 22.18; 24.11
3(3)(a) 10.5
3(3)(b) 5.104, 5.105; 22.13
3(4) 5.107; 22.3, 22.19; 24.14
3(5). 5.108; 22.19; 24.15
3(6) . . 5.118, 5.119, 5.120, 5.121; 6.82;
8.1, 8.9; 21.14; 22.19; 27.21
4. . . . . 1.23; 4.1; 5.108; 22.3; 24.15
4(1). 5.109, 5.115; 6.9; 12.4; 24.16
4(2) 5.110; 24.16
4(3). 5.108, 5.111; 24.16
4(4) 2.11; 5.115; 22.3; 24.16
5 . . 1.23; 5.118; 6.1, 6.3; 7.1, 7.30; 9.3;
12.14, 12.53, 12.58; 16.4; 21.25
5(1) 6.5, 6.7–.9, 6.14, 6.53–54,
6.63, 6.72–73, 6.81,
6.82–83; 7.27, 12.2–4
5(1)(a) 9.4
5(2). . . . 5.72; 6.5, 6.7, 6.12, 6.14, 6.15,
6.17, 6.18, 6.19, 6.21, 6.26,
6.29, 6.30, 6.32, 6.33, 6.37,

Trade Marks Act 1994–*contd*
  s 5(2). . 6.45, 6.46, 6.50, 6.53, 6.54, 6.57,
    6.58, 6.70, 6.72, 6.73, 6.78, 6.81,
    6.82; 7.27; 8.9; 12.2, 12.14; 24.19
  5(3). 6.5, 6.6, 6.7, 6.53, **6.55**, 6.57,
    6.58, 6.61, 6.63, 6.68, 6.70, 6.71,
    6.72, 6.73, 6.75, 6.78, 6.81; 7.27,
    7.30; 8.9; 12.2, 12.14, 12.17,
    12.54; 23.11; 24.20
  5(4) 6.6, 6.53, 6.61, 6.62, 6.70,
    6.74, 6.75, 6.76, 6.81, 6.83;
    7.27; 8.9; 12.58
  5(4)(a) 6.76, 6.77, 6.78; 24.22
  5(4)(b) 6.79; 24.23; 27.23
  5(5). 2.4; 6.1, 6.55
  6 . . . . 7.27; 12.53, 12.58; 21.37;
    22.40; 23.11; 24.18
  6(1) **6.3**, 6.72
  6(1)(a)–(b). **6.3**, 6.4
  6(1)(c) 5.118; **6.3**; 12.2
  6(2) 6.4; 12.2
  6(3). 6.4
  7 . . . . 6.6, 6.80, 6.81, 6.82, 6.83;
    16.14; 17.12; 26.14
  7(2). 6.82; 16.14, 16.15
  8 . . . . 6.2, 6.81; 8.21; 16.11,
    16.12; 17.12
  8(1). 6.2
  8(2). 6.2
  8(a), (b) 16.11
  8(3). 16.11
  8(5) 6.2; 16.11
  8(6). 6.2
  9 . . . . 11.9; 12.1, 12.3, 12.5, 12.16,
    12.50;18.99, 18.111; 19.100; 20.10,
    20.97, 20.99; 21.22; 24.26, 24.30
  8(1) 12.4, 12.7, 12.17, 12.40
  8(2). 12.4
  8(3) 11.1; 12.4
  8(3)(a) 16.17
  10. . . . . 1.24; 2.6; 6.9; 12.1, 12.2, 12.3,
    12.4, 12.7, 12.16, 12.40, 12.50,
    12.58;18.99, 18.111; 19.100, 19.132;
    20.10, 20.97, 20.99; 21.22; 24.26
  10(1) 6.7, 6.25, 6.28; 12.2, 12.6,
    12.10, 2.11, 12.13, 12.14; 18.3,
    18.35; 19.37; 20.10,
    20.92; 24.17; 24.29
  10(2) . 6.7, 6.21, 6.25, 6.28, 6.29, 6.30,
    6.32, 6.33, 6.35, 6.36, 6.37, 6.45,
    6.46, 6.57; 12.2, 12.6,12.11, 12.13,
    12.14, 12.50; 16.52; 18.3, 18.35;
    19.37; 20.2, 20.10; 24.17, 24.29

Trade Marks Act 1994–*contd*
  s 10(2)(a) 18.41; 19.41
  10(3) 6.7, 6.25, 6.28, 6.46, 6.50,
    6.57, 6.58, 6.60, 6.62; 12.2, 12.6,
    12.10, 12.11, 12.13, 12.14, 12.17,
    12.28, 12.50,12.54;16.52;18.3;
    20.2, 20.92, 22.45; 24.17, 24.29
  10(3 (a). 6.57
  10(4) . . . 12.6, 12.7, 12.9, 12.13, 20.35,
    20.37; 24.17, 24.29
  10(4)(a), (b) 12.9
  10(5). 10.9, 10.16, 12.15
  10(6). 12.3, 12.17, 12.18, 12.19,
    12.20,12.21; 12.24, 12.25, 12.40;
    15.17; 20.103, 20.104, 20.106;
    22.31, 22.46
  11 . . . . . . 5.8; 12.1, 12.3, 12.50, 12.51;
    20.10, 20.97, 20.99, 20.103,
    20.106, 21.22; 24.26
  11(1). 6.82; 12.22, 12.23, 12.58;
    24.35, 24.37
  11(2) . 6.46; 12.11, 12.14, 12.17, 12.24,
    2.27, 12.29; 22.31, 22.46; 24.31
  11(2)(a) 5.41; 12.25
  11(2)(b) 5.10, 5.12; 12.11, 12.26,
    12.27; 18.76
  11(2)(c) 12.26, 12.29, 12.30
  11(3) 12.31; 24.32
  12 . . . 12.1, 12.34, 12.35, 12.50; 14.55;
    20.29; 21.22; 24.26, 24.33
  12(1). 12.35
  12(2). **12.35**
  13 . . . . 2.9; 5.54; 6.11; 12.1, 12.3,
    12.18,12.49, 21.23
  13(1). 12.49
  13(1)(a), (b) 2.4
  13(2). 2.11; 5.108, 5.117
  13(3). 5.117
  14 . . . . 12.50; 21.22
  15 . . . . 21.22
  16 . . . . 12.4; 21.22
  17 . . . . 20.41; 21.22; 23.19
  17(2), (3) 18.3
  18 . . . . 21.22
  19 . . . . 21.22
  19(2) 10.9, 10.16
  19(3). 2.14
  20 . . . . 21.22
  21 . . . . . . 13.3, 13.4, 13.5, 13.7, 13.12,
    13.18; 21.9, 21.24; 23.12; 31.4
  21(1) 13.13, 13.23
  21(1)(a)–(c). 13.6, 13.14
  21(2). 13.5, 13.17, 13.18

Trade Marks Act 1994–*contd*
s 21(2)(a)–(c) 13.18
 21(3) 13.17; 21.24
 21(4). . . . . 13..11; 21.24
 22 . . . . 11.1; 21.25
 22(2). 11.4
 23. . . . . 11.1, 11.2; 11.4; 21.25
 23(1). 11.2
 23(3) 11.2, 11.3
 24(4), (5) 11.2
 24(6). 11.3
 23A. 11.4
 24 . . . . 11.1, 11.4, 11.5; 21.25,
    22.13; 24.51
 24(1), (2) 11.4
 24(3) 11.4; 24.51
 24(4)–(6) 11.4
 25 . . . 2.9, 2 19; 9.14; 11.1, 11.5, 11.10,
    11.11, 11.15, 11.16, 11.17, 11.18;
    12.5; 16.29; 21.27
 25(1) 2.19, 2.20; 11.11,
    11.17, 11.18
 25(2). 2.19; 11.1; **11.16**
 25(2)(a)–(e) **11.16**
 25(3) 2.19; 11.1, 11.21; 21.27
 25(4) 11.1, 11.21; 21.27
 25(5), (6) 2.11, 11.22
 26 . . . . 7.2; 11.1, 11.6; 12.5; 21.25
 27 . . . . 11.1, 11.6, 11.16; 21.25
 27(1). 11.1
 27(2). 11.2
 27(3) 11.1, 11.2, 11.17, 11.18
 28 . . . . 11.1, 11.11; 21.26
 28(1). 21.26
 28(3) 11.10, 11.21
 28(12). 11.9
 29 . . . . 11.1, 11.10; 21.26
 29(2) 11.10, 11.11
 30. . . . 10.16; 11.1, 11.10, 11.14, 11.21;
    18.78; 19.80; 21.26, 21.27; 31.14
 30(2)–(6) 11.14
 31 . . . . 11.1, 11.10, 11.11, 11.14, 11.21;
    21.26, 21.27; 31.14
 32 . . . . 5.120; 7.2; 8.1; 16.5, 16.6,
    16.7; 21.14
 32(1). 16.5
 32(2) 8.1, 8.3
 32(1)(a)–(d) 16.5
 32(3). 8.1; 16.5; 21.14
 32(4). 8.1
 33 . . . . 8.3; 21.14
 34 . . . . 21.14

Trade Marks Act 1994–*contd*
s 34(1). 2.5
 34(2). 2.8
 35 . . . . 2.4; 8.4, 8.5, 8.6, 8.7, 8.8;
    9.13; 21.15; 22.3, 22.8; 25.5,
    25.6, 25.7, 15.10
 35(1) 8.5; 16.6
 35(1)(c), (d) 11.22
 35(2). 8.5
 35(2)(a) 25.10
 35(3). 8.5
 35(4). 8.5
 35(5). 2.11, 8.5; 21.15
 35(6). 8.5
 36. . . . . 2.4; 8.4, 8.6, 8.7; 22.3
 36(1). 16.6
 36(2) 8.6; 16.6
 36(3). 8.6
 37 . . . . 5.5; 6.2; 8.9; 10.6, 10.14;
    16.7, 16.11
 37(1). 16.7
 37(2) 6.2; 16.7
 37(3) 5.5; 21.35
 37(4) 5.5; 16.8
 35(5). 5.5
 38 . . . . 8.10; 10.6, 10.14
 38(1) 2.9; 16.10
 38(2) 3.8; 8.13; 9.1; 16.10; 21.35
 38(3) 9.1; 16.13; 16.33; 21.18
 39 . . . . 16.39
 39(1) 8.15; 16.16
 39(2). 5.107; 8.15; 10.4
 39(3) 2.11; 8.15
 40(1) 8.20; 16.16
 40(2). 8.20
 40(3) 2.4; 7.31; 8.20; 9.8; 11.1;
    12.4; 25.10
 40(4). 8.20
 41 . . . . 2.13; 8.16
 41(1). 2.11, 2.25; 9.3
 41(2). 8.16
 41(3). 2.11
 42(1), (2) 9.8
 43 . . . . 9.8, 9.9; 23.15
 43(2) 2.11; 9.9
 43(3). 7.31; 9.10, 9.11
 43(5) 2.11, 9.11
 43(6). 9.11
 44 . . . . 2.9, 2.36; 9.12, 16.29
 44(1). 9.12
 44(2). 9.12
 44(3) 2.11, 9.12

Trade Marks Act 1994–*contd*

s 45 . . . . 2.9; 9.14; 23.15
  45(2) 2.11; 9.14
  46 . . . . . 1.23, 2.28, 2.38; 3.8; 7.1, 7.12,
    7.20, 7.23; 9.15, 9.20; 10.10, 10.17;
    11.8, 12.22; 16.29, 16.42; 18.46,
    18.111; 19.124, 20.101; 21.28;
    22.47; 23.15
  46(1) 7.2, 7.3, 7.4, 7.13; 9.13;
    12.22, 21.28; 27.11, 27.13
  46(1)(a) . . . 2.8; 5.121; 7.5, 7.10, **7.11**,
    7.17; 9.16; 11.9; 12.5;
    16.41; 22.9; 24.38
  46(1)(b) 2.8; 5.121; 7.5, 7.10,
    7.11, 7.17; 9.16; 11.9;
    12.5; 16.41; 22.9; 24.38
  46(1)(c) 7.18, 7.22; 24.27; 27.16
  46(1)(d) 7.19, 7.20, 7.21, 7.22;
    11.3, 22.13; 27.17
  46(2) 7.2, 7.9, 7.20; 9.13; 12.22;
    21.28; 22.9; 24.38
  46(3) 7.2, **7.11**, 7.12
  46(4) 2.38; 16.39, 16.44
  46(4)(a) 16.39; 18.46
  46(4)(b) 9.19; 16.39
  46(5) 7.2, 7.3, 7.13, 7.19,
    7.22; 21.28
  46(6) 7.2, 7.16, 7.22, 7.23; 12.4;
    21.28; 27.29
  47 . . . . . 1.23, 2.28, 2.38; 3.8; 6.80; 7.1,
    7.22, 7.24, 7.28, 7.30, 7.33; 9.16,
    9.20; 10.10, 10.17, 12.58; 16.11,
    16.29, 16.42; 18.46, 18.111, 18.117,
    19.124, 20.101; 21.28; 23.15
  47(1) 5.77, 5.79, 5.121; 6.81;
    7.5, 7.24, 7.25, 7.26, 7.31;
    21.14; 27.20
  47(1)(b), (c) 7.25
  47(1)(d) 5.104; 7.21, 7.25
  47(2) 1.23; 6.2, 6.75, 6.81; 7.24,
    7.27, 7.31, 7.33; 12.51
  47(3) 2.38; 6.2; 7.23; 16.39, 16.44
  47(3)(a) 16.39; 18.46
  47(3)(b) 9.19; 16.39
  47(4) 5.120; 6.81
  47(5) 6.81; 7.23, 7.24, 7.28; 27.25
  47(6) 7.23, 7.29; 12.4, 12.22; 27.30
  48 . . . . 6.81; 7.33; 12.22, 12.58;
    21.29; 27.26
  48(1)(b) 12.58
  48(2) 12.59; 27.28
  49 . . . . 4.2; 10.11; 22.26; 30.1
  49(1), (2) 10.11

Trade Marks Act 1994–*contd*

s 50 . . . . 4.2; 10.2; 16.29; 30.3
  50(1) 10.3
  50(2) 10.2, 10.3
  51 . . . . 6.3; 23.1
  52 . . . . 2.14; 12.23
  52(1) 23.11
  52(2) 20.2; 23.11, 23.13
  52(2)(a) 23.14
  52(2)(c) 23.16
  52(3) 23.11, 23.12, 23.13
  52(3)(a), (b) 23.12, 23.22
  52(4) 23.11
  53 . . . . 6.3; 21.1
  53(3) 20.155
  54 . . . . 2.14; 21.10
  54(1) 21.7
  54(2) 21.7, **21.8**
  54(3) 21.7, 21.9
  54(4) 21.7, 21.9
  55 . . . . 1.2; 8.5
  55(1) 6.72; 7.34; 8.5; 9.2
  55(1)(a) 16.6
  55(2) 8.5
  56 . . . . 1.2; 5.118; 6.3, 6.59, 6.72; 12.1;
    12.53, 12.55, 12.56, 12.58; 14.19;
    22.3, 22.40, 22.45
  56(1) 6.3; 12.53, 12.54
  56(2) 12.53, 12.54, 12.56,
    12.58, 12.59
  56(3) 12.56
  57 . . . . 1.2; 5.108, 5.111, 5.112;
    22.3; 24.16
  57(1)–(5) 5.112, 5.113
  57(6) 5.111
  58 1.2; 5.108, 5.111, 5.113; 22.3; 24.16
  58(1), (2) 5.113, 5.114
  58(4) 5.111
  58(5) 5.113
  59 . . . . 1.2; 5.111, 5.112, 5.113
  59(2) 16.38
  59(4) 5.111
  60 . . . . 1.2; 5.118; 7.1, 7.34; 9.2;
    22.3, 22.24; 24.21
  60(2) 9.2
  60(3) 3.8; 7.34; 9.15, 9.16
  60(4) 9.2
  60(5), (6) 7.34; 9.16
  62 . . . . 16.3
  63 . . . . 2.1; 3.10; 9.21
  63(1) 2.4; 16.16
  63(2) 16.16
  63(2)(a) 2.4

Trade Marks Act 1994–*contd*

s 63(3). 2.18
64. . . . . 2.28, 2.38; 3.8; 7.1, 7.35; 9.16,
     9.20; 16.29, 16.39, 16.42; 21.30
64(1) 7.35, 7.38
64(2). 2.38; 16.39, 16.44
64(2)(b) 9.19
64(3) 7.35, 7.38
64(4). 7.35, 7.37, 7.38
64(5). 7.35, 7.38; 11.22
65. . . . . 2.6, 2.11
65(1), (2) 2.6
65(3). 2.6, 2.7; 16.29
65(4) 2.6, 2.7
65(5). 2.6
66. . . . . 2.15
67 . . . . 11.18; 21.40
67(1). 2.19
67(2) 2.19; 21.41
67(3). 21.40
68. . . . . 2.36, 2.40; 16.34
68(1) 2.11; 5.83
68(2). 2.36
68(3). 2.11
69 . . . . 2.11, 2.24, 2.30, 2.40; 9.6, 9.19
69(a) 2.30; 9.4
69(b), (c). 2.32; 9.6
70 . . . . 2.2; 21.40
70(1)–(2) 2.2
71. . . . . 2.1
71(2). 2.1
72. . . . . 11.20; 21.40; 23.15
73 . . . . 2.9; 21.30
74. . . . . 2.42; 21.30; 23.15
74(2). 2.42
74(3). 16.3
75 . . . . 16.36; 18.123; 19.124
75(a) 18.46
76. . . . 2.37, 2.39, 2.41; 7.4, 7.38; 8.12;
     16.24, 16.25, 16.36; 23.15
76(1). 2.7, 2.11, 2.39; 9.18; 16.22
76(2). 2.40, 2.41; 8.12
76(3) 2.40, 2.41; 16.25, 16.36
76(a)–(c). 16.25
76(4). 2.40; 8.12; 16.24
76(5) 2.40; 8.12
77. . . . . . . 1.18, 1.25; 2.40; 3.10; 16.24
77(1). 16.24
77(2)–(4) 2.40
78 . . . . 2.10, 2.12; 3.1; 8.21
78(2). 2.10; 3.8; 8.21
78(3). 2.11
79 . . . . 2.11, 2.14; 8.1

Trade Marks Act 1994–*contd*

s 80. . . . . 2.26
80(1). 2.11
80(2). 2.16
80(3) 2.11, 2.16
81 . . . . 2.9, 2.11; 8.13
82 . . . . 2.11; 3.1; 16.29; 21.40
83 . . . . 2.11; 3.3
83(2), (3) 3.3
84 . . . . 3.3, 3.4, 3.5; 23.12, 23.22
84(4). 3.3
85 . . . 2.11; 3.3, 3.4, 3.11; 23.12, 23.22
85(2), (4) 3.4
86 . . . . 3.11; 23.12, 23.22
86(1), (2) 3.11
87 . . . . 3.13, 3.15; 23.12, 23.22
87(2). 23.22
87(2)(b) 3.15
88 . . . . 2.11; 3.5; 23.12
88(1). 3.5
89 . . . . . 10.16; 18.1, 18.3, 18.6, 18.35,
     18.74, 18.75, 18.81, 18.83,
     18.84, 18.86, 18.87, 18.88, 18.89,
     18.92, 18.95, 18.96, 18.99, 18.107,
     18.108, 18.113, 18.120; 19.3, 19.35;
     21.9, 21.31; 23.12, 23.19, 23.22
89(1) 18.81, 18.82
89(1)(a) 18.81, 18.88
89(1)(b). 18.49, 18.81, 18.84,
     18.88, 18.92
89(1)(b)(i), (ii) 18.83
89(1)(c) 18.81, 18.88
89(1)(d) 18.81
89(2). 18.49, 18.83, **18.91**, 18.94,
     18.102; 19.102, 19.103
89(3). 18.75, 18.83; 19.84
90 . . . . 18.80; 21.9; 23.12, 23.19
90(1). 18.82
90(1)(a), (b) 18.82
90(2)(a)–(c) 18.82
90(4). 18.82
91 . . . . 21.9; 23.12, 23.19
92 . . . 12.4; 16.63, 16.64; 18.118; 20.6,
     20.7, 20.11, 20.13, 20.14,
     20.20, 20.21, 20.32, 20.38,
     20.40, 20.41, 20.42, 20.45, 20.46,
     20.59, 20.92, 20.96, 20.97, 20.100,
     20.101, 20.107, 20.112, 20.114,
     20.115, 20.129, 20.145, 20.148,
     20.154; 21.9, 21.32; 22.29; 23.12,
     23.19, 23.20
92(1). **20.14**, 20.15, 20.17, 20.30,
     20.96, 20.97, 20.98

Trade Marks Act 1994–*contd*

s 92(1)(a) **20.31**, 20.35, 20.36,
20.37, 20.38, 20.39, 20.40,
20.46, 20.61, 20.70
92(1)(b) **20.31**, 20.33, 20.36,
20.37, 20.40, 20.46, 20.70
92(1)(c) 20.31, 20.34, 20.40, 20.46
92(2) 20.35, 20.41, 20.96,
20.97, 20.98
90(3) 20.35, 20.42, 20.96,
20.97, 20.98
90(3)(a) 20.70
90(4) **20.91**, 20.96
90(4)(b) 20.92, 20.93, 20.94
90(5) 20.19, 20.30, 20.93, 20.94,
20.95, **20.96**, 20.98, 20.102
90(6) 20.107
90(6)(a) 20.107
93 . . . . 21.9; 23.12, 23.20
93(1) 20.129
93(1)(b)(i), (ii) 18.75
93(2) 20.129
94 . . . . . 20.13, 20.101, 20.129, 20.138
95 . . . . 20.13; 21.9, 21.33; 23.12, 23.21
95(2), (3) 23.21
96 . . . . 21.9; 23.12
96(2)(b) 20.107
97 . . . . 23.20
98 . . . . 23.20
100 . . . . 1.23; 9.16, 16.41; 21.28; 24.43
103(1) 11.14
103(2) 1.24; 4.4; 12.4, **12.8**; 20.37
104 . . . . 3.1
106(1), (2) 3.13
Sch 1 . . . . . . 4.2; 10.11, 10.14; 30.1, 30.4
para 1 . . . . 10.11
2, 3 . . . . 10.12
4 . . . . 10.12
4(1) 10.17; 30.7
4(2) 30.7
5 . . . . 10.13
5(1), (2) 10.13, 10.17
6 . . . . 10.13
6(1) 10.14, 10.15, 10.17
7 . . . . 10.13, 10.14
8 . . . . 10.13, 10.14
9 . . . . 10.13
10 . . . . 10.13, 10.15
10(1)–(3) 10.15
11(1) 10.16
12 . . . . 10.16
12(2), (3), (5), (6) 10.16

Trade Marks Act 1994–*contd*

Sch 1, para 13, 14 . . . . 10.17
Sch 2 . . . . 4.2; 10.2, 10.3, 10.6; 30.3
para 1, 2 . . . . 10.3
3 . . . . 10.4
4 . . . . 10.4, 10.10
5 . . . . 10.4
5(1) 10.10
6 . . . . 10.5, 10.8
6(1), (2) 10.5, 10.10
7 . . . . 10.5
7(1) 10.5, 10.6, 10.7, 10.10
7(2) 10.5
8, 9 . . . . 10.5, 10.6
10 . . . . 10.5
11 . . . . 10.7
11(1)–(3) 10.7
12 . . . . 10.4
13 . . . . 10.9
14 . . . . 10.9; 10.16
15, 16 . . . . 10.10
Sch 3 . . . . 1.10; 7.29; 9.7; 11.11,
11.17; 12.56
para 1 . . . . 12.50
1(1) 2.1
2 . . . . 7.2
2(3) 11.4
3 . . . . 2.1
3(2) 12.49
3(3) 5.104
4(1) 12.50
4(2) 12.50, 12.51, 12.52, 12.56
4(2)(b) 12.50
6 . . . . 11.14
6(2) 10.9
7 . . . . 11.2
8 . . . . 11.11, 11.17
8(1)–(6) 11.5
9(1) 11.11
9(2), (3) 11.11, 11.17
9(4) 11.11
9(5) 11.22
10(1) 2.1
10(2) 2.11; 8.21
10(3) 8.21
11 . . . . 2.1, 2.20; 8.21; 9.8
12 . . . . 2.11
13 . . . . 8.5, 8.21
14 . . . . 8.8
14(5) 2.11
15(1), (2) 9.8
16 . . . . 9.13

Trade Marks Act 1994–*contd*
  Sch 3, para 17(1) 7.2, 7.17
  para 17(2) 7.17
    18(1) 7.2, 7.30
    18(2) 7.23, 7.30
    18(4) 7.2
    19 . . . . 10.8
    22(1) 3.3, 3.4
  Sch 4
  para 8 . . . . 3.13
  Sch 5 . . . . 3.13
Trade Marks (Amendment) Act 1937 . . 1.10
Trade Marks (Amendment) Act 1984 . . . 1.1
  s 1(7) 4.1

Trade Marks Registration Act 1875 . . . . . 1.9
Trade Marks Registration Amendment
  Act 1876 . . . . 1.9
Trade Marks Registration Extension
  Act 1877 . . . . 1.9
Trading with the Enemy Act 1939 . . . . 15.20
Unfair Contract Terms Act 1977 . . . . . 20.90
Weights and Measures Act 1985 . . . 20.129,
                                 20.135
  s 69 . . . . **20.129**, 20.135
    72 . . . . 20.136

Table of statutory instruments

*References on the right-hand side are to paragraph numbers. Those paragraph numbers in **bold** indicate where the statutory material is set out in full or in part.*

Civil Procedure Rules 1998,
SI 1998/3132. . . . . . . 2.14; 9.20; 16.53;
 18.16, 18.31, 18.122
Pt 1
  r 1.1(2). 16.50
Pt 6 . . . . 3.10; 9.21
  r 6.5 . . . . 3.10; 9.21
Pt 7. . . . . 18.40
  r 7.2(1). 16.53
  7.4(1)(b) 16.46
Pt 8. . . . . 9.20; 18.40; 31.9
Pt 10. . . . . 31.9
  r 3(1)(a), (b). 16.46
Pt 11 . . . . 31.9
Pt 15
  r 15.4(1)(a), (b) 16.46
  15.9. . . . . 16.46
Pt 16
  r 16.5(2)(a), (b) 16.46
Pt 17
  r 17.1(2)(a), (b) 16.48
Pt 18
  r 18 . . . . 16.48
Pt 20. . . . . 13.3; 16.45, 16.48
  r 20.2(1). 16.48
  20.4(2). 16.48
Pt 22
  r 22.1(1)(a), (b) 16.47
  22.1(6)(a) 16.47
  22.2(2). 16.47
Pt 23
  r 23 . . . . 16.46
Pt 24

Civil Procedure Rules 1998
SI 1998/3132–*contd*
  r 24.2(a), (b) 16.54
Pt 25
  r 25.1. . . . . 3.10
  25.1(b). 18.104
  25.1(h). 18.55
  25.2 . . . . 25.3, 3.10
Pt 26. . . . . 18.35
  r 26.1 . . . . 18.34
  26(2)(a)–(c). 18.34
  26.3 . . . . 18.34
  26.3(1) 16.49; 18.40
  26.4 . . . . 16.54
  26.5(1). 18.34
  26.5(4) 16.49; 18.34
  26.6 . . . . 18.34
  26.7(1) 18.34, 18.35
  26.8 . . . . 18.34, 18.35
  26.8(1)(a) 18.32
Pt 27
  r 27 . . . . 16.49
  27.4(1). 18.34
  27.6(1). 18.34
Pt 28
  r 28.2(1). 18.34
  28.5 . . . . 16.49
  28.5(1). 18.34
  28.5(3)(c) 18.34
Pt 29
  r 29.2. 16.49
  29.2(1). 18.34
  29.2(b). 18.34

Civil Procedure Rules 1998
SI 1998/3132–*contd*
    r 29.2(3)(b) 16.49
       29.6(1). 18.34
    Pt 30 . . . . 18.33
    r 30.2(2), (4) 18.37
       30.3(1), (2) 18.37
    Pt 31 . . . . . . 2.32; 3.14; 9.6; 16.28; 18.41
    r 31.6 . . . . 16.50; 18.41
       31.6(c). 18.41
       31.7 . . . . 16.50
       31.8 . . . . 18.42
       31.12 . . . . 16.50; 18.41
    Pt 32 . . . . 16.28
    r 32.6 . . . . 16.54
       32.14 . . . . 16.46
    Pt 33 . . . . 16.28
    Pt 34 . . . . 16.28
    r 34.1 . . . . 16.28
       34.2 . . . . 16.28
       34.2(1)(a), (b) 16.28
       34.4(1). 18.55
       34.5(1), (2) 16.28
       34.8(1). 16.29
       34.13 . . . . 16.29
    Pt 35 . . . . 16.28
    r 35.8 . . . . 16.46
       35.8(2). 16.46
    Pt 44 . . . . 16.54; 18.71
    r 44.3 . . . . 18.71
       44.3(1)–(3) **18.43**
       44(4). 16.54; **18.43**
       44(5) **18.43**
    Pt 49 . . . . 2.14, 2.41, 2.42; 3.10;
       9.15, 9.19, 9.20; 16.36; 31.17
    r 49.1 . . . . 16.36
       49.2(d)(ii), (iii) 16.36
       49.7(4). 16.36
       49.22(1). 16.36
       49.23(1). 16.36
       49.23(3). 16.20, 16.22, 16.36
       49.23(4). 16.36
       49.23(5). 16.44
       49.23(6). 16.36
       49.24(1)–(3) 16.45
    Pt 50 . . . . 2.37
    Sch . . . . 1, RSC
    Ord 3 r 12. . . . . 14.75
    Ord 15 r 12. . . . . 14.75
    Ord 52 . . . . 16.37
    Ord 53 . . . . 18.102
    Ord 53 r 3. . . . . 16.21
    Ord 53 r 4(1) 16.20

Civil Procedure Rules 1998
SI 1998/3132–*contd*
    Ord 55 r 4(1)(b). 16.23
    Ord 55 r 4(2) 2.41
    Ord 55 r 7. . . . . 16.23
    Ord 100 . . . . 2.42
    Sch 2, CCR
    Ord 5 r 5. . . . . 14.75

Community Trade Mark (Fees) Regulations
1995, SI 1995/3175 . . . . 2.14; 23.14

Community Trade Mark Regulations
    1996, SI 1996/1908 . . . . 2.14; 12.23;
       23.13; 24.35, 24.37; 31.3
    reg 2 . . . . 23.15
       3 . . . . 23.15, 23.23; 25.16
       3(1)–(4) 23.15
       4 . . . . 13.5; 23.18; 31.4
       5 . . . . 23.22
       7 . . . . 20.3; 23.20
       7(2). 23.20
       8 . . . . 23.21
       8(1). 23.21
       9 . . . . 17.28; 23.17, 23.24
       10. . . . . 23.16, 23.23
       11. . . . . 23.15, 23.23

Copyright, Designs and Patents Act 1988
    (Commencement No 1) Order 1989,
    SI 1989/816 . . . . 20.9
    art 2. . . . . 20.9

Copyright, Designs and Patents Act 1988 . .
    (Commencement No 5)Order 1990,
    SI 1990/1400 . . . . 3.2

Counterfeit and Pirated Goods (Customs)
    Regulations 1995, SI 1995,
    SI 1995/1430 . . . . 19.3
    reg 1(1). 19.3

Counterfeit and Pirated Goods
    (Consequential Provisions) Regulations
    1995, SI 1995/1447. . . . . 18.5; 19.3
    reg 1(1). 19.3

County Court Rules 1981,
    SI 1981/1687 . . . . 18.40
    Ord 4. . . . . 18.37
    r 2(1)(a), (b). 18.37
    Ord 16
    r 2 . . . . 18.37

County Court Rules
1981,SI 1981/1687–*contd*
  Ord 19. . . . . 16.59, 16.62, 16.66

Criminal Procedure and Investigations Act
  1996 (Defence Disclosure Time Limits)
  Regulations 1997, SI 1997/684 . . 20.174
  reg 2 . . . . 20.174

Crown Court (Criminal Procedure and
  Investigations Act 1996) (Disclosure)
  Rules 1997, SI 1997/698 . . . . 20.173

European Communities (Definition of
  Treaties) (The Agreement Establishing
  the World Trade Organisation) Order
  1995, SI 1995/265 . . . . 22.39

European Communities (Designation)
  (No 2) Order 1995, SI 1995/751 . . 19.93
  art 2. . . . . 19.93
  Schedule 19.93

European Communities (Enforcement of
  Community Judgments) Order 1972,
  SI 1972/1590 . . . . 31.20

European Communities (Enforcement of
  Community Judgments) (Amendment)
  Order 1998, SI 1998/1259 . . . . 31.20

Good Infringing Intellectual Property Rights
  (Consequential Provisions) Regulations
  1999, SI 1999/1618 . . . . . . 19.3, 19.84,
                       19.96; 19.101, 19.106
  reg 1 . . . . 19.3
  1(2). 19.97
  2. . . . . 19.101, 19.103
  3. . . . . 19.97, 19.101, 19.102, 19.157
  3(1)(a) 19.100
  4. . . . . . 19.98, 19.99, 19.101, 19.102
  4(1)(a), (b) 19.98
  4(1)(c) 19.98, 19.99
  5 . . . . 19.103
  5(1). 19.103
  5(1)(a), (b) 19.103
  5(2). 19.104
  6(1). 19.161
  9 . . . . 19.3

Goods Infringing Intellectual Property
  Rights (Customs) Regulations 1999,
  SI 1999/1601 . . . . 19.3, 19.59, 19.84,
                       19.95, 19.96, 19.106
  reg 2 . . . . 19.101
  5 . . . . 19.94
  7. . . . . **19.89**, 19.94
  8 . . . . 19.91

High Court and County Courts Jurisdiction
  Order 1991, SI 1991/724 . . . . 18.30
  art 7. . . . . 18.31
  7(2) 18.33
  7(5). **18.33**, 18.34
  9 . . . . 18.31
  9(b)(i), (ii) 18.32
  10 . . . . 18.31

Local Government (Wales) Act 1994
  (Commencement No 4)Order 1995,
  SI 1995/852
  art 9. . . . . 20.129

Magistrates' Courts (Advance Information)
  Rules 1985, SI 1985/601 . . . . 20.120
  r 3 . . . . 20.120

Magistrates' Courts (Forms) (Amendment)
  Rules 1983, SI 1983/524 . . . . 18.52

Magistrates' Courts (Forms) Rules 1981,
  SI 1981/553 . . . . 18.52
  r 2 . . . . 18.52
  Sch 2. . . . . 18.52
  Form 99, 105, 108, 112 . . . . 18.52

Magistrates' Courts Rules 1981,
  SI 1981/552
  r 98 . . . . 18.52

Olympic Association Right (Appointment
  of Proprietor) Order 1995,
  SI 1995/2473 . . . . 5.117

Olympic Symbol etc (Protection) Act
  1995 (Commencement)Order 1995,
  SI 1995/2472 . . . . 5.108

Olympic Association Right (Infringement
  Proceedings)Regulations 1995,
  SI 1995/3325
  reg 5 . . . . 2.14

Patents Agents (Non-recognition of Certain
Agents by Comptroller) Rules 1990,
SI 1990/1454 . . . . 3.6

Patents and Trade Marks (World Trade
Organisation) Regulations 1999,
SI 1999/1899. . . . . 1.1; 8.5; 12.53;
22.39, 22.40
reg 13. . . . . 12.53; 22.40
13(1). 6.3
13(2), (3) 8.5
14 . . . . 22.40

Patents Office (Address) (Revocation)
Rules 1999, SI 1999/1993 . . . . 2.3

Patent Office (Address) Rules 1991,
SI 1991/675 . . . . 2.3

Register of Patent Agents and the Register
of Trade Marks (Amendment) Rules
1999, SI 1999/983. . . . . 3.3, 3.6

Register of Patents Agents Rules 1990,
SI 1990/1457 . . . . 3.6
r 8 . . . . 3.6

Register of Trade Mark Agents Rules
1990, SI 1990/1458 . . . . 3.3
r 9 . . . . 3.6, 3.7
9(2) 3.6
10 . . . . 3.7, 3.8, 3.10
10(1). 3.8, 3.10
10(3). 3.7, 3.9
10(5), (6) 3.8, 3.9
14 . . . . 3.7

Registered Trade Mark Agents (Mixed
Partnership and Bodies Corporate)
Rules 1994, SI 1994/363 . . . . 3.4

Rules of the Supreme Court 1965,
SI 1965/1776 . . . . . . 18.28, 18.29, 18.40
Ord 2 r 1(3). 18.27
Ord 5 r 4(1). 18.27
Ord 5 r 4(2)(a), (b) 18.27
Ord 23. . . . . 2.37
Ord 24 r 5 . . . . 3.14
Ord 55 r 2 . . . . 16.22
Ord 62 r 7(4)(b) 18.44
Ord 100 r 2 (2) 9.15
Ord 114. . . . . 16.59, 16.62, 16.66

Trade Marks (Amendment) Rules 1998,
SI 1998/925   1.1, 2.12; 4.6; 6.9,
6.10; 8.15; 10.15;
16.36; 21.12; 23.15
r 4 . . . . 8.1
6 . . . . 8.15; 9.3, 9.17
7 . . . . 8.15
9 . . . . 9.12; 10.7
10 . . . . 9.9
10(c) 10.15
11. . . . . 9.10
14 . . . . 2.20
16 . . . . 2.25
17 . . . . 2.27
17(c) 9.12

Trade Marks and Service Marks (Relevant
Countries) Order 1986,
SI 1986/1303 . . . . 8.6

Trade Marks and Service Marks Rules
1986, SI 1986/1319. . . . . 2.13; 5.108
r 10, 13 . . . . 3.10
16–18 . . . . 5.108
21 . . . . 5.121
31(5) 9.18

Trade Marks and Service Marks Rules
1986, SI 1986/1319
r 56 . . . . 2.37
121 . . . . 2.25

Trade Marks (Claims to Priority from
Relevant Countries) (Amendment) Order
1995, SI 1995/2997 . . . . 16.6

Trade Marks (Claims to Priority from
Relevant Countries) Order 1994,
SI 1994/2803. . . . . 8.6; 16.6

Trade Marks (Customs) Regulations 1994,
SI 1994/2625. . . . . . 18.80, 18.87, 18.88,
18.89, 18.108; 19.85; 21.31; 23.19
reg 1 . . . . 18.80
2. . . . . 18.88, 18.89
3 . . . . 18.88; 19.85
4 . . . . 19.85
5 . . . . 18.88; 19.87
6 . . . . 18.88, **18.106**; 19.54
6(1) 18.106, 18.108
6(2) 18.90, 18.108
6(3). 19.88
Schedule 18.83

Trade Marks (EC Measures Relating to
  Counterfeit Goods) Regulations 1995,
  SI 1995/1444 . . . . 18.83; 19.84
  reg 1 . . . . 18.83
      2 . . . . 18.75

Trade Marks (Fees) Rules 1994,
  SI 1994/2584 . . . . 2.14

Trade Marks (Fees) Rules 1996,
  SI 1996/1942 . . . . 2.14

Trade Marks (Fees) Rules 1998,
  SI 1998/1776 . . . . 2.14, 8.1

Trade Marks (International Registration)
  (Fees) Rules 1996,
  SI 1996/715 . . . . 2.14; 21.10

Trade Marks (International Registration)
  Order 1996, SI 1996/714 . . . . . 1.2; 2.14,
                                   21.10, 21.11
  art 1 . . . . 21.11, 21.12
      2 . . . . 21.11, 21.12, 21.27
      3 . . . . 21.11, 21.14, 21.16
      4 . . . . 21.11, 21.14
      4(2) 21.15, 21.22
      4(3) 21.22
      4(4), (5) 21.23
      4(6) 21.24
      5 . . . . 21.11, 21.14, 21.16, 21.25
      6 . . . . 21.11, 21.14, 21.27, 21.40
      6(1)–(3) 21.27
      6(4), (5) 21.28
      6(6) 21.27
      7 . . . . 21.11, 21.14, 21.26
      8 . . . . 21.11, 21.14
      8(1), (2) 21.15
      9 . . . 21.11, 21.14, 21.16, 21.19, 21.27
      9(3) 21.16, 21.17, 21.35
      9(4) 21.16, 21.19
      9(5) 21.16
      10 . . . . 21.11, 21.14, 21.19
      10(1) 21.17, 21.18, 21.35, 21.40
      10(2) 21.40
      10(3) 21.17
      10(4) 21.17, 21.19
      10(6) 21.17, 21.18
      11 . . . . 21.11, 21.14
      11(1) 21.16, 21.18
      11(2) 21.17, 21.20
      11(3) 21.16, 21.17
      11(4), (5) 21.16, 21.17, 21.19

Trade Marks (International Registration)
  Order 1996, SI 1996/714–*contd*
  art 11(6) 21.16, 21.17
      12 . . . . 21.11, 21.14, 21.18,
                            21.19, 21.22, 21.35
      12(2) 21.21, 21.36
      12(3) 21.21, 21.32
      13 . . . . 21.11, 21.20, 21.28
      13(3) 21.28
      14 . . . . 21.11, 21.29
      15 . . . . 21.11
      15(1), (2) 21.30
      16 . . . . 21.11, 21.31
      17 . . . . 21.11, 21.32
      17(3) 21.32
      18 . . . . 21.11, 21.33
      19 . . . . 21.6, 21.11, 21.34
      19(1), (3) 21.34
      20 . . . . 21.11, 21.34, 21.35
      20(3) 21.35
      21 . . . . . . 21.11, 21.21, 21.22, 21.36
      21(2)–(6) 21.37
      22 . . . . 21.11, 21.38
      22(6) 21.38
      23 . . . . 21.11, 21.38, 21.39
      23(3) 21.39
      24 . . . . . . 21.11, 21.12, 21.27, 21.40
      25 . . . . 21.11, 21.40
      25(3) 21.40
      26–28 . . . . 21.11, 21.40
      29 . . . . 21.11, 21.28, 21.40
      30, 31 . . . . 21.11, 21.40
      32 . . . . 21.11; 21.34
      34(1) 21.17

Trade Marks Rules 1994,
  SI 1994/2583 . . . . 1.1, 2.12; 4.5;
                             6.9; 20.155; 23.23
  r 1 . . . . 9.7
    2 . . . . 8.13
    2(1) 7.38
    3 . . . . 2.15, 2.23
    3(6) 8.9
    4 . . . . 2.13
    5 . . . . . . 2.13; 4.6; 8.1, 8.2, 8.7; 16.5
    5(1) 8.1
    5(2) 4.6; 8.2, 8 7, 8.9
    5(3) 4.6; **6.10**; 8 2, 8.9
    5(4) 4.7; **6.9**; 8 2, 8.9
    6 . . . . 8.7
    6(1), (2) 16.7
    9 . . . . 5.115
    9(4)(a)(iv) 21.15

Trade Marks Rules 1994,
  SI 1994/2583–*contd*
  r 10 . . . . 2.4; 7.37; 9.21; 21.14
    10(6) 2.27
    11 . . . . 2.27; 21.14
    12 . . . . 2.27; 8.13; 9.3; 16.9
    13 . . . . 2.24, 2.27, 2.28;
               8.15; 9.3, 9.4, 9.16,
               9.17, 9.18; 21.17
    13(1) 2.27, 2.28; 8.13; 9.3,
               9.12; 16.9, 16.10
    13(2) 2.27, 2.28; 9.3, 9.12;
               10.7, 10.15; 16.10
    13(3) 2.28; 8.13; 9.3; 16.10
    13(4), (5) 9.4, 9.12; 10.7,
               10.15; 16.10, 16.29
    13(6) . . . 9.4, 9.12; 10.7, 10.15; 16.29
    13(7) 9.4, 9.6, 9.12; 10.7,
               10.15; 16.29, 16.31
    13(8) 2.31; 9.5, 9.12, 9.16,
               9.17; 10.7, 10.15
    13(9) . . 9.12, 9.17; 10.7, 10.15; 16.33
    14(1), (2) 16.33
    15 . . . . 16.33
    18 . . . . 2.27; 8.15
    19 . . . . 2.13; 8.16, 8.19
    19(1)–(3) 8.17
    20 . . . . 2.13; 8.16, 8.17, 8.18
    20(1)–(5) 8.18
    21 . . . . 2.9; 8.16, 8.19
    21(2), (3), (4) 8.19
    22 . . . . 10.5, 10.13
    23 . . . . 2.27; 10.7, 10.15
    23(1) 10.7, 10.15
    23(2) 10.7, 10.15
    23(3) 10.7, 10.15
    23(4) 2.27; 10.10, 10.15
    23(5) 10.7, 10.15
    24 . . . . 2.9
    25 . . . . 2.9, 2.27
    25(1) 16.29
    25(3) 2.27; 9.12; 21.40
    25(6) 21.40
    26 . . . . 2.9; 21.40
    26(1) 9.14
    26(2) 9.14; 21.40
    26(3) 9.14
    27(1), (2) 9.9; 21.40
    27(6) 21.40
    28 . . . . 9.9; 21.40
    29 . . . . 2.27; 9.11
    29(1)–(3) 9.10
    29(4), (5) 9.11

Trade Marks Rules 1994,
  SI 1994/2583–*contd*
  r 30 . . . . 2.27; 9.10, 9.11; 21.41
    31 . . . . 2.24; 7.37; 9.16, 9.18;
          16.39; 21.28, 21.41; 23.15
    31(1) 9.16, 16.40
    31(2) 9.16, 9.17; 16.41
    31(3) 2.28; 9.16, 16.29, 16.41
    31(4) . . . 2.28, 2.31; 9.16, 9.17; 16.41
    31(5) 3.8, 9.18, 16.42
    31(6) 9.17; 16.42
    31(7) 9.17
    32 . . . . 2.4; 20.155; 21.12
    33 . . . . 2.1, 2.4
    33(f), (g) 8.17
    34 . . . . . . 2.9; 3.8; 7.37; 11.1, 11.18,
             11.20; 21.12, 21.27
    35 . . . . . . 2.9, 2.19; 8.18; 11.1; 21.12
    35(1) 11.18
    35(1)(a)–(e) 11.18
    35(2) 11.18; 16.29
    35(3) 11.19
    35(4) 11.18
    36 . . . . 2.19; 8.18, 20.157; 21.12
    36(1) 2.6
    37 . . . . 2.19; 8.9; 21.12
    37(4) 8.9
    38 . . . . 7.37; 21.12
    39 . . . . 7.38; 11.22; 21.12
    39(1)–(3) 7.38
    40 . . . . 2.5, 2.7, 2.39; 8.12
    40(1) 2.7
    40(2), (3) 2.7
    40(4) 2.7
    41 . . . . 2.7, 2.27, 2.39; 8.12
    42 . . . . 2.22; 11.18
    43 . . . . 2.19; 11.18
    44 . . . . 5.4; 11.18
    44(1) 2.20
    44(2) 2.20, 2.21; 21.40
    44(3) 2.20, 2.22; 21.40
    44(3)(e), (f) 2.23
    44(4) . . . 2.20, 2.39; 5.90; 9.7; 21.40
    44(5) 21.40
    45 . . . . 2.23, 2.24; 21.40
    45(1)–(3) 2.23
    46 . . . . 3.1
    46(1), (2) 3.1
    46(3) 3.1; 16.29
    47 . . . . 3.5
    48 . . . . 2.35; 9.1, 9.10, 9.19
    48(1) 2.27; 8.11; 16.8
    48(2) . . . 2.35, 2.41; 8.11; 16.8, 16.26

Trade Marks Rules 1994,
SI 1994/2583–*contd*
r 48(2)(a), (b). 2.27
48(3) 2.27
49 . . . . . 2.30, 2.41; 9.4; 16.26, 16.30
49(1). 2.30; 16.29
49(2) 2.30
50 . . . . 2.30, 2.41
50(1) 2.30
51 . . . . . . 2.30, 2.31, 2.41; 9.6; 16.28
52 . . . . 2.24, 2.30, 2.32, 2.41; 9.6
52(1) 16.28
52(2) 16.28
53 . . . . 2.41; 16.26, 16.32
54 . . . . 2.36, 2.41; 16.26
55 . . . . 2.36, 2.37, 2.41; 16.26, 16.34
55(1) 16.34
55(2) 2.37
56(1), (2) 2.35; 16.36
57 . . . . 2.41; 16.24
57(1), (2) 16.24
57(3). 2.41; 16.24
58 . . . . 2.41
58(1)–(6) 16.25
59 . . . . 2.41
59(1) 16.26
59(1)(a), (b). 16.26
59(2). 16.26, 16.27
59(4) 16.26
60 . . . . 2.25, 2.27; 16.39
60(1). 2.25, 2.27
60(2) 2.25, 2.27, 2.29
60(3). 2.25, 2.27
61(3), (4). 2.26

Trade Marks Rules 1994,
SI 1994/2583–*contd*
62 . . . . 2.7, 2.25, 2.27, 2.29;
7.38; 8.7, 8.15; 9.5, 9.12, 9.17;
10.5, 10.7, 10.13, 10.15, 21.34
62(1). 2.28, 2.29; 9.3; 21.17
62(2) 2.28
62(3) 2.27, 2.28, 2.29; 3.8;
8.13; 9.3, 9.10, 9.11, 9.12;
9.16; 10.15; 21.17
62(4) 2.27
62(5). 2.27, 2.29
62(6). 2.27, 2.28
62(7). 2.25, 2.28, 2.29; 9.3
63 . . . . 2.16
64 . . . . 2.15, 2.26
65 . . . . 2.9
66 . . . . 2.18
67 . . . . 9.3

Trade Marks Rules 1994,
SI 1994/2583–*contd*
r 68 . . . . 8.21
69(1) 2.13, 2.26; 9.7
69(2) 2.26
Sch 2. . . . . 8.21
Sch 3 . . . . 2.5, 2.5, 2.6, 2.7
Sch 4 . . . . 2.5, 2.7

Unfair Terms in Consumer Contracts
Regulations 1994, SI 1994/3159 . . 20.90

Table of European legislation

References on the right-hand side are to paragraph numbers. Those paragraph numbers in bold indicate where the legislation is set out in full or in part.

DIRECTIVES

Directive 84/450/EEC (OJ L250, 19.9.84,
  p 17) (relating to the approximation
  of the laws etc of the member
  states concerning misleading
  advertising). 12.17

Directive 89/104/EEC (OJ L40, 11.2.89.
  p 1) (to approximate the laws of
  the Member States relating to trade
  marks) 1.1, 1.18; 5.3, 5.41;
              16.64;18.115; 22.16
Preamble. 4.11
art 2 . . . . **4.1**; 5.23, 5.26, 5.41; 24.2
  3 . . . . 5.1, 5.5, 5.15, 5.34, 5.91; 7.24;
                 18.116; 20.101
  3(1)(a) **5.13**, 5.14, 5.19, 5.33
  3(1)(b). **5.13**, 5.14, 5.19, 5.24,
        5.26, 5.33, 5.34, 5.38, 5.41,
             5.81, 5.82; 22.17
  3(1)(c) . . 5.10, 5.11, 5.12, **5.13**, 5.14,
        5.19, 5.38, 5.57, 5.60, 5.61,
            5.62, 5.82; 22.17
  3(1)(d) 5.13, **5.13**, 5.14,
            5.38, 5.82; 22.17
  3(1)(e) **5.92**, 5.96, 5.101; 22.19
  3(1)(f). 5.103; 22.18
  3(1)(g) 22.13, 22.18
  3(1)(h). 24.15
  3(2) 24.14
  3(2)(a) 22.19
  3(2)(c) 24.15
  3(2)(d) 5.118; 8.1; 22.19; 27.21

Directive 89/104/EEC (OJ L40, 11.2.89.
  p 1)–*contd*
art 3(3) 5.10, 5.14, 5.19, 5.63,
          5.81, 5.82, 5.83, 7.25
  4 . . . 6.1; 7.24; 18.116; 20.101: 24.17
  4(1). **6.27**: 24.19
  4(1)(b). 6.21, 6.37, 6.38, 6.39,
         6.40, 6.41, 6.43, 6.44
  4(2) 6.30
  4(3). 6.58, 24.20
  4(4)(a) 6.43, 6.58, 24.20
  4(4)(b) 6.75; 24.22
  4(4)(c) 27.23
  5 . . . . 6.28; 12.11; 20.10, 20.94,
         20.99, 20.100; 24.26
  5(1). 6.30; 24.29
  5(1)(a) 6.28; 20.10
  5(1)(b) 6.21, 6.28, 6.37; 20.10
  5(2) . . . 6.28, 6.59, 6.60; 24.20, 24.29
  5(2)(d). 6.59
  5(3). 6.60; 24.29
  5(4) 6.77; **12.50**, 12.52
  5(5) 12.17
  6 . . . . 5.10; 20.94. 20.98,
         20.99, 20.100; 24.26
  6(1) 12.17; 12.24; 22.31; 24.31
  6(1)(a) 5.41
  6(1)(b) 5.10, 5.11, 5.12
  6(1)(c) 12.30
  6(2). 12.31; 24.32
  7 . . . . 12.30, 12.34, 12.35, 12.36,
        12.37, 12.42, 12.43; 20.93,
        20.94, 20.100; 24.26, 24.33

Directive 89/104/EEC (OJ L40, 11.2.89.
 p 1)–*contd*
  art 7(1) 12.38
    7(2). 12.42, 12.48
    9 . . . . 7.31; 12.58; 27.26
    9(3) 27.28
    10(1) 7.3
    12 . . . . 7.3
    12(1). 7.3, 7.4
    12(1)(a), (b). 7.3
    12(2)(a) 24.27; 27.16
    12(2)(b). 22.13; 24.50; 27.17
    12(5) 7.3
    13 . . . . 1.18; 5.2; 7.3
    15(1). 10.4, 10.10, 10.12, 10.17
    15(2). 5.61; 10.4, 10.12, 10.17
  recital 5 . . . . 20.101
    6 . . . . 20.92, 20.99
    7 . . . . 5.5; 20.101
    7(b) 5.16
    7(10)(a) 5.16
    8 . . . . 18.111; 20.101
  annex. 4.14; 5.94; 6.21; 24.19
  para 2(a) 4.3
    2(b). 4.3
    7 . . . . 12.25

Directive 97/55/EC (OJ L290,
 23.10.97, p 18) (amending
 Directive 84/450) 12.17

REGULATIONS
Regulation 802/68/EEC (OJ L148, 27.6.68,
 p 1) (on the common definition of the
 concept of the origin of goods) . . 19.112
  art 5. . . . . 19.112
    14. . . . . 19.112

Regulation 823/87/EEC (OJ L84, 27.3.87,
 p 59) (laying down special provisions
 relating to quality wines produced in
 specified regions) 5.107

Regulation 2658/87/EEC (OJ L256, 7.9.87,
 p 1) (on the tariff and Statistical nomenclature and on the CCT) 19.10
  annex I 19.10

Regulation 2081/92/EEC (OJ L208, 24.7.92,
 p 1) (on the protection of geographical
 indications and designations of origin
 for agricultural products and
 foodstuffs) 5.86, 5.107; 22.49

Regulation 2913/92/EEC (OJ L302,
 19.10.92, p 1) (establishing the
 community Customs Code). . 18.77; 19.5
  art 84(1)(a) 18.77

Regulation 2454/93/EEC (OJ L253,
 11.11.93, p 1) (laying down provision
 for the implementation of 2913/92
 establishing the Community
 Customs Code) 19.5, 19.22
  art 1 . . . . 19.48, 19.106
    2 . . . . 19.107
    2(a) 19.48
    2(b) 19.49
    2(c) 19.49, 19.50, 19.107
    3 . . . . 19.50, 19.51, 19.55
    4 . . . . 19.90
    14(1) 19.22
    78(6) 19.22
    79 . . . . 19.22
    106(5) 19.22
    183 . . . . 19.22
    189 . . . . 19.16
    240 . . . . 19.22
    241(1), (2). 19.22
    804 . . . . 19.22
    813(1) 19.16
    813(2) 19.22
    877(1)(c). 19.22
    885(1) 19.22
    915 . . . . 19.5

Regulation 40/94/EEC (OJ L11, 14.1.94,
 p 1) (on the Community Trade
 Mark). 1.3, 1.19, 1.22; 4.5; 5.3,
      5.91; 6.59; 13.7; 20.3; 22.13,
      22.17, 22.35; 23.1, 23.3, 23.27,
      23.28; 24.2, 24.26; 25.1, 25.6
  art 1(1) **23.1**, 23.22; 24.4
    1(2) **23.2**
    2 . . . . 23.1, 23.26
    3 . . . . 23.26
    3(3) 27.20
    4 . . . . **24.2**, 24.3; 30.2
    5 . . . . 14.56; 23.26; 24.5, 24.7;
      26.3, 26.7, 26.8, 26.11, 26.14;
      27.11, 27.18, 27.20, 27.29
    5(1)(d). 27.18
    5(2), (3). 24.6
    6 24,7
    7 . . . . 5.1; 14.55, 14.56; 17.22;
      23.26; 24.11, 24.13; 26.4,
      26.11; 27.20; 30.4

Regulation 40/94/EEC (OJ L11, 14.1.94,
  p 1)–*contd*
  art 7(1) 24.9, 24.13, 24.14
  7(1)(a) **24.11**
  7(1)(b) 5.38, 5.47; **24.11**; 27.20
  7(1)(c) 5.38; **24.11**; 27.20; 30.4
  7(1)(d) **24.11**; 27.20
  7(1)(e)–(g) **24.11**
  7(1)(h), (i) 24.15; 24.16
  7(1)(j) 24.14
  7(2) 24.9, 24.13
  7(3) 24.12; 30.4
  8 . . . . 6.1; 17.4; 24.23, 24.37;
                25.10; 26.7, 26.8, 26.16
  8(1) 24.18, 24.19; 26.18; 27.37
  8(2) 6.59; 24.18; 26.18,
                26.24; 27.27, 27.37
  8(2)(a) 26.27
  8(2)(b) 26.31
  8(2)(c) 26.21
  8(3) 24.21, 24.54; 26.18; 27.37
  8(4) 24.22; 26.18, 26.24; 27.27, 27.37
  8(5) 24.18, 24.20; 26.18,
                26.21, 26.24; 27.37
  9 . . . . 24.28, 24.33; 31.11
  9(1) 24.29
  9(1)(a)–(c) 24.29
  9(2) 24.29
  9(3) 21.16; 24.30; 31.2, 31.4,
                31.5, 31.12, 31.19
  9(4) 21.16
  10 . . . . 24.27, 24.28
  11 . . . . 23.15; 24.21
  12 . . . . 24.31, 24.39
  13 . . . . 24.33
  14 . . . . 17.28
  14(1)–(3) 24.36
  15 . . . . 24.38; 27.13, 27.15
  15(1) 24.38, 24.41
  15(2), (3) 26.29
  16 . . . . . . 24.45, 24.49, 24.50, 24.51,
                24.54, 24.55, 24.57, 24.59
  16(1)–(3) 24.46, 24.47, 24.48
  16(4) 24.59
  17 . . . . . . 24.45, 24.49, 24.50, 24.54
  17(1), (2) 24.51
  17(3) 24.51, 24.54
  17(4), (5) 24.52
  17(6) 24.52, 24.53
  17(8) 24.53
  18 . . . . 24.45, 24.49, 24.54
  19 . . 24.45, 24.49, 24.54, 24.55; 27.8
  19(2) 27.1

Regulation 40/94/EEC (OJ L11, 14.1.94,
  p 1)–*contd*
  art 20 . . 24.45, 24.49, 24.54, 24.55; 27.8
  20(1), (2) 24.55
  20(3) 27.1
  21 . . . . 24.45, 24.49, 24.54,
                24.55, 24.56, 24.56; 27.8
  21(1) 24.59; 27.1
  22 . . 24.45, 24.49, 24.54; 27.8; 31.14
  22(1), (2) 24.57
  22(3), (4) 24.58; 30.10
  22(5) 24.57; 27.1
  23 . . . . 24.45, 24.49, 24.54
  23(1)–(3) 24.59
  24 . . . . 24.45, 24.49, 24.54
  25 . . . . 17.2; 24.45
  25(1) 25.1
  25(1)(b) 23.14; 25.4; 28.6
  25(2)–(4) 25.1
  26 . . . . 17.2; 25.2, 25.3
  26(1) 25.2, 25.4
  26(2), (3) 25.2
  27 . . . . 17.2; 25.4; 26.2
  28 . . . . 17.2; 25.3
  29 . . . . 17.2, 17.8; 23.26; 25.6, 25.12
  29(1) 25.8; 28.29
  29(3) 25.7, 25.10
  29(5) 25.6
  28(8) 25.8
  30 . . . . 17.2, 17.8; 25.9
  31 . . . . 17.2, 17.8; 25.10, 25.12
  32 . . . . 17.2, 17.8; 24.24; 25.11
  33 . . . . 17.2, 17.8; 25.12
  33(2), (3) 25.12
  34 . . . . 6.3; 17.2, 17.8; 23.15;
                24.18, 24.24; 25.13,
                25.14, 25.15; 27.7
  34(1) 25.13
  34(2) 24.18: 25.16
  34(3) 23.15; 25.16: 25.16
  35 . . . . 6.3; 17.2, 17.8; 23.15;
                24.24; 25.4, 25.13,
                25.14, 25.15; 27.7
  35(2) 25.16
  36 . . . . . . 17.2, 17.4; 26.1, 26.2; 30.7
  36(2)–(7) 26.2
  37 . . . . 17.2, 17.4; 26.1, 26.3,
                26.4, 26.8, 26.11
  38 . 17.2, 17.4; 26.1, 26.4, 26.11; 30.7
  38(1) 17.10
  38(2) 17.10,17.11; 24.34; 26.4
  38(3) 17.10; 26.4
  38(6) 17.10

Regulation 40/94/EEC (OJ L11, 14.1.94,
  p 1)–*contd*
  art 39 .... 17.2, 17.10; 26.1, 26.7, 26.10
    39(1) 17.10; 26.7, 26.9
    39(2)............... 17.10; 26.8
    39(3) 17.10; 26.8, 26.9
    39(4)............ 26.8, 26.10
    39(5) 26.9
    39(6) 17.10; 26.9, 26.11
    39(7) 26.10
    40 .... 17.2, 26.1
    40(1), (2)............... 26.11
    41 .... 17.2, 17.4; 23.3; 26.1,
              26.11, 26.14, 26.15;
              27.19; 30.7
    41(1) 29.3
    41(2) 17.22; 26.14, 26.15
    42 .... 17.2, 17.4, 17.12, 17.23;
              26.1, 26.16, 26.24
    42(1)......... 17.23; 26.18, 26.27,
              26.35; 27.37; 28.29
    42(1)(a)–(c)............... 17.23
    42(2)............... 26.12, 26.18
    42(3) 26.18, 26.19, 26.20
    43 .... 17.2, 17.4; 26.1, 26.16,
              26.26; 29.10
    43(1)............... 26.26; 29.10
    43(2), (3) 24.43; 26.17, 26.26,
              26.27, 26.29, 26.30; 27.49
    43(4) 26.30; 27.50; 29.10
    43(5), (6)................. 26.31
    44 .... 4.4; 17.2; 26.1, 26.12
    44(1)............... 26.12, 26.31
    44(2)...... 26.12, 26.13, 26.18; 30.7
    45 .... 17.2; 26.1, 26.35
    46................... 17.2; 27.1
    47 .... 17.2; 27.1, 27.2
    47(2) 27.1
    47(3) 27.1, 27.2; 28.28
    47(4)............... 27.1; 28.28
    47(5).............. 27.1, 27.2
    47(6) 27.2
    48 .... 17.2
    48(1), (2)................. 27.3
    48(3) 27.4
    49 .... 17.4, 17.25; 27.8
    49(1)–(3)................. 27.8
    50 .... 7.3; 17.4; 24.38; 27.10,
              27.11, 27.15, 27.16,
              27.29; 30.11
    50(1)(a) 17.26; 24.41; 27.13,
              27.14, 27.29
    50(1)(b) .. 17.26; 24.27; 27.16, 27.29

Regulation 40/94/EEC (OJ L11, 14.1.94,
  p 1)–*contd*
  art 50(1)(c) .. 17.26; 24.50; 27.17, 27.29
    50(1)(d)....... 17.26; 27.18, 27.29
    50(2) 27.11
    51 ... 17.4; 24.9; 27.20, 27.35; 30.12
    51(1)(b) 27.21, 27.26
    51(2) 27.20
    51(3) 27.22, 27.25, 27.22
    52 ...... 17.4; 25.10; 27.23, 27.37,
              27.35; 30.12
    52(1) 27.24, 27.37, 27.39
    52(1)(a)................. 27.23
    52(1)(b)................. 24.21
    52(2) 24.23, 24.37; 27.23, 27.24,
              27.37, 27.39; 29.3
    52(3)............. 27.23, 27.50
    52(4). 27.24, 27.38
    52(5).............. 27.25, 27.50
    53 .... 17.4; 24.35, 24.37; 27.26
    53(1) 27.26
    53(2)............. 12.23; 27.27
    53(3)............. 24.35; 27.28
    54 .... 17.4
    54(1) 27.29
    54(2) 27.30
    54(3) 27.30, 27.32, 27.34
    54(3)(a), (b)............... 27.33
    55 .... 17.4; 27.35, 27.35,
              27.39, 27.46; 31.15
    55(1)(c) 27.39
    55(2) 27.38, 27.43, 27.46
    55(3)............. 27.38, 27.38
    56 .... 17.4; 24.53; 27.10, 27.35,
              27.47; 29.10
    56(1)..... 27.47, 27.48, 27.49; 29.10
    56(2) 24.43; 26.27; 27.49
    56(3) 24.43; 27.49; 31.15
    56(4) 27.50; 29.10; 31.15
    56(5), (6) 27.50; 31.15
    57 ...... 17.2, 17.4; 29.1, 29.3, 29.4
    57(1) 29.2
    57(2) 17.16; 29.2, 29.4
    58, 59 .... 17.2, 17.4, 17.27;
              29.1, 29.3, 29.4
    60 ..... 17.2, 17.4; 29.1, 29.8, 29.15
    60(2) 29.8
    61 .... 17.2, 17.4; 29.1
    61(1) 29.9
    61(2) 29.10
    62 .... 17.2, 17.4; 29.1, 29.12, 29.13
    62(1), (2)................. 29.12
    62(3) 29.14

Regulation 40/94/EEC (OJ L11, 14.1.94,
p 1)–*contd*
art 63 . . . . 1.22; 17.2, 17.4, 17.34,
                27.21; 29.1
63(1)–(4). 29.16
63(5). 29.14, 29.16
63(6) 29.16
64 . . . . 17.2; 30.1, 30.7
64(1). 30.2, 30.3
64(2). 30.4, 30.6
64(3) 30.2
65 . . . . 17.2; 30.1, 30.2, 30.7,
                30.9, 30.11
65(1) 30.5
65(2). 30.4, 30.6
66 . . . . 17.2, 17.4; 30.1, 30.2,
           30.9, 30.7, 30.11, 30.12
66(2), (3) 30.7, 30.11
67 . . . . . . 17.2; 30.1, 30.2, 30.7, 30.9
68 . . . . 17.2; 30.1, 30.2, 30.8
69 . . . . 17.2; 30.1, 30.2
69(1) 30.9
69(2). 30.9, 30.11
69(3), (4). 30.9
70 . . . . 17.2; 30.1, 30.2, 30.10
70(1), (2). 30.10
71 . . . . . 17.2, 17.4; 30.1, 30.2, 30.11
71(b), (c) 30.11
72 . . . . 17.2; 30.1, 30.2, 30.12
73 . . . . 17.2, 17.3, 17.4, 17.14,
         17.20; 28.1, 28.9, 28.10
74 . . . . . . 17.2, 17.3, 17.4; 28.1, 28.9
74(1) 17.15; 28.11, 28.12
74(2) 28.11
75 . . . . 17.2, 17.3, 17.4; 26.3,
        26.4; 28.1, 28.9, 28.13
75(2), (3). 17.17
76 . . 17.2, 17.3, 17.4;28.1, 28.9, 28.13
76(1)(f) 26.28
76(2) 17.16
77 . . . . 17.2, 17.3, 17.4; 24.53;
      28.1, 28.9, 28.10, 28.14
78 . . . . 17.2, 17.3, 17.4, 17.19;
      28.1, 28.9, 28.28, 28.31
78(1) 28.28
78(2). 28.27, 28.28
78(3) 28.27
78(6), (7). 28.30
78(8) 28.31
79 . . . . 17.2, 17.3, 17.4; 28.1,
      28.9, 28.12, 28.32
80 . . . . 17.2, 17.3, 17.4; 28.1,
      28.9, 28.33

Regulation 40/94/EEC (OJ L11, 14.1.94,
p 1)–*contd*
art 81 . . . . 17.2; 26.25; 28.1, 28.34
81(1), (2). 17.21
81(3). 17.21; 28.34
81(4) 17.21; 26.33; 28.34
81(6). 17.21; 28.34
82 . . . . 17.2 28.1
83 . . . . 17.2; 28.1, 28.35
84 . . . . 17.2; 28.1, 28.35, 28.40
84(1) 28.36
84(2). 26.35; 28.36
84(3) 28.36
85 . . . . 17.2; 28.1, 28.35, 28.35
86 . . . . 17.2; 28.1, 28.35, 28.40
87 . . . . 17.2; 28.1, 28.35
88 . . . . 17.2; 28.1, 28.7
88(1) 28.41
88(2). 28.7, 28.18, 28.20, 28.41
88(3) 28.41
89 . . . . 17.2; 23.8, 23.12, 23.22;
      28.7, 28.41, 28.42
90 . . . . 17.2, 17.32; 31.1, 31.2
90(1) 31.10
90(2). 17.33; 31.2
90(2)(a) 31.2
91. . . . . 17.2; 23.1, 23.17;
      24.28; 31.1, 31.3
91(1) 17.28
91(1)(c) 31.30
91(2)–(4). 31.3
91(5). 17.28; 31.3
92 . . . . . . 17.2, **17.30**, **17.33**; 24.28;
     31.1, 31.2, 31.3, 31.4, 31.5,
     31.6, 31.10, 31.21, 31.23
93 . . . . 17.2, 17.33; 31.1, 31.3, 31.19
93(1) . . 17.33; 31.5, 31.9, 31.11, 31.24
93(2) 17.33; 31.5, 31.7, 31.9,
     31.11, 31.19, 31.24
93(3). 17.33; 31.5, 31.8,
     31.9, 31.11, 31.19
93(4). 31.5, 31.9, 31.11, 31.19
93(5). 17.33; 31.5, 31.11,
     31.19, 31.24
94 . . . . 17.2, 17.33; 31.1, 31.3, 31.18
94(1) 31.11
94(2) 17.33
95 . . . . 17.2, 17.29; 31.1, 31.3
95(1)–(3). 31.12
96 . . . . 27.24; 17.2, 17.29; 31.1,
     31.2, 31.3, 31.4
96(1), (2). 31.13
96(3), (4) 31.14, 31.15

Regulation 40/94/EEC (OJ L11, 14.1.94,
  p 1)–*contd*
  art 96(5), (6) 31.15
    96(7) 31.16, 31.25
    97 . . . . 17.2, 17.29; 24.36; 31.1, 31.3
    97(1), (2) 17.31; 31.17
    97(3) 17.31; 24.36; 31.17
    98 . . . 17.2, 17.29; 24.36; 31.1, 31.11
    98(1), (2) 31.18
    99 . . . . 17.2, 17.29; 24.30; 31.1,
                          31.3, 31.11, 31.19
    99(1) 24.30; 31.19
    99(2) 31.18, 31.19
    100 . . . . 17.2; 31.1, 31.3
    100(1) 17.30
    100(2) 17.30; 31.25
    100(3) 17.30; 31.16, 31.25
    101 . . . . 17.2, 17.28; 31.1, 31.3
    101(1)–(3) 31.10, 31.21, 31.23
    102 . . . . 17.2; 24.28; 31.1, 31.10
    103 . . . . 17.2; 31.1
    104 . . . . 31.1
    105 . . . . 31.1, 31.26, 31.33
    105(1) 31.26
    105(1)(a) 31.28, 31.30, 31.32
    105(1)(b) 31.29, 31.32
    105(2), (3) 31.26, 31.30
    105(4) 31.32
    106 . . . . 24.37
    106(1) 12.23
    106(2) 24.37
    107 . . . . 24.32; 24.37
    107(1), (2) 24.32
    108 . . . . . . 2.14; 23.16; 24.24, 24.40,
                        24.41; 26.3, 26.11,
                        26.34; 27.51
    108(1) 24.40
    108(2) 24.24, 24.40, 24.41
    108(2)(a) 24.40, 24.41
    108(3)–(7) 24.24
    109 . . . . 23.16; 24.24, 24.25
    109(2) 24.25
    110 . . . . 23.1, 23.16; 24.24, 24.25
    111–114 . . . . 23.4
    115 . . . . 23.5; 25.9; 27.41, 27.43,
                        27.44; 28.45
    115(2) 17.18
    115(3) 25.3; 27.41, 27.42, 27.43
    115(4) 17.18
    115(5) 27.41, 27.42
    115(6) 17.18; **27.41**, 27.43
    115(7) 17.18; 23.5; 26.23;
                          27.42, 27.45

Regulation 40/94/EEC (OJ L11, 14.1.94,
  p 1)–*contd*
  art 116, 117 . . . . 23.7
    118 . . . . 23.4
    119–124 . . . . 23.8
    125 . . . . 17.3; 23.8; 29.1
    126 . . . . 17.4; 23.8; 29.1
    127 . . . . 17.4; 23.8; 29.1
    128 . . . . 17.4, 17.24; 23.8; 29.1
    129 . . . . 23.8; 29.1
    130, 131 . . . . 17.4; 23.8; 29.1
    132 . . . . 23.8; 28.36; 29.1
    132(1), (3) 28.13
    133–139 . . . . 23.8
    140, 141 . . . . 23.9
    143(1)–(4) 23.1
    annex 1.19; 23.25
  para 3(a) 4.4
    4 . . . . 24.3
    4(a), (b) 4.3
    5(b) 6.32

Regulation 3288/94/EC (OJ L349,
  31.12.94, p 83) (amending Regulation
  40/94) 1.3; 17.2; 23.26; 24.14

Regulation 3295/94/EEC (OJ L341,
  30.12.94, p 14) (on certain procedures
  for applying the Europe Agreement
  establishing an association between
  the EC and their Member States,
  of the one part, and the Czech
  Republic, of the other
  part) 1.4, 18.74; 19.3
  art 1(1) 19.73
    1(1)(a) 19.7, 19.19, 19.20, 19.21,
                      19.22, 19.34, 19.35, 19.42,
                      19.44, 19.60, 19.77,
                      19.139, 19.158
    1(1)(b) 19.5, 19.43
    1(2) 19.42
    1(2)(a) 19.5, 19.7, 19.20,
                      19.60, 19.67, 19.73,
                      19.75, 9.97, 19.100,
                      19.101, 19.124
    1(2)(b) 19.80, 19.101,
                      19.106, 19.107
    1(2)(c) 19.118
    1(3) 19.38, 19.39, 19.42, 19.101
    1(4) 18.77; 19.4, 19.42
    2 . . . . 19.36, 19.44, 19.71,
                      19.106, 19.128, 19.139
    2(b), (c) 19.106

Regulation 3295/94/EEC (OJ L341,
30.12.94, p 14)–*contd*
art 3 ...... 19.44, 19.68, 19.69, 19.70,
19.71, 19.72, 19.73, 19.74,
19.75, 19.76, 19.77, 19.85,
19.88, 19.95, 19.97, 19.99,
19.100, 19.101, 19.102,
19.106, 19.118, 19.124,
19.131, 19.132, 19.135, 19.139
3(1) 19.44, 19.68, 19.107
3(2)........... 19.48, 19.51, 19.53,
19.71, 19.85, 19.116
3(3) 19.53, 19.56, 19.68
3(4) 19.57, 19.68, 19.72
3(5)........... 19.56, 19.58, 19.68,
19.70, 19.72, 19.132
3(6)..... 19.68, 19.72, 19.85, 19.85
3(7) 19.69
4 .... 19.61, 19.100, 19.101,
19.102, 19.124
5 .... 19.37, 19.70, 19.71,
19.72, 19.124
5(1), (2) 19.70, 19.72
6 ...... 19.73, 19.74, 19.75, 19.78,
19.79, 19.85, 19.101, 19.101,
19.105, 19.106, 19.118, 19.119,
19.124, 19.127, 19.128,
19.142, 19.161
6(1) **19.73**, 19.74, 19.75, 19.76,
19.77, 19.78, 19.80, 19.90,
19.100, 19.102, 19.118,
19.120, 19.127
6(2)........... 19.80, 19.83, 19.90,
19.118, **19.122**, 19.123, 19.125
6(2)(a) 19.84, 19.127, 153
6(2)(b) 19.83, 19.84
7 .... 19.79, 19.84, 19.105,
19.106, 19.123, 19.124,
19.125, 19.126, 19.127,
19.142, 19.150
7(1)....... 19.142, 19.144, 19.149,
19.150, 19.152, 19.153,
19.156, 19.157, 19.158,
19.159, 19.160
7(2)............. 19.126, 19.150
8 .... 19.79, 19.84, 19.130
8(1)(a), (b)................ 19.130
8(2), (3) 19.130
9 .... 19.130, 19.134
9(1)............... 19.131, 19.133
9(3) 19.134

Regulation 3295/94/EEC (OJ L341,
30.12.94, p 14)–*contd*
art 10 .... 19.14, 19.130, 19.137
11......... 19.130, 19.138, 19.139
12 ... 19.109, 19.124, 19.130, 19.141
13 ... 19.108, 19.124, 19.130, 19.141
13(1), (2)................. 19.108
13(3) 19.108, 19.109,
19.110, 19.115
13(4) 19.109, 19.111, 19.115
14 .... 19.130
15, 16............. 19.130, 19.141
17 .... 19.141
recital 5..................... 19.124
6 .... 19.145, 19.152
7..................... 19.124
12.................... 19.14

Regulation 1367/95/EEC (OJ L133, 17.6.95,
p 2) (laying down provisions for the
implementation of 3295/94 laying down
measures to prohibit the release for free
circulation, export,re-export or entry for
a suspensive procedure of counterfeit
and pirated goods) 19.3

Regulation 2868/95/EEC (OJ L303,
15.12.95, p 1) (implementing 40/94
on the Community
trade mark).......... 13.7; 17.2; 20.3
rule 1 .... 25.2, 25.4
1(1)(a) 17.8
1(1)(b) 17.8; 29.3
1(1)(c), (d) 17.8
1(1)(e) 17.8; 27.39; 28.25; 29.3
1(1)(f) 17.8; 25.9, 25.10
1(1)(g) 17.8; 25.12
1(1)(h) 17.8; 25.15
1(1)(i)–(k) 17.8
2................ 17.8; 25.3, 25.4
2(1)–(4)................... 25.3
3 .... 17.8; 25.3, 25.4; 26.12
5.................... 17.8; 25.1
6............... 17.8; 25 4, 25.9
6(1), (2).................. 25.9
6(3)................. 25.9, 25.15
6(4) 25.9
7........................ 25.4
7(1), (2).................. 25.12
7(3) 25.15
8 .... 25.4, 25.15

Regulation 2868/95/EEC (OJ L303,
    15.12.95, p 1)–*contd*
rule 8(1), (4) 25.15
    9 . . . . 17.4, 17.8
    9(1) 25.4
    9(1)(b) 26.2
    9(2) 25.4
    9(3) 25.4
    9(3)(a)–(d) 25.4
    9(4)–(7) 25.4; 26.2
    9(8) 25.4
    10 . . . . 17.4, 17.9
    11 . . . . 17.4; 26.4
    11(1)–(3) 17.11; 26.4
    12 . . . . 17.12; 26.11
    13(1) 26.12
    13(2) 26.12, 26.13
    13(3)–(5) 26.12
    14 . . . . 26.13
    14(1), (3), (4) 26.13
    15 . . . . 17.4, 17.23; 26.12,
        26.13, 26.16, 26.19; 27.4
    15(2) 26.20
    15(2)(b), (c) 26.19
    16 . . . . . . 17.4; 26.12, 26.13, 26.16,
        26.20; 27.4
    16(1) 17.23; 26.20, 26.21,
        26.23, 26.31
    16(2) 26.20, **26.21**, 26.22,
        26.23, 26.31
    16(3) 26.20, 26.23
    17 . . . . . . 17.4; 26.12, 26.13, 26.16,
        26.23; 27.4
    17(1)–(3) 26.23, 26.24
    18 . . . . . . 17.4; 26.12, 26.13, 26.16,
        26.17, 26.24, 26.25; 27.4
    18(1)–(3) 26.24
    19 . . . . . . 17.4, 17.23; 26.12, 26.13,
        26.16, 26.17 26.20,
        26.31; 27.4
    19(1) 26.23, 26.25, 26.26, 26.31
    19(2), (3) 26.23, 26.25
    20 . . . . . . 17.4; 26.12, 26.13, 26.16,
        26.26, 26.30; 27.4; 29.10
    20(1) 26.31
    20(2) 26.20, 26.22, 26.31
    20(3), (4), (6) 26.31
    21 . . . . . . 17.4; 26.12, 26.13, 26.16,
        26.33; 27.4
    21(1) 26.33
    21(2)–(4) 26.33; 27.49
    22 . . . . . . 17.4, 17.23; 26.12, 26.13,
        26.16; 27.4, 27.49

Regulation 2868/95/EEC (OJ L303,
    15.12.95, p 1)–*contd*
rule 22(1) 26.28
    22(2) 26.28, 26.29
    22(3), (4) 26.28
    23 . . . . 26.35
    23(2), (4) 17.13
    24 . . . . 26.35
    25(2)–(5) 27.4
    26 . . . . 27.6
    26(1), (2), (4)–(7) 27.5
    27(1)–(3) 27.6
    28 . . . . 27.7
    28(1) 27.7
    29 . . . . 27.1
    30 . . . . 27.2
    30(2)–(6) 27.2
    31, 32 . . . . 24.52
    33 . . . . 24.56, 24.58
    34 . . . . 24.56, 24.57, 24.58
    35 . . . . 24.56, 24.58
    36 . . . . 27.8
    36(1)–(3) 27.9
    37 . . . . 17.4, 17.26; 27.35,
        27.39, 27.46
    37(b) 27.39
    37(b)(i), (ii) 27.39
    37(b)(iii) 27.40
    37(b)(iv) 27.39, 27.40
    37(c) 27.39
    38 . . . . 17.4, 17.26; 27.35,
        27.40, 27.46
    38(1) 27.41, 27.43, 27.46
    38(2) 27.44, 27.46
    38(3) 27.45
    39 . . . . 17.4; 27.35, 27.45,
        27.46, 27.47
    39(1)–(3) 27.46
    40 . 17.4, 17.26; 27.35, 27.47; 29.10
    40(1) 27.45, 27.47
    40(2) 27.47
    40(3) 27.47, 27.48
    40(5) 27.47, 27.49
    41 . . . . 17.4, 17.22; 27.35
    42 . . . . 30.1
    43 . . . . 30.1
    43(1) 30.5
    43(2) 30.6, 30.9
    43(2)(a)–(f) 30.6
    43(3) 30.6
    44–46 . . . . 24.24, 24.25
    48 . . . . 17.4, 17.27
    48(1) 29.3, 29.5

Regulation 2868/95/EEC (OJ L303,
15.12.95, p 1)–*contd*
rule 48(1)(a), (b)................ 29.5
48(1)(c)................... 29.4
48(2)........... 29.3, 29.4, 29.5
49................... 17.4; 29.4
49(1)..................... 29.4
49(2)..................... 29.5
49(3)..................... 29.3
50 .... 17.4; 29.12, 29.13
50(1)........ 29.10, 29.11, 29.13
50(3)..................... 29.15
51 .... 17.4, 17.27; 29.15
52 .... 26.3, 26.4; 28.1, 28.9,
28.10, 29.11, 29.13
52(1)................... 17.20
52(2)................... 29.14
53 .... 26.3, 26.4; 28.1, 28.9,
28.10, 29.11
54 .... 26.3, 26.4; 28.1, 28.9, 29.11
54(1), (2) 28.10
55 .... 26.3, 26.4; 28.1, 28.9,
28.10, 28.15, 29.11
56 .... 26.3, 26.4; 28.1, 28.9,
28.13; 29.10, 29.11
57 .... 26.3, 26.4; 28.1, 28.9,
28.13; 29.10, 29.11
58 .... 26.3, 26.4; 28.1, 28.9,
28.13; 29.10, 29.11
58(3), (4) 28.13
59, 60 ...... 26.3, 26.4; 28.1, 28.9,
28.13; 29.10, 29.11
61 .... 17.7; 26.3, 26.4; 28.1,
28.9, 28.14; 29.10, 29.11
61(1) 28.15, 28.23
61(2) 28.16, 28.23
62 .... 17.7; 26.3, 26.4; 28.1,
28.9, 28.14, 28.16, 28.17,
28.21; 29.10, 29.11
62(1)........ 28.17, 28.20, 28.24
62(2) 28.18, 28.20
62(3), (4) 28.19, 28.20
62(5)................... 28.20
63 .... 17.7; 26.3, 26.4; 28.1,
28.9, 28.14, 28.16, 28.21;
29.10, 29.11
64 .... 17.7; 26.3, 26.4; 28.1,
28.9, 28.14, 28.16, 28.22;
29.10, 29.11
65 .... 17.7; 26.3, 26.4; 28.1,
28.9, 28.14, 28.16;
29.10, 29.11

Regulation 2868/95/EEC (OJ L303,
15.12.95, p 1)–*contd*
rule 65(1).................... 28.23
66 .... 17.7; 26.3, 26.4; 28.1,
28.9, 28.14, 28.16,
28.24; 29.11
66(1), (2) 28.24; 29.10
67 .... 17.7; 26.3, 26.4; 28.1,
28.9, 28.14, 28.25;
29.10, 29.11
67(2), (3) 28.25
68 .... 17.7; 26.3, 26.4; 28.1,
28.9, 28.14, 28.26;
29.10, 29.11
69 .... 17.7; 26.3, 26.4; 28.1,
28.9, 28.14, 28.26;
29.10. 29.11
70 .... 17.6; 26.3, 26.4; 28.1,
28.2, 28.5; 29.10. 29.11
70(1)–(5) 28.5
71 .... 17.6; 25.4, 25.9; 26.1,
26.3, 26.4, 26.4, 26.12, 26.25,
26.31; 27.44; 28.1, 28.2;
29.10, 29.11; 30.5
71(1)...... **17.6**; 26.1, 26.3, 26.18,
26.20, 26.24, 26.28, 26.35;
27.4, 27.6, 27.7, 27.9, 27.43,
27.46; **28.2**, 28.3, 28.5; 29.3,
29.5, 29.11; 30.5
71(2)...... **17.6**; 26.1, 26.3, 26.24;
28.2, 28.3, 28.5
72 .... 17.6; 26.3, 26.4; 28.1,
28.2, 28.6; 29.10, 29.11
72(1)–(4) 28.6
73 .... 26.3, 26.4, 26.33; 28.1,
28.2, 28.7, 28.8;
29.10, 29.11
72(1)–(3) 28.7
74 .... 26.3, 26.4; 28.1, 28.33;
29.10, 29.11
75 .... 26.3, 26.4; 28.1, 28.41;
29.10, 29.11
75(1).................... 28.25
76 .... 26.3, 26.4; 28.1. 28.41,
28.42; 29.10, 29.11
75(2)–(5) 28.42
77 .... 26.3, 26.4; 28.1. 28.43;
29.10, 29.11
78............. 26.3, 26.4; 28.1;
29.10, 29.11
79 .... 17.7; 26.3, 26.4; 28.1,
28.44; 29.10, 29.11

Regulation 2868/95/EEC (OJ L303,
  15.12.95, p 1)–*contd*
rule 79(a) 17.7
    80–82 . . . . . . 17.7; 26.3, 26.4; 28.1,
                28.44; 29.10, 29.11
    83 . . . . 26.3, 26.4; 28.1, 28.44;
                29.10, 29.11
    83(4), (7) 17.5
    84 . . . . 26.3, 26.4; 28.1, 28.35;
                29.10, 29.11
    84(2) 17.13
    84(3)(n), (m) 31.15
    85 . . . . 26.3, 26.4; 28.1, 28.35,
                28.38; 29.10, 29.11
    85(1), (2) 17.12
    86, 87 . . . . . 26.3, 26.4; 28.1, 28.35,
                28.38; 29.10, 29.11
    88 . . . . 26.3, 26.4; 28.1, 28.35;
                29.10, 29.11
    89–91 . . . . . 26.3, 26.4; 28.1, 28.35,
                28.37; 29.10, 29.11
    92, 93 . . . . . 26.3, 26.4; 28.1, 28.35,
                28.40; 29.10, 29.11
    94 . . . . 26.3, 26.4; 28.1, 28.34;
                29.10, 29.11, 29.15
    94(1), (2), (4) 17.21
    95 . . . . 26.3, 26.4; 28.1, 28.45;
                29.10, 29.11
    95(a) 17.18
    96 . . . . 26.3, 26.4; 28.1, 28.45;
                29.10, 29.11
    97 . . . . 26.3, 26.4; 28.1, 28.45;
                29.10, 29.11
    97(1), (4) 28.45
    98, 99 . . . . . . 26.3, 26.4; 28.1, 28.45;
                29.10, 29.11
    100 . . . . 29.10, 29.11

Regulation 2869/95/EEC (OJ L303,
  15.12.95, p 33) (on the fees payable to
  the Office for Harmonisation in the
  Internal Market (Trade Marks and
  Designs) 17.2; 23.9
art 2 . . . . 25.2

Regulation 216/96/EC (OJ L28, 6.2.96)
  laying down procedure rules of the
  Boards of Appeal of the Office for
  Harmonisation in the Internet
  Market) 23.9; 29.1
art 7 . . . . 29.6
  7(2) 29.6
  8 . . . . 29.7
  9 . . . . 29.11
  11 . . . . 29.9

Regulation 2261/98 OJ L292, 30.10.98,
  p 1) (amending annex 1 to Regulation
  2658/87) 19.10
art 1 . . . . 19.10
  1(7) 19.70
annex 19.10

Regulation 241/99/EC (OJ L027, 2.2.99,
  p 1) (amending Regulation
  3295/94) 19.3, 18.74; 19.60
art 1(6) 19.60

TREATIES

Treaty of Rome (as amended by the Treaty
  of Amsterdam, and renamed Treaty
  on European Union,
TEU) 1.3; 12.34; 22.42
art 12(25) 19.15, 19.22
  14 . . . . 19.93
  25 . . . . 19.15
  28 . . . . 19.28
  36(30) 12.42
  86(82) 7.21; 12.7
  110 . . . . 19.93
  155(211) 19.108, 19.114
  165(221) 16.61
  177(234) 19.155; 23.24
  189(249) 19.108
  228(300) 22.38, 22.39
  234(307) 16.1, **16.58**, **16.59**,
                16.66; 17.1
  234(307)(2) 16.59
  234(307)(3) 16.59, 16.60
  235(308) 23.1; 25.7

Table of international conventions and treaties

References on the right-hand side are to paragraph numbers. Those paragraph numbers in **bold** *indicate where the material is set out in full or in part.*

AGREEMENTS

Madrid Agreement Concerning the International Registration of Marks,
14 April 1894 ....11.2; 21.1, 21.3, 21.6
Madrid Protocol 1.2; 2.14; 21.1, 21.6, 21.40, 21.41; 23.28
art 1..21.3
    1(2), (3) 21.3
    2 ....21.4, 21.6
    2(1) 21.38
    3...21.3, 21.6, 21.16
    3(4) 21.34
    3^{bi} 21.3, 21.6
    3ter 21.3, 21.6, 21.34
    3ter(1), (2) 21.12
    4 ....21.3, 21.6
    5 ....21.3, 21.6
    5(2)(b) 21.6
    5(2)(c) 21.6
        (i) 21.17
        (ii) 21.6
    5(2)(d) 21.6
    5(3) 21.17
    6 ....21.4, 21.6
    6(2) 21.4
    6(3)...21.4, 21.39
    6(4) 21.34
    7 ....21.4, 21.6
    8...21.4
    9..21.16
    9bis 21.4
    10..21.13
Nice Agreement concerning the International Classification of Goods and Services for the
purposes of the Registration of Marks, 15 June 1957 ....2.5; 25.3

Marrakech Agreement (establishing the World Trade Organisation, 15 April 1994)................
    1.2; 12.53; 22.38, 22.40; 24.5;25.6
    art 2 ....**12.54**
    Annex1C 1.2; 18.76
Agreement Relating to Trade Related Aspects of Intellectual Property
      (TRIPS) 1.1, 1.2;.12.47; 18.5; 19.63, 19.145;
                                        22.1, 22.38; 23.26; 24.5; 25.7
  Pt I 22.41
    art 1 ....22.41
    art 1(1) 22.42
    art 2 ....17.2; 22.41, 22.42, 22.43
    arts 3, 4..22.41, 22.43, 22.44
    art 5 ....22.41, 22.43
    art 6 ....22.41, 22.44
    arts 7, 8...22.41
    art 15 ....22.45
    art 16 ....12.47
    art 16(2), (3)...22.45
    art 17 ....12.47; 22.46
    arts18, 19..22.47
    art 20 ....22.48
    art 21 ....22.46, 22.48
  Pt II..22.42, 22.45
    arts22-24 ....22.49
    art 41 ....22.50
    art 41(1)-(3) 19.159
    arts 42-48 ....19.151, 19.152; 22.50
    art 49 ....**9.151**, 19.152; 22.50
  Pt III 22.42,22.50, 22.51
    art 50 ....**19.146**, 19.147, 19.149, 19.151, 19.152; 22.51
    art 50(6) 19.150, 19.159
    art 50(8)..19.151, 19.152
    art 51 ....18.76; 19.63; 19.64; 22.51
    art 52 ....19.63; 22.51
    arts 53, 54...22.51
    art 55 ....**19.148**, 19.149,19.150,19.152;22.51
    art 56, 57 ....22.51
    art 58 ....**19.65**, 19.66; 22.51
    art 59. 60 ....22.51
    art 61 ....20.6; 22.51
  Pt IV 22.42, 22.52
    art 62 ....22.52
  Pt V 22.53
    arts 63, 64...22.53
  Pt VI   22.54
    art 66   22.54
  Pt VII...22.53, 22.55
    arts 68-73 ....22.53, 22.55

CONVENTIONS

Bern Copyright Convention 22.42
Brussels Convention, 1968, on the Jurisdiction and Enforcement Of Judgments in Civil and
    Commercial Matters.. 17.32; 31.6, 31.20

Brussels Convention, 1968, on the Jurisdiction and Enforcement Of Judgments in Civil and
    Commercial Matters–*contd*
    arts 2, 4 ....17.33; 31.2
    art 5 ....17.33; 31.2
    art 5(1), (3)-(5) 17.33; 31.2
    arts17, 18 ....17.33; 31.2, 31.9
    art 24 ....17.33; 31.2
    art 52 ....17.33
Paris Convention for the Protection of IndustrialProperty, 20 March, 1883....1.2; 5.113; 5.60;
    .30, 7.34; 8.5;9.2; 10.11; 12.54 12.54;
    16.6; 22.1, 22.5,22.42, 22.45;
    24.5, 24.13; 25.6

GATT Agreement 12.47; 19.63, 19.145; 20.6; 22.53
    art1 ....22.4, 22.6
    art1(1)-(3) 22.6
    art2 ....22.4, 22.7
    art 2(1) ....22.4, 22.
    art 2(2), (3) 22.7
    art 3 ....22.4, 22.7, 22.11
    art 4 ....22.3, 22.4, 22.8, 22.22, 22.35, 22.52
    art 5 ....22.4, 22.9
    art 5(1) 22.9
    art 5(1)(d) 27.18
    art 5(2), (3) 22.9
    art 5C 22.9, 22.47
    art 5D 22.9
    art 6 ....22.4, 22.11
    art 6(1)-(3) 22.11
    art 6*ter* 5.111; 22.3, 22.12, 22.19; 24.15, 24.16
    art 6*ter*(3) 5.111
    art 6*bis* 6.59, 6.72; 12.1, 12.14, 12.53, 12.54, 12.58;
    22.3, 22.12, 22.45; 24.18
    art 6*sexies* 22.23
    art 6*septies* 7.34; 22.3, 22.24; 24.21
    art 6*quater* 22.13
    art 6*quater*(1), (2) 22.13
    art 6*quinquie*s 22.14
    art 6*quinquies*(A) 22.22
    art 6*quinquies*(A1) 22.14, 22.16
    art 6*quinquies*(A2) 22.15
    art 6*quinquies*(B2) 22.16, 22.17, 22.21
    art 6*quinquies*(C1), (C2) 22.21
    art 6*quinquies*(D)-(F) 22.22
    art 7 ....22.4, 22.25
    art 7*bis* 10.11; 22.26
    art 7*bis*(1)-(3) 22.26
    art 8 ....22.4, 22.27
    art 9 ....22.4, 22.28, 22.30, 22.34, 22.51
    art 9(1)-(6) 22.28
    art 10 ....22.4, 22.30, 22.34, 22.51
    art 10(1)-(3) 22.30

art 10bis 22.20, 22.31, 22.33

art 10bis(1)..22.31

art 10bis(2) 12.17; 22.31

art 10bis(3)...22.32

art 10ter 22.33, 22.34

art 10ter(1)-(3)...22.34

art 10bis 22.33, 22.34

arts 11, 12 ....22.4, 22.35

art 19 ....22.4

art 29(1)(b) 22.1

art 33 ....22.35

Table of cases

A

ACF Chemiefarma NV v EC Commission: 41/69 [1970] ECR 661, ECJ 19.115
AD 2000 Trade Mark [1997] RPC 168 .... 5.7, 5.8, 5.21, 5.26, 5.30, 5.37, 5.41
ADIDAS SARL's Trade Mark [1983] RPC 262 .... 2.39
Academy Trade Mark, Re (27 November 1998, unreported) New Law Digest
    1 March 1999, 699031803 .... 7.5, 7.12, 7.14
Academy Trade Mark Revocation, Re (10 May 1999, unreported) New Law
    Digest 699067101 .... 2.40
Ad-Lib Club Ltd v Granville [1971] 2 All ER 300, [1971] FSR 1, [1972] RPC 673,
    115 Sol Jo 74.. 14.20
Adams v R [1995] 1 WLR 52, [1995] 2 Cr App Rep 295, [1995] Crim LR 561,
    [1995] 2 BCLC 17, [1995] BCC 376, PC................................ 20.87
Adidas, Re (14 October 1999, unreported), ECJ......................... 19.6, 19.160
Adjustment Tax on Petrol, Re [1966] CMLR 409 .... 16.61
Akhtar v Grout (1998) 162 JP 714..................................... 20.154
Albatros v SOPECO: 20/64 [1965] ECR 29, [1965] CMLR 159 .... 16.60
Algemene Transport-en Expeditie Onderneming van Gend en Loos NV v Nederlandse
    Belastingadministratie: 26/62 [1963] ECR 1, [1963] CMLR 105, ECJ 16.60
Alpi Pietro e Figlio & Co v Wright (John) & Sons (Veneers) [1971] FSR 510,
    [1972] RPC 125 .... 13.15
American Greetings Corpn's Application, Re, (Re Holly Hobbie Trade Mark)
    [1983] 2 All ER 609, [1983] 1 WLR 912, [1983] FSR 581, [1984] RPC 329,
    127 Sol Jo 424, CA; affd [1984] 1 All ER 426, [1984] 1 WLR 189, [1984] FSR 199,
    [1984] RPC 329, 128 Sol Jo 99, [1985] EIPR 6, HL 11.7
Amministrazione delle Finanze dello Stato v SpA San Giorgio: 199/82 [1983] ECR 3595,
    [1985] 2 CMLR 658, ECJ.. 20.26
Amp Inc v Utilux Pty Ltd [1971] FSR 572, [1972] RPC 103, HL 5.98
Anciens Établissements Panhard et Levassor, SA des v Panhard Levassor Motor Co Ltd
    [1901] 2 Ch 513, 70 LJ Ch 738, 18 RPC 405, 50 WR 74, [1900-3] All ER Rep 477,
    45 Sol Jo 671, 85 LT 20, 17 TLR 680 .... 14.17, 14.61
Anheuser-Busch Inc v Budejovicky Budvar Narodni Podnik, Budweiser
    Case [1984] FSR 413, 128 Sol Jo 398, [1984] LS Gaz
    R 1369, CA 12.53, 14.15, 14.16, 14.18

Anns v Merton London Borough Council [1978] AC 728, [1977] 2 All ER 492,
   [1977] 2 WLR 1024, 75 LGR 555, 141 JP 526, 121 Sol Jo 377, 5 BLR 1,
   243 Estates Gazette 523, 591, [1977] JPL 514, HL 19.131
Antec International Ltd v South Western Chicks (Warren) Ltd [1997] FSR 278 . . . . 13.3
Anthony O'Gorman's Trade Mark Application, Re
   (15 February 1999, unreported) 6.16, 6.78
Argyllshire Weavers Ltd v A Macaulay (Tweeds) Ltd [1964] RPC 477,
   1965 SLT 21 . . . . 14.61
Aristoc Ltd v Rysta Ltd. See Rysta Ltd's Application, Re, Re Aristoc Ltd's Opposition
Athletes Foot Marketing Associates Inc v Cobra Sports Ltd [1980] RPC 343 . . . . 14.15
Atterton v Browne [1945] KB 122, 43 LGR 13, 109 JP 25, 114 LJKB 68,
   173 LT 13, 61 TLR 70, DC 18.68
A-G's Reference (No 1 of 1975) [1975] QB 773, [1975] 2 All ER 684, [1975] 3 WLR 11,
   [1975] RTR 473, 61 Cr App Rep 118, 139 JP 569, 119 Sol Jo 373, CA 20.50, 20.58
A-G's Reference (No 1 of 1992) [1993] 2 All ER 190, [1993] 1 WLR 274, 96 Cr App
   Rep 298, 157 JP 753, [1993] Crim LR 274, [1992] 41 LS Gaz R 36, CA 20.74
Audi-Med Trade Mark, Re [1998] RPC 863 . . . . 6.68
Automotive Network Exchange Trade Mark, Re [1998] RPC 885 . . . . 5.72
Avnet Inc v Isoact Ltd [1998] FSR 16 . . . . 6.13
Azrak-Hamway International Inc's Licence of Right (Design Right and
   Copyright) Application [1997] RPC 134 . . . . 22.38

B
BASF plc v CEP (UK) plc [1996] ETMR 51, 19(4) IPD 9 . . . . 6.57, 20.92
Bach and Bach Flower Remedies Trade Marks, Re [1999] RPC 1; on appeal
   (21 October 1999, unreported), CA 5.21, 5.66, 5.72
Balabel v Air India [1988] Ch 317, [1988] 2 All ER 246, [1988] 2 WLR 1036,
   132 Sol Jo 699, [1988] NLJR 85, CA 3.15
Bale and Church Ltd v Sutton, Parsons and Sutton and Astrah Products (1934)
   51 RPC 129, CA 6.34
Barclays Bank plc v Homan [1993] BCLC 680, [1992] BCC 757; affd [1993] BCLC 680,
   [1992] BCC 757, CA 13.21
Barclays Bank plc v RBS Advanta [1996] RPC 307 . . . . 12.18, 20.104
Baume & Co Ltd v A H Moore Ltd [1958] Ch 137, [1957] 3 All ER 416, [1957] 3 WLR
   870, [1957] RPC 459, 101 Sol Jo 903; on appeal [1958] Ch 907, [1958] 2 All ER 113,
   [1958] 2 WLR 797, [1958] RPC 226, 102 Sol Jo 329, CA 5.120, 12.25
Bayerische Motorenwerke AG (BMW) v Deenik: C-63/97 [1999] All ER (EC) 235,
   [1999] 1 CMLR 1099, ECJ 12.30
Baywatch Production Co Inc v Home Video Channel [1997] FSR 22 . . . . . 6.25, 6.57, 20.92
Beautimatic International Ltd v Mitchell International Pharmaceuticals Ltd
   (1999) Times, 8 July 12.7
Beck, Koller & Co (England) Ltd's Application, Re (1947) 64 RPC 76 . . . . 6.52
Belegging-en Exploitatiemaatschappij Lavender BV v Witten Industrial Diamonds Ltd
   [1979] FSR 59, CA 14.63, 20.43
Bell Atlantic Corpn v Bell Atlantic Communications plc (21 December
   1998, unreported) 6.12
Berlei (UK) Ltd v Bali Brassiere Co Inc [1969] 2 All ER 812, [1969] 1 WLR 1306,
   [1969] RPC 472, 113 Sol Jo 720, HL 6.76
Bernardin (Alain) et Cie v Pavilion Properties Ltd [1967] FSR 341,
   [1967] RPC 581 . . . . 14.18
Bestobell Paints Ltd v Bigg [1975] FSR 421, 119 Sol Jo 679 . . . . 15.5
Bestuur der Sociale Verzekeringsbank v Van der Vecht: 19/67
   [1967] ECR 345, [1968] CMLR 151 . . . . 16.61, 19.154

Betts v Willmott (1871) 6 Ch App 239, 19 WR 369, Goodeve's Patent Cases 61,
  25 LT 188, CA 14.53, 20.27
Birmingham Vinegar Brewery Co Ltd v Powell [1897] AC 710, 66 LJ Ch 763,
  14 RPC 720, 76 LT 792, HL 4.11
Bismag Ltd v Amblins (Chemists) Ltd [1940] Ch 667, [1940] 2 All ER 608,
  109 LJ Ch 305, 57 RPC 209, 84 Sol Jo 381, 163 LT 127, 56 TLR 721, CA 6.37
Blackbaud, Re, Trade Marks Registry, 19 December 1997; CIPA Journal,
  March 1998, p 210 . . . . 5.72
Blanchard v Hill (1742) 2 Atk 484 . . . . 1.6
Blue Bottle's Trade Mark Application (12 July 1999, unreported) 4.10
Blue Metal Industries Ltd v Dilley [1970] AC 827, [1969] 3 All ER 437,
  [1969] 3 WLR 357, 113 Sol Jo 448, [1969] ALR 595, PC 18 108
Blue Paraffin Trade Mark [1977] RPC 473, CA 4.12, 5.18
Blunden v Gravelle Ltd (1986) 151 JP 701, [1987] BTLC 344 . . . . 20 100
Body paint, Re Trade Marks Registry, 31 March 1998; CIPA Journal,
  September 1998, p 728 . . . . 5.72
Bognor Regis UDC v Campion [1972] 2 QB 169, [1972] 2 All ER 61,
  [1972] 2 WLR 983, 70 LGR 313, 116 Sol Jo 354 . . . . 15.13
Bollinger v Costa Brava Wine Co Ltd [1960] Ch 262, [1959] 3 All ER 800,
  [1959] 3 WLR 966, [1960] RPC 16, 103 Sol Jo 1028 . . . . 14.5, 14.68, 14.72, 14.74
Bon Matin Trade Mark [1989] RPC 537 . . . . 7.5, 7.31, 24.42
Boneham and Hart v Hirst Bros & Co Ltd (1917) 34 RPC 209 . . . . 13.8
Bonnington Castings Ltd v Wardlaw [1956] AC 613, [1956] 1 All ER 615, [1956] 2 WLR
  707, 54 LGR 153, 100 Sol Jo 207, 1956 SC (HL) 26, 1956 SLT 135 . . . . 13.14, 15.15
Bonus Gold, Re Trade Marks Registry, 22 December 1997; CIPA Journal,
  March 1998, p 210 . . . . 5.72
Bostitch Trade Mark [1963] RPC 183 . . . . 11.7
Bowden Controls Ltd v Acco Cable Controls Ltd [1990] RPC 427 . . . . 13.8
Brain v Ingledew Brown Bennison and Garrett (a firm) (No 3) [1997] FSR 511 . . 13.9, 13.13
Bravado Merchandising Services Ltd v Mainstream Publishing (Edinburgh) Ltd
  [1996] FSR 205, 1996 SLT 597, OH 6.9, 12.11
Brian v Ingledew Brown Bennison & Garrett (a firm) [1996] FSR 341, CA 13.10, 13.13
Bristol Conservatories Ltd v Conservatories Custom Built Ltd
  [1989] RPC 455, CA 14.50, 14.52
Bristol-Myers Squibb v Paranova A/S: C-427, 429, 436/93 [1996] ECR I-3457,
  [1997] 1 CMLR 1151, 34 BMLR 59, ECJ 12.43
British Diabetic Association v Diabetic Society Ltd [1995] 4 All ER 812,
  [1996] FSR 1 . . . . 14.36
British Sugar plc v James Robertson and Sons Ltd [1996] RPC 281 . . . . 1.18, 5.4, 5.5,
            5.16, 5.19, 5.25, 5.71, 5.75, 5.77, 5.84, 6.12, 6.28, 7.7, 7.26, 12.4, 12.11, 20.2
British Telecommunications plc v One in a Million Ltd [1998] 4 All ER 476,
  [1999] 1 WLR 903, [1999] FSR 1, [1998] NLJR 1179, CA 14.11, 14.59
Browne v DC Thomson & Co (1912) 49 SLR 285, 1912 SC 359, 1 SLT 123 . . . . 15.12
Bulmer (HP) Ltd v J Bollinger SA [1974] Ch 401, [1974] 2 All ER 1226, [1974]
  3 WLR 202, [1974] 2 CMLR 91, [1975] RPC 321, 118 Sol Jo 404, CA 16.59
Button v Jenkins [1975] 3 All ER 585, 139 JP 828, 119 Sol Jo 697 . . . . 18.84
Byrd (AA) & Co Ltd's Application, Re (1953) 70 RPC 212 . . . . 2.8
Byrne v Deane [1937] 1 KB 818, [1937] 2 All ER 204, 106 LJKB 533,
  81 Sol Jo 236, 157 LT 10, 53 TLR 469, CA 15.8

C

CBS Songs Ltd v Amstrad Consumer Electronics plc [1988] AC 1013, [1988] 2 All ER
  484, [1988] 2 WLR 1191, [1988] RPC 567, 132 Sol Jo 789, HL 14.63, 19.134, 20.43

CDX Trade Mark (21 October 1998, unreported) New Law Digest 698102001 . . . 5.36, 6.51
CHC Software Care Ltd v Hopkins & Wood [1993] FSR 241 . . . . 15.3
CILFIT Srl and Lanificio di Gavardo v Ministry of Health: 283/81 [1982] ECR 3415,
    [1983] 1 CMLR 472, ECJ. 19.154
CJ & Device, Re Trade Marks Registry, 16 June 1997; CIPA Journal,
    August 1997, p 625 . . . . 5.72
CNL-Sucal NV SA v HAG GF AG: C-10/89 [1990] ECR I-3711,
    [1990] 3 CMLR 571, [1991] FSR 99, ECJ 6.36, 12.34
CREOLA Trade Mark [1997] RPC 507 . . . . 8.14
Cable & Wireless plc v British Telecommunications plc [1998] FSR 383 . . . . 12.21
Cacique Trade Mark (1989) unreported 3.10
Cadbury Ltd v Ulmer GmbH [1988] FSR 385 . . . . 14.61, 14.63
Cadbury-Schweppes Pty Ltd v Pub Squash Co Pty Ltd
    [1981] 1 All ER 213, [1981] 1 WLR 193, [1981] RPC 429, 125 Sol Jo 96,
    [1980] 2 NSWLR 851, PC 14.11, 14.39, 14.40
Canon Kabushiki Kaisha v Metro-Goldwyn-Mayer Inc (formerly Pathé
    Communications Corpn: C-39/97 [1998] ECR I-5507, [1998] All ER (EC) 934,
    [1999] RPC 117, ECJ 6.31, 6.37, 6.41, 6.43, 6.49, 6.53, 6.58, 12.14, 20.2
Caparo Industries plc v Dickman [1990] 2 AC 605, [1990] 1 All ER 568, [1990]
    2 WLR 358, [1990] BCLC 273, [1990] BCC 164, 134 Sol Jo 494, [1990] 12 LS
    Gaz R 42, [1990] NLJR 248, HL 19.131
Carflow Products (UK) Ltd v Linwood Securities (Birmingham) Ltd
    [1998] FSR 691 . . . . 13.14
Cars v Bland Light Syndicate Ltd (1910) 28 RPC 33 . . . . 13.8
Cassidy v Daily Mirror Newspapers Ltd [1929] 2 KB 331, 98 LJKB 595, [1929]
    All ER Rep 117, 73 Sol Jo 348, 141 LT 404, 45 TLR 485, CA 15.11
Castrol Ltd v Automotive Oil Supplies Ltd [1983] RPC 315 . . . . 12.39, 14.54
Celine SA's Trade Mark [1985] RPC 381 . . . . 6.16
Cellular Clothing Co v Maxton and Murray [1899] AC 326, 68 LJPC 72,
    16 RPC 397, 80 LT 809, HL. 14.31
Centrafarm BV v American Home Products Corpn: 3/78 [1978] ECR 1823,
    [1979] 1 CMLR 326, [1979] FSR 189, CMR 8475, ECJ. 12.34
Cepravin, Re Trade Marks Registry, 4 April 1997; CIPA Journal, June 1997, p 448 . . . . 7.14
Champagne Heidsieck et Cie Monopole SA v Buxton [1930] 1 Ch 330,
    99 LJ Ch 149, 47 RPC 28, 142 LT 324, 46 TLR 36 . . . . 12.34
Chan Wing-Siu v R [1985] AC 168, [1984] 3 All ER 877, [1984] 3 WLR 677, 80 Cr App
    Rep 117, [1984] Crim LR 549, 128 Sol Jo 685, [1984] LS Gaz R 216, PC. 20.62
Chanel Ltd v L'Arome (UK) Ltd [1991] RPC 335; affd sub nom Chanel Ltd v Triton
    Packaging Ltd (formerly L'Arome (UK) Ltd) [1993] RPC 32, CA 12.20
Charleston v News Group Newspapers Ltd [1995] 2 AC 65, [1995] 2 All ER 313,
    [1995] 2 WLR 450, [1995] NLJR 490, 139 Sol Jo LB 100, [1995] EMLR 129, HL. 15.17
China-Therm Trade Mark [1980] FSR 21 . . . . 5.102
Chocosuisse Union des Fabricants Suisses de Chocolat v Cadbury Ltd
    [1998] RPC 117, Times, 25 November, [1998] ETMR 205; on appeal (1999)
    Times, 15 March, CA. 14.65, 14.69, 14.73, 22.49
Churchill v Walton [1967] 2 AC 224, [1967] 1 All ER 497, [1967] 2 WLR 682,
    51 Cr App Rep 212, 131 JP 277, 111 Sol Jo 112, HL. 20.82
Clark v Associated Newspapers Ltd [1998] 1 All ER 959, [1998] 1 WLR 1558,
    [1998] RPC 261, [1998] 07 LS Gaz R 31, [1998] NLJR 157 . . . . 14.25, 14.29
Clay, Re, Clay v Booth, Re Deed of Indemnity [1919] 1 Ch 66, 88 LJ Ch 40, [1918–19]
    All ER Rep 94, 63 Sol Jo 23, 119 LT 754, CA. 13.20
Club Europe Trade Mark, Re [1999] 33 LS Gaz R 32 . . . . 2.34, 16.23

Club Soda Trade Mark (4 December 1998, unreported) New Law Digest 10 March
  1999, 699032103. . . . . 7.14
Coca Cola Trade Marks [1985] FSR 315, [1986] RPC 421, CA; affd sub nom
  Coca-Cola Co's Applications, Re [1986] 2 All ER 274, sub nom Coca-Cola Co, Re
  [1986] 1 WLR 695, [1986] FSR 472, [1986] RPC 421, 130 Sol Jo 429,
  [1986] LS Gaz R 2090, [1986] NLJ Rep 463, HL. 4.3, 5.16
Coffeemix Trade Mark, Re [1998] RPC 717 . . . . 5.72
Colgate-Palmolive Ltd v Markwell Finance Ltd
  [1989] RPC 497, CA. 12.39, 14.53, 14.54, 20.26, 20.27
Colorcoat Trade Mark [1990] RPC 511 . . . . 5.8
Combe International v Scholl (UK) Ltd [1977] FSR 464, [1980] RPC 1 . . . . 14.7
Comer v Bloomfield [1971] RTR 49, 55 Cr App Rep 305, [1971] Crim LR 230 . . . . . . 20.71
Concord Trade Mark [1987] FSR 209 . . . . 2.38, 7.5
Coney v Choyce [1975] 1 All ER 979, [1975] 1 WLR 422, 119 Sol Jo 202 . . . . 18.84
Conran v Mean Fiddler Holdings Ltd [1997] FSR 856 . . . . 6.25
Consorzio del Prosciutto di Parma v Asda Stores Ltd and Hygrade Foods Ltd
  [1998] 2 CMLR 215, [1999] 02 LS Gaz R 29; affd (1998) 143 Sol Jo LB 46,
  [1999] ETMR 319, CA 5.86, 22.49
Consorzio del Prosciutto di Parma v Marks & Spencer plc [1991] RPC 351, CA 14.6
Corgi Trade Mark, Re [1999] RPC 549 . . . . 6.58
Cousin (criminal proceedings against): 162/82 [1983] ECR 1101,
  [1984] 2 CMLR 780, ECJ. 19.112
Co-venture, Re Trade Marks Registry, 13 June 1997; CIPA Journal, July 1997, p 539. . . 5.72
Cruttwell (or Crutwell) v Lye (1810) 1 Rose 123, 17 Ves 335. 1.7
Cullimore v Lyme Regis Corpn [1962] 1 QB 718, [1961] 3 All ER 1008, [1961]
  3 WLR 1340, 60 LGR 55, 13 P & CR 142, 126 JP 13, 105 Sol Jo 117 . . . . 18.84
Customs and Excise Comrs v Air Canada [1991] 2 QB 446, [1991] 1 All ER 570,
  [1991] 2 WLR 344, CA. 18.8
Customs and Excise Comrs v Anchor Foods Ltd [1999] 3 All ER 268,
  [1999] 1 WLR 1139, 143 Sol Jo LB 96 . . . . 18.104
Customs and Excise Comrs v Top High Developments Ltd
  [1998] FSR 464. . . . . 18.92, 18.121, 19.48
Cyberpub, Re Trade Marks Registry, 26 September 1996; CIPA Journal,
  October 1996, p 851 . . . . 5.72

D

DUCATI Trade Mark [1998] RPC 227 . . . . 2.25, 9.3
Da Costa en Schaake NV v Nederlandse Belastingadministratie:
  28-30/62 [1963] ECR 31, [1963] CMLR 224, ECJ. 16.59, 16.61
Dalgety Spillers Foods Ltd v Food Brokers Ltd [1994] FSR 504 . . . . 14.29
Davies v DPP [1954] AC 378, [1954] 1 All ER 507, [1954] 2 WLR 343,
  38 Cr App Rep 11, 118 JP 222, 98 Sol Jo 161, HL. 20.61
Davies v Sumner [1984] 1 WLR 405, 148 JP 134, 128 Sol Jo 18; affd [1984] 3 All ER
  831, [1984] 1 WLR 1301, 83 LGR 123, [1985] RTR 95, 149 JP 110, 128 Sol Jo 814,
  [1985] LS Gaz R 45, 4 Tr L 1, HL 20.34
Day v Day (1816) Digest 21. . . . . 1.8
Day by day, Re Trade Marks Registry, 18 June 1997; CIPA Journal, July 1997, p 539;
  upheld CIPA Journal, March 1998, p 212, New Law Digest 698058204. . . . . 5.72
Dead Sea Mineral Therapy & Device, Re Trade Marks Registry,
  26 November 1997; CIPA Journal, March 1998, p 210 . . . . 5.72
De Beers Abrasive Products Ltd v International General Electric Co of New York Ltd
  [1975] 2 All ER 599, [1975] 1 WLR 972, 119 Sol Jo 439 . . . . 15.18
De Cordova v Vick Chemical Co (1951) 68 RPC 103, 95 Sol Jo 316, PC 6.16

Dee Corpn plc, Re [1989] 3 All ER 948, [1990] RPC 159, CA 4.11, 4.14

Denkavit Internationaal BV, VITIC Amsterdam BV and Voormeer BV v
　Bundesamt für Finanzen: C-283/94, C-291/94 and C-292/94 [1996] ECR I-5063,
　[1996] STC 1445, ECJ 19.154

Derbyshire County Council v Times Newspapers Ltd [1992] QB 770, [1992] 3 All ER
　65, [1992] 3 WLR 28, 90 LGR 221, [1992] NLJR 276, CA; revsd [1993] AC 534,
　[1993] 1 All ER 1011, [1993] 2 WLR 449, 91 LGR 179, [1993] 14 LS Gaz R 46,
　[1993] NLJR 283, 137 Sol Jo LB 52, 81, HL 15.3, 15.13

Deutsche Grammophon GmbH v Metro-SB-Grossmärkte GmbH & Co KG: 78/70
　[1971] ECR 487, [1971] CMLR 631, CMR 8106, ECJ 16.60

Deutsche Renault AG v Audi AG: C-317/91 [1993] ECR I-6227,
　[1995] 1 CMLR 461, [1995] FSR 738, ECJ 6.36

Device of Coffee Beans/Leaves, Re Trade Marks Registry, 1 November;
　CIPA Journal, December 1996, p 1017. . . . . 5.72

DPP v Stonehouse [1978] AC 55, [1977] 2 All ER 909, [1977] 3 WLR 143, 65 Cr App
　Rep 192, 141 JP 473, [1977] Crim LR 544, 121 Sol Jo 491, HL 20.71, 20.73

DPP for Northern Ireland v Lynch [1975] AC 653, [1975] 2 WLR 641,
　61 Cr App Rep 6, 119 Sol Jo 233, sub nom Lynch v DPP for Northern Ireland
　[1975] NI 35, [1975] 1 All ER 913, 139 JP 312, [1975] Crim LR 707, HL 20.54

DPP for Northern Ireland v Maxwell [1978] NI 42, [1978] 3 All ER 1140, [1978] 1
　WLR 1350, 68 Cr App Rep 128, 143 JP 63, 122 Sol Jo 758, HL. 20.60

Doe d France v Andrews (1850) 15 QB 756 . . . . 20.157

Dolan v O'Hara [1975] NI 125 . . . . 18.84

Dolland & Aitchinson Ltd's Trade Mark Application (30 April 1998, unreported)
　New Law Digest 698102002. . . . . 6.51

Donnelly v Marrickville Municipal Council [1973] 2 NSWLR 390 . . . . 18.84

Dormeuil Frères SA v Dormire Menswear Ltd [1983] RPC 131, 126 Sol Jo 770. . . . . . . 3.12

Drummond-Jackson v British Medical Association [1970] 1 All ER 1094,
　[1970] 1 WLR 688, 114 Sol Jo 152, CA. 15.3

Dualit Ltd's (Toaster Shapes) Trade Mark Applications, Re [1999] RPC 304; on appeal
　sub nom Dualit Ltd, Re (1999) Times, 19 July 5.7, 5.72, 5.96, 8.19

Du Cros v Lambourne [1907] 1 KB 40, 5 LGR 120, 70 JP 525, 76 LJKB 50,
　21 Cox CC 311, 95 LT 782, 23 TLR 3 . . . . 20.53

Dyson v A-G [1911] 1 KB 410, 80 LJKB 531, 55 Sol Jo 168, 103 LT 707,
　27 TLR 143, CA 13.20

E

EC Commission v Belgium: 237/84 [1986] ECR 1247, [1988] 2 CMLR 865, ECJ 1.20

EC Commission v Greece: C-306/89 [1991] ECR I-5863, [1994] 1 CMLR 803, ECJ . . . 1.20

EC Commission v Nederlands: 49/82 [1983] ECR 1195, [1983] 2 CMLR 476, ECJ . . . 19.19

EUROLAMB Trade Mark [1997] RPC 279 . . . . 5.5, 5.71

Ebony Maritime SA v Prefetto della Provincia di Brindisi: C-177/95
　[1997] ECR I-1111, [1997] 2 CMLR 24, ECJ 19.154

Edor Handelsonderneming BV v General Mills Fun Group 24 June 1977,
　NederlandseJurisprudentie 1978, 83. . . . . 6.18

Electrolux Ltd v Electrix Ltd (1954) 71 RPC 23, CA. 7.5, 7.12

Elle Trade Marks, Re [1997] FSR 529 . . . . 7.5, 7.7

Elvis Presley Trade Marks, Re [1997] RPC 543; affd [1999] RPC 567, CA. 5.50

Emaco Ltd v Dyson Appliances Ltd (1999) Times, 8 February. 12.21

Enamelize Trade Mark Case R 29/1998-3, OJ 10/98, p 1070 . . . . 26.6

Ener-Cap Trade Mark, Re [1999] RPC 362 . . . . 6.17

Esso Petroleum Co Ltd v Kingswood Motors (Addlestone) Ltd [1974] QB 142,
　[1973] 3 All ER 1057, [1973] 3 WLR 780, [1973] CMLR 665, 117 Sol Jo 852 . . . . 16.61

Eurim-Pharm Arzneimittel GmbH v Beiersdorf AG: C 71-73/94 [1997] 1 CMLR 1222,
34 BMLR 59, ECJ. 12.44
European Ltd v Economist Newspapers Ltd [1996] FSR 431, [1996] EMLR 394;
affd [1998] FSR 283, [1998] EMLR 536, CA 6.46, 12.25, 14.25
Europemballage Corpn and Continental Can Co Inc v EC Commission:
6/72 [1973] ECR 215, [1973] CMLR 199, ECJ 7.21, 12.7
Export of Oat Flakes, Re [1969] CMLR 85. . . . . 16.61

F

Fabrica de Queijo Eru Portuguesa Lda v Subdirector-Geral das Alfândegas:
C-325/96 [1997] ECR I-7249, ECJ. 19.19
Farina v Silverlock (1855) 1 K & J 509, 24 LJ Ch 632, 3 Eq Rep 883,
3 WR 532, 25 LTOS 211. . . . . 14.60
Ferriere Nord v EC Commission: C-219/95P [1997] ECR I-4411, ECJ 19.154
Firma Rheinmuhlen-Düsseldorf v Einfuhr- und Vorratsstelle für Getreide und
Futtermittel: 146/73 [1974] ECR 139, [1974] 1 CMLR 523, ECJ 16.59
Flexible Reserve, Re Trade Marks Registry, 31 January 1997; CIPA Journal,
March 1997, p 217. . . . . 5.72
Floradix Trade Mark [1974] RPC 583 . . . . 6.20
Foglia v Novello (No 2): 244/80 [1981] ECR 3045, [1982] 1 CMLR 585, ECJ. 16.65
Ford Motor Co Ltd (Nastas's) Application [1968] RPC 220 . . . . 16.31
France v EC Commission: C-327/91 [1994] ECR I-3641,
[1994] 5 CMLR 517, ECJ. 19.154
Francovich and Bonifaci v Italy: C-6, 9/90 [1991] ECR I-5357,
[1993] 2 CMLR 66, [1995] ICR 722, [1992] IRLR 84, ECJ 17.28
Fratelli Grassi fu Davide v Administrazione delle Finanze: 5/72 [1972] ECR 443,
[1973] CMLR 322, ECJ 16.60
French Widow's Pension Settlement, Re [1971] CMLR 530. . . . . 16.61
Fresh Banking Trade Mark, Re [1998] RPC 605 . . . . 5.72
Froot Loops Trade Mark [1998] RPC 240 . . . . 5.71

G

GE Trade Mark, Re. See General Electric Co v General Electric Co Ltd
Gallotti, Criminal proceedings against: C-58, 75, 112, 119, 123, 135, 140, 141, 154
and 157/95 [1996] ECR I-4345, [1997] 1 CMLR 32, ECJ. 20.10
Galoo Ltd (in liquidation) v Bright Grahame Murray (a firm) [1995] 1 All ER 16,
[1994] 1 WLR 1360, [1994] 2 BCLC 492, [1994] BCC 319, CA. 13.14, 15.15
Gardinol Chemical Co Ltd's Application, Re, Re Cyclo Chemicals Ltd's
Application (1948) 65 RPC 455 . . . . 9.18
Garfield v Maddocks [1974] QB 7, [1973] 2 All ER 303, [1973] 2 WLR 888,
57 Cr App Rep 372, 137 JP 461, 117 Sol Jo 145, DC. 18.57
General Electric Co v General Electric Co Ltd [1972] 2 All ER 507, [1972] 1 WLR 729,
116 Sol Jo 412, sub nom GE Trade Mark, Re [1973] RPC 297, HL. 7.21, 14.38
General Motors Corpn v Yplon SA [1999] ETMR 122. . . . . 6.58, 6.60, 12.14, 24.20
General Nutrition Investment Co's Application, Re Trade Marks Registry,
23 January 1998, New Law Digest 698058209 . . . . 5.72
Genesis Trade Mark (2 February 1998, unreported) 7.36
George v Secretary of State for the Environment (1979) 77 LGR 689, 38 P & CR 609,
[1978] RVR 215, 250 Estates Gazette 339, [1979] JPL 382, CA 18.84
Gibson, Re Trade Marks Registry, 24 October 1996; CIPA Journal,
December 1996, p 107 . . . . 5.72
Golden Pages Trade Mark [1985] FSR 27. . . . . 4.14
Graham v A-G [1966] NZLR 937 . . . . 18.84

Gromax Plasticulture Ltd v Don & Low Nonwovens Ltd [1999] RPC 367 .. 5.119, 6.9, 7.21
Grunwick Processing Laboratories Ltd v Advisory Conciliation and Arbitration Service
    [1978] AC 655, [1978] 1 All ER 338, [1978] 2 WLR 277, [1978] ICR 231, CA;
    affd [1978] AC 655, [1978] 1 All ER 338, [1978] 2 WLR 277, [1978] ICR 231,
    122 Sol Jo 46, sub nom Advisory Conciliation and Arbitration Service v Grunwick
    Processing Laboratories Ltd [1977] IRLR 38, HL 18.84
Guaranty Trust Co of New York v Hannay & Co [1915] 2 KB 536, 84 LJKB 1465,
    21 Com Cas 67, [1914-15] All ER Rep 24, 113 LT 98, CA 13.20
Gucci (Guccio) SpA v Paolo Gucci [1991] FSR 89 . . . . 14.29

H

HFC Bank plc v Midland Bank plc (1999) Times, 28 September 14.30
Habib Bank Ltd v Habib Bank AG Zurich [1981] 2 All ER 650,
    [1981] 1 WLR 1265, [1982] RPC 1, 125 Sol Jo 512, CA 7.32, 12.57
Hallelujah Trade Mark [1976] RPC 605 . . . . 5.102
Hammermill Paper Co's Opposition to Application for Registration by Alex Pirie
    & Sons Ltd, Re. See Pirie (Alexander) & Sons Ltd's Trade Mark, Re Harrods Ltd v
    Harrodian School Ltd [1996] RPC 697, CA 14.7, 14.25, 14.32, 14.43, 14.46, 14.48
Harrods Ltd v R Harrod Ltd (1923) 41 RPC 74, 40 TLR 195, CA 14.21, 14.43
Havering London Borough v Stevenson [1970] 3 All ER 609, [1970]
    1 WLR 1375, [1971] RTR 58, 134 JP 689, 114 Sol Jo 664 . . . . 20.34
Hedley Byrne & Co Ltd v Heller & Partners Ltd [1964] AC 465, [1963] 2 All ER 575,
    [1963] 3 WLR 101, [1963] 1 Lloyd's Rep 485, 107 Sol Jo 454, HL 19.135
Henderson v Henderson (1843) 3 Hare 100, [1843-60] All ER Rep 378, 1 LTOS 410. . 27.24
Henderson & Son v Munro & Co (1905) 7 F (Ct of Sess) 636, Ct of Sess 14.52
Henn and Darby v DPP [1981] AC 850, [1980] 2 All ER 166, [1980] 2 WLR 597,
    71 Cr App Rep 44, 124 Sol Jo 290, ECJ. 20.101
Henri Julien BV v Norbert Verschuere 20 May 1983, A 82/5 Nederlandse
    Jurisprudentie 1984, 72. . . . . 6.18
Hermes Trade Mark [1982] Com LR 98, [1982] RPC 425 . . . . 7.12
Hessische Knappschaft v Maison Singer et fils: 44/65 [1965] ECR 965,
    [1966] CMLR 82, ECJ 16.60
History Live, Re Trade Marks Registry, 31 December 1997; CIPA Journal,
    March 1998,p 211 . . . . 5.72
Hodgkinson and Corby Ltd v Wards Mobility Services Ltd [1994] 1 WLR 1564,
    [1995] FSR 169 . . . . 14.6, 14.7, 14.24, 27.24
Hoffmann-La Roche & Co AG v Centrafarm Vertriebsgesellschaft Pharmazeutischer
    Erzeugnisse mbH: 102/77 [1978] ECR 1139, [1978] 3 CMLR 217,
    [1978] FSR 598, CMR 8466, ECJ 12.34
Holdijk: 141-143/81 [1982] ECR 1299, [1983] 2 CMLR 635, ECJ 16.65
Holly Hobby Trade Mark, Re. See American Greetings Corpn's Application, Re
Homework Helpers Trade Mark Application, Re Trade Marks Registry, 6 October 1998,
    New Law Digest 699010201. . . . . 5.72
Horrocks v Lowe [1975] AC 135, [1974] 1 All ER 662, [1974] 2 WLR 282,
    72 LGR 251, 118 Sol Jo 149, HL 15.16
"Hospital World" Trade Mark [1967] RPC 595 . . . . 4.14
Hough v London Express Newspaper Ltd [1940] 2 KB 507, [1940] 3 All ER 31,
    109 LJKB 524, 84 Sol Jo 573, 163 LT 162, 56 TLR 758, CA 15.9
Howard v Bodington (1877) 2 PD 203 . . . . 18.84
Howard v Secretary of State for the Environment [1975] QB 235,
    [1974] 1 All ER 644, [1974] 2 WLR 459, 27 P & CR 131, 138 JP 203,
    117 Sol Jo 853, 228 Estates Gazette 2271, CA. 18.84

Hulton (E) & Co v Jones [1910] AC 20, 79 LJKB 198, [1908–10] All ER Rep 29,
    54 Sol Jo 116, 101 LT 831, 26 TLR 128, HL 15.14
Hunter v Coombs [1962] 1 All ER 904, [1962] 1 WLR 573, 60 LGR 506,
    126 JP 300, 106 Sol Jo 287, DC 18.60
Hyam v DPP [1975] AC 55, [1974] 2 All ER 41, [1974] 2 WLR 607,
    59 Cr App Rep 91, 138 JP 374, 118 Sol Jo 311, HL......................... 20.16

I

IHT Internationale Heiztechnik GmbH and Danziger v Ideal-Standard GmbH
    and Wabco Standard GmbH: C-9/93 [1994] ECR I-2789, [1994] 3 CMLR 857,
    [1995] FSR 59, ECJ 12.34
Ide Line AG v Philips Electronics NV [1997] ETMR 377, Sweden CA 5.96
Imperial Group Ltd v Philip Morris & Co Ltd [1982] FSR 72, CA................. 5.121
Imperial Group Ltd v Philip Morris & Co [1984] RPC 293 .... 14.28
Import Licence for Oats, Re [1968] CMLR 103 .... 16.61
Import of Powdered Milk Goods, Re (No 3) [1967] CMLR 326 (Bundesfinanzhof) ... 16.61
IRC v Muller & Co's Margarine Ltd [1901] AC 217, 70 LJKB 677, 49 WR 603,
    [1900–3] All ER Rep 413, 84 LT 729, 17 TLR 530, HL 14.12
Interlego AG's Trade Mark Application, Re [1998] RPC 69..................... 2.13
Invermont Trade Mark [1997] RPC 125 .... 7.4
Irish Creamery Milk Suppliers Association v Ireland: 36, 71/80 [1981] ECR 735,
    [1981] 2 CMLR 455, ECJ.. 16.65

J

J3 Learning, Re Trade Marks Registry,1 November 1996; CIPA
    Journal December 1996, p 1017... 5.72
Jameson (John) & Son Ltd v R S Johnston & Co Ltd (1909) 18 RPC 259 .... 14.61
Jellinek's Application, Re (1946) 63 RPC 59................................. 6.20
Jeryl Lynn Trade Mark, Re (1998) 49 BMLR 92.............................. 5.21
Jian Tools for Sales Ltd v Roderick Manhattan Group Ltd [1995] FSR 924.......... 14.19
Jimmy Nicks Property Co Ltd's Application [1999] ETMR 445................... 2.40
John v Humphreys [1955] 1 All ER 793, [1955] 1 WLR 325, 53 LGR 321,
    119 JP 309, 99 Sol Jo 222, DC 20.24
Johnson v Youden [1950] 1 KB 544, [1950] 1 All ER 300, 48 LGR 276,
    114 JP 136, 94 Sol Jo 115, 66 (pt 1) TLR 395 .... 20.59
Johnson & Johnson's Application [1991] RPC 1 .... 3.10
Johnston & Co v Orr Ewing & Co (1882) 7 App Cas 219, 51 LJ Ch 797,
    30 WR 417, 46 LT 216, HL.. 14.62
Jones v Department of Employment [1989] QB 1, [1988] 1 All ER 725, [1988]
    2 WLR 493, 132 Sol Jo 128, [1988] 4 LS Gaz R 35, [1987] NLJ Rep 1182, CA .. 19.132
Joyce v Sengupta [1993] 1 All ER 897, [1993] 1 WLR 337, [1992] 39 LS Gaz R 35,
    [1992] NLJR 1306, 136 Sol Jo LB 274, CA.............................. 15.3

K

Karo Step Trade Mark, Re [1977] RPC 255 .... 6.79
Kaye v Robertson [1991] FSR 62, CA...................................... 15.15
Keary Developments Ltd v Tarmac Construction Ltd [1995] 3 All ER 534,
    [1995] 2 BCLC 395, CA 16.34, 18.16
Knupffer v London Express Newspaper Ltd [1944] AC 116, [1944] 1 All ER 495,
    113 LJKB 251, 88 Sol Jo 143, 170 LT 362, 60 TLR 310, HL 15.12
Kodiak Trade Mark [1987] RPC 269, CA 9.18
Konservenfabrik Lulbella Friedrich Büker GmbH & Co. KG v Hauptzollamt Cottbus:
    C-64/95 [1996] ECR I-5105, ECJ....................................... 19.154

L

Laboratoire Garnier et Cie v Ste Copar [1998] ETMR 114 . . . . 6.48
Ladd v Marshall [1954] 3 All ER 745, [1954] 1 WLR 1489, 98 Sol Jo 870, CA 16.23
Ladney and Hendry's International Application, Re [1998] RPC 319, CA 16.36
Lambert & Howarth & Sons Ltd's Application, Re (12 December 1997, unreported)
    New Law Digest 698058207 . . . . 5.72
Lapeyre v Administration Des Douanes [1967] CMLR 362 . . . . 16.61
Laurie v Raglan Building Co Ltd [1942] 1 KB 152, [1941] 3 All ER 332,
    111 LJKB 292, 86 Sol Jo 69, 166 LT 63, CA 18.123
Lego Systems A/S v Lego M Lemelstrich [1983] FSR 155. . 6.72, 12.54, 14.34, 14.43, 14.45
Lerose Ltd v Hawick Jersey International Ltd [1973] CMLR 83, [1973] FSR 15,
    [1974] RPC 42 . . . . 16.61
Lever v Goodwin (1887) 36 Ch D 1, [1887] WN 107, 4 RPC 492, 36 WR 177,
    [1886–90] All ER Rep 427, 57 LT 583, 3 TLR 650, CA 14.61
Levy's (A J & M A) Trade Mark, Re [1999] RPC 291 . . . . 8.12, 9.5
Levy's (A J & M A) Trade Mark (No 2), Re [1999] RPC 358 . . . . 2.40, 7.4
Lifesavers Trade Mark, Re [1997] RPC 563 . . . . 9.6
Lilley v Pettit [1946] KB 401, sub nom Pettit v Lilley [1946] 1 All ER 593, 44 LGR 171,
    110 JP 218, 115 LJKB 385, 90 Sol Jo 380, 175 LT 119, 62 TLR 359, DC 20.157
Liquid Force Trade Mark, Re [1999] RPC 429 . . . . 8.12, 9.5
Little World, Re CIPA Journal, December 1998, p 982 . . . . 5.72
Lloyd Schuhfabrik Meyer & Co GmbH v Klijsen Handel BV: C-342/97 [1999] All ER
    (EC) 587, [1999] 2 CMLR 1343, [1999] ETMR 10, ECJ 6.52
Loughans v Odhams Press Ltd [1963] 1 QB 299, [1962] 1 All ER 404,
    [1962] 2 WLR 692, 106 Sol Jo 262, CA 15.11
Löwenbräu München v Grünhalle Lager International Ltd [1974] 1 CMLR 1,
    [1974] FSR 1, [1974] RPC 492, 118 Sol Jo 50 . . . . 16.61
Luna Advertising Co Ltd v Burnham & Co (1928) 45 RPC 258 . . . . 13.9

M

M, Re [1994] 1 AC 377, [1993] 3 WLR 433, [1993] 37 LS Gaz R 50, [1993] NLJR 1099,
    137 Sol Jo LB 199, sub nom M v Home Office [1993] 3 All ER 537, HL 18.97
MB RM's Trade Mark Application Registry, 3 June 1999, noted in New Law Digest,
    2 November 1999, 699118301 . . . . 8.16
MICKEY DEES (NIGHTCLUB) Trade Mark [1998] RPC 359 . . . . 5.120
McGregor Clothing Co's Trade Mark [1978] FSR 353, [1979] RPC 36 . . . . 3.12
MacMillan Magazines Ltd v RCN Publishing Co Ltd [1998] FSR 9 . . . . . 12.11, 12.21, 15.5
Madame Trade Mark [1966] FSR 324, [1966] RPC 541 . . . . 5.4
Mai Consultant Ltd's Trade Mark Application, Re (7 December 1998, unreported) 5.72
Maid's Trade Mark Application, Re (9 December 1998, unreported) 8.12
Maintainit, Re Trade Marks Registry, 20 March 1998; CIPA Journal,
    September 1998, p 725 . . . . 5.72
Marcus Publishing plc v Hutton-Wild Communications Ltd [1990] RPC 576 . . . . 14.30
Marengo v Daily Sketch and Daily Graphic Ltd (1946) [1992] FSR 1, CA 14.30
Marks & Spencer plc v One in a Million Ltd [1999] 1 WLR 903, [1998] FSR 265,
    [1999] FSR 1, ITCLR 2; on appeal [1999] FSR 1, CA 6.46, 6.58
Mayfair Brassware Ltd v Aqualine International Ltd (costs order)
    [1998] FSR 135, CA 18.44
Meek v Powell [1952] 1 KB 164, [1952] 1 All ER 347, 50 LGR 247, 116 JP 116,
    96 Sol Jo 91, [1952] 1 TLR 358, DC 18.61
Memory Lock, Re Trade Marks Registry, 22 January 1998; CIPA Journal,
    May 1998, p 377 . . . . 5.72

Mercer v Denne [1905] 2 Ch 538, 3 LGR 1293, 70 JP 65, 74 LJ Ch 723,
   54 WR 303, [1904–7] All ER Rep, 93 LT 412, 21 TLR 760, CA 20.157
Mercury Communications Ltd v Mercury Interactive (UK) Ltd
   [1995] FSR 850 . . . . 5.121, 12.25, 19.69
Milchwerke Heinz Wöhrmann & Sohn KG v EEC Commission: 31, 33/62
   [1962] ECR 501, [1963] CMLR 152 . . . . 16.59
Milk Marketing Board v Cricket St Thomas Estate: C-372/88 [1990] ECR I-1345,
   [1990] 2 CMLR 800, [1990] 41 LS Gaz R 33, ECJ; refd sub nom Milk
   Marketing Board v Cricket St Thomas Estate [1991] 3 CMLR 123 . . . . 19.154
Millington v Fox (1838) 3 My & Cr 338 . . . . 1.7
Minilite, Re (17 November, 1998, unreported) 5.79
Ministry of Housing and Local Government v Sharp [1970] 2 QB 223,
   [1970] 1 All ER 1009, [1970] 2 WLR 802, 68 LGR 187, 21 P & CR 166,
   134 JP 358, 114 Sol Jo 109, 213 Estates Gazette 1145, CA 19.135
Minnesota Mining and Manufacturing Co v Geerpres Europe [1973] CMLR 259,
   [1973] FSR 133, [1974] RPC 35 . . . . 16.61
Mister Long Trade Mark, Re [1998] RPC 401 . . . . 1.18, 5.2, 5.41, 5.45, 12.49
Moments in time, Re Trade Marks Registry, 9 February 1998; CIPA Journal,
   June 1998, p 471 . . . . 5.72
Monson v Tussauds Ltd [1894] 1 QB 671, 58 JP 524, 63 LJQB 454, 9 R 177,
   [1891–4] All ER Rep 1051, 70 LT 335, 10 TLR 227, CA 15.10
Monster Munch Trade Mark, Re [1997] RPC 721 . . . . 2.29
Morgan v Odhams Press Ltd [1971] 2 All ER 1156, [1971] 1 WLR 1239,
   115 Sol Jo 587, HL 15.9
Morny Ltd's Trade Marks, Re (1951) 68 RPC 131, CA 6.9
Moseley v Victoria Rubber Co (1886) 3 RPC 351, 55 LT 482, Griffin's Patent
   Cases 163 . . . . 3.12
Mothercare UK Ltd v Penguin Books Ltd [1988] RPC 113, CA 5.68, 14.29
Moulijn v EC Commission: 6/74 [1974] ECR 1287, ECJ 19.154
Murphy v Brentwood District Council [1991] 1 AC 398, [1990] 2 All ER 269,
   [1990] 2 WLR 944, 88 LGR 333, 20 Con LR 1, 134 Sol Jo 458, [1990] 5 LS
   Gaz R 42, CA; revsd [1991] 1 AC 398, [1990] 2 All ER 908, [1990] 3 WLR 414,
   89 LGR 24, [1990] 2 Lloyd's Rep 467, 22 HLR 502, 21 Con LR 1, 134 Sol Jo 1076,
   [1990] NLJR 1111, 50 BLR 1, HL 19.131
My Kinda Town (t/a Chicago Pizza Pie Factory) v Soll and Grunts Investments
   [1983] RPC 407, CA 14.31

N

National Phonograph Co of Australia Ltd v Menck [1911] AC 336, 80 LJPC 105,
   28 RPC 229, 104 LT 5, 27 TLR 239, PC 14.53, 20.27
Nationale Raad van de Orde van Architecten v Egle: C-310/90 [1992] ECR I-177,
   [1992] 2 CMLR 113, ECJ 1.20
Neutrogena Corpn v Golden Ltd [1996] RPC 473; affd [1996] RPC 473, CA . . . 14.25, 14.38
New Southgate Metals Ltd v Islington London Borough Council
   [1996] Crim LR 334 . . . . 13.63
New Zealand Lotteries Commission's Application [1998] ETMR 569 . . . . 5.38
Newham London Borough v Singh [1988] RTR 359, 152 JP 239 . . . . 20.100
Next Generation, Re Trade Marks Registry, 19 February 1997; CIPA Journal,
   May 1997, p 365 . . . . 5.72
Nightwatch, Re (19 August 1996, unreported), CIPA Journal 1996 p 850 . . . . 7.10
Nimmo v Alexander Cowan & Sons Ltd [1968] AC 107, [1967] 3 All ER 187,
   [1967] 3 WLR 1169, 111 Sol Jo 668, 1967 SC (HL) 79, 1967 SLT 277 . . . . 20.22

Norman v Bennett [1974] 3 All ER 351, [1974] 1 WLR 1229, 72 LGR 676,
  [1974] RTR 441, 59 Cr App Rep 277, 138 JP 746, [1974] Crim LR 559,
  118 Sol Jo 697, [1974] CLY 3448 . . . . 20.100
North Kerry Milk Products Ltd v Minister for Agriculture and Fisheries:
  80/76 [1977] ECR 425, [1977] 2 CMLR 769, ECJ 19.154

O
Oasis Stores Ltd's Trade Mark Application, Re [1998] RPC 631 . . . . 6.63, 6.78
Odpo, Re Trade Marks Registry, 15 May 1998; CIPA Journal, October 1998, p 807 . . . . 5.72
Office Cleaning Services Ltd v Westminster Office Cleaning Association
  [1946] 1 All ER 320n, 63 RPC 39, 174 LT 229, HL 14.31, 14.36
Office-pack, Re Trade Marks Registry, 15 August 1996; CIPA Journal,
  September 1996, p 673 . . . . 5.72
Open cad, Re Trade Marks Registry, 1 November 1996; CIPA Journal,
  December 196, 1017 . . . . 5.72
Orient Express Trade Mark [1996] RPC 25 . . . . 2.34
Origins Natural Resources Inc v Origin Clothing Ltd [1995] FSR 280 . . . . 6.9, 12.14

P
POSTPERFECT Trade Mark [1998] RPC 255 . . . . 8.9
PREDATOR Trade Mark [1982] RPC 387 . . . . 2.39
PREPARE Trademark, Re [1997] RPC 884 . . . . 5.35
Padfield v Minister of Agriculture, Fisheries and Food [1968] AC 997,
  [1968] 2 WLR 924, 110 Sol Jo 604, CA; revsd [1968] AC 997,
  [1968] 1 All ER 694, [1968] 2 WLR 924, 112 Sol Jo 171, HL 18.97
Parisienne Basket Shoes Pty Ltd v Whyte (1938) 59 CLR 369 . . . . 18.84
Parker-Knoll Ltd v Knoll International Ltd [1961] RPC 31; on appeal
  [1961] RPC 346, CA; affd [1962] RPC 265, HL 12.25
Parkins v Scott (1862) 1 H & C 153, 31 LJ Ex 331, 8 Jur NS 593,
  10 WR 562, 6 LT 394 . . . . 15.9
Parmiter v Coupland (1840) 9 LJ Ex 202, 4 Jur 701, 6 M & W 105 . . . . 15.7
Pastelline, Re Trade Marks Registry, 11 January 1996; CIPA Journal,
  February 1996, p 128 . . . . 5.72
Peckitt's Application, Re [1999] RPC 337 . . . . 16.31
Perfection Trade Mark (1909) 26 RPC 837, CA 5.9, 5.18
Perfectionists, The, Re Trade Marks Registry, 14 July 1997; CIPA Journal,
  August 1997, p 626 . . . . 5.27
Perry v Truefitt (1842) 6 Beav 66 . . . . 14.1
Petch v Gurney (Inspector of Taxes) [1994] 3 All ER 731, [1994] STC 689,
  66 TC 743, [1994] 27 LS Gaz R 37, CA 18.84, 18.85
Philips Electronics BV v Remington Consumer Products [1998] RPC 283; on appeal
  [1999] ETMR 816, CA 4.3, 5.14, 5.26, 5.33, 5.34, 5.71, 5.78, 5.96, 7.26, 12.11
Pianotist Co's Application, Re (1906) 23 RPC 774 . . . . 6.16
Pirie (Alexander) & Sons Ltd's Trade Mark, Re (1932) 49 RPC 195, sub nom
  Hammermill Paper Co's Opposition to Application for Registration by Alex Pirie
  & Sons Ltd, Re, Re Pirie (Alex) & Sons Ltd 146 LT 493, CA; affd sub nom Re
  Hammermill Paper Co's Opposition to Application for Registration by Alex Pirie
  & Sons Ltd (1933) 50 RPC 147, [1933] All ER Rep 956, 149 LT 199, HL 6.81
Pitman Training Ltd v Nominet UK [1997] FSR 797, ITCLR 11 . . . . 13.22
Plastus Kreativ AB v Minnesota Mining and Manufacturing Co
  [1995] RPC 438 . . . . 13.21, 13.22
Plomien Fuel Economiser Co Ltd v National School of Salesmanship Ltd
  (1943) 60 RPC 209, CA 14.51, 14.52

Pointing (Martin) v Customs and Excise Comrs
  [1999] FSR 394 . . . . 19.79, 19.123, 19.127, 19.128, 19.129, 19.150, 19.160
Poly Pads Trade Mark Case R 68/1998-3, OJ 10/98, p 1079 . . . . 26.6
Portafloor Trade Mark (29 August 1997, unreported) 9.5
Portakabin Ltd v Powerblast Ltd [1990] RPC 471 . . . . 12.27
Portfolio Trade Mark Application, Re (31 May 1996, unreported) CIPA Journal,
  July 1996, p 522 . . . . 5.120
Potato Flour Tax, Re [1964] CMLR 96 . . . . 16.61
Powell v Birmingham Vinegar Brewery Co [1894] AC 8, 58 JP 296,
  63 LJ Ch 152, 11 RPC 4, 6 R 52, 70 LT 1, 10 TLR 84, HL 2.38
Power Fuel, Re Trade Marks Registry, 7 July 1998, CIPA Journal,
  October 1998, p 809 . . . . 5.72
Practice Note [1977] 2 All ER 540, sub nom Practice Direction [1977] 1 WLR 537,
  64 Cr App Rep 258, DC 20.80
Practice Note [1990] 3 All ER 979, [1990] 1 WLR 1439, [1990] NLJR 1534 . . . . 20.120
Prince plc v Prince Sports Group Ltd [1998] FSR 21 . . . . 13.10, 13.13, 13.18, 13.19
Processed Vegetable Growers Association Ltd v Customs and Excise Comrs
  [1974] 1 CMLR 113 . . . . 16.61
Procter and Gamble's Trade Mark Application, Re [1998] RPC 710; on appeal
  [1999] RPC 673, [1999] ETMR 375, CA 5.5, 5.27, 5.34, 5.45, 5.72

Q
Queen's Club Trade Mark Application [1997] ETMR 345 . . . . 6.50

R
R v Adam [1998] 2 Cr App Rep (S) 403, CA 20.111, 20.112
R v Adamson (1875) 1 QBD 201, 45 LJMC 46, 24 WR 250, sub nom
  R v Tynemouth Justices 40 JP 182, 33 LT 840 . . . . 18.52, 20.118
R v Allan [1965] 1 QB 130, [1963] 2 All ER 897, [1963] 3 WLR 677,
  47 Cr App Rep 243, 127 JP 511, 107 Sol Jo 596, CCA 20.52
R v Anderson [1966] 2 QB 110, [1966] 2 WLR 1195, 110 Sol Jo 369, sub nom
  R v Anderson and Morris [1966] 2 All ER 644, 50 Cr App Rep 216,
  130 JP 318, CCA 20.61
R v Anderson [1986] AC 27, [1985] 2 All ER 961, [1985] 3 WLR 268,
  81 Cr App Rep 253, [1985] Crim LR 651, 129 Sol Jo 522, [1985] LS Gaz
  R 3172, [1985] NLJ Rep 727, HL 20.82
R v Ansari, Horner, Ling and Ansari (11 May 1999, unreported), CA 20.114
R v Bainbridge [1960] 1 QB 129, [1959] 3 All ER 200, [1959] 3 WLR 656,
  43 Cr App Rep 194, 123 JP 499, CCA 20.60
R v Becerra (1975) 62 Cr App Rep 212, CA 20.63
R v Belfon [1976] 3 All ER 46, [1976] 1 WLR 741, 63 Cr App Rep 59,
  140 JP 523, 120 Sol Jo 329, CA 20.16
R v Bhad [1999] 2 Cr App Rep (S) 139, CA 20.111, 20.112
R v Birt (8 June 1999, unreported), CA 20.114
R v Bishop [1975] QB 274, [1974] 2 All ER 1206, [1974] 3 WLR 308,
  59 Cr App Rep 246, 138 JP 654, 118 Sol Jo 515, CA 15.7
R v Bouchereau: 30/77 [1978] QB 732, [1981] 2 All ER 924n,
  [1978] 2 WLR 250, [1977] ECR 1999, [1977] 2 CMLR 800,
  66 Cr App Rep 202, 122 Sol Jo 79, ECJ 19.154
R v Brentford Justices, ex p Catlin [1975] QB 455, [1975] 2 All ER 201,
  [1975] 2 WLR 506, 139 JP 516, 119 Sol Jo 221 . . . . 20.118
R v Brighton Gaming Licensing Committee, ex p Cotedale Ltd [1978] 3 All ER 897,
  [1978] 1 WLR 1140, 143 JP 98, 122 Sol Jo 487, CA 18.84

R v Brisac (1803) 4 East 164 . . . . 20.78

R v Bros (1901) 66 JP 54, 20 Cox CC 89, 85 LT 581, 18 TLR 39, DC 18.52, 20.118

R v Byrde and Pontypool Gas Co, ex p Williams (1890) 55 JP 310, 60 LJMC 17,
    17 Cox CC 187, 39 WR 171, 63 LT 645, 7 TLR 79, DC. 18.52, 20.118

R v Carroll (Clarkson) [1971] 3 All ER 344, [1971] 1 WLR 1402,
    55 Cr App Rep 445, 135 JP 533, 115 Sol Jo 654 . . . . 20.53

R v Chief Metropolitan Stipendiary Magistrate, ex p Choudhury
    [1991] 1 QB 429, [1991] 1 All ER 306, [1990] 3 WLR 986, 91 Cr App Rep 393,
    [1990] Crim LR 711, [1990] NLJR 702. . . . . 18.52, 20.118

R v Comptroller-General, ex p Cyclo Chemicals Ltd (1949) 66 RPC 225, DC 9.18

R v Coney (1882) 8 QBD 534, 46 JP 404, 51 LJMC 66, 15 Cox CC 46,
    30 WR 678, 46 LT 307, CCR 20.52

R v Customs and Excise Comrs, ex p EMU Tabac SARL (Imperial Tobacco intervening):
    C-296/95 [1998] QB 791, [1998] All ER (EC) 402, [1998] 3 WLR 298,
    [1998] ECR I-1605, [1998] 2 CMLR 1205, [1997] Eu LR 153, ECJ. 19.155

R v Dacorum Gaming Licensing Committee, ex p EMI Cinemas and Leisure Ltd
    [1971] 3 All ER 666, 135 JP 610, 115 Sol Jo 810. . . . . 18.84

R v Davis [1993] 2 All ER 643, [1993] 1 WLR 613, 97 Cr App Rep 110,
    [1993] 10 LS Gaz R 35, [1993] NLJR 330, 137 Sol Jo LB 19, CA 20.163, 20.167

R v Eagleton (1855) 19 JP 546, Dears CC 376, 515, 24 LJMC 158, 6 Cox CC 559,
    1 Jur NS 940, 4 WR 17, [1843-60] All ER Rep 363, 3 CLR 1145,
    26 LTOS 7, CCR 20.71, 20.73

R v Edwards [1975] QB 27, [1974] 2 All ER 1085, [1974] 3 WLR 285,
    59 Cr App Rep 213, 138 JP 621, 118 Sol Jo 582, CA. 20.21

R v Ewing [1983] QB 1039, [1983] 2 All ER 645, [1983] 3 WLR 1,
    77 Cr App Rep 47, [1983] Crim LR 472, 127 Sol Jo 390, CA 20.23

R v Flynn (11 March 1999, unreported), CA 20.114

R v Foxley [1995] 2 Cr App Rep 523, 16 Cr App Rep (S) 879, CA 20.153

R v Fretwell (1862) 26 JP 499, Le & Ca 161, 31 LJMC 145, 9 Cox CC 152,
    8 Jur NS 466, 10 WR 545, 6 LT 333, CCR. 20.57

R v Ghosh [1982] QB 1053, [1982] 2 All ER 689, [1982] 3 WLR 110, 75 Cr App Rep
    154, 146 JP 376, [1982] Crim LR 608, 126 Sol Jo 429, CA. 20.105

R v Goodwin and Unstead [1997] STC 22, CA 20.114

R v Grundy [1977] Crim LR 543, CA 20.64

R v Gullefer [1990] 3 All ER 882, [1990] 1 WLR 1063n, 91 Cr App Rep 356n,
    [1987] Crim LR 195, CA 20.73

R v Halpin [1975] QB 907, [1975] 2 All ER 1124, [1975] 3 WLR 260,
    61 Cr App Rep 97, 119 Sol Jo 541, CA 20.157

R v Hammertons Cars Ltd [1976] 3 All ER 758, [1976] 1 WLR 1243, 75 LGR 4,
    [1976] RTR 516, 63 Cr App Rep 234, [1976] Crim LR 775, 120 Sol Jo 553,
    [1976] CLY 2470, CA. 20.100

R v Hancock [1986] AC 455, [1986] 1 All ER 641, [1986] 3 WLR 1014, 82 Cr App Rep
    264, 150 JP 33, [1986] Crim LR 180, 129 Sol Jo 793, [1985] NLJ Rep 1208, CA;
    affd [1986] AC 455, [1986] 1 All ER 641, [1986] 2 WLR 357, 82 Cr App Rep 264,
    150 JP 203, [1986] Crim LR 400, 130 Sol Jo 184, [1986] LS Gaz R 967,
    [1986] NLJ Rep 214, HL 20.16

R v Howe [1987] AC 417, [1987] 1 All ER 771, [1987] 2 WLR 568, 85 Cr App Rep 32,
    151 JP 265, [1987] Crim LR 480, 131 Sol Jo 258, [1987] LS Gaz R 900,
    [1987] NLJ Rep 197, HL 20.67

R v Hunt [1987] AC 352, [1987] 1 All ER 1, [1986] 3 WLR 1115,
    84 Cr App Rep 163, [1987] Crim LR 263, 130 Sol Jo 984, [1987] LS Gaz
    R 417, [1986] NLJ Rep 1183, HL 20.22, 20.104

R v Immigration Appeal Tribunal, ex p Antonissen: C-292/89 [1991] ECR I-745,
[1991] 2 CMLR 373, ECJ..1.20
R v IRC, ex p Rossminster Ltd [1980] AC 952, [1979] 3 All ER 385, [1980] 2 WLR 1,
[1977] STC 677, 52 TC 160, [1979] TR 287, 123 Sol Jo 554; on appeal [1980] AC
952, [1979] 3 All ER 385, [1980] 2 WLR 1, [1979] STC 677, 52 TC 160, 170,
[1979] TR 309, 123 Sol Jo 586, CA; revsd sub nom IRC v Rossminster Ltd [1980]
AC 952, [1980] 1 All ER 80, [1980] 2 WLR 1, 70 Cr App Rep 157, [1980] STC 42,
52 TC 160, 191, [1979] TR 309, 124 Sol Jo 18, L(TC) 2753, HL..............18.101
R v Inner London Area (West Central Division) Betting Licensing Committee, ex p Pearcy
[1972] 1 All ER 932, 136 JP 273, sub nom R v Inner London Betting Licensing
Committee, ex p Pearcy [1972] 1 WLR 421, 116 Sol Jo 143, DC...............18.84
R v Inspector of Taxes, ex p Clarke [1974] QB 220, [1972] 1 All ER 545, [1973]
3 WLR 673, 117 Sol Jo 815, sub nom R v Freshwell General Comrs for Income
Tax, ex p Clarke 47 TC 691, 50 ATC 389, L(TC) 2431, CA 18.84
R v Jones [1990] 3 All ER 886, [1990] 1 WLR 1057, 91 Cr App Rep 351, 154 JP 413,
[1990] Crim LR 800, [1990] 24 LS Gaz R 40, CA.........................20.74
R v Keane [1994] 2 All ER 478, [1994] 1 WLR 746, 99 Cr App Rep 1,
[1995] Crim LR 225, 138 Sol Jo LB 76, CA........................20.170, 20.171
R v Kelly [1996] 1 Cr App Rep (S) 61, CA...........................20.111, 20.112
R v Kennedy (1902) 20 Cox CC 230, 50 WR 633, 86 LT 753, 18 TLR 557 ... 18.52, 20.118
R v Leak [1976] QB 217, [1975] 2 All ER 1059, [1975] 3 WLR 316, 61 Cr App Rep
217, 139 JP 608, [1975] Crim LR 584, 119 Sol Jo 473, CA...................20.67
R v Leicester Gaming Licensing Committee, ex p Shine [1971] 3 All ER 1082,
[1971] 1 WLR 1648, 115 Sol Jo 722, CA..................................18.84
R v Liverpool City Council, ex p Liverpool Taxi Fleet Operators' Association [1975]
1 All ER 379, [1975] 1 WLR 701, 73 LGR 143, 139 JP 171, 119 Sol Jo 166 ......18.84
R v McMillan Aviation Ltd and McMillan [1981] Crim LR 785..................20.100
R v Manchester Stipendiary Magistrate, ex p Hill [1983] 1 AC 328, [1982] 3 WLR 331,
[1982] RTR 449, 126 Sol Jo 526, sub nom Hill v Anderton [1982] 2 All ER 963,
75 Cr App Rep 346, 146 JP 348, [1982] Crim LR 755, HL..............18.52, 20.118
R v Mead, ex p National Health Insurance Comrs (1916) 14 LGR 688, 80 JP 332,
85 LJKB 1065. 114 LT 1172, DC..................................18.52, 20.118
R v Melton and Belvoir Justices, ex p Tynan (1977) 75 LGR 544, 33 P & CR 214,
242 Estates Gazette 205 ....18.84
R v Mohan [1976] QB 1, [1975] 2 All ER 193, [1975] 2 WLR 859, [1975] RTR 337,
60 Cr App Rep 272, 139 JP 523, 119 Sol Jo 219, CA.......................20.16
R v Moloney [1985] AC 905, [1985] 1 All ER 1025, [1985] 2 WLR 648,
81 Cr App Rep 93, 149 JP 369, [1985] Crim LR 378, 129 Sol Jo 220,
[1985] LS Gaz R 1637, [1985] NLJ Rep 315, HL..........................20.16
R v Moses and Ansbro [1991] Crim LR 617, CA..............................20.86
R v Newcastle-upon-Tyne Gaming Licensing Committee, ex p White Hart Enterprises
Ltd [1977] 1 WLR 1135, 121 Sol Jo 460; revsd [1977] 3 All ER 961, [1977] 1 WLR
1135, 142 JP 81, 121 Sol Jo 460, CA 18.84
R v Newcastle-upon-Tyne Justices, ex p John Bryce (Contractors) Ltd [1976] 2 All ER
611, [1976] 1 WLR 517, [1976] RTR 325, 140 JP 440, [1976] Crim LR 134,
120 Sol Jo 64, DC...18.64
R v Pontypool Gaming Licensing Committee, ex p Risca Cinemas Ltd [1970] 3 All ER
241, [1970] 1 WLR 1299, 134 JP 648, 114 Sol Jo 705....................18.84
R v Reed [1982] Crim LR 819, CA...20.58
R v Registrar of Trade Marks, ex p Interturbine Germany GmbH
(22 February 1999, unreported) 2.13
R v Richards [1974] QB 776, [1973] 3 All ER 1088, [1973] 3 WLR 888, 58 Cr App Rep
60, 138 JP 69, 117 Sol Jo 852, CA 20.67

R v Robinson [1915] 2 KB 342, 11 Cr App Rep 124, 79 JP 303, 84 LJKB 1149,
24 Cox CC 726, 59 Sol Jo 366, 113 LT 379, 31 TLR 313, [1916-17] All ER
Rep Ext 1299, CCA 20.71
R v Sandwell Justices, ex p West Midlands Passenger Transport Executive
[1979] RTR 17, [1979] Crim LR 56, DC 18.59
R v Saunders and Archer (1573) Fost 371, 2 Plowd 473 . . . . 20.61
R v Scunthorpe Justices, ex p McPhee and Gallagher (1998) 162 JP 635 . . . . 18.62
R v Secretary of State for Transport, ex p Factortame Ltd [1990] 2 AC 85, [1989] 2
WLR 997, [1989] 3 CMLR 1, 133 Sol Jo 724, [1989] 27 LS Gaz R 41, [1989]
NLJR 715, sub nom Factortame Ltd v Secretary of State for Transport [1989]
2 All ER 692, HL; refd sub nom R v Secretary of State for Transport, ex p
Factortame Ltd (No 2): C-213/89 [1991] 1 AC 603, [1990] 3 WLR 818, [1990]
ECR I-2433, [1990] 3 CMLR 1, [1990] 2 Lloyd's Rep 351, [1990] 41 LS Gaz R 33,
sub nom Factortame Ltd v Secretary of State for Transport (No 2) [1991] 1 All ER 70,
[1990] NLJR 927, ECJ; apld sub nom R v Secretary of State for Transport, ex p
Factortame Ltd (No 2) [1991] 1 AC 603, [1990] 3 WLR 818, [1990] 3 CMLR 375,
[1990] 2 Lloyd's Rep 365n, [1991] 1 Lloyd's Rep 10, 134 Sol Jo 1189, [1990] 41
LS Gaz R 36, [1990] NLJR 1457, sub nom Factortame Ltd v Secretary of State for
Transport (No 2) [1991] 1 All ER 70, HL 18.96, 18.98
R v Slack [1989] QB 775, [1989] 3 All ER 90, [1989] 3 WLR 513, 89 Cr App Rep 252,
[1989] Crim LR 903, [1989] 31 LS Gaz R 44, [1989] NLJR 1075, CA 20.63
R v Swallow (14 October 1997, unreported), CA 20.114
R v Taylor (1875) LR 2 CCR 147, 39 JP 484, 44 LJMC 67, 13 Cox CC 68,
23 WR 616, 32 LT 409 . . . . 20.56
R v Titus (20 January 1998, unreported), CA. 20.114
R v Torbay District Council, ex p Singh (1999) Times, 5 July 20.92, 20.102, 20.134
R v Urbanowski [1976] 1 All ER 679, [1976] 1 WLR 455, 62 Cr App Rep 229,
140 JP 270, 120 Sol Jo 148, CA 18.84
R v Ward [1993] 2 All ER 577, [1993] 1 WLR 619, 96 Cr App Rep 1, [1993] Crim LR
312, [1992] 27 LS Gaz R 34, [1992] NLJR 859, 136 Sol Jo LB 191, CA 20.160
R v West London Justices, ex p Klahn [1979] 2 All ER 221, 143 JP 390, sub nom R v
West London Metropolitan Stipendiary Magistrate, ex p Klahn [1979] 1 WLR 933,
123 Sol Jo 251, DC 18.52, 20.118
R v Whitefield (1984) 79 Cr App Rep 36, [1984] Crim LR 97, [1983] LS Gaz R
3077, CA. 20.64
R v Woollin [1999] AC 82, [1998] 4 All ER 103, [1998] 3 WLR 382, [1999] 1 Cr App
Rep 8, [1998] Crim LR 890, [1998] 34 LS Gaz R 32, [1998] NLJR 1178,
142 Sol Jo LB 230, HL. 20.16
R v Yanko [1996] 1 Cr App Rep (S) 217, CA 20.111
Ratcliffe v Evans [1892] 2 QB 524, 56 JP 837, 61 LJQB 535, 40 WR 578,
[1891–4] All ER Rep 699, 36 Sol Jo 539, 66 LT 794, 8 TLR 597, CA 15.3
Ravenhead Brick Co Ltd v Ruabon Brick and Terra Cotta Co Ltd (1937) 54 RPC 341 . . 6.34
React and Device Trade Mark, Re [1999] RPC 529 . . . . 6.54
Reckitt & Colman Products Ltd v Borden Inc [1990] RPC 341; on appeal [1988] FSR 601,
[1990] RPC 341, CA; affd [1990] 1 All ER 873, [1990] 1 WLR 491, [1990] RPC 341,
134 Sol Jo 784, [1990] 16 LS Gaz R 42, HL 6.77, 14.6, 14.10, 14.13, 14.21, 14.22, 14.24,
14.26, 14.27, 14.28, 14.35, 14.38
Red Stripe Trade Mark Application, Re Trade Marks Registry, 12 October 1998,
New Law Digest 699010205. . . . . 5.72
Reddaway (Frank) & Co Ltd v George Banham & Co Ltd [1896] AC 199, 65 LJQB 381,
13 RPC 218, 44 WR 638, [1895-9] All ER Rep 313, 74 LT 289, 12 TLR 295, HL. . 14.37
Revlon Inc v Cripps and Lee Ltd [1980] FSR 85, 124 Sol Jo 184, CA 12.34, 14.53,
20.26, 20.27

Rey Soda v Cassa Conguaglio Zucchero: 23/75 [1975] ECR 1279, [1976] 1 CMLR
   185, ECJ 19.114, 19.115
Reymes-Cole v Elite Hosiery Co Ltd [1965] RPC 102, CA 13.13
Rheinmühlen Düsseldorf v Einfuhr-und Vorratsstelle für Getreide und Futtermittel:
   166/73 [1974] ECR 33, [1974] 1 CMLR 523, ECJ 16.59
Rich (Marc) & Co AG v Bishop Rock Marine Co Ltd, The Nicholas H [1996] AC 211,
   [1995] 3 All ER 307, [1995] 3 WLR 227, [1995] 2 Lloyd's Rep 299, [1995] 31 LS
   Gaz R 34, [1995] NLJR 1033, 139 Sol Jo LB 165, HL 19.131
Richardt and Les Accessoires Scientifiques SNC, Re: C-367/89 [1991] ECR I-4621,
   sub nom Ministre des Finances v Richardt [1992] 1 CMLR 61, ECJ 19.15
Road Tech Computer Systems Ltd v Unison Software (UK) Ltd
   [1996] FSR 805 . . . . 6.82, 16.15
Roburn Construction Ltd v William Irwin (South) & Co Ltd [1991] BCC 726,
   [1991] CILL 700, CA 18.16
Rockfon A/S v Specialarbejderforbundet i Danmark: C-449/93 [1995] ECR I-4291,
   [1996] ICR 673, [1996] IRLR 168, ECJ. 19.154
Roho Inc's Applications, Re Trade Marks Registry, 18 August 1998,
   IPD (October 1998) 21113 . . . . 5.72
Roudolff, Re: 803/79 [1980] ECR 2015, ECJ 19.154
Roussel Uclaf SA v Hockley International Ltd [1996] RPC 441 . . . . 14.53, 20.26, 20.27
Rover Group Ltd's Trade Mark Application, Re (13 July 1998, unreported)
   New Law Digest 698102001. . . . . 5.36
Rubber Improvement Ltd v Daily Telegraph Ltd [1964] AC 234, [1963] 2 WLR 1063,
   107 Sol Jo 356, sub nom Lewis v Daily Telegraph Ltd [1963] 2 All ER 151, HL . . . 15.17
Rysta Ltd's Application, Re, Re Aristoc Ltd's Opposition [1943] 1 All ER 400, 60 RPC
   87, CA; revsd sub nom Aristoc Ltd v Rysta Ltd [1945] AC 68, [1945] 1 All ER 34,
   114 LJ Ch 52, 62 RPC 65, 89 Sol Jo 10, 172 LT 69, 61 TLR 121, HL . . 1.12, 6.16, 12.13

S
SDS Biotech UK Ltd v Power Agrichemicals [1995] FSR 797. . . . . 14.9
SIOT v Ministero delle Finanze: 266/81 [1983] ECR 731, [1984] 2 CMLR 231 . . . . . . 19.15
Sabel BV v Puma AG and Rudolf Dassler Sport: C-251/95 [1998] 1 CMLR 445,
   [1998] RPC 199, [1998] ETMR 1, ECJ 1.14, 1.20, 6.18, 6.31, 6.37, 6.38, 6.41, 6.43,
                                                     6.48, 6.49, 6.53, 6.58, 12.14, 24.19
Salgoil SpA v Italian Ministry for Foreign Trade: 13/68 [1968] ECR 453,
   [1969] CMLR 181. . . . . 16.61
Samuelson v Producers Distributing Co Ltd [1932] 1 Ch 201, 101 LJ Ch 168,
   48 RPC 580, [1931] All ER Rep 74, 146 LT 37, CA 14.52
Scandecor Development AB v Scandecor Marketing Ltd [1998] FSR 500, [1998] 12
   LS Gaz R 28; on appeal [1999] FSR 26, CA 7.21, 13.8, 14.13
Schulke & Mayr UK Ltd v Alkapharm UK Ltd
   (1997) 21 (11) IPD 20106, Pat Ct. 12.21
Scott v Metropolitan Police Comr [1975] AC 819, [1974] 3 All ER 1032,
   [1974] 3 WLR 741, 60 Cr App Rep 124, 139 JP 121, 118 Sol Jo 863, HL 20.86
Scragg (Ernest) & Sons' Application [1972] FSR 219, [1972] RPC 679 . . . . 16.31
Scurr v Brisbane City Council (1975) 133 CLR 242. . . . . 18.84
Sebago Inc and Ancienne Maison Dubois et Fils SA v GB-UNIC SA: C-173/98 [1999]
   All ER (EC) 575, [1999] 2 CMLR 1317, [1999] ETMR 467, ECJ . . 12.38, 20,25, 20.103
Second Sight Ltd v Novell UK Ltd and Novell Inc [1995] RPC 423 . . . . 7.29
Secretary of State for Trade and Industry v Langridge [1991] Ch 402,
   [1991] 3 All ER 591, [1991] 2 WLR 1343, [1991] BCLC 543, [1991] BCC 148,
   [1991] 22 LS Gaz R 35, CA 13.84

Seldun (or Seldon) Transport Services Ltd v Baker [1978] ICR 1035, 13 ITR 494,
  122 Sol Jo 456, EAT 18.84
Selsdon Fountain Pen Co Ltd v Miles Martin Pen Co Ltd (1949) 66 RPC 193 . . . . 13.8
Senior, Re Trade Marks Registry, 6 January; CIPA Journal, May 1998, p 378 . . . . 5.72
Sheffield City Council v Graingers Wines Ltd [1978] 2 All ER 70, [1977] 1 WLR 1119,
  75 LGR 743, [1977] RA 127, 20 RRC 286, 121 Sol Jo 271, 242 Estates Gazette 687,
  [1977] JPL 789, CA 18.84
Sheraton Corpn of America v Sheraton Motels Ltd [1964] RPC 202 . . . . 14.18
Silhouette International Schmied GmbH & Co KG v Hartlauer Handelsgesellschaft mbH:
  C-355/96 [1999] Ch 77, [1998] All ER (EC) 769, [1998] 3 WLR 1218, [1998] ECR
  I-4799, [1998] 2 CMLR 953, [1998] FSR 474, 729 ECJ 12.37, 14.56, 19.124, 20.25,
  . . . . 20.26, 20.27, 20.94, 24.33
Sim v Stretch [1936] 2 All ER 1237, 80 Sol Jo 703, 52 TLR 669, HL 15.7
Simmenthal SpA v EC Commission: 92/78 [1979] ECR 777,
  [1980] 1 CMLR 25, ECJ 19.113
Singer Manufacturing Co v Loog (1882) 8 App Cas 15, 52 LJ Ch 481, 31 WR 325,
  49 LT 3, HL 14.58
Sirena Srl v Eda Srl: 40/70 [1971] ECR 69, [1971] CMLR 260, CMR 8101, ECJ 16.61
Skuse v Granada Television Ltd [1996] EMLR 278, CA. 15.18
Slim v Daily Telegraph Ltd [1968] 2 QB 157, [1968] 1 All ER 497, [1968] 2 WLR 599,
  112 Sol Jo 97, CA. 13.11, 15.17
Smith Hayden & Co Ltd's Application (Ovax), Re (1945) 63 RPC 97 . . . . 6.9
Smith, Kline & French Laboratories Ltd v Sterling-Winthrop Group Ltd
  [1975] 2 All ER 578, [1975] 1 WLR 914, [1975] FSR 298, [1976] RPC 511,
  119 Sol Jo 422, HL. 4.3, 4.12
Société des Pétroles Shell-Berre, Re [1964] CMLR 462 . . . . 16.61
Sorrento, Re Trade Marks Registry, 9 June 1998; CIPA Journal, October 1998, p 808. . . 5.72
Spalding (A G) & Bros v A W Gamage Ltd and Benetfink & Co Ltd (1915)
  84 LJ Ch 449, 32 RPC 273, 113 LT 198, 31 TLR 328, HL 14.2, 14.21, 14.25, 14.42
Speedmaster, Re Trade Marks Registry, 9 March 1998; CIPA Journal,
  June 1998, p 470 . . . . 5.72
Spicer v Holt [1977] AC 987, [1976] 3 All ER 71, [1976] 3 WLR 398, [1976] RTR 389,
  63 Cr App Rep 270, 140 JP 545, [1977] Crim LR 364, 120 Sol Jo 572, HL 18.84
Spring v Guardian Assurance plc [1993] 2 All ER 273, [1993] ICR 412,
  [1993] IRLR 122, [1993] NLJR 365, 137 Sol Jo LB 47, CA; revsd [1995] 2 AC 296,
  [1994] 3 All ER 129, [1994] 3 WLR 354, [1994] ICR 596, [1994] IRLR 460,
  [1994] 40 LS Gaz R 36, [1994] NLJR 971, 138 Sol Jo LB 183, HL. 15.16, 19.135
Standard Woven Fabric Co's Application, Re (1918) 35 RPC 53 . . . . 5.32
Star Industrial Co Ltd v Yap Kwee Kor (t/a New Star Industrial Co)
  [1976] FSR 256, PC 14.14
Stilton Trade Mark [1967] RPC 173 . . . . 2.43
Stringfellow v McCain Foods (GB) Ltd [1984] FSR 175, [1984] RPC 501;
  revsd [1984] PC 501, 128 Sol Jo 701, CA. 14.33, 14.44
Sturla v Freccia (1880) 5 App Cas 623, 44 JP 812, 50 LJ Ch 86, 29 WR 217,
  [1874–80] All ER Rep 657, 43 LT 209, HL. 20.155, 20.157
Summers (John) & Sons Ltd v Cold Metal Process Co (1947) 65 RPC 75 . . . . 13.13
Svenska Akt Gasaccumulator's Application, Re [1962] 1 All ER 886, [1962] 1 WLR
  657, [1962] RPC 106, 106 Sol Jo 219, CA. 2.43
Swizzels Matlow Ltd's Trade Mark Application [1998] RPC 244 . . . . 4.8
Sykes v Sykes (1824) 3 B & C 541, 3 LJOSKB 46, 5 Dow & Ry KB 292 . . . . 1.7

T

TV Shop, Re Trade Marks Registry, 14 April 1998; CIPA Journal,
    September 1998, p 729 .... 5.72
Taittinger v Allbev Ltd [1994] 4 All ER 75, [1993] 2 CMLR 741,
    [1993] FSR 641, CA 5.107, 14.47
Tarleton Engineering Co Ltd v Nattrass [1973] 3 All ER 699, [1973] 1 WLR 1261,
    72 LGR 56, [1973] RTR 435, 137 JP 837, [1973] Crim LR 647,
    117 Sol Jo 745, DC 20.100
Taw Manufacturing Co Ltd v Notek Engineering Co Ltd (1951) 68 RPC 271 .... 6.16
Taylor v Director of the Serious Fraud Office [1997] 4 All ER 887, [1997] 36 LS Gaz R
    44, [1997] NLJR 1309, 141 Sol Jo LB 216, [1998] EMLR 463, CA; affd [1999] 2 AC
    177, [1998] 4 All ER 801, [1998] 3 WLR 1040, [1999] EMLR 1, HL 19.134
Taylor v Smith [1974] RTR 190, [1974] Crim LR 200, DC 20.100
Team Lotus Trade Mark Application, Re [1999] ETMR 669, Trade Marks Registry,
    23 October 1998, New Law Digest 699010202 .... 5.119, 6.79
Teint Vitalite Trade Mark Application (10 December 1998, unreported)
    New Law Digest 699021202. .... 6.12
Teknek Electronics Ltd v KSM International Ltd (19 December 1997, unreported),
    CIPA Journal, May 1998, p 380 .... 12.21
Thornton v Mitchell [1940] 1 All ER 339, 38 LGR 168, 104 JP 108, 84 Sol Jo 257,
    162 LT 296, 56 TLR 296. .... 20.656
Three Card Poker, Re Trade Marks Registry, 20 May 1998; CIPA Journal,
    October 1998, p 807 .... 5.72
Today's Gourmet, Re Trade Marks Registry, 2 July 1998; CIPA Journal,
    October 1998, p 809 .... 5.72
Torbay Council v Singh (1999) 163 JP 744, [1999] NLJR 1002 .... 20.30
Trade Marks Registrar v W and G Du Cros Ltd [1913] AC 624, 83 LJ Ch 1, 30 RPC
    660, 57 Sol Jo 728, 109 LT 687, 29 TLR 772, HL. 4.12, 5.29
Trebor Bassett Ltd v Football Association [1997] FSR 211. .... 12.9
Ty Nant Spring Water Ltd's Trade Mark Application, Re [1999] RPC 392. .... 5.72

U

UPDATE Trade Mark [1979] RPC 166 .... 4.14
Unilever plc v Gillette (UK) Ltd [1989] RPC 583; on appeal [1989] RPC 583, CA. . . 19.134
Unilever plc v Procter and Gamble Co [1999] 2 All ER 691, [1999] 1 WLR 1630,
    [1999] NLJR 370, [1999] FSR 849; affd (1999) Times, 4 November 13.16
Union Laitière Normande v French Dairy Farmers Ltd: 244/78 [1979] ECR 2663,
    [1980] 1 CMLR 314, ECJ. 16.65
United Biscuits (UK) Ltd v Asda Stores Ltd [1997] RPC 513 .... 6.49, 7.4
University of London v American University of London (12 November 1993,
    unreported) 14.38
Upjohn SA, Danmark v Paranova A/S [1999] ETMR 97 .... 12.45
Uruguay Round Treaties, Re [1995] 1 CMLR 205, ECJ. 19.66, 19.152
Uultraclear, Re Trade Marks Registry, 9 January 1997; CIPA Journal,
    February 1997, p 144 .... 5.72

V

Van Duyn v Home Office [1974] 3 All ER 178, [1974] 1 WLR 1107,
    [1974] CMLR 347, 118 Sol Jo 548. .... 16.61
Vereniging van Fabrikanten en Importeurs van Verbruiksartikelen (FIVA) v Mertens
    [1963] CMLR 141. .... 16.61
Vernootschap onder Firma Senta Aromatic Marketing's Application: R 156/1998-2
    [1999] ETMR 429 .... 4.10

Vodafone Group plc v Orange Personal Communications Services Ltd
  [1997] FSR 34, [1997] EMLR 84 . . . . 12.21, 15.17, 20.105
Volvo AB v Heritage Leicester Ltd (7 May 1999, unreported) 12.30

W

Wagamama Ltd v City Centre Restaurants
  [1995] FSR 713 . . . . 1.14, 1.19, 4.14, 5.94, 6.16, 6.32, 6.45, 12.14, 24.19
Wai Yu-tsang v R [1992] 1 AC 269, [1991] 4 All ER 664, [1991] 3 WLR 1006,
  94 Cr App Rep 264, 135 Sol Jo LB 164, PC 20.86, 20.88, 20.89
Walker (John) & Sons Ltd v Henry Ost & Co Ltd [1970] 2 All ER 106,
  [1970] 1 WLR 917, [1970] RPC 489, 114 Sol Jo 417 . . . . 14.62
Wallabee, Re Trade Marks Registry, 29 October 1996; CIPA Journal,
  December 1996, p 107 . . . . 5.72
Waltham Forest London Borough Council v T G Wheatley (Central Garage) Ltd
  (1977) 76 LGR 195 . . . . 20.100
Warnink (Erven) BV v J Townend & Sons (Hull) Ltd [1980] RPC 31; on appeal
  [1978] FSR 473, [1980] RPC 31, CA; revsd [1979] AC 731, [1979] 2 All ER 927,
  [1979] 3 WLR 68, [1979] FSR 397, [1980] RPC 31, 123 Sol Jo 472, HL 6.77, 14.1,
       14.5, 14.7, 14.8, 14.9, 14.11, 14.43, 14.64, 14.65, 14.67, 14.68, 14.70, 14.72
Waterman (Pete) Ltd v CBS United Kingdom Ltd [1993] EMLR 27 . . . . 14.19
We set the hire standard, Re Trade Marks Registry, 5 January 1996; CIPA Journal,
  1996, p128 . . . . 5.72
Weblink, Re Trade Marks Registry, 4 July 1997; CIPA Journal, August 1997, p 625 . . . . 5.27
Weldmesh Trade Mark, Re [1966] RPC 220, CA 5.19
Welham v DPP [1961] AC 103, [1960] 1 All ER 805, [1960] 2 WLR 669, 44 Cr App
  Rep 124, 124 JP 280, 104 Sol Jo 308, HL 20.89
Wheeler v Le Marchant (1881) 17 Ch D 675, 45 JP 728, 50 LJ Ch 793,
  30 WR 235, 44 LT 632, CA 3.12
Wiener SI GmbH v Hauptzollamt Emmerich: C-338/95 [1997] ECR I-6495,
  [1998] 1 CMLR 1110, ECJ 19.154
Wild Child Trade Mark, Re [1998] RPC 455 . . . . 2.31, 6.77, 9.3
Wilden Pump and Engineering Co v Fusfield [1985] FSR 159, CA 3.12
Windsurfing Chiemsee Produktions- und Vertriebs GmbH v Boot- und Segel-zubehör
  Walter Huber: C-108, 109/97 (1999) Times, 18 May, ECJ 5.10, 10.4, 10.12
Woolmington v DPP [1935] AC 462, 25 Cr App Rep 72, 104 LJKB 433, 30
  Cox CC 234, [1935] All ER Rep 1, 79 Sol Jo 401, 153 LT 232, 51 TLR 446, HL . . 20.22
Wörsdorfer (née Koschniske) v Raad van Arbeid: 9/79 [1979] ECR 2717,
  [1980] 1 CMLR 87, ECJ 19.154
Worth Trade Marks, Re [1998] RPC 875 . . . . 7.4, 7.10
Wright v Nicholson [1970] 1 All ER 12, [1970] 1 WLR 142, 54 Cr App Rep 38,
  134 JP 85, 113 Sol Jo 939, DC 18.65
Wyko Group plc v Cooper Roller Bearings Co Ltd (1995) Times, 4 December 13.21
Wyllie v Crown Prosecution Service [1988] Crim LR 753 . . . . 18.66

X

XTRA Trade Mark Case R 20/97, OJ 10/98, p 1045 . . . . 26.6
Xpresslink, Re Trade Marks Registry, 6 March 1996; CIPA Journal April 1996, p 287 72

Y

York Trade Mark, Re [1984] RPC 231, HL 4.12, 5.9
Yorkshire Copper Works Ltd v Trade Marks Registrar [1954] 1 All ER 570,
  [1954] 1 WLR 554, 71 RPC 150, 98 Sol Jo 211, HL 4.12, 5.8

Yoshida GmbH v Industrie- und Handelskammer Kassel: 114/78 [1979] ECR 151,
   [1979] 2 CMLR 747, ECJ 19.112
Yoshida Nederland BV v Kamer van Koophandel en Fabrieken voor Friesland: 34/78
   [1979] ECR 115, [1979] 2 CMLR 747, ECJ 19.112
Youssoupoff v Metro-Goldwyn-Mayer Pictures Ltd (1934) 78 Sol Jo 617,
   50 TLR 581, CA 15.7

Z
Zamoyski Trade Mark, Re (14 December 1998, unreported) 7.14
Zawadski v Sleigh [1975] RTR 113, [1975] Crim LR 180, 119 Sol Jo 318 . . . . 20.100
Zimmer Inc's Trade Mark Application, Re (30 April 1998, unreported)
   New Law Digest 698081304 . . . . 5.105, 6.51
Zino Davidoff SA v A & G Imports Ltd [1999] 3 All ER 711, [1999] 3 WLR 849, [1999]
   2 CMLR 1056, [1999] RPC 631 . . . . . . 12.41, 14.53, 20.27, 20.28, 20.29, 20.103, 24.33
Zippo Trade Mark, Re [1999] RPC 173 . . . . 7.4

*Decisions of the European Court of Justice are listed below numerically. These decisions
are also included in the preceding alphabetical list.*

26/62: Algemene Transport-en Expeditie Onderneming van Gend en Loos NV v
   Nederlandse Belastingadministratie [1963] ECR 1, [1963] CMLR 105, ECJ 16.60
28-30/62: Da Costa en Schaake NV v Nederlandse Belastingadministratie
   [1963]ECR 31, [1963] CMLR 224, ECJ 16.59, 16.61
31, 33/62: Milchwerke Heinz Wöhrmann & Sohn KG v EEC Commission
   [1962]ECR 501, [1963] CMLR 152 . . . . 16.59
20/64: Albatros v SOPECO [1965] ECR 29, [1965] CMLR 159 . . . . 16.60
44/65: Hessische Knappschaft v Maison Singer et fils [1965] ECR 965,
   [1966]CMLR 82, ECJ 16.60
19/67: Bestuur der Sociale Verzekeringsbank v Van der Vecht [1967] ECR 345,
   [1968] CMLR 151 . . . . 16.61, 19.154
13/68: Salgoil SpA v Italian Ministry for Foreign Trade [1968] ECR 453,
   [1969] CMLR 181 . . . . 16.61
41/69: ACF Chemiefarma NV v EC Commission [1970] ECR 661, ECJ 19.115
40/70: Sirena Srl v Eda Srl [1971] ECR 69, [1971] CMLR 260, CMR 8101, ECJ 16.61
78/70: Deutsche Grammophon GmbH v Metro-SB-Grossmärkte GmbH & Co KG
   [1971] ECR 487, [1971] CMLR 631, CMR 8106, ECJ 16.60
5/72: Fratelli Grassi fu Davide v Administrazione delle Finanze [1972] ECR 443,
   [1973] CMLR 322, ECJ 16.60
6/72: Europemballage Corpn and Continental Can Co Inc v EC Commission
   [1973]ECR 215, [1973] CMLR 199, ECJ 7.21, 12.7
146/73: Firma Rheinmuhlen-Düsseldorf v Einfuhr- und Vorratsstelle für Getreide und
   Futtermittel [1974] ECR 139, [1974] 1 CMLR 523, ECJ 16.59
166/73: Rheinmühlen Düsseldorf v Einfuhr-und Vorratsstelle für Getreide und
   Futtermittel [1974] ECR 33, [1974] 1 CMLR 523, ECJ 16.59
6/74: Moulijn v EC Commission [1974] ECR 1287, ECJ 19.154
23/75: Rey Soda v Cassa Conguaglio Zucchero [1975] ECR 1279,
   [1976] 1 CMLR 185, ECJ 19.114, 19.115
80/76: North Kerry Milk Products Ltd v Minister for Agriculture and Fisheries
   [1977] ECR 425, [1977] 2 CMLR 769, ECJ 19.154
30/77: R v Bouchereau [1978] QB 732, [1981] 2 All ER 924n, [1978] 2 WLR 250, [1977]
   ECR 1999, [1977] 2 CMLR 800, 66 Cr App Rep 202, 122 Sol Jo 79, ECJ 19.154

102/77: Hoffmann-La Roche & Co AG v Centrafarm Vertriebsgesellschaft
Pharmazeutischer Erzeugnisse mbH [1978] ECR 1139, [1978] 3 CMLR 217,
[1978] FSR 598, CMR 8466, ECJ 12.34
3/78: Centrafarm BV v American Home Products Corpn [1978] ECR 1823,
[1979] 1 CMLR 326, [1979] FSR 189, CMR 8475, ECJ 12.34
34/78: Yoshida Nederland BV v Kamer van Koophandel en Fabrieken voor Friesland
[1979] ECR 115, [1979] 2 CMLR 747, ECJ 19.112
92/78: Simmenthal SpA v EC Commission [1979] ECR 777,
[1980] 1 CMLR 25, ECJ 19.113
114/78: Yoshida GmbH v Industrie- und Handelskammer Kassel [1979] ECR 151,
[1979] 2 CMLR 747, ECJ 19.112
244/78: Union Laitière Normande v French Dairy Farmers Ltd [1979] ECR 2663,
[1980] 1 CMLR 314, ECJ 16.65
9/79: Wörsdorfer (née Koschniske) v Raad van Arbeid [1979] ECR 2717,
[1980] 1 CMLR 87, ECJ 19.154
803/79: Re Roudolff [1980] ECR 2015, ECJ 19.154
36, 71/80: Irish Creamery Milk Suppliers Association v Ireland [1981] ECR 735,
[1981] 2 CMLR 455, ECJ 16.65
244/80: Foglia v Novello (No 2) [1981] ECR 3045, [1982] 1 CMLR 585, ECJ 16.65
141-143/81: Holdijk [1982] ECR 1299, [1983] 2 CMLR 635, ECJ 16.65
283/81: CILFIT Srl and Lanificio di Gavardo v Ministry of Health [1982] ECR 3415,
[1983] 1 CMLR 472, ECJ 19.154
49/82: EC Commission v Nederlands [1983] ECR 1195, [1983] 2 CMLR 476, ECJ . . . 19.19
162/82: Criminal proceedings against Cousin [1983] ECR 1101,
[1984] 2 CMLR 780, ECJ 19.112
199/82: Amministrazione delle Finanze dello Stato v SpA San Giorgio [1983] ECR
3595, [1985] 2 CMLR 658, ECJ 20.26
237/84: EC Commission v Belgium [1986] ECR 1247, [1988] 2 CMLR 865, ECJ 1.20
C-372/88: Milk Marketing Board v Cricket St Thomas Estate [1990] ECR I-1345,
[1990] 2 CMLR 800, [1990] 41 LS Gaz R 33, ECJ 19.154
C-10/89: CNL-Sucal NV SA v HAG GF AG [1990] ECR I-3711, [1990] 3 CMLR 571,
[1991] FSR 99, ECJ 6.36, 12.34
C-292/89: R v Immigration Appeal Tribunal, ex p Antonissen [1991] ECR I-745,
[1991] 2 CMLR 373, ECJ 1.20
C-306/89: EC Commission v Greece [1991] ECR I-5863, [1994] 1 CMLR 803,
ECJ 1.20
C-367/89: Richardt and Les Accessoires Scientifiques SNC, Re [1991] ECR I-4621,
sub nom Ministre des Finances v Richardt [1992] 1 CMLR 61, ECJ 19.15
C-6, 9/90: Francovich and Bonifaci v Italy [1991] ECR I-5357, [1993] 2 CMLR 66,
[1995] ICR 722, [1992] IRLR 84, ECJ 17.28
C-310/90: Nationale Raad van de Orde van Architecten v Egle [1992] ECR I-177,
[1992] 2 CMLR 113, ECJ 1.20
C-317/91: Deutsche Renault AG v Audi AG [1993] ECR I-6227, [1995] 1 CMLR 461,
[1995] FSR 738, ECJ 6.36
C-327/91: France v EC Commission [1994] ECR I-3641,
[1994] 5 CMLR 517, ECJ 19.154
C-9/93: IHT Internationale Heiztechnik GmbH and Danziger v Ideal-Standard GmbH
and Wabco Standard GmbH [1994] ECR I-2789, [1994] 3 CMLR 857,
[1995] FSR 59, ECJ 12.34
C-427, 429, 436/93: Bristol-Myers Squibb v Paranova A/S [1996] ECR I-3457,
[1997] 1 CMLR 1151, 34 BMLR 59, ECJ 12.43
C-449/93: Rockfon A/S v Specialarbejderforbundet i Danmark [1995] ECR I-4291,
[1996] ICR 673, [1996] IRLR 168, ECJ 19.154

C 71-73/94: Eurim-Pharm Arzneimittel GmbH v Beiersdorf AG [1997] 1 CMLR 1222,
  34 BMLR 59, ECJ. 12.44
C-283/94, C-291/94 and C-292/94: Denkavit Internationaal BV, VITIC Amsterdam
  BV and Voormeer BV v Bundesamt für Finanzen [1996] ECR I-5063,
  [1996] STC 1445, ECJ 19.154
C-58, 75, 112,119, 123, 135, 140, 141, 154 and 157/95: Criminal proceedings against
  Gallotti [1996] ECR I-4345, [1997] 1 CMLR 32, ECJ. 20.10
C-64/95: Konservenfabrik Lubella Friedrich Büker GmbH & Co. KG v Hauptzollamt
  Cottbus [1996] ECR I-5105, ECJ 19.154
C-177/95: Ebony Maritime SA v Prefetto della Provincia di Brindisi [1997] ECR
  I-1111, [1997] 2 CMLR 24, ECJ. 19.154
C-219/95P: Ferriere Nord v EC Commission [1997] ECR I-4411, ECJ 19.154
C-251/95: Sabel BV v Puma AG and Rudolf Dassler Sport [1998] 1 CMLR 445,
  [1998] RPC 199, [1998] ETMR 1, ECJ. 1.14, 1.20, 6.18, 6.31, 6.37, 6.38, 6.41,
                                                                6.43, 6.48, 6.49, 6.53, 6.58, 12.14, 24.19
C-296/95: R v Customs and Excise Comrs, ex p EMU Tabac SARL (Imperial Tobacco
  intervening) [1998] QB 791, [1998] All ER (EC) 402, [1998] 3 WLR 298,
  [1998] ECR I-1605, [1998] 2 CMLR 1205, ECJ 19.155
C-338/95: Wiener SI GmbH v Hauptzollamt Emmerich [1997] ECR I-6495,
  [1998] 1 CMLR 1110, ECJ. 19.154
C-325/96: Fabrica de Queijo Eru Portuguesa Lda v Subdirector-Geral das Alfândegas
  [1997] ECR I-7249, ECJ. 19.19
C-355/96: Silhouette International Schmied GmbH & Co KG v Hartlauer
  Handelsgesellschaft mbH [1999] Ch 77, [1998] All ER (EC) 769,
  [1998] 3 WLR 1218, [1998] ECR I-4799, [1998] 2 CMLR 953, [1998] FSR 474,
  ECJ1 . . . . 2.37, 14.56, 19.124,20.25, 20.26, 20.27, 20.94, 24.33
C-39/97: Canon Kabushiki Kaisha v Metro-Goldwyn-Mayer Inc (formerly Pathé
  Communications Corpn) [1998] ECR I-5507, [1998] All ER (EC) 934,
  [1999] RPC 117, ECJ 6.31, 6.37, 6.41, 6.43, 6.49, 6.53, 6.58, 12.14, 20.2
C-63/97: Bayerische Motorenwerke AG (BMW) v Deenik [1999] All ER (EC) 235,
  [1999] 1 CMLR 1099, ECJ. 12.30
C-108, 109/97: Windsurfing Chiemsee Produktions- und Vertriebs GmbH v Boot- und
  Segel-zubehör Walter Huber (1999) Times, 18 May, ECJ 5.10, 10.4, 10.12
C-342/97: Lloyd Schuhfabrik Meyer & Co GmbH v Klijsen Handel BV
  [1999] All ER (EC) 587, [1999] 2 CMLR 1343, ECJ. 6.52
C-173/98: Sebago Inc and Ancienne Maison Dubois et Fils SA v GB-UNIC SA [1999]
  All ER (EC) 575, [1999] 2 CMLR 1317, [1999] ETMR 467, ECJ . . 12.38, 20.25, 20.103

Acknowledgments

Appendix 4 is reproduced with kind permission of the World Trade Organisation.

Decision EX-96-3 and the Guidelines for Opposition Proceedings in Appendix 5 are reproduced with kind permission of OHIM.

Appendix 6 and the International Classification of Goods and Services in Appendix 7 are reproduced with kind permission of the World Intellectual Property Organisation.

Trade Marks Registry Guide to the Cross Searching of Trade Marks in the UK and the Trade Marks Forms in Appendix 7 are reproduced with kind permission of the Patent Office.

Part I

General introduction

Chapter 1

Subject matter and history of the law

1 Subject matter and arrangement of this book

1.1 This book is concerned with all aspects of the protection of trade marks. The law governing registered trade marks is now to be found in the Trade Marks Act 1994 ('TMA 1994').[1] Under the previous law, it was necessary in some respects to treat the law relating to 'trade marks' and that relating to 'service marks' separately. This was because of the way in which service marks were brought within the scope of the Trade Marks Act 1938 ('TMA 1938').[2] Although in many countries the term 'trade mark' has for some time been used to denote both what have been traditionally known as trade marks in this country, that is marks used for goods, and marks for services, the UK legislature in 1986 decided to use the separate terms 'trade mark' and 'service mark', except in some instances where the word 'mark' could be used for both. This was unnecessarily complicated, and led to the need to use two 'versions' of the amended TMA 1938, one dealing with trade marks and the other dealing with service marks. Fortunately, the TMA 1994, which repealed the old law with effect from 31 October 1994, avoids this difficulty and follows the EC Directive[3] (referred to as 'the Directive') in using the one term, 'trade mark', to denote marks for goods and marks for services, and that term is used accordingly in this book. The TMA 1994 is in Appendix 1, and the two versions of the amended TMA 1938, to which reference still needs to be made for some purposes, are also in Appendix 1. The applicable rules, which govern practice and procedure in the registry, The Trade Marks Rules 1994[4] as amended by the Trade Marks (Amendment) Rules 1998[5] (referred to in this book as 'the Rules') are set out in Appendix 2. Other rules, dealing with fees, international registration, Community trade marks ('CTMs'), and a number of other topics, are also in the Appendices.

1 The TMA 1994 has already been amended in some respects. Amendments are referred to in the relevant places in this book. For example amendments have been introduced by the Olympic Symbol, etc (Protection) Act 1995, providing for the protection of the Olympic symbol and other signs associated with the Olympic games. Certain amendments have also been made in connection with the Agreement relating to Trade Related Aspects of Intellectual Property (the 'TRIPS Agreement'), by the Patents and Trade Marks (World Trade Organisation) Regulations 1999 (SI 1999/1899) made under the European Communities Act 1972, s 2(2).
2 By the Trade Marks (Amendment) Act 1984 and the Patents, Designs and Marks Act 1986, which amended the law with effect from 1 October 1986.
3 First Council Directive to approximate the laws of the Member States relating to trade marks (89/104/EEC) OJ L40 11.2.89, p 1. See Appendix 5.
4 SI 1994/2583 and 1998/925.
5 SI 1998/925.

1.2   After this introduction, which includes a brief history of the law, there follow two main parts. Part II deals with registered trade marks. Part III deals with the law of passing off, which includes what is sometimes called the law relating to 'unregistered marks', and various miscellaneous matters. Part IV covers proceedings for infringement and passing off, and Part V deals with customs procedures and criminal offences. Part VI is concerned with certain international treaties which affect trade marks. Of particular importance is the Madrid Protocol[1] for international registration of trade marks. The Protocol, like its predecessor the Madrid Agreement,[2] establishes procedural rules for obtaining trade mark registrations internationally by a single application; registrations once obtained are national or (in the case of the Benelux countries) regional registrations and subject to the applicable local laws. Also included in Part VI are the Paris Convention,[3] some of the provisions of which have only very recently been specifically enacted in the UK, by ss 55–60 of the TMA 1994, and the TRIPS Agreement[4] which, as mentioned above, has necessitated amendments to the TMA 1994.

1 Protocol Relating to the Madrid Agreement Concerning the International Registration of Marks, 27 June 1989. Appendix 6. See also Commission Regulation 2868/95/ECof 13 December 1995 implementing Council Regulation 40/94/EC on the CTM and the Trade Marks (International Registration) Order 1996, SI 1996/714, Appendix 2.
2 Madrid Agreement Concerning the International Registration of Marks, of 14 April 1891, as subsequently revised. Appendix 6.
3 The Paris Convention for the Protection of Industrial Property of 20 March 1883, as revised and amended from time to time. See Appendix 6 for the trade mark and other general provisions.
4 Annex 1C of the Marrakesh Agreement establishing the World Trade Organisation, which was concluded on 15 April 1994 and came into force on 1 January 1995. The provisions which affect trade marks are set out in Appendix 4.

1.3   The CTM, a unitary trade mark system established in the European Union and administered by the Office for Harmonisation in the Internal Market ('OHIM') in Alicante, Spain, and introduced by a Council regulation adopted on 20 December 1993 ('the CTM Regulation'),[1] is covered in a separate part, Part VII. Also included, in Appendix 5 are the implementing regulations governing the procedures in the Office, fees and appeals.

1 Council Regulation 40/94/EEC OJ L11 14.1.1994, p 1, as amended by Council Regulation 3288/94/EC OJ L 349/83, 22.12.1994. See Appendix 5.

1.4   The Directive and CTM Regulation apart, European Community (now European Union) laws have had a very significant effect on the domestic laws relating to trade marks and passing off since the UK became a member. The Treaty of Rome and subsequent treaties involving Member States and other countries in the European Economic Area ('EEA') continue to affect such national laws and the national rights obtained under them. There are also several other EU regulations, such as those concerned with counterfeit goods[1] and geographical indications of origin,[2] which are of some relevance to trade marks. These matters are mentioned in the appropriate places in this book.

1 Council Regulation 3295/94/EC laying down measures to prohibit the release for free circulation, export, re-export or entry for a suspension of counterfeit and pirated goods as amended by Council Regulation 241/99/EC. See Appendix 5.
2 Council Regulations 2081/92/EEC (see Appendix 5) and 2082/92/EEC.

1.5   Other areas of the law, in which trade mark related problems sometimes arise, are defamation and malicious falsehood and plant varieties; these are dealt with in Part III. Emergency legislation which, though generally of academic interest only, was nevertheless extended to service marks by the Patents, Designs and Marks Act 1986 and is still in force. It is mentioned briefly in the same chapter.

2 Historical development of the law

Pre-registration law

1.6 Although it was a practice from very early times for merchants to distinguish the goods of their manufacture from those of their competitors by marking them with some special symbol or other device, it is only in comparatively recent years that an exclusive right to a particular trade mark came to be recognised by the courts as a kind of property capable of being protected against misuse. As late as 1742, one Lord Chancellor, Lord Hardwicke, in the case of *Blanchard v Hill*[1] refused to grant an injunction at the suit of a manufacturer of playing cards, to restrain the defendant from making and selling cards bearing a counterfeit of the plaintiff's mark, on the ground (inter alia) that he knew of no instance of the granting of an injunction to restrain one trader from using the same mark as another, observing that to impose such restraint would be 'fraught with mischievous consequence'. However this observation was qualified by the remark that if the use of the mark were done with fraudulent design or to draw away customers from the other trader, whose mark was thus appropriated, that might be sufficient to maintain an action.

1 1742 2 Atk 484.

1.7 From the early part of the 19th century there are several reported cases in the Courts of Chancery, in which defendants were restrained from misrepresenting that their goods were the plaintiff's goods, or connected with the plaintiff.[1] An early example of a case of infringement in the Courts of Chancery was *Day v Day*.[2] However the Courts of Chancery, in which the development of remedies against the infringement of trade marks mainly took place, continued for some time to maintain the view that a fraudulent intention was a necessary ingredient of an action for infringement of a trade mark. The Courts of Chancery gradually abandoned the doctrine that fraudulent intention was required, and it became accepted that the owner of a trade mark had a genuine proprietary right in his mark, which he was entitled to have protected against invasion like any other right of property. The first case, in which this was definitely established, was *Millington v Fox*.[3] In the earliest reported instance of a successful attempt in a common law court to restrain trade mark piracy, the case of *Sykes v Sykes*,[4] fraud was the basis of the action. The view, that fraud had to be proved, continued to prevail in the common law courts until the Judicature Act 1873 brought them into line with the Courts of Chancery. The common law action, which did not require proof of fraud after 1873, has continued to exist as the action for 'passing off'.

1 See for example *Cruttwell v Lye* (1810) Ves 335.
2 (1816) Digest 21.
3 (1834) 3 M & Cr 333.
4 (1824) 3 B & C 541; 3 LJOSBKB 46.

Legislation

1.8 Although remedies became available in the courts for traders whose marks had been taken by other traders, nevertheless a plaintiff had in every case to prove that his mark had acquired a public reputation and that goods bearing it were associated in the mind of the public with goods of the plaintiff's manufacture as distinct from those of all other manufacturers. Trade mark litigation was very lengthy and expensive and there was much complaint that the burden on traders, who sought to protect their legitimate rights, was a great hardship. The matter was considered in 1862 by a Select Committee of the House of Commons but a proposal for the establishment of a register of trade marks was not accepted. The Merchandise Marks Act of 1862 was passed in the same year, but registration of trade marks, giving a statutory right against infringement, did not become possible until 1875.

1.9 An important purpose of registration of trade marks was to afford protection to the trader without the need of establishing his title to his trade mark by evidence. The entry of a trade mark on the register was presumptive evidence of the right of the registered proprietor to the exclusive use of the mark for the goods specified. At the same time the public would be better protected against deception and rival traders were given notice, by the register, of the rights claimed in the registered mark. The first statute providing for registration of trade marks was the Trade Marks Registration Act 1875. After amendments in 1876 and 1877, the law was replaced by the Patents, Designs and Trade Marks Act 1883. The part of the 1883 Act dealing with trade marks was amended in 1888. The Trade Marks Act 1905 repealed the trade mark provisions of the 1883 and 1888 Acts. The Trade Marks Act 1919 made a number of amendments to the 1905 Act, including the introduction of Part B of the register.

1.10 Major changes were made by the TMA 1938,[1] which implemented most of the recommendations of the Goschen Committee.[2] However many of the basic principles, in particular those concerned with registrability of trade marks, remained unchanged. The TMA 1938 was amended on a number of occasions. Much the of most important amendments were those introducing the provisions for the registration of service marks.[3] In this book, the 1938 Act, in its most recently amended form, is referred to as 'the TMA 1938'. As mentioned above, it was necessary for practical reasons to have two 'versions' of the Act, one for trade marks and the other for service marks. The TMA 1938 is still applicable in some respects to marks registered or applied for before the TMA 1994 came into force, and reference may also have to be made to it for other purposes, under the TMA 1994. The numbers of cases being prosecuted under the old law is decreasing, being limited mainly to some applications for registration dated prior to 31 October 1994, to oppositions to such applications and to rectification proceedings which were pending at that date, and to certain other situations arising under the transitional provisions of Sch 3 to the TMA 1994.

1 The changes were actually made by the Trade Marks Amendment Act 1937, which was immediately repealed and replaced by a consolidating act, the TMA 1938. This legislative history is now probably only of academic interest.
2 (1934) Cmd 4568.
3 See para **1.1**, n 2 above.

1.11 The 1875–77 legislation and the subsequent trade mark legislation prior to the TMA 1938 might conceivably still have some relevance on occasions, in interpreting the TMA 1938 in so far as any of its provisions continue to be applicable. This possibility is considered to be of little, if any, importance, and it is therefore unnecessary to include texts of these previous laws.

The role of trade marks today

1.12 The traditional function of a trade mark was the indication of the origin, or trade source, of goods. This was emphasised, for instance, by the House of Lords in *Aristoc Ltd v Rysta Ltd.*[1] The emphasis no doubt changed somewhat, owing to the relaxation of the very strict rules, which before 27 July 1938 applied to the licensing of any trade mark, or its assignment separately from the business in which it was used, and also owing to the frequency of company takeovers, in which the effective ownership of trade mark rights can be transferred without any actual assignment. Nevertheless the function of a trade mark has remained essentially the same. As it was put in the *Memorandum on the creation of an EEC trade mark*:[2]

> 'Both economically and legally the function of the trade mark as an indication of origin is paramount. It follows directly from the concept of a trade mark as a distinctive sign, that it serves to distinguish trade marked products originating from a particular firm or group of firms from the products of other firms. From this basic function of the trade mark are derived all the other functions which the trade mark fulfils in economic life. If the trade mark guarantees that the commercial origin is the same, the consumer can count on a similarity of composition and quality of goods bearing the trade mark; and the advertising value of the trade mark requires that between the trade marked goods and the owner of the trade mark there is a definite legal relationship. Although the quality function predominates in the mind of the consumer and the publicity function predominates in the mind of the producer, so far as the legal aspect is concerned the decisive criterion is the function of the mark as an indication of origin. Only if the proper purpose of the trade mark is maintained, namely to distinguish the trade marked goods from goods of different origin, can it fulfil its further role as an instrument of sales promotion and consumer information; and only then does the trade mark right perform its function of protecting the proprietor against injury to the reputation of his trade mark.'

1 (1945) 62 RPC 65. See in particular per Viscount Maugham at 74 line 31 and per Lord Wright at 82 line 36.
2 *Bulletin of the European Communities*, Supplement 8/76, adopted by the Commission on 6 July 1976—see para 68.

1.13 These observations apply equally to service marks, and they point also to the role of the trade mark in commerce, a matter mentioned earlier in the Memorandum:[1]

> 'The consumer is faced ... with a large and ... considerable number of consumer goods of the same kind; and these are not distinguished, like raw materials and many agricultural products, by natural or technical features alone, but have numerous variations and differences in quality, special properties, taste and appearance. To make the right choice, the consumer needs to be able to identify and distinguish these goods according to their origin and to recognise a connection between a particular product, its quality and its reputation.
> Trade marks facilitate this process of identification and choice... The consumer needs a clear and unambiguous distinguishing mark for each required article. Thus trade marks assist the consumer in the first instance when consumer goods of the same kind are offered for sale, facilitate a further purchase of the same article and enable the consumer to distinguish, according to his wishes, between the various goods offered for sale. The same is true in respect of the provision of services.

To an economic system directed towards the needs of consumers, trade marks are thus indispensable. They play an important role in the public interest in the distribution of goods and services, and should therefore be given legal protection.'

1 Paragraphs 11–13.

1.14 By removing all restrictions on the licensing and assignment of trade marks the TMA 1994 goes even further than did the TMA 1938. However, given the obvious reasons for having trade marks at all, and the strong incentive upon traders to preserve the distinguishing power and thus the value of their trade marks, it was not to be expected that the TMA 1994, and the Directive on which its main provisions are based, would lead to a fundamental change in the traditional function of a trade mark. This has already been confirmed by decisions of the English High Court and the European Court of Justice ('ECJ'),[1] both courts deriving assistance from the recitals in the Directive, which emphasise the original function of trade marks.

1 *Wagamama Ltd v City Centre Restaurants plc* [1995] FSR 713 (Laddie J); *Sabel BV v Puma AG* [1998] ETMR 1, [1998] RPC 199, ECJ.

1.15 It is but a short step from the foregoing passages in the Memorandum to the conclusion, again expressed in the Memorandum, that trade marks stimulate trade. It is observed[1] that:

'By virtue of their role as an indicator of origin and quality and as a means of advertising, trade marks are indeed an indispensable means of promoting trade and in doing so assist the further interpenetration of national markets. They help manufacturers to acquire new markets and thus help to promote the expansion of economic activity beyond national borders.'

1 Paragraph 21.

1.16 It follows that, if it is desired to abolish altogether trade in any particular product, one means of accelerating this is to prohibit the use of trade marks for such products. This principle can be illustrated by some recent national laws aimed at curbing trade in tobacco products; in some countries these are coming close to a prohibition of the use of trade marks and proposals have been made in some countries which do go that far. Similarly, a recent Canadian law has prohibited (with few exceptions) the use of the same trade mark for tobacco products as for other goods, and vice versa. It is hard to imagine any clearer demonstration of the role of trade marks.

1.17 One result of the recognition of the importance of trade marks in stimulating trade, is the growing practice of placing substantial values on brand names in the balance sheets of companies. This interesting, but still controversial, development is outside the scope of this book, but is mentioned here because it represents another demonstration of the continuing, indeed increasing, importance of trade marks in modern business.

The Directive and the TMA 1994

1.18 It is of considerable practical importance that a major purpose of the TMA 1994 is to implement the EC Directive. As already pointed out, the Directive itself can be the subject of interpretation by the ECJ. Although this procedure may not always be of direct relevance in instances in which the TMA 1994. is not in identical terms to the Directive, it is to be noted that the draughtsman of the Act has generally kept very close to the wording of the Directive; in many instances the wording is identical or virtually so. Furthermore, where the wording of the Act does differ from the corresponding provision of the Directive, the court will refer to the latter for the purpose of construing the statutory provision based on it.[1] Even a provision of the Directive which has not been incorporated into the Act may have binding effect.[2] Therefore it is inevitable, as a practical matter, that courts in the UK will need to pay close attention to the interpretation placed on provisions of the Directive by the ECJ, and to be ready to request rulings from the Court of Justice.

1 See for example the observations of Jacob J in *British Sugar plc v James Robertson & Sons Ltd* [1996] RPC 281 at 291.
2 Thus, in the case of *Mister Long Trade Mark* [1998] RPC 401 Geoffrey Hobbs QC (sitting as the appointed person under the TMA 1994, s 77), held (at 406) that art 13 of the Directive is binding on the registrar.

1.19   On the question of interpretation, some mention should be made of another document, which has been claimed to be relevant when interpreting certain provisions of the Directive. This document, which was originally considered as being confidential[1] but has now been published in the Official Journal of the OHIM,[2] (but not in the Official Journal of the EC), is headed 'Annex'; its sub-heading is 'Statements for entry in the minutes of the Council meeting at which the Directive is adopted'. In this book it is referred to as 'the Annex to the Directive', and the similar document relating to the CTM Regulation as 'the Annex to the Regulation'. Each paragraph commences with the words 'The Council and the Commission consider that ...', followed by statements as to the meaning and effect of a number of the provisions of the Directive, not necessarily obvious from the provisions themselves. The precise nature, status and origin of these documents are unclear. It has been rumoured that the 'Council minutes' do not exist as such, in the form of some book or other formal record. It is understood that the documents came into being as a compromise following disagreements among Member States as to how the provisions in question should be worded, perhaps being recorded by way of some kind of reassurance to Member States who were unhappy with the form proposed. If this understanding is correct, then it would seem unfortunate if the courts cannot take any notice of the documents at all, even if it is recognised, as it must be in any event, that the Annexes can only be regarded as guides in interpreting and applying the statutory provisions based upon the Directive, and the CTM Regulation, as the case may be, and not in any way conclusive. It is thought that, in relation to the Regulation, OHIM regard these statements of opinion as binding on them. However in an early decision of an English court, in the *Wagamama* case,[3] an infringement action brought under the TMA 1994, in which the plaintiff sought to rely upon a concept of Benelux trade mark law, referred to in the Annex, Laddie J held that it was not permissible to refer to confidential Council minutes, and declined to rely upon the Annex to the Directive for the purpose of construing the Directive. In his judgment, Laddie J observed:

'Minutes of Council meetings are confidential. Directives become part of the law which affects all citizens of the European Union. Those citizens and their lawyers must be able to discover from open material what the laws are that bind them. It would strike at the heart of this principle if the meaning of legislation was to be determined by reference to minutes which citizens and their advisers cannot inspect. In my view that is so even if the European Court of Justice has power to call for the minutes. What counts to citizens is the meaning of the law now, not what might be found out about it after confidential material is made public some time in the future.'

Laddie J also referred to the fact that *Halsbury's Laws of England*[4] points out that it is not certain that the Annex accurately represents what was actually entered in the confidential minutes. He said that it would be wrong for the court to draw any conclusions as to the meaning of a directive on the basis of what is said in the minutes when the minutes themselves are closed to inspection. It seems clear, from the passage of his judgment just quoted, that Laddie J's view would not be altered by the subsequent publication of the Annex to the Directive.

1 Notwithstanding that it had been the subject of fairly wide circulation by at least early 1994.
2 5/96 at 606–611, together with a similar document concerning the CTM Regulation.
3 [1995] FSR 713.
4 Volume 48, p 6.

1.20 In the first case to come before the ECJ in which the relevance of the Annex to the Directive could have been considered,[1] it was not even mentioned. Decisions of the court in cases concerned with other Council minutes do not disclose a consistent view.[2] The general approach of Laddie J can hardly be criticised, although it may be asked how many citizens or even how many of their advisers in fact have access to '*travaux preparatoires*', to which, as the learned judge acknowledges, reference is permissible as an aid to construction. Nevertheless the observations—and other parts of his judgment which shed an interesting light on the history of the Directive—do provide support for the view that the current position, including the manner in which Community legislation is formulated and enacted, is unsatisfactory. If the inclusion in Council minutes of opinions as to the meaning of provisions in directives and regulations is justifiable at all, there seems to be no real justification for maintaining their confidentiality and there are strong arguments for publishing them with the legislation and taking any other steps needed to establish their status clearly.

1 *Sabel BV v Puma AG* [1998] ETMR 1, [1998] RPC 199, ECJ.
2 *Nationale Raad van de Orde van Architecten v Egle* [1992] ECR I-177; *Re the Business Transfer Directive: EC Commission v Belgium* [1986] 2 ECR 1247; *R v Immigration Appeal Tribunal, ex p Antonissen* [1991] ECR I-745; *Re Transport Workers: EC Commission v Greece* [1991] ECR I-586?.

1.21 It is convenient to mention here two alternative ways in which the plaintiff in the *Wagamama* case sought to persuade the court to follow the Benelux route, both of which were rejected by Laddie J. The first submission was based on the proposition that it was a matter of common knowledge that the words referring to 'association' were inserted in the Directive for the purpose of introducing the Benelux concept. The second was that since the Benelux courts have construed their equivalent trade mark law derived from the Directive[1] to cover non-origin association, the British courts should do likewise as a matter of comity and to help deliver the harmony which the Directive hoped to secure. The learned judge observed:

'In any event, the obligation of the English court is to decide what the proper construction is. If that construction differs from that adopted in the Benelux countries, one, at least, is wrong. It would not be right for an English court to follow the route adopted by the courts of another Member State if it is firmly of a different view

simply because the other court expressed a view first. The scope of European legislation is too important to be decided on a "first past the post" basis'.

1 As a matter of fact the so-called principle of non-origin association is not derived from the Directive,
but was developed before the Directive was adopted. As Laddie J pointed out ([1995] FSR at p 728) the
Benelux courts have simply assumed that the Directive made no alteration to their domestic laws, an
assumption which may well have been wrong.

1.22   As matters stand, this approach must clearly be correct. The nature of the
arguments put forward in the *Wagamama* case demonstrate clearly that the proper
interpretation of the provisions of the Directive, and the admissibility and relevance, if any, of the Annex to the Directive, is a matter which may ultimately have
to be resolved by the ECJ, if the question is raised again. This might happen on an
appeal in relation to the CTM Regulation, to the Court of First Instance of the ECJ,[1]
if OHIM maintains the view that the Annexes have binding effect.

1 Under art 63 of the CTM Regulation.

General comment on the new law

1.23   As well as adding to the kinds of trade mark which may be registered. by
providing for registration of certification marks for services and of collective
marks, and by broadening the definition of a 'trade mark', the TMA 1994 is in a
number of respects significantly different from the old law in its general approach
to trade marks. First of all, whereas the onus under the TMA 1938 was on the applicant for registration to show that his mark ought to be registered, the new law[1]
follows the Directive in adopting the opposite approach, by setting out grounds for
refusal or invalidity, creating a presumption that a mark ought to be registered
unless there is some specific objection to it.[2] The same general approach applies to
grounds for refusal (or invalidation) based on prior rights.[3] It should also be noted
that the registrar's discretion, which has been part of the law since 1883, to refuse
registration where there is no statutory ground for objection, or to refuse to remove
a mark from the register even when statutory grounds for removal are established,
has ceased to exist; all the grounds for refusal or invalidation are set out in the
TMA 1994.[4] In the case of revocation on grounds of non-use,[5] the TMA 1994[6] now
places the burden of proving use, in the relevant period, on the proprietor, whereas
under the old law the party alleging the non-use had to establish it. This is a welcome reform. Another difference of approach concerns the treatment of concurrent
use. The new law[7] still provides for refusal on grounds of conflict with prior rights,
including prior registrations and applications, both by the registrar ex officio, and in
opposition or rectification proceedings. In the Bill as originally published there was
no provision corresponding to s 12(2) of the TMA 1938, enabling an objection,
based upon a prior registration or application, to be overcome by establishing 'honest concurrent use' or 'other special circumstances'. As a result of representations
made at a later stage a new clause, now s 7, was introduced, to allow reliance on
honest concurrent use (but not other special circumstances) to a limited extent.
However, as explained below, this provision appears to give the user no actual *right*
to registration as against the owner of the earlier trade mark.

1 TMA 1994, ss 3, 4 and 47.
2 See the White Paper, paras 3.06 and 3.07.
3 TMA 1994, ss 5 and 46.
4 See the White Paper, paras 3.10–3.12.

5 TMA 1994, s 46(1).
6 TMA 1994, s 100.
7 TMA 1994, ss 5 and 47(2).

1.24   There are significant changes in the scope of the rights obtained by registration of a trade mark. Whereas under the old law there could only be infringement by the use of an identical or nearly resembling mark in relation to goods or services actually covered by the registration, the TMA 1994 [1] extends the potential scope of protection to use of an identical or similar mark, in relation to similar goods or services or even, in the case of a mark having a reputation, to dissimilar goods or services. Furthermore, infringement is no longer restricted to visual use, as it has been previously, and there may be infringement (eg) by oral use.[2] Finally, a notable improvement resulting from the form of the TMA 1994 is that where it is possible to succeed in opposing an application for registration of a trade mark on any relative grounds there will be the possibility of preventing use of the mark for the goods or services in question. This was often not the case under the old law.

1 TMA 1994, s 10.
2 TMA 1994, s 103(2).

1.25   Turning to procedural matters, there are again a number of significant changes, which will be seen as improvements. These include the possibility of multi-class applications and of dividing or merging applications and merging registrations; also the relaxation of the restrictions on assignments and licensing and the facilitation of the granting of security interests over registered trade marks. Another improvement is the extension of the provisions for appeals to an appointed person,[1] as an alternative to appealing to the court, to oppositions and revocation and invalidation proceedings, as well as to cases of refusal by the registrar ex officio.

1 By the Lord Chancellor under the TMA 1994, s 77, replacing the old 'Board of Trade' appeal.

Part II

Registered marks

Chapter 2

The Comptroller-General and the registry

1 The Comptroller-General

2.1   Under s 63 of the TMA 1994 the registrar, who is the Comptroller-General of Patents, Designs and Trade Marks,[1] continues to have responsibility to maintain a register of trade marks ('the register'). Under para 2 of Sch 3, the transitional provisions, all 'existing registered marks' were transferred to the register kept under the Act upon commencement of the Act.[2] 'Existing registered mark' means[3] a trade mark, certification trade mark or service mark registered under the TMA 1938 immediately before commencement. Under para 10(1), marks registered pursuant to applications for registration made under the TMA 1938, save in the case of an application converted under para 11 for determination under the TMA 1994, are treated as existing registered marks. Existing registered marks include the marks for textile goods formerly entered on the duplicate register (the Manchester Record) kept by the Keeper of the Manchester Branch of the registry and Sheffield Marks, which were recorded on the register kept by the Cutlers' Company. Under the TMA 1938 the registrar was appointed by the Board of Trade. The functions of the Board of Trade, which continued to be referred to as such in the TMA 1938, are now exercised by the Secretary of State for Trade, who is also the 'President of the Board of Trade'. In practice the registrar's functions are largely delegated to an assistant registrar and his or her staff. Under TMA 1994, s 71 the Comptroller must, in his annual report under the Patents Act 1977, s 121 include a report on the execution of the Act, including the discharge of his functions under the Madrid Protocol. Section 71(2) provides that the report shall include an account of all money received and paid by him under or by virtue of the Act during the previous year.

1 TMA 1994, s 62.
2 The Rules, r 3 sets out the particulars of registered trade marks which are to be entered in the register. See para **2.4** below.
3 Schedule 3, para 1(1).

2.2   Section 70 protects the registrar against liability in respect of official acts. Sub-section (1) provides that the registrar shall not be taken to warrant the validity of the registration of a trade mark under the Act or under any treaty, convention arrangement or engagement to which the UK is a party. By virtue of sub-s (2) the registrar is not subject to any liability by reason of, or in connection with, any examination required or authorised by the Act, or any such treaty, convention, arrangement or engagement, or any report or other proceedings consequent on such examination. Thus, for example, the registrar is not liable for the consequences of a failure to cite a relevant prior registration or application during the examination of an application. Under sub-s (3) protection against proceedings in respect of any matter for which, by virtue of the above provisions, the registrar is not liable, is extended to officers of the registrar.

2 The registry

2.3 The Patent Office, which includes the Trade Marks Registry, is an 'executive agency' of the Department of Trade and Industry. Since early 1989, the Trade Marks Registry has been located in Newport, Gwent, but for some purposes, including hearings, offices in London are retained.[1] The Patent Office has an internal management board made up of its senior managers, and a Steering Board, which has an advisory role and is comprised largely of non-civil servants having relevant commercial experience.

1 As to the address of the Patent Office, see the Patent Office (Address) (Revocation) Rules 1999 (SI 1999/1993) repealing the Patent Office (Address) Rules 1991 (SI 1991/675).

The register

2.4 Preserving a change made in 1986, r 32 of the Rules provides that the register required to be maintained under s 63(1) need not be kept in documentary form. Rule 33 sets out the particulars which are to be entered in the register in respect of each registered trade mark, in addition to the entries required by s 63(2)(a) (the registered trade marks, prescribed particulars of registrable transactions and other prescribed particulars). These are:

(a) the date of registration under s 40(3), that is the date of filing of the application for registration;
(b) the actual date of entry in the register;
(c) any priority date accorded pursuant to a claim under ss 35 or 36;
(d) the name and address of the proprietor;
(e) the address for service;[1]
(f) any disclaimer or limitation of rights under s 13(1)(a) or (b);
(g) any memorandum or statement of the effect of any memorandum relating to a trade mark;[2]
(h) the goods or services in respect of which the mark is registered;
(i) where the mark is a collective or certification mark, that fact; and
(j) where the mark is registered with the consent of the proprietor of an earlier trade mark or other earlier right,[3] that fact.

1 Furnished under r 10.
2 Notified on Form TM24.
3 Pursuant to the TMA 1994, s 5(5).

Classification of goods and services

2.5 The TMA 1994 has not changed the system for classification of goods and services. Under s 34(1) goods and services are to be classified for the purposes of registration, according to a prescribed system of classification. The current

International Classification of Goods and Services originated with the new classification drawn up in 1934, which was introduced in the UK as Sch 4 to the Trade Marks Rules 1938 and which has been amended from time to time.[1] Rule 7 prescribes the classification systems for the purposes of s 34(1). For the purposes of registrations for goods dated before 27 July 1938 (services not then being included), goods are classified in accordance with Sch 3 to the Rules, except where the specification has been converted, whether under the old law or under r 40, to Sch 4, which sets out the current version of the classes of the International Classification. Accordingly, for all registrations for goods dated on or after 27 July 1938, as well as any registrations dated before that date which have been converted, and for all registrations for services, goods and services are classified in accordance with Sch 4. There are now 42 classes of goods and services. Classes 1 to 34 inclusive are for goods; classes 35 to 42 inclusive are for services.

1 The International Classification is drawn up under the Nice Agreement concerning the International Classification of Goods and Services for the purposes of the Registration of marks of 15 June 1957 (as last revised on 13 May 1977) (Cmnd 6898). The current version is the Seventh Edition, which came into force on 1 January 1997.

2.6 Although the old law[1] clearly provided for the possibility of compulsory conversion of specifications, that never in fact happened, and it was left to individual proprietors to apply for conversion. The intention of the TMA 1994 and the Rules is to re-classify all old registrations which are still classified in accordance with Sch 3. Section 65(1) enables provision to be made by rules empowering the registrar to do such things as he considers necessary to implement any amended or substituted classification for the purposes of the registration of trade marks, and under sub-s (2) provision may in particular be made for the amendment of existing entries on the register so as to accord with the new classification. Sub-section (3) provides that any power of amendment shall not be exercised so as to extend the rights conferred by the registration. However there is an exception to this, where it appears to the registrar that compliance would involve undue complexity and that any extension would not be substantial and would not adversely affect the rights of any person. Given that the definition of infringement[2] now extends the scope of the rights of the proprietor of a registered trade mark to goods and services which are similar, and even in certain circumstances to goods which are not similar, to those covered by the registration, it is unlikely that an extension which is not substantial would adversely affect the rights of any person. With a view to speeding up the process of re-classification, sub-s (4) provides for the rules to empower the registrar to require the proprietor of a registered trade mark, within such time as may be prescribed, to file a proposal for amendment of the register, and to cancel or refuse to renew the registration if this is not done. Sub-section (5) requires any proposal for amendment to be advertised, and allows for opposition in such manner as may be prescribed. Rule 40 contains the provisions, under s 65, for effecting changes of classification for registrations for goods which are still classified under the old classification.

1 TMA 1938, s 36(1).
2 In the TMA 1994, s 10.

2.7 It is of interest to note that r 40 does not follow s 65(4) in enabling the registrar to require the proprietor to file a proposal for amendment. Subject to s 65(3), r 40(1) empowers the registrar, in order to reclassify a specification of a registered trade mark founded on Sch 3 to one founded on Sch 4, or consequent upon an amendment of the International Classification, to 'make such amendments to entries on the register as he considers necessary for the purpose of re-classifying the specification'. Before doing this, the registrar is required by para (2) of r 40 to give written notice to the proprietor of his proposals for amendment, at the same time advising him that he may make written objections to the proposals within three months[1] of the date of the notice, stating his grounds, and that if no written objections are received within the period specified the registrar will publish the proposals and that the proprietor will not then be entitled to make any objections. Accordingly para (3) provides that if the proprietor makes no written objections within the period specified or at any time before expiry of that period gives the registrar written notice of his intention not to make any objections, the registrar shall as soon as practicable publish the proposals. Under para (4), where the proprietor does make written objections within the period specified, the registrar shall, as soon as practicable after he has considered the objections, publish the proposals or, where he has amended the proposals, publish the proposals as amended. The decision is final and not subject to appeal.[2] Rule 41 allows for notice of opposition to be given[3] within three months of the date of publication of the proposals under r 40, stating the grounds of opposition. Paragraph (2) allows the registrar to admit or require evidence directed to the questions in issue and requires him to give the opponent the opportunity to be heard before deciding the matter. Under para (3) if there is no opposition or any opposition has been determined, the registrar is to make the amendments and enter in the register the date when they were made. Again the decision is final and not subject to appeal. It is understood that the registry has now almost completed the work of re-classification under these provisions, and that there have been no oppositions.

1 This period is extendable under r 62.
2 An exception to the general rule under the TMA 1994, s 76(1).
3 On Form TM7.

2.8 Classes 1 to 34 are comprehensive in that each class has a heading describing the specific categories of goods allocated to the class. Similarly in the case of classes 35 to 41 the categories of services in each are specified in a heading. On the other hand class 42 is an 'omnibus' class, headed 'Miscellaneous' and including all services not allocated to any other class. In all cases it is the duty and the exclusive function of the registrar to determine the appropriate class. Section 34(2) of the TMA 1994 provides that 'Any question arising as to the class within which any goods or services fall shall be determined by the registrar, whose decision shall be final.' In recent years the registrar had adopted a practice of requiring the words 'all included in class X' to be added at the end of specifications of goods and services. It is understood that this practice has ceased to be followed, as a general practice. In most cases the practice was unlikely to give rise to any difficulty in practice. However it is not impossible that the registry might allocate goods or services to the wrong class, and if that were to happen the result of qualifying the specification by reference to the class could be a registration which was open to revocation under s 46(1)(a) or (b) of the TMA 1994, on grounds of non-use.[1] Each case will depend upon its own circumstances. It might be appropriate in some instances to raise the argument that s 34(2) goes further than providing that the registrar alone is to determine classification and indeed places an obligation on him to determine in which class the goods or services fall. If that be so, then it could have been said that, by insisting on the qualification by reference to class the registrar was not meeting his obligation under the Act. A further point arises here, in relation to goods or services which are not specifically listed in the International Classification. Clearly the registrar must place any goods or services in some class. Of particular interest is the much debated case of 'retailing services'. These are not listed, but in view of the fact that class 42 is an omnibus class including all services not allocated to any other class, if 'retailing' is properly described as a service, then it is arguable that the registrar must allocate an application for 'retailing services' to that class. This point is further mentioned below.[2]

1 As an example of the consequences of incorrect classification, see *AA Byrd and Co's Application for the Rectification of the Register* (1953) 70 RPC 212.
2 See ch 4, para **4.14** below.

The Trade Marks Journal

2.9 Every week the Trade Marks Journal[1] is published, which is the Patent Office's official journal for trade mark matters—referred to as 'the Journal' in the Rules.[2] The Journal is required to contain particulars of any application for the registration of a trade mark (including a representation of the mark) and such other information relating to trade marks as the registrar thinks fit. All applications for registration are advertised in the Journal when they have been accepted by the registrar.[3] Other matters published in the Journal include proposals for alteration of a trade mark,[4] surrender of a trade mark,[5] entry in the register of disclaimers or limitations,[6] the granting of a certificate of validity[7] and registration of transactions affecting registered trade marks and applications for registration.[8] There is no longer any provision for Court orders made under the Act to be published in the Journal.

1 Provided for by the TMA 1994, s 81.
2 See rr 2(1) and 65.
3 This is the 'prescribed manner' for the purposes of the TMA 1994, s 38(1).
4 Under the TMA 1994, s 44 – see r 25.
5 Under the TMA 1994, s 45 – see r 26.
6 Under the TMA 1994, s 13 – see r 24.
7 Under the TMA 1994, s 73 of the Act.
8 Under the TMA 1994, s 25; see r 34 and 35.

3 Rules

2.10 Procedure in the registry is governed by the Rules, in accordance with a number of provisions of the TMA 1994. The main rule-making provision is s 78, which empowers the Secretary of State to make rules (a) for the purposes of any provision of the Act authorising the making of rules with respect to any matter, and (b) for prescribing anything authorised or required by any provision of the Act to be prescribed, and generally for regulating practice and procedure under the Act. By way of example s 78(2) says that provision may, in particular, be made (a) as to the manner of filing of applications and other documents; (b) requiring and regulating the translation of documents and the filing and authentication of any translation; (c) as to the service of documents; (d) authorising the rectification of irregularities of procedure; (e) prescribing time limits for anything required to be done in connection with any proceeding under the Act; and (f) providing for the extension of any such limit, whether or not it has already expired.

2.11 Other provisions of the TMA 1994 authorising the making of rules or the giving of directions are as follows:

(a) s 4(4) (prohibition on registration of mark consisting of arms);
(b) s 13(2) (publication and entry in the register of any disclaimer or limitation);
(c) s 25(5) and (6) (amendment or removal of particulars of transactions affecting registered trade marks);
(d) s 35(5) (provision as to manner of claiming Convention priority);
(e) s 39(3) (publication of amendment of an application);
(f) s 41(1) and (3) (division of applications, merging of applications and registrations and the registration of a series of marks);
(g) s 43(2) and (5) (renewal and restoration of registration);
(h) s 44(3) (publication of alteration of a registered trade mark);
(i) s 45(2) (surrender of registered trade mark);
(j) s 65 (adaptation of entries in the register to a new classification);
(k) s 68(1) and (3) (provisions regarding costs and security for costs);
(l) s 69 (provisions relating to evidence and discovery);
(m) s 76(1) (exclusion of right of appeal);
(n) s 79 (fees);
(o) s 80(1) and (3) (directions as to hours of business and business days);
(p) s 81 (the Trade Marks Journal);
(q) ss 82, 83, 85 and 88 (register of trade mark agents and related matters);
(r) paras 10(2), 12 and 14(5) of Sch 3 (transitional provisions relating to applications pending at 31 October 1994, re-classification and priority claims.

Rules are to be made by statutory instrument, subject to annulment in pursuance of a resolution of either House of Parliament.[1]

1 TMA 1994, s 78(3).

2.12 The Rules, made under s 78 and many of the other provisions mentioned above, are the Trade Marks Rules 1994,[1] as amended by the Trade Marks (Amendment) Rules 1998,[2] set out in Appendix 2.

1 SI 1994/2583.
2 SI 1998/925.

2.13 A question has arisen in some cases as to whether the Rules apply to applications for registration made before 31 October 1994 and to oppositions to such applications, or whether such proceedings remain subject to the 1986 Rules. It is to be noted that the Rules expressly provide[1] that the old rules are revoked. Moreover, where procedural matters are concerned, changes are normally treated as retrospective in effect. Consistently with this, the 1998 amendments, with the exception of r 4,[2] are intended to apply to all applications whenever made. The question was considered by the court in the case of *Re Interlego AG's Trade Mark Application*,[3] in which the applicant sought to divide several applications into two, covering goods for which the registry had held that the marks were acceptable and those for which the registry (the court agreeing) had held were not acceptable. The judge held that the provisions of the TMA 1994 and Rules[4] applied to the applications in question. In an unreported decision[5] on an application for judicial review in opposition proceedings involving an application for registration under the TMA 1938, Laddie J has held that the Rules are applicable to such applications. The point will become of less significance as outstanding applications under the old law are disposed of, but is still of importance in some opposition proceedings, for example where a party wishes to seek discovery of documents.

1 Rule 69(1).
2 Amending r 5 of the Rules (applications for registration). See r 20.
3 [1998] RPC 69 (Neuberger J).
4 See TMA 1994, s 41 and r 19 respectively – see ch 8.
5 *R v Registrar of Trade Marks, ex p Interturbine Germany GmbH*; (22 February 1999, unreported).

2.14 Fees are the subject of separate rules, made under s 79. The current fees rules are the Trade Marks (Fees) Rules 1998.[1] Some matters, such as provisions under s 19(3) of the TMA 1994 or the Olympic Association Right (Infringement Proceedings) Regulations 1995,[2] reg 5, as to service of notice on persons having an interest in any goods, articles or materials in respect of which an order for disposal is sought, are dealt with in the Civil Procedure Rules 1998 ('CPR 1998').[3] Procedures in the registry relating to CTMs[4] and applications under the Madrid Protocol designating the UK, are governed respectively by regulations under s 52[5] and orders under s 54.[6]

1 SI 1998/1776, revoking the Trade Marks (Fees) Rules 1996 (SI 1996/1942), to be construed as one with The Trade Marks (Fees) Rules 1994 (1994/2584) and The Trade Marks (International Registration) (Fees) Rules 1996 (1996/715).
2 SI 1995/3325.
3 Part 49, para 23.10. Appendix 3.]
4 Including applications resulting from conversion of a CTM or a CTM application under art 108 of the CTM Regulation into an application for registration under the Act. See ch 23, paras **23.24–23.25**
5 The Community Trade Mark (Fees) Regulations 1995 (SI 1995/3175) and the Community Trade Mark Regulations 1996 (SI 1996/1908) – see Part VII.
6 The Trade Marks (International Registration) Order 1996 (SI 1996/714) – see ch 20.

2.15 Forms no longer have to be prescribed by rules. Section 66 simply provides that the registrar may require the use of such forms as he may direct, and the only requirement is that the forms be published in the prescribed manner. Rule 3 provides for the forms to be published[1] and allows the use of the replica of a form or of a form acceptable to the registrar containing the information required by the published form and complying with any directions as to the use of the published form. The forms are to be found in Appendix 7.

1 The original forms for the TMA 1994 were published in the special edition of the Trade Marks Journal dated 31 October 1994. Further forms have been published from time to time.

Transaction of business at the registry

Hours of business and business days

2.16 Under s 80 of the TMA 1994, the registrar is empowered to give directions specifying the hours of business of the Patent Office for the purpose of the transaction by the public of business under the Act and the days which are business days for that purpose. Sub-section (2) provides that any business done on any day after the specified hours of business, or on a day which is not a business day, is to be deemed to have been done on the next business day. Where the time for doing anything under the TMA 1994 expires on a day which is not a business day, the time is extended to the next business day. Directions under this section, which may make different provision for different classes of business, are required to be published in the prescribed manner.[1] Directions were published in the special edition of the Trade Marks Journal dated 31 October 1994, published under r 64 of the Rules. Subject to certain days being excluded, the Office is open for all classes of business from Monday to Friday inclusive, from 10.00 am to 4.00 pm. In addition, notices, applications and other documents may be filed up to midnight from Monday to Friday. In addition, applications which do not claim Convention (or other) priority (under ss 35 and 36 of the TMA 1994) may be filed on Saturday from 10.00 am to 10.00 pm. Sundays, Good Friday, Christmas Day and bank holidays are not business days. Saturdays, if immediately preceded by any of the above, are also excluded as business days.

1 Sub-section (3).

Filing of documents and translation

2.17 In the past the normal means of filing applications, notices and other documents at the registry has been by post or delivery at the Office. Filing by facsimile is also permitted. Rule 63 enables the registrar, at his discretion, to permit as an alternative to those means, filing by electronic means subject to such terms or conditions as he may specify. This may be done generally by published notice,[1] or in any particular case by written notice to the person desiring to file any document by such means. To date no such notice has been given, but it is understood that the registrar will accept letters by e-mail, and skeleton arguments, but not pleadings or evidence sent by such means.

1 In the Trade Marks Journal.

2.18 Rule 66 deals with translation of documents. Where any document or part thereof which is in a language other than English is filed or sent to the registrar in pursuance of the TMA 1994 or the Rules, the registrar may require that there be furnished a translation into English of the document or that part, verified to his satisfaction as corresponding to the original text. The registrar may refuse any translation which is in his opinion inaccurate, and in such a case another duly verified translation must be furnished.

Inspection of documents and confidentiality

Inspection

2.19 In accordance with s 63(3) of the TMA 1994, rr 36 and 37 make provision for the public inspection of the register and for the supply[1] of certified or uncertified copies or extracts of entries in the register. The TMA 1994 contains new provisions for the obtaining of information about applications and registered trade marks and the inspection of documents. Although restrictions may still be imposed in appropriate circumstances, generally speaking much more material is now open to inspection than under the old law. Section 67 makes different provision for two situations: one where an application for registration has been published and the other when the application has not been published. Once an application has been published, sub-s (1) requires the registrar, subject to any prescribed restrictions, to provide a person on request with such information and permit him to inspect such documents relating to the application, or to any registered trade mark resulting from it, as may be specified in the request. The request must be made in the prescribed manner and be accompanied by any appropriate fee. Sub-section (2) imposes some restriction upon disclosure of information relating to unpublished applications for registration. In respect of such applications, the registrar may not publish, or communicate to any person, any documents or information constituting or relating to the application, except in such cases and to such extent as may be prescribed, or with the applicant's consent. Rule 43 specifies the documents which may be inspected prior to publication of an application; these are the application itself, any amendments made to it, and any particulars contained in a notice under r 35 (that is particulars of a registrable transaction to which s 25 of the TMA 1994 applies). Notwithstanding the restriction under sub-s (2), sub-s (3) applies the provisions of sub-s (1) in favour of a person who has been notified that the application has been made and that the applicant will, if the application is granted, bring proceedings against him in respect of acts done after publication of the application.

1 Pursuant to a request on Form TM31R.

2.20 These provisions are notably different from the previous provisions for inspection of documents, the emphasis being much more on general disclosure of information and documents, as opposed to disclosure only of certain specified classes of documents. Under s 25(1) it will normally be possible to inspect evidence filed by an applicant in response to official objections, as well as the correspondence between his agent and the registrar. Rule 44(1) requires the registrar to permit inspection of all documents filed or kept in relation to a published application for registration or a registered trade mark, subject only to paras (2) and (3) of the rule and to possible application of para (4), which excludes from the right of inspection any document or information filed at or sent to or by the Office before 31 October 1994 or filed at or sent to or by the Office after that date and relating to an application for registration under the TMA 1938,[1] and any document or part of a document which in the registrar's opinion disparages any person in a way likely to damage him. This last-mentioned provision is presumably intended to avoid the publication of defamatory material, but would not, it is thought, permit the registrar to refuse inspection of a document merely because it was critical of him or one of his officers. It is to be noted that r 44(4) does not in terms prohibit the registrar from allowing inspection; it only says that he has no duty to make the material referred to available for public inspection. It may therefore be the case that the registrar has a discretion to make such material if the circumstances justify it. A request for information relating to an application or a registered mark must be made on Form TM31C.

1 These provisions are as amended by the Trade Marks (Amendment) Rules 1998, r 14. The reference to an application under the TMA 1938 does not, it is thought, apply to an application converted for determination under the TMA 1994, under para 11 of Sch 3.

2.21 The first exception to the right of inspection is provided by r 44(2), where the registrar has not completed any procedure, or the stage in the procedure which is relevant to the document in question, which he is required or permitted to carry out under the TMA or the Rules. This exception seems more likely to arise in relation to applications than in relation to registered marks. In such cases the registrar is not obliged to permit inspection, but he is not expressly obliged to refuse inspection. So it is possible that he may still allow inspection if this seems appropriate in any particular case.

2.22 Rule 44(3) sets out a number of instances in which the right of inspection does not apply. There is no right of inspection of a document until 14 days after it has been filed, of a document prepared in the Office solely for use therein, of any document sent to the Office (whether at its request or otherwise) for inspection and subsequent return to the sender, or of a request for information made under rule 42. Again it does not appear that the registrar must refuse inspection in these instances. While there is no right of inspection, there may be sufficient reason for permitting inspection in some circumstances.

Confidentiality

2.23 In addition to the exceptions referred to above, rr 44(3)(e) and (f) exclude the right of inspection in respect of any document issued by the Office which the registrar considers should be treated as confidential, and any document in respect of which the registrar issues directions under r 45 that it be treated as confidential. It is understood that a number of applications have been made to the registrar, for the application of r 44(3)(f) to matters contained in evidence, and that directions have been given where the registrar was satisfied that there was a proper case for confidentiality. The registrar is unlikely to give a direction where the information is of a kind which is regularly given openly in evidence in court. In principle a direction ought not to be given, save in exceptional circumstances, if the effect would be that a party would be unable to answer material evidence or would be deprived of information which was material to his case. Attempts to invoke r 45 merit careful scrutiny because of the possibility of its provisions being exploited by a party to the detriment of another party to whose case it is relevant. Rule 45 does not apply at all to a document which is one of the official forms required by the registrar and published under r 3. But in the case of any other document, where the person filing the document requests, at the time of filing or within 14 days of filing, that it, or a specified part of it, be treated as confidential, giving his reasons, the registrar may direct that it, or part of it, as the case may be, be treated as confidential. If the registrar does so direct, the document is not open to public inspection while the matter is being determined by the registrar. Where such direction is given and is not withdrawn, para (2) provides that nothing in the rule shall be taken to authorise or require any person to be allowed to inspect the document or part of it to which the direction relates, except by leave of the registrar. Paragraph (3) prevents withdrawal of a direction without prior consultation with the person at whose request the direction was given, unless the registrar is satisfied that such prior consultation is not reasonably practical. Thus, under r 45 the registrar is given a discretion in several respects. First, under para (1), the use of the words 'may direct' indicates that the registrar has a discretion as to whether or not to give the direction sought. Second, under para (2) it is clear that the registrar has a discretion to give leave to inspect even where a direction under para (1) has not been withdrawn. Thirdly, it is implicit in para (3) that the registrar has a discretion to withdraw a direction, subject to the requirement to consult the party concerned, even if that party objects, as well as being permitted to proceed without consultation if he is satisfied that it is not practical. On the last point, apart from the non-availability of the party, it is possible to envisage cases in which a third party needs inspection as a matter of urgency, and time does not allow for consultation with the party who obtained the direction.[1]

1 See also r 45(4).

2.24 As for the general approach to be adopted, it is submitted that the registrar ought not to be too ready to give a confidentiality direction whenever requested to do so. For example, if the document is a declaration containing matter of a kind which is frequently used in evidence in court proceedings without restriction as to disclosure, such as details of sales and advertising under a trade mark, then prima facie a direction should not be given. Furthermore, it is to be noted that r 45 is concerned only with the limitation to a right of *public* inspection. In any proceedings in the registry any party should be given a clear idea of the case to be answered, and a party's advisers must be in a position to obtain proper instructions from their clientTherefore it cannot justify a direction which would prevent a party to proceedings from receiving the whole of any evidence filed by another party. This would be contrary to the requirements of rr 13 and 31 to send copies of evidence, in opposition, revocation, invalidation and rectification proceedings, to the other party. Moreover the TMA 1994 and the Rules[1] contain provisions for the discovery and production of documents in any proceedings before the registrar. Unless it appears that there would be grounds, such as have been recognised and applied by the courts, for restricting disclosure of relevant documents, those provisions should prevail even if the documents concerned are the subject of a confidentiality direction.

1 TMA 1994, s 69 and r 52 – see below.

Correction of irregularities, calculation and extension of time

Correction of irregularities

2.25 Rule 60, as amended,[1] gives the registrar general powers to rectify any irregularity in procedure in or before the Office or the registrar, on such terms as he may direct. Originally these powers, under r 60(1) of the 1994 Rules, were subject to para (2). This provided that in the case of an irregularity or prospective irregularity: (a) which consisted of a failure to comply with any limitation as to times or periods specified in the TMA 1994, the Rules or the old law as that law continued to apply, and which had occurred or appeared to the registrar as likely to occur in the absence of a direction under the r 60; and (b) which was attributable wholly or in part to an error, default or omission on the part of the Office or the registrar and which it appeared to him should be rectified, the registrar might direct the time or period in question to be altered in such manner as he might specify. By the amendment in 1998, sub-para (2) has been removed, and also sub-para (3), by which sub-para (2) was without prejudice to the registrar's powers to extend times or periods under r 62, and essentially the same provision now appears as r 62(7). The powers given to the registrar under r 60 are now only 'subject to' r 62, which deals with time extensions. It appears that where the 'irregularity' results in a failure to comply with a time limitation, r 60 has no application, and an extension must be justified under r 62 before the matter can be rectified. Rule 62 is considered more fully below. It may be remarked that r 60 does not appear to permit amendment of documents such as grounds of opposition, revocation, invalidation or rectification, which was possible under the old rules.[2] Failure to plead a possible ground, for instance, cannot properly be called an 'irregularity in procedure'. In a decision of the registry, in the case of *Ducati Trade Mark*,[3] it was held that there was no power, under r 60, to rectify an 'irregularity in procedure' once the application procedure had been completed and the mark in question was on the register. This may be too narrow a basis for not exercising the powers given by r 60. For example, if a trade mark is mistakenly placed on the register when an opposition is still pending, there would clearly have been an irregularity in procedure in the Office, and it is submitted that r 60 must allow it to be rectified;[4] it seems implicit in the decision itself that it would have been rectified if the notice of opposition had been validly filed.

1 The Trade Marks (Amendment) Rules 1998 (1998/925), r16.
2 The Trade Marks and Service Marks Rules 1986, r 121.
3 [1998] RPC 227. The original application for registration had been divided into two, under s 41(1), the application number being replaced by the same number with added suffixes A and B for the two resulting applications. The notice of opposition was filed under the original number without the appropriate suffix A designating the first divisional application, and the mark proceeded to registration in the class covered by such application. It was held that the notice of opposition was not validly filed.
4 See for example the decision of another Hearing Officer, in O/150/97 (24 August 1997) noted in CIPA Journal, September 1997, at p 712.

Calculation of times and periods

2.26   Where on any day there is a general interruption or subsequent dislocation in the postal services of the UK, or an event or circumstances causing an interruption in the normal operation of the Office, r 61(1) empowers the registrar to certify the day as being one on which there is an 'interruption'. Under para (2) the certificate must be posted in the Office. Where any period of time specified in the TMA 1994 or the Rules for the giving, making or filing of any notice, application or other document expires on a day of 'interruption', the period is extended to the next following day (not being an excluded day[1]) which is not so certified. Rule 61(3) makes provision for the situation in which the registrar is satisfied, in any particular case, that the failure to give, make or file any notice, application or other document within any period of time specified in the TMA 1994 or the Rules was wholly or mainly attributable to a failure or undue delay in the postal services in the UK. In such case the registrar may, if he thinks fit, extend the period so that it ends on the day of the receipt by the addressee of the document or, if that is an excluded day, on the first following day which is not an excluded day, upon such notice to other parties and upon such terms as he may direct.

1 Under para (4), a day which is not a business day of the office under the registrar's direction pursuant to s 80, as published in accordance with r 64.

Extensions of time

2.27   As mentioned above, the current r 60 makes it clear that the power to rectify an irregularity in procedure is subject to the registrar's power to extend any time or period under r 62. Under the old law there was general provision for the extension of a time specified in the rules or by the registrar. The power given by r 62[1] is in some respects not as general. Although para (1) is general in its terms it is subject to some important exceptions. Any time or period prescribed by the Rules, *other than the times or periods prescribed by the rules mentioned in para (3)*, or specified by the registrar for doing any act or taking any proceedings, subject to para (2) may at the written request of the person or party concerned, be extended by the registrar as he thinks fit and upon such terms as he may order. The express requirement for a 'written' request, introduced by amendment, was always intended. It is to be noted that the original provision, that extension should be 'upon such notice to any other person or party affected ... ', has been removed. However the registrar will presumably direct such notice where appropriate, as one of the terms which he will direct, for example where a party is not present or represented at a hearing where an extension is granted. In any event, r 48(1), which requires the registrar to give any party to any proceedings, to whom any decision is or may be adverse, an opportunity to be heard, would usually require notice of the extension to be given to a party to the proceedings concerned. Under sub-para (2)(a), if the extension is sought in respect of a time or periods prescribed by rr 13, 18, 23 or 25 (dealing with opposition proceedings, advertisement of an application after publication, amendment of regulations of collective and certification marks, and alteration of registered trade marks), the party seeking the extension must send a copy of the request to each person who is a party to the proceedings. Under sub-para (2)(b), where an application has already been published,[2] any request for the extension of a period prescribed by the Rules filed after publication must be on Form TM9, which is also to be used in other cases if the registrar so directs. The rules excepted by para (3) are r 10(6) (failure to file an address for service), r 11 (deficiencies in application), r 13(1) (time for filing opposition), r 13(2) (time for filing counter-statement), r 23(4) (time for filing opposition), r 25(3) (time for filing opposition), r 29 (delayed renewal), r 30 (restoration of registration), and r 41 (time for filing opposition). Rules 23(4), 25(3) and 41, prescribe times for opposing, respectively, applications to amend regulations of collective and certification marks, alterations of registered trade marks, and proposals for changes of classification of goods and services. In all the cases to which r 62(3) now applies, the times prescribed by the rules referred to are non-extendable. An important change of practice is to be found in para (4). Under the old law there was a general provision allowing the time to be extended notwithstanding that it had expired and an application for an extension could be made after such expiry. Paragraph (4) alters the position by providing that, subject to para (5), a request for extension shall be filed before the time or period in question has expired. Where the request is made after expiry of the time or period, para (5) gives the registrar a discretion to allow an extension, but only if he is satisfied with the explanation for the delay in requesting the extension *and* it appears to him that it is just and equitable to do so. This second requirement replaces the original requirement, that it must appear to him that any extension would not disadvantage any other person or party affected by it. Any party to the proceedings could argue that the extension would 'disadvantage' him in a sense, and other persons not actually party to the proceedings might also claim to be disadvantaged in some circumstances. Now the emphasis is on the extension being 'just and equitable'; so long as that is so on an overall assessment of the case, taking into consideration any 'disadvantage' to any other person or party affected, any such disadvantage is not an overriding factor, as it appears it may have been under the original sub-para (5). Lastly, mention should be made here of sub-para (6), which enables the overall period for the filing of evidence to be shortened. Where the period within which any party to any proceedings before the registrar may file evidence is to begin upon the expiry of any period in which the other party may file evidence, and that other party notifies the registrar that he does not wish to file any, or any further, evidence, the registrar may direct that the period within which the first-mentioned party may file evidence may begin on such date as may be specified in the direction. All parties to the dispute are to be notified of the date.

1 The 1994 Rules (SI 1994/2583), r 62 as amended by of the 1998 Rules (SI 1998/925), r 17.
2 Under r 12.

2.28   It is generally known that in recent years the registrar has become increasingly stricter in matters of extension of times. These changes, and other changes in the Rules,[1] may be seen as a continuation of the process of reducing delays in registry proceedings. One point, which may be mentioned here, concerns the time specified in r 31(3) for the filing by a proprietor of a counter-statement in proceedings for revocation, declarations of invalidity and rectification[2] and, in a non-use case, evidence of use. Rule 31(3) is not mentioned in r 62(3), as one of the rules excepted from r 62(1), and it would therefore be expected that the period of three months was to be regarded as extendable. However the registry have insisted that it is not. The basis for this view is that the time for a counter-statement in opposition proceedings, under r 13(3), is not extendable, since that provision is excepted by r 62(3), and that, subject to paras (2), (6) and (7), r 31(4) applies 'the provisions of rule 13' to proceedings under r 31 'as they apply to opposition proceedings'. The difficulty in this approach is that the purpose of r 31(4) appears to be to save the need to include specific provisions for the periods for filing evidence; r 13(2) clearly does not apply because r 31(3) prescribes the time for filing a counterstatement in the proceedings covered by that rule. Therefore in principle the time under r 31(3) should be extendible simply because it is not expressly mentioned in rule 62(3) and it cannot properly be said that the time is one 'prescribed by r 13(2)'. However until the position is clarified by the courts, it is important to observe the time limit of three months as specified in r 31(3).

1 Eg the shorter period set by rr 13 and 31 for filing evidence in opposition, revocation, invalidation and rectification proceedings.
2 Under the TMA 1994, ss 46, 47 and 64 respectively.

2.29   Reference has already been made to r 62(7), which repeats essentially the same provision as that formerly incorporated in the Rules as part of r 60(2). This applies in the case of an 'irregularity or prospective irregularity' in or before the Office or the registrar which consists of a failure to comply with any limitation as to times or periods specified in the TMA 1994, the Rules or the old law as that law continues to apply and which has occurred or appears to the registrar as likely to occur in the absence of a direction under the rule *and* is attributable wholly, or in part, to an error, default or omission on the part of the Office or the registrar and which it appears to him should be rectified. The registrar may in such cases direct that the time or period in question shall be altered in such manner as he may specify and upon such terms as he may direct. The provision is expressed to be without prejudice to the preceding provisions of r 62, so it may be possible to obtain an extension without needing to resort to sub-para (7). The importance of the provision, which may apply even where the party concerned is in part responsible for the failure to comply with the limitation, is that the matter may be rectified where the time or period has already expired, without having to satisfy the requirements of sub-para (5), or if the time or period in question is one which is excluded from extension under para (1), by para (3). It is sufficient, for invoking this provision, that at least *a* contributory cause of the failure to comply with the limitation was some kind of mistake on the part of the Office or the registrar, but the operation of the rule is limited to irregularities within the Office. This is demonstrated clearly by a registry decision in the case of *Re Monster Munch Trade Mark*,[1] in which the mistaken use by an agent, of a fax number which had not been generally available for public use and had been discontinued, instead of using published numbers, resulting in missing the three-month opposition period, was held not to be the result of an irregularity of procedure 'in or before the Office, or the registrar'.

1 [1997] RPC 721.

Evidence and discovery

2.30 Section 69 of the TMA 1994 provides for the making of some potentially important changes regarding evidence before the registrar.[1] The provisions, which have been made, are to be found in rr 49 to 52 inclusive. In accordance with s 69(a), r 49(1) provides that where under the Rules evidence may be admitted by the registrar in any proceedings before him, it shall be by the filing of a statutory declaration or affidavit. Under the old law[2] the general rule was that evidence should be by statutory declaration. Rule 50 sets out the formal requirements for the making and subscribing of statutory declarations and affidavits. Rule 49(2) empowers the registrar in any particular case to take oral evidence in lieu of or in addition to evidence by statutory declaration or affidavit and provides that he *shall, unless he otherwise directs, allow any witness to be cross-examined on his declaration, affidavit or oral evidence.* The italicised part of r 49(2) seems at first sight to create difficulty, because its literal effect might be understood as being that, prima facie, the registrar must allow any witness to be cross-examined on his declaration or affidavit, subject only to a direction to the contrary by the registrar. The potential inconvenience of this is obvious, because it could mean that witnesses had to attend the hearing of the proceedings. It is submitted that such a construction of r 49(2) is incorrect. The purpose of the provision is to make it clear that if a witness does give oral evidence, then cross-examination of him must be allowed, unless the registrar directs otherwise, not only on his oral evidence, but on any other evidence which he has already given by declaration or affidavit. It should be noted that the terms 'statutory declaration' and 'affidavit' are used in their strict sense,[3] so that an unsworn document will not comply with the Rules, which in their present form do not allow for the practice often followed in the courts, of permitting an approved but unsworn affidavit to be served and read, so long as an undertaking is given that it will be sworn. This can have important implications where there is a 'final' extension of time or a period for filing evidence is non-extendable

1 See further, ch 16, paras **16.28** et seq.
2 TMA 1938, s 55.
3 See r 50(1).

2.31 Rule 51 gives the registrar additional powers. At any stage of any proceedings before him, he may direct that such documents, information or evidence as he may reasonably require shall be filed within such period as he may specify. The registrar may exercise this power of his own motion.[1] It should also be noted that r 13(8), which by r 31(4) applies to proceedings under that rule, makes general provision for the filing of further evidence by either party, with the leave of the registrar, upon such terms as he may think fit. This may provide some flexibility where the time for filing evidence has expired or cannot be extended, and has been used for this purpose in appropriate circumstances.

1 *Re WILD CHILD Trade Mark* [1998] RPC 455 (appointed person) (Geoffrey Hobbs QC).

2.32   In accordance with s 69(b) and (c), r 52 provides that the registrar shall, in relation to the examination of witnesses on oath and the discovery and production of documents, have all the powers of an official referee of the Supreme Court,[1] and that the rules applicable to the attendance of witnesses before an official referee are applicable to the attendance of witnesses in proceedings before the registrar. The provision for discovery and production of documents is new in trade mark proceedings in the Office. Although the Comptroller in patent and registered design proceedings before the Office had for many years had these powers, the powers in trade mark cases were confined to requiring the attendance of witnesses and taking evidence on oath.[2] There was no provision for discovery in trade mark proceedings in the Office. It was a practical disadvantage, in cross-examining witnesses, that there was no means of obtaining relevant documents from the party concerned.

1 See now the new CPR 1998, Part 31 (Disclosure and Inspection of Documents). Official Referees are now Judges of the Technology and Construction Court.
2 TMA 1938, s 55.

2.33   These provisions relate only to the form of the evidence and not to its content. Certain aspects of admissibility of evidence, in proceedings before the registry, are considered elsewhere.

Cross-examination of witnesses

2.34   In the past, little advantage has been taken of the power of the registrar to take evidence *viva voce*, which included the power to direct cross-examination, whether in lieu of or in addition to evidence by declaration. This may well have been due to the fact that cross-examination was often ineffective owing to the non-availability of discovery. However applications for cross-examination of witnesses, because of principles laid down by the courts in cases in which cross-examination was sought on appeal,[1] of witnesses who had made statutory declarations for proceedings before the registrar, are made from time to time, and are sometimes granted. As a general rule, the court will not permit cross-examination on appeal, where cross-examination was not requested before the registrar, unless the conditions for adducing fresh evidence on appeal are met.[2]

1 See for example the decision of Mummery J in *Orient Express Trade Mark* [1996] RPC 25.
2 As to additional evidence on appeal, see the recent decision of Sir Richard Scott V-C in *Re CLUB EUROPE Trade Mark* [1999] 33 LS Gaz R 32, noted in IPD (October 1999) 22101.

Decision of the registrar

2.35   Rule 48 requires the registrar, before taking any decision on any matter under the TMA 1994 or the Rules which is or may be adverse to any party to any proceedings before him, to give that party an opportunity to be heard. This requirement is without prejudice to any provisions of the Act or Rules requiring the registrar to hear any party or to give such party an opportunity to be heard. Under para (2) the registrar must give the party at least 14 days' notice of the time when he may be heard, unless the party consents to shorter notice. Once the registrar has made a decision in any proceedings, following a hearing or, if a hearing has not been requested, after considering any submission in writing, r 56(1) requires the registrar to send notice of his decision in writing to each party. Under r 56(2) where the notice does not include a statement of the reasons for the decision, any party may within one month of the date on which the notice was sent request the registrar on Form TM5 to send a statement of the reasons. The registrar must then send such a statement. For the purposes of an appeal from the decision, the date on which the notice of the decision is sent is the date of the decision; but if the notice does not include a statement of the reasons for the decision, the date on which the registrar sends such a statement, pursuant to a request under para (2) is deemed to be the date of the decision.

Costs and security for costs before the registrar

2.36   Under the TMA 1938[1] the registrar was given a general power to award any party, in proceedings before him, such costs as he considered reasonable, and provision was made for enforcement of orders by the court. Costs were awarded, on the basis of established scales, and awards have never represented more than a contribution, usually being small compared to the actual costs incurred. Rules also made provision for security for costs. Section 68 of the TMA 1994 leaves the making of provisions for awards of costs, and for the giving of security for costs, to rules. The provisions are to be found in rr 54 and 55. Under r 54 the registrar may, in any proceedings before him under the Act or Rules, by order award to any party such costs as he may consider reasonable, and direct how and by what parties they are to be paid. This does not represent any change in practice, and it is expected that the same scales will be used as before. Section 68(2) provides for enforcement of costs orders in the same way as court orders.

1 TMA 1994, s 44.

2.37   The provision for security for costs, in r 55, is broader than the old rule,[1] under which security could only be awarded against foreign parties. Rule 55 gives a general power to the registrar to require any party in any proceedings before him under the TMA 1994 or the Rules to give security for costs in relation to the proceedings, and he may also require security for the costs of any appeal from his decision. No guidance is given as to how the registrar is to order security in any given case, but it may be appropriate to proceed on generally similar principles to those applied by the courts.[2] Thus, security might be ordered in appropriate circumstances against a foreign party or an insolvent corporate party. In all cases an important consideration must be the likelihood or otherwise of the successful party actually recovering the costs ordered to be paid, and the amount of the security ordered should reflect the amount likely to be assessed in each case. Where a party fails to comply with the order to give security, r 55(2) allows the registrar (or in the case of an appeal the person appointed under s 76) to treat the party in default as having withdrawn his application, opposition, objection or intervention, as the case may be.

1 Trade Marks and Service Marks Rules 1986, r 56. See also ch 16, para **16.34** below.
2 See the Rules of the Supreme Court 1965, Ord 23, retained under Part 50 of the CPR 1998.

The court as an alternative tribunal to the registrar

2.38   Sections 46 (revocation of registration), 47 (grounds for invalidity of registration) and 64 (rectification or correction of the register) of the Act give an option of making applications under those provisions to the registrar or the court. It should be noted that, under ss 46 and 47, such applications may be made by *any* person, not only by a 'person aggrieved' as under the cancellation and rectification provisions of the TMA 1938. An application under s 64 can only be made by 'any person having a sufficient interest', which is probably the same as a 'person aggrieved'.[1] In each case it is provided[2] (a) that the application must be to the court if proceedings[3] concerning the trade mark in question are pending in the court, and (b) that the registrar may at any stage refer the application to the court. So far as (a) is concerned, proceedings for passing off in respect of the trade mark could well be regarded as 'concerning the trade mark in question'; even if this is not so, the registrar might be readily persuaded to refer the application to the court. A pending appeal to an appointed person[4] is not a proceeding in the court.

1 In particular under the TMA 1938, ss 26 and 32. See for example *Powell v Birmingham Vinegar Brewery Co* [1894] AC 8 and *Concord Trade Mark* [1987] FSR 209.
2 By the TMA 1994, ss 46(4), 47(3) and 64(2).
3 Note that the word 'action' was used in the corresponding provision of the 1938 Act, s 54(a). It was not entirely clear whether other proceedings, such as rectification proceedings before the court, were included, although in such cases no doubt the registrar would have been likely to refer the matter to the court under s 54(b). At all events the word 'proceedings' avoids any difficulty in this respect.
4 See para **2.40** below.

Appeals from decisions of the registrar

2.39   Under the TMA 1938 the position regarding appeals from decisions of the registrar was complex. There were a number of separate provisions for appeal against final decisions, but in interlocutory decisions the only possible way of challenging a decision was by way of judicial review.[1] The TMA 1994 introduces several very significant changes. Firstly, s 76(1) provides that an appeal lies from any decision of the registrar under the Act, except as expressly provided by rules. Under the Rules, the only instances in which an appeal under s 76(1) is excluded are a decision on change of classification (under rr 40 and 41) and a decision under r 44(4) not to make a document or part of a document available for public inspection. In these instances there might, in an exceptional case, be a possibility of applying for judicial review. But apart from this the appropriate way of challenging a decision of the registrar is an appeal under s 76.

1 See *ADIDAS SARL's Trade Mark* [1983] RPC 262 (QBD). The Court referred to the decision of Slade J in *PREDATOR Trade Mark* [1982] RPC 387 that there is no appeal against interlocutory decisions of the registrar and confirmed that the proper, indeed the only, procedure for challenging an interlocutory decision of the registry was by way of judicial review.

2.40   The second change, which is more procedural than one of substance, is that the previous alternative under the TMA 1938, of appealing to the 'Board of Trade' instead of to the court is replaced by the alternative of appeal to an 'appointed person'.[1] An 'appointed person' is defined by s 77 as a person appointed by the Lord Chancellor to hear and decide appeals under the Act; sub-ss (2)–(4) deal with the qualification and appointment of an appointed person. Under s 76(3) an appointed person may refer the appeal to the court if it appears to him that a point of general legal importance is involved, or if requested to do so by the registrar or a party to the proceedings in question.[2] Before doing so the appointed person is required to give the parties an opportunity to make representations as to whether the appeal should be referred to the court; this does not appear to require the appointed person to hold an oral hearing. If the appeal is not referred to the court, under s 76(4) the decision of an appointed person is final, subject only to the possibility of judicial review where a point of law is involved. A more major change is that an appointed person may now hear appeals from any decision of the registrar, including decisions in oppositions and applications for revocation, invalidity and rectification. This provides the opportunity for considerable savings, in terms of time and expense, in appealing against decisions in cases in which it is unlikely that the matter would go to a higher court. Section 76(5) applies the provisions of ss 68 and 69, as to costs and security for costs and evidence, to proceedings before an appointed person.

1 TMA 1994, s 76(2) .See further ch 16, paras **16.24–16.26.**
2 For examples of the exercise of this power, see the decisions of MG Clarke QC in *A J and M A Levy's Trade Mark (No 2)* [1999] RPC 358 and *Jimmy Nicks Property Co Ltd's Application* [1999] ETMR 445. In *Re Academy Trade Mark Revocation*, S refused referral (10 May 1999, noted in New Law Digest 699067101).

2.41 The procedure under s 76 is regulated by rr 57–59. The notice of appeal must be sent to the registrar within one month[1] of the date of the decision, accompanied by a statement of the appellant's grounds of appeal and his case in support of the appeal. The registrar is required by para (2) to send the notice and statement to the appointed person, and by para (3) to send copies to any other party to the proceedings. Under r 58 a period of one month, from the date which the registrar sends the notice of appeal under r 57(3), is allowed for the registrar or a party to request reference to the court. Rule 59 deals with the hearing of the appeal and applies the rules governing proceedings before the registrar, r 48(2) and rr 49–55, to the appeal.

1 Note that this period is one calendar month; the period for an appeal to the court is four weeks. See now Part 49 of the CPR 1998, para 23.3, and Ord 55, r 4(2), retained under Part 50. It is expected that the period for appealing to the appointed person will be reduced to four weeks.

Appearance of the registrar in court proceedings

2.42 In any proceedings where no other party is involved, the registrar appears by counsel in court proceedings concerning registration or other matters concerned with trade marks under the TMA 1994. Where another party is involved, as in revocation or invalidation proceeding, or appeals from the registrar's decisions in oppositions or revocation or invalidation proceedings, he does not usually appear. However s 74 of the TMA 1994 provides that in any proceedings before the court involving an application for the revocation of a registration of a trade mark, a declaration of invalidity of a registration, or the rectification of the register, he is entitled to appear and be heard if he so wishes, and must appear if so directed by the court. If the court does not direct otherwise, s 74(2) permits the registrar, instead of appearing, to submit a written statement. A statement submitted in accordance with s 74(2), which may give particulars of any proceedings before him in relation to the matter in issue, the grounds of any decision given by him affecting it, the practice of the Patent Office in like cases, and such matters relevant to the issues and within his knowledge as registrar as he thinks fit, is deemed to form part of the evidence in the proceedings. In the case of any application, including an appeal, to the court, or any counterclaim for revocation or a declaration of invalidity of a registration, the registrar must be served with the proceedings.[1]

1 Until 26 April 1999 court procedure in trade mark mark cases was governed by RSC 1965 Ord 100. See now the Part 49 of the CPR 1998.

4   Costs and the registrar

Registrar's costs and liability for costs

2.43   The questions of the registrar's costs in court proceedings and payment of costs by the registrar are not expressly covered by the TMA 1994. They were expressly provided for in the TMA 1938, in s 48. Sub-section (1) provided that in all proceedings before the court under the Act the registrar's costs should be in the discretion of the court, but that, in any proceedings in England or Northern Ireland the registrar should not, except in accordance with the provisions of sub-s (2) in a case in which he had appeared in the proceedings, be ordered to pay the costs of any other party. Thus, in any case in which the registrar appeared, if he was successful he was entitled to his costs as much as any other party would be. Sub-section (2), for the purpose of any proceedings in which the registrar appeared before the court in England or Northern Ireland under the Act, applied s 7 of the Administration of Justice (Miscellaneous Provisions) Act 1933 as it had effect in relation to other proceedings to which the Crown was a party in a court having power to award costs in cases between subjects. For many years it was the practice for a successful party to be ordered to pay the registrar's costs. Although in the case of *Re Svenska AKT Gasaccumulator's Application*[1] it was conceded by the registrar that costs should follow the event, a concession considered by Upjohn LJ[2] to be a proper one having regard to the terms of the 1938 Act, it appears that the previous practice was continued, at least in some cases of appeals against refusal of applications for registration, until late 1966.[3] Since then the registrar was treated as being in exactly the same position as any other litigant. The 1994 Act contains no provisions regarding the payment of the registrar's costs or the payment by the registrar of an applicant's costs. However there is no reason to believe that the practice followed since 1966 will not be followed.

1 [1962] RPC 106.
2 At 117 line 42.
3 See *Stilton Trade Mark* [1967] RPC 173 at 182 line 35.

Chapter 3

Representation at the registry

Agents

3.1 Under s 82, except as otherwise provided by rules,[1] any act required or authorised by the TMA 1994 to be done by or to a person in connection with the registration of a trade mark, or any procedure relating to a registered trade mark, may be done by or to an agent authorised by that person orally or in writing. Provisions relating to agents are to be found in r 46. Where an agent has been authorised under s 82, r 46(1) permits the registrar in any particular case to require the personal signature or presence of the agent or the person authorising him to act as agent. Under r 46(2), where after a person has become a party to any proceedings before the registrar he appoints an agent for the first time or appoints one agent in substitution for another, the newly appointed agent must file Form TM 33. Any act required or authorised by the Act in connection with the registration of a trade mark or any procedure relating to a trade mark may not be done by or to the newly appointed agent until on after the date on which he files that form. Rule 46(3) empowers the registrar to require an agent, by notice in writing sent to him, to produce evidence of his authority.

1 Ie the Rules made under the TMA 1994, s 78 – see the definition of 'rules' in s 104.

Register of trade mark attorneys

3.2 Although there was a register of Patent Agents for many years, prior to the coming into force of s 282 of the Copyright, Designs and Patents Act 1988 ('CDPA 1988')[1] there was no register of trade mark agents. Representation at the registry was undertaken by anyone with whom the registrar was prepared to deal. Grounds, on which the registrar might decline to recognise any person as an agent, were set out in the rules. Generally applicants and proprietors have been represented by patent agents or trade mark agents, but the latter were not required to be Members of the Institute of Trade Mark Agents or to have any other qualification. In addition solicitors can and do act as agents in the registry. The creation, by the CDPA 1988, of a register of trade mark agents, which is continued under the TMA 1994, is an important step in the regulation of agents. However it should be emphasised that the register is not exclusive; a party to proceedings before the registry may still be represented by any agent with whom the registrar will deal, and who need not be on the register.

1 CDPA 1988 s 282 and other provisions relating to patent agents and trade mark agents were brought into operation on 13 August 1990 by the Copyright, Designs and Patents Act 1988 (Commencement No 5) Order 1990, (SI 1990/1400).

3.3   Sections 282–284 of the CDPA 1988, which were concerned with trade mark agents, have now been replaced by ss 83–85 of the TMA 1994, which are in very similar terms. Section 83 empowers the Secretary of State to make rules requiring the keeping of a register of persons who act as agent for others for the purpose of applying for or obtaining the registration of trade marks. A person whose name is entered on such a register is called a 'registered trade mark agent'. Under s 83(2) the rules may contain such provisions as the Secretary of State thinks fit regulating the registration of persons, and specifies certain particular matters, namely payment of fees and erasure from the register or suspension of registration, which may be covered. Section 83(3) enables the rules to delegate the keeping of the register to another person and to confer on such person the power to make regulations with respect to matters such as fees and any other matter which could be regulated by the rules. Disciplinary and other functions may also be delegated. Section 84 prohibits a person who is not a registered trade mark agent from carrying on a business (other than in partnership) under any name or other description which contains the words 'registered trade mark agent' or, in the course of business, from otherwise describing himself or holding himself out, or permitting himself to be described or held out, as a registered trade mark agent. There are like restrictions on a partnership, unless all the partners are registered trade mark agents or the partnership satisfies prescribed conditions, and on a body corporate, unless all the directors are registered trade mark agents or the body satisfies prescribed conditions. Contravention of s 84 is a criminal offence, punishable by a fine.[1] Proceedings must be commenced within a year from the date of the offence. The current rules[2] were made under s 282 of the CDPA 1988. The register is still called 'the register of trade mark agents' notwithstanding the change of the name of the Institute.

1 Not exceeding level 5 on the standard scale – TMA 1994, s 84(4).
2 The Register of Trade Mark Agents Rules 1990 – (SI 1990/1458), which came into force on 1 October 1990 and applied by Sch 3, para 22(1) of the TMA 1994. This has now been amended, by the Register (of Patent Agents and the Register of Trade Mark Agents (Amendment) Rules 1999, (SI 1999/983), reflecting the change of name of the 'Institute of Trade Mark Agents' to the 'Institute of Trade Mark Attorneys'.

3.4   For many years it was not possible to form mixed partnerships between, for example, patent agents or trade mark agents. It was common for trade mark agents to be employed by firms of patent agents, but they could not become partners. The law was changed by ss 279 and 283(4) of the CDPA 1988, which have now been replaced by s 85 of the TMA 1994, which is entitled 'Power to prescribe conditions for mixed partnerships and bodies corporate'. The Secretary of State may make rules prescribing the conditions to be satisfied for the purposes of s 84, in relation to a partnership where not all the partners are qualified persons, or in relation to a body corporate where not all the directors are qualified persons. For this purpose 'qualified person' means a registered trade mark agent.[1] Section 85(2) stipulates some matters in particular which such rules may provide for. These include the number or proportion of partners or directors who must be qualified persons, the imposition of requirements for identifying qualified and unqualified persons in advertisements, circulars and letters relating to the business of the partnership or body corporate and as to the securing of a sufficient degree of control by qualified persons over unqualified persons. The current rules, the Registered Trade Mark

Agents (Mixed Partnerships and Bodies Corporate) Rules 1994,[2] were made under s 283(4) of the CPDA 1988. and continue in force under the TMA 1994.[3]

1 Section 85(4).
2 (SI 1994/363).
3 By virtue of Sch 3 para 22(1).

3.5 Section 88 of the TMA 1994 enables the Secretary of State to make rules authorising the registrar to refuse to recognise certain persons as agents in respect of any business under the Act. The registrar may refuse recognition in the cases set out in sub-s (1), which are simply repeated in r 47. In the case of an individual, recognition may be refused on three grounds: conviction of an offence under s 84 of the Act; erasure (the name not having been restored) or suspension from the register of trade mark agents for misconduct; and a finding by the Secretary of State of conduct which would, in the case of a registered trade mark agent, render the individual liable to have his name erased from the register on the ground of misconduct. The registrar may also refuse to recognise as agent any partnership or body corporate of which one of the partners or directors is a person whom the registrar could refuse to recognise on any of the above grounds.

Qualification for entry on register of trade mark agents

3.6 Rule 9 of the Register of Trade Mark Agents Rules 1990 sets out the categories of persons who qualify for registration. These include persons who have passed the qualifying examinations of the Institute of Trade Mark Agents and who have completed the prescribed period of appropriate full-time practice. Also included are Fellows and ordinary members of the Institute and others having appropriate experience of trade mark agency work, but these persons must register before the expiry of the periods specified in r 9(2). Among those who may be qualified by virtue of appropriate experience, is a 'registered patent agent'. That term is defined by reference to the register kept under s 275 of the CDPA 1988.[1]

1 See the Register cf Patent Agents Rules 1990, (SI 1990/1457) and the Patent Agents (Non-recognition of Certain Agents by Comptroller) Rules 1990, (SI 1990/1454), which came into force on 13 August 1990. R 8 of (SI 1990/1457) (qualifying examinations) has been amended by the Register of Patent Agents and the Register of Trade Mark Agents (Amendment) Rules 1999, (SI 1999/983).

3.7 Under r 10 of the Register of Trade Mark Agents Rules 1990, subject to the production of the evidence of qualification and to payment of the prescribed fee, any person who qualifies for registration under r 9 is entitled to have his name entered in the register unless a direction in relation to him, under r 10(3) is in force. Such a direction may be given, after due inquiry, if the Secretary of State is satisfied that a person has been guilty of misconduct. Misconduct is also a ground for erasure from the register under r 14.

Address for service

3.8 Service of documents is one of the matters specifically mentioned, in s 78(2) of the TMA 1994, as to which rules may provide. Rule 10 of the Rules contains provisions for the filing of an address for service. For the purpose of any proceedings before the registrar under the rules or any appeal from a decision of the registrar under the TMA 1994 or the Rules, an address for service must be filed by any applicant for registration of a trade mark, any person opposing an application for registration, any applicant for revocation or invalidation, or rectification, of the registration of a trade mark,[1] a person granted leave to intervene,[2] and any proprietor of a registered trade mark which is the subject of an application for revocation, invalidation or rectification of the registration. On registration of a trade mark, an address for service of the applicant for registration is deemed to be the address for service of the registered proprietor.[3] Rule 10(6) imposes sanctions in cases of failure to file an address for service. The registrar is required to give notice to the person concerned, to file an address for service. If that person fails to do so within two months of the date of the notice, in the case of an applicant for registration, revocation, invalidation or rectification the application is treated as abandoned; in the case of an opponent to an application, or an intervenor, he is deemed to have withdrawn from the proceedings; and in the case of the proprietor, whose registration is the subject of an application for revocation, invalidation or intervention, he will not be permitted to take part in the proceedings. It is important to note that the two-month period is non-extendable.[4] The address for service is to be filed on Form TM33, except where a form required under r 3 which requires the furnishing of an address for service, in which case the address should be filed on that form. Rule 10(5) provides for voluntary filing of an address for service by a proprietor of a registered trade mark and by any person having an interest in or a charge on a registered trade mark, which is registered.[5]

1 Under the TMA 1994, s 46 (revocation), s 47 (invalidation) or s 64 (rectification).
2 Under r 31(5), in revocation, invalidation or rectification proceedings.
3 Subject to any filing to the contrary under r 10(1) or r 38(2).
4 See r 62(3).
5 Under r 34.

3.9   Rule 10(4) provides that anything sent to any applicant, opponent, intervenor or registered proprietor at his address for service shall be deemed to be properly sent. Furthermore, where no address for service is filed, the registrar may treat as the address for service of the person concerned his trade or business address in the UK, if any. This would enable service to be effected if necessary, where a notice under r 10(6) had been given but had not expired. Rule 10(4) does not mention the case of an address for service filed[1] by a person having an interest in or a charge on a registered trade mark, but the clear intention of the rule seems to be that service at that address would be effective and, probably, that service at any other address would not be.

1 Voluntarily under r 10(5) .

3.10   A principal purpose of the requirement to file an address for service in the UK has of course always been to facilitate the work of the registry when dealing with parties who are abroad. However the provisions of r 10 apply generally, and are not limited to foreign parties. The rule enables service to be effected regardless of a change of address by the party concerned or, it would appear, even if the party was a company in liquidation.[1] Questions have arisen as to whether such an address may be used as an address for service of court proceedings and other documents. In the past there has been no specific provision for service in trade mark cases, in the Rules of the Supreme Court. In the case of an appeal from a decision of the registrar, the matter seems clear; r 10(1) refers to 'any appeal from a decision of the registrar under the Act or these rules', which includes appeals to the court or to a person appointed under s 77. Therefore it is no longer necessary to rely upon decisions under the old law.[2] In the case of an application to the court for revocation, invalidation, or rectification, the matter is not (and could not be) covered by the rules. In a decision under the old law,[3] it was held that service of rectification proceedings could validly be effected under r 13 of the Trade Marks and Service Marks Rules 1986, but the wording of the rule was differently worded from the present r 10, which plainly does not extend to court proceedings other than appeals from the registrar. For court proceedings the position is now covered by Part 49 of the new Civil Procedure Rules 1998. Paragraph 25 of Part 49 concerns service of documents. Para 25.1 provides that the rules apply to the service of any document on a party until such time as that party has provided an address for service in accordance with CPR 6.5. Under para 25.2, subject to para 25.3 which says that nothing in para 25.2 shall prevent service being effected on the proprietor of a trade mark in accordance with the provisions of CPR Part 6,[4] express provision is made for service, in the manner authorised by Part 6 of the CPR, on a proprietor at his address for service given in the register kept under s 63 of the TMA 1994 , which is the address filed under r 10. This applies to any proceedings relating to a registered trade mark.

1 However the requirements of the legislation affecting proceedings against a company in liquidation should be noted. See the Insolvency Act 1986, s 126.
2 See eg *Johnson & Johnson's Application* [1991] RPC 1, Mummery J, subject of a Case Comment in [1990] 8 EIPR 303.
3 *Cacique Trade Mark* , unreported (1989), (Harman J).
4 This includes general rules regarding service of documents.

Use of the term 'trade mark attorney'

3.11   Section 86 of the TMA 1994 contains a new provision concerning the use of the designation 'trade mark attorney'. Until some time in the 1970s, it appears that the word 'attorney' was associated in this country with someone having a legal qualification, although it was not used very much. There was a fairly strong view, held in some quarters, that the use of the word by a person who was not a solicitor could constitute an offence under the Solicitors Act 1974 and corresponding statutes applying to Scotland and Northern Ireland. In a number of countries in Europe, however, a practice grew up whereby persons who were not lawyers, but were qualified as patent agents or trade mark agents began to use the designation 'European Patent/Trade Mark Attorney'. There was pressure to bring the situation in the UK into line with that existing in Europe. After some debate, a provision was included in the Patents Act 1977[1] permitting patent agents to use the designation 'European Patent Attorney'. The issue was raised again when the Trade Marks Bill came before the House of Commons in 1994. Section 86(1) now provides that no offence is committed under the enactments restricting the use of certain expressions in reference to persons not qualified to act as solicitors by the use of the term 'trade mark attorney' in reference to a registered trade mark agent. Those enactments are identified in s 86(2) as the acts just mentioned. As already mentioned, the Institute of Trade Mark Agents has changed its name to 'Institute of Trade Mark Attorneys'.

1 Section 85. See now CPDA 1988, ss 276–278.

Professional privilege

Privilege at common law

3.12   Until comparatively recently, there was in general no privilege attaching to communications between any person and his trade mark agent. The same applied to patent agents dealing with trade mark matters. This had been widely assumed to be the case since the decision of Chitty J in *Moseley v Victoria Rubber Co.*[1] The question arose in the case of *McGregor Clothing Co Ltd's Trade Mark.*[2] However in that case the document in question was plainly privileged, as Whitford J held, because it was a letter from a party's American attorney containing legal advice; the fact that it was sent to the party's trade mark agent instead of the party itself did not deprive it of privilege. Section 15 of the Civil Evidence Act 1968 had conferred a privilege, in certain circumstances, in respect of communications between patent agents and their clients. That provision was replaced by ss 104–105 of the Patents Act 1977. However the privilege only applied to *patent agents* dealing with *patent* matters. That there was no privilege in the case of communications between a person and his trade mark agent was confirmed by Nourse J, in *Dormeuil Frères SA v Dormire Menswear Ltd,*[3] applying the decision of the Court of Appeal in *Wheeler v Le Marchant*[4] and holding that it was an established rule that legal professional privilege was afforded only to communications between a client and his legally qualified advisers. The Court of Appeal reached the same conclusion, in a case of a patent agent dealing with a copyright matter, in *Wilden Pump Engineering Co v Fusfield.*[5]

In *Dormeuil*[6] Nourse J made it clear that he was not ordering production of any correspondence which might already in one way or another be covered by the legal professional privilege. Such an example was provided by *McGregor*, and another instance might arise where the trade mark agent (or patent agent) was acting on instructions from solicitors in a situation in which legal proceedings were pending or contemplated. Furthermore it is thought that in any event legal professional privilege attached in the normal way to counsel's advice obtained by an agent and to correspondence recording or commenting upon such advice.

1   (1886) 55 LT 482.
2   [1979] RPC 361.
3   [1983] RPC 131.
4   (1881) 17 ChD 675.
5   [1985] FSR 1959.
6   [1983] RPC 131 at 136 line 41.

Privilege since 13 August 1990

3.13   Section 284 of the CDPA 1988, which came into force on 13 August 1990, extended privilege in certain circumstances to communications with registered trade mark agents, as to any matter relating to the protection of any design, trade mark or service mark, or as to any matter involving passing off. Under s 280,[1] which came into force at the same time, a similar privilege was conferred on communications with patent agents, as to any of the above matters and also any matter relating to the protection of any invention or technical information. Sections 104 and 105 of the Patents Act 1977 were repealed.[2] Section 87 of the TMA 1994 substantially re-enacts s 284 of the CDPA 1988, which is repealed.[3]

Any communication as to any of the above-mentioned matters, between a person and his trade mark agent or[4] patent agent, as the case may be, or for the purpose of obtaining, or in response to a request for, information which a person is seeking for the purpose of instructing such agent, is privileged from (or, in Scotland, protected against) disclosure in legal proceedings in England, Wales or Northern Ireland *in the same way* as a communication between a person and his solicitor or, as the case may be, a communication for the purpose of obtaining, or in a response to a request for, information which a person seeks for the purposes of instructing his solicitor.

1 Now amended by the TMA 1994, s 106(1) and Sch 4, para 8.
2 CDPA 1988, s 303(2) and Sch 8.
3 TMA 1994, S 106(2) and Sch 5.
4 Under the CDPA 1988, s 280.

3.14   The effect of these provisions is thus determined by the general common law rules as to legal professional privilege. A detailed discussion of these rules was included in the Supreme Court Practice, under Ord 24, r 5 of the Rules of the Supreme Court. The principles applied are now discussed in several of the currently available guides to the new CPR 1988, under Part 31.[1] The rules are only summarised here. Briefly, where no litigation is contemplated or pending, letters and other communications passing between a party, or his predecessors in title, and his, or their solicitors are privileged from production, provided that they are and are sworn to be, confidential, and written to, or by, the solicitor in his professional capacity, and for the purpose of getting legal advice or assistance for the client. Communications through an agent are included, as are communications with a lawyer employed by the party relating to legal, as opposed to administrative, matters. The scope of the privilege is broader when, at the time of the communication, litigation was contemplated or pending. It extends to communications between a solicitor and a non-professional agent or a third party, directly, or through an agent, which come into existence after litigation is contemplated or commenced and made with a view to such litigation, either for the purpose of obtaining or giving advice in regard to it, or of obtaining or collecting evidence to be used in it, or obtaining information which may lead to the obtaining of such evidence.

1 See eg the Civil Court Practice 1999 (Butterworths), 1/CPR/31.15/1 at p 341.

3.15   It is not clear what, for the purposes of s 280 of the CDPA 1988 Act and s 87 of the TMA 1994, is the nature of the advice sought or the business as to which advice is sought, which may be the basis of a claim for privilege. However, since it is well established that legal professional privilege does extend to non-litigious business,[1] it is submitted that any advice of a legal nature, on matters as to the protection of trade marks or service marks or involving passing off, should be covered if it is confidential. Another question is whether 'litigation', which must be contemplated or pending under the second head of privilege, is confined to legal proceedings in the courts. It is submitted that, having regard to the context and purpose of the provisions, and to the general wording of sub-s (2)(b) in each provision, contemplated or pending proceedings in the Trade Marks Registry ought to be sufficient. Probably the question whether a document is privileged is to be determined as at the date on which the obligation of disclosure arose. Finally, it should be emphasised that, as before with communications with lawyers, the privilege in all cases is the privilege of the client, not of the trade mark agent or the patent agent.

1 See eg *Balabel v Air India* [1988] Ch 317; [1988] 2 All ER 246, CA.

Chapter 4

Definition of a trade mark

Trade mark

4.1 In contrast to the TMA 1938, which defined 'mark' and 'trade mark' (and, when amended, 'service mark') separately[1] and which contained separate provisions in ss 9 and 10 laying down what marks were registrable, the TMA 1994 contains a comprehensive definition of 'trade mark' in s 1, covering marks for both goods and services, followed by provisions in ss 3 and 4 setting out what is not registrable. Section 1(1), which follows closely the wording of art 2 of the Directive, is as follows:

> 'In this Act a "trade mark" means any sign capable of being represented graphically which is capable of distinguishing goods or services of one undertaking from those of other undertakings.
>
> A trade mark may, in particular, consist of words (including personal names), designs, letters, numerals or the shape of goods or their packaging.'

1 The TMA 1938, s 68(1) of and the Trade Marks (Amendment) Act 1984, s 1(7) (as amended by the Patents, Designs and Marks Act 1986).

4.2 Section 1(2) provides that references in the TMA 1994 to a trade mark include, unless the context otherwise requires, references to a collective mark or certification mark. The special provisions for these two kinds of mark, which are to be found respectively in s 49 and Sch 1, and s 50 and Sch 2, are discussed in Chapter 10.

'Any sign' – qualification for registration as a trade mark

4.3 The expression 'sign' is very broad. As it has been put by Jacob J,[1] a sign is anything which can convey information; the learned judge appreciated that this was extremely wide, but could see no reason to limit the meaning of the word, the only qualification being that it be capable of being represented graphically. The words 'may, in particular consist of … ' indicate that the list of examples of trade marks is not intended to be exhaustive. As is pointed out in the White Paper[2] the definition is a flexible definition intended to serve the needs of commerce and is open-ended so as to be capable of adapting to changes in trading practices. The categories of signs specifically mentioned confirm that a trade mark may be three-dimensional. In addition to signs in these categories, devices and logos, and indeed everything that

43

could be a 'mark' for the purposes of TMA 1938 will be a 'sign' for the purposes of the definition. For instance colour combinations, such as those which were held to be 'marks' in the case of *Smith, Kline and French Laboratories Ltd v Sterling-Winthrop Group Ltd*[3] may also qualify as trade marks under the new law.[4] The inclusion of the shape of goods or their packaging makes it clear[5] that the decision of the House of Lords in *Re Coca-Cola Co*,[6] that the distinctive shape of a bottle was not a 'mark' for the purposes of the TMA 1938, is no longer applicable. There is nothing in the definition to suggest – any more than there was in the TMA 1938[7] – that anything capable of protection under design law is excluded. In each case the guiding principle, endorsed in the White Paper,[8] is that if a sign functions in the market place as a trade mark, it is to be regarded as a trade mark.

1 In *Philips Electronics NBV v Remington Consumer Products* [1998] RPC 283 at 298. Note that this case has now been heard by the Court of Appeal: see [1999] ETMR 816. The decision of the Court of Appeal, which is subject to the ruling of the European Court of Justice on a number of questions, does not affect Jacob J's interpretation of the word 'sign'.
2 Paragraph 2.06.
3 [1975] 1 WLR 914, [1976] RPC 511, HL.
4 This is in fact stated in the Annex to the Directive, para 2(a); cf para 4(a) of the Annex to the Regulation.
5 This is also stated in the Annex to the Directive, para 2(b); cf para 4(b) of the Annex to the Regulation.
6 [1986] RPC 421.
7 See *Smith, Kline and French Laboratories Ltd* [1976] RPC 511 at 537.
8 See n 2 above.

'Capable of being represented graphically'

4.4   There has been discussion about some other things not specifically listed in the definition which might, now or in the future, be held to be 'signs' and therefore capable of being trade marks. Three instances are sounds, smells and tastes, which are mentioned in the Commission's Explanatory Memorandum.[1] The Trade Marks Bill, in its original form, did not expressly extend the protection given by registration to use of a sign in other than visual form. Section 103(2) of the TMA 1994[2] greatly extends the meaning of 'use' of a mark beyond visual representations. Without such a provision, registration of a sound or a smell, or a taste, if obtainable, would probably have had little if any practical use, because the registration could not have been infringed. The possibility of sounds, at least, being properly registered as trade marks must be considered a reality. Smells and taste pose more difficult problems, from the point of view of representation on the register. In determining whether such things can come within the definition of a trade mark,[3] an essential issue is whether the 'sign' is capable of being represented graphically. One question is what is the meaning of 'represented'? Of the number of meanings of 'represent'[4] the relevant ones are: 'to serve or use as a means of expressing'; 'portray'; 'to set forth in words; state or explain'. The second of these is narrower than the other two, and might well exclude smells and tastes, and perhaps also sounds, altogether. If one follows the principle that anything which functions in the market place as a trade mark is to be regarded as a trade mark, then the first and third meanings of 'represent', which are broader, are more appropriate. What in particular is required, it is suggested, is that the sign should be capable of being 'represented' in such a manner that other traders can see for themselves precisely what the trade mark is. If this is not the case, then the registrar may be entitled to take the view that the mark is not shown to be 'capable of being represented graphically'. On this point of principle, reference may be made to a decision of a Board of Appeal at OHIM in dealing with a CTM application for a colour mark,[5] in which it was observed, after stating the legal requirements:

> 'These legal requirements also conform with the principle of certainty, which is a guiding principle in the system of law governing the Community trade mark, since the latter is based on registration. According to this principle, the content of a trade mark application must be determined unequivocally from the outset, that is to say, it must reveal what, according to the intention of the applicant, is to be subject matter of the protection flowing from the requested trade mark. Notwithstanding Article 44 CTMR, the trade mark itself constitutes a single and indivisible unity from the application date on. From this follows further that, as a rule, the trade mark must be pictorially represented if the applicant claims any special graphic feature or, as in the present case, a colour. This is an imperative necessity for conducting the examination and registration procedure, including the search, and is commanded by the interests of the public and all owners of registered rights such as, for example, the owners of earlier trade mark rights who wish to determine the scope of protection of the application and, finally, with regard to possible opposition proceedings.'

1 Bulletin of the European Communities, Supplement No 5/80, p 56. So far as sounds are concerned, they are also mentioned in the Annex to the Directive, para 2(a), which states that art 2 of the Directive does not rule out the possibility of registering sounds as trade marks in the future; smells are not mentioned; see also para 3(a) of the Annex to the Regulation.
2 Introduced during the passage of the Bill through the House of Lords.
3 The potential problems in overcoming absolute grounds for refusal and invalidity, which are separate, are discussed below.
4 References here are to *Collins English Dictionary*, 3rd Edition (1991).
5 Case R 7/97-3 reported in Official Journal of OHIM 5/98 at p 641.

4.5 These observations seem equally apt when considering trade marks under the TMA 1994, since the relevant provisions come from the Directive, which are virtually identical to the corresponding provisions of the CTM Regulation. It is considered that the definition of a trade mark necessarily requires the applicant to make clear what kind of trade mark is sought to be registered and to define it properly. This is indeed the registry's practice. Although the original Rules[1] contained no requirements as to manner of representation, the registry's Work Manual in its successive editions[2] has contained guidance as to how trade marks should be represented for the purpose of applications for registration. The current view of the registrar, as to acceptable forms of graphical representation[3], is that a sign is graphically represented when:

(a) it is possible to determine from the graphical representation precisely what the sign is that the applicant uses or proposes to use without the need for supporting samples etc;

(b) the graphical representation can stand in place of the sign used or proposed to be used by the applicant because it represents that sign and no other;

(c) it is reasonably practicable for persons inspecting the register, or reading the Trade Marks Journal, to understand from the graphical representation what the trade mark is.

1 The Trade Marks Rules 1994 (SI 1994/2583).
2 The current edition was published in August 1998. See ch 5, para **5.3** for details of the current and earlier editions.
3 Work Manual, ch 6, para 2.3.

4.6 The amendment made to the Rules in 1998[1] contains new provisions covering, in particular, three-dimensional and colour marks. The new r 5(2) provides that an application for registration of a three-dimensional mark shall not be treated as such unless the application contains a statement to that effect. Similarly under r 5(3), where colour is claimed as an element of the trade mark, it shall not be treated as such unless the application contains a statement to that effect and specifies the colour. This also appears to be in line with the general principles set out in the Work Manual and with the approach adopted by the Board of Appeal at OHIM, in the decision referred to above.[2] Although the Board in that decision stated that the colour in question should be 'pictorially represented', another way in which a colour may be specified is by reference to a standard, such as Pantone, from which the actual colour can be identified. That should suffice under r 5(3). The reason why colours must be specified is well explained in the decision of the Board of Appeal which, after referring to the applicant's failure to comply with the statutory requirements, said:[3]

> 'This applies especially to colours since an unaccountable number of different colour shades, ranging in the specific case from dark to light and from the yellowish to the reddish tones, are conceivable which would all fall under the wide generic term "orange". This is true not only for the colour reproduction of a figurative trade mark or a word mark, but also and above all for an application which only consists of the colour per se and which hence does not possess any other identifying characteristics beyond the colour shade as such.'

1 The Trade Mark (Amendment) Rules 1998, SI 1998/925, substituting a new r 5.
2 See para **4.4**, n 5 above.
3 At p 649.

4.7 Rule 5(4) concerns applications to register word marks. Any such application is treated as an application to register the word in the graphical form in which it is shown in the application, unless the applicant includes a statement that the application is for registration of the word without regard to its graphical form. This will have a bearing on the scope of protection given to the registration, if granted;[1] it may also have a corresponding effect on registrability, in that a word in graphical form may be more distinctive than the plain word. The requirements of r 5(4) provide just another illustration of the principle of certainty referred to above.

1 See chs 6 and 12 below.

4.8 A recently reported example, which demonstrates the importance of certainty in the representation of trade marks, is the decision of one of the registry's Hearing Officers in *Swizzels Matlow Ltd's Trade Mark Application*.[1] The applicant applied to register for 'non-medicated confectionery' a mark defined by the words 'the trade mark consists of a chewy sweet on a stick'. The application met with a number of objections, including an objection that the sign applied for was not a sign which satisfied the requirements of s 1(1), being a sign not capable of being represented graphically which is capable of distinguishing goods or services of one undertaking from those of other undertakings. This objection was maintained after a hearing, on the ground that the sign did not comply with the registrar's practice in relation to acceptable forms of graphical representation, which required a mark to be defined with sufficient precision so that infringement rights can be determined. It was pointed out in the decision that 'sweets' and 'sticks' come in many sizes, shapes, colours and compositions, and that the use of the words in combination suggested an infinite variety of marks, all of which would be covered by the description. Moreover 'chewy' was difficult to define with accuracy. The application also failed to comply with other requirements of the registrar, that the graphical representation should be capable of standing in place of the trade mark, without the need to refer to samples, and that it should be reasonably practicable for persons inspecting the register, or reading the Journal, to understand from the graphical representation what the trade mark is.

1 [1998] RPC 244. For a decision of the appointed person, Mr S Thorley QC (29 January 1999), on the question of adequacy of 'geographical representation' on an application by the same applicant, see New Law Digest, 28 July 1999, 699076102.

Sounds

4.9 Similar principles apply to applications to register sounds. Such an application should include confirmation that this is the type of mark applied for; otherwise the application may be treated as an application for a device mark. It is clear that there are at least some sounds which are capable of graphical representation. For example the Work Manual[1] says that musical notation will be accepted as a graphical description of a sound mark; if the instrument(s) on which the sound is played forms part of the mark, then this should be stated. The title of a piece is not acceptable, being regarded as too imprecise. The acceptability of a sound as a mark may well depend upon how complex it is and on whether it comprises definable musical notes. As a simple example of representation by musical notation one may take the first three notes of 'Three Blind Mice', which could be represented either by the notes E, D and C shown on a musical stave, or even perhaps by 'Me-Ray-Doh'. Sounds represented by descriptions, such as for example 'the sound of a dog barking' (an actual case) or 'the sound of a gun-shot' may encounter two difficulties. The first question, is whether this would be a 'graphical representation' for the purposes of s 1(1). In the broader senses mentioned above it could be. The second question is whether the representation is sufficiently precise for the registry's requirements. It is understood that the application to register 'the sound of a dog barking' has been rejected on the ground that the mark was not sufficiently defined.

1 Chapter 6, para 2.3.6.

Smells

4.10 Turning to the case of smells, their graphical representation appears to give rise to rather greater difficulty because, to judge from some of the descriptions in pending applications, other traders could well find it impossible to determine precisely what the trade mark was and what other 'signs' might be regarded as 'similar'. The same applies to tastes. The Work Manual[1] says that it is unlikely that a description of a smell, in words, will be precise enough to be accepted as a graphical representation, and indicates that unless a smell can be defined precisely by some other form of representation which is consistent with the principles already mentioned, it may not be possible to represent it graphically. However the registry has accepted two applications for smells described solely by words, namely, 'the strong smell of bitter beer applied to flights for darts'. A similar approach was adopted by a Board of Appeal at OHIM, in concluding that 'the smell of fresh cut grass' was an acceptable description of a trademark for tennis balls.[2] Consistently with the principles as stated in the Work Manual, it was said in an earlier edition of the Work Manual that the applicant must show (inter alia) that the mark can be represented graphically in such a way as to allow an ordinary member of the public inspecting the register to obtain an accurate understanding of what the mark is. The reference here to a member of the public may be too broad; at least in the perfume trade the main concern is that competitors or potential competitors (whether manufacturers or sellers) should know what the protected mark is. Ultimately the courts, including the ECJ, are likely to be asked to decide on some of the issues raised by applications and registrations for smells and tastes.

1 Chapter 6, para 2.3.8.
2 See *Vernootschap onder Firma Senta Aromatic Marketing's Application* Case R 156/19998-2, [1999] ETMR 429, referred to in *Re Blue Bottle Trade Mark Application* (11 July 1999) by the appointed person (Mr Geoffrey Hobbs QC), New Law Digest 699086303, on appeal from the registry decision reported at [1999] RPC 392.

The function of a trade mark

4.11 Some further comment is appropriate on the function of a trade mark under the new law. Although, as already mentioned[1] the traditional object of a trade mark was to denote the trade origin of goods, it was never necessary that the identity of the proprietor of the mark should be known.[2] This was expressly confirmed in the definition of a 'trade mark' in s 68(1) of the TMA 1938. There is no reason to suppose that the new law changes the position in this respect. The earliest trade mark statutes did not attempt to define a trade mark in terms of its function. This was first done in the Trade Marks Act 1905 Act, s 3, which referred to use 'upon or in connexion with goods for the purpose of indicating that they are the goods of the proprietor'; particular kinds of relationship with the goods (manufacture, selection, certification, dealing with, or offering for sale) were specified. The TMA 1938 definition adopted the general term 'connection in the course of trade', which included all the kinds of connections previously specified. When the law was extended in 1986 to cover service marks, the definition of 'service mark'[3] required an indication 'that a particular person is connected in the course of business, with the provision of those services'. 'Provision' in this context was defined as 'provision for money or money's worth'; this itself gave rise to certain difficulties, which are mentioned below. The concept of distinguishing goods or services of the proprietor from those of others was to be found in the requirements for a mark to be registrable.[4] Essentially, whatever the wording used, a trade mark or a service mark was an indication which enabled the goods or services from a particular source to be indentified and thus distinguished from goods or services from other sources. In adopting a definition of 'trade mark' which simply describes the function in terms of capability of 'distinguishing the goods or services of one undertaking from those of other undertakings' the new law is really saying precisely the same thing.[5]

1 Chapter 1, para **1.12**.
2 See *Birmingham Vinegar Brewery V Powell* [1897] AC 710 at 715, 14 RPC 720 at 729 and 750; also the observations of Slade LJ in *Re Dee plc Corpn* [1990] RPC 159 at 181, line 26 to 182 line 4.
3 See para **4.1**, n 1, above.
4 Trade Marks Act 1938, ss 9 and 10.
5 This is confirmed by the Preamble to the Directive, para 14.

'Capable of distinguishing the goods or services of one undertaking from those of other undertakings'

4.12   Although the words 'capable of distinguishing' are familiar enough to trade mark practitioners, in the context of the requirement for registration of a trade mark in Part B of the register under s 10 of the TMA 1938, the effect of the words in the new definition of a trade mark in TMA 1994 is significantly different. In the TMA 1938, the term 'capable of distinguishing' and the corresponding requirement for a Part A registration, in s 9, of being 'adapted to distinguish' were defined with reference not only to factual distinctiveness, acquired through use, but also to 'inherent' distinctiveness, which had to be present in the mark to at least some extent.[1] Successive decisions of the courts resulted in the conclusion[2] that the meaning of the references to the inherent qualities of the mark was that, in order to be registrable at all (however distinctive in fact) a mark must be adapted to distinguish or capable of distinguishing (as the case might be) *in law* – a concept which businessmen have, not surprisingly, found hard to comprehend. This conclusion was equated with the requirement that the right to registration should:

> 'largely depend upon whether other traders are likely, in the ordinary course of their business and without any improper motive, to desire to use the same mark, or some mark nearly resembling it, upon or in connection with their own goods.'[3]

1 See *Yorkshire Copper Works Ltd's Trade Marks Register* (1954) 71 RPC 156 at 156 per Lord Asquith and *Blue Paraffin Trade Mark* [1977] RPC 473 at 501, per Buckley LJ.
2 See eg the decision of the House of Lords in *Re York Trade Mark* [1984] RPC 231 at 254.
3 Per Lord Parker in *Trade Marks Register v W & G du Cros Ltd* (1913) 30 RPC 660, approved (eg) by Lord Diplock in *Smith, Kline & French Ltd* [1976] RPC 511.

4.13   The intention of the Directive and the new law, in using the term 'capable of distinguishing' in place of the more complex wording of the TMA 1938, is to abolish the requirement that a mark be registrable in law. That is not to say that the interests of other bona fide traders will be ignored. The TMA 1994 contains several provisions designed to safeguard honest traders in the use of non-distinctive matter and in certain other respects. These include the 'absolute grounds' for refusal of registration, set out in s 3, and other provisions set out in ss 10(6) and 11, limiting the effect of a registered trade mark. In future, subject only to the absolute grounds, any trade mark which is shown to be distinctive in fact will be regarded as distinctive in law and thus capable of registration.[1] The approach to be adopted in considering whether a sign is 'capable of distinguishing' is considered further below in relation to 'absolute' grounds for refusal.[2]

1 This view was stated in the White Paper at para 3.08.
2 See Ch 5, paras **5.15** et seq.

The nature of the proprietor's trade or business activity

4.14   Another question, which arose under the previous law, was whether, in order to be trading in goods or providing services in the course of business, there had to be any payment of money. The original TMA 1938 said nothing about whether trading in goods must necessarily involve some kind of consideration, monetary or otherwise. Some decisions supported the view that there could be no trade in goods without there being some monetary consideration.[1] However the position changed following a decision of the Supreme Court of Ireland in *Golden Pages Trade Mark,*[2] in which the goods concerned were a classified telephone directory issued free of charge, the applicants receiving their revenues from the advertising, as did the applicants in *Update.*[3] Subsequently it became the registrar's practice to accept that marks used for 'free' publications could be 'trade marks'. Nevertheless it probably remained the case that there must be some monetary or equivalent consideration in order to constitute a 'trade', although it did not matter who provided such consideration. By contrast, the amendment to the TMA 1938 in 1986, for service marks, introduced a specific requirement of provision for 'money or money's worth' in the case of services. In *Re Dee Corpn plc*[4] the Court of Appeal held that this means the services have to be charged for as such. Accordingly, it was held, a mark could not be registered for 'retail services', athough the Court of Appeal appeared to accept that 'retailing' could properly be described as a 'service' in the ordinary sense of the word. The definition of a trade mark in the new law, which only refers to distinguishing of goods or services, and makes no mention of 'money or money's worth', or any other reference to consideration, seems to leave it open to argue that the position has now changed and that so long as there are 'services' in the ordinary sense of the word, marks can be registered for such services. It must be noted that in the Annex to the Regulation, the opinion is stated that 'the activity of retail trading in goods is not as such a service for which a Community trade mark may be registered ... '. However no such statement is to be found in the Annex to the Directive and, as already suggested, these opinions are to be considered, at most, as guides in interpretation and not in any way binding on the courts, which have the task of construing the words of the Directive. Indeed, the Annex to the Directive has been rejected by the High Court,[5] as having no bearing at all on interpretation of the TMA 1994. In the end, unless the registrar accepts that 'retailing sevices' are 'services' within the definition of a trade mark in s 1 of the TMA 1994, the matter will have to be determined by the courts. But if retail services are 'services', then as pointed out above,[6] classification presents no problem.

1 See *'Hospital World' Trade Mark* [1967] RPC 595 (Registry) and *UPDATE Trade Mark* [1979] RPC 166 (Board of Trade, Douglas Falconer QC). In both cases the goods were printed publications distributed free of charge, but in *UPDATE* there was a difference; in that case the applicants received revenues from the advertisers instead of the readers.
2 [1985] FSR 27.
3 See n 1 above.
4 [1989] 3 All ER 948, [1990] RPC 159.
5 *Wagamama Ltd v City Centre Restaurants* [1995] FSR 713 (Laddie J). See also ch 1, paras **1.19–1.22** above.
6 Chapter 2, para **2.8**.

4.15 Another aspect, which needs mentioning, is the position of charities, which have sometimes had difficulty in registering trade marks and service marks under the old law. No problem ever seems to have arisen where a charity has established a separate trading 'arm', perhaps a company, selling goods. But in other cases, especially when the law was extended to services in 1986, there have been difficulties for the reasons already explained. However that may have been, there does not appear to be any special difficulty, under the TMA 1994, in the way of charities in registering trade marks for goods or services.

Chapter 5

Registrability

Absolute grounds for refusal of registration

5.1   The term 'absolute grounds' is to be found in art 7 of the CTM Regulation, which sets out grounds for refusal of registration in essentially the same terms as art 3 of the Directive, on which s 3 of the TMA 1994 is based. The term does not mean that the grounds are all 'absolute' in the sense that they cannot be overcome, but simply denotes grounds which are related to the mark or application itself, as opposed to grounds based on conflict with rights of other parties. The absolute grounds for refusal, set out in s 3 of the TMA 1994, fall into six categories. The first comprises basic grounds, directed primarily at lack of distinctiveness, which may be applied to any kind of mark. A second category comprises objections applicable only to marks consisting of shapes of goods. The third relates to matters of public policy or morality, and deceptiveness. Fourth, registration may be refused in the case of marks whose use is prohibited by law. The fifth category comprises certain other specified cases, called 'specially protected emblems'. Finally, there is a ground of objection in cases of applications made in bad faith.

5.2   The TMA 1994 itself is silent on the position which arises, as is often the case, where an objection only applies to some of the goods or services covered by the application. However it is necessary to have regard, on this point, to art 13 of the Directive, which is as follows:

> 'Where grounds for refusal of registration or for revocation or invalidity of a trade mark exist in respect only of some of the goods or services for which that trade mark has been applied for or registered, refusal of registration or revocation or invalidity shall cover those goods or services only.'

In an appeal to the appointed person, in *Re Mister Long Trade Mark*,[1] it has been held that this provision, although not enacted in the TMA 1994, is binding on the registrar, and has the effect that no ground for refusal or revocation or invalidity should exist in respect of any of the goods or services for which a mark is applied for or registered. This confirms what has long been the registrar's practice, both under the old law and under the TMA 1994. Conversely, the registrar must not refuse an application in respect of any goods or services to which the ground for refusal does not apply.

1 [1998] RPC 401 (Geoffrey Hobbs QC).

5.3   Inevitably registry practice under the TMA 1994 is still developing. For some years the registry has been publishing a Work Manual, divided into a series of volumes called 'Chapters'. The first version published after the passing of the Act was, not surprisingly, entitled 'Draft Work Manual'. 'Examination and Practice' are covered in chapter 6, to which there is also an Addendum. Since 1994 two editions of chapter 6 have been published, the most recent in August 1998.[1] Changes have been made, and are expected to be made in the future, as a result of experience and decisions on appeals. Decisions of the ECJ, relating to provisions of both the Directive and the CTM Regulation, also taken into consideration, and decisions of the Boards of Appeal at OHIM may also need to be considered; exchange of views between the registry and OHIM is a part of the process of the development of registry practice. It is important that the status of the Work Manuals should be clearly understood. They are guides to the registry's thinking, not necessarily statements of the law. This is well summarised in the Foreword to chapter 6:

> 'Registry practice reflects and interprets current law, but just as the law evolves, particularly when a new Act comes into force, so practice must change to take new factors into account.
>
> 'Occasionally an application referred to as an example to illustrate a point suggests that the decision regarding acceptability was not in line with current practice. Given the constantly changing significance of certain words, phrases or signs in general use, it may be decided in retrospect that a given mark should not have been accepted for registration. An expression of opinion relating to such marks is not intended to determine or affect the registrability of any mark or any rights arising under the Trade Marks Act.
>
> 'It should be remembered that the practice stated in this chapter should not be applied rigidly and without regard to the circumstances of the application. Each case must be considered on its own merits. An Examiner should not disregard practice but the particular circumstances may suggest that a departure from practice would be justified.'

1   The current Addendum to ch 6, which is understood to be under revision, was published in June 1996.

5.4   The question of the relevance of 'precedents' in the registry, that is marks previously accepted for registration, has arisen from time to time. This was considered by Geoffrey Tookey QC (Board of Trade) in the *Madame* case in 1966,[1] a decision to which Jacob J referred in the *Treat* case[2] as follows:

> 'In particular the state of the register does not tell you what is actually happening out in the market and in any event one has no idea what the circumstances were which led the registrar to put the marks concerned on the register. It has long been held under the old Act that comparison with other marks on the register is in principle irrelevant when considering a particular mark tendered for registration, see eg *MadameTrade Mark* ([1966] RPC 541) and the same must be true under the 1994 Act.'

Although, as a matter of general principle, this must be correct, it may sometimes be legitimate to refer to recently accepted marks, particularly where the acceptance of a mark under the TMA 1994 may be illustrative of the way in which the law has actually been correctly applied, perhaps in the light of evidence filed in support of the application for registration and observations made in correspondence with the registry, these documents normally being available for inspection under r 44.

1   [1966] RPC 541.
2   *British Sugar plc v James Robertson and Sons Ltd* [1996] RPC 281 at 305.

5.5   While recognising that changes in practice have been made and that further changes will continue to occur, some mention should be made of certain aspects of the practice at the registry since the TMA 1994 came into force. In some respects there has been a tendency to adopt the approach followed under the old law. While this may no doubt be appropriate in many cases, in others it may not be in accordance with the Directive and the TMA 1994. In some objections to registration raised soon after the Act came into force, it was asserted (for example) that the mark 'does not satisfy the requirements of s 3(1)(b) or (c)'. This was, as now appears to be accepted, an incorrect approach. Unlike the position under s 9(1) of the TMA 1938, the trade mark does not have to *satisfy* the requirements of s 3(1) of the TMA 1994. Section 3 sets out grounds on which a mark should be refused registration. However that does not necessarily mean that there is no burden on an applicant for registration. Section 37 of the TMA 1994 requires the registrar to examine whether an application for registration satisfies the requirements of the Act, and for that purpose to carry out a search of earlier trade marks, to such extent as he considers necessary. If it appears to the registrar that the requirements are not met, sub-s (3) requires him to inform the applicant and give him an opportunity to make representations or to amend the application. Sub-section (4) provides that if the applicant fails to satisfy the registrar that the requirements are met, or amend the application so as to meet them, he shall refuse to accept the application. If however it appears to the registrar that the requirements for registration are met, then sub-s (5) requires him to accept the application. The matter was considered by the appointed person (Geoffrey Hobbs QC) in the case of *EUROLAMB Trade Mark*.[1] He held that there was no presumption either way in favour of or against registration, and that each application had to be considered on its own merits; the combined effect of s 37(4) and (5) of the TMA 1994 was, he said, to eliminate the discretion which the registrar had previously had under the old law and required him to decide positively that the mark either was or was not registrable. The decision does not directly answer the question, what is the position where the registrar is in doubt as to whether the mark is registrable. Under the old law, he would have refused it.

The understanding of art 3 of the Directive, from which the relevant provisions of the TMA 1994 are expressed in the White Paper,[2] compared the position with that existing under the old law:

> 'Article 3 of the Directive adopts the opposite approach by setting out grounds for refusal or invalidity of registration, thus creating a presumption that a mark ought to be registered unless there is some specific objection to it.'

Although the White Paper is not to be regarded as a guide in construing the statutory provisions,[3] nevertheless the Directive itself must be referred to when interpreting provisions based upon it. If art 3 is considered together with the seventh Recital of the Directive, it is submitted that the understanding expressed in the White Paper and set out above is correct. In practice, however, any discussion of the incidence of the burden of proof in this context is of no real relevance. On this point reference should also be made to the decision of the Court of Appeal in *Procter and Gamble Ltd v Registrar of Trade Marks*.[4] Accordingly the position is that the registrar must make a decision one way or the other, as stated by Geoffrey Hobbs QC.

1 [1998] RPC 279.
2 Cm 1203 at paras 3.06–3.07.

3 See for example the observations of Jacob J in *British Sugar plc v James Robertson & Sons Ltd* [1996] RPC 281 at 292.
4 Reported, as *Re Procter and Gamble's Trade Mark Application* [1999] ETMR 375, [1999] 3 RPC 673, on appeal from Chadwick J (25 July, unreported). See further para **5.27** below.

5.6   Another common form of objection under the TMA 1994, which merits some general discussion, has been that a mark is such that other traders would or might wish to use it, the objection usually being raised under either or both of sub-paragraphs (b) and (c) of s 3(1),[1] under which a large number of objections to registration are raised. In the case of s 3(1)(c) the actual reference is to 'trade marks which consist exclusively of signs or indications *which may serve, in trade, to designate* ... characteristics of goods or services', and it is preferable to use the actual language of the statute rather than trying to paraphrase it. In the case of s 3(1)(b) the objection is that the trade mark 'is devoid of any distinctive character.' Until this provision is interpreted by the ECJ, the only guidance available is from decisions of the courts and of the registrar. The question posed is, has the mark *any* (the word tends to be omitted in objections) distinctive character? One approach might have been simply to apply the language used and to ask, of the mark in question, can it be said not to have any distinctive character at all. Although a consideration of what other traders might wish to use may sometimes be of assistance, there may be a danger of going back to the old requirement of 'inherent capability of distinguishing'. First, it is necessary to consider the words 'capable of distinguishing', in s 1(1), in the context of the new law.

1 For the text, see para **5.13** below.

5.7   In Chapter 6 of the Work Manual[1] it is remarked that the phrase 'capable of distinguishing', which appears in the definition of a trade mark in s 1(1) of the TMA 1994, is similar to the wording used in s 10 of the TMA 1938, which was concerned with registrability (in Part B of the register), not with the definition of a trade mark. As a matter of words the observation is of course correct. But as explained above,[2] it was not the intention of the legislation that the words should be construed in the same way. The Work Manual now puts the matter thus:

> '"*Capable of distinguishing*" is similar to the wording used in section 10 of the 1938 Act. However it is used in section 1 of the 1994 Act as a definition of what may be a trade mark rather than as a prima facie requirement for registrability. Geoffrey Hobbs QC, sitting as the Lord Chancellor's Appointed Person for the first time, referring to the meaning of section 1(1) in his decision relating to the trade mark *AD2000* [1997] RPC 168 said:
>
> > "*From the proviso to section 3(1) it is apparent that section 3(1)(b), 3(1)(c) and 3(1)(d) prohibit the registration of signs which satisfy the requirements of section 1(1), but nonetheless lack a distinctive character in the absence of appropriate use. This implies that the requirements of Section 1(1) are satisfied even in cases where a sign represented graphically is only 'capable' to the limited extent of 'not incapable' of distinguishing goods or services of one undertaking from those of other undertakings.*"'

This seems to be the correct approach.[3] The separate question of the relevance of considering what other traders might wish to use, has now been considered by the Court of Appeal, in *Procter & Gamble*.[4] The point is further discussed below, in relation to the specific grounds of objection under s 3(1)(b) and (c).

1 Paragraph 2.3.9.
2 Paragraph 4.12.

3. See also *Dualit LTD's (Toaster Shapes) Trade Mark Application* [1999] RPC 304 (Registry). On appeal, Lloyd J (5 July 1999) did not uphold the objection under s 3(1)(a).
4 Paragraph **5.5**, n 4 above.

5.8   Another general question, which has arisen under the previous Trade Marks Acts and under the TMA 1994, is the relevance, to the issue of registrability, of the fact that there are provisions excluding from the scope of infringement the use of certain matter, such as a person's own name or the description of goods or services. Such provisions, sometimes called 'saving provisions' are now to be found in s 11 of the TMA 1994. In his decision in *AD 2000 Trade Mark*, referred to in the last paragraph, Geoffrey Hobbs QC dealt with the question in the following terms:

> 'Although Section 11 of the Act contains various provisions designed to protect the legitimate interests of honest traders, the first line of protection is to refuse the registration of signs which are excluded from registration by the provisions of Section 3. In this regard, I consider that the approach to be adopted with regard to registrability under the 1994 Act is the same as the approach adopted under the old Act. This was summarised by Robin Jacob Esq QC in his decision on behalf of the Secretary of State in *Colorcoat Trade Mark* [1990] RPC 511 at 517 in the following terms: "That possible defences (and in particular that the use is merely as a bona fide description) should not be taken into account when considering registration is very well settled, see eg *Yorkshire Copper Works Ltd v Trade Marks Registrar* (1954) 71 RPC 150 at 154 lines 20–25 per Viscount Simonds LC. Essentially the reason is that the privilege of a monopoly should not be conferred where it might require honest men to look for a defence."'

5.9   Thus, although in a sense the decisions under the old law are to be treated as 'water under the bridge', nevertheless the registrar and the courts are still applying a number of the old rules. Even before 1994 it could perhaps be said that the approach was a little confusing. In a number of cases[1] over many years, full approval has been given to the well-known judgment of Fletcher-Moulton LJ in *Perfection*,[2] in which at two places he appears to accept the relevance of s 44 of the Trade Marks Act 1905, which was a 'saving provision' in that Act. The approach approved under the old law was applied even where the mark applied for was proved to be 100% distinctive of the applicant's goods. However, whatever the previous position, it is submitted that the approach under the Directive and the TMA 1994 is not necessarily the same. Under the old law the burden of proving entitlement to registration was clearly on the applicant, and the approach was conditioned by the existence of the registrar's 'discretion'. This discretion no longer exists, and the scheme of the Directive is such that registration should be granted unless one of the grounds for refusal exists.

1 See eg the speech of Lord Wilberforce in *Re York Trade Mark* [1984] RPC 231 at 254.
2 *Perfection Trade Mark* (1909) 26 RPC 837 at 856.

5.10   The relevance of the 'saving provisions', in art 6(1)(b) of the Directive, to which s 11(2)(b) of the TMA 1994 corresponds, to the interpretation of art 3(1)(c) of the Directive, from which s 3(1)(c) originates, has now been considered by the ECJ in two cases heard together.[1] The court also had to consider art 3(3) of the Directive, under which some objections may be overcome by evidence of distinctive character acquired through use.[2] The first question referred to the court included the question 'Is it of significance for a broader or narrower interpretation of art 3(1)(c) with respect to geographical indications of origin that the effects of the mark are restricted under art 6(1)(b)?' According to an English translation of the Opinion of the Advocate-General, it appeared that he concluded that art 6 'does not directly affect the interpretation of [art 3(1)(c)].' However, earlier in the Opinion, when considering the question whether it is necessary to approach the provisions of art 3(1)(c) on the basis that geographical designations had to remain free for other traders to use, he made the following observations:[3]

> '... how is it possible to refuse, on grounds of principle, to allow the person who first thought of it to use a geographical term *now*, so that the same geographical term can remain available to possible competitors *in future*?

> 'If, however, "availability" is understood to mean that the geographical term remains available to any interested party for *other* lawful uses, and not for use as a trade mark, then the matter is fully dealt with by Article 6(1)(b) of the Directive. ... . In this case, however, it is a question of limiting the effects of an already existing right to a trade mark. In other words, the need for other uses of the geographical term by competitors, excluding its use as a trade mark, in no way constitutes a reason for refusing the holder the right to the trade mark.'

1 *WSC Windsurfing Chiemsee Produktions und Vertriebs GmbH v Boots and Segelzubehör Walter Huber* and *WSC Windsurfing Chiemsee Produktions und Vertriebs GmbH v Franz Attenberger* (C-108/97 and C-109/97); Opinion of Advocate-General, 5 May 1998; judgment of the Court [1999] ETMR 585.
2 See below, paras **5.82** et seq, for a discussion of the proviso to s 3(1) of the TMA 1994, which corresponds to art 3(3).
3 At paras 53–54.

5.11   Although it is not entirely clear, the Advocate General did appear to be expressing the opinion that there was no need to keep a geographical name 'free' for use by other traders *as a trade mark*, and that the need to keep it free for non-trade mark use was sufficiently met by art 6(1)(b). In its decision the ECJ, in its final answers to the questions referred to it by the German court, does not actually mention art 6(1)(b). It is however referred to in the judgment, in the context of the court's consideration of the public interest underlying art 3(1)(c), in the following terms:[1]

> '... Article 6(1)(b) of the Directive, to which the national court refers in its questions, does not run counter to what has been stated as to the objective of Article 3(1)(c), nor does it have a decisive bearing on the interpretation of that provision. Indeed, Article 6(1)(b), which aims, inter alia, to resolve the problems posed by registration of a mark consisting wholly or partly of a geographical name, does not confer on third parties the right to use the name as a trade mark but merely guarantees their right to use it descriptively, that is to say, as an indication of geographical origin, provided that it is used in accordance with honest practices in industrial or commercial matters.'

1 Paragraph 28.

5.12   This is not a direct answer to the question referred by the German court. The court, in saying that art 6(1)(b) does not have a *decisive bearing on the interpretation* of art 3(1)(c), is not necessarily saying that it is wholly irrelevant. It may be that what the court is actually saying is that if the mark applied for is open to objection under art 3(1)(c), as consisting exclusively of an indication of characteristics of goods or services, then in the absence of evidence of acquired distinctive character the application must be refused and that art 6(1)(b) cannot

not be used as a basis for allowing the application. Nevertheless it is submitted that the decision implicitly accepts that, even if no account can be taken of art 6(1)(b) in determining whether a mark is prima facie registrable, account may be taken of it, and hence s 11(2)(b), where the mark applied for has been in substantial use and has thereby acquired a distinctive character. To refuse to do so would seem to be reintroducing the principle of distinctiveness in law, which is no longer applicable.

The basic grounds for refusal of registration

5.13   Section 3(1) sets out the four basic grounds; if any of these are applicable the mark must be refused registration. These four grounds adopt the wording of art 3(1)(a)–(d) inclusive of the Directive, and provide:

> 'The following shall not be registered–
>
> (a) signs which do not satisfy the requirements of section 1(1),
> (b) trade marks which are devoid of any distinctive character,
> (c) trade marks which consist exclusively of signs or indications which may serve, in trade, to designate the kind, quality, quantity, intended purpose, value, geographical origin, the time of production of goods or of rendering of services, or other characteristics of goods or services,
> (d) trade marks which consist exclusively of signs or indications which have become customary in the current language or in the *bona fide* and established practices of the trade.
>
> Provided that, a trade mark shall not be refused registration by virtue of paragraph (b), (c) or (d) above if, before the date of application for registration, it has in fact acquired a distinctive character as a result of the use made of it.'

5.14   The four grounds need to be considered separately. It should be noted at once that, although the words 'shall not be registered' are used, the proviso applies to each of grounds (b)–(d), so that ground (a) is the only one which, according to the proviso, is incapable of being overcome by proof of acquired distinctive character. It will sometimes be the case, in practice, that evidence of use of a sign may serve to demonstrate that the sign in fact performs the function of a trade mark. It might thus be thought that such evidence could overcome an objection under s 3(1)(a), but the decision of the Court of Appeal in *Philips Electronics BV v Remington Consumer Products Ltd*[1] indicates that this may not be so. The proviso follows the first part of art 3(3) of the Directive; the second part of that art, in so far as it says that Member States may permit reliance on acquisition of distinctive character *after* the date of application for registration, has not been adopted here.

1 Considered in detail below at paras **5.19** et seq. See [1998] RPC 283 for the decision of Jacob J at first instance.

'Signs which do not satisfy the requirements of s 1(1)'

5.15   This provision is simply a confirmation that a sign must, in order to be registrable, fall within the definition of a 'trade mark' in s 1(1). If in some respect the requirements of the definition are not met, for example if the 'sign' is not one which can be represented graphically, then it cannot be registered, regardless of any distinctive character which is claimed to have resulted from use. The first decision of a court in the UK on the meaning and effect of s 1(1) is that of Jacob J in *Philips v Remington,* which, as mentioned in the last paragraph, has now been the subject of a decision of the Court of Appeal. However that decision itself is subject to the views of the ECJ, to which a number of questions under art 3 of the Directive have been referred by the Court of Appeal. The registered trade mark in question was a pictorial representation, in two dimensions, of the face of the plaintiff's three-headed rotary shaver, and the registration was for 'electric shavers'. The plaintiff's three-headed rotary shavers had been sold for many years, under the trade mark 'Philishave'. In an infringement action, brought against the defendant in respect of its sale of a three-headed rotary shaver under its 'Remington' trade mark, t   h   e defendant counterclaimed for a declaration of invalidity. Among the grounds of invalidity raised,[1] the defendant relied upon s 3(1)(a) of the Act, alleging that the registered mark was not a sign capable of distinguishing goods of one undertaking from those of another.

1 Other grounds of invalidity were raised under the TMA 1994, s 3(1)(b) and (c), s 3(2) and s 3(3); these are discussed at the appropriate places below.

5.16   After some consideration of the old law, Jacob J referred to Recital 7(b) of the Directive which, as he said, emphasises that capability of distinguishing is a fundamental requirement of the sort of sign which can be registered, and said that did not think that one could disregard this. He also mentioned Recital 10(a), which places particular importance on the purpose of a trade mark, to guarantee trade origin, observing:

> 'If that is what trade marks are for, then a sign which can never fully do that is not, in my judgment, to be regarded as capable of distinguishing.'

The learned judge continued:

> 'I think that is the case here. Philips can never get away from the fact that the sign primarily denotes function. More use could not make difference. The sign can never only denote shavers made by Philips and no-one else because it primarily says "here is a three-headed rotary shaver". It is not "capable" of denoting only Philips goods. That is why the public's reaction to [the defendant's shaver] was essentially there is a three-headed shaver "put out by Remington". The reaction would have been different if the shaver had been marked "Philishave" as well as "Remington". This shows the "sign" is not distinctive in the sense of a true trade mark such as Philishave.

> 'I do not think in so holding I am resurrecting the old British law. On the contrary I think there is a difference between this sort of case and the *Yorkshire* sort. In the latter the word has truly come to denote the goods of the undertaking. True it also meant a county, but not when used for copper tubing. For copper tubing it had come to say "here is tubing made by the Yorkshire Copper Works" and nothing else. "Yorkshire" would be registrable now. It is the sort of trade mark "devoid of distinctive character" which can be saved by proof of factual distinctiveness. The same goes for the shape of the Coca-Cola bottle (unregistrable under the old law, *C-C Trade Marks* [1986] RPC 421). This says "my contents are from the Coca-Cola company" and really conveys no other message.'

The judge then quoted a part of his own judgment in *British Sugar plc v James Robertson and Sons Ltd*,[1] in which he had said that '*capable of distinguishing*' means whether the mark can in fact do the job of distinguishing, and continued:

> 'Thus I think the real question here is whether there is factual bar preventing the sign from really being distinctive. I think the test for this is to ask whether, no matter how much the sign may be used and recognised, it can really serve to convey in substance only the message: "here are a particular trader's goods". The point is important because the sign conveys the primary message "here is a three-headed rotary shaver – from what you see you know how this device works".'

1 [1996] RPC 281 at 305.

5.17 In his comparison of the case before him with the *Yorkshire* and *C-C* cases, it is submitted that the learned judge was not clearly distinguishing between the two separate questions which he was considering in this part of his judgment, namely whether the sign in question is a 'trade mark' and whether it has sufficient distinctive character to be registrable. It was never suggested that 'Yorkshire' was not a trade mark; registration was only rejected on the ground that the mark was not inherently distinctive. On the other hand the application to register the shape of the Coca-Cola bottle was rejected on the ground that what was sought to be registered was not a 'mark', and was therefore not a 'trade mark' for the purposes of the TMA 1938, a ground which has been removed by the TMA 1994; in the Court of Appeal it was accepted that if it was a 'mark', then it had been shown to be distinctive.[1] Under the 1994 Act the question whether a mark is 'capable of distinguishing' within the meaning of s 1(1), so as to qualify as a trade mark, and the question whether the sign applied for is 'devoid of any distinctive character' within s 3(1)(b) are separate questions, even if both objections might apply in some cases. Taking the same examples, 'Yorkshire' probably would not be the subject of an objection under ss 1(1) and 3(1)(a), even before filing of evidence of acquired distinctiveness; the real objection, now capable of being overcome, would be under s 3(1)(c). Neither, probably, would the Coca-Cola bottle have been the subject of an objection under ss 1(1) and 3(1)(a), but it is thought that evidence was required to meet an objection under s 3(1)(b). So neither of the cases referred to really had anything directly to do with the first question.

1 Accordingly a two-dimensional representation of the bottle, which had been refused registration by the registrar and by Falconer J, was allowed to proceed to registration.

5.18 Another aspect of the decision in *Philips* is the judge's view, expressed also in the passage from *British Sugar* set out above, that a sign must be excluded from registration if it cannot serve to convey *only* the message 'here are a particular trader's goods'. Leading counsel for Philips had relied upon the well known observations of Fletcher Moulton LJ in *Perfection Trade Mark*[1] to the effect that the assumption that there was a natural and innate antagonism between distinctive and descriptive (applied to words) was a fallacy. The learned judge's reply was that the argument can be taken too far, giving the example of 'soap', which could of course never be a trade mark for soap. This is obviously correct; but whether or not the *Philips* decision is correct as regards the particular mark in suit, there would be a danger in approaching cases where the applicability of s 3(1)(a) or (b) was in issue, on the basis that a descriptive sign cannot be registered unless it *only* conveys the message that the goods are a particular trader's goods. To take one example, of a mark which was held to be registrable under the old law, in Part A of the register, *Blue Paraffin*[2] would probably fail Jacob J's test, were it to be applied rigidly. To do so would, it is submitted, resurrect the old requirement of inherent distinctiveness, or distinctiveness *in law*,[3] which is not a part of the TMA 1994. There are many marks, which are very descriptive, but have in fact become registered on the basis of evidence. But that does not of course mean that they cease to be descriptive; they serve as trade marks, and *also* convey a message to the public, for example as to some characteristic of the goods or services. Thus many perfectly good registered trade marks would fail Jacob J's test, because they do not serve *only* to convey the message 'here are a particular trader's goods'.

1 (1909) 26 RPC 837 at 857, set out in Jacob J's judgment at [1998] RPC 301.
2 *Blue Paraffin Trade Mark* [1977] RPC 473.
3 A requirement which, as the Court of Appeal reminded us, at [1977] RPC 473 at 501, only had to be satisfied to a small degree.

5.19 In the Court of Appeal the judgment of the court was given by Aldous LJ, who emphasised at the outset that the function of a trade mark is to identify the trade origin of goods or services, such function being important to protect both traders and consumers. He observed that this is a requirement of European law, just as much as it has been under UK law, this function of a trade mark being recognised in the Recital 10 of the Directive. In his consideration of s 3(1)(a), Aldous LJ accepted that a substantial portion of traders and the general public recognised the registered mark as being a representation of the head of the Philips three-headed rotary shaver and that if they saw a shaver with a head as shown in the mark or a picture of such a shaver they would, absent a statement to the contrary, believe that it came from Philips. In a very helpful discussion, which needs to be set out in full, he continued:

> 'They associate the shape of such a head with a rotary shaver made by Philips and nobody else. That is not surprising because Philips had, up to 1995, been the only company selling rotary shavers in the United Kingdom and their rotary shavers have been the most popular type of shaver in the United Kingdom and the majority of sales in recent times had a head as shown in the trade mark. In fact Philips have had a monopoly in the United Kingdom in rotary shavers and the public's perception reflects that fact. It is against that background that the court must decide whether the trade mark is capable of distinguishing one trader's goods from those of another trader.

> 'I do not believe that the fact that a trade mark has by use become such as to denote goods of a particular trader necessarily means that it is capable of distinguishing as required by section 1 (Article 2). I have already pointed out that use is relevant when deciding registrability under section 3(1)(b), (c) and (d), but not under section 3(1)(a) (see Articles 3(1)(a), (b), (c) and 3(3)). That suggests that the capability of distinguishing depends upon the features of the trade mark itself, not on the result of its use. Thus a person who has had monopoly use of a trade mark for many years may be able to establish that it does in fact denote his goods exclusively, but that does not mean that it has a feature which will distinguish his goods from those of a rival who comes into the market. The more the trade mark describes the goods, whether it consists of a word or a shape, the less likely it will be capable of distinguishing those goods from similar goods of another trader. An example of a trade mark which is capable of distinguishing is Weldmesh,[1] whereas Welded Mesh would not be. The former, despite its primary descriptive meaning, has sufficient capricious alteration to enable it to acquire a secondary meaning, thereby demonstrating it is capable of distinguishing.

The latter has no such alteration. Whatever the extent of use, whether or not it be monopoly use and whether or not there is evidence that the trade and the public associate it with one person, it retains its primary meaning, namely mesh that is welded. It does not have any feature which renders it capable of distinguishing one trader's welded mesh from another trader's welded mesh.

'Shapes such as shown in the trade mark are pictorial descriptions of products. The test of registrability is the same for such shapes as that for word marks. The trade mark shows the head of a particular three-headed rotary shaver and it would be recognised by the trade and public as such, albeit as one made by Philips. Even though there are a number of other designs of three-headed rotary shavers that could be produced, the shape shown in the trade mark is a shape which, absent patent, registered design, copyright or unfair trading protection, another trader is entitled to make. It is not capable of distinguishing Philips' shavers of that shape from those of other traders who produce shavers with a similar shaped head. I believe that is accepted by Philips; but they contend that such use of the shape by another trader is unlawful in that it would result in infringement of a valid trade mark registration. But that submission avoids the question of whether a picture of a three-dimensional article which is purely descriptive of the article is registrable. In my view the definition in the Act and the Directive prevents that happening. No doubt an application to register a picture of a reel for cotton or a flag for coffee would succeed as they are not descriptive of the goods for which registration is sought; but that does not mean that a shape of an article is registrable in respect of the article shown in the application. To so hold would enable a few traders to obtain registrations of all the best designs of an article and thereby monopolise those designs. In my view a shape of an article cannot be registered in respect of goods of that shape unless it contains some addition to the shape of the article which has trade mark significance. It is that addition which makes it capable of distinguishing the trade mark owner's goods from the same sort of goods sold by another trader.

'The judge was right to conclude that the trade mark did not constitute a registrable trade mark as required by s (art) 3(1)(a). However I do not believe that my reasoning is consistent with all that he said in *British Sugar plc v James Robertson and Sons Ltd* [1996] RPC 281.'

1 This is a reference to a mark which was the subject of a decision of the Court of Appeal under the old law. See *Re Weldmesh Trade Mark* [1966] RPC 220.

5.20   In essence, what Aldous LJ is saying is that a picture or a shape of a three-dimensional article is not registrable as a trade mark in respect of such an article if it is *purely* descriptive of the article, and no more. In particular his view is not consistent with the line of reasoning of Jacob J in *British Sugar*,[1] that a sign must be excluded from registration is it cannot serve to convey *only* the message, 'here are a particular trader's goods.'

1 See para **5.19**, r. 1 above.

5.21   In practice, therefore, the judgment of Aldous LJ seems to suggest that the objection under the TMA 1994, s 3(1)(a), is of comparatively limited scope. Essentially, it requires consideration of the question whether the sign applied for is capable at all of performing the function of a trade mark, which is to distinguish the goods or services of one undertaking from those of other undertakings. As Geoffrey Hobbs QC put it,[1] the sign should be 'not incapable' of distinguishing. Apart from obvious cases,[2] such as those where the sign applied for is nothing more than the description of the goods or services, the provision can be applied to other signs, such as the basic shape of some goods or containers, which are completely incapable of distinguishing the applicant's goods or services, although such cases would normally fall also under s 3(1)(b).[3] Of course there will be many signs which pass this test but, because of their descriptiveness will be open to objection under s 3(1)(b), (c) or (d). Slogans provide a good example. Some slogans may be the subject of an objection under s 3(1)(a), unless they contain an existing trade mark, but it, submitted that in most cases slogans are not such that it can be said that they are 'not incapable' of distinguishing, and that the real objection will be under s 3(1)(b) or (c).

1 In *AD 2000*, see para **5.7** above.

2 The recent decision of Laddie J in *Re Registered Trade Mark 'Jeryl Lynn'* (1998) 49 BMLR 92, holding a trade mark, registered for medicinal and pharmaceutical preparations, invalid on the ground that it was merely the name for a particular strain of mumps virus, is an example. See also the decision of the Court of Appeal in *Bach Flower Remedies Ltd*, 21 October 1999. Judgment at first instance reported at [1999] RPC 1.

3 The registrar previously indicated that objections under s 3(1)(a) would not be raised only because the sign consists of the shape of goods or their packaging. However it seems that such objections are being raised on this basis, since the *Remington* decision. A recent example is a decision in opposition proceedings, where the marks in question were shapes of toasters of particular designs – *Dualit Ltd's Application* [1999] RPC 304. However, on appeal, Lloyd J (5 July 1999) decided the applications should not have been rejected under s 3(1)(a).

Colours, sounds and smells

5.22   Particular instances in which the TMA 1994, s 3(1)(a) may be invoked by the registry are colours, sounds and smells, which have already been considered in Chapter 4.[1] Colours are used for all kinds of purposes, and a single colour or even a combination of colours is not necessarily a trade mark. Evidence will usually be required to show that such a sign is in fact a trade mark.[2] The same is likely to apply to sounds and smells. Of sounds, the Work Manual[3] states that provided that they can be represented graphically, they are not excluded from registration. Some sounds may be acceptable without evidence, but in many instances evidence will be required, to demonstrate that the sound is a trade mark and is registrable. In the case of smells, as the Work Manual[4] correctly states, many products have scents, the purpose of which is to make the use of the products more pleasant or attractive. In such cases, as the Manual points out, it may be difficult to show that a particular smell indicates the goods of a particular trader. The Manual continues:

> *'There will be a case for registering the mark if the applicant can show that:*
>
> (1)   the smell is used as a trade mark;
> (2)   it is not an inherent or natural characteristic of the goods but is added by the applicant to identify his goods;
> (3)   the public regard the smell as a sign which identifies the applicant's goods;
> (4)   the mark is represented graphically.'

This seems reasonable enough as a general approach, but it may perhaps be going too far to state, generally, that a smell mark which is an inherent or natural characteristic of the goods can never be registered. It is not necessarily beyond the bounds of possibility, for example, that a perfume might be shown to be completely different and distinguishable from all previous perfumes, and so well-known and established, and hence distinctive, that it can properly be concluded that its smell functions as a trade mark in the market place. In practice, subject to the question whether evidence is admissible to show that something is a 'trade mark', evidence that the smell serves as a trade mark will be required, as well as evidence of factual distinctiveness. In most cases, it is likely that the same evidence will suffice for both purposes.

1 See **4.4–4.5** and **4.8–4.9**.
2 As an example of the registry's approach to colours, an attempt by the vacuum cleaner company, Dyson, to protect the colours yellow and silver failed, in spite of the filing of voluminous evidence. See CIPA Journal, March 1998, p 211.
3 Chapter 6, para 5.2.
4 Chapter 6, para 5.3.

'Trade marks which are devoid of any distinctive character'

5.23 There is a statement in the Annex to the Directive, to the effect that a trade mark is devoid of any distinctive character if it is not capable of distinguishing the goods or services of one undertaking from those of other undertakings. Even if it were subsequently to be decided that the Annex had any effect at all, which is unlikely, this statement is singularly unhelpful, being merely a repetition of the definition of a 'trade mark' in art 2 of the Directive and in s 1(1) of the TMA 1994. Although there is the possibility of some overlap with s 3(1)(a) in some cases, it is important that s 3(1)(b) is considered separately. The provision may also overlap in some cases with sub-s (c), which is considered below, but it is capable of covering signs which would not necessarily be caught by that provision.

5.24 At first sight it would appear that the important words in s 3(1)(b) might be 'devoid' and 'any'; so long as there is *some* distinctive character a mark ought not to be refused registration under this head. Thus trade marks which are 'devoid of any distinctive character' might include the generic names of goods and words which are purely laudatory, such as 'good' and 'perfect', as well as descriptions such as 'all wool'. Other examples of marks which might be refused under this head include 'king size' and 'international' for cigarettes, and single letters and simple devices, such as squares, circles and oval borders. Furthermore, there is no doubt that the provisions of the Directive were not framed with the intention that the words of art 3(1)(b), from which s 3(1)(b) of the TMA 1994 is derived, should be equated with the old concept of 'lacking in inherent distinctiveness'. For example, marks which were refused under the old law as being mere phonetic equivalents of descriptive words, such as 'Orlwoola', may not necessarily be regarded as '*devoid* of *any* distinctive character'. The Work Manual[1] mentions a number of types of marks which, under sub-s (b), may not be considered acceptable prima facie, and there is a helpful discussion of the registrar's current approach. Some aspects merit further comment, but reference should first be made to some of the decisions.

1 Chapter 6, s 3.

5.25 The first reported case, in which s 3(1)(b) was considered, was *British Sugar*;[1] this concerned the trade mark 'Treat', which had been registered for 'dessert sauces and syrups'. The validity of the registration was attacked under each of the provisions of s 3(1)(a), (b), (c) and (d) of the TMA 1994. Jacob J expressed no conclusion under s 3(1)(a) regarding the mark in suit. As to s 3(1)(b) he said:[2]

'What does *devoid of any distinctive character* mean? I think the phrase requires consideration of the mark on its own, assuming no use. Is it the sort of word (or other sign) which cannot do the job of distinguishing without first educating the public that it is a trade mark? A meaningless word or a word inappropriate for the goods concerned ("North Pole" for bananas) can clearly do. But a common laudatory word such as "Treat" is, absent use and recognition as a trade mark in itself (I hesitate to borrow the word from the old Act but the idea is much the same) devoid of any *inherently* distinctive character.'

1 [1996] RPC 281.
2 [1996] RPC 281 at 306.

5.26 The learned judge referred to this passage in *Philips*.[1] After concluding that 'when a word is so descriptive that it is incapable of distinguishing properly, even if it does so partially', it is 'incapable of distinguishing' within the meaning of art 2 of the Directive, he continued:

'And likewise the mark is then devoid of distinctive character. Other, less descriptive, words may not be in that class: they may, given use and recognition as a trade mark, come in substance to say: here are the goods of a particular trader. Such words become trade marks "by nurture, not nature" to use the happy conjunction of words borrowed from other fields of learning by Mr Hobbs QC in *AD 2000 Trade Mark* [1997] RPC 168. It is this sort of word which is contemplated by Article 3(1)(b).'

After referring to his decision in *British Sugar*, set out above, the judge continued:

'What I have said about word marks is also true of picture marks. They too may be more or less descriptive. A picture of an article is equivalent to a description of it – both convey information. If the picture is simply of an artefact which traders might legitimately wish to manufacture then to my mind it is just like the common word for it and, like the word for it, incapable of distinguishing.'

1 [1998] RPC 283 at 302.

5.27 It is submitted that here again the learned judge was not clearly distinguishing between the two objections, under s 3(1)(a) and (b). If the applicant has passed the first hurdle, in that the sign applied for is not incapable of performing the function of a trade mark, then this difficulty might be avoided by looking at the sign and asking the question, has it any distinctive character? The first case in which s 3(1)(b) has been considered by the Court of Appeal is *Procter & Gamble Ltd v Registrar of Trade Marks*.[1]

1 Reported as *Re Procter and Gamble's Trade Mark Application* [1999] RPC 673, [1999] RPC 673, affirming the decision of Chadwick J (unreported) 25 July 1997; noted in New Law Digest at 699021002.

5.28 *Procter & Gamble*[1] was also the first case in which the applicability of s 3(1)(b) to a 'pictorial' mark had been considered by any court. There were three applications, for registration of three-dimensional signs each comprising a bottle of the same shape, bearing a label.[2] In each case the colours of the bottles and the different colours of the labels were specified. There was no objection under s 3(1)(a); originally the registry had raised objections under s 3(1)(b) and (c), but the objection under s 3(1)(c) had been withdrawn. The applicant appealed to the court against the refusal of the applications under s 3(1)(b).

1 [1999] ETMR 375.
2 The case is mentioned as an example in the Work Manual, ch 6, para 3.10.

5.29 In reaching her decision, the registrar's Hearing Officer had considered separately each of the constituents of the marks applied for, namely the shape of the bottles, the patterns on the labels (which depicted a kitchen sink, a bath, tiled floors, etc, the goods being cleaning preparations), and the colours applied to both. Applying the test laid down by Lord Parker in the case of *Trade Marks Registrar v W and G Du Cros Ltd's Application*,[1] that is whether the component parts or marks resembling them were unlikely to be required without improper motive by other traders, she concluded that each was devoid of any distinctive character. While accepting that it was necessary to consider the marks as wholes, and to consider whether other traders were unlikely, without improper motive, to want to use the components in the particular way appearing in the applications, she concluded in each case that they were devoid of any distinctive character.

1 (1913) 30 RPC 660 at 372, a decision under the Trade Marks Act 1905 and consistently applied by the courts in a number of decisions under the TMA 1938.

5.30 On appeal from the decision of the registrar's Hearing Officer, Chadwick J accepted that the enactment of the TMA 1994 for the express purpose of implementing the EC Directive makes it necessary to look afresh at matters which might otherwise be thought to have been determined by decisions under the TMA 1938 and earlier legislation. After setting out ss 1(1) and 3(1) and making some observations on the relationship between ss 1(1) and 3(1)(a), the learned judge said:

'Paragraph (b) of s 3(1), read in conjunction with the proviso to that subsection, contains recognition that a mark may be capable of distinguishing goods or services of one undertaking from those of another undertaking notwithstanding that it is devoid of any distinctive character. But if it is devoid of any inherent distinctive character then it cannot be registered as a trade mark unless, before the date of application for registration, it has in fact acquired a distinctive character as a result of the use made of it.'

Referring to the decision of Geoffrey Hobbs QC in *AD 2000 Trade Mark*,[1] the learned judge said that the dichotomy between distinctive by nature and distinctive by nurture appeared to him to be a helpful way of identifying the point, and adopted it with gratitude. He also cited, with approval, the passage from Jacob J's decision in *British Sugar* set out above.[2] After setting out the relevant parts of the Hearing Officer's decisions, he concluded that she identified correctly the question which she had to decide, applied the correct test and reached conclusions which could not be faulted, adding at the end of his judgment that 'I do not differ from her view as to inherent distinctiveness.'

1 See para **5.7** above.
2 See para **5.25**.

5.31 In upholding the decision of the Hearing Officer and Chadwick J, Robert Walker LJ, with whose judgment the other members of the Court of Appeal agreed, after referring to the Opinion of Advocate General Cosmos in the *Windsurfing Chiemsee* case,[1] considered the applicability of Lord Parker's test in *W&G* in the following passage:

'I would accept that Lord Parker's observations about distinctiveness must since the 1994 Act be treated with considerable caution, especially so far as they refer to what is capable in law of distinguishing one product from another. The passage in Lord Parker's speech immediately following that quoted above is concerned with adaptation in law, and stands at the beginning of a line of authority which leads to *York Trailer*. If the European Court of Justice follows the opinion of the Advocate General in the *Windsurfing* cases and *York Trailer* is shown to be incompatible with the Trade Marks Directive, the range within which Lord Parker's observations continue to apply will be restricted. However it appears to me that the passage was referred to (both by the hearing officer and the Judge) for little more than its description of the context in which the meaning of 'distinctive character' has to be determined: that is, of traders who are in competition with each other in the marketplace, and to whom Parliament wishes to accord proper protection but not an exorbitant monopoly.'

1 See para **5.10**, n 1.

5.32   After referring to passages from *British Sugar*, and from *Philips*, Robert Walker LJ continued:

'Despite the fairly strong language of s 3(1)(b), "devoid of any distinctive character" – and Mr Morcom emphasised the word "any" – that provision must in my judgment be directed to a visible sign or combination of signs which can by itself readily distinguish one trader's product – in this case an ordinary, inexpensive household product – from that of another competing trader. Product A and Product B may be different in their outward appearance and packaging, but if the differences become apparent only on close examination and comparison, neither can be said to be distinctive (unless, of course, one constitutes an unlawful infringement of some existing registered trade mark). An objection on those grounds cannot in my judgment be treated (in the words of Younger J in the *Standard Woven Fabric* case (1918) 35 RPC 53, 58 as being on "Grounds which were fanciful and which, in a business sense, were insubstantial." On the contrary, any objection on those grounds would be a practical and businesslike objection.'

The Lord Justice concluded that, taking the three elements together, shape, 'ghosted' label and colours, and treating them as a combination, he found that they were not distinctive but typical of the get-up of products used for cleaning different kitchen and bathroom surfaces; typical, that was, in every respect except that there was no identification by any distinctive product name or device.

5.33   In the Court of Appeal in *Philips*,[1] with reference to the words 'devoid of any distinctive character', Aldous LJ observed that it would seem to follow that it is the character of the trade mark that has to be considered at the date of registration. Much of the discussion, in the short passage of the judgment dealing with the objection under s 3(1)(b), on which Aldous LJ agreed with Jacob J's conclusion, is concerned with the claim of the proprietor, invoking the proviso, that the mark had acquired a distinctive character as a result of use and not of general application. But the following passages should be mentioned:

'The scheme of the Directive and the Act appears to require that signs which are not capable of distinguishing are excluded for registration at the initial stage. Those which are capable of distinguishing will be excluded unless they have or have acquired some distinctive character. An example is Weldmesh to which I have referred. It is capable of distinguishing, but without use would retain its primary meaning of, welded mesh. It would therefore be devoid of any character that was distinctive. However use could provide a secondary meaning, namely that the welded mesh to which the trade mark was applied came from a particular trader. Upon that being established it would become registrable as it would pass the dual test laid down by section (Article) 3(1)(a) and (b).

'The requirement under section (Article) 3(1)(b) is that the mark must have a distinctive character to be registrable. Thus it must have a character which enables it to be distinctive of one trader's goods in the sense that it has a meaning denoting the origin of the goods.'

1 [1999] ETMR 816.

5.34   As mentioned above, the Court of Appeal in *Philips*[1] has referred certain questions to the ECJ under art 3 of the Directive, and that court will give its ruling on the interpretation of art 3(1)(b) of the Directive, to which s 3(1)(b) corresponds. Any further comment on this approach and the difference, if any, between the approaches of Robert Walker LJ and Aldous LJ respectively in *Procter & Gamble*[2] and *Philips*, must await the ruling of the ECJ. For the moment no firm conclusions can be put forward, but the views of Robert Walker LJ and Aldous LJ should be used as guidance.

1 [1999] ETMR 816.
2 [1999] RPC 673, [1999] ETMR 375.

Other kinds of marks mentioned in the Work Manual

5.35   It is clear from the Work Manual[1] that a mark comprising prima facie non-distinctive elements may be registrable if added matter gives it sufficient distinctiveness when seen as a whole. In the case of a word presented in a stylised form or with a graphical background, the registrar will consider:

'a) How strongly the meaning of the word(s) point away from the sign being a trade mark (usually how descriptive it is);
  b) How strongly the stylisation or graphical background points toward the sign being a trade mark'.

Although the general approach here seems sensible, there is perhaps a risk that thinking in terms of whether or not the sign is a trade mark involves some confusion with the separate objection under s 3(1)(a), and tends to lead away from the essential question which s 3(1)(b) raises, namely whether the sign, as a whole, possesses any distinctive character. An example of a mark comprising a non-distinctive word with additional matter, which was held to be devoid of any distinctive character, is *P.R.E.P.A.R.E*,[2] which was sought to be registered for printed matter for use in education.

1 Chapter 6, paras 3.2–3.8.
2 [1997] RPC 884 (Geoffrey Hobbs QC, sitting as the appointed person).

5.36   The Work Manual adopts a similar approach to single letters and otherwise non-distinctive combinations of letters presented in a stylised form or with a graphical background. Single letters are regarded as devoid of any distinctive character, and therefore unregistrable unless supported by evidence of acquired distinctive character. In the case of two letter marks,[1] these may be acceptable prima facie if they form a recognisable word which is not otherwise open to objection, for example as being descriptive abbreviations or acronyms. Marks consisting of two random letters will usually meet an objection that they are devoid of any distinctive character, because of the tendency, in trade, to use letters as model or catalogue references, and also because of the limited number of possible combinations of two letters. However marks consisting of two letters, which are not recognisable as words, may be acceptable, even prima facie, for some goods if they are of a kind, such as foods and beverages, which are not indexed in this way.[2] Three letter marks are generally regarded as prima facie registrable, but not if they are open to objection as being descriptive words or acronyms.[3]

1 See ch 6, para 3.11.2.
2 See eg *Re Rover Group Ltd's Trade Mark Application*, Trade Marks Registry 13 July 1998, New Law Digest 698102001, where an application to register the mark 'Xe' was refused, on the basis that it was unlikely to be recognised as a word.
3 See eg *CDX Trade Mark*, Trade Marks Registry in opposition proceedings, 21 October 1998, New Law Digest 6990110104.

5.37 Marks consisting of numerals, or a combination of letters and numerals, may meet with objections on a number of grounds, which are set out in the Work Manual.[1] The position depends first of all on the number of digits and letters; the more there are, the more likely they are to be acceptable. Numbers written as words are treated in the same way as the numbers themselves. Single digit numbers are always regarded as devoid of any distinctive character and thus prima facie unregistrable. The same generally applies to two digit numbers, and also to marks consisting of a single letter and a single digit. Three digit numbers will not normally be regarded as devoid of any distinctive character, unless they are 'round numbers' ie ending in one or two zeros; but even these may be acceptable prima facie for goods or services not usually sold or provided under a model or product number. Generally speaking combinations of two letters and one number are acceptable. Four digit numbers are usually acceptable, but as with three digit numbers, 'round' numbers may meet with objections if they are such as might be used as model or product numbers. Current or shortly forthcoming dates are regarded as devoid of any distinctive character.[2] Five digit numbers are not normally regarded as being devoid of any distinctive character. It must be emphasised that these rules are only guidelines; there are several grounds on which numbers may be open to objection, the most usual being that they are dates, or indications of size or quantity. The general approach of the registrar to all letter/number combinations is that they will be regarded as acceptable so long as they are unlikely to be required for use by other honest traders in the goods or services concerned.

1 See ch 6, paras 3.11.4–3.11.10.
2 *AD 2000* [1997] RPC 168, was refused on a similar basis.

5.38 It is to be noted that in many of the instances discussed above there may also be a basis for objections under s 3(1)(c). There are some indications that OHIM may be adopting a rather narrower interpretation of the corresponding provision of art 7(1)(b) of the CTM Regulation, when examining CTM applications, than the registrar does of s 3(1)(b). On this point a recent decision of a Board of Appeal of OHIM is of interest. In *New Zealand Lotteries Commission's Application*[1] the examiner had objected to an application to register the mark Telebingo for games, games of chance and related products and services, under art 7(1)(b) of the CTM Regulation, on the ground that it was devoid of any distinctive character. On appeal, the Board held that this objection was not well founded, but instead decided that it was open to objection under art 7(1)(c). In the *Windsurfing Chiemsee* case,[2] the opinion of the Advocate General was that art 3(1)(c) and (d) cover examples of what the general words of art 3(1)(b) covers. The Court of Justice did not specifically deal with this point. But the approach of the Board of Appeal in the *New Zealand Lotteries* cases seems inconsistent with the Advocate General's opinion. Possibly the ruling of the ECJ in *Philips* will clarify the position.

1 [1998] ETMR 569.
2 Para **5.10** above.

Geographical names

5.39 Geographical names would normally fall to be considered under sub-s (1)(c), although an objection under sub-s (1)(b) is sometimes raised as well. However, if a geographical mark is not such as to be prima facie objectionable under that sub-section,[1] it seems unlikely that it should be properly regarded as being devoid of any distinctive character unless such an objection arises from another meaning of the word.

1 See the Work Manual, ch 6 paras 4.9.1–4.9.14, and paras **5.7** et seq below.

Surnames and forenames

5.40 Surnames are in a different category, because they cannot (as such) be the subject of an objection under sub-s (c). So far, the registrar's general practice has been to raise an objection, subject to certain exceptions mentioned in the Work Manual,[1] under s 3(1)(b), to 'common surnames', on the ground that they are 'devoid of any distinctive character'. For this purpose, a surname is regarded as 'common' if there are more than 100 entries in the London Telephone Directory. It is understood that the registrar also consults other 'appropriate regional directories', for Scotland, Wales and Ireland). Entries in foreign directories are, however, no longer considered, as they were under the TMA 1938.

1 See ch 6.

5.41 Before considering the registrar's practice in further detail, reference should be made to a recent decision on appeal from the registry, in the case of *Re Mister Long Trade Mark*.[1] The applicant had sought registration of the trade mark for ice cream and water ices, etc, but the application was refused on the ground that the mark was devoid of any distinctive character, on the basis that it was of obvious surnominal significance. The applicant intended to use the mark for water ices which were of an elongated appearance. On appeal, the application was allowed to proceed subject to disclaimers in respect of both 'Mister' and 'Long', and to a satisfactory limitation of the specification of goods. On the approach to be adopted for surname marks, Mr Hobbs said:

'The conditions which a sign must satisfy in order to be registrable under the 1994 Act are drawn from the Council Directive 89/104 of 21 December, 1988. Section 1(1) of the Act (implementing Article 2 of the Directive) confirms that personal names are eligible to be regarded as signs capable of registration. Different persons having the same name nevertheless share the right to use it in accordance with honest practices in industrial or commercial matters under section 11(2)(a) of the Act (which gives effect to Article 6(1)(a) of the Directive). And section 3(1)(b) of the Act (which implements Article 3(1)(b) of the Directive) prohibits the registration of trade marks which are devoid of any distinctive character. These provisions indicate to my mind that surnames are neither automatically eligible nor automatically ineligible for registration under the Act. In each case the question to be determined is whether the surname put forward for registration possesses the qualities identified in section 1(1) of the Act and none of the defects identified in section 3. For the reasons I gave at greater length in *AD 2000 Trade Mark* [1997] RPC 168, I think that in order to be registrable a surname or any other sign must possess the capacity to communicate the fact that the goods or services with reference to which it is to be used recurrently by the applicant are those of one and the same undertaking. When assessing whether a surname possessed that capacity at the relevant date (the date of the application) it is, of course, necessary to bear in mind that surnames, as such, are naturally adapted to identify all individuals so named.

'It seems to me (and the disclaimer offered on behalf of the applicant would appear to recognise) that the surname LONG did not possess the capacity to distinguish the goods of interest to the applicant from those of other suppliers at the date of the application for registration. LONG is a common surname (it is noted in the Hearing Officer's decision that the name appears about 800 times in the London Telephone Directory) and it is by no means unlikely that persons having that surname would be interested, engaged or concerned in businesses supplying ice creams, water ices or frozen confectionery. These factors combine to make it unlikely that people in the world at large would be united in thinking that such goods emanated from one *and* the same undertaking simply because they were supplied under or by reference to the surname LONG. It takes time for a consensus of that kind to develop in relation to an ordinary surname. And there was no opportunity for such a consensus to develop as a result of use prior to the date of the application in the present case.'

1 [1998] RPC 401 (Geoffrey Hobbs QC sitting as an appointed person).

5.42 The Work Manual[1] indicates that the current practice is framed in the light of this decision. The registrar will not accept words which are surnames for registration prima facie, unless having regard to:

(1) the commonness of the surname;
(2) the size of the market (in terms of traders in it) in the goods or services specified in the application;
(3) the nature of the goods or services,

it is likely that the trade mark will be taken as a sign identifying goods or services originating from a single source.

1 Chapter 6, para 3.12.1.

5.43 After stating the general approach, that a surname will be regarded as common if there are more than 100 entries in the London Telephone Directory, the Work Manual continues with situations coming under (b) above, in these terms:

'Where the market in the goods or services is small, more common surnames may be capable of distinguishing goods or services. Where the market is very small, eg airline services, even very common surnames may be capable of distinguishing.

'Where a word, which is also a surname, is likely to be taken as a fanciful allusion to the nature of the goods or services (as per MISTER LONG), the trade mark may be capable of distinguishing, even though it is a common surname. However, a common surname should not be accepted simply because it has another meaning, eg WALKER or READ.

'Every case should be decided on its own merits taking account of the above guidance.'

5.44 Under the registrar's practice, objections may also be raised to signs which are phonetic equivalents of surnames. Where the mark applied for is merely the phonetic equivalent of a common surname (eg 'Dugglass') it may be accepted unless it is a recognised alternative spelling of the common surname. The idea of a 'recognised alternative spelling' of any surname is perhaps a little strange, and it is also unclear how this is to be distinguished from a 'mere phonetic equivalent'. In a later paragraph of the Work Manual, examiners are instructed to take account of entries appearing in the possessive form and the plural form, as well as any *obvious* spellings of the same name. The example given is Brown (including the forms Brown's, Browns and Browne). The Work Manual continues with the case of surnames with initials. It is stated that similar conditions apply as for surnames. However it is then accepted that a surname with initials may (leaving aside any other considerations) have a slightly higher capacity to distinguish goods or services from a single source, and may be accepted even if the surname is a little more common than the figure mentioned above (ie 100 entries in the London Telephone Directory). Finally, it should be mentioned that the registry accepts that combinations of two or more surnames may be accepted prima facie.

5.45 It is submitted that there are difficulties with the registry's current approach to surnames. It will be noted that the words 'capable of distinguishing' are used several times in this part of the Work Manual. Yet, as mentioned earlier these words, although they were important to the question of registrability under the TMA 1938,[1] appear in the definition of a trade mark, in s 1(1) of the TMA 1994. Thus, although the words are relevant if the objection is under s 3(1)(a), they should not be involved in construing s 3(1)(b). Some passages from the decision in *Mister Long,* are also really paraphrasing the requirements of s 1(1). But surnames, even if very common, are not being objected to by the registry under s 3(1)(a). That must be because they are recognised as having the *capacity* to function in the manner defined in s 1(1), and of course surnames were not objected to under the old law on the ground that they were not 'trade marks'. As already mentioned, some of the phraseology in the Work Manual, and in previous editions, indicates that considerations of 'what other traders may require to use' still play a large part, as they did under the old law, and this approach has been endorsed to some extent by the Court of Appeal in *Procter & Gamble,*[3] although the court was not considering a surname case.

1 Section 10, concerned with registration of trade marks in Part B of the register.
2 [1998] RPC 401.
3 Paragraphs **5.27–5.31** above.

5.46 It may also be remarked that the rules applied by the registry are very arbitrary. Why, it can be asked, should a surname be devoid of any distinctive character if it appears 100 times in the London Telephone Directory, but not if it appears only 80 times, or if it appears 500 times in the Madrid, Paris or Berlin directories? In the current context of international trade it does not seem logical to treat common English surnames differently from common foreign surnames. Even less justifiable is the exclusion of marks which are 'phonetic equivalents' of so-called common surnames. Why should the mere fact that they sound like surnames rob them of all distinctive character? It could be said that any surname possesses *some* 'distinctive character'. Again, further guidance from the courts, including the ECJ, will clarify the matter.

5.47 It is understood that OHIM is not refusing applications to accept surnames as CTM under the equivalent provision of the Regulation,[1] and it is submitted that the same approach should be adopted under s 3(1)(b) of the TMA 1994, on the basis that no surname can be said to be truly *devoid* of *any* distinctive character.

1 Article 7(1)(b).

Forenames

5.48 In regard to forenames, the registry's approach differs as between goods and services. In the case of certain services, the registry takes the view that objection should be raised under s 3(1)(b). This is on the basis that for such services ie restaurants, teashops, hairdressers and beauty salons, male and female names are frequently used as the names of the establishments. The registry considers that it is therefore inappropriate to grant nationwide rights for these services without evidence of distinctiveness, and indicates that applications to register forenames for other services should be considered on their merits. In the case of goods, the registry takes a different view, on the basis that there is no comparable use of forenames on goods and that there seems to be no reason to refuse to accept them. Therefore applications to register forenames as trade marks for goods will be accepted prima facie. In the case of marks consisting of two or more forenames, these are considered to be acceptable for any goods or services.

Full names

5.49 The basic approach of the registry[1] is that full names have, by their nature, a greater capacity to distinguish the goods/services of one undertaking than a surname per se. Unless the full name is extremely common (John Smith being cited as an obvious example) *and* the number of traders involved in the relevant market is very large, the registrar will usually accept such marks prima facie, on the basis that the likelihood of a number of different traders using the same full name as a badge of origin is sufficiently remote that the public are likely to take a full name as a sign which indicates goods or services from a single source. On the assumption that the general approach to surname marks is correct, the practice for full names seems reasonable. However it is to be noted that here again the Manual uses the language appropriate to s 3(1)(a), rather than asking the question, is the sign devoid of any distinctive character?

1 Work Manual, ch 6, para 3.12.8.

Names and pictures of famous persons

5.50 The current edition of the Work Manual has two new paragraphs[1] dealing with the cases of names and pictures of famous persons (living and deceased). This addition to the Work Manual appears to have resulted from the decision concerning trade mark applications by the estate of the late Elvis Presley[2] and perhaps certain applications to register the name and photographs of the late Diana Princess of Wales. The Work Manual, in both these paragraphs, includes the advice 'Such cases raise complex issues. Unit Managers should be consulted in all such cases.' This suggests that the situation was not considered to be settled. However, the

Elvis Presley decision has been upheld on appeal.[3] The decision, under the TMA 1938, was to the effect that the marks applied for, 'Elvis', 'Elvis Presley' and a signature of Elvis Presley, were neither distinctive of, nor capable of distinguishing, the applicants goods (cosmetics and other goods in Class 3), as required by s 9 and 10 of the 1938 Act. The Work Manual says:

> 'Where a famous name is concerned (and where the reputation does not stem from trade in the goods/services applied for) there is a greater requirement to consider whether the name is likely to be taken as a badge of origin for the goods/services. See the *Elvis Presley* case ... for useful guidance. The deciding factor is whether the sign is likely to be taken as an indication that the goods/services are supplied *by or under the control* of the person whose name it is, or whether they will simply be seen as goods/services *about* the person whose name it is, irrespective of trade origin.'

1 Chapter 6, paras 3.12.9 and 3.12.10.
2 *Re Elvis Presley Trade Mark* s[1997] RPC 543 (Laddie J).
3 [1999] RPC 567.

5.51 As a general statement, this requires further examination. It is now common for well known people, particularly sports personalities but others also, to exploit their names and pictures of themselves, for example through companies controlled by them. It may well be that members of the public, when seeing the name or picture of a well-known personality used in connection with goods or services, will assume that the personality is connected in some way with the goods or services, even where there is no reputation stemming from trade in the goods or services. Furthermore, the *Elvis Presley* case was decided under the old law, and it is by no means settled that the position under the TMA 1994 is the same. Although the registrar appears to be raising these objections under s 3(1)(b) and also (c), yet again the language used in the Work Manual is more apt for an objection under s 3(1)(a). As regards s 3(1)(c), which is considered further below, an objection under this provision may be more appropriate in the cases of some deceased persons, but it is rather harder to see how the name of a living person, merely because it is such a name, would serve to designate any characteristic of goods or services. In the case of souvenirs and memorabilia, particularly where other traders were producing these before the application date, the Work Manual indicates that there may possibly be an objection also under s 3(1)(d), which again is considered below.

The proviso

5.52 Even if a mark does fall within the ground of objection under s 3(1)(b) it will in many cases, if not in every case, be possible to obtain registration under the proviso if the mark has in fact acquired a distinctive character as a result of the use made of it. The proviso is considered further below.

Signs designating characteristics of goods or services

5.53 Section 3(1)(c) covers many signs which were excluded from qualifying for registration under s 9(1)(d) of the TMA 1938, as being marks having 'direct reference to the character or quality' of the goods or services, or being, according to their ordinary signification, geographical names. The kinds of marks excluded by s 3(1)(c) will include some marks which under the 1938 Act would have been rejected as being non-distinctive *in law*. However that objection, as such, is no longer applicable. As explained below, the wording of s 3(1)(c) indicates that it is narrower than the old law as applied to descriptive and geographical marks. As mentioned above,[1] surnames are not included.

1 Paragraph **5.40**.

5.54 The first point to emphasise is that, in order for the objection to be applicable, the mark must 'consist exclusively' of the offending sign. If there is other matter in the mark, which is not itself open to objection under the same provision, then the objection is not applicable.[1] Therefore composite marks, such as labels, will not be excluded by this provision although, while disclaimers of non-registrable matter will not now be required by the registrar, by virtue of s 13, registration will by no means necessarily give rights to the non-registrable matter. If the mark consists exclusively of a sign of any of the kinds specified, or if such a sign is in essence the mark sought to be registered, then, as mentioned above, it will nevertheless be open to the applicant to file evidence in order to obtain registration under the proviso, by proving that the mark has acquired a distinctive character..

1 See ch 6 of the Work Manual, s 4, and the observations of the Advocate-General in *Windsurfing Chiemsee*, mentioned at para **5.10** above, at para 31 of the Opinion.

5.55 As to what signs fall within the provision, the important words are '… which may serve, in trade, to designate … ', and no doubt require the registrar to consider whether the sign is one which other traders are likely to need to use; so to that extent the approach is similar to the approach to words inherent distinctiveness and capability of distinguishing under the old law. However it is important to compare the wording of the provision with the statement of Lord Parker,[1] which defined what became known as inherent distinctiveness. Under Lord Parker's test, it was necessary to consider whether other traders are likely, without any improper motive, to desire to use the mark applied for, or *some mark resembling it*, upon or in connection with their own goods. Section 3(1)(c) is in terms directed solely to the trade mark applied for, and is thus not concerned with the question, whether other traders might wish to use a *similar* mark. The registry's general approach seems to recognise this. The Work Manual[2] states that there must exist a *reasonable likelihood* that other honest traders will wish to use the sign to designate characteristics of the goods or services. The provision should not be interpreted as meaning that other traders *must* use the sign, in the sense that there are no, or are few, alternatives. On the other hand a theoretical possibility will not be enough if there is no real likelihood. This, it is submitted, is a correct interpretation of the words 'may serve in trade … '. Although to the extent indicated above the approach may be similar to that adopted under the TMA 1938, an important difference is that, because of the proviso to s 3(1) of the TMA 1994, evidence of acquired distinctive character can overcome the objection even if the sign is something which other honest traders might have been thought to be likely to wish to use to designate characteristics of the goods or services.

1 See para **5.29** above, n 1.
2 Chapter 6, para 4.1.

5.56   As for the examples specified in s 3(1)(c), 'kind' clearly covers general descriptions of goods or services, or of types of goods or services. The Work Manual[1] cites 'Jumbo' and 'Mini', and 'Personal' (for computers); 'Multi' and 'Maxi' may be other examples. As instances of indications of 'quality' the Manual mentions 'Good' or 'Best' and, for some goods 'Classic; 'Perfection' would be another example. Indications as to 'quantity' may cover numbers. 'Intended purpose' needs no special comment.[2] Under 'value', the Manual[3] indicates, that words or symbols which merely serve to indicate the worth, merit or importance of the goods or services are not acceptable. 'Two for one' is given as an example. Another: 'worth their weight in gold' a statement which is probably never literally true, should not perhaps fall within this exclusion at all. It remains to be seen how this approach is applied. It is by no means clear that 'value' should be equated with 'merit' or 'importance', although such matters may well be within 'other characteristics'.

1   Chapter 6, para 4.8.1.
2   Chapter 6, para 4.8.4 gives some instances.
3   Chapter 6, para 4.8.5.

Geographical names

5.57   In the context of s 3(1)(c) geographical names require special consideration. Under s 9(1)(c) of the TMA 1938, the only question was whether the word or words were geographical names, 'according to their ordinary signification'. If so, registration could not be allowed in the absence of evidence of distinctiveness, although in some cases registration under s 10, in the old Part B of the register, might be allowed. At first sight the words of s 3(1)(c), 'may serve in trade to designate the ... geographical origin ... of goods or services' would seem to be narrower. The corresponding provision of the Directive, art 3(1)(c), must now be considered in the light of the decision of the ECJ in the *Windsurfing Chiemsee* case.[1] Before referring in detail to that case, it is helpful to review the registrar's current approach to geographical names.

1   See para **5.10**, n 1 above.

5.58   In the Work Manual, applications to register marks consisting exclusively of geographical names are, as under the TMA 1938, subject to certain guidelines[1] based upon factors such as population and the nature of local industries, but it must be emphasised that the population figures mentioned are only guides, not hard and fast rules. Generally speaking, the guidelines relax the restriction in the case of names of small places, the registrar indicating that a judgment must be made 'that the mark applied for is not likely to be required for use in trade to denote geographical origin before he can accept *prima facie.*' As a general approach this seems correct, except that under s 3 – in contrast to the provisions of the TMA 1938 – in order to refuse the application it may be[2] that the registrar must be satisfied that the mark may be required (or rather, 'may serve in trade') to denote geographical origin, as opposed to being satisfied that it is not likely to be required for such purpose before he can accept the application. Under this provision, an important consideration is whether the particular place has a reputation for the goods or services; in such cases registration will be refused without sufficient evidence of distinctive character, except where such reputation has arisen because the place grew up around the business of the applicant or his predecessor and adopted the same name;[3] Bournville, for chocolate, might be an example. The guidelines indicate that names of places with populations under 2000 in the UK will normally be acceptable prima facie, it being thought that the likelihood of traders wishing to use such place names in relation to goods is so remote that it can be ignored. Much higher figures are set for overseas names: 100,000 for industrialised countries such as the USA, Japan and Europe, and 250,000 for China and South America. The Manual also indicates that, as before, geographical marks used fancifully, such as 'North Pole' for bananas, can be acceptable, and that in many instances names of rivers, seas and deserts, etc, can be accepted prima facie so long as the products concerned are not associated with these geographical features. Again this approach is clearly correct for s 3(1)(c), being consistent with the words 'may serve, in trade, to designate ... geographical origin'. Names of streets and roads are generally acceptable unless the name is associated with the goods; the same approach applies to foreign names of streets and roads. So also with names of districts which do not have a reputation for the goods. Names of some London districts are treated differently, in the same way as towns.[4] Provided, however, that use of the name is likely to be seen as fanciful, as opposed to a plausible indication of geographical origin, it should be acceptable. Names of counties in the USA need special mention. In the past, these met with objections in the same way as other geographical names. However the Registrar now accepts, as a result of evidence filed in cases under the old law, that in formal or legal usage the word 'county' is never omitted, and that the name of an American county denotes only the administrative area and is not used in postal addresses. Therefore geographical objections will not normally be taken to such names.[5] It can be added that there are some names in the UK which may be capable of being treated similarly because, although they appear as such in gazetteers, they may actually be used in the area concerned in conjunction with other words.

1 Work Manual, ch 6, para 4.9.
2 See para **5.5** above.
3 Work Manual, ch 6, para 4.9.8.
4 Work Manual, ch 6, para 4.9.7.
5 Work Manual, ch 6, para 4.9.9.

5.59 In the case of marks for services, the names of places with populations under 2000 are also generally considered acceptable prima facie, but for places with larger populations a distinction may be drawn between services which are international or national and those which are of a local nature. The names of larger places may be acceptable for services of a local nature, but subject to an appropriate area exclusion.[1] For services which are of a kind provided nationally or internationally, the names of well-known places with populations in excess of 2000, are not accepted prima facie, but if sufficient factual distinctiveness is proved, registration will be allowed without any geographical limitation. Where a mark is a combination of two geographical names, it is considered to be acceptable regardless of size, unless both names have a reputation for the services concerned. Foreign geographical names are treated differently.[2] Whatever the population, the matter depends upon whether the name has a reputation for the services. The Manual notes that in many cases the use of foreign names as trade marks for services would be fanciful. Particular circumstances may justify (or indeed merit) different levels, and of course refusal may be justified where the place has a reputation for the goods or services concerned.

1 Work Manual, ch 6, paras 4.9.10–11.
2 Work Manual, ch 6, para 4.9.14.

5.60 The ruling of the ECJ (though not the Opinion of the Advocate General) in the *Windsurfing Chiemsee*[1] case was given after the current edition of the Work Manual was completed. It is the first decision of the court on the interpretation of art 3(1)(c) of the Directive. Before referring to the decision itself, some passages from the Opinion of the Advocate General[2] are worthy of mention. These suggest that the words of art 3(1)(c), 'which may serve, in trade, to designate the ... geographical origin ... of goods or services' may be rather narrower in scope than had been thought to be the case. His view is that the provision cannot exclude all geographical terms in their entirety. Thus far this is not inconsistent with the registry's approach. However the essence of the Advocate General's Opinion[3] is that the provision only excludes signs which are or could constitute 'indications or origin' or 'designations of origin' in the particular sense in which such terms are used in Community law. After considering the use of these terms in certain Community Regulations and some decisions of the ECJ, he concludes:[4]

'The above shows that when, in Community law, and especially in the field of distinguishing marks, which includes trade marks, the concept of the "indication of geographical origin" is a specific legal concept and signifies that there is a direct, necessary, causal relationship between a product and the place from which that product originates. This causal relationship is due to the fact that the product has specific properties, characteristics or qualities which are connected with its origin. These special characteristics may be due to natural factors (eg raw materials, soil, regional climate), to the method of manufacture or preparation of the product (eg traditional production methods), or to other human factors (eg a concentration of similar businesses in the same region, specialisation in the production or preparation of certain products and the maintaining of certain quality levels). If these products are more widely known, the place in which the products are produced also acquires a reputation so that as a result, in the circles involved, a reference to the place also describes the produce or product that is produced there (eg "Limoges" or "Meissen" for items of porcelain, "Bordeaux" for wines etc). If the above-mentioned causal relationship between the place and the product has become established, the name of the place becomes the common property of the producers who are established in that area, which gives them the exclusive right to use that name. This right is usually recognized at national level, but is protected at Community level".

'In view of this, as the plaintiff rightly maintains, art 3(1)(c) of the Directive means that a geographical indication has a distinctive character and may lawfully constitute a trade mark for the products of a certain company, provided that the choice of that designation is "arbitrary", in the sense that has already been explained, ie that it does not and *cannot* constitute an indication of origin or a designation of origin. This is because of the awareness of the geographical term, in this case, does not give rise to any special connection in the public imagination, but has the same effect that the choice of any other invented term or name would have.'

1 Paragraph **5.10**, n 1 above.
2 Paragraphs 33 et seq.
3 Paragraph 37.
4 Paragraphs 45 to 46.

5.61 The ruling of the ECJ does not appear to give quite such a narrow meaning to the words of art 3(1)(c). The plaintiff had contended for a very narrow scope to the provision, suggesting that it only applied where several undertakings manufactured the goods in question in the place of the name sought to be registered and the name was habitually used to designate the geographical origin of the goods. This view was rejected by the court, which observed that art 3(1)(c) pursues an aim which is in the public interest, namely that descriptive signs or indications relating to the categories of goods or services in respect of which registration is applied for may be freely used by all, including as collective marks or as part of complex or graphic marks. Article 3(1)(c) therefore prevented such signs from being reserved to one undertaking alone because they have been registered as trade marks. The court continued:

> 'As regards, more particularly, signs or indications which may serve to designate the geographical origin of the categories of goods in relation to which registration is applied for, especially geographical names, it is in the public interest that they remain available, not least because they may be an indication of the quality and other characteristics of the categories of goods concerned, and may also, in various ways, influence consumer tastes by, for instance, associating the goods with a place that may give rise to a favourable response.

> 'The public interest underlying the provision which the national court has asked the Court to interpret is also evident in the fact that it is open to the Member States, under Article 15(2) of the Directive, to provide, by way of derogation from Article 3(1)(c),[1] that signs or indications which may serve to designate the geographical origin of the goods may constitute collective marks.'

1 On this point, and on the similar derogation in respect of certification marks, also permitted by art 15(2) see ch 10.

5.62   The court's ruling on the questions raised was as follows:

(1)   Article 3(1)(c) of First Council Directive 89/104/EEC of 21 December 1988 to approximate the laws of the Member States relating to trade marks is to be interpreted as meaning that:

    (a)   it does not prohibit the registration of geographical names as trade marks solely where the names designate places which are, in the mind of the relevant class of persons, currently associated with the category of goods in question; it also applied to geographical names which are liable to be used in future by the undertakings concerned as an indication of the geographical origin of that category of goods;

    (b)   where there is currently no association in the mind of the relevant class of persons between the geographical name and the category of goods in question, the competent authority must assess whether it is reasonable to assume that such a name is, in the mind of the relevant class of persons, capable of designating the geographical origin of that category of goods;

    (c)   in making that assessment, particular consideration should be given to the degree of familiarity amongst the relevant class of persons with the geographical name in question, with the characteristics of the place designated by that name, and with the category of goods concerned;

    (d)   it is not necessary for goods to be manufactured in the geographical location in order for them to be associated with it.

5.63 Although it is not clear from the terms of this ruling, it may well be that the court is using the term 'geographical origin' in the technical sense suggested by the Advocate General. If this is so, then the registrar's approach as set out in the Work Manual may not require any substantial changes in the light of the court's decision. The application of the proviso, and the evidence required to overcome an objection under s 3(1)(c) where it is claimed that the mark applied for has acquired a distinctive character through use, are considered below in the light of the court's ruling on the second question, regarding art 3(3) of the Directive.[1] It should also be kept in mind that an applicant is not restricted, so far as evidence is concerned, to proving acquired distinctive character under the proviso. Evidence may also serve to prove that the goods in question are not likely to be made or designed in the place concerned, or that for some other reason the name is not likely in the future to be used as an indication of geographical origin for the goods. Furthermore the decision does not deal with marks applied for in respect of services. Here the registry's guidelines would appear to represent a reasonable and practical approach.

1 Paragraphs **5.81–5.84**..

5.64   One point worth mentioning briefly, which is not in the latest version of the Work Manual, is the position regarding words which are similar to geographical names, or phonetically close. It was said in a previous version that: 'Such marks should generally prove to be acceptable unless the reference is very close. Clearly if the area concerned has a reputation for the goods at issue then a stronger line should be taken'. Presumably, however, such objections will no longer be taken. The approach would seem to have ignored what s 3(1)(c) actually says, which is set out above.[1] Before a geographical objection can be taken, it must be the case that *the sign* 'may serve, in trade, to designate geographical origin'. Unless, perhaps, the difference from the name, such as the mere addition of a letter 's' can be regarded as *de minimis*, or unnoticeable to ordinary members of the public, this would not be so. It is not sufficient to say that something similar may serve such purpose. The same applies to misspellings of descriptive words. The Work Manual correctly says[2] that misspellings of descriptive words excluded from registration by s 3(1)(c) cannot be said to consist *exclusively* of signs that may be used in trade to designate characteristics of the goods/services. It indicates, however, that misspellings commonly used in trade may be excluded from registration by s 3(1)(b) and (c). This is correct so far as s 3(1)(c) is concerned, because such words are clearly such as 'may serve in trade' to designate characteristics of the goods or services, although it may be doubted whether such marks are necessarily devoid of any distinctive character on any other basis, for the purposes of s 3(1)(b), and the examples given in the Work Manual do indicate some flexibility.

1 Paragraph **5.13**. See also para **5.54**..
2 Chapter 6, para 4.12.

Definitions of other matters

5.65   Signs which may serve to designate the 'time of production of goods or rendering of services' really need little comment. Typical examples mentioned in the Manual are vintage years for wines, 'overnight delivery' (for transport services) and '24 hour service' for (eg) plumbing services. The TMA 1994 gives no guidance on 'other characteristics of goods or services'. The Manual cites 'Gold Cap' and 'Red Cap' for wines and spirits, on the ground that it is common practice for wine or whisky bottles to have a cap on them coloured red or gold. However these signs may not necessarily indicate 'characteristics' of the goods mentioned, and any objection might be better founded under s 3(1)(b). 'Gold Cap' might be more aptly objected to under the 'other characteristics' provision of s 3(1)(c) if the goods were milk. Other examples given in the Manual, such as signs describing the subject matter of a publication, computer programmes, etc, need no further comment.

5.66 As has already been noted, surnames are not specifically mentioned in s 3(1)(c). Since they would not usually be considered to designate any 'characteristics' of goods or services, it is difficult to see how there is any scope for refusing registration of surnames under s 3(1)(c), and the Work Manual does not suggest that objections to surnames should be raised under this provision. An objection could arise in the case of a surname which had acquired another meaning as an indication of some characteristic of products, for example through association with some inventor of a product of the kind concerned or some process applied to such product. The name Bach, which was in issue in the *Bach and Bach Flower Remedies* case,[1] is an example.

1 [1999] RPC 1 (Neuberger J). Now upheld by the Court of Appeal, 21 October 1999, noted in New Law Digest 699107802.

5.67 Words in foreign languages may sometimes be the subject of objections under s 3(1)(c).[1] In the case of languages which are likely to be known to a reasonable (and increasing) number of UK residents, namely French, German, Italian and Spanish, objections may be taken of the word(s) in English would be the subject of an objection under s 3(1)(c). The approach for services is different from that for goods. For services of kinds provided internationally, or for particular services for which it is common to use a foreign language, such as French for restaurant or beauty care services, descriptive words may be the subject of objection under s 3(1)(c). On the other hand, where the services are local in nature, no objection will normally be taken. In the case of less well-known languages, the registrar may raise objections as with the better known languages if the country has a reputation for any of the goods covered by the application; for services, only if these are international in nature, will objection be raised to descriptive words. Languages used by significant ethnic minorities in the UK are generally treated like commonly spoken languages.

1 See Work Manual, ch 6, para 4.13.

The 'Penguin' practice

5.68 The so-called 'Penguin' practice, which derived its name from a case concerning the mark 'Penguin' for books, should be mentioned here. The practice was developed under the TMA 1938 to meet the case in which an objection based on non-distinctiveness which only applied to some goods within a category contained in the specification. Thus the applicant was required to exclude 'books about birds'. Similarly an application for registration of 'Hamlet' for audio recordings was restricted by the exclusion of 'recordings of Shakespeare's plays'. The practice was also applied to applications in Class 28 (for toys) and to confectionery. The practice was fairly widely criticised, on the basis that it was normally clear what was trade mark (and thus potentially infringing) use and what was a mere description, a point well illustrated by the decision of the Court of Appeal in the *Mothercare* case.[1] The previous version of the Work Manual, while acknowledging that the basis for the practice is not as clear under the TMA 1994, because it could be argued that excluding for example 'books about marine birds' from an application for Penguin for books would still leave the proprietor with rights in respect of similar goods, which could include books about penguins. Nonetheless it was indicated that the Penguin practice would still be applied, apparently on the basis that (for example) the word 'Penguin' is devoid of any distinctive character in relation to books about

penguins and also (see s 3(1)(c) below) a word which may be used in trade to indicate a characteristic about such goods. The current version of the Work Manual
does not refer to the Penguin practice in the section devoted specifically to objections under s 3(1)(c), but discusses it in some detail in another section[2] concerned
with overcoming objections under s 3(1), in particular by restricting the specification of the application.

1 [1988] RPC 113. However the fact of the decision at first instance, in favour of the plaintiff, might be
said to have provided some justification for the need of the Penguin practice.
2 Section 7: 'Overcoming s 3(1) objections'. See para **5.73** below.

'Generic' signs

5.69 Section 3(1)(d) is intended to enable applications, for signs which have
become generic or have come into general use in the trade, to be refused. Objection
is required to be taken where the mark applied for consists exclusively of 'signs or
indications' which have become customary in the current language or in the bona
fide and established practices of the trade. As with s 3(1)(c), the word 'exclusively'
is important. The objection does not apply if there is other matter included in the
mark applied for. Objection may be raised where a sign has always been generic, as
well as where a sign, once exclusively used by the applicant, has fallen into generic
use. The exclusion from registration is not confined to word marks. Examples mentioned in the Work Manual,[1] are devices of grapes for wine, star devices for brandy
and hotel services and simple devices of chefs for restaurant services. An important
question is whether the words 'of the trade' qualify the words 'which have become
customary in the current language', as well as 'the bona fide and established practices'. The arrangement of the words suggests that they do not. Therefore where, as
not infrequently happens with some well-known trade marks which were first
adopted for a new product, a trade mark is 'misused' by members of the public in
the sense of being used as the name of the product, it could well be found that such
a mark is 'customary in the current language' for the purposes of s 3(1)(d).
However in such cases evidence of distinctive character acquired through use will
often suffice for the proviso to be applicable so that registration can be granted. If
the trade mark has fallen into descriptive use in the trade, for example through failure on the part of the proprietor to police it effectively, then again registration will
be refused under this provision. Although the proviso may again be relied upon, an
objection based upon customary use in the trade may in practice be considerably
harder to overcome, unless the effect of the evidence of use is to demonstrate that
the original objection was in fact unfounded.

1 Chapter 6, s 5.

Some decisions under the TMA 1994

5.70 There have been many decisions applying the provisions of s 3(1) to
applications and registrations under the TMA 1994. Generally speaking the more
important ones have been reported in the specialist series of reports; others have
been mentioned briefly in various other publications.[1] Some of the decisions have
already been mentioned in connection with s 3(1)(a) and (b). Comparatively few of
the reported decisions have been concerned with the application of s 3(1)(c) or (d).
These are referred to below, and some examples from the other publications are
also given.

1 Such as New Law Digest, the ITMA Newsletter, CIPA Magazine, and Intellectual Property Decisions.

5.71   In the *Philips* case[1] Jacob J also held that the registration was invalid under s 3(1)(c), on the basis that the picture of the shaver head was a sign which 'may serve, in trade' to designate the kind of goods or their intended purpose. In *British Sugar*,[2] the same judge held that 'Treat', for dessert sauces and syrups, as well as being devoid of any distinctive character, also fell foul of s 3(1)(c) as being a sign which might serve to designate the kind, quality and intended purpose of the product, and probably of s 3(1)(d), being a sign which had become customary in the current language. Another mark, held on appeal to have been rightly refused under s 3(1)(b) and (c), was 'Froot Loops'[3] for cereals and cereal preparations, on the basis that it described a loop shaped cereal containing fruit. One example of a mark being refused under s 3(1)(c) as being a sign which might serve to designate geographical origin (and also under s 3(1)(b) as being devoid of any distinctive character) was 'Eurolamb',[4] because it would be understood simply as an abbreviation of 'European lamb'.

1 [1998] RPC 283 at 304. The decision of the Court of Appeal has upheld the decision of Jacob J on this point.
2 [1996] RPC 281 at 306.
3 *Froot Loops Trade Mark* [1997] RPC 240, before an appointed person (Simon Thorley QC).
4 *EUROLAMB Trade Mark* [1997] RPC 279, before an appointed person (Geoffrey Hobbs QC).

5.72   Other examples of applications refused by the registry under s 3(1) are noted here by way of example. It must be emphasised that the registry's practice has been changing in some respects and is likely to change further in the future. The decisions may give some idea of the way in which the registry has been applying the provisions, but should not be used as precedents.

— *We set the hire standard*:[1] application for hire of motor and land vehicles, refused under s 3(1)(b) and (c);
— *Pastelline*:[2] refused under s 3(1)(b) for steel strip and steel sheet, all having a coloured protective coating of plastics or paint. The correctness of this decision seems to be open to question;
— *Xpresslink*:[3] refused registration for electromedical apparatus and devices for telecommunications, in Class 9, under s 3(1)(b) and (c), as being devoid of any distinctive character and only consisting of words to show the purpose of the goods;
— *Office-pack*:[4] refused registration for adhesives and adhesive materials, in Classes 1 and 16;
— *Cyberpub*:[5] refused registration in Class 42 for (inter alia) restaurant and catering services, on the ground that it was a word which other traders (particularly those on the Internet) might legitimately want to use. Even if it is right to take into account the position of other traders under s 3(1)(b), this decision seems unduly cautious;
— *Gibson*:[6] refused for restaurant and bar services, although the mark had a reputation for guitars. The correctness of this decision may need to be examined in the light of future decisions on surname marks;
— *Wallabee*:[7] refused under s 3(1)(b) for ice cream, water ices, etc, in the shape of wallabies. This would appear to have been an example of the application of the 'Penguin' practice;
— *Open Cad*:[8] refused under s 3(1)(b) for computers for use in computer aided design;
Device of coffee beans/leaves:[9] the mark applied for was a device comprising three coffee beans and six leaves, and was refused under s 3(1)(b) in respect of coffee and mixtures of coffee and chicory;

— *J3 Learning*:[10] An application to register this mark, in stylised form, in Classes 9, 16 and 41, was rejected under s 3(1)(b) on the ground that the individual elements were devoid of distinctive character and that their combination did not alter that fact;

— *Ultraclear*:[1] refused under s 3(1)(c) in Class 16 for paper, especially self-adhesive paper, on the basis that it described a characteristic of the goods;

— *Flexible Reserve*:[12] an application for registration in Class 36, for financial services, loan and mortgage services, was refused on the grounds that the mark was devoid of distinctive character and consisted of words which other traders might legitimately wish to use;

— *Next Generation*:[13] refused under s 3(1)(b) for mortgage and insurance services, etc, in Class 36;

— *Procter & Gamble Ltd's Application*:[14] an application to register a particular shape of a bar of soap, in Class 3, was refused under s 3(1)(b);

— *Co-venture*:[15] refused, presumably under s 3(1)(c), in Class 35 for business management consulting services relating to a process of implementing productivity and changing management techniques for clients;

— *Day by Day*:[16] refused, for milk and milk products and other goods in Class 29;

— *CJ (and Device)*:[17] a device of a four-wheel drive vehicle with the letters 'CJ' was refused registration in Classes 12, 16 and 37 for (inter alia) motor vehicles and repair services, as being devoid of distinctive character;

— *Weblink*:[18] the mark, in stylised form, was refused registration in Class 9, for computer software for use in connection with the Internet, on the ground that it was devoid of distinctive character;

— *The perfectionists*:[19] an application to register this mark in Class 25 for, inter alia, underclothing, was refused under ss 3(1)(b) and (c);

— *Dead Sea Mineral Therapy (and Device)*:[20] the application, in Class 3 for non-medicated toilet preparations containing ingredients from the Dead Sea, was allowed to proceed; notwithstanding that the words were descriptive, the combination of the whole had a striking impact and was acceptable;

— *Footlites*:[21] This mark was sought to be registered for footwear. In opposition proceedings, in which the opponents contended that the application should be refused under s 3(1)(b) and (c), as being devoid of distinctive character and descriptive, it was held that although the words Foot and Lite each had no capacity to distinguish, the combination was unusual and traders did not need the particular combination in order to describe their goods. The application was allowed;

— *Bonus Gold*:[22] refused registration under s 3(1)(b) and (c), in Class 36 for investment account services, on the ground that the meaning which the mark would convey was that of an investment account which paid a superior or higher level of bonus;

— *Blackbaud*:[23] the application, in Classes 9, 16 and 41, for (inter alia) computer software, paper and education services, was refused in opposition proceedings. In addition to upholding the opposition under s 5(2) on the ground of conflict with the opponent's prior registration of a similar mark, the application was refused under s 3(1)(b), (c) and (d). Unless the word was actually used in the trade with its particular spelling, the decision under s 3(1)(c) and (d), at least, seems surprising;

— *History Live*:[24] an application to register this mark in Class 41, for education and entertainment services for radio and TV, was refused as the mark indicated the content of the programme;

— *Herbal Plus*:[25] The mark applied for was a device comprising a picture of a bunch of herbs together with the words 'Herbal Plus – Saw Palmetto – 30 softgel capsules'. The device was an illustration of the 'Saw Palmetto' plant. It was held that the individual elements of the mark did not add up to a distinctive whole. The application was refused under s 3(1)(b) and (c);

— *Senior*:[26] an application to register the mark in Classes 9 and 16 for computer programs, etc, and printed forms for computers was opposed under s 3(1)(a), (b),(c) and (d). The objections under s 3(1)(a) and (b) failed. The objections under s 3(1)(c) and (d) would have succeeded in full, on the basis of the opponent's evidence as to use of the words 'junior' and 'senior' in the industry; however the applicant filed substantial evidence of use for some goods, and the application was allowed for a limited specification of goods;

— *Memory Lock*:[27] application for registration in Class 9 for remote controls, refused under s 3(1)(b) because the mark was used in relation to technology that protected device codes programmed into remote controls;

— *Moments in Time*:[28] application refused under s 3(1)(b) and (c), for education and entertainment services for radio and television, on the basis that the mark was clearly intended to convey that the programme would be about significant moments in time, and that other traders should remain free to use this combination of words;

— *Speedmaster*:[29] in opposition proceedings, it was held that the mark, applied for in Class 2 in respect of (inter alia) paints and preservatives, did not offend against s 3(1)(b) or (c), being a devised word and not designating any characteristics of the goods;

— *Bach Flower Remedies*:[30] on an application for a declaration of invalidity, it was held that the mark, which had been registered in Classes 5 and 16 for, respectively, preparations for medicinal purposes derived from herbs and flowers, and publications relating to such products, was registered contrary to s 3(1)(c), being the name of a type of product. The judge declined to decide on objections under s 3(1)(a), (b) and (d). But the Court of Appeal has upheld the objection under s 3(1)(9).

— *Maintainit*:[31] refused registration in Class 9 for computer programs and in Class 16 for printed matter including computer manuals, because it consisted of a trivial combination of two ordinary words, presumably under s 3(1)(b);

— *Body Paint*:[32] an application in Class 30, for confectionery, etc, was refused under s 3(1)(b) and (c);

— *TV Shop*:[33] an application to register a device mark incorporating the words TV SHOP in Class 35, for preparation of advertisements and commercials for television transmission, was refused under s 3(1)(b) and (c);

— *Homework Helpers*:[34] the application, for electronic publications, educational books, and entertainment services, was refused in opposition proceedings; although capable of distinguishing, it was held that the application must be refused under s 3(1)(b) and (c), because the words formed a natural and apt term for use in trade to describe books or other media designed to help students with their homework;

—*Red Stripe*:[35] The application was for registration of a trade mark consisting of a red stripe, for printed matter and intellectual property services. The mark was used as a line down the right hand margin of the goods in question, but the mark as applied for was not limited to this positioning. It was held that the mark was devoid of any distinctive character, and the evidence of use relied upon was unsatisfactory; the application was accordingly refused;

— *Little World*:[36] a decision of the registry in opposition proceedings, that the mark was not devoid of distinctive character for toys and playthings (in Class 28), globes being excluded, was upheld on appeal;

— *Fresh Banking*:[37] this mark was refused for goods in Classes 9 and 16, and services in Class 36, relating to banking;

— *Odpo*:[38] an application to register the mark Odpo for insulating materials and non-metallic building materials (in Classes 17 and 19 respectively) was refused (in opposition proceedings) under s 3(1)(b), (c) and (d), because it was a known abbreviation in the industry, meaning 'Ozone Depletion Potential';

— *Three Card Poker*:[39] the application was for registration of a series of three marks in Class 41, for casino services. The marks were, a fan of three playing cards, a fan of three playing cards each with a diamond on it, and the fan with the diamonds and the words 'Three card poker'. The application was refused under s 3(1)(b) and (c);

— *Coffeemix*:[40] was refused under s 3(1)(b) for coffee preparations, in Class 32;

— *Sorrento*:[41] this was an unsuccessful opposition to an application to register the mark Sorrento in Class 25, for articles of clothing. Although Sorrento is an Italian town and Italy is famous for fashion clothing and shoes, there was nothing in the evidence to show that the mark might serve in trade to designate geographical origin when used in relation to clothing. This decision was given soon after the delivery of the Advocate General's Opinion in *Windsurfer Chiemsee*[42] and is consistent with the views which he expressed;

— *Today's Gourmet*:[43] an application to register 'Today's Ggourmet' for preserved vegetables, fruits and meals, was refused under s 3(1)(b) and (c), on the ground that it indicated foodstuffs fit for a gourmet;

— *Automotive Network eXchange*:[44] an application to register this mark, in Class 35 for 'business information for the automotive industry by means of a private communication system', had been refused under s 3(1)(b) and (c). On appeal it was held that, although the component words individually were unregistrable, the expression as a whole said nothing in particular about the services in question and was therefore registrable;

— *Power Fuel*:[45] a mark comprising the words 'Power Fuel' and a striped 'M' device was held, in opposition proceedings, not to be devoid of any distinctive character, for non-alcoholic drinks, in Class 32;

— *Roho Inc's Applications*:[46] two applications, filed in respect of the shape of an item of medical apparatus and the shape of one of its component parts, were refused under s 3(1)(a) and (b), as well as s 3(2)(b) (see also below);

— *As$et*:[47] an application to register the mark As$et, for computer software relating to cost modelling in the oil industry, was refused under s 3(1)(b). Although it was doubted whether the mark was exclusively descriptive for the purposes of s 3(1)(c), it was held that the use of the '$' sign was insufficient to overcome the objection that the mark was devoid of any distinctive character;

— *Ty-Nant Spring Water Ltd's Trade Mark Application*:[48] an application to register a 'blue bottle' in Class 32 for bottled water and similar goods, was refused under s 3(1)(a) and (b); See also the decision of the appointed person (Geoffrey Hobbs QC) 12 July 1999, New Law Digest 699086303;

— *Dualit Ltd's (Toaster Shapes) Trade Mark Applications*:[49] applications for registration of shapes of electric toasters, refused in opposition proceedings, under s 3(1)(b) and (c). The objections were not overcome by evidence of use.

1 Trade Marks Registry, 5 January 1996; CIPA Journal, February 1996, p 128.
2 Trade Marks Registry, 11 January 1996; CIPA Journal, February 1996, p 128.
3 Trade Marks Registry, 6 March 1996; CIPA Journal, April 1996, p 287.
4 Trade Marks Registry, 15 August 1996; CIPA Journal, September 1996, p 673.
5 Trade Marks Registry, 26 September 1996; CIPA Journal, October 1996, p 851.
6 Trade Marks Registry, 24 October 1996; CIPA Journal December 1996 p 1017. See **5.27–5.34** above.
7 Trade Marks Registry, 29 October 1996; CIPA Journal, December 1996, p 1017.
8 Trade Marks Registry, 1 November 1996; CIPA Journal, December 1996, p 1017.

9   Trade Marks Registry, 1 November 1996; CIPA Journal, December 1996, p 1017.

10   Trade Marks Registry, 1 November 1996; CIPA Journal, December 1996, p 1017.

11   Trade Marks Registry, 9 January 1997; CIPA Journal, February 1997, p 144.

12   Trade Marks Registry, 31 January 1997; CIPA Journal, March 1997, p 217.

13   Trade Marks Registry, 19 February 1997; CIPA Journal, May 1997, p 365.

14   Trade Marks Registry, 13 February 1997; [1998] RPC 710.

15   Trade Marks Registry, 13 June 1997; CIPA Journal, July 1997, p 539.

16   Trade Marks Registry, 18 June 1997; CIPA Journal, July 1997, p 539. The decision was upheld on appeal (Simon Thorley QC sitting as the appointed person) – see CIPA Journal, March 1998, p 212; New Law Digest 698058204.

17   Trade Marks Registry, 16 June 1997; CIPA Journal, August 1997, p 625.

18   Trade Marks Registry, 4 July 1997; CIPA Journal, August 1997, p 626. See also the registrar's practice regarding the word 'Link', Work Manual, ch 6.

19   Trade Marks Registry, 14 July 1997; CIPA Journal, August 1997, p 626.

20   Trade Marks Registry, 26 November 1997; CIPA Journal, March 1998, p 210.

21   *Re Lambert & Howarth & Sons Ltd's Application*; Trade Marks Registry, 12 December 1997, New Law Digest 698058207.

22   Trade Marks Registry, 22 December 1997; CIPA Journal, March 1998, p 210.

23   Trade Marks Registry, 19 December 1997; CIPA Journal, March 1998, p 210.

24   Trade Marks Registry, 31 December 1997; CIPA Journal, March 1998, p 211.

25   *Re General Nutrition Investment Co's Application*; Trade Marks Registry 23 January 1998, New Law Digest 698058209.

26   Trade Marks Registry, 6 January; CIPA Journal, May 1998, p 378.

27   Trade Marks Registry, 22 January 1998; CIPA Journal, May 1998, p 377.

28   Trade Marks Registry, 9 February 1998; CIPA Journal, June 1998, p 471

29   Trade Marks Registry, 9 March 1998; CIPA Journal, June 1998, p 470.

30   [1999] RPC 1 (Neuberger J), Court of Appeal 21 October 1999, noted in New Law Digest 699107802.

31   Trade Marks Registry, 20 March 1998; CIPA Journal, September 1998, p 725.

32   Trade Marks Registry, 31 March 1998; CIPA Journal, September 1998, p 728.

33   Trade Marks Registry, 14 April 1998; CIPA Journal, September 1998, p 729.

34   *Re Homework Helpers Trade Mark Application*; Trade Marks Registry, 6 October 1998, New Law Digest 699010201.

35   *Re Red Stripe Trade Mark Application*; Trade Marks Registry, 12 October 1998, New Law Digest 699010205.

36   MG Clarke QC (an appointed person); CIPA Journal, December 1998, p 982.

37   [1998] RPC 605 (Simon Thorley QC sitting as an appointed person).

38   Trade Marks Registry, 15 May 1998; CIPA Journal, October 1998, p 807.

39   Trade Marks Registry, 20 May 1998; CIPA Journal, October 1998, p 807.

[1998] RPC 717 (Simon Thorley QC sitting as an appointed person).

41   Trade Marks Registry, 9 June 1998; CIPA Journal, October 1998, p 808.

42   See para **5.48** above.

43   Trade Marks Registry, 2 July 1998; CIPA Journal, October 1998, p 809.

44   [1998] RPC 885 (Geoffrey Hobbs QC, sitting as an Appointed Person).

45   Trade Mark Registry, 7 July 1998; CIPA Journal, October 1998, p 809.

46   Trade Marks Registry, 18 August 1998, IPD (October 1998) 21113.

47   *Re Mai Consultant Ltd's Trade Mark Application*, 7 December 1998, New Law Digest.

48   [1999] RPC 392; upheld on appeal (Geoffrey Hobbs QC) 12 July 1999, noted in New Law Digest, 11 August 1999.

49   Trade Mark Registry [1999] RPC 304. On appeal,Lloyd J upheld the pbjection under s 3(1)(b) but did not consider s 3(1)(c) separately, 5 July 1999..

Overcoming objections under section 3(1)

5.73   The Work Manual[1] indicates that objections under s 3(1) may be overcome in three ways, namely by evidence of acquired distinctiveness, prior rights, and restricting the specification. The first of these is expressly mentioned, in the form of the proviso to s 3(1). The other two reflect a continuation of registry practice applied under the old law. Disclaimers are not mentioned and may not be imposed by the registrar under s 13, although they may be offered bt the applicant and may assist in obtaining acceptance in special cases offered.[2]

1 Chapter 6, Section 7.
2 *MISTER LONG Trade Mark* discussed at para **5.41** above.

The proviso – acquired distinctive character

5.74 This is an important provision. It makes it clear that any objection under s 3(1)(b)–(d) is capable of being overcome by evidence demonstrating that the mark has acquired a distinctive character as a result of the use made of it before the date of application for registration. The Work Manual also indicates[1] that evidence may overcome an objection under s 3(1)(a), that the sign applied for does not satisfy the requirements of s 1(1); this falls outside the scope of the proviso, but is clearly correct. The Manual points out, if a sign is shown to be distinctive in fact, the objection that it is incapable of distinguishing must be wrong. However, as mentioned above[2] Aldous LJ, in his judgment in *Philips*, as suggested that evidence is not admissible on this point. Although it is undoubtedly true that an applicant cannot overcome an objection, that the sign applied for is not a 'trade mark', by evidence of acquired distinctive character under the proviso to s 3(1), it is submitted that as a matter of principle an applicant ought not to be barred from challenging the registry's initial reaction, that the sign is not a trade mark, by demonstrating that such a reaction was wrong, and from filing evidence for that purpose.

1 Chapter 6, para 7.1.
2 Paragraph **5.14**.
3 On this point, see the observations in the Court of Appeal in Bach Flower Remedies Ltd (21 October 1999) per Morrit LJ (para 35).

5.75 The effect of the proviso is that most marks (provided that they are 'trade marks') will be registrable, although in some cases substantial evidence, including trade evidence, will be necessary. It is clear, from sub-s (1) itself, that once an objection is made out the onus is on the applicant or proprietor to show that the requirements of the proviso are satisfied.[1] Clearly, as the Manual also indicates, the evidence necessary will vary, depending on the facts of each case, and the burden of establishing factual distinctiveness will generally be proportionate to the strength of the prima facie objection.

1 See *British Sugar plc v James Robertson and Sons Ltd*[1996] RPC 281 at 302.

5.76 As to what amount of acquired distinctive character is necessary to bring a case within the proviso, to some extent this will depend upon the facts of each case, in particular the nature of the mark and the goods and services concerned, as well as the period and amount of use.[1] Clearly an applicant will have some difficulty if he cannot prove distinctive character acquired through use *as a trade mark*.[2] The necessary distinctive character may also be harder to establish, particularly with very non-distinctive marks, where the use has been mainly in conjunction with another trade mark. However it is suggested that applicants should not be required to go as far, in every case, as was often necessary under the TMA 1938. The filing of a main declaration of use should suffice in many cases, and it is hoped that the requirement of filing extensive trade evidence will eventually be found to be the exception, particularly bearing in mind that the old requirement of 'inherent' capability of distinguishing no longer exists.

1 Detailed information on dealing with and evaluating evidence is given in ch 6, s 7 of the Work Manual.
2 The cases of *Jeryl Lynn* – see para **5.21**, n 2 above – and *Bach Flower Remedies* – see para **5.72**, n 25 above – illustrate the difficulties.

5.77 Although there have been a number decisions of the registry, in the first instance only cases in which the application is unsuccessful will be reported, and then only if a written decision, giving the grounds of refusal, is requested and given. Apart from a few opposition cases, in which absolute grounds for refusal have been relied upon, the only guidance from the courts has come from cases in which the validity of registrations has been challenged by way of counterclaim in infringement proceedings or in proceedings under s 47(1) for declarations of invalidity. The two principal decisions in which the proviso has been considered, both of Jacob J, are *British Sugar* and *Philips*,[1] and involved counterclaims for declarations of invalidity in infringement proceedings. In *British Sugar*, Jacob J was critical of the evidence of distinctiveness relied upon by the plaintiff, and considered that the registrar was wrong to have allowed registration under the TMA 1938, on the basis of the evidence that was filed. In particular the evidence did not make it explicit that all the use of 'Treat' had been accompanied by prominent use of the plaintiff's mark 'Silver Spoon'. The judge said that 'mere evidence of use of a highly descriptive or laudatory word will not suffice, without more, to prove that it is distinctive of one particular trader – is taken by the public as a badge of origin'. This was all the more so, he said, when the use had been accompanied by what was undoubtedly a distinctive and well-recognised trade mark. He considered the evidence in some detail,[2] referring to the unspoken and illogical assumption that 'use equals distinctiveness'. He concluded that the word had achieved some minor degree of distinctiveness in fact, but fell far short of universal or near universal acceptance as a trade mark for ice cream toppings. Turning to the law, he concluded that sufficient distinctive character had not been established:

> 'Is my finding that to some but not most people "Treat" has some trade mark significance enough? This depends on what is meant by a *distinctive character*. Neither the Directive nor Act throw any light on this. So I have to use what I at least regard as my common sense. Take a very descriptive or laudatory word. Suppose the proprietor can educate 10% of the public into recognising the word as his trade mark. Can that really be enough to say it has a *distinctive character* and so enough to let the proprietor lay claim to the word as a trade mark altogether? The character at this stage is part distinctive but mainly not. I do not think it would be fair to regard the character of the word as *distinctive* in that state of affairs. But if the matter were the other way round, so that to 90% of people it was taken as a trade mark, then I think it would be fair so to regard it. This all suggests that the question of factual *distinctive character* is one of degree. The proviso really means "has the mark acquired a sufficiently distinctive character that the mark has really become a trade mark." In the case of common or apt descriptive or laudatory words compelling evidence is needed to establish this. And in particular mere evidence of extensive use is unlikely to be enough on its own. Of course the power of advertising may be able to turn almost anything (save a pure description) into a trade mark, but it must be shown in a case of this sort that the mark has really become accepted by a substantial majority of persons as a trade mark – is or is almost a household word.

'My findings on the facts here fall a long way short of this. Indeed even the suggested 60% figure put forward for British Sugar falls short. I do not think the mark has been shown to have a *distinctive character* and accordingly I propose to declare the registration invalid pursuant to the provisions of section 47(1).'

1 See para **5.4**, n 3 and para **5.14**, n 1 above. Subject to the views of the ECJ, the Court of Appeal has upheld the decision of Jacob J under s 3(1) in *Philips*.
2 [1996] RPC 281 at p 302–305. As permitted by the proviso to s 47(1) of the TMA 1994, the plaintiff also relied upon evidence of use after the date of the registration.

5.78   In the *Philips* case, Jacob J only alluded to the proviso itself at one point,[1] in a citation from his decision in *British Sugar*. Strictly speaking, in view of his finding that the sign was not a 'trade mark' within the definition in s 1(1), he did not need to consider the proviso. In summary, his view, which has been confirmed by the judgment of Aldous LJ in the Court of Appeal, appears to have been that the nature of the use of the picture of the shaver head was not such as to overcome the objections under s 3(1)(b), (c) and (d), because it was not shown that it was recognised as an indication that the goods were from a particular trader. This is essentially the same as his approach in *British Sugar*.

1 [1998] RPC 283 at 300.

5.79   The case of the mark '*Senior*'[1] provides an example of an opposed application succeeding for some goods, on the basis of evidence of acquired distinctive character. Another recent decision of interest is in the case of the trade mark '*Minilite*', registered in respect of lightweight magnesium or aluminium wheels for motorcars.[2] In proceedings under s 47(1) of the TMA 1994, for a declaration of invalidity, the mark was held to have been devoid of any distinctive character at the date of the original registration, but on the evidence the Hearing Officer concluded that it had become distinctive in fact by the date of the proceedings.

1 See above, para **5.72**, n 26.
2 Trade Marks Registry, 17 November 1998; New Law Digest, 24 November 1998.

5.80   It remains for future decisions to determine just what degree of acquired distinctiveness will be required in order to satisfy the requirements of the proviso. *British Sugar*[1] and *Philips*[2] were perhaps extreme cases. The insistence that the applicant or proprietor must prove that the sign is recognised as a trade mark, when *ex hypothesi* (in most cases, including *British Sugar*) it has not been objected to under s 3(1)(a), does not necessarily accord with the intention of the Directive, and it may be that in less extreme cases not so much evidence of use will in practice be required. The remarks of Jacob J in *Philips*, in particular, appear to require 100% or something approaching it. Nevertheless it seems clear that the use required must be use as a trade mark, not merely descriptive use, and this was an important factor in these cases.

1 [1996] RPC 281.
2 [1998] RPC 283.

5.81   The *Windsurfer Chiemsee* case, already considered on the interpretation of art 3(1)(b) of the Directive,[1] provides further guidance on the application of the proviso, contained in art 3(3). One of the questions referred to the ECJ concerned the requirements of the provision as regards level of distinctive character. The Advocate General considered this aspect in his Opinion,[2] although he only dealt with this aspect for the sake of completeness, having already expressed the view that the marks in question had a distinctive character to begin with, and only suggested an approach in very general terms. First of all, he said, the use must have lasted for a period of time which is reasonable in the opinion of the national court. Secondly, the 'commercial public', which he said consists mainly of the consumers of the product concerned, but also includes dealers and shops which sell similar products and the manufacturers and producers of such products, must have been convinced that the mark characterises the products of a specific company. However he indicated the need for care, particularly with the manufacturers and producers, since they may have a special interest in the registration or rejection of the mark. Turning to the question of percentage recognition required, the Advocate General said that this must in principle be left to the national court to decide on a case by case basis, according to circumstances. However he emphasised that art 3(3) is an exceptional provision and must be interpreted fairly strictly. He continued:

> 'Since what is being sought here is the extent and degree of the impression which the trade mark makes on the mind of the public to which it is addressed, in addition to its assessment in terms of value, quality and general substance, it is also necessary to take quantitative criteria seriously into consideration. From this point of view, I am of the opinion that a percentage of at least 50% is an appropriate limit, below which the trade mark cannot be said to have become established in the market.

> 'Finally, as far as the degree of impression that the trade mark makes is concerned, we must assume that it is not enough merely for the general public to have noticed that there is another trade mark in the market. It is also necessary to have created the conviction that the products bearing that trade mark are connected with a specific company.'

1 See paras **5.10** and **5.60–5.63** above.
2 See paras 22.2 and 66–77.

5.82 The ECJ adopted the same general approach, also emphasising that art 3(3) constitutes a major exception to the rule laid down in art 3(1)(b), (c) and (d) and that, just as distinctive character is one of the general conditions for registering a trade mark under art 3(1)(b), distinctive character acquired through use means that the mark must serve to identify the product in respect of which registration is applied for nas originating from a particular undertaking, and thus to distinguish that product from goods of other undertakings. The court accepted[1] the contention of the plaintiff, also supported by the Commission, that art 3(3) does not permit any differentiation as regards distinctiveness by reference to the perceived importance of keeping the geographical name available for use by other undertakings. The court's ruling was as follows:

(2) The first sentence of art 3(3) of the First Directive 89/104/EEC is to be interpreted as meaning that:

  (a) a trade mark acquires distinctive character following the use which has been made of it where the mark has come to identify the product in respect of which registration is applied for as originating from a particular undertaking and thus to distinguish that product from goods of other undertakings;

  (b) precludes differentiation as regards distinctiveness by reference to the perceived importance of keeping the geographical name available for use by other undertakings;

(c) in determining whether a trade mark has acquired distinctive character following the use which has been made of it, the competent authority must make an overall assessment of the evidence that the mark has come to identify the product as originating from a particular undertaking and thus to distinguish that product from goods of other undertakings;

(d) if the competent authority finds that a significant proportion of the relevant class of persons identify the goods as originating from a particular undertaking because of the trade mark, it must hold the requirement for registering the mark to be satisfied;

(e) where the competent authority has particular difficulty in assessing the distinctive character of a mark in respect of which registration is applied for, Community law does not preclude it from having recourse, under the conditions laid down by its own national law, to an opinion poll as guidance for its judgment.

1 At Para 48.

5.83 In essence, what this means is that the assessment of distinctive character is ultimately for the national courts (or of course registries, where they are dealing with the matter). It is clear from the penultimate paragraph of the ruling that the discretionary aspect, that is the old requirement of distinctiveness in law, no longer applies. One factor which is not specifically mentioned is the nature of the mark; clearly the more non-distinctive a mark, the less readily is it likely to become established as a trade mark. A second factor is the manner in which it has been used. If it has not been used in a clearly trade mark manner, it will be more difficult to demonstrate that it has in fact acquired a sufficient distinctive character. The picture of a three-headed razor in *Philips v Remington*[1] provides an example of a mark which is of such a nature that it would require evidence of a very specific character, ie unmistakably as a trade mark, before it would be accepted as having acquired a 'distinctive character'. For this reason the observation that art 3(3) is an 'exceptional provision' must be considered in its context, having regard to all the circumstances including the nature of the mark. There should be a difference for this purpose, between a mark which is near to the borderline of prima facie registrability, and one which is very far to the wrong side of the borderline. Another point is that it would seem that the requirement of identifying products bearing the trade mark as originating from a particular undertaking should not be equated with a requirement that the relevant public should know the identity of that company. There is no reason to suppose that the principles established by the common law in this respect, and recognised expressly in the TMA 1938 definition of a 'trade mark'[2] has disappeared. The definition of a 'trade mark' in the Directive and in s 1(1) of the TMA 1994, is consistent with this view. After all, it is frequently the case that members of the public are not aware of the identity of owners of trade marks, but nevertheless associate the marks with products having a particular trade origin. Finally, it is to be noted that the court did not suggest a particular of recognition of the mark, preferring the requirement of identification by a 'significant proportion' of the relevant class of persons. Here again all the circumstances of the case have to be considered, and while a figure of 50%, as suggested by the Advocate General, might be justifiable for a very descriptive mark, a rather lower percentage might be appropriate in more marginal cases. As the court appears to recognise, it would be wrong for the national courts and registries to be fettered by arbitrary rules and prevented from dealing with each case on its merits.

1 Para **5.14** above, n 1.
2 Section 68(1).

5.84   The Advocate General also made some observations about evidence and proof of acquired distinctive character. Basically as he said, the means of proving distinctive character will depend upon the national provisions governing such matters. Nevertheless he considered that it must be accepted that at least some general rules arise from the general context of the Directive. First, he emphasises that the means of proof must be 'appropriate'. For example, he said that where the question is not the commercial success of the product but the impression that the trade mark has made on the public, the means of proof would have to make it possible to evaluate the breadth and extent of that impression. Thus merely to give evidence of use, with turnover figures is not, he said, sufficient, thereby echoing the remarks of Jacob J in *British Sugar Corpn plc v James Robertson and Sons Ltd.*[1] He favoured the kind of evidence suggested by the Commission, such as the opinions of the appropriate Board of Trade, trade organisations, and experts. As a general approach this must be correct, but there will always be some cases in which the extent of use of a mark, measured in terms of turnover, combined with the amount and the nature of the advertising of the products under the mark, must be such that it can be assumed that distinctive character has resulted. Again this may depend upon the nature of the mark. The Advocate General was also against a rigid adherence to a particular means of proof, where several means are available, citing as an example the tendency in German courts to base their findings only or mainly on demoscopic survey reports. He also suggested that surveys should be used sparingly and carefully, particularly with regard to their representativeness and objectivity.

1 [1996] RPC 281 at 286.

5.85   The Work Manual[1] gives detailed guidance on the registry's current approach to cases in which it is sought to overcome objections under s 3(1) by means of evidence of acquired distinctive character. No doubt the registry will also now take account of the decision of the ECJ in *Windsurfer Chiemsee*[2], and perhaps also of the Advocate General's remarks about evidence, with which the court did not disagree and which seem helpful for general guidance. While recognising that everything that is said is subject to the observations made in the Foreword,[3] some aspects of the current practice as set out in the Work Manual should be mentioned.

1 Chapter 6, paras 7.2–7.4.
2 [1999] ETMR 585.
3 See para **5.3** above.

Protected indications of geographical origin

5.86   There is a general statement in the Work Manual, that indications of geographical origin for foods and beverages protected under Council Regulation 2081/92 are inherently incapable of distinguishing the goods of one trader from those of another, and cannot, therefore, fall within the definition of a trade mark in s 1(1) of the TMA 1994. This must be taken as referring to the goods covered by the protection under the Regulation. But the status of the Regulation itself is not yet clear. The Court of Appeal has recently held[1] that the Regulation does not have direct effect in the UK. Until the position is clarified, where a mark is an indication or designation of geographical origin, in the sense in which these terms are used in the Opinion of the Advocate General in *Windsurfer Chiemsee*,[2] the registry may be on safer ground in raising objection under s 3(1)(c) rather than relying on matters done under the Regulation.

1 In *Consorzio dei Proscuitto di Parma v Asda Stores Ltd* and Hygrade Foods Ltd [1998] 2 CMLR 215.
2 See para **5.60** above.

Signs 'incapable of distinguishing'

5.87 The Work Manual then deals with 'signs which appear to be *incapable* of distinguishing and unregistrable', saying that as a rule of thumb these can be identified as the sort of signs that would not have been registrable under the old law, because they have no inherent distinctiveness', and gives some examples. But in view of the fact that the old doctrine of lack of inherent distinctiveness is no longer part of the law, and that many marks which were unregistrable under the old law, (geographical marks are a particular example), this approach is unsound as a general approach, even if it may lead to a correct result in some cases. The phrase 'incapable of distinguishing' should no longer enter into discussions as to registrability once a sign is accepted as a 'trade mark', and attention must be turned to s 3(1)(b), (c) and (d); objections under these provisions are all presumably to be regarded as being potentially capable of being overcome by evidence of acquired distinctive character. The overriding requirement must be that each case should be determined on its own facts. Even a highly descriptive term may, if used over a sufficiently long period in an unmistakably trade mark sense, may acquire sufficient distinctive character to become registrable.

5.88 The Work Manual also deals with 'signs which appear to be *incapable* of distinguishing used with another distinctive mark', and again gives examples. The *Treat* case,[1] in which the evidence showed that the mark had been accompanied in use by a distinctive and well recognised trade mark ('Silver spoon'), is cited. But here again a general approach may be dangerous. In each case the position may depend not only in what manner and in what context the mark has been used, but on how it has been perceived by the public.

1 *British Sugar Corpn* case – see para **5.4**, n 2 above.

Prior rights

5.89 One question which may arise from time to time, but which is not specifically covered by the TMA 1994, is whether the registrar can take into consideration, in favour of an applicant, the fact that he has a previous registration of the same mark for similar goods or services, or a similar mark for the same or similar goods or services. Under ss 9(3)(b) and 10(2)(b) of the TMA 1938, such matters could be taken into account as 'other circumstances'. Where for example an application is for a sign such as a label or a logo, or some other combined mark, incorporating a well established mark which is already on the register in the name of the applicant, there can be little if any justification for requiring the applicant to file voluminous evidence of acquired distinctive character. In some instances, which would usually be cases involving objections under s 3(1)(b) or (c), the prior registration may properly be regarded as an indication that the mark is not 'devoid of any distinctive character' or that the sign is not such as 'may serve, in trade', to designate any characteristics of the goods or services.[1] Alternatively another possible approach, where there is an existing registration, which was obtained by filing evidence of distinctiveness, may enable the registrar to allow the new application on the basis of a formal short declaration confirming that use has continued since the date of the existing registration.

1 There are instances appearing in the Journal, of applications under the TMA 1994 advertised as 'proceeding because of prior rights in Registration No. ....'.

5.90   The registrar will now take earlier registrations into consideration in certain circumstances. The current practice is set out in detail in the Work Manual.[1] The first situation is that of a new trade mark which includes an existing registered mark or a minor variation of it, and which is sought to be registered by the same proprietor for the same goods or services. If the new mark contains the earlier mark or that mark without differences in elements which do not affect its distinctive character, and the presence of such mark in the new mark is not *de minimis*, ie insignificant, and is not included in such a way as to take away any distinctive character of the earlier mark when viewed alone, then the registrar will accept the later application. The second situation is where the application being considered is in respect of similar goods or services to those covered by an existing registration of the same proprietor. Here the registrar is prepared to accept that although the proviso, strictly interpreted, requires factual distinctiveness resulting from use for the goods or services covered by the application, nevertheless it is common practice for there to be a progression in trade, over time, and that marks which are factually distinctive for one range of goods/services can quickly become distinctive for similar goods/services. Accordingly, subject to the same requirements as to the relationship of the later mark as compared to the earlier mark, as mentioned above, and to the further requirement that the earlier mark must have been registered on the basis of evidence of acquired distinctiveness, the registrar will take this into account when examining the later application. Acceptance in such cases is not automatic and each case will be determined on its own merits in all the circumstances. The Work Manual indicates the factors to be taken into consideration and gives some helpful examples. There is an important safeguard for third parties. Where the registrar takes into account earlier registrations based on evidence of acquired distinctiveness (whether under the old or the new law), the applicant will be required to agree *in writing* that the evidence filed in the earlier case be copied and regarded as having been filed on the later application also, *and the evidence be made available for public inspection* as if it had been so filed. This is particularly important where the earlier application was under the old law and inspection would otherwise be precluded by rule 44(4). In all these cases there will be a clause in the Journal in the terms set out above.[2]

1 Chapter 6, s 7.5.
2 Paragraph 5.89, n 1 above.

5.91   Another important matter mentioned in the Work Manual is the question of the relevance of acceptance of the same mark by OHIM for the same goods or services. This is raised, quite understandably, because the absolute grounds for refusal under the CTM Regulation are in the same terms as art 3 of the Directive. The registrar's position is that acceptance by OHIM is not binding on him and that he must decide for himself whether the mark meets the requirements of the TMA Act. In the absence of guidance from the ECJ with which any practice of the registry is inconsistent, this approach seems correct. Nevertheless the registrar may be prepared to treat acceptance by OHIM as of persuasive value in marginal cases. Where acceptance by OHIM was based upon evidence of acquired distinctive character, the registrar will consider any evidence received in support of the UK application according to the usual criteria. A similar approach is adopted where the same mark has been accepted in other Member States for the same goods or services. Such acceptance may be given persuasive value in marginal cases, where the objection is on one of the absolute grounds for refusal. The matter will depend upon how many acceptances or registrations there are in other Member States, whether the countries concerned examine on absolute grounds, and whether the objections are based on UK practice in interpreting the Directive or on the facts of the case. Language differences may also be material. Of course, if registration in other Member States was obtained on the basis of evidence of acquired distinctiveness in those countries, then this would not assist overcoming an objection to prima facie registrability in the UK. Furthermore the applicant must provide full information about the acceptances or registrations in the other countries, so that the weight to be given to them may be assessed. Finally, the Work Manual makes it clear that registrations outside the EU are, in principle, considered irrelevant.

Restricting the specification

5.92 Restricting the specification of goods or services for which registration is sought has always been a possible means of overcoming objections, both on absolute and relative grounds. This aspect of the practice in the registry is covered in full in Chapter 6 of the Work Manual.[1] It is not necessary here to set out the practice in all its detail. Essentially, the 'Penguin' practice is still being applied where the mark is seen as descriptive of some goods or services contained in the specification, although the objection will be overcome by evidence of sufficient acquired distinctive character. In some cases there will be an objection of deceptiveness, under s 3(3), in respect of the goods or services for which the mark is not descriptive. For the time being at least the practice will be maintained, although it has met with some criticism and may require modification in the light of any guidance from the courts, including the ECJ.

1 Paragraph 7.6.

Objections relating to shapes of goods and their packaging

5.93 Section 3(2) of the TMA 1994, the wording of which follows art 3.1(e) of the Directive, contains grounds of objection which relate to marks which consist of shapes of goods; it provides that

'a sign shall not be registered as a trade mark if it consists exclusively of–

(a) the shape which results from the nature of the goods themselves,
(b) the shape of good which is necessary to obtain a technical result,
(c) the shape which gives substantial value to goods.'

5.94 As with s 3(1)(c) and (d) the word 'exclusively' should be emphasised. Marks are not precluded from registration under these provisions where they comprise a combination of a shape with other matter such as words or devices. It should be noted that, although these provisions do not apply in terms to the shape of packaging, the matter may not be as straightforward as that. On this point, a statement in the Annex to the Directive says that, where goods are packaged, the expression 'shape of goods' includes the shape of the packaging.[1] Statements in the Annex have been held inadmissible[2] for the purpose of construing the provisions of the Directive to which they relate. Even in the absence of such a statement, the courts may well apply s 3(2) to 'packaging' comprising a container which is an essential part of the 'goods' in the sense that they could not be marketed other than in a container. Liquids, such as beverages, provide an obvious example.

1 Cf para 4 of 'the Annex' to the Regulation (see para **1.9** above)
2 *Wagamama Ltd v City Restaurants plc* [1995] FSR 713 – see paras **1.20–1.21** above.

5.95 It is to be observed that an application must be refused if the shape in question falls within any of paras (a)–(c). The objection, if well-founded, cannot be overcome by proving acquired distinctive character, although evidence will be permissible to show that the ground of objection is not applicable. Under s 3(2)(a) an ordinary shaped bottle or other container, required to contain a liquid product, might be regarded as a shape which 'results from the nature of the goods themselves'; so also might a basic handle of an utilitarian article, such as a tool. The Work Manual[1] previously gave the example of the shape of an egg cup. On the other hand a container of distinctive appearance would not be so regarded. The Work Manual[2] illustrates some unusually shaped bottles as examples of prima facie acceptable shapes. Under s 3(2)(b) the important word seems to be 'necessary'. The Manual provides the example of the shape of a wheel which must be round. But if the product or container can be made in a number of possible shapes, as well as that claimed by the applicant, and still have the same function, it is at least arguable that the shape is not one which results from the nature of the goods and is not 'necessary' to achieve a technical result. The third ground of objection, contained in s 3(2)(c), is not so straightforward to apply. It would appear to be contrary to the purpose of the Directive to exclude shapes under this head merely because they are more attractive to customers, which might in a sense be said to give 'substantial value to the goods'. One possible view is that the objection should be understood as applying to something that makes a product a better product, in the functional sense. The example given in the Work Manual is the cut of a diamond, without which it is useless in an item of jewellery and of substantially less value. In general, looking at the overall purpose of the provisions, they are clearly designed to exclude the basic or fundamental shape of an article, even if it is capable of being made in other shapes, and probably go further than that. On the other hand, a shape adopted for the purpose of distinguishing goods, ie to serve the function of a trade mark, should not be refused on this ground. The foregoing remarks are only put forward as tentative suggestions, as to what those who framed the Directive may have had in mind. The matter must now be considered in the light of some decisions which have been given on the scope of the provisions of s 3(2).

1 September 1994 edns ch 6, page 20, para 4.1.3.
2 Chapter 6, para 6.4, pp 59–60..

5.96 The only reported decisions of courts on s 3(2) is that of Jacob J in *Philips,*[1] discussed above in relation to the provisions of s 3(1). The case is of interest not only because it is the first decision of an English court which deals with s 3(2) but because there is a conflicting decision of a Swedish court on the same trade mark.[2] In *Philips* the plaintiff's registration was attacked under all three of the sub-paragraphs of s 3(2). There is another decision of the court[3] on appeal from the registry, in which an objection under s 3(2)(c) was upheld in opposition proceedings, the application for registration having been accepted and advertised. In that case, Lloyd J did not find it necessary to decide the point. The *Philips* case has now been the subject of a decision by the Court of Appeal,[4] which is considered below. However it should be noted that the court has referred several questions to the ECJ for interpretation of the relevant provisions of the Directive, including art 3(1)(e).

1 [1998] RPC 283 at 304–310.
2 *Ide Line AG v Philips Electronics NV* [1997] ETMR 377 (Swedish Court of Appeal).
3 *Re Dualit Ltd's (Toaster Shapes) Trade Mark Applications* [1999] RPC 304 (Registry) 5 July 1999, Lloyd J.
4 [1999] ETMR 816.

5.97   At first instance Jacob J, dealing with sub-para (a), which applies to a sign which consists exclusively of 'the shape which results from the nature of the goods themselves', the learned judge first considered the question, what are 'the goods themselves'? If one regarded 'the goods' as 'rotary shavers having three equilateral heads and a face plate' then, as the judge said, the shape results from the nature of the goods. If on the other hand 'the goods' are regarded as just rotary shavers, or more generally electric shavers, or even more generally shavers, electrical or otherwise, then, he said, the shape does not result from the nature of the goods. In determining how one should define 'the goods' for this purpose, he considered that one should not simply take the specification of goods covered by the registration, which was 'electric shavers', for that would be partly adventitious. One must ask what the goods are, he said, as a practical business matter, the answer depending on how they are viewed in practice as articles of commerce. He concluded that the goods were 'electric shavers', and on that basis rejected the attack under s 3(2)(a). On appeal, Aldous LJ (with whose judgment the other Lords Justices agreed), agreed with Jacob J, holding that 'the goods' were the goods for which the mark was registered. The mark was registered in repect of 'electric shavers' and, as he put it, there is no one shape, let alone that depicted in the trade mark, which results from the nature of the goods.

5.98   Sub-paragraph (b) was the provision to which the argument was mainly directed. It was submitted on behalf of the plaintiff that because you can get an equally good shave from rotary shavers, even three-headed rotary shavers, of shapes other than that shown in the picture which constituted the registered sign. Thus, it was claimed, if the proprietor can show that some other shape will do the job, his 'sign' is not within the exclusion, no matter how functional it may be. As the judge observed, it was this argument that found favour with the majority of the Swedish Court of Appeal. After considering the Swedish decision, he decided that he must form his own view and, with some qualification, agreed broadly with the dissenting judgment. He referred to the speech of Lord Reid in decision of the House of Lords in *Amp Inc v Utilux Pty Ltd*,[1] in which the House of Lords was concerned with the meaning[2] of the phrase 'features of shape or consideration which are dictated solely by the function which the article to be made in that shape or configuration has to perform'. In a passage set out in the judgment of Jacob J, Lord Reid rejected the proposition that this meant that the article had to have the particular shape to work. Adopting the same approach, Jacob J concluded that the question to be answered, under s 3(2)(b), was: in substance, does the shape solely achieve a technical result? Applying that test, he held that the shape registered as a trade mark in the case before him consisted exclusively of a shape which is necessary to obtain a technical result. In the Court of Appeal, Aldous LJ agreed with the conclusion of Jacob J. He said that the subsection must be construed so that its ambit coincides with its purpose, which was to exclude from registration shapes which are merely functional in the sense that they are motivated by and are the result of technical considerations. He concluded that the restriction on registration, imposed by the words 'which is necessary to obtain a technical result' is not overcome by establishing that there are other shapes which can obtain the same technical result. All that had to be shown, he said, was that the essential features of the shape were attributable only to the technical result.

1 [1972] RPC 103 at 109.
2 In the Registered Designs Act 1949, s 1.

5.99 As regards the objection under s 3(2)(c), which excludes a shape which gives substantial value to the goods, Jacob J observed that good trade marks add value to goods, so that one must not take the exclusion too literally. He thought that what was meant was an exclusion of shapes which exclusively add some sort of value (design or functional appearance or perhaps something else) to the goods *disregarding* any value attributable to a trade mark function. He concluded that the registration came within the exclusion. On this issue, Aldous LJ disagreed with Jacob J. He said that the sub-section, being only concerned with shapes having 'substantial value', requires a conclusion as to whether the value of the shape is substantial, which in his view requires that a comparison has to be made between the shape sought to be registered and shapes of equivalent articles. It was only if the shape sought to be registered had, in relative terms, substantial value that it would be excluded from registration. The learned Lord Justice concluded, considering the shape as a shape, regardless of the reputation which Philips had built up, that the evidence did not establish that the registered shape had any more value than other shapes which were established to be as good as and as cheap to produce as that which was registered.

5.100 As is clear from the provisions themselves, Jacob J held that the exclusions under s 3(2) could and did overlap with other exclusions, such as those under s 3(1). There does not appear to have been any argument over this point in the Court of Appeal. Thus in cases in which the shape is essentially the fundamental shape of an article, or the goods are of a kind in which there is not much difference in design as between different manufacturers, objections may equally well be raised, for example, under s 3(1)(a) as being incapable of distinguishing, and s 3(1)(b), on the ground that the shape is devoid of any distinctive character.

5.101 Until the ECJ has ruled on the questions of the interpretation of art 3(1)(e), no clear conclusions can be reached on the precise scope of the provisions. The conclusions of Jacob J and Aldous LJ on s 3(2)(a) would seem to be correct as, it is submitted, would the views of Aldous LJ on s 3(2)(c). Section 3(2)(b) raises difficult questions, as is perhaps demonstrated by the fact that the Swedish and English courts have come to different conclusions. However it should be emphasised that each case must be determined on its own facts. Although the conclusion of the English courts may well be upheld by the ECJ, the decision is not necessarily applicable to shapes which, while having features which are functional, incorporate other features which are definitely not functional, but are part of the design. In many instances, the word 'exclusively' in sub-s (2) may be crucial.

Marks contrary to public policy or morality, and deceptive marks

5.102   Section 3(3) provides that a trade mark

'shall not be registered if it is–

(a) contrary to public policy or to accepted principles of morality, or
(b) of such a nature as to deceive the public (for instance as to the nature, quality or geographical origin of the goods or service).'

In some respects this provision is quite similar to s 11 of the TMA 1938, to the extent that objections under it were raised by the registrar at the examination stage. The ground of objection, as an 'absolute' ground for refusal, cannot be invoked on the basis of earlier rights. Section 11 prohibited the registration of marks 'the use of which would be disentitled to protection in a court of justice, by reason of its use being likely to deceive or cause confusion or otherwise, or would be contrary to law or morality'. Also excluded was 'any scandalous design'. Some marks were refused registration on the ground of deceptiveness as to such matters as the nature of the goods[1] but objections of this kind were usually readily overcome by evidence of use, without any deception occurring, or any complaint being made, for example under consumer legislation. A few applications were also refused under the TMA 1938 provision, it seems, as being contrary to morality[2] although in some of the cases it is not always clear whether refusal was on that ground or merely in the exercise of the registrar's discretion, which (for the purpose of refusing registration where none of the substantive grounds set out in the TMA 1994 are established) now no longer exists.

1 See for example *China-Therm Trade Mark* [1980] FSR 32.
2 See eg *Hallelujah Trade Mark* [1976] RPC 605. 'Jesus' is understood to have been refused, for jeans, on this ground; also 'Orgasm' and 'Poison' for perfume.

5.103   The Work Manual[1] gives detailed guidance on the application of s 3(3). As to what is 'contrary to public policy or to accepted principles of morality' it is stated that it is not possible to define this, and that the registrar must exercise his judgment on each case. Examples given include a mark which might be seen as promoting misuse of drugs, or counterfeiting, pornography or murder, and bad language. However marks have been accepted which only incorporate 'mild' bad language, or language which is regarded as only 'fairly' or 'relatively' inoffensive. Generally speaking, it does not appear that the practice in this respect is any different from that followed under s 11 of the TMA 1938 as mentioned above, although the registrar accepts that public susceptibilities and taste do change and it is presumably necessary in any case that the mark should be offensive to a substantial section of the public. In practice it is unlikely that this provision will be applied very often. The approach adopted by OHIM under the equivalent provision of the Regulation may need to be considered. It is quite possible that the ECJ, in any rulings on art 3(1)(f) of the Directive, or on appeal from decisions of OHIM under the Regulation, will adopt a fairly broad-minded approach.

1 Chapter 6, para 9.

5.104   Under s 3(1)(b) the registry previously indicated[1] that it would follow essentially the same practice as under s 11 of the TMA 1938. It was said that objection would be raised 'if the mark gives rise to an expectation that the goods services are of a certain quality, type etc when the specification clearly indicates that this will not always be the case'. Under the previous practice, one criterion was whether the descriptive element could reasonably be expected to influence the public's interest in the goods. These tests seem quite fair, although it is a little difficult to see how they would be applied to exclude a mark such as 'Chinatherm',[2] which probably would not in fact deceive anyone into believing that the goods were made of china or influence the public's interest in any material sense. The Work Manual[3] no longer mentions s 11 of the TMA 1938 and adopts a much more realistic approach. It is pointed out that the verb 'to deceive' is defined as 'to mislead by deliberate misrepresentation or lies'. It is also recognised that objections had in the past been raised to trade marks where there was no realistic possibility of deception, but where the specification was too wide. The example is given of Hartley's strawberry jam, which might have been the subject of an objection unless the goods were limited to 'strawberry jam', and it is acknowledged that there would be little possibility that the applicant would use such a mark for anything else, and that an application to register for 'jams' would not now be regarded as involving any 'deliberate misrepresentation'. It should be noted that conditions of registration, which were in the past used to overcome objections of deceptiveness in some marks, may no longer be imposed, and also that where a mark was registered under the TMA 1938 with a condition as to use, such condition will have ceased to have effect.[4] Any deceptive use of a trade mark will fall to be dealt with under the revocation provisions of s 47(1)(d) of the TMA 1994, or under consumer protection legislation. The Manual now states that in future, an objection under s 3(3)(b) will only be raised if in the examiner's view there is a real potential for deception of the public. The examiner should, it continues, consider whether there would be any possible advantage to any trader, not specifically the applicant, from using the mark on anything other than goods with the characteristics conveyed by the mark. Thus, objection will be taken where the mark is or includes the name of, or a device indicating, a place which has a reputation for the goods or services in question. Objection will also be taken to marks which indicate a particular (desirable) quality of the goods. The Manual includes a helpful list of examples of marks which will not now meet an objection under s 3(3)(b), with indications of what would have happened under the old law.[5] The usual way of overcoming an objection under the provision is to restrict the specification of goods to reflect their composition, so long as there is not also another objection, for example under s 3(1). However, where the applicant already has a registration for the same mark, or a variation of it which is no more objectionable, for the same unrestricted specification of goods or services, no objection will be raised under s 3(1)(b). In the case of marks of one particular kind, namely marks that are evocative of Scotland and are sought to be registered for goods which include whisky and whisky based liqueurs, the registry has a specific practice, which is set out in the Manual.[6] A further means of overcoming an objection is by filing evidence of use to demonstrate that the secondary meaning of the mark, as the applicant's trade mark, has become the primary meaning so far as the public is concerned. The nature of the evidence required will depend upon the strength of the objection in each case.

1 Work Manual, ch 6, September 1994.
2 Paragraph **5.102**, n 1 above.
3 Chapter 6, paras 9.2–9.6.
4 On 31 October 1994 – see the TMA 1994, Sch 3, para 3(3).
5 Chapter 6, para 9.6.
6 Chapter 6, para 9.4.

5.105 There have been no decisions of the courts on s 3(3) of the TMA 1994 . A decision of the registry in opposition proceedings illustrates the current approach as described in the Work Manual. The mark concerned was 'Ecofix', which had been accepted for orthopaedic devices. The objection under s 3(3)(b) was that the prefix Eco- suggested that the goods were environmentally friendly. It was held that the prefix was fanciful in relation to orthopaedic devices, that no-one expected the goods to be environmentally friendly and that the public was not being deceived.[1]

1 *Re Zimmer Inc's Trade Mark Application*, 30 April 1998;New Law Digest 698081304.

5.106 It should also be mentioned that there were several means of overcoming objections under s 11 of the TMA 1938 Act, which are not now available under the 1994 Act. In addition to the condition of use, to which reference has already been made, 'variation clauses', which required that the mark be varied in use in a manner specified, so as to avoid deception, cannot now be used. Another means, of amending the mark to remove descriptive matter, is excluded under s 39(2) of the TMA 1994.

Marks, the use of which is contrary to law

5.107 Section 3(4) prohibits registration of a trade mark 'if or to the extent that its use is prohibited in the United Kingdom by any enactment of rule of law or by any provision of Community law'. To some extent this provision may cover cases in which applications might have encountered objections under s 11 of the TMA 1938. UK enactments, which may be relevant for this purpose, include various consumer protection statutes, such as the Trade Descriptions Act 1968 and the Hallmarking Act 1973, and certain laws implementing international obligations, such as the Anglo-Portuguese Commercial Treaty Acts 1914 and 1916, the 'Anzac' (Restriction on Trade Use of Word) Act 1916 and the Geneva Conventions Act 1957. 'Rule of law' could perhaps cover a common law rule, although it is difficult to identify any such rule as might apply here; for example it probably is not intended to exclude a trade mark the use of which might constitute passing-off, since that would come under 'relative grounds' for refusal, considered below in Chapter 6. Also included among 'rules of law' for this purpose might be subordinate legislation such as statutory instruments. The term 'any provision of Community law' is potentially very broad, covering not only the Treaty of Rome and the subsequent treaties, but also the many directives and regulations adopted by the Council. So far as trade marks are concerned, particular instances which come to mind include the wine regulations[1] and the recent regulation 'on the protection of geographical indications and designations of origin for agricultural products and foodstuffs'.[2] Objections under s 3(4) may be overcome in appropriate cases by similar means to those described in relation to s 3(3).

1 Eg Council Regulation 823/87 EEC, applied by the Court of Appeal in the 'Elderflower Champagne' case, *Taittinger v Allbev Ltd* [1993] 2 CMLR 741, [1993] FSR 641.
2 Council Regulation 2081/92/EEC; OJ L208, 24.7.92, p 1. This however has to be considered in the light of the decision of the Court of Appeal in the *Parma Ham* case. See para **5.86** n 1 above.

Specially protected emblems

5.108   Section 3(5) provides that 'a trade mark shall not be registered in the cases specified, or referred to, in section 4, (specially protected emblems)'. Under the TMA 1938, the main provisions for refusal of registration of marks in these categories were contained in the Trade Marks and Service Marks Rules[1] 1986, rr 16–18. Under the TMA 1994 the main provisions are to be found in the Act itself. The categories of emblems are set out in detail in s 4, sub-s (3) of which in turn refers to ss 57 and 58. It is not necessary to set out the provisions in detail here; they appear in full in Appendix [1][2]. They are also discussed in detail in the Work Manual.[3] A further category was added by the Olympic Symbol etc (Protection) Act 1995.[4] This is discussed below.

1 SI 1986/1319 (as amended).
2 Chapter 6, para 10.8.
3 By s 13(2). This was brought into force on 20 September 1995, by The Olympic Symbol etc (Protection) Act 1995 (Commencement) Order 1995, SI 1995/2472.
4 Paragraphs **5.116–5.117**.

Marks concerning the Royal Family

5.109   Section 4(1) is concerned with matters affecting the Royal Family and specifies categories of trade marks which must not be registered unless it appears to the registrar that consent has been given by or on behalf of Her Majesty or, as the case may be, the relevant Member of the Royal Family. For this purpose it seems to be clear that 'Royal Family' must be a reference to the British Royal Family, and the registry has been provided with a list of those regarded as members.[1] Such trade marks are those consisting of or containing (a) the Royal arms, or any of the principal armorial bearings of the Royal arms, or any insignia or device so nearly resembling the Royal arms or any such armorial bearing as to be likely to be mistaken for them or it, (b) a representation of the Royal crown or any of the Royal flags, (c) a representation of Her Majesty or any member of the Royal family, or any colourable imitation thereof, or (d) words, letters or devices likely to lead persons to think that the applicant either has or recently has had Royal patronage or authorisation. The question whether a device so nearly resembles the Royal arms or any armorial bearing as to be likely to be mistaken for them or it, or whether any words, letters or devices might suggest Royal patronage or authorisation is one of fact. It is thought that mere similarity, which in the case of a trade mark might give rise to a finding of infringement, would not suffice here, and that there must be a fairly close similarity.

1   Chapter 6, para 10.2 and Appendix 4.

UK flags

5.110   Section 4(2) prohibits registration of trade marks consisting of or containing any representation of (a) the Union Jack or (b) the flags of England, Wales, Scotland, Northern Ireland or the Isle of Man, but only if it appears to the registrar that the use of the trade mark would be 'misleading or grossly offensive'. The subsection enables provision to be made by rules identifying the flags to which (b) applies, but no such provision has been made. No guidance is offered as to the meaning of these words, but it is not thought that they are likely to be applied in many cases. The Work Manual give examples of some ways in which a mark incorporating a UK flag might be regarded as misleading, namely if it suggests that goods are made in the UK when they are not, or if it suggests some kind of official or Royal endorsement when there is not. In some respects there may thus be overlap with s 3(3). The giving of consent is not mentioned, but may presumably have some bearing on whether the use would in fact be misleading or grossly offensive.

National emblems and emblems of international organisations

5.111 The provisions of ss 57 and 58, referred to in s 4(3), are included in compliance with the UK's obligations under art 6*ter* of the Paris Convention,[1] and relate respectively to flags, national emblems, official signs and hallmarks of Convention countries and to emblems, abbreviations and names of certain international intergovernmental organisations. In the cases covered by these provisions registration of the flags and emblems, etc, is prohibited. Section 59 imposes certain conditions which must be met before the restrictions of ss 57 and 58 can be invoked. Under both sections[2] the relevant authorities may restrain by injunction the unauthorised use of a trade mark for the registration of which their authorisation would be required. For the purposes of s 57, except in the case of flags, the country in question must notify the UK, in accordance with art 6*ter* (3) of the Convention, that it desires to protect the emblem, sign or hallmark in question, the notification must still be in force, and any objection by the UK to the notification must have been withdrawn. The same conditions apply, as to notifications, for the purposes of s 58, in respect of the emblems, abbreviations and names of the international organisations in question. In either case notifications have effect only in relation to applications for registration made more than two months after receipt of the notification. Section 59(4) requires the registrar to keep and make available for public inspection a list of the state emblems, abbreviations and hallmarks, and the emblems, abbreviations and names of international organisations, which are for the time being protected by virtue of notification under art 6*ter* (3).

1 Sections 57–59 have been amended by the Patents and Trade Marks (World Trade Organisation) Regulations 1999, SI 1899/1999, to incorporate references to the WTO agreement as well as the Paris Convention.
2 Sections 57(6) and 58(4).

Section 57

5.112 Section 57(1) provides that where a trade mark consists of or contains the flag of a Convention country, it shall not be registered without the authorisation of the competent authorities, unless it appears to the registrar that use of the flag in the manner proposed is permitted without such authorisation. Such permission would normally, it is thought, be granted if at all by the law or the competent authorities of the country concerned. Under sub-s (2) registration of a trade mark consisting of or containing the armorial bearings or any other state emblem of a Convention country, which is protected under the Paris Convention,[1] requires the authorisation of the competent authorities. A like authorisation is required, under sub-s (3) for registration of a trade mark consisting of or containing an official sign or hallmark adopted by a Convention country and indicating control and warranty, which is protected under the Paris Convention, *in relation to goods or services of a similar kind as those in relation to which it indicates control and warranty*. Sub-section (4) applies all these provisions to anything 'which from a heraldic point of view imitates any such flag or other emblem, or sign or hallmark'. Where any question arises as to any trade mark under these provisions, no doubt the registrar will consult the appropriate heraldic authorities in London or Edinburgh. However it would appear that a likelihood of confusion, such as might give rise to a finding of infringement, is not necessarily sufficient for the purposes of sub-s (4), and the Work Manual[2] confirms that the word 'imitates' is narrower. Section 57(5) makes it clear that similarity to an emblem, etc of one country, is not sufficient ground to prevent registration of a trade mark by a national of a country who is authorised to use a state emblem, etc of his country.

1 As to which, see s 59.
2 Chapter 6, para 10.6 at p 116.

Section 58

5.113 Section 58 applies to the armorial bearings, flags or other emblems, and the abbreviations and names, of 'international intergovernmental organisations of which one or more Convention countries are members'.[1] It is thus not necessary, for the purposes of this provision, that all members of the intergovernmental organisation be Convention countries. Sub-section (5) provides a saving for the rights of a person whose bona fide use of the trade mark in question began before 4 January 1962, which is the date on which the relevant provisions of the Paris Convention came into force in relation to the UK. Under sub-s (2) a trade mark consisting of or containing any such emblem, abbreviation or name – or in the case of an emblem, anything which from a heraldic point of view imitates any such emblem[2] – which is protected under the Paris Convention,[3] must not be registered, unless it appears to the registrar that use of the emblem, abbreviation or name in the manner proposed:

> (a) is not such as to suggest to the public that a connection exists between the organisation and the trade mark, or

> (b) is not likely to mislead the public as to the existence of a connection between the user and the organisation.

1 Sub-section (1).
2 See the reference to s 57(4) above at para **5.112**.
3 See TMA 1994, s 59.

5.114 In spite of the use of the word 'or', it seems clear that an applicant must satisfy both limbs of sub-s (2). Their purpose is to ensure that the organisations do not have a monopoly in all use of any emblem, name or abbreviation falling within sub-s (1) if there is in fact no likelihood of deception or confusion as to any connection with the organisation concerned.

Arms and insignia

5.115 Section 4(4) enables provision to be made by rules for the prohibition, in such cases as may be prescribed, of the registration, without the appropriate consent, of a trade mark consisting of, or containing, arms to which a person is entitled by virtue of a grant of arms from the Crown, or insignia so nearly resembling such arms as to be likely to be mistaken for them. Rule 9 requires the registrar to refuse to accept an application to register a mark, on which a representation of any such arms or insignia appears, unless satisfied that the consent of the person entitled to the arms has been obtained. Even if such a mark is accepted for registration, s 4(4) contains a provision that nothing in the Act is to be construed as authorising its use in any way contrary to the law of arms. As in the case of the Royal arms, etc,[1] it is thought that the words 'likely to be mistaken' require a closer similarity than might suffice for the purpose of the infringement provisions, and that the fact that a mark might be open to objection from a heraldic point of view is not necessarily sufficient basis for an objection under r 9.

1 See para **5.109**, above.

The Olympic Symbol

5.116 The Olympic Symbol etc (Protection) Act 1995 'OS(P)A 1995' created the Olympics association right, which applies to the Olympic symbol, the Olympic motto and the 'protected words'.[1] Section 3(1) uses the term 'a controlled representation' to refer to a representation of any of these, and also includes 'a representation of something so similar to the Olympic symbol or the Olympic motto as to be likely to create in the public mind an association with it'.

1 Defined in the TMA 1994, s 18(1) and (2). The Olympic symbol is the symbol of the International Olympic Committee, consisting of five interlocking rings, and the Olympic motto is the motto of the Committee, 'Citius, altius, fortius'. The protected words are Olympiad, Olympiads, Olympian, Olympian, Olympic and Olympics.

5.117 Section 13(2) added a new sub-s (5) to s 4 of the OS(P)A 1995. The new sub-s (5)(a) requires the registrar to refuse registration of a trade mark which consists of or contains a controlled representation, unless it appears to him (a) that the application is made by the person for the time being appointed under s 1(2) of the OS(P)A 1995[1] as the proprietor of the Olympics Association right, or (b) that consent has been given by or on behalf of that person. The registrar's practice is to raise the objection unless the applicant can show that it has the written consent of the British Olympic Association, which has indicated that it would not normally grant such consent.[2] By virtue of s 13(3), this provision only applies to applications for registration made on or after the Act came into force, that is 20 September 1995.

1 By The Olympic Association Right (Appointment of Proprietor) Order 1995, SI 1995/2473, The British Olympic Association was appointed as the proprietor of the right.
2 Work Manual, ch 6, para 10.1.

Applications made in bad faith

5.118 Section 3(6) requires registration to be refused 'if or to the extent that the application is made in bad faith'. This provision is based upon art 3(2)(d) of the Directive, but neither there nor anywhere in the TMA 1994 is there any actual indication of what is 'bad faith' for these purposes. The term is capable of covering cases in which the applicant seeks to register a trade mark which he knows does not belong to him, although such cases may well be covered also by s 5[1] or by the provisions of s 60 relating to 'acts of agent or representative'. It might have been thought that s 3(6), coming under the heading of 'absolute grounds' for refusal, was not intended to cover objections based on matters in the nature of relative grounds. However there have been some decisions in which the provision has been applied to cases in which the applicants' claim of entitlement to the mark has been impugned.[2] On the other hand, where a mark was coined in good faith and the applicant only learned of the opponent's mark a few days before making the application, an opposition under s 3(6) failed.[3]

1 See TMA 1994, s 6(1)(c) and s 56, relating to 'well-known' trade marks.
2 See for example: *Yoohoo Trade Mark* 30 May 1995, noted in CIPA Journal, July 1997, p 538, in which a registration was declared invalid; *Travelpro Trade Mark* 25 June 1997, noted in CIPA Journal, August 1997, p 625, in which a registration obtained by a US company's UK distributor was declared invalid; *3K Trade Mark* 30 March 1998, noted in CIPA Journal, September 1998, p 725, in which a registration obtained by a UK distributor was declared invalid and *Re C A Shiever's Trade Mark Application (No 2)* (Geoffrey Hobbs QC) 28 September 1999, noted in New Law Digest 5 October 1999, 699107001.
3 *Attaboy Application* 28 August 1997, noted in CIPA Journal, October 1997, at p 782.

5.119 The interpretation placed on s 3(6) seems by implication to have been approved by the High Court. In proceedings relating to a dispute between a manufacturer and a distributor, *Gromax Plasticulture Ltd v Don & Low Nonwovens Ltd,*[1] Lindsay J considered the meaning of 'bad faith' where a registration was attacked under s 3(6). He held that bad faith clearly included dishonesty, but also included some dealings which fell short of the standards of acceptable commercial behaviour observed by reasonable and experienced men in the field under consideration. In the particular case, bad faith on the part of a distributor was not established. In another case, before the registry,[2] the adoption of a trade mark which was obviously an imitation of the opponent's logo, was held to be sufficient as a basis for a finding of bad faith. Copyright objections will normally be left to opposition, but the registry may raise objection, under s 3(3), to applications to register the names or pictures of famous individuals. Such objections may be overcome by obtaining the appropriate consents. The registry's current practice is set out in the Work Manual.[3]

1 [1999] RPC 367.
2 *Re Team Lotus Trade Mark Application* 23 October 1998, noted in New Law Digest, 699010202.
3 Chapter 6, para 9.11.

5.120 The registry itself has said that applications made without any bona fide intention to use the mark applied for would be covered by s 3(6), and objections on this ground have been raised in a number of cases where the specification of goods or services has been considered by the registry to be over broad. There are several examples of decisions on this basis.[1] This aspect needs further examination. It is to be noted that s 32 (Application for registration) requires an applicant to state that the trade mark is being used, by the applicant or with his consent, in relation to the goods or services concerned, or that he has a bona fide intention that it should be so used; also that s 47(4) gives the registrar himself the right to apply to the court for a declaration of invalidity in case of bad faith in the registration of a trade mark. The term 'in bad faith' would appear to mean dishonest conduct, or at least recklessness. For an understanding of the opposite term 'bona fide' in a provision of the TMA 1938, the decision of the Court of Appeal in *Baume and Co Ltd v AH Moore Ltd*[2] is helpful.

1 See eg *MICKEY DEES (NIGHTCLUB) Trade Mark* [1998] RPC 359 and *Portfolio Trade Mark Application* 31 May 1996, noted in CIPA Journal, July 1996, p 522.
2 [1958] RPC 226, the TMA 1938, s 5(8)(a).

5.121 It is likely that applications for registration of 'ghost' trade marks,[1] with a view to securing protection against the use of some other unregistrable mark, would be regarded as having made in bad faith within the meaning of s 3(6). On the other hand the mere fact that registration is sought for a specification of goods or services which is broader than those in which the applicant is specifically interested ought not, it is submitted, be regarded as evidence of bad faith on the part of the applicant. For example it is a common practice in the UK,[2] to seek registration of marks for 'computer programs' without any limitation as to type or purpose. In a recent decision of the High Court,[3] it was said that there was a strong argument 'that a registration of a mark simply for 'computer software' will normally be too wide'. This was in the context of an application for summary judgment in an action for infringement, in which there was a claim for partial cancellation on the ground of non-use. It may well be that, except where a trade mark is a house mark of a company trading in a variety of computer programs, an application for revocation on grounds of non-use[4] would succeed in part where a mark had only been used for a particular type of program. However the issue of 'bad faith', which, as suggested above, is essentially dishonesty, involves different considerations. It would be hard to say that anyone seeking registration for computer programs generally, even when he is interested in only one particular type of program, is necessarily being dishonest. Similar comments can be made of applications for 'pharmaceutical preparations and substances'; such applications have long been and still are quite normal in the pharmaceutical industry, and it would be going to far to categorise such applications in general as 'dishonest'. In approaching applications for registration covering a broad specification of goods or services, such as a whole class, it should be noted that the Rules contain no equivalent to rule 21 of the 1986 Rules, under which apparently broad specifications were quite often challenged. However in some cases the registry may have sufficient doubt, to justify asking applicants as to their true intentions. If an untrue answer is given, that could be a basis for finding bad faith, either for the purposes of refusal or for a subsequent application for a declaration of invalidity under s 47(1) of the TMA 1994. Apart from this kind of situation it is considered that it will usually be very difficult for the Office to justify a charge of bad faith simply by reason of a claim for what is said to be an unnecessarily broad specification of goods or services. From experience so far it seems likely that issues of bad faith will more usually arise in opposition or invalidation proceedings, rather than at the pre-acceptance stage.

1 See eg the Nerit case, *Imperial Group Ltd v Philip Morris & Co Ltd* [1982] FSR 72, CA.
2 Although not, it is understood, permitted in the USA.
3 Laddie J in *Mercury Communications Ltd v Mercury Interactive (UK) Ltd* [1995] FSR 850 at 865.
4 Under s 46(1)(a) or (b) see below, ch 7.

Chapter 6

Conflict with earlier rights

1   Relative grounds for refusal

Meaning of 'relative grounds'

6.1   The term 'relative grounds', on which a trade mark may be refused registration, again has its origin in the CTM Regulation,[1] and refers to grounds based upon some conflict with the rights of another party. Article 4 of the Directive, on which relative grounds for refusal under the TMA 1994 are based, sets out similar grounds to those provided by the Regulation. Under the TMA 1938 and previous Acts, the registrar was required to raise objections based on conflict with earlier registrations and pending applications. There has been considerable discussion, for many years, of the question whether the registrar should have any power at all to refuse registration of a trade mark on such grounds. In a number of countries, and now also under the CTM Regulation, there is no such power. Under the TMA 1994, for the time being at least, such grounds for refusal may be raised not only in opposition proceedings but by the registrar himself as was the case under the TMA 1938. The grounds are set out in s 5 and are based either upon an 'earlier trade mark' or on some other 'earlier right'. A very important change however is that, under s 5(5), the registrar cannot now refuse registration on any relative ground if the proprietor of the earlier trade mark or other earlier right concerned consents to the registration. Previously the registrar might take consent into consideration in deciding whether or not to allow registration, but was never bound by it.

1 Article 8.

Possible removal of registrar's powers to refuse on relative grounds

6.2   Section 8,[1] entitled 'Power to require that relative grounds be raised in opposition proceedings' provides for the ultimate removal of the registrar's power to refuse an application, ex officio, on relative grounds. By virtue of sub-s (5), the powers conferred by the section cannot be invoked until after the end of the period of ten years from the day on which applications for CTMs may first be filed.[2] Under sub-s (1) it will then be possible for the Secretary of State to provide, by order,[3] that registration of a trade mark may not be refused on relative grounds, other than following opposition by the proprietor of the earlier trade mark or other earlier right. It could be that the registrar's obligation to make a search for earlier trade marks will be continued, and consequential provisions may be made, under sub-s (2), for that purpose; and also as to the persons who may apply for a declaration of invalidity on relative grounds, under s 47(2). However sub-s (3) will enable the order to direct that the requirement to search[3] shall cease to have effect. Unless and until that happens, the registrar is obliged to examine applications and for that purpose to carry out a search of earlier trade marks, although it should be noted that the latter obligation is qualified by the words 'to such extent as he considers necessary'.[4] It remains to be seen what searches the registrar will carry out, and there may be practical limits beyond which he cannot search. There is probably a need already for proprietors of earlier trade marks to be more vigilant than before.

1 See also ch 16, paras **16.11** and **16.12**.
2 This was subsequently fixed at 1 April 1996.
3 Ie by statutory instrument – see sub-s (5), which requires a draft to be laid before and approved by a resolution of each House of Parliament. Under sub-s (6), transitional provisions may be included.
4 Under s 37.
5 Section 37(2).

Refusal based on an 'earlier trade mark'

Meaning of 'earlier trade mark'

6.3   The earlier trade marks, on which refusal of registration under s 5 may be based, are defined in s 6. In accordance with s 6(1) these are:

(a)   a registered trade mark, an international trade mark (UK)[1] and a CTM,[2] all of which must have application dates earlier than that of the trade mark applied for (taking into account priorities claimed, where appropriate);
(b)   a CTM having a valid claim to seniority[3] from an earlier registered trade mark or international trade mark (UK); and
(c)   a trade mark which, at the date of application (or priority claimed) was entitled to protection under the Paris Convention or the WTO Agreement as a well-known trade mark.[4]

1 A trade mark entitled to protection in the UK under the Madrid Protocol – see s 53.
2 As defined in s 51.
3 Under arts 34 and 35 of the CTM Regulation.
4 See s 56. See further **6.72–6.73** below. It is clear from s 56(1) that the mark must be shown to be 'well-known' in the UK. The reference to the WTO agreement has been added by The Patents and Trade Marks (World Trade Organisation) Regulations 1999 (SI 1999/1899) reg 13(1).

5 See ITMA Information 2/99. The change took effect on 1 July 1999.

6.4   Also included, under s 6(2), are trade marks which have been applied for and which, if registered, would be earlier trade marks under sub-s (1)(a) or (b), but subject to their being registered. The Rules are silent as to the procedure to be adopted where a relative ground of objection is based on an earlier application. In such cases the application under objection may be suspended until the earlier application is finally granted (if it is), after which the refusal could be confirmed. A recent notice of 'practice change' of the registry has confirmed that this will be the normal case where the objection based on an earlier pending application is the only objection. But if it is not, the other objections need to be met by the applicant before the registrar will suspend the application. Under sub-s (3), where an earlier trade mark under sub-s (1)(a) or (b) has expired, it remains a possible basis for refusal for a year, unless the registrar is satisfied that there was no bona fide use of the mark in the two years before the expiry. The actual words used: '... shall continue to be taken into account ... for a period of one year ...' suggest that the ground then goes, even if the application was made within the one year period.

1 See ITMA Information 2/99. The change took effect on 1 July 1999.

6.5 It is clear from these provisions that there can be no objection, under s 5(1)–(3), on the basis of an application having the same filing or priority date, and the registry[1] has confirmed this. The TMA 1994 contains no provision for cross-citation or for determining conflicts on the basis of priority of use.[2] In such cases applicants will be notified of the potential conflict and their attention drawn to the caveat procedure. The Manual indicates that they will also be informed that the registrar does not intend to take any further action, and that the parties must determine any conflict through opposition proceedings.

1 Work Manual, ch 6, para 11.10.
2 As could be done under the TMA 1938, s 12(3). See now the Work Manual at the reference cited above, n1.

6.6 The TMA 1994 has significantly changed the position regarding the relevance of priority of use to conflicting pending applications. Under the TMA 1938 Act, when there were two conflicting applications pending at the same time, s 12(3) contained special provisions for dealing with them, and the 'vested rights' provision of s 7 made clear the superior position of the prior user. In practice the party which could establish continuous prior use over the other would succeed. Under the TMA 1994 the position of the prior user is very much weaker. Where there is a pending application (or registration) of an earlier date, it is not enough for him simply to prove use of his mark continuously from a date before the earlier applicant's use commenced. 'Honest concurrent use' may enable him to overcome a citation by the registrar[1] and, as will be seen below, may have some relevance in cases in which an application is opposed under s 5(3) or (4). Otherwise, the applicant must make good his case in opposition proceedings (or in proceedings for a declaration of invalidity where the earlier mark is registered) on the basis of a valid claim in passing off, or perhaps copyright infringement in some cases, under s 5(4) of the Act.[2] The position is summarised in the Work Manual.[3]

1 Under the TMA 1994 s 7 – see paras **6.80–6.83** below.
2 See paras **6.74–6.79** below.
3 Chapter 6, para 11.11.

2 The grounds

6.7 It should be noted that the grounds for refusal based on earlier trade marks, set out in s 5(1)–(3), are reflected in the definition of infringement in s 10(1)–(3). Thus, where registration is refused on the ground of conflict with an earlier registered trade mark, or an international trade mark (UK), there will also be infringement. That was not always the case under the TMA 1938. Accordingly decided cases under the infringement provisions should be referred to for the purposes of construing s 5(1)–(3), and vice versa. There are three different situations in which registration must be refused, unless consent is given by the proprietor of the earlier trade mark. These need to be considered in some detail.

Identical marks and identical goods or services

6.8   Section 5(1) applies where the trade mark applied for is identical to the earlier mark and the goods or services are identical to those for which the earlier mark is protected. If the specifications are not identical, the objection will apply to the items which are the same. In these cases there is no need for any likelihood of confusion. In the absence of consent registration must be refused.

Identity of marks

6.9   A question which will arise quite frequently is, what is an 'identical' mark? It seems clear that only small differences will prevent the marks from being treated as identical. For example the singular and plural forms of a noun are not identical; neither are, probably, two words joined by a hyphen and the same words without a hyphen.[1] A less straightforward situation, perhaps, is the case of the same word in different forms of lettering. In such a case, are the two marks only similar, or are they to be regarded as identical for the purposes of s 5(1)? Under the definition of infringement in the TMA 1938,[2] registration of a word in block capitals was considered to cover use in any form of lettering, on the basis that the law required assessment of the likelihood of confusion on the assumption that the cited registered mark might be used in any normal and fair manner, and the same approach was adopted when comparing marks in opposition and rectification proceedings.[3] For the purposes of the corresponding provisions in s 10 of the TMA 1994 it would seem that two marks in different lettering should not be regarded as identical.[4] The Trade Marks Rules 1996 have been amended by the Trade Marks (Amendment) Rules 1998,[5] which introduces a new r 5, para (4) of which provides:

> 'An application to register a trade mark which is a word shall be treated as an application to register that word in the graphical form shown in the application, unless the applicant includes a statement that the application is for registration of the word without regard to its graphical form.'

It is not clear whether this provision has any real effect in applying s 5, although it serves to emphasise that, in the case of marks already on the register, in the absence of a statement such as is required by r 5(4), any form of a word which is not in the graphical form of the word shown on the application form should not be treated as identical to the registered mark. As for new applications, it can hardly be the case that the mere making of the statement on the application form can make two signs identical if they are not, and the Act does not allow 'claims' to a variety of forms of a sign, especially an unlimited variety. Be that as it may, the matter will normally be academic for practical purposes, because of the obvious likelihood of confusion where the form of the lettering is the only difference. The importance of considering whether two marks, or in infringement proceedings a mark and a sign, are or are not identical is that where they are not, or may not be, it is necessary to give some thought to the question of obtaining evidence as to likelihood of confusion. It may also be said that there could be some advantage in registering word marks as a series of marks, in block letters and in other graphic forms.

1 See *Origins Natural Resources Inc v Origin Clothing Ltd* [1995] FSR 280 and *Gromax Plasticulture Ltd v Don & Low Nonwovens Ltd* [1999] RPC 367 Lindsay J.
2 Section 4(1).

3 See eg *Re Smith Hayden & Co Application* (1948) 63 RPC 97 and *Re Morny Ltd's Trade Marks* (1951) 65 RPC 131.
4 However in a Scottish case, *Bravado Merchandising Services Ltd v Mainstream Publishing (Edinburgh) Ltd* [1996] FSR 205 (Outer House, Lord McCluskey) the court appears to have decided otherwise.
5 SI 1998/925, which came into force on 27 April 1998.

6.10   The question of colour raises a different problem. The TMA 1938[1] provided for limitations as to colour, and further provided that a mark registered without limitation of colour was to be deemed to be registered for all colours. The TMA 1994 contains no such provision. It would therefore appear that a mark registered in black and white is to be regarded not as identical to the same mark registered in specific colours, but only as being similar. The registry practice, regarding the registration of marks in colour, has undergone some change since the TMA 1994 came into force. The 1994 Rules contained no specific requirements for the application form. But following the coming into force of the Trade Marks (Amendment) Rules 1998,[2] the new r 5(3) provides:

> 'Where colour is claimed as an element of the trade mark, it shall not be treated as such unless the application contains a statement to that effect and specifies the colour.'

The effect of this provision is not entirely clear. If there is no statement that colour is claimed as an element of the mark, but the representation is in a colour or several colours, it can hardly be that colour should be ignored. It would seem wrong that, if the colour is not specified, the mark should be treated as if it had been registered in all colours. Because there is no provision in the TMA 1994 corresponding to s 16 of the TMA 1938, it must be doubtful whether the new rule 5(3) can have the effect of re-introducing it into the legislation. In practice, where the difference between the applicant's sign and the earlier trade mark is only in respect of colour, this should not raise serious difficulties, because the registrar or the court must continue to assess the likelihood of confusion on the basis of any 'normal and fair manner of use' of the earlier mark. Thus, normal and fair use of a mark, registered in black and white, should include use in other colours, and presumably the same should be the case where the representation is in colour but there is no statement that colour is claimed as an element. Nevertheless there may be something to be said, in some cases, for registering a series of marks in black and white and other colours, or combinations of colours, which may be of interest to the applicant.

1 Section. 16.
2 See para **6.9**, n 5 above.

6.11   Related to the issue of colours in registered marks is the question of the effect of limitations in respect of colour, which may be voluntarily accepted in accordance with s 13 of the TMA 1994 . Quite clearly, where there is an express limitation, the mark in different colours cannot be regarded as identical. The effect of colour limitations is further discussed under infringement.[1]

1 Chapter 12.

6.12   Another situation, which is likely to arise quite often, is where the mark applied for includes the earlier registered mark but with added matter. The added matter may be a device, or a word or words. The question has arisen in an infringement action, in the case of *British Sugar plc v James Robertson and Sons Ltd,*[1] in which the registered mark was the word 'treat' and the allegedly infringing product was called Robertson's *toffee treat.* Jacob J held that this amounted to use of a sign identical to the registered mark, because the word 'treat' was there for all to see. On the particular facts of the case, this seems correct, because the word 'treat' was used in different lettering from the word 'toffee'. However this may not necessarily be the right approach where the word that is a registered mark is used as part of a term or phrase comprising two or more words. There is something to be said for the view that where the allegedly conflicting mark combines a registered mark with another word, or other words, so as to make a term or phrase which conveys its own idea, there is no 'identity' with the registered mark. This was the approach of a Hearing Officer at the registry, in a case in which the proprietor of the trade mark 'joy', registered in Class 3 for perfume, was unsuccessful in opposing an application to register 'comfort & joy' in Class 3. It was held that the mark applied for was more than a mere collocation of two words, being a phrase in its own right.[2] However if the additional material is descriptive or otherwise non-distinctive, a likelihood of confusion may readily be found under s 5(2).[3] Also, merely incorporating a registered mark in a device should not avoid a finding of identity. This follows from the general principle that 'added matter' is not taken into account when comparing two marks for the purpose of determining whether there is infringement.

1   [1996] RPC 281 (Jacob J).
2   25 July 1997, noted in CIPA Journal, September 1997, p 710.
3   See for example the registry decision in *Teint Vitalite Trade Mark Application,* 10 December 1998, noted in New Law Digest, 699021202; an application for 'Teint Vitalite' was refused on the basis of a prior registration of 'vitalite' in the same Class. Similarly, in *Bell Atlantic Corpn v Bell Atlantic Communications plc* (Deputy Judge Hazel Williamson QC)(21 December 1998); unreported, but noted in CIPA Journal, February 1999, p 147, it was held that use of 'Bell Atlantic' involved use of an identical mark to the registered mark 'BELL', because the added word did not distinguish the defendant's sign from that of the plaintiff.

Identity of goods or services

6.13   The question whether there is any identity between the goods or services for which registration is sought, and those covered by the earlier mark, should not give rise to many difficulties. The point has however been raised in a few cases. For example, in *Avnet Inc v Isoact Ltd*[1] the plaintiff's mark was 'Avnet', registered, inter alia, for 'advertising and promotional services', included in Class 35. The defendant had used the same mark for Internet services, particularly for the aviation industry; these services included a facility to allow its customers to advertise on the customers' own web pages. In so doing, the defendant had merely provided spaces where the customers could display their own advertisements. In determining whether these services fell within the specification of the plaintiff's registration, Jacob J said that in his view, specifications for services should be considered carefully and they should not be given a wide construction covering a wide range of activities. They should, he said, be confined to the substance, as it were, the core of the possible meanings attributable to the rather general phrase. Accordingly the words 'advertising and promotional services' required one to look at the essence of what the defendant is doing. The judge concluded that the defendant was not, in substance, providing advertising and promotional services. He also thought, after considering views expressed by the registry, that the defendant's services did not fall within Class 35. Thus there was no identity of services.

1 [1998] FSR 16.

No identity of marks and goods or services, but goods or services identical or similar and marks identical or similar

6.14 Section 5(2) covers cases where there is no identity of both the marks and of the goods or services, but there is similarity, if not identity, of goods or services. Here the trade marks may be the same and the goods or services similar, but not identical, to those for which the earlier trade mark is protected; or the trade marks may be similar and the goods or services identical or only similar, to those for which the earlier trade mark is protected. The word 'protected' is used in sub-s (2), as also in sub-s (1) to cover the case of a well-known trade mark, which is not registered in the UK. Under sub-s (2), refusal can only be justified where 'there exists a likelihood of confusion in the part of the public which includes the likelihood of association with the earlier trade mark'.

6.15 Several points arise in relation to the application of sub-s (2). First, when are marks similar? And when is there similarity in respect of goods or services? Are these matters to be considered separately, or is it the case that the likelihood of confusion is to be determined in the light of all the relevant factors, which include the identity or similarity of the marks and the identity or similarity of the goods or services? Finally, what kind of confusion must be likely?

Similarity of marks

6.16 Under the TMA 1938, if the mark applied for was identical or confusingly similar to the earlier trade mark and there was the required overlap of goods or services,[1] then registration would be refused.[2] There is no guidance in the TMA 1994 as to when marks are similar, nor as to when goods or services are to be regarded as 'similar'. Under the 1938 Act, for the prohibition on registration to apply, it was necessary that the mark applied for so nearly resembled the earlier mark as to be likely to deceive or cause confusion. This question had to be determined in the light of all the circumstances of each case, including the degree of similarity between the marks, the nature of the marks and the nature of the goods or services. Generally speaking, the rules of comparison developed under the 1938 Act are still apt as guidance under the TMA 1994, and have been applied in a number of cases. For instance, in *Wagamama Ltd v City Centre Restaurants*,[3] Laddie J referred to a number of well-known decisions under the old law, apparently treating the principles laid down in them as still applicable under the TMA 1994 .[4] In some cases the registry has applied the well-known test laid down by Parker J in *Re Pianotist Co's Application*.[5] It will now be necessary to apply decisions of the courts, including the ECJ, on the interpretation of the relevant provisions of the Directive. However, subject to this, Parker J's test still offers useful general guidance in comparing marks:

> 'You must take the two words. You must judge of them, both by their look and by their sound. You must consider the goods to which they are to be applied. You must consider the nature and kind of customer who would be likely to buy those goods. In fact, you must consider all the surrounding circumstances; and you must further consider what is likely to happen if each of those trade marks is used in a normal way as a

trade mark for the goods of the respective owners of the marks. If, considering all those circumstances, you come to the conclusion that there will be a confusion – that is to say, not necessarily that one man will be injured and the other will gain illicit benefit, but that there will be a confusion in the mind of the public which will lead to confusion in the goods, then you may refuse the registration, or rather you must refuse the registration in that case.'

1 Ie goods or services the same or of the same description, or goods and services 'associated' – see the TMA 1938 Act (as amended), s 12.
2 Unless the applicant could rely upon s 12(2), on the basis of honest concurrent use or other special circumstances.
3 [1995] FSR 713.
4 Eg the 'imperfect recollection' test of Luxmoore LJ in *Aristoc Ltd v Rysta Ltd* (1945) 60 RPC 87 at 108; approved by the House of Lords (1945) 62 RPC 65 and the 'essential feature' principle applied by the Privy Council in *De Cordova v Vick Chemical Co* (1951) 68 RPC 103 and by Lloyd-Jacob J in *Taw Manufacturing Co Ltd v Notek Engineering Co Ltd* (1951) 68 RPC 271. A recent example of the application of these principles is the registry decision in *Re Anthony O'Gorman's Trade Mark Application.*
5 (1906) 23 RPC 774 at 777. This has also been held to provide a proper approach for comparing device marks: see *Celine SA's Trade Mark* [1985] RPC 381 (Falconer J).

6.17   A few examples of decisions under the TMA 1994 will illustrate the general approach adopted in comparing marks for the purposes of s 5(2).

— 'BLUE ZONE'/'BLUONE', for goods in Class 25, held similar;
— 'CLAVUMIX'/'CLAVAMOX', for pharmaceutical preparations, held similar;[1]
— 'VARIA'/'VARTA' held to be similar;
— 'MANU'/'MANI', held to be similar;
— 'HYPERSORB'/'HYDROSORB' held to be similar;[2]
— 'ORIENTAL PEARL'/'PEARL',[3] for soaps, held in proceedings for a declaration of invalidity to be similar;
— 'DICOFLAM'/'DICOFLEX'[4] both for pharmaceutical preparations, held similar;
— 'TATERBABIES'/'TATERTOTS', for preserved, dried, frozen and cooked potatoes, held similar;
— 'RASTAPLAST'/'ELASTOPLAST', for medical and surgical plasters, held similar;
— 'CIDER JACK'/'SCRUMPY JACK', both for cider, held similar in view of the fact that 'scrumpy' and 'cider' have the same meanings;[5]
— 'Blackbaud'/'Carbon Blackboard',[6] an application to register 'BLACKBAUD' in Classes 9,16 and 41 covering, inter alia, software, paper and education services, was rejected under s 5(2), as well as under s 3(1), because of a registration of 'CARBON BLACKBOARD' for technical bulletins relating to carbon black;
— 'MASTERS'/'CODEMASTERS',[7] an application to register a mark comprising 'Master's and a device of a brush stroke, in Class 9 for a wide range of electronic goods and in Class 28 for electronic toys, was successfully opposed by the proprietors of two marks comprising 'CODEMASTERS' and a stylised brush stroke device indicating a letter M, in Classes 9 and 28. Although the two words were not considered similar, the brush stroke was the dominant feature of the mark applied for;
— 'FOUNTAIN'/'FONT FOUNTAIN',[8] the mark 'FOUNTAIN' and device, sought to be registered in Class 9, was held to be similar to 'FONT' registered in the same Class, notwithstanding that the earlier registration was subject to disclaimers in respect of both 'FONT' and 'FOUNTAIN';
— 'RUN/WALK FOR LIFE'; 'WORKING FOR LIFE',[9] an application to register

'RUN/WALK FOR LIFE', with a picture of a runner in place of the 'I', for recreation and fitness services, was successfully opposed by the proprietors of a registration of 'WORKING FOR LIFE', registered in Class 41 for health club services and in Class 42 for medical health and fitness services, which enjoyed some notoriety through extensive use;

— 'ANUCCI'/'YANUCCI',[10] an application to register a mark comprising the letter 'A' in a lozenge, with the word 'YANUCCI' below, in Class 3 for fragrances, perfumery, cosmetics and soaps, was refused on the basis of registrations of 'YANUCCI', in Class 3 and 21;

— Kangaroo devices[11] An application to register the word 'Classic' with a device of a silhouetted kangaroo, within an ellipse, for football jerseys and shirts, etc, was successfully opposed by the proprietor of the mark 'KangaROOS' with a device of a silhouetted kangaroo, registered in Class 25. It was held that the word 'Classic' contributed little and that the essential and dominant feature of both marks was the silhouetted kangaroo;

— 'SPEEDMASTER'/'WICKES MASTER' and 'MASTER'[12] The application and the opponent's registrations covered, inter alia, paints. It was held that the mark applied for was not similar to 'WICKES MASTER', but was similar to 'MASTER';

— 'FRUIT CAKE'/'FRIUT', 'FRUIT BRAND' and 'FRUIT OF THE LOOM', for inter alia outer clothing, held similar;

— 'WATER KING'/'SK   ALE KING', for water treatment apparatus, held not similar, but 'WATER KING', with a device if a fallen water drop resembling a crown, held similar to 'SKALE KING' with a crown device, registered in the opponent's name;

'BODYLISS/'BABYLISS' for non-medicated toilet preparations, held similar;[13] Device of two 'E's back-to-back with Elizabeth Emanuel/Device of two 'E's back-to-back, for jewellery and watches in Class 14, held similar because of strong conceptual link of the double 'E' devices, being essential features of both marks;

— 'HURRY CURRY'/'HURRY ME A CURRY' and elephant device for curry powder and Indian meals respectively, held similar;

— 'ORADENT'/'ORAL-B' for goods in Class 3, held not similar;[14]

— 'ENER-CAP'/'ENERING' and 'ENERSEAL', for seals in Class 17, held on appeal not to be similar;[15]

— 'LAURA'/'LAURA ASHLEY',[16] application to register 'LAURA' for paints, varnishes and lacquers, refused by the Registry on basis of a registration of 'LAURA ASHLEY' for identical goods;

— 'SYNT'/'SYNTEX' and 'SYNTEL'; both for pharmaceutical preparations, held similar; — 'PASSION ATTACK'/'PASSIONATA', both for aerated water, held dissimilar;

— 'JUMELLE'/'JONELLE', both for toiletries, held similar;

— 'LEATHER-WOOD'/'LEATHER', for soap, held similar;

— 'SOLERASE'/'TOLERASE' for pharmaceutical preparations, held similar;

— 'JACK & DANNY'S ROCK CAFE' (and device)/'HARD ROCK CAFE', both for restaurant services, held similar;

— 'ISENBECK'/'BECK'S', both for beer, held not similar.[17]

---

1 Decisions of registry, noted in CIPA Journal, March 1997, at 217.
2 Registry decisions, noted in CIPA Journal, June 1997, at 449.
3 Registry, 27 May 1997, noted in CIPA Journal, July 1997, at 538.
4 Registry, 14 October 1997, noted in CIPA Journal, December 1997, at 934.
5 Registry decisions in November 1997, all noted in CIPA Journal, February 1998, at 125–126.
6 Registry, 19 December 1997, noted in CIPA Journal, March 1998, at 210.

7 Registry, 30 December 1997, noted in CIPA Journal, March 1998, at 211.

8 12 December 1998; The appointed person (Geoffrey Hobbs QC), on appeal from the registrar's Hearing Officer. Noted in CIPA Journal, February 1999, at 148.

9 Registry, 13 January 1998; noted in CIPA Journal, May 1998, at 377.

10 Registry, 10 February 1998, noted in CIPA Journal, June 1998, at 469.

11 Registry, 2 February 1998, noted in CIPA Journal, June 1998, at 469.

12 Registry, 9 March 1998, noted in CIPA Journal, June 1998, at 470.

13 Decisions of registry in March/April 1998, noted in CIPA Journal, September 1998, at 726–728.

14 Decisions of registry, June 1998, noted in CIPA Journal, October 1998, at 807–9.

15 [1999] RPC 362, The appointed person (Simon Thorley QC), reversing the registry decision.

16 4 November 1998, New Law Digest, 699010103.

17 These decisions of the registry are all noted in CIPA Journal, December 1998, at 979–980.

6.18 Clearly the matter will continue to depend upon all the circumstances of each case. As appears below, the suggestion that the provision of the Directive, on which s 5(2) is based, is derived from Benelux law, has been questioned. Nevertheless it is of interest to quote some observations of the Benelux Court of Justice in one leading case,[1] which has been cited as following the Benelux concept of 'association' discussed further below, although on the face of them they do not seem to suggest an approach so very different from that adopted in some decisions under the TMA 1938:[2]

> 'There is similarity between a mark and a sign when, taking into account the particular circumstances of the case, such as the distinctive power of the mark, the mark and the sign, each looked at as a whole and in correlation, show such a resemblance phonetically, visually or conceptually that by this resemblance alone, associations between the sign and the mark are evoked.'

1 Decision of 20 May 1983, case A 82/5, Nederlandse Jurisprudentie 1984, 72 *Henri Julien BV v Norbert Verschuere.*

2 As an example of this approach reference may also be made to a decision of the Dutch Supreme Court, in which it was decided, applying the concept of likelihood of association, that anti-monopoly (used for a game) was an infringement of a registration of monopoly, because of the simple fact that the public when seeing or hearing anti-monopoly in connection with a game would think of monopoly. See decision of 24 June 1977, Nederlandse Jurisprudentie 1978, 83, *Edor Handelsonderneming B.v General Mills Fun Group.* However it appears that the court in fact found that there was a significant likelihood of confusion. See the observations of Advocate-General Jacobs in *Sabel BV v Puma AG* [1998] RPC 199 at 212.

6.19 Although the old tests are still being used, nevertheless, as already indicated above, it is necessary now to consider the application of s 5(2) in the light in particular of decisions of the ECJ, which are concerned not just with the issue of similarity between marks, but with the overall question of likelihood of confusion.

Similarity between goods and services

6.20 When the TMA 1994 came into effect, the registry's initial approach was to say that the question of similarity of goods and services should be determined in the same way as the question, under the old law, whether the goods or services were 'of the same description' as any of those covered by the earlier trade mark, unless or until the courts directed otherwise. Reference was made to the decision of Romer J in *Re Jellinek's Application,*[1] which was generally relied upon as being the correct approach, and to *Floradix.*[2] So far as goods are concerned, the matters to be considered were:

(1) the nature and composition of the goods;
(2) the purposes for which the goods are used;
(3) the channels of trade for the goods.

The test for goods was adapted for services, as follows:

(1) the nature of the services;
(2) the purpose of the services;
(3) the users of the services;
(4) the normal business relationships.

1 (1946) 63 RPC 59.
2 [1974] RPC 583.

6.21 Even applying these tests could never have provided a complete answer to the question of similarity between goods or services. Although goods or services, which were goods or services 'of the same description' for the purposes of the TMA 1938, may well be properly regarded in many instances as 'similar' for the purposes of the TMA 1994 , the concept of similarity under s 5(2) is not necessarily the same. Moreover the tests set out above take no account of the possibility of similarity between goods and services, which was introduced into the TMA 1938 as 'association' between goods and services.[1] There is a statement in 'the Annex'[2] to the effect that for the purpose of art 4(1)(b) of the Directive (referred to above) and art 5(1)(b) (corresponding to s 10(2) of the TMA 1994), goods may be considered to be similar to services in appropriate circumstances. That statement is probably not admissible material for interpreting any part of the Directive.[3] However it is clear from the wording of the provisions of the Directive and of s 5(2) itself that the possibility of similarity between goods and services is contemplated, and this should be regarded as being the effect of the words used.

1 Defined in the TMA 1938 s 68(2A) as amended.
2 Paragraph 5(a).
3 See generally the *Wagamama* decision, para **6.16**, n 3 above.

6.22 The question of similarity of goods arose in infringement proceedings, in *British Sugar plc v James Robertson & Sons Ltd.*[1] Jacob J adopted a fairly cautious approach because of the broader protection conferred on registered trade marks by the TMA 1994 as compared with the TMA 1938. He said that the term 'similar goods' was the same sort of phrase as 'goods of the same description', and thought that the court must have in mind similar considerations to those arising under the 1938 Act in relation to 'goods of the same description'. Accordingly Jacob J put forward the following considerations:

(a) The respective uses of the respective goods or services;
(b) The respective users of the respective goods or services;
(c) The physical nature of the goods or acts of service;
(d) The respective trade channels through which the goods or services reach the market;
(e) In the case of self-serve consumer items, where in practice they are respectively found or likely to be found in supermarkets and in particular whether they are, or are likely to be, found on the same or different shelves;
(f) The extent to which the respective goods or services are competitive. This inquiry may take into account how those in trade classify goods, for instance

whether market research companies, who of course act for industry, put the goods or services in the same or different sectors.

1 Paragraph **6.12**, n 1 above.

6.23 These seem to be helpful practical general guidelines which, as Jacob J said, seek to take account of present day marketing methods. He added that he saw no reason in principle why, in some cases, goods should not be similar to services, giving the case of a repair service and the goods repaired as a suggested instance, thus confirming the view expressed above. With this in mind perhaps a seventh consideration might, it is suggested, be added:

(g)   Whether there is, in trade, any relationship or nexus between goods and services claimed to be similar.

On this basis, for example, computer software and computer software writing services could be regarded as similar, and food products such as beefburgers might be similar to restaurant services. The test is thus similar to that for 'associated' goods and services under the amended the TMA1938.[1]

1 Section 68(2A).

6.24 There have been several decisions under the TMA 1994 , on the issue of similarity between goods and services, which can be summarised here.

— 'ABRA'[1] The application was for registration of the mark in Classes 9, 37 and 42, for computer hardware and software, repair of computer hardware and IT consultancy services, respectively. The opponent's mark, 'DAS ABRA', to which, perhaps a little surprisingly, 'ABRA' was held not to be similar, was registered for industrial design services and, inter alia, designing trade marks. It was held that the applicant's services were not similar to these;
— 'MAXAM',[2] the application to register this mark in Classes 6, 19 and 37, in relation, inter alia, to doors, windows and security fixings and related services, was successfully opposed by the proprietor of the same mark, registered for 'adhesive-backed films of plastic material for window repairs and the like purposes'. The Hearing Officer held that the application covered goods and services which were similar to those covered by the prior mark, on the basis that the uses and the end users were likely to be the same;
— 'BALMORAL',[3] the application to register the mark for wines was successfully opposed by the proprietors of the same mark, registered for whisky in Class 31, and for hotel and bar services, etc., in Class 42. It was held that there was similarity between the wines and both the goods and services of the earlier marks, even they might not be directly in competition, because the uses, users, physical nature, and trade channels were the same;
— 'ANUCCI',[4] in the case of the objection to the application, to register the mark for fragrances, perfumery, cosmetics and soaps, based on the registration of yanucci in Class 21 for cosmetic utensils, perfume sprayers, etc, it was held that the goods were similar, although 'at the margin of similarity';
— 'ESPIRIT',[5] the application to register the mark for motor land vehicles and parts/fittings was unsuccessfully opposed by the proprietor of the mark 'ESPRIT' (to which it was held to be similar), registered for bicycles and parts/fittings. It was held that the goods were not similar, because they do not compete and do not reach the market through the same trade channels;

— 'BELL',[6] in this case, on an application for summary judgment, the deputy judge held that there was a triable issue as to whether telecommunications equipment and computer equipment were similar goods.

1 Registry, 11 April 1997, noted in CIPA Journal, June 1997, at 449.
2 Registry, 13 November 1997, noted in CIPA Journal, at 126.
3 Registry, 22 January 1998, noted in CIPA Journal, May 1998, at 377.
4 Paragraph **6.17**, n 10 above.
5 Registry, 2 July 1998, noted in CIPA Journal, October 1998, at p 809
6 Paragraph **6.12**, n 3 above.

6.25 Before leaving the subject of similarity, reference should be made to two decisions of the High Court, which merit further examination. The first of these is *Baywatch Production Co Inc v Home Video Channel*,[1] which is also considered below in connection with s 5(3) of the TMA 1994. The plaintiff's registered trade mark was 'Baywatch', which was the subject of a number of registrations, including one in Class 9 for, inter alia, video tapes and video discs, all featuring music, action-adventure, comedy, animation, sports or exercise. The defendant produced an adult entertainment television channel. The plaintiff sought an interlocutory injunction, and relied upon s 10(2) of the TMA 1994, alternatively on s 10(3). The deputy judge found that there was no arguable case of infringement. As regards s 10(2) he held that the defendant's services were not similar to the goods for which the plaintiff's mark was registered. On an interlocutory application this seems surprising. It is submitted that there was an arguable case on this issue, on the basis of Jacob J's decision in *British Sugar*. The uses and users are likely to overlap and there is competition between pre-recorded video tapes and films broadcast by television. The other decision, in the case of *Sir Terence Conran v Mean Fiddler Holdings Ltd*[2] was on an application for summary judgment, in which it is not clear whether or not the court considered the question of similarity between the defendant's services and those covered by the registered mark. The plaintiff, a well-known designer and restauranteur, was the proprietor of the trade mark 'Zinc', registered for planning, design and interior of restaurants, cafés, cafeterias, bistros, wine bars, etc. The plaintiff planned to open restaurants called the 'Zinc Bar and Grill', in London and Glasgow, but neither had been opened at the time of the hearing. The defendant had opened a bar in Kilburn under the name 'Zincbar'. On the facia of the premises the symbol for the element zinc, 'Zn' appeared, as well as the name 'Zincbar'. The judge held that there had been infringement of the plaintiff's registration, but the judgment does not indicate the basis on which this conclusion was reached, and in particular does not refer expressly to either s 10(2) or (3) of the Act. On the facts stated in the judgement, it does not appear that there was any basis for a claim under s 10(3), and, plainly, neither 'Zincbar' nor 'Zn' was identical to the registered mark, although they were, as the judge concluded, similar; so there was no question of infringement under s 10(1). It may be that the reason why the judge did not consider this aspect in his judgment was that, it appeared, the defendant accepted that there had been infringement and was only disputing the scope of the monopoly claimed by the plaintiff. It is submitted that on the basis of Jacob J's decision in *British Sugar*, it would have at least been open to the defendant, particularly on an application for summary judgment, to argue with some force that wine bar services were not in fact similar to the planning and design services for which the plaintiff's mark was registered.

1 [1997] FSR 22 (Deputy High Court Judge Michael Crystal QC).
2 [1997] FSR 856 (Robert Walker J).

Should identity/similarity of marks, and of goods or services, be considered separately?

6.26 There is a difference between the wording of the TMA 1994 and the wording of the Directive. As already mentioned, s 5(2) provides that a trade mark 'shall not be registered if because:

(a) it is identical with an earlier mark and is to be registered for goods or services similar to those for which the earlier trade mark is protected, or

(b) it is similar to an earlier trade mark and is to be registered for goods or services identical with or similar to those for which the earlier trade mark is protected,

there exists a likelihood of confusion …'.

6.27 Article 4.1 of the Directive provides that a trade mark 'shall not be registered … —

(b) if because of its identity with, or similarity to, the earlier trade mark and the identity or similarity of the goods or services covered by the trade marks, there exists a likelihood of confusion …'

6.28 It appears from Hansard[1] that the form of wording ultimately adopted was used in the interest of better drafting or a greater elegance of language. Therefore it should be assumed that no change of meaning was intended. The question of the relationship between similarity and confusion arose in *British Sugar*.[2] On behalf of the plaintiff it was argued that the two were linked, but Jacob J rejected this approach. He said:

> 'British Sugar seek to elide the questions of confusion and similarity. Their skeleton argument contends that there is "use in relation to a product so similar to a dessert sauce that there exists a likelihood of confusion because the product may or will be used for identical purposes." I do not think it is legitimate to elide the question in this way. The sub-section does not merely ask "will there be confusion?"; it asks "is there similarity of goods?", if so, "is there a likelihood of confusion?" The point is important. For if one elides the two questions, then a "strong" mark would get protection for a greater range of goods than a "weak" mark. For instance "Kodak" for socks or bicycles might well cause confusion, yet these goods are plainly dissimilar from films or cameras. I think the question of similarity of goods is wholly independent of the particular mark the subject of registration or the defendant's sign.

> 'I think there is confirmation for this view in a recital to the Directive. It says:

>> "Whereas the protection afforded by the registered trade mark, the function of which in particular is to guarantee the trade mark as an indication of origin, is absolute in the case of identity between the mark and the sign and goods and services;

> (This is the precursor to Article 5(1)(a) – the basis of s 10(1) of the 1994 Act)

>> "whereas the protection applies also in case of similarity between the mark and the sign and the goods or services"

'This recital relates to the *protection* to be given. It is the precursor to Article 5(1)(b) and thus is the basis of s 10(2). The question of similarity is separated in the recital from the question of confusion. The recital goes on to deal with confusion later and in particular notes that it may depend upon the degree of similarity. But at that point it is not dealing with the scope of protection. So I think the recital makes it clear that questions of similarity are independent of a particular likelihood of confusion.

'It is true that the recital goes on to say:

> "whereas it is indispensable to give an interpretation of the concept of similarity in relation to the likelihood of confusion"

'I do not think it is here saying more than in judging the question of similarity one should bear in mind the fact that the purpose to be considered is trade mark purposes. It is not saying that goods are similar if there is confusion, no matter how dissimilar the goods may be. That is a matter for Article 5(2) (which is the basis of our s 10(3)).'

1 See Committee Stage, 13 January 1994 (15) and 18 January 1994 (25); Report Stage, 24 February 1994 (730/1 and 735).
2 Paragraph **6.12**, n 1 above.

6.29   It is clearly right that the mere existence of a likelihood of confusion does not mean that there is infringement under s 10(2) (or a ground for refusal under s 5(2)); that cannot be so unless the good or services are 'similar'. But whether it is correct to regard the questions of similarity and likelihood of confusion as independent is another matter. The learned judge's treatment of the recital to the Directive is not easy to follow. The parts which he quotes are all part of one paragraph of the recitals, which (after the quoted passages) continues:

> 'whereas the likelihood of confusion, the appreciation of which depends upon numerous elements and, in particular, on the recognition of the trade mark on the market, of the association which can be made with the used or registered sign, of the degree of similarity between the trade mark and the sign and between the goods or services identified, constitutes the specific condition for such protection; whereas the ways in which likelihood of confusion may be established, and in particular the onus of proof, are a matter for national and procedural rules which are not prejudiced by the Directive;'

6.30   While there can be no likelihood of confusion unless the mark or sign in question is at least 'similar' to some extent to the registered mark, and while for ss 10(2) or 5(2) to apply there must be at least some similarity between the goods or services, the question of a likelihood of confusion cannot be entirely separate, but must depend on the combination of the identity/similarity of the marks or signs, on the one hand, and of the goods or services on the other. That this is the intention of the Directive seems clear from the wording of arts 4(2) and 5(1), and confirmed by the recitals (which are concerned with both the grounds for refusal and the rights conferred by registration) when read as a whole. What the new provisions require is an appraisal of the likelihood of confusion of the public in all the circumstances of each case, which includes the identity or the degree of similarity of the marks and of the goods or services.

6.31   That this is indeed the correct approach has now been confirmed by two decisions of the ECJ, *Sabel BV v Puma AG*[1] and *Canon KK v Metro-Goldwyn-Mayer Inc.*[2] Before considering these cases in detail, some mention should be made of the background to the question of likelihood of confusion and to the decision in *Wagamama*[3] on the meaning of the term and the effect of the reference to 'likelihood of association'.

1 [1998] RPC 199.
2 [1999] RPC 117.
3 See para **6.16**, n 3 above.

The meaning of 'likelihood of confusion'

6.32   As mentioned above, the ground of objection under s 5(2), and the definition of infringement under s 10(2), require the existence of 'a likelihood of confusion on the part of the public, which includes the likelihood of association with the trade mark'. The reference to 'likelihood of association' has been the subject of a considerable amount of discussion. According to 'the Annex'[1] this is a concept which in particular has been developed by Benelux case-law. In fact, that could only be a reference to infringement cases, there having been no provision for refusal or opposition on relative grounds under the Benelux law. Be that as it may, there is considerable dispute as to whether it was intended to introduce any concept of Benelux law into the Directive, and reference to such law has been rejected in the *Wagamama* case.[3] That case, which was the first reported decision on the particular point,[4] merits further detailed consideration.

1 Paragraph 5(b); cf para 5 of 'the Annex' to the Regulation.
2 See para **6.16**, n 3 above.
3 The decision was on the issue of infringement under the TMA 1994, s 10(2), which is essentially the same as s 5(2).

The Wagamama decision

6.33   The case was concerned with infringement (and also passing off), rather than objections to registration on relative grounds. However the decision is relevant to both since, as already mentioned, the words under consideration are the same in ss 10(2) as in s 5(2). Laddie J considered in some detail the question whether the kind of confusion required by the TMA 1938 has been extended by the provisions of the TMA 1994 . Although the result of the case did not depend on the distinction between 'origin confusion' and the broader 'non-origin association', said to be a concept of Benelux law and contended for by the plaintiff, the distinction may be crucial in other cases. As already mentioned above,[1] Laddie J declined to take the statement in the 'Annex' into consideration, and also rejected other submissions based on the proposition that it was a matter of common knowledge that the words referring to 'association' were inserted in the Directive for the purpose of introducing the Benelux concept, and in the interests of harmony and comity.

1 See para **1.19** above.

6.34   Having dealt thus with the attempt to introduce the Benelux concept of 'non-origin association', the learned judge concluded[1] that it was necessary to approach the Directive and the TMA 1994 from first principles. He said that the case law in which the previous definitions of infringement, in s 4(1) of the TMA 1938 Act and its predecessors, were considered, made clear that what counted was confusion as to the source of the goods or services bearing the offensive mark, ie whether such goods or services were likely to be derived from or connected with the proprietor of the registered mark. He referred to some of the cases which illustrated the principles applied by the courts in comparing marks, such as the doctrine of imperfect recollection and consideration of whether the 'idea' of the mark is similar, or whether an 'essential feature' of the registered mark has been taken.[2] The judge accepted that if, in accordance with these principles, the marks were too similar, usually infringement would be found, even if in the market place the infringer took steps to prevent confusion in fact occurring.[3] He also referred to a case of infringement by suggestion that the defendant's and the proprietor's goods were associated.[4] but pointed out that even in such cases the association had to be an association as to source or origin.

1 [1995] FSR at 728.
2 Paragraph **6.16**, n 3 above.
3 *Taw Manufacturing Co Ltd v Notek Ltd*, para **6.16**, n 4 above, provides an example. See also *Bale and Church Ltd v Sutton, Parsons and Sutton and Astrah Products* (1934) 51 RPC 129.
4 *Ravenhead Brick Co Ltd v Ruabon Brick and Terra Cotta Co Ltd* (1937) 54 RPC 341.

6.35 There was no dispute between the parties that such 'classic infringement', as he termed it, would also constitute infringement under the TMA 1994 . However the plaintiff argued that the Act, particularly s 10(2), covered confusion in a much broader sense, and that there would now be infringement if, on seeing the defendant's mark, the registered mark would be 'called to mind' by customers, even if there was no possibility of the customer being under any misapprehension as to the origin of the goods. For this purpose the plaintiff relied upon the reference to 'association' in s 10(2). This 'non-origin association', the learned judge said, was a new concept to those steeped in British trade mark law. The essence of the plaintiff's argument, as to what the judgment calls the 'domestic interpretation route', was that the words at the end of s 10(2), 'which includes the likelihood or association with the trade mark' must do more than merely repeat what was already covered by the earlier words referring to a likelihood of confusion on the part of the public. The judge rejected this argument. Referring to the legislative context of the TMA 1994 , he remarked:

> 'It would be wrong to apply rules of construction developed during a period when one philosophy of draftsmanship was prevalent to a statute drafted when an entirely different philosophy applied. In particular it is quite artificial for the court to pretend that each word of a modern statute which has been lifted more or less verbatim from an EC directive was chosen with the economy which was believed to have been applied to the drafting of British statutes of purely domestic origin. There is no basis upon which the court can assume that the original Directive was drafted so as to avoid tautology'.

6.36 The judge continued by saying that, viewed solely linguistically, s 10(2) pointed away from the plaintiff's construction. If, he said, the words 'likelihood of association with the trade mark' covered non-origin confusion, they covered 'classical infringement' also. However, the learned judge continued, if this were so, there would not be any point in including the reference in s 10(2) to 'likelihood of confusion', since it was comprehended within 'likelihood of association'. He then considered, and rejected, the European construction route[1] and concluded, after considering some of the ECJ decisions[2] emphasising the origin function of trade marks, and the preamble to the Directive itself, that the rights given by s 10(2) were limited to 'classic infringement'. He remarked that, if the broader scope were to be adopted, the Directive and the TMA 1994 would be creating a new type of monopoly 'not related to the proprietor's trade but in the trade mark itself'.

1 See paras **1.19–1.22** above.
2 *SA CNL-Sucal NV SA v HAG GF AG* [1990] ECR I-3711 ('HAG II') and *Deutsche Renault AG v Audi AG* [1993] ECR I-6227.

6.37 It may be open to question whether the Directive is so much less economic with words than British laws,[1] and no doubt the debate will continue as to what really was the intention in adding the references to 'likelihood of association'. The courts may perhaps, when considering other cases under the Directive, have to determine whether a more 'European' approach to interpretation might be appropriate. However the position regarding 'likelihood of confusion' has now been clarified by the decisions of the ECJ in *Sabel* and *Canon* mentioned above.[2] These decisions both concern, primarily, the interpretation of art 4(1)(b) of the Directive, to which s 5(2) corresponds, although they are also relevant to the interpretation of art 5(1)(b), on which s 10(2) is based.

1 A comparison with the words used in the definition of infringement in the TMA 1938, s 4(1) is instructive. See also the remarks of Sir Wilfrid Greene MR in *Bismag Ltd v Amblins (Chemists) Ltd* [1940] Ch 667; (1940) 57 RPC 209, at 232 line 36.
2 [1998] RPC 199 and [1999] RPC 117 respectively.

6.38 *Sabel* was a case of opposition to registration. Sabel applied to register a device mark comprising a bounding cheetah together with the name 'sabel', for inter alia leather and imitation leather goods and for clothing. Puma opposed the applications on their earlier registered mark, which was a device of a bounding puma. The question referred by the German Court to the ECJ was as follows:

'With reference to the interpretation of Article 4(1)(b) of [the Directive] is it sufficient for a finding that there is a likelihood of confusion between a sign composed of text and picture and a sign consisting merely of a picture, which is registered for identical and similar goods and is not especially well known to the public, that the two signs coincide as to their semantic content (in this case, a bounding feline)?'

6.39 The governments of the Benelux countries contended that there were three sets of circumstances in which a likelihood of association could arise, and that art 4(1)(b) applied in all three cases. The first was where the public confuses the sign and the mark in question ('likelihood of direct confusion') and the second was where the public makes a connection between the proprietors of the sign and those of the mark and confuses them ('likelihood of indirect confusion or association'). The third was where the public considers the sign to be similar to the mark and perception of the sign calls to mind the memory of the mark, although the two are not confused ('likelihood of association in the strict sense'). The UK government and the Commission contested the inclusion of the third case.

6.40 The ECJ rejected the Benelux approach, observing that it followed from the wording of art 4(1)(b) that the concept of association was not an alternative to that if likelihood of confusion, but served to define its scope, and that the terms of the provision itself excluded its application where there was no likelihood of confusion on the part of the public. As to the requirement of a likelihood of confusion, the court continued:

'In that respect, it is clear from the tenth recital in the preamble to the Directive that the appreciation of the likelihood of confusion "depends on numerous elements and, in particular, on the recognition of the trade mark on the market, of the association which can be made with the used or registered sign, of the degree of similarity between the trade mark and the sign and between the goods or services identified". The likelihood of confusion must therefore be appreciated globally, taking into account all factors relevant to the circumstances of the case.

'That global appreciation of the visual, aural or conceptual similarity of the marks in question, must be based on the overall impression given by the marks, bearing in mind, in particular, their distinctive and dominant components. The wording of Article 4(1)(b) of the Directive –" ... there exists a likelihood of confusion on the part of the public ..." – shows that the perception of marks in the mind of the average consumer of the type of goods or services in question plays a decisive role in the global appreciation of the likelihood of confusion. The average consumer normally perceives a mark as a whole and does not proceed to analyse its various details.

'In that perspective, the more distinctive the earlier mark, the greater will be the likelihood of confusion. It is therefore not impossible that the conceptual similarity resulting from the fact that two marks use images with analogous semantic content may give rise to a likelihood of confusion where the earlier mark has a particularly distinctive character, either *per se* or because of the reputation it enjoys with the public.

'However, in circumstances such as those in point in the main proceedings, where the earlier mark is not especially well known to the public and consists of an image with little imaginative content, the mere fact that the two marks are conceptually similar is not sufficient to give rise to a likelihood of confusion.'

The court accordingly concluded that the criterion of likelihood of confusion which includes the likelihood of association with the earlier mark contained in art 4(1)(b) is to be interpreted as meaning that the mere association that the public might make between two trade marks as a result of their analogous semantic content is not in itself a sufficient ground for concluding that there is a likelihood of confusion within the meaning of that provision.

6.41 The question, whether reputation should be taken into account should be taken into account in assessing similarity, which was not directly in point in *Sabel*, was further considered by the ECJ in *Canon*. This was another opposition case. MGM sought to register, in Germany, the trade mark 'Cannon' for 'films recorded on video cassettes (video film cassettes); production, distribution and projection of films for cinemas and television organisations'. The application was opposed by Canon, whose 'Canon' mark was registered in Germany for (inter alia) still motion picture cameras and projectors; television filming and recording devices, television re-transmission devices, television receiving and reproduction devices, including tape and disc devices for television recording and reproduction. The 'canon' mark had a reputation in Germany. The question referred to the ECJ was as follows:

'May account be taken, when assessing the similarity of the goods or services covered by the two marks, of the distinctive character, in particular the reputation, of the mark with earlier priority ... so that, in particular, likelihood of confusion within the meaning of Article 4(1)(b) of [the Directive] must be taken to exist even if the public attributes the goods to different places of origin?'

6.42   The form of the question was such as might suggest that the German court considered that reputation might have some bearing on the issue of similarity of goods or services, an idea which would seem surprising. However the Court of Justice treated the question as in substance raising the issue whether the reputation of the earlier mark was relevant in determining whether the similarity between the goods or services was sufficient for there to exist a likelihood of confusion.

6.43   The ECJ referred to its earlier decision in *Sabel*, that the likelihood of confusion, for the purposes of art 4(1)(b) must be appreciated globally, taking into account all factors relevant to the circumstances of the case. The judgment continued as follows:

> '17. A global assessment of the likelihood of confusion implies some interdependence between the relevant factors, and in particular a similarity between the trade marks and between these goods or services. Accordingly a lesser degree of similarity between these goods or services may be offset by a greater degree of similarity between the marks, and vice versa. The interdependence of these factors is expressly mentioned in the tenth recital of the preamble to the Directive, which states that it is indispensable to give an interpretation of the concept of similarity in relation to the likelihood of confusion, the appreciation of which depends, in particular, on the recognition of the trade mark on the market and the degree of similarity between the mark and the sign and between the goods or services identified.

> '18. Furthermore, according to the case-law of the Court, the more distinctive the earlier mark, the greater the risk of confusion (*sabel*, paragraph 24). Since protection of a trade mark depends, in accordance with Article 4(1)(b) of the Directive, on there being a likelihood of confusion, marks with a highly distinctive character, either *per se*, or because of the reputation they possess on the market, enjoy broader protection than marks with a less distinctive character.

> '19. It follows that, for the purposes of Article 4(1)(b) of the Directive, registration of a trade mark may have to be refused, despite a lesser degree of similarity between the goods or services covered, where the marks are very similar and the earlier mark, in particular its reputation, is highly distinctive.

> ...

> ...

> '22. It is, however, important to stress that, for the purposes of applying Article 4(1)(b), even where a mark is identical to another with a highly distinctive character, it is still necessary to adduce evidence of similarity between the goods or services covered. In contrast to Article 4(4)(a), which expressly refers to the situation in which the goods or services are not similar, Article 4(1)(b) provides that the likelihood of confusion presupposes that the goods or services covered are identical or similar.

> '23. In assessing the similarity of the goods or services concerned, as the French and United Kingdom Governments and the Commission have pointed out, all the relevant factors relating to those goods or services should be taken into account. Those factors include, inter alia, their nature, their end users and their method of use and whether they are in competition with each other or are complimentary.

> '24. In the light of the foregoing, the answer to be given to the first part of the question must be that, on a proper construction of Article 4(1)(b) of the Directive, the distinctive character of the earlier trade mark, and in particular its reputation, must be

taken into account when determining whether the similarity between the goods or services covered by the two trade marks is sufficient to give rise to the likelihood of confusion.'

6.44   On the second part of the question referred to the court, the judgment is equally clear. It was held that the risk that the public might believe that the goods or services in question came from the same undertaking or, as the case might be. from economically-linked undertakings, constitutes a likelihood of confusion within the meaning of art 4(1)(b). Accordingly, in order to demonstrate that there is no likelihood of confusion, it is not sufficient to show simply that there is no likelihood of the public being confused as to the place of production of the goods or services.

6.45   These two decisions have considerably clarified the approach to be adopted when considering cases, under ss 5(2) and 10(2) of the TMA 1994 , where the overriding issue is whether there is a likelihood of confusion. It is now necessary to examine some of the decisions of the courts and of the registry, to see how, so far, these are consistent with the principles which have been laid down by the ECJ. As *Wagamama,*[1] which seems consistent with the views of the ECJ, demonstrates, where the goods or services concerned are identical, the issue of likelihood of confusion depends essentially on the degree of similarity between the two marks. This is likely to remain the case, and the rules developed under the old law will continue to serve as guides in applying the provisions of the TMA 1994 .

1   Paragraph **6.16**, n 3 above.

6.46   The only reported decision of the Court of Appeal on the question of likelihood of confusion under the TMA 1994 is that of *European Ltd v Economist Newspapers Ltd,*[1] which concerned infringement under s 10(2) of the TMA 1994, but which is of course also relevant to s 5(2). The plaintiff's mark, registered for 'newspapers', was the masthead of The European newspaper, comprising the words 'The European' (the word 'the' being very much less prominent); below the 'o' of 'European' was a representation of a hemisphere and, on the top, a dove holding a copy of 'The European' newspaper in its beak; and there was a heavy black line below the words. The mark had been registered under the 1938 Act and, on the basis of evidence of distinctiveness, had been registered without any disclaimer in respect of the word 'European'. The defendant's mark was the masthead of a new newspaper published by the defendant, named 'European Voice', with a heavy black line below the words. The two mastheads are reproduced in the judgment of Rattee J.[2] Since the defendant's goods were identical to those for which the plaintiff's mark was registered, the principal issues[3] were whether the defendant's mark was similar to the plaintiff's registered mark and whether there existed a likelihood of confusion on the part of the public.

1   [1998] FSR 283. There is also a decision of the Court of Appeal, in the case of *Marks & Spencer plc v One in a Million Ltd* [1999] FSR 1, reported at first instance at [1998] FSR 265, which is concerned principally with s 10(3).
2   [1996] FSR 431 at 433, 434.
3   There was a defence raised by the defendant, under the TMA 1994, s 11(2) which is considered in ch 12 below.

6.47   At first instance, Rattee J's own comparison of the marks failed to satisfy him that they were similar, and the evidence did not persuade him to depart from his initial conclusion. He added that, if he was wrong, and the defendant's sign was to be regarded as similar to the plaintiff's mark because of the inclusion of the word 'European', he did not consider that the plaintiff had established any likelihood of resultant confusion on any significant scale on the part of the public. In the Court of Appeal, Millett LJ made these observations as to the general approach to be adopted:

> 'Although the judge cannot be criticised for the way in which he described the issues, it should be borne in mind that there is only one question to be decided in a case of the present kind: is there a likelihood of confusion of the public because of the similarity between the defendant's sign and the plaintiff's registered trade mark and the identity of the goods in relation to which they are used? Similarity is a matter of degree; and except in the case in which there is absolutely no similarity between the sign and mark (which is not this case) the question is whether the similarity is such as to be likely to cause confusion in the mind of the public. A degree of similarity is tolerable; the question is whether there is a confusing similarity.'

Millett LJ agreed with Rattee J in rejecting the plaintiff's submission that the word 'European' was the essential feature of the registered trade mark. He said:

> 'The judge rejected this submission, and in my judgment he was right to do so. He accepted, of course, that the word "European" is the most prominent feature of the plaintiff's mark, but he pointed out that it is not a made-up or invented word but an ordinary word in common use, capable of being used most naturally in a descriptive manner, and in the case of the defendant's newspaper used to describe its character and contents.

> 'In my judgment the plaintiff's contention that the word "European" forms the essential feature of its registered trade mark does not sit comfortably with its disclaimer of any monopoly of the word even as the title of a newspaper. If the plaintiff disclaims such a monopoly, it must be because it recognises that the word is not of itself distinctive of the trade origin of its newspaper. The function of a trade mark is to serve as an indication of the trade origin of the goods to which it is applied. I do not understand the concept of a trade mark which has as its essential feature a word or phrase which does not perform this function because it is not in itself distinctive of the origin of the goods.

> 'I accept, of course, that while the defendant's use of the word "European" in its masthead is descriptive rather than distinctive of the trade origin of its newspaper, the plaintiff's use of the word is different. It is not used descriptively but as a prominent part of its distinctive trade mark. But in my judgment any contention on behalf of the plaintiff that the word "European" forms an essential feature of its registered trade mark which distinguishes the origin of its newspaper would almost inevitably lead to the very monopoly which it disclaims, and the judge was rightly reluctant to accept this. Where descriptive words are included in a registered trade mark, the courts have always and rightly been exceedingly wary of granting a monopoly in their use.'

6.48 Millett LJ cited some passages from the decision of the ECJ in *Sabel*, which had just been given, including the observation that the more distinctive the earlier mark, the greater will be the likelihood of confusion, saying that the converse followed, that the more descriptive and the less distinctive the major feature of the mark, the less the likelihood of confusion. A good illustration of this approach can be found in an earlier French decision, *Laboratoire Garnier et Cie v Ste Copar*,[1] in which the use by the defendant of the term 'Ultra Doux', with its own trade mark, was held not to infringe two registrations of composite marks, containing the words 'Ultra Doux' as a prominent feature but with the name 'Garnier' also included.

1 [1998] ETMR 114 (Tribunal de Grande Instance de Paris).

6.49 Essentially, the Court of Appeal in *The European* followed the approach of the ECJ in *Sabel* and later in *Canon*. It may be wondered whether, on the basis of those decisions, the result might have been different if the plaintiff had adduced substantial evidence, of the kind which had been put before the registrar in order to overcome the initial requirement of a disclaimer in respect of 'European', demonstrating that the word had itself acquired a distinctive character as an indication of the trade origin of the plaintiff's newspaper. On this point, the later decision in the case of *United Biscuits (UK) Ltd v Asda Stores Ltd*[1] is of interest. One issue which the court had to consider was whether the defendant's use of a the word 'puffin' was an infringement of the plaintiff's registration of the trade mark 'Penguin'. As a result of the defendant's counterclaim for revocation of certain of the plaintiff's trade mark registrations, the plaintiff was not able to rely upon any registrations of devices of penguins. Although the judge had remarked, earlier in his judgment[2] that the word 'puffin' is not very different from 'penguin', he concluded[3] that there was no infringement. He said:

> 'As regards the word mark penguin I am not persuaded that its fair use is infringed by the use of the sign puffin, once surrounding added matter is disregarded, as it must be.'

If, as has now been established by the ECJ in *Sabel* and *Canon*, the reputation of the plaintiff's mark is relevant in considering the global question of likelihood of confusion, it would seem to be proper to consider the matter surrounding the use of the registered mark. On that basis, it might possibly have been concluded that there was a likelihood of confusion arising from the use of the mark 'Puffin', in a manner which was found to constitute passing off.

1 [1997] RPC 513 (Robert Walker J).
2 [1997] RPC at 526.
3 At 540.

6.50 There are several reported decisions of cases under ss 5(2) and 10(3) adopting the principles of the decisions of the ECJ, and also some under the corresponding provisions in the trade marks laws of other EU Member States. Even before those decisions, a similar approach is to be found in other Member States. One example is a decision of the German Bundespatentgericht,[1] upholding an opposition to an application to register 'Queen's Club' for mineral waters, because of an earlier registration of 'Queen's Garden' for non-alcoholic drinks.

1 *Queen's Club Trade Mark Application* [1997] ETMR 345.

6.51 A recent application of the *Sabel* case by the registry is the decision, in opposition proceedings, in *Re Zimmer Inc's Trade Mark Application*.[1] The applicant sought to register the mark 'Ecofix' for orthopaedic devices. The opposition was based on an earlier registration of 'Endofix' for materials and apparatus for ligament and joint fixation. Although the goods were found to be similar, it was held that because of the specialised nature of the goods and because the prefixes were different, both visually and aurally, the marks were not similar and there was no likelihood of confusion. Another decision of interest, where the marks had the same prefixes, is *Re Dollond & Aitchison Ltd's Trade Mark Application*,[2] in which an application to register 'Polaclip' for lenses and spectacles was unsuccessfully opposed by the proprietors of the mark 'Polaroid', registered for identical goods. The same general approach was adopted in a case involving letter marks, *Re CDX Trade Mark Application*,[3] where an application to register the mark 'CDX' for footwear was unsuccessfully opposed by the proprietors of the mark 'CD' for identical goods. It was held that the issue of conceptual similarity did not arise in relation to letter combinations which had no discernible meaning in relation to the goods. The mark 'CD' had some reputation, but a low level of inherent distinctiveness and the difference between the marks was such that there was no likelihood of confusion.

1 30 April 1998. New Law Digest 698081304.
2 16 July 1998. New Law Digest 698102002. See also *GTR Group's Application; Opposition by Jean Patou* [1999] ETMR – Jois & Jo allowed for goods in Classes 3, 9, 18 and 25; held, no likelihood of confusion with the opponent's mark 'Joy'.
3 21 October 1998. New Law Digest 699010104.

6.52   The ECJ has also considered the question of likelihood of confusion, in a case where the goods concerned were identical, on a reference from a German court, in *Lloyd Schuhfabrik Meyeer & Co GmbH v Klijsen Handel BV.*[1] This was an infringement action, in which the plaintiff's mark 'Lloyd' was registered for footwear, and the defendant's mark is 'Loint's', used for shoes and footwear. The plaintiff sought to rely upon the enhanced distinctive character of its mark, because of the lack of any descriptive element in the mark and on its high degree of recognition. Repeating the need[2] for the question to be considered globally, the Advocate-General had expressed the view that, in assessing the likelihood of confusion, between a mark and a sign used for identical goods, the national court must consider whether there is a genuine and properly substantiated likelihood of confusion for an average consumer of the particular type of goods in the Member State concerned. All the relevant factors must be assessed, including the degree of aural, visual or conceptual similarity between the mark and the sign and the distinctiveness which the mark has either *per se* or by virtue of the degree of recognition of the mark. The Advocate-General again emphasised that the concept of the likelihood of association is not an alternative to that of likelihood of confusion,[3] and said that the Directive does not lay down a threshold above which a mark automatically acquires, by virtue of its degree of recognition, a particular distinctive character and enjoys greater protection; the degree of recognition is just one factor to be taken into account in the overall assessment of the likelihood of confusion. Finally, he said that the fact that a mark has no descriptive elements may be a factor in assessing the distinctiveness of a mark but does not itself increase the likelihood of confusion. The decision of the court essentially follows the Advocate-General's opinion.

1 Advocate-General's Opinion delivered 29 October 1998 – [1999] ETMR 10. Judgment of the court, 22 June 1999, [1999] All ER (EC) 587.
2 Emphasised in the court's earlier decisions, mentioned above.
3 See the *Wagamama* case, at paras **6.33–6.36** above, and *Sabel*, at paras **6.38–6.40** above.

'Families' of marks

6.53   Under the old law, an opponent to the registration of a trade mark sometimes relied upon the fact that he had several trade marks which all contained a feature such as a prefix, which was also present in the mark applied for. Because of the wording of s 12 of the TAM 1938, which governed objections based upon earlier registered marks, it was held[1] that such an objection, sometimes called a 'series' objection or an objection based upon a 'family' of marks, could not be established under that provision, but depended upon use of the marks with the common feature. Therefore objections of this nature were dealt with under s 11 of the 1938 Act. It might have been thought that the position would be the same under the TMA 1994, so that such objections would arise, if at all, under s 5(3) or (4), considered below, rather than under s 5(1) or (2), although the registry's position on this point is not clear.[2] However in view of the approach which must now be adopted under s 5(2), as a result of the decisions of the ECJ in *Sabel* and *Canon*,[3] which may involve consideration of the reputation of an opponent's mark or marks, it possible that the position may have changed. It is possible now that the fact that an opponent owns several registrations with the common feature, and uses them all, will be regarded as one of the matters to be considered in the global assessment of the likelihood of confusion.

1 In *Re Beck, Koller & Co (England) Ltd's Application* (1947) 64 RPC 76.
2 See Work Manual, ch 6, para 11.4.
3 Paragraphs **6.38–6.45** above.

Marks identical or similar, but goods or services dissimilar

6.54 It is clear that for the purposes of objections under s 5(1) and (2), the cited mark need not have been used. The tribunal must, as under the old law, consider the matter on the basis of normal and fair use of the cited mark and the mark applied for. This has been confirmed, for example, in a registry decision in *React Trade Mark and Device*.[1] However, as seen above, in opposition proceedings use may assist an opponent.

1 [1999] RPC 529.

6.55 Under s 5(3), an application to register a trade mark will be refused if it is identical with or similar to the earlier mark, notwithstanding that the goods or services are not similar to those covered by the earlier mark. The sub-section is as follows:

'(3)   A trade mark which—

(a) is identical with or similar to an earlier trade mark, and
(b) is to be registered for goods or services which are not similar to those for which the earlier trade mark is protected,

shall not be registered if, or to the extent that, the earlier trade mark has a reputation in the United Kingdom (or, in the case of a Community trade mark, in the European Community) and the use of the later mark without due cause would take unfair advantage of, or be detrimental to, the distinctive character or the repute of the earlier trade mark'.

Because of the requirement that the earlier trade mark should have a reputation, it is impracticable for the registrar to raise objections under this sub-section, and the registrar will not deal with this at the examination stage, so that it is up to proprietors to raise it in opposition proceedings. Therefore, although the provision is subject to sub-s (5), by which registration cannot be refused under s 5 where the proprietor of an earlier trade mark consents to the registration, this is of no practical significance for the purpose of sub-s (3).

6.56 It would appear from the words of the provision that it is concerned with what, in some jurisdictions, is sometimes called 'dilution' of trade marks. The purpose of the words 'without due cause' is not clear; they may simply mean in the absence of authority, such as some form of licence, or perhaps the absence of some otherwise legally justifiable reason for adopting the mark for the goods or services in question. For example if the similarity of the mark applied for lay in the incorporation of the applicant's own name into the mark, that might provide due cause. Previous substantial use by the applicant without any confusion might also provide due cause. Guidance must be awaited from the courts.

Whether section 5(3) requires a likelihood of confusion

6.57 Before considering the reputation that must be proved under this provision, and the meaning of the terms 'unfair advantage' and 'detrimental', it is necessary to mention another question which has been raised in several cases, which is whether there is an additional requirement to be read into the sub-section, that is a likelihood of confusion as specified in sub-s (2). The first suggestion that this might be the case was made by Knox J in interlocutory proceedings, in *BASF plc v CEP (UK) plc*.[1] This was followed by a decision in another interlocutory application in the High Court, in *Baywatch Production Co Inc v Home Video Channel*.[2] In that case, the plaintiff, which was the producer of a weekly television series called 'Baywatch' and the proprietor of a registration of the name as a trade mark for, inter alia, video tapes and video discs, all featuring music, action-adventure, comedy, animation, sports or exercise, sought to restrain the defendant from transmitting an entertainment television programme under the name 'Babewatch'. The plaintiff relied in particular on s 10(3) of the TMA 1994, corresponding to s 5(3), the defendant having argued and the judge having accepted that its services were not similar to the goods covered by the registration. The deputy judge took the view that the use of the concept of similarity in s 10(3)(a) introduced the ingredient of a likelihood of confusion on the part of the public into s 10(3). He continued:

> 'Section 10(2) protection is given in relation to similar goods or services where, because of the similarity, there exists a likelihood of confusion on the part of the public. It would, it seems to me, be illogical for section 10(3) to give a greater protection in relation to non-similar goods or services by dispensing with the ingredient of a likelihood of confusion than the protection afforded to similar goods under s 10(2).'

1 [1996] ETMR 51.
2 [1997] FSR 22 (Deputy High Court Judge Michael Crystal QC).

6.58 This suggestion came as something of a surprise to many people. It may be that the seeming illogicality referred to by the deputy judge would have been seen a little differently, had the decisions of the ECJ in *Sabel* and *Canon*,[1] which explained the relevance of reputation to the issue of likelihoods of confusion, been available. In *Sabel*,[2] the ECJ referred in passing to art 4(3) and (4)(a) of the Directive, which s 5(3) implemented, in terms which made it reasonably clear that the provision did not require proof of a likelihood of confusion. English courts have continued to avoid deciding the question,[3] and it may be that the point will be decided by the ECJ. However in a case on appeal from a decision of the registry,[4] Geoffrey Hobbs QC, sitting as the appointed person, has provided a careful analysis of the question, concluding that the requirement for a likelihood of confusion was deliberately included in the provisions of the Directive implemented by s 5(2) and deliberately omitted from the provisions of the Directive implemented by s 5(3). He also indicated that this is the view held in the registry.

1 Paragraphs **6.38–6.45** above.
2 [1998] RPC 199 at 223. See also now the reaffirmation of the position in the Opinion of the Advocate General in *General Motors Corpn v Yplon SA* [1999] ETMR 122 at 129, para 26.
3 Thus, in *Marks & Spencer plc v One in a Million Ltd* [1998] FSR 265 at 272–273, the deputy judge (Jonathan Sumption QC) regarded the observations in *Sabel* as less than conclusive, and did not need to decide the point because, in the case before him, a likelihood of confusion was established. On appeal, [1999] FSR 1, at 25, Aldous LJ said that he was not satisfied that s 10(3) did not require the use to be confusing use, but was prepared to assume that it did.
4 *Re Corgi Trade Mark* [1999] RPC 549.

Reputation

6.59 Neither the Directive nor the TMA 1994 offer any direct guidance as to what amount of reputation needs to be demonstrated under the sub-section. It has been suggested that it might be necessary to show that the earlier trade mark is 'well-known' in the sense of art 6bis of the Paris Convention.[1] However this seems unlikely, because both the Directive[2] and the CTM Regulation[3] contain separate provisions referring expressly to marks which are 'well-known' within art 6bis, and it is clear that 'reputation' in the provisions of the Directive under consideration here, and in the Regulation, was intended to mean something different. It is thought that the provision does not require proof of any particular degree of reputation, although it seems clear that the reputation must arise from use in relation to goods or services for which the earlier mark is registered. Where the objection is based on a CTM it is not clear whether there need be any reputation in the UK, so long as that the trade mark has a reputation in the Community. However it would be rather surprising if no UK reputation was needed, since the sub-section is concerned with the possible consequences if the mark applied for is used in the UK. In each case, it is suggested that what has to be considered is whether, having regard to the marks themselves and to the nature of the goods or services covered by the earlier mark and by the application, the reputation of the earlier mark is such that either of the consequences, of unfair advantage or detriment, can be expected to follow. This, generally, is the aproach of the ECJ in the case referred to in the next paragraph.

1 See also the TMA 1994, s 56 .
2 Article 4(2)(d).
3 Article 8(2).

6.60 The interpretation of art 5(3) of the Directive, on which s 10(3) of the TMA 1994 is based, has been the subject of a decision of the ECJ[1] from the Commercial Court in Tournai, in a case under the uniform Benelux trade marks law concerning use by the defendant of the plaintiff's registered trade mark 'Chevy'. The questions referred to the court (as rephrased by the Advocate-General to raise issues of Community law, rather than national law) were as follows:

'(1) How is the concept of a trade mark with a 'reputation' within the meaning of Article 5(2) of the Directive to be interpreted?
(2) Must the reputation of the trade mark extend throughout the Benelux countries or is it sufficient that its reputation is established in one of those countries or part thereof?

The Advocate-General advised the court as follows:

'(1) For a trade mark to have a 'reputation' within the meaning of Article 5(2) of Directive 89/104, it must be established that the mark is known to a significant part of the relevant sectors of the public;

(2) It is sufficient that such reputation extends to a substantial part of the Benelux territory, which may be part only of one of the Benelux countries.'

The ECJ endorsed their views. Thus, it would appear that the views expressed in the previous paragraph are consistent with the decision of the ECJ. In particular, the effect of the decision is that the requirement than that for a mark to be 'well-known' within the meaning of the Paris Convention.[2]

1 *General Motors Corpn v Yplon SA*, Case C-375/97. The Opinion of the Advocate-General, delivered on 26 November 1998, is reported at [1999] ETMR 122, and the decision of the ECJ (14 September 1999) is not yet reported.
2 [1999] ETMR 122 at 130–132, paras 30–37 and para 31 of the decison..

The requirements of unfair advantage or detriment

6.61 The requirements of taking 'unfair advantage of' or being 'detrimental to' the distinctive character or the repute of the earlier trade mark are clearly alternatives. It is not necessary to meet both of them. Geoffrey Hobbs QC in the *Corgi* case[1] put the matter thus:

'Section 5(3) provides protection to an earlier trade mark where (i) it can be shown to possess distinctive character enhanced by a reputation acquired through use in relation to goods or services for which it is registered; and (ii) it can be shown that use of the later mark in relation to goods or services for which it is registered (or sought to be registered) would without due cause capture the distinctive character or repute of the earlier trade mark and exploit it positively (by taking unfair advantage of it) or negatively (subjecting it to the effects of detrimental use).'

1 See para **6.58**, n 4 above.

6.62 Section 5(3) has now been the subject of several decisions in the registry, although there are as yet no reported decisions of the English courts on the provision. The *One in a Million* case[1] was the first reported case in which a plaintiff established infringement under s 10(3), to which s 5(3) corresponds. The case concerned 'domain name grabbing', involving the registration of Internet domain names containing well-known trade marks and then trying to sell them to the trade mark proprietors. The greater part of the decision of the Court of Appeal is concerned with the claim in passing off, which also succeeded, but the court, in addition, held that there had been infringement. The decision is not of any great assistance in interpreting s 10(3) or s 5(3) because the court assumed that a likelihood of confusion was required and, moreover, it could not be disputed that the trade marks concerned had 'reputations' in the UK, being mostly household names.

1 See para **6.58**, n 3 above.

6.63 The first fully reported decision of the registry under s 5(3) is in *Oasis Stores Ltd's Trade Mark Application,*[1] where the opponent, the owner of the trade mark 'Ever Ready', registered for, inter alia, batteries, torches, plugs and smoke alarms, opposed an application to register the almost identical mark 'Eveready' for contraceptives and condoms. There was of course no difficulty in concluding that the opponent's trade mark 'Ever Ready' enjoyed a reputation in the UK, and the Hearing Officer also accepted that such reputation extended beyond the opponent's actual goods. The Hearing Officer also held, having considered the Directive and some decisions, including the observations of the ECJ in *Sabel*, that it was possible for an opposition under s 5(3) to succeed without there being any likelihood of confusion. Nevertheless he dismissed the opposition. On the issue of unfair advantage, he was prepared to accept that the applicant's mark might remind some people of the opponent's mark, although he said that there was no reliable evidence on the point. However he considered that this was not enough. He said:

'I do not consider that simply being reminded of a similar trade mark with a reputation for dissimilar goods necessarily amounts to taking unfair advantage of the repute of that mark. The opponents chances of success may have been better if they were able to point to some specific aspect of the reputation for batteries etc sold under their mar which was likely, through (non-origin) association, to benefit the applicants' mark to some significant extent. However, in my judgement, the opponents have not established any such conceptual connection between their reputation for batteries, etc. and the goods in respect of which the applicants' mark is to be used.

'Where the applicants' mark consists substantially of dictionary words which allude to (but do not directly describe) the nature of the goods in respect of which it is proposed to be registered, I think that the registrar should be slow to infer that the use of the mark will take unfair advantage of the distinctive character of the earlier mark consisting of the same dictionary words. The most that can be said here is that the applicants' mark makes a vaguely similar allusion to the nature of the applicants' goods as the opponents' mark to theirs. The link is tenuous and unsurprising given that dictionary words are concerned. In these circumstances the "bringing to mind" of the opponents' trade mark insofar as it occurs, is likely to be no more than word association.'

1 [1998] RPC 631.

6.64   On the issue whether there would be detriment to the distinctive character of the opponent's mark, the Hearing Officer said that any use of the same or similar mark for dissimilar goods or services is liable, to some extent, to dilute the distinctiveness of the earlier mark, but that the provision was clearly not intended to have the sweeping effect of preventing the registration of any mark which is the same as, or similar to, a trade mark with a reputation. He continued:

'It therefore appears to be a matter of degree. In considering detriment under this heading it appears to me appropriate to consider:
1   The inherent distinctiveness of the earlier trade mark;
2   The extent of the reputation that the earlier mark enjoys;
3   The range of goods or services for which the earlier mark enjoys a reputation;
4   The uniqueness or otherwise of the mark in the market place;
5   Whether the respective goods/services, although dissimilar, are in some way related or likely to be sold through the same outlets;
6   Whether the earlier trade mark will be any less distinctive for the goods/services for which it has a reputation than it was before.'

6.65   The Hearing Officer observed that the opponent's mark had a substantial reputation, but was a one product mark and, on their own evidence, was not unique in the market place; although the goods in question might sometimes be sold through the same outlets, the opponent's and the applicant's goods were wholly unrelated, and he concluded that there would be no detriment to the distinctive character of the opponent's mark for the goods for which it had a reputation.

6.66   The Hearing Officer dealt separately with the question of detriment to the repute of the opponent's mark, saying that the provision required that the mark was likely to be damaged or tarnished in some significant way, ie that it would be affected in such a way that the value added to the goods sold under the earlier trade mark because of its repute was, or was likely to be, reduced on a scale that is more than *de minimis*. After referring to some earlier cases, and to the evidence, he concluded that there was not shown to be any likelihood of detriment to the opponents' mark. He added, with reference to a particular concern expressed by the opponents, that if he thought that there was a likelihood of the opponents' mark becoming a butt of misplaced humour or ridicule, he would have felt inclined to accept that the repute of their mark could be at risk. However, in the absence of what he called 'any conceptual connection' between the respective goods, he thought that this result was unlikely.

6.67 It is to be noted that the Hearing Officer did not specifically deal in his decision with the relevance of the words 'without due cause'. Although generally speaking his approach to the issues seems reasonable, those words are important in some circumstances. For example, the fact that the mark in question comprises ordinary dictionary words, particularly if they are descriptive, may be a reason for concluding that there would be 'due cause' for their use.

6.68 The registry also had to consider the effect of s 5(3) in *AUDI-MED Trade Mark*,[1] in which the application was opposed by the German car company which owns the 'AUDI' trade mark, which is registered, inter alia, for motor cars, parts and fittings, and financial services relating to motor cars. The application was for the registration of 'audi med' in respect of hearing aids, etc. There was a dispute between the parties as to where the onus of proof lay in cases under s 5(3), and the Hearing Officer held that it was for the opponents to show unfair advantage or detriment to their mark or its reputation and that, if this was shown, it was for the applicants to show that they had due cause to use the mark. Although this conclusion may be correct in the practical result, it would seem from the wording of the provision that it is for the opponent to show that, prima facie, there is no good cause; at the end of the day, if there is good cause, the opposition must be rejected.

1 [1998] RPC 863.

6.69 The Hearing Officer adopted the same approach as he had followed in the *Eveready* case. He accepted that the opponents' mark had a substantial reputation, although there was no evidence on this apart from the evidence from the opponents themselves, and also that the mark had a high level of inherent distinctiveness. However it was not disputed that the word 'audi' was likely to be seen as descriptive of the applicants' goods. Furthermore, as with *Ever ready*, 'AUDI' was a one-product mark and the respective goods were completely unrelated. and unlikely to be sold through the same outlets. It was held that any effect on the distinctive character of the trade mark was de minimis, if indeed there was any effect at all, and that there was nothing in the evidence to support the argument that use of the applicant's mark was likely to take advantage of the opponents' reputation. The opposition was accordingly dismissed.

6.70 Two other decisions of the registry under s 5(3) may be mentioned briefly, by was of example. In the first,[1] an application to register the mark 'CLUB 240' in Class 25, for articles of clothing etc, was unsuccessfully opposed by the proprietor of the mark 'CLUB TWENTY FOUR' for financing (securing funds for others) services and other services in Class 36. The opposition, under s 5(2), (3) and (4), was rejected. The second case,[2] by way of contrast, was one in which an opposition under s 5(3) succeeded. The applicant had sought to register the mark 'VISA' for condoms and contraceptive devices. The case is an interesting contrast with the *Eveready* case mentioned above. The opponent was the proprietor of the same mark, registered for, inter alia, financial services related to bank cards. The Hearing Officer held, on the evidence, held that a substantial number of people would be caused to wonder whether the applicant's products were in some way connected with the services provided by the opponent. He also considered that the use of 'VISA' in shop windows to advertise products such as condoms was bound to have a detrimental effect on the distinctive character of the opponent's mark, which depended to some extent on its ability to function on shop windows and at points of sale as an indication that the visa credit card was accepted at the retail outlet. The mark would be less effective if some members of the public came to see it as a trade mark for condoms.

1 *Club 240* Trade Mark Application, 4 March 1998, noted in CIPA Journal, June 1998, p 470.
2 *Visa Trade Mark Application*, 31 July 1997, noted in CIPA Journal, November 1998, p 898. The decision has been upheld on appeal to the appointed person, Mr Geoffrey Hobbs QC (28 September 1999) cited in New Law Digest, 5 October 1999, 699107001.

6.71 It should be emphasised that, as the decisions referred to above demonstrate, that each case will be determined on its particular facts, in the light of the evidence. Clearly the nature of the mark is a crucial factor. An invented mark or another distinctive mark is more likely to be the basis of a successful opposition under s 5(3) than a descriptive mark, and the existence of some nexus between the respective goods or services of the parties is also important. If the applicant has used the mark, whether in the UK or elsewhere, the manner of use may well be relevant as showing that the applicant intended to trade off the reputation of the opponent's mark.

Refusal on the ground of conflict with a 'well-known' trade mark

6.72 The special position of trade marks, which are protected as well known trade marks within art 6[bis] of the Paris Convention, and which are included as such in the definition of 'earlier trade mark' in s 6(1), requires separate consideration. The owners of such well known trade marks are entitled to invoke the protection conferred by art 6[bis] under s 56 of the TMA 1994 , which is considered below. Section 56 follows the wording of the Convention fairly closely. For the purposes of refusal under s 5(1)-(3) the proprietor of the well known mark must be a person who (a) is a national of a Convention Country (ie a country which is a party to the Paris Convention, *other than the UK*),[1] or (b) is domiciled, or has a real and effective industrial or commercial establishment in, a Convention Country, but need not carry on business, or have any goodwill, in the UK. The requirement is that the trade mark be 'well-known in the United Kingdom as being the mark of [such a] person'. Although a UK national cannot, as such, claim the protection of a well-known trade mark, it would seem that he can do so if he is either domiciled in, or has a real and effective industrial or commercial establishment in, a Convention Country. It remains to be seen how far a UK company, whose main business is in the UK, will be able to claim the protection of his 'well-known' trade mark on the basis that he also has a lesser industrial or commercial establishment in a Convention Country. In principle the possibility does not appear to be excluded. The question, what constitutes a well-known trade mark for these purposes, is discussed

139

further below.[2] It is perhaps sufficient to say here that it is not sufficient merely that the mark should have a 'reputation' in the UK; much more than that is necessary. A trade mark which is properly to be regarded as a 'household name'[3] would clearly qualify; on the other hand it should not be necessary to show that the mark is 100% distinctive in the sense that use of it by someone else would amount to passing off.

1 Section 55(1).
2 Chapter 12, para **12.53–12.57**.
3 See eg *A/S Legod Systems A/S v Lego M Lemelstrich* [1983] FSR 155, at 161–162 (Falconer J).

6.73   Where a trade mark is shown to be well known within art 6[bis], refusal may be justifiable under any of the provisions of s 5(1)–(3), according to whether the marks are identical or similar, and whether the goods or services concerned are identical, similar or dissimilar. The general approach in determining oppositions, in which a well-known trade mark is invoked, will therefore be as for objections founded on registered marks. Since the registrar will not normally be in a position to judge, in the absence of evidence, whether or not a mark, to which a mark applied for is identical or similar, it is not expected that the registrar will himself raise an objection founded on a well-known trade mark, at the examination stage.

Refusal based upon other earlier rights

6.74   Section 5(4) provides that a trade mark shall not be registered 'if, or to the extent that, its use in the UK is liable to be prevented:

   (a) by virtue of any rule of law (in particular the law of passing off) protecting an unregistered trade mark or other sign used in the course of trade, or

   (b) by virtue of an earlier right other than those referred to in subsections (1) to (3) or paragraph (a) above, in particular by virtue of the law of copyright, design right or registered designs.'

A person thus entitled to prevent use of the mark is referred to as the proprietor of an 'earlier right'.

6.75   This provision is derived from art 4(4)(b) of the Directive. As with refusal on the basis of trade marks having a reputation, under s 5(3), or of conflict with well-known trade marks, the registrar is not in a position to raise objections under s 5(4), because he does not have the necessary information. These grounds will be left to be raised in opposition proceedings, or in applications under s 47(2) of the TMA 1994, for declarations of invalidity.

6.76   The first point of significance about s 5(4)(a) is that it is considerably narrower in scope than the previous ground of objection based upon prior use of a conflicting mark, under s 11 of the TMA 1938. As was clear from the authorities,[1] it was not necessary for an opponent, or an applicant for rectification, relying on section 11 of the 1938 Act, to make out a case for passing off. Established use of the conflicting trade mark, even over quite a short period, was sufficient. Thus, s 5(4) serves to underline the importance of registering trade marks under the TMA 1994 , if one wishes to be in the best position to prevent registration of later conflicting marks. Some of the cases, decided in opposition and invalidation proceedings, illustrate well the change in the law which s 5(4)(a) represents, now requiring, as it does, sufficient evidence to persuade the registrar that use of the mark applied for in a normal and fair manner will amount to a misrepresentation that the applicant's goods or services are those of the owner of the earlier right or are in some way connected with him. In some of the recent cases, the evidence put forward by the opponent might perhaps have sufficed to establish an objection under s 11 of the TMA 1938 but was not enough to prove that passing off would occur.

1 See in particular the decision of the House of Lords in *Berlei (UK) Ltd v Bali Brasserie Co Inc* [1969] 2 All ER 812, [1969] RPC 472.

6.77 The effect of s 5(4)(a) was considered, on appeal to the appointed person, in the case of *Wild child Trade Mark*.[1] The opposed application was for registration of the mark 'Wild Child' in respect of complete articles of outer clothing, footwear and headgear. The application date was 4 March 1995 and the opponent claimed to have used the same mark for clothing since the end of 1993. For the purposes of the appeal, Mr Hobbs took the summary of the necessary elements of an action for passing off, from *Halsbury's Laws of England*.[2] He concluded that the evidence of the opponent, which comprised a main declaration and a further declaration from the opponent's Managing Director, and which did not clearly show use of the mark in question as a trade mark, was an insufficient basis for a claim for passing off. He said that he was not willing to regard assertions without any real substantiation as sufficient to sustain an objection to registration under s 5(4). What this case demonstrates is that save in plain cases in which the likelihood of deception is fairly clear, an opponent invoking this provision must be prepared to obtain rather more evidence than his own declaration or declarations establishing use of a mark which is the same as or similar to the mark applied for. Reference may also be made to another decision of Mr. Hobbs, in *Re Corgi Trade Mark*.[3]

1 [1998] RPC 455 (Geoffrey Hobbs QC).
2 (4th Edition) Vol 48 (1995 reissue) at para 165, derived from decisions of the House of Lords in *Reckitt & Colman Products Ltd v Borden Inc* [1990] RPC 341 and *Erven Warnink BV v J Townend & Sons (Hull) Ltd* [1979] AC 731.
3 See para **6.58**, n 4 above.

6.78 Other decisions under the TMA 1994 confirm this view, although it should be emphasised that each case will depend upon its particular facts. One reported case, in which an objection under s 5(4)(a) failed, is *Oasis Stores Ltd's Trade Mark Application*,[1] in which an application to register 'eveready' for condoms was unsuccessfully opposed by the proprietors of the 'ever ready' mark for batteries. The following are further examples:
— 'Knobwyp',[2] an application to register the mark for non-medicated wipes, in Classes 6 and 24, was unsuccessfully opposed by the owner of the unregistered mark 'knobwipes', because it could not be shown that a passing off claim would succeed;
— 'Foot lites',[3] an application to register this mark for footwear, the word 'foot' appearing above 'lites', was unsuccessfully opposes under, inter alia, s 5(4)(a), by the owners of the unregistered mark 'comfortlites';
— 'BMF',[4] an application to register the mark for casual wear for men, women and children, was successfully opposed by the British Motorcyclists Federation under s 5(4)(a). Although the opponent's reputation had been built up in a fairly specialised market, it was sufficient that a section of the public would be confused;
— 'club 240',[5] an application to register the mark for, inter alia, articles of clothing, was unsuccessfully opposed by the proprietors of the proprietor of the mark 'club twenty four' for financing services, who relied upon s 5(4)(a) as well as s 5(2) and (3);
— 'Little world',[6] an application to register this mark for toys and playthings was

unsuccessfully opposed by the opponent, who with considerable effort had developed a cartoon character named Spinny – The Little World, but had not generated a sufficient reputation to support a passing off action;

— 'DESKTALK',[7] an opposition under s 5(4)(a) succeeded against an application to register this mark in Class 9 for, inter alia, computers and computer programs and in Class 16 for stationery and printed matter, the opponent having established a reputation in the mark 'DECtalk' for computers and computer programs incorporated in communication aids;

— 'Espirit',[8] an application for registration in Class 12, for bicycles, and parts and fittings, was unsuccessfully opposed by the proprietor of the mark 'esprit' registered and used for motor land vehicles, and parts and fittings, who relied upon s 5(4), as well as s 5(2) and (3);

— ‚Manhattan bagel company',[9] the application was to register a device of a silhouette of the Manhattan skyline together with these words, for, inter alia, restaurant services. It was unsuccessfully opposed, under s 5(4)(a), by the owners of an unregistered mark comprising a device of the Statue of Liberty with the words 'New York Bagel Company', which supplied bagels to retail outlets such as supermarkets;

— 'Man O man',[10] an application to register this mark for soaps and other goods in Class 3 was unsuccessfully opposed under s 5(4)(a), by the producers of the television show of the same name;

— 'Demon' device,[11] an application to register a device of a demon with a trident, for articles of clothing for leisure and sporting activities, was successfully opposed by Manchester United Merchandising Ltd under, inter alia, s 5(4)(a) on the basis of use of a devil and trident device which, although different, was found to be similar.

1 [1998] RPC 631 (Registry). See paras **6.62–6.66** above.
2 Registry, 14 May 1997, noted in CIPA Journal, July 1997, at 538.
3 Registry, 12 December 1997. New Law Digest , 698058207.
4 Registry, 4 March 1998, noted in CIPA Journal, June 1998, at 470.
5 Registry, 4 March 1998, noted in CIPA Journal, June 1998, at 470.
6 Registry, 13 March 1998, noted in CIPA Journal, September 1998, at 725.
7 Registry, 29 April 1998, noted in CIPA Journal, September 1998, at 728.
8 Registry, 2 July 1998, noted in CIPA Journal, October 1998, at 808.
9 Registry, 20 November 1998, New Law Digest, 698112602.
10 Registry, 24 September 1998, noted in CIPA Journal, December 1998, at 982.
11 *In the Matter of Anthony O'Gormanr's Trade Mark Application* Registry, (15 February 1999 unreported).

6.79 Section 5(4)(b) needs little comment, and probably represents no change in the law, because it was established under the old law that a mark could be refused registration under s 11 of the TMA 1938, if it infringed a third party's copyright.[1] There was no reason to suppose that the same would not have applied to a mark which infringed some other right such as a registered design or a design right. An example of the application of s 5(4)(b) is the case of *Re Team Lotus Trade Mark Application,*[2] in which it was sought to register a 'lotus' device as a trade mark for advertising services. The opponent, Group Lotus, successfully opposed the application on the ground that it owned the copyright in the device, as well as on the ground of bad faith.[3]

1 See *'Karo Step Trade Mark* [1977] RPC 255, decided under TMA 1938, s 11.
2 Trade Marks Registry, [1999] ETMR 669.
3 The mark was also strikingly similar to the opponent's own registered mark, covering land vehicles, but the registrar was unable on the evidence to determine whether or not advertising services were similar to land vehicles.

Honest concurrent use

6.80 The UK concept of 'honest concurrent use' (see s 12(2) of the TMA 1938) which could be invoked by applicants to register marks where there was an objection based on an earlier registration, is not mentioned in the Directive and had no place in the Bill as originally published. However as a result of representations made at a later stage, a new clause, now s 7, was introduced to allow reliance on honest concurrent use to a limited extent. It is important that the words 'to a limited extent' should be emphasised. The provision has no effect on the substantive law, and is in essence no more than a procedural device, which enables an applicant faced with an otherwise potentially fatal citation of a prior registration, to proceed to the stage of advertisement of his application for opposition purposes. It does not give a right to registration merely by establishing honest concurrent, and will not save the application if an opponent has a valid ground for opposition. If there is no opposition and the mark becomes registered, honest concurrent use for the purposes of s 7 will not of itself protect the registration if a third party has a valid ground for attacking the registration under s 47 on the basis of prior rights.

6.81 Section 7 can apply to any case where it appears to the registrar that there is an objection under s 5(1), (2) or (3) based on an earlier trade mark, or under s 5(4) on the basis of another earlier right. Where honest concurrent use, which by sub-s (3) is such use, by the applicant or with his consent, as would have amounted to honest concurrent use of the purposes of s 12(2) of the TMA 1938,[1] is established to the satisfaction of the registrar, the registrar cannot refuse registration by reason of the earlier trade mark or other earlier right, 'unless objection on that ground is raised in opposition proceedings by the proprietor of that earlier trade mark or other earlier right'. In practice the references to sub-ss (3) and (4) will not be significant, because objections under those provisions will not normally be raised by the registrar.[2] Sub-section (2) explains the true nature of the provision as described above, and shows that the provision is likely to be of rather limited practical use, although it will enable the application to proceed to registration if the owner of the earlier right fails to see the publication of the application in time to oppose. The limited use of the provision is further emphasised by sub-s (4), which says that refusal on the absolute grounds, mentioned in s 3 of the Act, is unaffected, and that the making of an application for a declaration of invalidity under s 47(2) (application on relative grounds where no consent to registration) is also unaffected. So far as absolute grounds for refusal are concerned, sub-s (4) does not in terms provide that the making of a declaration of invalidity on absolute grounds, under s 47(1), is unaffected, although if there has been sufficient use to be accepted as 'honest concurrent use', it may well be that any absolute grounds for refusal will also have been overcome or be capable of being overcome if raised. In the case of relative grounds for refusal, if the owner of the earlier right allows more than five years to pass after registration, before seeking a declaration of invalidity under s 47(2), then he may in any event be barred from seeking such a declaration.[3] It should also be mentioned that, by virtue of sub-s (5) the provision will cease to apply if there is a statutory instrument in force under s 8.[4]

1 Previous decisions such as *Pirie & Sons Ltd's Trade Mark* (1933) 50 RPC 147 at 294 per Tomlin J should be referred to – see also Kerly's Law of Trade Marks and Trade Names, 12th edn, para 10–18. Note that 'other special circumstances' which could be taken into account under s 12(2), are not mentioned in the TMA 1994, s 7.
2 See paras **6.55** and **6.75** above.
3 See s 48 (effect of acquiescence) which is in terms confined to acquiescence in use of a registered trade mark.
4 See para **6.2** above.

6.82 The effect of s 7 has been considered in one reported case which came before the court. This is *Road Tech Computer Systems Ltd v Unison Software (UK) Ltd*.[1] The plaintiff was the proprietor of a registration of the trade mark 'Roadrunner', for 'consumer software and programs; all included in Class 9; but not including any such goods relating to birds'.[2] The defendant used the mark 'Road-Runner' for certain computer software, which was different from the software sold by the plaintiff under its trade mark. The plaintiff sued for infringement and passing off, and sought summary judgment on the claim for infringement, asserting that there was no defence to the claim. The defendant counterclaimed for a declaration of invalidity, alleging that the plaintiff's application for registration had been made in bad faith, relying on s 3(6) of the TMA 1994.[3] The defendant also sought to rely, under s 7, upon honest concurrent use of its own mark in support of its application for registration of its mark which would, if successful, have provided a defence.[4] On this point, the judge considered the provision and concluded that 'refusal of registration is mandatory under s 7(2) if the proprietor of the earlier registered mark objects'. Of course this should not be taken too literally; the proprietor must have a *valid* objection. On the facts of the case, the defendant's mark, although very similar to the registered mark, was not identical. If it had been, and if there had been no arguable basis for challenging the validity of the registration, then there would have been no defence to an opposition to registration under s 5(1) of the Act and in such a case at least, refusal of registration on the later application would be 'mandatory'. In the case in question, the parties' marks were so similar that in all probability there was a likelihood of confusion sufficient to justify refusal under s 5(2). However in many cases where the similarity is not so great, an applicant may be in a position to argue that his honest concurrent use demonstrates that there is in fact no likelihood of confusion.

1 [1996] FSR 805 (Robert Walker J). We expand upon the procedural implications in more detail at para **16.15** below.
2 The limitation, which is not relevant here, would have been required under the registrar's 'Penguin' practice. See para **5.26** and **5.92** above.
3 See paras **5.118–121** above.
4 Under the TMA 1994, s 11(1).

6.83 It would seem therefore that in cases in which the applicant's honest concurrent use of his mark has been found acceptable for the purposes of s 7, but the application is opposed on the basis of an earlier rights, the procedure to be followed will depend upon the facts of the case. If there is an earlier trade mark to which the mark applied for is identical, and the specification of the application includes goods or services which are identical to goods or services covered by the earlier registration, then the registrar must refuse registration under s 5(1). If however the marks are not identical, or there is only similarity of goods or services, then refusal is not mandatory and the registrar must proceed with the opposition in the normal way, with the filing of evidence and a hearing if requested, before reaching a decision. The same applies if the goods or services concerned are dissimilar or if the opposition is under s 5(4), on the basis of an earlier right.[1]

1 This is confirmed by the registrar's notice in Journal No 6171, noted in the Work Manual, ch 6, at 11.17.3.

Chapter 7

Loss of rights and rectification

Introduction

7.1   Under the TMA 1994, the proprietor of a trade mark registration may lose his rights in several ways. Under s 46 a registration may be revoked, on a number of grounds arising after registration. Under s 47, a registration may be declared invalid, on any of the 'absolute' and 'relative' grounds on which registration might have been refused, under ss 3 and 5 of the TMA 1994. Section 60 makes further provision for rectification of the register in certain circumstances. Finally, s 64 permits rectification or correction of the register in certain circumstances not involving validity. These provisions each require separate detailed consideration.

Revocation

General remarks

7.2   Under the TMA 1938 there were provisions[1] for rectification of the register, which covered both objections to the validity of the original registration and objections arising from matters occurring after registration, with the exception of non-use, which was the subject of a separate provision.[2] Under the TMA 1994 there is a clear distinction between invalidation of the registration of a trade mark, on grounds which applied to the original registration, and revocation of a registered trade mark on grounds which arise after registration. Section 46(1) of the TMA 1994 sets out four grounds on which the registration of a trade mark may be revoked. The first two involve non-use, or interruption of use, for five years, the other two apply in certain cases where the mark becomes generic or misleading. Sub-section (2) contains further provisions relating to these grounds and sub-s (3) deals with non-use cases in which use is commenced or re-commenced at a time when grounds for revocation exist. Generally speaking, all registered trade marks, including 'existing registered marks' registered under the old law, are treated, after commencement of the TMA 1994, as if registered under the Act[3] and thus subject to the new provisions. Under Sch 3, para 17(1) applications under s 26 of the TMA 1938, for removal of registrations on grounds of non-use, pending at 31 October 1994, are determined under the old law. Schedule 3, para 18(1) makes similar provisions in respect of pending applications for rectification or correction of the register.[4] Under sub-s (4) an application may be made by any person. There is no longer the requirement for an applicant to be a 'person aggrieved', as was the case under ss 26 and 32 of the TMA 1938, although in practice he usually will be; as before, the application may, with two exceptions, be made to the registrar or to the court at the applicant's option. The exceptions are the same as in s 54 of the TMA 1938. When proceedings concerning the trade mark in question are pending in the court, the application must be made to the court; and in any other case, if an application is made to the registrar, he may at any stage refer the application to the court. Under s 46(5), where grounds for revocation exist only in respect of some of the goods or services covered by the registration, revocation will relate only to those goods or services. Section 46(6) provides that revocation, whether in whole or only to the extent of some goods or services, has the effect that the rights of the proprietor shall be deemed to have ceased at the date of the application for revocation or at an earlier date if the tribunal is satisfied that the grounds existed then.

1 TMA 1938, s 32.
2 TMA 1938, s 26.
3 Schedule 3, para **2**.
4 TMA 1938, ss. 32 and 34.

Is there a discretion not to revoke?

7.3 One question, which has not yet been resolved, is whether the use of the words '*may* be revoked' import any discretion not to revoke where any of the grounds specified is established, or whether in that event the tribunal must order revocation. The word 'may'[1] perhaps suggests that there could be a residual discretion. However, art 12 of the Directive uses the words 'shall be liable to revocation', and it should be presumed that the legislation was intended to comply with the Directive. Moreover there are indications in the section itself that there is no discretion. For example, the references to 'proper reasons for non-use' in s 46(1)(a) and (b) suggest that if there are no such reasons there should be no discretion to allow a registration to remain once the necessary non-use is proved. In addition the use of the word 'shall' in s 46(5), with reference to partial revocation,[2] supports the view that 'may' is to be construed as meaning 'shall' in s 46(1).[3] Furthermore, the corresponding wording of the non-use provision in the CTM Regulation[4] appears, prima facie, to exclude any discretion not to revoke when non-use is established, in the absence of proper reasons for the non-use.

1 Which was also used in the TMA 1938, ss 26 and 32, under which there was always a discretion not to remove or rectify in appropriate circumstances
2 See also the Directive, art 13.
3 See also para **7.24** below regarding the same question in connection with the invalidation provisions of s 47.
4 Council Regulation 40/94/EC, art 50.

7.4 There have been several decisions, of both the registry and the courts, in which this question of discretion has arisen. One of the earlier cases before the registry is *Invermont Trade Mark,*[1] in which a Hearing Officer considered the point, with specific reference to art 12(1) of the Directive, and concluded that the wording of the provisions in the Directive was compatible with a residual discretion not to revoke. Reference was made to the corresponding wording of the CTM Regulation. The question was also mentioned in an infringement action in the High Court, *United Biscuits (UK) Ltd v Asda Stores Ltd,*[2] on a counterclaim for revocation, where the judge appeared to assume that there was a discretion not to remove even if non-use for five years was established, although there is no indication that there was any argument on the point. On the other hand, in another decision of the registry, *Zippo Trade Mark*,[3] it was held that there was no such discretion. The matter is now to be considered by the court. In *A J & MA Levy's Trade Mark (No 2)*.[4] On an appeal to the appointed person (MG Clarke QC) under s 76 of the TMA 1994,[5] the Hearing Officer had held that he had residual discretion, under s 46(1) – which he exercised in the proprietor's favour – to retain a registration in spite of non-use and the absence of any reason for the non-use. A request by the registrar, to refer the appeal to the court on the ground that it raised an important point of law, was allowed.

1 [1997] RPC 125. See also *Worth Trade Marks* [1998] RPC 875, in which another Hearing Officer referred to *Invermont* and assumed that there was a discretion not to revoke.
2 [1997] RPC 513, at 540 (Robert Walker J).
3 [1999] RPC 173.
4 [1999] RPC 358.
5 See ch 2, paras **2.39–2.41** above.

Non-use

7.5 Section 46(1)(a) and (b) relate to two different non-use situations. The ground for removal under (a) is that 'within the period of five years following the date of completion of the registration procedure' (ie the date on which the trade mark was actually put on the register), the trade mark has not been put to genuine use in the UK, by the proprietor or with his consent, in relation to the goods or services for which it is registered, and there are no proper reasons for non-use. It will be seen that, unlike s 26(1)(a) of the TMA 1938, there is no requirement to establish a lack of bona fide intention to use, which may possibly be the subject of an application for invalidation under s 47(1).[1] Under s 46(1)(b) the ground is that genuine use of the trade mark (by the proprietor or with his consent) has been suspended for an uninterrupted period of five years, and there are no proper reasons for non-use. The term 'genuine use' is probably the same as 'bona fide use', in the sense in which the latter term has been interpreted by the courts under the TMA 1938. This was the approach of the registrar's Hearing Officer in *Re Academy Trade Mark*,[2] where the actual amount of use of the trade mark by the proprietor for the goods in question, articles of clothing, was very small but held to be genuine.[3] The use must be real commercial use, ie use with a specific commercial purpose in itself; if the use is merely for trade mark protection purposes, in particular if it is not intended to continue once any threat of revocation has receded, then it is unlikely to be regarded as 'genuine'[4] for the purposes of sub-s (1)(a) or (b).

1 On the ground that the application was made in bad faith, within the meaning of s 3(6). See paras **5.118–5.121** above.
2 27 November 1998, unreported, but noted in New Law Digest, 1 March 1999, 699031803.
3 See also the decision of Lloyd J in *Re Elle Trade Marks* [1997] FSR 529 (Lloyd J).
4 See for example *Concord Trade Mark* [1987] FSR 209, decided under the TMA 1938, s 26, distinguishing on the facts the decision of the Court of Appeal in *Electrolux Ltd v Electrix Ltd* (1954) 71 RPC 23. Compare the decision of Whitford J in *Bon Matin Trade Mark* [1989] RPC 537, mentioned in the *Academy Trade Mark* decision.

7.6 It should be noted that 'use' is not, as was the case under the TMA 1938,[1] confined to printed or visual use; by virtue of s 103(2) a reference to use includes use otherwise than by means of a graphic representation. Use 'by the proprietor or with his consent' covers any form of consent, not just written consent. This will include any use under a licence or, probably, a sub-licence, and also any other use by consent, such as use by a subsidiary or other company in the same group.

Another important change in the law relating to non-use cases is made by s 100, under which, in any civil proceedings in which a question arises as to the use to which a registered trade mark has been put, the burden of showing what use has been made of it is placed on the proprietor. This is a great improvement over the unsatisfactory position under the old law, under which an applicant claiming non-use had the burden, which was often difficult to discharge, of proving that the mark had not been the subject of any bona fide use during the whole of the relevant five-year period.

1 TMA 1938, s 68(2).

7.7 It is clear from sub-s (2) that the use does not have to be precisely in the form of the registered mark. Under this provision, use 'in a form differing in elements which do not alter the distinctive character of the mark in the form in which it was registered' is sufficient. The effect of this provision may in many instances be the same as that of s 30(1) of the TMA 1938,[1] which uses the words 'additions or alterations not substantially affecting the identity [of the trade mark],' but not necessarily so. For example, if a registered mark is 'X', it is doubtful whether use of a mark 'X&Y' would have been treated as use of 'X' under the TMA 1938. On the other hand, under s 46(2) of the TMA 1938 the position could be different, because the form of 'X' is not itself altered.[2] The provision was considered by the court in *Elle Trade Marks,*[3] where the proprietor was unsuccessful in a claim that use of the word 'ELLE' in block capitals should be treated as use of the registered mark, which comprised the word 'elle' in lower case letters within a device of a circle and cross, being the symbol for the female sex. More recently,[4] a Hearing Officer at the registry has held that the use of the word mark 'Club', for soft drinks, should not be regarded as being use of 'Club Soda' in a form 'differing in elements which do not alter the distinctive character of the mark'.

1 See also the TMA 1938, s 34(1)(e), relating to alteration of a registered trade mark.
2 On this point, the observations of Jacob J in *British Sugar plc v James Robertson and Sons Ltd* [1996] RPC 281 at 293–294, discussed in para **6.12** above, may be relevant.
3 [1997] FSR 529 (Lloyd J).
4 17 November 1998, unreported, noted in New Law Digest, 10 March 1999, 699032103.

7.8 Sub-section (2) also provides that applying the mark to goods or their packaging in the UK, solely for export, is included in use for the purposes of sub-s (1). Section 30(2) of the TMA 1938 contained a similar provision.

7.9 It appears that, whereas under s 30(1) of the TMA 1938 the tribunal had a discretion in the matter, ie as to whether it was right to treat the use as use of the registered mark notwithstanding that the identity was not substantially affected, s 46(2) confers no discretion at all. Proof of genuine use of a variation of the registered mark falling within the provision will defeat an application for revocation.

7.10 There is no guidance in the TMA 1994 as to what are 'proper reasons for non-use' for the purposes of s 46(1)(a) and (b). The phrase may be contrasted with s 26(3) of the TMA 1938, which made an exception where the non-use was shown to have been due to 'special circumstances in the trade' and not to any intention not to use, or to abandon the trade mark. This was interpreted as referring to circumstances affecting the trade generally, as opposed to circumstances affecting only the proprietor and his trade. The new wording seems to be broader, and should permit justification of non-use on the basis of circumstances peculiar to the proprietor. For example, if an exclusive licensee ceased using the licensed mark, but refused to give up his exclusive rights under the licence, such situation might well be considered as providing a proper reason for non-use. The issue of proper reasons for non-use was raised in the case of *Nightwatch,*[1] where the proprietor claimed that it took a long time to develop and launch a new product in the field of alcoholic beverages, and that it remained his intention to use the mark. Such delay – clearly more than five years – within the control of the proprietor was held not to constitute 'proper reasons' for the non-use and the registration was revoked. The question of proper reasons for non-use was also considered in the registry in *Worth Trade Marks.*[2] The Hearing Officer adopted the approach suggested in the earlier decision in *Invermont Trade Mark,*[3] that 'proper' should be understood as meaning apt, reasonable, justifiable in all the circumstances. On the evidence before him, which showed that the proprietor had been negotiating for some years to licence the trade marks in suit, and had continued throughout the period during which the registrations had been under threat, he held that there were proper reasons for non-use, in that the proprietor had been unable to conclude any licence until the proceedings, which included not only the proceedings before him, but previous proceedings under the TMA 1938 determined in the proprietor's favour only a few weeks before the TMA 1994 proceedings were commenced. Essentially, the Hearing Officer's view was that it was reasonable for potential licensees not to conclude an agreement while the marks were under threat and that it was not reasonable to expect the proprietor to give an open-ended warranty to a would-be licensee. The decision seems to be entirely correct, and supports the view that the term 'proper reasons' should receive a fairly broad interpretation. It may be said that this is a reasonable result, particularly if the registrar no longer has a residual discretion, which may well be found to be the case. In a sense, the concept of proper reasons, fairly applied, can be regarded as a replacement for the residual discretion under the old law.

1 (19 August 1996, unreported) but noted in CIPA Journal, October 1996, p 850.
2 [1998] RPC 875.
3 See para **7.4**, n 1 above.

7.11 Section 46(3) of the TMA 1994 makes special provision regarding cases in which use of a trade mark is commenced or resumed after the expiry of the five-year period referred to in sub-s (1)(a) or (b). Sub-section (3) is as follows:

> '(3) The registration of a trade mark shall not be revoked on the ground mentioned in subsection (1)(a) or (b), if such use as is referred to in that paragraph is commenced or resumed after the expiry of the five year period and before the application for revocation is made:
>
> Provided that, any such commencement or resumption of use after the expiry of the five year period but within the period of three months before the making of the application shall be disregarded unless preparations for the commencement or resumption began before the proprietor became aware that the application might be made.'

7.12 The position under s 46(3) should be compared with that of s 26 of the TMA 1938, under which the question of commencement or resumption of use was dealt with by counting the five-year period up to the date one month before the date of the application for removal. If the use was commenced or resumed more than a month before the application, and was bona fide, then the application failed, even if the use was made with a view to defeating the application.[1] Under s 46(3) the general rule is that, where genuine use is commenced or resumed before the application for revocation is made, the registration will not then be revoked on the ground of non-use. However commencement or resumption of use after the expiry of the five-year period but within three months before the making of an application for revocation is treated differently. Such use is to be disregarded, unless preparations for the commencement or resumption began before the proprietor became aware that the application might be made. Clearly, it is for the proprietor to show that he was unaware that an application for revocation might be made. If, as in the normal kind of situation, an intending applicant or someone on his behalf makes inquiries as to use of the mark by communicating with the proprietor or his attorney, then of course he will not succeed in defeating the application. A less clear case might be one in which the proprietor sends a letter before action, complaining of infringement, when he knows that his registration is vulnerable because the mark has not been used for more than five years. It may not be unreasonable in the circumstances to conclude that he was aware that an application 'might be made', particularly if he had obtained legal advice. The case against him could well be even stronger if infringement proceedings were actually commenced. In each case the question is one of fact, depending upon all the circumstances. A good example of a case in which the resumption of use would not have been disregarded, so that revocation would have been refused under s 46, is provided by the case of *Hermes Trade Mark,*[2] had the preparations in that case not been themselves held to constitute bona fide use.

1 As happened in *Electrolux Ltd v Electrix Ltd* (1954) 71 RPC 23.
2 [1982] RPC 425.

7.13 Issues concerning partial cancellation are more likely to arise in non-use cases than in other applications for revocation under s 46(1) of the TMA 1994. It has been quite common in the past, particularly under the old law when a claim for infringement was confined to goods or services actually covered by the registration, to register trade marks for as broad a specification as the registry will accept. As already mentioned, the position under s 46(5) is that where grounds for revocation exist in respect of only some of the goods or services for which the trade mark is registered, revocation shall relate to those goods or services only. Subject to the question, which is not entirely straightforward in every case, what are the goods or services in respect of which the non-use ground 'exists', it is clear that there is no possibility for the proprietor to retain the mark for any of those goods or services, merely because he has used the mark for similar goods or services.[1] Where the specification of the registration lists a number of different descriptions of goods or services, there will normally be no difficulty in simply striking out those categories in which there has been no use during the relevant five-year period. However the matter may be more difficult in some cases in which the proprietor has only used the mark for a specific product within a broad general description. What is the position, for example, where a mark is registered for 'pharmaceutical preparations and substances' but has been used only for one particular preparation, where the proprietor of a mark registered for 'computer software' has only used the mark for software for a particular application or where a mark registered for 'non-medicated confectionery' has only been used for chocolate?

1 Cf TMA 1938, s 26(2).

7.14 It is helpful to refer to some cases decided under the TMA 1994 in which only partial revocation has been ordered. In *Cepravin*[1] the specification of a registration of a mark which had only be used for two veterinary medicine products during the relevant period, was reduced from 'pharmaceutical and veterinary preparations and substances', to 'antibiotic preparations for use in veterinary treatments'.

In *Academy*[2] the mark was registered for articles of clothing and, on evidence that the mark had been used for leisurewear during the relevant period, was only amended by excluding footwear. In *Re Zamoyski Trade Mark*,[3] a stricter approach was adopted. The registration of the mark 'Zamoyski' in respect of wines, spirits and liqueurs, which had only been used for vodka, was revoked for all goods except vodka. In the case of *Club Soda*,[4] registrations of marks covering non-alcoholic drinks and preparations for making such drinks, which had only been used for non-alcoholic drinks, were revoked for preparations for making such drinks. In the same case, a registration for 'beverages containing not more than 2% (by volume) of alcohol' was partially revoked, by limiting the specification to non-alcoholic beverages.

1 Registry, 4 April 1997, unreported, but noted in CIPA Journal, June 1997, p 448.
2 27 November 1998, unreported, but noted in New Law Digest, 1 March 1999, 699031803.
3 Registry, 4 December 1998, unreported, but noted in New Law Digest, 10 March 1999, 699032101. The note does not indicate whether the proprietor sought to argue that he should be permitted to retain the registration for 'spirits'.
4 17 November 1998, unreported, but noted in New Law Digest, 10 March 1999, 699032103.

7.15 In the absence of decisions of the court on these questions of partial rectification, or any clear rulings from the registry, the present position is somewhat uncertain. It is submitted that a proprietor ought in general, as a matter of principle, to be allowed to retain a registration for a broader description of goods or services than his specific product or products. For example, in the *Zamoyski* case,[1] there might well have been some justification in allowing the registration to remain for 'spirits' and not just 'vodka'; in the *Cepravin* case,[2] although it was right to revoke the registration for pharmaceutical preparations and substances, there might have been an argument in favour of retention for veterinary preparations generally. However each case must be judged on its merits having regard to all the circumstances, including the nature of the goods or services concerned and of the trade mark, and any particular factors relating to the trade in such goods or services.

1 Paragraph **7.14**, n3 above.
2 Paragraph **7.14**, n1 above.

7.16 The effect of s 46(6) of the TMA 1994, which has already been mentioned, is that prima facie the rights of the proprietor only cease as from the date of the application for revocation. However it is open to the applicant to seek to satisfy the tribunal that the grounds for revocation existed at an earlier date, and if he succeeds, the proprietor's rights cease from that earlier date, by virtue of sub-para (b) of the sub-section. There is no guidance as yet, from the registry or the courts, as to when a ground for revocation 'exists' for these purposes. In non-use cases there seems to be no reason why the ground of non-use should not be held to have existed at the end of the earliest continuous five-year period of non-use. Thus if there was no use of the mark in suit for ten years prior to the application for revocation, the rights of the proprietor could be held to have ceased five years prior to the application date. In many cases this point may be academic, but it could be important where there was a claim for damages for infringement in respect of use prior to the date of the application for revocation.

7.17 Finally, reference should be made to the transitional provisions in Sch 3. Whereas, under para 17(1) an application pending at the commencement of the TMA 1994 for removal on grounds of non-use under s 26 of the TMA1938[1] will be dealt with under the old law, para 17(2) enables a new application to be made, under s 46(1)(a) or (b), at any time after commencement, in respect of an existing registered mark. Thus it is open to a person who has made an application for revocation under the old law, also to make a fresh application under the TMA 1994, which may be advantageous in some cases because of the change of the burden of proof. The only exception to the operation of the transitional provision here is in favour of defensive registrations,[2] in respect of which no application may be made until after five years from commencement.

1 Under the TMA 1938, s 26.
2 Under the TMA 1938, s 27.

Use of a trade mark as a common name in the trade.

7.18   The third ground for revocation, under s 46(1)(c), is that in consequence of acts or inactivity of the proprietor, the mark has become the common name in the trade for a product or service for which it is registered. As yet there have been no decisions of the registrar or the courts providing guidance in the application of this provision. The words 'in the trade' should be emphasised; as under s 15 of the TMA 1938, mere descriptive use by members of the public, as opposed to traders, will not suffice. But the mere fact of generic use, even in the trade, will not of itself lead to revocation under sub-s (1)(c). Such a result must be the consequence of acts or inactivity of the proprietor. In some comparatively rare cases, a proprietor has invalidated his trade mark rights by his own generic use; more usually this will result from inactivity, in particular a failure to police the use of the mark effectively. Such conduct is clearly capable of amounting to 'inactivity' for these purposes; on the other hand a failure to take steps against misuse by traders, of which the proprietor was not even aware would not, it is thought, be found to be inactivity, 'in consequence of which' the misuse had occurred.

7.19   By virtue of s 46(5) the registration will not, it seems, be revoked for any other goods or services on this ground, although in some situations the registration might perhaps be open to revocation on the next ground, ie under sub-s (1)(d). As for the date on which the proprietor's rights cease, the matter is purely one of fact on the evidence. It is for the applicant for revocation to adduce evidence to show when it is proper to conclude that the mark had 'become' the common name for a product or services. The collection of such evidence may not be justified where there is no claim for damages; in most cases the date of the application for revocation should be sufficient for the applicant's purposes.

Trade mark becoming misleading

7.20   Section 46(1)(d) provides for revocation where, in consequence of the use made of the mark by the proprietor or with his consent, in relation to the goods or services for which it is registered, it is liable to mislead the public, particularly as to the nature, quality or geographical origin of those goods or services. Sub-section (2), which has already been considered in relation to non-use[1] applies generally to the whole of s 46. Consequently, for the purposes of sub-s (1)(d) it is clear that the use of the mark, which has rendered it liable to mislead, need not be use of the mark in precisely the form in which it is registered, but may be use in a form differing in elements which do not alter the distinctive character of the mark.

1 See also paras **7.7–7.9** above.

7.21 There has been little guidance from the registry[1] or the courts on the application of this provision. The requirement that the liability to mislead the public must be 'in consequence of the use by the proprietor or with his consent' probably amounts to the same as the requirement under s 11 of the TMA 1938, as applied by the courts[2] in cases in which a mark was alleged to have become deceptive after registration, of some 'blameworthy conduct' on the part of the proprietor. Use by licensees or sub-licensees, and use with consent in other cases, such as use by subsidiary companies, is covered. The liability to mislead the public must, it is submitted, be a liability among a significant section of the relevant public, or (as it was put in decisions under the TMA 1938) a likelihood among a substantial number of persons. There is no requirement, as there was in s 11 of the TMA 1938, that the use of the mark be 'disentitled to protection in a court of justice'. Whether there is a likelihood of misleading the public is a question of fact; if it exists, then the ground for revocation is established. Although the provision only actually specifies a liability of the public being misled as to nature, quality or geographical origin, it may be that revocation can be ordered if a mark becomes liable to mislead in other respects, such as the identity of the manufacturer. It is understood that this view is not universally accepted in Europe. However, the use of the word 'particularly', which has been interpreted as meaning 'inter alia',[3] does provide a basis for arguing that the list of examples, of ways in which a mark may become liable to mislead for the purposes of s 46(1)(d), is not exhaustive. The only case in which the provision has been applied is *Scandecor Development AB v Scandecor Marketing AB*, a decision of the Court of Appeal.[4] The facts of the case are complex; essentially the dispute involved certain companies which had originally been part of the same group, the group becoming split on largely territorial lines. As a result, the trade marks in the UK had been used for some time by companies which were unrelated to the registered proprietor. Although the registrations were ordered to be revoked, there appears to have been no argument on the point, the unsuccessful respondent to the appeal having conceded that the trade marks should be revoked as being no longer distinctive of the origin of the registered proprietor and liable to deceive the public.[5] Thus, it seems that the Court of Appeal ordered revocation under s 46(1)(d) on the basis that the provision is not exhaustive and applies to marks which have become liable to mislead as to trade origin. The position is far from clear, and it may be that further guidance will be given by the House of Lords in due course.

1 One case in which a mark was revoked under s 47(1)(d) is *OKO Trade Mark*, Registry, 10 September 1997, noted in CIPA Journal, October 1997, p 783.
2 See *GE Trade Mark* [1973] RPC 297.
3 See *Europemballage Corpn and Continental Can Co Inc v EC Commission* [1973] CMLR 199 at 224 [26] on art 86 of the EC Treaty.
4 [1999] FSR 26. Leave has been granted for an appeal to the House of Lords. The provision was also relied upon, unsuccessfully, in another case in the court, *Gromax Plasticulture Ltd v Don & Low Nonwovens Ltd* [1999] RPC 367 (Lindsay J).
5 [1999] FSR 26, at 45.

7.22 What does, however, seem to emerge from a consideration of the provision is that, generally speaking, although the new law has relaxed considerably the restrictions on licensing and assignment of trade marks and use of jointly owned trade marks, the need to maintain effective control, and in some cases of assignment to take steps to reduce any risks of trade marks becoming misleading, may well be no less than under the TMA 1938. Indeed it may be easier for an application for revocation to succeed under s 46(1)(d) than it would have been under s 11 of the TMA 1938. In accordance with s 46(5) revocation will only be ordered in respect of goods or services for which the mark has become liable to mislead the public. So far as the date of cessation of the proprietor's rights are concerned, under s 46(6) this will normally be the date of the application for revocation. As with revocation under s 46(1)(c) it is a question of fact, to be determined on the evidence if the matter is raised, whether the ground for revocation existed at an earlier date.

Declarations of invalidity

7.23   Section 47 of the TMA 1994 contains a comprehensive code setting out all the grounds on which the registration of a trade mark, whether registered before or after the commencement of the Act,[1] may be declared invalid. The grounds are the same as the absolute and relative grounds for refusal of registration, which have been considered in detail in Chapters 5 and 6. As with revocation under s 46, an application may be made by any person; there is no requirement that the applicant must be a 'person aggrieved',[2] and the application may be made to the registrar or to the court. As under s 46, s 47(3) provides that the application must be made to the court if proceedings concerning the trade mark in question are pending in the court, and the registrar may refer an application made to him to the court at any stage of the proceedings. In addition to the right given to any person to seek a declaration of invalidity, the sub-section gives the registrar, in the case of bad faith in the registration of a trade mark, to apply to the court for a declaration of invalidity of the registration. The question what amounts to bad faith has been considered in Chapter 5.[3] Sub-section (5) provides that where the grounds of invalidity exist only in respect of some of the goods or services for which the trade mark is registered, the trade mark shall be declared invalid as regards those goods or services only. Under sub-s (6) where the registration of a trade mark is declared invalid to any extent, the registration shall to that extent be deemed never to have been made,[4] but there is a proviso that 'this shall not affect transactions past and closed'. These provisions are discussed below.

1 See Sch 3, para 18(2).
2 See para **7.2** above.
3 See paras **5.118–5.121** above.
4 Note the difference from the effect of revocation, under the TMA 1994, s 46(6).

7.24   As with s 46,[1] the question also arises under s 47 whether the tribunal has any discretion to refuse a declaration of invalidity when any grounds for such a declaration are established, because of the use of the words 'may be declared invalid' in sub-ss (1) and (2). Similar arguments, for the view that there is no discretion, can be founded in arts 3 and 4 of the Directive and sub-s (5) of s 47. So far the question has not arisen in any reported cases under s 47.

1 See paras **7.3–7.4** above.

The grounds for invalidity of a registration

7.25   Section 47(1) of the TMA 1994 deals with the absolute grounds. It provides that a registration of a trade mark may be declared invalid on the ground that the trade mark was registered in breach of s 3 or any of the provisions referred to in that section, ie if any of the absolute grounds for refusal applied at the date of the registration. It is not necessary to discuss those grounds further here. There is an important proviso to s 47(1), under which a registration can be saved from invalidation nothwithstanding that the trade mark should not have been registered in the first place. Where the trade mark was registered in breach of s 47(1)(b), (c) or (d) (not s 3(1)(a), which requires refusal of a sign which did not constitute a trade mark), then it is not to be declared invalid if, in consequence of the use which has been made of it, it has after registration acquired a distinctive character in relation to the goods or services for which it is registered. The similar proviso to s 3(1) is discussed in Chapter 5 and the same general approach is appropriate under the proviso to s 47(1). In cases in which registration was obtained without any evidence of acquired distinctive character, it is open to the proprietor to rely upon evidence of use made prior to the date of the application for registration. But even where there was no such use, the effect of the proviso to s 47(1) is that an application for a declaration of invalidity may be defeated by sufficient evidence of use of the mark after the application date. This is in accordance with art 3(3) of the Directive.[1]

1 The legislature could have extended the proviso to s 3(1) to allow an applicant for registration to rely upon use of the mark after the application, but the matter was optional under the Directive, and this was not done.

7.26   The decisions on refusal of registration, which are discussed in detail in Chapter 5, may all be referred to for the purposes of s 47(1). Two decisions of the court provide good examples of the application of the provision, both on counter-claims to infringement claims. In *British Sugar plc v James Robertson and Sons Ltd,*[1] a registration of the mark 'Treat', for dessert sauces and syrups, was declared invalid as having been registered contrary to s 3(1)(b) and (c) and, probably, (d). The judge considered that the use of the mark relied upon by the plaintiff, both before and after the registration date was, having regard to its extent and nature, insufficient to justify the application of the proviso to s 47(1) of the TMA 1994. In a rather different case, *Philips Electronics BV v Remington Consumer Products,*[2] a registration of a mark comprising a representation of the head of a three-headed rotary shaver was declared invalid, not only under s 3(1)(b), but also under s 3(1)(a) on the ground that the mark was not a trade mark, and under s 3(2)(b) and (c), because of the nature of the shape of the article represented by the mark.

1 [1996] RPC 281 (Jacob J).
2 [1998] RPC 283. The Court of Appeal has upheld the decision on invalidity on several grounds, but certain questions have been referred to the ECJ.

7.27   Sub-section (2) is concerned with relative grounds. The registration of a trade mark may be declared invalid on the ground of a conflict with an 'earlier trade mark' in relation to which the conditions set out in s 5(1), (2) or (3) obtain, or that there is an earlier right in relation to which the condition set out in s 5(4) is satisfied, unless the proprietor of the earlier trade mark or right has consented to the registration. Whether there has been consent must be a question of fact. Such consent may be express, but it could also be implied from the conduct of the proprietor of the right. It would appear that consent given after registration would suffice for these purposes. It seems probable that the applicability of the provisions based on s 5(1), (2) and (3) must be determined as at the date of the application for the registration under attack, because an 'earlier trade mark' must be protected as at a date prior to that date.[1] The same must apply to s 5(4). But that is not to say that evidence of use of the mark after – or before – registration is to be ignored. Except in cases where the marks and the goods or services are identical, so that s 5(1) applies, evidence of use without confusion occurring may well demonstrate that there was in fact no likelihood of confusion within s 5(2), or no 'unfair advantage' or 'detriment' for the purposes of s 5(3), or no passing off for the purposes of s 5(4).

1 See the TMA 1994, s 6.

7.28 As already mentioned, s 47(5) provides that the trade mark shall be declared invalid only as regards the goods or services in respect of the grounds of invalidity exist. In most cases there will be no difficulty in determining the specification of goods or services, if any, for which the registration may be retained. The principles applicable are the same as for determining the scope of the specification of goods or services that is permitted where an application for registration meets with absolute or relative grounds of objection. In applications under s 47 before the registrar, the Hearing Officer would decide the matter; in the case of applications before the court, if there is any difficulty it would be open to the court to seek the registrar's view.

7.29 Section 47(6) provides expressly that where the registration of a trade mark is declared invalid to any extent, the registration is, to that extent, deemed never to have been made. Thus no question of awarding damages for any period of use of an otherwise infringing mark will arise. The position is therefore much clearer and hence more satisfactory than it was under the TMA 1938, where it was held that an order for rectification only took effect on the date of the order.[1] As already mentioned, the proviso states that the sub-section shall not 'affect transactions past and closed'. No specific guidance is given as to the effect of the proviso. Presumably it means, for example, that a previous assignment, or other transaction affecting the trade mark, such as a licence, would not be regarded as void as between the parties, by reason only of the declaration of invalidity. Of course such a declaration might have some consequences under the contract governing the transaction, but this will depend upon the terms of each contract.

1 *Second Sight Ltd v Novell UK Ltd and Novell Inc* [1995] RPC 423 (Lightman J). An appeal to the Court of Appeal was filed, but never decided.

7.30 The transitional provisions in Sch 3 need little mention. Apart from the case of pending applications under ss 32 and 34 of the TMA 1938, which continue to be dealt with under that Act, in accordance with para 18(1), under sub-para (2), s 47 applies to existing registered marks as if the provisions of the TMA 1994 had been in force at all material times. This relates in particular to the grounds for refusal under ss 3 and 5. The only exception under para 18(2) is that the relative ground specified in s 5(3), which is based on conflict with a trade mark registered or applied for in respect of different goods or services, cannot be relied upon in respect of an existing registered mark. It should be noted however that an objection based not on an existing registered mark but on a trade mark entitled to protection under the Paris Convention as a well-known trade mark, is not excluded.

Acquiescence

7.31 Section 48 of the TMA 1994 contains a special provision regarding acquiescence, which is virtually identical to art 9 of the Directive, and which is relevant to applications for a declaration of invalidity under s 47(2).[1] It is by its terms limited to cases of acquiescence in the use of a registered trade mark in the UK. It is not absolutely clear whether the five-year period can run from the date of the application for registration, from which date the proprietor's rights commence,[2] or whether the period can only start to run once the mark is placed on the register. Under the TMA 1938, a 'registered trade mark' was defined as 'a trade mark which is actually on the register',[3] with the consequence that the five-year period for a non-use attack could not start to run until the mark was placed on the register.[4] There is no definition of a 'registered trade mark' in the TMA 1994, and s 40(3) provides that:

> 'A trade mark when registered shall be registered as of the date of the filing of the application for registration; and that date shall be deemed for the purposes of this Act to be the date of registration'.

In the circumstances it is probable that, for the purpose of s 48, the acquiescence period can start to run from the application date.

1 Not on absolute grounds, under the TMA 1994, s 47(1).
2 TMA 1994, s 40(3).
3 TMA 1938, s 68(1).
4 *BON MATIN Trade Mark* [1989] RPC 537.

7.32 There is no provision for acquiescence in use of a trade mark which is not registered; in such a case the common law doctrine of acquiescence can still apply in appropriate circumstances.[1]

1 See for example the decision of the Court of Appeal in *Habib Bank Ltd v Habib Bank AG Zurich* [1981] 2 All ER 650, [1982] RPC 1.

7.33 Under s 48, the acquiescence required is for a continuous period of five years, the proprietor of the earlier trade mark or right being aware of such use, which must mean awareness of the use for the whole five-year period. It seems likely that the common law rule requiring reliance on the acquiescence will not apply as such, and that it will suffice for the purposes of s 48 that the proprietor is aware of the use for five years and does nothing about it. If on the other hand he makes a complaint but delays taking proceedings under s 47 until a five-year period has passed, then so long as he has clearly reserved his rights, he may be held not to have acquiesced within s 48. If acquiescence is established, then, unless the registration in question was applied for in bad faith,[1] the owner of the earlier trade mark or other right may not seek a declaration of invalidity under s 47(2). It is probable that this only applies to invalidity in respect of the goods or services for which the mark has been used during the requisite period.

1 See paras **5.118–5.121** above.

Rectification under s 60

7.34 Rectification of the register is one of the remedies available under s 60 of the TMA 1994, which implements the UK's obligations under art 6*septies* of the Paris Convention. Section 60 applies in cases where an application for registration is made by a person who is an agent or representative of a person who is the proprietor of the mark in a Convention country. For this purpose 'Convention country' means a country other than the UK, which is a member of the Paris Convention.[1] Where s 60(1) applies, under s 60(2) the application will be refused if the proprietor opposes it. Under s 60(3), where the application is granted, such proprietor may apply for a declaration of the invalidity of the registration. It should be noted that the proprietor has an alternative remedy, which may often (for reasons of priority) be more valuable, which is to apply for the rectification of the register so as to substitute his name as the proprietor of the registered trade mark. In providing these remedies s 60 deals with a situation (which has arisen from time to time in the past and is often difficult to resolve because it has not been covered expressly in any agreement between the parties), in which a trade mark of an overseas proprietor is registered by an agent or distributor who owns the rights to the trade mark in his own country. The application of these provisions is excluded by sub-s (5) if, or to the extent that the agent or representative justifies his action, ie his action in registering the mark. Such justification might arise where the proprietor had consented to the registration, unless it appeared that such consent was conditional upon the relationship of principle and agent continuing. The remedy is excluded by sub-s (6) if the application for a declaration of invalidity is made after the proprietor has been aware of the registration for three years or longer. An application for rectification under s 60 may be made to the court, but it is not clear whether an application may also be made to the registrar.[2]

1 TMA 1994, s 55(1).
2 See para **9.15** below.

Rectification or correction of the register

7.35 Section 64 of the TMA 1994 makes provision for rectification or correction of the register, in respect of matters not affecting the validity of the registration of a trade mark. Under sub-s (1) any person having a sufficient interest may apply for the rectification of an error or omission in the register. As with applications for revocation or declarations of invalidity, the application may be to the registrar or the court,[1] subject to the same exception, where proceedings concerning the trade mark are pending in the court, in which case the application must be made to the court, and subject to the registrar's right to refer the application to the court at any stage. Under sub-s (3) the effect of rectification is that the error or omission shall be deemed never to have been made, except where the tribunal directs otherwise. Subsection (4) makes separate provision for requests by a proprietor or a licensee to enter any change in his name or address as recorded. Under sub-s (5) the registrar may remove from the register any matter appearing to him to have ceased to have effect. This is a general provision, separate from the earlier parts of the section, and enables the registrar to keep the register clear of any clearly 'dead matter'.

1 As to procedure in the court, see paras **9.20-9.21** below.

7.36 The provision is not thought to have been much used. One instance was a case in which an application for rectification[1] to show that a registration in Class 11 covered goods in Classes 7 and 11, was unsuccessful. The Hearing Officer held that the application for registration was granted as filed and the goods fell appropriately into Class 11. There were therefore no errors or omissions to correct.. The amendment sought was appropriate for an application under s 64(1).

1 *GENESISTrade Mark*, 2 February 1998, noted in CIPA Journal, June 1998, p 471.

The Registrar's powers under the Rules

7.37 The procedures for rectification, which are laid down by r 31, are discussed in Chapter 9, paras 9.15-9.17. For change of a name or address under s 64(4), r 38 requires the request to be made on Form TM21. The right to make such a request is given not only to a proprietor or licensee, in accordance with s 64(4), but is extended to any person having an interest in or a charge on a registered trade mark which has been registered under r 34. Rule 38 also provides for the change of an address for service furnished under r 10.

7.38 The powers given to the registrar under s 64(5), to remove from the register matter appearing to him to have ceased to have effect, are governed by r 39. In such a case, r 39(1) provides that he may, when he considers it appropriate, publish[1] his intention to remove the matter concerned, and requires him, where any person appears to him to be affected by the removal, to send notice of his intention to that person. Under r 39(2) within three months of the publication of the registrar's intention, or of the sending of notice of the registrar's intention (as the case may be) any person may file notice of opposition to the removal on Form TM7, and any person to whom a notice is sent may file (in writing) his objections, if any, to the removal or a request to have his objections heard orally. The three months' period is extendable under r 62. Under para (4), if there is no response to the registrar's notice the registrar may remove the matter. Rule 39(3) provides that if the registrar is satisfied after considering any objections or opposition to the removal that the matter has not ceased to have effect, he shall not remove it. Under para (4), where representations objecting to the removal have been made (whether in writing or orally), the registrar may, if he is of the view after considering the objections that the entry or any part thereof has ceased to have effect, remove it or, as appropriate, the part thereof. The relationship between paras (3) and (4) is not entirely clear, but it would seem that if the registrar is in any doubt, as to whether or not the matter in question has ceased to have effect, he should not remove it. In general it may be said that caution should be observed in exercising these new powers of the registrar. Although there is much to be said for removing 'dead wood' from the register, removal of any matter without sufficient cause could have very serious consequences, and the registrar will no doubt be particularly careful not to be too ready to act on the request of a third party who may have some commercial interest in having the matter removed. Although s 64(5) is not qualified by a requirement that the matter must not affect the validity of the registration of a trade mark (as is the case under sub-s (1)), it is important that the provision should not be used as a 'back-door' means for revocation or invalidation. Finally, it should be noted that an unsuccessful objector to a proposal to remove any matter has a right of appeal under s 76 of the TMA 1994.

1 Ie in the Trade Marks Journal – see r 2(1).

Chapter 8

The application for registration

The application

8.1 Section 32 contains provisions as to what information must be in the application form. In addition to the obvious particulars required by sub-s (2) (which include a statement of the goods or services and a representation of the mark), sub-s (3) requires that the application state that the trade mark is being used, by the applicant or with his consent, in relation to the goods or services, or that he has a bona fide intention that it should be so used. This represents a change in the practice followed under the TMA 1938 in recent years, and is said to have been included because of the provision of the Directive (art 3(2)(d), which was implemented by s 3(6) of the TMA 1994) that registration may be refused where an application is made in bad faith.[1] Section 32(4) provides for the payment of an application fee and such class fees as may be appropriate.[2] Rule 5(1)[3] provides that the application shall be filed on Form TM3 and shall be subject to the payment of the application fee. An important feature of the new law is that it will now be possible to apply to register a trade mark in a number of different classes of goods and services. Rule 5(1) also requires payment of the appropriate class fees. The operation of the system of classification of goods and services is discussed in Chapter 2 above, and needs no further mention here.

1 Section 3(6) is discussed in ch 5 , paras **5.118–5.121**.
2 The fees are now prescribed by the Trade Marks (Fees) Rules 1998, SI 1998/1776, made under s 79.
3 Rule 5 of the Trade Marks Rules 1994 (SI 1994/2583) has been substituted by a new r 5, by r 4 of the Trade Marks (Amendment) Rules 1998 (SI 1998/925).

8.2 The new r 5 includes some specific requirements for certain categories of marks. Paragraph (2) provides that an application for the registration of a three-dimensional mark shall not be treated as such unless the application contains a statement to that effect. Paragraph (3) requires that, where colour is claimed as an element of the trade mark, it shall not be treated as such unless the application contains a statement to that effect and specifies the colour. The mere description of the colour in words (eg 'navy blue') will not comply with this requirement, and the attachment of a sample may not suffice either. Paragraph (4) concerns word marks, and provides that an application to register a trade mark which is a word shall be treated as an application to register that word in the graphical form shown in the application, unless the applicant includes a statement that the application is for registration of the word without regard to its graphical form.

Date of filing

8.3   Under s 33, the date of filing of an application is the date on which documents containing everything required by s 32(2) are furnished to the registrar; if the documents are furnished on different days, the filing date is the last of those days. Under sub-s (2) references to the date of an application for registration are to the date of filing; this represents no change in the law.

Priority

8.4   Claims to priority of applications, based on applications made previously in other countries,[1] are the subject of ss 35 and 36. Section 35 relates to priority claimed from applications in countries which are parties to the Paris Convention. Section 36 is concerned with priority claimed from other relevant overseas applications.

See further ch 16, para **16.6**.

8.5   For the purposes of s 35 a 'Convention country' is defined (in s 55) as a country, *other than the UK*, which is a party to the Paris Convention, or the WTO Agreement[1] and 'Convention application' is to be construed accordingly, as an application made in a 'Convention country'. The definition of 'Convention country' thus excludes the possibility of claiming 'internal priority', on the basis of an earlier UK application. A person who has duly filed a Convention application to register a trade mark, has a right of priority, for the purposes of registering the same mark under the TMA 1994 for some or all of the same goods or services, for a period of six months from the date of filing of the first Convention application. If the application under the TMA 1994 is made within the six-month period, then under sub-s (2), the date of filing of the first Convention application is the relevant date for establishing which rights take precedence, and registrability is not affected by any use of the mark in the UK between the date of the first Convention application and the date of the application in the UK. Sub-section (3) sets the requirements for a Convention application to serve as a basis for claiming the right of priority. For this purpose the term 'regular national filing' is defined as meaning a filing which is adequate to establish the date of filing in the country concerned, whatever the fate of the application. Any filing which, in a Convention country is equivalent to a regular national filing, under its domestic legislation or an international agreement, is treated as giving rise to the right of priority. Sub-section (3) makes it clear that the claim to priority, once properly made, is independent from the Convention application. It is not necessary that the Convention application be successful. The significance of the term 'first such application' in sub-s (1) appears from sub-s (4). It is not permitted simply to extend the time for claiming priority under s 35 simply by filing further applications in the same Convention country. However a subsequent Convention application concerning the same subject as the first application filed in the same Convention country may serve as the first Convention application (of which the filing date is the starting date of the period of priority); this is subject to two conditions. These are that at the time of the subsequent application (a) the previous application has been withdrawn abandoned or refused, without having been laid open to public inspection and without leaving any rights outstanding, and (b) it (ie the subsequent application) has not yet served as a basis for claiming a right of priority. To ensure that the first of these conditions is not circumvented by reinstating the previous application, if this is possible, sub-s (4) provides that the previous application may not thereafter serve as a basis for claiming a priority right. It should be noted that by virtue of Sch 3, para 13, an application made after commencement may claim priority from a Convention application made before commencement. Sub-section (5) allows provision to be made by rules as to the manner of claiming a right to priority on the basis of a Convention application.[2] Subsection (6) provides for the possibility of assignment or transmission of a right of priority, either with the application or independently.

1 References to the WTO Agreement have been added to s 55 (1) and (2) by The Patents and Trade Marks (World Trade Organisation) Regulations 1999 (SI 1999/1899, reg(2) and (3)).
2 See para **8.7** below.

8.6 Under s 36, Her Majesty, by Order in Council, may provide for persons to claim priority from applications in certain other territories, for the purposes of registering the same trade mark under the TMA 1994 for some or all of the same goods or services, for a specified period from the date of filing of the application. These are (a) any of the Channel Islands or a colony, and (b) a country or territory in relation to which the Government has entered into a treaty, convention, arrangement or engagement for the reciprocal protection of trade marks. This requirement as to reciprocal protection does not apply to the Channel Islands or colonies. Sub-section (2) provides that the Order in Council[1] may make provision corresponding to that made by s 35 for Convention countries, or such other provision as appropriate. The previous Order, ie the Trade Marks and Service Marks (Relevant Countries) Order[2] as subsequently amended on a number of occasions, continues to be in force in relation to the countries to which it applies.[3] The Trade Marks (Claims to Priority from Relevant Countries) Order 1994,[4] covers Ecuador and Hong Kong, and contains provisions essentially the same as those contained in s 35.

1 Under sub-s (3) a statutory instrument containing an Order in Council under the section is subject to annulment in pursuance of a resolution of either House of Parliament.
2 SI 1986/1303.
3 Interpretation Act 1978, ss 17(2)(b), 22(1), Sch 2.
4 SI 1994/2803.

8.7 Rule 6 makes provisions as to information to be given in applications claiming priority, by reason of an application for protection duly filed in a Convention country or in another country or territory, under ss 35 and 36 respectively. The application for registration, under r 5, must include particulars of the claim to priority. The particulars must include the country or countries and the date or dates of filing, but these only have to be given if a certificate, as referred to in para (2), is not filed with the application. Unless it has been filed at the time of the filing of the application for registration, para (2) requires the filing, within three months of the filing of the application under r 5, of a certificate by the registering or other competent authority of the country certifying, or verifying to the satisfaction of the registrar, the date of the filing of the application, the country or registering or competent authority, the representation of the mark, and the goods or services covered by the application. The three-month period is extendable under r 62 in appropriate cases.

8.8 In the case of applications filed before commencement in a relevant overseas country within the meaning of s 39A of the TMA 1938, which is not a Convention country (a 'relevant overseas application'), para 14 of the Transitional Provisions, in Sch 3, makes detailed provisions, which follow the provisions of s 35 of the TMA 1994.

Registration procedure

8.9   Section 37 requires the registrar to examine whether an application satisfies the requirements of the TMA 1994, including any requirements imposed by rules. For this purpose he must carry out a search of earlier trade marks. As already mentioned this is qualified by the words 'to such extent as he considers necessary'. It is not yet known how extensive the search will continue to be, although it would seem that in practice the registrar is not generally going to be an a position to raise objections under s 5(3) (marks having a reputation), or of course under s 5(4). If it appears to the registrar that the requirements for registration are not met, he must inform the applicant and give him an opportunity to make representations or to amend the application. If the applicant fails to satisfy the registrar, or to amend the application so as to meet the requirements, or does not respond within the time specified, then the registrar must refuse the application. If the requirements are met, he will accept the application. It should be noted that where the registrar raises objections, setting a time for response, responses to all the objections are required. It is not sufficient to respond only to one objection. Therefore in a case in which objections had been raised regarding a claim to convention priority and also under ss 3(6) (based on the width of the specification) and 5(2), the applicant having responded only to the first objection but not to the others, refusal under s 37(4) was mandatory once the time for responding had expired.[1]

1   *POSTPERFECT Trade Mark* [1998] RPC 255 (Geoffrey Hobbs QC as an appointed person).

8.10   One matter which should be mentioned here, is the receipt by the registrar of objections from third parties before an application has been accepted. Under the TMA 1938 there was no provision at all for 'observations' by third parties, but the registrar – presumably on the basis that he was required to have regard to the public interest and had wide discretionary powers, not only received such objections but in some cases acted upon them. From the applicant's point of view the difficulty was that he was frequently not informed of the identity of the objector, nor even given full details of the material on which the objection was based. The registrar was normally not prepared to release such information unless the third party consented. It is probable that the practice was open to challenge by way of judicial review, on the grounds of contravention of the rules of natural justice. But in most cases it was not practicable – for reasons of cost among others – for applicants to seek judicial review. Under the TMA 1994 the position is different. It is now for the registrar to justify refusal of an application, and the Act makes express provision, in s 38, for written observations by third parties, but only after an application has been advertised. If such observations are received, the registrar is now obliged to inform the applicant of the observations, which would seem to involve disclosure of the material on which they are based and the identity of the party submitting the observations. In these circumstances it is arguable that the registrar has no power to receive observations prior to the advertisement of the application, still less to act on them and to refuse to disclose the relevant information to the applicant. It is submitted that the proper course, if objections are sent to the registrar before an application has been accepted, is for the registrar to refuse to take them into consideration, at least if the objector does not agree to his identity, and the relevant material, being disclosed to the applicant, and to inform the objector of his right to oppose or make written objections if the application is accepted.

Ex parte hearings

8.11   Under the Rules, the right of an applicant to have a hearing at which to attempt to overcome objections raised by the registrar, is continued. Rule 48(1) provides that, without prejudice to any provisions of the TMA 1994 or the Rules requiring the registrar to hear any party to any proceedings under the Act or Rule, or to give such a party an opportunity to be heard, the registrar shall, before taking any decision on any matter under the Act or Rules which is or may be adverse to any party to any proceedings before him, give that party an opportunity to be heard. Under para (2) such party must be given at least 14 days' notice of the time when he may be heard, unless he consents to shorter notice. In practice the registry will communicate with the party's representative and arrange a convenient time.

Appeal against refusal

8.12   As under the TMA 1938, the TMA 1994 provides for a right of appeal against refusal of an application for registration,[1] but there are significant changes. Section 76 now provides that an appeal lies from any decision of the registrar under the TMA 1994 except as otherwise expressly provided by rules. 'Decision' includes any act of the registrar in exercise of a discretion vested in him by or under the Act. This extends the right of appeal to interlocutory decisions, as well as final decisions, which represents a change from the position under the old law. Accordingly there will generally no longer be cases in which application for judicial review would be necessary or appropriate. As before there are alternative routes of appeal. The Rules only exclude the right of appeal in very few instances.[2] However it is likely, notwithstanding the much greater possibilities for appeal, that the person appointed, or the court, will not readily interfere with interlocutory decisions of the registrar, for example in matters of extensions of time, unless a point of principle is involved.[3] Under sub-s (2) any appeal may be brought either to an 'appointed person' or to the court, such person being appointed by the Lord Chancellor,[4] (who must consult with the Lord Advocate) for the purpose. Where an appeal is made to an appointed person, it is open to him to refer the appeal to the court in specified circumstances. In the case of an ex parte appeal against refusal the appeal might be referred to the court if it appeared to the appointed person that a point of general legal importance is involved. The appointed person must give the appellant an opportunity to make representations as to whether the appeal should be referred to the court. A decision of a Hearing Officer may be discharged if the registrar consents, and the application remitted to the registry for further consideration, in appropriate circumstances.[5] Under sub-ss (4) and (5), if the appeal is not referred to the court, the appointed person hears and determines the appeal, his decision being final.[6]

1 See generally chs 5 and 6 as to grounds for refusal.
2 See r 40 (Change of classification) and r 41 (Opposition to proposals for change of classification.
3 See for example the decisions of appointed persons in revocation and opposition proceedings, in *A J & M A Levy's Trade Mark* [1999] RPC 291 and *LIQUID FORCE Trade Mark* [1999] RPC 429.
4 Instead of the Board of Trade, which had this responsibility under the TMA 1938.
5 *Re MAID's Trade Mark Application* (9 December 1998) (Geoffrey Hobbs QC sitting as an appointed person), noted in New Law Digest, 30 September 1998, 698123501. After notice of appeal had been given the registry agreed to proceed on a restricted specification.
6 Although the decision is described as 'final' it would be open to judicial review on a point of law.

Procedure following acceptance

8.13   If the application is accepted, under s 38 the next step, as under the TMA 1938, is for the application to be published in the Trade Marks Journal in accordance with r 12 (see r 2 and s 81). Section 38(2) provides that any person may give notice of opposition within the prescribed time from publication. Under r 13(1) the period is three months and the period is, in contrast to the position under the old law, *non-extendable*.[1] As before, the notice must be in writing and must include a statement of the grounds of opposition. Sub-section (3) introduces a new practice, which, as mentioned above, was sometimes followed informally under the TMA 1938, and under which, after publication and at any time before registration, any person may make written observations to the registrar as to whether the mark should be registered. The registrar must inform the applicant of any such observations. A person making any such observations does not become a party to the proceedings.

1 Rule 62(3).

8.14   The registrar has in some instances, where he has taken the view that the publication in the Journal is not sufficiently clear as to the representation of the mark, caused the application to be re-advertised. A challenge to this practice, by way of judicial review, was rejected by Laddie J in *CREOLA Trade Mark*,[1] on the basis that, because of the defects in representation of the marks concerned, the application was not properly published. The application had not originally been opposed, but notice of opposition was filed in time after the second advertisement. Only if the first advertisement had been correct could the second advertisement have been regarded as a nullity.

1 [1997] RPC 507.

8.15   Section 39(1) provides for withdrawal of the application, or restriction of the goods or services, at any time. In the case of restrictions to goods or services, re-publication is required if the application has already been published. Sub-section (2) makes provision for amendment of the application, but only in very limited respects, considerably narrower than under the previous practice. The only amendments allowed are correction of the applicant's name or address, errors of wording or copying, or obvious mistakes, but even then the amendment must not substantially affect the identity of the trade mark or extend the goods or services covered.[1] In accordance with sub-s (3), r 18 provides for publication of any amendment which affects the representation of the mark or the goods or services covered by the application, and for the making of objections by any person claiming to be affected by it. Objections are made by a notice of opposition under para (2); this must be filed on Form TM7,[2] within one month[3] of the publication of the application as amended, and must include a statement of the grounds of objection and, in particular, how the amendments would be contrary to s 39(2). Para (3) applies r 13,[4] which governs ordinary oppositions, to the proceedings.

1 For an example of a proposed amendment which was not permitted, see a decision of the registry, O/155/98 (24 July 1998), noted in CIPA Journal, November 1998, p 899.
2 See r 18, as amended by r 7 of the Trade Marks (Amendment) Rules 1998,(SI 1998/925).
3 It would appear that this period is extendable in appropriate circumstances, under r 62.
4 This has been amended by the 1998 Rules, r 6.

Division, merger and registration of a series of marks

8.16 Section 41 relates to the division of applications, the merging of applications or registrations, and to the registration of a series of trade marks, and contains important new provisions. Registration of a series of trade marks was possible under s 21(1) of the TMA 1938. The definition of a series, in s 41(2) of the TMA 1994, is less detailed than the corresponding provision of the TMA 1938, simply specifying that the marks should 'resemble each other as to their material particulars and differ only as to matters of a non-distinctive character not substantially affecting the identity of the trade mark'.[1] Probably there is no significant change involved here. The provisions relating to division and merger are completely new and introduce a welcome flexibility into the procedure. Section 41 is implemented by rr 19–21.

1 For a recent instance of two marks being held not to constitute a 'series', see *Re MB RM Trade Mark Application* Registry, 3 June 1999, noted in New Law Digest, 2 November 1999, 699118301.

8.17 Under r 19(1), at any time before registration an applicant may request the registrar, on Form TM12, for division of the original application into two or more separate divisional applications. Each divisional application is treated as a separate application with the same filing date as the original application. Under r 19(2), if the request for division is made after publication of the application, any objections in respect of, or opposition to, the original application are to be taken to apply to each divisional application. Under r 19(3) the same applies to a request for division of an application in respect of which notice has been given of particulars of the grant of a licence, or of a security interest or any right in or under it; ie the notice applies to each of the divisional applications. The provisions for division will be particularly useful in a situation in which the registrar maintains objections against an application in respect of some, but not all, of the goods or services for which registration is sought. It will now be possible to divide out the application for the goods or services in respect of which the objection is raised, and to proceed to publication and registration with the remaining part. Where an application is opposed, division may still be useful in some cases, notwithstanding r 19(2), since it may be possible to isolate the goods or services with which the opponent is really concerned, leaving the way open to withdrawal of the opposition to the other divisional application(s). It should be noted that a registration cannot be similarly divided, although the same result could be achieved, if wished, by a partial assignment.

8.18 Rule 20 relates to merger of applications or registrations. Merger is only possible where the applications or registrations are for the same trade mark. A request for merger must be filed on Form TM17.[1] In the case of applications, r 20(1) provides that the request must be made before preparations for the publication of any of the applications have been completed by the office, and under r 20(2) they must bear the same application date and be in the name of the same person at the time of the request. In the case of registrations, they do not have to bear the same dates, but where they bear different dates, r 20(6) provides that the merged registration will bear the latest of such dates. Although it is not stated, the registrations must clearly be in the same name. Rule 20(4) and (5) contain provisions for the cases where any of the registrations to be merged is subject to a disclaimer or a limitation, or has had registered in relation to it particulars relating to the grant of a licence or a security interest or any right in or under it, or any memorandum or statement of the effect of a memorandum.[2] The merged registration is restricted in accordance with the disclaimer or limitation, and the particulars are registered in relation to the merged registration, as the case may be.

1 Rule 20(1) and (3).
2 See the TMA 1994, ss 25 and 27 and rr 33(f) and (g), 35 and 36.

8.19 Rule 21 governs registration of a series of trade marks in a single registration. The application is made on Form TM3. A representation of each mark must be included and the registrar must accept the application if satisfied that the marks constitute a series. Where the registrar objects that any of the marks do not constitute a series, it is open to the applicant, under r 21(2) to request (on Form TM12) the division of the application into two or more separate divisional applications. Under this provision, division can only be requested before preparations for publication of the application have been completed by the office. It has been held,[1] in opposition proceedings, that r 19 is not applicable to series applications and that because r 21(2) is not available after publication of an application to register a series of marks, to divide the application into separate applications for each of the marks, there is no possibility for division of such an application after publication. Rule 21(4) requires the payment of a divisional fee and such application and class fees as are appropriate. Rule 21(3) permits an applicant, for registration of a series of marks, at any time to request deletion of a mark from the series, and the registrar must then delete that mark.

1 Re *Dualit Ltd's Trade Mark Applications (Toaster Shapes)* [1999] RPC 304. This decision has been upheld on appeal by Lloyd J (5 July 1999).Times, 19 July.

8.20 As under the TMA 1938, once an application has been accepted and no notice of opposition has been given within the prescribed time or all opposition proceedings are withdrawn or decided in the applicant's favour, s 40(1) provides that the registrar must register the mark unless it appears to him that the application was accepted in error. However there appears to be a material difference from the TMA 1938, in that the registrar can only come to the view that the application was accepted in error 'having regard to matters coming to his notice since he accepted the application'. It is likely that he cannot now change his mind, on the basis of a change of opinion as to the relevance of an earlier registered mark, because all registered marks are within his knowledge. Although there may be cases where new facts are discovered which go to registrability from the point of view of absolute grounds, there should generally be very much less scope, after acceptance, for one official in the registry to overturn a decision reached by another official. Sub-section (2) provides that the appropriate fee must be paid before a trade mark can be registered; if it is not paid within the period prescribed the application is deemed to be withdrawn. Sub-section (3) provides that the trade mark shall be registered as at the date of the application for registration, which is deemed to be the date of registration; this is the same as under the TMA 1938. Under sub-s (4) the registration is published and a certificate of registration issued to the applicant.

Applications pending at commencement

8.21 In the case of applications for registration which were pending at commencement, ie 31 October 1994, applicants were permitted, under Sch 3, para 11, to have the registrability of their marks determined in accordance with the provisions of the

TMA 1994. This was only possible where the application had not then been advertised under s 18 of the TMA 1938, and notice to the registrar[1] had to be given no
later than six months after commencement. The notice was irrevocable. In cases in
which such notice was duly given, the applications and resulting registrations are to
be treated as if the applications were made immediately after commencement. It is
to be noted that although the original date was lost on conversion, the effect of Sch
3, para 13, appears to be that priority, based upon a Convention application made
not more than six months before commencement, would have been retained.
Applications pending at commencement, which were not converted under Sch 3,
para 11, were required by Sch 3 to be dealt with under the TMA 1938, but this was
subject to rules made under s 8 of the TMA 1994 and to para 10(3), which provided
that s 23 of the TMA 1938 (requirements for associated marks) should be disregarded. Schedule 3, para 10(2), provides that the rule-making power of the
Secretary of State under s 78, and as to the matters mentioned in sub-s (2), was
exercisable in relation to applications pending at commencement, and that different
provision might be made for such applications from that made for other
applications.

1 In the form set out in Sch 2 to the Rules – see r 68.

Chapter 9

Procedures after acceptance and registration

1 Opposition to registration

The grounds

9.1 If an application for registration is accepted by the registrar and published in the Trade Marks Journal, it may be opposed by any person,[1] on any of the absolute or relative grounds set out in the TMA 1994.[2] In the case of relative grounds based upon an 'earlier trade mark' or other 'earlier right' it is not necessary for the opponent to be the owner of such rights, although in practice he usually will be the owner or a related company, or some other person such as a licensee, having an interest in the earlier mark or right. Opposition under s 38(2) is to be distinguished from the making of written observations under s 38(3);[3] any ground may be raised in this way, but the person making the observations does not become a party to the proceedings on the application and is not entitled to be heard on the matter. The applicant, who must be informed of the observations, is of course entitled to be heard [4]before any decision is or may be taken which is adverse to him.

1 Section 38(2).
2 See chs 5 and 6 above.
3 See ch 8 above.
4 See r 48.

9.2 An additional ground for opposition is provided by s 60 of the TMA 1994, where the opponent is the proprietor of the mark applied for in a Convention country,[1] if the applicant is an agent or representative of the opponent. By virtue of sub-s (2) such proprietor (but no-one else) may oppose the application, and will succeed unless the applicant can justify his action, in seeking registration, under sub-s (4). Any such justification would usually, it is thought, be based on some agreement or other relationship between the parties.

1 Ie a country, other than the UK, which is a party to the Paris Convention – see s 55(1) and para **8.5** above.

Procedure

9.3 The procedure for oppositions is laid down in the Rules. There are several significant differences from the procedure under the TMA 1938, one being that the onus is now on the opponent to establish his case. Opposition procedures are laid down by r 13.[1] Any person may oppose, and it is not necessary that the opponent be the proprietor of prior rights relied upon under s 5.[2] Under r 13(1) the notice of opposition must be sent to the registrar, on Form TM7, within three months of the date on which the application was published under r 12. It should be noted that where an application has been divided pursuant to s 41(1) of the Act, the notice of opposition must refer to the new number of the resulting application or applications opposed, which have suffixes 'A', 'B', etc added after the original number; a notice referring to the original number has been held invalid.[3] The notice must include a statement of the grounds of opposition[4] and the registrar is required to send a copy of the notice and the statement to the applicant. By virtue of sub-para (2) of r 13 the applicant may, within three months of the date on which a copy of the statement of grounds is sent to him by the registrar, file, in conjunction with notice of the same on Form TM8, a counterstatement, and the registrar is required to send a copy of this to the applicant. The first point to emphasise is that the times for opposing and filing a counterstatement are not extendable.[5] It is also important to note that in the amended r 13, para (3) provides that where a notice and counterstatement are not filed by the applicant within the three month period prescribed, he shall be deemed to have withdrawn his application for registration. In the original r 13 there was no sanction for such failure. So far as the time for opposing is concerned, the same applies to applications under the TMA 1938 which are advertised after 31 October 1994;[6] although it appears that the time for filing a counterstatement may be extendable, the position is not entirely clear and it is safer to observe the three-month period here also. Consistent with the restriction of the period for opposition to three months is the omission of the possibility of amending grounds of opposition. Rule 62(7), which makes provision for extension of times by way of correction of irregularities of procedure in or before the office in certain circumstances,[7] might for example be used to obtain an extension of the time for filing a notice of opposition or a counterstatement where the failure resulted from a mistake on the part of the office (for example in sending the notice of opposition and statement of grounds to an address for service which had been superseded). However a failure to include a ground for opposition, which might have been relied upon, cannot, it is submitted, be termed an 'irregularity of procedure'.

1 Of the Trade Mark Rules 1994, SI 1994/2583, replaced by the Trade Marks (Amendment) Rules 1998, (SI 1998/925), r 6.
2 *WILD CHILD Trade Mark* [1998] RPC 455 (Geoffrey Hobbs QC sitting as appointed person).
3 *DUCATI Trade Mark* [1998] RPC 227.
4 It appears that a statement of grounds relying on earlier trade marks, under s 5, may be treated as ineffective if full details, including the specifications of goods or services covered by the earlier marks. See notice No 6162 in the Journal, and the registry decision in *ORADENT* (2 July 1998) noted in the CIPA Journal, October 1998, p 808.
5 See r 62(1) and (3).
6 See r 67.
7 See para **2.25** above.

9.4 Rule 13 (as amended) also lays down, in paras (4)–(7), the timetable for filing of evidence. There is now a choice for the form of the evidence; either a statutory declaration or an affidavit may be used.[1] Whereas under the previous rules initial periods of six months were allowed for each stage of the evidence (evidence in support, in answer and in reply), the new rules reduce these periods to three months at each stage. As before, evidence in reply must be confined to matters strictly in reply to the applicant's evidence. If the opponent files no evidence in support of the opposition, then under r 13(5) he is deemed to have abandoned the opposition unless the registrar otherwise directs. There may be cases in which the matter is considered to be so clear that no evidence is required. This is less likely now that the onus of proof is on the opponent, but can happen, for example where the marks and the goods or services concerned are identical, so that a likelihood of confusion need not be established,[2] or it is obvious that the mark applied for is too similar to an earlier mark. Since it is necessary to obtain a direction from the registrar if the opposition is to be continued, there will often be much to be said in any event, for filing some evidence, even if it is only formal evidence of registrations or pending applications relied upon.

1 See also s 69(a) and r 49.
1 TMA 1994, s 5(1).

9.5 Although the periods for the evidence are extendable under rule 62, the fact that they have been shortened, and that the periods of opposition and counterstatement are not extendable, are indications of the registrar's intention to reduce the overall time taken for oppositions to be heard. Extensions of time for evidence have been becoming more difficult to obtain in recent years, and any party seeking an extension is expected to provide justification for the request. Two decisions of appointed persons on appeal,[1] illustrate the current approach. In another registry decision[2] the Hearing Officer, in allowing an extension of time for filing evidence, did not accept an argument that the period of three months, from the filing of the notice of opposition to the receipt of the applicant's counterstatement, should be taken into account as time during which the opponent should have been preparing evidence. The fact that the grounds for opposition and invalidation are now identical and that the incidence of the onus of proof is the same in both kinds of proceeding, is perhaps another reason for being stricter in the matter of extensions of time and, in appropriate circumstances, leaving an opponent to the alternative remedy of applying for a declaration of invalidity once the mark is registered. As previously, it is possible, under r 13(8), for a party to seek leave to file further evidence, which may be given upon such terms as the registrar may think fit. Here again, it has been noted that the registrar has been exercising the discretion, given by the Rules, quite strictly. Further evidence is much less likely to be allowed if it has been available for some time or if the other party is given insufficient time to consider and (if necessary) respond to it. Accordingly fresh evidence submitted at or shortly before the hearing stands a very high chance of being rejected.

1 *A J & M A Levy's Trade Mark* [1999] RPC 291 and *LIQUID FORCE Force Trade Mark* [1999] RPC 429.
2 *PORTAFLOOR Trade Mark* (29 August 1997) noted in CIPA Journal, September 1997, p 712.

9.6 Reference has already been made to the powers of the registrar to hear oral evidence and to order cross-examination of witnesses, and to the new provisions regarding discovery and production of documents.[1] As to cross-examination of witnesses, the registrar may be fairly sympathetic to an application for leave to cross-examine a witness if the application is made in good time before the hearing, and he would normally also be expected to give leave for cross-examination of the other party's witness or witnesses on the same issue. However he will be likely to take all matters into consideration, including matters such as cost and convenience, and balance these against the importance of the evidence in question.[2] It is expected that the courts will continue to apply the rule that cross-examination of a witness on appeal will not be allowed if no request to cross-examine the witness was made to the registrar before the hearing, on the basis that the request amounts to a request to adduce fresh evidence.[3] A request to the registrar to receive oral evidence at the hearing would seem to amount to an application to introduce further evidence which should be treated in the same way as an application to file further evidence under r 13(7). It would be unusual for the registrar to agree to receive such evidence if the application was only made at the hearing or a short time before, or if the evidence had been available for some time. As regards discovery and production of documents, r 52[4] gives to the registrar all the powers of an official referee of the Supreme Court. This matter is now regulated by the CPR 1998.[5] Again applications ought where possible to be made well before the hearing. Although clearly the powers are given to be used, some decisions[6] indicate that the registrar's new powers will be exercised with some restraint, so as to avoid unnecessary escalation of costs. It may well be appropriate in most cases to direct orders to specific documents or categories of documents, or to specific issues, rather than to make general orders for discovery. Such approach is consistent with the CPR 1998.

1 Section 69(b) and (c) and r 51 and 52. See also ch 2, paras **2.30–2.34**.
2 See also ch 2, para **2.30** above.
3 See para **2.34**.
4 Made under the TMA 1994, s 69.
5 See Part 31; official referees are now judges of the Technology and Construction Court.
6 See for example *LIFESAVERS Trade Mark* [1997] RPC 563.

9.7   One question, which has arisen, is whether the powers under the TMA 1994 and Rules are available in oppositions commenced before 31 October 1994, or whether they are restricted to use in oppositions to applications advertised after that date. The Rules make no specific provision on this question, but (subject only to the transitional provisions in Sch 3) the TMA 1938 is repealed with effect from 31 October 1994 and the Rules, which came into force on that date,[1] do expressly revoke the 1986 Rules.[2] Furthermore, there is a presumption that procedural provisions are retrospective and apply to existing proceedings. It seems now to have been established that, except where the Rules specifically provide otherwise,[3] they apply to applications made before 31 October 1994, and to oppositions to such applications, as well as to new applications.[4]

1 Rule 1.
2 Rule 69(1)
3 See for example r 44(4).
4 See ch 2, para **2.13** above.

2   Duration, renewal and alteration

Duration

9.8   Under s 42(1) of the TMA 19994, a trade mark is registered, in the first place, for ten years from the date of registration, that is the application date.[1] By sub-s (2) renewal, in accordance with s 43, is for further successive terms of ten years. This is simpler than under the old law, under which registration was for a first term of seven years, with renewals for 14-year terms. The transitional provisions, in para 15(1) of Sch 3, provide that s 42(1) applies in relation to registration of a mark applied for after commencement; this will include an application converted under para 11 of the Schedule. In the case of old applications, the original period remained at seven years, but the renewal period of ten years has applied to all registrations where the renewal fell due after 31 October 1994.[2]

1 Section 40(3).
2 By para 15(2) of the transitional provisions in Sch 3, which provides that, where renewal falls due on or after commencement, ss 42(2) and 43 apply; but that in other cases the old law applies.

Renewal

9.9 Under s 43 a registration may be renewed at the request of the proprietor, subject to payment of a renewal fee. Sub-section (2) requires provision to be made by rules for the registrar to inform the proprietor of a registered trade mark, before the expiry of the registration, of the date of expiry and the manner in which the registration may be renewed. Under r 28, renewal must be effected by filing a request for renewal on Form TM11, at any time within the period of six months ending on the date of the expiration of the registration. By sub-s (4) renewal takes effect from the expiry date. In accordance with sub-s (2), amended r 27(1)[1] provides, subject to r 27(2), for the registrar to send to the registered proprietor notice of the approaching expiration, informing him that the registration may be renewed in the manner described in rule 28. This may be done at any time not earlier than six months nor later than one month before the expiration of the last registration, but need not be done where renewal has already been effected. In order to cover a situation which sometimes arises, rule 27(2) now provides that if it appears to the registrar that a trade mark may be registered under s 40 at any time within six months before or after the date on which renewal would be due (by reference to the date of application for registration), the registrar shall be taken to have complied with rule 27(1) if he sends to the applicant notice thereof within one month following the date of actual registration.

1 The original r 27 has been amended by the Trade Marks (Amendment) Rules 1998 (SI 1998/925). r 10.

9.10 Section 43(3) requires the request for renewal to be made, and the fee paid, before the expiry date, but allows for renewal within such further period (of not less than six months) as may be prescribed, and an additional renewal fee must also be paid within that period. Under r 29(1), if on the expiration of the last registration of a trade mark, the renewal fee has not been paid, the registrar must publish that fact; and if, within six months,[1] which is the minimum period under sub-s (3), from the date of expiration the request for renewal is filed on Form TM 11 accompanied by the appropriate renewal fee and the additional renewal fee, the registrar is required to renew the registration without removing it from the register. By r 29(2), where no request for renewal is filed in accordance with these provisions, the registrar must, subject to r 30, remove the mark from the register. The original rr 29(3) and (4), relating to the situation in which a mark is not registered until shortly before or after the renewal date, as calculated from the date of the application for registration, have been replaced[2] by a new r 29(3). Under this provision, if a mark is due to be registered after the date on which it is due for renewal (by reference to the date of application for registration), the request for renewal is to be filed together with the renewal fee and additional renewal fee within six months[3] after the date of actual registration.

1 This period is not extendable – see the Rules, r 62(3).
2 Trade Marks (Amendment) Rules 1998 (SI 1998/925), r 11.
3 This period is not extendable – see r 62 as amended.

9.11   If a registration is not renewed in accordance with sub-s (3), s 43(5) requires the registrar to remove the trade mark from the register, and amended r 29(4)[1] requires the removal to be published in the Journal. However for the proprietor that is not necessarily the end of the matter, since under s 43(5) rules may provide for restoration, subject to such conditions (if any) as may be prescribed. Rule 30 deals with restoration. Where a registration is removed for failure to renew it in accordance with r 29, the registrar may, upon a request filed on Form TM13 within six months[2] of the date of the removal, accompanied by the appropriate renewal fee and appropriate restoration fee, renew the registration if, having regard to the circumstances of the failure to renew, he is satisfied that it is just to do so. The new law is thus stricter than the old law, under which it was possible to restore a lapsed registration rather more than six months after the expiry. It is clear that restoration, even within the six-months period, is discretionary and will not be allowed as of right. For example, if a proprietor deliberately fails to renew, and then only decides to seek restoration because he has discovered that another party is using the same or a similar mark and wants to make a claim for infringement, it is likely that restoration will not be granted. Sub-section (6) requires the renewal or restoration to be published in the prescribed manner.

1 Which is the same as the original r 29(5).
2 This period is not extendable – see the Rules, r 62(3).

Alteration

9.12   Under the old law it was never easy to alter a registered trade mark, although it was possible, subject to the requirement[1] that the change must not substantially affect the identity of the mark. Section 44 of the TMA 1994 is very much stricter even than that. Under sub-s (1) it is provided that a registered trade mark shall not be altered in the register, during the period of registration or on renewal. Nevertheless under sub-s (2) the registrar can, at the request of the proprietor, allow alteration where the mark includes the proprietor's name or address, if (and only if) the alteration is limited to altering that name or address and does not substantially affect the identity of the mark. In accordance with sub-s (3) r 25, which requires a request for alteration of a registered mark to be made on Form TM25 and allows the registrar to require evidence as to the circumstances of the application, provides for publication of any alteration and for the making of objections by persons claiming to be affected. The notice of opposition to the alteration, including a statement of the grounds, must be sent to the registrar, on Form TM 7, within three months of publication. Rules 13(2) and (4)–(9)[2] apply to the proceedings. Originally, the period for opposition was extendable under r 62, since r 13(1) was not applied, although the period for filing a counterstatement was not extendable, because r 13(2) was applied. However, r 62 has been amended,[3] and the amended r 62(3) now also excludes any extension of time under r 25(3).

1 TMA 1938, s 35.
2 Of the 1994 Rules as amended by the Trade Marks (Amendment) Rules 1998 (SI 1998/925), r 9.
3 By the Trade Marks (Amendment) Rules 1998 (SI 1998/925), r 17(c).

9.13   It will be seen that in most cases alteration of a registered trade mark will be impossible. Where a proprietor alters a registered trade mark in use, then he will have the choice of relying on existing registrations if the alteration is not substantial, since they will not be likely to be open to attack on the ground of non-use,[1] or obtaining new registrations of the altered form, perhaps keeping the old registrations in force for at least some time afterwards. It should be noted that, under para 16 of Sch 3, an application[2] for alteration of a registered trade mark, pending at commencement, was dealt with under the old law.

1 Under s 46(1) –because of sub-s (2).
2 TMA 1994, S 35.

Surrender

9.14 Section 45 of the TMA 1994 provides that a registered trade mark may be surrendered by the proprietor, in respect of some, or all, of the goods or services for which it is registered. In accordance with sub-s (2) provision has been made by r 26 as to the manner and effect of a surrender and for protecting the interests of other persons having a right in the registered mark. This provision may be of considerable practical importance, not only because of the broader rights which licensees, particularly exclusive licensees, may have under the new law, but because of the new possibilities for using registered marks as security interests, registrable under s 25. Under r 26 the proprietor must give notice of surrender to the registrar on Form TM22 if the surrender is in respect of all the goods or services for which the mark is registered, or on Form TM23 if the surrender is in respect of only some of the goods or services. Presumably, where under the new provisions of the TMA 1994, the registration is a multi-class registration covering goods and services, Form TM22 will only be used if the surrender is in respect of all the goods and all the services. Rule 26(2) contains the provisions intended to ensure that any persons affected by the surrender are notified and consent to the surrender. Under this rule, a notice under para (1) is of no effect unless the proprietor in the notice gives the name and address of any person having a registered interest in the mark and certifies that any such person either has been sent not less than three months' notice of the proprietor's intention to surrender the mark, or is not affected, or if affected consents thereto. Under para (3) of r 26 the registrar, upon the surrender taking effect, will make the appropriate entry in the register and publish the same. It remains to be seen whether these provisions are satisfactory or sufficient in practice. The position of persons whose interests are not registered should not be of particular concern because, it can be said, they may reasonably be expected to accept the risks of non-registration. But in the case of persons whose interests are registered it is not clear that even they are adequately protected. Moreover the position of third parties may be affected. The Rules make no provision for opposition, or for any objection to be made by a person interested, who has not been given the necessary notice or believes that he is prejudiced by the proposed surrender. It may be that if the proprietor does not comply with r 26(2), the surrender is to be treated as a nullity, by virtue of the words 'shall be of no effect' in para (1), but that may be of no comfort to a third party who has obtained a registration, or commenced use, of a conflicting mark on the basis that the surrender was effective. It is not clear whether the registrar will check the register to ensure that any persons having a registered interest in the mark are named in the notice. Furthermore, a notice, even if certified to have been sent, may not be received, and the proprietor's view as to whether the person concerned is 'affected' by the surrender may not necessarily be correct. At all events it might have been better to require the registrar to notify them of any proposed surrender, rather than leave this to the proprietor, who might have reasons for not giving notice to such person, or simply omits to do so.

3 Proceedings for revocation, invalidation and rectification or correction of the register

Proceedings before the registrar

9.15   Where an application is made to the registrar the procedure is governed by the Rules. At present, r 31 applies to all applications for revocation under s 46, for declarations of invalidity under s 47 and for rectification or correction of the register under s 64. No specific provision appears to be made for applications, under s 60(3) of the TMA 1994, for a declaration of invalidity of a registration obtained by an agent or representative of the proprietor of the mark in a convention country, or for rectification of the register so as to substitute such proprietor's name as proprietor of the trade mark. In the absence of any such provision, it is clearly permissible to apply to the court.[1] It may also be that the intention is that an application for a declaration of invalidity under s 60(3) should be made in accordance with s 47 and an application for rectification should be made in accordance with s 64. That would mean that the application could be made to the registrar or to the court. However, until the position is clarified by the registry, or by amendment of the Rules, it may be safer to make the application to the court.

1 Formerly under the procedure laid down in RSC 1965, Ord 100 r 2(2). See now the Civil Procedure Rules 1998 Practice Direction under Part 49, para 23.5.

9.16   Rule 31 provides that the application shall be made on Form TM26 together with a statement of grounds on which the application is made. If the procedure is applicable to applications under s 60(3), it should be noted that sub-s (6) requires such applications to be made within three years of the proprietor becoming aware of the registration. As with oppositions, there appears to be no possibility of amending a statement under r 31(1), to add new grounds.[1] Under r 31(2) a copy of the application and statement must be sent by the registrar to the proprietor, where he is not the applicant. Within three months of the date on which these documents are sent to the proprietor, r 31(3) provides that the proprietor may file a counterstatement together with Form TM8, and a copy is to be sent to the applicant. Although r 31(3) is not included among the provisions specifically excluded by r 62(3) from the general powers to extend times, the registry has treated the period under r 31(3) as non extendable, on the basis of the application, by r 31(4), of the provisions of r 13.[2] Rule 31(3) also contains a new provision to meet the new situation created by s 100, which provides that where, in any civil proceedings under the TMA 1994, a question arises as to the use to which a registered trade mark has been put, it is for the proprietor to show what use has been made of it. Where an application for revocation is based on non-use under s 46(1)(a) or (b), the proprietor must file, within the period allowed for the filing of a counterstatement, evidence of the use by him of the mark. If he fails to do so, then the registrar may treat his opposition to the application as having been withdrawn. Although the word 'may' suggests that the registrar might have a discretion, it is difficult to see how in practice the proprietor could continue to defend the proceedings if he failed to file the evidence of use required by r 31(3).[3] And while the word 'may' in r 31(3) might appear to suggest that the filing of a counterstatement is optional, in practice the proprietor must file a counterstatement in non-use cases because, if he does not do so, under r 31(4) the application for revocation must be granted. These provisions may be very important in cases in which an applicant for revocation, on grounds of non-use, files an application and enters into negotiations with the proprietor with a view to taking an assignment of the registration. In such a situation the proprietor should always file a counterstatement; otherwise the application for revocation will automatically be granted under r 31(4) and the registration will be removed and the purpose of the negotiations will be defeated.

1 See para **9.3** above.
2 See ch 2, para **2.28** above.
3 In exceptional circumstances it is possible that the registrar might accept the evidence under the general provisions of the amended Rules. r 13(8).

9.17 The next stage is the filing of evidence by the applicant, and in accordance with r 31(4) the provisions of r 13[1] apply to the proceedings, subject to r 31(2) and to paras (6) and (7) relating to intervention by third parties. Thus, from the date on which a copy of the counterstatement is sent to the applicant, there are successive periods of three months for each stage, which periods are again extendable under r 62. Also applicable are the provisions of r 13(8) regarding the filing of further evidence and r 13(9) requiring a date to be set for a hearing if required by any party. The observations in this chapter in relation to opposition procedures, including those as to extensions of time and filing of further evidence, and as to cross-examination, the receiving of oral evidence and discovery and production of documents, apply similarly to revocation proceedings before the registrar.[2] It should be noted that if a party fails to comply with an order for discovery, this may lead to his application failing or to him being debarred from defending the application, as the case may be.[3]

1 Ie. r 13 of the Trade Marks Rules 1994 (SI 1994/2583) as substituted by r 6 of the Trade Marks (Amendment) Rules 1998 (SI 1998/925).
2 See paras **9.4–9.6** above.
3 See the registry decision O/44/98 (4 February 1998) noted in CIPA Journal, June 1998, p 471.

Intervention

9.18 Rule 31(5) makes provision for intervention by third parties in revocation proceedings. Any person other than the registered proprietor, claiming to have an interest in proceedings on an application under r 31, may file an application to the registrar on Form TM27 for leave to intervene, stating the nature of his interest. The registrar may, after hearing the parties if so required, refuse such leave, or grant leave upon such terms and conditions (including any undertaking as to costs) as he thinks fit. The words 'claiming to have an interest in proceedings ... ' appear to have a broader effect than the corresponding words of r 84 of the 1986 Rules and earlier rules, which were interpreted as requiring a claim to an interest in the trade mark which is the subject of the application.[1] Rule 31(5) may be sufficiently broad in its scope to allow a person having an interest in a conflicting mark relied upon in the statement of grounds, in using a conflicting mark, or in using a description which is the same as a mark claimed in the proceedings to have become generic, to intervene. Under the TMA 1938, if a party was refused leave to intervene he could not usually take the matter further, the decision being at the registrar's discretion. Under the TMA 1994 there is now the possibility of an interlocutory appeal under s 76(1). Under r 31(6) a person granted leave to intervene is, subject to the terms and conditions imposed in respect of the intervention, to be treated as a party for the purposes of the application of r 13 to the proceedings.

1 See eg *Application by Gardinol Chemical Co Ltd for Rectification of the Register and Application by Cyclo Chemicals Ltd to intervene* (1948) 65 RPC 455 and 66 RPC 225. Cf *Kodiak Trade Mark* [1987] RPC 269.

Reference to the court

9.19   As already mentioned, the registrar may at any stage of the proceedings refer the matter to the court.[1] The Rules make no provision as to the procedure to be followed. The registrar will normally inform the parties if he is minded to refer the application to the court; it is also possible for one of the parties to request a reference, which would be done informally by letter. If either party objected to the application being referred, he would presumably be entitled to a hearing under r 48, on the basis that a decision to refer would or might be adverse to him. The usual situation, in which reference to the court may often be appropriate, is where subsequent proceedings are commenced in the court concerning the trade mark in question. Other reasons sometimes advanced, such as the need for discovery or cross-examination of witnesses making the court a more appropriate tribunal, would have rather less force in view of the new powers given to the registrar under s 69. Where the application is referred, the procedure is governed by Rules of Court.[2]

1 Under the TMA 1994, ss 46(4)(b), 47(3)(b) and 64(2)(b).
2 See the Civil Procedure Rules, Part 49, set out in Appendix 3, paras 23 and 24, and para **9.20** below.

Proceedings before the court

9.20   Applications to the court under ss 46, 47 and 64 are now made by the issue of a claim form or by way of an application notice in existing proceedings; in infringement proceedings the application is made by counterclaim. The procedure is laid down by the CPR 1998,[1] which also deal with applications referred to the court by the registrar. In cases where validity of a registration is put in issue in the defence or an application is made by counterclaim for revocation, a declaration of invalidity or for rectification, the CPR 1998 require service of particulars of the objections relied upon. All claim forms, application notices and counterclaims with particulars of objections, must be served on the registrar.[2] Where an application is referred to the court by the registrar, then the applicant must, within one month after receiving notification of the decision to refer, make to the court the application referred; otherwise he will be deemed to have abandoned it.

1 See now the Civil Procedure Rules, Part 8, and Part 49, paras 23.5 and 23.7.
2 Part 49, paras 23.6 and 24.3. A party in whose favour a court order is made must serve an office copy on the registrar.

9.21   Under the TMA 1938, the question of service of proceedings under the Act was sometimes a cause of difficulty. There were decisions of the court upholding service of proceedings at the address for service filed with the registrar under the rules. Under the CPR 1998 the position is clarified by a provision that until an address for service has been provided in accordance with r 6.5, for the purposes of any proceedings under the TMA 1938 or the TMA 1994 (including proceedings for revocation, declaration of invalidity or non-infringement or groundless threats of infringement proceedings) where any document is served, in such manner as complies with the requirements of Part 61 of the CPR 1998, at an address for service given in the register kept under s 63 of the TMA 1994,[2] service shall be deemed to have been effected on the registered proprietor on the date at which the document was served at such address. For the purposes of any provisions of the rules of court specifying a time-limit for responding to the document served, the party on whom such service is deemed to have been effected is to be treated as having been served on the seventh day after the date on which the document was served at the address for service. It is further provided that nothing in this rule shall prevent service being effected on the proprietor in accordance with Part 6. However although service on the proprietor direct in accordance with the provisions of the CPR 1998 is thus retained as an alternative, with foreign proprietors service at an address for service provided under the TMA 1994 is obviously much easier.

1 The general rules for service of court proceedings.
2 Ie an address of the proprietor filed pursuant to the Trade Marks Rules 1994, r 10 or any rules previously made under the TMA 1938.

Chapter 10

Special categories of trade marks

1 Certification marks

The origin of certification trade marks in the UK

10.1   Certification trade marks were introduced into UK law under s 62 of the Trade Marks Act 1905 as 'standardisation marks' Act and continued, as certification trade marks, under the provisions of s 37 of, and Sch 1 to the TMA 1938. When the TMA 1938 was amended in 1986 to allow for the first time, for the registration of service marks, the provisions relating to certification marks were not extended to services.

The new provisions

10.2   Under s 1 of the TMA 1994, references in the Act to a trade mark include references to a certification mark unless the context otherwise requires. In the TMA 1994 certification marks are dealt with by s 50 and Sch 2; under s 50(2) the provisions of the TMA 1994 are applied to certification marks, subject to the provisions of Sch 2, and the new provisions cover services as well as goods. A significant change is that the whole responsibility, for all aspects of the registration and maintenance of certification marks, is now given to the registrar, whereas under the previous law matters such as the approval and alteration of the regulations governing use of certification marks were dealt with by the Department of Trade and Industry (formerly the Board of Trade).

Definition of a certification mark

10.3   Section 50(1) defines a certification mark as 'a mark indicating that the goods or services in connection with which it is used are certified by the proprietor of the mark in respect of origin, material, mode of manufacture of goods or performance of services, quality, accuracy or other characteristics'. Sub-section (2) refers to Sch 2 which, in para 1, applies the provisions of the TMA 1994 generally, subject only to the following provisions of the Schedule. In relation to a certification mark the reference, in the definition of a 'trade mark' in s 1(1), to 'distinguishing goods or services of one undertaking from those of another undertaking', is to be construed[1] as a reference to 'distinguishing goods or services which are certified from those which are not'. Subject to this, the requirement of capability of distinguishing, in s 1(1), applies. Applications to register certification marks are subject to examination as to absolute and relative grounds for refusal under the TMA 1994, in the same way as other applications for registration of trade marks, subject only to any differences provided for in Sch 2. In considering absolute grounds it must be emphasised that the previous definition of a 'certification trade mark',[2] including the requirement of inherent distinctiveness, no longer applies, and that the general approach to registrability[3] must be the same as for other trade marks. Subject to this, and to the extension to services, the function of a certification mark is essentially the same as it was under the TMA 1938.

1 Schedule 2, para 2.
2 TMA 1938, s 37(1).
3 See ch 5 above.

Differences from ordinary trade marks under the TMA 1994

10.4 The kinds of signs which may qualify as certification marks are therefore the same as those set out in the definition of a 'trade mark' in s 1 of the TMA 1994, subject to the different requirement that they be capable of distinguishing goods or services which are certified from those which are not. Similarly to the provisions of the TMA 1938, Sch 2, para 4 prohibits registration of a certification mark if the proprietor carries on a business involving the supply of goods or services of the kind certified. Paragraph 3 excludes from the absolute grounds for refusal the provisions of s 3(1)(c)[1] in so far as they refer to signs or indications which may serve to designate the geographical origin of goods or services, but adds a provision that the proprietor is 'not entitled to prohibit the use of the signs or indications in accordance with honest practices in industrial or commercial matters (in particular by a person who is entitled to use a geographical name)'. The purpose of this last part is not clear; it could be understood as referring to established use of such a name, but it is general in its terms and could cover any kind of entitlement to use a name, including specific entitlement under a statute or, perhaps a right arising from having a business established in the place concerned. An additional provision, which may be regarded as an absolute ground for refusal,[2] is contained in Sch 2, para 5, which prohibits registration where the public is liable to be misled as to the character or significance of the mark, in particular if it is likely to be taken as something other than a certification mark. Accordingly the registrar may require inclusion in the mark of an indication that it is a certification mark, and this may involve amendment in the course of the registration procedure, which is accordingly expressly permitted, notwithstanding s 39(2) of the TMA 1994. Another notable difference, in Sch 2, para 12, is that the registrar's consent must be given before any assignment or transmission can take effect.

1 See paras **5.57–5.64** above and the decision of the ECJ in *Windsurfing Chiemsee Produktions- und Vertriebs GmbH v Huber and Attenberger* [1999] ETMR 585. This exception is permitted by the Directive, art 15(2) from which para 3 is derived.
2 And therefore permitted under the exception provided by the Directive, art 15(1).

The regulations

10.5 Continuing the policy of the TMA 1938, an applicant for registration of a certification mark is required to file regulations governing the use of the mark. The provisions governing the filing, approval and amendment of the regulations, are contained in Sch 2, paras 6–10. Paragraph 6(1) imposes the requirement to file the regulations. Under para 10 the regulations are open to public inspection. Under para 7(2) and r 22 the applicant must file Form TM 35 with a copy of the regulations, and pay the prescribed fee, within nine months[1] of the date of the application for registration; otherwise the application will be deemed to be withdrawn. In accordance with para 6(2) the regulations must indicate who is authorised to use the mark, the characteristics to be certified by the mark, how the certifying body is to test those characteristics and to supervise the use of the mark, the fees (if any) to be paid in connection with the operation of the mark and the procedures for resolving disputes. Further requirements may be imposed by rules.[2] Paragraph 7(1) prohibits registration of a certification mark unless (a) the regulations comply with these requirements and are not contrary to public policy or accepted principles of morality and (b) the applicant is competent to certify the goods or services concerned. The references to public policy and accepted principles of morality are no doubt intended to be understood in the same sense as under s 3(3)(a).[3]

1 This period may be extended under r 62.
2 No further requirements are imposed by the current Rules.
3 See paras **5.102–5.103** above.

Examination of the application and the regulations

10.6 Schedule 2 makes no special provisions as to searching and examination for registrability, and for this purpose the general provisions of s 37 apply. Under para 8, the registrar is to consider whether the requirements of para 7(1) are met; the applicant must be informed of any objections and be given an opportunity to make representations or to file amended regulations. If the applicant fails to satisfy the registrar that the requirements are met, or to file regulations amended so as to meet them, or to respond before the end of the period specified by the registrar, then the registrar must refuse the application. It is to be noted that, so far as the regulations are concerned, the onus is on the applicant to satisfy the registrar. If the requirements regarding the regulations, and the other requirements for registration, are met, then the application is accepted and the registrar proceeds in accordance with the general provisions of s 38, as to publication of the application, opposition and the making of observations. Paragraph 9 provides for the publication of the regulations, and notice of opposition may be given and observations made, in respect of the matters mentioned in para 7(1), as well as other grounds for opposition.

Amendment of the regulations

10.7 Schedule 2 para 11 makes provision regarding amendment of the regulations governing the use of a registered certification mark. The procedure to be followed is set out in r 23. Under para 11(1) an amendment of the regulations is not effective unless and until the amended regulations are filed[1] with the registrar and approved by him. Under para 11(2) the registrar may, in any case where it appears expedient to him to do so, publish the amended regulations before accepting them, and r 23(2) requires him to publish a notice indicating where copies of the amended regulations may be inspected. If he does publish the amended regulations, then under para 11(3) notice of opposition may be given, and observations made, relating to the matters mentioned in para 7(1). Rule 23(3) and (4) deals with observations and opposition respectively, to applications to amend the regulations. In either case the observations or notice are to be filed within three months of the date of publication of notice under r 23(2). Copies of the observations, or the notice of opposition and statement of grounds, must be sent to the proprietor.[2] Under r 23(5)[3] the procedure in amended r 13(2) and (4)–(9) applies as for opposition to an application for registration. The period for opposition is not now extendable under the provisions of r 62 (as amended) and the period for filing a counterstatement, which is governed by r 13(2), is similarly non-extendable.

1 On Form TM36 – see r 23(1).
2 Rule 23(3) and (5).
3 As amended by the Trade Marks (Amendment) Rules 1998 (SI 1998/925), r 9.

Existing certification marks and pending applications under the TMA 1938

10.8 Regulations governing the use of an existing certification mark, registered under the TMA 1938, are to be treated after commencement as if filed under Sch 2, para 6.[1] Any requests for the amendment of regulations, pending at commencement, will be dealt with under the TMA 1938 provisions.

1 See TMA 1994, Sch 3, para 19.

Infringement

10.9 The provisions of the TMA 1994, concerning infringement are generally applicable to certification marks. However Sch 2, para 13 makes certain additions, which place an authorised user in the position of a licensee for the purposes of some provisions.[1] Paragraph 14 requires any loss suffered or likely to be suffered by authorised users to be taken into account in infringement proceedings, and the court may give directions as to the holding of the proceeds of any pecuniary remedy on behalf of such users. By virtue of Sch 3, para 6(2) this only applies to infringements committed after commencement of the Act.

1 TMA 1994, s 10(5) (definition of infringement: unauthorised application of mark to certain material); s 19(2) (order as to disposal of infringing goods, material or articles: adequacy of other remedies; and s 89 (prohibition of importation of infringing goods, material or articles: request to Commissioners of Customs and Excise).

Revocation and invalidity

10.10 In addition to the grounds for revocation provided for in s 46, further possible grounds are contained in Sch 2, para 15.[1] They are: (a) that the proprietor has started to carry on business involving the supply of goods or services of the kind certified; (b) that the mark has been used by the proprietor so as to become liable to mislead the public within the meaning of para 5(1); (c) that the proprietor has failed to observe, or to secure the observance of, the regulations governing the use of the mark; (d) that an amendment of the regulations has been made so that they no longer comply with para 6(2) and any further conditions imposed by rules; or (e) are contrary to public policy or to accepted principles of morality; or that the proprietor is no longer competent to certify the goods or services. With regard to invalidity of the registration Sch 2, para 16 adds a further ground to those available under s 47, namely that the mark was registered in breach of paras 4, 5(1) or 7(1) of Sch 2.[2]

1 These are permitted under the Directive, art 15(1).
2 These also are permitted under the Directive, art 15(1).

2   Collective marks

The new provisions for registered collective marks

10.11   Collective marks – or 'association marks' as they are sometimes called, have never previously been registrable in the UK. In its original form the Paris Convention of 1883 contained no provision for the protection of collective marks. Such a provision was introduced subsequently, by art 7^{bis1}. Such protection as has hitherto been available in the UK was obtained, in practice, under the law of passing off. Collective marks differ from certification marks in that they are protected in the name of an association, the members of which do carry on business supplying the goods or services concerned. Only members of the association are entitled to use the marks. The new provisions, which make such registration possible, are contained in s 49, with further detailed provisions, on similar lines to those for certification marks, being set out in Sch 1. Section 49 (1) defines a collective mark as a mark 'distinguishing the goods or services of members of the association which is the proprietor of the mark from those of other undertakings'. By sub-s (2), the provisions of the TMA 1994 are applied, subject to the provisions of Sch 1; this is repeated in Sch 1, para 1, which applies the provisions of the Act generally to collective marks, subject to the following provisions of the Schedule.

1 Under an amendment introduced at the Washington Conference of 1911, subsequently amended at London in 1934.

Differences from other trade marks under the TMA 1994

10.12   The kinds of signs which may qualify as collective marks are the same as for ordinary trade marks, which are set out in s 1 of the TMA 1994, but Sch 1, para 2 provides that the reference to 'distinguishing goods or services of one undertaking from those of other undertakings' is to be construed as a reference to distinguishing goods or services of members of the association which is the proprietor, from those of other undertakings. As with certification marks, the general provisions for refusal on absolute and relative grounds apply, and Sch 1, para 3 excludes from the absolute grounds for refusal the provisions of s 3(1)(c) insofar as they refer to signs or indications which may serve to designate the geographical origin of goods or services, adding the same provision, that the proprietor is not entitled to prohibit use the signs or indications in accordance with honest practices in industrial or commercial matters – in particular by a person who is entitled to use a geographical name.[1] There is also, as for certification marks, an additional absolute ground for refusal,[2] contained in Sch 1, para 4, which prohibits registration where the public is liable to be misled as to the character or significance of the mark, in particular if it is likely to be taken as something other than a certification mark, and again the registrar may require inclusion in the mark of an indication that it is a certification mark, with amendment if necessary during the course of the registration procedure. Unlike the case of certification marks, there is no provision restricting assignment or transmission without the registrar's consent.

1 See the Directive, art 15(2) which permits this derogation, and the decision of the ECJ in Cases : C 108, 109/97 *Windsurfing Chiemsee Produktions- und Vertriebs GmbH (1999) Times, 18 May.* See also para **10.4** above.
2 Permitted under the Directive, art 15(1).

The regulations

10.13   Like certification marks, collective marks are required to be subject to regulations governing use. The provisions regarding the filing, approval and amendment of the regulations, are contained in Sch 1, paras 5–10. Paragraph 5(1) imposes the requirement to file the regulations. Under para 5(2) the regulations must specify the persons authorised to use the mark, the conditions of membership of the association and, where they exist, any conditions of use of the mark, including any sanctions against misuse. Paragraph 9 provides that the regulations are to be open to public inspection. Paragraph 6 prohibits registration unless the regulations comply with the requirements of para 5(2), including further requirements imposed by rules,[1] and are not contrary to public policy or accepted principles of morality. There are provisions in para 8 for opposition, and for the making of observations. Under para 6(2) and r 22 the applicant must file Form TM 35 with a copy of the regulations, within nine months[2] of the date of the application for registration, and pay the prescribed fee; otherwise the application will be deemed to be withdrawn.

1 As permitted by para 5(2). None are imposed by the current Rules.
2 This period may be extended under r 62.

Examination of the application and regulations

10.14   The procedure to be followed for collective marks is essentially the same as for certification marks. There are no special provisions in Sch 1 as to searching and examination for registrability, and for this purpose the general provisions of s 37 apply. Under para 7 the registrar is to consider whether the requirements of para 6(1) are met; the applicant must be informed of any objections and be given an opportunity to make representations or to file amended regulations. If the applicant fails to satisfy the registrar that the requirements are met, or to file regulations amended so as to meet them, or to respond before the end of the period specified by the registrar, then the registrar must refuse the application. As with certification marks it should be noted that, so far as the regulations are concerned, it is for the applicant to satisfy the registrar. If the requirements regarding the regulations, and the other requirements for registration, are met, then the application is accepted and the registrar proceeds in accordance with s 38 (publication, opposition proceedings and observations). Paragraph 8 provides for the publication of the regulations, and notice of opposition may be given and observations made, in respect of the matters mentioned in para 6(1), as well as other grounds for opposition or making observations, ie under the main general provisions of the TMA 1994.

Amendment of the regulations

10.15   As with certification marks, Sch 1, para 10 makes provision regarding amendment of the regulations governing the use of a registered collective mark. Again the procedure is set out in r 23. Paragraph 10(1) provides that an amendment of the regulations is not effective unless and until the amended regulations are filed[1] with the registrar and approved by him. Under para 10(2) the registrar may, in any case where it appears expedient to him to do so, cause the amended regulations to be published before accepting them, and r 23(2) requires him to publish a notice indicating where copies of the amended regulations may be inspected. If he publishes the amended regulations, then under para 10(3) notice of opposition may be given, and observations made, relating to the matters mentioned in para 6(1). As for certification marks, r 23(3) and (4) deals with observations and opposition, respectively, to amendment of the regulations. In both cases the observations or notice are to be filed within three months of the date of publication of notice under r 23(2). Copies of the observations, or the notice of opposition and statement of grounds, must be sent to the proprietor.[2] Under r 23(5) as amended, the procedure in amended r 13(2) and (4)–(9)[3] applies as for opposition to an application for registration. Under the original Rules it appears that the period for opposition was extendable under the general provisions of r 62, because r 62(3) did not mention the period under r 23(4) as being non-extendable, although the period for filing a counterstatement, being set by r 13(2), could not be extended. As with certification marks, the amended r 62(3)[4] now specifically excludes the period under r 23(4) from any extension, and the period for filing a counterstatement remains non-extendable.

1 On Form TM36 – see r 23(1).
2 Rule 23(3) and (5).
3 For the amendments, see the Trade Marks (Amendment) Rules 1998 (SI 1998/ 925).
4 See the Trade Marks (Amendment) Rules 1998, r 10(c).

Infringement

10.16   The provisions of the TMA 1994 concerning infringement are generally applicable to collective marks, but Sch 1, para 11(1) makes identical additions, treating an authorised user as a licensee for the purposes of ss 10(5), 19(2) and 89 of the Act, to those made in respect of authorised users of certification marks.[1] Schedule 1, para 12 gives authorised users similar rights, to take proceedings in their own names, to those provided for licensees by s 30 of the TMA 1994. These rights arise automatically, but subject to any agreement to the contrary between the authorised user and the proprietor, and under paras 12(2) and (3) the authorised user having such right may call on the proprietor to take infringement proceedings in respect of any matter which affects his interests. It is likely that this reference to the interests of the authorised user will be construed fairly broadly, covering any claim that the mark is being infringed, and any situation in which the authorised user might have made a claim in passing off under the common law. If the proprietor refuses to take proceedings or fails to do so within two months of being called upon, the authorised user may bring the proceedings in his own name as is he were the proprietor. The authorised user may not proceed with the action, without the leave of the court, unless the proprietor is either joined as a plaintiff or added as a defendant, but the granting of interlocutory relief on an application by the authorised user alone, is not affected.[2]. Under para 12(5) a proprietor added as defendant is not liable for any costs unless he takes part in the proceedings. Paragraph 12(6) contains provisions, corresponding to Sch 2, para 14, requiring any loss suffered or likely to be suffered by authorised users to be taken into account in infringement proceedings, and the court may give directions as to the holding of the proceeds of any pecuniary remedy on behalf of such users.

1 See para **10.9** above.
2 Paragraph 12(4) of Sch 1.

Revocation and invalidity

10.17   As with certification marks, there are further grounds for revocation, in addition to those available under s 46 of the TMA 1994.[1] They are contained in Sch 1, para 13, and are: (a) that the manner in which the mark has been used by the proprietor has caused it to become liable to mislead the public in the manner referred to in para 4(1); (b) that the proprietor has failed to observe, or secure the observance of, the regulations governing the use of the mark; (c) that an amendment of the regulations has been made so that they no longer comply with para 5(2) and further conditions imposed by rules, or are contrary to public policy or accepted principles of morality. With regard to invalidity of registration, para 14 adds a further ground in addition to those provided by s 47 of the TMA 1994, namely that the mark was registered in breach of Sch 1, paras 4(1) or 6(1).[2]

1 These additional grounds are permitted by the Directive, art 15(1).
2 These are also permitted by the Directive, art 15(1).

Chapter 11

Registered trade marks as property

The new provisions

11.1   In the past, there has been a fair amount of discussion as to whether a trade mark is a right of property. The TMA 1994 finally settles the question. Section 2(1) confirms that a registered trade mark is a property right obtained by registration of the trade mark under the Act. Section 22 states that a registered trade mark is personal property (in Scotland, incorporeal moveable property). Section 22 is followed by a series of provisions, in ss 23 to 27, which are concerned with registered trade marks and applications for registration as objects of property rights. Sections 28–31 relate to licensing. Sections 22–31 thus cover all aspects cf the ownership of and dealings with trade mark rights. One consequence of these provisions is that the use of a trade mark as a security interest, which was generally a difficult and complex matter under the old law, is now much more straightforward, as far as the registry is concerned. The question, which parties considering accepting registered trade marks as security will always consider in each case, namely whether the trade mark is a sufficient security, is outside the scope of this book. Section 27, which relates to pending applications, is an important new provision. It states that the provisions of ss 22–26 apply, with the necessary modifications, in relation to an application for the registration of a trade mark as in relation to a registered trade mark. Under the TMA 1938 there were difficulties involved in dealing with trade marks which were subject to pending applications for registration. For example, because such a trade mark was to be regarded as an unregistered trade mark,[1] it could not be assigned (unless it was assigned together with a registered trade mark which was used in the same business).[2] Section 27 of the TMA 1994 removes this difficulty; although, as will be seen below, the procedure for registration of transactions[3] does not appear to allow an assignee actually to be registered as the applicant for registration of the trade mark, this does not appear to be of any practical significance. Some comment must be made as to the positioning of the licensing provisions. It might have been expected that ss 28–31 would have been in the part of the TMA 1994 entitled 'Registered trade mark as object of property'. This would have been the case in an earlier form of the Trade Marks Bill, but some amendments made in the House of Lords resulted in the licensing provisions being moved to their present position, after s 27. Section 27(1) does not apply the provisions of ss 28–31 to pending applications. There could thus be a question about the status of a licence of a trade mark which is subject to a pending application. It is hoped that there will be no difficulty in practice. If the mark becomes registered, the registration will date back to the date of the

191

application for registration;[4] in any case there is nothing to prevent the licensing of even an unregistered trade mark, which is the contractual granting of permission to the licensee to use the trade mark. It is to be noted that s 25(2) (definition of 'registrable transactions') includes licences, and that the provisions in the Rules,[5] which relate to applications to register, or (in the case of pending applications for registration)[6] to give notice of, particulars of transactions, cover licences as well as other transactions. Clearly the registrar will be accepting notices of particulars of licences in respect of pending applications. There appears to be no basis on which a court would find that such a licence was not effective as between the parties. So far as effectiveness against third parties is concerned, perhaps the important point is that s 27(1) does apply s 25 to pending applications, and s 25 covers licences as well as other transactions. The courts can be expected to be reluctant to hold that, where an application has been duly made, to give notice in accordance with r 35, of particulars of a licence of a trade mark which is the subject of a pending application, is not as effective under s 25(3) and (4) as it would be in respect of other transactions. The provisions concerning registration of transactions, and the consequences of non-registration, are considered further below.[7]

1 Since a 'registered trade mark' was defined, in TMA 1938, s 68(1) the, as 'a trade mark which is actually on the register'.
2 See the TMA 1938, s 22(2).
3 Under s 25 – see paras **11–15** to **11–18** below.
4 TMA 1994, ss 40(3) and 9(3).
5 Rules 34 and 35; see paras **11.15–11.17** below.
6 Under s 27(3).
7 See paras **11.15–11.21**.

Co-ownership

11.2   Section 23 makes potentially quite significant changes in respect of co-ownership of registered trade marks. Under s 63 of the TMA 1938 (as amended) joint registration was only possible where the relationship between the applicants was such that no one of them was entitled as between himself and the other or others of them to use the mark except (a) on behalf of both or all of them or (b) in relation to goods with which both or all of them were connected in the course of trade or (as the case might be) services with the provision of which both or all of them were connected in the course of business. Section 23(1) provides that where a registered trade mark is granted to two or more persons jointly, each of them is entitled, subject to any agreement to the contrary, to an equal undivided share in the registered trade mark; by s 27(2) this also applies to cases of joint applications for registration. Sub-section (2) applies the provisions that follow to cases of joint ownership; these impose some restrictions upon the exercise of rights by the joint owners. Under sub-s (3) (again subject to any agreement to the contrary) each co-proprietor is entitled, by himself or his agents, to do for his own benefit and without the consent of or the need to account to the other(s), any act which would otherwise amount to an infringement of the registered trade mark. In the case of registrations in joint names under the old law, Sch 3, para 7 of the TMA 1994 provides that s 23 shall apply, but so long as the relations between the joint proprietors are such as are described in s 63 of the TMA 1938, there is deemed to be an agreement to exclude the operation of sub-ss (1) and (3) of s 23. Under sub-s (4), one co-proprietor cannot, without the consent of the other or others, licence the use of the trade mark or assign or charge his share in it (or in Scotland, cause or permit security to be granted over it). Sub-section (5) ensures that, unless the leave of the court is given, all co-proprietors are parties to any infringement proceedings, and thus bound by any decision in the proceedings, although a single proprietor may apply for inter-locutory relief. If a co-proprietor does not agree to be joined as a plaintiff, he must be made a defendant, although he will not be liable for any costs unless he actually takes part in the proceedings.

11.3 It is clear from s 23(3) that, notwithstanding the restrictions on transactions affecting the mark, each co-proprietor may use the trade mark freely without refer-ence to the other(s), unless both or all of them agree otherwise. In practice, there may be risks involved if co-proprietors do exercise their rights independently of one another, in such a way that the trade mark becomes liable to mislead.[1] In order to avoid complications in any situation in which a registered trade mark becomes vested in personal representatives, sub-s (6) provides that nothing in the section affects the mutual rights and obligations of such persons or their rights and obliga-tions as personal representatives or trustees.

1 See s 46(1)(d), discussed in ch 7.

Assignment

11.4 In clear (and intentional) contrast with the position under the TMA 1938, the TMA 1994 places no restrictions on the assignment of registered trade marks or applications for registration. Furthermore, where under the TMA 1938 (as amended) registered marks were 'associated' (under s 23 or 23A of that Act), which prevented their assignment other than together, the associations are removed by the transitional provisions of Sch 3, para 2(3).[1] Section 24 (which as mentioned above applies also to applications for registration) provides, in sub-s (1), that a registered trade mark is transmissible by assignment, testamentary disposition or operation of law in the same way as any other personal or moveable property, and whether in connection with the goodwill of a business or separately. Sub-section (2) permits a partial assignment or transmission, limited to some only of the goods or services covered by the registration, and in relation to the use of the mark in a particular manner or in a particular locality. Under sub-s (3) the assignment (or assent) must be in writing and signed by or on behalf of the assignor (or personal representative); it does not however need to be signed by the assignee or transferee. Except in Scotland,[2] the requirement may be satisfied where the assignor or personal representative is a body corporate, by the affixing of its seal. Sub-section (4) confirms that the provisions apply to an assignment by way of security as in relation to any other assignment. Under sub-s (5), a regis-tered trade mark may be the subject of a charge (in Scotland, security) in the same way as other personal or moveable property. Finally, sub-s (6) provides that nothing in the TMA 1994 is to be construed as affecting the assignment or other transmission of an unregistered trade mark as part of the goodwill of a business. This confirms the common law position, that the transfer of the goodwill of a busi-ness included the trade marks used in the business. In one respect the provisions regarding assignment are more restrictive than those of s 22 of the TMA 1938. Under s 22(2) of that Act it was possible to assign an unregistered trade mark if it was assigned at the same time as a registered trade mark used in the same busi-ness. Since there is no such provision in the TMA 1994, it would appear that a trade mark which is not registered (or applied for) can now only be assigned with the goodwill of the business in which it is used, as was the case before the TMA 1938.

Presumably it was thought that under the TMA 1994 there would rarely be significant trade marks in use, which could not be registered. In any case in which it is wished to assign an unregistered trade mark separately from the business, it will be necessary to make an application for registration before executing the assignment. It should, however, be noted that if the application for registration is unsuccessful, then the assignment does not transfer any rights of property in the trade mark. In such a situation it is probable that the assignment would have the effect (whether by an implied term or by estoppel) of preventing the assignor from using the trade mark without a licence from the assignee and from challenging the assignee's right to use the trade mark or to register it; however it may be preferable to make the position clear by express provisions as to what is to happen if the mark does not become registered.

1 This does not apply to a series of marks registered in a single registration.
2 As to which, see the Companies Act 1985, s 36B.

11.5   Schedule 3, para 8(1) provides that s 24 applies, and applies only, to transactions and events occurring after commencement, ie 31 October 1994; assignments made before that date are governed by the old law and are thus unaffected by the new provisions. Under para 8(2), existing entries of assignments (under s 25 of the TMA 1938) were transferred on commencement to the register kept under the TMA 1994 and have effect as if made under s 25 of that Act. By virtue of para 8(3) applications made before commencement to record assignments have been treated as applications under s 25 of the TMA 1994,[1] and will have proceeded accordingly; the registrar was given power to require the applicant to amend his application to conform with the requirements of the Act. Under para 8(4), para 8(2) was applied to pending applications to register assignments under s 25 of the TMA 1938, which had been determined by the registrar but not finally determined (meaning, presumably, accepted but not completed) before commencement; these were to continue to be dealt with under the TMA 1938, but the resulting entries are now treated as if made under s 25 of the TMA 1994. In the case of assignments or transmissions taking effect before commencement, where the person entitled had not registered his title, para 8(5) required an application for registration after commencement to be made under s 25 of the TMA 1994. By virtue of para 8(6) however, the consequences of failure to register title in such cases, or in the case of pending applications subject to para 8(3), are subject to s 25(3) of the TMA 1938 and not s 25 of the TMA 1994.

1 See paras **11.15–11.17** below.

Trusts and equities

11.6   Section 26 provides that no notice of any trust shall be entered in the register, and the registrar shall not be affected by any such notice. But this does not affect the enforcement of equities (or in Scotland, rights) in a registered trade mark as for other personal or moveable property, subject to the provisions of the TMA 1994. Essentially the position under this provision is the same as under s 64 of the TMA 1938, but by s 27, s 26 is also expressly applied to applications for registration. The effect is that, if a situation arises where a proprietor or applicant for registration is to be regarded as holding the registration or application in trust for another party, then the trust can be enforced by that party against him, even though the there is no notice of the trust on the register.

Licensing of registered trade marks

11.7 The trade marks statutes before the TMA 1938 made no provision for the licensing of registered trade marks. In 1938 there was introduced the possibility of recording other parties, who were licensees although not so described, as 'registered users' of registered trade marks. Under the TMA 1938, some degree of control was required, by the proprietor over the use of the mark by the registered user,[1] and if this was absent, the registrar might refuse to record the user, on the ground that to do so might tend to facilitate 'trafficking' in a trade mark.[2] In the case of *BOSTITCH Trade Mark*[3] it was held that the requirements of s 28 of the TMA 1938 were only optional, not mandatory, so that use of a trade mark could be licensed; so long as the proprietor exercised sufficient control over the use, the registration of the mark was not invalidated.

1 TMA 1994, s 28(4).
2 Section 28(6), and see eg *HOLLY HOBBIE Trade Mark* [1984] RPC 329.
3 [1963] RPC 183.

11.8 The approach of the new law to licensing is in accordance with the general intention of the 1994 legislation, to leave trade mark proprietors to take care of their marks, rather than providing for the law or the registrar do it for them. Therefore, the TMA 1994 repeals all the previous provisions and imposes no restrictions on the licensing of registered trade marks. In general the relationship between licensor and licensee, and the right to take proceedings for infringement, are subject to the terms of the licence. Nevertheless, while it is certain that the old rules regarding 'trafficking' have been abolished,[1] it should not be assumed that licensing can never involve any risk to the validity of a registration of the licensed mark, and it may be that the new provisions relating to revocation[2] mean that as much if not more care will need to be taken to ensure that use of a registered mark by a licensee is properly controlled.

1 Note also the White Paper, paras 4.40–4.43.
2 Section 46 – see ch 7.

The basic provisions for licensing

11.9 Section 28(1) provides that a licence to use a registered trade mark may be general or limited. A limited licence may, in particular,[1] apply in relation to some but not all of the goods or services covered by the registration, or in relation to use of the mark in a particular manner or in a particular locality. The only formal requirement[2] (under sub-s (2)) is that, in order to be effective, the licence must be in writing, signed by the grantor (the licensor). Except in Scotland,[3] this requirement may be satisfied, where the proprietor is a body corporate, by the affixing of its seal. It is to be noted that 'licence' is to be distinguished from mere 'consent' to the use of a trade mark, which for some purposes[4] may be oral or implied, as for instance between a holding company and a subsidiary. In such instances it may be that some proprietors will wish to consider the possibility of formal written licences with subsidiaries, in order to take advantage of the new provisions. An important provision, in sub-s (3) is that, unless the licence otherwise provides, it is binding on a successor in title to the grantor's interest. It is generally better, from a licensee's point of view, if his licence continues notwithstanding that the registered trade mark is assigned to a new proprietor. If the licensor does not want this to happen automatically, then he will need to ensure that the terms of the licence are drawn to provide otherwise. Sub-section (3) further says that references in the Act to doing anything with, or without, the consent of the proprietor of a registered trade mark shall be 'construed accordingly'. This means that where a licence is binding on a new proprietor under the subsection, use of the mark by the licensee will be treated as being use by the new proprietor. Another new provision is sub-s (4), relating to sub-licensing, something which was discouraged under the TMA 1938, if not prohibited.[5] References in the TMA 1994 (eg in ss 25 and 29–31) to licence or licensee include a sub-licence or sub-licensee.

1 These words appear to be intended to have the same meaning as the Latin term 'inter alia', thus indicating that other kinds of limited licence are possible.
2 Apart from the registration of the licence, discussed at paras **15.15–15.18** below, which while being voluntary may generally be regarded as advisable.
3 As to which see the Companies Act 1985 s 36B, added by the Companies Act 1989, s 130(2).
4 Eg s 9 (infringement), s 12 (exhaustion of rights), s 46(1)(a) and (b) (revocation for non-use).
5 See s 28(12). This may have been intended simply to make sure that recordal of a registered user under s 28 could not have the effect of permitting sub-licensing. However the assistant registrar in HOLLY HOBBIE – see para **11.7**, n 2 above – decided that it actually prohibited sub-licensing.

11.10   The TMA 1994 makes special provision for exclusive licences. For the purposes of the Act, s 29 provides that 'exclusive licence' means a licence (whether general or limited) authorising the licensee to the exclusion of all other persons, including the grantor, to use the trade mark in the manner authorised by the licence. This represents what has long been understood as the meaning of 'exclusive licence' in relation to intellectual property rights. Section 29(2) should be noted; it states that an exclusive licensee has the same rights against a successor in title who is bound by the licence as he has against the grantor. This would seem to follow from s 28(3), whether the licence is exclusive or non-exclusive, but the provision is perhaps included to make it clear that the licence remains exclusive, after assignment of the registered trade mark, as against the new proprietor.

11.11   Schedule 3, para 9(1) makes it clear that ss 28 and 29(2) only apply to licences granted after commencement. Paragraph 9(1) further provides that the old law continues to apply to licences granted before commencement. Therefore if the parties to a licence granted before 31 October 1994 wish to take advantage of any aspect of the new law, including the provisions of s 31,[1] a new licence will be required. The other transitional provisions relating to licences are similar to those of Sch 3, para 8 which apply to assignments. Schedule 3, para 9(2) provided for existing entries of registered users (under s 28 of the TMA 1938) to be transferred on commencement to the register kept under the TMA 1994 and to have effect as if made under s 25 of that Act. By virtue of Sch 3, para 9(3), applications for registration of registered users made before commencement were treated as applications under s 25 of the the TMA 1994,[2] and will have proceeded accordingly; as with assignments the registrar was given power to require the applicant to amend his application to conform with the requirements of the TMA 1994. Under para 9(4), para 9(2) was applied to entries resulting from pending applications under s 28 of the TMA 1938, which had been determined by the registrar but not finally determined (again presumably meaning not completed) before commencement; these were to continue to be dealt with under the TMA 1938. Where there is no written licence (as would be required by s 28 of the TMA 1994), which may be the case where, for example, a company had applied to record a subsidiary as a registered user, it would seem that this provision will still have the effect that the application to register particulars of the licence is to be treated as made under s 25(1). It is to be noted that Sch 3 contains no specific provision as to the consequences of failure to apply to register a licence. It would appear that s 25 of the TMA 1994 does not apply in this respect to a failure to register a registered user before commencement; it may be arguable that continued failure to apply after 31 October 1994 would carry the consequences set out in s 25, although this seems contrary to the intention of para 9(1) of Sch 3. Finally, Sch 3, para 9(5) provides that any proceedings, pending at commencement, to vary or cancel a registration of a registered user (under s 28(8) or (10) of the TMA 1938) are to be dealt with under the old law, any necessary alteration being made to the new register.

1 This is not the case with the general provisions of s 30: see Sch 3, para 6(1) and paras **15.13** and **15.14** below.
2 See paras **11.15–11.17** below.

Exclusive licences

11.12 The TMA 1994 creates greater possibility for exclusive licensees to take their own action to protect their interests in the licensed trade marks, but the extent of their rights is dependent upon the terms of their licences. Under s 31(1) an exclusive licence *may* provide that the licensee shall have, 'to such extent as may be provided by the licence, the same rights and remedies in respect of matters occurring after the grant of the licence as if the licence had been an assignment'. Where or to the extent that such provision is made, the exclusive licensee is entitled to bring infringement proceedings, against any person other than the proprietor, in his own name. This, however, is further subject to the provisions of the licence and to the other provisions of s 31. Under s 103(1) 'infringement proceedings' includes proceedings for delivery up, under s 16. Section 31(2) provides that the rights and remedies of the exclusive licensee are concurrent with those of the proprietor, and that references in the TMA 1994 to infringement are to be construed accordingly. As would be expected, by sub-s (3) any defendant to an action for infringement brought under these provisions can avail himself of any defence which would have been available to him if the action had been brought by the proprietor. Sub-section (4) aims to ensure that the proprietor and the exclusive licensee, where their rights are concurrent, are bound by any decision. Under this sub-section neither of them may proceed with the action without the leave of the court, unless the other is joined as a plaintiff or added as a defendant (except for the purposes of the granting of interlocutory relief). Under sub-s (5) the proprietor or licensee, if added as a defendant, is not liable for any costs unless he takes part in the proceedings. In any case where an action for infringement relates wholly or partly to an infringement in respect of which the proprietor and an exclusive licensee have or have had a concurrent right of action, sub-s (6) requires the court, in assessing damages, to take into account the terms of the licence and any pecuniary remedy already awarded or available to either of them in respect of the infringement. The reference to a remedy being 'available' would cover the case in which an inquiry as to damages or an account of profits had been ordered but no assessment had taken place. Sub-section (6) also excludes the directing of an account of profits where there has already been a pecuniary remedy ordered in favour of the other party (whether an award of damages or an account of profits) and the court is required to apportion any profits between them as it considers just, subject to any agreement between them. These provisions apply whether or not the proprietor and the exclusive licensee are both parties to the action; if they are not, the court is empowered to direct the one party to hold the proceeds of any pecuniary remedy on behalf of the other, to such extent as the court thinks fit. Sub-section (7) makes separate provision in the case of an application for delivery up under s 16; the proprietor must notify an exclusive licensee having a concurrent right of action, before making an application, and the licensee is entitled to apply to the court, which may make such order as it thinks fit, having regard to the terms of the licence. Finally, sub-s (8) states that the provisions of sub-ss (4)–(7) have effect 'subject to any agreement to the contrary between the exclusive licensee and the proprietor'. To the extent that those provisions appear to be intended to ensure that any decisions regarding the registered trade mark are binding on both the proprietor and the exclusive licensee, and any assessment of damages or profits is made between all the parties, so as to avoid the possibility of defendants being made to pay twice over, the giving of a general right to the proprietor and licensee to nullify the provisions, either in the licence or by subsequent agreement, seems surprising. It remains to be seen how the courts will deal with any situations which may arise, where proprietors and exclusive licensees seek to exclude any of these provisions.

General provisions as to rights of licensees

11.13   Section 30 of the TMA 1994 contains general provisions concerned with the rights of licensees in case of infringement. The relationship of these provisions with s 31, regarding the rights of exclusive licensees, is not entirely clear. Sub-section (1), which says that the section has effect with respect to the rights of a licensee in relation to infringement of a registered trade mark, continues by stating that the provisions do not apply where or to the extent that, by virtue of s 31(1), the licensee has a right to bring proceedings in his own name. Sub-section (7), however, seems, at first sight at least, to say the opposite. It says that 'the provisions of the section apply in relation to an exclusive licensee if or to the extent that he has, by virtue of s 31(1), the rights and remedies of an assignee as if he were the proprietor'. It has been suggested that the purpose of sub-s (7) is to cover the position of the exclusive licensee as putative assignee (under s 31(1)) so that if, for example, he grants a licence to a third party the relationship between him and that third party is governed by the provisions of s 30(2)–(6). It would seem that this suggestion is correct, although it cannot be said that the matter is altogether clear.

11.14   Turning to the provisions of s 30(2)–(6) it is to be noted that, whereas in the case of s 31(1) the licence must make express provision for the exclusive licensee to have any of the rights set out, s 30(2) entitles the licensee to take infringement proceedings in his own name in the circumstances indicated, *unless* his licence (or any licence through which his interest is derived) provides otherwise. Thus, if the grantor does not wish the licensee to be in a position to take proceedings in his own name, he must ensure that the licence excludes the rights set out in s 30. The right given to the licensee by sub-s (2) is to call on the proprietor to take infringement proceedings, (which, by virtue of s 103(1), includes proceedings under s 16 for delivery up) in respect of any matter which affects his (ie the licensee's) interests. By virtue of Sch 3, para 6, s 30 applies to licences granted before commencement, but only in respect of infringements committed after commencement. Under sub-s (3) the licensee can bring proceedings in his own name, as if he were the proprietor, if the proprietor refuses to take proceedings or fails to do so within two months after being called upon. A notable difference between this provision and the similar provision in s 28(3) of the TMA 1938 is that the right to take proceedings arises immediately if the proprietor expressly refuses to do so; previously the licensee had in any event to wait until the end of the two-month period specified. As in the case of exclusive licensees, the licensee may not proceed with the action, without the leave of the court, unless the proprietor is joined as a plaintiff or added as a defendant (in the latter case sub-s (5) exempting him from liability for any costs unless he takes part), although interlocutory relief may be granted on an application by the licensee alone. Sub-section (6) requires the court, in any infringement proceedings brought by a proprietor, to take into account any loss suffered or likely to be suffered by licensees; the court is also given power to give directions as to the extent to which the proprietor is to hold the proceeds of any pecuniary remedy on behalf of licensees.

Registration of transactions affecting registered trade marks

11.15   While dealings in registered trade marks, including in particular assignment and licensing, have been made considerably easier, and much of the formality has been removed, the TMA 1994 contains provisions, in s 25, for the registration of transactions affecting registered trade marks. Although registration under s 25 is voluntary, it is clear that there may in practice be significant risks involved, or at least disadvantages of a financial nature, if a transaction is not registered.

Definition of registrable transaction

11.16   Registrable transactions are defined in s 25(2). They are—

'(a)   an assignment of a registered trade mark of any right in it;
(b)   the grant of a licence under a registered trade mark;1
(c)   the grant of a security interest (whether fixed or floating) over a registered trade mark or any right in or under it;
(d)   the making by personal representatives of an assent in relation to a registered trade mark or any right in or under it;
(e)   an order of a court or other competent authority transferring a registered trade mark or any right in or under it.'

As already mentioned, s 27 applies the provisions of s 25 to applications for registration. This is further considered below.

1   Which includes a sub-licence.

Applications to register transactions

11.17   Section 25(1) specifies who may apply to register a transaction. For this purpose it is necessary to have in mind s 27(3), which provides that in s 25 as it applies in relation to a transaction affecting an application for registration of a trade mark, the reference to the entry of particulars in the register, and to the making of an application to register particulars, shall be construed as references to the giving of notice to the registrar of those particulars. Under s 25(1) the persons who may apply to the registrar for particulars of a registrable transaction to be entered in the register or, by virtue of s 27(3), give notice to the registrar of such particulars, are a person claiming to be entitled to an interest in or under a registered trade mark by virtue of a registrable transaction or a person claiming to be affected by such a transaction. The transitional provisions in Sch 3, which have already been mentioned,[1] should be noted. Paragraph 8 makes provisions regarding previously recorded assignments and pending applications to record assignments, treating them generally as if made under s 25 of the TMA 1994. Under Sch 3, para 9(2) existing entries of registered users (under s 28 of the TMA 1938) have been transferred to the register and have effect as if made under s 25. Under Sch 3, para 9(3), pending applications to record registered users are treated as applications to register under s 25.

1 Paras **11.5** and **11.11** above.

11.18   Rule 34 sets out the particulars of each kind of registrable transaction which is to be entered in the register upon application to the registrar by a person under s 25(1). The procedure under s 25 is laid down in r 35, sub-para (1) of which says how an application to register particulars of a transaction to which s 25 applies, or to give notice to the registrar of particulars of a transaction to which s 27(3) applies, is to be made. By r 35(1)(b)–(d), an application relating to the grant of a licence is to be made on Form TM50; Form TM51 is prescribed for an application relating to an amendment to, or termination of, a licence; and an application relating to the grant, amendment or termination of any security interest is to be made on Form TM24. In the case of an application relating to any other transaction, including an assignment, r 35(1)(a) requires Form TM16 to be used. By r 35(1)(e) any application relating to the making by personal representatives of an assent or to an order of a court or other competent authority is to be made on Form TM24. Rule 35(2) sets out procedural requirements. There are two possibilities. If the transaction is an assignment, the application may be signed by or on behalf of the parties to the assignment. In the case of the other transactions specifically mentioned (in r 35(1)(b)–(d)), the application may be signed by, or on behalf of, the grantor of the licence or security interest. The advantage of this provision is that it is not necessary that the document effecting the transaction be produced, and it may therefore be useful if the document is abroad and payment of stamp duty would be required if it were brought into the UK. As an alternative, if for some reason it is not possible to comply with these requirements as to signature, the application must 'be accompanied by such documentary evidence as sufficient to establish the transaction'. This, for instance, enables an interested party to register a transaction where the other party will not sign the necessary application. No guidance is given as to what evidence is to be regarded as sufficing to establish the transaction. It is possible that the actual assignment or other document need not be produced, if the transaction can be established by other means. Rule 35(4) relates to transactions affecting applications for registration of trade marks, and provides that where an application to give notice to the registrar has been made of particulars relating to an application for registration, upon registration of the trade mark, the registrar shall enter those particulars in the register. The effect of this is that, in the case of an application for registration, the entry of the transaction cannot actually be made unless and until the mark is placed on the register. However, in view of the new provisions regarding inspection,[1] the relevant information will normally be available to others.

1 Section 67 and rr 42–44.

11.19   Rule 35(3) concerns stamp duty, and provides that where the transaction is effected by an instrument chargeable with duty, the application shall be subject to the registrar being satisfied that the instrument has been duly stamped. The relevant forms originally incorporated a declaration to such effect. This has given rise to some concern in cases in which a document, having been executed abroad and not having been brought into the jurisdiction, is not liable to be stamped, even though it may be technically 'chargeable'. It may be that the word 'duly' means there must be a liability. The current Form TM16 requires a signed confirmation that stamp duty 'has been paid' or 'is not payable'. This seems to present no problems. However, it is thought that the issue of stamp duty may not have been finally resolved.

11.20 One question, which requires mention, is whether any problems could arise in cases in which an assignment of a registered trade mark covers several countries and a separate 'confirmatory' assignment is executed, for recordal purposes, in respect of each country. One reason for this may be to avoid a liability for stamp duty, which would arise if the original assignment was brought into the UK. On this question the case of *Coflexip Stena Offshore Ltd's Patent*[1] – the facts of which gave rise to the dispute, rather than the decision itself – has caused concern. The case raises the issue whether the title of the assignee may be invalid, on the basis that once the trade mark is assigned by the original document, the confirmatory assignment which is recorded has no effect. It is possible that some cases may arise, of assignments under the old law, which need consideration on their particular facts in the light of the law governing the transactions. However it unlikely that problems will arise under the TMA 1994, because under the new rules particulars of the transaction are recorded, and not the transaction itself; and, at least where signature of the form by or on behalf of all the parties can be obtained, no assignment document needs to be produced. The particulars required, by r 34, to be entered in the register, are the name and address of the assignee, the date of the assignment, and a description of any rights in respect of the trade mark, which were assigned; no other information is required. Finally it should be observed that a court will not normally be concerned as to how the assignee's title came to be recorded[2] in the register. Section 72 provides that in all legal proceedings relating to a trade mark, the registration of a person as proprietor of a trade mark shall be prima facie evidence of the validity of the original registration and any subsequent assignment or other transmission of it.

1 [1997] RPC 179 (Jacob J).
2 See the remarks of Jacob J in *Coflexip Stena* [1997] RPC 179 at 193 line 21.

The consequences of non-registration or delayed registration

11.21 Section 25(3) emphasises the importance of promptness in applying to register the particulars of a registrable transaction. Until that is done, the transaction *is ineffective* as against a person acquiring a conflicting interest in or under the registered trade mark in ignorance of it, and any person claiming to be a licensee by virtue of the transaction does not have the rights and remedies which would otherwise be available to him under ss 30 and 31. The consequence of this provision is that, for example, if A assigns a registered trade mark to B and subsequently, before B has applied to register the assignment to him, A executes an assignment in favour of C, who was then unaware of the earlier assignment, then C will take free of B's interest, so long as he himself applies to register his title and does so before B applies. Or if X grants a licence to Y, who does not apply to register the licence, and then X assigns the registered trade mark to Z, Z is not bound by the licence to Y if at the date of the assignment to him Z was unaware of the licence. Although it might seem that s 28(3), which provides that a licence (unless it provides otherwise) is binding on a successor in title to the grantor's interest, conflicts with s 25(3) it would appear that the latter provision is intended to prevail. In the case of licensees' rights to take action in their own name, under ss 30 or 31, the effect of s 25(3) is not so serious, although it is still advisable for licensees to apply to register their interests. Sub-section (4) imposes a further disadvantage in infringement proceedings, on the person who becomes proprietor or a licensee of a registered trade mark by virtue of a registrable transaction but fails to apply to register the particulars of the transaction within six months. Unless he satisfies the court that it was not practicable to apply before the end of the six-month period and an application was made as soon as practicable thereafter, such person is not entitled to damages or an account of profits in respect of any infringement occurring after the date of the transaction and before the particulars of the transaction are registered. Clearly sub-s (4) makes it advisable for an assignee or licensee to make the application to register within six months of the transaction, but because of sub-s (3) the application should generally be made even earlier.

Other provisions which may be made by rules

11.22 Section 25(5) enables provision to be made by rules for the amendment of particulars relating to a licence, to reflect any alteration of the terms of the licence and for the removal of the particulars if the licence, being for a fixed period, appears to the registrar to have expired or where the registrar has notified the parties of his intention to remove the particulars after a prescribed period. Sub-section (6) enables provision to be made for amendment or removal of particulars relating to a security interest, on the application of or with the consent of the person who is entitled to the benefit of such interest. Apart from r 39 (removal of matter from register),[1] which would enable the registrar to delete an entry relating to a licence which had expired, the only provisions under s 25(5) are to be found in r 35(1)(c) and (d) in so far as they relate to amendment of entries. As already mentioned above,[2] Sch 3, para 9(5) provides that any proceedings pending at commencement, for variation or cancellation of registration of a registered user, are to be dealt with under the old law.

1 Under s 64(5).
2 Paragraph **11.11**.

Chapter 12

Infringement and protection of well-known marks

The arrangement of the provisions

12.1 The basic provisions, defining the rights conferred by a registered trade mark and the acts which constitute infringement, are contained in ss 9 and 10 of the TMA 1994. Section 11 contains certain provisions limiting the effects of a registered trade mark and s 12 concerns 'exhaustion' of trade mark rights. Section 13 deals with registrations which are subject to disclaimers or limitations. Protection of well-known trade marks, within art 6bis of the Paris Convention, is provided under s 56 of the Act.

12.2 As already explained above,[1] the provisions for refusal of registration of a trade mark on the relative grounds set out in s 5(1), (2) and (3) of the TMA 1994, based on 'earlier trade marks', are reflected in the provisions defining infringement of a registered trade mark, in s 10(1), (2) and (3) of the Act. There are two main differences. One is that the provisions in s 10 refer to goods or services for which the trade mark is *registered*, since the question of infringement of course only arises where there is a registered trade mark, and not where a trade mark is 'protected' in some other way.[2] The other, which may well be very significant, is that s 10 refers to use of a 'sign', not a 'trade mark'. This point is discussed below. Subject to these differences, the parts of Chapter 7, in which the provisions of s 5(1)–(3) are discussed, are generally applicable to s 10(1)–(3) and will not be repeated here.

1 Paragraph **6.7**.
2 Eg by a pending application for registration, or as a 'well-known' trade mark. See ss 5(1)–(3) and 6(1)(c) and (2).

12.3 Infringement is defined in ss 9 and 10. Section 9 confers the basic right, referring to s 10 for the acts which constitute infringement.[1] Section 10 also includes, in sub-s (6), one limitation on the scope of the preceding provisions, which is in addition to the further limitations provided by ss 11–13, which are considered in detail below.

1 In a limited sense this follows the idea of the TMA 1938, s 4(1), which conferred the right in general terms and then specified two kinds of infringing act.

Rights conferred by a registered trade mark

12.4   Section 9(1) provides that the proprietor of a registered trade mark has 'exclusive rights' in the trade mark, which are infringed by use of the trade mark in the UK without his consent. Consent for this purpose clearly does not have to be written, as would be required for a formal licence, and may for example be oral. Even an implied consent would appear to suffice to avoid infringement. The sub-section refers to s 10 for the acts which constitute infringement, if done without the proprietor's consent. It is to be noted that s 9(1) does not have any exact equivalent in the Directive, a matter which was the subject of comment by Jacob J in *British Sugar plc v James Robertson and Sons Ltd*.[1] Section 9(2), provides that references in the TMA 1994 to infringement are to 'any such infringement' of the rights of the proprietor. However, by s 103(2), proceedings under s 16, for delivery up of infringing goods, etc, are 'infringement proceedings'. As under the TMA 1938, the rights of the proprietor have effect from the date of registration, which is the date of filing of the application for registration[2] but it is expressly provided, in s 9(3), that no infringement proceedings may be commenced, and no offence can be committed under s 92 (the anti-counterfeiting provision) in respect of 'unauthorised use', until the trade mark is actually registered. It appears that it is necessary that the trade mark is *validly* registered. Although this is not specifically stated (as it was in the TMA 1938[3]), in the case of revocation or invalidation it would seem to follow that, as from the date with effect from which a registered trade mark is revoked[4] or declared invalid[5] there can be no infringement.

1 [1996] RPC 281 at 291 line 38.
2 TMA 1994, s 40(3).
3 TMA 1938, s 4(1).
4 TMA 1994, s 46(6).
5 TMA 1994, s 47(6). The wording here is particularly clear, in that it is stated that a registration which is declared invalid shall be deemed never to have been made. See ch 7, paras **7.7–7.29**.

12.5   A question, which may arise under s 9 and certain other provisions of the TMA 1994, is whether 'proprietor' means registered proprietor or whether a person who is the beneficial owner of a registered trade mark – for example an assignee whose title has not yet been registered under s 25 – may bring proceedings for infringement. Under the TMA 1938[1] the words used suggested strongly that only a *registered* proprietor could take proceedings for infringement. Section 9 is not so explicit, and it might therefore be suggested that it could be open to a different interpretation. Under the TMA 1938 there were decisions[2] that 'proprietor' was not restricted to a registered proprietor. However it is unlikely that it was the intention that anyone not actually on the register as proprietor could commence infringement proceedings. This may not matter so much now that assignments can be much more speedily registered than was the case under the old law, but could perhaps be important if a new proprietor wished to make immediate application for an injunction and the assignor was not willing to commence the proceedings.

1 Section 4(1).
2 Eg under the non-use provisions of s 26; the same question could also arise under the provisions of s 46(1)(a) and (b) relating to revocation for non-use.

What constitutes infringement?

12.6   Each of the kinds of infringing act defined in s 10(1)–(3) involves use of a 'sign' in the course of trade in relation to goods or services. This raises several questions. First, what is meant by 'use'? This is answered by s 10(4). But a second question then arises, which is, what is use 'in relation to' goods or services? Another question is, what does the word 'sign' mean here? Yet another is, what is the effect of the words 'in the course of trade'? As will be seen, some of these questions may be interrelated.

'Use' of a sign

12.7 The definition of 'use' of a sign, in s 10(4) of the TMA 1994, raises no particular difficulty. Sub-section (4) specifies certain examples of what is 'use' of a sign for the purposes of s 10. By providing that a person uses a sign 'if, in particular' he does any of the acts specified, the sub-section indicates that the list is not exhaustive.[1] The examples listed are: affixing it to goods or their packaging; offering or exposing goods for sale, putting them on the market or stocking them for those purposes under the sign; offering or supplying services under the sign, importing or exporting goods under the sign, or using the sign on business papers or in advertising. A recent decision of Neuberger J, in *Beautimatic International Ltd v Mitchell International Ltd,*[2] on an application for summary judgment, provides helpful guidance in the application of these provisions. So far as affixing to packaging is concerned, this means that the goods must be in the packaging at the time. Exporting goods under the sign requires that the goods must be marked, or in marked packaging at the time of export, or perhaps be in documents accompanying the goods. In all the examples given in s 10(4), the effect of section 9(1), when read with the provisions of s 10, is that there must be such 'use' in relation to goods, taking place in the UK.

1 See for example the interpretation of art 86 of the EC Treaty by the Court of Justice in *Europemballage Corp and Continental Can Co Inc v EC Commission* [1973] CMLR 199 at 224 para [26].
2 *Beautimatic International Ltd v Mitchell International Ltd* (1999) Times, 8 July.

12.8 An important change in the law, which should be emphasised, is effected by s 103(2) of the TMA 1994, which provides that:

'References in this Act to use (or any particular description of use) of a trade mark, or a sign identical with, similar to, or likely to be mistaken for a trade mark, include use (or that description of use) otherwise than by means of a graphic representation.'

This makes it clear that infringing use does not have to be visual, or 'graphical', but may for example be oral and may also, it would seem, include use by storing in a computer memory. This provision is probably not as far reaching in its effect as might be thought, because infringement claims will rarely relate only to non-graphic use, but it could be of use in some cases of counterfeits of goods which do not actually bear a registered trade mark, where the trader makes an oral representation that they are 'X' goods. However, where the only use relied upon by a plaintiff is oral, a court is likely to require clear proof of the use.

Use of a sign in relation to goods or services

12.9 Section 10(4) only seeks to define 'use'. It does not necessarily follow, for example, that a sign is used 'in relation to' goods merely because it is affixed to them. That there are limits on the word 'use' is well illustrated by a decision of

Rattee J in *Trebor Bassett Ltd v Football Assocn.*[1] There were two actions, one by the plaintiff claiming relief for unjustified threats of infringement proceedings, and a separate but related action by the defendant in the first action, against the plaintiff, alleging infringement of a registration of the crest of the England football team, covering, inter alia, 'printed matter' in Class 16. The alleged infringement was the inclusion, in packets of candy sticks, of cards bearing the photographs of famous footballers, some of whom were members of the England team, shown wearing shirts on which the registered mark could be seen. In giving summary judgment in the threats action and striking out the defendant's infringement action, Rattee J held that the reproduction of the crest was not even arguably 'using' it in any real sense of the word, and was certainly not using it as a sign in respect of (the judge could equally well have used the words 'in relation to') the cards. Furthermore, he held that the plaintiff in the threats action was not in any real sense affixing the sign in question to the cards, nor had it put the cards on the market under the sign, within the meaning of s 10(4)(a) and (b) of the TMA 1994.

1   [1997] FSR 211.

12.10   It is suggested that the question, whether use of a sign is in relation to goods or services, may be considered as part of the other question posed above, that is whether the use is *in the course of trade* in relation to the goods or services. This approach may be important when considering the third question mentioned above, which is what is the meaning of 'sign' in s 10(1)–(3). This will be considered next.

12.11   On the face of it, the word 'sign' should not be restricted, because its use must be taken to have been deliberate; in particular it ought not to be interpreted as meaning 'trade mark'. The word is used in the definition of a trade mark in s 1(1) and is clearly intended there to be very broad, covering anything which might serve as a trade mark. In *British Sugar*[1] Jacob J held that use, which may infringe under these provisions, is not restricted to trade mark use in relation to the defendant's goods or services.[2] He pointed to the fact that there are other possible reasons why use other than as a trade mark may not infringe, including the exceptions provided by s 11(2), which are considered below. However the matter does not seem as straightforward as this. While it seems probable that the framers of art 5 of the Directive, which contains the provisions on which s 10(1)–(3) are based, intended that 'use' of a sign should cover generic use of a registered trade mark, there are examples of non-trade mark use which do not necessarily have the benefit of s 11(2). In particular, use of ordinary words, or even punctuation marks such as '!' or '?', which may be the subject of trade mark registration, would not qualify as use of a descriptive indication falling within s 11(2)(b). The point arose again in *Philips Electronics BV v Remington Consumer Products.*[3] However the judge did not find it necessary to express any conclusion, because of his firm decision on the issues of invalidity; moreover he held that in any event the defendant's use, ie of the 'sign' in the form of the head of the shaver with three rotary cutters, was descriptive use and protected by s 11(2)(b). The case has now been the subject of a decision of the Court of Appeal.[4] In his judgment, with which the other two Lords Justices agreed, Aldous LJ gave his views on this point and others raised in the case, but it must be emphasised that these are subject to the views of the ECJ, to which the matter has been referred. It is sufficient to note that Aldous LJ held that the decision of Jacob J on this point, in *British Sugar,*[5] was correct.

1 [1996] RPC 281 at 290–293.
2 In so holding, Jacob J disagreed with the contrary view expressed by Lord McCluskey in the Scottish Court of Scotland, in *Bravado Merchandising Services Ltd v Mainstream Publishing (Edinburgn) Ltd* [1996] FSR 205, accepting a concession by Counsel for the plaintiff.
3 [1998] RPC 283 at 311–312.
4 [1999] ETMR 816.
5 See n 1 above.

12.12 It is suggested that one possible approach, which could protect the position of the honest trader using non-descriptive, but non trade mark, matter, is to place some restriction on the words 'uses in the course of trade a sign ... in relation to goods or services', as did Rattee J in effect, in the *Trebor Bassett* case.[1] Where there is only incidental use of ordinary words or other signs, which are to be regarded as wholly open to traders to use, in a completely non trade mark sense, there is, it is submitted, a proper basis for finding that the use is not truly 'in relation to' the goods or services concerned.

1 Paragraph **12.9** above.

12.13 There is a further restriction which, it is submitted, ought to be placed on the provisions of s 10(1)-(3) of the Act. The point is best illustrated by an example. Suppose that P has a registration of a trade mark 'X' in Class 16, which covers printed matter, including posters, and that D uses posters to advertise completely different goods, say sunglasses, under the same mark. Thus the identical mark 'X' is 'affixed', in the sense of s 10(4), to the posters. But no court would hold that this sufficed for the use to constitute an infringement under s 10(1), which, as will be seen, applies where the sign used is identical to the registered mark and is used in relation to goods or services which are identical to goods or services covered by the registration, without any requirement of a likelihood of confusion. Such a finding would have possibly alarming implications, in that anyone adopting a trade mark for any product would have to have regard to possibly conflicting registrations in Class 16. Other examples could arise with other classes. If the matter is approached on the basis that the words 'in the course of trade ... in relation to goods or services' mean, in the course of *a trade in the goods or services in question,*[1] then the difficulty is avoided. The proprietor of the registration is not precluded from arguing that the goods being advertised are 'similar' to goods covered by the registration for the purposes of a claim under s 10(2), or that there is infringement under s.10(3), which applies where there is no identity or even similarity of goods or services. The suggested approach avoids a result, which the legislators cannot have intended, that a party can infringe a registration where he is not in any sense trading in any goods covered by the registration.

1 See for example the decision of the House of Lords in *Aristoc Ltd v Rysta Ltd* (1945) 62 RPC 65.

Infringement under s 10(1)–(3)

12.14 Since, as has already been pointed out, the provisions of s 10(1)–(3) reflect the provisions for refusal of registration on relative grounds, in s 5(1)–(3) respectively, decisions on the relative grounds are applicable to infringement cases, and vice versa. Therefore in interpreting the infringement provisions, reference may be made here to the considerations discussed in Chapter 6,[1] and to any cases decided in the future under the corresponding provisions of s 5. Some of the basic principles may be summarised here.

(a) In order to fall within s 10(1)–(3) the defendant's use of the sign need not be use as a trade mark for his goods or services,[2] although if it is not, he may well have a defence under s 11(2), and in any case the use must fairly be capable of being regarded as 'in relation to' the goods or services in question.

(b) If the sign used by the defendant is identical to the registered mark and is used in relation to goods or services falling within the specification of goods or services covered by the registered mark, then (subject to revocation or invalidation) there is infringement. No proof of any likelihood of confusion is required – s 10(1).

(c) In the absence of such identity, where there is at least similarity of goods or services and either identity or similarity between the defendant's sign and the registered mark, there is infringement if (and only if) there exists a likelihood of confusion on the part of the public (which includes the likelihood of association with the trade mark) – s 10(2).

(d) The registered trade mark need not have been used for infringement to occur under s 10(1) or (2). The court will assume normal and fair use of the registered mark,[3] and (in the case of s 10(2)), assess the likelihood of confusion on that basis. By similar reasoning it may be seen that the court is not confined to a consideration of the actual use of the mark which has been made by the proprietor. Since the comparison is of sign with mark, it matters not that the proprietor has used the mark with a particular get-up, or for a particular type of product; nor that the proprietor is a retailer who has used his mark only at his own retail outlets. Subject to the possibility of an application by counterclaim, to cut down the specification of goods or services, in revocation or invalidation proceedings, the court should consider the matter on the basis of normal and fair use in relation to any of the goods or services covered by the registration. Moreover, a defendant does not avoid infringement merely by the use of added matter which prevents actual confusion from occurring.

(e) The kind of confusion required by s 10(2) is 'classic' confusion, that is confusion as to trade origin,[4] the reference to a likelihood of association adding nothing, and in particular not introducing a concept of infringement by association other than as to origin.

(f) Whether there exists a likelihood of confusion depends on all the circumstances of each case, including the identity or the degree of similarity of the sign to the registered mark and of the goods or services. The reputation of the registered mark, in respect of the goods or services for which is is registered, may also be taken into account.[5]

(g) The test for infringement under s 10(2) is not the same as for passing off,[6] which involves deception or a likelihood of deception and requires consideration of all the circumstances of each case, not just comparison of sign with mark.

(h) Where there is no similarity of goods or services, there can be infringement under s 10(3), but only where the registered mark has a reputation. Whether the mark has a reputation is a question of fact; it is not necessary that the mark should be 'well known' within the meaning of art 6[bis] of the Paris Convention and the reputation need not be in the whole of the UK.[7] Nor is there any requirement of a likelihood of confusion[8] under s 10(3). The requirement that the use be 'without due cause' appears to involve the absence of any objective justification for the use complained of.[9] Whether the use is such as to take unfair advantage of, or be detrimental to, the distinctive character or the repute of the registered mark is to be determined on the facts of each case. The proof of actual damage to the proprietor of the mark is probably not necessary.

1 See paras **6.7–6.70**1
2 See *British Sugar*, para **12.11**, n 1 above and *Philips*, para **12.11**, n 4 above.
3 *Origins Natural Resources Inc v Origin Clothing Ltd* [1995] FSR 280.
4 *Wagamama Ltd v City Centre Restaurants* [1995] FSR 713 (Laddie J) and the decision of the ECJ in *Sabel BV v Puma AG* [1998] RPC 199.
5 See the *Sabel* decision, and also the decision of the ECJ in *Canon KK v Metro-Goldwyn-Mayer Inc* [1999] RPC 117.
6 This was the case under the TMA 1938 and there is no basis for finding that the Directive or the TMA 1994 was intended to change the law in this respect. See for example *Origins*, n 2 above, and *Wagamama* [1995] FSR at 720–721.
7 See the opinion of Advocate-General Francis Jacobs QC in *General Motors v Yplon SA* [1999] ETMR 122 and the decision of the Court of Justice (unreported) 14 September 1999.
8 See the discussion of this point in relation to s 5(3) at **6.56–6.58**
9 See para **6.56**.

Infringement in relation to labelling or packaging materials

12.15 Sub-section (5) contains a new provision under which a person who applies a registered trade mark to material intended to be used for labelling or packaging goods, as business paper, or for advertising goods or services, is to be treated as a party to any use of the material which infringes the registered trade mark in certain circumstances. These are that when he applied the mark he knew or had reason to believe that the application of the mark was not duly authorised by the proprietor or a licensee. Each case will depend upon its own facts, but a printer of such material may well be found to have reason to believe that the application of the mark was not duly authorised if the order comes from someone who is clearly not the proprietor or some person who might reasonably be thought to be an authorised agent – this may particularly be the case where the trade mark is very well-known, and in some cases 'one-off' orders may well in themselves be found to be a sufficient reason for believing that the application was not duly authorised. This provision has been held to be limited to cases in which the material is intended to be used in the UK.[1] It should however be observed that this provision is of comparatively limited use, because it only applies to application of the actual mark as registered to the material, and does not cover use of even a very similar mark, unless perhaps the differences are so slight as not to be noticeable in the market place. It is most likely to be of use in counterfeiting cases.

1 See *Beautimatic*, para **12.7**, n 2 above.

What is not infringement

12.16 The TMA 1994 does not follow the basic definition of infringement in the TMA 1938[1] in defining any particular manner of use which is necessary in order to constitute infringement. Instead, as has already been seen, the TMA 1994 defines infringing use in quite general terms, as use of a 'sign', which is identical with or similar to the registered mark, but then adds a number of provisions which limit the scope of infringement under ss 9 and 10. Some of these are similar to limitations on the scope of infringement under the old law, but others are new.

1 TMA s 4(1)(a) and (b).

Use in relation to the goods or services of the proprietor or a licensee

12.17 Section 4(1) of the TMA 1938 specified that infringement could only occur where the goods or services were not connected in the course of trade or business with the proprietor. Section 9(1) of the TMA 1994 implies this, by requiring an absence of consent, but was apparently not thought to go far enough in this respect. Section 10(6), which has no equivalent in the Directive, excludes, from the scope of infringement, use in relation to what have often been called 'genuine' goods or services of the proprietor of a registered trade mark, or a licensee. Thus it is similar in some respects to the corresponding provision of the old law,[1] but extends also into the area of 'comparative advertising', which is not covered in any other provision.[2] The subsection states that nothing in the preceding provisions is to be construed as preventing the use of a registered trade mark by any person for the purposes of identifying goods or services as those of the proprietor or a licensee. However there are limitations on the kind of use which is to be protected under this provision. The protection will be lost if two requirements are satisfied. If the use is otherwise than in accordance with honest practices in industrial or commercial matters, then it is treated as infringing, if also the use without due cause takes unfair advantage of, or is detrimental to, the distinctive character or repute of the trade mark. The reference to honest practices in industrial or commercial matters is to be found also in s 11(2) – see paras **12.24** et seq below, which is in turn derived from a provision of the Directive.[3] These words originate in the definition of 'unfair competition' in art 10bis (2) of the Paris Convention. The application of these words in s 10(6) will depend upon the facts of each case. The second requirement echoes the 'anti-dilution' provisions of ss 5(3) and 10(3), and is itself derived from another provision of the Directive.[4] It is thus clear from the form of s 10(6) that the aim of identifying goods or services of the proprietor or a licensee is to be considered as prima facie legitimate and that the onus is on the proprietor to show that the acts of the alleged infringer are outside the protection of the sub-section.

1 See TMA 1938, s 4(3)(a) as amended.
2 There is now an EU Directive, 97/55/EC, amending Directive 84/450/EEC concerning misleading advertising, so as to include comparative advertising. Subject to any decisions of the ECJ, this does not appear to affect the interpretation which has been placed on s 10(6).
3 Article 6.1.
4 See art 5.5.

12.18 The application of s 10(6) in cases of 'genuine' goods or services, not involving comparative advertising, has not yet been considered by a court. This aspect is further discussed below, in connection with 'exhaustion' of rights under s 13. In the area of comparative advertising the provision was considered in some detail by Laddie J on an application for an interlocutory injunction, in the case of *Barclays Bank plc v RBS Advanta*.[1]

1 [1996] RPC 307.

Barclays Bank plc v RBS Advanta

12.19   In the *Barclays Bank* case the plaintiff complained of infringement of its registered trade marks 'BARCLAY(S)' and 'BARCLAYCARD'. The use complained of consisted of use of the mark 'barclaycard' in advertising material for promoting a new VISA card of the defendant. The judge, and counsel for both parties, were in agreement in criticising the wording of s 10(6), which the judge described as a mess. He had no difficulty in finding that the first part of the subsection allows comparative advertising. On the other hand the construction of the proviso gave rise to considerable problems. The judge proceeded on the basis that the proviso should not be construed in a way which effectively prohibits all comparative advertising, and accepted the defence argument that the onus was on the registered proprietor to show that the factors indicated in the proviso exist. He said that there would be no infringement unless the use of the registered mark was not in accordance with honest practices; this is clearly right, since the proprietor must satisfy both parts of the proviso. It was agreed by counsel, and the judge, that the test involved was objective. As the judge said, this part of the proviso simply means that if the use is considered honest by members of a reasonable audience, it will not infringe. If, on the other hand, a reasonable reader was likely to say, on being given the full facts, that the advertisement was not honest, for example because it was significantly misleading, then the protection from trade mark infringement was removed. Strictly speaking, this conclusion may not follow, because of the other requirement, that the use 'without due cause takes unfair advantage of, or is detrimental to, the distinctive character or repute of the trade mark'. However, as the judge said, these words in most cases add nothing of significance to the first part of the proviso, since an advertisement which makes use of a registered trade mark in a way which is not honest will almost always take unfair advantage of it and vice versa. The effect of the words, suggested by the judge, is that the use of the registered mark must either give some advantage to the defendant or inflict some harm on the character or repute of the registered mark which is above the level of *de minimis*.

12.20   This approach seems generally right, although reference should also be made to the words 'without due cause'. Their effect is not clear, but whether any particular use is without due cause may itself depend upon whether there is any 'unfair advantage' or 'detriment' as required by the sub-section. It will be a question of fact, depending upon the nature of the mark, its reputation, the nature of the goods or services, whether the use takes 'unfair advantage', or is 'detrimental' for these purposes. Looking at the proviso as a whole, it may well be that the requirements as to 'unfair advantage' or 'detriment' should be treated as being linked with the idea of 'honest practices', thus perhaps introducing an overall concept of 'fairness' in the use of a registered trade mark of another party. It is suggested that the case of *Chanel Ltd v Triton Packaging Ltd*,[1] decided under the old law, may be regarded as providing a good example of the kind of conduct which would constitute infringement, notwithstanding s 10(6); in that case Millett J described[2] the defendants' material as 'freighted with the goodwill attached to the [plaintiffs'] brand names'.

1 [1993] RPC 32 (Court of Appeal), affirming the decision of Millett J sub nom *Chanel Ltd v L'Arome (UK) Ltd* [1991] RPC 335.
2 [1991] RPC 335 at 345 line 8.

12.21   Section 10(6) of the TMA 1994 has been considered in some other cases since *Barclays*, but the decisions have for the most part been against the trade mark proprietors.[1] However, in a recent decision,[2] in a case in which two competitors brought claims for infringement and malicious falsehood against each other in respect of comparative advertising, which advertising included uses of the other party's registered trade marks, the court found for both proprietors on the trade mark infringement claims. The claims, on both sides, for malicious falsehood were rejected. The basis for the findings of infringement was that each party had made false representations about the other's products which, although not made 'maliciously', were not in accordance with the test of 'honest practices', were without due cause, and took unfair advantage of, or were detrimental to, the distinctive character or the repute of the other party's trade mark.

1 See for example *Vodatone Group plc v Orange Personal Communications Services Ltd* [1997] FSR 34; *MacMillan Magazines Ltd v RCN Publishing Co Ltd,* [1998] FSR 9 (Neuberger J); *Schulke & Mayr UK Ltd v Alkapharm UK Ltd* [1999] FSR 161 (Jacob J); and *Cable & Wireless plc v British Telecommunications plc* [1998] FSR 383. An instance of an interlocutory decision in Scotland, in favour of a plaintiff, is *Teknek Electronics Ltd v KSM International Ltd*, 19 December 1997 (Lord Penrose), noted in CIPA Journal, May 1998, p 380.
2 *Emaco Ltd v Dyson Appliances Ltd* (1999) Times, 8 February (Jonathan Parker J).

Use of own registered trade mark

12.22   At first sight, s 11(1) needs little explanation. As under the old law,[1] a registered trade mark cannot be infringed by the use of another registered trade mark which is validly registered for the goods or services in question. The express reference to s 47(6), which provides that a declaration of invalidity has the effect that the registration (to the extent of the declaration) is to be deemed never to have been made, prompts the question why is there no reference to revocation under s 46? Whatever the reason, it would seem clear that s 11(1) cannot apply to any use of a previously registered trade mark, which takes place *after* it ceases to have effect. Although the provision seems otherwise simple, it could give rise to some difficulties, at least of a technical nature, if the use in question is of a mark differing from the mark as registered. First, because of the absence in the TMA 1994 of any provision that a registration without limitation as to colour is to be treated as extending to all colours and combinations of colour,[2] use of a mark in colour when it is registered in black and white is, strictly, not use of the registered mark. Secondly, there is no general provision allowing use of a registered trade mark, with additions or alterations not substantially affecting its identity.[3] Perhaps both these difficulties, if such they are, can be overcome by construing the subsection as covering any normal and fair use of the registered mark, which would at least allow for variations of colour and forms of lettering. In many cases the matter may be academic, because in practice it is likely that the plaintiff will seek invalidation of the defendant's registration, or vice versa, unless barred by acquiescence.[4] However the point should be noted.

1 TMA 1938, s 4(4).
2 TMA 1938, s 16.
3 TMA 1938, ss 30(1). A similar provision in s 46(2) only applies in cases where revocation is sought under s 46(1).
4 Under TMA 1994, s 48 – see paras **12.58–12.59** below.

12.23 A further point to mention is the position of a CTM under s 11(1). This provision is not mentioned in s 52 and is not applied to CTMs by the CTM Regulaitions 1996.[1] Moreover art 106.1 of the CTM Regulation makes it clear that use of a CTM may infringe an earlier national trade mark unless the proprietor of that mark is barred by acquiescence, under art 53.2, from applying for a declaration that the CTM is invalid.

1 SI 1996/1908 – see ch 22 below.

Use of own name, etc and descriptive and other indications

12.24 Section 11(2), which is derived wholly from the Directive,[1] is similar to provisions in the old law[2] protecting bona fide use by any person of his name or address, or bona fide use of a description of the character or quality of goods or services. Three categories of use are covered, namely (a) use by a person of his own name or address; (b) the use of indications of various characteristics of goods or services; (c) the use of the trade mark where it is necessary to indicate the intended purpose of a product or service (in particular as accessories or spare parts). Each category is governed by the overriding proviso that the use be in accordance with honest practices in industrial or commercial matters, which has already been considered above in connection with s 10(6), and which, it is submitted, similarly imposes an objective test.

1 Article 6.1.
2 TMA 1938 (as amended), s 8.

Use by a person of his own name or address

12.25 The application of s 11 (2)(a) would appear to be fairly straightforward, although for reasons appearing below this may not necessarily be the case. It is thought that, as under s 8(a) of the TMA 1938, the question what is a person's name is one of fact. If the evidence shows that the allegedly infringing sign is the name by which the defendant is known in the market, then the use is capable of being protected by the sub-section.[1] Comment should be made here on para 7 of the Annex to the Directive, in which the view is expressed that the words 'his own name' apply only in respect of natural persons. Having regard to the rule under English law, that 'person' includes any body of persons corporate or unincorporate,[2] it seems most unlikely that the courts would accept the view expressed. If the provision does apply to company names, then there is no reason for doubting that it will cover the use of the corporate name without the words 'ltd' or 'plc' as was the case under the TMA 1938.[3] So far as the requirement that the use be in accordance with 'honest practices' is concerned, it might be thought that this is essentially the same as the requirement of 'bona fide' use under s 8(a) of the TMA 1938. Clearly the onus of proof in each case is on the alleged infringer. However in *Baume v Moore*[4] it was held that 'bona fide' meant not dishonest, which is a subjective test. As already mentioned, Laddie J held, in *Barclays Bank,*[5] that the test in applying the same words in s 10(6) of the TMA 1994 is objective, and this view has been endorsed by Rattee J in *The European Ltd v Economist Newspapers Ltd.*[6] One question, which arose under the TMA 1938, was whether s 8(a) protected use of a name as a trade mark. In *Baume v Moore* it was held that it did, and this view was upheld by the House of Lords in *Parker-Knoll.* In principle the position should, it is suggested, be the same under the TMA 1994, so long as the requirement of use in accordance with 'honest practices' is met. Although in general use of a name as a trade mark should be acceptable, it could be otherwise if the name were used, for instance, in a similar type face or colour to that used by the proprietor of the registered mark.

1 See *Mercury Communications Ltd v Mercury Interactive (UK) Ltd* [1995] FSR 851, a decision of Laddie J on the TMA 1938, as amended, s 8(a).
2 See the Interpretation Act 1978, s 5 and Sch 1
3 See *Baume & Coy Ltd v AH Moore Ltd* [1957] RPC 459 (Danckwerts J) and [1958] RPC 226 (CA); approved by the House of Lords in *Parker-Knoll Ltd v Knoll International Ltd* [1962] RPC 265.
4 *Baume & Coy Ltd v AH Moore Ltd* [1957] RPC 459.
6 [1996] RPC 307.
6 [1996] RPC 431; affirmed by the Court of Appeal, who expressed no concluded view on the point – [1998] FSR 283.
7 *Parker-Knoll Ltd v Knoll International Ltd* [1962] RPC 243.

Use of descriptive matter

12.26   Sub-section 11(2)(b) is very similar to s 3(1)(c) of the TMA 1994, containing grounds for refusal of registration of descriptive matter. The sub-section protects, again subject to the requirement of use in accordance with honest practices, 'use of indications concerning the kind, quality, quantity, intended purpose, value, geographical origin, the time of production of goods or of rendering of services, or other characteristics of goods or services'. The reference to 'intended purpose' might seem, at first sight, to overlap with sub-s (2)(c), discussed below. However, it should probably be limited to such use in the sense of a description of the purpose for which the goods or services are intended to be used, from a functional point of view, and not with reference to use as spare parts or accessories for a trade mark proprietor's product, which is covered by sub-s (2)(c).

12.27   It is necessary to consider a further question, which has already been referred to in two decisions,[1] namely whether an alleged infringer can rely upon s 11(2)(b) of the TMA 1994 where the description concerned is used as a trade mark for his goods or services. Under the amended TMA 1938, it had been held that for the purposes of the similar provision of s 8(b), which protected bona fide use of descriptions of the character or quality of goods or services, the protection was excluded where the defendant was using the 'description' as a trade mark.[2] In *British Sugar*, Jacob J considered that s 11(2)(b) of the TMA 1994 would not have assisted the defendant if the words in question had been used as a trade mark for the defendant's goods, which the judge held not to be the case. He said:

> 'Thirdly there is the question of use of the sign for the defendant's goods. I considered the question of comparative advertising first to test the proposition that the sign can only be used as a "pure descriptor". I reject that because it can be used as part of a description when used for the plaintiff's goods. But use of the sign for the defendant's goods is something different. That seems to me to be inconsistent with the mark being used as a description or performing any of the other functions. If a mark is used as a trade mark for the defendant's goods, then it is not used as a description. This conclusion may have important implications where a semi-descriptive mark is validly registered. In particular if the defendant's mark is descriptive to some but has a trade mark significance to others, he will not be within the section.'

Later on, the judge concluded:

> 'Section 11(2) does not cover the case where a word, outside the context of the use, is descriptive if, in context, it is part of trade mark use for the defendant's goods.'

1 *British Sugar* and *The European* – see para **12.6** n 1 and para **12.25**, n 6 above.
2 Per Mummery . in *Portakabin Ltd v Powerblast Ltd* [1990] RPC 471 at 483.

12.28　This approach seems a reasonable one, and is consistent with the decision of Mummery J in *Portakabin*.[1] It was also accepted by Rattee J in *The European*.[2] It may be remarked that the same result might be reached through a different route if, as suggested above,[3] the test under the proviso is objective. Given that a descriptive word is identical with or similar to a registered mark, and that there is a likelihood of confusion or (where the goods or services are dissimilar) the requirements of s 10(3) are met, it can be argued that use of the descriptive word as a trade mark for another party's goods or services is not in accordance with 'honest practices', viewing the matter objectively. This was the view expressed by Rottee J in *The European*.

1 Paragraph **12.27**, n 2.
2 Paragraph **12.25**, n 6.
3 Paragraph **12.24**.

Use necessary to indicate the intended purpose of a product or service

12.29　Sub-section 11(2)(c) is quite similar to s 4(3)(b) of the TMA 1938. The provision protects a third party using the registered trade mark where 'it is necessary to indicate the intended purpose of a product or service (in particular as accessories or spare parts)'. It seems clear, from the reference to services and the words 'in particular', that the subsection allows for other 'intended purposes', where use of the trade mark is 'necessary', and not only use for spare parts or accessories, and one example is provided by the decision of the ECJ referred to in the next paragraph. Section 4(3)(b) of the TMA 1938 used the word 'reasonably necessary' but it is doubtful whether the absence of the word 'reasonably' ' will make any practical difference. If the goods of the defendant are intended to be capable of being used as accessories or spare parts for a product sold under a trade mark, then it is plainly necessary to refer to the trade mark to indicate that this is the case. As with the other parts of s 11(2), sub-s (2)(c) is subject to the requirement of use in accordance with honest practices in industrial or commercial matters, and thus any kind of use which suggested that the defendant's goods or services were those of the proprietor or in some way commercially connected with him would probably be outside the protection of the subsection.

12.30　Article 6(1)(c) of the Directive, from which s 11(2)(c) is derived, has been considered by the Court of Justice in the case of *Bayerische Motorenwerke AG (BMW) v Deenik*[1], which concerned the use of the mark BMW by a dealer specialising in the sale of second-hand BMW cars and in repairing and maintaining 'BMW' cars, who was not an authorised dealer in such cars. The court had also to consider the application of art 7 of the Directive, concerning exhaustion of rights. As to art 6(1)(c), the Court said that the use of the trade mark to inform the public that the advertiser repairs and maintains trade-marked goods must be held

215

to constitute use indicating the intended purpose of the service within the meaning of art 6(1)(c), adding that like the use of a trade mark intended to identify the vehicles which a non-original spare part will fit, the use in question is intended to identify the goods in respect of which the service is provided. The court referred to the Opinion of the Advocate-General, who had pointed out that if an independent trader carries out the maintenance and repair of BMW cars, or is in fact a specialist in that field, that fact cannot in practice be communicated to his customers without using the 'BMW' mark. Thus use of the mark was necessary to indicate the intended purpose. However, in applying the provision, questions as to whether the particular uses are in accordance with honest practices in industrial or commercial matters are questions for the national court deciding the case.

1 [1999] All ER (EC) 235. See also the decision of Rattee J in *AB Volvo v Heritage Leicester Ltd* (7 May 1999, unreported), giving summary judgment against a former dealer.

Use of an earlier right applying only in a particular locality

12.31   Section 11(3) of the TMA 1994 provides that a registered trade mark is is not infringed 'by the use in the course of trade in a particular locality of an earlier right which applies only in that locality'. This provision is derived from art 6.2 of the Directive but does not use exactly the same wording, which is understood to have been aimed at a particular kind of local situation which arises under German law. 'Earlier right' and 'applying in a particular locality are defined as follows:

> 'For this purpose an "earlier right" means an unregistered trade mark or other sign continuously used in relation to goods or services by a person or a predecessor in title of his from a date prior to whichever is the earlier of—
>
> (a) the use of the first-mentioned trade mark in relation to those goods or services by the proprietor or a predecessor in title of his, or
> (b) the registration of the first-mentioned trade mark in respect of those goods or services in the name of those goods or services in the name of the proprietor or a predecessor in title of his;
>
> and an earlier right shall be regarded as applying in a particular locality if, or to the extent that, its use in that locality is protected by virtue of any rule of law (in particular the law of passing off.'

12.32   The definition of earlier right is similar to the 'vested rights' provision of s 7 of the TMA 1938, in requiring proof of continuous use prior to both the registration and the first use of the registered trade mark. It would appear that the use must precede the use of the registered trade mark by the proprietor (or a predecessor in title of his) in any part of the UK, not merely in the 'particular locality' concerned.

12.33   It is not immediately obvious how far the sub-section will be applicable in the UK. It is thought that the provision is unlikely to be of much practical application to marks used for goods, since such use is not normally local in character. It might apply to some cases of marks used for certain services of a local nature, such as launderettes, public houses and village stores. It is fairly clear that the owner of the 'earlier right' would not be permitted to expand the area of use outside the particular locality, and still avoid infringement. In view of this, and the uncertainty as to the scope of this provision, it may well be advisable for owners of such rights to consider opposition to any application to register trade marks, which they may infringe, and perhaps to apply to register their own trade marks.

Exhaustion of rights

12.34   Under the TMA 1938 and under the common law the courts have developed a doctrine of 'exhaustion of rights' in cases where a trade mark proprietor seeks to restrain the importation and sale in the UK of its own goods or the goods of an associated company, by means of an action for infringement or passing off. Reference may be made to such cases as *Champagne Heidsieck et Cie Monopole SA v Buxton* and *Revlon Inc v Cripps and Lee Ltd.*[2] In more recent years there has been a parallel development of a doctrine of exhaustion of rights within the EU, under the provisions of the Treaty of Rome relating to free movement of goods. After a period in which there was some doubt as to how far the ECJ would countenance the enforcement of any intellectual property rights to prevent imports of goods from one Member State into another, it was finally established[3] that trade mark rights would generally be enforced in such cases unless the goods in question had been placed on the market in a Member State by the proprietor or with his consent. Other decisions of the ECJ[4] defined circumstances, with particular reference to repackaged pharmaceutical products, in which a trade mark proprietor might object to the imports notwithstanding the fact that the goods had been marketed in the Member State of export by him or with his consent. Article 7 of the Directive made a specific provision for exhaustion of trade mark rights within the Community. In accordance with the Agreement on the European Economic Area ('EEA')of 2 May 1992[5] the doctrine was effectively extended to the whole of the EEA. Article 7 of the Directive is implemented, and extended to the EEA, by s 12 of the TMA 1994.

1 [1930] 1 Ch 330; 47 RPC 28.
2 [1980] FSR 85, CA.
3 See *CNL-Sucal NV v HAG GF AG ('Hag II')* [1990] ECR I-3711 and *IHT Internationale Heiztechnik GmbH v Ideal Standard GmbH* [1994] ECR I-27897.
4 See in particular *Hoffmann-La Roche & Co AG v Centrafarm BV* [1978] 3 CMLR 2.7 and *Centrafarm BV v American Home Products Corpn* [1979] 1 CMLR 326.
5 OJ L1 3.1.94, p1.

Section 12 of the TMA 1994

12.35   In accordance with art 7 of the Directive, s 12 of the TMA 1994 provides that a registered trade mark is not infringed by the use of the trade mark in relation to goods put on the market in the EEA under the trade mark by the proprietor or with his consent. This is likely to be applied to goods marketed by another related company, as well as goods of licensees, on the basis that there is consent to their marketing of the goods. Sub-section (2) makes an exception to the general principle of exhaustion, by providing that:

> 'Subsection (1) does not apply where there exist legitimate reasons for the proprietor to oppose further dealings in the goods (in particular where the condition of the goods has been changed or impaired after they have been put on the market).'

12.36 Before discussing some of the cases concerning the application of art 7 of the Directive, it is necessary to consider whether there is now any scope for a doctrine of international exhaustion of trade mark rights, applying to goods coming from outside the EEA.

International exhaustion

12.37 The ECJ has held, in the case of *Silhouette International Schmied GmbH & Co KG v Hartlauer Handelsgesellschaft mbH,*[1] that the effect of the Directive is that it is not open to Member States to apply a doctrine of international exhaustion in cases where the goods in question come from outside the EEA. The court specifically held that any national rules providing for exhaustion of trade mark rights in respect of products put on the market outside the EEA under a trade mark by the proprietor or with his consent, was contrary to art 7.

1 [1999] Ch 77.

12.38 It seems clear that the *Silhouette*[1] decision will not be confined to the facts of the particular case. It involved the sale in Austria of spectacle frames under the trade mark 'Silhouette'. A consignment of the goods, of a design which was no longer considered fashionable, had been sold and delivered by Silhouette to a firm in Bulgaria. The transaction had been arranged by Silhouette's Middle East representative, who had been instructed by Silhouette to sell them on in Bulgaria or the States of the former Soviet Union and not to export them to other countries. The defendant subsequently acquired the goods and offered them for sale in Austria. A subsequent Opinion of the Advocate-General[2] has reaffirmed the *Silhouette* decision as being of general application and rejects an attempt to circumvent it by arguing that the proprietor of a trade mark must be taken to have consented to the marketing in the EEA of a batch of his products imported from outside the EEA if he has consented to the marketing within the EEA of other batches of identical or similar articles. After reviewing the arguments the Advocate-General observes:

> '28. To say that once a trade-mark proprietor has consented to the marketing of one particular batch of products within the EEA he must be deemed to have consented to the marketing of other identical (or similar) batches would accordingly deprive the court's limitation of the exhaustion principle to EEA-wide exhaustion of much of its practical effect. It would for most practical purposes effectively impose a rule of international exhaustion since, in the absence of a legitimate reason, all parallel imports would necessarily have to be admitted into the EEA.

> '29. Such a limitation upon the effect of the Directive as interpreted in the court's judgment in *Silhouette* may seem desirable and would no doubt be welcomed in many circles. However, as the court observed in *Silhouette*, no argument has been presented to the court that the Directive could be interpreted as *imposing* a rule of international exhaustion. The dispute centred only on whether the Directive left the matter to the discretion of the Member States. The imposition of international exhaustion in the way suggested by GB-Unic does not follow easily from the wording of Article 7(1). Nor does it appear to have been the intention of the Community legislature.

The views of the Advocate-General were followed by the ECJ in its decision.[3]

1 [1998] ETMR 539–628.
2 In *Sebago Inc v GB-UNIC SA* [1999] All ER (EC) 575, Case C-173/98.
3 [1999] ETMR 681.

The effect of the Silhouette decision on the previous English cases

12.39   In the English cases,[1] the doctrine of international exhaustion was applied to passing off claims as well as those of infringement. Since the action for passing off is expressly preserved by s 2(2) of the TMA 1994, it seems clear that the doctrine of international exhaustion, as developed by the courts in passing off cases,[2] will continue to be applied in appropriate situations. No further comment is necessary here.

1 See para **12.34** above.
2 Subject to the recognised exceptions, in particular where there is a misrepresentation as to the nature or quality of the goods. See for example *Castrol Ltd v Automotive Oil Supplies Ltd* [1983] RPC 315 and *Colgate-Palmolive Ltd v Markwell Finance Ltd* [1989] RPC 497.

12.40   One provision of the TMA 1994, which requires further consideration in the light of the *Silhouette*[1] decision, is s 10(6). As already mentioned, s 9(1) of the TMA 1994 defines infringement by reference to acts done without the proprietor's consent. That might be thought to have been sufficient for a court to reject a claim for infringement where the trade mark in question is used in relation to 'genuine' goods or services of the proprietor. However s 10(6) expresses the position in this respect[2] fairly clearly, in that it provides that nothing in s 10 shall be construed as preventing the use of a registered trade mark by any person for the purpose of identifying goods or services as those of the proprietor or a licensee. Because s 9(1) refers to use of the trade mark in the UK, it would appear that the consent must be to use in the UK. If that is so, then s 9(1) does not provide any basis for an argument of international exhaustion. Even if, read literally, it might otherwise allow a finding of international exhaustion in some cases, such an interpretation was thought to have been ruled out by the *Silhouette* and *Sebago* decisions. Nevertheless some questions remain to be revolved

1 [1998] ETMR 539–628.
2 Subject to the difficulties arising from the second para, discussed above in paras **12.17–12.21**.

12.41   A recent decision of the High Court, in *Zino Davidoff SA v A & G Imports Ltd*[1] raises another question related to international exhaustion, which is whether a trade mark owner may in some circumstances be found to have consented to the sale of parallel imported goods coming from outside the EEA, and thus be precluded from enforcing his rights by a claim for infringement or passing off. The decision was on an application for summary judgment, so the judge only had to decide whether the defendant had an arguable defence. The judge found that the goods in question, which were the genuine goods of the plaintiff and indistinguishable from goods sold under the same trade mark in the UK and elsewhere, did in fact come from outside the EEA. While accepting that the effect of the *Silhouette* decision was that international exhaustion could not be *imposed* by Member States of the EU, that did not preclude a trade mark owner from being found to have consented to the sale of the goods in question within the EEA. On the evidence, he held that the defendant had an arguable case on this issue. He also held that there was an arguable defence to the plaintiff's contention that there were legitimate reasons for opposing the use complained of. However it should be noted that the judge has referred the matter to the ECJ for their interpretation of the relevant provisions of the Directive.

1 (Laddie J.) [1999] RPC 631. Similar questions, also raising the issue of 'consent' under art 5 of the Directive, have been referred to the ECJ by Pawfrey J in two cases, Levi Strauss & Co v Costco UK Ltd and Levi Strauss & Co v Tesco Stores Ltd (22 July 1999).

Exhaustion of rights within the EEA

12.42 Since the adoption of the Directive, a number of cases concerning art 7 and provisions of national laws implementing it, and in particular the effect of para (2) relating to 'legitimate reasons' for opposing further commercialisation of the goods, have come before the ECJ. The most important decisions have related to pharmaceutical products and in particular their repackaging, and represent a significant development in the area of repackaging, beyond the principles established by previous rulings of the ECJ in parallel import cases interpreting art 36 of the EC Treaty.[1] Nevertheless, the decisions establish that, while the national laws concerned have to be assessed in the light of art 7, that article must itself be interpreted in the light of the Treaty rules on the free movement of goods, and in particular art 36.

1 Paragraph **12.34**, n 4 above.

12.43 Among the first cases on art 7 to come before the court, were three repackaging cases, by different plaintiffs against the same defendant, *Bristol-Myers v Paranova*[1]. The principle laid down by the court in these cases was that a trade mark owner may legitimately oppose the marketing of his own pharmaceutical products under his trade mark where the importer has repackaged the products and reaffixed the trade mark, unless it is established that reliance of the trade mark rights for this purpose would contribute to the artificial partitioning of the markets between Member States. The court ruled that such is the case, in particular, where the owner has put an identical pharmaceutical product on the market in several Member States in various forms of packaging, and the repackaging carried out by the importer is necessary in order to market the product in the Member State of importation, and is carried out in such conditions that the original condition of the product cannot be affected by it. The court emphasised that this did not imply that it must be established that the trade mark owner deliberately sought to partition the markets between Member States.

1 Cases C 427/93, C 429/93 and C 436//93, (from the Danish Court) [1996] ECR I-3457.

12.44 A further three cases, on references from a German court, again concerning repackaging, are *Eurim-Pharm Arzneimittel GmbH v Beiersdorf AG*[1]. The repackaging was carried out in order the comply with national standard sizes conforming to the prescribing practices of medical practitioners in Germany. The decision in the *Paranova* cases[2] was followed. Answering the questions referred, the court responded in the form of a general acceptance of the proposition that a trade mark owner was entitled to rely on his rights to prevent an importer from marketing a pharmaceutical product put on the market in another Member State by the proprietor or with his consent, where the importer has repackaged the product in new external packaging through which the trade mark affixed to the original packaging has been made visible, or where he has modified the contents and the appearance of the original packaging whilst preserving the trade mark affixed by the manufacturer, *unless* certain conditions apply. The first condition, as in the decision in the *Paranova* cases, was that it must be established that the reliance on trade mark rights to oppose the marketing of the repackaged products would contribute to the artificial partitioning of the markets between Member States which, the court said, was the case where the proprietor had put an identical pharmaceutical product on the market in several Member States in various forms of packaging, and the repackaging is necessary in order to market the product in the State of importation, and also carried out in such conditions that the original condition of the product cannot be affected. Again the court emphasised that the requirement did not imply that it must be established that the trade mark owner deliberately sought to partition the markets between Member States. Next, the court elaborated on the requirement that it must be shown that the repackaging cannot affect the original condition of the product inside the packaging, and gave some indications as to matters which national courts should determine. The court added other requirements, which have been stated in earlier decisions, that the new packaging must clearly state who repackaged the product and the name of the manufacturer, and that the importer must give notice to the trade mark owner before the repackaged product is put on sale and, on demand, provide a sample. The court however pointed out that it is not necessary to state that the repackaging has been carried out without the authorisation of the trade mark owner. Furthermore, the court said that the presentation of the repackaged product must not be such as to be liable to damage the reputation of the trade mark and of its owner, for example where the packaging is defective, of poor quality, or untidy, these being matters for the national court to determine.

1 Cases C 71–73/94, [1997] 1 CMLR 1222.
2 Paragraph **12.43**, n1 above.

12.45   The cases on repackaging of pharmaceutical products were recently comprehensively reviewed again in the Opinion of Advocate-General Francis Jacobs in another case before the ECJ, *Upjohn SA, Danmark v Paranova A/S*[1]. This case raises the question whether the importer is permitted to apply to the goods a trade mark used by the trade mark owner for the product in the country of importation, where this is different from the trade mark which the owner affixed to the product for sale in the Member State in which the product was originally put on the market. Such situations can arise where there are reasons, for example because of conflicting rights of third parties, why the same mark cannot be used in the Member State of importation. Changes of trade mark may also be dictated by local national regulations or preferences. It had previously been widely thought that the trade mark owner could prevent the remarking of the product in such circumstances, unless he had adopted the different marks for the purpose of partitioning the markets. The Advocate-General in *Upjohn v Paranova* expressed the opinion that this was not the correct view.

1 [1999] ETMR 97.

12.46   The Advocate-General pointed out that the scope of a parallel importer's right to repackage where the trade mark owner markets goods in different forms of packaging in different Member States is, since *Bristol-Myers*,[1] now governed by a body of coherent and clearly articulated principles hinging on objective factors. He expressed the view that it would be anomalous and illogical for the scope of the importer's right to affix a different trade mark were the trade mark owner markets goods under different marks in different Member States to continue to be governed by a separate set of principles dependent upon the subjective element of intention. He therefore proposed that the new criteria laid down by the court in *Bristol-Myers* should be applied equally to such cases. After giving his reasons, he referred to the requirement of necessity, ie that the power of the trade mark owner to oppose the marketing of repackaged products should be limited only in so far as the repackaging is necessary in order to market the product in the State of importation, and proposed that the criterion of necessity should apply in re-branding cases. Referring to the guidance found in *Bristol-Myers*, as to the circumstances in which repackaging is to be regarded as 'necessary', he said:

'Certainly where such circumstances also rendered marketing impossible without re-branding, re-branding would similarly be regarded as necessary: thus if any such practices or rules in the Member States of import have the effect that the importer cannot market the products under the trade mark they bear in the State of export, the trade mark owner will not be able to rely on his trade mark rights to prevent the importer from affixing the trade mark used by the owner for identical goods in the State of import.'

After further discussions of the factors involved, the Advocate General concluded by saying that he considered that the criteria established by the court in *Bristol-Myers* for determining the scope of a parallel importer's right to repackage should be extended so as to determine the scope of a parallel importer's right to change the mark. The crucial part of the Advocate General's conclusion is that the trade mark owner can exercise his rights to prevent the importation of the re-branded product unless (inter alia):

'Changing the mark is necessary in order to market the product in the Member State of import, in the sense that prohibiting the importer from rebranding would constitute an obstacle to effective access by him to the markets of the State of import.'

12.47 In its decision[1] the ECJ has essentially followed the Advocate-General's opinion It therefore appears that it is for the national courts to determine whether changing the trade mark is 'necessary'. If the conclusion of the Court is interpreted literally, it is open to a national court to find that changing the mark is not necessary, because the importer can always use the official generic name of the product, instead of the trade mark. Such approach might not seem entirely consistent with the Advocate-General's observations or with those of the Court. However, the ECJ did not go so far as to say that re-branding is 'necessary' even where the generic name could have been used to gain access to the market. Indeed, the Court stated that 'the condition of necessity will not be satisfied if replacement of the trade mark is explicable solely by the parallel importer's attempt to secure a commercial advantage'. Such considerations may be particularly relevant where, as is thought to be the case with a number of pharmaceutical products in the UK, a large majority of medical prescriptions use the generic name of the product rather than the brand name. A further question arises under the TRIPS provisions of the GATT.[2] Article 16 sets out the rights conferred by a registered trade mark in terms which are essentially the same as the relevant provisions of the TMA 1994. Article 17, entitled 'exceptions' is as follows:

'Members may provide limited exceptions to the rights conferred by a trademark, such as fair use of descriptive terms, provided that such exceptions take account of the legitimate interests of the owner of the trademark and of third parties.'

This wording does not suggest that there should be an over liberal interpretation of the term 'limited exceptions', and it may be arguable, if the ruling of the Court were to be interpreted as compelling national courts to hold that re-branding is not 'necessary' in the circumstances discussed above, that the ruling offends against art 17 of TRIPS. This question might have to be considered by the court on some future occasion.

1 Judgment 12 October 1999.
2 See Appendix 4.

12.48 It must be emphasised that whatever the decision of the ECJ in the *Upjohn*[1] case, there will still be room for national courts to make their own decisions on what are, or are not 'legitimate reasons' for opposing further commercialisation of the goods, for the purposes of art 7(2). The decision of Laddie J in *Davidoff*,[2] albeit on an application for summary judgment, provides a good example of a case in which the court considered the reasons not to be legitimate.

1 Paragraph **12.45** above.
2 Paragraph **12.41**, n 1 above

Disclaimers

12.49 Although, as appears from s 13 of the TMA 1994, the registrar will no longer be able to insist on disclaimers of non-distinctive matter appearing in a trade mark which is sought to be registered, sub-s (1) does provide for applicants for registration voluntarily to accept a disclaimer of any right to the exclusive use of any specified element of the trade mark applied for, or a territorial or other limitation on the rights conferred by registration. Such disclaimers and limitations will usually only exist if they are accepted by applicants following objection by third parties or opposition, as a result of a term of settlement of a dispute, although there will be some cases in which the registrar may be persuaded to waive objections if an appropriate disclaimer or limitation is agreed to be the applicant[1]. However disclaimers and limitations imposed under the old law will continue to apply – see the transitional provisions in Sch 3 to the TMA 1994, para 3(2) – and have effect as if entered on the register in pursuance of s 13. Where, whether under the old law or the TMA 1994, a registration is subject to a disclaimer, the rights of the proprietor are accordingly limited by s 13(1).

1 See for example *MISTER LONG Trade Mark* [1998] RPC 401.

Transitional provisions affecting infringement

12.50 From commencement, para 4(1) of the transitional provisions of Sch 3 to the TMA 1994 provides that ss 9–12 (effects of registration) apply in relation to existing registered marks, and that s 14 (action for infringement) applies in relation to infringements committed after commencement. Paragraph 4(2) contains some protection for continued use of a sign after commencement of the TMA 1994, if the use did not constitute an infringement under the old law. However this may be seriously limited, because para 4(2) only protects the continued use from a claim of infringement in respect of either an 'existing' registered trade mark[1] or a registered trade mark of which the distinctive elements are the same or substantially the same as those of an existing registered mark and which is registered for the same goods or services. The last mentioned part of the provision prevents a proprietor from circumventing the first part by simply re-registering an existing registered trade mark under the new law. However if the registered trade mark allegedly infringed is a mark which could not be or was not registered under the old law but is registered under the TMA 1994, then the transitional provision seems to offer no protection to the continuing user, and it appears that he will be left to defend the claim on the basis that if there has been no confusion, or unfair advantage or detriment, arising from his previous use, then there is no likelihood of confusion, and no unfair advantage or detriment within s 10(2) and (3) respectively, as the case may be. It may in fact be doubted whether this provision complies with art 5(4) of the Directive, which is as follows:

> 'Where, under the law of the Member State, the use of a sign under the conditions referred to in 1(b) or 2[2] could not be prohibited before the date on which the provisions necessary to comply with this Directive entered into force in the Member State concerned, the rights conferred by the trade mark may not be relied on to prevent the continued use of the sign.'

It seems fairly clear that the purpose of the Directive was to protect continuing users against infringement claims in respect of any trade marks, whether they were registered before or after implementation of the Directive. However it is to be hoped that courts will try to mitigate any unjust effects by making appropriate findings of fact in relation to the claim for infringement. The only situation in which, it would seem, this cannot be done, except in the case of existing registered trade marks or other trade marks falling within para 4(2)(b) of Sch 3, is where the mark, and the goods or services, are identical to those for which the trade mark is registered.

1 Defined in Sch 3, para. 1.
2 Ie in cases in which there is not identity in respect of both mark and sign, and goods or services.

12.51   Some consideration is also necessary of the words, in para 4(2) of Sch 3, 'to continue after commencement any use which did not amount to infringement of the existing registered mark under the old law'. For this purpose reference must be made to ss 4 and 5 of the amended TMA 1938, which defined the rights conferred by registration of a trade mark in Part A and Part B of the register respectively. It is clear that continuation of any use, which was not an infringement under s 4(1) for any reason, for example because the marks were not confusingly similar or because the use was for goods or services not covered by the specification of the registration, will be protected. Similarly, use protected by s 7 or s 8 of the old law (respectively protecting vested rights and bona fide use of a name or address, or a description) was not an infringement under s 4(1) and would fall within the transitional provision. The same applies to any use which was not an infringement by virtue of the other sub-sections of s 4. A further instance, in which there was no infringement under the old law, is where the registration was invalid under that law[1]. This may be important for a user who was not sued for infringement, because the proprietor did not wish to risk a claim for rectification.

1 See the words 'if valid' in s 4(1). Examples of cases in which a registration might have been invalid under the old law but would not be open to attack under the TMA 1994, are trade marks which were distinctive in fact but inherently non-distinctive, and registrations which offended against s 11 but could not now be attacked under ss 47(2)/5(4).

12.52   A further issue may arise in cases of marks which were registered in Part B of the register, where a user of an identical or a confusingly similar mark for goods or services covered by a registration would have been entitled to rely upon s 5(2) of the amended TMA 1938. The difficulty, for an alleged infringer under the TMA 1994, is that s 5(2) only protected a defendant against the granting of any injunction or other relief, and did not in terms have the effect that there was no 'infringement'. There is thus a case for denying the benefit of para 4(2) of Sch 3 to a defendant in such a case. However the courts can be expected to be reluctant to reach this conclusion. The terms of art 5.4 of the Directive may assist here, because the words 'could not be prohibited' plainly extend beyond uses which were not, strictly speaking, 'infringement'. It may be open to the courts to construe the words 'did not amount to infringement' in para 4(2) fairly broadly, on the basis that the provision must be taken to have been intended to comply with the Directive.

Protection of well kn-wn trade marks – sect

12.53   Section 56 of the TMA 1994[1] represents a belated compliance with art 6*bis* of the Paris Convention. Before this provision was enacted, a well-known trade mark, which was not the subject of a trade mark registration, could not obtain protection against the use of even the identical mark for identical or similar goods or services for which the mark was used and known, if the owner did not have a business in the UK.[2] Subsection (1) defines a trade mark which is entitled to protection under the Paris Convention or the WTO ('WTO') agreement[3] as a well-known trade mark, for the purposes of the TMA 1994, as 'a mark which is well-known in the UK as being the mark of a person who (a) is a national of a Convention country, or (b) is domiciled in, or has a real and effective industrial or commercial establishment in, a Convention country, whether or not that person carries on business, or has any goodwill, in the UK'. As pointed out in Chapter 8, the UK is excluded from the definition of 'Convention country'.

1 Together with the provisions of TMA 1994, ss 5 and 6, discussed in ch 6 – see paras **6.72–6.73**.
2 *Anheuser-Busch Inc v Budejovicky Budvar NP* [1984] FSR 413.
3 References to the WTO agreement have been added to s 56(1) and (2) by reg 13 of The Patents and Trade Marks (World Trade Organisation) Regulations 1999 (SI 1999/1899).

12.54   There are no decisions of any courts in the UK as to the requirements for a mark to be 'well known' within the meaning of the Paris Convention. Clearly the requirement is considerably greater than the requirement, under ss 5(3) and 10(3), that a mark have a 'reputation' in the UK. There are some trade marks which would be expected to be found to be well known without much difficulty. For example the mark 'LEGO' was held to be a 'household' word in the UK,[1] and there is little doubt that, given sufficient evidence, it would be held to be well known for these purposes. In every case the question will be one of fact, to be determined on the evidence, although more evidence may be required where the mark is less obviously well known. On the basis of decisions in other countries criteria have been put forward in Draft Provisions on Well-Known Marks, by WIPO[2]. Article 2 is as follows:

Article 2

Conditions of Protection

(1)   [*Protection Without Registration or Use*] For the purposes of determining whether a mark is to be protected as a well-known mark, registration or use of the mark in, or in respect of, the territory in which it is to be protected as a well-known trade mark may not be required.

(2) [*Territory in Which and Persons by Whom the Mark is to be well-known*] For the purposes of determining whether a mark is to be protected as a well-known trade mark, it shall suffice that the mark be well-known by the relevant sector of the public in the territory in which it is to be protected as a well-known mark.

(3) [*Criteria*] For the purposes of determining whether a mark is to be protected as a well-known mark, at least the following shall be taken into account:

(i) the potential customers of the goods and/or services to which the mark applies;

(ii) the channels of distribution of the goods and/or services to which the mark applies;

(iii) the duration, extent, and geographical area of any use of the mark;

(iv) the duration, extent, and geographical area of any advertising of the mark;

(v) the market share, in the territory in which the mark is to be protected as a well-known mark and in other territories, of the goods and/or services to which the mark applies.

1 By Falconer J in *Lego System A/S v Lego M Lemelstrich Ltd* [1983] FSR 155, at 161.
2 The Draft Provisions are set out in Appendix 20 of 'Famous and Well-Known Marks' by FW Mostert (Butterworths 1997).

12.55 No comment is necessary on para (1), which seems to accord with the position under s 56 of the TMA 1994 and art 6[bis] itself. Paragraph (2) may well represent the likely approach of courts in applying s 56. The criteria set out in para (3) seem fairly obvious and in accordance with what would appear to be a correct approach, with the possible exception of (v) to the extent that it refers to market shares in other territories. However such matters could be relevant, because the extent to which a mark is known to the relevant public in the UK may be dependent on the extent of use in other countries, to which members of the public travel and where they may be exposed to the mark, as well as that of use in the UK.

12.56 One question, which is not explicitly covered by s 56, is, at what date must the trade mark be shown to be well known in the UK? Clearly it must be well known when the claim is made. But there is a further question that may arise, which is what is the position where the defendant's use commenced at a time when the mark was not well known in the UK, or perhaps had not even commenced anywhere? Sub-section (3) deals with one particular situation, by providing that nothing in sub-s (2) affects the continuation of any bona fide use of a trade mark begun before the commencement of the section, that is 31 October 1994. This provision was necessary because para 4(2) of the transitional provisions in Sch 3 of the TMA 1994 (right to continuing use)[1] only applies as against a claim for infringement, and a claim under s 56 is not a claim for infringement. But sub-s (3) does not cover any case in which the use in question commenced after 31 October 1994. It would seem likely that a court would be very reluctant to reach a decision which would involve a wholly innocent party being compelled to cease use of a mark which was lawfully used from inception, on the basis of a later acquired right. It may be that the question could be resolved, should it arise, in the same way as in passing off cases. As confirmed by the Court of Appeal in the *Anheuser-Busch* case[2], a case of passing off must be established as at the date on which the conduct complained of commenced. Against this, it might be argued that such a conclusion would make sub-s (3) redundant. However that would not necessarily be so, because sub-s (3) meets a different kind of situation, in which the use in question was commenced in good faith before 31 October 1994 but after the claimant's trade mark had become 'well known', so that an existing honest user would not be defeated by a change in the law.

1 Paragraphs **12.48–12.52** above.
2 Paragraph **12.53**, n 2 above.

12.57 In order to succeed in a claim under s 56, the proprietor must establish that the defendant's mark, or the essential part of it, is identical or similar to his well-known mark, that it is used in relation to identical or similar goods services (ie, presumably, to those for which the mark is well known[1]), and that the use is likely to cause confusion. The courts will probably adopt the same approach, in determining whether the use is likely to cause confusion, as for ss 5 and 10 of the Act. The remedies available for the protection of a well-known trade mark are limited by s 56(2), to an injunction. It would seem to be likely that the court could also grant other relief, such as delivery up or destruction, or the obliteration of offending marks, where the purpose is to enhance the efficacy of injunctive relief. Under sub-s (2) the right given by s 56 is subject to the acquiescence provisions of s. 48. These are discussed below.

1 See art 6[bis] itself.

Acquiescence

12.58 The TMA 1994 contains a special provision regarding acquiescence, s 48, which is virtually identical to a provision in the Directive.[1] It is in terms limited to cases of acquiescence in the use of a *registered* trade mark in the UK, by the proprietor of an earlier trade mark or other earlier right. The terms 'earlier trade mark' and 'earlier right' are defined in s 6 and s 5(4) of the TMA 1994 respectively.[2] For a discussion of the provision, and in particular of the question whether for these purposes the period of acquiescence can run from the date of the original application for registration, as opposed to the date on which the mark is actually registered, reference may be made to Chapter 7.[3] There is no provision for acquiescence in use of a trade mark which is not registered; in such a case the common law doctrine of acquiescence[4] will still apply. Under s 48, the acquiescence required is for a continuous period of five years, the proprietor of the earlier trade mark or right being aware of such use. This must require awareness of the use for the whole five-year period, although if a proprietor became aware of the use and then did not bother to make any inquiries or investigations for more than five years, it is submitted that s 48 should be applied. It seems that the common law rule requiring reliance by the defendant on the acquiescence will not apply as such, and that it will suffice for the purposes of s 48 that the proprietor is aware of the use for five years and does nothing about it. If on the other hand he makes a complaint but delays taking proceedings under s 47 until a five-year period has passed, then so long as he has clearly reserved his rights, it may be that he will not be held to have acquiesced within s 48. The consequences of a finding of acquiescence, unless the registration in question was applied for in bad faith, are that the owner of the earlier trade mark or other right may not seek a declaration of invalidity under s 47, and that he may not oppose the use of the later trade mark for the goods or services for which it has been used for the requisite period. The last mentioned provision is unnecessary in so far as it relates to opposing use by infringement proceedings, because s 11(1) provides a defence so long as the registration cannot be invalidated. Having regard to the fact that s 48 applies against a proprietor of an earlier trade mark or other earlier right, it is likely that the reference to opposing use includes opposing it by means of a passing-off action. Although s 2(2) of the TMA 1994 preserves the action for passing off, the wording of s 48(1)(b) seems unambiguous and should prevail over s 2(2). As already mentioned, a claim under s 56, based on a well-known trade mark, is expressly made[5] subject to s 48.

1 Article 9.
2 See paras **6.3** and **6.74** above.
3 Paragraphs **7.31–7.33**.
4 See for example the decision of the Court of Appeal in *Habib Bank Ltd v Habib Bank AG Zurich* [1982] RPC 1.
5 Section 56(2).

12.59   Finally, s 48(2) makes it clear that, even though the proprietor of an earlier trade mark or other earlier right may be barred from opposing the use of a later registered trade mark, the proprietor of the later trade mark is not entitled to oppose the use of the earlier trade mark or the exploitation of the earlier right.

Chapter 13

Threats

The rationale and objectives

13.1 The justification for the threats jurisdiction is that of deterrence and protection Traders are to be protected against the heavy-handed proprietor of trade mark registrations since an action can be brought to restrain unjustified threats. It is submitted, however, that the threats jurisdiction offers little practical protection to the weak and poor. It is likely to be as expensive and inconvenient to bring threats proceedings as it would be to defend trade mark infringement proceedings.

13.2 The minister responsible for the passage of the Trade Marks Bill in the House of Lords (Lord Strathclyde) said:[1]

> '... [O]ne of the main purposes of this provision, ... is to allow a company whose customers are the object of an unjustified threat of infringement proceedings to protect itself. If the company producing the alleged infringing goods is itself threatened, it can take a view on whether to defend the action. The customers have, however, no interest in so doing. Faced with a threat of legal proceedings, the course of least resistance is simply to stop buying that company's goods. That is why that company needs to be able to protect itself by an action for unjustified threats.'

1 House of Lords Debates, Public Bill Committee, 3rd Sitting, 19 January 1994, Col 66.

13.3 Where threats are made, the threatened party can take the initiative and bring the matter before the court without further ado, though more often than not, a threats action will result in a counterclaim[1] for infringement.

In relation to registered trade marks, the position is governed by a statutory regime and the purpose of these statutory provisions is to prevent abuse of these monopolies since the mere threat to sue may give the owner of the monopoly a power over others. Indeed, this was alluded to by Laddie J in the case of *Antec International Ltd* v *South Western Chicks (Warren) Ltd*,[2] where he said:

> '[Counsel for the Plaintiff] ... readily conceded that any assertion of registered trade-mark infringement was unarguable. In my view it is quite unacceptable that professional men should make wild and unsupportable allegations of trade mark infringement and that they should refuse to disclose the identity of the registered right on which they are threatening their client's competitors. Whether the actions of the plaintiff's agents amounts to an unjustified threat under section 21 of the Trade Marks Act 1994 is not in issue before me, nor is it an issue before me whether it amounts to an even more serious tort. It is sufficient for present purposes to say that it is not accept-

able for those who have the status of expert professional men in the trade-mark field to use the weight of their professional qualifications to make clearly unsupportable allegations of trade-mark infringement against a trader.'

1 That is a part 20 claim under the CPR 1998.
2 [1997] FSR 278, 281.

13.4 An action may be brought pursuant to s 21 of the TMA 1994 for relief in respect of unjustified registered trade mark threats. Similar provisions exist in respect of threats to bring patent and registered and unregistered design rights infringement proceedings. There is some authority which suggests that there is a common law jurisdiction which empowers the court to decide questions by way of an appropriate declaration where any adverse assertion of right is made, though the extent of this jurisdiction is unclear.

Actionable threats

13.5 Section 21 of the TMA 1994 provides that, subject to specific exceptions, where a person threatens another with proceedings for infringement of a registered trade mark, a person aggrieved may bring proceedings for relief. The onus then shifts onto the defendant to justify the threat.[1] The defendant must show that the acts in respect of which proceedings were threatened constitute, or if done would constitute, an infringement of the registered trade mark concerned. However, nothing precludes the claimant from raising the issue of validity and if he successfully impugns the registered trade marks in question so that at the time of the making of the threat (or the time to which the threat relates) there is no valid registered trade mark in existence, then the defendant is unable to justify his threat.

1 TMA 1994, s 21(2) which deems the claimant as being entitled to relief unless the defendant proves otherwise.

13.6 Proceedings cannot be brought in respect of threats concerning the application of the mark to goods or their packaging,[1] the importation of goods to which, or to the packaging of which, the mark has been applied,[2] or the supply of services under the mark.[3] These activities are presumably unobjectionable because it is probably more acceptable to threaten the maker or supplier of the goods than the customers for and sellers of the goods, since the former is less likely to be unduly influenced by the threat whereas the latter is more likely to stop its activities at the merest hint of litigation.

The threat must be to bring proceedings for infringement of the rights given by the registration of the UK trade mark. Threats confined to the bringing of proceedings for passing off or infringement of foreign trade marks are not actionable under the TMA 1994, though the effect of these is discussed below.[4]

1 TMA 1994, s 21(1)(a).
2 TMA 1994, s 21(1)(b).
3 TMA 1994, s 21(1)(c).
4 See para **13.14** below.

13.7 It is to be observed that the threats jurisdiction exists only in relation to 'registered trade marks', that much appears from the wording of s 21 of the TMA 1994 which should be taken to mean trade marks which are registered *under the TMA 1994* (see s 2 of the TMA 1994) and no other type of trade mark registered or unregistered. Further, the threats jurisdiction is not directive based but appears to be domestic in origin and there is no harmony with our European partners since save for the Republic of Ireland[1] no other county in the EU has such a statutory provision under their Trade Mark legislation, though it may be that other sources of law cater for unjustified threats. Likewise there is no jurisdiction either domestic or European under the CTM Regulations[2] or under the Commission Regulation implementing the CTM[3] in relation to CTMs. Nevertheless, Parliament has provided that CTMs shall, insofar as threats are concerned have the same status as UK registered trade marks.[4] It may be that threats relating to registered trade marks are not considered to be as serious in other European countries or by the EU as a whole. It is unclear and untested as to whether there is any right in our national legislature to 'invent' a threats jurisdiction in the absence of any Community requirement that one be set up, though it is to be observed that since the Directive only provides for partial harmonisation of the Community-wide trade marks regime (with, presumably more to follow) it is likely that Parliament was free to place s 21 of the TMA 1994 on the statute book.

1 Irish Trade Marks Act 1996, s 24, which is in substantially similar terms the TMA 1994, s 21.
2 Council Regulation 40/94/EC of 20 December 1994. OJ L11 14.1.94 p.1.
3 Commission Regulation 2868/95/EC of 13 December 1995 implementing Council Regulation 40/94/EC. OJ L303 15.12.95, p.1.
4 See the CTM Regulations 1996 (SI 1996/1908), reg 4.

13.8 A threat may be made orally or in writing and there appears to be no reason why a threat should not be implied as well as express. Aldous J (as he then was) said as much in *Bowden Controls Ltd v Acco Cable Controls Ltd*:[1]

'... a threat can be veiled or implied just as much as it can be explicit.'

Which received the approbation of the Court of Appeal in *Scandecor Development Aktiebolag v Scandecor Marketing Aktiebolag*[2]. The true test is that a threat is made if what is communicated (by whatever means) would be understood by the ordinary recipient in the position of the claimant as constituting a threat by the defendant of proceedings for the infringement of a UK registered trade mark.[3]

1 [1990] RPC 427, 431.
2 [1999] FSR 26, 47.
3 See *Selsdon Fountain Pen Co v Miles Martin Co* (1949) RPC 193; *Boneham and Hart v Hirst Brother and Co* (1917) 34 RPC 209 and *Cars v Bland Light Syndicate Ltd* (1911) 28 RPC 33.

13.9 Threats actions have recently been considered by both the High Court and the Court of Appeal in a series of actions between one Patrick Brain and a firm of solicitors called Ingledew Brown Bennington & Garrett. In *Brain v Ingledew Brown Bennington & Garrett (a firm)*[1] *(No 3)* Laddie J said in relation to a written threat:

'There is no dispute between the parties that the meaning and impact of the letter in issue has to be decided in accordance with how they would be understood by an ordinary reader. See *Luna Advertising Co Ltd v Burnham & Co* (1928) 45 RPC 258. What is particularly important is the initial impression which the letters would have on a reasonable addressee. During court proceedings it is inevitable that the lawyers, parties and the judge will read and reread the offending passage with ever closer attention. Such meticulous analysis is not what would happen in the real world and the court must guard against being led down a path of forensic analysis to a meaning which is narrower or broader than would occur to the ordinary recipient reading the letter, circular or other document, in the normal course of business.'

1 [1997] FSR 511 at 521.

13.10   Although Laddie J was considering the threats provisions under the Patents Act 1977, this reasoning was applied by Neuberger J in *Prince plc v Prince Sports Group Ltd*[1] in relation to trade mark threats. It is an objective test. An alleged threat must, however, be read in the context of the correspondence or series of communications as a whole. In *Brainv Ingledew Brown Bennington & Garret (a firm)*[2] Aldous LJ said:

> '... the conclusion as to whether a document amounts to threat of patent proceedings is essentially one of fact. It is a jury-type decision to be decided against the appropriate matrix of fact. Thus a letter or a statement may on its face seem innocuous, but when placed in context it could be a threat of proceedings. The contrary is less likely but could happen.'

1 [1998] FSR 21 at 28.
2 [1996] FSR 341 at 349.

13.11   Aldous LJ therefore considered it might be possible for the sting of a threatening statement to be drawn by reference to other correspondence. Where, however, a threat has been made in a letter, it is not possible to re-construe the letter in the light of subsequent correspondence so that it no longer constitutes a threat (see *Prince plc v Prince Sports Group Inc*[1]). When deciding whether a threat has been made the court should avoid over detailed or legalistic analysis of the contents of the documents since it is unlikely that they will be initially (at least) read by lawyers. The point that it is not lawyers who read letters was highlighted in the libel case of *Slim v Daily Telegraph Ltd*[2], per Diplock LJ, where he said in a different context:

> 'Everyone outside a court of law recognises that words are imprecise instruments for communicating the thoughts of one man to another. The same words may be understood by one man in a different meaning from that in which they are understood by another and both meanings may be different from that which the author of the words intended to convey; but the notion that the same words should bear different meanings to different men, and that more than one meaning should be "right", conflicts with the whole training of a lawyer. Words are the tools of his trade. He uses them to define legal rights and duties. They do not achieve that purpose unless there can be attributed to them a single meaning as the "right" meaning. And so the argument between lawyers as to the meaning of words starts with the unexpressed major premise that any particular combination of words has one meaning, which is not necessarily the same as that intended by him who published them or understood by any of those who read them, but is capable of ascertainment as being the "right" meaning by the adjudicator to whom the law confides the responsibility of determining it'.

But caution should be exercised in over-reliance upon this part of Diplock LJ's judgment, not least because he was deciding a completely different question, relating to libel, where it is necessary to extract a single meaning from a given statement. The passage is cited merely to show that statements mean different things to different people and is, at the very least, highly dependent upon context.

Section 21(4) of the TMA 1994 provides that a mere notification that a trade mark is registered, or that an application for registration has been made, does not constitute a threat of proceedings. To go beyond a mere notification is to risk making a threat.

1 See para **13.10**, n 1 above at 27.
2 [1968] 1 All ER 497 at 504–506; [1968] 2 QB 157 at 171–174.

Aggrieved person

13.12   A threats action[1] may be brought by any party aggrieved by the threats. The threats may be made directly or indirectly. Where the threats are made to the claimant himself, that will generally be sufficient to make him an aggrieved person. If the threat is not made directly to the claimant, then he will generally need to lead evidence to show that the threats have been or a likely to be damaging and that the damage is not minimal.

1 See TMA 1994, s 21(1).

13.13   In *Brain v Ingledew Brown Bennison and Garrett (a firm)*[1] Aldous LJ said:

'The ambit of the word "aggrieved" is a question of law, but whether or not a person is aggrieved by a threat is a question of fact. That was made clear by the Court of Appeal in *Reymes-Cole v Elite Hosiery Co Ltd* [1965] RPC 102'.

Aldous LJ referred to a passage from that decision of Wilmer LJ at 111 and continued:

'As is apparent from the reasoning of Wilmer LJ, the question of whether or not a person is aggrieved by a threat is in the main a question of fact to be established by evidence. If the threat is not made to the person himself, then he must establish by evidence that the threats have or are likely to cause him damage which is not minimal.'

Brain v Ingledew Brown Benninson & Garrett (a firm) (No 3)[2] Laddie J said that in the absence of binding authority he would be inclined to take the view that:

'The legislative intent behind the inclusion of "person aggrieved" in section 70(1) [of the Patents Act 1977] is to exclude frivolous applications or applications by busybodies who have no real personal interest in the threats.'

Laddie J then considered the above authorities and said:[3]

'For the purpose of demonstrating that he has status to sue, what Mr Brain [the claimant] has to do is show that his commercial interests are or are likely to be adversely affected in a real as opposed to a fanciful or minimal way. Where the threats are made against him directly, following *Summers*,[4] the court will infer such adverse effect. Where the threats are made indirectly, he will need to demonstrate it. But I do not think that the court should be astute to find that a complainant has not been affected in his commercial activities where it is clear that the purpose of the threat was to do so.'

In *Prince plc v Prince Sports Group Ltd*[5] Neuberger J reviewed these authorities and said that to his mind they established that:

'Save perhaps in very exceptional circumstances, where a threat of the sort contemplated by section 21(1) is made directly to the person who is alleged to be the infringer, that person may bring proceedings as an "aggrieved person" without further ado.'

1 [1996] FSR 341 at 350.
2 [1997] FSR 511 at 519.
3 At 520.
4 *John Summers & Sons v The Cold Metal Process Co* (1947) 65 RPC 75.
5 [1998] FSR 21 at 34.

When is a threat not a threat?

13.14   Or more correctly, when is a threat not an *actionable* threat? As discussed above, a threat is not actionable if it is within the exceptions contained within s 21(1)(a)–(c) of the TMA 1994. In *Carflow Products (UK) Ltd v Linwood Securities (Birmingham) Ltd*[1] Laddie J considered the threats jurisdiction in relation to registered designs. In that case an actionable threat had been made (which would entitle the plaintiff to an injunction) and shortly afterwards a writ was issued. The evidence showed that it was the writ which stopped the threatened party from selling its goods and not the letters before action, which contained the threat. It was conceded and accepted between the parties (and accepted by the court to be a proper concession) that threats made by bringing proceedings per se were not actionable since the damage caused by the threat of the proceedings was not recoverable. Laddie J said:[2]

> "There is no dispute between the parties as to the relevant law. The claimant must adduce evidence that it is more likely than not that the wrongful conduct of which complaint is made in fact resulted in the damage of which he complains. He must establish a link, a *prima facie* connection, between the wrongdoing and the relevant damage. The burden of proving the required causal link between wrongdoing and damage rests on the claimant *Clerk & Lindsell* 17th Ed par 2–03. As Lord Reid said in *Bonnington Castings Ltd v Wardlaw* [1956] AC 613:
>
> > "the plaintiff must prove ... that such fault caused or materially contributed to [the plaintiff's] injury"
>
> 'It is necessary to look at the breach and decide what flowed from it. If the breach is an effective or dominant cause of the loss then the defendant will be liable. That issue must be determined by the application of common sense; see *Galoo Ltd v Bright Grahame Murray* [1994] 1 WLR 1360.'

1 [1998] FSR 691.
2 At 693.

13.15   This follows on from *Alpi Pietro E Figlio & Co v John Wright & Sons (Veneers) Ltd*[1] (a patent threats action) where Whitford J held that general warnings to the trade were not adequate to give rise to an actionable threat. Also in *Alpi* a threat was made by the defendant to W, an agent of the first plaintiff in the course of a discussion where W asked the defendant what its reaction would be if W and the first plaintiff carried out certain supposedly infringing acts. The defendant replied that proceedings would follow. Whitford J doubted (on an interlocutory motion to seek an order to restrain threats) whether a response to questions put which was a statement that proceedings would follow could amount to threats under the prevailing patent legislation.

1 [1972] RPC 125.

13.16 Recently it has been suggested that where threats are made in the course of settlement, the substance of which is privileged from disclosure, then they are not actionable. In *Unilever plc v Procter and Gamble Co*[1], a case involving a declaration of non-infringement where the adverse assertions of right made by the defendant patentee in settlement negotiations were relied upon, Laddie J said:[2]

> 'It seems to me that the rule against the subsequent use of without prejudice discussions is wide enough to cover all statements made by each party touching upon the strength or weakness of its own and its opponent's case and any valuation, for whatever reason, it places on its or its opponent's rights. These are the issues which go to the heart of any attempt to compromise litigation. Parties should be free to discuss them without fear of their words coming back to haunt them in court proceedings. For these reasons, I have come to the conclusion that the without prejudice rule covers not only admissions but assertions also, that [the defendant's] ... statement [that the plaintiff infringed their Patent and that they might sue in the United Kingdom] is covered by it ...'

Though no threats action was asserted by the plaintiff, the judge nevertheless held that the principles applied to threats actions as well as to declarations of non-infringement.

1 [1999] 2 All ER 691, [1999] 1 WLR 1630, [1999] NLJR 370, [1999] FSR 849; affd (1999) Times, 4 November.
2 [1999] FSR 849 at 857.

Defences

13.17 Section 21(2) of the TMA 1994 provides that once the claimant has established that the threat has been made and that he is an aggrieved person, the claimant is entitled to relief unless the defendant shows that the threat is justified. The defendant must show that the acts in respect of which the threats were made constitute (or if done would constitute) an infringement of the registered trade mark concerned.

The claimant will be entitled to relief, pursuant to s 21(3), if he shows that the registration of the trade mark is invalid or liable to be revoked in a relevant respect; (see Chapter 7, above).

Remedies

13.18 Relief in the following manner may be applied pursuant to s 21(2):

(a) a declaration that the threats are unjustified.[1]
(b) an injunction against the continuance of the threats.[2]
(c) damages in respect of any loss he has sustained by the threats.[3]

Where the court has determined that there have been unjustified threats, injunctions and declarations are generally ordered and made. In *Prince plc v Prince Sports Group Ltd*[4] Neuberger J said that once the court has concluded that an unjustified threat falling within s 21 has been made, then absent special circumstances, an injunction should be granted to prevent repetition of the threat and declarations made in respect of past threats.

1 TMA 1994, s 21(2)(*a*).
2 TMA 1994, s 21(2)(*b*).
3 TMA 1994, s 21(2)(*c*).
4 [1998] FSR 21 at 36.

13.19   A damages inquiry should be ordered where the claimant has suffered loss or damage as a result of the threats. The claimant must, however, produce some evidence to show a prima facie case that he has suffered some damage.[1] This damage must have been caused by the unjustified threat.

1 See *Prince plc v Prince Sports Group Inc* [1998] FSR 21 at 36–37.

Adverse assertions of right and claim for declaration of non-infringement

13.20   Another aspect of the threats issue arises where a claim is made by a person against whom an adverse assertion of right has been made and who wishes the court to declare there is no cause of action against him or that the assertion is unfounded. *In Re Clay, Clay v Booth*[1] Swinfen Eady MR reviewed the relevant authorities and considered the judgment of Pickford LJ in *Guaranty Trust Co of New York v Hannay & Co.* Swinfen Eady MR said:

> 'But reliance was mainly placed upon what was said by Pickford LJ in *Guaranty Trust Co of New York v Hannay & Co* [1915] 2 KB 536 Pickford LJ there first came to the conclusion that there was no necessity in order to invoke proceedings under the rules that we are now considering that there should be an existing cause of action. Then he went on to consider whether the rule could be invoked only by the person claiming the right and intending to assert it. And, again, he negatived that. But no inference whatever can be drawn from that in favour of the petitioners here to the effect that the proceedings can be invoked not only where there is no cause of action and the person instituting the proceedings does not assert the right, but where there is no claim at all by anyone ' by the plaintiff against the defendant, or vice versa. Here the position of the parties is that no claim is made by the defendant Booth as against the petitioners, and the petitioners by their petition make no claim against the defendant Booth. The observations that were made by Cozens-Hardy MR in *Dyson v A-G* [1911] KB 410, 417 may properly be referred to. He there said:
>
> > "But I desire to guard myself against the supposition that I hold that a person who expects to be made defendant, and who prefers to be plaintiff, can, as a matter of right, attain his object by commencing an action to obtain a declaration that his opponent has no good cause of action against him. The Court may well say: "Wait until you are attacked and then raise your defence," and may dismiss the action with costs."
>
> 'This is really the position in the present case. The petitioners have not been attacked. No claim has been made against them; but they launched these proceedings to have it determined that someone who has not made a claim and who has not asserted any right has no claim and has no right. In my opinion they are not entitled to do that. As has been pointed out by Duke LJ during the course of the argument, with regard to rights under contracts there are certain statutory limitations which fix the time during which actions may be brought, and a party to a simple contract has the full statutory period to determine whether or not he will bring an action. And it is not open to a person, certainly to one against whom no claim in fact has been made, to cut the matter short by bringing an action at his own option, and saying, "I wish to have it determined that you have no claim whatever against me." That really is the nature of the proceedings in the present case.'

1 [1919] 1 Ch 66.
2 [1915] 2 KB 536 at 77.

13.21   In *Plastus Kreativ Aktiebolag v Minnesota Mining and Manufacturing Co[1]*
Aldous J (as he then was) said:

'I believe that *In Re Clay* is a good authority and binding upon me for the proposition

"... that a party against whom no claim has been formulated cannot sue for a declaration of non-liability. Subject to limitation periods and laches, the prospective
plaintiff is entitled to decide for himself when he will bring his action."

(Per Hoffmann J in *Barclays Bank plc v Homan* [1993] BCLC 680 at page 693.)'

Also the case of *Wyko Group plc v Cooper Roller Bearings Co Ltd[2]* supports this
stance and the repeated upholding of this position by the appellate courts.

1 [1995] RPC 438 at 443 line 17.
2 (1995) Times, 4 December.

13.22   However, it is unclear whether in the context of intellectual property rights
where there is a statutory threats jurisdiction, the *Re Clay*[1] doctrine has any status at
all. It is certainly used a great deal in patent cases and indeed Aldous J in *Plastus
Kreativ Aktiebolag v Minnesota Mining and Manufacturing Co*[2] held that he would
have been able to entertain an application for a declaration of non-infringement of a
patent had the facts allowed him to do so (though on the facts in *Plastus* he found
that he could not do so). It is, however, to be noted, that a mere threat to bring proceedings, per se is not to be regarded as an abuse of process, though the threatened
party may still nevertheless seek an appropriate declaration. In *Pitman Training Ltd
v Nominet UK,*[3] Sir Richard Scott V-C said:

'There never has been a case, so far as the researches of counsel have shown or so far
as my own knowledge goes, in which the tort of abuse of process has been found to be
committed simply by a threat of proceedings. In every case where the tort has been
found to be committed there has been the actual institution of the process said and
held to have been abused.'

1 See para **13.20** above.
2 [1995] RPC 438.
3 [1997] FSR 797, 810.

13.23   The extent of this doctrine is unclear. Can a disgruntled defendant seek a
declaration of non-infringement (ie that the adverse assertion of right is unjustified)
if trade mark infringement proceedings have been discontinued against him without
a decision on the merits? Further, if the doctrine as expounded in *re Clay*[1] is
allowed to run its full length then it would appear that threats which were not
actionable under s 21(1) of the TMA 1994, would be actionable at least in a
declaratory sense. Given that the common law jurisdiction to declare rights is often
used in patent proceedings, notwithstanding that there is a statutory scheme in
place relating to threats and indeed non-infringement, there appears to be no reason
in principle why the same should not be true for trade marks.

1 See para **13.20** above.

Part III

Passing off and miscellaneous

Chapter 14

Passing off

Development of the tort of passing off – individual causes of action

14.1   The history of the action for passing off was explained by Lord Diplock in the well-known case of *Warnink (Erven) Besloten Vennootschap v J Townend & Sons (Hull) Ltd* [1] in which he noted that in the 19th century passing off actions were confined to the deceptive use of trade names, marks, letters and other indicia. The principle underlying these actions had been stated by Lord Langdale MR in *Perry v Truefittt*:[2]

> 'A man is not to sell his own goods under the pretence that they are the goods of another man'.

and that statement has as much truth in the modern law of passing off as it had 1842 when it was made, even though the context might be different.

1 [1980] RPC 31 HL.
2 (1842) 6 Beav 66, 73.

14.2   Actions were all of the kind characterised by Lord Diplock in *Warnink* [1] as the 'classic form' of misrepresentation of one's own goods as the goods of someone else. It was (according to Lord Diplock) Lord Parker in *A G Spalding & Brothers v A W Gamage Ltd* [2] who laid the foundation for the development of the modern tort of passing off when he identified the legal nature of the right protected by a passing off action as:

> 'The property in the business or goodwill likely to be injured by the misrepresentation'.

In so finding, Lord Parker rejected the suggestion (presented in some earlier cases) that it was the proprietary rights of the trader in the mark, name or get-up improperly used which were themselves protected. Though that is not to say that the *effect* of the modern law of passing off is to deny protection to a mark, name or get-up but rather that the modern law of passing off is not *focussed* upon those indicia as such but rather is *aimed* at something different. It is this distinction which is often lost and hence the many judicial dicta aimed at explaining what is, in truth, a relatively simple legal concept.

1 See para **14.1**, n 1 above.
2 (1915) 32 RPC 273 (HL).

14.3   In *A G Spalding & Brothers v A W Gamage Ltd*[1] it was held that a manufacturer's goodwill could be injured by someone else who sells goods made by that manufacturer of a certain class or quality but misrepresents that they are goods of that manufacturer, of a *superior* class or quality. This decision is therefore significant as an extension of the older forms of the tort of passing off beyond the misrepresentation of one's goods as someone else's, though in reality and through the eyes of the law of passing off, goods of differing quality are as distinct from each other as are goods from different sources.

1 See para **14.2**, n 2 above.

14.4   However, in modern times the tort has been described as comprising two elements (not wholly divorced from each other and not wholly distinct). Those two strands have been described as the classic (or classical) form of passing off and the extended form of passing off. In the so-called classic form, private traders do battle in relation to their distinctive and identifiable goodwill. In the so-called extended form (or champagne type of case[2]), classes of traders who trade under common indicia are able to identify a sort of collective goodwill. The epaulets of 'classical' and 'extended' are not particularly helpful to identify the characteristics of these two strands of the tort. Nevertheless, they are the terms commonly used. For present purposes the two strands will be loosely referred to as individual and group actions or actions based upon individual and group goodwill since this better describes the differences, such as they are, between the two.

   Lord Diplock explained that it was *A G Spalding & Brothers v AW Gamage Ltd*[1] and later cases which enabled him to identify the five characteristics which must be present in order to found a cause of action, on a pleadable basis at least, for passing off. These five characteristics are discussed below.

1 See para **14.2**, n 2 above.
2 This type of passing off was first recognised by Danckwerts J in *J Bollinger v Costa Brava Wine Company Ltd* [1960] Ch 262. Actions of this type differ in certain respects from the classic form of passing off and are considered at paras **14.64–14.75**.

Ingredients of the tort

14.5   The characteristics necessary in order to found a cause of action for passing off were identified by Lord Diplock in *Warnink (Erven) Besloten Vennootschap v J Townend & Sons (Hull) Ltd* (a goodwill case) where he said that there must be:[1]

(1)   a misrepresentation;
(2)   made by a trader in the course of trade;
(3)   to prospective customers of his or ultimate consumers of goods or services supplied by him;
(4)   which is calculated to injure the business or goodwill of another trader (in the sense that this is a reasonably foreseeable consequence); and
(5)   which causes actual damage to a business or goodwill of the trader by whom the action is brought or (in a *quia timet* action) will probably do so.

In *Warnink*, Lord Fraser of Tullybelton also formulated the essential facts that a claimant must show in a passing off case. Lord Fraser of Tullybelton's formulation[2] is particularly apt in relation to group actions or the champagne types of case[3] where the goodwill is owned by a class of traders.

1 [1980] RPC 31 (HL).
2 At lines 28–34.2.
3 See para **14.65** below.

14.6 In *Reckitt & Colman Products Ltd v Borden Inc, Suzy International Naamloze Vennootschap and Paterson Jenks plc.*[1] Lord Oliver of Aylmerton explained that the principles of the law of passing off were well established in that no man was to sell his goods as those of another. He reduced the elements which a claimant had to prove to the following three :

'First, he must establish a goodwill or reputation attached to the goods or services which he supplied in the mind of the purchasing public by association with the identifying "get-up" (whether it consists simply of a brand name or a trade description, or the individual features of labelling or packaging) under which his particular goods or services are offered to the public, such that the get-up is recognised to by the public as distinctive specifically of the [claimant's] ... goods or services.

'Secondly, he must demonstrate a misrepresentation by the defendant to the public (whether or not intentional) leading or likely to lead the public to believe that the goods or services offered by him are the goods or services of the [claimant] . ... Whether the public is aware of the [claimant's] ... identity as the manufacturer or supplier of the goods or services is immaterial, as long as they are identified with a particular source which is in fact the [claimant]. ... For example, if the public is accustomed to rely upon a particular brand name in purchasing goods of a particular description, it matters not at all that there is little or no public awareness of the identity of the proprietor of the brand name.

'Thirdly, he must demonstrate that he suffers or, in a *quia timet* action that he is likely to suffer, damage by reason of the erroneous belief engendered by the defendant's misrepresentation that the source of the defendant's goods or services is the same as the source of those offered by the [claimant]. ...'

This has been described as the 'classical trinity'[2] of passing off, namely goodwill, misrepresentation and damage which must be established to found a cause of action for passing off.

1 [1990] RPC 341, 406 HL.
2 From the dicta of Nourse LJ in *Consorzio del Prosciutto di Parma v Marks & Spencer plc* [1991] RPC 351, 368 line 45 as applied by Jacob J in *Hodgkinson & Corby Ltd v Wards Mobility Services Ltd* [1995] FSR 169, 177.

14.7 In *Harrods Ltd v Harrodian School Ltd*,[1] Millett LJ (as he then was) set out these passages and said that he found the approach of Lord Oliver of Aylmerton more helpful than that of Lord Diplock in two regards. First, Lord Oliver of Aylmerton made it clear that the claimant must show not a goodwill or reputation in his brand name or get-up but a goodwill or reputation attaching to the goods or services which he supplies by association with the identifying name or get-up. Secondly, since it was generally neither desirable nor possible to consider whether there has been a misrepresentation separately from the effect on the minds of the public of the use of the mark or get-up adopted by the defendant, it was appropriate to take the first of Lord Diplock's elements ('misrepresentation') and the fourth element ('calculated to injure') together. To extend the ambit of the law of passing off beyond (the relevant type of) deception could stifle competition, as Jacob J observed in *Hodgkinson and Corby Ltd v Wards Mobility Services Ltd*[2] where he said:

'I turn to consider the law and begin by identifying what is not the law. There is no tort of copying. There is no tort of taking a man's market or customers. Neither the market nor the customers are the [claimant's] ... to own. There is no tort of making use of another's goodwill as such. There is no tort of competition. I say this because at times the [claimants] ... seemed close to relying on such torts. For instance, [counsel for the claimants] ... reminded me of the old adage "Anything worth copying is worth protecting".

'At the heart of passing off lies deception or its likelihood, deception of the ultimate consumer in particular. Over the years passing off has developed from the classic case of the defendant selling his goods as and for those of the [claimant] ... to cover other kinds of deception, eg that the defendant's goods are the same as those of the [claimant] ... when they are not, eg *Combe International Ltd v Scholl (UK) Ltd* [1980] RPC 1; or that the defendant's goods are the same as goods sold by a class of persons of which the [claimant] ... is a member when. they are not, eg *Warnink (Erven) Besloten Vennootschap v J Townend & Sons (Hull) Ltd* [1980] RPC 30. Never has the tort shown even a slight tendency to stray beyond cases of deception. Were it to do so it would enter the field of honest competition, declared unlawful for some reason other than deceptiveness. Why there should be any such reason I cannot imagine. It would serve only to stifle competition.'

1 [1996] RPC 697, at 711.
2 [1995] FSR 169, 174, 175. Jacob J,(a distinguished and highly experienced practitioner in relation to the law of passing off), in saying that 'There is no tort of copying' was literally wrong–of course there is a tort of copying via the law of copyright. Jacob J should not be understood as saying what he literally said, but rather that there is no tort of copying as such.

The 'logical fallacy of the undistributed middle'

14.8 Not all factual situations in which these characteristics are present give rise to a cause of action for passing off. Lord Diplock characterised this as the 'logical fallacy of the undistributed middle'. Although Lord Diplock did not specify the precise ambit of the fallacy, he indicated that the purpose of the tort was not to hamper competition:[1]

'The market in which the action for passing off originated was no place for the mealy mouthed; advertisements are not on affidavit; exaggerated claims by a trader about the quality of his wares, assertions that they are better than those of his rivals, even though he knows this to be untrue, have been permitted by the common law as venial "puffing" which gives no cause of action to a competitor even though he can show that he has suffered actual damage in his business as a result.'

and that in exceptional circumstances a remedy could be withheld on public policy grounds.[2]

1 *Warnink (Erven) Besloten Vennootschap v J Townend & Sons (Hull) Ltd* [1980] RPC 31, 93, 94.
2 See n 1 above, at 99.

14.9 Although it remains a theoretical possibility that relief might be refused despite the presence of the characteristics formulated by Lord Diplock, Lord Fraser of Tullybelton or Lord Oliver of Aylmerton, a review of the decided cases shows that where relief has been refused it is usually because one of these characteristics was absent not because the case fell into the 'undistributed middle'. However, in *SDS Biotech UK Ltd v Power Agrichemicals,*[1] Aldous J (as he then was) in refusing the claimant's application for summary judgment, held that it was possible, in that case, that the claimant's complaint fell within the undistributed middle referred to by Lord Diplock. In that case the claimant marketed a fungicide for which it had obtained regulatory approval from the relevant government regulatory body (the Ministry of Agriculture, Fisheries and Food, or MAFF for short). Consequently the claimant was entitled to use a MAFF number in relation to its product. The defendant sold a similar product but had not obtained MAFF approval, though it did cite a MAFF number which (deceptively) gave the impression of MAFF approbation. The claimant complained that the use of a MAFF number by the defendant amounted to passing off. It was arguable or at least argued in such circumstances that any goodwill arising out of the use of MAFF numbers was the property of the government and the claimant had no right to bring an action to restrain the unauthorised use of MAFF numbers. Aldous J said :[2]

> 'Even if the [claimants] ... are was right that they fall within the principles set out by their Lordships [in *Warnink (Erven) Besloten Vennootschap v J Townend & Sons (Hull) Ltd* [1980] RPC 31], it does not mean their complaint does not fall within the undistributed middle that Lord Diplock referred to.'

The law of passing off was consequently not to be extended to include such actions upon an application for summary judgment at least, and the issue has not yet arisen in a case which has reached trial.

1 [1995] FSR 797.
2 At 804.

Passing off – a question of fact

14.10   As was stated by Lord Oliver of Aylmerton in *Reckitt & Colman Products Ltd v Borden Inc, Suzy International Naamloze Vennootschap and Paterson Jenks plc*,[1] the law of passing off may be summarised in one short proposition – no one may pass off his goods as those of another. Though to rely upon that proposition as being the basis for what the claimant has to prove is clearly wrong. Decided cases are therefore only of assistance by way of analogy as the questions which arise are in general questions of fact.[2] Nevertheless decided cases are of assistance to determine the scope of the tort and the manner in which the legal principles may be applied.

1 [1990] 1 All ER 873, 880-F.
2 As most passing off cases turn out to be.

14.11   Although the tort of passing off is very old, it is not, as we have observed, anchored in its early formulation. In the nineteenth century it protected the name or trade mark of a product or business. Over time the protection has been extended. Descriptions such as slogans or visual images which have as a result of advertising become part of the goodwill of the product may be the subject of passing off actions (see *Cadbury-Schweppes Pty Ltd v Pub Squash Co Pty Ltd*[1]). The tort also continues to evolve to meet the changes in the methods of trade and communication. In *British Telecommunications plc v One In A Million Ltd*[2] Aldous LJ said:

> "The cause of action called passing-off is of ancient origin. It has developed over time. As Lord Diplock pointed out in the *Warnink* case,[3] Parliament has over the years progressively intervened in the interests of consumers and traders so as to impose standards of conduct and to ensure commercial honesty. It is therefore not

surprising that the courts have recognised that the common law, in that particular field, should proceed upon a parallel course rather than a diverging one. Lord Diplock explained how the cause of action had moved from the classical form over the years. His five characteristics were those he identified in 1980 from previously decided cases, but I do not believe that he was thereby confining for ever the cause of action to every detail of such characteristics, as to do so would prevent the common law evolving to meet changes in methods of trade and communication as it had in the past.'

1 [1981] RPC 429 (PC) per Lord Scarman at 218.
2 [1999] FSR 1 CA at 11.
3 *Warnink (Erven) Besloten Vennootschap v J Townend & Sons (Hull) Ltd* [1980] RPC 31 (HL).

Goodwill

14.12   Goodwill is a broad concept. It is defined in one way by Lord Macnaghten in *IRC v Muller & Co's Margarine Ltd*[1] as:

'the benefit and advantage of the good name, reputation, and connection of a business. It is the attractive force which brings in custom'.

However, that is not to say that what a valuer of a business or an accountant might call goodwill, ie the difference between the price which a willing purchaser might pay for a business and its intrinsic asset value, is the kind of goodwill necessary to maintain an action for passing off. The goodwill needed to maintain an action for passing off and 'accountant's' goodwill are not unrelated. What the law of passing of describes as goodwill is not susceptible to the same analysis or abstraction as might be appropriate in an accountancy exercise.

1 [1901] AC 217, 223–224.

14.13   Under our current law goodwill in a passing off sense may be assigned like any other chose in action or business asset. In *Reckitt & Colman Products Ltd v Borden Inc, Suzy International Naamloze Vennootschap and Paterson Jenks plc*[1] the House of Lords said that the owner of such goodwill could be a manufacturer or a distributor provided that there was association with a particular source which source is in fact the claimant, though how that works in practice is a matter of debate. It is questionable whether trading entities are able to deal with goodwill in a manner which is inconsistent with or different from public perception of reputation (and thus attachment of goodwill) or indeed common sense. This question was posed to a certain extent in the case of *Scandecor Development AB v Scandecor Marketing Ltd.*[2]

1 [1990] RPC 341, at 406 lines 35–37.
2 [1999] FSR 26, CA, currently on apeal to the HL.

14.14   A trader does not get a monopoly in a trade mark or get-up as such under the law of passing off. In this regard the protection afforded to the owner of goodwill in a unregistered trade mark differs to that afforded to the proprietor of a registered trade mark. Under the law of passing off, it is the traders' business(which is likely to be harmed by the defendant's misrepresentation) which is to be protected. By contrast, the owner of a registered trade mark is given the exclusive rights to exploitation[1] and damage does not found the gist of the cause of action. In *Star Industrial Co Ltd v Yap Kwee Kor*[2] Lord Diplock said:

'A passing off action is a remedy for the invasion of a right of property not in the mark, name or get-up improperly used,[3] but in the business or goodwill likely to be injured by the misrepresentation made by passing off one person's goods as the goods of another. Goodwill, as the subject of proprietary rights, is incapable of subsisting by itself. It has no independent existence apart from the business to which it is attached. It is local in character and divisible; if the business is carried on in several countries a separate goodwill attaches to each. So when the business is abandoned in one country in which it has acquired a goodwill, the goodwill in that country perishes with it although the business may continue to be carried on in other countries.'

1 The scope of these rights is set out in TMA 1994, ss 9–11.
2 [1976] FSR 256, 269.
3 To which we would add the words 'as such'.

Goodwill in the UK

14.15   It is necessary to show goodwill in the UK. More specifically there must be a business which is carried on in this country. Not every activity in this country qualifies as carrying on a business. In *Anheuser-Busch Inc v Budejovicky Budvar Narodini Podnik*[1] Oliver LJ (as he then was) said that the mere existence of trading reputation in this country in the absence of customers is not sufficient. This, Oliver LJ said, was illustrated by *Athletes Foot Marketing Associates Inc v Cobra Sports Ltd*[2] in which despite an awareness of the claimant's trade name as a result of the circulation of American journals in the UK, there were no customers and so no goodwill here. The term 'customers' is not to be construed to require a direct contractual relationship with the claimant. It is necessary only that the claimant's goods are on the market in the UK. It does not matter whether they are sold by the claimant or through an agent.

1 [1984] FSR 413 CA at 465–467.
2 [1980] RPC 343.

14.16   In *Anheuser-Busch Inc v Budejovicky Budvar Narodini Podnik*[1] the claimant (an American company) sought to rely upon the quite significant sales of its beer at US military and diplomatic establishments in the UK. This did not amount to the carrying on of a business over here since ordinary members of the public could not buy the claimant's beer. Thus the claimant lacked the requisite goodwill. Also the defendant's activities would not damage the claimant; there was no potential for lost sales in the postal exchanges where the claimant's beer was sold since the defendant's Czech beer was not sold there and in the rest of the country the claimant made no sales. However it is apparent that the relevant goodwill was perhaps improperly pleaded or there was no overlap in markets. *Anheuser-Busch* is certainly not authority for the proposition that a claimant must prove goodwill in the *whole* of the UK, passing off is as parochial as any other right though the parochial nature of passing off could lead to parochial injunctions.

1 [1984] FSR 413 CA.

14.17   In *Anciens Établissements Panhard et Levassor SA v Panhard-Levassor Motor Co Ltd*[1] although the French claimant did not have a place of business in the UK its motors were frequently imported either through an importer who bought cars for resale or by customers from this country going to France and buying the cars there. The French company was found to have goodwill in this country which gave rise to a cause of action in passing off.

1 [1901] 2 Ch 513.

14.18   In *Sheraton Corpn of America v Sheraton Motels Ltd*[1] an interlocutory injunction was granted to restrain passing off even though the claimants had no business in the UK save for a booking office in London for their hotels abroad. This decision was referred to by Oliver LJ in *Anheuser-Busch Inc v Budejovicky Budvar Narodini Podnik*[2] as the high-water mark and explained by him as having really been decided on the balance of convenience rather than its merits. In *Bernadin (Alain) et Cie v Pavilion Properties Ltd*[3] the claimant was the proprietor of a restaurant in Paris called 'The Crazy Horse Saloon'. Publicity material for this establishment was distributed through the tourist board and hotels in the UK. Pennycuick J considered that the claimant might acquire a reputation in the wider sense of travellers returning from Paris in France speaking highly of the establishment. This was held or found not to amount to goodwill such as to form the basis of a passing off action since there was no real connection with the UK.

1 [1964] RPC 202.
2 [1984] FSR 413.
3 [1967] RPC 581.

14.19   Although *Bernadin (Alain) et Cie v Pavilion Properties Ltd*[1] was cited and seemingly approved of by the Court of Appeal in *Anheuser-Busch Inc v Budejovicky Budvar Narodini Podnik*[2] it was distinguished or not followed by Browne Wilkinson V-C in *Waterman (Pete) v CBS United Kingdom Ltd*.[3] In that case, 'The Hit Factory' was a nickname attributed by some members of the public to the claimant, a well known and extremely successful contemporary song writer. It was also the name of a recording studio in New York which had licensed the defendant to use the name in the UK. Although the New York studio had customers worldwide including the UK, it had no place of business in the UK. Browne Wilkinson V-C considered that the presence of customers in this country was sufficient to constitute the carrying on of business here to which the local goodwill could be attached. From this it has to be commented that the law upon the necessity of a place of business in the UK is awkwardly uncertain. In *Jian Tools for Sales Ltd v Roderick Manhattan Group Ltd*[4] Knox J considered that the presence of customers in the UK was sufficient for the grant of an interlocutory injunction but that it was inappropriate at an interlocutory stage to reconcile the conflicts between *Bernadin (Alain)* and later cases.

This uncertainty may be of less practical importance as a result of the protection afforded to well known marks pursuant to s 56 of the TMA 1994. This protection is discussed in Chapter 12, although the interpretation of these provisions is yet to be determined by the courts, it may well be that on the facts in *Anheuser-Busch,* the American claimant's mark would be protected as a well-known mark.

1 Paragraph **14.18**, n 3 above.
2 See para **14.18**, n 2 above.
3 [1993] EMLR 27.
4 [1995] FSR 924 Knox J.

Duration of goodwill

14.20   Goodwill must be attached to a business. It is established through the use of a name or mark in relation to a business. In order to bring a passing off action it must be shown that the business is carried on and that the mark is used. Where, however, the mark or name is no longer used or the business has ceased there will be residual goodwill in the mark or name provided that it has not been abandoned.

In *Ad-Lib Club Ltd v Granville*,[1] Pennycuick V-C considered that although the claimant had ceased to run a night club under the name 'Ad-Lib Club' for five years there was residual goodwill in the name. This residual goodwill was an asset of value which the claimant was entitled to exploit if it chose to and which it had not abandoned.

1 [1972] RPC 673.

Misrepresentation

14.21 The first of Lord Diplock's and the fifth of Lord Fraser of Tullybelton's characteristics is misrepresentation. The majority of cases refer to a situation where the allegation of misrepresentation is that the defendant's goods are those of the claimant (see eg *Reckitt & Colman Products Ltd v Borden Inc, Suzy International Naamloze Vennootschap and Paterson Jenks plc*[1]) when they are not. The goodwill of a manufacturer may also be damaged by someone else who sells goods which are correctly described as being made by that manufacturer but which are of an inferior class or quality are which are thereby misrepresented as goods of his manufacture of a superior class or quality (see *A G Spalding & Bros v A W Gamage Ltd*[2]). The misrepresentation may alternatively be that the defendant is associated in some way with the claimant. When the claimant and the defendant are not competing traders in the same line of business, a false suggestion by the defendant that the businesses are connected with one another may damage the reputation and thus the goodwill of the claimant's business (see for example *Harrods Ltd v R Harrod Ltd*.[3]

1 [1990] RPC 341.
2 (1915) 32 RPC 273 (HL).
3 (1923) 41 RPC 74.

14.22 Although the misrepresentation may take many forms, it must always be a misrepresentation as to *origin* as opposed to mere quality unless, it is submitted, a particular quality can be attributed in a passing off sense to a particular source. In *Reckitt & Colman*[1] the defendant sold lemon juice in containers so fashioned to suggest that the juice emanated from the source with which the containers of those particular configurations had become associated by the public. The misrepresentation was that the defendants's juice was Jif juice. It was not the sale of plastic lemons or the dimpled containers per se which was objectionable. In practice, however, the law of passing off may, upon proof of the correct elements, enable traders, in effect, to obtain a monopoly in descriptive elements or in trade marks or trade dress even though it has been repeatedly said that it is such things which the law of passing off does not protect. As a result although the law of passing off *protects* goodwill, in *effect* it is the ability of other traders to use certain indicia of trade which is controlled.

1 [1990] RPC 341.

Confusion

14.23 It must be shown that on the balance of probabilities it is likely that a number of members of the public will be deceived as a result of the misrepresentation. In an action between traders (as opposed to class type actions) the confusion will be the mistaken purchase of the defendant's goods in the belief that they are the claimant's goods. Thus in *Reckitt & Colman Products Ltd v Borden Incorporated, Suzy International Naamloze Vennootschap and Paterson Jenks plc*[1] the question was whether on the balance of probability a substantial number of members of the public would be misled into purchasing the defendant's lemon juice in the belief that it was the claimant's Jif juice because of its packaging.

1 See para **14.22**, n 1 above.

14.24   This is a question of fact for the court and not for the witnesses to decide. It must be determined taking account of all relevant circumstances. These may include:

— similarities between the claimant's and defendant's respective marks and get ups. The comparison is both phonetic and visual.
— the nature of the market place and circumstances in which the goods are sold or services supplied (eg in a self-service where customers pick goods from the shelves, by mail order or via the Internet);
— the habits of ordinary purchasers (informed eg *Hodgkinson & Corby Ltd v Wards Mobility Services Ltd*[1] or casual eg *Reckitt & Colman Products Ltd v Borden Incorporated, Suzy International Naamloze Vennootschap and Paterson Jenks plc*;[2] or even repeat business);
— the nature of the goods themselves (cost, technical specification etc).

1 [1995] FSR 169.
2 [1990] RPC 341.

Evidence of confusion

14.25   The court must look at all the circumstances and decide if confusion is likely to occur or has occurred and is attributable to damage of goodwill. Evidence of actual confusion on the part of relevant and rational members of the public should be adduced if possible but sometimes this is not easy or possible since the extent of confusion may lead to total deception. As we shall discuss further below, and in more detail, it is also necessary to adduce evidence of the right sort of confusion, being confusion as to origin as opposed to confusion arising for some other reason.[1] As a result, witnesses may be hard to find because they believe that they have purchased the real thing. Where there has been no such confusion, despite the carrying out of the activities complained of for a considerable period of time, the lack of confusion may be very telling against the claimant (see *Harrods Ltd v Harrodian School Ltd*).[2] Often survey evidence will be produced and the significance to be attached to the results of a survey will depend largely upon its reliability as an indication of the actual likelihood of confusion, though such evidence is often deprecated and sometimes roundly condemned. In *Alan Kenneth McKenzie Clark v Associated Newspapers Ltd*[3] the issue before the court was whether a substantial (or large) number of readers[4] of a daily London newspaper called the Evening Standard had been misled or were likely to be misled that Alan Clark was the author of a column entitled 'Alan Clark's Secret Political Diary'.[5] According to Lightman J at 271:

'The judge has the sole responsibility for determining the issue [namely the likelihood of deception]: he may be assisted by evidence of rational men that they have been misled and (to a lesser degree) by evidence of rational men that they have not been misled, but he must not surrender his own independent judgment to any witness or number of witnesses (see *A G Spalding & Bros v A W Gamage Ltd* (1915) 32 RPC 273 at 283–4 per Lord Parker). The judge may also be assisted by the evidence of experts explaining special features of the relevant "market" of which he may otherwise be ignorant and which are relevant to the likelihood of deception or damage (see *European Ltd v Economist Newspapers Ltd* [1998] FSR 283)'.

1 See, for an example of how the wrong sort of confusion was dealt with by the court, *HFC Bank plc v Midland Bank plc* (unreported 30 July 1999) Lloyd J.
2 [1996] RPC 697, 710.
3 [1998] RPC 261.
4 Ie it is, we submit, that a large number of the intended recipients or likely recipients are deceived (or likely to be so). Thus, we submit, that where the relevant market comprises a small number of buyers then the tort is made out even if only a small number of them are deceived or confused since that connotes damage to goodwill. To this extent the judge was wrong, we respectfully submit, to say that a 'large' number of readers have been misled or are likely to be misled before the action gets off the ground – what is important is the *effect* on goodwill. See the dicta of Morritt LJ in *Neutrogena Corp v Golden Ltd* [1996] RPC 473, 493, 494.
5 There was also the question of false authorship under the Copyright, Designs and Patents Act 1988, s 84.

14.26   Although the court is concerned with the evidence that rational men would be or would be likely to be deceived, there is no principle of law that customers must be assumed to be literate or careful. According to Lord Oliver of Aylmerton in *Reckitt & Colman:Products Ltd v Borden Inc, Suzy International Naamdoze Vennootschap and Paterson Jenks plc*[1]

'The essence of the action for passing off is the deceit practised on the public and it can be no answer, in a case where it is demonstrable that the public has or will be deceived, that they would not have been if they had been more literate or more careful or more perspicacious. Customers have to be taken as they are found'

1 [1990] RPC 341, 415.

14.27   The question of deception is to be considered in all the circumstances in which the goods are sold. Thus in *Reckitt & Colman Products Ltd v Borden Incorporated, Suzy International Naamloze Vennootschap and Paterson Jenks plc*,[1] although on a side-by-side comparison the differences between the respective marks were clearly apparent and careful shopper, would have no difficulty in differentiating them, the evidence showed that the buying public would be confused and a diversion of trade would result. As Lord Oliver of Aylmerton concluded at 416:

'the law of passing off does not rest solely upon the deceit of those whom it is difficult to deceive.'

1 [1990] RPC 341.

14.28   As to whether survey evidence is at all useful in this regard, see *Imperial Group Ltd v Philip Morris & Co* where Whitford J said:[1]

'If survey evidence is to be of any weight at all it can only be of weight if in any case where, as here, a number of surveys have been carried out the [claimants] ... give – and they must give this to the Defendants before ever the action comes on – the fullest possible disclosure of exactly how many surveys they have carried out, exactly how those surveys were conducted and the totality of the number of persons involved, because otherwise it is impossible to draw any reliable inference that answers given by one or two or three people in one survey might conceivably be said to indicate that similar answers would be given if a survey covering the entire smoking population or the entirety of retail tobacconists were carried out.

'It is also important that the totality of all answers given to all surveys should be disclosed and made available to the defendants. Unfortunately in some of the surveys which were here conducted provision was made for objection to be entered by any person interviewed to the use of the answers to the questions for some purposes without his consent, as a result of which only a limited disclosure on one survey was or could be offered.

'Great importance inevitably attaches to the way in which the questions are cast. It is very difficult in connection with an exercise such as this to think of questions which, even if they are free from the objection of being leading, are not in fact going to direct the person answering the question into a field of speculation upon which that person would never have embarked had the question not be put. It must necessarily be the case that the exact answers given and not some sort of abbreviation or digest of the exact answer should be recorded. For the purpose of an analysis coding is in general carried out, as is well known, and it is of vital importance that any such coding should be accurately carried out. Of course one has to know exactly what instructions were given to persons carrying out the interviews upon which answers to questionnaires are secured, and indeed, in the instance of those surveys upon which reliance was placed, we have got information as to the instructions given, the way in which the interviews were carried out and the coding. What emerges at the end of the evidence is that there may be doubt as to whether in fact in all cases the answers which were given correctly recorded. There may be doubt as to whether the instructions in all cases were sufficiently carefully followed by those carrying out the interviews. There is no doubt whatsoever that, so far as the coding is concerned, in some cases it must be considered to have been incorrect and in other cases it might be considered to be misleading.

'I make these comments about these surveys, not because I think it is of vital importance to the final decision in this case, but there is increasing reliance upon the material of this character which results in a vast amount of paper being brought before the court, which in fact if it is to be of any value should be even larger than was the amount brought in this case, I have found the results of the plaintiffs, save and in so far as what is in fact established is that one would reasonably expect to find established, of very little value."

See also the dicta of Walton J in *Reckitt & Colman*:[2]

'Now when considering this [survey] evidence I bear very much in mind the warning indicated by [Counsel for the Defendants] ... to the effect that the Courts are accustomed to treat evidence of the general nature here in question with some degree of suspicion, mindful of the fact that it is often possible by means of questions to indicate to the person being questioned the precise answer that one wants, or even to frame one's questions in such a manner as to provide untruthful or exaggerated answers (as happened historically in the case of "The Lyon in Mourning"). But in the present case firstly, both sides have presented such evidence. Second, the [Claimant] ... tendered for examination by the Defendants the whole segment of witnesses, starting with the professional organisers of their surveys , through the persons who conducted their interviews down to a fair sample, so far as it was possible for the Court to judge, of the persons who had been interviewed. These persons ranged from fairly humble housewives, doubtless noted for their kind hearts and passion for jif lemon with pancakes, but with no other great claim to fame, to some extremely intelligent shoppers, who, immediately they were put on notice that there might be some doubt as to the product they had purchased, did not require very long to appreciate the exact position of things.

'Third, the [Claimant] ... supplied the Defendants with the names of their, or at any rate, some of their, potential witnesses, and the defendants did indeed, in the interlocutory stages of the first action, interview them. They did not interview any of such potential witnesses in relation to the second action . As a result of the interviews that were carried out, there was no complaint whatsoever as to the views of those witnesses having been misrepresented, or exaggerated, in the slightest.

'Accordingly, whilst fully realising that for this aspect of the matter, I must decide the case for myself and not merely accept the evidence of such witnesses, I find it impossible to ignore such a formidable body of opinion. It must be highly unusual for a Judge in a *quia timet* action; of course I fully accept that it is not entitled to the same weight as would have been attached thereto if the lemons had actually come onto the market and the expressions were the expressions of the views of the witnesses after actually having bought the Defendants' lemons. But, at least, I feel that I am now fully instructed in the way in which shoppers who shop, as the vast majority of us willy nilly have to shop, in self service stores of some description, do so shop and of what their apprehension of the jif lemon really is.'

1 [1984] RPC 292, 302.RPC 341.

14.29 But for instances where such evidence has been roundly rejected, see the dicta of Dillon LJ in *Mothercare UK Ltd v Penguin Books Ltd*:[1]

'It has become rather a fashion latterly for large companies involved in passing off actions to have surveys carried out to show public reaction to the Defendant's product. I do not for may part find such surveys helpful.'

In certain circumstances it may, however, be necessary for the court to be educated (notwithstanding what Lightman J said in *Alan Kenneth McKenzie Clark v Associated Newspapers Ltd*[2]) where one is talking about a special market, as was the case in *Guccio Gucci SpA v Paolo Gucci*.[3]

In *Dalgety Spillers Foods Ltd v Food Brokers Ltd*[4] Blackburne J said when ruling that certain survey evidence was not admissible in helping him determine whether there was confusion in a normal market which a judge could be normally be expected to understand:

'In cases where the goods were of a kind which were sold to the public for consumption ... , evidence of persons accustomed to deal in that market as to the likelihood of deception or confusion may be admissible. The test must be whether the experience which a judge must be taken to possess as an ordinary ... consumer would enable him ... to assess the likelihood of confusion. If it would, then the evidence would not be admissible. If it would not, then such evidence would be admissible. The weight the court then attaches to such evidence would of course depend on its nature and quality.'

and then at 528:

'In all cases evidence will be admissible to prove the circumstances and the places in which the goods are sold, the kind of persons who buy them, and the manner in which the public are accustomed to ask for those goods.'

1 [1988] RPC 113,117.
2 [1998] RPC 261.
3 [1991] FSR 89.
4 [1994] FSR 504, 527.

The right kind of confusion

14.30   Confusion alone is not conclusive of passing off. It must be confusion arising from a relevant misrepresentation. Mere confusion between two traders' products does not provide the basis for a passing off action unless established goodwill
in relation to one of the products can be shown.[1] In *Marengo v Daily Sketch*, Lord
Greene MR said:[2]

> 'No one is entitled to be protected against confusion as such. Confusion may result
> from the collision of two independent rights or liberties, and where that is the case
> neither party can complain; they must put up with the results of the conufsion as one
> of the misfortunes which occur in life. The protection to which a man is entitled to
> against passing off, which is quite a different thing from mere confusion.'

Where the buying public, that is the relevant public are either not concerned or not
mistaken as to the origin of the goods or services in question, there is no actionable
passing off.

1 See Marcus Publishing plc v Hutton-Wild Communications Ltd [1990] RPC 576. See also HFC Bank
plc v Midland Bank plc (1999) Times, 28 September.
2 (1946) [1992] FSR 1 at 2.

14.31   The adoption by a trader of an accepted trade description or an ordinary
English word for his goods or services may result in confusion and in the right circumstances he may be stopped. Such confusion is all the more likely where this
description was only previously used by one other trader. Thus the application to
the defendant's clothing of the ordinary English word 'cellular' (*Cellular Clothing
Co v Maxton & Murray*),[1] or the use of the name 'office cleaning' in relation to
such service (*Office Cleaning Services Ltd v Westminster and Window and General
Cleaners Ltd (trading as Office Cleaners Association)*[2] or the use of the descriptive
name 'Chicago Pizza' in relation to pizzas (*My Kinda Town Ltd v Soll*)[3] was held
not to result in actionable misrepresentation, even though it was accepted that there
was confusion. In *Office Cleaning Services* it was held that such an increased risk
of confusion was something that the public had to suffer (the tort of passing off
never being concerned with consumer protection) and it was held that the distinction between 'services' and 'association' was sufficiently distinct for such damage
to be minimal. We look at this question in a slightly different way below.[4]

1 (1899) 16 RPC 397.
2 (1946) 63 RPC 39).
3 [1983] RPC 407 CA
4 Paragraph **14.36**.

Misrepresentation – the relevant connection

14.32   The classic form of misrepresentation arises where the claimant and defendant are competing traders in the same line of business. In such circumstances an
actionable misrepresentation will result in the diversion of trade or a likelihood of
such a diversion. Where the claimant's and defendant's businesses are not competing traders, a false suggestion that the claimant's and defendant's businesses are
associated may be actionable. The false suggestion must be that the claimant is
responsible in some way for the quality of the defendant's goods or services not
just that the claimant is behind the defendant in some way. In *Harrods Ltd v*

Harrodian School Ltd[1] a mere representation that the famous store sponsored the defendant's school would not have been sufficient to cause the public to believe that it was responsible for the quality of the teaching even though the school was so named because it had taken over the old sports ground (in Barnes in south west London) of the claimant.

1 [1996] RPC 697.

Common field of activity

14.33   There is no requirement to show that the defendant is carrying on a business which competes with the claimant's business or with any natural extension of the claimant's business in any exact sense. The presence or absence of a common field of activity between the claimant and defendant is a highly relevant but not conclusive consideration when deciding whether there is a likelihood of confusion (see *Harrods Ltd v Harrodian School Ltd).*[1] The further removed the respective fields of activity are from one another, the less likely it will be that a member of the public could reasonably be confused into thinking that one business is connected with the other. In *Stringfellow v McCain Foods (GB) Ltd,*[2] the only tenuous overlap was that the claimant sold food in his upmarket restaurant at his nightclub and the defendant's sold frozen potato chips. The lack of a common field of activity was a matter to be borne in mind when considering whether use of the word 'Stringfellows' on the packaging of the defendant's chipped potato products was likely to lead members of the public to the reasonable belief that the claimant (one Mr Stringfellow) or his club (called Stringfellows) were associated with chipped potatoes in any way.

1 See para **14.32**, n1 above, at 714.
2 [1984] RPC 501 CA.

14.34   Where the mark in question is a household word, the degree of overlap between the fields of activity of the parties' respective businesses may be less important when assessing the likelihood of confusion or deception. In *Lego Systems A/S v Lego M Lemelstrich Ltd*[1] Falconer J considered that the word 'Lego' was a household word in the sense that everyone associated it with the manufacturer of the toy bricks. The association with the defendant's irrigation equipment (including garden sprinklers made of coloured plastic material) was therefore easier to assume and prove. This gives more apparent power to stronger marks or trade dress, however, in reality, it is the goodwill which has the power.

1 [1983] FSR 155, 160.

Descriptive marks

14.35   Where a claimant adopts a name or mark which is an ordinary English word in common use and which is apt to describe the goods sold or services rendered by him, the essential matter in issue remains unchanged[1] – is the use by the defendant of its name or mark or other indicia likely to lead to the belief that the defendant's business is the business of the claimant? A claimant does not acquire a monopoly in a descriptive mark by mere use of that mark even for an extensive period of time. What must be shown is that the mark has become associated in the minds of the buying public with the goods of the first trader and none other.

1 That much was made clear, at least impliedly by Lord Oliver of Aylmerton in *Reckitt & Colman Products Ltd v Borden Inc, Suzy International Naamloze Vennootschap and Paterson Jenks plc* [1990] RPC 341.

14.36   There are two consequences of the adoption of such a descriptive mark. First, there may be confusion but no actionable misrepresentation if a defendant adopts a similar mark. Second, the court will accept that small differences between the respective marks of the claimant and defendant will serve to differentiate the two.

In *Office Cleaning Services Ltd v Westminster and Window and General Cleaners Ltd (trading as Office Cleaners Association) per* Lord Simonds:[1]

> 'Where a trader adopts words in common use for his trade name, some risk of confusion is inevitable. But that risk must be run unless the first trader is allowed to unfairly monopolise the words. The Court will accept comparatively small differences as sufficient to avert confusion. A greater degree of discrimination may fairly be expected from the public where a trade name consists wholly or in part of words descriptive of the articles to be sold or the services rendered.'

In that case the claimants carried on a business under the name 'Office Cleaning Services Ltd' and the defendant had adopted the name 'Office Cleaning Association'. It was held that the distinctive words were 'Services' in the claimant's title and 'Association' in the defendant's title and that these were sufficiently differentiated to avert any confusion that might otherwise arise from the use of ordinary descriptive words. However to sail any closer to the wind than the defendant in *Office Cleaning Services* is to risk trouble as may be seen in the case of *British Diabetic Association v Diabetic Society*[2] where 'Society' was held to be too close to 'Association'.[3]

1 (1946) 63 RPC 39 HL, 43.
2 [1996] FSR 1.
3 Though the claimant in that case also contended that it had an exclusive reputation in the word 'diabetic society' and that as a result all donations made to the defendants were as a result of deception – the judge held that this was not the case but rather the defendant's use of 'society' was confusing when compared to the claimant's 'association'.

Descriptive marks – secondary meaning

14.37   Where the mark in question is an ordinary English word or apt to describe the goods sold or services provided then it is not sufficient to demonstrate sole use of it. The mere fact that a trader has been the sole provider of goods of that type under that description may lead the public to believe that all such goods must emanate from him simply because they know of no other. Rather it must be shown that the mark has become so closely associated with this trader's goods or services that it has acquired a secondary meaning not simply as goods of that description but goods or services of which he alone is the source. In other words that he has an exclusive reputation.

These principles are explained by Lord Hershell in *Reddaway v Banham*:[1]

> 'The name of a person, or words forming part of the common stock of language, may become so far associated with the goods of a particular maker that it is capable of

proof that the use of them by themselves without explanation or qualification by another manufacturer would deceive a purchaser into the belief that he was getting the goods of A when he was really getting the goods of B. In a case of this description the mere proof by the [claimant] ... that the defendant was using a name, word or device which he had adopted to distinguish his goods would not entitle him to any relief. He would only obtain it by proving further that the defendant was using it under such circumstances or in such a manner as to put off his goods as the goods of the [claimant] . ... If he could succeed in proving this I think he would, on well established principles, be entitled to an injunction.'

1 [1896] AC 199 at 210.

Momentary and inconsequential deception

14.38   It is said to be necessary that a substantial number of customers or potential customers to be misled or deceived. This, in truth, it is submitted, is the wrong test if that is all it is. Rather it is better to look at the effect on goodwill and damage thereto and to bear in mind that the law tolerates behaviour of minimal effect. In *Neutrogena Corpn v Golden Ltd* Jacob J (whose views were endorsed by the Court of Appeal) said:[1]

'There is no dispute as to the applicable law. The question is whether the [defendants'] ... mark ... so nearly resembles the [claimants'] mark ... as to be likely to deceive or cause confusion. (I take this from [counsel for the defendants'] ... skeleton argument ...). There is in this case no real difference between deception and confusion – if people think [that the defendants' mark] ... is connected with the [claimants] ... , or mistake one for the other, or in other ways mix one with another that is enough. Another way of putting the question is to ask whether the goodwill of [the claimants] ... is damaged by any form of misrepresentation caused by [the defendants] ... .

'It is, of course, the effect on the goodwill of [the claimant] ... which matters. It is not a defence to passing off that many of a defendant's sales do not cause deception or confusion. There is passing off even if most of the people are not fooled most of the time but enough are for enough of the time. By "enough" I mean a substantial number of the [claimants'] ... customers or potential customers deceived for there to be a real effect on the [claimants'] ... trade or goodwill. In this case (where most of these are probably not confused) the crucial question is whether or not the [claimants] ... have established a sufficient degree of confusion and deception to take the case above a *de minimis* level.[2] For there are always some people who are confused and even when products and names are well differentiated, mistakes do occur.

'[Counsel for the defendants] ... formulation relates to the, words [used by the parties – Neutrogena of the claimants as opposed to Neutralia of the defendants] as such. There were, at some points in the evidence, suggestions that there were other factors (eg differences in packaging or the use of [the defendants] ...) which might reduce the chances of passing off, even if the names were confusingly similar. I do not think they amounted to anything significant. Indeed the point on the packaging seems to have struck some witnesses one way and others the other.

[*His lordship then referred briefly to certain evidence and continued*]
'The proper approach of the court to the question was not in dispute. The judge must consider the evidence adduced and use his own common sense and his own opinion as to the likelihood of deception. It is an overall "jury" assessment involving a combination of

all these factors, see *GE Trade Mark* [1973] RPC 297 at 321. Ultimately the question is one for the court, not for the witnesses. It follows that if the judge's own opinion is that the case is marginal, one where he cannot be sure whether there is a likelihood of sufficient deception, the case will fail in the absence of enough evidence of the likelihood of deception. But if that opinion of the judge is supplemented by such evidence then it will succeed. And even if one's own opinion is that deception is unlikely though possible, convincing evidence of deception will carry the day. The *Jif lemon* case (*Reckitt & Colman Products Ltd v Borden Incorporated, Suzy International Naamloze Vennootschap and Paterson Jenks plc* [1990] RPC 341) is a recent example where overwhelming evidence of deception had that effect. It was certainly my experience in practice that my own view as to the likelihood of deception was not always reliable. As I grew more experienced I said more and more "it depends on the evidence".'

Which we submit supports this proposition – anything more than minimal damage will do.

1 [1996] RPC 473, 481 line 37 to 482 line 32.
2 Though it must be observed that Morritt LJ in the same case on appeal deprecated the use of the expressions like 'more than *de minimis*' and 'above a trivial level' by Jacob J. In relation to that passage Morritt LJ said at 494 lines 8 to 15 said this:
    'Nevertheless, for my part, I think that references, in this context, to "more than *de minimis*" and "above a trivial level" are best avoided notwithstanding this court's reference to the former in *University of London v American University of London* (unreported 12 November 1993). It seems to me that such expressions are open to misinterpretation for they do not necessarily connote the opposite of substantial and their use may be thought to reverse the proper emphasis and concentrate on the quantitative to the exclusion of the qualitative aspect of confusion.'

It is submitted that Morritt LJ was saying that whilst the law tolerates trivialities is true, the damage must be substantial, though what constitutes substance is a matter for each case and it does not necessarily follow that mere force of numbers will win the day.

14.39   There is no actionable passing off if the confusion which might arise would be corrected. Thus were the defendant's rather than the claimant's goods might in some instances be offered to the prospective customers, if the purchaser was aware of the error prior to the purchase then the defendant's goods are sufficiently distinguished and there is no passing off (see *Cadbury-Schweppes Pty Ltd v Pub Squash Co Pty Ltd*).[1]

1 [1981] RPC 429 at 491–492.

Taking advantage of a market developed by the another

14.40   In *Cadbury-Schweppes Pty Ltd v Pub Squash Co Pty Ltd*[1] it was held that taking advantage of the market developed by another trader was not actionable as such. The claimant had promoted its 'Solo' lemonade drink using advertisements with a heroically masculine theme and as the sort of 'real lemon squash that the pubs used to make'. The defendant took advantage of the claimant's advertising campaign. It sold its 'Pub Squash' lemonade in cans which were not dissimilar to those used by the claimant. The defendant's own advertising campaign featured stalwart men and evoked the memory of pubs squashes of the past. This did not amount to passing off. The public was not deceived or misled by the get-up, the formula of the drink or the advertising of 'Pub Squash' into thinking that it was manufactured by the claimant.

1 [1981] RPC 429.

Damage

14.41   The misrepresentation must be such that injury is suffered to the claimant's identifiable goodwill (or in a *quia timet* action that such damage is a reasonably foreseeable consequence). The damage must be actual or real. Where the claimant and defendant are rival traders and the defendant misrepresents his goods or services as being those of the claimant, the damage is often the diversion of sales.

14.42   The claimant's goodwill will also be damaged where the defendant has led the purchasing public to believe that his inferior goods might be those of the claimant. The damage may even be caused by selling a manufacturer's genuine goods but misrepresenting them to be goods of his manufacture of a superior class or quality (see *A G Spalding & Brothers v A W Gamage Ltd*).[1]

1   (1915) 32 RPC 273 HL.

14.43   Where the claimant and defendant are not competing traders in the same line of business, a false suggestion by the defendant that their businesses are connected with one another may also damage the claimant's goodwill (see *Warnink (Erven) Besloten Vennootschap v J Townend & Sons (Hull) Ltd*, per Lord Diplock,[1] referring to *Harrods Ltd v R Harrod Ltd*,[2] the money lending case as an illustration of this.) In *Lego Systems A/S v Lego M Lemelstrich Ltd*[3] as explained by Millett LJ in *Harrods Ltd v Harrodian School Ltd*,[4] a customer who was dissatisfied with the plastic irrigation equipment manufactured by the defendant might be dissuaded from buying the claimant's toy bricks in the belief that the toy bricks were made by the defendant. The danger in such a case is that the claimant cannot control the quality of the defendant's goods and so loses control over his own reputation.

1   [1980] RPC 31 HL at 93.
2   (1923) 41 RPC 74.
3   [1983] FSR 155.
4   [1996] RPC 697 CA at 715.

14.44   The court will, however, be less ready to infer that damage is the likely consequence in the absence of common field of activity. In such cases the claimant has the burden of showing not only that there will be a misrepresentation but also that damage will result. In *Stringfellow v McCain Foods (GB) Ltd*[1] Slade LJ said:

> 'Even if it considers that there is a limited risk of confusion of this nature, the court should not, in my opinion, readily infer the likelihood of resulting damage to the [claimants] … as against an innocent defendant in a completely different line of business. In such a case the onus falling on the [claimants] … to show that damage to their business reputation is in truth likely to ensue and to cause them more than minimal loss is in my opinion a heavy one'.

1   [1984] RPC 501 CA at 545.

14.45   The claimant may choose to exploit its goodwill by licensing or franchising it to other traders or by expanding into other markets. Damage of this kind was found to be the likely consequence of the intended activities of the defendant in *Lego Systems A/S v Lego M Lemelstrich Ltd*[1] Falconer J considered that this potentiality of the claimant, the manufacturer of the 'Lego' toy bricks, to exploit the goodwill in the area of garden equipment would be, Falconer J considered, likely to be lost if the defendant was allowed to sell such goods under the mark 'Lego'. Although there was no evidence that the claimant intended to enter the garden equipment field, Falconer J found that their reputation in the mark 'Lego' extended beyond the field in which it had hitherto engaged and was so extensive that a very substantial number of members of the public would mistakenly believe that the coloured plastic garden sprinklers bearing the mark would be the claimant's goods or have some association or connection with it.

1 [1983] FSR 155.

14.46 In *Harrods Ltd v Harrodian School Ltd*[1] Millett LJ said that 'damage to reputation without damage to goodwill is not sufficient to support an action for passing off'. He considered hypothetically the consequence of a scandal at the defendant's school. The attendant publicity might temporarily tarnish Harrods' good name but he did not consider that there was any real likelihood of danger that Harrods' customers would withdraw their custom as a result. But this is a case where the robustness of the claimant's reputation makes it less prone to an indirect assault.

1 [1996] RPC 697 at 718.

Erosion of goodwill

14.47 Where the passing off is in the extended or class action form, such as in the Champagne cases, then the damage may take the form of the dilution or erosion or debasement of the goodwill (see for example *Taitinger v Allbev Ltd*[1] 'the Elderflower Champagne Case', although the sales of the defendant's non-alcoholic cordial would not be likely to reduce the sales of the Tattinger champagne the exclusive reputation and goodwill in the name 'champagne' would nevertheless be damaged) . This extended or class action form of passing off is discussed below.

1 [1993] FSR 641.

14.48 It is doubtful that erosion of goodwill on its own is a sufficient head of damage in the more traditional type of passing off action. In *Harrods Ltd v Harrodian School Ltd*[1] Millett LJ considered that it would be an unacceptable extension of the tort of passing off to recognise erosion of distinctiveness as an actionable head of damage. It may be that there is no absolute rule against damage of this type being actionable but rather that it is a matter of fact and degree. Millett LJ said:[2]

> 'To date the law has not sought to protect the value of the brand name as such, but the value of the goodwill which it generates; and it insists on proof of confusion to justify its intervention. But the erosion of distinctiveness of a brand name which occurs by reason of its degeneration into common use as a generic term is not necessarily dependent on confusion at all.'

1 [1996] RPC 697 at 715–716.
2 See n 1 above at 716.

Reverse passing off

14.49 So called reverse passing off[1] occurs not when a defendant represents that his own goods are the goods of somebody else but when the defendant asserts that the goods of somebody else are his. A misrepresentation by a defendant that the services of somebody else are his is equally tortious.

1 Or, amongst practitioners 'passing on'.

14.50 In *Bristol Conservatories Ltd v Conservatories Custom Built Ltd*[1] the court was concerned with an application to strike out such a reverse passing off claim. The claimant designed, manufactured and constructed ornamental conservatories. The defendant was a retailer of ornamental conservatories. One of the claimant's salesmen went to work for the defendant and, after starting work with the defendant, used a portfolio of photographs to assist him in his work. The portfolio contained photographs of conservatories designed and constructed by the claimant. Nothing in the portfolio suggested that the conservatories were not designed and built by the defendant and there was no reference to the claimant in the portfolio.

The misrepresentation was that if one was to order a conservatory from the defendant one would get a conservatory designed and built by the commercial source that had designed, manufactured and constructed the conservatories shown in the photographs. In fact if one ordered a conservatory from the defendant in response to the misrepresentation (as the defendant hoped one would) then the defendant would supply a conservatory not of the stated commercial source but of their own manufacture. This would amount to passing off.

1 [1989] RPC 455, CA.

14.51 It does not matter that the person who is deceived or confused by the misrepresentation does not know the claimant's name. In *Plomien Fuel Economiser Co Ltd v National School of Salesmanship Ltd,*[1] Lord Greene said:

'It is perfectly true that there is no evidence that a single person who purchased an economiser from the defendants had ever heard of the plaintiffs; but in passing off there is no necessity that the person who is deceived should have known the name of the person who complains of the passing off. In many cases the name is not known at all. It is quite sufficient, in my opinion, to constitute passing off in fact, if a person being minded to obtain goods which are identified in his mind with a definite commercial source is led by false statements to accept goods coming from a different commercial source.'

1 (1943) 60 RPC 209 CA at 214.

14.52 It may be that it is the defendant himself who identifies the claimant and demonstrates the claimant's goodwill. In *Bristol Conservatories Ltd v Conservatories Custom Built Ltd* Gibson LJ considered that it was not necessary in order to establish passing off to show that any member of the public, looking at any of the photographs, would associate any conservatory with the plaintiffs. He said:[1]

'No person affected by the misrepresentation in *Samuelson's* case,[2] or in the *Plomien* case,[3] or in the *Henderson* case[4] would have known who the plaintiff in any of those cases was. That did not stop the plaintiff being injured in his property rights in his business or goodwill. Nor would it matter if there was nothing in any photograph to link the conservatory there depicted with the plaintiffs in any way. Next, it would not matter that there was no allegation that there would be any confusion in the minds of the public. The concept of confusion, in my view, is irrelevant when the misrepresentation leaves no room for confusion. The prospective customer here is not left to perceive the difference between two allegedly similar products, he is told simply and untruthfully that Custom Built design and constructed the conservatories which provide the evidence for the experience, skill and reputation of the plaintiffs. Lastly, the judge was wrong, I think, to proceed on the basis that the plaintiffs were not alleging that they have a goodwill which was affected by the use of the photographs. In truth, as Mr Prescott submitted, the goodwill was asserted and demonstrated as the photographs were shown and was at the same moment misappropriated by Custom Built.'

1 [1989] RPC 455, 464 line 46, 465.
2 *Samuelson v Producers Distributing Co Ltd* (1932) 48 RPC 580 CA.
3 *Plomien Fuel Economiser Co Ltd v National School of Salesmanship Ltd* (1943) 60 RPC 209 CA.
4 *Henderson & Son Ltd v Munro & Co* (1905) 7 F (Ct of Sess) 636.

International exhaustion of rights

14.53 Cases such as *Revlon Inc v Cripps and Lee Ltd*[1] show that there exists a doctrine of international exhaustion of rights in relation to passing off – at least in form if not in substance. Under this doctrine a trader may only control the initial marketing and release of his goods. He cannot restrain subsequent dealing in the goods under the law of passing off. From the reasoning of their lordships in *Revlon Inc* and the comments of the judges in cases such as *Zino Davidoff SA v A & G Imports Ltd*,[2] *Roussel Uclaf SA v Hockley International Ltd*,[3] *Colgate-Palmolive Ltd v Markwell Finance Ltd*[4] and *Betts v Willmott*[5] as approved of and applied in *National Phonograph Co of Australia Ltd v Walter T Menck*[6] it would appear that there is or was in place not so much a doctrine of international exhaustion of rights as an evidential presumption that a trade mark owner or a person having rights of action to protect his goodwill must take positive steps to limit his markets (which he may be perfectly at liberty to do).[7]

In *Revlon* Templeman LJ (as he then was) said:[8]

'In my judgment where a parent company chooses to manufacture and sell wholly or partly through a group of subsidiary companies in different parts of the world, products bearing the same trade mark and attract an international reputation, neither the parent nor any subsidiary can complain in the United Kingdom if those products are used, sold and re-sold under that trade mark. A purchaser of a Revlon product from a Revlon company in the United States or the United Kingdom or in any other part of the world, whether a Revlon company operates in that part of the world or not, is at least entitled to assume that he will not be sued by a Revlon company in the United Kingdom or Venezuela or New York or anywhere else, merely because of the place of manufacture of the product which he has acquired under the name REVLON. The purchaser may have no idea of the place of manufacture of the Revlon product or the name of the Revlon company responsible for production or distribution, and he will only know that he is buying a Revlon product derived from a Revlon company. The legal ownership of the trade mark enables the proprietor in the interests of the Revlon group in general and Revlon Inc. in particular to protect in the United Kingdom the group Revlon reputation and goodwill by ensuring that no goods are sold under the name REVLON unless they are produced and labelled by a Revlon company. The legal ownership of the trade mark does not go further and enable a Swiss, American or Bermudan subsidiary Revlon company to ensure that the Revlon products of its American parent or other Revlon company are not sold within the territory of the United Kingdom.'

1 [1980] FSR 85 CA.
2 [1999] RPC 631.
3 [1996] RPC 441.
4 [1989] RPC 497 CA.
5 (1871) 6 Ch App 239 CA.

6 [1911] AC 336 HL.
7 Though he might be prohibited from doing so on the grounds that such behaviour is anti-competitive.
8 At 144.

14.54 This doctrine (if a doctrine it be) is subject to limitation where the characteristics of the goods are altered (see eg *Colgate-Palmolive Ltd v Markwell Finance Ltd*[1]; see also the trade mark infringement case of *Castrol Ltd v Automotive Oil Supplies Ltd).*[2] Passing off may therefore arise where there is a misrepresentation as to the commercial origin, class or quality of the goods. In *Colgate-Palmolive* Lloyd LJ (as he then was) said[3] that in a case where a manufacturer manufactures goods of two different qualities and:

> 'where a defendant expressly represents that the lower quality is the higher quality, he is clearly liable in passing off, even though both qualities are manufactured by the same manufacturer, provided the other ingredients of a successful passing off action are present. I do not see why the instances of implied representation should be limited to those I have mentioned, namely, switching of labels, alteration of packaging, or deterioration of contents. These are obvious examples where a representation is easily implied. But they are not the only examples. Where the United Kingdom market has come to expect goods of one particular quality manufactured by a particular manufacturer then a defendant who markets indistinguishable goods impliedly represents that they are goods of the same quality.'

1 [1989] RPC 497 CA.
2 [1983] RPC 315.
3 At 530.

14.55 A registered trade mark is not infringed by use of the mark in relation to goods which have been put on the market in the Community under that trade mark by the proprietor or with his consent.[1] The doctrine (if there is or was such a doctrine) of exhaustion has therefore been modified in relation to registered trade marks.

1 See art 7 of Directive and the TMA 1994, s 12.

14.56 The recitals to the Directive however, allow for the preservation of national common law rights as follows:

> 'Whereas the Directive does not deprive the Member States of the right to continue to protect trade marks acquired through use but takes them into account only in regard to the relationship between them and trade marks acquired by registration'

and s 2 (1) of the TMA 1994 specifically provides that:

> '... nothing in this Act affects the law relating to passing off'.

It would therefore seem that the doctrine of exhaustion should continue to apply in relation to passing off. Although the Advocate-General's opinion in *Silhouette International Schmied GmbH & Co KG v Hartlauer Handelsgellshaft mbH*[1] indicated that the Directive precluded Member States from adopting the principle of international exhaustion, the decision of the ECJ was not expressed so broadly. In *Silhouette International Schmied GmbH & Co KG v Hartlauer Handelsgellshaft mbH*[2] the ECJ determined that the rights of the proprietor of a registered trade mark were defined by arts 5 and 7. It is submitted therefore that the ECJ was limiting its consideration to the rights of the owners of registered trade marks.

1 [1998] FSR 474 at 489.
2 [1998] FSR 474..

14.57   The law of trade marks insofar as it concerns international exhaustion is in a state of flux. In *Zino Davidoff SA v A & G Imports Ltd*[1] Laddie J thought that it was more appropriate to consider the question as an evidential presumption of consent. But a reference to the ECJ was made in this case and the answers to the questions posed may resolve this uncertainty.

1 See para **14.53**, n 2 above.

Instruments of deception

14.58   Injunctions may be granted to restrain a party who is not himself passing off where he is equipped with or intending to equip another with an instrument of fraud. There are two kinds of deception (see *Singer Manufacturing Co v Loog*.[1] First, where fraudulent use is intended, second where a name is inherently deceptive or readily and easily lends itself to fraud.

1 (1882) 8 App Cas 15 at 21.

14.59   In *British Telecom plc v One In A Million Ltd*[1] Aldous LJ said:

'In my view there can be discerned from the cases a jurisdiction to grant injunctive relief where a defendant is equipped with or intending to equip another with an instrument of fraud. Whether any name is an instrument of fraud will depend upon all the circumstances. A name which will, by reason of its similarity to the name of another, inherently lead to passing off is such an instrument. If it would not inherently lead to passing off, it does not follow that it is not an instrument of fraud. The court should consider the similarity of the names, the intention of the defendant, the type of trade and all the surrounding circumstances. If it be the intention of the defendant to appropriate the goodwill of another or enable others to do so, I can see no reason why the court should not infer that it will happen, even if there is a possibility that such an appropriation would not take place. If, taking all the circumstances into account the court should conclude that the name was produced to enable passing off, is adapted to be used for passing off and, if used, is likely to be fraudulently used, an injunction will be appropriate.'

'It follows that a court will intervene by way of injunction in passing-off cases in three types of case. First, where there is passing off established or it is threatened. Secondly, where the defendant is a joint tortfeasor with another in passing off either actual or threatened. Thirdly, where the defendant has equipped himself with or intends to equip another with an instrument of fraud. This third type is probably a mere *quia timet* action.'

1 [1999] FSR 1 CA at 18.

14.60   Relief may be granted where the defendant has produced goods which would or could be used by others to pass off. It is not necessary for the claimant to wait until the completion of the fraud by the sale of the goods. The court has the power to grant an injunction to 'arrest the evil at its source' (see *Farina v Silverlock*,[1] an interim injunction was initially granted and then overturned on appeal but renewed following the trial of the action).

1 (1855) 1 K & J 509.

14.61   Where a manufacturer sells instruments of deception, it is no defence to say that the party to whom the instruments are sold is not himself deceived if the end consumer is likely to be deceived. Where, however, the goods are capable of being sold legitimately but some other party chooses to pass them off, the supplier is not liable. In *Cadbury Ltd v Ulmer GmbH*[1] Falconer J said:

'... where the [claimant's] ... case is that the ultimate retail purchaser will be deceived through the intervening middleman, but the trade customers will not be, there has to be a "badge of fraud" and that has to be supplied so as to assist in the deception of the ultimate purchaser. It has either got to be on the goods supplied to the middleman or has got to be supplied separately as counterfeit labels, as in the *Jameson*[2] case, or in the *Harris Tweed*[3] case or the goods themselves have got to go to a middleman bearing a deceptive get-up or a deceptive mark, as in *Lever v Goodwin*.'[4]

Relief may also be granted where the defendant has equipped himself with means of identification similar to that of the claimant. In *Panhard et Levassor v Panhard Levassor Motor Company Ltd*[5] a French motor company claimant with goodwill in this country was granted an injunction preventing the defendant from trading and requiring it to change its company's name.

1 [1988] FSR 385 at 410.
2 *John Jameson & Son Ltd v RS Johnston & Co Ltd* (1901) 18 RPC 259.
3 *Argyllshire Weavers Ltd v A Macaulay (Tweeds) Ltd* [1964] RPC 477.
4 *Lever v Goodwin* (1887) 4 RPC 492.
5 [1901] 2 Ch 513.

14.62   The supplier of an instrument of deception does not escape liability where the instrument is used or intended to be used outside the UK (see *R Johnston & Co v Archibald Orr Ewing & Co*).[1] In *John Walker & Sons Ltd v Henry Ost & Co Ltd*[2] Foster J said:

'I would be slow to decide that if a trader in England sells goods and labels which are true and has no knowledge of any improper use of those goods in a foreign country, such trader has committed a tort in England. But when I have already held as a fact that Mr. Jindrich Ost, the proprietor of the first defendant, not only knew that the second was going to add cane spirit and sell it as Scotch Whisky but intended that the whisky which was supplied should be admixed, bottled and have the labels put on the bottle describing it as Scotch Whisky, then in my judgment the first defendant's acts in selling those instruments amount to tortious acts done in England.'

1 (1882) 7 App Cas 219, HL.
2 [1970] RPC 489.

14.63   Where there is a common design by two or more parties to pass off they are liable as joint tortfeasors. There must, however, be concerted action by them in relation to the commission of the tort. A party who merely facilitates, rather than procures, a tort is not a joint tortfeasor. In *CBS Songs Ltd v Amstrad Consumer Electronics plc*[1] Lord Templeman said:

'My Lords, I accept that a defendant who procures a breach of copyright is liable jointly and severally with the infringer for the damages suffered by the plaintiff as a result of the infringement. The defendant is a joint infringer; he intends and procures and shares a common design that infringement shall take place. A defendant may procure an infringement by inducement, incitement or persuasion. But in the present case Amstrad do not procure infringement by offering for sale a machine which may be used for lawful or unlawful copying and they do not procure infringement by advertising the attractions of their machine to any purchaser who may decide to copy unlawfully. Amstrad are not concerned to procure and cannot procure unlawful copying. The purchaser will not make unlawful copies because he has been induced or incited or persuaded to do so by Amstrad. The purchaser will make unlawful copies for his own use because he chooses to do so. Amstrad's advertisements may persuade the purchaser to buy an Amstrad machine but will not influence the purchaser's later decision to infringe copyright. Buckley LJ observed in *Belegging-en Exploitatiemaatschappij Lavender BV v Witten Industrial Diamonds Ltd*,[2] at p. 65, that "Facilitating the doing of an act is obviously different from procuring the doing of the act." Sales and advertisements to the public generally of a machine which may be used for lawful or unlawful purposes, including infringement of copyright, cannot be said to "procure" all breaches of copyright thereafter by members of the public who use the machine. Generally speaking, inducement, incitement or persuasion to infringe must be by a defendant to an individual infringer and must identifiably procure a particular infringement in order to make the defendant liable as a joint infringer.'

Although *CBS Songs* was concerned with the infringement of copyright, the principles are equally applicable to torts such as passing off (see *Cadbury Ltd v Ulmer GmbH*).[3]

1 [1988] AC 1013, at 1058 HL.
2 [1979] FSR 59, CA.
3 [1988] FSR 385 at 404 , 405.

Passing off – the group or class type action – the necessary characteristics

14.64 A trade name may come to denote goods of a particular type or class. Traders who sell these goods do not have the exclusive rights in the name. The goodwill in the name is shared by all of the traders who sell this type or class of goods. A passing off action may be brought by one or more of these traders to protect the goodwill in the name.

In *Warnink (Erven) Besloten Vennootschap v J Townend & Sons (Hull) Ltd*[1] Lord Diplock said that this was:

> '... an action for "passing off", not in its classic form of a trader representing his goods as goods of somebody else, but in an extended form first recognised and applied by Danckwerts J in the ... [case of *J Bollinger v Costa Brava Wine Company Ltd* [1960] Ch 262].'

1 [1980] RPC 31, 89 HL.

14.65 Although the five characteristics identified by Lord Diplock as being necessary in order to create a valid cause of action are applicable to the extended form of passing off (indeed *Warnink*[1] was such a case) Lord Fraser of Tullybelton's formulation of the ingredients of the tort is particularly apt for this type of action. Lord Fraser of Tullybelton said the claimant must show:[2]

(1) that his business consists of, or includes, selling in England a class of goods to which the particular trade name applies;

(2) that the class of goods is clearly defined, and that in the minds of the public, or a section of the public, in England, the trade name distinguishes that class from other similar goods;

(3) because of the reputation of the goods, there is goodwill attached to the name;

(4) that he, the claimant, as a member of the class of those who sell the goods, is the owner of goodwill in England which is of substantial value;

(5) that he has suffered, or is really likely to suffer, substantial damage to his property in the goodwill by reason of the defendants selling goods which are falsely described by the trade name to which the goodwill is attached.

This formulation was recently applied in *Chocosuisse Union des Fabricants Suisses de Chocolat v Cadbury Ltd* both at trial[3] before Laddie J and on appeal[4] however the Court of Appeal raised the additional question as to the classes of person who might sue and obtain damages (or suffer damages for that matter since it was held that a mere trade association suffered no damage to its goodwill as opposed to representative traders from a group of traders).

1 [1980] RPC 31.
2 At 105–106.
3 [1998] RPC 117.
4 (1999) Times, 15 March.

Comparison with passing off where traders sue one another (the usual form)

14.66 As set out in the following table, the class action differs from the usual form of passing off in a number of significant respects.

Comparison of the usual and class action form of passing off

USUAL FORM	CLASS TYPE ACTION
Protection is given to indicia which are distinctive of the source of the products or services (ie it has come to indicate the products or services of a particular trader).	Protection is may be given to indicia which are distinctive of goods or services (ie the indicia are descriptive of the goods possessing certain recognised and general properties but not the goods of a particular trader. There must, however, be a class which is certain and associated goodwill.
The indicia will have come to signify a product or service from a particular source by reason of the particular reputation arising therefrom and associated goodwill.	The indicia will have come to signify a particular class of product or service by reason of the particular reputation arising therefrom and the associated goodwill.

USUAL FORM	CLASS TYPE ACTION
Goodwill is owned by a trader (or traders) who has (or have) used the indications in the UK.	Goodwill is owned by the group or class of traders who market this type or class of product using the class indication in the UK.
Owners of goodwill may prevent use of the name by new competitors.	Owners of goodwill may prevent use of the name in relation to goods for which it is not a proper description or designation.
Damage is typically measured by lost sales.	Damage is typically measured the reduction of the distinctiveness of a descriptive term or other indicia. The damage could be lost sales.

Defined class of goods

14.67   The mark may be descriptive of goods manufactured in a specific geographic area or otherwise descriptive of a particular type of product. The class of goods must, however, be clearly defined so that all the members of the class may be identified with reasonable precision. It is often easier to identify the members of a class defined by reference to the geographical area in which the goods are produced but the class may be defined by reference to the qualities of the product. As Lord Diplock said in *Warnink (Erven) Besloten Vennootschap v J Townend & Sons (Hull) Ltd*:[1]

> 'Of course it is necessary to be able to identify with reasonable precision the members of the class of traders of whose products a particular word or name has become so distinctive as to make their right to use it truthfully as descriptive of their product a valuable part of the goodwill of each of them; but it is the reputation that type of product itself has gained in the market by reason of its recognisable and distinctive qualities that has generated the relevant goodwill. So if one can define with reasonable precision the type of product that has acquired the reputation, one can identify the members of the class entitled to share in the goodwill as being all those traders who have supplied and still supply to the English market a product which possesses those recognisable and distinctive qualities'.

1 [1980] RPC 31 at 98, lines 15–24.

14.68   In *J Bollinger v Costa Brava Wine Co Ltd*[1] the goodwill was said to belong to a class producing goods in a certain locality. More specifically the class comprised the traders selling a wine made in the Champagne region, under the name 'champagne' by the correct process and from grapes grown there.

The class therefore consisted of all those who market in England the product genuinely indicated by a particular name. In *Warnink (erven) Besloten Vennootschap v J Townend & Sons (Hull) Ltd*[2] the members of the class were defined by reference to the ingredients irrespective of their origin. The class consisted of those who supplied and were supplying an egg and spirit drink in England in broad conformity with an identifiable recipe under the name 'Advocaat'.

1 [1960] Ch 262.

2 [1980] RPC 31.

14.69 In *Chocosuisse Union des Fabricants Suisses de Chocolat v Cadbury Ltd*[1] the class of persons entitled to use the name 'Swiss Chocolate' was in issue. Chadwick LJ said :

> 'The words "Swiss chocolate" are, as the judge pointed out, [1998] RPC 117, at page 129 line 31, descriptive in nature. They are clearly apt to describe chocolate made in Switzerland. But they are also apt to describe chocolate made to a Swiss recipe with Swiss expertise by a Swiss manufacturer. If the words are no more than descriptive – whether of the place of manufacture or of the identity of the manufacturer – they cannot found an action in passing-off. The judge identified the point, correctly in my view, in the following passage of his judgment, [1998] RPC 117, at page 129 lines 31 to 36:
>
>> 'It is only if they [the words 'Swiss chocolate'] are taken by a significant part of the public to be used in relation to and indicating a particular group of products having a discreet reputation as a group that a case of passing off can get off the ground. I have had to bear this in mind when assessing the evidence of what the words mean to members of the public. If they convey nothing more than their descriptive meaning the action must fail".'

1 (1999) Times, 15 March.

14.70 The class may be large or small but it may be harder to show that the members of a large class are clearly identifiable. In *Warnink (Erven) Besloten Vennootschap V J Townend & Sons (Hull) Ltd* Lord Diplock said:[1]

> 'The larger [the class] … is the broader must be the range and quality of products to which the descriptive term used by the members of the class has been applied, and the more difficult it must be to show that the term has acquired a public reputation and goodwill as denoting a product endowed with recognisable qualities which distinguish it from others of inferior reputation that compete with it in the same market. The larger the class the more difficult it must also be for an individual member to show that the goodwill of his own business has sustained more than minimal damage …'

1 [1980] RPC 31 at 95 lines 19–21.

Misrepresentation

14.71 The misrepresentation is not that the goods sold by the defendant are the claimant's goods but that the defendant's goods sold are falsely described by the trade name or indication to which the goodwill is attached. It is the use of the mark on products for which it is not a proper description which is objectionable. A new trader is therefore not prevented from using the mark or indication on his goods provided they are accurately described by the mark.

14.72 In *J Bollinger v Costa Brava Wine Co Ltd*[1] the defendants were the makers of a Spanish sparkling wine which they had begun to sell in England under the name 'Spanish Champagne'. The claimants were shippers of genuine champagne into England and so some of the owners of the goodwill attached to the name champagne. The misrepresentation was not that the defendant's product was the product of the claimants manufactured in France. The misrepresentation was that 'Spanish Champagne' was wine of the type that enjoyed the reputation and goodwill which attached to genuine Champagne. According to Dankwerts J in *J Bollinger*, as approved by Lord Diplock in *Warnink (Erven) Besloten Vennootschap v J Townend & Sons (Hull) Ltd*:[2]

> 'There seems to be no reason why ... licence should be given to a person, competing in trade, who seeks to attach to his product a name or description with which it has no natural association so as to make use of the reputation and goodwill which has been gained by a product genuinely indicated by the name or description.'

1 [1960] Ch 262.
2 [1980] RPC 31.

14.73   The misrepresentation is actionable if a significant section of members of the public is consequently led to believe that the defendant's products possess some attribute or attributes which they do not truly possess (see *Chocosuisse Union des Fabricants Suisses de Chocolat v Cadbury Ltd*.[1]

1 (1999) Times, 15 March.

Who may sue?

14.74   As discussed above it is necessary to define with reasonable precision the type of product that has acquired the reputation. Once this has been done, the members of the class entitled to share in that goodwill can be identified with similar precision. The class whose goodwill is protected comprises those traders (and only those traders) who have supplied and still supply in England and Wales products which possess those recognisable and distinctive qualities. The claimants must be members of that class. Although this class must be ascertainable, all the members of the class need not be joined in a passing off action.

In *J Bollinger v Costa Brava Wine Co Ltd*[1] there were 12 claimants. They were shippers of genuine champagne to England. Although there were 200 champagne houses only those who exported to England were potential claimants. Nevertheless it is plain that the claimants formed only a small part of the class of shippers who together owned the goodwill in England.

1 [1960] Ch 262.

Representative proceedings

14.75   The action is brought in a representative capacity. The procedural requirements for representative actions brought in the High Court are set out in CPR 1998, Sch 1, RSC Ord 15, r 12 The equivalent county court procedural is set out in CPR 1998, Sch 1, CCR Ord 5, r 5).

The parties bringing the proceedings and the parties on whose behalf the proceedings are brought must have the same interest in the proceedings. Consequently where goodwill is owned by the members of a trade association, the associations cannot bring an action on the behalf of its members. Such actions must be brought by one or more members of the association on the behalf of some or all of the other members of the association.

Chapter 15

Malicious falsehood, trade libel, defamation and emergency legislation

Introduction

15.1 Somewhat conveniently, the heads of malicious falsehood, trade libel and defamation fall to be considered in a trade mark context under the same broad heading which can be classed as actionable statements, negligence apart.[1] Emergency legislation is very terse in its scope and effect and we consider it in some short detail below, though our analysis will be brief.

1 About which we are not concerned.

Malicious falsehood and trade libel v defamation

15.2 We start in our analysis by looking at the law of defamation proper (ie not strictly within the context as might be required by our readers). The reason for this is because most of the development of this area of the law or this related area of law is in the field of defamation and there are sufficient parallels between defamation, malicious falsehood and trade libel[1] for an extensive analysis of the former to be undertaken, even in a text such at this. Before doing this, however, we should start by making some general statements about similarities and differences between malicious falsehood, trade libel and defamation.

1 To which we would add slander of title which warrants separate, short, consideration.

15.3 First, trade libel is about statements made about a person's trade, the goods which they sell and the services which they provide and the *effect* that those statements have upon the repute of the trader concerned.

Second, defamation is about the protection of a person's reputation, no matter how impugned (ie whether statements are made about them directly or about the things they sell or provide). In other words, a statement that 'Harry sells stolen cars' is (upon proof of certain other elements) prima facie an actionable defamatory statement because it implies that Harry is dishonest (though the statement may still be actionable even if true and if Harry had no idea what he was selling). This is the case even though the statement is directed to Harry's goods and not him – it is the same or can, in the correct circumstances, be said to be the same as saying that Harry is dishonest, which, of course, is ex facie actionable. Thus a trade libel really only means a libel (or in fact slander) made about traders such as Harry by, perhaps, a rival car dealer or by somebody else.

Third, trade libel essentially governs the position where statements are made about traders whether it sounds in defamation or in malicious falsehood – it is an imprecise label.

Fourth, malicious falsehood makes actionable statements which are false, made with malice[1] and from which, generally, but not specifically speaking, special damage flows. The distinction between malicious falsehood and defamation is that malicious falsehood seeks to protect either (i) the claimant's interest in his property (by making statements such as 'Harry sells stolen cars' and thereby impugning Harry's title to those cars) or (ii) the claimant's interest in his goodwill or trade as was explained by Mummery J (as he then was) in *CHC Software Care Ltd v Hopkins & Wood*,[2] citing with approval what Bowen LJ said in the case of *Ratcliffe v Evans*:[3]

> 'An action will lie for written or oral falsehoods, not actionable *per se* or even defamatory, where they are maliciously published, where they are calculated in the ordinary course of things to produce, and where they do produce, actual damage.
>
> ...
>
> 'Such an action is not one of libel or of slander, but an action on the case for damage wilfully and intentionally done without just occasion or excuse, analogous to an action for slander of title.'

Fifth, malicious falsehoods enjoy a six-year limitation, defamation only three.[4]

Sixth, the burden of proof is on the claimant whereas in defamation, the claimant needs to prove nothing, the presumption being in his favour. Indeed in *Derbyshire County Council v Times Newspapers Ltd* Balcombe LJ said:[5]

> 'The distinction between the torts of defamation and malicious falsehood is conveniently summarised in *Duncan and Neill on Defamation* (2nd edn, 1983) para 2.03. The essential differences are: (1) the shift in the burden of proof: in defamation the defendant has to prove that the defamatory words were true; in malicious falsehood the plaintiff must prove that the words are false; (2) in an action for malicious falsehood the plaintiff has to prove malice as part of his cause of action; this is not so in the case of defamation; (3) damage is not presumed in the case of malicious falsehood as it is in libel. However the severity of this rule is mitigated by s 3 of the Defamation Act 1952, which provides that in an action for malicious falsehood it shall not be necessary to allege or prove special damage if the words upon which the action is founded are calculated to cause pecuniary damage to the plaintiff and are published in writing or other permanent form.'

and in *Drummond-Jackson v British Medical Association* per Lord Denning MR:[6]

> 'These two actions [of libel and malicious falsehood] must be kept distinct. They have very different consequences. In *libel* the law presumes everything against the writer; the words presumed to be false and malicious; and it is for the writer to prove, if he can, that the words were true and the comment was fair, or otherwise make good his defence. But in *malicious falsehood* the boot is on the other foot. The writer is presumed to be acting honestly and without malice; and it is for the plaintiff to prove, if he can, that the words were written by the defendant falsely and maliciously and were calculated to damage the plaintiff in his calling; see s 3(1) of the Defamation Act 1952.'

Finally, the difference between defamation and malicious falsehood was summarised by Sir Donald Nicholls V-C in *Joyce v Sengupta*:[7]

'... I should comment briefly on the difference between defamation and malicious falsehood. The remedy provided by the law for words which injure a person's reputation is defamation. Words may also injure a person without damaging his reputation. An example would be a claim that the seller of goods or land is not the true owner. Another example would be a false assertion that a person has closed down his business. Such claims would not necessarily damage the reputation of those concerned. The remedy provided for this is malicious falsehood, sometimes called injurious falsehood or trade libel. This cause of action embraces particular types of malicious falsehood such as slander of title and slander of goods, but it is not confined to those headings.'[8]

However there is much in common.

1 Which has a special meaning as we shall see.
2 [1993] FSR 241, 247.
3 [1892] 2 QB 524, 527.
4 Limitation Act 1980, ss 2 and 4A.
5 [1992] 3 All ER 65, 81, 82 CA.
6 [1970] 1 All ER 1094, 1099.
7 [1993] 1 WLR 337, 341.
8 To which one could add, perhaps an eighth difference which is that assistance under the Legal Aid Act 1988 is available for cases relating to malicious falsehood whereas it is not available for taking of defending defamation proceedings unless it is to defend a counterclaim.

15.4   Defamation is not a tort as such but is rather the generic term used to describe two closely related torts, that of slander (the spoken word) and that of libel (the written words, or permanent form). Defamation is a common law tort which is supplemented, extended (or limited) and regulated by statute. The distinction is blurred since, for instance, it is statute law that a broadcast is to be treated as a libel despite there being no permanent form as such.[1] However the distinction between libel and slander is also one of effective actionability since slander is only actionable upon proof of special damage,[2] though even then certain forms of slanderous statement are actionable without proof of special damage if made about a person's calling or profession.[3]

1 Broadcasting Act 1990, s 166, though this was culled from the pre-existing common law on the subject. The initial illogicality of the distinction may, perhaps, be explained on the basis that it is one thing to whisper something to somebody in a pub but quite another to shout it from the rooftops.
2 And the rationale for this is perhaps that people forget what they have heard but can re-read that which they have read.
3 Defamation Act 1952, s 2.

15.5   Libel and slander protect the interests that a person has in relation to the views of others, ie reputation but it does not cover insults (an affront to dignity), trading rights or invasions into privacy (the right to deal with personal matters personally). However, one instantly sees that two conflicting and important constitutional doctrines or principles come into play, that of protection of reputation from unwarranted or unjustified attack and that of freedom of speech.[1] It is to be noted that this latter right is now to be enshrined in our national law as the Human Rights Act 1998 and so it might have more significance, though it is too early to say at present. In a trade mark context the relevance lies in the fact that rival traders sometimes want to say rude, uncomplimentary or denigratory things about their competitors. Sometimes people take these things seriously.

1 See *Bestobel Paints Ltd v Bigg* [1975] FSR 421 and *Macmillan Magazines Ltd v RCN Publishing Co Ltd* [1998] FSR 9.

15.6 The requirements for defamation are that (i) the statement must be defamatory; (ii) the statement must refer to the claimant; (iii) the statement must be published; and (iv) in cases of slander the claimant must show special damage. To which there are essentially four defences[1] being (i) that there was an unintentional, innocent defamation;[2] (ii) the defendant was telling the truth;[3] (iii) the publication was fair comment on a matter of public interest and (iv) privilege of which there are two varieties being (a) absolute, where anything can be said, ie in judicial proceedings and, to a certain extent parliament and (b) qualified, provided that the defendant is innocent of any malice and the communication is made between persons having a duty to give and receive such communications, pursuant to a legal or moral duty to do so or in reply to a public attack and fair and accurate reporting of what has been said by others.

1 Though Halsbury's Laws of England (4th Ed – Reissue, volume 28) in fact sets out 16 defences, many of which are procedural, see para 21.
2 Defamation Act 1952, s 4.
3 Often called justification.

15.7 How then does one determine the defamatory nature of a statement? Simply stated (though almost impossible to apply in practice) when a statement is defamatory it has the tendency to injure the reputation of the person to whom it is referred.[1] This is admittedly a loose definition and there have been attempts to refine it. In *Parminter v Coupland*[2] Park B said there was a defamation to cause an injury to reputation if it exposed the victim to hatred, contempt and ridicule – this is called the positive identification test. In *Sim v Stretch*[3] Park's B definition was extended or explained as being the loss of esteem of right-thinking members of society. This wider test is still not complete. What of the situation where somebody is labelled insane of that he has a contagious disease but this does not cause the lessening of esteem? If somebody is labelled a homosexual, what then? In *R v Bishop*[4] the trial judge said that it was a defamation to call somebody a homosexual in this day and age.[5]

In the land mark case of *Youssoupoff v Metro-Goldwyn-Mayer Pictures Ltd*[6] – a film intimated that a young Russian princess had involuntarily had a sexual encounter with a confidente of the monarch queen who was seen as a person who pursued his own ruthless agenda, exerting a profound influence over the queen. The claim by the princess (who was depicted in the film but whose identity was disguised) managed to claim damages for libel, despite the oblique reference.

1 Though this is subject to the defences.
2 (1840) 6 M & W 105.
3 [1936] 2 All ER 1237.
4 [1975] QB 274.
5 Though 'this day and age' was in fact that day and age (being 1974) and it is doubted whether to call a heterosexual a homosexual now would be treated in the same way. However this is a debate we cannot engage in since we are not qualified to do so and we perceive that the arguments are potentially fierce. We do not cite this authority for the purposes of engaging in such a debate but in order to show that much depends upon current thinking.
6 (1934) 50 TLR 581.

15.8 One question or series of questions which may be asked is whether the test is objective or subjective (in the eyes of the claimant). This matters where society is not homogenous, ie in the proper context of this chapter, where a trade is divided. To call somebody a communist[1] may be complimentary or derogatory depending upon the society. This was highlighted in the case of *Byrne v Deane*[2] where the claimant sued the committee of a golf club after a notice had been placed on the club notice board saying that the claimant had reported the club to the police because there was an illegal gaming machine on the golf club's premises, which was true – the implication was that the claimant was not fit to be a member of the club. The court at first instance allowed the claimant's claim but this was reversed by the Court of Appeal, where it was said that society should applaud the reporting of crime or wrongdoing to the police.

1 Or for that matter a homosexual.
2 [1937] 1 KB 818.

15.9 What if nobody believes what is said and that the claimant is not directly identified? In *Morgan v Odhams Press Ltd*[1] Lord Reid held that in such circumstances there was still a defamation. In *Hough v London Express Newspaper Ltd*[2] a newspaper interviewed the wife of a famous sportsman. It turned out that the wife who was interviewed was in fact another woman who the boxer was living with. The real wife sued as she claimed that she had lost reputation with her neighbours since they might have thought that whatever the impropriety of her husband's behaviour she was unmarried (which she was not). The neighbours were brought in to testify – they did so but said they did not believe a word of what was published. It was held that the claimant was still defamed. It is submitted that what matters is whether the statement is expressed in a way which people would take seriously and whether something points to the claimant. This first point is the rationale behind not allowing insults to be actionable as in *Parkins v Scott*,[3] ie abuse is not the same as defamation.

1 [1971] 1 WLR 1239.
2 [1940] 2 KB 507.
3 [1862] 1 H & C 153.

15.10 A defamatory statement does not have to be written or spoken it may be a picture or a statue as in *Monson v Tussauds Ltd*.[1]

1 [1894] 1 QB 671.

15.11 The face value of the defamation must be examined. There may also, however, be defamation by implication as in a second meaning. Words may carry this meaning in one of three ways:

(1) There is an unusual second meaning for the words, ie 'you are a pansy.'
(2) Reading between the lines – there is an actionable defamation when pieces of text taken on their own are harmless in themselves but become defamatory when taken as a whole. In *Loughans v Odhams Press Ltd*,[1] a barrister in his memoirs intimated that the only reason why the claimant had been acquitted in a criminal trial which the barrister was involved in was because certain evidence was mistakenly not admitted at trial – this was taken as intimating that the claimant was a criminal notwithstanding his acquittal.
(3) The statement along with an extrinsic fact or statement makes the statement defamatory. Ie showing a picture of a woman which is a mock up of her being pregnant and the woman is not pregnant and is unmarried. In *Cassidy v Daily Mirror Newspapers Ltd*[2] the defendant published a photograph of a man and a woman suggesting that the woman (the claimant) was his purported fiancée. The man was in fact married to the claimant. The photograph therefore suggested that the claimant and the man were living out of wedlock.

This last class of statement is termed a true or legal innuendo and the first two classes are termed false or popular innuendos. The distinction is used from the point of view of pleadings but each founds a cause of action.

1 [1963] 1 QB 299.
2 [1929] 2 KB 331.

15.12   Statements published about a group is one principal area where traders are likely to be less prone to attack. Statements like 'you've seen the rest now try the best, X is the only product which is safe' – implying that other traders are not safe. As a general allegation it might be regarded by the pubic as merely being puff. However if there is only one other person in the relevant market then an action may lie.

However, much depends upon the size and characteristics of the group. If, for instance, it is a very small group then a cause of action may accrue as in *Browne v Thompson*,[1] where some Scottish clergymen were accused of being oppressive and there were only seven possible clergymen in the group and they successfully brought an action. It is necessary to show that the claimant was aimed at personally – if the group is small enough then there will be liability.

The group may be too large as in *Knupffer v London Express Newspaper Ltd*.[2] A paper published an article that a certain group (numbering 2000 worldwide) were political extremists. The UK section were 24 in number and the UK leader sued. The House of Lords held that there was no liability for the group as it was too large to enable a person to pick out an individual. The House of Lords attempted to lay down a test:

    i) were the words capable of referring to the claimant? and
    ii) did reasonable people who knew the claimant reasonably believe the words to refer to him?

Accordingly, it is necessary to see the nature of the defamation, charge, size of class, generality of accusation and the extravagance of the claim before deciding whether a class statement is actionable. Statements made about a class as a whole, identify each member of that class and so, potentially at least, gives each member of that class a several cause of action.

1 1912 SC 359.
2 [1944] AC 116.

15.13   A corporation is a legal entity and it is discrete from it members and can be defamed as it has its own personality. In *Bognor Regis Urban District Council v Campion*,[1] it was suggested by Browne J that it is not really in the nature of corporations to sue in these matters but that they could do so. The law has now changed direction since it is a matter of public policy that elected governmental bodies should be open to uninhibited public criticism (of the highest public importance) and to give lie to defamation actions at the suit of governmental bodies would inhibit such criticism, see *Derbyshire County Council v Times Newspapers Ltd*.[2]

1 [1972] 2 QB 169.
2 [1993] 2 WLR 449 HL.

15.14   Hence there are many different ways in which a claimant may be defamed such as:

    i) expressly – 'Joe Bloggs is a thief.'

ii) impliedly – 'Joe Bloggs is not known for his honesty.'
iii) *Browne v Thompson*[1] where a small group is defamed of which the claimant is a part.

It does not matter, therefore, that the defendant intended to refer to the claimant since it is the claimant's relationship with the public that matters. This led to the reasoning in the case of *E Hulton & Co v Jones*[2] where it was made clear that there was no need to show the defendant's intention. The facts of this case are illuminating and are as follows: the defendant's newspaper published a totally fictitious story about a man called A Jones and it portrayed him as an adulterer. An A Jones, unrelated to the story, came out of the woodwork and sued. The defendant claimed that there was no intention to defame such a person – this was rejected. This led to the Defamation Act 1952 where innocence furnished a defence provided that it is coupled with an offer of amends (ie a right to publish a correction) and an apology. However, the publisher must have exercised reasonable care in relation to the publ cation.

1 See para **15.12**, n 1.
2 [1910] AC 534.

Malicious falsehood on its own

15.15   As we have said above[1] the claimant must establish (1) that the defendant has published words about him which were false, (2) that they were published maliciously and (3) that the result of the publication has been to cause special damage. Special damage is either actual financial loss (lost sales which are causally attributable to the statement)[2] or that the words in question are calculated to cause financial loss (see s 3(1) of the Defamation Act 1952).

Indeed as Glidewell LJ said in *Kaye v Robertson* :[3]

'The essentials of [the tort of malicious falsehood] are that the defendant has published about the ... [claimant] words which are false, that they were published maliciously, and that special damage has followed as the direct and natural result of their publication. As to special damage, the effect of section 3(1) of the Defamation Act 1952 is that it is sufficient if the words published in writing are calculated to cause pecuniary damage to the ... [claimant]. Malice will be inferred if it is proved that the words were calculated to produce damage and that the defendant knew when he published the words that they were false or was reckless as to whether they were false or not.'

1 See para **15.6**.
2 As Lord Reid said in *Bonnington Castings Ltd v Wardlaw* [1956] AC 613:
  'the ... [claimant] must prove ... that such fault caused or materially contributed to [the claimant's] injury,'
See also *Galoo Ltd v Bright Grahame Murray* [1994] 1 WLR 1360.
3 [1991] FSR 62, 67.

15.16   There is much reported authority upon what is meant by 'malice'. The most recent is *Spring v Guardian Assurance plc*,[1] which was a case where the claimant was given a reference in such terms[2] that he could not obtain employment elsewhere.

The claimant said (or claimed) that the reference had been prepared maliciously. Glidewell LJ held in the Court of Appeal (at 288$_f$) that malice in the tort of malicious falsehood is the same as in relation to defamation. In other words it must be the same sort as will defeat a defence of qualified privilige. Glidewell LJ referred to the speech of Lord Diplock in *Horrocks v Lowe*:[3]

'... what is required on the part of the defamer to entitle him to the protection of the privilege is positive belief in the truth of what he published or, as it is generally though tautologously termed, "honest belief." If he publishes untrue defamatory matter recklessly, without considering or caring whether it be true or not, he is in this, as in other breaches of the law, treated as if he knew it to be false. But indifference to the truth of what he publishes is not to be equated with carelessness, impulsiveness or irrationality in arriving at a positive belief that it is true. The freedom of speech protected by the law of qualified privilege may be availed of by all sorts and conditions of men. In affording to them immunity from suit if they have acted in good faith in compliance with a legal or moral duty or in protection of a legitimate interest the law must take them as it finds them. In ordinary life it is rare indeed for people to form their beliefs by a process of logical deduction from facts ascertained by rigorous search for all available evidence and a judicious assessment of its probative value. In greater or in less degree according to their temperaments, their training, their intelligence, they are swayed by prejudice, rely of intuition instead of reasoning, leap to conclusions on inadequate evidence and fail to recognise the cogency of material which might cast doubt on the validity of the conclusions they reach. But despite the imperfection of the mental process by which the belief is arrived at it may still be "honest," that is, a positive belief that the conclusions they have reached are true. The law demands no more.

'Even a positive belief in the truth of what is published on a privileged occasion – which is presumed unless the contrary is proved – may not be sufficient to negate express malice if it can be proved that the defendant misused the occasion for some purpose other than that for which the privilege is accorded by the law. The commonest case is where the dominant motive which actuates the defendant is not a desire to perform the relevant duty or to protect the relevant interest, but to give vent to his personal spite or ill will towards the person he defames. If this is proved, then even positive belief in the truth of what is published will not enable the defamer to avail himself of the protection of the privilege to which he would otherwise have been entitled. There may be instances of improper motives which destroy the privilege apart from personal spite. A defendant's dominant motive may have been to obtain some private advantage unconnected with the duty or the interest which constitutes the reason for the privilege. If so, he loses the benefit of the privilege despite his positive belief that what he said or wrote was true.

'Judges and juries should, however, be very slow to draw the inference that a defendant was so far actuated by improper motives as to deprive him of the protection of the privilege unless they are satisfied that he did not believe that what he said or wrote was true or that he was indifferent to its truth or falsity. The motives with which human beings act are mixed. They find it difficult to hate the sin but love the sinner. Qualified privilege would be illusory, and the public interest that it is meant to serve defeated, if the protection which it affords were lost merely because a person, although acting in compliance with a duty or in protection of a legitimate interest, disliked the person whom he defamed or was indignant at what he believed to be that person's conduct and welcomed the opportunity of exposing it. It is only where his desire to comply with the relevant duty or to protect the relevant interest plays no significant part in his motives for publishing what he believes to be true that "express malice" can properly be found.'

Accordingly, to prove malice it must be shown that the defendant either (1) did not believe what was said or (2) did not care.

1 [1993] 2 All ER 273.
2 Some of which were untrue.
3 [1975] AC 135 at 150.

Malicious falsehood in a trade mark context

15.17   A number of cases have been decided where complaint has been made about comparative advertising (something made possible by the operation of s 10(6) of the TMA 1994) and the dicta on this subject has been useful, see especially, the case of *Vodafone Group plc v Orange Personal Communication Services Ltd*[1] where Jacob . raised two points of interest, the first is the 'one meaning rule' which is that best explained by Jacob J (at 37) where he said that such a meaning:

'is not one of construction in the legal sense. The ordinary man does not live in an ivory tower and he is not inhibited by the rules of construction. So he can-and does read between the lines in the light of his general knowledge and experience of worldly affairs … What the ordinary man would infer without special knowledge has generally been called the natural and ordinary meaning of the words. But that expression is rather misleading in that it conceals the fact that there are two elements in it. Sometimes it is not necessary to go beyond the words themselves, as where the [claimant] has been called a thief or a murderer. But more often the sting is not so much in the words themselves as in what the ordinary man will infer from them, and that is also regarded as part of their natural and ordinary meaning', *per* Lord Reid in *Lewis v The Daily Telegraph*[2]

Jacob J went on to say:

'That case was one of libel but the principle must be the same for malicious falsehood: for the question both in libel and malicious falsehood is, "what is the meaning to the ordinary man?"'

'The legal construct of the ordinary man … may in reality take a given set of words in different ways. Different people may react in different ways to a statement – and in particular may draw different "stings" from it. But it is settled, as was accepted by both sides, that I must look for the single natural and ordinary meaning. In *Charleston v News Group Newspapers Ltd*[3] [1995] 2 All ER 313 Lord Bridge (with whom the other members of the House agreed) referred at 317 to "two principles which are basic to the law of libel":

"The first is that, where no legal innuendo is alleged to arise from extrinsic circumstances known to some readers, the "natural and ordinary meaning" to be ascribed to the words of an allegedly defamatory publication is the meaning, including any inferential meaning, which the words would convey to the mind of the ordinary, reasonable, fair-minded reader. This proposition is too well established to require citation of authority. The second principle, which is perhaps a corollary of the first, is that, although a combination of words may in fact convey different meanings to the minds of different readers, the jury in a libel action, applying the criterion which the first principle dictates, is required to determine the single meaning which the publication conveyed to the notional reasonable reader and to base its verdict and any award of damages on the assumption that this was the one sense in which all readers would have understood it. The origins and the implications of this second principle are the subject of a characteristically penetrating analysis in the judgment of Diplock LJ in *Slim v Daily Telegraph Ltd*[4] [1968] 1 All ER 497 at 504–506, [1968]2 QB 157 at 171–174, from which it will, 1 think, be sufficient to cite the following passages:

'Everyone outside a court of law recognises that words are imprecise instruments for communicating the thoughts of one man to another. The same words may be understood by one man in a different meaning from that in which they are understood by another and both meanings may be different from that which the author of the words intended to convey; but the notion that the same words should bear different meanings to different men, and that more than one meaning should be "right", conflicts with the whole training of a lawyer. Words are the tools of his trade. He uses them to define legal rights and duties. They do not achieve that purpose unless there can be attributed to them a single meaning as the 'right' meaning. And so the argument between lawyers as to the meaning of words starts with the unexpressed major premise that any particular combination of words has one meaning, which is not necessarily the same as that intended by him who published them or understood by any of those who read them, but is capable of ascertainment as being the 'right' meaning by the adjudicator to whom the law confides the responsibility of determining it ... Where, as in the present case, words are published to the millions of readers of a popular newspaper, the chances are that if the words are reasonably capable of being understood as bearing more than one meaning, some readers will have understood them as bearing one of those meanings and some will have understood them as bearing others of those meanings. But none of this matters. What does matter is what the adjudicator at the trial thinks is the one and only meaning that the readers as reasonable men should have collectively understood the words to bear. That is 'the natural and ordinary meaning' of words in an action for libel ... Juries, in theory, must be unanimous on every issue on which they have to adjudicate; and, since the damages that they award must depend on the defamatory meaning that they attribute to the words, they must all agree on a single meaning as being the "right" meaning. So the unexpressed major premise that any particular combination of words can bear but a single "natural and ordinary meaning" which is "right", survived the transfer from judge to jury of the function of adjudicating on the meaning of words in civil actions for libel.'

'...

'The reason for the libel rule in part relates to the entitlement of jury trial for libel (as Diplock LJ explained in *Slim*[5]). Save in exceptional circumstances the right to jury trial remains for libel and slander (see section 69(1) of the Supreme Court Act 1981) but there is no such right in relation to malicious falsehood. So it by no means follows that that historical reason for the rule in libel should apply to malicious falsehood. Another reason for the rule relates to the function of a Jury in awarding damages for defamation: unless one has settled on a particular meaning one cannot judge the extent of the defamation. But in malicious falsehood damages are rather different: they are essentially compensatory for pecuniary loss as for most other torts. So again it does not seem necessarily to follow that the libel rule should apply to the tort. However, as I say, the parties were agreed that I should proceed on the basis that I am a notional jury identifying the single meaning of the words complained of. That is what I will do, and, as will be seen, in this case the point is academic.'

The one meaning rule is therefore the meaning which the jury must find the statement complained of to mean. That meaning has already been decided upon by the judge even before the jury get to decide upon it and their task is to look at the statement complained of and to see whether it has the judicially-stated meaning. If it does then the statement will be actionable depending upon whether the statement has to fall within or without the meaning to be actionable, ie if it has the one meaning then it is true and thus not actionable and if it does not then it is false and is actionable.

1 [1997] FSR 34.
2 sub nom *Rubber Improvement Ltd v Daily Telegraph Ltd [1964] AC 234, 258.*
3 [1995] 2 All ER 313.
4 [1968] 1 All ER 497 at 504–506, [1968] 2 QB 157 at 171–174.
5 See n 4 above.

15.18 The second point Jacob J made was that one must look at the facts to ensure that the statements were being taken seriously. Jacob J continued:

> 'But I must add a general comment. This is a case about advertising. The public are used to the ways of advertisers and expect a certain amount of hyperbole. In particular the public are used to advertisers claiming the good points of a product and ignoring others, advertisements claiming that you can "save £££££ ..." are common, carrying with them the notion that "savings" are related to amount of spend, and the public are reasonably used to comparisons- "knocking copy" as it is called in the advertising world. This is important in considering what the ordinary meaning may be. The test is whether a reasonable man would take the claim being made as one made seriously, *De Beers Abrasive Products Ltd v International General Electric Co of New York Ltd*:[1] the more precise the claim the more it is likely to be so taken-the more general or, fuzzy the less so.'

We cannot better Jacob J's exposition of the law in this area and indeed was echoed in the case of *Skuse v Granada Television Ltd*,[2] which was a libel case.

1 [1975] 1 WLR 972.
2 [1996] EMLR 278.

Slander of title

15.19 Put shortly, no person may maliciously impugn the title to goods or property of another without justification.

Emergency legislation

15.20 In certain circumstances it may be necessary, during times of emergency, for the Crown to take over intellectual property rights for the purposes of dealing with that emergency though it is difficult to see how the use of trade marks would assist in the fighting of, say, a war. However, the stance which the government took in the last war was that it enacted specific emergency legislation:[1] which it then repealed and it is expected that this is what would happen in the event of any subsequent war.

Trading with the enemy is another branch of emergency law which remains in force today. It is both a common law and statutory offence to trade with the enemy. The statute form of the offence derives from the Trading With the Enemy Act 1939 and (now) the Emergency Laws (Miscellaneous Provisions) Act 1953.

The main impact as far as the Trading With the Enemy Act 1939 is concerned is in dealing with enemy property which becomes the property of a custodian appointed for that purpose.

Specifically however, trade marks are dealt with in accordance with the provisions of the Patents, Designs, Copyright and Trade Marks (Emergency) Act 1939 where a person may use a trade mark owned by an enemy with the consent of the Comptroller-General (s 3 of the Patents, Designs, Copyright and Trade Marks (Emergency) Act 1939) though it must be shown that it is difficult to refer to the goods without using the trade mark in question. The Comptroller-General's order has the effect of suspending the rights given by the registered trade mark so that the national can use the trade mark with impunity.

Trade marks may be granted to enemies but the property in the trade mark passes to the custodian of enemy property.

1 Such as the Emergency Powers (Defence) Acts 1939–1945 (repealed). The Emergency Powers (Defence) Act 1940, s 1 empowered the making of regulations for 'requiring persons to place themselves, their services and their property at the disposal of His Majesty'. Provision was made for compensation of such persons, though most of the regulations and enactments have been repealed.

15.21 As regards time limits for doing acts under the TMA 1994, s 6 of the Patents, Designs, Copyright and Trade Marks (Emergency) Act 1939 allows the Comptroller-General to extend prescribed times.

Part IV

Civil proceedings

Chapter 16

Domestic procedure

Introduction

16.1 There are two places where disputes relating to trade marks are heard: the trade marks registry (so called) and the High Court. When reference is made in this part to proceedings relating to trade marks it is intended to mean proceedings relating to trade marks registered or seeking to be registered under the TMA 1994. The community position will be considered further below in a separate section as will the position pertaining to the now relatively small number of proceedings taking place under the TMA 1938. There is also an elaborate domestic appeal procedure as well as the possibility of making a reference to the ECJ under art 234[1] of the Treaty of Rome. As we have dealt with criminal and condemnation procedure extensively elsewhere, we confine our comments to civil proceedings proper.

1 Formerly art 177.

Prosecution

16.2 The process of prosecution is the process where a person applies for and seeks to obtain registration for a trade mark. The only place this can happen is in the trade marks registry which has exclusive original jurisdiction in relation to the prosecution of application for registration of UK trade marks.

16.3 The term 'registry', though used extensively in practice, does not in fact exist in strict legal terms. It is understood to mean that part of the office of the Patent Office which deals with the prosecution of applications for trade marks, one outcome of which is registration – it is the place you go to in order to get a trade mark registered (if possible). The registrar of trade marks is defined by s 62 of the TMA 1994 as being the Comptroller-General of patents, designs and trade marks. It is apparent from the TMA 1994 taken as a whole that the registrar has many functions to perform, such as the scrutinising of applications for trade marks and the hearing of oral representations and the consideration of written representations. To require the registrar individually to perform each and every function in the TMA 1994 is clearly onerous, burdensome, impossible and not envisaged by Parliament. Accordingly (as would be expected) there is an express power to delegate such functions which the registrar would otherwise have to perform himself.[1] We pause to note, with a sigh of relief, that this has been done, since the law relating to whether the registrar is entitled to delegate his functions (or, for that matter any person entrusted with such functions) was in considerable disarray. Luckily, the TMA 1994 makes clear reference to the permissibility and existence of delegates in s 74(3).[2] However we shall continue to refer to the 'registrar' which should be taken to mean him or his duly authorised officers.

1 In fact at the time of writing the registrar is a female and we hope that readers will understand such gender specific references to be personal references as opposed to identificatory ones and done for matters of convenience only. References to 'him' or 'he' should not mean that the person being referred to is male or individual any more than they may be female or corporate.
2 'Anything which the registrar is or may be authorised or required to do under this section may be done on his behalf by a duly authorised officer.'

The application procedure

16.4   Broadly speaking, the application is made by a person wishing to protect the trade mark.[1] The application is made in a prescribed form, in accordance with the relevant forms as are determined by the registry and must be accompanied by the relevant fee. Upon the application being sent to the registrar, the applicant will be notified of receipt of the application and thereafter it will be examined for registrability. There are essentially three aspects of registrability: formal, absolute and relative. Those three aspects of registrability are intended to ensure that the application is in the correct *form* and that it satisfies the requirements of ss 3 and 5 of the TMA 1994.[2] If the registrar is satisfied, he will notify the applicant accordingly and will advertise the application in the normal way, ie he will ensure it is published in the Trade Marks Journal which is open to public inspection.[3]

1 See generally ch 8.
2 Discussed in detail in chs 5 and 6.
3 See http://www.patent.gov.uk

16.5   The manner of application is governed by s 32 of the TMA 1994 which requires an application for registration be made to the registrar[1] and that certain particulars be included such as a request for registration of a trade mark,[2] the name and address of the applicant,[3] a statement of the goods or services in relation to which it is sought to register the trade mark[4] and a representation of the trade mark.[5] Further, it is necessary to state that the trade mark is being used by the applicant or with his consent, in relation to those goods or services, or that he has a bôna fide intention that it should be so used.[6] This requirement is presumably put in so as to deal with the problem which arose in relation to disputes under s 17 of the TMA 1938[7] where it was (and probably still is) unclear as to whether a person could merely apply for a trade mark without more. It is understood that in at least other European countries it is no objection to an entitlement to apply that the applicant has no intention to use the trade mark in question, the proper remedy being revocation after five years non-use. Further, r 5 of the Trade Mark Rules 1994[8] provides that an application shall be filed on Form TM3 and shall be subject to the payment of the application fee and class fees as may be appropriate. If the application is for a three-dimensional mark then it is necessary to make a statement to that effect, similarly with colour.[9]

1 TMA 1994, s 43(1).
2 TMA 1994, s 32(2)(a).
3 TMA 1994, s 32(2)(b).
4 TMA 1994, s 32(2)(c).
5 TMA 1994, s 32(2)(d).
6 TMA 1994, s 33(3).
7 See *Al Bassam Trade Mark* [1995] RPC 511 CA.
8 SI 1998/2583.
9 See ch 4, para **4.6**.

16.6 In many cases the date of registration is or can be an important and critical date for the purposes of assessing whether upon relative grounds there is an earlier mark on the register or there is an earlier right in existence. For that reason there is a limited procedure in place where priority can be obtained from earlier applications made in other countries,[1] that is an earlier date (up to a maximum of six months)[2] than the date of application which can be used as the date of assessment. The priority date is the date upon which the convention application has been made. In addition, priority may be obtained from applications made in countries specified in any Order in Council made by Her Majesty. This power is conferred by s 36(1) and (2) of the TMA 1994 and is fairly wide in its ambit.[3] In either case if priority is claimed then it must be expressly claimed[4] and the priority application must be proved.

1 Being countries defined by the TMA 1994, s 55(1)(a), which are signatories to the Paris Convention for the Protection of Industrial Property of the 20 March 1883. At the time of writing those countries are: Albania, Argentina, Armenia, Australia, Austria, Azerbaijan, Bahamas, Bahrain, Bangladesh, Barbados, Belarus, Belgium, Benin, Bolivia, Bosnia and Herzegovina, Botswana, Brazil, Bulgaria, Burkina Faso, Burundi, Cambodia, Cameroon, Canada, Central African Republic, Chad, Chile, China, Colombia, Congo, Costa Rica, Côte d'Ivoire, Croatia, Cuba, Cyprus, Czech Republic, Democratic People's Republic of Korea, Democratic Republic of the Congo, Denmark, Dominica, Dominican Republic, Ecuador, Egypt, El Salvador, Equatorial Guinea, Estonia, Finland, France, Gabon, Gambia, Georgia, Germany, Ghana, Greece, Grenada, Guatemala, Guinea, Guinea-Bissau, Guyana, Haiti, Holy See, Honduras, Hungary, Iceland, India, Indonesia, Iran (Islamic Republic of), Iraq, Ireland, Israel, Italy, Japan, Jordan, Kazakhstan, Kenya, Kyrgyzstan, Lao People's Democratic Republic, Latvia, Lebanon, Lesotho, Liberia, Libyan Arab Jamahiriya, Liechtenstein, Lithuania, Luxembourg, Madagascar, Malawi, Malaysia, Mali, Malta, Mauritania, Mauritius, Mexico, Monaco, Mongolia, Morocco, Mozambique, Netherlands, New Zealand, Nicaragua, Niger, Nigeria, Norway, Oman, Panama, Papua New Guinea, Paraguay, Peru, Philippines, Poland, Portugal, Republic of Korea, Republic of Moldova, Romania, Russian Federation, Rwanda, Saint Kitts and Nevis, Saint Lucia, Saint Vincent and the Grenadines, San Marino, Sao Tome and Principe, Senegal, Sierra Leone, Singapore, Slovakia, Slovenia, South Africa, Spain, Sri Lanka, Sudan, Suriname, Swaziland, Sweden, Switzerland, Syrian Arab Republic, Tajikistan, The former Yugoslav Republic of Macedonia, Togo, Trinidad and Tobago, Tunisia, Turkey, Turkmenistan, Uganda, Ukraine, United Arab Emirates, UK, United Republic of Tanzania, United States of America, Uruguay, Uzbekistan, Venezuela, Viet Nam, Yugoslavia, Zambia and Zimbabwe. The up-to-date position may be obtained from the website of the World Intellectual Property Organisation at http://www.wipo.org/eng/main.htm
2 TMA 1994, s 35(1).
3 Which extends the right to priority to applications made in Antigua and Barbuda, Bahrain, Belize, Bolivia, Botswana, Brunei, Darussalam , Colombia, Djibouti, Dominica, Ecuador, Guatemala, Hong Kong, India, Jamaica, Kuwait, Macau, Maldives, Mozambique, Myanmar, Namibia, Nicaragua, Pakistan, Sierra Leone and Thailand, in accordance with art 3 of the Trade Marks (Claims to Priority From Relevant Countries) Order 1994 (SI 1994/2803) as amended by the Trade Marks (Claims to Priority from Relevant Countries) (Amendment) Order 1995 (SI 1995/2997) which gives six months' grace.
4 Trade Marks Rules 1994 (SI 1998/2583) rr 6(1) and 6(2) provides that a formal certificate must be filed within three months of the application being made.

Examination

16.7 Once an application is made under s 32 of the TMA 1994 then under s 37 of the Act the registrar is bound to examine it for all forms of validity,[1] carrying out such searches as may be necessary, presumably for the purposes of establishing whether the rules relating to relative validity have been satisfied.[2]

1 TMA 1994, s 37(1).
2 TMA 1994, s 37(2).

What if the registrar objects?

16.8   Objections are dealt with by the registrar in two ways, either in correspondence or by way of a hearing.[1] Objections have to be notified to the applicant.[2] Obviously such hearings will be as between the registrar and the applicant. Usually the registrar will make his position clear in correspondence in the first instance and will then continue the correspondence until the matter is resolved or if it is not resolved and neither party is prepared to change their respective positions then the applicant can appeal. The registrar is bound to accede to an application that there be an oral hearing[3] before he makes a decision adverse to the applicant. The registrar will inevitably impose a time limit for representations and if the registrar is not satisfied or fails to respond before the end of the specified period, the application is refused.[4] Accordingly, the situation may arise where the applicant ends up with a decision of the registrar with which he is dissatisfied and which he wishes to appeal against. We examine the appeal process below.

1 Though in all cases where an adverse decision is to be made the party against whom the decision is to be made must be given the opportunity to be heard, which we submit it a rule of natural justice which cannot be breached but, nevertheless it is enshrined in the Trade Marks Rules 1994, r 48 (1), r 48(2) of which requires 14 days notice to be given of such a hearing unless consent is given to a shorter period.
2 TMA 1994, s 37(3).
3 Trade Marks Rules 1994 (SI 1998/2583), r 48(1) .
4 TMA 1994, s 37(4).

What if the registrar does not object?

16.9   If the registrar does not object, then he accepts the application and it must be published (unless withdrawn).[1] After publication there is then a period of three months[2] during which any person may object.[3] Opposition may be entered by the opponent in one of two ways as discussed below.

1 TMA 1994, s 38(1) and the Trade Marks Rules 1994, r 12.
2 TMA 1994, s 38(2) and the Trade Marks Rules 1994, r 13(1), which prescribes the three month period.
3 The manner of publication has been discussed above.

Formal opposition

16.10   In most (but by no means all) cases the opponent will be a competitor of the applicant and he will enter a formal opposition. This is done by way of notice of opposition[1] which must include grounds of opposition and this is sent by the registrar to the applicant who then has three months in which to put in his counter-notice,[2] failing which his application is deemed to be withdrawn.[3] Then comes the evidence stage and the opponent has three months in which to file his evidence in support of his opposition[4] failing which his opposition is deemed to be withdrawn unless the registrar otherwise directs.[5] Thereafter three months are available apiece for evidence in answer and reply (though not compulsory).

1 Trade Marks Rules 1994, r 13(1).
2 Trade Marks Rules 1994, r 13(2).
3 Trade Marks Rules 1994, r 13(3).
4 Trade Marks Rules 1994, r 13(4). However there will inevitably be cases where evidence is not required and in such cases the opponent will need to get a direction from the registrar to that effect.
5 Trade Marks Rules 1994, r 13(5).

Section 8 of the TMA 1994

16.11 It is at this point we pause to discuss the procedural effects of s 8 of the TMA 1994,[1] despite it being not yet applicable and pending on the operation of art 1 of Decision No CA-95–19 of the Administrative Board of the Office for the Harmonisation in the Internal Market (Trade Marks and Designs) of 11 July 1995[2] concerning the date from which applications may be filed at the office. This speci-fies that application for a CTM may be made on or after 1 April 1996 meaning that an order under s 8 of the TMA 1994 cannot be in force until 1 April 2006.[3] There does not seem to be any logic to this save that the effect of s 8 of the TMA 1994 coming into force is to make the exercise of assessing relative validity unnecessary unless the question is raised in opposition proceedings.[4] Section 8(3) of the TMA 1994 provides that such commencement order may also make provision that the requirement to conduct relative searches (as is currently required by s 37 of the TMA 1994) may be modified or indeed extinguished.

1 See also ch 6, para **6.2**.
2 OJ (OHIM) 1/95 p13.
3 See TMA 1994.
4 This despite the fact there is nothing to stop the question from being raised in an application to have the trade mark declared invalid either as an original claim or as a counterclaim pursuant to the TMA 1994, s 47. The position of a potential opponent who does not avail himself of the opportunity to oppose on the grounds (at least) that *his* trade mark is the prior mark in question is unclear. This point raises the question whether an applicant, not being opposed when an order under the TMA 1994, s 8 has been made, is immune to opposition by that potential opponent under the TMA 1994, s 47 in subsequent cancellation proceedings.

16.12 The existence of s 8 of the TMA 1994 would tend to suggest two things. Firstly the rival trade mark owner must be vigilant and police his trade mark cther-wise he faces dilution and loss of brand image. Secondly (and we have discussed this in the criminal context) it is proof (if proof be needed) of the fact that the TMA 1994 is nothing to do with the protection of the consumer *in* the market place[1] but rather is orientated towards the regulation of the rights of traders com-peting, in the broadest sense of the expression, *on* the market place. The TMA1994 may use the consumer (as a notional entity) to assess confusion but in reality, the TMA 1994 cares little about the consumer as such – there is other legis-lation to deal with that.[2]

1 Hence, the sixth Recital of the Directive leaving consumer protection to the national legislatures.
2 Such as the TDA 1968.

Informal opposition

16.13 In some cases, the opponent may wish to make a simple observation or may wish to make multiple observations. It may be that he is content for his cbser-vations to be made and considered by the applicant and registrar without him having any opportunity of replying to any points made in answer by the applicant or the registrar. In such cases, the opponent may make his observations without becoming a party to any proceedings (and thus becoming liable for costs).[1] This may be done at any time up to registration.

1 TMA 1994, s 38(3).

Opposition and concurrent use

16.14   Section 7(2)[1] of the TMA 1994 provides the application shall not be refused if the mark in suit has been used honestly and concurrently with the earlier trade mark or right. It would appear from the wording of s 7 of the TMA 1994 that 'concurrent' does not require the mark in suit and the earlier mark to have been used at all times at the same time but rather that there has been some concurrent use. One instantly sees that there is a dividing line to be drawn – when does the concurrency have to take place? However it would perhaps be foolish to say anything other than that such use has to be measured at the time of the filing of the application since it is registrability that is being considered.

1 See also ch 6, para **6.80–6.82**.

16.15   If the registrar is satisfied that there has been honest concurrent use, then by s 7(2) of the TMA 1994 the application shall not be refused by reason of that earlier trade mark or right unless objection on that ground is raised in opposition proceedings by the proprietor of the earlier right or trade mark.

This provision has been the subject of some intense debate and in the case of *Road Tech Computer Systems Ltd v Unison Software (UK) Ltd (Road Runner* TM)[1] Mr Robert Walker J (as he then was) suggested that in cases where s 7(2) of the TMA 1994 applied, registrar was bound to refuse an application for a trade mark where honest concurrent use was being claimed if the owner of the earlier trade mark or right objected in opposition proceedings. However, two questions arise namely (1) what happens if the opponent is not acting *bona fide* and (2) even if he is, what if his opposition is misconceived. We submit that the interpretation of Mr Justice Robert Walker's judgment as being that if anybody who purports to be the proprietor of the earlier mark or right objects then the registrar is bound to refuse the application in suit, then such an interpretation must be wrong since such a procedure is highly amenable to abuse or (in cases where *bona fides* are not in doubt) injustice.

1 [1996] FSR 805. See the discussion in ch 6, paras **6.80-6.82**.

Registration

16.16   The opposition process may be completely successful in which case the application is rejected by the registrar, or it may be partially successful in which case the scope of the application in suit (but, not the mark in suit itself) may be amended and the amendment also needs to be published.[1] Thereafter, the mark must be registered,[2] and it would appear that this is a positive act which has to be carried out, as defined in s 63(1) of the TMA 1994 as being the 'registration in … [the United Kingdom Trade Marks] register' which means placing the trade mark itself upon the register in some publically amenable form along with certain pertinent information.[3] Once the mark is registered it is said to be a registered trade mark and the *effect* of registration is to give the trade mark the status of a registered trade mark from the date that the application in question was filed (though not its priority date). Thus pre *grant* infringers are caught if their acts post-date the effective date on which the trade mark was *registered*. It is better to speak of registration as opposed to grant and to the date upon which the trade mark was registered as opposed to the effective date of registration.

1 TMA 1994, s 39(1).
2 TMA 1994, s 40(1).
3 TMA 1994, s 63(2).

16.17 The date upon which the trade mark was registered (referred to in s 9(3)(a) of the TMA 1994 as 'the date on which the trade mark is in fact registered') is the earliest time that infringement proceedings may be commenced.

Appeals from and impugning the decisions of the registrar

16.18 Often the registrar will make a decision which either party wishes to appeal. There are three ways of doing this.

Judicial Review

16.19 The registrar, when sitting as a tribunal (usually through a hearing officer) tends to conduct proceedings before him in much the same way as court proceedings, though the tribunal is an inferior court not of record and as such is amenable to the supervision of the Divisional Court. The jurisdiction of the Divisional Court is too well known to require re-description save to say that the Divisional Court route, by way of judicial review, is usually used where the inferior tribunal has acted in excess of jurisdiction. Cases where this happens in relation to trade marks are likely to be rare, particularly in view of the possibility for appeal against many interlocutory decisions. The Divisional Court is a single entity and although usually populated and staffed by judges from the Queen's Bench Division and that side of the Court of Appeal, in trade mark matters, the usual chancery judges are used, though there have to be two.[1]

1 Supreme Court Act 1981, s 60(3).

16.20 An application by way of judicial review must be made within three months of the decision complained of,[1] though relief being discretionary will not be granted if there has been a delay within that period; the period may be extended in appropriate circumstances. The relief sought is of three prerogative types (being mandamus, prohibition and certiorari), one equitable type (being injunction) and two common law types (being declaration and damages). The prerogative orders are usually made where an inferior tribunal governmental department is concerned. Mandamus is an order directing that an act be done, prohibition is an order prohibiting that an act be done and certiorari is an order that a decision be removed from the authority concerned in order for it to be dealt with by the Divisional Court – usually reversing the decision concerned and quashing the order in question.

1 CPR 1998, Sch 1, RSC 1965 Ord 53, r 4 (1).

16.21 An important feature for judicial review is that the leave of the Divisional Court is needed before an application for judicial review may be made.[1]

There is no real test for whether a decision ought to be reviewed or appealed against since wrongfully applying the law is to act outside it and hence the authority to decide, being the jurisdiction, is lost by the inferior tribunal. Generally speaking, where factual matters are very much in issue then the matter is more appropriate for appeal than for review.

An appeal to the Court of Appeal follows in the usual way, now with leave.

1 CPR 1998. Sch 1, RSC 1965, Ord 53, r 3(1).

Appeal to the High Court

16.22   Appeals from any decision (including the exercise of any discretion) of the registrar may be appealed[1] to the High Court.[2] An appeal must be made (ie issued from a court office) within 28 days of the decision complained of,[3] the notice of appeal may be in an approved form.[4] It is probable that practitioners are unlikely to go wrong if the format of notices of appeal to the Court of Appeal is used, ie reciting the order made (and appealed against), the grounds upon which the appeal is made and is the order sought by the appellant.

1 TMA 1994, s 76(1).
2 Order 55, r 2 specifies that subject to any other enactment it shall be the Queen's Bench Division, though the Supreme Court Act 1981, Sch 1 assigns all matters relating to trade marks to the Chancery Division, thus it is the Chancery Division in which such appeals are brought.
3 Paragraph 23.3 of the Part 49 CPR Practice Direction.
4 Though at the time of writing no approved forms have been promulgated.

16.23   The notice of appeal should, after issue, be served on all other parties in the proceedings as well the registrar.[1] The appeal is by way of re-hearing and although the court has the power to receive further evidence[2] and although the rules relating to further evidence in the court on appeal[3] are more relaxed, following the advent of the Civil Procedure Rules ('CPR')(which require the consideration of the overriding objective to be the principle basis for decision making)[4] the courts are likely to exercise some degree of control, though it is too early to say how much.

An appeal to the Court of Appeal follows in the usual way with leave.

1 RSC 1965, Ord 55, r 4(1)(b).
2 RSC 1965, Ord 55, r 7.
3 See *Ladd v Marshall* [1954] 1 W.L.R. 1489.
4 See *In Re Club Europe TM* [1999] 33 LS Gaz R32.

Appeal to the appointed person under s 77 of the TMA 1994

16.24   The third route is by way of an appeal to what is called the appointed person, which is usually a senior counsel with experience in trade marks. The appointed person is a person who has been appointed to that office by the Lord Chancellor.[1] The decision of the appointed person is final[2] (though probably reviewable) and it is also quick to obtain which is one of the attractions of making an appeal to the appointed person. The provisions relating to appeals to the appointed person are governed by the Trade Mark Rules 1994, specifically rule 57 which requires that a notice of appeal should be sent to the registrar within one month of the date of the registrar's decision accompanied by grounds and a case in support of appeal[3] (which, presumably means skeleton argument). Thereafter, the documents are sent to the appointed person under s 76 of the TMA 1994[4] as well as any other party[5] (if there is one).

1 TMA 1994, s 77(1). See also ch 2, paras **2.40** and **2.41**.
2 TMA 1994, s 76(4).
3 Trade Marks Rules 1994, r 57(1).
4 Trade Marks Rules 1994, r 57(2).
5 Trade Marks Rules 1994, r 57(3).

16.25 In some cases the appointed person may decide that the matter ought to be referred to the court if it appears to him that a point of general legal importance is involved,[1] the registrar requests that it be so referred,[2] or such a request is made by any party to the proceedings before the registrar in which the decision appealed against was made.[3] As can be seen, the decision as to whether to refer rests with the appointed person and he has a discretion which can only be exercised upon one or more of the three foregoing events occurring, though he is obliged to give an opportunity to other parties to be heard before he so refers.[4] The request to refer must be made within one month from the date on which the appeal documents were sent to the appointed person,[5] though where the registrar makes a request then he shall send a copy of that request to the other parties[6] and where any party makes a request then he shall send his request to the registrar who shall then send it to the other parties and the appointed person.[7] Thereafter, representations may be made but must be made within one month of the date upon which the request was sent to the parties by the registrar[8] and if the appointed person comes to the view that a point of general public importance is involved, then he may himself refer and give notice to the other parties of his intention to do so[9]. The parties then have one month in which to make representations.[10]

1 TMA 1994, s 76(3)(a). see also ch 2, paras **2.40** and **2.41**.
2 TMA 1994, s 76(3)(b).
3 TMA 1994, s 76(3)(c).
4 TMA 1994, s 76(3).
5 Trade Marks Rules 1994, r 58(1).
6 Trade Marks Rules 1994, r 58(2).
7 Trade Marks Rules 1994, r 58(3).
8 Trade Marks Rules 1994, r 58(4).
9 Trade Marks Rules 1994, r 58(5).
10 Trade Marks Rules 1994, r 58(6).

16.26 If the matter remains in the hands of the appointed person then he shall hear the appeal and shall give notice of the time and place of the hearing[1] to all concerned, including the registrar,[2] though a minimum of 14 days' notice must be given.[3] The rules relating to evidence,[4] hearings,[5] costs[6] and security for costs[7] apply to the appointed person as they apply to the registrar.

Once the appointed person has heard the appeal, he shall give a copy of his decision to all parties.[8]

1 Trade Marks Rules 1994, r 59(1).
2 Trade Marks Rules 1994, r 59(1)(a) and (b).
3 Trade Marks Rules 1994, rr 59(2) and 48(2).
4 Trade Marks Rules 1994, rr 49–52 and 48(2).
5 Trade Marks Rules 1994, rr 53 and 48(2).
6 Trade Marks Rules 1994, rr 54 and 48(2).
7 Trade Marks Rules 1994, rr 55 and 48(2).
8 Trade Marks Rules 1994, r 59(4).

Procedure in relation to oral hearings before the registrar or appointed person

16.27 There are three matters which fall for consideration in relation to the conduct of oral proceedings before the registrar or appointed person. Since, by the operation of r 59(2) of the Trade Marks Rules 1994 the appointed person is subject to the same rules of procedure, then we shall refer merely to the registrar. The three matters are evidence, conduct of hearings and costs and security for costs.

Evidence

16.28   In relation to the examination of witnesses upon oath and the discovery and production of documents the registrar has all of the powers of an official referee,[1] which presumably means that he may exercise those powers as if he were subject to, and entitled to take advantage of, parts 31–35 of the Civil Procedure Rules 1998 ('CPR 1998') *insofar as they relate to the examination of witnesses on oath and the disclosure of documents.* Specifically therefore, as concerns disclosure, the registrar is entitled to take advantage of, and be subject to, not only rule 51 of the Trade Marks Rules 1994 which entitles him to direct the production of documents and the provision of information or evidence as he may reasonably require and within such time period as he may specify, but also to the parts of part 31 of the CPR 1998 relating to disclosure (ie discovery by another name) and production. This would tend to preclude any jurisdiction relating to inspection as such, the duty being to produce a certain document if required to do so, though it is unclear whether this duty is imposable inter partes (ie that one party produce a document to another) or to the registrar. It is well understood in the law generally that production of a document means production to the court and, in fact, no court has original jurisdiction to simply order production of a document unless it is in relation to the ordering of a witness summons under r 34.2(1)(b) of the CPR 1998, which must be at the behest of a party.[2] Difficulty arises as to whether the registrar has original[3] jurisdiction to make orders under r 34.2(1)(b) of the CPR 1998 to compel the production of documents.[4] Further if the registrar is empowered under r 34.2(1)(b) of the CPR 1998 to compel the attendance of a witness to produce documents (as an official referee would be entitled to do) then he can only do so on the application of a party in accordance with CPR 34.3(2) and then in accordance with proper procedure such as the requirement that the summons be served seven days before attendance.[5] The same must apply in relation to compelling witnesses to give oral evidence. In conclusion, on the basis of r 52(1) of the Trade Mark Rules 1994, the registrar has no right to order the production of documents or the attendance of witnesses as such, but only on the application of a party and then only by the witness summons route. The registrar does have the right to order disclosure[6] but not inspection. However, r 51 of the Trade Marks Rules 1994 does entitle the registrar to simply direct that such documents, information or evidence as *he may reasonably require* be filed within a time that he specifies.[7] It does not appear that the class of persons to whom this rule is directed is limited in any way but the circumstances where a third party were to be the subject of such a direction would be, it is submitted, rare indeed.

1 Trade Marks Rules 1994, r 52(1) the official referee is now known as a judge of the Technology and Construction Court.
2 See the CPR 1998, r 34.4 (1).
3 By the use of the word 'original' in this sense we mean originating from the Trade Mark Rules 1994 as opposed to relying upon the aid of a superior court to give aid to an otherwise inferior tribunal.
4 Though it is clear that he certainly has power under the CPR 1998, r 34.2(1)(a) which is applied by the operation of the Trade Marks Rules 1994, r 52(2) to compel the attendance of witnesses, but not on his own motion.
5 Pursuant to the CPR 1998, r 34.5(1) unless the court otherwise directs, r 34.5(2) thereof.
6 Which we understand to mean disclosure by description (ie by list) as opposed to actual disclosure (iepresenting the original or copy of a document to another party).
7 Which exceeds the jurisdiction of the High Court.

16.29   A further original power is the power in relation to the examination of witnesses upon oath. It would appear, therefore, that the registrar can order depositions to be taken by an examiner[1] and overseas[2] if necessary though it appears that the letter of request must be issued from the High Court and it is unclear what the procedure is for this. Further, the position is complicated by the operation of r 49(1) of the Trade Marks Rules 1994 which enables the registrar to receive evidence by way of affidavit or statutory declaration if under the Trade Marks Rules 1994 the registrar is otherwise entitled to admit evidence. There are six circumstances where evidence may be admitted by the registrar, which are:

— Opposition proceedings under rr 13(4), (6) and (7) of the Trade Marks Rules 1994 which specify that such evidence may be by way of affidavit or statutory declaration.[3]
— Applications to alter a trade mark (limited to the alteration of names and addresses if they form part of the mark and the alteration makes little difference to the mark) under s 44 of the TMA 1994 and in accordance with r 25(1) of the Trade Marks Rules 1994 which requires evidence (if required by the registrar) by statutory declaration or as otherwise required.
— Applications for revocation, declaration of invalidity and rectification of the register under ss 46, 47 and 64 of the TMA 1994 and r 31(3) of the Trade Marks Rules 1994 which specifies that if objection is taken on the grounds of non-use then the proprietor may put in evidence of use.
— Applications for registration of a recordable transaction under s 25 of the TMA 1994 and r 35(2) of the Trade Marks Rules 1994 in cases where documentation which evidences the establishment of a registerable transaction must be provided.
— Applications relating to the change in goods or services classification and related proposals of any proprietor to alter the scope of his registration so as not to widen his rights under s 65(3) of the TMA 1994 and r 11(2) of the Trade Marks Rules 1994 which allows the registrar to require or admit evidence directed at the questions in issue to be given.
— Where an agent acts for a principal in relation to trade mark matters under s 82 of the TMA 1994 and r 46(3) of the Trade Marks Rules 1994 which allows the registrar to require evidence of authority.

1 CPR 1998, r 34.8(1).
2 CPR 1998, r 34.13.
3 The making of which is governed by the Trade Marks Rules 1994, r 50 which requires a justice of the peace or any commissioner or other officer authorised by law in any part of the UK to administer an oath for the purpose of any legal proceedings to administer such oath in the UK; or before any court, judge, justice of the peace or any officer authorised by law to administer an oath there for the purpose of any legal proceedings in any other part of Her Majesty's dominions or in the Republic of Ireland; and before a commissioner for oaths, notary public, judge or magistrate elsewhere. Further, any document purporting to have affixed, impressed or subscribed the seal or signature of any person so authorised to take a declaration may be admitted by the registrar without proof of the of the seal or signature, or of the official character of the person or his authority to take the declaration.

16.30 Thus in one case (opposition) the use of statutory declarations or affidavits is the only way that such evidence may be given, on another case (alteration) evidence the use of statutory declarations or otherwise is required and in the other cases (revocation, invalidity and rectification proceedings, registerable transactions, opposition to proposed changes in scope and agent's authority) the references to evidence are nebulous and presumably r 49 of the Trade Mark Rules 1994 is intended to cater for that. The effect of this is to allow evidence which is otherwise inadmissible to be admissible if it is contained in a statutory declaration or affidavit, ie it is as if the affidavit or statutory declaration is doing the speaking rather than the deponent. The position in civil proceedings and very probably in the registry is that almost all evidence is admissible (subject to weight) save for irrelevant evidence and evidence not strictly in reply when it is required to be.

16.31   One of the points relating to evidence in reply is that in the registry, the registrar is very insistent that evidence in reply is just that, dealing with points raised for the first time in answer. However, to look at the position through a magnifying glass is dangerous since inevitably something not strictly in reply will be presented in reply evidence. In many cases, such evidence is mere repetition of evidence already presented, comment upon evidence in answer (which is not, strictly speaking, evidence at all and so, strictly speaking, is not admissible) and argument (the same comments follow). The relevant rule (relating only to opposition proceedings)[1] speaks of 'evidence *strictly* in reply'[2] as opposed (we presume) to evidence *merely* in reply. There is some authority on this point, specifically to the issue of what kind of evidence constitutes evidence in reply. It must be the case now (if ever it was not before) that following the CPR 1998, objection taken on the point that the so-called reply evidence consists of that which is more than strictly in reply, will only succeed if the extra part comprises more than evidence in reply, comment, repetition and argument. Indeed in *Peckitt's Application*[3] the Hearing Officer accepted that proposition to be correct. Accordingly, given that the attitude of the courts in relation to reply evidence generally is lax to the point, it is wondered what the word 'strictly' adds. Indeed, the previous authorities (*Ford Motor Co (Nastas') Application*[4] and *Ernest Scragg & Sons Application*)[5] would tend to indicate that what is really in issue is a wholesale change of case.[6]

1 And indeed opposition proceedings are the only proceedings where evidence in reply (or, as the Trade Mark Rules 1994 would have it, strictly in reply) is expressly permitted.
2 Trade Marks Rules 1994, r 13(7).
3 [1999] RPC 337.
4 [1968] RPC 220.
5 [1972] RPC 679.
6 To which we would add that an attempt to bolster a case in chief with extra corroboration, thus changing the *strength* of the case which has to be met, effectively in answer, might also be disallowed. The question, as ever, comes down to where one draws the line.

Conduct of hearings

16.32   All hearings before the registrar which are heard inter partes must, in accordance with r 53 of the Trade Mark Rules 1994, be in public unless directed otherwise.

Hearings are usually conducted in much the same way that hearings are conducted in court proceedings, comprising opening, evidence for both sides, closing and reply or, if the evidence is read or there is no evidence, then opening, answer and reply.

16.33   In the case of opposition proceedings (which form the bulk of the work which the Hearing Officers have to deal with) the opposition is *presumed* to be dealt with on paper unless the parties request a hearing upon being notified of their option to have an oral hearing by the registrar.[1] In cases where a formal opposition is not mounted, by reason of the fact that observations have been submitted pursuant to s 38(3) of the TMA 1994, the applicant is still entitled to see the observations[2] (and, though it does not appear to be provided for, the applicant must be given an opportunity to reply thereto). In all cases, in opposition proceedings the registrar must provide written reasons for his decision[3] and time for appealing starts to run from the date on which the decision is sent to the party concerned.[4]

1 Trade Marks Rules 1994, r 13(9).
2 Trade Marks Rules 1994, r 15.

3 Trade Marks Rules 1994, r 14(1).
4 Trade Marks Rules 1994, r 14(2).

Security for costs

16.34 The original jurisdiction to make rules relating to an order for the provision of security for costs (and the consequences for the failure to make such an order) is contained in s 68 of the TMA 1994 and the corresponding rule is to be found in r 55 of the Trade Marks Rules 1994. The registrar has a complete discretion as to whether to award security for costs and in what amount. Further, the registrar is entitled to order security for costs in relation to any appeal from any decision of his.[1] The domicile, pecuniosity and legal status of the respondent to an application for security for costs, though important in the exercise of discretion, do not form a principal basis for the activation of the jurisdiction.[2] It is also right to say that *any* one party may seek security for costs as against the other, so an opponent could seek security for costs as against the applicant and vice versa. A party defaulting in the provision of security is deemed to have withdrawn his application. A fuller guide to the principles which, it is suggested, ought to apply in the registry as they do in the High Court, are to be found in the case of *Keary Developments Ltd v Tarmac Construction Ltd.*[3]

1 Trade Marks Rules 1994, r 55(1).
2 As they do in relation to proceedings in court at first instance.
3 [1995] 3 All ER 534.

The High Court[1]

16.35 The High Court has three separate jurisdictions in relation to trade marks, being appellate, original and supervisory. We have already discussed the supervisory and appellate jurisdiction in some detail above, though we shall discuss them in a more procedural sense below. It is the original jurisdiction which shall form the primary element of this chapter.

1 Though in relation to the original jurisdiction we would, with some trepidation, include the county courts since it does, at least insofar as infringement is concerned, appear to have jurisdiction, though the county courts have no power to impugn the validity of any registered trade mark – this is odd to say the least.

The appellate jurisdiction

16.36 Under s 76 of the TMA 1994, an appeal lies from any decision of the registrar to the court or the appointed person,[1] which is the High Court[2] and which must be heard in the Chancery Division[3] (as must all trade mark matters except for applications for judicial review). The appeal procedure is governed by Part 49(1) and (2)(d)(ii) & (iii) of the CPR 1998 which really does no more than refer the litigant to the Part 49 practice direction, part B (directions 21–25). The appeal is heard by a single judge[4] whether under the TMA 1938 or the TMA 1994 and the appeal must be brought by way of a notice of appeal in a form approved by the court[5] which must be issued (ie stamped by the court office, which includes the payment of the relevant fee) within 28 days of the decision being appealed from.[6] The decision is deemed to have been made on the date on which the notice containing the decision is sent to the parties[7] though in some cases reasons are not given and either party may request[8] that written reasons be given, thereafter time for appealing starts to run from the date that written reasons were sent to the parties.

Thereafter the appellant has 21 days in which to serve his issued notice of appeal on the other parties, including the registrar[9] and the clerk of the Chancery List.[10]

1 The Appointed Person may refer the matter to the court if there is either a point of general legal importance involved. The registrar makes a request or one of the parties before the registrar so requests – TMA 1994, s 76(3), though the appointed person may hear representations.
2 See the TMA 1994, s 75.
3 See the Supreme Court Act 1981 s 61(1) Sch 1, para 1(i) and para 22.1 of the Part 49 Civil Procedure Rules 1998 Practice Direction part B (which are strictly speaking otiose).
4 Paragraph 23.1 of the Part 49 of the Civil Procedure Rules Practice Direction part B.
5 At the time of writing no form has been approved by the court, though it is submitted that such an appeal notice would be in the same form as a notice of appeal from the High Court in its original jurisdiction since in such a context the High Court is, in effect the Court of Appeal. See, by analogy, in relation to appeals from the Comptroller of Patents the case of *Ladney and Hendry's International Application* [1998] RPC 319, 330 lines 21–47.
6 Paragraph 23.3 of the Part 49 of the Civil Procedure Rules Practice Direction part B.
7 Trade Mark Rules 1994, r 56(1) as amended by the Trade Mark (Amendment) Rules 1998 (SI 1998/925) as from 27 April 1998.
8 Trade Mark Rules 1994, r 56(2).
9 Paragraph 23.4 and repeated at para 23.6 of the Part 49 of the Civil Procedure Rules Practice Direction part B.
10 Paragraph 23.4 of the Part 49 of the Civil Procedure Rules 1998 Practice Direction part B.

The supervisory jurisdiction

16.37 This is simply judicial review, the procedure for which is explained at Order 52 of the Rules of the Supreme Court 1965 ('RSC 1965').

The original jurisdiction

16.38 Only the High Court (though possibly the county courts) has original jurisdiction to hear and determine civil disputes relating to infringement of a registered trade mark, that is infringement of the rights which the registration of a trade mark in this country cedes.[1] The High Court does, however, share original jurisdiction in relation to questions of validity[2]. We shall advert firstly to the original jurisdiction of the registry and thereafter the High Court.

1 TMA 1994, s 9(2).
2 See ch 9, paras **9.20** and **9.21**, ch 2, para **2.38**.

The original jurisdiction of the registry

16.39 This is ceded by s 46(4) (revocation) and 47(3) (invalidity) of the TMA 1994 save that where proceedings are on foot in court and in relation to that trade mark (irrespective, it appears, of who the parties to the proceedings are) then the application must be made to the court[1] and in any event the registrar has the option to refer if he so wishes.[2] To this original jurisdiction we should add that any person may also apply under s 64 of the TMA 1994 (provided he has sufficient interest) for the rectification of an error or omission of the registrar. This jurisdiction, though relatively untested, is potentially very powerful if, say a proprietor has been given rights which have been ceded to him unlawfully.[3] Like provisions exist under this 'corrective' jurisdiction for references to the court in relation to invalidity and revocation proceedings.[4]

1 TMA 1994, ss 46(4)(a) and 47(3)(a).
2 TMA 1994, ss 46(4)(b) and 47(3)(b).
3 Such as broadening of the scope of the registration contrary to the TMA 1994, s 39, although it is debatable whether the registrar or court *has* to rectify the error or whether it (or he) has a discretion to do so – see, for instance, the Trade Marks Rules 1994, r 60. It is doubtful whether scope-widening could be said to be procedural as such.
4 TMA 1994, s 64(2), cf ss 46(4)(b) and 47(3)(b).

16.40 The procedure before the registrar is governed by r 31 of the Trade Marks Rules 1994. The applicant makes his opening gambit in Form TM26 much the same way a claim for revocation or invalidity is made in the High Court by claim form.[1] Form TM26 must contain a statement of the grounds upon which the application is made.

1 Trade Mark Rules 1994, r 31(1).

16.41 In cases where the application is being made by a person other than the proprietor, then the registrar is obliged to send the notice (that is the application and the statement of grounds) to the proprietor[1] although there is no stated time by which this should be done. Presumably proceedings in the Divisional Court can be brought if the registrar refuses to do so. Cases where the proprietor makes the application are merely between the proprietor and the registry (those cases will usually, but not always, be corrective, though it is not unknown for a trade mark proprietor to impugn his own mark); other cases are between the applicant, proprietor and the registry and will usually be cases relating to validity. In such cases the proprietor may file a counter-statement on Form TM8 with the registry and this is also sent to the applicant. If the application is for revocation for non use[2] then the proprietor must file evidence of use.[3] If he does not do so, then the registrar may[4] treat the opposition to the application as being withdrawn. However, where no counterstatement is filed then the registrar must[5] allow the application.[6] Thereafter (subject to what is discussed below) the rules relating to opposition proceedings apply *mutatis mundatis*.[7]

1 Trade Mark Rules 1994, r 31(2).
2 TMA 1994, s 46(1)(a) or (b).
3 Since the onus is upon him to prove use – the TMA 1994, s 100.
4 The word 'may' is in the language of the Trade Mark Rules 1994, r 31(3).
5 Which is from the language of the Trade Mark Rules 1994, r 31(4).
6 It would appear that this is so even if the application is inadmissible because it asks the registry to do something it cannot do. Although that is not to say that even if it *does* that thing, it is a thing which the law recognises as having been done, since things done in excess of jurisdiction are to be treated as if not done at all.
7 Trade Mark Rules 1994, r 31(4).

16.42 It is a special of applications to the registrar under ss 46, 47 or 64 of the TMA 1994 that interested persons may under r 31(5) of the Trade Mark Rules apply to the registrar for leave to intervene and the registrar may hear the parties and grant leave to intervene on such terms (including as to costs) as shall be thought fit[1]. Such an intervener shall be treated as a party to the application[2] and any decision (which must include reasons) on the application shall be sent to the parties, the time for appealing running from the date upon which the notice of the decision is sent.

1 See also ch 9, para **9.18**.
2 Trade Mark Rules 1994, r 31(6).

The original jurisdiction of the High Court

16.43   There are a number of ways in which the High Court exercises its jurisdiction in relation to trade marks. There is the reference jurisdiction, that is the jurisdiction which originally exercised by the registrar but referred by him to the High Court, there is the original jurisdiction which arises because proceedings are already on foot and therefore references which would or could go to the registrar have to go to the High Court and then there is the original jurisdiction of the High Court (which properly only relates to infringement since the other questions which the court may decide are also decidable by the registrar).

16.44   In all events, where the original or the reference jurisdiction is exercised or arises, the procedure is the same, being either the claim form or application notice if in existing proceedings.[1] However, it must be pointed out that the reference powers of the registrar or the provisions which lock out the registrar under ss 46(4), 47(3) and 64(2) of the TMA 1994 do not make any application in or to existing High Court proceedings, mandatory, though it is likely that the court will order consolidation or some other way of hearings to be heard together to save costs. This will result in the likelihood of adverse orders for costs if some independent route is taken, although that, in turn, may depend upon the nature of the pre-existing proceedings.

1 Paragraph 23.5 of the Part 49 Civil Procedure Rules 1998 Practice Direction part B.

16.45   The claim form route, whether in relation to a claim seeking relief with regards to infringement or validity involves all of the usual incidents relating to claims under the CPR with Part 20 type claims being permissible (usually a counterclaim impugning the validity of the mark concerned)[1] but only if accompanied by particulars of the objections[2] and the registrar must be served and may take part in the proceedings.[3] It appears odd, however, that the right to make a counterclaim impugning the validity of a mark may only be made if an allegation of infringement is made in a claim whilst there is no reason why the basis for a counterclaim cannot exist independently of a claim for infringement. It would appear that paras 24.2 and 24.3 of the Part 49 Civil Procedure Rules 1998 Practice Direction part B does not expressly cover all cases in which a defendant may wish to challenge validity.

1 Paragraph 24.1 of the Part 49 Civil Procedure Rules 1998 Practice Direction part B.
2 Paragraph 24.2 of the Part 49 Civil Procedure Rules 1998 Practice Direction part B.
3 Paragraph 24.3 of the Part 49 Civil Procedure Rules 1998 Practice Direction part B.

16.46   Thereafter the claimant must serve within 14 days his particulars of claim (if not served with his claim form).[1] If a claim form is served with particulars of claim then the defendant(s) may acknowledge service within 14 days[2] and if particulars of claim are served later on, then such acknowledgment must be served within 14 days thereafter.[3] Failure to serve a claim form may result in the claim being struck out, whereas failure to acknowledge service may result in judgment in default.[4] The position is the same for judgment in default of defence. Otherwise the defendant(s) have 14 days in which to file a defence[5] or 28 days if an acknowledgment of service has been filed.[6] Thereafter the claimant may reply and such reply must be served with the allocation questionnaire,[7] thereafter no further pleadings are allowed without permission.[8] Where denials are made in a defence, the defendant must state the basis for such denial.[9]

1 See the CPR 1998, r 7.4 (1)(b).
2 See the CPR 1998, r 10.3 (1)(b).
3 See the CPR 1998, r 10.3 (1)(a).
4 Which will, if injunctive relief is sought, involve an application to the court under. See the CPR, r 23.
5 See the CPR 1998, r 15.4 (1)(a).
6 See the CPR 1998. r 15.4 (1)(b).
7 See the CPR 1998, r 35.8 (a)
8 See the CPR 1998, r 15.9.
9 See the CPR 1998, r 16.5 (2) (a) and (b).

16.47   All pleadings, if they are to be relied upon as evidence in the proceedings (as they may be) must be accompanied by a statement of truth[1] signed either by the party concerned (or its relevant officer).[2] Further, a pleading not accompanied by a statement of truth may not be evidence and could be struck out.[3] The penalty for not holding an honest belief in the truth of statements made and verified by a statement of truth is committal or sequestration,[4] though not criminal proceedings for perjury (since the statements are not sworn).

1 See the CPR 1998, r 22.1(1) (a) and (b).
2 See the CPR 1998, r 22.1 (6)(a).
3 See the CPR 1998, r 22.2 (2).
4 See the CPR 1998, r 32.14, though the permission of the court be sought unless proceedings are brought by the Attorney-General.

16.48   Parties may seek further information from each other[1] and parties may also make amendments to their statements of case (which basically means pleadings) with permission[2] or by agreement with the other parties.[3] If counterclaims are to be made[4] then these are termed 'Part 20 claims' though Part 20 claims include certain other types of claim such as claims in contribution, for indemnity and against third parties generally.[5] Counterclaims are usually included with a defence and if so, no permission is required,[6] otherwise, permission is required. In trade mark matters counterclaims are obviously necessary where the relief sought is relief impugning the validity of the trade marks being relied upon.

1 See the CPR 1998, r 18 as to this generally.
2 See the CPR 1998, r 17.1 (2)(b).
3 See the CPR 1998, r 17.1 (2)(a).
4 See the CPR 1998, r 20.
5 See the CPR 1998, r 20.2 (1).
6 See the CPR 1998, r 20.4 (2).

16.49   Thereafter and once a defence has been filed, an allocation questionnaire will be filed[1] which will be used by the court to assign the case to a track. In cases of difficulty, the court will hear the parties[2] if necessary (called an allocation hearing). Allocation is the process whereby the court decides which track the matter should be heard and the rules we have adverted to above apply.

Thereafter the parties will be allocated and in the small claims track, the parties follow automatic directions[3] whereas in the fast track and multi-track listing, questionnaires are sent out by the court upon allocation[4] although in the case of the multi track there will be directions given first or a conference or pre-trial reviews will be held.[5] It is only after the directions process that a listing questionnaire must be submitted.[6] Upon the listing questionnaire being submitted, the court will fix a date for hearing.

1 See the CPR 1998, r 26.3 (1).
2 See the CPR 1998, r 26.5 (4).
3 See, generally, the CPR 1998, r 27.
4 See the CPR 1998, rr 28.5 and 29.2.
5 See the CPR 1998, r 29.2.
6 See the CPR 1998, r 29.2 (3)(b).

16.50 The usual rules of disclosure and inspection of documents apply, and applications may be made for specific disclosure.[1] Otherwise the parties must disclose all documents upon which they rely and those which do or might help their opponents or damage their own case.[2] There is a duty to search for documents and declare the outcome of that search.[3]

In relation to all proceedings in court, the court will have regard to the overriding objective, which is to deal with cases justly.[4]

1 See the CPR 1998, r 31.12.
2 See the CPR 1998, r 31.6.
3 See the CPR 1998, r 31.7.
4 Which means: '... so far as is practicable —
    (a) ensuring that the parties are on an equal footing;
    (b) saving expense;
    (c) dealing with the case in ways which are proportionate —
        (i) to the amount of money involved;
        (ii) to the importance of the case;
        (iii) to the complexity of the issues; and
        (iv) to the financial position of each party;
    (d) ensuring that it is dealt with expeditiously and fairly; and
    (e) allotting to it an appropriate share of the court's resources, while taking into account the need to allot resources to other cases." (taken from CPR 1998 Part 1.1(2).)

16.51 In pleading an allegation of trade mark infringement it is important to set out the bare basis of a claim, being (1) the parties, (2) identification of the rights relied upon , (3) the acts carried out by the defendant, (4) the allegation of infringement, (5) particulars of damage and (6) claim for interest, although in relation to infringement it will only be necessary to plead one instance of infringement provided that the door is left open should further information come to light and it is clear on the pleading or is made clear either by order, direction or conduct that there will be a split trial on liability and quantum.

Passing off

16.52 It is now difficult to see what extra relief a claimant is likely to get in an action for passing off that he would not get in proceedings for infringement of his (corresponding) registered trade mark. Obviously the position is wholly different if there is no corresponding registered trade mark.

The procedure for passing off actions in court is the same as for trade mark infringement save that instead of proving the rights relied upon (ie by reliance upon the trade mark registration certificate) it is necessary to prove reputation and goodwill. This is normally done by particularising sales of articles or services under some trade badge or dress over a period of three or more years.

Since damage is an important part of the cause of action in passing off, it is also necessary to plead it and (if possible) particularise it.

The CPR 1998

16.53 Whilst we have made extensive reference to the Civil Procedure Rules 1998 (CPR 1998) we have not discussed them in any independent detail – it has always been in a trade marks context. Whilst it would be far beyond the scope of this chapter or indeed book to say anything extensive about the CPR 1998 we feel that a short summary of their operation and effect would be of assistance.

The principal feature of the CPR 1998 is the notion of case management. Previously, judges would only do as they were asked but now the parties must do as they are told and the judge is encouraged to be more interventionist.

Another central theme is the notion of tracks, being the small claims, fast and multi track. The case is allocated to a track once the parties have submitted their answers to an allocation questionnaire to the court.

The small claims track is for cases where the value of the action is not more than £5,000[1] and must be heard in the county courts.[2] Expert evidence is not allowed and the court can give summary judgment, strike out a statement of case and deal with a case without a hearing.

The fast track is for cases where the value of the action is not more than £15,000 and the court will give directions for the future conduct of the case. Fast track cases will always be heard in the county courts.[3]

The multi track is the catchall and the procedures are more flexible.

1 Not, we observe, impossible in relation to certain trade mark cases.
2 Paragraph 2.1 of Part 7 of the Civil Procedure Rules 1998 Practice Direction.
3 Paragraph 2.1 of Part 7 of the Civil Procedure Rules 1998 Practice Direction.

16.54 Once the defendant has entered his defence, either party may ask the court for a stay to enable settlement negotiations or some other procedure such as alternative dispute resolution to take place.[1] If the court believes that a stay is appropriate it may itself order a stay.

Further, almost all of the evidence is now simply exchanged by way of witness statements (as opposed to affidavits), similarly verified by a statement of truth.[2]

There is one way of striking out an opponent's case based upon whether the opponent has any real prospect of success,[3] though there is some residual jurisdiction to deal with cases which ought not otherwise to go to trial.[4]

One major aspect where the court will wield the most power is in expressing its displeasure in relation costs, and the conduct of the proceedings is an important factor.[5]

1 The CPR 1998, r 26.4 .
2 The CPR 1998, r 32.6.
3 The CPR 1998, r 24.2(a).
4 The CPR 1998, r 24.2(b).
5 The CPR 1998, r 44.3(4).

The High Court and the county courts

16.55 In the chapter on condemnation a fair amount is said about the difference in jurisdiction between the High Court and the county court. At this point we simply observe that s 15 of the county courts Act 1984 confers like jurisdiction onto the county court as relates to contract and tort cases in the High Court. Accordingly it is theoretically possible for small claims, fast track and multi-track litigation to take place in the county court for infringement of trade marks, though no question may be raised in relation to their validity.

16.56 If one accepts (as one must) that the High Court is a multi-track only court and that it is conceivable that some trade mark litigation might, by reason of its value, likely to be classified as small track or multi-track litigation, then the upshot of this could be that in small track and fast track litigation the defendant is deprived of the right to impugn the marks in suit which is a right guaranteed him by the Directive. However, this cannot have been intended. Any difficulty in this respect is avoided if all trade mark litigation is treated as multi-track.

Appeals to the Court of Appeal and beyond

16.57 Appeal may be made to the Court of Appeal from any order of the High Court with leave (now required in all cases, though it is only in the clearest cases that leave will be refused after trial). The procedure in the Court of Appeal is best understood by consulting the relevant rules of court.

Appeal may also be made from the Court of Appeal to the House of Lords, though such appeals are rare and will be entertained only in cases of public importance.

The ECJ

16.58 There is not, strictly speaking, any appeal to the ECJ, which is merely a referring court for deciding questions of interpretation of EC law – it has no power in this context to make compulsive orders as such, this is within the preserve of the domestic courts and to that extent, at least, national sovereignty has been preserved. Article 234 of the Treaty of Rome, which governs this jurisdiction reads:

> 'Article 234. The Court of Justice shall have jurisdiction to give preliminary rulings concerning:
>
> (a) the interpretation of this Treaty;
> (b) the validity and interpretation of acts of the institutions of the Community and of the ECJ;
> (c) the interpretation of the statutes of bodies established by an act of the Council, where those statutes so provide.
>
> Where such a question is raised before any court or tribunal of a Member State, that court or tribunal may, if it considers that a decision on the question is necessary to enable it to give judgment, request the Court of Justice to give a ruling thereon.
>
> Where any such question is raised in a case pending before a court or tribunal of a Member State against whose decisions there is no judicial remedy under national law, that court or tribunal shall bring the matter before the Court of Justice.'

16.59 The position of the court in relation to a reference under art 234 of the Treaty is governed by Ord 114 of the RSC and Order 19 of the CCR. How then does the court decide if there is a case of interpretation of Community law which needs deciding upon? In *H P Bulmer Ltd v J Bollinger SA*[1] [1974] Ch 401, 419 CA where Master of the Rolls (Lord Denning) said:

'6. *By what courts is the treaty to be interpreted?*
It is important to distinguish between the task of interpreting the Treaty – to see what it means – and the task of applying it – to apply its provisions to the case in hand. Let me put on one side the task of applying the Treaty. On this matter in our courts, the English judges have the final word. They are the only judges who are empowered to decide the case itself. They have to find the facts, to state the issues, to give judgment for one side or the other, and to see that the judgment is enforced.

'Before the English judges can apply the Treaty, they have to see what it means and what is its effect. In the task of interpreting the Treaty, the English judges are no longer the final authority. They no longer carry the law in their breasts. They are no longer in a position to give rulings which are of binding force. The supreme tribunal for interpreting the Treaty is the European Court of Justice, at Luxembourg. Our Parliament has so decreed. Section 3 of the European Communities Act 1972 says:

"(1) For the purposes of all legal proceedings any question as to the meaning or effect of any of the Treaties, or as to the validity, meaning or effect of any community instrument, shall be treated as a question of law (and, if not referred to the European court, be for determination as such in accordance with the principles laid down by and any relevant decision of the European court). (2) Judicial notice shall be taken of the Treaties, of the Official Journal of the Communities and of any decision of, or expression of opinion by, the European court on any such question as aforesaid; … "

'Coupled with that section, we must read article … [234] of the Treaty. It says:

(1) "The Court of Justice" (*ie* the European Court of Justice) "shall have jurisdiction to give preliminary rulings concerning: (a) the interpretation of this Treaty; (b) the validity and interpretation of acts of the institutions of the community; (c) the interpretation of the statutes of bodies established by an act of the Council, where those statutes so provide."

(2) "Where such a question is raised before any court or tribunal of a member state, that court or tribunal may, if it considers that a decision on the question is necessary to enable it to give judgment, request the Court of Justice to give a ruling thereon."

(3) "Where any such question is raised in a case pending before a court or tribunal of a member state, against whose decisions there is no judicial remedy under national law, that court or tribunal shall bring the matter before the Court of Justice."

'That article shows that, if a question of interpretation or validity is raised, the European court is supreme. It is the ultimate authority. Even the House of Lords has to bow down to it. If a question is raised before the House of Lords on the interpretation of the Treaty – on which it is necessary to give a ruling – the House of Lords is bound to refer it to the European court. Article … [234] (3) uses that emphatic word "shall." The House has no option. It must refer the matter to the European court, and, having done so, it is bound to follow the ruling in that particular case in which the point arises. But the ruling in that case does not bind other cases. The European court is not absolutely bound by its previous decisions: see *Da Costa en Schaake NV v*

Nederlandse Belastingadministratie [1963] CMLR 224. It has no doctrine of stare decisis. Its decisions are much influenced by considerations of policy and economics: and, as these change, so may their rulings change. It follows from this that, if the House of Lords in a subsequent case thinks that a previous ruling of the European court was wrong – or should not be followed – it can refer the point again to the European court: and the European court can reconsider it. On reconsideration it can make a ruling which will bind that particular case. But not subsequent cases. And so on.'

The Master of the Rolls was saying that all courts but the House of Lords may not must refer. He then went on to say that there must therefore be a discretion[2]:

'*7. The discretion to refer or not to refer*
But short of the House of Lords, no other English court is bound to refer a question to the European court at Luxembourg. Not even a question on the interpretation of the Treaty. Article ... [234] (2) uses the permissive word "may" in contrast to "shall" in article ... [234] (3). In England the trial judge has complete discretion. If a question arises on the interpretation of the Treaty, an English judge can decide it for himself, He need not refer it to the court at Luxembourg unless he wishes. He can say: "It will be too costly," or "it will take too long to get an answer," or "I am well able to decide it myself." If he does decide it himself, the European court cannot interfere. None of the parties can go off to the European court and complain. The European court would not listen to any party who went moaning to them. The European court take the view that the trial judge has a complete discretion to refer or not to refer: see *Rheinmühlen-Düsseldorf (Firma) v Einfuhr und Vorratsstelle für Getreide und Futtermittel* [1974] 1 CMLR 523 – with which they cannot interfere: see *Milchwerke Heinz Wöhrmann & Sohn KG v EEC Commission* [1963] CMLR 152. If a party wishes to challenge the decision of the trial judge in England – to refer or not to refer – he must appeal to the Court of Appeal in England. (If the judge makes an order referring the question to Luxembourg, the party can appeal without leave: see RSC, Ord 114. If the judge refuses to make an order, he needs leave, because it is an interlocutory order: section 31 of the Supreme Court of Judicature (Consolidation) Act 1925.) The judges of the Court of Appeal, in their turn, have complete discretion. They can interpret the Treaty themselves if they think fit. If the Court of Appeal do interpret it themselves, the European court will not rebuke them for doing so. If a party wishes to challenge the decision of the Court of Appeal – to refer or not to refer – he must get leave to go to the House of Lords and go there. It is only in that August place that there is no discretion. If the point of interpretation is one which is "necessary" to give a ruling, the House must refer it to the European court at Luxembourg. The reason behind this imperative is this: the cases which get to the House of Lords are substantial cases of the first importance. If a point of interpretation arises there, it is assumed to be worthy of reference to the European court at Luxembourg. Whereas the points in the lower courts may not be worth troubling the European court about: see the judgment of the German Court of Appeal at Frankfurt in *Re Export of Oat Flakes* [1969] CMLR 85, 97.[2]

1 [1974] Ch 401, 419 CA.
2 At 420.

16.60 Then one asks how that discretion is to be exercised, see what the Master of the Rolls said at 421:

'*8. The condition precedent to a reference. It must be "necessary"*
Whenever any English court thinks it would be helpful to get the view of the European court – on the interpretation of the Treaty – there is a condition precedent to

be fulfilled. It is a condition which applies to the House of Lords as well as to the lower courts. It is contained in the same paragraph of article … [234] (2) and applies in article … [234] (3) as well. It is this: an English court can only refer the matter to the European court "if it considers that a decision on the question is necessary to enable it to give judgment." Note the words "if it considers." That is, "if the English court considers." On this point again the opinion of the English courts is final, just as it is on the matter of discretion. An English judge can say either "I consider it necessary" or "I do not consider it necessary." His discretion in that respect is final. Let me take the two in order.

"(1) If the English judge considers it necessary to refer the matter, no one can gainsay it save the Court of Appeal. The European court will accept his opinion. It will not go into the grounds on which he based it. The European court so held in *Algemene Transpoort en Expeditie Onderneming van Gend en Loos NV v Nederlandse Tariefcommissie* [1963] CMLR 105, 128, 129 and *Albatros SARL v Société des Petroles et des Combustibles Liquides (SOPECO)* [1965] CMLR 159, 177. It will accept the question as he formulates it: *Fratelli Grassi v Amministrazione delle Finanze* [1973] CMLR 322, 335. It will not alter it or send it back. Even if it is a faulty question, it will do the best it can with it: see *Deutsche Grammophon GmbH* v. *Metro-SB-Grossmärkte GmbH & Co KG* [1971] CMLR 631, 656. The European court treats it as a matter between the English courts and themselves – to be dealt with in a spirit of co-operation – in which the parties have no place save that they are invited to be heard. It was so held in *Hessische Knappschaft v Maison Singer et Fils* [1966] CMLR 82, 94.

"(ii) If the English judge considers it 'not necessary' to refer a question of interpretation to the European court – but instead decides it itself – that is the end of the matter. It is no good a party going off to the European court. They would not listen to him. They are conscious that the Treaty gives the final word in this respect to the English courts. From all I have read of their cases, they are very careful not to exceed their jurisdiction. They never do anything to trespass on any ground which is properly the province of the national courts.'"

1 [1974] Ch 401, at 421.

16.61 So the test is whether it is necessary, how does one satisfy or otherwise consider this test? See what the Master of the Rolls said[1]:

'9. *The guidelines*
Seeing that these matters of "necessary" and "discretion" are the concern of the English courts, it will fall to the English judges to rule upon them. Likewise the national courts of other member states have to rule on them. They are matters on which guidance is needed. It may not be out of place, therefore, to draw attention to the way in which other national courts have dealt with them.

'(1) Guidelines as to whether a decision is necessary

(i) The point must be conclusive.
The English court has to consider whether "a decision on the question is necessary to enable it to give judgment." That means judgment in the very case which is before the court. The judge must have got to the stage when he says to himself: "This clause of the Treaty is capable of two or more meanings. If it means this, I give judgment for the plaintiff. If it means that, I give judgment for the defendant." In short, the point must be such that, whichever way the point is decided, it is conclusive of the case. Nothing more remains but to give judgment. The Hamburg court stressed the necessity

in *In re Adjustment Tax on Petrol* [1966] CMLR 409, 416. In *Van Duyn v Home Office* [1974] 1 WLR 1107, in England Pennycuick V-C said: "it would be quite impossible to give judgment without such a decision."

'(ii) Previous ruling.
In some cases, however, it may be found that the same point – or substantially the same point – has already been decided by the European court in a previous case. In that event it is not necessary for the English court to decide it. It can follow the previous decision without troubling the European court. But, as I have said, the European court is not bound by its previous decisions. So if the English court thinks that a previous decision of the European court may have been wrong – or if there are new factors which ought to be brought to the notice of the European court – the English court may consider it necessary to re-submit the point to the European court. In that event, the European court will consider the point again. It was so held by the European court itself in the *Da Costa* case [1963] CMLR 224; in Holland in *Vereniging van Fabrikanten en Importeurs van Verbruiksartikelen (FIVA) v Mertens* [1963] CMLR 141, and in Germany in *Re Import of Powdered Milk (No 3)* [1967] CMLR 326, 336.

'(iii) *Acte claire*.
In other cases the English court may consider the point is reasonably clear and free from doubt. In that event there is no need to interpret the Treaty but only to apply it: and that is the task of the English court. It was so submitted by the Advocate-General to the European Court of Justice in the *Da Costa* case [1963] CMLR 224, 234. It has been so held by the highest courts in France. By the Conseil d'Etat in *Re Société des Petroles Shell-Berre* [1964] CMLR 462, 481, and by the Cour de Cassation in *State v Cornet* [1967] CMLR 351 and *Lapeyre v Administration des Douanes* [1967] CMLR 362, 368. Also by a superior court in Germany in *Re French Widow's Pension Settlement* [1971] CMLR 530.

'(iv) Decide the facts first.
It is to be noticed, too, that the word is "necessary." This is much stronger than "desirable" or "convenient." There are some cases where the point, if decided one way, would shorten the trial greatly. But, if decided the other way, it would mean that the trial would have to go its full length. In such a case it might be "convenient" or "desirable" to take it as a preliminary point because it might save much time and expense. But it would not be "necessary" at that stage. When the facts were investigated, it might turn out to have been quite unnecessary. The case would be determined on another ground altogether. As a rule you cannot tell whether it is necessary to decide a point until all the facts are ascertained. So in general it is best to decide the facts first.

'(2) Guide lines as to the exercise of discretion
Assuming that the condition about "necessary" is fulfilled, there remains the matter of discretion. This only applies to the trial judge or the Court of Appeal, not to the House of Lords. The English court has a discretion either to decide the point itself or to refer it to the European court. The national courts of the various member countries have had to consider how to exercise this discretion. The cases show that they have taken into account such matters as the following:

'(i) The time to get a ruling.
The length of time which may elapse before a ruling can be obtained from the European court. This may take months and months. The lawyers have to prepare their briefs; the Advocate-General has to prepare his submissions; the case has to be argued; the court has to give its decision. The average length of time at present seems

to be between six and nine months. Meanwhile, the whole action in the English court is stayed until the ruling is obtained. This may be very unfortunate, especially in a case where an injunction is sought or there are other reasons for expedition. This was very much in the mind of the German Court of Appeal of Frankfurt in *Re Export of Oat Flakes* [1969] CMLR 85, 97. It said that it was important "to prevent undue protraction of both the proceedings before the European court and trial before the national courts." On that ground it decided a point of interpretation itself, rather than submit it to the European court.

'(ii) Do not overload the court.
The importance of not overwhelming the European court by references to it. If it were overloaded, it could not get through its work. There are nine judges of that court. All nine must sit in plenary sessions on these cases, as well as many other important cases: see article 165. They cannot split up into divisions of three or five judges. All nine must sit. So do not put too much on them. The Court of Appeal in Frankfurt took this view pointedly in *Re Import Licence for Oats* [1968] CMLR 103, 117:

"the European court must not be overwhelmed by requests for rulings. ... This viewpoint should induce courts to exercise their right sparingly. A reference to the European court must not become an automatic reaction, and ought only to be made if serious difficulties of interpretation occur, ..."

'(iii) Formulate the question clearly.
The need to formulate the question clearly. It must be a question of interpretation only of the Treaty. It must not be mixed up with the facts. It is the task of the national courts to find the facts and apply the Treaty. The European court must not take that task on themselves. In fairness to them, it is desirable to find the facts and state them clearly before referring the question. That appears from *Salgoil SpA v Foreign Trade Ministry of the Italian Republic* [1969] CMLR 181, 193 and *Sirena Srl v Eda Srl* [1971] CMLR 260, 263. In any case, the task of interpretation is better done with the facts in mind rather than in ignorance of them.

(iv) Difficulty and importance.
The difficulty and importance of the point. Unless the point is really difficult and important, it would seem better for the English judge to decide it himself. For in so doing, much delay and expense will be saved. So far the English judges have not shirked their responsibilities. They have decided several points of interpretation on the Treaty to the satisfaction, I hope, of the parties. At any rate, there has been no appeal from them. I refer to the decision of Whitford J in *Lerose Ltd v Hawick Jersey International Ltd* [1973] CMLR 83; Graham J in *Minnesota Mining and Manufacturing Co v Geerpres Europe Ltd* [1973] CMLR 259; Bridge J in *Esso Petroleum v Kingswood Motors (Addlestone) Ltd* [1974] QB 142; [1973] CMLR 665; Graham J in *Löwenbräu München v Grunhalle Lager International Ltd* [1974] 1 CMLR 1 and Mr Suenson-Taylor QC in *Processed Vegetable Growers Association Ltd v Customs and Excise Commrs* [1974] 1 CMLR 113.

'(v) Expense.
The expense to the parties of getting a ruling from the European court. That influenced a Nuremberg court in *In re Potato Flour Tax* [1964] CMLR 96, 106. On a request for interpretation, the European court does not as a rule award costs, and for a simple reason. It does not decide the case. It only gives advice on the meaning of the Treaty. If either party wishes to get the costs of the reference, he must get it from the English court, when it eventually decides the case: see *Bestur derk Sociale Verzekeringsbank v Van der Vecht* [1968] CMLR 151, 167.

'(vi) Wishes of the parties.
The wishes of the parties. If both parties want the point to be referred to the European court, the English court should have regard to their wishes, but it should not give them undue weight. The English court should hesitate before making a reference against the wishes of one of the parties, seeing the expense and delay which it involves.'

1 [1974] Ch 401 at 402.

Mechanics of the reference

16.62 The courts, which are minded or compelled to make a reference, simply draft questions for the court which are then lodged with the domestic court in accordance with RSC Ord 114 or CCR Ord 19. Considerable care must be exercised in relation to drafting questions, which should be sufficiently clear and sufficiently precise so as to avoid the danger of there being any misunderstanding. Specifically, reference needs to be made to Community legislation and also any specific or general principles. It should be observed (even if this is a matter of opinion) that the tendency of the ECJ in the past has been to deprecate *specific* reliance on its past decisions in the way that we do in the UK but there is a perception that this is changing and accordingly, reference to authority may well be apposite.

16.63 Two important interrelated matters fall for consideration in the drafting of questions which are the interrelationship between questions of the interpretation of community law on its own (ie what does this specific regulation say?) and questions upon the validity of implementation (ie have we correctly transposed the TMA 1994 from the Directive?). Out of those two points comes a third which is that given that it is now a principal rule or cannon of construction of domestic statutes that they be consistent with our Community obligations, at least insofar as relate to implementing statutes,[1] so questions of domestic construction fall to be decided (albeit indirectly) by the ECJ if it is asked to look at directives.

1 Though we submit that the rule should go wider if it does not do so.

16.64 Further, no matter what one's view is of Europe, the fact is that the ECJ is very sensitive to the jurisdiction and rights of national courts and will not willingly trespass upon it. The ECJ's job is to interpret Community law. What it does not do is say anything about the interpretation of national measures or the conformity of those measures with Community law when viewed from a national construction perspective – it would not be competent to do so since such is within the province of the domestic interpretation of statutes. Accordingly. a question such as 'Is s 92 of the UK TMA 1994 compatible with the Trade Marks Directive insofar as the said s 92 gives no direct right to the defendant in criminal proceedings to impugn the rights in relation to which he has been charged?' will not do since it looks as if the ECJ is being asked to construe s 92 of the TMA 1994. To the ECJ, on this score, appearances are (understandably) everything. If, however, the question was posed 'Is the Trade Marks Directive to be interpreted as meaning that a Member State may not make laws which, when relating to criminal proceedings for infringement of a registered trade mark[1] deprive the defendant of any direct right to impugn the registrations relied upon?' then the court would prefer such a question.

1 Though that is not to say we concede by any means that the test for criminal liability under the TMA 1994, s 92 is the same as or is to be looked upon in the same way as the test for infringement – we would rather leave the question open for a reference. To that extent the example is not devoid of controversy, but no example would be.

16.65   As well as questions, matters of fact are also important to place the question in the correct context. Indeed in the case of *Foglia v Novello (No 2)*[1] the ECJ was asked by the domestic referring court 'why they consider that a reply to their question is necessary to enable them to give judgment'[2] and indeed in *Irish Creamery Milk Suppliers Association v Republic of Ireland*[3] the court opined that it should be placed in a such a position:

> 'To take cognizance of all the features of fact and law which may be relevant to the interpretation of Community law which it is called upon to give'

This makes sense from two perspectives, firstly and obviously because no real question can be decided in a vacuum and secondly because interveners (such as the European Commission) need to have some idea of what the proceedings are about.

1 [1981] ECR 3045, 3062, line 17.
2 See also *(Case 244/78) Union Laitière Normande v French Dairy Farmers Ltd* [1979] ECR 2663, 2681, line 5; [1980] 1 CMLR 314 and *(Joined Cases 141–143/81) Holdij* [1982] ECR 1299, 311, line 5; [1983] 2 CMLR 635.
3 Joined cases 36 and 76/98; [1981] ECR 735, 748, line 6; [1981] 2 CMLR 455

16.66   Once the court has decided to make a reference[1] and the questions have been formulated the application must be forwarded to the Senior Master of the Queen's Bench Division[2] who will transmit the questions to the ECJ. Thereafter the rules of the ECJ take over.[3]

1 In the case of the House of Lords it has to make a reference – there is apparently no discretion, though it is submitted that frivolous applications for a reference ought to be rejected.
2 RSC, Ord 114, r 5 (though no provision is actually made for transmission to the Senior Master) and the County Court Rules, Ord 19, r 15(5).
3 Codified version of the Rules of Procedure, the latest version of which may be found at (1999/C 65/01), O. C65 6 March 1999, p 1–36, though generally see http://europa.eu.int/cj/en/txts for the range of regulations governing the procedure of the ECJ.

Chapter 17

European procedure

Introduction

17.1 When we speak of European Procedure we mean the procedure in the rather oddly-named Office for the Harmonisation of the Internal Market (or OHIM for short) based at Alicante, Spain, where questions of prosecution of CTMs are decided and determined. We do not intend to cover or re-cover the question of references to the ECJ under art 234 of the Treaty of Rome.

OHIM

17.2 Despite its Kafkaesque name, OHIM[1] is the CTM registry and its existence and procedure is governed by two basic instruments being (as far as substance is concerned) Council Regulation of 20 December 1993 on the Community trade mark,[2] specifically arts 25–48, 57–63 and 90–103 (which we shall call the Basic Regulation) and Commission Regulation of 13 December 1995 implementing the Basic Regulation[3] (which we have called the CTM Implementing Regulation) which perform the same sort of function as the Trade Mark Rules 1994 do for national trade marks. Confusingly (or perhaps not so) regulations within the Implementing Regulation are called 'rules' whereas in the Basic Regulation they are called 'articles'. Hereinafter, (in the context of CTM procedure) when we refer to a rule it is the corresponding rule in the Implementing Regulation and likewise when we refer to an article it is the corresponding article in the Basic Regulation. The rules and articles are a magnitude more fastidious than are the corresponding domestic Trade Mark Rules 1994 and as such they require more attention to detail than has been afforded to the Trade Mark Rules 1994. For completeness, the Basic Regulation was amended by Council Regulation 3288/94 EC[4] to take account of certain obligations arising from the Uruguay Round and TRIPS Agreement with effect from 1 January 1996 (art 2).

1 Whose presence may be detected at http://www.oami.eu.int./en/default.htm. OAMI is the Spanish for OHIM.
2 (40/94/EEC), OJL 11 of 14 January 1994 pp 1-36 and http://www.oami.eu.int/en/aspects/reg40-94/reg.htm
3 (2868/95/EEC), OJL 303 of 15 December 1995 pp 1-32 and http://www.oami.eu.int/en/aspects/reg 2868/reg.htm.
4 Of 22 December 1994.

OHIM in practice

17.3   The law of the CTM and the practice of OHIM are fully discussed in Chapters 23-31 of this book. The rôle of OHIM is very similar to that of the registry in that it determines questions of registrability (including opposition), revocation and invalidity, all, theoretically the same as under the Directive though the jurisdiction runs parallel to it as opposed to being derived from it. Accordingly, one would hope that the rules relating to absolute and relative grounds of refusal would be the same – we will have to wait and see whether this is so in practice. Appeals from OHIM are determined in the first place by the CFI of the ECJ at first instance as opposed to the full ECJ. Procedure is generally dealt with in arts 73–80.

17.4   OHIM is divided up into five logical areas of competency where decision making is allowed. Those five areas are defined by art 125 as being:

1   Examiners[1]
2   Opposition divisions[2]
3   An administration of trade marks and legal division[3]
4   Cancellation divisions[4]
5   Boards of appeal[5]

which form the logical basis for the existence of OHIM. Procedure generally is to be found in arts 73–80 and the Implementing Regulation is basically one large instrument on procedure.

The procedure for registration can be conveniently broken down into seven stages, which we cover below.

1 Articles 36–38, 66 and 126; r 9–11.
2 Articles 8, 41–43 and 127; r 15–21 and 22 (relating to proof of use).
3 Article 128.
4 Articles 49–56 and 71; r 37–41.
5 Articles 57–63, 130 and 131; r 48–51.

Filing of the application and other minor procedural matters

17.5   An application is filed (though not via e-mail – yet) by the completion of an application form (OHIM Form 1.1 EN).[1]

Form filing procedure is not dependent upon the form being filed, though the place of filing may vary. Forms are, and have to be, available free of charge,[2] though they must (as with all correspondence) be in such a form as to permit an automated input of their content into a computer.[3]

All documents may (upon the absence of any provision to the contrary) be communicated to OHIM via facsimile or other means (as explained in more detail below) and upon receipt, an application is given an application number which is the number that the application has for the remainder of its prosecution.

1 This form (as with all forms) is to be found electronically at http://www.oami.eu.int/en/marque/form.htm in PDF format.
2 Rule 83(4).
3 Rule 83(7).

Time Limits

17.6   Rule 71 (1) states that with the exception of the periods expressly specified in either the Basic or Implementing Regulations, any period specified by OHIM may not:

> '... when the party concerned has its domicile or its principal place of business or an establishment within the Community, be less than one month or greater than six months or, when those conditions are not fulfilled, be less than two months or more than six months'.

Extensions may be granted under r 71 (1) and (2) if circumstances dictate it but the request must be made before expiry of the period. In cases where there are more than two parties to the proceedings, time may be extended by agreement between them.
   OHIM has stated that:

> 'In practice, with the exception of the expressly specified cases and in order to prevent the proceedings from being unnecessarily protracted, the periods specified by the Office shall, in principle, be two months. This rule shall nevertheless be subject to variation in accordance with the specific case, and the Office will take the respective situations of the parties into consideration during proceedings.

> 'Moreover, the periods specified by the Office shall generally be expressed in months.'[1]

Rules relating to the computation of time may be found in rr 70–72 and importantly r 71 provides for extensions granted by OHIM in the case where there is no opponent and by agreement in inter partes matters.[2]

1 Taken from 'Guidelines concerning proceedings before the Office for Harmonization in the Internal Market (Trade Marks and Designs)', part A, s 1(2) OJ OHIM 12/96, p 1790.
2 Time limits and extensions of time are further considered in ch 28, paras **28.2-28.6**.

Communicating with OHIM

17.7   There are a large number of detailed rules relating to communications with and by OHIM, generally to be found in rr 61–69 and 79–82. Under r 79, all documents, including the documents introducing the proceedings, may, in the absence of any provision to the contrary, be communicated to the Office by facsimile or other electronic means (though there is, at present, no e-mail), by post, by telegram or by any other means, including personal delivery. Mere acceptance of these documents is not to be taken to mean that they are admissible. Under r 79 (a) if a document is served by post, service or personal delivery then only signed originals of the documents shall be admissible by OHIM, though this is not the case with electronic communications.

Preliminary examination and according a date of filing

17.8   The application, once filed must undergo a preliminary examination, that is an examination under r 9 so as to ascertain the filing date, which is either the date of actual filing or such other date under r 6 and art 29–35 (priority and seniority from national marks) as the priority or seniority rules determine. Further, the preliminary examination is more of an administrative act than a substantive one and relates to things such as ensuring that the correct forms are filled in and that the application complies with r 1 which determines the necessary content of any application of a CTM. The information generally required is information such as a request for registration[1] the name and address of the applicant,[2] a representation of the trade mark,[3] the list of goods and services applied for,[4] the name and address of the representative (if any),[5] the declaration basis and existence of any seniority or priority claimed[6] whether a collective mark is claimed,[7] the language and second language[8] and the signature of the applicant.[9]

1 Rule 1(1)(a).
2 Rule 1(1)(b).
3 Rule 1(1)(d), see also r 3.
4 Rule 1(1)(c), see also r 2.
5 Rule 1(1)(e).
6 Rule 1(1)(f), (g) and (h).
7 Rule 1(1)(i).
8 Rule 1(1)(j).
9 Rule 1(1)(k).

Examination as to other formalities (fees, classification, priority, seniority, etc)

17.9 Thereafter, the application form is scrutinised and if any seniority or priority is claimed then a filing date is accorded. Otherwise the date of filing of the application is the filing date. Further, the fee is checked as is the integrity of the classification claimed (eg a claim to a trade mark covering thoughts would not be allowed). Further, the applicant's entitlement to use the mark applied for is also examined pursuant to r 10.

Examination of relative grounds of refusal

17.10 Once a filing date has been accorded a search of CTMs and applications is carried out [1] There is also provision for sending requests to national offices, for searching of their registries for CTM applications,[2] in such event the local registries are required to respond within three months.[3] Thereafter OHIM must notify the proprietors of any conflicts which arise on relative grounds, though it is apparent that OHIM does not itself take any action of its own motion on relative grounds[4] it being a matter for the opposition division and opposition proceedings in the event of opposition being filed.

1 Article 39(1).
2 Article 39(2).
3 Article 39(3).
4 Article 39(6).

Examination as to absolute grounds for refusal

17.11 The application is scrutinised to ensure that it is a registrable trade mark (for all the usual reasons). Under r 11(1) OHIM can cite its objections on absolute grounds and give the applicant time within which to withdraw or amend the application or in which to make observations, though non-distinctive elements of a particular trade mark may be specifically disclaimed under art 38(2) and r 11(2). If the objection is not overcome within the time limit, the application shall be refused in whole or in part (as the case may be).[1]

1 Rule 11(3).

Publication of the application

17.12 Thereafter the application is published in the Community Trade Mark Bulletin pursuant to r 85(1) and (2) and in accordance with the form set out in r 12 (which provides for a depiction of the mark, the specification and various other particulars). It is at this stage that an opponent can get involved under art 42 which provides that within three months from publication the opponent can object on relative grounds. He can only do so if he is the proprietor of the earlier trade mark or right in questionor in some instances if he is a licensee. In OHIM it is this way and only this way that relative grounds may be raised against any application.[1] We cover opposition proceedings in more detail below.

1 The TMA 1994, *Cf* ss 7 and 8.

Granting of the right and registration in the register of Community trade marks

17.13 If the opposition proceedings are unsuccessful or only partially successful, the mark or that part of it which survives either OHIM objection or opposition[1] may preceed to registration following the request by OHIM to pay registration fees. Once the fee is registered then the mark and other details[2] shall be recorded on the register (ie the register of CTMs) pursuant to r 23(4) and published in the Community Trade Marks Bulletin.

1 Rule 23(2).
2 Rule 84(2).

General procedural matters

Form of applications

17.14 The basic rule is that most of the procedural actions will take place in OHIM without the necessity for a hearing and the correspondence and representations will take place on paper. There is a fundamental principle in OHIM that every person who is party to a proceding shall have the opportunity of making representations and of being heard.[1]

1 Article 73.

17.15 An important principle in relation to relative grounds for refusal is that the tribunal must limit itself to the evidence provided by the parties and the submissions of the parties.[1] This would appear to preclude presumptive rules of evidence and matters of judicial notice. In other cases, the Office shall examine facts of its own motion[2] and shall scrutinise evidence according to whether the proceedings are adversarial or whether the enquiry is into relative or absolute grounds.

1 Article 74(1).
2 Article 74(1).

Evidence

17.16   Evidence may be taken from witnesses,[1] documents, experts, written statements and real evidence. There do not appear, however, to be any rules relating to evidence at all save that OHIM may issue a summons (of apparently little coercive effect). Indeed it is to be observed that there does not appear to be any provision for compelling the attendance of witnesses, though oral evidence has been described by OHIM as 'exceptional'.

1 Though only orally if OHIM approves – art 76(3) which is only appealable with a final appeal – art 57(2).

Hearings not necessarily in public

17.17   Oddly, under art 75 (2) oral proceedings in OHIM before examiners, in oppositions, administration departments and legal divisions shall not be in public but under art 75(3) those before the cancellation division and the Boards of Appeal shall be in public if not decided otherwise. Such proceedings may be held in private where the admission of the public could have serious and unjustified disadvantages - where for instance, confidential information such as sales information is being divulged.

Language

17.18   Under art 115(2) there are five languages of OHIM being Spanish, German, English, French and Italian though in the case of filing, all the official languages of the EEC may be used. The language of a set of proceedings is determined in accordance with a pre-set procedure. The applicant must specify a second language on the application form. Under art 115(4) if the applicant for a Community trade mark remains the sole party throughout the proceedings before the Office, the language of proceedings shall be the language in which the application was filed, which may therefore be any of the official languages of the Community. Thereafter in accordance with r 95(a) other procedures in the prosecution may be filed in either laguage. However, under art 115 (6) if a notice of opposition or an application to impugn is filed in the primary or secondary language then that language becomes the language of the proceedings. Under art 115(7) the parties in opposition, revocation or invalidity proceedings may agree upon any of the official languages of the Community.[1]

1 The question of language is further discussed in ch 23, paras **23.5-23.7**.

Extension of time limits

17.19   In some cases a party to proceedings might not be able to comply with a time limit for reasons outside his control. OHIM refers to the remedy procedure as *restitutio in integrum* which allows the proprietor of a CTM to avoid a sanction containing time limits if his failure to observe that time limit was due to circumstances beyond his control providing he had taken care to observe the time limit.[1]

1 Article 78.

Form of decisions

17.20 In giving a decision, OHIM shall '... state the reasons on which they are based'[1] and 'shall be based only on reasons or evidence on which the parties have had an opportunity to present their comments'.[2]

1 Rule 52(1).
2 Article 73.

Costs

17.21 Costs are governed by art 81(1) and (2) and r 94(1) and the general rule is that the losing party shall pay the costs. However, apportionment is possible if both sides come away with something.[1]

In cases of withdrawal, where a decision is not made, costs can be awarded against the terminating party[2] though the practice is that a bill of costs is required.

1 Article 81(3) and (4) and r 94 (2).
2 Article 81(6) and r 94(4).

Opposition

17.22 'Opposition' means objection to an application on relative grounds as contrasted with the impugning of an already registered CTM. This latter means of 'opposition', though effectively the same (in some respects at least) as the former, is more commonly referred to as 'cancellation' and we cover it separately. There are two types of opponents – active (in the sense that they become parties to any opposition proceedings) and passive (in that they are mere observers). Passive observers (who in accordance with art 41 can be anybody) may make observations raising grounds under art 7 (absolute grounds) on which the applicant is entitled to comment.[1] The observations can be made *at any time* after the publication of the application. The fact that there is no time limit is confusing since it is apparent that no such observation can be entertained once the trade mark is registered.

1 Article 41(2).

Opposition – the time to object and the procedure

17.23 An opponent may enter opposition within three months of the publication of the application.[1] The opponent must be the owner of an earlier mark or right[2] or may, in some circumstances, be a licensee. The opposition must state the grounds upon which opposition is made as well as complying with other formalities laid down by r 15 and art 42. Such opposition is entered on the requisite form from OHIM – Form 2.1. The opposition notice must contain all the facts asserted as well as evidence and arguments[3] in support. The opposition is examined as to admissibility and is then sent to the applicant who must reply, within a specified time limit under r 19. OHIM then considers the opposition and any reply and will rule upon it or call for a hearing and then rule. In cases where use of an earlier trade mark relied upon by an opponent needs to be proved, r 22 places the onus upon the opponent.

Thereafter, the opposition either fails or succeeds in whole or in part and the mark is accorded registration if the opposition is in any respect unsuccessful.

1 Article 42(1).
2 Article 42(1)(a), (b) and (c).
3 Rule 16(1).

Administrative decisions

17.24   In some cases, decisions are made which are not decisions relating to applications, oppositions or cancellation These are dealt with under art 128 by a special division called the 'administration of trade marks and legal division'[1].

1 See para **17.5** above.

Cancellation

17.25   Cancellation means the process of surrender, revocation or invalidity in OHIM. Surrender is governed by art 49 and simply relates to the position where a proprietor wishes not to own his trade mark any more or wishes to restrict the goods or services. The effect is to remove the trade mark from the register or restricted scope from the date upon which the surrender was entered onto the register. A surrender may be whole or partial with regards scope but may not involve the alteration of any part of the mark in question.

Revocation and invalidity

17.26   The procedure is, relating to revocation and invalidity identical.

Revocation is the process where a registered trade mark is revoked from a certain date, usually on the grounds of non-use (for five years)[1] but it may also cover situations where the mark has become descriptive through misuse,[2] deceptive by use[3] or the proprietor is no longer a person entitled to own a CTM.[4]

Revocation proceedings may be brought in the cancellation division of OHIM in accordance with r 37, and under r 38, applications for revocation which do not comply with the requirements set down are to be rejected. The requirements include a statement of grounds and *an indication of* the evidence, facts and arguments in support. It is important to comply with r 37 in full. If the application for revocation is in order then the application is communicated, under r 40, to the proprietor who must supply observations within a specified time period. If no observations are made then OHIM shall decide the question on the basis of materials before it.[5] The applicant for revocation may reply to any observations made within any further time as may be specified.[6]

1 Article 50(1)(a).
2 Article 50(1)(b).
3 Article 50(1)(c).
4 Article 50(1)(d).
5 Rule 40(2).
6 Rule 40(3).

Appeals

17.27 Boards of appeal exist to which appeals may be made. Appeals are made by way of notice of appeal under r 48 which has to contain certain relevant information including the identification of the decision appealed against. This must be lodged within two months of the decision being appealed against though grounds need not be lodged for another two months;[1] the grounds are likely to be detailed and have to include summaries of legal argument as well as factual matters relied upon in support of the grounds.[2]

Only parties adversely affected by a decision may appeal.[3]

1 Article 59.
2 Rule 51.
3 Article 58.

Infringement and related counterclaims

17.28 Infringement of a CTM is governed by art 14 (ie our national law which is in fact Community law because our national law stems from the Directive) but is decided by CTM courts in the UK. The procedure for infringement of a CTM is the same as relates to domestic trade marks save that there is only one level of appeal allowed for in the Basic Regulation[1] and none allowed for expressly in the statutory instrument which creates such courts.[2] The basic designated court is the High Court and it is submitted that since no second level or tier court is designated, the effect of art 91(5) is that any appeal is to the Court of Appeal.

As far as the procedures relating to appeals and further appeals are concerned this is a matter of national law.[4]

1 Article 91(1).
2 See The CTM Regulations 1996 (SI 1996/1908), reg 9.
3 Article 101.

17.29 Articles 95 and 96 allow counterclaims to be made in relation to revocation and invalidity, though those questions are to be decided by reference to the Basic Regulation as opposed to questions of infringement which are to be decided by reference to national law

In seeking to remedy infringements, the national CTM court follows its own procedures[1] and has all the usual tools in its armoury[2] including interim relief.[3]

1 Article 97.
2 Article 98.
3 Article 99.

Jurisdiction and law

17.30 The jurisdiction of the CTM courts is defined in art 92 as being:

'… exclusive jurisdiction-

    (a) for all infringement actions and-if they are permitted under national law-actions in respect of threatened infringement relating to Community trade marks;

(b) for actions for declaration of non-infringement, if they are permitted under national law;

(c) for all actions brought as a result of acts referred to in Article 9(3), second sentence,[1]

(d) for counterclaims for revocation or for a declaration of invalidity of the Community trade mark pursuant to Article 96'.[2]

That said (and simply stated) the question of jurisdiction is fraught. Firstly, jurisdiction has to be ceded under art 100(1) to other courts (or OHIM if the validity of the trade mark is already in issue) – this only happens, however, upon the application of one of the parties or upon the court's own motion. Similarly where proceedings are on foot in OHIM and prior validity proceedings are also on foot in a CTM court then under art 100(2) the OHIM proceedings may be stayed or the parties may apply to the CTM court to stay those proceedings. Article 100(3) enables provisional and protective measures to be granted in appropriate circumstances.

1 Which reads:
'The rights conferred by a Community trade mark shall prevail against third parties from the date of publication of registration of the trade mark. Reasonable compensation may, however, be claimed in respect of matters arising after the date of publication of a Community trade mark application, which matters would, after publication of the registration of the trade mark, be prohibited by virtue of that publication. The court seized of the case may not decide the merits of the case until the registration has been published.'
2 Which relates to counterclaims for invalidity based upon grounds only appearing in the Basic Regulation – which are, incidentally, the only grounds upon which the Community trade marks court is entitled to decide such questions.

17.31   Secondly, the CTM courts are obliged to apply the law as it appears in the Basic Regulation[1] except where the Basic Regulation does not provide, in which case national law shall prevail (such as the law of infringement).[2] Private international law, insofar as left alone by the Basic Regulation, remains national.[3] The procedures (already discussed) are identical to the ordinary national procedures of the CTM court.[4]

1 Article 97(1).
2 Article 97(2).
3 Article 97(2).
4 Article 97(3).

17.32   Thirdly, the question, when looked at from the Brussels Convention perspective, is difficult, since on one reading, the Basic Regulation purports to exclude parts of the Brussels Convention – which it cannot do since the Brussels Convention is not an EU measure as such but is rather a multilateral treaty – the EU has no right to interfere with it as such. However, what the Basic Regulation appears to do is to remove questions of CTM law from the hands of the Brussels Convention and then to say that questions of CTM law shall be decided *as if* the Brussels Convention applied *save that* certain changes shall apply – we submit that this is the better way to look at the position and such is indeed the effect of art 90.

17.33   In relation to proceedings in CTM courts, those courts shall proceed, in relation to disputes over which it is given jurisdiction from art 92, as if it were bound by the Brussels Convention save that:

'In the case of proceedings in respect of the actions and claims referred to in Article 92-

(a) Articles 2, 4, 5(1), (3), (4) and (5) and Article 24 of the [Brussels] Convention … shall not apply;
(b) Articles 17 and 18 of that Convention shall apply subject to the limitations in Article 93(4) … ;
(c) the provisions of Title II of th[e] … [Brussels] Convention which are applicable to persons domiciled in a Member State shall also be applicable to persons who do not have a domicile in any Member State but have an establishment therein.'[1]

It should be recalled that arts 2, 4, 5 and 24 of the Brussels Convention are jurisdiction conferring articles, and do not rquire repetition here. Articles 17 and 18 of that Convention relate to prorogation of jurisdiction and jurisdiction arising by appearance. Each of those articles is limited by the Basic Regulation so as only to allow prorogation to different CTM courts or appearance before those courts.

Article 93 then provides that a defendant shall be sued in the Member State in which he is domiciled or has establishment[2] and in accordance with art 52 of the Brussels Convention, the question of whether a person is domiciled is to be determined in accordance with national law – there is no guidance upon what is meant by 'establishment'. If the defendant is neither domiciled nor established within a Member State then the courts of the place where the claimant is domiciled or has establishment is chosen as the place to sue,[3] leaving Spain[4] under art 93(3) or the place where the act took place.[5]

Once seized of a matter, a CTM court has jurisdiction over all acts within the EU.[6]

1 Article 90(2).
2 Article 93(1).
3 Article 93(2).
4 The seat of OHIM.
5 Article 93(5), save for declarations of non-infringement.
6 Article 94 – though there is only parochial jurisdiction for courts whose jurisdiction is based upon the place where the infringing act took place – art 94(2).

Final appeals

17.34 By 'final appeals' we mean appeals to the Court of First Instance ('CFI') at the ECJ. OHIM is subject to the judicial control of the CFI. This is governed by art 63 which provides that (1) the CFI has jurisdiction in relation to matters brought before the boards of appeal on appeal, (2) the grounds may be lack of competence, procedural impropriety (provided essential), substantive impropriety (ie non-compliance with a substantive Community obligation), (3) the remedy is annulment of the contested decision, (4) the parties with *locus standi* to appeal to the CFI are parties who are adversely affected by any decision of the board of appeal. Once the decision is made by the board of appeal there is a period of two months where an appeal may be made to the CFI and OHIM must take all steps necessary to comply with a judgment of the CFI. The detailed procedure of the CFI is outside the scope of this chapter and readers are invited to consult the specialist texts.

Part V

Customs and criminal offences

Chapter 18

Border controls – domestic procedure and proceedings

1   The rationale and objectives

18.1   One of the major difficulties which faces the proprietor of a UK
(or Community) registered trade mark is the restraining of activities carried out by
others which are infringing or counterfeit. It could be said that one of the major
purposes of this book is to examine in detail the rights of such a proprietor in relation to such activities and it is only towards one aspect of this that this chapter is
devoted. There are two distinct strands to this problem: (1) the proliferation of
counterfeit goods where the goods concerned do not originate from the proprietor
or are not marked with his consent which can properly be described as counterfeit;
and (2) the proliferation of goods which although produced by the proprietor by or
with his consent should not by the operation of a domestic law or European measure, be sold in the UK and which can properly be described as infringing. It is
obvious that all goods which are counterfeit are so marked in infringement of the
rights of the proprietor. The converse does not necessarily follow, that goods which
are infringing goods are necessarily counterfeit. It should be noted that whilst in
infringement or counterfeiting cases the goods themselves are not to be described
as infringing since their making or production usually, but not always, infringes no
rights arising by way of the law of registered trade marks, it has become common
practice to refer to such goods as are *marked* in infringement of the proprietor's
rights as infringing goods. It should also be noted that in a purely civil sense
infringing articles may be dealt with by the remedy of delivery up, destruction on
oath or obliteration of the trade mark in question whereas there are certain proceedings (which form the scope and subject matter of this chapter) where the only remedy available is a form of delivery up. These distinctions will be discussed and
expanded upon below. We also pause to observe that although in terms of trade
marks law, this area, though potentially very powerful and certainly expanding in
use, is still something of a backwater in relation to the law of trade marks proper.

18.2   The problems which the proprietor faces in relation to goods which are
imported into the UK either from outside the EEA or from within the EEA can be
massive. In the usual course, the proprietor, upon discovering the activities of a
counterfeiter or infringer in the UK will take the appropriate civil measures provided for the protection of his rights. However, this can be difficult where there are
a large number of counterfeiters or infringers and very often these people are difficult to track down. The proprietor will usually go as far up the chain as he can since
there is a resultant saving in costs and he can stem the sources of supply (and thus
the supplies themselves) with the minimum use of civil remedies. The reasons for
the expediency and desirability of this course are obvious.

One means whereby a proprietor may stem the flow of infringing or counterfeit goods into the United Kingdom is to take advantage of an array of domestic laws and European measures which enable him to cause the importation of such goods as bear the marks in question to be prohibited and to take advantage of a relatively straightforward set of proceedings to ensure that the goods are never made available for sale in the United Kingdom. That such proceedings are described as 'relatively simple' acknowledges that, in some cases (but by no means all), trade mark litigation, in a purely civil sense,[1] can be lengthy, time consuming and very complex and that the juridical basis for the existence of the prohibition is not, as yet, well established as part of our domestic law or our body of law relating to the interpretation and application of any appropriate or corresponding European measure.

1 That is by way of claim form in the High Court.

18.3   The insidious nature of the activities of counterfeiters and infringers means that the trade mark proprietor is in weak position if all he can stop is the importation of infringing goods. He must also be entitled and able to stop the secondary means of enablement such as the importation of dyes, patterns, packaging, labels and other means for the production of infringing goods.[1] It should also be noted that in many senses the rights of a potential or actual claimant are powerful, if costly, and we would wish to make clear that whilst it is the rights of a trade mark proprietor that forms the basis of trade mark legislation in its widest sense, defendants have rights too.

1 Goods falling within the scope of the United Kingdom registered trade mark registration and marked in an infringing way (within the meaning of TMA 1994, s 10(1), (2) or (3)) are termed infringing goods, TMA 1994, s 17(2). Packaging and business papers for advertising such goods are termed infringing material, TMA 1994, s 17(3). Specially adapted means such as dies, knitting or sewing patterns are termed infringing material, TMA 1994, s 17(3), *quare* whether a programmable pattern sewing machine is specifically adapted or even whether the software used to programme it is so adapted.

18.4   As presently developed, both domestic law and certain European measures make provision for the use of a *quasi* civil set of proceedings which are (or can be) summary in nature, quick and relatively inexpensive and allow infringing and/or counterfeit goods to be dealt with in much the same way that certain other goods are dealt with at the border.[1] However, as we shall see, there are a number of profound constitutional issues which may make the questions to be considered far more protracted than the relevant legislation intended. Those laws and measures also provide certain safeguards for the importer so that he may have an opportunity of being heard.

1 Such as certain alcohol-based products.

18.5   The basis for such laws and measures stems in part from the provisions of the General Agreement on Tarrifs and, annexed thereto (Annex 1c), the Agreement on Trade-Related Aspects of Intellectual Property Rights, Including Trade in Counterfeit Goods[1] ('the TRIPS agreement'). The TRIPS agreement was signed in Marrakesh, in April 1994, as an annex to the agreement establishing the World Trade Organisation although, as shall be seen, there were already in place a number of measures which provided similar protection to those set out in TRIPS.[2] In certain respects, an understanding of TRIPS and its rationale is important in construing certain of the European legislation. However, as will become clear the drafting of certain of the relevant provisions of TRIPS in fact post dates certain other European measures and it is these measures which provided the basis for the current version not only of TRIPS but also of the current body of European and domestic law.

1 The drafting history of the Agreement on Trade-Related Aspects of Intellectual Property Rights, Including Trade in Counterfeit Goods is outside the scope of this chapter but an excellent guide to this can be found in D Gervais *The TRIPS Agreement – Drafting History and Analysis* (Sweet & Maxwell 1998).
2 Such as the Berne or Paris Conventions.

2 The means

18.6 The regime currently (and, we stress purportedly) in force in the UK has force by way of the Customs and Excise Management Act 1978 ('CEMA 1979') by whichever route one chooses to stem supply (and there is more then one) at least that appears to be the intention of the UK Government and the European Commission. The CEMA 1979 provides a wide range of powers which may be exercised by Her Majesty's Commissioners of Her Majesty's Customs and Excise ('the Commissioners' and 'HMC&E') in relation to a large number of matters.[1] An important feature of the CEMA 1979 is that in order to check the many wide ranging powers which are vested in the Commissioners or the officers of HMC&E there is also provision whereby the defendant or person in the position of a defendant can be heard.

1 Obviously, the Commissioners themselves perform no such function directly but, rather, delegate (upon express authority) their powers, functions and duties onto officers of HMC&E by the operation of the CEMA 1979 s 8(1)(b) the CEMA 1979 or such officers have such powers, functions and duties imposed upon them direct by various sections of the CEMA 1979.

18.7 An important and central concept in relation to the operation of the CEMA 1979 is the notion or concept of prohibited goods. Prohibited goods are those goods which are prohibited either by the operation of the CEMA 1979 itself or by any other enactment, though the precise scope of this is unclear. Prohibition in this sense means prohibition against importation, landing or unloading.[1] Once it is established that goods are likely to be prohibited goods then upon their importation, landing or unloading, they become liable to forfeiture.[2] The means by which goods may be or become described as prohibited and the manner in which the CEMA 1979 is applied will be discussed further below. Goods which are liable to forfeiture are not to be treated automatically as seized without more but are either seized or detained as liable for forfeiture. Once the goods are seized or detained as liable for forfeiture (either by an officer of HMC&E or by a constable or any member of the armed forces or any coast guard)[3] then they must be delivered to the nearest office of HMC&E or if such delivery is not practicable then written particulars must be furnished to that office.[4] If the person making the seizure or the detention is a constable then if the goods concerned are to be used in evidence in proceedings other than proceedings under the CEMA 1979 or related statutes then the goods may be kept at a police station[5] though the police must give the Commissioners written notice of the keeping of such goods and must allow inspection of such goods.[6]

1 CEMA 1979, s 40(1)(b).
2 CEMA 1979, s 40(1).
3 CEMA 1979, s 139(1).
4 CEMA 1979, s 139(2) (a) and (b).
5 CEMA 1979, s 139(3).
6 CEMA 1979, s 139(4).

18.8   However, it is not just the goods which are liable to be forfeit. The things that they are bound up, mixed or packed with and any means whatsoever which has been used for the transportation of those goods are also liable to be forfeit.[1] Gavin McFarlane in his book *Customs and Excise Law and Practice*[2] describes the breath of this liability as 'breathtaking' and that expression is tame to say the least,[3] though some distinction may be drawn between cases where goods are mixed or packed with each other and where they form discrete batches.

1 CEMA 1979 s 141(1) .
2 Sweet & Maxwell, 1993.
3 For a particularly draconian example of how this works see *Customs and Excise Comrs v Air Canada* [1991] 2 QB 446 where an aeroplane carrying cannabis resin was seized even though the carriers had no idea what was on board. The Court of Appeal held that knowledge did not matter. CEMA 1979, s 142(1) provides for situations where a ship is over 250 tons register which lessens the draconian effects of these provisions.

18.9   Another important concept prevalent in the CEMA 1979 is the concept of seizure or detention of goods as liable to forfeiture. In this context, seized goods simply mean that such goods are being held temporarily pending determination as to whether those goods are forfeit and accordingly there is little distinction between the word 'seize' and the expression 'detain as liable for forfeiture' and, it is submitted, there is in fact no distinction, the latter words being intended to explain the scope of the former. When goods which have been seized or detained as liable to forfeiture (on the grounds that they are prohibited goods either by the operation of the CEMA 1979 or by some other (normally judicial) process (set out in the CEMA 1979)) are determined as truly prohibited the goods are said to be condemned as forfeit and any judicial proceedings where the nature and, therefore, the legality of the prohibition or detention is in issue (usually as a matter of fact) are termed condemnation proceedings.

18.10   Goods which are condemned as forfeit then become forfeit and title to those goods, or at least the right to dispose of the goods in such manner as the Commissioners direct, vests in the Commissioners.[1] This will usually (but not always) mean that the goods are destroyed.

1 CEMA 1979, s 139(5).

3   Procedure

18.11   On the assumption that the importer of the goods in question is attempting to import goods which are prohibited, then, as discussed above, the Commissioners or any relevant officer or other person may, upon completion of the relevant formalities, seize the goods or detain them as liable for forfeiture. The Commissioners must then initiate the condemnation procedure.[1] It is not a necessary consequence of the condemnation procedure that condemnation proceedings result but rather a possible consequence. the CEMA 1979, Sch 3 sets out the condemnation procedure. the CEMA 1979, Sch 3 has force in relation to condemnation proceedings by the operation of the CEMA 1979, s 145.[2] Firstly, the Commissioners must notify the person who is to their knowledge the owner or one of the owners of the seized or detained goods that those goods are liable to forfeiture and must also specify the grounds of such liability[3] though such notice need not be given if the seizure was made in the presence of: (a) the person whose offence or suspected offence occasioned the seizure; or (b) the owner or any of the owners of the thing seized or any servant or agent of his; (c) in the case of anything seized in any ship or aircraft, the master or commander.[4] However, absent such circumstances, such notice shall be given by the Commissioners to the owner or part owner in writing and shall be deemed to have been duly served on that person: (a) if delivered to him personally; or (b) if addressed to him and left or forwarded by post to him at his usual or last known place of abode or business or, in the case of a body corporate, at its registered or principal office; or (c) where he has no address within the UK or the Isle of Man, or his address is unknown, by publication of notice of the seizure in the London, Edinburgh or Belfast Gazette.[5]

1 CEMA 1979, s 139(6) and Sch 3.
2 Which is mainly administrative in effect providing that the CEMA 1979, Sch 3 applies to condemnation proceedings (s 145(1)), that such proceedings may only be commenced by order of the Commissioners (s 145(1)), that where proceedings are commenced in a Magistrates' Court then they must be in the name of an officer (s 145(2)), that where an officer in whose name proceedings are constituted dies, is discharged, removed or is absent then he may be substituted by an officer authorised by the Commissioners (s 145(4)), and where a person is in custody in relation to a Customs and Excise Act offence then the court can deal with him notwithstanding that no proceedings have been instituted by the order of the Commissioners (s 145(6)) or have not been commenced in the name of an officer.
3 CEMA 1979, Sch 3, para 1(1).
4 CEMA 1979, Sch 3, para 1(2).
5 CEMA 1979, Sch 3, para 2.

18.12   Thereafter, the owner or part owner is termed 'the claimant' and he must within one month of the service of such notice or (if no such notice is served upon him) within one month[1] of the date of seizure[2] give notice in writing to the Commissioners at any office of HMC&E of his claim that the seized or detained goods are not prohibited and are thereby not liable to forfeiture. There is no requirement that such a notice be in any particular form though it is necessary to set out 'the name and address of the claimant and, in the case of a claimant who is outside the UK and the Isle of Man, shall specify, the name and address of a solicitor in the UK who is authorised to accept service of process and to act on behalf of the claimant'.[3] Service on any such solicitor is thereafter deemed to be service on the claimant.[4] This is to be contrasted with the rules relating to the service of process, ie a claim form or other process issued anywhere in the UK, which is governed by the CEMA 1979, s 146 which requires that service be effected in the UK without further endorsement,[5] that service is effected by delivering the process personally[6] or leaving the process at his last known place of abode, business address or (in the case of bodies corporate) registered or principal office[7] or such process is left on board any aircraft or vessel to which he may belong or have lately belonged.[8] Further the CEMA 1979, s 146(2) allows service of any subsequent process such as a summons, notice, order or other document issued for the purposes of the proceedings or any appeal to be effected by an officer, though there is no prohibition on such an officer effecting service of originating process under the CEMA 1979, s 146(1).

1 Which is one calendar month, Interpretation Act 1978, s 5 and Sch 1.
2 CEMA 1979, Sch 3, para 3.
3 CEMA 1979, Sch 3, para 4(1).
4 CEMA 1979, Sch 3, para 4(2).
5 CEMA 1979, s 146(1).
6 CEMA 1979, s 146(1)(a).
7 CEMA 1979, s 146(1)(b).
8 CEMA 1979, s 146(1)(c).

18.13 If the claimant or his solicitor (as the case may be) has not served a notice of claim[1] within the relevant time or such notice is defective, then the goods shall be automatically deemed to be condemned as forfeit and such forfeiture runs retrospectively from the date of seizure or detention (which is the date from which the liability to forfeiture arose).[2]

1 Not to be confused with a claim form.
2 CEMA 1979, Sch 3, para 7.

18.14 If, however, the claimant has served a notice of claim within the relevant time which complies with the required form, the Commissioners are under a mandatory obligation to institute condemnation proceedings in relation to the condemnation of those goods as forfeit by the court[1] and the court will consider on the facts whether the goods are to be condemned as forfeit. However, the mandatory requirement is somewhat abrogated by the effects of the CEMA 1979, s 152 which confers a power onto the Commissioners to mitigate penalties and the like. the CEMA 1979, s 152 provides:

> 'The Commissioners may, as they see fit:
> (a) stay, sist or compound any proceedings ... for the condemnation of any thing as being forfeited under the customs and excise Acts; or
> (b) restore, subject to such conditions (if any) as they think proper, any thing forfeited or seized under those Acts;
> ...'

1 The expression 'court' is defined in the CEMA 1979, Sch 3, para 8 as:
'8. Proceedings for condemnation shall be civil proceedings and may be instituted-
(a) in England or Wales either in the High Court or in a magistrates' court;
(b) in Scotland either in the Court of Session of the sherrif court ;
(c) in Northern Ireland either in the High Court or in a court of summary jurisdiction.
9. Proceedings for the condemnation of any thing instituted in a magistrates' court in England or Wales, in the sheriff court in Scotland or in a court of summary jurisdiction in Northern Ireland may he so instituted-
(a) in any such court having jurisdiction in the place where any offence in connection with that thing was committed or where any proceedings for such an offence are instituted; or
(b) in any such court having jurisdiction in the place where the claimant resides or, if the claimant has specified a solicitor under paragraph 4 above [because he, the claimant, is outside the UK or the Isle of Man and has specified a solicitor to act for him], in the place where that solicitor has his office; or
(c) in any such court having jurisdiction in the place where that thing was found, detained or seized or to which it is first brought after being found, detained or seized.'

18.15 As can be seen, the Commissioners have a fairly wide discretion to stay proceedings and to return the goods (though we submit that it would be on terms as to costs). Further, the mandatory requirement that condemnation proceedings be *instituted* as opposed to *continued* is not really abrogated by the effect of the CEMA 1979, s 152 which relates to the position where proceedings are on foot. However, it is submitted that the CEMA 1979, s 152 is of use where the importer and proprietor have come to terms in relation to further dealing in the goods.[1] However, since the Commissioners appear to have an absolute discretion it is unlikely they will exercise that discretion in the importer's favour if it would be contrary to its public law duty or would interfere with the private rights of others including the proprietor. However, even where the importer and the proprietor do not come to terms but the importer is able to deal with the goods in such a way that does not interfere with the private rights of the proprietor (or at least put them at risk) nor interfere with the Commissioners' public duty then it is at least open to the Commissioners to stay the proceedings in question and return the goods, on whatever terms they stipulate. This emphasises the fact that there is nothing penal in the CEMA 1979 relating to condemnation.[2]

1 Which could well be the case in relation to parallel imports.
2 Though there are the allied penal provisions under the TMA 1994, s 92 or the TDA 1968,SI.

18.16 It is an important and often overlooked condition precedent in condemnation proceedings 'instituted in England, Wales or Northern Ireland, that the claimant or his solicitor shall make oath that the thing seized was, or was to the best of his knowledge and belief, the property of the claimant at the time of the seizure'[1] and, where proceedings are instituted in the High Court (of England and Wales or of Northern Ireland), then the claimant shall also be required to give security for the Commissioner's legal costs. It is submitted that, although the requirement to give security for costs is mandatory, the other incidents relating to the court's discretion as to the amount and the manner of provision of such security would follow the normal procedure in the High Court in, at least England and Wales, pursuant to the relevant procedural rules[2] though it is submitted that it is likely that the court in considering the amount of security that it ought to order will always bear in mind that it can order any amount up to the full amount claimed by way of security, and though it ought to be more than a simply nominal amount; it is not bound to make an order of a substantial amount.[3]

1 CEMA 1979, Sch 3, para 10(1).
2 Pursuant to the RSC 1965 Ord 23 (as amended), which is not echoed in the CPR 1998.
3 *Roburn Construction Ltd v William Irwin (South) and Co Ltd* [1991] BCC 726 as approved by the Court of Appeal in *Keary Developments Ltd v Tarmac Construction Ltd* [1995] 3 All ER 534.

18.17 In the event that the claimant does not assert title or provide such security as is determined by the court then the court shall give judgment for the Commissioners and shall thereby condemn the goods as forfeit.[1] It is to be noted that in condemnation proceedings the court has no other powers save to condemn and as such, for instance, the court cannot order obliteration of the relevant trade marks from the goods.[2]

1 CEMA 1979, Sch 3, para 10(3).
2 Though, as we shall see, HMC&E does have the power and right to deal with the goods in any manner they see fit.

18.18 Because condemnation proceedings can be instituted in two wholly different kinds of courts exercising civil jurisdiction[1] it is important to examine with some degree of detail the relative procedure in each of those courts. Apart from the manner of appeal (which is dealt with below), the procedure in the High Court follows the same procedural route as any other civil claim[2] though the rules of evidence are modified by the CEMA 1979 in that the burden of proof is shifted entirely upon the defendant insofar as relates to pleaded facts.[3] All the Commissioners need do is state the nature of their claim or complaint and the facts upon which they rely without the necessity of formally proving them.[4] This does not mean that the Commissioners need merely make a formal claim without any factual allegations accompanying them since it is only pleaded facts which cause the legal burden to shift to the defendant. There is no presumption that the goods in question shall be forfeit and if a pleading is factually deficient to a material degree then prima facie the pleading falls to be struck out or ignored. The distinction is important since it effectively levels the scales and only provides an easy route for the proof of facts which are not within the knowledge of the defendant.

1 That is the High Court and the Magistrates' Court.
2 Or, as in the Magistrates' Court, complaint.
3 CEMA 1979, Sch 3, para 13.
4 Though to take this course would be unwise since any claimant defending condemnation proceedings would put in his own evidence which (if believed) would shift the evidential burden back onto the Commissioners who would fail in the absence of any evidence of their own.

18.19   Furthermore, the Commissioners have the benefit of certain other statutory provisions relating to evidence such as there being a rebuttable presumption that any document purporting to be signed by the Commissioners or by their order shall be presumed to have been so signed and may be proved by the production of a copy of that document.[1] Such a presumption also applies in relation to any proclamation, order, or regulation: (1) issued by the Commissioners;[2] or (2) issued before the 1 April 1909 by the Commissioners or themselves and the Commissioners of Inland Revenue acting jointly[3] or by the Commissioners of Inland Revenue acting alone[4] by either:

(i)   the production of a copy of the Gazette purporting to contain such proclamation, order, or regulation;[5]
(ii)   the production of a copy of such proclamation, order, or regulation, purporting to be printed by the Government printer.[6]

1 CEMA 1979,s 153(1).
2 CEMA 1979, s 153(2)(a).
3 CEMA 1979, s 153(2)(b).
4 CEMA 1979, s 153(2)(c).
5 Documentary Evidence Act 1868, s 2(1), as incorporated by reference by the operation of CEMA 1979, s 153(2).
6 Documentary Evidence Act 1868, s 2(2), as incorporated by reference by the operation of CEMA 1979, s 153(2).

18.20   The effect is that '[no] proof shall be required of the handwriting or official position of any person certifying, in pursuance of … the Documentary Evidence Act 1868, to the truth of any copy of or extract from any proclamation, order, or regulation'[1] provided that the document is signed or purports to be signed by the Commissioners or any secretary or assistant secretary to the Commissioners or the Commissioners of Inland Revenue as the case may be.[2] the CEMA 1979, s 153, and the Documentary Evidence Act 1868 create rebuttable presumptions that certain official documents need not be proved and neither is it necessary to prove that they have been signed.

1 Documentary Evidence Act 1868, s 2.
2 CEMA 1979, s 153(3).

18.21   Certified photographs of documents which have been delivered to the Commissioners for any customs and excise purpose shall be admissible to the same extent as the original.[1]

1 CEMA 1979 s 153(4).

18.22   Of more value to the Commissioners in condemnation proceedings is the effect of the CEMA 1979, s 154, which creates certain other rebuttable presumptions. The relevant presumptions we list below, ie that the following shall be rebuttably presumed to be true where made by an averment in any process in condemnation proceedings under the CEMA 1979:

— that those proceedings were instituted by the order of the Commissioners;[1]
— that any person is or was a Commissioner, officer or constable, or a member of Her Majesty's armed forces or coastguard;[2]
— that any person is or was appointed or authorised by the Commissioners to discharge, or was engaged by the orders or with the concurrence of the Commissioners in the discharge of, any duty;[3]
— that the Commissioners have or have not been satisfied as to any matter as to which they are required by any provision of the Customs and Excise Acts to be satisfied;[4]
— that any ship is a British ship;[5]
— that any goods thrown overboard, staved or destroyed were so dealt with in order to prevent or avoid the seizure of those goods.[6]

1 CEMA 1979, s 154(1)(a).
2 CEMA 1979, s 154(1)(b).
3 CEMA 1979, s 154(1)(c).
4 CEMA 1979, s 154(1)(d).
5 CEMA 1979, s 154(1)(e).
6 CEMA 1979, s 154(1)(f).

18.23   The presumption under the CEMA 1979, s 155(1)(d), is, we submit, available to the Commissioners in relation to condemnation proceedings so far as the domestic route is concerned and where trade marks are concerned since the enactment which requires the Commissioners to be satisfied is the TMA 1994, the relevant parts of which are, for the purposes of condemnation proceedings, a customs and excise act.[1] However, this is limited in its scope since there are no matters so far as the domestic route is concerned about which the Commissioners have to be dissatisfied (as opposed to satisfied, and the presumption does not work in the converse).

1 See CEMA 1979. s 1(1), where the expression 'customs and excise acts' is defined as including 'any other enactment for the time being in force relating to customs or excise'.

18.24   The CEMA 1979, s 154(2), in relation to proceedings relating to condemnation and where those proceedings are either: (1) brought against any person not in the next class; or (2) by or against the Commissioners, a law officer of the Crown or an officer, causes the burden of proof to lie on the other party insofar as respects 'anything purporting to have been done in pursuance of any power or duty conferred or imposed on him by or under the Customs and Excise Acts'. He, the other party, has (insofar as the question arises) to establish the following questions in his favour as:

— to the place from which any goods have been brought;[1]
— whether or not any goods or other things whatsoever are of the description or nature alleged in the information, writ or other process;[2]
— whether or not any goods have been lawfully imported or lawfully unloaded from any ship or aircraft;[3]
— whether or not any goods are or were subject to any prohibition of or restriction on their importation or exportation[4].

1 CEMA 1979, s 154(2).
2 CEMA 1979, s 154(2)(b).
3 CEMA 1979, s 154(2)(c).
4 CEMA 1979, s 154(2)(f).

18.25 The placing of the burden of proof on the other party has the effect in condemnation proceedings of effectively placing the burden on him of *disproving* those matters if the issue is raised by HMC&E against the importer and of *proving* those matters if the issue is raised by him against HMC&E. Importantly, the burden of proving that certain goods are not the subject of a prohibition in proceedings to which HMC&E is a party is upon the importer, whether or not he is the claimant or complainant.

18.26 We add that insofar as proceedings before Magistrates' Courts are concerned, authorised officers or persons or in-house solicitors who have been admitted but do not hold a practising certificate may conduct those proceedings whether or not they are legally qualified.[1]

1 CEMA 1979, s 155(1) and (2).

The High Court

18.27 Until the CPR 1998 came into force in April 1999, proceedings in the High Court were usually commenced by writ of summons but could also be commenced by originating summons.[1] The originating summons procedure was apt where there were unlikely to be any substantial issues of fact for the court to determine and the questions were really ones of construction or of law.[2] Experience has shown that there were as many sets of High Court condemnation proceedings where there was no dispute as to fact (and where the issues turned on matters of construction or of law) as there were where the facts were in dispute. However, since it was unlikely in all but the clearest cases that the Commissioners would know whether the totality of the facts or any smaller number of them were in dispute the preferred procedure would usually have been by way of writ of summons. If and in the event that the Commissioners decided upon one route or another whether by way of writ of summons or originating summons and the route of origination was or turned out to be incorrect, then the court would, in any event, either of its own motion or upon that of one of the parties, give appropriate directions. It was certainly not fatal to the proceedings for them to have been incorrectly constituted.[3] A full treatise on the manner and conduct of civil proceedings is outside the scope of this chapter and the reader is directed to the Civil Court Practice. However, given that the legal burden is, in certain respects, on the claimant it would be likely at the very least that the claimant would want to take advantage of the discovery (or now 'disclosure') process which an action commenced by writ of summons now (Part 7 or Part 8 claim form) afforded.

1 RSC 1965 Ord 5, r 4(1)(as amended).
2 RSC 1965 Ord 5, r 4(2)(a) and (b) (as amended).
3 RSC 1965 Ord 2, r 1(3) (as amended).

18.28 The CPR 1998 swept away the different ways of initiating proceedings in the High Court and county courts and left us with only one type of procedure which is akin to the writ of summons procedure, though, as we shall see, there are limits upon the discovery process.

18.29 Further, the introduction of the CPR 1998 is not and is not intended to be (at least at present) a complete replacement of the pre-existing rules of procedure in the High Court.

The county court

18.30 Proceedings in the county court are subject to all of the usual incidents of the rules relating to county court procedure. However it is possible that by the operation of the CEMA 1979, Sch 3, para 8(a) the county courts have no jurisdiction in relation to condemnation proceedings under the CEMA 1979. However, to say that is to ignore the effects of s 1 of the Courts and Legal Services Act 1990 which provides (at s 1(1)(b)) for the conference of jurisdiction existing solely on the High Court to be exercised by the county courts. Thus, it is strongly arguable that notwithstanding the strongly implied exclusion of the jurisdiction of the county courts by means of the operation of the CEMA 1979, Sch 3, para 8(a), jurisdiction has been conferred by means of orders made under s 1 of the Courts and Legal Services Act 1990 (being the High Court and County Courts Jurisdiction Order 1991[1] as variously amended, 'the jurisdiction order').

1 SI 1991/724, coming into force on 1 July 1991, art 1.

The High Court and county courts financial limits

18.31 Because of the way that the track system (explained below) works in accordance with the CPR 1998 and in relation to the jurisdiction order it is important to assess, insofar as possible, the value of the action. The basic rules are set out in the jurisdiction order. Article 7 of the jurisdiction order sets out the limitations upon the court in which an action should be tried regardless of where it has been commenced and there is a rebuttable presumption that where the value of the action is less than £25,000 then it shall be heard in a county court and those where the value of the action is more than £50,000 (or £200,000 for actions in the Central London County Court Business List) then the action shall be heard in the High Court. The limits are not, however, to be regarded as rigid and the remaining provisions of the jurisdiction order must be looked at to determine whether trial of the action is suitable for the county court or the High Court. The court in deciding whether to transfer a case from or to the county court or High Court, upon application of one of the parties or upon the court's own motion, will firstly determine the value of the action in accordance with arts 9 and 10 of the jurisdiction order. In the cases where liquidated demands are made, then the exercise is simple enough and indeed (on one view) in condemnation proceedings the value of the action is unlikely to be difficult to determine since the value of the action is likely to be referable to the value of the goods concerned and the importer will usually have had to make a declaration of value pursuant to the CEMA 1979, s 77.

18.32 Since the essence of the proceedings is to attain title in goods, in that the Commissioners, following determination in their favour, have the right to dispose of those goods as they see fit[1] ascertaining the value of the action by reference to the equivalent value of the goods in question, (ie the declared value of the goods in question), is consistent with the use of the expression 'inancial value' in Part 26.8(1)(a) of the CPR 1998 since that is what the defendant is likely to lose. However, under art 9(b)(i) of the jurisdiction order, the approach is different in that it speaks not of what the defendant will loose but is specifically referable to what the claimant will win. One manner of disposal of the goods in question might be to simply throw them away or destroy them, in which case they represent goods of no value at all and so have no value within the meaning of

337

art 9(b)(i) of the jurisdiction order. If that be right then the value of the goods is always nill (since they are of no value to the Commissioners) and, therefore, by the operation of art 9(b)(ii) of the order, the action is deemed to be of no quantifiable value. This absurd inconsistency of approach between the operation of the CPR 1998 and the jurisdiction order is, it is submitted, an artificial and ill considered distinction (if ever it was the subject of consideration) which is unnecessary.

1 Pursuant to CEMA 1979, s 139(5).

18.33   In most, if not all, cases the value of the action will be of no quantifiable value unless the Commissioners intend to dispose of the goods in some other way than destruction[1] in which case they will have to either rely upon the importer's declaration or upon their own reckoning of the value of the goods. On the assumption (as will arise in most cases) that the value of the goods is unquantified then the limits of £25,000, £50,000 or £200,000 (as the case may be) are clearly of no application and indeed, by the operation of art 7(2) of the jurisdiction order, are disapplied. In such cases, the court in deciding whether the action should be determined (and transferred) to the corresponding lower or higher court will have regard to the provisions of art 7(5) of the order, which states:

'The High Court and the county courts, when considering whether to exercise their powers under sections 40(2),[2] 41(1)[3] or 42(2)[4] of the County Courts Act 1984 (Transfer) shall have regard to the following criteria:
(a) the financial substance of the action, including the value of any counterclaim,
(b) whether the action is otherwise important and, in particular, whether it raises questions of importance to persons who are not parties or questions of general public interest,
(c) the complexity of the facts, legal issues, remedies or procedures involved, and
(d) whether transfer is likely to result in a more speedy trial of the action,
but no transfer shall be made on the grounds of sub-paragraph (d) alone.'[5]

1 Which may arise if the Commissioners are able to sell the goods with the relevant trade marks obliterated.
2 Jurisdiction of the High Court to transfer the proceedings to the county court.
3 Jurisdiction of the High Court to transfer proceedings from the county court.
4 Jurisdiction of the county court to transfer the proceedings to the High Court. It should be noted that the county court has no corresponding jurisdiction to order transfer from the High Court to itself as the High Court does under of the County Courts Act 1984, s 40(2).
5 This is echoed in part 30 of the CPR 1998.

18.34   One aspect of the CPR 1998 is to change the way in which cases are selected for which type of determination by the courts whether in the High Court or the county courts. This is governed by Part 26.1(2)(a)–(c) and 26.6 of the CPR 1998[1] which sets up and defines the existence of the tracks for litigation, the small claims track, the fast track and the multi-track.[2] Once defences have been entered the parties in an action will have to fill in a track allocation questionnaire.[3] At that stage the court will have to give directions as to which track the case travels along[4] and as to the future determination of the action. Such directions may be automatically given,[5] a hearing may be held if needed, necessary or as is seen fit.[6] Further upon allocation and in relation to the fast track the parties have to complete a listing questionnaire giving certain information which will enable the court to make the appropriate listing arrangements (Part 28.5(1) of the CPR 1998) and the same applies for the multi-track (Part 29.6(1) of the CPR 1998) but not the small claims track. The track is determined by certain financial limits such as £5,000 or less for the small claims track, between £5,000 and £15,000 for the fast track and for claim of a value of more than £15,000 the multi-track procedure applies. However, as has been discussed above, where the claim is of unquantifiable value then the court may have regard to matters such as the complexity and the nature of the relief sought[7] in much the same way that art 7(5) of the jurisdiction order applies. The net result of this is that, in assessing the track, the court will have regard to the value of the action by reference to the value of the goods in suit (whether to the claimant or the defendant) whereas, in assessing which court (county or High) ought to hear and determine the matter, the court immediately seized of jurisdiction and the one giving the appropriate directions will only have regard to the value of the goods by reference to the claimant which, as has been said above is likely to be negligible or nil.

1 Case Management Preliminary Stage.
2 CPR 26.1.
3 CPR 26.3.
4 CPR 26.5(1).
5 CPR 27.4(1) for the small claims track, CPR 28.2(1) for the fast track, CPR 29.2(1) for the multi-track.
6 CPR 26.5(4) in relation to allocation, CPR 27.6(1) for the small claims track, CPR 28.5(3)(c) for the fast track and CPR 29.2(1)(b) for the multi-track. Though what constitutes what is needed, is necessary or fit for this purpose is difficult to say, it is submitted that this may include (but not be limited to) the position where the answers to the questionnaires submitted by the parties are at odds with one another in such a way as to make determination by the court as to the most appropriate track impossible.
7 CPR 26.7(1). and CPR 26.8.

18.35   Further, it is unclear whether Part 26 of the CPR 1998 will apply in its entirety to High Court proceedings since logic dictates that small claims and fast track litigation will inevitably (but not necessarily) be dealt with in the county courts because of the way that the jurisdiction order works, leaving the High Court to deal with multi-track cases of complexity or importance in accordance with the criterion of the jurisdiction order, the corresponding provisions of the CPR 1998[1] and ss 40–42 of the County Courts Act 1981. However, for complex cases (which would include some types of condemnation proceedings, as will be amply demonstrated below) it is certainly desirable for the High Court to be the appropriate forum.

1 CPR 26.7(1) and CPR 26.8.

18.36   In summary, the county courts will probably take on the bulk of the small claims and fast track litigation leaving the valuable, complex litigation to the High Court.

The High Court and county courts' territorial jurisdiction

18.37   An action may be commenced in the court for the district in which the defendant or one of the defendants resides or carries on business or in the court for the district in which the cause of action wholly or in part arose.[1] Districts are defined from time to time by the Lord Chancellor and are set out in the Civil Court Practice to which the reader is referred. Where proceedings have been commenced at the wrong venue then the court either of its own motion or upon application of one of the parties has the right to transfer the proceedings to the correct venue.[2] In the High Court, the claimant has a compete discretion as to where it may wish to commence proceedings, though a defendant may apply subsequent to the issue of proceedings to have the proceedings transferred to a local district registry.[3]

1 CPR 1998 Sch 1, CCR Ord 4, r 2(1) (a) and (b); CPR 30.2(2) thereof.
2 CPR 1998 Sch 1, CCR Ord 16, r 2; CPR 30.3(1) and (2) thereof.
3 CPR 30.2(4).

4   Condemnation

18.38   Proceedings in the courts for condemnation of goods as forfeit are the same for proceedings under the domestic and European regimes. Aspects of the latter will be covered in due course but the matters relating to condemnation itself need not be repeated later on.

Mode of beginning condemnation proceedings in the High Court and county courts

18.39   The mode of commencing proceedings in the High Court and the county courts are now, following the implementation of the CPR 1998 the same, which is essentially akin to the old writ of summons procedure (save that there is an additional requirement that all pleadings are accompanied by a statement of truth).

Procedure following issue of originating process

18.40   Once the condemnation proceedings are commenced by way of the originating process procedure,[1] namely the claim form, then the defendant is under the usual obligation to serve a defence (which is also, confusingly and indirectly, referred to in the CPR 1998 as a statement of case). Once the defence is served, and the allocation questionnaire[2] is dealt with and the track and venue determined, then the court will give directions as to the future conduct of the action including directions relating to the disclosure of documents. It should be noted that a special procedure is available where facts are unlikely to be in issue or dispute and this is set out in Part 8 of the CPR 1998 which provides for a procedure which is akin to the old originating summons procedure. The expression 'disclosure' relates to the process which was known under the RSC 1965 and the CCR 1981 as discovery in that the existence of the documents in question is disclosed though not (at that stage) its contents (save in bare summary form, for the purposes of identification only).

1 CPR, Part 7.
2 CPR, Part 26.3(1).

18.41   The CPR 1998 set out two types of disclosure, standard and specific. In relation to standard disclosure CPR 31.6 of the CPR 1998:

> 'Standard disclosure requires a party to disclose:
> (a) all documents on which he relies; and
> (b) all documents which could-
>   (i) adversely affect his own case;

      (ii) adversely affect another party's case; or

      (iii) support another party's case; and

(c) all documents which he is required to disclose by a relevant practice direction.'

This is done by list and the manner of the disclosure as set out in CPR 1998 as is supplemented by the CPR Pt 31 practice direction. At present the Part 31 Practice Direction says nothing about Part 31.6(c) type disclosure. There are important additional requirements in the Part 31 practice direction which are that the person compiling the list must certify what he has not included in the list and he must also certify that he has carried out a reasonable and proportional search for the documents concerned, though there is nothing in the rules which limits the ambit of any search to what is reasonable or proportional, this appears in the practice direction. Any party dissatisfied with the extent of the disclosure may apply for specific disclosure.[1]

1 CPR, Part 31.12.

18.42 A couple of comments about the ambit of the disclosure (in the new sense of the expression) are worth making. Firstly, it is apparent that as far as the standard disclosure process is concerned there appears to be no obligation on a party to disclose documents which, although supportive of his case, are not intended (by him) to be relied upon in support of his case. This, it is submitted, is short-sighted and too narrow an obligation since wide and almost universal experience dictates that the relevance of a document and its importance as a document supporting a party's case is often not clear until, during or just before trial by which time there is a serious danger of the other party being taken by surprise, which is what the disclosure process is intended and designed to prevent. Secondly, it is apparent that the disclosure process works in a clearer way,[1] the definition is far more lucid than the old 'power, possession, custody or control' test and is to be welcomed.

    For reasons which shall become clear the disclosure process is very important for a defendant defending condemnation proceedings, though it is less so for HMC&E since it has less to prove evidentially at least.

1 CPR, r 31.8 states:

'(1) A party's duty to disclose documents is limited to documents which are or have been in his control.

(2) For this purpose a party has or has had a document in his control if -

    (a) it is or was in his physical possession;

    (b) he has or has had a right to possession of it; or

    (c) he has or has had a right to inspect or take copies of it.'

The High Court, county courts and costs

18.43 The CPR 1998 provide[1] for the making of an award of costs and rr 44.3(1)–(5) state:

'(1) The court has discretion as to:

(a) whether costs are payable by one party to another;

(b) the amount of those costs; and

(c) when they are to be paid.

(2) If the court decides to make an order about costs:

(a) the general rule is that the unsuccessful party will be ordered to pay the costs of the successful party; but

(b) the court may make a different order.

(3) The general rule does not apply to the following proceedings:

(a) proceedings in the Court of Appeal on an application or appeal made in connection with proceedings in the Family Division; or

(b) proceedings in the Court of Appeal from a judgment, direction, decision or order given or made in probate proceedings or family proceedings.

(4) In deciding what order (if any) to make about costs, the court must have regard to all the circumstances, including:

(a) the conduct of all the parties;

(b) whether a party has succeeded on part of his case, even if he has not been wholly successful; and

(c) any payment into court or admissible offer to settle made by a party which is drawn to the court's attention (whether or not made in accordance with Part 36).

(Part 36 contains further provisions about how the court's discretion is to be exercised where a payment into court or an offer to settle is made under that Part)

(5) The conduct of the parties includes:

(a) conduct before, as well as during, the proceedings and in particular the extent to which the parties followed any relevant pre-action protocol;

(b) whether it was reasonable for a party to raise, pursue or contest a particular allegation or issue;

(c) the manner in which a party has pursued or defended his case or a particular allegation or issue; and

(d) whether a claimant who has succeeded in his claim, in whole or in part, exaggerated his claim.'

18.44   As can be seen there is provision whereby the court can make an award of costs itself[1] and this procedure is appropriate for condemnation proceedings in the High Court and county courts.

1 As was the case under the old RSC 1965 Ord 62, r 7(4)(b), where the Court could award costs by way of a gross sum rather than ordering taxation. This procedure was approved, in appropriate cases, by the Court of Appeal in *Mayfair Brassware Ltd v Aqualine International Ltd* [1998] FSR 135.

5   Procedure in the Magistrates' Courts – general

18.45   Despite the clear procedural advantages to be gained from using the traditional civil courts[1] the practice of the Commissioners is to institute condemnation proceedings in the local Magistrates' Court. There are advantages for the Commissioners in that there is no or little discovery and the proceedings are determined more quickly and presumably (but we speculate) they choose such a route not only on the grounds of costs but also, it is perceived that the exercise of determining whether goods ought to be condemned is relatively simple being a mere comparison between the signs and the relevant trade mark registration certificate. We submit, as experience has shown in the High Court in infringement proceedings, that nothing could be further from the truth! On the other hand, there is no obligation on the defendant to serve a defence. Against this is the fact that in condemnation proceedings relating to trade marks, legally technical questions can be raised which are outside the experience of bench and clerk alike whose undoubted experience in certain legal matters does not generally extend to issues of trade mark law. Like the county courts, the magistrates' courts are parochial in jurisdiction and the usual court will be the magistrates' court covering the port of entry as being within that court's commission area. Commission areas are determined from time to time by the Lord Chancellor by way of statutory instrument. However, the jurisdiction of the magistrates' courts is determined by the operation of the CEMA 1979 itself and not by reference to the commission area.[2]

1 Such as the mandatory requirement that security for costs be provided and the mandatory requirement that a defence be served.
2 The CEMA 1979, Sch 3, para reads:
'9.   Proceedings for the condemnation of any thing instituted in a magistrates' court in England or Wales, in the sheriff court in Scotland or in a court of summary jurisdiction in Northern Ireland may be so instituted:
(a)   in any such court having jurisdiction in the place where any offence in connection with that thing was committed or where any proceedings for such an offence are instituted; or
(b)   in any such court having jurisdiction in the place where the claimant resides or, if the claimant has specified a solicitor under paragraph 4 above, in the place where that solicitor has his office; or
(c)   in any such court having jurisdiction in the place where that thing was found, detained or seized or to which it is first brought after being found, detained or seized.'

18.46   Another important and, as yet, untested issue in relation to the magistrates' courts and the county courts is whether apart from what has been said above those courts have jurisdiction to conduct condemnation proceedings at all. It is well known that in proceedings for the infringement of a registered trade mark a defendant will often put the validity of the registered trade mark in issue. Indeed, in many cases the issue of validity will usually be the only real issue for determination. Issues of validity, revocation or declaration of invalidity are dealt with elsewhere in this book. However, it is clear that only the High Court has jurisdiction under ss 46 (revocation) and 47 (declaration of invalidity) of the TMA 1994 where otherwise there are proceedings on foot in relation to the trade mark in question.[1] Hence, if condemnation proceedings were instituted in the High Court then it would be open to the defendant to claim that the registered trade mark in question ought never to have been on the register or that its scope ought to be limited in some way such as to enable the defendant to escape the consequences of condemnation. It is clear that since the High Court is the only tribunal which has the power to impugn the registration of trade marks, the inferior courts do not have such jurisdiction. In other words, where condemnation proceedings are instituted in the magistrates' courts and the county courts then the defendant is deprived of a defence, though the defence might be of limited assistance if the only attack on validity is by way of revocation since the effect of revocation is to cause the trade mark registration to be expunged from the register effective from a date which might postdate the date on which the goods were seized or detained as liable to forfeiture.

It is submitted that this raises an important procedural issue and an important and fundamental constitutional issue.

1 TMA 1994, ss 46(4)(a) and 47(3)(a), which cedes sole jurisdiction to the court (where proceedings are otherwise on foot which will always be the case in relation to condemnation proceedings), and the court is defined in TMA 1994, s 75(a), as the High Court.

18.47   The procedural issue turns upon the scope of the court's enquiry, ie whether, if the defendant in condemnation proceedings is ever able or entitled to impugn the registered trade mark in issue. The test for seizure or detention as liable for forfeiture of goods in this context is whether they are prohibited by the operation of the CEMA 1979, s 49(1)(b), which provides:

'(1) Where—

...

(*b*)   any goods are imported, landed or unloaded contrary to any prohibition or restriction for the time being in force with respect thereto under or by virtue of any enactment;

...

those goods shall, subject to subsection (2) below, be liable to forfeiture.'

18.48   The test which has to be applied by the judicial mind of whether those goods are prohibited is whether the goods sought to be imported are (to quote TMA 1994, s 89(2)):

'goods to which the notice relates ...'

18.49   One view has been to say that if a notice is in force (whether or not it relates to a trade mark which ought or ought not to be on the register or which is over wide in scope) then if it is found that the goods do fall within the scope or meaning of the notice that is enough. However, that, it is submitted, is an over simplistic view and is only right upon a restricted reading of TMA 1994, s 89(2), since the proprietor is required to state that the goods concerned are infringing goods (in accordance with of the TMA 1994, s 89(1)(b)), and it is those (infringing) goods to which the notice relates. Further, if the test is infringement then the defendant must be able to say in condemnation that the goods are not infringing and hence the notice does not relate to them.

18.50   This leads us to the second issue of constitutional importance which relates to the kinds of defences which a defendant can run in an infringement action, this is dealt with below under the heading of defences.

Civil procedure the magistrates' court

18.51   This is dealt with by Part II of the MCA 1980[1] ('MCA'), though this part of MCA 1980 primarily deals with enforcement of certain civil debts, domestic proceedings and certain other residual civil matters such as restraining breaches of the peace. Generally, save for certain specific matters such as licensing, the civil jurisdiction of the magistrates' courts are limited. It is clear that by the operation of s 1(1)(a), (b) and (c) of the Civil Procedure Act 1997, magistrates' courts are not intended to be within the ambit of the Civil Procedure Rules though given that the purpose of the Civil Procedure Rules is to provide a uniform set of rules for all civil proceedings it is submitted that it ought to do so. That, however, is a matter for parliament.

1   MCA, ss 51–74.

18.52 Civil proceedings in the magistrates' court are initiated by way of a complaint which is made to a Justice of the Peace or the court clerk (as opposed to an information being laid as is the case in criminal matters). The complaint needs to be in a particular form[1] and should set out concisely the facts which the complainant (that is in this context, the relevant officer of HMC&E) seeks to prove and should state the relief sought. Once the complaint is made then the Justice of the Peace has a discretion as to whether to issue a summons based upon that complaint which has the effect of compelling the defendant (ie the person to whom the summons is addressed) to attend to answer the complaint. Such a discretion is to be exercised judicially[2] and although the decision process is reviewable the Divisional Court will not intervene unless the discretion has been exercised as a result of a legal misdirection or if unreasonable[3] in the legally accepted sense of the expression.[4] The same applies to the justices' clerk if it is he who is being asked to issue the summons[5] and, in either case, theJustice of the Peace or his clerk may hear representations from the proposed defendant,[6] though this is rare.

1 See The Magistrates' Courts Rules 1981 (SI 1981/552), r 98 and also the Magistrates' Courts (Forms) Rules 1981 (SI 1981/553 as amended by SI 1983/524), r 2, Sch 2 and Forms 99, 105, 108 and 112.
2 *R v Adamson* (1875) 1 QBD 201; 45 LJMC 46; *R v Byrde and Pontypool Gas Co, ex p Williams* (1890) 60 LJMC 17; 63 LT 645; *R v Bros* (1901) 85 LT 581; 66 JP 54; *R v Kennedy* (1902) 86 LT 753; 50 WR 633; *R v Mead, ex p National Health Insurance Comrs* (1916) 85 LJKB 1065; 114 LT 1172; *R v Brentford Justices, ex p Catlin* [1975] QB 455; 2 All ER 201; and *R v Manchester Stipendiary Magistrates, ex p Hill*, sub nom *Hill v Anderton* [1983] AC 328, [1982] 2 All ER 963.
3 *R v Bow Street Magistrates' Court, ex p Choudhury* [1991] 1 QB 429; [1991] 1 All ER 306, 311.
4 Ie being a decision which no reasonable person could possibly come to.
5 *R v Manchester Stipendiary Magistrate, ex p Hill* [1983] 1 AC 328, [1982] 2 All ER 963.
6 *R v West London Justices, ex p Klahn* [1979] 2 All ER 221, [1979] 1 WLR 933.

18.53 Once the summons is issued, it will state upon its face a time for the defendant to appear to answer the complaint, the defendant must then be served with the summons to attend the first hearing. There is nothing in the rules or statutes which govern magistrates' courts procedure that states that the first hearing shall not be the trial though usually the first hearing is a pre-trial hearing and directions will be given as to the future conduct of the action and, although there is no compulsive provision providing for compliance with such directions, the complainant runs the risk of having his complaint dismissed as an abuse of process and both parties may be in peril as to costs if they do not comply with such directions.

18.54 There is no absolute obligation on the complainant to provide any witness statements or proofs of evidence at all although there are two powerful (if unwieldly) methods of obtaining evidence or documents from the other party. As we shall see, the production of the relevant documentation is a vital necessity as far as the defendant is concerned. Further, there is no obligation on the defendant to disclose his defence to the complainant in any way and indeed the magistrates' courts civil jurisdiction appears not only to allow for what is effectively trial by ambush but could be said to condone it.

18.55 The jurisdiction in relation to obtaining documents arises in two ways which are:
(a) *Subpœna deuces tecum* which is now called a witness summons to produce document and which is dealt with in Part 33 of the CPR 1998, particularly Part 34.4(1) thereof relating to inferior tribunals. The procedure is difficult since the witness summons to produce documents must be properly directed, properly served and served in compliance with the rules and must specify the documents

with a degree of accuracy which the complainant (or respondent) may not possess. Failure to obey such a witness summons is a contempt of court and the court may make a search order[1] to remedy the wrong done to the applicant by reason of the contempt.[2] The same rules apply *mutatis mutandis* to cases where it is desired to get a witness to come to court to give *viva voce* evidence pursuant to a witness summons requiring attendance to give evidence.

(b)   order for production as is set out in MCA 1980, Part IV. The MCA 1980, s 97 sets out the rule which is that where the justices are satisfied that a person can produce a document or can give evidence in relation to inter alia a complaint and he will not voluntarily do so then they can order attendance or production.

If the justices are satisfied by sworn evidence that the witness will not attend or produce the required document notwithstanding the issuing of the above summons then there is no civil jurisdiction to make an immediate order for the arrest of that person. Instead, the justices have firstly to issue a summons directed to the witness to attend or produce the required documents and then only upon failure to attend on the part of the person who has the evidence concerned. Once there has been a failure to respond to a summons, the justices can issue a warrant for the arrest of that person pursuant to the MCA 1980, s 97(3), provided that the justices are satisfied that the person in question can give the evidence or produce the document, that he was duly served with the first summons and there is no just excuse for non-attendance.

The penalty for not attendance the second time is seven days imprisonment or such sooner time as the evidence is given or the documents produced. It is open to question whether repeated orders can be made under MCA, s 97, for successive periods of imprisonment.[3]

1 CPR, Part 25.1(h).
2 There is currently no known case where this has happened though the commentary to the relevant rule suggests that it can happen in theory, though it does not mention magistrates' courts specifically.
3 It is worth adding that MCA, s 55(1), gives the justices the power to compel attendance by the issuing of a warrant of arrest in certain circumstances.

18.56   We cannot leave our discussion in certain procedural aspects relating to civil proceedings in the magistrates' courts without mentioning the powers and rights attaining to amendment of the complaint section 123 MCA states:-

'123.–(1) No objection shall be allowed to any ... complaint, or to any summons or warrant to procure the presence of the defendant, for any defect in it in substance or in form, or for any variance between it and the evidence adduced on behalf of the ... complainant at the hearing of the ... complaint.
(2) If it appears to a magistrates' court that any variance between a summons or warrant and the evidence adduced on behalf of the ... complainant is such that the defendant has been misled by the variance, the court shall, on the application of the defendant, adjourn the hearing.'

18.57   A literal reading of the MCA 1980, s 123, would tend to imply that defects in the complaint should be ignored by the justices no matter how gross the defect in question, the only 'remedy' being that an adjournment will be granted on the defendant's application. Specifically, there is no means whereby the complainant can be compelled to amend his complaint. However, the courts have not allowed the section to have such a severe effect. In the case of *Garfield v Maddocks*,[1] the Lord Chief Justice, Lord Widgery, stated that:

'Those extremely wide words, which on their face seem to legalise almost any discrepancy between the evidence and the information, have in fact always been given a more restricted meaning, and in modern times the section is construed in this way, that if the variance between the evidence and the information is slight and does no injustice to the defence, the information may be allowed to stand notwithstanding the variance which occurred. On the other hand, if the variance is so substantial that it is unjust to the defendant to allow it to be adopted without a proper amendment of the information, then the practice is for the court to require the prosecution to amend in order to bring their information into line. Once they do that, of course, there is provision in ... [MCA, s 123(2)] whereby an adjournment can be ordered in the interests of the defence '

1 [1974] QB 7 at 12.

18.58 Obviously the question arises as to where one draws the line between a 'slight' variation and a 'substantial' one, though the authorities seem to set out three classes of defect in the complaint (though all of the cases are in fact to do with informations in criminal cases but the reasoning and principles to be applied must be the same).

18.59 The first class encompasses minor defects of such a trivial nature that they do not require amendment at all. In the case of *Sandwell Justices, ex p West Midlands Passenger Transport Executive*,[1] the Divisional Court held that a variation between the information and the evidence (defective rear nearside as alleged as opposed to a defective rear offside tyre as adduced) was trivial and the conviction would be upheld, though in that case the amendment was actually made since it was clear what the subject of the complaint was because the tyre in question was brought to court – there being no issue as to which position the tyre had been used. These defects can be described as de minimis and are no more than a true statement of the law which is that the law is not concerned with trivialities.

1 [1979] RTR 17.

18.60 The second class is defects, not being de minimis, that may still be such as to cause no real prejudice (which we submit is the class of defects falling within Lord Widgery's first category in his judgment in the case of *Garfield v Maddocks*) is where amendment is required but are not so bad as to be incurable. Usually, if an amendment is sought then it will be allowed although if the defendant has been misled by the defect then he will be entitled to an adjournment to re-prepare his case if it is in the interests of justice to do so. In such circumstances where the complainant fails to seek an amendment or where an adjournment ought to have been granted but is not, then the Divisional Court will intervene and quash the conviction by certiorari. So, in the case of *Hunter v Coombs*,[1] the defendant was convicted when nowhere in the summons was the correct statutory provision mentioned and the facts were not fully set out either. Fenton Atkinson J stated that though the correct amendment would have entitled the justices to convict, that they had convicted on the basis of information which was incorrect meant that the conviction had to be quashed.

1 [1962] 1 WLR 573.

18.61 Also in the case of *Meek v Powell*,[1] the defendant was convicted under a repealed statutory provision (though re-enacted elsewhere in an identical fashion). The court held that the amendment could and should have been made, an adjournment could be granted but also the justices were free to dismiss the information as well (though the prosecutor could have set up the correct information under the correct statutory provision) but it was not open to them to convict on the unamended information.

1 [1952] 1 KB 164.

18.62   In *R v Scunthorpe Justices, ex p McPhee*,[1] the defendant was charged with robbery, but a guilty plea was accepted by the Crown as to theft and common assault. An application to amend the information so as to reflect the plea was granted but because of an objection by the clerk of the court an amendment to allege common assault was refused because the six-month time limit had expired. In relation to the six-month rule, the Divisional Court held that amendment was allowable in such circumstances so as to substitute a different offence because it was all tied up in the same course of wrongdoing. In other words to prove the lesser offence would necessarily involve adducing the same or substantially the same evidence as related to the greater and the interests of justice were served by allowing the amendment.

1 (1998) 162 JP 635.

18.63   In *New Southgate Metals Ltd v London Borough of Islington*[1] a 1988 statute was referred to in the information as being a 1991 statute but the defendant did not take the point below and on appeal the argument was advanced that the offence disclosed in the summons was not known in law. This odd decision does not sit well with *Hunter v Coombes* and the Divisional Court held that the difference between the two cases was because in the *New Southgate Metals* case the summons accurately set out the full particulars of the offence and no point was made to the prosecution in the court below.

1 [1996] Crim LR 334.

18.64   In *R v Newcastle-upon-Tyne Justices, ex p John Bryce (Contractors) Ltd*,[1] an amendment in relation to an overladen lorry changed an allegation from permitted use to use per se six months after the alleged offence had been committed. The Divisional Court held that the defence were neither misled nor taken by surprise because the prosecution case on the facts as set out in the summons had been clear from the outset.

1 [1976] 1 WLR 517.

18.65   In *Wright v Nicholson*,[1] an information which specified that a particular act had taken place on a certain date (for which the defendant had an alibi), though it transpired on the evidence that the incident could have occurred on some other date, resulted in the defendant's conviction. The Divisional Court held that the conviction ought to be quashed because the variation between the evidence and the information was such as to mislead the defendant. The Divisional Court observed that if the information had been amended and the defence granted an adjournment then the conviction would have been safe.

1 [1970] 1 WLR 142.

18.66   In *Wyllie v Crown Prosecution Service*,[1] information relating to failure to provide a urine specimen was correctly amended to allege a failure to supply a specimen of blood because the defence had not been misled and the evidence would have been the same.

1 [1988] Crim LR 753.

18.67 The foregoing authorities show that there are a wide variety of circumstances where amendment would be allowed, on terms as to an adjournment.

18.68 The third category relates to situations where the error is fundamental as being incapable of amendment. In *Atterton v Browne*,[1] the defect was so gross as to represent a serious departure from the true factual situation as set out in the prosecution evidence. Humphreys J said:

'There have been, however, many decisions under that section ... [being the equivalent s 123 of the MCA in force at the time] which show that the section does not operate to prevent an objection being effective where the error alleged is fundamental, such as, for instance, where one offence is charged in the information and a different offence is found in the conviction recorded by the justices, even though the two matters may seem to be very much the same thing'.[2]

1 [1945] KB 122.
1 [1945] KB 122 at 270.

Magistrates' courts and costs

18.69 Orders for costs in the magistrates' courts pursuant to its civil jurisdiction are governed by the MCA 1980, s 64:

'64.-(1) On the hearing of a complaint, a magistrates' court shall have power in its discretion to make such order as to costs'
(a) on making the order for which the complaint is made, to be paid by the defendant to the complainant;
(b) on dismissing the complaint, to be paid by the complainant to the defendant,
as it thinks just and reasonable but if the complaint is for an order for the periodical payment of money, or for the revocation, revival or variation of such an order. or for the enforcement of such an order, the court may, whatever adjudication it makes, order either party to pay the whole or any part of the other's costs.
(2) The amount of any sum ordered to be paid under sub-section (1) above shall be specified in the order, or order of dismissal, as the case may be.
(3) Subject to sub-section (4) below, costs ordered to be paid under this section shall be enforceable as a civil debt.
(4) Any costs awarded on a complaint for an affiliation order or order enforceable as an affiliation order, or for the enforcement, variation, revocation, discharge or revival of such an order, against the person liable to make payments under the order shall be enforceable as a sum ordered to be paid by an affiliation order.
(5) The preceding provisions of this section shall have effect subject to any other Act enabling a magistrates' court to order a successful party to pay the other party's costs.'

18.70 The issue therefore turns on the exercise of a discretion. It is submitted that there is only one discretion in relation to civil costs in the magistrates' courts which is how much and not whether to order the payment of costs at all.

18.71 The procedure to be followed in such circumstances is for the winning party to bring a draft bill of costs to the court. However, questions will often arise as to the particularity of that bill and it is submitted that the most expedient course is to bring a bill of costs to court which is particularised in the same way and to the same extent as a draft bill would be presented in a security for costs application or upon taxation though it is submitted that the summary taxation practice under Part 44.3 of the CPR 1998 and Part 44 of the Practice Direction (para 4) should be adopted in such cases.

18.72 In exercising the discretion as to the level of costs, there are a number of principles which it is submitted are to be applied. The court should award those costs at a level in its discretion just and reasonable. An award of the whole of the costs is clearly contemplated by the MCA 1980, s 64(1)(a). In the consideration or resolution of doubts as to whether costs are reasonably incurred, the discretion should be exercised in favour of the paying party unless it is just to do otherwise. The hearing as to costs should be simple and not protracted. If no specific form of bill of costs is specified and there is no reason to doubt the accuracy or particularity of the draft bill, the draft bill of the receiving party should be accepted at face value. In case of real doubt as to the accuracy or particularity of the draft bill then the receiving party should be given an opportunity to submit a more detailed bill or supporting documentation in relation to the bill. The discretion, being a discretion, should not be subject to fetter. However, its exercise should not be illogical. The court should also have regard to the entire circumstances of the case. However, where a party succeeds in an action on one of several grounds he should not be unduly penalised because he has not been successful on the other grounds. In other words, the real winner should get all of his costs. This is particularly the case where the justices have not unequivocally ruled against that party in their finding on a particular issue.

6 Procedure – two regimes, the domestic and European–comparisons and contrasts

18.73 Before the condemnation proceedings are instituted, there are a number of procedures which have to be complied with. The position is made more complex by the existence of two separate regimes which govern such questions, though they are tied together to a certain extent by the operation of the CEMA 1979.

18.74 The two regimes are firstly the operation of s 89 of the TMA 1994 and secondly the operation of amended Council Regulation 3295/94/EC[1] of 22 December 1994, laying down measures concerning the entry into the Community and the export and re-export from the Community of goods infringing certain intellectual property rights ('the Basic Regulation') as implemented by Commission Regulation 1367/95/EC[2] of 16 June 1995 ('the Implementing Regulation'). The Basic and Implementing Regulations will be referred to together as the European Regulations.[3]

1 OJ L 341, 30.12.1994 p 8.
2 OJ L133, 17.6.1995 p 2.
3 The Basic Regulation has been amended by Council Regulation 241/99/EC of 25 January 1999 ('the Amending Regulation') with effect from 3 February 1999 or 1 July 1999 (see Amending Regulation, art 2, which suggest two dates of commencement). References in this Chapter to the Basic Regulation should be taken as references to the amended Basic Regulation.

18.75 The distinction between the regime under s 89 of the TMA 1994 ('the domestic regime') and the European Regulations regime ('the European regime') is that the domestic regime seeks to stop the importation into the UK of infringing goods originating either from outside the EEA[1] or from within the EEA but, where there has been no free circulation of those goods in the state from which the goods have been exported,[2] further the domestic regime is specifically excluded where the European regime applies,[3] in other words, one cannot, in respect of one consignment of goods, proceed under both though that would not preclude proceeding in the alternative if the position is sufficiently uncertain, as we shall see this may lead to a procedural nightmare! The European regime, on the other hand relates to a narrower class of goods, namely those which are counterfeit. Accordingly, there are circumstances where the domestic regime would apply to, say, goods originating from the proprietor which could be described as infringing (since they are being imported or being sought to be imported without authority) though not counterfeit (since no misrepresentation is being made as to origin). The Basic Regulation describes counterfeit goods as being:

'— goods, including the packaging thereof, bearing without authorisation a trade mark which is identical to the trade mark validly registered in respect of the same type of goods, or which cannot be distinguished in its essential aspects from such trade mark, and which thereby infringes the rights of the holder of the trade mark in question under Community law or the law of the Member State where the application for action by the customs authorities is made,
— any trade mark symbol (logo, label, sticker, brochure, instructions for use, guarantee document) whether presented separately or not, in the same circumstances as the goods referred to in the first indent,
— packaging materials bearing the trade marks of counterfeit goods, presented separately in the same circumstances as the goods referred to in the first indent;'.[4]

1 TMA 1994, s 93(1)(b)(i).
2 TMA 1994, s 93(1)(b)(ii).
3 TMA 1994, s 89(3) as amended by The Trade Marks (EC Measures Relating to Counterfeit Goods) Regulations 1995, reg 2 (SI 1995/1444) with effect from 1 July 1995, reg 1; ss 2(2) and 2(4) of the European Communities Act 1972.
4 Basic Regulation, art 1(2)(a).

18.76 It is submitted that the words 'without authorisation' apply to cases where either unmarked goods originating from the proprietor are marked with the relevant trade marks without authorisation or where goods not originating from the proprietor are marked with his marks. It appears too that the classification of counterfeit goods within the meaning of the Basic Regulation is too wide since it would cover situations where an importer was legitimately importing goods purchased overseas (not bearing any trade marks) but marked them as originating from the proprietor in a descriptive sense, as is allowed and condoned in accordance with the TMA 1994, s 11(2)(b). The note to art 51 of TRIPS[1] also defines what is understood by the expression counterfeit as being:

'counterfeit trademark goods shall mean any goods, including packaging, bearing without authorization a trademark which is identical to the trademark validly registered in respect of such goods, or which cannot be distinguished in its essential aspects from such a trademark, and which thereby infringes the rights of the owner of the trademark in question under the law of the country of importation;'

though this definition is taken from the definition which is familiar to customs officials because it was drafted by the Brussels-based customs co-operation council, latterly the World Customs Organisation long before TRIPS.

1 Itself being part of TRIPS since it appears in annex 1c.

18.77 What must be emphasised is that without more, the European regime would appear to cover almost all of the situations catered for by the domestic regime. However, in accordance with art 1 (4) of the Basic Regulation the European regime does not apply:

> '... to goods which bear a trade mark with the consent of the holder of that trade mark ... and which have been manufactured with the consent of the holder of the right but are placed in one of the situations referred to in paragraph 1(a)[1] [of the Basic regulation] without the latter's consent.'

1 That is where goods suspected of being counterfeit or pirated are:
— entered for free circulation, export or re-export,
— found when checks are made on goods placed under a suspensive procedure within the meaning of art 84 (1) (a) of Council Regulation 2913/92/EEC of 12 October 1992 establishing the Community Customs Code ... [OJ L302 19.10.92 p 1], or re-exported subject to notification ; ...'

18.78 In other words, the European regime applies to goods which are truly counterfeit in the sense that the goods concerned do not originate from the proprietor at all whereas the domestic regime applies to all other situations where infringing goods are concerned.

Another common feature

18.79 One important common feature which is seemingly apparent in both regimes[1] is the distinction between prospective and retrospective applications to the customs authorities by the proprietor. The prospective regime (the mechanics of which will be explained in much more detail below) essentially allows a proprietor to put the customs authorities on notice to seize or detain as liable for forfeiture any prohibited goods which are entered after the date of the acceptance of such notice. The retrospective regime caters for the situation where the Commissioners, in the course of checks being made on goods which are being imported into the UK, have suspicions as to whether the goods are infringing but are not on notice to stop them. In such cases, there are procedures whereby the Commissioners can notify the proprietor of their suspicions and a notice can be given by the proprietor which has retrospective effect, though, as we shall see in the following chapter, this is subject to time limits and there is doubt in relation to the domestic route as whether such a procedure exists at all.

1 Though as we shall see from paras **19.61** et seq this is not in fact the case.

The domestic regime

18.80 The Commissioners have a direct power pursuant to the TMA 1994, s 90, to make rules relating to the procedure to be followed in relation to cases where there has been seizure or detention of goods which are liable to forfeiture. The regulations currently in force are contained in the Trade Marks (Customs) Regulations 1994[1] ('TM(C)R 1994') and are the only regulations which have been made under the TMA 1994, s 90. We intend to cover the position and procedure governing the making of a prospective application and the subsequent practice and procedures of HMC&E firstly followed by the position in relation to the retrospective procedure under the European regime since they differ only in a few subtle respects.

1 SI 1994/2625, which took effect on 31 October 1994 (reg 1).

The prospective procedure

18.81 A trade mark proprietor may perceive that generally a person is intending to import his goods into the UK which are infringing goods or counterfeit goods, he may have burned his fingers on previous occasions or he may have become aware of a potential threat. In any event, he may simply wish to protect his position especially where he does not wish to involve himself in costly litigation. His first recourse is to make an application under the TMA 1994, s 89. Only the proprietor of a registered trade mark or his licensee can do this and if he wishes to do so he must give notice in writing to the Commissioners:[1]

> '(a) that he is the proprietor or, as the case may be, a licensee of the registered trade mark,
> (b) that, at a time and place specified in the notice, goods which are, in relation to that registered trade mark, infringing goods, material or articles are expected to arrive in the UK-
>   (i) from outside the European Economic Area, or
>   (ii) from within that Area but not having been entered for free circulation, and
> (c) that he requests the Commissioners to treat them as prohibited goods.'[2]

1 TMA 1994, s 89(1).
2 TMA 1994, s 89(1)(a)–(c).

18.82 Section 90(1) of the TMA 1994 gives power to the Commissioners to make regulations prescribing the form of a notice given under TMA 1994, s 89(1) ('a section 89 notice'). The power to make regulations also includes the power to require an applicant under a section 89 notice to provide certain evidence at certain times (such as evidence of ownership or existence of the registered trade marks in question),[1] to comply with any other conditions as the regulations may impose,[2] to pay such fees as may be specified in the regulations,[3] to give such security as may be specified in the regulations,[4] or to indemnify against any liability in respect of any liability or expense as may arise as a result of the actions of the Commissioners in acting upon the section 89 notice.[5] The Commissioners are entitled simply to make the regulations without any accountability for that although they can be annulled by a resolution by either House of Parliament.[6]

1 TMA 1994, s 90(1)(a).
2 TMA 1994, s 90(1)(b).
3 TMA 1994, s 90(2)(a).
4 TMA 1994, s 90(2)(b),4.
5 TMA 1994, s 90(2)(c).
6 TMA 1994, s 90(4).

18.83 As can be seen the TMA 1994, s 89(1)(b)(i) and (ii) makes it clear that the TMA 1994, s 89 applies to a limited class of cases and is expressly excluded in its effect where other European measures apply.[1] It is worth adding at this stage that the section 89 notice is only effective in relation to goods which are not imported by a person for his private or domestic use.

1 TMA 1994, s 89(3), as amended by reg 2 of the Trade Marks (EC Measures Relating to Counterfeit Goods) Regulations 1995 (SI 1995/1444) as from 1 July 1995, reg 1.
2 TMA 1994, s 89(2).

The notice

18.84   Although under the TMA 1994, s 89(1)(b) it is a requirement that the section 89 notice specifies the time and place when goods which are infringing goods, materials or articles[1] are expected to arrive in the UK, this requirement is honoured more in the breach than in the observance. This is so because it is seldom known when such goods will enter the UK and although, in order to assist HMC&E, the applicant under the section 89 notice should give as much detail as possible, failure to provide such information is, it is submitted, a breach of a directory provision rather than the infringement of a mandatory provision which would render the section 89 notice void or voidable and thereby a nullity. There are two reasons for this. Firstly, if the failure to specify the time and place of importation was an infringement of a mandatory requirement then that would almost completely nullify the effect of the TMA 1994, s 89 since its purpose is to provide a firm and effective remedy against the importation of infringing goods. Secondly, there is no real reason for making such a requirement mandatory but rather the provision of such information is intended to assist HMC&E and there is certainly no prejudice to the importer (over and above having his goods seized or detained as liable for forfeiture). The principles governing whether such requirements are directory or mandatory are to be found in *DeSmith's Judicial Review of Administrative Action*[2] subsequently approved by the Court of Appeal:[3]

> 'When Parliament prescribes the manner or form in which a duty is to be performed or a power exercised, it seldom lays down what will be the legal consequences of failure to observe its prescriptions. The courts must therefore formulate their own criteria for determining whether the procedural rules are to be regarded as mandatory, in which case disobedience will render void or voidable what has been done, or as directory, in which case disobedience will be treated as an irregularity not affecting the validity of what has been done (though in some cases it has been said that there must be "substantial compliance" with the statutory provisions if the deviation is to be excused as a mere irregularity).[4] Judges have often stressed the impracticability of specifying exact rules for the assignment of a procedural provision to the appropriate category. The whole scope and purpose of the enactment must be considered, and one must assess "the importance of the provision that has been disregarded, and the relation of that provision to the general object intended to be secured by the Act."[5] In assessing the importance of the provision, particular regard may be had to its significance as a protection of individual rights, the relative value that is normally attached to the rights that may be adversely affected by the decision and the importance of the procedural requirement in the overall administrative scheme established by the statute. Furthermore, much may depend upon the particular circumstances of the case in hand. Although "nullification is the natural and usual consequence of disobedience,"[6] breach of procedural or formal rules is likely to be treated as a mere irregularity if the departure from the terms of the Act is of a trivial nature,[7] or if no substantial prejudice has been suffered by those for whose benefit the requirements were introduced,[8] or if serious public inconvenience would be caused by holding them to be mandatory, or if the court is for any reason disinclined to interfere with the act or decision that is impugned.'

1   'Goods' are the goods themselves, 'materials' would refer to such items as labels and 'articles' to such marking items as stamps and dies. These three classes of object are effectively considered as one type of object and for the remainder of this chapter we shall simply refer to them as goods.
2   4th Edition, (Stevens, 1980) at pp 142–145.
3   In *Secretary of State for Trade and Industry v Langridge* Ch 402. See also *Petch v Gurney* [1994] 3 All ER 731 at 736.
4   *Coney v Choyce* [1975] 1 WLR 422 (where the attempt bona fide to comply and the absence of prejudice from the non-compliance are also emphasised). And see *Scurr v Brisbane City Council* (1975) 133

CLR 242. See also *Grunwick Processing Laboratories Ltd v ACAS* [1978] AC 655, 691–692, where mandatory duties in absolute form were contrasted with duties to be performed 'as far as reasonably practicable'. See also *Donnelly v Marrickville Municipal Council* [1973] 2 NSWLR 390 at 398. For general surveys of this intractable topic, see Craies Statute Law (7th Edition), Chap 12; Maxwell *Interpretation of Statutes* (12th Edition), 314–322; 36 *Halsbury's Laws* (3rd Edition) paras 443–446. Authorities are reviewed in *Cullimore v Lyme Regis Corpn* [1962] 1 QB 718; *Graham v The Attorney-General* [1966] NZLR 937 at 953–961; and *Parisienne Basket Shoes Pty Ltd v Whyte* (1938) 59 CLR 369.

5 *Howard v Bodington* (1877) 2 PD 203 at 211; and see *Spicer v Holt* [1977] AC 987 (compliance with procedure for administering breath tests, a condition precedent for valid conviction). See *Grunwick Processing* (n 4 above) for a recent important statement of the relevant principles; see also *Sheffield City Council v Graingers Wines Ltd* [1978] 2 All ER 70.

6 Maxwell *Interpretation of Statutes* (11th Edition) at p 364. (This phrase is not reproduced in the 12th edition, possibly because it was thought to be over emphatic.) Nullification does not necessarily imply that the act successfully impugned was null and void *ab initio*; and breach of a directory provision may render an act voidable.

7 *R v Dacorum Gaming Licensing Committee, ex p EMI Cinemas and Leisure Ltd* [1971] 3 All ER 666 (minor typographical error in notice of application for licence could be disregarded, despite general strictness of statutory requirements); *R v Inner London Betting Licensing Committee, ex p Pearcy* [1972] 1 WLR 421 (unimportant additional words added to advertisement and notice of application). See also *R v Pontypool Gaming Licensing Committee, ex p Risca Cinemas Ltd* [1970] 1 WLR 1299 (time limit for submitting advertisement of bingo licence application exceeded); *Howard v Secretary of State for the Environment* [1975] QB 235; *Seldun Transport Services Ltd v Baker* [1978] ICR 1035; *R v Inspector of Taxes, ex p Clarke* [1974] QB 220; *R v Melton and Belvoir Justices ex p Tynan* (1977) 75 LGR 544; *Dolan v O'Hara* [1975] NI 125; *Button v Jenkins* [1975] 3 All ER 585; *R v Urbanowski* [1976] 1 WLR 455 (time limitations within which magistrates must state a case and accused person be tried only directory: judge of Crown Court may extend time); *R v Leicester Gaming Licensing Committee, ex p Shine* [1971] 1 WLR 1648 (additional wording invalidated application because of express negative wording in Act distinguished in *R v Inner London Betting Licensing Committee, ex p Pearcy* decided under a different Act); *R v Newcastle-upon-Tyne Gaming Licensing Committee, ex p White Hart Enterprises Ltd* [1977] 1 WLR 1135 and *R v Brighton Gaming Licensing Committee, ex p Cotedale Ltd* [1978] 1 WLR 1140.

8 See, eg *R v Liverpool City Council* [1975] 1 WLR 701; *Coney v Choyce* (n 4 above); *George v Secretary of State for the Environment* (1979) 77LGR 689.

18.85   Further, Millett LJ in *Petch v Gurney*[1] (a case concerning appeals from income tax assessments) said:

'Where statute requires an act to be done in a particular manner, it may be possible to regard the requirement that the act be done as mandatory but the requirement that it be done in a particular manner directory. In such a case; the statutory requirement can be treated as substantially complied with if the act is done in a manner which is not less satisfactory having regard to the purpose of the legislature in imposing the requirement'.

1 [1994] 3 All ER 731 at 738.

18.86   In the case of a section 89 notice, the act is the act of notification, ie the act of notifying the Commissioners. The manner of doing the act is to specify the time and place of entry which on occasion, indeed usually, as has been said above, the proprietor or his licensee will not know.

18.87   Notwithstanding the foregoing, it is apparent that the schedule to TM(C)R 1994 specifies the following in the recitals to the section 89 notice form:

'Please note that in Part 3 it is not mandatory to provide details other than the time and place of expected arrival of infringing goods but it will greatly increase the prospect of intercepting the consignment concerned if all the details requested are given.'

18.88   So whether strict compliance with s 89(1)(b) of the TMA 1994, is or is not necessary, it appears that the Commissioners have placed upon themselves the mandatory requirement that the place and time of importation be specified.[1] This, it is submitted, is absurd since it places a greater burden on the proprietor or his licensee, a greater burden upon HMC&E and provides an additional and highly technical defence to an otherwise red-handed unlawful importer. Whether strict compliance with s 89(1)(b) of the TMA 1994 is mandatory and whether regulation 2 and compliance with the conditions set out in the schedule[2] to the TM(C)R 1994 is mandatory we do suggest that it is necessary and mandatory for s 89(1)(a) and (c) of the TMA 1994 to be complied with since otherwise there will be considerable doubt as to whether a section 89 notice is being served on the Commissioners at all.

1 And indeed this they are entitled to do pursuant to their rule-making powers under the TMA 1994, s 90(1)(b).
2 The schedule specifies in the Recitals that the notice may only be given by the proprietor or his licensee (this provision also appears in the TMA 1994, s 89(1)(a) and the body of the TM(C)R 1994 as well as the schedule thereto), that it is not mandatory to provide details other than the time and place of importation (which provisions also appear as directory provisions in the TMA 1994, s 89(1)(b) but appears nowhere else), that a cheque payable to the Commissioners for the prescribed sum (being £30 at present, though this is liable to change) should be enclosed with the section 89 notice (TM(C)R 1994, reg 3 (though it is probably a directory provision) but appears nowhere else), that a copy of the certificate of registration for the trade mark in question be provided with the section 89 notice or at the time of importation as well as a certificate of renewal (TM(C)R, reg 6 but nowhere else) and that an indemnity be provided with security therefor (which liability for an indemnity also appears in the body of TM(C)R, reg 5 but nowhere else).

18.89   The Notice has to comply with TM(C)R and in particular has to be in the form set out in the schedule to the TM(C)R 1994[1] and each section 89 notice relates to one consignment only, once a consignment has been seized or detained as liable to forfeiture, then the section 89 notice is spent.

1 See the TM(C)R 1994, reg 2.

18.90   Whilst the directory/mandatory debate rages it is clear that by the operation of regulation 6(2) of the TM(C)R 1994 provision of the certificates of registration and relevant renewal certificates is mandatory which has the effect of rendering the section 89 notice of no effect. The words 'of no effect' appear in regulation 6(2) of the TM(C)R 1994 and there is uncertainty as to their meaning and (more importantly) their scope and effect.

7   The prohibition and seizure or detention as liable for forfeiture

18.91   Once a notice has been validly filled out and served, the fees paid and all of the aforementioned formalities completed, the proprietor then sits and waits for the goods to be imported. The effect of the notice is that such goods as are specified in the notice become prohibited and upon their importation are liable to be seized or detained as liable to forfeiture pursuant to the CEMA 1979, s 40. The test, which we repeat for the sake of convenience is set out in s 89(2) of the TMA 1994, which reads:

'When a notice is in force under this section, the importation of the goods to which the notice relates, otherwise than by a person for his private and domestic use, is prohibited; but a person is not by reason of the prohibition liable to any penalty other than forfeiture of the goods.'

18.92 It is to be noted, first, that private and domestic use is excluded and, second, that in any other case the only penalty which can be meted out on the importer is forfeiture. The possible reason for this second limitation is that importers are very often unwilling links in the chain and in many cases have little idea about what is being imported. The test then is whether the goods (which expression includes material or articles) which are sought to be imported are goods to which the section 89 notice relates. However, it is submitted that such a literal reading of the sub-section would produce harsh results especially where it turns out (as is sometimes the case) that the goods are not infringing goods at all. Accordingly, the test is to ask whether the goods in question are the infringing goods to which the notice relates since the notice itself relates to infringing goods. This is borne out by s 89(1)(b) of the TMA 1994 (which requires the section 89 notice to specify that *infringing* goods are about to be imported) and by one of the few authorities on the matter (if authority it be).[1] An importer who can show that the goods are not infringing goods should, it is submitted, escape liability even though the goods are goods to which the notice relates. This provides a valuable, if controversial, defence.

1 *Customs and Excise Comrsv Top High Development Ltd* [1998] FSR 464, Mr Inigo Bing, Stipendiary Magistrate, thought that was a case under the corresponding European regime though, it is submitted, that since the prohibition is dealt with in the same ways the case is good authority on the point.

18.93 Further, as we shall see, the Commissioners are not necessarily liable if they seize or detain as liable for forfeiture in good faith goods which ought not to have been seized or detained as liable for forfeiture.

18.94 From the wording of the TMA 1994 s 89(2), goods which are not otherwise prohibited (but would be so prohibited if such a notice had been in force) cannot be seized or detained as liable for forfeiture by HMC&E. This is so even if HMC&E suspect that the goods would be prohibited if a notice had been in force.

18.95 The corresponding European measures do provide for such a situation, ie detention or suspension from further release without the existence of the requisite notice. However, the domestic legislation does not. The question is, then, as sometimes happens, what is the position where HMC&E seizes or detains as liable for forfeiture goods where no section 89 notice is in force, and then notifies the proprietor that they are holding such goods and await the receipt of a section 89 notice from him? Seizure in such circumstances is clearly unlawful but the question remains whether HMC&E can make lawful that which is unlawful. In making the decision to seize or detain HMC&E is exercising a jurisdiction which in a public law sense means 'authority to decide'.[1] The question that arises is whether in exercising its jurisdiction, ie its authority to decide, to seize or detain the goods, it is doing so within that jurisdiction or authority, in which case the decision is said to be intra vires or is doing so outside that jurisdiction or authority, in which case the decision is said to be ultra vires and void.

Voidness is to be distinguished from voidability and the distinction is very blurred, the authorities are unclear and conflict, but for present purposes we shall assume that the distinction is between invalidity and temporary validity. However, an examination of this distinction does not matter for present purposes because if a decision is made ultra vires then it is void. The difficulty faced is that if the seizure or detention is carried out in excess of jurisdiction because a valid section 89 notice has not been proffered then HMC&E has no right to carry out such seizure or detention and the decision to do so is void and HMC&E are bound to return or release the goods in question (all other formalities being complied with). In that instance, the importer can simply make a demand for the release of the goods and if release is refused then he can seek appropriate relief from the court. Whether the court can or will grant such relief is another question and given that the period between purported seizure or detention and the proper service of a section 89 notice is likely to be short, there is a respectable argument for saying that there is in effect a retrospective procedure in operation under s 89 of the TMA 1994. This is so because goods to which no section 89 notice relates can effectively be seized or detained, the proprietor can be notified and encouraged to serve a section 89 notice and the service thereof can effectively make lawful that which is unlawful by HMC&E re-seizing the goods once the notice is in force.

1 See DM Gordon 'The Relation of Facts to Jurisdiction' (1929) 45 LQR 459.

18.96 Is such conduct allowed? Can a Crown body which has acted unlawfully subsequently make lawful that which was unlawful? The obvious answer is no but in reality the question is vexed and devoid of authority and it is submitted that cases where HMC&E deliberately embarks upon such conduct will be rare indeed if such ever happens. However, because the corresponding European measures specifically allow for a retrospective application to be made, it is possible that by inadvertence rather than by design, purported seizure or detention takes place when there is no section 89 notice in force because confusion may arise as to the correct procedure, though it may be noted that there appears to be no justification for the distinction. In such circumstance, any purported seizure will be void so the HMC&E will hold such goods as constructive bailees and are liable to return them upon demand. What happens if, however, such demand is made and HMC&E refuse to return the goods on the grounds that a section 89 notice is in the pipeline? The importer could apply to the court for interlocutory relief but that is said by some commentators to be a fruitless exercise since the granting of injunctions and prerogative orders are useless against the Crown.[1] Certiorari is unlikely to be available on an interlocutory basis and was we have said an injunction does not lie against the Crown in any event either in a public law sense (save where there is a conflict with a European measure)[2] or a private law sense.[3]

1 Though it may be possible to enjoin the officer concerned.
2 *Secretary of State for Transport, ex parte Factortame* [1990] 2 AC 85; [1989] 2 All ER 692.
3 Crown Proceedings Act 1947, s 21.

18.97 However those stark sentiments belie two extremely important principles, the first being that for many years the Crown Office has sought to impose prerogative orders on Crown servants without demur from above, the public or the Crown. Indeed the Crown itself has conceded as much,[1] though strictly speaking this concession was made by the minister, the subject of the review and not the Crown itself. The second principle is to be found in the short speech of Lord Templeman in the case of *In Re M*,[2] which was a case concerning whether or not the Secretary of State for the Home Department could be in contempt for breaching an order directed at him though he was acting in his capacity as Crown minister:

'... the argument that there is no power to enforce the law by injunction or contempt proceedings against a minister in his official capacity would, if upheld, establish the proposition that the executive obey the law as a matter of grace and not as a matter of necessity, a proposition which would reverse the result of the Civil War.'

1 See *Padfield v Minister for Agriculture Fisheries and Food* [1968] AC 997; [1968] 2 WLR 924, where the record shows that no suggestion was made that there was a want of jurisdiction to order *mandamus* directed at the minister and counsel for the minister in that case is recorded as having submitted at 1021 D–E:

> 'As to the question whether the court can intervene to control the exercise by the minister of the discretion conferred on him by statute, it is salutary that, when ministers have misconceived their powers, they should be subject to judicial correction.'

2 [1993] 3 WLR 433 at 437[H].

18.98   Now it must be accepted that HMC&E is conterminous with the Crown so any person seeking relief against the Crown as such will fail since the Crown is virtually immune from suit (or more properly, the remedies flowing therefrom). However, if suit were directed to the Commissioners as opposed to the Crown then no such difficulty would arise and accordingly it is to be contended (and submitted) that there is (or at least there is more likely to be) jurisdiction to grant injunctions or coercive orders against the Commissioners at least in Crown proceedings.[1] However, seeking judicial review of a decision of the Commissioners may be fruitless even then because the grant of relief, being discretionary, may be withheld if the Commissioners undertake to regularise the position and the resulting damages (because of a few days of not having the goods in question) are likely to be small.[2]

1 Since it appears from Crown Proceedings Act 1947, s 21 that injunctive relief against an officer of the Crown is precluded if the effect is to achieve the same result as would have been achieved if relief were granted against the Crown. The notes to this section in the Supreme Court Practice suggest that such relief is not available against the minister (or Commissioners), citing *R v Secretary of State for Transport, ex p Factortame Ltd* [1990] 2 AC 85; [1989] 2 WLR 997 *sub nom Factortame Ltd v Secretary of State for Transport* [1989] 2 All ER 692 HL, where Lord Bridge emphatically said that no such injunction lies, at least in an interim sense. However, as Lord Woolf explains in *In Re M* (para 18.97 above), Lord Bridge's analysis (and necessarily his conclusions) is tainted by the fact that the House in *Factortame* was not referred to certain important statutory provisions and that in any event Lord Bridge's analysis was not accepted by the ECJ in *R v Secretary of State for Transport, ex p Factortame Ltd (No 2)* (Case C-213/89) [1991] 1 AC 603; [1990] 3 WLR 818; [1990] 3 CMLR 1; [1990] 2 Lloyds Rep 351; (1990) 41 LS Gaz R 33 *sub nom Factortame Ltd v Secretary of State for Transport (No 2)* [1991] 1 All ER 70; [1990] NJLR 927, ECJ. but only on the issue of whether injunctions could be so granted to ensure continuity of community law. Importantly, s 38(1) of the Crown Proceedings Act 1947 expressly disapplies the effects of s 21 in relation to proceedings on the Crown Office side, ie in judicial review proceedings.

2 But query the position where the owner has a vital contract to service, failing which he could be liable to suit for breach of contract – in such circumstances the position might be different. Much will depend upon the facts of each case.

18.99   Having discussed at some length the position in relation to public law there also remains the position in private law. Under public law, the decision of the Commissioners to retain the goods notwithstanding the absence of a section 89 notice and absent any power to do so, is a decision made for want of jurisdiction and hence is reviewable, that is what gives the Crown Office the power to intervene.

18.100   Notwithstanding the apparent immunity of the Commissioners, their servants and HMC&E (at least in some senses) from injunctive type remedies in private proceedings,[1] there is some argument for suggesting that the private law route is not bound to fail, even in an interlocutory sense (and it is the interlocutory sense that we are discussing here). The private law and indeed the public law route will or could produce final results by way of an order of mandamus or declaration and (in the Crown office by way of injunction). Section 21(1)(a) of the Crown Proceedings Act 1947 ('CPA 1947') makes it clear that in any case where a coercive injunctive order is to be made then the court shall make a declaration instead and the same must apply to servants of the Crown. Even though s 21 of the CPA 1947 does not say so, it would be illogical if declarations in *lieu* of injunctive relief could be made against the Crown but not its servants.

It is submitted that logic dictates that declarations are equally available against Crown servants as they are against the Crown.

1 Which would, presumably be brought as interference with goods or conversion, provided that the Commissioners or HMC&E had either acted in a way that was inconsistent with the property rights of the importer or owner or had refused to accede to a demand for their return.

18.101 What s 21 of the CPA 1947 does not say is that no interlocutory declaration may be made. We accept that to draw this to the attention of the reader is to set alarm bells ringing as it is odd, to say the least, to make an interlocutory declaration going one way and a final one going the other. Indeed, as Lord Scarman said in *R v Her Majesty's Commissioners of the Inland Revenue, ex p Rossminster Ltd*:[1]

> 'I find absurd the posture of a court declaring one day in interlocutory proceedings that an applicant has certain rights and upon a later day that he has not. Something less risible must be devised.'

1 [1980] AC 952 at 1027E.

18.102 The problem which the courts have perceived appears to reside in the idea that a declaration is only something which may be given as a form of final relief. Whether those who hold such a view do so strongly does not deny the fact that it has its detractors. Indeed the Law Commission in its Report on Remedies in Administrative Law[1] appended clause 3(2) to a draft bill which would have amended s 21 of the CPA 1947 so as to enable the court, in *lieu* of the grant of an interim injunction against the Crown, to 'declare the terms of the interim injunction that it would have made'. The suggested bill never reached the statute book. However, what followed the Law Commission Report was the new Ord 53 of the RSC 1965, made in 1977, which was validated (there being doubts as to whether delegated legislation was powerful enough to confer such a jurisdiction onto the court) by s 31 of the SCA 1981. The Israeli Supreme Court, in *Yotvin v State of Israel*,[2] has disagreed with the line of thought (in England at least) as regards interim declarations. Cohn J said:

> 'I fail to find any logical or legal contradiction between the declaration of a certain right or obligation and the temporary nature of such declaration: the meaning of the impermanence is that the declaration refers to a right or obligation that exists *prima facie* ...'[2]

1 (1976, Cmnd 6407).
2 As quoted in Supperstone & Gouldie on Judicial Review, Butterworths 1996, para 10.9.

18.103 We also submit that the jurisdiction to grant an interim declaration against the Crown in *private law* proceedings is (or at least may already be) available by statute if one accepts the true construction of s 21(1) of the CPA 1947, which states:

> 'In any civil proceedings by or against the Crown, the court shall ... have power to make all such orders as it has power to make in proceedings between subjects, and otherwise to give such appropriate relief as the case may require; provided that:

(*a*) where in any proceedings against the Crown any such relief is sought as might in proceedings between subjects be granted by way of injunction or specific performance, the court shall not grant an injunction or make an order for specific performance, but may in *lieu* thereof make an order declaratory of the rights of the parties: ... '.

18.104 Hence, any party seeking interim relief against the Crown or its servants needs simply preface the order (for injunctive relief) which they would otherwise seek for the return of goods the words 'This court doth declare that but for the provisions of s 21(1) [or (2)] of the CPA 1947 it would have ordered that ...'.[1] Whether the Commissioners would pay heed to such a declaration is anybody's guess[2] since they may justify prolonged detention on the grounds that no final determination had been made. Further, there seems to be added strength for the existence of interim declarations since mention is made of them in Part 25.1(b) of the CPR 1998,[3] though there is, as yet, no practice direction or case law. Given that the CPR 1998 are procedural there may be doubts as to whether such an interim declaration is available on a substantive law basis by the mere existence of the rules since they can only ever be procedural. Again apart from the difficulties relating to jurisdiction, a claimant would have to satisfy the court in relation to all of the other requirements relating to interim relief, which are too well known to require repetition here.[4]

1 It is accepted that in reality this is likely to be a point which will need to be decided by the House of Lords.
2 Though it is not being suggested that the Commissioners would simply ignore the effect of any declaration which the court might make.
3 CPR, Part 25.1(b) states 'The court may grant the following interim remedies— ... (b) an interim declaration ...'.
4 It is interesting to note that in relation to interlocutory proceedings taken at the behest of the Crown (to obtain a freezing injunction), the court has required the Crown to provide a cross undertaking in damages (though we accept that this does not imply that there is thereby a power to grant injunctions) which would suggest that there is some coercive power in the court which it is prepared to exercise, see *Customs and Excise Comrs v Anchor Foods Ltd* [1999] 1 WLR 1139.

18.105 It ought to be added that if an importer takes exception to the operation of an unauthorised seizure or detention because HMC&E have been operating an unlawful retrospective notice procedure, then it is likely that such will (by this time) have come to the attention of the proprietor. If he gets wind of the fact that declaratory proceedings are on foot, he may, of course, apply for an interlocutory injunction to restrain dissemination as a private law matter between himself and the importer.

18.106 If the prospective procedure has been correctly carried out in the sense that an actual or purported section 89 notice has been validly served then, HMC&E have authority to seize or detain the relevant imported goods as liable for forfeiture. However, the notice must be valid and must conform with the requirements as to form. In some cases, the form and formality of the section 89 notice is probably directory but in others the formal requirements are mandatory, particularly in relation to the requirements of TM(C)R 1994 reg 6, which states:

'(1) The person giving the notice shall, either on giving notice or when the goods are imported, furnish the Commissioners with the certificate of registration (or a copy of it) issued by the Registrar of Trade Marks on the registration of the trade mark specified in the notice, together with evidence that such registration was duly renewed at all such times as it may have expired.

(2) If such a certificate or copy and, where applicable, evidence of renewal is not furnished in accordance with paragraph (1) above then the goods shall not be detained,
or, if detained, shall be released, and (but without prejudice to the operation of regulation 5 above) any notice given in respect of them shall have no effect.'

18.107   The requirements of reg 6(1) are clear. The trade mark registration certificate must be provided as well as evidence of renewal, though that evidence can
be provided either when the section 89 notice is proffered to HMC&E or when the
goods are imported. It would appear that compliance with such a requirement as is
set out in reg 6(1) is a relatively simple one to satisfy but it is, as experience has
shown, a requirement which is honoured more in the breach than in the
observance.

18.108   A second and perhaps more far reaching issue which arises in practice is
whether a section 89 notice can only specify one registered trade mark or whether
(as a reflection of commercial practice and reality) it can relate to more than one
registered trade mark. It is trite to observe that many proprietors mark their goods
with more than one trade mark.[1] It is accepted that s 6(c) of the Interpretation Act
1978 provides that '[i]n any Act, unless the contrary intention appears, ... words in
the singular include the plural and words in the plural include the singular' and that
s 23 of the Interpretation Act 1978 provides that statutory instruments such as the
TM(C)R 1994 shall be construed likewise. However, it is trite law that there need
not be an express limitation as to whether a word is intended to embrace the singular or plural – it depends upon the legislative intention and whether if in applying s
6(c) of the Interpretation Act 1978 the effect is to change the character of the legislative intent.[2] It is submitted that the effect of s 89 of the TMA 1994 and the
TM(C)R 1994 is that the proprietor may indeed rely upon more than one registered
trade mark when he completes his s 89 notice since to rely upon more than one registration does make any difference to the working of section 89 of the TMA 1994.
However, what is unclear is whether a failure to provide the information required
by the TM(C)R 1994 reg 6(1), in relation to one of the registered trade marks relied
upon is sufficient to render the entire notice of 'no effect' within the meaning of the
TM(C)R 1994 reg 6(2), or whether the notice is ineffective only in relation to the
registration in question.

1 Eg the Microsoft Corporation often marks its goods with more than one registered trade mark such as
'Microsoft' and 'Windows'.
2 See *Blue Metal Industries Ltd v RW Dilley* [1970] AC 827 at 848, *per* Lord Morris of Borth-y-Gest.

18.109   This leads us to our final word on the domestic seizure or detention route
which is that once a valid notice is in force and the goods (materials or articles) correspond with what is set out in the notice, in the sense that they are goods (articles
or materials) which were marked or made by a person other than the proprietor,
without his consent and fall within the scope of the registrations concerned in such
a way as to infringe the rights given by such registration then HMC&E can seize
those goods, material or articles or detain them as liable for forfeiture. Once this
happens and objection is made to such seizure or detention by the owner then
HMC&E is obliged to refer the matter to one of the appropriate courts for determination as to whether the goods seized or detained correspond with what is in the
notice and if they do then the court is bound to order the goods condemned as
forfeit.

18.110 In cases where the goods are either not counterfeit or the relevant formalities have not been complied with or otherwise the court refuses to order that the goods be condemned as forfeit, the court will dismiss the application. Interestingly, there is no compulsive power requiring the delivery up of the goods in question (consistent with the principle that compulsive orders will not be made against the Crown) though in the (unlikely) event that the goods are detained even after condemnation proceedings have been dismissed then the owner can seek a declaration that the goods ought to be returned. Where an appeal is being made against the dismissal of an application to condemn or at the suit of the owner then the goods have to be kept by HMC&E pending resolution of that appeal.[1]

1 CEMA 1979, Sch 3, para 12.

8 Defences

18.111 This leads us to the second issue of constitutional importance which relates to the kinds of defences which a defendant can run in an infringement action namely:

— that the goods are not infringing within the meaning of s 10 of the TMA 1994;
— that the proprietor has given his consent within the meaning of s 9 of the TMA 1994;
— that the trade mark registration (or scope thereof) in question ought to be revoked wholly or partially within the meaning of s 46 of the TMA 1994;
— that the trade mark registration (or scope thereof) in question ought to be declared invalid wholly or partially within the meaning of s 47 of the TMA 1994.

18.112 The first two of these defences may be categorised as primary defences whilst the second two may be described as secondary defences in the sense that the defendant in an infringement action can say 'true, I would be infringing the rights given by your UK trade mark registration if it were valid but it is invalid'.

18.113 Having established that it is a valid defence in condemnation proceedings to say that the goods to which the section 89 notice relates are not infringing goods, it must follow that avoiding infringement may be done by way of a primary or a secondary defence, yet the secondary defences are not available to the defendant in the Magistrates' Courts or apparently in the county courts. The question is whether, therefore, because such defences are not available in the Magistrates' Courts and county courts, they have jurisdiction in relation to condemnation proceedings (insofar as s 89 of the TMA 1994 is concerned) at all.

18.114 The rationale for this objection lies in the fact that nobody ought to have a monopoly unless they qualify for it or deserve it and that because monopolies (however they work) can be against the public interest, compliance with the rules relating to their existence and conference must be observed strictly and the rules relating to their existence must be interpreted strictly. The existence of a monopoly in trade dress (by way of the law of registered trade marks) does provide some public benefit in that there is guarantee of origin and therefore quality (which justifies the monopoly) and some commercial benefit[1] by way of strengthened brand image allowing for product diversity and specific identity which inevitably leads to prosperity.

1 Though we do not say that this is the ratioale or raison d' etre for the TMA at all.

18.115   The first Council Directive 89/104/EEC of 21 December 1988 to approximate the laws of the Member States relating to trade marks[1] ('the Directive'), which is extensively discussed elsewhere in this book provides at the eighth Recital:

> 'Whereas in order to reduce the total number of trade marks registered and protected in the Community and, consequently, the number of conflicts which arise between them, it is essential to require that registered trade marks must … , if not used, be subject to revocation; … whereas … Member States remain free to … provide that a trade mark may not be successfully invoked in infringement proceedings if it is established as a result of a plea that the trade mark could be revoked; …'

1 OJ L40 11.2.1989 p 1.

18.116   What is odd is that whilst the recitals state that non-used registered trade marks ought to be revoked, there is no like recital in relation to registered trade marks which ought (apart from non-use) never to have got onto the register at all. However, the Directive must be stronger than its recitals and indeed arts 3 and 4 of the Directive state that trade marks ought to be declared invalid if they should never have been on the register in the first place. Though it is true that the effects of invalidity and the procedure for attaining a declaration of invalidity are matters for each Member State, it is submitted that all that the Member State can do is decide the manner in which procedures are to be followed, not that there should or should not be a procedure at all nor that there should be no final result. The same goes for revocation.

18.117   Accordingly, whenever a registered trade mark is in issue in any proceedings it must always be an option for the defendant, or person in the position of a defendant, to be able to say that the registered trade mark is invalid or ought to be revoked. The fact that ss 46 and 47 of the TMA 1994 only cede power to the High Court or registrar to determine such matters would tend to imply that, therefore, the county courts and Magistrates' Courts have no such power and as such the defendant is constitutionally deprived of a guaranteed right to impugn the existence of the monopoly which he is alleged to have infringed or practically speaking (in the case of seizure or detention on import) has attempted to infringe.

18.118   Whether this defence is one which is complete remains to be seen, since even if a submission of lack of jurisdiction is successfully made to the county court or to the Magistrates' Courts, there is nothing to stop the Commissioners from taking the matter up again in the High Court (though costs would, of course, be an issue). This issue, though of only partial assistance in relation to condemnation proceedings, burns very bright in the context of criminal proceedings within the meaning of s 92 of the TMA 1994 and the European route (discussed below)[1] where the rules are a degree (or two) more complex.

1 See ch 19.

18.119 Finally, in relation to defences it has to be acknowledged that many defences are run on the basis of a defect in procedure and this is something which can only be ascertained if the internal documentation of HMC&E is turned up since, given the various presumptions which favour HMC&E and the Commissioners there is little obligation on them to furnish such documentation to the court. Because of the operation of the presumptions, the defendant would have little to lose in seeking to get hold of such documentation by the disclosure cr witness summons route.

9 Further proceedings

18.120 In some cases, seizure or detention will take place and the resultant condemnation proceedings will be dismissed. In such cases, HMC&E are liable to pay damages for conversion (or, more properly, trespass to goods). Despite the fact that HMC&E will almost always seek an indemnity from the proprietor in respect of such proceedings as a condition before agreeing to accept a section 89 notice, there are cases where, notwithstanding the wrongful seizure or detention, the behaviour of HMC&E was, in the circumstances, reasonable. If the court agrees then it can issue a certificate under the CEMA 1979 s 144, certifying such and thereafter HMC&E are immune from further suit in respect of that seizure or detention. The court has a discretion as to whether to issue a certificate under the CEMA 1979 1979 s 144, and indeed there is nothing to stop HMC&E from raising the s 144 issue in any subsequent proceedings brought at the suit of the owner for conversion damages (subject to any issue estoppel or *res judicata*, though if the s 144 issue was not raised below then it can be raised in the fresh proceedings).

18.121 Instances where a s 144 certificate has been refused are where, for instance, HMC&E has failed in some respect to an easy-to-follow procedure such as was the case in *Customs and Excise Comrs v Top High Development Ltd*[1] where the Commissioners, being required to satisfy themselves as to the existence of certain UK trade mark registrations mistakenly relied upon application forms when, in fact, there had been no registration and the Commissioners themselves had in fact stated that their practice was that they would only accept registration certificates (such statement not, in that case, being communicated to the relevant officer concerned). Experience has also shown that where HMC&E have failed to follow the (mandatory) letter of delegated legislation which the Commissioners are empowered to draft, then little sympathy will be given to a plea that the legislation is complex and difficult to follow.

1 [1998] FSR 464

10 The court process itself

18.122 Condemnation proceedings in the High Court or the county court will proceed and be conducted in accordance with the CPR 1998 and practice directions under them and an intimate discussion of them is outside the scope of this chapter.

18.123 In relation to Magistrates' Court proceedings, there are no real rules of procedure and each case works its own way to trial. The usual procedure is for there to be one or two initial hearings so that non-binding directions can be given as to the further conduct of the action, default simply leads to further adjournments and wasted costs (in every sense of the expression). At trial, the proceedings are conducted very much as if they were a summary trial before the justices on a criminal information with live witnesses and no witness statements in place of examination in chief (though the complainant will usually serve witness statements in any event). It is, however, unclear whether a submission of no case to answer at the close of the complainant's case precludes the defendant from adducing evidence.[1]

1 As it does in High Court proceedings, see *Laurie v Raglan Building Co* Ltd [1942] 1 KB 152.

Chapter 19

Border controls – the European procedure

1 The rationale and objectives

19.1 There is little need to amplify or extend what is said about the rationale and objectives of the European route save to say that in addition to the section 89 route[1] there is also in operation a system of European regulations which governs the position relating to those who import goods to which the equivalent of a section 89 notice is in force. It is not right to say, however, that the domestic rules or European regulations do the same thing twice, they do not, as we have seen, and indeed the section 89 rules are expressly exclusive in relation to the European Regulations.

1 See ch 18.

19.2 By far the most important features of the European regime are, firstly, the fact that there is a system in place for the making of retrospective applications and, secondly, that the European regime applies to goods, material or articles which bear Community as well as domestic trade marks, whereas the domestic regime purely relates to domestic marks, is not enshrined in the Directive and is (it is thought) derived from previous domestic law on the subject.[1]

1 TMA 1938, s 64.

19.3 The European regime is a degree more complex and comes in two forms being the European regulations as amended[1] and the uamended European Regulations. The European Regulations overlap with each other to a certain extent in that they are both procedural in their nature and the Basic regulation interlocks with the CEMA 1979 via a number of statutory instruments, initially the Counterfeit and Pirated Goods (Consequential Provisions) Regulations having effect from 1 July 1995,[2] though this has now been revoked and replaced by the Goods Infringing Intellectual Property Rights (Consequential Provisions) Regulations 1999 ('(CP)R 1999') which has effect from 1 July 1999.[3] The effect of the (CP)R 1999 is to cause CEMA 1979 to have effect in relation to goods which offend (ie fall within the meaning of) the appropriate notice under the Basic regulation (which is akin to but not identical to the section 89 notice). As well as (CP)R 1999 there is also the Counterfeit and Pirated Goods (Customs) Regulations 1995 (SI 1995/1430) also having effect from 1 July 1995,[4] though this has now been revoked and replaced by The Goods Infringing Intellectual Property Rights (Customs) Regulations 1999[5] ('(C)R 1999') and the effect of the (C)R 1999 is to provide the notification procedure which is to be followed when calling the Basic

Regulation and the CEMA 1979 into play.

1 Namely Council Regulation 3295/94/EC (the 'Basic Regulation'), as implemented by Commission Regulation 1367/95/EC and as amended by Council Regulation 241/99/EC. See para **18.72**.
2 (SI 1995/1447) made pursuant to the ECA 1972, s 2(2) and having effect by the operation of reg 1(1).
3 (SI 1999/1618) see (CP)R 1999, reg 1 for commencement and reg 9 for revocation.
4 (SI 1995/1430) made pursuant to s 2(2) of the ECA 1972 and having effect by the operation of reg 1(1).
5 (SI 1999/160). See the (CP)R 1999, reg 1 for commencement and reg 9 for revocation.

2   The means

19.4   The Basic Regulation applies only to counterfeit goods, ie goods not manufactured by the proprietor of the relevant registered trade mark. It does not apply to goods which are manufactured by the proprietor but which are placed on a particular market without his consent, or are marked without his consent in circumstances where he has given his consent for such goods to be marked.[1]

1 Basic Regulation, art 1(4).

19.5   Goods entering any country in the EU are governed by the Community Customs Code ('CCC')[1] which empowers the customs authority of each member state to hold goods to establish their status under the CCC, art 37 and also requires the importer (often termed the declarant) to file papers identifying the goods.[2] Where in the course of making such checks or in the course of considering such paperwork there is a suspicion that the goods concerned are counterfeit within the meaning of art 1(2)(a) of the Basic Regulation then under art 1(1)(b) of the Basic Regulation, the customs authorities may take action (and the expression 'take action' is defined as the actions or measures which the customs authorities are empowered to take in accordance with the Basic Regulation).

1 The Community Customs Code is in fact made up of two very large regulations, the first, is Council Regulation 2913/92/EEC of 12 October 1992 establishing the CCC comprising some 253 articles and 8 recitals, OJ L 302 19.10.92 p 1 as variously amended which we shall hereinafter simply call the CCC since it is by far the nost substantial in effect. The, second, implementing regulation is Commission Regulation 2454/93/EEC of 2 July 1993 comprising some 915 articles, 113 annexes and 6 recitals; OJ L 253 11.10.93 p 1 (the CCC Implementing Regulation). Both regulations came into force on 1 January 1994 (CCC, arts 253 and 915 of the CCC Implementing Regulation).
2 CCC, art 61.

19.6   Thus far, there is no need for the filing of the equivalent of a section 89 notice though in order to understand the manner in which applications under the Basic Regulation are processed it is necessary to have some understanding of who the players are in a scenario involving the attempted importation of counterfeit goods. Firstly, there is the competent customs service or authority (which in this country is HMC&E) and HMC&E will be divided into a central administrative office or unit (though organs of such an office may be geographically disparate) and various port offices. The expression 'service' is often used to denote the part of the customs authority which processes applications whereas the expression 'authority' means the whole of the customs unit in each member state. Secondly, the port offices are referred to in the Basic Regulation as the customs office liable to be concerned, which is self explanatory. Thirdly, there is the applicant who is the proprietor of the registered trade mark in question (or his licensee or their respective representatives). Fourthly, there is the declarant who is usually the importer and is also the person who declares the goods to HMC&E pursuant to CCC, art 61. Fifthly, there is the consignee whose position is self explanatory and, finally, there is the authority competent whose position, existence and status is entirely unclear.[1]

1 Though now suspected to be the domestic court having jurisdiction in relation to registered trade amrk infringement disputes – see *Re Adidas*, (14 October 1999, unreported), ECJ.

19.7   In order to enable HMC&E to take action under the Basic Regulation the conditions set out in art 1(1)(a) of the Basic Regulation must be satisfied, those conditions are:

(1)   the goods in question:
   (a) are entered into the Member State; and
   (b) are declared to the customs authorities by the declarant in the manner set out in the CCC, art 6; and
(2)   those goods are entered for the purposes of:
   (a) free circulation;
   (b) export; or
   (c) re-export; or
(3)   those goods are found in the course of checks on:
   (a) goods under customs supervision;
   (b) placed under a suspensive procedure;
   (c) re-exported subject to notification; or
   (d) placed in a free zone or free warehouse.

It is a condition precedent that the goods in question are suspected of being counterfeit goods within the meaning of art 1(2)(a) of the Basic Regulation.

3   The CCC

19.8   It is important to examine with care what each of these conditions entails but firstly it is important to say a little about the operation of the CCC generally.

19.9   The EU has as its basis a customs union which is concerned with all trade in goods. This customs union seeks to eliminate customs duties on imports and exports (or like measures) and seeks to set out common tariffs in relation to non-EEA countries. This should lead to the abolition of charges and duties of a customs nature in relation to trade between Member States. The effect of this is to outlaw discriminatory taxation within the EEA. It is only recently (in relation to the life of the EU as a whole) that significant progress has been made towards this goal. The Agreement on the EEA signed at Oporto on 2 May 1992 (which was adjusted by the Protocol signed at Brussels on 17 March 1993) had the effect of moving the Member States of the EEA much closer to this goal. The Oporto Agreement on the EEA was designed to simplify border controls and formalities and that the Member States of the EEA have to provide each other with mutual assistance in order to achieve this goal. One means of achieving this is the imposition and creation of a common customs tariff which seeks to classify goods and then determines the duty chargeable on them, a complex area in its own right and far beyond the scope of this book. However, a basic understanding of the tariff system is important.

19.10   The tariff[1] consists of:

(1)   the combined nomenclature of goods, ie a means of classifying goods (as opposed to services) into certain defined classes which as most trade mark lawyers know is an area which is not beyond controversy;

(2)   any other nomenclature which supplements and is wholly or partly based upon (1) as adopted by the Community;

(3)   charges to be made in relation to goods covered by the nomenclatures referred to in (1) and (2) above;

(4)   charges to be made in relation to goods covered by the nomenclatures referred to in (1) and (2) above but reduced (also forming part of the preferential tariff measures) by reason of unilateral treaties or action in relation to non-EEA states or groups of them;

(5)   charges to be made in relation to goods covered by the nomenclatures referred to in (1) and (2) above but reduced (called preferential tariff measures) by reason of bilateral agreements with certain non-EEA states;[2]

(6)   suspension (by way of reduction or relief) of duties chargeable on goods determined by the Community as deserving such suspension (known as autonomous suspensive measures or favourable tariff treatment); and

(7)   anything else relating to tariff measures where the Community so decrees, for instance trade embargoes or anti-dumping measures.

1 To be found in Council Regulation 2658/87/EEC, Annex I, as substituted by Commission Regulation 2261/98/EEC, OJ L 292 30.10.98 p 1, art 1 and Annex thereto.
2 The Customs Union with Turkey.

19.11   The effect of this is that goods are classified and charged in accordance with a tariff. It can be determined whether any reductions or reliefs apply and accordingly and ultimately, what charges are to be made. The rules relating to the application of the tariff system along with other customs procedures are contained in the CCC and its implementing regulation.

19.12   The normal charge is presumed to apply as under (3) above. However, the declarant may ask HMC&E to treat the goods on a preferential basis as under (4)–(6) above provided that he can satisfy the relevant conditions. Applications may be prospective or retrospective, though certain additional conditions apply to retrospective applications. In many cases, preferential charges apply to set quotas.

19.13   Once goods arrive in the territory they are, from that time subject to what is called 'customs supervision'. Customs supervision is defined by the CCC, art 4(13) as being:

> 'action taken in general by those [local customs] authorities with a view to ensuring that customs rules and, where appropriate, other provisions applicable to goods subject to customs supervision are observed.'

19.14   Merely because goods are the subject of customs supervision does not mean that they are the subject of customs control, which is a different thing altogether and is defined as:

'the performance of specific acts such as examining goods, verifying the existence and authenticity of documents, examining the accounts of undertakings and other records, inspecting means of transport, inspecting luggage and other goods carried by or on persons[1] and carrying out official inquiries and other similar acts with a view to ensuring that customs rules and, where appropriate, other provisions applicable to goods subject to customs supervision are observed.'[2]

1 Though it is to be noted that the Basic Regulation does not apply to personal luggage or imports 'of a non-commercial nature' since it would be too difficult to enforce, see the 12th recital to and art 10 of the Basic Regulation.
2 CCC, art 4(14).

19.15 The control may be exercised in accordance with Community provisions or national provisions.[1] When goods are the subject of customs supervision they remain so for as long as may be necessary and appropriate to determine their status.[2] Imported Community goods may be freely entered into a EEA Member State of the Community from any other[3] though there may be specific restrictions in force for certain types of goods and very different rules apply in relation to Community goods sought to be exported from the EEA. If the status of the goods is that they are Community goods then they travel on unimpeded, though there may at any time be movement restrictions or special duties chargeable. For non-community goods, they remain under customs supervision until they are re-exported or destroyed or they enter a free zone or a free warehouse, or their status is changed (ie from non-Community to Community status).

1 Obviously national provisions cannot be incompatible with Community provisions and, it is submitted, they must be proportionate.
2 CCC, art 37(2). 'Customs status' means whether they are Community or non-Community goods, CCC, art 4(6). CCC, art 4(7) defines community goods as being goods: (1) wholly obtained in the customs territory of the Community under the conditions referred to in CCC, art 23 (basically raw, processed and products derived from animals, minerals and vegetable originating from within the territory) and not incorporating goods which have been imported from non-EEA states, or (2) imported from non-EEA countries but which have been released for free circulation; or (3) obtained or produced in the EEA, either from (2) alone or from goods falling within (1) and (2). 'Non-Community goods' is defined by CCC, art 4(6) as being everything else not being Community goods.
Goods obtained from goods placed under a suspensive arrangement do not have Community status where there are special economic rules in force.
3 See Case T-266/81 *Societa Italiana per l'Oleodotto Transalpino (SIOT) v Ministero delle Finanze* [1983] ECR 731 and (Case C367/89) *Richardt and Les Accessoires Scientifiques SNC* [1991] ECR I-4621. See also the EC Treaty, art 25 as amended by the Treaty of Amsterdam which states that 'customs duties on imports and exports and charges having equivalent effect shall be prohibited between member states.' whereas the original text, the Treaty of Rome, art 12 speaks of no new duties between Member States being introduced or increased. This represents a significant change in position.

19.16 Goods arriving into the EEA from outside must be conveyed to such place and by such route as customs may specify, usually a customs office and usually the office is situated at the port of importation.[1] Thereafter the goods must be 'presented' to the customs office by the importer or such person who assumes responsibility for those goods such as a freight forwarder.[2] Presentation refers to the process of notifying the customs authorities (HMC&E in the case of the UK) of their arrival[3] and such notice must be in the prescribed form[4] and it is at this point that a declaration must be made (called a summary declaration) by the importer, the person assuming responsibility for importation or the persons they represent.[5]

1 CCC, art 38(1)(a) and (b).
2 CCC, art 40 and art 189 of the CCC Implementing Regulation.
3 CCC, art 170(2).

4 Article 813(1) of the CCC implementing regulation. Though nowhere is it expressly specified what this prescribed form is. It is assumed to be the summary declaration which *must* accompany presented goods; see CCC, art 43.
5 CCC, art 44(2).

19.17 It is at this point that the goods concerned must be assigned a 'customs-approved treatment or use' which is defined by art 4(15) CCC as being:

'(a) the placing of goods under a customs procedure;
(b) their entry into a free zone or free warehouse;
(c) their re-exportation from the customs territory of the Community;
(d) their destruction;
(e) their abandonment to the Exchequer.'

19.18 Until such assignment, the goods are deemed to be in temporary storage.[1] It should be noted that by the operation of CCC, art 164 Community goods sought to be imported shall not be the subject of a customs procedure, though they are, until their status, is determined, subject to customs supervision.[2] The assignment is something for the declarant[3] or other person interested in such assignment, there is no absolute rule that it need be the declarant. The assignment may include the placing of the goods under a customs procedure or one of the other five means of assignment.

1 CCC, art 50.
2 CCC, art 37(1).
3 CCC, arts 48 and 49.

First indent of the Basic Regulation, art 1(1)(a)

19.19 It is at this point that the CCC, art 61 comes into play. Article 61 of the CCC determines how declarations[1] may be made to the customs authorities where it is intended to place the goods under a customs procedure.[2] Indeed, it is important to define with a little more precision what the CCC means when it refers to a declarant, since that is defined in the CCC, art 4(18) as being the person who makes the customs declaration, that is the declaration necessary for the goods to be placed under a customs procedure. A customs procedure is defined in the CCC, art 4(16) as being:

'(a) release for free circulation;
(b) transit;
(c) customs warehousing;
(d) inward processing;
(e) processing under customs control;
(f) temporary admission;
(g) outward processing;
(h) exportation'

and relates to the procedures to be followed when classifying the goods in one of the eight categories of customs processing. Since all such goods are the subject of customs supervision, provided the goods entered are entered for free circulation, export or re-export and a customs declaration has been made, then the first indent of art 1(a) of the Basic Regulation is satisfied. However, the first indent is not satisfied in relation to goods where the customs procedure is sought to deal with goods which are: in transit, or subject to customs warehousing, inward processing,[3] processing under customs control,⁴ temporary admission, outward processing⁵ or exportation.

1 Called a 'customs declaration', CCC, art 4(17).
2 CCC, art 59(1).
3 That is industrial processing in the member state concerned for re-export out of the EEA – eg because the goods are in a partially complete state or are to be incorporated with others. See Case T 49/82*EC Commission v Nederlands* [1985] ECR 1195 at 1209; [1983] 2 CMLR 476 at 482, per Advocats General Slynn and Case C-325/96 *Fabrica del Queijo Eru Portugesa Lda v Subdirector-General das Alfandegas* [1997] ECR I-7249, ECJ.
4 That is industrial processing in the Member State concerned using the goods in such a way as to alter their nature of state (such as raw materials) but under the supervision of customs for the resultant goods to be exported or re-exported or assigned to a customs-approved treatment or use.
5 The converse of inward processing – ie the goods are leaving but they will come back, usually in an altered state.

19.20 It should be noted that goods which are under customs supervision may be checked pursuant to national law in accordance with the CEMA 1979, s 159(1),¹ though the customs declaration may also be used to tell HMC&E what the goods are and hence would or might enable HMC&E to determine whether the goods are counterfeit within the meaning of art 1(2)(a) of the Basic Regulation. It is, as we have noted, a condition precedent for the operation of art 1(1)(a) of the Basic Regulation that the goods in question are suspected of being counterfeit within the meaning of art 1(2)(a) of the Basic Regulation and that they have been checked in accordance with the procedures set out in art 1(1)(a) of the Basic Regulation. Both conditions must be satisfied.

1 Which empowers HMC&E to make checks on goods.

19.21 Thus, there are a wide range of goods which are not captured by the first indent of art 1(1)(a) of the Basic Regulation the goods are either not the subject of a customs declaration or, if they are, are not entered for free circulation, export or re-export pursuant to a customs procedure. Further, this provision only applies to non-Community goods since only non-Community goods need to be placed under a customs procedure (in order to turn them into Community goods or something else).

Second indent of the Basic Regulation, art 1(1)(a)

19.22 This takes us to the second indent of art 1(1)(a) of the Basic Regulation. There are three separate disjunctive conditions which need to be satisfied and we cover each in turn below, however what is important is that the goods are found in the course of checks – ie there must be a check made upon the goods, either in accordance with the CCC or the CEMA 1979, s 159(1).¹

1 The right to check or examine goods is conferred in specified circumstances by the CCC Implementing Regulation, arts 14(1), 78(6), 79, 106(5), 813(2), 877(1)(c) and 885(1) of the CCC implementing regulation, usually for the purposes of ensuring forms have been filled in correctly or declarations are accurate. Article 183 of the CCC implementing regulation enable checks to be made on goods for export and is akin to the power conferred by the CEMA 1979, s 159(1). Article 168(4) of the CCC enables checks to be made on goods entering or leaving free-zones or free-warehouses but only where reasonable doubts are held, art 804 of the CCC implementing regulation. The most far-reaching provision is art CCC, 4(14) which provides a general power to examine and is regulation by art 240 and 241(1)–(2) of the CCC implementing regulation. A general right akin to the CEMA 1979, s 159(1) right to examine, pervades the CCC and the CCC implementing regulation. See eg CCC, arts 65(a), 66, 68(b) and 78(2).

Goods under customs supervision

19.23   All goods entering the customs territory are subject to customs supervision within the meaning of the CCC, art 37. Hence, it does not apply to goods for export, which though under customs supervision, are not under customs supervision by virtue of the CCC, art 37 but rather by virtue of the CCC, art 59(2). The goods may not be detained merely for the purpose of checking to see whether they are counterfeit since the power to subject the goods to customs supervision ceases once it has been determined what the status of the goods is. Thus, if it is readily apparent that the goods are Community goods and it is unnecessary to make a check on the goods to ascertain that fact then the goods cannot be checked solely to see if they are counterfeit.

19.24   It should be added that once Community goods are exported from the customs union then if they are returned to the union, relief may be sought on duty, though they lose their status as being Community goods[1] and movement of Community goods within the customs union is also subject to transit procedures.[2]

1 CCC, art 4(8).
2 CCC, art 164.

19.25   Article 37(2) of CCC states that the goods which are the subject of customs supervision:

> '... shall remain under such supervision for as long as necessary to determine their customs status, if appropriate, and in the case of non-Community goods and without prejudice to Article 82(1), until their customs status is changed, they enter a free zone or free warehouse or they are re-exported or destroyed in accordance with Article 182.'

19.26   So, once the goods are found to be Community goods or if non-Community goods, until they become Community goods or enter a free zone or free warehouse, are re- exported or destroyed, then they are no longer subject to customs supervision. Hence, once goods are no longer under customs supervision then there is no right to check the goods and even then there appears to be no absolute right to check goods merely because they are suspected of being counterfeit. The check must be for some other reason since if goods are cleared of all other formalities (save in the case of non-Community goods which are not entered into a free zone or free warehouse or are re-exported or destroyed) then supervision ceases.

Goods placed under a suspensive procedure

19.27   The suspensive procedure, so called, but not well defined in the CCC, forms the subject matter of section 3(A) of Chapter 2 of Title IV ('Customs approved treatment or use') of the CCC 'Suspensive arrangements and customs procedures with economic impact'. The CCC, art 84(1)(a) simply defines, for the purposes of s 3 what is meant by 'procedure' in relation to non-Community goods as applying to the following arrangements:

> '—   external transit;
> —   customs warehousing;
> —   inward processing in the form of a system of suspension;

— processing under customs control;
— temporary importation.'

19.28 Suspensive arrangements or procedures are those which are designed to provide relief or reduction from import duty and as such a suspensive procedure in the context of the Basic Regulation can only ever apply to non-Community goods.[1] The word 'suspensive' and 'suspension' in the context of the CCC and the Basic Regulation is intended to refer to situations where autonomous common customs tariff duties imposed pursuant to art 28 (now art 26)[2] of the Treaty of Rome is suspended temporarily to meet the needs of the user industries of the Community.[3] Given that the Treaty of Amsterdam has removed the right to suspend duties and has replaced it with a right to fix duties we are frankly unclear whether the change in wording of art 28 (now art 26 of the Treaty of Rome) has the effect of abolishing suspension of duties – we rather suspect that it does in which case there is no longer a suspensive procedure within the meaning of the CCC. To say such a thing, however, is bold since one would have expected that once the Treaty of Amsterdam came into force the suspensive procedures in the CCC would have been deleted, yet, as at the time of writing, there is no proposal to remove the suspensive arrangements. However, that said, the first recital to the CCC derives its authority from the old art 28 and now that the basis of that authority has changed from *suspension* to *fixing* and this is as a result of the fact that article 12 (now art 25 of the Treaty of Rome) now prohibits customs duties on movements between member states as opposed to limiting their effect. All we can say at present is that the position is incredibly unclear. It is probably better to proceed on the footing that, despite our submissions as to the effective abolition of the suspensive procedure, it is still in force. In relation to the suspensive procedures all that we have said above in relation to the checking of goods applies equally to goods which are the subject of a suspensive procedure.

1 Since CCC, art 84(1)(a) applies exclusively to non-Community goods.
2 Though the original text of art 28 of the Treaty of Rome spoke of the Council being entitled to *suspend* duties, the amended article (now art 26) speaks of the Council *fixing* duties.

19.29 Further a suspensive procedure only applies to goods which are imported into the territory, save for outward processing.

19.30 A declarant wishing to take advantage of a suspensive procedure must expressly avail himself of it by way of the appropriate manner of making a declaration (if in writing, called a Single Administrative Document) and accordingly, if there has been no such declaration then there is no suspensive procedure.

Re-exportation subject to notification or placed in a free zone or free warehouse

19.31 The CCC, art 166 defines free-zones or free warehouses (which are really mini free zones) as being places within the EEA separate from the rest of it where non-Community goods are considered for the purposes of duty and import measures as not being on Community territory. These places are akin to bonded warehouses. Community goods may also reside in free zones or warehouses and if they do so, they qualify for measures normally relating to the export of goods.

19.32 Re-exportation always requires notification[1] and it is usually the case that goods which are sought to be re-exported reside in a free-zone or free warehouse though there is no hard and fast rule that this is so. However, where goods are sought to be re-exported then they are liable to be checked or examined. Further, since re-exportation is a customs-approved treatment or use, which can only apply to non-Community goods, this rule does not apply to Community goods.

1 CCC, art 182(3).

19.33 Any goods which reside for whatever reason in a free-zone or free warehouse may be checked, whether Community or non-Community goods.

The Basic Regulation, art 1(1)(a) taken as a whole

19.34 Once the provisions of art 1(1)(a) are satisfied then, as we have said, a suspicion needs to be formed that the goods are counterfeit. Once that test is satisfied then HMC&E may exercise the measures set out in the rest of the Basic Regulation.

19.35 We should add that the matters in the second indent of art 1(1)(a) of the Basic Regulation do allow for persons to move Community goods around the Community, even if they are counterfeit without fear of sanction from the Basic Regulation. It is for this purpose, we submit, that the TMA 1994, s 89 was enacted. Accordingly, a right owner would be well advised to consider using both procedures.

19.36 Further we have suggested that the Basic Regulation only applies to non-Community goods, which, we submit is beyond doubt but further that it only relates to imported goods as art 2 of the Basic Regulation makes clear.

Are the goods counterfeit?

19.37 It is of interest to note that the test as to whether the goods are counterfeit is somewhat different to the test for infringement which is set out in the TMA 1994, ss 10(1) and (2) or indeed art 5 of the Directive, the test being necessarily narrower. Thus there are three classes of circumstance whereby goods may be described as counterfeit: where the goods themselves are counterfeit; or, where a logo, label, sticker, brochure, instructions for use or a guarantee document is sought to be imported; or, where packaging materials are sought to be imported. In both of the latter cases it is submitted that the expression '… in the same circumstances as the goods referred to in the first indent' means that their existence must be such as to make them counterfeit goods in themselves (as materials or articles as opposed to goods to borrow the terminology of the Directive and the TMA 1994). We shall return to this further below.

19.38 Interestingly, the list referred to above is not exhaustive in that art 1(3) of the Basic Regulation provides that any mould or matrix which is specifically designed or adapted for the manufacture of a counterfeit trade mark is also to be treated as counterfeit goods provided that the *use* of such mould or matrix infringes the rights of the proprietor either under national or CTM law. This extension to cover specially adapted articles is made unnecessarily unclear by the language which the Basic Regulation uses to express itself. For instance the mere possession of an article specially adapted to infringe registered trade marks (for instance a dye) is in fact not an infringing act (though in an action for domestic trade mark infringement, the court may order the delivery up of that thing as well) under both national and CTM law and use of the thing specially adapted might not necessarily be used in an infringing manner (say, for instance a mould for making tyres with the mark 'Butterworths' affixed). It remains to be seen whether this extension of the definition of counterfeit goods really adds anything.

19.39 Further, the width of art 1(3) of the Basic Regulation possibly goes far further than is necessary to protect the interests of the proprietor since the mould or matrix itself, though it may be used to make goods to which a trade mark is to be applied become counterfeit, can also fall within the ambit of the meaning of counterfeit goods. What is odd is that whilst the first part of art 1(3) of the Basic Regulation apparently widens the class of items which may be determined as counterfeit goods, it then almost immediately narrows the class by requiring that the use of such moulds or matrices infringes the rights of the proprietor (under domestic or Community law), which on any view they would not.

19.40 The test for whether goods are counterfeit is whether the goods sought to be imported are goods which:

(1)   bear (on the goods themselves or their packaging) a trade mark (which, in order to be consistent with the TMA 1994 and the directive we shall refer to hereinafter as a sign); and

(2)   the sign is borne (which must mean affixed or imported when affixed) without the authorisation of the trade mark proprietor; and

(3)   the sign is either:
  (a)   identical to the trade mark in question; or
  (b)   cannot be distinguished in its essential aspects from the registered trade mark; and

(4)   the goods concerned fall within the scope of the trade mark registration: and

(5)   the trade mark is validly registered; and

(6)   the affixation of the trade mark (if taking place within the relevant Member State of the EU) would be an infringement of the rights accorded by registration (either as Community or domestic registered trade marks).

19.41 As can be seen the test is cumbersome and exhaustive, though it cannot be said to be unclear. It would appear that where there is a 'similar goods' type argument (as one might find in the TMA 1994, s 10(2)(a)) then the test fails and the goods do not fall to be treated in accordance with the remaining provisions of the Basic Regulation. The distinction between similar goods and similar marks, the latter falling within the ambit of the test and the former without, is it is submitted, heterodox and illogical since sailing close to the wind in a scope sense is or can be just as pernicious as sailing close to the wind in a perceptive sense.

19.42 However, there are some important derogations from the class of things which constitute counterfeit goods within the meaning of art 1(2) and 1(3) of the Basic Regulation such as that goods shall not be said to be counterfeit if they have been marked and/or manufactured by the proprietor but have been placed in the relevant market (or, more properly that attempts have been made to so place by importation) without consent, or, other conditions relating to manufacture or affixation have been breached.[1]

1 See the Basic Regulation, art 1(4).

19.43 The 'event' which enables HMC&E to take further action is uncertain. In art 1(1)(a) of the Basic Regulation it is said that a mere suspicion that the goods in question are counterfeit is sufficient (and this governs the 'conditions' under which the customs authorities, HMC&E, shall take action) whereas art 1(1)(b) of the Basic Regulation speaks of the requirement that it has indeed been established that the goods are counterfeit (and this governs the 'measures' which shall be taken by the competent authorities). This distinction, between 'conditions' and 'measures' on the one hand and between the existence of suspicion that the goods are counterfeit and indeed establishing that fact on the other hand are, it is submitted, fundamental and important distinctions which have, or could have the effect of drastically altering the way in which the scheme set out in the Basic Regulation works.

4 Procedure

19.44 Before examining the detail of the distinction referred to above it is important to examine the procedure which has to be followed in relation to goods entered into the Community, released for free circulation, exported or re-exported. It is worth noting that once the goods have been found to be counterfeit then the entry into the Community, release for free circulation, export, re-export or placing under a suspensive procedure (whatever that means) is prohibited.[1] We shall return to the meaning of the expression 'prohibited' later on in this chapter.

1 Basic Regulation, art 2.

19.45 The main procedural provisions are set out in art 3 of the Basic Regulation. Article 3(1) provides that the proprietor may lodge an application for action ('AA') with the competent service of the Customs Authority for action by the customs authority where the goods fall within art 1(1)(a) of the Basic Regulation (discussed above).

19.46 Goods may be placed under customs supervision if it is sought to: (1) import them for circulation; (2) export them from the territory, having been originated in the customs territory concerned; (3) export them from the territory, having been imported from another territory, not necessarily being an EU territory and their appearance in the current territory is transitory; or (4) hold the goods in a free warehouse. The CCC, art 37, simply says that all goods brought into the customs territory concerned shall be subject to customs supervision for as long as necessary to determine their customs status whereas the CCC, art 59(2) says that goods declared for export, outward processing, transit or customs warehousing procedure shall be subject to customs supervision. Thus, it is irrelevant what the customs status of the goods is – HMC&E can act where a border crossing is contemplated.

19.47 Subject to the meaning of the word 'action', which will be referred to further below a person[1] who holds a CTM may seek 'action' by way of an AA in many Member States and further such AAs may be communicated electronically if

Member States make legislative provision for such to be possible or allowed. It should be noted that the right to make an AA covers two classes of person, the proprietor and the person entitled under him (such as his licensee) or any of their representatives.

1 See para **19.73** below.

19.48 It is at this stage that the implementing regulation becomes involved since it governs (inter alia) the manner in which AAs may be made. The implementing regulation lays down a number of conditions such as the fact that the proprietor may be represented by any person (including a collecting society).[1] When the proprietor applies for 'action' to be taken, he must, in accordance with art 3(2) of the Basic Regulation provide a sufficiently detailed description of the goods so that HMC&E can identify them, as well as proof of the fact that the trade mark rights relied upon exist as registered rights. In accordance with art 2 of the Implementing Regulation this can be done in a variety of ways. A bare reading of art 2(a) of the Implementing Regulation suggests that proof of the proprietor's entitlement (or the applicant making the AA, who must be the proprietor) may be achieved by either producing the relevant registration documentation (though not any renewal information) or by the production that an application for registration has been lodged. It is submitted that this is an unreal way of approaching the provision of proof of current registration since: (1) proof of past registration is no proof of current registration unless the relevant renewal documentation is also included; and (2) a mere application for a trade mark registration confers no rights and there is always the possibility that the application will not ripen into a registered trade mark. Thus, an applicant lodging an AA can simply produce the application form along with evidence that it has been lodged in order to make a valid AA. It may be that art 3(2) of the Basic Regulation deals with this problem by making it a requirement that the proprietor must provide 'all other pertinent information available to … [the proprietor] to enable the competent customs service [(ie the branch of HMC&E which deals with AAs)] to take a decision in full knowledge of the facts' which would presumably include the provision of renewal documentation or statements to the effect that though the trade mark rights in question had been applied for they had not been granted. From the foregoing quoted wording it would seem that there is duty of full and frank disclosure incumbent upon the applicant lodging an AA. However, the remaining wording appears to qualify that assumption since it is, thereafter, stated that the duty to provide such information shall not be 'a condition of admissibility of the … [AA]'. This problem came to be decided in the case of *Customs and Excise Comrs v Top High Development Ltd*[2] where the applicant making the AA produced an application form which revealed that there were in fact no registered rights at the time of lodging the AA. The stipendiary magistrate held that to enable a person to provide proof of the existence of his registered trade mark rights by mere production of an application form would be wrong. Firstly, the Basic Regulation expressly requires proof that the applicant making the AA is the holder of the rights in question (presumably at the time that the goods were brought into the country) and no amount of subordinate legislation (or the European equivalent, being the Implementing Regulation) could abrogate that requirement. Secondly, the wording of the Implementing Regulation does not inevitably lead to conflict with the Basic Regulation since there may be circumstances in other Member States where rights are conferred on deposit of an application form[3] and it is to those situations that the Implementing Regulation is directed. Thirdly, to construe the *Implementing Regulation as allowing a person to assert a powerful and in many* *respects unstoppable legal process by mere assertion that a particular form which confers no rights is contrary to common sense, nobody can enforce a right they do not have.* Finally, HMC&E have acknowledged that they will only accept AAs which are accompanied by proof of extant rights. It is, therefore, submitted that to be valid an AA must be accompanied by proof that the trade mark is registered and was registered at the time that the goods entered the country.

1 Implementing Regulation, art 1.
2 [1998] FSR 464.
3 This is possible in principle since the trade marks directive does not make provision as to when during the prosecution process an application ripens into an enforceable right. Some laws of other Member States, Finland and France, for instance, appear to cede rights upon filing.

19.49 The foregoing requirements of proof apply where the proprietor makes the AA himself. However, the Implementing Regulation envisages that the proprietor may be represented by someone else. In such circumstances, the applicant (making the AA on the proprietor or licensee's behalf) must also prove that he is an authorised representative[1] and where a licensee makes the AA then he too must prove his entitlement[2] by provision of his licence in writing.

1 Implementing Regulation, art 2(c).
2 Implementing Regulation, art 2(b).

19.50 Where a person makes an AA as a representative of either the proprietor or the licensee, then in addition to the foregoing matters, the representative must provide proof of authority to act, though it is not clear whether such proof need be in documentary form.[1]

1 Implementing Regulation, art 2(c).

19.51 In accordance with art 3 of the Implementing Regulation when an AA is submitted then it must provide 'pertinent information' (as referred to in art 3(2) of the Basic Regulation), which shall include:

'(i)   particulars of the goods, notably their value and their packaging; and
(ii)   any information that could help distinguish the goods sought to be imported from the genuine article (referred to in art 3 of the Implementing Regulation as 'goods for which there is a protected right.'

19.52 Article 3 of the Implementing Regulation provides that the information:

'should be as detailed as possible to enable the customs authorities, using risk analysis, to identify suspect consignments accurately and without excessive effort.'

19.53 It is unclear precisely what degree of particularity is required, though it is clear that the more detailed the information, the easier it will be for the customs authorities to take action. Thus, it is in the interests of the applicant to provide as much information as possible. An unusual feature of the Basic Regulation is that there appears to be no mandatory requirement that details of the whereabouts and expected entry of the consignment in question be provided (as there is in the case of pirated goods and goods the existence or making of which infringe patents).[1]

Finally, it is to be noted that a failure to provide the 'pertinent information' is not a bar to the admissibility of the AA.[2] This raises some important issues.

1 Basic Regulation, art 3(2), para 3, which states:
'By way of indication, in the case of pirated goods or of goods infringing patents or certificates, that information shall, wherever possible, include:
— the place where the goods are situated or the intended destination,
— particulars identifying the consignment or packages,
— the scheduled date of arrival or departure of the goods,
— the means of transport used,
— the identity of the importer, exporter or holder.'
2 Basic Regulation, art 3(2), para 2.

19.54 It is fairly apparent from admissibility considerations arising in a domestic procedure[1] that provision of certain material is mandatory. In the case of the domestic procedure, this is so because it is expressly stated. In the European procedure, the position appears to be stated in the reverse, ie what the consequences (or non-consequences) of non-compliance will be, in that the provision of pertinent information shall not wreck the admissibility of the corresponding AA. It is submitted that to say that provision of information other than the pertinent information is not a mandatory requirement would be wrong since it would be inconsistent with the application of the domestic rules under TM(C)R and would also provide a vehicle or avenue whereby no or incorrect information is provided and yet there is still a valid AA.

1 TM(C)R 1994, reg 6.

19.55 Moreover, the scheme of the Basic Regulation provides for the instances where the provision of certain information, being the pertinent information, is not mandatory. If this were so in relation to all of the information then surely the Basic Regulation would say so. However, there is a certain gloss on this in that art 3 of the Implementing Regulation allows the customs authorities to say that, on the basis of the information which they have been provided with, it is too expensive in terms of time or money to enforce the relevant AA. If, however, art 3 of the Implementing Regulation were so clear then there would be little more to say about it but the article requires the customs authorities to engage in something called 'risk analysis'. The question then arises, what is the 'risk' referred to? It could be that the 'risk' referred to is the risk to the owner of the relevant registered trade marks, ie how much damage to the proprietor are the customs authorities saving? On the other hand it could mean (either exclusively or additionally) the risk to the exchequer in terms of the resources expended as against the likelihood of seizure. It is submitted that because the closing words of art 3 of the Implementing Regulation speak of identifying suspect consignments accurately and without excessive effort, it must follow that the 'risk' is the risk to the exchequer rather then the risk to the proprietor. Since, however, there is no authority or learning on the subject, we express this view cautiously.

19.56 Once the requisite AA is prepared with all of the aforementioned required and pertinent information then it must also specify the period during which the customs authorities are to take action. However, the applicant is not required to specify a time limit where he is the proprietor of a CTM and seeks action in relation to that or those registered trade marks, though he must specify in which other Member States he wishes action to be taken.[1] The time limit for such applications is set at one year[2] though this can be renewed for an additional year and so on.

1 Basic Regulation, art 3(3).
2 Basic Regulation, art 3(5), para 4.

19.57 Thereafter, the applicant must pay a fee which must not be disproportionate (presumably) to the service which the customs authority is to provide,[1] though this fee is not set and is within the limits of proportionality within the discretion of the customs authorities.

1 Article 3(4) of the Basic Regulation.

19.58 Once the AA has been prepared and the formalities as regards the provision of information complied with, the AA should be submitted to the 'competent customs service' which is, presumably the relevant organ of the customs authority, in this country, a department of HMC&E. Article 3(5) of the Basic Regulation compels that department to process the application and to notify the applicant forthwith of the decision in relation to that AA. It is to be assumed that HMC&E cannot be compelled to process the application forthwith and that the word 'forthwith' as appears in art 3(5) refers to what is required to be done once a decision has been reached by HMC&E. Somewhat arbitrarily, HMC&E may specify how long it intends to take action in relation to the AA, though there is a right to extend that period.[1] A refusal to grant an application is subject to appeal[2] though since the Basic Regulation appears to be speaking about a decision and a decision-making process being made or carried out by an organ of the state, the most likely avenue of 'appeal' would be by way of judicial review.

1 Basic Regulation, art 3(5), para 2.
2 To use the language of Basic Regulation, art 3(5), para 3.

19.59 So far we have spoken in general terms about the position relating to the compilation and preparation of the AA. The manner of completion and form of the AA is specified by the Goods Infringing Intellectual Property Rights (Customs) Regulations 1999 ('(C)R 1999') which includes a form and checklist. The (C)R 1999 also includes, as we shall see, much more. However, for present purposes the question of the prospective and retrospective procedure comes into play. This was discussed in a slightly different context in relation to the domestic procedure but is more rigidly defined (and authorised) in the context of the European route.

The retrospective procedure

19.60 When goods are entered into this country and appear to be suspect but no AA is in force, perhaps because the proprietor was not aware of their importation, then HMC&E is entitled to detain the goods for a limited period of time if it (or more properly, their officers) believes them to be counterfeit. This is covered by art 4 of the Basic Regulation which we reproduce in full:

> 'Where, in the course of checks made under one of the customs procedures referred to in Article 1(1)(a) [of the Basic Regulation] and before an application by the holder of the right has been lodged or approved, it appears evident to the customs office that goods are [goods referred to in Article 1(2)(a)],[1] the customs authority may, in accordance with the rules in force in the Member States concerned, notify the holder of the right, where known, of a possible infringement thereof. The customs authority shall be authorized to suspend release of the goods or detain them for a period of three working days to enable the holder of the right to lodge an application for action in accordance with Article 3 [of the Basic Regulation].'

1 Words in square brackets were substituted by art 1(6) of Council Regulation 241/99/EC. Previous to this amendment, refence was made to 'counterfeit or pirated' goods.

19.61   Basically, HMC&E are entitled, once it 'appears evident' that the goods are counterfeit, to suspend release of the goods or detain them for three working days ('the three day rule'). The proprietor can then lodge an AA within that period. Article 4 of the Basic Regulation is odd in its apparent effect in that a proprietor who has lodged an unapproved AA (on a literal reading of the article) still appears to be under an obligation to lodge a further AA pursuant to the three day rule. It is submitted that this interpretation of art 4 is nonsensical since it would be pointless, once the wheels were in motion, to start turning them again. However, if the AA is not lodged in time then HMC&E are bound to release the goods provided the other, more usual, formalities have been complied with. Compelling HMC&E to do so in the face of a bare refusal to do so has been discussed elsewhere in Chapter 18 and need not be repeated. However, it also lies in the power of the proprietor to take a private law action in the event that HMC&E will not or cannot act. In cases where an AA has been lodged other than at the invitation of HMC&E under the three day rule then the prospective procedure applies. Elements which are common to both the prospective and retrospective procedure will be discussed when we look at the prospective route.

19.62   Once the three day rule is in operation and a properly completed AA, with accompanying and supporting documentation, has been lodged and accepted within the three days, then HMC&E are entitled to act further, since, thereafter the procedures are the same for the prospective and the retrospective routes.

19.63   However, before leaving the retrospective procedure we shall concentrate for a short time on the test to be applied by HMC&E in deciding whether the three day rule is to be applied. As we have said above HMC&E must be satisfied that it 'appears evident' that the goods sought to be imported are counterfeit. We wonder (rhetorically speaking) what this expression means. One reason why the Implementing and Basic Regulations exist is to provide some degree of adherence with GATT and TRIPS. But to mention these treaties in terms of their general effect and not to concentrate upon their specifics, is to confuse the question. Articles 51 and 52 of TRIPS state:

'Section 4: Special Requirements Related To Border Measures[1]

Article 51
'Members shall, in conformity with the provisions set out below, adopt procedures[2] to enable a right holder, who has valid grounds for suspecting that the importation of counterfeit trademark or pirated copyright goods[3] may take place, to lodge an application in writing with competent authorities, administrative or judicial, for the suspension by the customs authorities of the release into free circulation of such goods. Members may enable such an application to be made in respect of goods which involve other infringements of intellectual property rights, provided that the requirements of this Section are met. Members may also provide for corresponding procedures concerning the suspension by the customs authorities of the release of infringing goods destined for exportation from their territories.

Article 52: Application
Any right holder initiating the procedures under Article 51 above shall be required to provide adequate evidence to satisfy the competent authorities that, under the laws of the country of importation, there is *prima facie* an infringement of his intellectual

property right and to supply a sufficiently detailed description of the goods to make them readily recognisable by the customs authorities. The competent authorities shall inform the applicant within a reasonable period whether they have accepted the application and, where determined by the competent authorities, the period for which the customs authorities will take action.'

1 Where a Member State has dismantled substantially all controls over movement of goods across its border with another Member State with which it forms part of a customs union, it shall not be required to apply the provisions of this section at that border.

2 It is understood that there shall be no obligation to apply such procedures to imports of goods put on the market in another country by or with the consent of the right holder, or to goods in transit.

3 For the purposes of this Agreement:

— counterfeit trademark goods shall mean any goods, including packaging, bearing without authorisation a trademark which is identical to the trademark validly registered in respect of such goods, or which cannot be distinguished in its essential aspects from such a trademark, and which thereby infringes the rights of the owner of the trademark in question under the law of the country of importation;

— pirated copyright goods shall mean any goods which are copies made without the consent of the right holder or person duly authorised by him in the country of production and which are made directly or indirectly from an article where the making of that copy would have constituted an infringement of a copyright or a related right under the law of the country of importation.

19.64   Article 51 of TRIPS speaks of 'valid grounds' for suspecting, though this is clearly intended to relate to prospective applications. Article 52 of TRIPS speaks of a prima facie infringement but again this is to be understood as relating to the prospective rather than the retrospective procedure.

19.65   Article 58 of TRIPS states:

'*Article 58: Ex officio* action

Where Members require competent authorities to act upon their own initiative and to suspend the release of goods in respect of which they have acquired *prima facie* evidence that an intellectual property right is being infringed:

(a)   the competent authorities may at any time seek from the right holder any information that may assist them to exercise these powers;

(b)   the importer and the right holder shall be promptly notified of the suspension. Where the importer has lodged an appeal against the suspension with the competent authorities, the suspension shall be subject to the conditions, *mutatis mutandis*, set out at Article 55 above;

(c)   Members shall only exempt both public authorities and officials from liability to appropriate remedial measures where actions are taken or intended in good faith.'

19.66   As can be seen, the test under art 58 of TRIPS is that there must be a prima facie case as opposed to it simply appearing evident (as art 4 of the Basic Regulation would lead us to suppose). We submit that, although, there is a wholesale confrontation in the language which art 4 of the Basic Regulation uses ('appears evident that the goods are counterfeit', which appears to be a subjective test) as against that in art 58 of TRIPS ('prima facie evidence that [the right given by registration of a domestic or Community trade mark] … is being infringed', which is much more objective) the test of there being prima facie evidence that the goods are counterfeit (following art 58 of TRIPS) is the correct one since the purpose or one purpose of the Basic Regulation is to give effect to or take account of TRIPS (see the sixth Recital). Further, the EU as an institution independent, as it were, from the Member States, has associated itself with and adheres to TRIPS (being a signatory thereof in its own right).[1]

1 See, generally, on this question, *Re Uruguay Round Treaties* [1995] I CMLR 205 and specifically para 55 (at 318) of the opnion of the court where it stated that the Community had supremacy in relation to cross-border matters. Presumably the Community (*via* its organ the commission) intended to sign what it did.

19.67 This question is an important one because of the consequences which may ensue if the wrong test is employed in relation to the three day rule, the problem being, that nobody knows what the correct test is. If, as we have submitted, the correct test is that before the three day rule applies there must be *prima facie* evidence that '[the right given by registration of a domestic or Community trade mark] ... is being infringed' then even this may be going too far. By virtue of art 1(2)(a) of the Basic Regulation, infringement is only part of the test, there is also the other first limb to be considered which is much more restrictive. We submit that to impose a complex burden on HMC&E at that stage (ie before any representations have been made by the proprietor) is too much of a responsibility and that the three days in the three day rule was obviously considered to be the upshot of a balancing exercise between the prejudice of the rights of the importer and those of the proprietor. Accordingly, we submit that in its application or exploitation of the three day rule, HMC&E need be no more than satisfied that there is prima facie evidence that '[the right given by registration of a domestic or Community trade mark] ... is being infringed.'

The prospective procedure

19.68 The prospective route is the more usual of the two. The proprietor gets wind of the fact that goods are going to be imported so he alerts HMC&E that this is going to happen and they (HMC&E) then lay in wait for the goods to arrive. This is covered by art 3 of the Basic Regulation. Article 3(1) of the Basic Regulation provides that the AA (in the form discussed above) may be lodged with the relevant department of HMC&E and where a CTM is the subject of the AA then an application may be made in more then one member state. Further electronic lodgment of such applications is allowed, though it is uncertain whether such a procedure has been implemented. The procedures and requirements of art 3(3)-(5) of the Basic Regulation have been discussed above and there is a remaining obligation on the proprietor to provide a security, in instances where an AA has been granted[1] and becomes an art 3 notice or in instances where goods have actually been detained or suspended from further release. In calling for a security, HMC&E has a discretion as to when to call for it, either when the article 3 notice is in force or when there is an actual detention or suspension from release. The security[2] can be sought so as to cover HMC&E's costs (both legal and in relation to storage) and the costs and damages of the importer in the event that the detention or suspension from further release is found or held to be unlawful or wrongful.

1 And we shall refer to an AA which has ripened into a granted application as an article 3 notice.
2 From a reading of art 3(6) of the Basic Regulation it is clear that reference to security is in fact reference to an indemnity.

19.69 Once the article 3 notice is in force then there is, in accordance with art 3(7) of the Basic Regulation, a continuing obligation on the part of the proprietor to inform HMC&E or the relevant department therein if the registered trade mark ceases to be on the register or the registration has expired. The Basic Regulation is unclear as to what happens if only part of a registration is invalid (for instance where a registration is over wide in scope or the scope is limited such as to exclude goods which are of the sort sought to be imported)[1] though we submit that the purpose of art 3(7) of the Basic Regulation should be construed so as to cover such a situation.

1 As was the case, in a slightly different context *Mercury Communications Ltd v Mercury Interactive (UK) Ltd* [1995] FSR 850.

The AA and the article 3 notice

19.70   The procedure of HMC&E in processing an article 3 notice once a decision has been made to grant it pursuant to art 3(5) of the Basic Regulation, is governed by art 5 of the Basic Regulation. This article was almost entirely rewritten by art1(7) of Council Regulation 241/99/EC amending the Basic Regulation and is not much more comprehensive than before. The old article merely provided that the decision by HMC&E relating to the AA shall be forthwith communicated to the relevant branch office of HMC&E concerned and indeed art 5(1) of the Basic Regulation also provides for this. However, we now have the CTM and the amendment to art 5 is intended to cater for a situation where CTMs form the subject matter of the AA and the associated article 3 notice. Article 5(2) merely says (by reference to the CCC) art 250:

> 'Where a customs procedure is used in several member states:-
> 1.   the decisions, identification measures taken or agreed on, and the documents issued by the customs authorities of one member state shall have the same legal effects in other member states as such decisions, measures taken and documents issued by the customs authorities of each of those member states;
> 2.   the findings made at the time controls are carried out by the customs authorities of a member state shall have the same conclusive force in the other member states as the findings made by the customs authorities of each of those member states.'

19.71   Therefore, in relation to a CTM all that is required is for an application to be made in one member state for the article 3 notice to have effect in all *provided that* the applicant forwards the relevant decision to those other member states along with 'other useful information and translations'. Articles 2 and 3 of the Implementing Regulation and art 3(2) of the Basic Regulation refer to such information, in particular, information relating to entitlement to submit an AA and information relating to the rights forming the subject matter of the AA. If HMC&E and the proprietor agree then HMC&E can forward the relevant information to the customs authorities of other member states, though in relation to the execution of decisions taken in one member state (the granting state), the other state (the executing state) may request further information to enable it to execute the article 3 notice. Where the article 3 notice specifies a period during which the customs authorities of the granting state shall take action then the same period applies to the executing state and the granting state which is also an executing state. The customs authorities of the executing state must then forward the article 3 notice (or, to use the language of art 5 of the Basic Regulation, the decision, which is understood as being the article 3 notice). Further, if any extension of time is granted then a similar set of rules apply.

19.72 The procedure under art 5 of the Basic Regulation is as follows:

(1) The purpose of art 5 of the Basic Regulation is to determine what happens to an AA which has turned into an article 3 notice.

(2) Where an AA is turned into an article 3 notice (by means of a decision by the relevant department of HMC&E) then the local customs offices in all of the relevant Member States shall be informed immediately.[1]

(3) Decisions and findings made by the relevant department of HMC&E shall bind other Member States.[2]

(4) If a decision relates to a CTM then the onus is on the applicant making the AA to forward it to the other Member States customs authorities, translated if necessary, together with 'any other useful information' though this can by arrangement be facilitated by the domestic customs office. If non-domestic customs authorities request additional information then they shall have it..[3]

(5) Where a CTM is involved then the article 3 notice shall run for one year[4] and that shall be from the date when the AA turns into an article 3 notice but:

    (a) it shall not take effect in a member state until submitted to that member state; and

    (b) the fee chargeable under art 3(4) of the Basic Regulation has been paid; and

    (c) any required security which the person making the AA is bound to pay (which is discretionary under art 3(6) of the Basic Regulation) has been paid; and

    (d) article 3 notice shall only ever run for one year from the date the AA was turned into an article 3 notice unless renewed; and

    (e) the article 3 notice must be forwarded to the other member states immediately[5]

6. A decision may be made to extend an article 3 notice[6.]

1 Basic Regulation, art 5(1).
2 Basic Regulation, art 5(2), para 1 and the CCC, art 250.
3 Basic Regulation, art 5(2), para 2.
4 Basic Regulation, art 3(5), para 4.
5 Basic Regulation, art 5(2), paras 3–4.
6 Basic Regulation, art 5(2), para 5.

The effects of an article 3 notice

19.73 Simply stated the effect of an article 3 notice is to render goods imported and to which the notice applies being as prohibited and thus forfeit.[1] However, that does not mean that if HMC&E detain or suspend from further release goods which it believes fall within the article 3 notice then the goods are prohibited. At that stage, they are only detained or suspended from release. The test for whether imported goods fall within the scope of an article 3 notice is set out in art 6 of the Basic Regulation. This test is to be applied by the branch office of HMC&E (ie the port office) which has been sent an article 3 notice by the relevant HMC&E processing department. The port office (or the relevant officer) must be satisfied after consulting the applicant where necessary, that:

(1) The imported goods are goods which are placed in one of the situations referred to in art 1(1)(a) of the Basic Regulation, ie they are:

      (a) entered for free circulation, export or re-export, in accordance with the CCC, art 61;[2] or

      (b) are found in the course of checks on goods under customs supervision within the meaning of the CCC, art 37;[3] or

      (c) are placed under a suspensive procedure within the meaning of the CCC, art 84(1)(a);[4] or

      (d) are re-exported subject to notification or placed in a free zone or free warehouse within the meaning of the CCC, art 166;[5]

(2)   Those goods are counterfeit in that they are either:-

      (a) goods, including the packaging thereof, bearing, without authorisation, a trade mark which is identical to the trade mark validly registered in respect of the same type of goods; or

      (b) goods, including the packaging thereof, bearing, without authorisation, a trade mark which cannot be distinguished in its essential aspects from the trade mark validly registered in respect of the same type of goods; or

      (c) any physical embodiment of any trade mark symbol (logo, label, sticker, brochure, instructions for use, guarantee document) whether presented separately or not; or

      (d) packaging materials bearing the trade mark of counterfeit goods, presented separately; and

      (e) in any of the four cases above, which affixation or presentation infringes the rights of the holder of the trade mark in question under Community law or the law of the member state where the application for action by the customs authorities is made.

(3)   Those goods, that packaging or those other embodiments correspond to the description of the goods referred to in Article 1(2)(a)

contained in that decision, it shall suspend release of the goods or detain them.

The foregoing is the effect of the first paragraph of art 6(1) of the Basic Regulation.

1 Basic Regulation, art 2.

2 The goods sought to be imported are placed under a customs procedure and the declaration by the importer is the formal notification that such is to happen – this is mandatory (see CCC, art 59).

3 Which merely provides that:

    '1. Goods brought into the customs territory of the Community shall, from the time of their entry, be subject to customs supervision. They may be subject to control by the customs authority in accordance with the provisions in force.

    2. They shall remain under such supervision for as long as necessary to determine their customs status, if appropriate, and in the case of non-Community goods and without prejudice to (1) CCC, art 82, [which provides that by reason of their end-use certain reduced or zero rated goods shall remain under customs supervision until the rules relating to such reduction or extinction of duty cease to apply, where the goods are exported or destroyed or higher duties are paid or payable by reason of the change in the end-use], until their customs status is changed, they enter a free zone or free warehouse or they are re-exported or destroyed in accordance with CCC, art 182, [which provides that non-Community goods may be re-exported out of the Community, destroyed or surrendered. In the case of re-exportation this is subject to certain formalities, including formalities that they not be re-exported if they fall within an article 3 notice].'

    4. Which provides that:-

    'where the term "procedure" is used, it is understood as applying, in the case of non-Community goods, to the following arrangements:

    –   external transit;

    –   customs warehousing;

    –   inward processing in the form of a system of suspension;

    –   processing under customs control;

    –   temporary importation;'.

5. Which provides that:
 Free zones and free warehouses shall be parts of the customs territory of the Community or premises situated in that territory and separated from the rest of it in which:
 (a) Community goods are considered, for the purpose of import duties and commercial policy import measures, as not being on Community customs territory, provided they are not released for free circulation or placed under another customs procedure or used or consumed under conditions other than those provided for in customs regulations;
 (b) Community goods for which such provision is made under Community legislation governing specific fields qualify, by virtue of being placed in a free zone or free warehouse, for measures normally attaching to the export of goods.'

19.74   The essential and central feature of the Basic Regulation, art 6 is the test which must be applied by the person, being the relevant customs officer, who is checking the goods which are sought to be imported. He will or should have in front of him the goods in question and the article 3 notice. According to Basic Regulation, art 6(1) the customs office which has been sent the article 3 notice must 'be satisfied, after consulting the applicant where necessary that ... [the] goods ... correspond to the description of the goods ... contained in that decision ... ' before the goods are suspended from release or detained.

19.75   This test appears to be very different, at least insofar as words are concerned, to the test which must be applied in the domestic context ('goods to which the notice relates') but despite the textual differences in wording, it is submitted that the two tests are not so different. Under the Basic Regulation the customs office is entitled to consult the person making the AA (or article 3 notice) and it is apparent from the art 6 test per se that the customs office is not expressly obliged to ask whether the goods which are sought to be imported fall within the specification of the trade mark registrations in question. It would, however, be a serious abrogation of the rights of the importer if it were not to be implied that such is the case and indeed by explicit reference to art 1(2)(a) in art 6 it puts it beyond doubt that there is an express obligation to ask whether the goods are counterfeit, ie whether they fall within the scope of art 1(2)(a) of the Basic Regulation.

19.76   Once it has been determined by the customs office that the goods which are sought to be imported do correspond to the description of those goods as set ut in the article 3 notice then, firstly, the goods must be detained or suspended from further release and, secondly, art 6(1), para 2, of the Basic Regulation kicks in. In accordance with that para 2, the customs office must immediately inform the part of HMC&E which issued the article 3 notice that the goods sought to be imported have been detained or suspended from further release. Thereafter, either the issuing section of the local customs office must inform the declarant (that is the person who sought to import the goods in question or otherwise declared them on entry) and also the applicant (either the lawyers making the application or the proprietor himself if he does so).

19.77   Interestingly, the proprietor may also independently be told, on request, of the detention or suspension from further release and must be informed of the name and address of the declarant and the consignee (if known). Such information must be imparted 'In accordance with national provisions on the protection of personal data, commercial and industrial secrecy and professional and administrative confidentiality ... '. This protective condition is confusing and we shall consider it further below. However, we wonder why it is that such information need be imparted to the proprietor and why he has to make a request for such information. Though tart 6(1), para 2 provides an answer in part ('so as to enable the holder of the right to ask the competent authorities to take a substantive decision'), it is unclear what is meant by 'substantive decision' or 'competent authorities'. Further it is apparent that the person making the AA and ' ... the persons involved in any of the operations referred to in art 1(1)(a)' of the Basic Regulation shall be given an 'opportunity to inspect the goods whose release has been suspended or which have been detained.', ie the importer or declarant. Again whilst it is relatively clear that the reason why the importer or declarant is entitled to inspect the goods in question is so as to ascertain whether they do correspond to the description as is set out in the art 3 notice so that it might be determined whether the customs office has made a mistake, there does not appear to be any valid reason as to why the applicant making the AA needs to examine the goods.

19.78   Article 6(1), para 3, of the Basic Regulation also provides that the customs office may take samples of the goods 'to expedite the procedure' and by this it is to be presumed that these samples may be sent out to the parties concerned rather than necessitating the attendance of them at a port or other place of entry.

19.79   The foregoing question leads us to a fundamental difficulty with the interpretation of art 6 of the Basic Regulation which we are unable to resolve.[1] In order to place this fundamental difficulty into the correct context it is necessary to consider the interplay between arts 6–8 of the Basic Regulation. Hence, we shall refrain from our analysis of this fundamental difficulty until we have considered that interplay.

1 Though it is true to say that one route is supported by one of the only authorities on the matter namely, *Martin Pointing v Customs and Excise Comrs* [1999] FSR 394.

19.80   We start by noting that art 6(1), para 2, of the Basic Regulation allows the proprietor, that is the holder of the right in question,[1] to inspect the goods (or samples thereof) and to be told, on request of the name and address of the importer or other relevant persons.

1 Which in accordance with art 1(2)(b) of the Basic Regulation includes the proprietor or any authorised user of the trade mark in question (whether a bare or exclusive licensee or indeed (arguably at least) a subsequent purchaser where the relevant trade mark rights have been exhausted) . We shall refer to that class as the proprietor for the sake of brevity ,though the TMA 1994, s 30 provides that a licensee may take proceedings if the proprietor neglects to do so and despite being called upon to do so. It is to be noted that the TMA 1994, s 30 is not echoed in the Directive, and it is therefore uncertain whether, in terms of the Directive, there is in fact any right vested or intended to be vested in licensees, let alone authorised users – this is yet another question for the ECJ to determine!

19.81   Article 6(2) of the Basic Regulation further provides that, firstly, the domestic law shall apply as relates to :

(1)   referral to the 'authority competent to take a substantive decision';
(2)   immediate notification of HMC&E or the customs office unless HMC&E has made such a reference itself.

19.82   This implies that a reference to 'the authority competent to take a substantive decision' may be undertaken by the proprietor or HMC&E or the customs office. It is suggested that, as a starting point, the 'authority competent to take a substantive decision' (the authority competent) can be one of three entities, either: (1) HMC&E itself; or (2) the condemnation court;[1] or (3) a court competent to decide issues of trade mark infringement.[2] We note that sch 1, para 1(i) of the Supreme Court Act 1981 speaks of 'all causes and matters relating to … trade marks … ', though we shall reserve comment on this to a later point in this chapter.

1 In accordance with the CEMA 1979, Sch 3, para 8(a), and some statutory instruments which we shall refer to in more detail later.
2 Which would be the Chancery Division of the High Court in accordance with the Supreme Court Act 1981, s 6(1) ans Sch 1, para 1(i).

19.83 Secondly, art 6(2) of the Basic Regulation also provides that the domestic law as relates to reaching the decision to be taken by the authority competent shall also apply. However, it is also provided that in the absence of Community rules in relation to the reaching of a decision (and there are, as at the time of writing, none):

> ' … the criteria to be used in reaching that decision shall be the same as those used to determine whether goods produced in the member state concerned infringe the rights of the holder. Reasons shall be given for decisions adopted by the competent authority. [1]

1 Basic Regulation, art 6(2)(b).

19.84 Before we turn to further consider arts 7 and 8 of the Basic Regulation, it is necessary to look at domestic measures which have been specifically taken (as opposed to generally existing) as far as art 6(2)(a) and (b) of the Basic Regulation is concerned. We have already made passing reference to the Trade Marks (EC Measures relating to Counterfeit Goods) Regulations 1995[1] which has the effect of substituting s 89(3) of the TMA 1994 with something new. We have also made passing reference to the (CP)R 1999 and the (C)R 1999 but the time has now come to consider them in detail.

1 SI 1995/1444.

The Goods Infringing Intellectual Property Rights (Customs) Regulations 1999

19.85 The (C)R 1999 provides the mechanics where an AA is to be made to HMC&E. Regulation 3 provides that an AA is made to the Commissioners in a set form or approved form containing the particulars set out in the form which accompanies the (C)R 1999. We have already discussed this above. The (C)R 1999, reg 4 augments art 3(6) of the Basic Regulation though art 3(6) speaks of security being provided: (1) to cover the applicant's liability if the procedure under art 6 of the Basic Regulation is discontinued because it is found that the goods are not counterfeit or due to some act or omission on the part of that AA applicant; and (2) to cover the storage costs of HMC&E. However, of the (C)R 1999, reg 4, requires security or further security to be given to the Commissioners 'within such time and in such manner, whether by deposit of a sum of money or guarantee as the Commissioners may require', in respect of:

> 'all actions, proceedings, claims and demands whatsoever which may be taken or made against, or costs and expenses which may be incurred by, the … [Commissioners] in consequence of the detention of any goods to which the application relates.'

19.86 Unless security of the type envisaged in art 3(6) of the Basic Regulation is provided (if requested) then the article 3 notice is of no effect. Article 3(6) of the

Basic Regulation appears to speak of security being provided for the applicant's liability to the importer and there would seem no logical reason why the applicant should provide security in relation to *his* liability to the importer. The requirement of art 3(6) of the Basic Regulation would make more sense if it referred to security being provided to cover the potential liability of HMC&E in the event that the goods are found not to fall within the ambit of the article 3 notice (notwithstanding their detention or suspension from further release) or because the condemnation proceedings were discontinued because of an act or omission on the part of the applicant. We suspect that art 3(6) envisages the position where the applicant might be liable to HMC&E in the event that HMC&E were found liable to the importer for trespass to goods because the goods were wrongfully detained or wrongfully suspended from further release.

19.87 The (C)R 1999, reg 5, provides that in any event the applicant shall, notwithstanding the provision by him of security, also give to HMC&E an indemnity in relation to the maters for which security should be given. It would appear that the obligation to provide an indemnity is not echoed in the Basic Regulation and the *vires* of the (C)R 1999, reg 5, is to be questioned.

19.88 The (C)R 1999, reg 6(3), provides a detailed schedule for the payment of fees in relation to the processing of applications and the currency of an article 3 notice.[1] Reference should be made to that regulation for specific amounts but currently to use the procedure for one year the amount to be paid is £1,200 excluding value added tax – though the scale is not linear.

1 £185 for the first month or part thereof and £165 for each subsequent month or part thereof of the period specified in the article 3 notice or for each month or part thereof for which the article 3 notice is extended in accordance with the Basic Regulation, para 2, both exclusive of value added tax.

19.89 The (C)R 1999, reg 7, provides that where the Commissioners:

(1) supply the applicant with a sample of the goods which have been detained or suspended from further release; and
(2) where that sample appears to the Commissioners both:
   (a) to correspond to the description of the goods contained in the art 3 notice; and
   (b) that they are offending goods within the meaning of art 1(3) of the Basic Regulation;

then:

> 'the applicant must, within ten days of being requested by the Commissioners, or within such further time as the Commissioners may allow, confirm to them in writing whether or not in his opinion the sample is comprised of offending goods, giving his reasons, by reference to characteristics of the sample or its packaging or otherwise.'

19.90 In relation to a prospective application, the time limit of ten days runs from the day when under Basic Regulation, art 6(1), para 2, the relevant parties are *informed* that detention or suspension from further release has happened. In relation to a retrospective application that time limit starts to run from the day that an AA is lodged.[1]

1 Implementing Regulation, art 4.

19.91 Finally, the (C)R 1999, reg 8, provides that an AA shall be of no further effect where any requirement of the (C)R 1999 is not complied with, where there is any change in ownership or authorised use of the trade mark in question and such is not communicated to the Commissioners and where the trade mark registration expires.

19.92 The (C)R 1999 is purportedly made in accordance with s 2(2) of the European Communities Act 1972 ('ECA 1972') which provides:

'(2) Subject to Schedule 2 to this Act, at any time after its passing Her Majesty may by Order in Council, and any designated Minister or department may by regulations, make provision—

(a) for the purpose of implementing any Community obligation of the United Kingdom, or enabling any such obligation to be implemented. or of enabling any rights enjoyed or to be enjoyed by the United Kingdom under or by virtue of the Treaties to be exercised; or
(b) for the purpose of dealing with matters arising out of or related to any such obligation or rights or the coming into force, or the operation from time to time, of subsection (1) above;

and in the exercise of any statutory power or duty, including any power to give directions or to legislate by means of orders, rules, regulations or other subordinate instrument, the person entrusted with the power or duty may have regard to the objects of the Communities and to any such obligation or rights as aforesaid.

In this subsection "designated Minister or department" means such Minister of the Crown or government department as may from time to time be designated by Order in Council in relation to any matter or for any purpose, but subject to such restrictions or conditions (if any) as may be specified by the Order in Council.'

19.93 The Commissioners are deemed to be a government department by virtue of art 2 of and the schedule to The European Communities (Designation) (No 2) Order 1985[1] in relation to counterfeit and pirated goods. The question is whether, in exercising such powers to give effect to the European Regulations, the Commissioners are entitled to over legislate, ie to bring in matters which are not expressly or impliedly mentioned in the relevant regulation. In this case, the (C)R 1999 provides for the giving of an indemnity on the part of the applicant whereas there is no such provision in either the basic or implementing regulations. There is no doubt that a certain amount of leeway has to be given. However, in this instance, the relevant subordinate legislation gives effect to the basic or implementing regulations which by their very nature as regulations already have direct effect by virtue of ss 1(2) and 2(1) of the ECA 1972 and EC Treaty art 108a(2).[2] It is therefore arguable that where the (C)R 1999 goes outside the basic or implementing regulations those provisions are *ultra vires* the Treaty of European Union and dependent legislation.

1 (SI 1995/751).
2 Shortly to be the Treaty of Rome (Now called the Treaty on European Union, 'TEU'), art 110(2) as amended by the 1997 Treaty of Amsterdam, signed on 2 October 1997 and having force in the United Kingdom by reason of the ECA 1972, s 1(2)(o) as amended by the European Communities (Amendment) Act 1998 with effect from royal assent, 11 June 1998, though the amendments shall not take effect until 2 months after the last member state deposits its instruments of ratification with the

Commission (art 14). This date was 1 March 1999 and the amendments take effect from 1 May 1999. For convenience we shall refer to the TEU but we shall refer to the old article number by the corresponding number of the unamended treaty with the new number (as set out in the Treaty of Amsterdam) in brackets. It is hoped that there is some logic to the renumbering scheme.

19.94 Whilst the requirement that an indemnity be provided under of the (C)R 1999, reg 5, is arguably *ultra vires* the ECA 1972, it might be regarded by some of minor importance in the general scheme of things. The effect of the (C)R 1999, reg 7, is more important since it does appear to envisage a scheme which not only is not in tune with the Basic Regulation but in many ways seems to run contrary to it. Further consideration of this conflict will be discussed below.

The (CP)R 1999

19.95 Whilst the (C)R 1999 relates to the manner in which an AA is prepared and deals with the procedure to be followed in relation to checking whether imported goods correspond to an art 3 notice, (CP)R 1999 is the instrument which brings the post importation machinery into play by using the procedure (already discussed) set out in to the CEMA 1979, s 139 and Sch 3. In essence, (CP)R 1999 says that the CEMA 1979 applies to goods which fall within the terms of an art 3 notice. However it would be misleading to say that both the domestic and European procedures, which are linked to the CEMA 1979, are identical.

19.96 As with the (C)R 1999, we propose to discuss the provisions of (CP)R 1999 in broad detail and leave consideration of its relationship with the Basic Regulation and the (C)R 1999 until later on in this text.[1]

1 See para **19.142** below.

19.97 The (CP)R 1999, reg 3, simply states that where goods fall within an article 3 notice *and* are counterfeit,[1] they shall be liable to forfeiture. As can be seen, the (CP)R 1999 is now starting to use the more traditional language of the CEMA 1979.

1 As defined by Basic Regulation, art 1(2)(a). See also the (CP)R 1999, reg 1(2).

19.98 The (CP)R 1999, reg 4, provides the machinery whereby the Commissioners can suspend release of the goods and detain them pursuant to a retrospective procedure and the Commissioners are empowered pursuant to the (CP)R 1999, reg 4, to notify the proprietor, that is the holder of the right of the possible infringement,[1] to suspend release of the goods or detain them[2] and to invite the proprietor to make an application within three days of the suspension or detention.[3]

1 (CP)R 1999, reg 4(1)(a).
2 (CP)R 1999, reg 4(1)(b).
3 (CP)R 1999, reg 4(1)(c).

19.99 The (CP)R 1999, reg 4, applies not only to situations where there is no article 3 notice in force but also where an AA has been made but has not yet turned into an article 3 notice. A literal reading of the (CP)R 1999, reg 4, would imply that it matters not whether an AA is in the pipeline, if there is no article 3 notice actually in force at the time of the checks which are being made then pursuant to the (CP)R 1999, reg 4(1)(c), the proprietor must make an AA afresh. Such a reading is absurd. However, the wording of the (CP)R 1999 is clear.

19.100 The right of the Commissioners under reg 3(1)(a) to inform the right holder of a possible *infringement* of his rights seems odd since the Basic Regulation is not intended to stop or deal with goods which merely *infringe* the rights of the proprietor[1] but is intended (insofar as registered trade marks are concerned) to deal with goods which fall within the meaning of Basic Regulation art 1(2)(a), ie those goods which are counterfeit. Counterfeit goods occupy a smaller class than infringing goods and indeed because of the restrictive meaning of Basic Regulation, art 1(2)(a), the class of goods which are counterfeit is small and wholly contained within the class of goods which are infringing. For goods to be counterfeit it is necessary but not sufficient that they are infringing, however, for goods to be infringing it is sufficient but not necessary for them to be counterfeit. Again, it would appear that the (CP)R 1999 over legislates as the ambit of Basic Regulation, art 6(1), is considerably narrower. However, that said, the objection is really linguistic since only counterfeit goods fall within the ambit of an article 3 notice and once that test is satisfied then the goods are necessarily infringing. The same difficulty applies in relation to art 4 of the Basic Regulation.

1 Within the full meaning of TMA 1994, ss 9 and 10.

19.101 The test as to whether the goods sought to be imported fall to be detained or suspended from further release is whether it 'appears evident' to the Commissioners that the goods are offending goods, that is goods which are counterfeit or are deemed to be counterfeit because they are moulds or matrices specifically adapted and, therefore, fall within Basic Regulation, art 1(3), and are deemed to fall within art 1(2)(a) thereof, though no article 3 notice is in fact in force. Further, the power to engage in a retrospective procedure (including detention or suspension from further release until the procedure has been carried out) under Basic Regulation art 4, or the power to suspend release of the goods under Basic Regulation, art 6, depends specifically and expressly upon the goods sought to be imported being goods which fall within Basic Regulation, art 1(2)(b). The (C)R 1999, reg 2, and the (CP)R 1999, regs 2 and 4, reflect this, though it is necessary for the (C)R 1999 or the (CP)R 1999 to do so. However, the upshot of this is that, if the goods sought to be imported are evidently counterfeit within the meaning of Basic Regulation, art 1(2)(a), expressly or by reference to Basic Regulation, art 1(3), then they are deemed to be offending goods, that is goods which, although not the subject of an article 3 notice, could be. The (CP)R 1999, reg 4, enables a retrospective application pursuant to Basic Regulation, art 3, and such application must be made within three days of the initial detention. It is thus clear that the (CP)R 1999, reg 4, applies only to instances where no article 3 notice is in force. If, during the period of initial detention or suspension from further release an AA (whether submitted before or during the period of initial detention or suspension from further release) ripens into an article 3 notice then the goods are dealt with under the (CP)R 1999, reg 3, which enables further detention and suspension from further release if the goods are counterfeit and correspond with the description of them in the article 3 notice. The words 'correspond with the description' are taken from the words contained in Basic Regulation, art 6.

19.102 Accordingly, where a retrospective procedure is involved then it must appear evident that the goods are counterfeit. This is set out in Basic Regulation, art 4, and also in the (CP)R 1999, reg 4, though in relation to the (CP)R 1999 the test is whether it appears that rights are being infringed. However, once an article 3 notice is in force then the test to be applied is whether the goods are counterfeit and correspond to the description of them as are set out in the article 3 notice, that is set out in art 6(1) of the Basic Regulation and reg 3 of (CP)R 1999. It is submitted that the test to see whether the goods are counterfeit and correspond to the description in the article 3 notice is a harder test to satisfy than the test which enables the Commissioners to justify short-term detention or suspension from further release under the (CP)R 1999, reg 4, or Basic Regulation, art 4, which requires it merely to be evident that the goods sought to be imported are counterfeit. This test should be compared to the single test which is required under the domestic route, which only admits for a retrospective procedure, that is whether the imported goods are ones 'to which the notice relates'.[1] It is unclear, whether this test is any different to the test set out in Basic Regulation, art 6(1), and the (CP)R 1999, reg 3, but we submit that the difference in wording is not sufficient to give rise to a difference in principle.

1 TMA 1994, s 89(2).

19.103   Article 5 of the (CP)R 1999 makes the CEMA 1979, s 139 and Sch 3, apply to goods which are found to be liable to forfeiture under the (CP)R 1999, reg 2, as they apply to goods which are liable to forfeiture under the CEMA 1979.[1] We have already discussed the CEMA 1979 procedure in relation to the domestic route and the same procedure applies to the European vents, though whether it *should* apply is a different question altogether ad is one which we consider below. Specifically, where goods are seized as liable to forfeiture then the issue as to whether they are so liable and should be condemned as forfeit is specifically subject to the CEMA 1979, s 139, Sch 3.[2] Further the CEMA 1979, s 144, applies in such cases[3] as do ss145 to146 and 152 to 155 the CEMA 1979.[4]

1 Specifically in relation to trade marks because those goods are prohibited by the operation of the TMA 1994, s 89(2), and, thus become liable to forfeiture by the operation of the CEMA 1979, s 49(1)(b).
2 (CP)R 1999, reg 5(1).
3 (CP)R 1999, reg 5(1)(a).
4 (CP)R 1999, reg 5(1)(b).

19.104   Regulation 5(2) of the (CP)R 1999 appears to create yet another burden of proof in favour of the Commissioners in that the importer must prove that the goods were not liable forfeiture. There appears to be no original power to do this

The Basic Regulation, arts 6 and 7

19.105   We have engaged in a complex and painstaking analysis of the provisions of the (C)R 1999 and (CP)R 1999 and we have done this because it is clear that the (C)R 1999 and (CP)R 1999 do not sit well together as pieces of legislation with the Basic Regulation. Before we consider the domestic statutory instruments in conjunction with arts 6 and 7 of the Basic Regulation we shall consider arts 6 and 7 alone.

19.106   An important feature of arts 6 and 7 of the Basic Regulation is the system of notification. In art 6, the customs office which detains the goods or suspends them from further release is obliged to *inform* a certain class of person as to what action has been taken. Those persons are the office in HMC&E which processed the AA and which granted the article 3 notice, the importer (termed the declarant since, strictly speaking in accordance with the CCC, that person need not necessarily be the importer) and the applicant making the AA. It is to be remembered that the applicant making the AA and the proprietor (by which we mean and have meant the holder of the relevant right as defined in Basic Regulation, art 1(2)(b)) may not necessarily be the same person since by the operation of art 2(b) of the Implementing Regulation, the AA may be made by a class of persons other than the right holder, namely legal representatives and collecting societies (and possibly agents, tough this is unclear).[1] In this regard, the Implementing Regulation appears to contradict itself since the words of art 2 of the Implementing Regulation states:

'The proof that the applicant holds one of the rights referred to in point ... (a) ... of Article 1(2) of the Basic Regulation, which must be submitted when ... [making an AA] shall be as follows ... '

It appears to envisage that the applicant and the holder of the relevant right must be one and the same, yet art 2(c) of the Implementing Regulation states:

'where a representative of the holder or of any other person authorized to use one of the rights referred to in point ... (a) ... of Article 1(2) of the Basic Regulation applies: in addition to the proof required under (a) and (b) hereof, proof of authorisation to act.'

1 Implementing Regulation, art 1.

19.107 This raises two interesting points. First, art 2(c) of the Implementing Regulation expressly and in apparent contradiction to the opening words of art 2 of that regulation makes it clear that the applicant making the AA does not have to be the holder of the right. Second, whereas art 3(1) of the Basic Regulation expressly states that the holder of a right (being the proprietor or the person authorised to use the trade mark or their representatives)[1] may make an AA, art 2(c) of the Implementing Regulation envisages that where the holder of the right is not the proprietor but is merely authorised to use the trade mark or is an authorised representative then he must have authority to make the AA or must prove how he derived his rights. It is clear that the Implementing Regulation has the effect of requiring things to be done in a way that is not strictly envisaged by the Basic Regulation which places no distinction between the proprietor, the person authorised to use the mark and their respective representatives. The question, therefore, is whether the European Commission was entitled to make the Implementing Regulation in the way that it did.

1 The Basic Regulation, art 1(2)(b).

19.108 Article 13 of the Basic Regulation gives some power to the European Commission which 'shall be assisted by the committee set up under [the CCC,] art 247[1] (which we shall hereinafter refer to as the 'CCC Committee'). The power of the CCC Committee is set out in art 13(2) of the Basic Regulation which enables the CCC Committee to examine *any* matter concerning implementation of the Basic Regulation which the chairman may raise (either himself or if asked to do so by a member state). Article 13(3) of the Basic Regulation sets out the procedure to be followed which is that the European Commission shall prepare a draft of the implementing measures, the CCC Committee shall deliver its (qualified) majority opinion on that draft (within time limits which can be set by the chairman of the CCC Committee if necessary). It is apparent from the EC Treaty, art 249,[3] that the European Parliament (acting jointly with the council), the Council and the

European Commission have the power to 'make regulations and issue directives, take decisions, make recommendations and deliver opinions' provided that this is done in accordance with the provisions of the EC Treaty. EC Treaty art 211,[4] sets out the powers of the European Commission in this regard which is to:

'exercise the powers conferred on ... [the European Commission] by the Council for the implementation of the rules laid down by the ... [Council]'

1 Basic Regulation, art 13(1).
2 Which states:
    '1. A customs code committee, hereinafter called "the committee", composed of representatives of the member states with a representative of the Commission as chairman, is hereby established.
    2. The committee shall adopt its rules of procedure.'
3 As mentioned by the Treaty of Amsterdam. Previously, EC Treaty, art 189.
4 As mentioned by the Treaty of Amsterdam. Previously, EC Treaty, art 155.

19.109 Therefore, it is apparent that the power to make the Implementing Regulation stems from the powers ceded to the European Commission by the Basic Regulation. There appears to be no overriding power in the EC Treaty for the European Commission to act independently of the Council in this regard. Article 12 of the Basic Regulation provides the machinery whereby this is done, stating that art 13(3) and (4) of the Basic Regulation provides the basis whereby implementing measures may be adopted.

19.110 The procedure under art 13(3) of the Basic Regulation is that draft rules are submitted to the CCC Committee, which provides an opinion thereon which is the opinion of the qualified majority. The opinion is 'delivered' ie given to the European Commission.

19.111 However, at the same time, if not before, the European Commission must adopt measures 'immediately'.[1] Those measures must be those which are necessary for the implementation of the Basic Regulation. Further, where the immediate measures differ with the opinion of the CCC Committee then that fact must be communicated 'forthwith' to the Council by the European Commission. In the event, that there is a difference between the CCC Committee opinion and the 'immediate' measures then the 'immediate' measures shall be deferred for not more than three months from the date upon which the European Commission tells the Council of the difference and the Council shall then, acting by qualified majority make its own regulations within the three month period. The last recital to the Implementing Regulation records that the Implementing Regulation is in accord with the opinion of the CCC Committee. It was, therefore, unnecessary for any divergence to be reported to the Council. However, there still remains the question as to whether the European Commission was entitled to make the Implementing Regulation and whether the CCC Committee was entitled to agree with it in its opinion.

1 That is when the Basic Regulation is in force namely, 1 July 1995. See also Basic Regulation, art 13(4).

19.112 There is some jurisprudence in this area. In Case T-162/82 *(criminal proceedings against) Cousin*,[1] the ECJ stated that:

' ... it must first be pointed out, as the Court has stated in its judgments of 31 January 1979 (Cases T-34/78 *Yoshida Nederland v Kamer van Koophandel en Fabrieken voor Friesland* [1979] ECR 151, [1979] 2 CMLR 747; and, T-114/78 *Yoshida GmbHv Industrie-und Handelskammer Kassel* [1979] ECR 151, [1979] 2 CMLR 747), that in adopting implementing provisions pursuant to Article 14 of Council Regulation 802/68/EEC, the Commission is obliged not to exceed the powers which the Council has conferred upon it for the implementation of the rules which it has promulgated in that regulation and, more precisely, that it must define specific criteria of origin which comply with the objective criteria of Article 5 of Council Regulation 802/68/EEC which is the legal basis of the Implementing Regulation and the source of the powers which the Commission exercises in adopting it.'

We understand this to mean that the European Commission can only do that which it is empowered to do by the corresponding Basic Regulation. Thus far, we submit, nothing is new or surprising about that.

1 [1984] 2 CMLR 780 at 794, para 15.

19.113 That jurisprudence is derived from the leading case on the subject namely, Case T-92/78 *Simmenthal Spa v EC Commission*[1] relating to levies to be charged on certain meat products sought to be imported into the EEC where such imports exceeded certain quotas to be set by the European Commission. The purpose of the underlying Council regulations was to protect the EEC meat processing industry but the European Commission had made implementing regulations which conferred that protection to a class of persons larger than the class of persons in the EEC meat processing sector. The European Court of Justice held that such went outside the Council regulations and was not permissible.

1 [1979] ECR 777

19.114 Finally, in Case T-23/75 *Rey Soda v Cassa Conguaglio Zucchero*,[1] a case involving the implementation of a Council regulation relating to the marketing of sugar, the European Court of Justice:

'Since the objective of Article 155 [now Article 211] of the Treaty is the preservation of the balance between the powers of the Council and the Commission, the powers conferred on the Commission by ... [the Basic Regulation] must be interpreted strictly.

When Article 155 [now Article 211] of the Treaty provides that the Commission shall exercise the powers conferred on it by the Council for the implementation of the rules laid down by the [Council], it follows from the context of the Treaty in which it must be placed and also from practical requirements that the concept of implementation must be given a wide interpretation.

Since the Commission alone is able continually to follow with attention trends on the agricultural markets and to act with urgency as the situation requires, the Council may be led in the sphere of the common agricultural policy, to confer on the Commission wide powers of discretion and action.

Further the provisions cited in Article 155 [now Article 211] allow the Council to determine any conditions to which it may subject the exercise by the Commission of the power granted to it.

The powers entrusted to the Commission under ... [the Basic Regulation] must be adopted under the so-called "Management Committee" procedure, a mechanism which allows the Council to give the Commission an appreciably wide power of implementation whilst reserving where necessary its own right to intervene.

When the Council has thus conferred extensive power on the Commission the limits of this power must be judged with regard to the basic general objectives of the organisation of the market and less in terms of the literal meaning of the enabling words.'

1   [1976]1 CMLR 185 at 208–209, paras 19–14.

19.115   Thus, we submit that art 2 of the Implementing Regulation, in providing that persons other than right owners (ie their authorised users and representatives) must provide proof of their authorisation falls within the ambit of the powers conferred by art 13(3) and (4) of the Basic Regulation since no wider class of person is affected and the requirement does not fall outside the objects of the Basic Regulation. Before leaving this point, we observe that there is an apparent contradiction in the judgment of the ECJ in *Rey Soda* since it appears that, on the one hand, the powers conferred on the Council and the Commission by the operation of EC Treaty, art 211[1]must be construed strictly. By this we understand that the European Commission can only do that which it is empowered to do. On the other hand and further on in the judgment; it is said that by the operation of the same provisions of the EC Treaty the powers of implementation must be construed widely and by this we understand that whilst the European Commission can only do that which it is empowered to do it has a fairly wide set of powers to exercise. Indeed, we find support for this not only in the opinion of Advocate-General Mayras in *Rey Soda*[2] but also in the case upon which he relies, namely, Case T-41/69 *ACF Chemiefarma NV v EC Commission:*[3]

'In article 24 of the ... [Implementing Regulation] the Council has conferred on the Commission power to adopt implementing provisions concerning such hearings [relating to investigations by the Commission in anti-trust maters].

Since the [delegated] principle that the persons concerned [in such anti-trust investigations] shall be given the opportunity of being heard by the Commission was adopted by the Council, the rules laying down the procedure to be followed in this connexion, however important they may be, constitute implementing provision within the meaning of the above-mentioned Article 155 [now Article 211].'

1   As renumbered by the Treaty of Amsterdam. Previously, EC Treaty, art 155.
2   [1976] 1 CMLR 185 at 196.
3   [1970] ECR 661 at 668, paras 64– 65

19.116   It would seem, therefore, that once the principle is enunciated by the Council then the European Commission has the power to legislate within the principle rather than being required to follow express powers. Indeed by the requirement of the provision of 'pertinent information' in Basic Regulation, art 3(2), and given a basic principle that it must be wrong to allow the Basic Regulation to become the subject of abuse by allowing a person *claiming* to be the proprietor or the persons deriving rights from the proprietor or their representatives to make an AA without *proving* their entitlement to do so, it is beyond doubt, we submit, that the Implementing Regulation was properly made.

19.117 The purpose of our analysis of the *locus* of the European Commission to make the Implementing Regulation is of importance since if our conclusions are right then it is clear that the person making the AA may be some person other than the proprietor and we hope that we have established that beyond doubt.

19.118 We now return to the basis upon which we conducted such analysis which was in relation to the question of notification. Article 6 of the Basic Regulation specified that the customs office which detains the goods or suspends them from further release is obliged to *inform*: (1) the office in HMC&E which processed the AA and which granted the article 3 notice; (2) the declarant; and, importantly (3) the applicant making the AA. It is the operation of the European Regulations in relation to the making of an AA and who may do so and the analysis we have engaged in above which establishes that this third class or this third person whilst being the applicant making the AA is not necessarily the same as the other persons who fall within the class of persons being defined as the holder of the right in Basic Regulation, art 1(2)(c).

19.119 The question of notification in the Basic Regulation, art 6(1), para 2, not only requires the classes of person falling within (1), (2) and (3) above to be *informed* but also and additionally requires the local customs office or the office in HMC&E which processed the AA and which granted the article 3 notice to *notify* the holder of the right (at his request) of the name and address of the declarant and consignee[1] 'so as to enable the holder of the right to ask the competent authorities to take a substantive decision'.[2] It is this difference between *informing* one class of persons and *notifying* another class of person, whether or not they happen also to fall into the first class that provides an essential key to the purpose and method of working of art 6 of the Basic Regulation.

1 'In accordance with national provisions on the protection of personal data, commercial and industrial secrecy and professional and administrative confidentiality ... ' as is cited further on in art 6(1), para 2.
2 Basic Regulation, art 6(1), para 2.

19.120 The holder of the right is notified of the name and address of the importer, declarant or consignee ' ... so as to enable the holder of the right to ask the competent authorities to take a substantive decision.'[1] Who the competent authority is remains uncertain.

1 Basic Regulation, art 6(1), para 2.

19.121 Furthermore, all parties also have the right to inspect the goods concerned or samples if expedient. This appears to be a right or a power which is additional to the power to check or examine as appears in the CCC or the CCC Implementing Regulation.

19.122 Article 6(2) of the Basic Regulation states that:

'The law in force in the member state within the territory of which the goods are placed in one of the situations referred to in Article 1(1)(a) shall apply as regards—

(a) referral to the authority competent to take a substantive decision and immediate notification of the customs service or office referred to in paragraph 1 of that referral, unless referral is effected by that service or office;

(b) reaching the decision to be taken by that authority. In the absence of Community rules in this regard, the criteria to be used in reaching that decision shall be the same as those used to determine whether goods produced in the member state concerned infringe the rights of the holder. Reasons shall be given for decisions adopted by the competent authority.'

19.123 It is an open question as to what the relevant law in this jurisdiction is and a great deal of argument centres on it. In the case of *Martin Pointing v Customs and Excise Comrs,*[1] this point, amongst others, was raised by the plaintiff who took proceedings for the return of goods which had been detained or suspended from further release. The plaintiff took such proceedings because some considerable time had elapsed between the importation of the goods in question (pots of cold cream) and the decision to take action by HMC&E.[2] The plaintiff took the point (amongst others) that the 'authority competent to take a substantive decision' could only be the court which was able to make a judicial finding as to infringement and since there had either been no referral to that authority within a period of ten days[3] and no 'interim' measures had been taken the goods were bound to be released. We shall return to art 7 of the Basic Regulation below, however held Carnwath J:

> 'It is clear that the authority competent to take a substantive decision is, in this country at any rate, the court, which alone is able to make a final decision as to whether the goods are counterfeit or not. Indeed, article 6(2) [of the Basic Regulation] makes it clear that that matter has to be dealt with according to the law of the member state concerned, and it is common ground I think that in this country it is the court which has the necessary power.'

1 [1999] FSR 394.
2 In fact this case was complicated by the fact that the goods were imported from Poland where the registered trade mark owner was an entity which was entirely different from the registered trade mark owner in the rest of the world.
3 As required by art 7 of the Basic Regulation.

19.124 It is submitted[1] that this reasoning is correct in so far as it goes though for the purposes of the point made in *Martin Pointing v Customs and Excise Comrs*[2] the judge did not need to go any further. However, we venture to suggest that in reality the only court which is able to determine matters of infringement (which is a necessary condition when the goods are counterfeit within the meaning of art 1(2)(a) of the Basic Regulation) is the High Court since the High Court is the only court which has jurisdiction in relation to questions of civil infringement.[2] Further, since the High Court is the only court which is able to revoke marks or declare them invalid pursuant to the TMA 1994, ss 46 and 47, then proceeding in any other court would deprive a defendant of his guaranteed right to impugn the validity of any trade mark as is set out in arts 3, 4, 12, 13 and 14 of and the fifth and seventh Recitals to the Directive[3] for if the defendant were not able to do so then the proprietor would have a very effective means (in part at least) of protecting an unjustified monopoly.

1 With some bias since one of the authors was counsel for the plaintiff.
2 [1999] FSR 394.
3 See the TMA 1994, s 75. The criminal side is, however a different matter and is one we shall consider in due course.
4 Though it should be pointed out that, so far, the ECJ in *Silhouette International Schmied GmbH & Co KG v Hartlauer Handelsgesellschaft mbH* [1998] FSR 729 at 735, para 25, has only gone so far as to say that arts 5–7 of the Directive constitute a complete code (or 'harmonisation' to use their words).

19.125 Article 7 of the Basic Regulation provides for the procedure to be followed once goods have been suspended from further release or detained. Within 10 working days of 'notification'[1] of suspension of release or detention, the customs office (that is the branch of HMC&E which is sent the decision of HMC&E in relation to an article 3 notice, usually the port office) must be informed:

  (a) 'that the matter has been referred to the authority competent to take a substantive decision on the case in accordance with Article 6 (2); or

  (b) that the duly empowered authority has adopted interim measures.'

1 Which should be 'informing the relevant parties'.

19.126 The goods which are the subject of the suspension from further release or detention must then be released pending compliance with other requirements under CCC or other domestic legislation 'and the detention order has been revoked'. The reference to a 'detention order' is odd and does not make sense since the first and last time reference is made in either CCC, the CCC Implementing Regulation, the Basic Regulation or the Implementing Regulation to a 'detention order' is in art 7 of the Basic Regulation.[1] However, this could be an interpretive slip since art 7(2) of the Basic Regulation makes reference to the revocation of detention as opposed to the revocation of a detention order.

1 Indeed the CCC and the CCC Implementing Regulation have no reference to "detention" or "detain" at all!

19.127 The 'authority competent to take a substantive decision' referred to in (a) above must be the same body as the body referred to in art 6(2)(a) of the Basic Regulation, ie the court or as we would have it the High Court.[1] However, reference to the 'authority' in (b) above is more cryptic. The point was made in *Martin Pointing*[2] where it was held and that the 'duly empowered authority' was one and the same as the 'authority competent'. We believe that this 'fundamental difficulty' which has precipitated our analysis of arts 6 and 7 along with the (C)R 1999 and the (CP)R 1999 is of extreme importance and we devote a section to this below

1 Or else why would the proprietor have the right to be *notified* of the names and addresses of the relevant persons as is set out in the second paragraph of art 6(1) of the Basic Regulation?
2 [1999] FSR 394.

19.128 Once one of the two events has taken place as set out in (a) and (b) above[1] and provided that it takes place within the ten days during which the parties have been informed of the suspension of release or detention[2] then there is no requirement to release the goods. The interim position can be maintained by way of interlocutory injunction via the court ('the authority competent to take a substantive decision') on the application of the relevant party or 'that the duly empowered authority' has adopted interim measures. HMC&E argued in *Martin Pointing* that in that case the 'interim' measure taken by the 'duly empowered authority' within the ten-day period (as was extended in that case) was seizure and that the power to seize is derived from the powers which the Commissioners had via the operation of the CEMA 1979, s 139, which allows seizure of goods which are prohibited and are liable to forfeiture under the CEMA 1979, s 49(1)(b).[3] The CEMA 1979, s 49(1)(b), causes difficulties since it refers to 'any enactment' as opposed to any provision or European regulation or the like. We leave it as an open question as to whether the section can be construed so widely so as to cover, in addition, something other than an enactment. It is certainly clear that art 2 of the Basic Regulation creates a prohibition once the procedure in art 6 of the Basic Regulation has been completed[4] and the general scheme of arts 6 and 7 of the Basic Regulation, taken with the CEMA 1979, s 139, envisages that a procedure might take place which is designed to determine whether the goods are actually prohibited or not whether by judicial or executive decision,[5] though the end result will, in the absence of abandonment by the importer, be judicial proceedings.

1 See para **19.125**.
2 Or 20 working days if extended 'in appropriate cases', though Carnwath J observed in *Martin Pointing v Customs and Excise Comrs* at 402:
'In principle, although the regulation does not in terms require any specific decision or notice in writing [that the initial 10 day period is to be extended by a further 10 days], it is implicit, as I see it, that the matter should be specifically addressed by someone properly authorised since a decision has to made whether the case is 'appropriate'. It is wrong in my view to regard it simply as a 20-day period since that is not how it is expressed. Furthermore, since the rights of the parties are directly affected by the time limits under article 7, there is a strong argument that fairness requires them to be informed.'
3 Which provides that:
'where ... any goods are imported, landed or unloaded contrary to any prohibition or restriction in force for the time being with respect thereto under or by virtue of any enactment ... , those goods shall be liable to forfeiture.'
4 Which must be construed liberally as meaning that the administrative process (if there is one) or the judicial avenues have been pursued to their ultimate end.
5 Though the Commissioners in *Martin Pointing v Customs and Excise Comrs* accepted that whether an interim judicial measure had been taken or an executive decision they would all result in the matter eventually ending up before a court either by way of condemnation proceedings or by way of infringement proceedings and indeed in that case there was a cross action for condemnation, it being accepted by the plaintiff that the cross-action automatically succeeded if the main action failed.

19.129   There appears to be little difference between seizure on the one hand and suspension from further release or detention on the other and we venture to suggest that the distinction is a fine one if it is there at all. However, in *Martin Pointing*[1] held that seizure was such an 'interim measure' and that HMC&E were entitled, as the duly empowered authority, to seize such goods.

1 [1999] FSR 394 at 401 and 403.

The Basic Regulation, arts 8–18

19.130   We finally and briefly comment upon arts 8 and 9 of the Basic Regulation. Article 8 of the Basic Regulation sets out the procedure once it is found that the goods are indeed counterfeit. Article 8 requires each member state to give the necessary powers to 'the competent authorities' to destroy the goods or dispose of those goods through non commercial channels (such as not to injure the proprietor and without compensation or cost to the Exchequer)[1] and/or to take measures to deprive the importer and other persons concerned of the economic benefits of the transaction.[2] Obliteration of the marks is not permissible save in exceptional circumstances. The goods can be turned over to the Exchequer but it must be such that the proprietor is not affected and there can be no compensation to the importer and others or cost to the Exchequer.[3] Finally, the proprietor has to be given the names and addresses of the consignor, importer, exporter and manufacturer and in addition he must be told of the quantity of goods concerned[4] – presumably so that he can sue them.

1 Basic Regulation, art 8(1)(a).
2 Basic Regulation, art 8(1)(b).

3 Basic Regulation, art 8(2).
4 Basic Regulation, art 8(3).

19.131 Article 9(1) of the Basic Regulation provides that if goods are missed then no action may be taken against the Commissioners by the proprietors for negligent (or even wilful) failure to spot them. The same applies where even though the goods are found and it is confirmed that they fall within the meaning of an article 3 notice and no detention or suspension from further release takes place. This, however is subject to the domestic law of the UK and our domestic law certainly does provide a remedy for negligent failure to perform a duty owed to another. It could therefore be argued that *Anns v Merton London Borough Council*[1] is still good law, it being overuled in *Murphy v Brentwood District Council*[2] on the basis that a statutory limitation regime had taken over in relation to a council's duty to ensure that houses were built properly and safely and had nothing to do with the test for proximity enunciated by Lord Wilberforce in *Anns*[3]. Notions of precedent aside, it is apparent that *Anns* is no longer considered to be good law but rather the test as enunciated in *Caparo Industries plc v Dickman*[4] as to whether it is fair, just and reasonable to impose a 'duty of a given scope'.[5] This test has had some quite surprising results such as in the case of *Marc Rich & Co v Bishop Rock Marine Co Ltd*[6] where an admittedly negligent defendant (who had stated that a ship was safe to sail when in fact it was not) escaped liability on the grounds that the plaintiff, being the owner of the cargo, had his remedy against the ship owners in contract and in accordance with certain maritime conventions and a finding of negligence would undermine that. Second, the ship surveyors would be more defensive in their survey and thus be less effective in their primary *role* of saving lives at sea. Thirdly, allowing the plaintiff to succeed would inevitably result in the work of people in the position of the defendant devoting time and resources to litigation when they ought to be devoting their duties to saving lives at sea.

1 [1978] AC 728.
2 [1991] 1 AC 398.
3 [1978] AC 728 at 751–752.
4 [1990] 2 AC 605.
5 [1990] 2 AC 605 at 617–618, per Lord Bridge.
6 [1996] AC 211.

19.132 In the case of failure by the Commissioners to spot counterfeit goods or deal with them once spotted many of the same considerations apply (though not to such a degree as saving lives – their function is almost, but not completely, economic in effect). The proprietor already has his remedy in infringement proceedings via the TMA 1994, s 10. With this and the possibility of proceedings against the Commissioner in mind, Commissioners would probably be likely to be more defensive in accepting AAs and turning them into article 3 notices (art 3(5) of the Basic Regulation seems to confer a complete discretion as to whether to transpose an AA into an article 3 notice). Further, the Commissioners are not litigators, they are there to provide funds for the Exchequer and provide certain other functions for the public good. In any event; *Jones v Department of Employment*[1] would tend to suggest that government departments are really only amenable to judicial review or to such appeal process as may exist in relation to the decision in question.

1 [1989] QB 1.

19.133 In addition to negligence there is also the possibility of a cause of action for breach of statutory duty but since *Jones v Department of Employment* was a

405

breach of statutory duty case we leave it there and conclude that art 9(1) of the Basic Regulation has its fullest effect.

19.134   Article 9(3) of the Basic Regulation makes it clear that the civil liability of the holder of the right shall be governed by domestic law. There is no guidance as to the meaning of this part of art 9 of the Basic Regulation but we venture to suggest that it is intended to cover the position whereby proceedings might be taken against the holder of the right in circumstances where false information has been provided to HMC&E in an action for malicious falsehood (provided that the relevant elements are made out being falsity, malice and special damage).[1] Cases such as *Taylor v Serious Fraud Office*,[2] which provide for immunity to persons assisting a criminal investigation or where there is some object on the part of the communicatee to further matters to their own ends. We submit that any such immunity in relation to persons who, for their own ends, communicate information to the relevant authority so that the communicator's position may be protected. As to whether proceedings might be taken against a proprietor who had acted in concert with HMC&E in depriving the declarant of his goods , thereby facing an allegation of trespass to goods, depends upon whether the elements as to joint tortfeasorship are made out[3] and it is irrelevant that HMC&E themselves might escape liability because a CEMA 1979, s 144 certificate has been issued in their favour since the essence of joint tortfeasorship is the common design to do the acts which go to the tort as opposed to the intention of committing the tort itself.

1 Though it is unlikely in trade disputes whether proof of special damage is required by virtue of the Defamation Act 1952, s 3(1)(a) and (b) if it can be proved that the words were calculated to cause pecuniary damage and are published in writing or other permanent form or that the words were calculated to cause pecuniary damage and they were so uttered in respect of a trade, calling or profession.
2 [1997] 4 All ER 887.
3 See *Unilever plc v Gillette (UK) Ltd* [1989] RPC 583 at 607–609, per Mustill LJ where he cites the speech of Lord Templeman in *CBS Songs Ltd v Amstrad Consumer Electronics plc* [1988] AC 1013; [1988] RPC 567.

19.135   We also consider that there may be a cause of action in negligence of the type encountered in the case of *Hedley Byrne and Co Ltd v Heller & Partners Ltd*[1] since the proprietor and the Commissioners could be said to have a special relationship. However, even if there is no special relationship of the type encountered in *Hedley Byrne*, it appears that such a doctrine has been extended as was established in *Ministry of Housing and Local Government v Sharp*.[2] In this case the plaintiff held a charge over some land which was registered at the local land charges registry. The defendant issued a certificate to a third party which failed to mention the charge and a purchaser bought the land and because of the way that the registration rules worked the purchaser bought free of the charge. The charge holder sued the defendant successfully, it being held that the defendant owed the plaintiff a duty of care not to make negligent statements to others which would interfere with the plaintiff's interest. We submit that as far as principles are concerned there is no distinction between *Ministry of Housing and Local Government* and the present case that the proprietor has made a representation via an AA to HMC&E relating to his trade marks and HMC&E will in all probability act on that representation thus producing an article 3 notice. Thus, if anything in the statement is untrue because of the neglect or, we submit, breach of duty which the proprietor owes to HMC&E and therefore the importer, then he will be liable for his breach. The position was re-visited in *Spring v Guardian Assurance plc*[3] where the defendant negligently gave a reference (which was unfavourable) to the plaintiff's prospective employers. The prospective employers declined to employ the plaintiff and the plaintiff successfully sued for damages. That damages can include economic loss of the type envisaged by the House of Lords in the *Hedley Byrne* case was made clear in *Spring v Guardian Assurance plc* since the reasoning in this case is derived from considerations of *Hedley Byrne*:

'The wide scope of the principle recognised in *Hedley Byrne and Company Limited v Heller & Partners Limited* is reflected in the broad statements of principle which I have quoted. All the members of the Appellate Committee in this case spoke in terms of the principle resting upon an assumption or undertaking of responsibility by the defendant towards the plaintiff, coupled with reliance by the plaintiff on the exercise by the defendant of due care and skill. Lord Devlin, in particular, stressed that the principle rested upon an assumption of responsibility when he said, at p 531, that—

'the essence of the matter in the present case and in others of the same type is the acceptance of responsibility.'

For the purpose of the case now before your Lordships it is, I consider, legitimate to proceed on the same basis. Furthermore, although *Hedley Byrne and Co Ltd v Heller & Partners Ltd* itself was concerned with the provision of information and advice, it is clear that the principle in the case is not so limited and extends to include the performance of other services, as for example the professional services rendered by a solicitor to his client (see, in particular, Lord Devlin, at pp 529–530). Accordingly where the plaintiff entrusts the defendant with the conduct of his affairs, in general or in particular, the defendant may be held to have assumed responsibility to the plaintiff, and the plaintiff to have relied on the defendant to exercise due skill and care, in respect of such conduct.

For present purposes, I wish also to refer to the nature of the "special skill" to which Lord Morris referred in his statement of principle. It is, I consider, clear from the facts of *Hedley Byrne and Co Lid v Heller & Partners Ltd* itself that the expression "special skill" is to be understood in a broad sense, certainly broad enough to embrace special knowledge. Furthermore, Lord Morris himself, when speaking of the provision of a statement in the form of information or advice, referred to the defendant's judgment or skill or ability to make careful inquiry, from which it appears that the principle may apply in a case in which the defendant has access to information and fails to exercise due care (and skill, to the extent that this is relevant) in drawing on that source of information for the purposes of communicating it to another.'[4]

1 [1964] AC 465
2 [1970] 2 QB 223.
3 [1994] 2 AC 296.
4 [1994] 3 WCR 354 at 369 A–F, per Lord Goff of Chievely.

19.136 Accordingly, in the right circumstances a cause of action will lie at the suit of the declarant where the proprietor makes negligent statements or statements in breach of a duty to tell the whole story.

19.137 Article 10 relates to the disapplication of the Basic Regulation to travellers luggage since it is envisaged by the twelfth Recital to the Basic Regulation which states:

'Whereas in order to avoid serious disruption to the clearing of goods contained in travellers' personal luggage, it is necessary to exclude from the scope of this Regulation goods which may be counterfeit or pirated which are imported from third countries within the limits laid down by Community rules in respect of relief from customs duty;'

and art 10 of the Basic Regulation has that effect.

19.138   Article 11 of the Basic Regulation provides:

'Moreover, each member state shall introduce penalties to apply in the event of infringements of Article 2 [of the Basic Regulation]. Such penalties shall be effective and proportionate and constitute an effective deterrent.'

19.139   We have already noted in Chapter 18 that insofar as the domestic route is concerned there is nothing penal in its operation and it appears that notwithstanding the operation of art 11 of the Basic Regulation there is a requirement that insofar as goods to which an article 3 notice relates fall within the meaning of art 1(1)(a) of the Basic Regulation then art 2 of the Basic Regulation will apply and the goods will become prohibited. It is to be presumed that once the goods are prohibited then penal sanctions will apply insofar as the same are effective, proportional and deterrent. It is an open question whether the mere vesting of the right to dispose in HMC&E is such a penalty – certainly the European Commission has taken no steps to force the UK to introduce such measures and we submit that this may be because there is sufficient criminal sanction for importing prohibited goods in the shape of the CEMA 1979, s 50, which states:

'(1) Subsection (2) below applies to goods of the following descriptions, that is to say—

(b)   goods the importation, landing or unloading of which is for the time being prohibited or restricted by or under any enactment.

(2) If any person with intent to defraud Her Majesty of any such duty or to evade any such prohibition or restriction as is mentioned in subsection (1) above–

(a)   unships or lands in any port or unloads from any aircraft in the United Kingdom or from any vehicle in Northern Ireland any goods to which this subsection applies, or assists or is otherwise concerned in such unshipping, landing or unloading; or
(b)   removes from their place of importation or from any approved wharf, examination station, transit shed or customs and excise station any goods to which this subsection applies or assists or is otherwise concerned in such removal,

he shall be guilty of an offence under this subsection and may be arrested.

(3) If any person imports or is concerned in importing any goods contrary to any prohibition or restriction for the time being in force under or by virtue of any enactment with respect to those goods, whether or not the goods are unloaded, and does so with intent to evade the prohibition or restriction, he shall be guilty of an offence under this subsection and may be arrested.

(4) … a person guilty of an offence under subsection (2) or (3) above shall be liable—

(a)   on summary conviction, to a penalty of the prescribed sum or of three times the value of the goods, whichever is the greater, or to imprisonment for a term not exceeding 6 months, or to both; or
(b)   on conviction on indictment, to a penalty of any amount, or to imprisonment for a term not exceeding 7 years, or to both.

…

(5A) In the case of an offence under subsection (2) or (3) above in connection with the prohibition contained in section 20 of the Forgery and Counterfeiting Act 1981,[1] subsection (4)(b) above shall have effect as if for the words "2 years" there were substituted the words "10 years".

    …

(7) In any case where a person would, apart from this subsection, be guilty of—

    (a)   an offence under this section in connection with the importation of goods contrary to a prohibition or restriction; and
    (b)   a corresponding offence under the enactment or other instrument imposing the prohibition or restriction, being an offence for which a fine or other penalty is expressly provided by that enactment or other instrument,

he shall not be guilty of the offence mentioned in paragraph (a) of this subsection.'

1 Which, despite its name applies only to forgeries of certain instruments and the like and to counterfeiting of coins and notes of legal tender and is not really anything to do with the law of trade marks.

19.140 As can be seen there is a requirement of *mens rea* whereas there is no such requirement in relation to the Basic Regulation – intention, in common with most of the law of trade marks, is irrelevant. Further, it is a moot point whether s 50(7) operates in cases where the Basic Regulation applies but that will depend upon whether the Basic Regulation can be described as penal. We submit that given that the current procedure under the Basic Regulation relating to condemnation is said to be governed by the CEMA 1979 (via the (CP)R 1999) and that, as we have already said, condemnation is not supposed to be penal, the CEMA 1979, s 50, applies with its full force.

19.141 Articles 12 and 13 of the Basic Regulation provide a basis upon which the Implementing Regulation may be brought into being and arts 15–17 of the Basic Regulation (1) provides a means whereby certain information relating to enforcement is to be communicated to the European Commission, (2) deals with repeals and (3) entry into force.

The Basic Regulation, arts 6 and 7, the (CP)R 1999 and TRIPS

19.142 During much of the commentary which we have made above we have highlighted a difficulty which we perceived in relation to the operation of art 7(1) of the Basic Regulation in this article envisages that during the ten day period, the local customs office must be told that the matter has been referred to the authority competent to take a substantive decision or that the duly empowered authority has adopted interim measures.

19.143 In *Martin Pointing v Customs and Excise Comrs*[1] Carnwath J held that the duly empowered authority taking interim measures can be HMC&E or the Commissioners and this may be effected by seizure. We examine whether HMC&E are entitled under the current domestic law to seize goods which fall within an article 3 notice. It is to be remembered that the CEMA 1979, s 49, relates to goods which are prohibited in accordance with any enactment and doubt is to be expressed as to whether this covers Community enforceable rights as is defined in s 2(1) of the ECA 1972 (as amended). Indeed the ECA 1972 makes great play between domestic legislation, on the one hand, and Community legislation, on the other. When goods fall within the CEMA 1979, s 49(1)(b), as being contrary to any prohibition under or by virtue of any enactment then they are liable to forfeiture and the CEMA 1979, s 139, provides that anything which is liable to forfeiture may be seized or detained. The working of art 3 of the (CP)R 1999 provides that goods falling within an article 3 notice shall be so liable (in other words it is doubtful whether the CEMA 1979, s 49, applies at all) and so the CEMA 1979, s 139, enables them to be seized.

1 [1999] FSR 394.

19.144 We submit that the scheme of the Basic Regulation and of TRIPS requires in both scenarios as set out in art 7(1) of the Basic Regulation, that the matter has to be referred to a court which is capable of deciding matters of trade mark infringement, which we submit is and can only be the High Court.

19.145 The Basic Regulation directly acknowledges that it has been implemented to conform with our international obligations under TRIPS[1] and it is, therefore, submitted that in construing the Basic Regulation one must refer back to TRIPS to understand what it is that TRIPS envisages.

1 See the sixth Recital, which reads:
'Whereas the Community takes into account the terms of the GATT agreement on trade-related intellectual property issues, including a trade in counterfeit goods in particular the measures to be taken at the frontier'.

19.146 Article 50 of TRIPS provides that:

'Section 3: Provisional Measures

Article 50
1. The judicial authorities shall have the authority to order prompt and effective provisional measures:

    (a)   to prevent an infringement of any intellectual property right from occur ring, and in particular to prevent the entry into the channels of commerce in their jurisdiction of goods, including imported goods immediately ,after customs clearance;

    (b)   to preserve relevant evidence in regard to the alleged infringement.

2. The judicial authorities shall have the authority to adopt provisional measures *inaudita altera parte*[1] where appropriate, in particular where any delay is likely to cause irreparable harm to the right holder, or where there is a demonstrable risk of evidence being destroyed.

3. The judicial authorities shall have the authority to require the applicant to provide any reasonably available evidence in order to satisfy themselves with a sufficient degree of certainty that the applicant is the right holder and that his right is being infringed or that such infringement is imminent, and to order the applicant to provide a security or equivalent assurance sufficient to protect the defendant and to prevent abuse.

4. Where provisional measures have been adopted *inaudita altera parte*, the parties affected shall be given notice, without delay after the execution of the measures at the latest. A review, including a right to be heard, shall take place upon request of the defendant with a view to deciding, within a reasonable period after the notification of the measures, whether these measures shall be modified, revoked or confirmed.

5. The applicant may be required to supply other information necessary for the identification of the goods concerned by the authority that will execute the provisional measures.

6. Without prejudice to paragraph 4 above, provisional measures taken on the basis of paragraphs 1 and 2 above shall, upon request by the defendant, be revoked or otherwise cease to have effect, if proceedings leading to a decision on the merits of the case are not initiated within a reasonable period, to be determined by the judicial authority ordering the measures where national law so permits or, in the absence of such a determination, not to exceed twenty working days or thirty-one calendar days, whichever is the longer.

7. Where the provisional measures are revoked or where they lapse due to any act or omission by the applicant, or where it is subsequently found that there has been no infringement or threat of infringement of an intellectual property right, the judicial authorities shall have the authority to order the applicant, upon request of the defendant, to provide the defendant appropriate compensation for any injury caused by these measures.

8. To the extent that any provisional measure can be ordered as a result of administrative procedures, such procedures shall conform to principles equivalent in substance to those set forth in this Section.'

1 Ie without hearing the other side or as English lawyers would have it ex parte or following the spirit of the implementation of the CPR 1998 an application without notice.

19.147   It is clear that our current domestic regime complies with s 3, art 50 of TRIPS. The important point about art 50 of TRIPS is that it envisages that provisional measures are those measures in relation to which application is made *to the court* or at least to a judicial authority (which in England is the court).

19.148   Next comes art 55 of TRIPS, which states:

'*Article 55*
Duration of Suspension
If, within a period not exceeding ten working days after the applicant has been served notice of the suspension, the customs authorities have not been informed that proceedings leading to a decision on the merits of the case have been initiated by a party other than the defendant, or that the duly empowered authority has taken provisional measures prolonging the suspension of the release of the goods, the goods shall be released, provided that all other conditions for importation or exportation have been complied with; in appropriate cases, this time-limit may be extended by another ten working days. If proceedings leading to a decision on the merits of the case have been initiated, a review, including a right to be heard, shall take place upon request of the defendant with a view to deciding, within a reasonable period, whether these measures shall be modified, revoked or confirmed. Notwithstanding the above, where the suspension of the release of goods is carried out or continued in accordance with a provisional judicial measure, the provisions of Article 50, paragraph 6 above shall apply.'

19.149   Thus, art 55 of TRIPS envisages that where notice of suspension [from further release] has been served on the applicant [for detention or suspension from further release, as defined by art 50 of TRIPS] then if within ten days the customs authorities, which is, we submit, not any office or branch of HMC&E but is HMC&E itself, have not been informed that proceedings are on foot or that no *provisional* measure has been taken by the 'duly empowered authority' then the goods shall be released. Since art 50 of TRIPS envisages, subject to the proviso in para 8 thereof which we deal with below, that the only authority which is entitled to grant provisional measures is the judicial authority, the court, then we submit that the effect of art 55 of TRIPS makes it clear that there are two situations referred to here. The first is where the customs authorities have been told that proceedings are on foot, in which case by the operation of art 55 of TRIPS and of art 7(1) of the Basic Regulation, HMC&E are entitled to retain the goods pending determination and the second is where provisional measures have been adopted ex parte by the court. In both cases, therefore, a reference to the court is envisaged.

19.150 In *Martin Pointing v Customs and Excise Comrs,* Carnwath J disagreed with this view and given his experience on matters relating to Community law his disagreement is not to be taken lightly. The nature of Carnwath J's disagreement in the following passage:[1]

> '[Counsel for the plaintiff] ... says that the duly empowered authority referred to in ... [art 7(2) of the Basic Regulation] should also be interpreted as the court, or in any event it is not apt to apply to an administrative agency such as ... [HMC&E]. With respect, I am unable to agree with that. It seems to me clear that article 7 [of the Basic Regulation] uses two different expressions. The measures which ... [HMC&E] has taken under ... [the CEMA 1979] are interim in the sense that they involve seizure pending the final decision of the court, and ... [HMC&E] are a duly empowered authority to take those measures. Accordingly I see no reason why they are not within the terms of article 7(1) [of the Basic Regulation]. Indeed, it is difficult to see what the purpose of that is if it is limited to the court authority because the first part of article 7(1) [of the Basic Regulation] deals with reference to a body competent to take the substantive decision, so reference to that body for interim measures would inevitably involve a reference to the court.
>
> The second point is I think more important. It is said that ... [HMC&E] is not "the duly empowered authority" for the purpose of article 7 [of the Basic Regulation]. The significance of this is that the ten-day period allowed is, in effect, overridden if the Customs office is informed that the matter has been referred to the authority competent to take a substantive decision or that "the duly empowered authority has adopted interim measures".
>
> ...
>
> [Counsel for the plaintiff] ... says that the duly empowered authority referred to in the second part of article 7 [of the Basic Regulation] should also be interpreted as the court, or in any event it is not apt to apply to an administrative agency such as ... [HMC&E]. With respect, I am unable to agree with that. It seems to me clear that article 7 [of the Basic Regulation] uses two different expressions. The measures which ... [HMC&E] has taken under ... [the CEMA 1979] are interim in the sense that they involve seizure pending the final decision of the court, and ... [HMC&E] are a duly empowered authority to take those measures. Accordingly, I see no reason why they are not within the terms of article 7(1) [of the Basic Regulation]. Indeed, it is difficult to see what the purpose of that is if it is limited to the court authority because the first part of article 7(1) [of the Basic Regulation] deals with reference to a body competent to take the substantive decision, so reference to that body for interim measures would inevitably involve a reference to the court.
>
> I was referred by way of background to what is called the TRIPS agreement ' that is the agreement on trade-related aspects of intellectual property and rights under GATT – because the provisions in the EC Regulation have many parallels in the proposals agreed under that. Article 55 [of TRIPS] deals with duration of suspension and con-

tains very similar provisions to article 7(1) [of the Basic Regulation], including the reference to "the duly empowered authority".

On the whole that article appears to support … [HMC&E's] case because later on in the same article there is a reference to what is called 'a provisional judicial measure', which is subject to special procedures in article 50, paragraph 6 [of TRIPS]. The reference to the 'duly empowered authority' seems in context to be intended to be broader, and if it had been intended to confine that to a judicial body then I am sure that could have been stated.

[Counsel for the plaintiff] … also makes the point that article 7 [of the Basic Regulation] on … [HMC&E's] interpretation is circular because it envisaged the Customs office being informed of the interim measures adopted by the duly empowered authority. Thus, in effect, … [HMC&E] would be informing themselves. But that is not a real objection because one sees from other parts of the regulation that reference to the Customs office is to the specific office which is dealing with the matter at the port of entry, so there is no difficulty in interpreting article 7 [of the Basic Regulation] as requiring notification to that office by the department or body which is actually responsible for authorising the interim measures. Accordingly, on this point I accept … [HMC&E's] argument.'

1 [1999] FSR 394 at 401.

19.151 This, however is to ignore the fact that arts 49 and 50 of TRIPS envisages at para 8 and art 49 that if an administrative authority has the power to order provisional measures then it shall conform to the principles in ss 2 and 3 of Part III of TRIPS and, accordingly, in any given jurisdiction if the relevant administrative authority is unable to conform with those sections then it has no right to power to order interim measures.[1] We submit that this is the case here since art 42 of TRIPS envisages representation by independent legal counsel and presentation of evidence, yet HMC&E has no procedure for hearing the declarant or his counsel or indeed receiving any evidence from the declarant whereas the court does. Secondly, art 43 of TRIPS envisages that the judicial [or administrative] authority shall be able to order each party to give evidence (akin to disclosure under the CPR 1998) yet HMC&E has no such procedure available to it but the court does. Thirdly, art 44 of TRIPS provides that the judicial [or administrative] authorities shall have the power to order a party to desist from infringement immediately after customs clearance, a power which HMC&E does not possess but the court does. Fourthly, art 45 of TRIPS provides that the judicial [or administrative] authorities shall have the power to order a party to pay damages to compensate for injury and costs, a power which HMC&E does not possess but the court does. Fifthly, art 47 of TRIPS provides that the judicial [or administrative] authorities shall have the power to order disclosure by the declarant to the proprietor of the names and addresses of other possibly infringing parties, a power which HMC&E does not possess but the court does. Finally, art 48 of TRIPS provides that the judicial [or administrative] authorities shall have the power to order a proprietor who has abused the system party to compensate the injured party, a power which HMC&E does not possess but which the court does via an action for malicious falsehood.

1 Article 49 of TRIPS reads:
  '*Article 49*
  Administrative Procedures
  To the extent that any civil remedy can be ordered as a result of administrative procedures on the merits of a case, such procedures shall conform to principles equivalent in substance to those set forth in this Section [that is arts 42–49 of TRIPS].'

19.152 Accordingly, we submit that in order for TRIPS, art 50, para 8, to have effect it is necessary to have an administrative authority which has all of the judicial powers as are set out in arts 42–49 of TRIPS. That HMC&E does not have any of those powers points to the likely conclusion that the 'duly empowered authority' is not HMC&E but is rather the authority which grants an ex parte provisional measure since that is what art 50 of TRIPS envisages a provisional measure to be. Therefore, if art 55 is to be construed in that light so is art 7(1) of the Basic Regulation since the sixth recital expressly states that the purpose of the Basic Regulation is to provide conformity with TRIPS. That the EU takes its obligations under TRIPS seriously is beyond doubt.[1]

1 See *Re Uruguay Round Treaties* [1995] 1 CMLR 205.

The European interpretation route

19.153   It is apparent that art 7(1) of the Basic Regulation is not, insofar as interpretation is concerned, without controversy since if the interpretation of Carnwath J in *Martin Pointing v Customs and Excise Comrs*[1] is correct then there is a great deal more scope for the use of condemnation proceedings and less scope for direct action by the proprietor whereas if, as we submit, there is really only scope for action by a court in adopting interim measures or in relation to referral[1] then if no interim measure or referral takes place within the ten day period (or twenty days if extended in 'appropriate cases')[2] the goods in question are bound to be released. The reason why the issue is of importance is because ten days is in fact a tight time period and is often ignored.

1 [1999] FSR 394.
2 Which must include the initiation of condemnation proceedings since art 6(2)(a) of the Basic Regulation envisages this by the use of the words ' ... unless referral [to the court] is initiated by that [customs] service [(HMC&E in the UK)] or [local customs] office;'.
3 Basic Regulation, art 7(1), para 2..

19.154   So far we have only considered the English language version of the Basic Regulation. It is beyond doubt, however, that each official language version of a Community measure is authentic[1] and where there is doubt, as here, as to the meaning of one text then others may be examined[2] though even if one particular language version is clear that does not preclude the examination of other language versions[3] to see whether there is consistency and in the case of such divergence[4] then the general principles which the measure in question seeks to address should be bourne in mind.[5] In Case C-338/95 *Wiener SI GmbH v Hauptzollamt Emmerich*[6] Advocate-General Jacobs said:

> 'The one point on which the *CILFIT* conditions might in my view be reconsidered or refined is the statement that
>
>> "an interpretation of a provision of Community law ... involves a comparison of the different language versions".
>
> Although the Court preceded that statement by pointing out that 'the different language versions are all equally authentic', I do not think that the *CILFIT* judgment should be regarded as requiring the national courts to examine any Community measure in every one of the official Community languages (now numbering 11 or 12, if the Treaties and certain other basic texts are in issue). That would involve in many cases a disproportionate effort on the part of the national courts; moreover, reference to all the language versions of Community provisions is a method which appears rarely to be applied by the Court of Justice itself, although it is far better placed to do so than the national courts. In fact, the very existence of many language versions is a

further reason for not adopting an excessively literal approach to the interpretation of Community provisions, and for putting greater weight on the context and general scheme of the provisions and on their object and purpose. The reference in the *CILFIT* judgment would be better regarded, in my view, as an essential caution against taking too literal an approach to the interpretation of Community provisions and as reinforcing the point that they must be interpreted in the light of their context and of their purposes as stated in the preamble rather than on the basis of the text alone. The text can be particularly misleading in the case of technical legal terms, which, as the Court goes on to point out, may not have the same meaning in Community law as they have in the legal systems of the Member States.'

1 Case C-19/67 *Eestuur der Sociale Verzekeringsbank v Van der Vecht* [1967] ECR 345 at 354; Case C-283/82 *CILFIT v Ministry of Health* [1982] ECR 3415 at para 18 and Case C-219/95P *Ferriere Nord v Commission* [1997] ECR I-4411 at para 15.
2 Case C-19/67 *Eestuur der Sociale Verzekeringsbank v Van der Vecht* [1967] ECR. 345 at 354, Case C-9/79 *Wörsdorfer v Raad van Arbeid* [1979] ECR 2717 at paras 5–9; Case C-327/91 *France v EC Commission* [1994] ECR I-3641 at paras 30–35; Case C-177/95 *Ebony Maritime SA v Prefecto della Provincia di Brindisi* [1997] ECR I-1111 at paras 30 and 31.
3 Case C-219/95P *Ferriere Nord v Commission* [1997] ECR. I-4411 at paras 13–15.
4 See Case C-64/95 *Lubella v Hauptzollamt Cottbus* [1996] ECR I-5105 at paras 17 and 18, where the ECJ resolved a divergence in one language version by reference to the other versions. See also Joined Cases C-283, C-291 and C-292/94 *Denkavit International v Bundesamt für Finanzen* [1996] ECR I 5063 at paras 24 and 25 and Case C-80/76 *North Kerry Milk Products v Minister for Agriculture and Fisheries* [1977] ECR 425 at para 11.
5 Case C-6/74 *Moulijn v EC Commission* [1974] ECR 1287 at paras 10 and 111; Case C-30/77 *R v Bouchereau* [1977] ECR 1999 at paras 13 and 14; Case C-449/93 *Rockfon AIS v Specialarbejderforbundet i Danmark* [1995] ECR I-4291 at paras 26–28 and at paras 33, 36 and 39 of the Opinion of Advocate-General Cosmas. See also Case C-80/76 *North Kerry Milk v Minister for Agriculture and Fisheries* [1977] ECR. 425 at para 11; Case 803/79 *Roudolff* [1980] ECR 2015 at para 7 and Case C-372/88 *Milk Marketing Board v Cricket St Thomas Estate* [1990] ECR I-1345 at paras 15–18.
6 [1998] 1 CMLR 1110 at 1133, para 65.

19.155 Regard should also be had to the approach advocated by the Court of Appeal in domestic proceedings[1] where it was suggested that it was seldom productive for the domestic court to consider differing language versions but where it is then translations should be provided with important questions being referred to the ECJ under art 177 (now art 234) of the EC Treaty.

1 In *R v Customs and Excise Comrs, ex p EMU Tabac SARL* [1997] Eu LR 153 at 160B-D.

19.156 However, there are some telling differences between the versions of art 7(1) of the Basic Regulation in other language. Take, for example, the French language version which, in its authentic text says:-

'Si, dans un délai de dix jours ouvrables à compter de la notification de la suspension de l'octroi de la mainlevée ou de la retenue, le bureau de douane visé à l'article 6 paragraphe 1 n'a pas été informé de la saisine de l'autorité compétente pour statuer au fond conformément à l'article 6 paragraphe 2 ou n'a pas eu communication de la prise de mesures conservatoires par l'autorité habilitée à cet effet, la mainlevée est octroyée sous réserve que toutes les formalités douanières aient été accomplies et la mesure de retenue est levée.'

19.157 The difference in wording between 'l'autorité compétente', on the one hand, and 'l'autorité habilitée', on the other, is the germane point. We suggest that the french word 'habilitée' means, in context, legal capacity or legal competency whereas the transitive verb 'habiliter' means to empower. Accordingly, the correct translation of the French version of art 7(1) of the Basic Regulation is that the customs office must either be told that the matter has been referred to 'l'autorité compétente', ie the court or that 'l'autorité habilitée', ie the legally competent authority has taken interim measures otherwise the goods are bound to be released. Taken in the context of condemnation, the former situation would apply where the proprietor issues a claim form (and in effect gets an automatic interim injunction because HMC&E are not bound to release the goods) or where HMC&E issue condemnation proceedings. However, under the CEMA 1979, without seizure *or detention* there can be no condemnation but we suggest that art 7(1) of the Basic Regulation empowers HMC&E to do what is necessary to bring condemnation proceedings about. In this context, if reg 3 of the (CP)R 1999 is to be construed as empowering seizure then it goes further than is necessary for the implementation of the Basic Regulation since, firstly, it does not limit itself to goods falling within art 1(1)(a) of the Basic Regulation and, secondly, seizure is unnecessary because the goods can be detained or suspended from further release until a substantive decision (ie by the court) is made. We, therefore, suggest that the proper interpretation of the (CP)R 1999 in the context of the CEMA 1979, s 139(1), is that detention continues and there is no need or requirement for the additional step of seizure. Therefore, if seizure is a redundant or unnecessary step it cannot be an interim remedy. So, in the latter situation, the detention or suspension from further release is superceded by an order of the court say, where the court concerned makes some other order which, though protecting the right of the proprietor, might also allow limited dealing in the goods subject to accounts being kept. This is, we suggest, the proper construction of art 7(1) of the Basic Regulation.

19.158   In the Italian version of art 7(1) of the Basic Regulation, the relevant authority is referred to throughout as the 'autorità competente' and the same applies in the Portuguese version where 'autoridade competente' is referred to throughout.

19.159   It appears that there is even in our rather cursory examination of the foreign language texts some divergence, We submit that in such a case it is the overriding objectives of the Basic Regulation which have to be looked at. If we are wrong as to our suggested construction of art 7(1) of the Basic Regulation then that would imply that if seizure by HMC&E takes place within the ten-day period there is no obligation on HMC&E to initiate condemnation proceedings – as indeed there is not. HMC&E can simply sit on the goods and do nothing.[1] However, that would be contrary to the rights guaranteed to the defendant via the sixth Recital of the Basic Regulation and art 41(1) of TRIPS which speaks of expeditious measures, art 41(2) of TRIPS which speaks of the need to avoid unwarranted delay, art 41(3) which speaks of the need to avoid undue delay, art 50(6) which speaks of a decision being made within a reasonable period.

1 Though if they do so for long enough then it could be argued that any subsequent condemnation proceedings constitute an abuse of process.

19.160   We submit, therefore, that in either of the cases envisaged in art 7(1) of the Basic Regulation there must be recourse to the court. This view was confirmed following the handing down of judgment in the case of *Re Adidas*[1] by the ECJ. In *Re Adidas*, the trade mark proprietor had managed to persuade the Swedish customs authorities to suspend from further release, or detain, certain goods. However, the Swedish customs authorities refused to divulge the news to the importer and consignee and as a result, Adidas could not refer the matter to the court and was therefore deprived of a remedy–the ECJ agreed with this. The judgment makes it clear that what must happen during the ten-day period, is referral to court. Thus, we submit that following *Re Adidas, Martin Pointing v Customs and Excise Comrs*[2] was wrongly decided.

1 (14 October 1999, unreported), ECJ.
2 [1999] FSR 394.

19.161 We further suggest that insofar as the (CP)R 1999 is concerned an interesting situation has arisen which is this: the Basic Regulation was amended in order to include a wider class of rights, such as patents and supplementary certificates. On any view, it would be a brave government or a brave commissioner of customs and excise that would allow a non-judicial body to decide questions of patent infringement. Indeed, the (CP)R 1999, reg 6(1), suggests that insofar as patents, supplementary protection certificates, registered designs and design right are concerned, it is the right owner in question who must refer the matter to the court within the ten day period – seizure is not an option.[1] The rational for this is obvious – only judicial authorities know what they are doing in this complex area of law. We fail to understand, however, how it is that the Commissioners can make an arbitrary decision as to whether to make the remedy of seizure available in respect of an arbitrary set of rights and not others. Further, there is no authority to define, in a statutory instrument purportedly deriving authority from the Basic Regulation via The ECA 1972, the authority competent to take a substantive decision as being one body for certain classes of right (arbitrarily chosen) and another in respect of other classes of right. There is simply no logic to it and we submit, strongly, that the commissioners themselves accept that art 6 of the Basic Regulation is capable of being construed in a way that is consistent with our suggested construction. At the time of writing, the (CP)R 1999 is still a very new piece of legislation, and it is therefore impossible to say how it will be construed, the fact that arbitrary distinctions have been made in the (CP)R 1999 which are not catered for in the Basic Regulation (at least insofar as patents and supplementary protection certificates are concerned – the position relating to design right and registered designs is somewhat different and a distinction may be justified, though, even then, that would mean giving two meanings to the single expression 'authority competent to take a substantive decision') would tend to suggest strongly that the distinction is not supported by substantive legislation and is outside its vires.

1 Though, even then, giving authority to a non-judicial body to decide, even prima facie and for an arbitrary period, questions of patent infringement is absurd and raises the question as to why our courts have an interim remedies procedure at all or indeed why we have a patents judge.

Chapter 20

Criminal aspects of the law of trade marks

1 Introduction

20.1 There is a growing perception that the deterrent effect of civil proceedings for trade mark infringement may not be so effective as to stop certain classes of infringer. Generally, the majority of cases of trade mark infringement are dealt with in the civil courts and this is dealt with elsewhere in this book. Sometimes the trade mark infringer will be difficult to track down and will not (by reason of his elusiveness) be easy to deter. Additionally, the public needs to be protected from deception of the sort practised by counterfeiters.[1] It is for these reasons that a number of criminal sanctions are imposed. We pause to note that there is in fact no real definition of the expression 'counterfeit' or 'counterfeiter' though the definition given in the European Regulations relating to detention and suspension from further release is a good starting point which is, to paraphrase, that goods are counterfeit if they are attempting to be genuine so that the consumer is deceived into thinking he thinks he knows what he is buying as opposed to being confused insofar as he is unsure what he is buying. We add that the criminal sanctions relating to trade marks would appear only to relate to goods and not services – though this is not clearly the case.

1 Though whether the criminal law of trade marks does this or is intended to do this, is a matter of debate.

20.2 It is also part of the received wisdom amongst trade mark owners that the elusive infringer is probably the one who is doing the most damage[1] if not to the trade mark owner then, possibly at least to the consumer. Whilst this chapter is not the place to start a political debate about the balance of rights between the proprietor and the infringer,[2] it has to be observed that in terms of civil remedies the trade mark proprietor already has a potentially vast array of remedies at his fingertips and one would wonder why he would want any more. On the other hand, it is also to be observed that the public is less protected under the civil regime of the TMA 1994 than it was under the TMA 1938 because it is now much easier to carry out transactions in trade marks as if they were an ordinary market commodity. Thus, there is at least a greater possibility of confusion which was something that was strongly deprecated under the TMA 1938. Whilst this has never been stated, it is quite clear that one of the guiding tenets of the Directive is that trade mark owners are better at regulating their position than is the state. Stronger marks lead to prosperity and a proprietor who deliberately weakens his trade mark by trafficking it, by purchasing a second-hand trade mark or selling low-quality goods is really acting against his own self interest. The modern law has never believed businessmen to be so obtuse, at least in relation to trade marks. It is also to be observed that a second unstated aim of the Directive is to encourage businessmen to develop stronger marks; stronger marks get greater protection, not only because they are inherently more registerable[3] but also because the class of potentially infringing acts is widened in the shape of ss 10(3) and 52(2) of the TMA 1994. It is also the case that following on from the judgment of the ECJ in *Canon Kabushiki Kaisha v Metro-Goldwyn-Mayer Inc, formerly Pathe Communications Corpn,*[4] the scope of s 10(2) of the TMA 1994 is also widened in respect of more powerful trade marks.[5] Whilst this may seem introverted, stronger marks also encourage the achievement of higher quality or maintenance of quality from the manufacturer which must, some would say, be of benefit to the public.

1   Though we doubt whether this is so, certainly in the cases of fashion clothing where persons who purchase infringing goods will only do so because of the low price which the infringer charges and would certainly not pay high street prices.
2   Or as some would say the 'free marketeer'.
3   Since objections under the TMA 1994, s 3(1)(a)–(c), can be overcome by use.
4   [1998] ECR I-5507; Case C-39/97.
5   Something which was strongly deprecated by Jacob J in *British Sugar plc v James Robertson & Sons Ltd* [1996] RPC 281, 294 lines 28–40.

20.3   As a result, the TMA 1994 has fashioned a set of crimes which seek to deter the infringer or at least the counterfeiter. In addition there are a number of inchoate offences such as conspiracy and the associated accessory crimes.[1] Those crimes relate to UK and CTMs,[2] though there appears to be no basis or authority for placing the question of CTMs on a criminal footing, governed as it is by a comprehensive European set of rules (which, we would say amounts to a code) via Council Regulation (40/94/EC) of 20 December 1993 on the Community trade mark[3] or under Commission Regulation (2868/95/EC) of 13 December 1995 implementing Council Regulation (40/94/EC) on the Community trade mark[4] which are, we submit, so comprehensive as to exclude the ambit of domestic criminal sanctions altogether.

1   Such as aiding, abetting, counselling and procuring.
2   See the CTM Regulations 1996 (SI 1996/1908), reg 7.
3   OJ L11 14.1.94 p 1.
4   OJ L303 15.12.95 p 1.

20.4   Before we leave our initial comments we would make one further observation which is this: criminal aspects of trade marks are not for the faint hearted, prosecutions can sometimes last for years without resolution, the legal argument can last for weeks and the costs can be astronomical.

20.5   In this chapter we propose to examine criminal aspects of trade mark infringement from four perspectives, being: general aspects of the crimes themselves, the position of the prosecution, the position of the defendant and the position of the court. This chapter is not intended to be a replacement or substitute for the leading practitioners' texts on the subject of crime and criminal procedure and the reader is strongly urged to consult these texts.

2   Legislative history

20.6   We start our analysis in this section with the comments of the minister, Lord Strathclyde in the debate on the second reading of Trade Marks Bill[1] where he said in introducing the bill:

> 'First, I turn to Clauses 86[2] to 88 which concern trade mark counterfeiting. Provisions making the fraudulent use of a trade mark were introduced into the 1938 Act in 1988 by the Copyright, Designs and Patents Act 1988. Those clauses replace those provisions with a widened scope. Section 58A of the 1938 Act was cast in terms of deception of the customer. Since that was enacted, there has been a dramatic growth in the sale of what are sometimes called 'brand copies"-garments, watches and so forth which feed on the reputation of famous trade marks while the trader is able to escape prosecution under the Trade Marks Act by admitting that they are fakes. It was thought in some quarters that such goods would still be caught by the Trade Descriptions Act, but a ruling earlier this year showed that that is not so. That prompted much lobbying of my department to change the law. Some of the lobbying came, as might be expected, from the owners of the famous marks being copied. However, we were particularly struck by letters from other traders who deal in the genuine goods and who complain of being undercut by market stalls or boot fair traders selling blatant copies.[3]

> 'Clause 86 is, as I say, broader in its scope, and the offence of trade mark counterfeiting is defined in much the same terms as trade mark infringement. I might add that there is an obligation to apply criminal sanctions against wilful counterfeiting under the intellectual property code being negotiated in GATT.'[4]

Then the Bill went to committee in the House of Lords and Lord Strathclyde said:[5]

> "We also propose making the defence under this provision less restrictive. As drafted, subsection (5) of Clause 86 requires a person charged to have a reasonable belief that the use was licensed by the proprietor of the mark. Even if 'licensed' is construed as simply meaning "permitted", the Government accept that, this is a very restricted defence. We therefore propose replacing it by a requirement for a reasonable belief that the use was not an infringement. This would cover the use of someone acting in ignorance, or in a genuine belief that what he was doing did not require the consent of the proprietor, rather than taking part in deliberate counterfeiting."

And when pressed by Lord Reay as to whether the defence was too weak, Lord Strathclyde said:[6]

> 'I return to subsection (6) and the use of the word "infringement". As far as I am concerned, the use of the word "infringement" is quite proper in subsection (6) because it refers to elements of offences which are infringements, which have now been set out in new subsections (1) to (3). An infringement is broader in scope than the offence under this clause. Moreover, the two ingredients in subsection (4) were in the original version of Clause 86. They are not new but they are grouped under 'fraudulently' which is now defined by the reference to these two ingredients.'

1 Debates of the House of Lords [550]: 6 December 1993 col 749, 754.
2 It is to be observed that Lord Strathclyde (and his department) chose mot to mention anything that consumers may have written – perhaps he did not get any letters from consumers.
3 Now the TMA1994, s 92 – a section or clause which did not survive unscathed.
4 See TRIPS, art 61.
5 House of Lords Public Bill Committee on the Trade Marks Bill, fourth sitting, 20 January 1994, col 96.
6 House of Lords Public Bill Committee on the Trade Marks Bill, fourth sitting, 20 January 1994, col 104.

20.7   Thereafter, the Bill went to the House of Commons and on the second reading the minister, Mr Patrick McLoughlin said this:[1]

'I should like to single out the provision dealing with trade marks and counterfeiting. That is a growing problem throughout the world and the UK is not immune from it. The offences trades on the reputation of famous and established trade marks. Unscrupulous traders copy goods sold under well known trade marks. That devalues the reputation of the trade mark, because the counterfeit goods are frequently of inferior quality and might even be dangerous. Moreover, it also harms traders in the genuine goods, who, consequently, lose business. The Bill, therefore, will strengthen the protection against trade mark counterfeiting.

'It is an essential ingredient of the offence under the current trade mark law that a trader intends that a consumer should believe that the goods were genuine. There has, however, been a dramatic growth in the practice of selling counterfeit goods clearly advertised as "brand copies".

'Until recently, it was believed that that was, none the less, an offence under the Trade Descriptions Act 1968. However, the Divisional Court held in a recent case '*Kent County Council v Price*[2] – that this was not so, observing that the Trade Descriptions Act [1968] existed to protect consumers and, as the defendant was advertising the goods as fake they were not deceived. There was, therefore, no offence.

'However this Bill is concerned with the protection of trade marks,[3] clause 87 defines the offence in terms of unauthorised use of the mark. That protects the legitimate rights of trade mark owners. Even if an unscrupulous trader sells the goods as "genuine fakes", it will still be an offence, because he will be deliberately exploiting someone's mark without their permission.

'Some concerns were expressed, both in another place and elsewhere, that the anti-counterfeiting provisions in the Bill went too far and could have made the person who inadvertently infringes someone else's trade mark liable to criminal charges. They felt such infringements should be left to the civil courts. The Government believe that the changes made in another place remove that danger and better focus the criminal sanctions on deliberate counterfeiting."

and from thence to be considered in committee where the minister Mr McLoughlin said:[4]

'... Clause 87 aims to tighten up the law against counterfeiting. For that reason, the Government consulted widely on the provision. Clause 87 makes it a criminal offence for anyone deliberately to use a registered mark without the permission of the owner of the trade mark intending to cause him loss. We have to be careful to provide a defence for someone acting in complete ignorance of the counterfeit nature of the goods Or in the genuine belief that what he is doing has the consent of the proprietor.

...

'The Government are not convinced that the re-enactment of that provision would meet the objective of focussing on deliberate counterfeiters while providing a defence for the innocent infringer.

...

422

'As it stands, the clause requires a belief on reasonable grounds that what the person was doing was not an infringement of the registered trade mark. That should, therefore, cover someone acting in ignorance of the infringing nature of the goods, or in a genuine belief that what he was doing had, or did not require, the consent of the proprietor. The Government and most professional groups with an interest in the subject believe that this is a fair and balanced provision as it stands, so I hope that it will receive. the Committee's support. There is no difference between us on what we want to achieve, and I think that the Bill, as worded, covers that point.'

The bill received royal assent in the House of Lords on the 21 July 1994.[4]

1 Hansard [241]: 18 April 1994, Trade Marks Bill, second reading, col 658, 661.
2 Reported at [1993] 9 EIPR D-225; (1993) 157 JP 1161.
3 And not, we observe (and will continue to observe) the protection of consumers – none of the statutes made in Parliament seem to emphasise this.
4 House of Commons Standing Committee B, 17 May 1994, col 16, 18.
5 Debates of the House of Lords [557]: 21 July 1994 col 351.

20.8 The Trade Marks Bill was enacted to implement the Directive and also to provide certain other functions not catered for in the Directive. The Bill was predicated by, first. the Directive and second, a Government White Paper entitled 'Reform of Trade Mark Law' (Cm 1203), September 1990. However neither the directive nor the white papers say anything about the ambit or purpose of s 92 of the TMA 1994. Further, the White Paper was predicated not only by the Directive but also by the Mathys Report of the Committee to Examine British Trade Mark Law and Practice (Cmnd 5601) Published in May 1974 which said nothing about the criminal aspects of trade mark law.

20.9 Indeed the first time that criminal sanctions for trade mark infringement existed (or related wrongs not being in the nature of Trade Descriptions Act 1968 ('TDA 1968') type offences) was from 1 August 1989 when s 58A of the TMA 1938 (entitled 'Fraudulent application or use of trade mark an offence') was inserted by s 300 of the Copyright, Designs and Patents Act 1988 ('CDPA 1988') and came into force on the 1 August 1989 by the operation of art 2 of the Copyright, Designs and Patents Act 1988 (Commencement No 1) Order 1989[1]. Section 58A of the TMA 1938 read:

'58A.–(1) It is an offence, subject to subsection (3) below, for a person-

(a) to apply a mark identical to or nearly resembling a registered trade mark to goods, or to material used or intended to be used for labelling, packaging or advertising goods, or
(b) to sell, let for hire, or offer or expose for sale or hire, or distribute
  (i) goods bearing such a mark, or
  (ii) material bearing such a mark which is used or intended to be used for labelling, packaging or advertising goods, or
(c) to use material bearing such a mark in the course of a business for labelling packaging or advertising goods, or
(d) to possess in the course of a business goods or material bearing such a mark with a view to doing any of the things mentioned in paragraphs (a) to (c),

when he is not entitled to use the mark in relation to the goods in question and the goods are not connected in the course of trade with a person who is so entitled.

(2) It is also an offence, subject to subsection (3) below, for a person to possess in the course of a business goods or material bearing a mark identical to or nearly resembling a registered trade mark with a view to enabling or assisting another person to do any of the things mentioned in subsection (1)(a) to (c), knowing or having reason to believe that the other person is not entitled to use the mark in relation to the goods in question and that the goods are not connected in the course of trade with a person who is so entitled.

(3) A person commits an offence under subsection (1) or (2) only if-

(a) he acts with a view to gain for himself or another, or with intent to cause loss to another, and
(b) he intends that the goods in question should be accepted as connected in the course of trade with a person entitled to use the mark in question;

and it is a defence for a person charged with an offence under subsection (1) to show that he believed on reasonable grounds that he was entitled to use the mark in relation to the goods in question.

(4) A person guilty of an offence under this section is liable-

(a) on summary conviction to imprisonment for a term not exceeding six months or a fine not exceeding the statutory maximum, or both;
(b) on conviction on indictment to a fine or imprisonment for a term not exceeding ten years, or both.

(5) Where an offence under this section committed by a body corporate is proved to have been committed with the consent or connivance of a director, manager. secretary or other similar officer of the body, or a person purporting to act in any such capacity, he as well as the body corporate is guilty of the offence and liable to be proceeded against and punished accordingly.

In relation to a body corporate whose affairs are managed by its members 'director' means a member of the body corporate.

(6) In this section 'business' includes a trade or profession.'

1 (SI 1989/816).

20.10 However, during the debates and considerations of the Copyright, Designs and Patents Bill, later the CDPA 1988, very little, if any, consideration was given to s 300 of that Act. What is apparent is that this aspect of the Trade Marks Bill was never compared, likened or intended to achieve any obligations under the Directive since (1) the test for criminal liability ('identical to or likely to be mistaken for') is not worded, at least, in the same way as ss 10(1) and (2) of the TMA 1994 or art 5(a) and (b) of the Directive; (2) the protection required by the Directive had already been enacted via ss 9 and 10 of the TMA 1994[1] – it makes no sense for it to be enacted twice; (3) the criminal defence requires a state of mind – the civil defence (insofar as s 11 of the TMA 1994 and art 6 of the Directive are concerned) does not so require; (4) criminal liability attaches to a much wider class of activity relating to materials and articles for making copies of registered trade marks whereas the civil provisions via s 10 of the TMA 1994 and art 5 of the Directive are more limited in scope; (5) nowhere in s 10 of the TMA 1994 or art 5 of the Directive is there any requirement for motive.

1 Although that is not to say that it is or would be wrong for the Government to have placed Registered Trade Mark infringement (within the meaning of art 5(a) and (b) of the Directive) on a criminal footing. Whether it be criminal or civil is a matter for each state to decide unless specifically directed – see Cases C 58, 75, 112, 119, 123, 135, 140, 154 & 157/95) *Sandro Gallotti* [1997] I CMLR 32, 51 (paras 17 and 18).

20.11   We discuss the implications of the foregoing below in the correct context, however before leaving this part, we note that it is extremely unclear what it was that the government was trying to achieve when it enacted s 92 of the TMA 1994.

3   Criminal aspects of the law of trade marks

20.12   There are three main aspects of the law of trade marks which are covered by criminal law, that of the TMA 1994 itself, that of the allied provisions of the TDA 1968 and the common law crime of conspiracy to defraud. We cover each in turn.

The TMA 1994

20.13   The criminal provisions of the TMA 1994 are contained in ss 92 (unauthorised user of trade mark, &c in relation to goods) and 95 (falsely representing trade mark as registered), though s 94 (falsification of register, &c) also relates to criminal behaviour, this section and its predecessors are so seldom used, if at all, that we do not propose to cover them in this chapter.

20.14   Section 92 of the TMA 1994 (entitled 'Unauthorised use of trade mark, &c in relation to goods') is the main criminal provision and has a number of distinctive features. Section 92(1) of the TMA 1994 states:

> '92.–(1) A person commits an offence who with a view to gain for himself or another, or with intent to cause loss to another, and without the consent of the proprietor–
>
> (a) applies to goods or their packaging a sign identical to, or likely to be mistaken for, a registered trade mark, or
> (b) sells or lets for hire, offers or exposes for sale or hire or distributes goods which bear, or the packaging of which bears, such a sign, or
> (c) has in his possession, custody or control in the course of a business any such goods with a view to the doing of anything, by himself or another, which would be an offence under paragraph (b).'

The primary mental elements

20.15   As can be seen there are a number of important elements, all of which must be proved (either conjunctively or disjunctively as the case may be) in order to secure a conviction. The first stopping point is the consideration of the word 'view' in contrast to the word 'intent' in the operative part of sub-s (1). Clearly the word 'view' envisages that the wrongdoer need not actually make a gain in relation to his criminal behaviour but that he must act with that object in mind or that such an object is the object to be achieved. But the real question is whether the wrongdoer needs to intend that there be gain or whether on the objective facts the acts can be said to be with a view to gain. Many criminal lawyers equate intention with outcome in that a person must have intended a certain outcome if that outcome is the consequence of his actions. However not all actions have one outcome and some outcomes are more probable than others. Indeed some outcomes can be so remote as to be discountable.[1] The difficulty is where does one draw the line? In most cases it is clear where the intention lies but in relation to the law of trade marks there may be cases where one straddles, or finds oneself on the wrong side of but close to, such line as may exist. Where a person desires the consequences of his actions (so called, direct, intent) then the law will deem that person to have the relevant intent. However there have been cases where the outcome, no matter how probable, is not what the wrongdoer intended. Where the outcome is virtually a certain outcome of the acts of the wrongdoer then no matter how little he wanted that outcome to result he must still be taken as intending that outcome. This sort of intent is often referred to as 'indirect' or 'oblique' intent.

1 Indeed certain well-known and oft used pharmaceutical drugs cause devastating injury to a very small class of persons in the global community. That class is almost impossible to identify in advance of administration. A doctor administering those drugs to an individual in that class could hardly be said to have intended that his patient should suffer the effects of the drug simply because there was a minute risk that the drug would have adverse effects. Obviously the position maybe different if the doctor was negligent.

20.16   The cases, unfortunately have not all gone one way and in *Hyam v DPP*[1] the House of Lords suggested that oblique intent was to be looked at from a very broad perspective so that whilst it may be proved beyond doubt[2] by a defendant that he did not desire certain consequences, if the consequences were 'highly probable' or even just 'probable' or even 'likely,' then that was enough. So for instance, a person who drove a car at a shop window and who started his journey from two metres away, can and must have realised that it was an inevitable consequence of his actions that the window would be damaged. But what if that same person started his journey 200 metres away? Can he, at the time of the commencement of his journey, be said to have intended that the shop window be damaged since the probability that the shop window would be damaged is far more remote even though it could be one of many likely outcomes? The wide approach of the House of Lords was deprecated by the Court of Appeal in *R v Mohan*[3] and *R v Belfon*.[4] These criticisms did not go unheeded and the House of Lords in *R v Moloney*[5] set down some guiding principles being, first that the criminal law would not serve its objects unless there was a consistent meaning of intent throughout[6] and second that foreseeability of the probability of a certain outcome, whilst being *evidence* of intention does not of itself amount to intention. These rules are important because the court needs to be very careful in how it directs the tribunal of fact. In *R v Hancock*[7] the proposed direction in *R v Moloney*, being in essence that the tribunal of fact *could* infer but would not *have* to infer that a person intended a certain outcome if it were the *natural* consequence of his actions. Lord Scarman in *R v Hancock*[8] said that the rules set down in *R v Moloney*:

> '... require a reference to probability. They also require an explanation that the greater the probability of a consequence the more likely it is that the consequence was foreseen and that if that consequence was foreseen the greater the probability is that that consequence was also intended. But juries also require to be reminded that the decision is theirs to be reached upon a consideration of all the evidence.

The result seems to be that:

    (a) Where there is clear evidence that the accused wanted the consequence to occur, the question of whether the accused intended that consequence can be left to the jury without further elaboration.

    (b) Where the accused may not have wanted the consequence for its own sake but may have foreseen it as a by-product of his action, a more detailed direction may be necessary which emphasises that 'the probability, however high, of a consequence is only a factor, though it may in some cases be a very significant factor, to be considered with all the other evidence in determining whether the accused intended to bring it about.'

What Lord Scarman was saying of course, was that whilst there may be clear cases where intention might be readily inferred there might also be cases which are not so clear and the tribunal of law directing the tribunal of fact might have to fashion more detailed directions. Lord Scarman's analysis in *R v Hancock* suggests that it is really up to the tribunal of fact to decides but that analysis has not escaped criticism since it is of crucial importance for the directions on intention to be given properly otherwise an appeal may lie.

1 [1975] AC 55.
2 Not the standard to which the defendant needs to achieve.
3 [1976] QB 1.
4 [1976] 1 WLR 741.
5 [1985] AC 905.
6 *Per* Lord Bridge of Harwich in *R v Moloney* [1985] AC 905, 920. But also see the speech of Lord Steyn in *R v Woollin* [1999] AC 82.
7 [1986] AC 455.
8 [1986] AC 455, 473 and 474.

20.17   Obviously the foregoing has some impact on the meaning of the phrase 'with a view' as appears in the first part of s 92(1) of the TMA 1994 since there appears to no real distinction between the use of 'view' and 'intent' as appears later on in the sub-section. In many cases a wrongdoer is caught in the act of preparation, in that his premises are raided by the relevant enforcement authorities and he is caught red-handed, so to speak, with the tools of his wrongdoing. If adequate evidence is found which establishes that if the wrongdoer were to carry out his objects then he would undoubtedly make a gain for himself, then he is doing the prohibited acts with a view to a gain. Further, we also submit that in some cases it could be argued that the wrongdoer, because he is a bad businessman, would make no profit for himself at all though he would be caught acting with a view to a profit. The position of a person who acts charitably would however be different since there would be no view to gain, though he might be caught by the fact that the mental element is disjunctive so that a person is caught if he intends to cause loss to another, though he may have a defence if he were able to prove that (a) he was acting charitably and (b) had no intention to cause loss to another.[1]

1 We are not aware of any case where this argument has been run.

20.18   As to the requirement that proof is necessary in relation to one or other (or even both) of the disjunctive elements relating to state of mind, this is obviously necessary but is as likely to be inferred from the facts as it is to be the subject of direct proof.

20.19   It may also be said however that the use of the word 'view' as opposed to 'intent' was intended by parliament to be much wider in that such a view need not be the view or the intent of the defendant because he is caught up in a chain even if he acts charitably (which is unlikely but not impossible). Rather the acts of the defendant when taken together with the way in which the goods are ultimately dealt with by another (him having a view to a profit) amount to acts which are done with a view to making a profit. It is submitted that this is a very wide interpretation of the expression since it would catch an otherwise unwitting and hapless employee who, having no intention to deceive or commit any wrongdoing is still criminally liable because he acted with somebody else's view in mind. However perhaps interpreting the word 'view' so widely is not so oppressive since the innocent and hapless employee may have a defence by saying that he believed that he was not doing anything wrong[1] and of course if he did think he was committing some wrongdoing then he ought to be liable. We submit that this wider interpretation of the word 'view' is not to be preferred even though the words which follow, 'gain for himself or another' clearly widen its scope. Since there is a choice of a narrow or wide interpretation of a penal provision, then in the absence of specific words of width (there are none), one view could be that the provision must be construed narrowly. To state the manner of statutory construction thus is to state the doctrine in its widest form and such has never been the law. Rather the court will not allow an individual to be imperiled upon an ambiguity, which is known as 'the rule against doubtful penalisation' but many commentators have referred to this as the 'strict constructional approach' simply because that is the effect of the rule against doubtful penalisation, Maxwell on 'The Interpretation of Statutes' says:[2]

> 'The strict construction of penal statutes seems to manifest itself in four ways: in the requirement of express language for the creation of an offence; in interpreting strictly word setting out the elements of an offence; in requiring the fulfilment to the letter of statutory conditions precedent to the infliction of punishment; and in insisting on the strict observance of technical provisions concerning criminal procedure and jurisdiction.'

though this was deprecated by Bennion on 'Statutory Interpretation'[3] since he could see no reason why it should be restricted to criminal statutes or penal measures. However, in reality the rule against doubtful penalisation is really a rule for enabling the court to ascertain whether a penalty was intended rather then a rule for establishing the classes of act which fall within an otherwise clearly extant penal provision.

1 And thus would if such a belief was reasonable, have a complete defence under the TMA 1994, s 92(5).
2 12th Edn, 1969, pp 239 and 240.
3 3rd Edn, 1997, p 638.

Consent

20.20   Additionally, it is also the requirement that the consent of the proprietor be lacking. The question of consent has to be considered from two angles, that of the parallel importer who has to source his goods from the proprietor but from a different market, and that of the person who is otherwise criminally liable. Whilst the question of consent is vexed we have to address it since it forms a fundamental part of the element of the offence. We also observe that the question of consent has and can have no special meaning for the purposes of s 92 of the TMA 1994 and cannot be considered in any different way to the way in which consent is considered for the purposes of civil registered trade mark infringement. To say otherwise would mean that the proprietor may be able to give his consent for the purposes of civil trade mark infringement but not for the corresponding crime or vice versa which would make a nonsense of the TMA 1994. Secondly, if parliament intended that something different should be meant then it would surely have used a different expression. However, in saying this we do not intend it to be the last word on the subject since there is the very vexed question of whether s 92 of the TMA 1994 derives its authority or existence from the Directive or from the domestic intention of Parliament. The context of this vexed question derives from the question as to whether or not, by the inclusion of an element of consent, s 92 of the TMA 1994 is a consumer protection measure or is no more than the sharp end of registered trade mark infringement. The relevance of and the answer to this question is vital and we shall consider it further later on in this chapter, as indeed we have considered it elsewhere in this book.

20.21   Also, as consent, or lack thereof, appears in the operative part of s 92 of the TMA 1994 it is uncertain whether this is a matter which has to be proved by the prosecution or the defence. Certainly it is arguable either way as to whether the burden is on the prosecution to prove lack of consent or upon the defendant to prove consent, lack of consent being on one view, rebuttably presumed. In the magistrates' courts the position is regulated by s 101 of the Magistrates' Courts Act 1980 ('MCA 1980') which states:

> '101. Where the defendant to an information relies for his defence on any exception, exemption, proviso, excuse or qualification, whether or not it accompanies the description of the offence or matter of complaint in the enactment creating the offence or on which the complaint is founded, the burden of proving the exception, exemption, proviso, excuse or qualification shall be on him; and this notwithstanding that the information or complaint contains an allegation negativing the exception, exemption, proviso, excuse or qualification.'

whereas there is no corresponding provision in relation to proceedings upon indictment. In *R v Edwards*[1] the Court of Appeal held that the exception was:

> '... limited to offences arising under enactments which prohibit the doing of an act save in specified circumstances or by persons of specified classes or with specified qualifications or with the licence or permission of specified authorities.'

1 [1975] QB 27; (1974) 59 Cr App R 213, CA.

20.22   In *R v Hunt*[1] the House of Lords considered what the Court of Appeal had said in *R v Edwards* and held that there was no rule which placed the burden of proving a statutory defence upon the defendant – each statutory provision must be read in accordance with its language, using established principles of statutory construction, though the court would be reluctant to place the burden of proving innocence on the defendant since that would break the 'golden strand' which pervades the conduct of criminal trials in this county, that the prosecution must prove that the defendant is guilty and not that the defendant has to prove he is innocent,[1] though even then statute may override this. In *R v Hunt* Lord Griffiths said:

'I have little doubt that the occasions on which a statute will be construed as imposing a burden of proof upon a defendant which do not fall into this formulation [as enunciated in *R v Edwards*] are likely to be rare. But I would find it difficult to fit *Nimmo v Alexander Cowan & Sons Ltd* [1968] AC 107 into this formula, and I would prefer to adopt the formula as an excellent guide to construction rather than as an exception to a rule. In the final analysis each case must turn on the construction of the particular piece of legislation to determine whether the defence is an exception within the meaning of section 101 [MCA] ... which the Court of Appeal rightly decided reflects the rule for trials on indictment. With this one qualification I regard *R v Edwards* as rightly decided.'

1 [1987] AC 352.
2 *Woolmington v DPP* [1935] AC 462 HL.
3 At 375 and 376.

20.23   It should be remembered that even though a legal burden might fall upon the defendant he only has to prove his case to the civil standard, on the balance of probabilities.[1]

1 *R v Ewing* [1983] QB 1039.

20.24   In *John v Humphreys*[1] a case turning on whether a government department had issued a vehicle licence to the defendant, the House of Lords held that the person best able to answer such a question as to whether there had or had not been a licence issued to the defendant was the defendant itself. However that is not to say that in trade mark cases the issue of consent falls to be proved in the same way. Very often consent can exist even though the defendant does not know about it, such as by way of estoppel or where there is an evidential presumption of consent or where consent *must* be given on the grounds of competition policy and since it has already been suggested that the issue of consent is the same in relation to civil and criminal matters, all of the usual arguments relating to consent may be deployed by the parties. Accordingly the case of *John v Humphreys* is really nothing to the point since in that case it was much easier for the defendant to prove that he had received a piece of paper, being in that case a certain type of vehicle licence, from the relevant government agency than it was for the relevant government agency to prove that it had granted the relevant licence and sent it.

1 [1955] 1 WLR 325.

Parallel imports

20.25   Our current law is uncertain in the light of *Silhouette International Schmied GmbH & Co KG v Hartlauer Handelsgesellschaft mbH*[1] where the ECJ held that there was no longer (if ever there was) a doctrine of international exhaustion of rights. The position has hardly been relieved by subsequent cases in the ECJ, such as *Sebago Inc and Aincienne Maison Dubois et Fils SA v BG-UNIC SA*.[2]

1 Case C-355/96, [1999] Ch 77.
2 [1999] ETMR 467.

20.26   Since the handing down of the judgment of the ECJ in the *Silhouette* case[1] and up until recently the attitude of the courts to the question of consent has been equivocal – perhaps because the question has never really arisen in a serious context. That it is a very live issue is beyond doubt, as the Advocate-General in the *Silhouette* case observed:[2]

'It should also be assumed for present purposes that Silhouette did not consent to its products being resold within the EEA. That is so even though the national court expresses some doubt as to whether the restrictions upon resale were passed on to the purchaser. If Silhouette had consented to marketing in the EEA, the answer to the first question referred would clearly be that Silhouette could not oppose the import of its products into Austria.'

Which we submit leaves the whole question of consent open and if there is an evidential presumption under national law which implies consent unless expressly negatived, then such will not detract from the requirements of Community law. It is well established that evidential presumptions are a matter of national law.[3] This argument supposes that the evidential presumption is that a trade mark proprietor is presumed to have consented to the importation of goods bearing his mark in the absence of an express export ban. The existence of the presumption under national law is supported by ample authority[4] though its existence appears to be denied by a wide range of commentators, not all of whom are best qualified to judge the issue. Such presumptions are, as a matter of European Law, invalid only if (1) better treatment is accorded to domestic nationals than may be accorded to nationals from fellow member states or (2) if it makes the working of the European Measure concerned (in this case the directive and the TMA 1994) unworkable. As a matter of common sense neither happens since there is nothing discriminatory and the presumption of consent does not make the trade mark laws unworkable, it merely places a relatively light burden on the trade mark proprietor to impose an export ban.

1 Case C-355/96, [1998] FSR 729.
2 [1998] FSR 474 at 482 line 27.
3 Case 199/82 *Amministrazione delle Finanze v San Giorgio* [1983] ECR 3595.
4 *Revlon Inc v Cripps and Lee Ltd* [1980] FSR 85, CA, *Roussel Uclaf v Hockley International Ltd* [1996] RPC 441 and *Colgate-Palmolive Ltd v Markwell Finance Ltd and Bak* [1989] RPC 497, CA.

20.27 Furthermore, in the light of the most recent authority on the subject, *Zino Davidoff SA v A & G Imports Ltd*[1] the question of consent is a real one to be considered on each set of facts. In *Zino Davidoff* the claimant, Davidoff, made perfumes under the name 'Cool Water' and owned certain trade marks. The defendant, A&G Imports Ltd, was engaged in the business of parallel importation of the claimant's perfumes and the claimant sued for registered trade mark infringement. The claimant applied for summary judgment conceding that there was no difference in quality but that the defendant was taking advantage of a price differential because of the way that the claimant divided up its markets. It was also accepted that some of the perfume had been imported from outside the European Economic Area (EEA) and that certain identification information had been removed which paved the way for the claimant to say that it had a right to object to further sales of the goods which were in the defendant's hands. The defendant primarily argued that it had the consent of the claimant. The judge found that the goods were placed on the market by the defendant in circumstances where the claimant could have taken action to stop such importation but did not do so and that the claimant's distributors appeared to be able to sell where they pleased. The judge said that the principle of exhaustion of rights applied as much to trade marks as it did to other intellectual property rights but Member States could not introduce a principle of international exhaustion for trade marks under their domestic law. We submit that to confuse the question of implied consent with the doctrine of international exhaustion of rights (which, if it exists would say that a trade mark owner's rights only extend so far as affixation, related activities and first marketing) is to fall into fundamental error. Accordingly trade mark proprietors could not object to the circulation of goods in the EEA being parallel imports if they had agreed to such circulation, or had arranged their distribution chains in such a way as to allow those distributors to sell where they pleased which was really no more than a matter of contractual construction. The judge then said that the law included a rebuttable presumption that, in the absence of a proper export ban or other effective restrictions being 'brought home' at the time of purchase, consent was to be implied. In this regard the cases of *Revlon Inc v Cripps and Lee Ltd*[2] and *Colgate-Palmolive Ltd v Markwell Finance Ltd*[3] were said to be good law, this despite the fact that since *Silhouette International Schmied GmbH & Co KG v Hartlauer Handelsgesellschaft mbH*[4] most thought that they were overridden, at least in terms of registered trade marks by the Directive. However, in *Betts v Willmott*[5] as approved of and applied in *National Phonograph Co of Australia Ltd v Walter T Menck*[6] and *Roussel Uclaf v Hockley International Ltd*[7] it was said that restrictions on further sale must be 'brought home' to the purchaser at the time of sale, though even if such were brought home at the time of sale it still might be regarded as an anti-competitive practice[8] and be disallowed.

1 [1999] RPC 631.
2 [1980] FSR 85.
3 [1989] RPC 497.
4 Case C-355/96, [1999[Ch 77.
6 [1911] AC 336.
7 [1996] RPC 441.
8 Either from a European or domestic perspective.

20.28   Further in *Zino Davidoff SA v A & G Imports Ltd*[1] the claimant did not have legitimate reasons for opposing the further sales of their perfume purchased outside the EEA and sold within the EEA. The mere removal of batch numbers (as happened) might make it difficult for the products to be recalled but, as the judge rightly observed, this had no effect upon the *quality* of the goods themselves. As a result the objection based upon impairment of quality was a bad one.

1 [1999] RPC 631.

20.29   Thus a parallel importer might have a real defence if he can show that he is able to come within the reasoning of Laddie J in the *Zino Davidoff*[1] case. That said, we ought to sound a note of caution. The decision in *Zino Davidoff* was on an application for summary judgment, necessarily interlocutory and is unsupported by any post-Directive authority. However, Laddie J is not known for his mistakes and, we submit, the Court of Appeal would be slow to interfere but, rather, would be more willing to refer the question to the ECJ. As at the date of writing the court in *Zino Davidoff* has referred the question to the ECJ and the parties are in the process of formulating questions.

We leave this part of this chapter by observing that a parallel importer is completely immune from prosecution if he sources his goods from within the EEA and they have initially been placed on the market in the EEA by the proprietor or with his consent, provided that there exist no legitimate reasons to oppose further dealing. That much is clear from s 12 of the TMA 1994.

1 [1999] RPC 631.

Cases not involving parallel imports

20.30 In most cases the wrongdoer is not a parallel importer at all, which is really a special case, but is alleged to be selling counterfeit goods. Obviously if he can show that he had the consent of the proprietor in relation to the goods, articles or materials in question then he has a defence, but (save for the defences which we discuss below) this is unlikely to occur in reality. The real question, which we posed above, is who has to prove it. The question is made the more complex by the fact that in many cases the wrongdoer will claim that he purchased his goods from a legitimate source – being the proprietor's licensee, the licensee overrun cases. We submit that it must be the prosecutor since if it were up to the defence to prove, there would be no requirement of proving objective reasons for believing in the existence of consent for the purposes of s 92(5) of the TMA 1994, which provides for the purposes of this section that a defendant has a defence if he is able to prove that he believed on reasonable grounds that he was not infringing the trade mark in question which is a defence open to the wrongdoer. Further it would be inconsistent with the provision of the defence in s 92(5) if there was one state of mind in s 92(5) of the TMA 1994, belief on reasonable grounds that there was consent, and another in s 92(1) of the TMA 1994, whether there is or was consent, no matter whether the wrongdoer believed it or not. Indeed this has recently been confirmed in the unreported case of *Torbay Council v Singh*[1] where Auld LJ said:

> 'In my view, the offence is made out if the prosecution prove:
>
> 1) the fact of registration of a trade mark to which a sign on goods which the defendant exposes for sale is identical or for which it is likely to be mistaken;
> 2) that he does so with view to gain for himself or another or with intent to cause loss to another; and
> 3) [he does so] without the consent of the proprietor.
>
> It is not necessary to prove knowledge of or intent to infringe a registered trade mark.'

1 (1999) 163 JP 744.

The actus reus

20.31 The acts which constitute the crime are set out in s 92(1)(a), (b) and (b) of the TMA 1994, being:

> '(a) applying to goods or their packaging a sign identical to, or likely to be mistaken for, a registered trade mark, or
> (b) selling, letting for hire, offering or exposing for sale or hire or distribution goods which bear, or the packaging of which bears, a sign identical to, or likely to be mistaken for, a registered trade mark, or
> (c) possessing or having in one's custody or control in the course of a business any goods with a view (either by himself or another) to selling them, letting them for hire, offering or exposing them for sale or hire or distribution which bear, or the packaging of which bears, a sign identical to, or likely to be mistaken for, a registered trade mark.'

20.32   As can be seen, mere possession without more is not caught. This is probably because the purpose of s 92 of the TMA 1994 is not to punish or deter the innocent individual purchaser but rather to punish and deter the dealers and markers. Hence the prosecution must prove that as far as possession is concerned this has to be done in the course of a business and with a view to the ultimate disposal of goods and as far as application is concerned that it was done with a view to gain or intention to cause loss to another.[1]

The three main disjunctive ingredients are therefore application, disposal and possession in the course of a business.

1 So it is doubted whether say, an art student,who printed on a t-shirt, which he alone intended to wear, a registered trade mark, would be caught by the section. If he were to sell his t-shirt then that might be another matter (though the trade mark registration would have to cover t-shirts).

20.33   However, insofar as the acts of disposal are concerned, there does not appear to be any restriction that such disposition must be in the course of a business. So an innocent purchaser who sells goods on would be caught even if it was a one-off transaction.[1]. Whilst we submit that this is unfair it clearly *is* the law since there does not appear to be any ambiguity in the construction of s 92(1)(b) of the TMA 1994.

1 Though it is unlikely that a prosecutor would prosecute on this basis since one factor which he must consider is whether the prosecution is in the public interest. It is unlikely that it would be in the public interest to prosecute a person who purchased one counterfeit item in good faith and, when he no longer wished to use that item, sold it on.

20.34   The course of business, for the purpose of s 92(1)(c) of the TMA 1994 must be the course of business that the possessor practices as opposed to the fact that *generally* he is acting in the course of his business. The distinction is important since it catches the person who is in the business of selling the goods concerned as opposed to the person whose business sells the goods concerned. This may arise where a business purchases an asset such as a computer which is counterfeit and then, some time later, because the computer is obsolete, it is sold on. In *Davies v Sumner*[1] (affirmed on appeal[2]) the defendant was charged as follows: that in the course of a trade or business he applied to a motor car a false trade description to the effect that the car had travelled a lower mileage than was in fact the case (the disparity being about 100,000 miles). The defendant was self-employed and worked as a courier. The car had become clocked because the odometer, which was a five figure odometer had travelled around the clock and the defendant knew that fact but did not disclose it. The defendant was convicted at first instance and he appealed. The Divisional Court held that since the sale of cars was not part of his normal business activities the sale was not in the course of a business, Forbes J, with whom the other member of the court agreed, said:[3]

> 'The justices, having had *Havering London Borough v Stevenson* [1970] 1 WLR 1375 drawn to their attention, have asked themselves the question, "Was the use of the car an integral part of the business?" and not, "Was the sale of the car an integral part of the business?"'

On appeal by the prosecutor to the House of Lords Lord Keith of Kinkel said:[4]

> 'The vital feature of the *Havering* case … [was] that the defendant's business, *as part of its normal practice*, bought and disposed of cars …

'In the present case it was sought to be inferred that the ... [defendant], covering as he did such a large regular mileage, was likely to have occasion to sell his car at regular intervals, so that he too would have a normal practice of buying and disposing of cars. But such a normal practice had not been established at the time of the alleged offence. The ... [defendant] might well revert to hiring a car, as he had previously done. Further, the ... [defendant's] car was a piece of equipment he used for providing his courier service. It was not something he exploited as stock in trade, which was what the defendant was in substance doing with his cars in the *Havering* case ... Where a person carried on the business of hiring out some description of goods to the public and had a practice of selling off those that were no longer in good enough condition, clearly the latter goods were offered or supplied in the course of his business within the meaning of s 1(1) of the [Trade Descriptions Act 1968] Act. But the occasional sale of some worn out piece of shop equipment would not fall within the enactment.'

1 [1984] 1 WLR 405; (1984) 148 JP 134, QBD.
2 [1984] 3 All ER 831; [1984] 1 WLR 1301, HL.
3 [1984] 1 WLR 405, 410, paras D–E.
4 [1984] 1 WLR 1301, 1305, para G.

The TMA 1994, s 92(1)(a) – application per se

20.35 As we have already observed it is essential to prove application and it must be done with a view to gain by the affixer with the intention to cause loss to another without consent. It is important to note that application need not be done in the course of a business – any type of application will do. However, though affixation is mentioned in s 10(4) of the TMA 1994, it is likely that application and what it constitutes is more properly to be considered in the same way that it is considered for the purposes of s 1(1)(a) of the TDA 1968. However this is only possibly true since the said s 1(1)(a) is augmented by s 4 of the TDA 1968 which sets out what amounts to application, whereas there is no such supplementary section for the purposes of the TMA 1994. It is submitted therefore that the ambit of application and what it constitutes must be construed narrowly, especially in the light of s 92(2) and (3) of the TMA 1994 since it appears to deal with other types of use.

20.36 Does the ambit of s 92(1)(a) of the TMA 1994 cover application where the mark affixed is permanent or temporary, or where the potential purchaser of the goods does not see the trade mark in question at the time of purchase? This question must be answered in the affirmative since the application in question must be of an identical mark or one which is likely to be mistaken for it. Given that the deception concerned (though the word 'mistake' is used) is an additional requirement, the act of mere application of an identical mark, irrespective of whether it is seen by the potential purchaser, falls within the ambit of s 92(1)(a) of the TMA 1994. Similarly it does not appear to matter that the application was temporary, that too on a literal reading of the paragraph is enough to be caught. However, as we shall see, though it does appear to be unarguable that such temporary or latent use is caught by para (a), if the section is so construed, there is a real danger of the section falling foul of the provisions and scheme of the Directive. We shall discuss this further below.

The TMA 1994, s 92(1)(a) – application to goods or their packaging

20.37   In relation to the act of application, it is relatively clear that this application must be to the goods in question or their packaging. It is in this context that application is to be distinguished from use which forms one of the essential elements for the purposes of s 10 of the TMA 1994. However, and lamentably, there is no definition of what is meant by 'application'. Would a person who used the mark in relation to the goods be caught even if the actual goods bore no mark? It cannot be doubted that such use is just as damaging and insidious yet para (a) does not appear to admit it. In other words is the word 'apply' to be construed as meaning to put on the goods or is it to be construed in much the same way that 'use' is defined in s 10(4) of the TMA 1994? Again, if Parliament had intended the words to have the same meaning then it would have used the same words. Unfortunately, s 103(2) of the TMA 1994, which states:

> 'References in this Act to use (or any particular description of use) of a trade mark, or of a sign identical with, similar to, or likely to be mistaken for a trade mark, include use (or that description of use) otherwise than by means of a graphic representation.'

does not appear to clarify the matter since that sub-section simply says that application other than by means of graphic representation is deemed as being application, it does not say what the scope of the word is. It is contradictory to say that one can apply a mark in a manner other than graphically since the word 'apply' has a very specific meaning. It is also the case that s 103(2) does not really deal with the case where there is graphic representation but only in relation to the goods and not by means of affixation since s 92(1)(a) of the TMA 1994 speaks of application of the mark to the goods.

20.38   The apparently narrow scope of s 92(1)(a) of the TMA 1994 and the fact that by reason of such narrow scope there are classes of activity which, though equally deceptive are not included within the scope of the *actus reus*, tends to imply that it is not the consumer who is sought to be protected but rather the trade mark proprietor. Even then, it is odd that the scope of s 92(1)(a) is so narrow since the trade mark proprietor is equally at peril by reason of proximate use as opposed to the application of the mark to the goods or its packaging. Furthermore, if it is accepted that s 92 of the TMA 1994 is a consumer protection measure[1] then the use should surely be such use as leads a consumer to be deceived – this will be a recurring theme in this chapter.[2] As we have noted, the absence of any element of confusion (which can on one view be just as damaging to the consumer) would tend to imply that the section is protective of the trade mark owners.

1   Though whether it *is* such a measure is one which we seriously doubt and debate below.
2   For which we make apology but the underlying point seems to justify it.

The TMA 1994, s 92(1)(a) – identical to or likely to be mistaken for

20.39   The identicality of the applied mark with the depiction in the trade mark registration is clearly going to cause deception. Also the fact that the consumer is mistaken would strongly imply that the test for liability under para (a) is deception, in one form or another. However, that conclusion would tend to suggest that in the absence of deception confusion is not enough since a person who makes a mistake as to a representation believes (wrongly) the truth of the representation being made, it does not appear to suggest that where a consumer is merely uncertain as to what he is buying there is liability under the paragraph.

The TMA 1994, s 92(1)(b) and (c) – disposal and keeping for disposal

20.40   If s 92(1)(a) of the TMA 1994 were to exist in isolation, the criminal provisions of the TMA 1994 would have little teeth since it is quite clear that counterfeiters organise themselves into distribution chains. Indeed it is the distribution of counterfeit products which causes the real damage to the trade mark owner and the consumer because they are deceived by the application of the mark onto the goods or their packaging by reason of identicality or consumer mistake. The words 'sells or lets for hire, offers or exposes for sale or hire or distributes' are standard terminology and are employed to cover not only dispositions by way of sale but also the invitation to treat and most other forms of disposition. However, what is apparent is that it is the disposition (or related activity) in relation to the goods which bear the identical mark, or one likely to be mistaken for it, that is caught by the paragraphs. Specifically, advertising such goods in relation to the marks in question is not caught by the paragraphs, though as we shall see, this is dealt with elsewhere in   s 92 of the TMA 1994.

The TMA 1994, s 92(2) – advertising and associated activities

20.41   Clearly s 92(1) of the TMA 1994 taken on its own would not stop advertising or selling in relation to the mark in question. The problems we posed in relation to sub-s (1) are dealt with in sub-s (2) which essentially prohibits the use of 'material' intended to be used for labelling, as a business paper and advertising. The distinction between 'goods' on the one hand and 'material' on the other is dealt with in s 17 of the TMA 1994 and though not exhaustively defined, tends to relate to things like posters, flyers and stickers or labels.

The TMA 1994, s 92(3) – the tools of deception

20.42   Sub-section (3) is the only part of s 92 which requires an extra element of knowledge on the part of the wrongdoer. This sub-section deals with the situation where a person makes or has in his possession an article which can be used for applying a mark, though that article must be specifically designed or adapted for making copies of the sign which is identical to or likely to be mistaken for a registered trade mark. It is suspected that the extra requirement of knowledge is there because a person who makes or keeps an 'article' of deception is sufficiently far removed from the consumer that mere possession on its own is not likely to cause deception.

20.43   However, it is worth posing the question as to what is meant by an article which is designed or specifically adapted to copy a registered trade mark. For instance this would probably include a mould or a stamping machine which contained a specific dye. However,r in the case where the dye could be removed, there is more doubt as to whether the stamping machine would fall within the sub-section since the fact that the dye could be removed would imply that the stamping machine was not specifically designed (by the designer) or adapted (by the adaptor)

with the object of deception in mind, it being apparent that something more permanent is required. This is especially the case where facilitating machinery is made
available, such as a programmable embroidering machine though it has no dedi-
cated embroidering function. The issue of whether such machinery can be said to
be specifically designed to copy registered trade marks is one that the House of
Lords looked at in *CBS Songs Ltd v Amstrad Consumer Electronics plc*[1] where the
defendant provided reel-to-reel tape recorders which *could* be used to infringe
rights in the nature of copyright. Lord Templeman said:[2]

> 'My Lords, I accept that a defendant who procures a[n] ... [infringement] of copyright
> is liable jointly and severally with the infringer for the damages suffered by the plain-
> tiff as a result of the infringement. The defendant is a joint infringer; he intends and
> procures and shares a common design that infringement shall take place. A defendant
> may procure an infringement by inducement, incitement or persuasion. But in the pre-
> sent case Amstrad do not procure infringement by offering for sale a machine which
> may be used for lawful or unlawful copying and they do not procure infringement by
> advertising the attractions of their machine to any purchaser who may decide to copy
> unlawfully. Amstrad are not concerned to procure and cannot procure unlawful copy-
> ing. The purchaser will not make unlawful copies because he has been induced or
> incited or persuaded to do so by Amstrad. The purchaser will make unlawful copies
> for his own use because he chooses to do so. Amstrad's advertisements may persuade
> the purchaser to buy an Amstrad machine but will not influence the purchaser's later
> decision to infringe copyright. Buckley LJ observed in *Belegging-en
> Exploitatiemaatschappij Lavender BV v Witten Industrial Diamonds Ltd* [1979]
> FSR 59, CA, at p 65, that "Facilitating the doing of an act is obviously different from
> procuring the doing of the act."'

1 [1988] AC 1013.
2 At 1207.

20.44 This raises the question as to whether programmable machinery is capable
of being an article specifically designed or adapted to copy registered trade marks.
We submit not. However, often such machines are digitally programmable by
means of a CD-ROM or floppy disk. In relation to a CD-ROM, the information is
etched on that medium in permanent (or semi-permanent) form so it could be said
that the CD-ROM is an article which is specifically adapted to make copies of the
registered trade mark in question. However it is also apparent that a floppy disk
which contains information which can be erased or changed is not specifically
adapted to perform a single function of providing information to an embroidering
machine or printer. However, as is obvious, this distinction is one without a difference since the evil is the same.

Inchoate and auxiliary offences

20.45 Our comments so far have concentrated upon the primary wrongdoer, that
is the person who actually does the acts concerned. Yet to restrict the scope of s 92
would be to allow a large number of persons who were at least as responsible to
escape liability. For this reason, as part of our general law, a person who, in general
terms, is somehow involved in the commission of a crime, is himself liable. So to is
the person who attempts to commit a crime. Furthermore, it is very often so in
counterfeiting cases that the wrongdoer will be caught in some sort of preparatory
act as opposed to carrying out the acts themselves.

20.46 In the context of s 92 of the TMA, we pose a scenario where counterfeit goods are made. A sold them, B made them and supplied them to A. A is directly responsible under s 92(1)(b) of the TMA 1994 for the supply to the public. B is directly responsible under s 92(1)(b) of the TMA 1994 for the supply to A and also under s 92(1)(a) for applying the mark to the goods. A and B are also probably liable under s 92(1)(c). However the question to be posed is to what extent is B responsible for the acts of A (whatever the independent position might be). B is also liable in the eyes of the criminal law since B has assisted and provided help in aid of the commission of a crime.

Aiding, abetting, counselling and procuring

20.47 Section 8 of The Accessories and Abettors Act 1861 ('AAA 1861') (as amended by the Criminal Law Act 1977 ('CLA 1977')) states:

> 'whosoever shall aid, abet, counsel or procure the commission of any indictable offence shall be liable to be tried, indicted and punished as a principal defendant.'

And s 1 of the Criminal Law Act 1967 ('CLA 1967') abolished the distinction between misdemeanours and felonies so that any criminal conduct whether indictable or triable on a summary basis is covered by s 8 of the AAA 1861.

20.48 Before 1967, the courts distinguished between principals. There was a first degree principal – the most immediate cause of the *actus reus* and who was the person who did the crime. Then there was the second degree principal who was somebody who helpe (ie supplied the counterfeit goods). The CLA 1967 abolished the distinction between the first and second degree, although subsequent cases still talk about first and second degree principals, and they do not, strictly speaking, exist.

20.49 The principal is a person who is directly responsible for the *actus reus*. This can be an individual or more than one person in which case they are *jointly* liable as principals; anybody more remote will not qualify. So that (to take an extreme example somewhat divorced from the law of trade marks) where A and B shoot C and it is not known who exactly killed C then A and B can be joint principals. A secondary party may however aid, abet, counsel or procure that act.

20.50 In *A-G's Reference (No 1 of 1975)*[1] the Court of Appeal looked at the issue of secondary parties and joint principals. D laced V's drinks and he drove home in contravention of s 56(1) of the Road Traffic Act 1972 (as was then in force) and was stopped by the police and charged with drunk driving. D was charged with aiding and abetting, counselling and procuring the commission of an offence within s 8 of the AAA 1861. D was initially acquitted on a motion of no case to answer because the trial court held there was no common intention. There was said to be no liability for the generous host at a party who supplies such drink, as there has been no surreptitious behaviour on the part of the host and no attempt on his part to procure the offence, even though he may know that if V takes any drink he will be breaking the law and since V knows this too and has a choice but the prosecution in this case argued that V did not have a choice and D knew V would drive home.

1 [1975] QB 773

20.51   The Court of Appeal approached s 8 of the AAA 1861 on the basis that the words should be given an ordinary meaning if possible and that if four words were employed then there should be a difference between them. If there was no such difference, the draftsman had wasted his time. The current view is that 'aid and abet' are words used in tandem but that 'counsel and procure' do have different meanings from each other as illustrated below.

20.52   A person who aids and abets another is therefore a secondary party and is usually a person who is present, assisting or encouraging the principal at the time of the offence. What is key is that assistance must be given at the time of the offence so that mere facilitating may not be enough. The person must be present in performance or as a result of an agreement that the crime will be committed. This person is still liable because he is helping and encouraging a commission. For instance in *R v Coney*[1] an illegal prize fight took place and the question arose as to whether the spectators were aiding and abetting the fight. The Court of Appeal said that proof of voluntary presence is prima facie evidence of aiding and abetting the battery in which the contestants were partaking. However in *R v Allan*[2] D was convicted of making an affray (which was a fight between two or more people likely to cause upset to local residents). The Court of Appeal held that somebody who remains present at an affray with the secret intention to help but does nothing does not become thereby become an abettor and that therefore, before conviction, the jury should be given evidence of encouragement to the participants by the secondary participants. Accordingly, encouragement is a minimal requirement before an accused person may properly be regarded as a principal in the second degree, though the temporal proximity between the encouragement and the criminal act is really a matter of fact and degree.

1 (1882) 8 QBD 534.
2 [1965] 1 QB 130.

20.53   In *Clarkson v Carroll*[1] some soldiers remained in a room where a crime was being committed. Those soldiers were charged with aiding and abetting the crime. They were convicted. The Court of Appeal held that the soldiers were not liable for aiding and abetting since they could not simply be guilty by the fact that they were in continuing non-accidental presence. However in *Du Cros v Lambourne*[2] D's car was driven at a dangerous speed. There was uncertainty as to whether D or E was driving but the car belonged to D and so D could be convicted because even if E had been driving, he was doing so in D's presence with his approval and D should have stopped E. The situation would be different if the car had been owned by E as D would have no right of control over the car. However, none of the cited cases seem to suggest that there is any necessity for a common purpose.

1 [1971] 1 WLR 1402.
2 [1907] 1 KB 40.

20.54   The House of Lords for Northern Ireland in *DPP for Northern Ireland v Lynch*[1] considered this question. D was forced to drive a car to a location where the passengers got out and committed a murder. D knew of this but took no part in the murder itself. The House of Lords said that D could still be a secondary principal and that there was no need for a common purpose for a person to be liable for aiding and abetting.

1 [1975] AC 653.

20.55 Furthermore, it is not necessary to have to agree with what is going on for there to be aiding and abetting, thus a person driving primary participants to the scene of a crime and keeping watch are all aiding and abetting.

Whilst the problem with aiding and abetting depends to a certain extent upon the proximity of the wrongdoer to the crime being committed, counselling and procuring is more distinct, hence the need to take them separately.

20.56 Somebody who before the commission of a crime conspires to commit it, endorses its commission or knowingly gives assistance to one of the principals, is said to counsel another on the commission of that crime. Counselling actually takes place before the crime itself. In *R v Taylor*,[1] A and B had an argument and agreed to fight it out. They each deposited £1 with a stakeholder, D and the winner was to take the total of quantum in winnings. They fought and A was fatally injured and D paid out to B, not knowing of A's fate. It was held that D was not liable because he had paid over the stake not knowing of A's death. This was a collateral transaction.

1 (1875) LR 2 CCR 147.

20.57 In *R v Fretwell*[1] the Court of Appeal heard that D had counselled Z to murder V, D and V being rivals. Z killed V and pleaded guilty and turned Queen's evidence. Z's position was that he had in fact decided not to murder V but for some reason went mad and killed her nonetheless. Accordingly, though V was killed it was not as a result of the plan. The appeal was pursued on the grounds that the judge had not put the defence to the jury that the plan never came about. Counselling required a causal connection and, it was argued, that there was no such connection here. The Court of Appeal held that 'counsel' had no requirement of causal connection with the offence ultimately committed and did not imply commission of an offence accordingly, the offence of counselling was established and the appeal dismissed.

1 (1862) 26 JP 499.

20.58 Likewise, procuring the commission of a crime has received some attention from the Court of Appeal. In *R v Reed*,[1] D belonged to a group which helped people to commit suicide. D was convicted of conspiring to aid and abet a suicide. The Court of Appeal looked at the meaning of procure and held that the definition of procure was the same as in *A-G's Reference (No 1 of 1975)*[2] that one is liable if one produces a result by endeavour, ie setting out to see that an event happens and taking appropriate steps to produce that result.

1 [1982] Crim LR 819.
2 [1975] QB 773.

20.59 What is odd, however, is that whilst there is a limited requirement of a state of mind for a person to be primarily liable within the meaning of s 92 of the TMA 1994 in order to be an accessory or secondary actor it must be that the secondary party has some idea of what he is getting involved in. This would tend to imply that a wholly different set of rules relating to state of mind is required in order to prove that a secondary party is liable for aiding, abetting, counselling or procuring. The question is, how much does such a party have to know before there is the requisite state of mind? In *Johnson v Youden*,[1] it was held by the Court of Appeal that before a person can be convicted for aiding and abetting an offence, he must be shown to know of the essential matters which constitute the offence and the circumstances.

1 [1950] 1 KB 544.

20.60   To illustrate, say A supplies some safe-breaking equipment to B, knowing that B is going to use that equipment in the commission of a crime but that the equipment is used for murder instead, can A claim lack of knowledge? Further, say A simply sells metal-cutting equipment from a hardware shop and has no idea what B is up to, A cannot be liable for B's acts. In *R v Bainbridge*[1] D (as case in point) bought oxygen-cutting equipment for another knowing that it was going to be used in the commission of a crime. It was indeed later used in the commission of a crime and D claimed that though he did know that the cutting equipment was to be used for the commission of a crime he did not know which one. The Court of Appeal held that it was essential that D knew the type of crime, but beyond that, the specific details did not have to be within the knowledge of D, the details are not necessary for guilt to be inferred. Similarly in *DPP for Northern Ireland v Maxwell*[2] D was a member of a proscribed organisation. D was told to drive past a pub in the country which he did. The car in front of him was driven by a bomber who threw a bomb into the pub. D was charged under the Explosive Substances Act 1883 with the intent to cause explosions, and possession of a bomb as a secondary party. D was convicted and appealed claiming that he had no idea why he was being asked to do what he did. D was in fact an officer of the organisation and thought that by going to the pub he might be partaking in a welfare evening. The House of Lords said that a person is guilty if he contemplated the commission of one of a limited number of crimes by the principal and intentionally lent him assistance and that D must have known that he was included in a terrorist attack and cannot have thought that the evening was a welfare evening – though this decision has not been blessed by favourable comment since it is not easy to decide whether one crime is the same as another. Say for instance D thought that the purpose of the visit had been to intimidate the pub's customers by going into the pub and proclaiming the terrorist cause then it cannot be said that D was involved in any acts involving endangering life and would not (or should not) be liable. The position would obviously be different where D thought that the customers were going to be shot at but were in fact bombed. *DPP for Northern Ireland v Maxwell* appears to be too wide or perhaps uncertain on this point but the law as currently stated comes down to whether the secondary party 'knew the principal would probably commit' the crime actually committed.

1 [1960] 1 QB 129.
2 [1978] NI 42.

20.61   However (and of much more relevance in the trade marks context), what is the situation where A accepts secondary liability for crime C1 but crime C2 is in fact committed where C2 exceeds C1? In the trade marks context, crime C1 could be the affixation of registered trade marks (without consent) for the purposes of export only[1] and C2 could be the disposal of the marked goods in the UK (which is when the real damage is felt). The difference being that a person guilty of crime C1 would most likely receive a lesser sentence upon conviction than he would if convicted of crime C2 because there is a likelihood of deception in the latter case whereas there is none in the former. In *Davies v DPP*,[2] there was a gang fight on Clapham Common and D was involved. A friend of D, X, had a knife and killed somebody. D was charged as a secondary accessory to murder. There was no evidence that D knew that X had a knife or that he intended to use it. The use of the knife was not part of the common design and this went beyond what D had contemplated – the appeal was allowed. In *R v Saunders and Archer*,[3] D1 decided to murder W. D1, on advice from D2, gave a poisoned apple to W but she gave it to her child in the presence of D1 who let the child eat it. The child died and the question of D2's liability was raised. D2 was not liable as an accessory to the murder of the child as D1's intention had changed from the one discussed with D2. Perhaps the leading case on the subject is *R v Anderson*[4] where A killed W with a knife in the company of M. M had no idea that A had a knife or was going to use it. The Court of Appeal was invited to consider the position on the basis that A and M were co actors but whether A went beyond what was agreed. The Court of Appeal held that if A had gone beyond what was agreed then M was not liable because A had departed completely from the common design, M could not have suspected A's behaviour and so M's conviction should be quashed.

1 Though we concede or submit that it is unclear whether this is an act of infringement, though it seems to fall square within the meaning of the TMA 1994, s 92(1)(a).
2 [1954] AC 378.
3 (1573) 2 Plowd 473.
4 [1966] 2 QB 110.

20.62 Similarly in *Chan Wing-Siu v R*,[1] three defendants were convicted in Hong Kong of murder and wounding with intent. D's went to V's flat to rob him and V was stabbed to death and V's wife was wounded. The trial judge told the jury that D could be convicted on both counts of murder and as an accessory of contemplation/knowledge that a knife was to be used by the others to cause death or serious bodily harm. The Privy Council said that if there was no contemplation by the particular person accused that serious bodily harm would be intentionally inflicted, then there was no party to murder.

1 [1985] AC 168.

20.63 Accordingly, it appears that the *mens rea* is subjective or subjective in part and is down to what the individual accused contemplated, which is what the appellate courts appear to say what matters. If there is a reasonable possibility that the accused did not contemplate the action, the accused is not guilty as a secondary principal of the primary act.

R v Slack[1] is consistent with this. D agreed with A to go to a flat and rob V. A murdered V in the absence of D but D was convicted and the appeal was dismissed. The Court of Appeal said that on trial for murder in the case of a joint enterprise, proof is necessary that the principal intended to kill or do serious harm and that even though the secondary party is not physically present, he is guilty of murder if he is part of a joint plan and it was understood (either expressly or tacitly) that it may be necessary that one of them would kill or do serious harm as part of the common enterprise. Accordingly it is still necessary (for the prosecution) to prove what the common design was. This is particularly difficult to do where D and E plan a crime but E withdraws and D goes on to commit the crime. In *R v Becerra*[2] a burglar gave a knife to a companion to use if there was an interruption to the burglary. D said, on interruption of the burglary, 'come on let's go' and fled but the companion stabbed the interrupter. D claimed that he was not liable but the Court of Appeal held that this was not sufficient to exempt D from complicity in the stabbing since it was clearly contemplated.

1 [1989] QB 775.
2 (1975) 62 Cr App Rep 212.

20.64 In cases where an initial participant realises the folly of his ways before the plan is carried out then his is not liable as a secondary party if he tries to stop the acts from being done (though he may be guilty of conspiracy), thus in *R v Grundy*,[1] D was tried for burglary. D had provided information to certain burglars who were to carry out the acts but on the day had tried to stop them from entering the premises in question. The Court of Appeal held that this was a good and valid defence. In *R v Whitefield*,[2] D told burglars that they could break into the flat next door using D's flat. D withdrew and the trial judge said that the communication of withdrawal was not enough for a defence. The Court of Appeal applied *Beccera* and *Grundy* holding that such communication is sufficient and may provide a defence.

1 [1977] Crim LR 543.
2 [1984] Crim LR 97.

20.65   What of the person who participates by way of assisting concealment after a crime has been committed? Sections 4 and 5 of the CLA 1967 deal with this and the reader is referred to the practitioners texts.

20.66   A secondary party may generally be convicted where principal has not been convicted. This situation often arises in cases where the principal has turned Queen's Evidence or has managed to avoid capture or even detection.

If the prosecution cannot produce the principal, then the second party can still be convicted provided that the prosecution can prove that there is the requisite *mens rea*. Similarly it follows that a second party can be convicted where a principal has been acquitted since there may be different evidence against the parties and the parties may be tried in different places by different juries and different rules relating to the admissibility of evidence as against each party may apply.[1] In *Thornton v Mitchell*[2] the driver of a bus was reversing on the guidance of the conductor. The driver drove into some bystanders and the driver was charged with driving without due care and attention and the conductor of aiding and abetting. The driver was acquitted and the court held that the conductor also must be acquitted as a second party. This clearly makes sense on the facts of that case since it is clear that the driver and the conductor were correctly before the court so that unless to driver was guilty of the offence his aider and abetter could not be so. In *R v Leak*[3] L terrorised his wife into consenting to having intercourse with C. This was in fact rape as the wife did not effectively consent. C was convicted but his conviction was quashed on the grounds that he clearly acted on an honest (albeit immoral) belief as to the wife's consent. L's conviction as an aider and abetter was maintained however. Commentators have suggested that *Leak* is illogical since L could only have been guilty as a second party if C had been guilty as a principal. Had L been charged for procuring the offence then the case might have some more logic to it however if, as most commentators have done, the case is viewed as one of principal and agent (where the agent is innocent) then the case is not so inexplicable.

1 Such as in the case of interviews conducted in the absence of the other party(ies). This evidence is only admissible as against the party being interviewed and no other even if it otherwise condemns the other.
2 [1940] 1 All ER 339.
3 [1976] QB 217.

20.67   Further before *R v Howe*[1] it was not possible to convict a second party of a crime greater than that committed by the principal. The old law is reflected in *R v Richards*.[2] D employed men to beat up H. The henchmen were convicted under s 20 of the Offences Against the Person Act 1861 but D was convicted under s 18 of that act (a far more serious offence). The appeal was allowed on the basis that D could not be charged with a greater offence. However in *Howe* (a particularly gruesome case of murder) the House of Lords disapproved of *Richards* and stated that it is possible to be convicted of an offence greater that with which the principal has been charged. *Howe* cannot be distinguished from *Richards* and so *Richards* must have been incorrectly decided. The *ratio* of their lordships in *Howe* was that where a person has been killed and the result is a result intended by one of the parties to that act, then the fact that the actual killer may only be convicted of manslaughter does not result in a compulsory reduction for the second party.

1 [1987] AC 417..
2 [1974] QB 776, CA.

Other inchoate offences

20.68 These are, for example, crimes where some form of preparation or planning is made but the complete crime is not necessarily accomplished. There is, however, a question as to how much preparation amounts to a crime. This may cover things such as conspiracy to commit an offence (as covered by s 1 of the CLA 1977), conspiracy to defraud (which we discuss in detail below under a separate heading) and attempts.

Attempts

20.69 Before 1981, an attempt to commit a crime was a common law offence but the Criminal Attempts Act 1981 ('CAA 1981') put this on a statutory footing. The Act was passed because the law had become confusing. Section 1 of the CAA 1981 sets out the *actus reus* which reads:

> '1.-(1) If with intent to commit an offence to which this section applies a person does any act which is more than merely preparatory to the commission of the offence then he is guilty of attempting to commit the offence.
>
> (2) A person may be guilty of attempting to commit an offence to which this section applies even though the facts are such that the commission of the offence is impossible
>
> (3) In any case where -
>
> > (a) apart from this subsection a person's intention would not be regarded as having amounted to an intent to commit an offence; but
> > (b) if the facts of the case had been as he believed them to be, his intention would be so regarded,
>
> then for the purposes of subsection (1) above, he shall be regarded as having an intent to commit that offence.
>
> (4) This section applies to any offence which, if it were completed, would be triable in England and Wales as an indictable offence, other than-
>
> > (a) conspiracy (at common law or under section 1 of the Criminal Law Act 1977 or any other enactment);
> > (b) aiding, abetting, counselling, procuring or suborning the commission of an offence;
> > (c) offences under section 4 (1) (assisting offenders) or 5 (1) (accepting or agreeing to accept consideration for not disclosing information about an arrestable offence) of the Criminal Law Act 1967.'

The statute does not define what 'more than merely preparatory' means and this has caused problems since one asks where does attempt begin? The law of inchoate offences and attempts in particular is of relevance in the context of trade marks since it is desirable to stop any potential offender as soon and as early as possible. It is obviously wrong to seek to make a person liable merely because he happened to have a passing thought of selling counterfeit clothing or because he does some act which goes further, such as consulting the trade marks register or, more realistically, makes enquiries about a pitch where he could sell his wares. Obviously if the law of attempts were to be developed in such an extreme fashion, this may introduce the concept of 'thought crime'.[1]

1 Redolent of certain popular literature emanating from the early 20th century.

20.70   We pose the following scenario for the purposes of analysis. Say D wishes to sell counterfeit goods, he purchases a t-shirt printing kit[1] and other paraphernalia. Then he creates the image on his computer and creates the transfers – he loses his nerve and does not transfer the images to the t-shirts. Where does the attempt to commit an offence under s 92(1)(a) or (b) of the TMA 1994 start? One would have to concede that so far as the creation of the transfers was concerned, an offence under s 92(3)(a) and (b) of the TMA 1994 is complete (other matters necessary for the commission of the offence being proved).

1 Usually a combination of a computer capable of generating images and a special printer which prints transfers which can be ironed onto the t-shirt.

20.71   The usual and general test is the old common law test. This test, like most legal tests has a history. In *R v Eagleton*,[1] a proximity test was proposed being that any act which remotely leads to an offence being committed is not to be considered to be an attempt whereas an act immediately connected with a crime is an attempt. This is sensible and superficially helpful but provides no real definition as to what constitutes remoteness.

In *DPP v Stonehouse*[2] the nature of the attempt was discussed. Lord Diplock in that case said that a person attempting to commit a crime must have crossed a river and burned his boats. Thus in *R v Robinson*[3] a jeweller tied himself up and told the police that he had been robbed. D was convicted of trying to obtain insurance money by fraud but the insurance claim had not actually taken place and the conviction was quashed because there was no false pretence. The situation was that when D was caught, he was in the preparatory stages and had *not* applied to the insurance company. Also in another insurance case, *Comer v Bloomfield*,[4] D's van crashed and he claimed that it had been stolen so that he could claim the value from his insurance. The defendant was exonerated on appeal as no substantive claim had been made from the insurance company (an initial enquiry had been made but nothing more). However it would appear that this line of cases suggests that where an insurance claim is contemplated then an insurance claim must be made (though the police do not have to wait for it to be paid out before the offence is complete).

1 (1855) Dears CC 376.
2 [1978] AC 55.
3 [1915] 2 KB 342.
4 [1971] RTR 49.

20.72   Another type of test has been proposed which is an equivocality test. That test, though now discredited, looks at the acts which are thus far complete and poses the question as to whether there is any further conduct, consistent with the acts which have been carried out which would lead to a final lawful act being carried out, If the final lawful conclusion culd result, then there can be no liability

20.73 The CAA 1981 uses the words 'more than mere preparation.' and there is some recent judicial *dicta* which has shed some light on the question of what more than mere preparation means. In *R v Gullefer*[1] D liked greyhound racing and waved his arms to distract the dogs to influence a race so that his stake would be repaid. D claimed his stake and was charged with attempted fraud and was eventually convicted. The conviction was quashed since there was insufficient evidence that D had gone beyond mere preparation. Section 1(1) and 4(3) of CAA 1981 were considered. Section 4(3) says that where sufficient evidence in law is used to support a finding that somebody comes within s 1(1) then the question as to whether D is caught by s 1(1) is a question of fact for the jury on the direction of the judge. However, by this stage there was no clear guidance as to whether the remote possibility test (as in *R v Eagleton*)[2] was the correct test or whether the boat-burning test (as in *DPP v Stonehouse*[3]) was the correct test.

1 [1990] 3 All ER 882.
2 (1855) Dears CC 376.
3 [1978] AC 5).

20.74 In *R v Jones*[1] D was charged with attempted murder as he pointed a gun at his victim. D claimed that he was merely preparing for the offence as he still had to undo the safety catch, put his finger on the trigger and pull it and that a true consideration of s 1(1) of the CAA 1981 proved that there was no attempt. D's conviction was upheld. The CAA 1981 was a codifying Act and forgot earlier case law 'more than merely preparatory without being the last act'. When deciding if a charge of attempted murder should be withdrawn, the trial judge has to decide if there was true evidence that a reasonable jury could conclude that D had done the acts which were more than merely preparatory.

This was all considered in *A-G's Reference (No 1 of 1992)*[2] where it was held that it is sufficient if there is evidence from which the intent can be inferred and there are proven acts which a jury could properly regard as more than merely preparatory to the commission of the offence. In other words, provided that a jury was capable of finding that the acts concerned were more than merely preparatory, there would be a case to answer. However this is unsatisfactory in a number of respects since there has to be a legal baseline beneath which a prosecution will fail and above which a prosecution is capable of succeeding. In short, the position in law about whether a person has attempted a crime is still unclear.

1 [1990] 1 WLR 1057.
2 [1993] 1 WLR 274.

20.75 As far as intention is concerned it is necessary to prove the specific intention to commit the offence concerned – which is always a matter of fact and there is little more that can be said about it.

Conspiracy

20.76 Conspiracy may be divided into two types – conspiracy to commit a crime (statutory conspiracy) and conspiracy to defraud. Both are of great importance in relation to the law of trade marks, being, as it is, concerned with deception.

20.77 Conspiracy itself involves the requirement that two or more people combine to do an act, they agree (in the loosest sense of the expression) that it should be done pursuant to a common design. Conspiracies may be of various types such as the wheel conspiracy where there is a central person or group at the hub who or which conspire with various individuals or groups separately. Then there is the chain conspiracy where one person conspires with another person or group who, in turn conspire with another person or group. Finally there is the group conspiracy where at all times a single group forms the basis of the conspiracy though individuals might peel off or join in at relevant times. Combinations and permutations of wheel, chain and group conspiracies are not unknown.

20.78 A person is not a party to a conspiracy if he either does not engage in any agreement to perform the prohibited act or he withdraws before the agreement is complete. Subsequent repentance is irrelevant since the crime is complete once the plot is hatched though it might make a difference in relation to mitigation of sentence, especially where the repenting party has informed the relevant authorities. It is often the case that a prosecutor will attempt to prove the evidence of a conspiracy by showing that the conspiracy came to fruition and since two or more people were involved in it there must have been a conspiracy. Indeed, experience shows that a charge of conspiracy proved in this way is very strong evidence indeed that there *was* a conspiracy[1] and this is also due to the fact that actual conspiracies, ie evidence of what was said and done during the agreement, are often very difficult to prove. Further since the essence of conspiracy is agreement (no matter how expressed) a mere secret desire that the conspiracy should come to fruition is never enough.

1 The existence of a conspiracy in evidential terms may be proved as 'a matter of inference, deduced from certain criminal acts of the parties accused, done in pursuance of an apparent criminal purpose in common between them': *R v Brisac* (1803) 4 East 164, 171.

20.79 However the prosecution must also prove that not only was there a combination with a specific object in mind but also that it was the intention of the conspirators to commit the acts concerned. What those acts are will depend upon the type of conspiracy being charged.

20.80 Finally a conspiracy charge is often preferable since it carries a greater penalty (10 years imprisonment), is viewed more seriously by the courts (since it amounts to organised crime) and is usually only reserved where the gravity of the ultimate offences require it. On the other side of the coin, it has time and time again been held to be wrong for a prosecutor to proceed on a conspiracy charges and upon any related substantive offences, unless it can be justified as being in the interests of justice[1] However, the relationship between conspiracy charges and their substantive counterparts is an uneasy one.

1 See Practice Direction (Conspiracy) [1977] I WLR 537.

Statutory conspiracy

20.81 This is governed by s 1 of the CLA 1977 as substituted by s 5 of the CAA 1981 which states:

'(1) Subject to the following provisions of this part of this Act, if a person agrees with any other person or persons that a course of conduct will be pursued which, if the agreement is carried out in accordance with their intentions, either

(a) will necessarily amount to or involve the commission of any offence or offences by one or more of the parties to the agreement or

(b) would do so but for the existence of facts which render the commission of the offence or any of the offences impossible,

he is guilty of conspiracy to commit the offence or offences in question.

(2) Where liability for any offence may be incurred without knowledge on the part of the person committing it of any particular fact or circumstance necessary for the commission of the offence, a person shall nevertheless not be guilty of conspiracy to commit that offence by virtue of subsection (1) above unless he and at least one other party to the agreement intend or know that the fact or circumstance shall or will exist at the time when the conduct constituting the offence is to take place.

...

(4) In this part of this Act 'offence' means an offence triable in England and Wales.'

20.82   The *actus reus* – this is the same under the common law and the pre-statute conditions are relevant. Further, conspiracy is an offence involving *mens rea* the Crown has to show agreement and intention. In *Churchill v Walton*,[1] D's were charged with conspiracy to use un-taxed fuel in their motor vehicles. The offence was a strict one (ie no *mens rea* was required for the substantive offence). The Court of Appeal that the prosecution had to prove that the conspirators knew the essential matters which constituted the offence. However at first sight this appears odd since if a strict liability crime is to be committed, independent of state of mind, then it matters not how honest or otherwise the perpetrators were or indeed whether the conspirators knew what they were doing was wrong. An examination and extension of the facts in *Churchill* tends to reveal the difficulty in this area. The substantive offence is committed even if the un-taxed fuel was used inadvertently. Therefore if one person asks another for some fuel and the other says 'use that fuel can over there' both believing that it is legal to use such fuel then nevertheless they are liable as conspirators. This would seem harsh (and indeed is so), though it is unlikely, on the basis of the authorities, that the conspirators would be sentenced any more severely because a conspiracy had taken place. Indeed this was acknowledged in a way in *R v Anderson*[2] where Lord Bridge of Harwich set out the requirements of conspiracy and *mens rea*, being:

(i) If a person agrees with any other person or persons that a course of conduct should be pursued,

(ii) which will necessarily amount to or involve the commission of an offence or offences by one or more of the parties to the agreement then,

(iii) the agreement must be carried out in accordance with the intentions.

1 [1967] 2 AC 224.
2 [1986] AC 27.

20.83   What then of intention? The *mens rea* of a crime is established if and only if it is shown that the accused, when he entered into the agreement intended to play some part in the agreed course of conduct in furtherance of the criminal purpose which the agreed course of conduct was intended to achieve – nothing more is required. It would appear to be the *intention* that a particular act be carried out rather then the intention to commit a crime which is important.

20.84 Conspiracy to commit the impossible is a crime if the acts are factually impossible to carry out so a person who conspires or indeed attempts to sell counterfeit goods believing that the trade mark in question is registered (when in fact it is not so) would be liable. However a person who conspires or attempts to sell counterfeit goods thinking that they are breaking the law because the trade mark in question is registered for a different class of goods, and they (wrongly) believe that a trade mark registration covers all goods and services, is said to misunderstand the law – which is a valid defence.

Conspiracy to defraud

20.85 Defraud has been defined as carrying out a fiddle and is often used by prosecutors who are dissatisfied with the remedies which substantive offences give them. In our experience it is not infrequently used in relation to trade mark type offences where the fiddle is the false representation. But to define it as a fiddle is to ignore the authorities. It is an important feature of the crime that the conspirators be proven to be dishonest, although that is often not all that difficult to prove.

20.86 The fact that the object of the conspiracy must be some right corporeal or incorporeal is not in doubt but care should be taken in looking at this with too powerful a magnifying glass, see *Scott v Metropolitan Police Comr*,[1] per Lord Diplock:

> '(i) Although at common law no clear distinction was originally drawn between conspiracies to "cheat" and conspiracies to "defraud", these terms being frequently used in combination, by the early years of the nineteenth century "conspiracy to defraud" had become a distinct species of criminal agreement independent of the old common law substantive offence of "cheating". The abolition of this substantive common law offence by section 32(1)(a) of the Theft Act 1968, except as regards offences relating to the public revenue, thus leaves surviving and intact the common law offence of conspiracy to defraud.
>
> (ii) Where the intended victim of a "conspiracy to defraud" is a private individual the purpose of the conspirators must be to cause the victim economic loss by depriving him of some property or right, corporeal or incorporeal, to which he is, or, would, or, might become entitled. The intended means by which the purpose is to be achieved must be dishonest. They need not involve fraudulent misrepresentation such as is needed to constitute the civil tort of deceit. Dishonesty of any kind is enough.
>
> (iii) Where the intended victim of a "conspiracy to defraud" is a person performing public duties as distinct from a private individual it is sufficient if the purpose is to cause him to act contrary to his public duty, and the intended means of achieving this purpose are dishonest. The purpose need not involve causing economic loss to anyone.'[2]

1 [1975] AC 819 at 840.
2 It is accepted that the width of (ii) (in that it was too narrow) has been criticised in *Wai Yu-tsang v R* [1992] 1 AC 269; [1991] 4 All ER 664 but the nature of the criticism was that for the allegation to be made out there was no necessity to prove an intention to cause economic loss. Lord Goff of Chieveley did not dissent from the proposition that the effect of the conspiracy (as opposed to the intention of those conspirators) is to cause (or put at risk) the economic interests of others – it is this narrow distinction which is of moment in this appeal and application for leave to appeal. See also *R. v Moses and Ansbro* [1991] Crim LR 617.

20.87 Also, more recently in *Adams v R*,[1] Lord Jauncey of Tullichettle opined :

> '[the victim] … can only suffer prejudice in relation to some right or interest which he possesses.'

1 [1995] 1 WLR 52 at 64 lines C–H.

20.88 However, *Wai Yu-tsang v R*[1] Lord Goff of Chieveley said in his opinion:

> '… the expression "intent to defraud" is not to be given a narrow meaning, involving an intention to cause economic loss to another. In broad terms, it means simply an intention to practise a fraud on another, or an intention to act to the prejudice of another man's right.'

Even Lord Goff of Chieveley was saying in his opinion that there had to be something in the nature of a right to be prejudiced or potentially prejudiced. Further the actual victim of the fraud (if successful and if coming to fruition) need not be the intended victim.

1 [1992] 1 AC 269 at 276.

20.89 It must be remembered that *Wai Yu-tsang v R*[1] was a case where the defendant said that there was (1) no intention to defraud the victim and (2) that the victim in fact suffered no loss. This, of course, does not avoid the allegation of conspiracy to defraud. However what Lord Goff of Chieveley was not saying was that one simply had to demonstrate a 'con' or a fiddle and indeed by endorsing what Lord Radcliffe said in *Welham v DPP*[2] of *Wai Yu-Tsang*:

> 'Lord Radcliffe agreed with the speech of Lord Denning, but went on to express in his own words his view of the meaning of the words "intent to defraud" in section 4(1) of the Act of 1913. He rejected the proposition that in ordinary speech 'to defraud' is confined to the idea of depriving a man by deceit of some economic advantage or inflicting upon him some economic loss, and continued, at p 124:
>
>> "Has the law ever so confined it? In my opinion there is no warrant for saying that it has. What it has looked for in considering the effect of cheating upon another person and so in defining the criminal intent is the prejudice of that person: what Blackstone (*Commentaries*, 18th ed, vol 4, at p 247) called 'to the prejudice of another man's right.' East, *Pleas of the Crown* (1803), vol 2, at pp 852, 854, makes the same point in the chapter on Forgery: 'in all cases of forgery, properly so called, it is immaterial whether any person be actually injured or not, provided any may be prejudiced by it.'"

He can be taken to have accepted that the 'other man's right' has to exist. That 'right' not only includes any right itself but also any potential right or the fact that that right might be put a risk. However, in-depth analysis of the law of conspiracy to defraud via the authorities should be avoided since if it were to be placed in any particular niche, it would be denuded of efficacy. The power of charging the crime of conspiracy to defraud is that it can cast a very wide net without the necessity of paying too much attention of the rights in question. It would appear that the practice of charging in relation to conspiracy to defraud is generally confined to cases where one looks at the case and comes away with the feeling that a con has been practised. The danger with using conspiracy to defraud too freely is that it can cause criminal proceedings to degenerate into muck-slinging exercises.

1 [1992]1 AC 269.
2 [1961] AC 103 at 276.

20.90   However this approach (as to whether a con has been practised) poses some difficulties in relation, at the very least, to the law of trade marks. It is very often the case that traders will disclaim the provenance of their wares by posting a disclaimer to the effect that no representation is being made as to whether the goods concerned are genuine or not or indeed, on occasion, that a representation is made that the goods are counterfeit. It might also be the case that written contracts are entered into where it is expressly stated that the vendor disclaims responsibility for provenance on the basis that he does not know, or indeed care. As matter of civil law and ignoring whether such a contractual term might be struck down and offending under the Unfair Contract Terms Act 1977 or the Unfair Terms in Consumer Contracts Regulations 1994[1] such a term is perfectly valid (though only, in effect, superficially so) since although contractual terms are created by reason of the operation of s 13 of the Sale of Goods Act 1979 ('SOGA 1979') (goods sold by description to correspond to description) and like sections, they can be contracted out[2]. Thus the clever (or perhaps unscrupulous) trader can, we submit, negative the existence of rights by means of the way in which he drafts his contract of sale, which would defeat an allegation of conspiracy to defraud since he could argue that the purchaser was acting (or was deemed to act) with his eyes wide open and therefore nobody was dishonest. It is for this reason that charging conspiracy to defraud is best done by reference to not only the immediate, final or intermediate purchaser but also to the trade mark owner too since no contractual term can defeat his rights (though the position might be different if he was only claiming rights arising by reason of goodwill). Whether as a matter of European law, this is permissible, is too fraught a topic to merit inclusion in this chapter.

1 (SI 1994/3159).
2 SOGA 1979, s 55.

The TMA 1994, s 92(4) – additional matters for the prosecution to prove

20.91   Section 92(4) of the TMA 1994 states:

'A person does not commit an offence under this section unless-

    (a) the goods are goods in respect of which the trade mark is registered, or
    (b) the trade mark has a reputation in the United Kingdom and the use of the sign takes or would take unfair advantage of; or is or would be detrimental to, the distinctive character or the repute of the trade mark.'

20.92   It is clear that notwithstanding what was said by Auld LJ in *R v Torbay Council, ex p Singh*[1] as to what constituted the elements of the offence in question, it is also necessary (if the question arises, which it did not in *Torbay District Council* for the prosecution to prove that the goods alleged to be counterfeit fell within the scope of the trade mark (akin, we submit, to s 10(1) of the TMA 1994 as far as scope is concerned). Further, insofar as s 92(4)(b) of the TMA 1994 is concerned (which, we submit, is akin to, and on many respects to be construed in the same way as, s 10(3) of the TMA 1994) two difficulties arise being (1) whether there is any necessity to prove confusion and something more,[2] though this has been discussed elsewhere[3] and (2) whether this part of s 92 of the TMA 1994 is intended to protect the consumer or the trade mark owner. This second distinction is of fundamental importance since if it is designed to protect the trade mark or trade mark owner and not the consumer then s 92(4)(b) of the TMA 1994 cannot be said to be a consumer protection measure and as such it is not a provision which is allowed in accordance with the sixth Recital of the Directive which reads:

'Whereas this Directive does not exclude the application to trade marks of provisions of law of the Member States other than trade mark law, such as the provisions relating to unfair competition, civil liability or consumer protection;'

1 (1999) Times, 5 July.
2 The authorities seem to suggest that likelihood of confusion is a minimum pre- requsite, see *Baywatch Production Co Inc v Home Video Channel* [1997] FSR 22 and *BASF plc v CEP (UK) plc* [1996] ETMR 51.
3 Though it would essentially be a jury question as to whether the goods in question fell within the scope of the registration in suit.

20.93 Whether we should have a criminal provision relating to trade mark infringement at all, at least in its current guise, is a matter of debate, which is dis,cussed below. However what is important is that when one reads s 92(4)(b) of the TMA 1994 with s 92(5), which we shall cover in more detail below, it is apparent that in order to avail oneself of a defence proper in criminal proceedings, one has to show a state of mind relating to one's belief in infringement – which is not a requirement of the Directive, in particular art 7 thereof, which states:

'1. The trade mark shall not entitle the proprietor to prohibit a third party from using, in the course of trade,

    (a) his own name or address;
    (b) indications concerning the kind, quality, quantity, intended purpose, value, geographical origin, the time of production of goods or of rendering of the service, or other characteristics of goods or services;
    (c) the trade mark where it is necessary to indicate the intended purpose of a product or service, in particular as accessories or spare parts; provided he uses them in accordance with honest practices in industrial or commercial matters.

2. The trade mark shall not entitle the proprietor to prohibit a third party from using, in the course of trade, an earlier right which only applies in a particular locality if that right is recognised by the laws of the Member State in question and within the limits of the territory in which it is recognised.'

20.94 Further in *Silhouette International Schmied GmbH & Co KG v Hartlauer Handelsgesellschaft mbH*[1] the ECJ stated:

' … Articles 5 to 7 of the Directive must be construed as embodying a complete harmonisation of the rules relating to the rights conferred by a trade mark.'

Which would seem to imply that insofar as intention is concerned, of which no mention is made in art 7 of the Directive, ss 92(4)(b) and 92(5) of the TMA 1994 ought not to be there in their present form. We say the foregoing in the face of what is said in the ninth Recital of the Directive which states:

'Whereas it is fundamental, in order to facilitate the free circulation of goods and services, to ensure that henceforth registered trade marks enjoy the same protection under the legal systems of all the Member States; whereas this should however not prevent the Member States from granting at their option extensive protection to those trade marks which have a reputation;'

Since it would appear that whatever freedom is given to the Member States to legislate in relation to reputation, the tenets of art 7 of the Directive must still stand, since there is no justification for this not to be so and the case of *Silhouette*, we submit, supports this.

1 [1998] FSR 729, 735, line 25.

The TMA 1994, s 92(5) – the defences

20.95 Obviously it is a defence for a defendant to say that one of the crucial elements of the offence either did not happen on the facts or has not been proved against him. It is also a defence for a defendant to say that his use was either not within the scope of the trade mark registration in suit or was not such as to impair the repute of the trade mark in suit – those are both negative defences and are only likely to be successful on a submission of no case to answer or if the jury or other tribunal of fact are sufficiently apprised of the position.

20.96 However s 92(5) of the TMA 1994 provides a positive defence, dependent upon state of mind, in a partially subjective sense at least. Section 92(5) of the TMA 1994 states:

> 'It is a defence for a person charged with an offence under this section to show that he believed on reasonable grounds that the use of the sign in the manner in which it was used, or was to be used, was not an infringement of the registered trade mark.'

This defence does not, to say the least, fit well with the first three sub-sections of s 92 of the TMA 1994 and it is quite apparent that the draughtsman, when drafting sub-ss (1)–(3) of s 92 of the TMA 1994 did not consider the effects of sub-ss (4) and (5) of that section.

20.97 Whilst there is no difficulty with the state of mind that the defendant must have (belief on reasonable grounds) in order to escape a charge under s 92 of the TMA 1994, since this is a fairly standard way of drafting a criminal statute,[1] the use of the word 'infringement' causes the most difficulty. Is it intended to mean, as Lord Strathclyde would have it) 'infringement' in the sense understood by ss 9–11 of the TMA 1994 and arts 5 and 6 of the Directive? Or is it intended to mean acts which fall within s 92(1)-(3) of the TMA 1994? This raises a whole host of difficulties since it is possible to envisage circumstances where a person might use a sign which is likely to be mistaken for a registered trade mark but does not cause confusion or association and thus a person who is not liable under the civil law might be criminally liable. Likewise a person who defeats a civil claim for infringement because he raises a defence under s 11 of the TMA 1994 might still be criminally liable if (a) he had no belief that he had such a defence at the time that the offence was committed or, more importantly (b) if his only defence related to the acts set out in s 92(1)–(3) of the TMA 1994.

1 Though that is not to say that it ought to be there at all, given what we say as to fidelity with the Directive.

20.98 We hope that in our analysis of the defence of s 92(5) of the TMA 1994 we have demonstrated that if the word 'infringement' is to be construed in the latter sense, that is within the meaning of s 92(1)–(3) of the TMA 1994, then this leads to absurdity so that a person making a legitimate and guaranteed use (via s 11 of the TMA 1994 and art 6 of the Directive) of another person's trade mark is nevertheless criminally liable, or at least potentially so. Accordingly we submit that the proper construction is whether the defendant is not infringing within the meaning of the civil provisions of the TMA 1994 – this is consistent with the Government's stance ('This would cover the use of someone acting in ignorance, or in a genuine belief that what he was doing did not require the consent of the proprietor, rather than taking part in deliberate counterfeiting'[1]).

1 House of Lords Public Bill Committee on the Trade Marks Bill, 4th sitting, 20 January 1994, col 96.

20.99 Even then this construction leads to difficulties since if the defence is to be looked at in this way, ie that the defendant has to have reasonable grounds for believing that he has a defence, then the defendant has more to prove in criminal proceedings (and may not be able to do so) than he is required to prove under the defence-type provisions of ss 9–11 of the TMA 1994 or under arts 5 and 6 of the Directive. If matters were left there then there might be an answer by a reading of the sixth recital which allows member states to protect consumers. But that is to ignore the government's motive in enacting the section where it has been expressly stated by the minister concerned that:

'... this Bill is concerned with the *protection of trade marks*, clause 87 defines the offence in terms of unauthorised use of the mark. That protects the *legitimate rights of trade mark owners*. Even if an unscrupulous trader sells the goods as "genuine fakes", it will still be an offence, because he will be *deliberately exploiting someone's mark* without their permission.'[1]

1 Hansard [241]:18.iv.1994. Trade Marks Bill, 2nd reading, col 658, 661.

20.100 We submit that it is a matter beyond doubt that the Government was not envisaging that s 92 of the TMA 1994 be considered a consumer protection measure and indeed it was enacted because of the failure of the pre-existent consumer protection measures, via the TDA 1968, to protect trade mark owners in cases where the disclaimer doctrine applied.[1] Though it must be accepted that following on from what Laddie J said in *Wagamama Ltd v City Centre Restaurants plc*.[2] that Parliamentary intention may, in the context of Directive derived law, be of less relevance than before. However, if this is so then the only power that the Government had to enact s 92 of the TMA 1994 was via the Directive since, given that it is clear that at least arts 5–7 of the Directive are a complete code to which all members of the Community must be subject, s 92 of the TMA 1994 imposed additional burdens over and above those envisaged by the Directive. Our present experience is that when this issue is raised in a criminal context the courts at first instance (that is the Crown and Magistrates' Courts) are reluctant to consider the matter but would rather leave the matter to the Court of Appeal, which, we submit is entirely sensible since an interim reference to the ECJ might be pointless if the defendant ended up being acquitted on other grounds. We would add and submit that in addition to the inchoate offences equal considerations ought to apply to the question of a reference to the ECJ.

1 In-depth discussion on this doctrine would make this a two or possibly three volume work, however reference should be made to *Tarleton Engineering Co Ltd v Nattrass* [1973] 3 All ER 699; [1973] 1 WLR 1261; *Taylor v Smith* [1974] RTR 190; *Norman v Bennet* [1974] 3 All ER 351; [1974] 1 WLR 1229; *Zawadski v Sleigh* [1975] RTR 113; *R v Hammertons Cars Ltd* [1976] 3 All ER 758; [1976] 1 WLR 1243; *R v T McMillan Aviation Ltd and McMillan* [1981] Crim LR 785; *Waltham Forest London Borough Council v TG Wheatley (Central Garage) Ltd* (1977) 76 LGR 195; *Blunden v Gravelle Ltd* (1986) 151 JP 701 and *Newham London Borough v Singh and Sandhu* (1988) 152 JP 239.
2 [1995] FSR 713, 722.

20.101   Finally, on the question of the legality of s 92 of the TMA 1994 there is in the criminal courts, no provision whereby the defendant can set up as a defence the fact that the rights relied upon are invalid or ought to be revoked in some material respect. Since the right to have a registered trade mark declared invalid (under s 47 of the TMA 1994) or revoked (under s 46 of the TMA 1994) is a right guaranteed by the Directive via the fifty, seventh and eighth Recitals and arts 3 and 4, which only give freedom to legislate as to the adjectival manner of applying for a declaration of invalidity and revocation and which do not displace the substantive right to apply for such remedies, the fact that a defendant in criminal proceedings has no such direct right is a matter of concern. Again, experience has shown that the criminal courts have taken mixed views as to how to deal with this problem. In some cases the criminal courts have granted lengthy adjournments (which cannot on any view be in the interests of justice) whilst the defendant can seek to have the registered trade marks in question impugned in the civil courts. In some cases the courts have suggested that they are simply not competent to decide the question and that it should be aired in the Court of Appeal. In some cases the problem has simply been ignored on the basis that such is what Parliament decided and in others, the criminal courts have held that s 92 of the TMA 1994 is a consumer protection measure and so falls outwith the Directive. We would not wish to express a view as to which procedure is correct (if any of them are) but we observe that on the basis of the analysis thus far presented it is wrong to say that s 92 of the TMA 1994 is a consumer protection measure. However it is to be observed that it is probably the case that such a question can only be decided by the ECJ and therefore having the question decided by the trial court is inappropriate as was suggested by Lord Diplock in *Henn and Darby* v *DPP*[1] since at first instance there was a always a chance that the defendant might be acquitted, thus making the need of a reference nugatory. That, one day there will be a reference on the question, is beyond doubt.

1 [1981] AC 850.

20.102   However absent considerations of the nature, legality and ambit of s 92(5) of the TMA 1994, it is quite clear that a defendant who says that he did not know that a certain trade mark was registered is going to have a difficult time if he has not consulted the register. That much was made clear by Auld LJ in *R v Torbay Council, ex p Singh*[1] where he said:

'That leaves the question whether a trader is entitled to take advantage of the statutory defence in section 92(5) on the basis that he believed on reasonable grounds that there was no registered trade mark to infringe. A trader who does not know of, or who is in doubt as to, the existence of a registered trade mark which he is in danger of infringing, can check the register. It will provide him with a definitive answer.[2] Even if the statutory defence had been modelled on the "due diligence" provisions to which I have referred, that a trader could not claim that he had exercised all due diligence without having consulted the register.

...

'It follows, in my judgment, that the statutory defence in section 92(5) can have no application to a defendant's state of mind as to whether at the material time there was or might have been a registered trade mark capable of infringement. Its wording makes plain that that is not its function. It does not speak of a reasonable belief in the absence of a registration. It speaks of a reasonable belief that the "manner" of use of the sign did not infringe "the registered trade mark". In my view, it presupposes an awareness by a defendant of the existence of the registration against which he can match his manner of use of the allegedly offending sign. The use of the definite article in the words "the registered trade mark" coupled with the reference to the "manner" of use of the sign makes plain that the draftsman intended that a defendant's reasonable belief of no infringement in the manner of use of the sign falls to be judged against his knowledge or deemed knowledge of the registered trade mark in question.'

This is, we submit, entirely correct. The register is there so that the public, but traders in particular can check to see what the forbidden territory is.

1 (1999), Times 5 July.
2 At least in relation to the question of whether the trade mark was registered. The interpretation of the scope of the registration is a question again and was not considered in this case.

20.103 Greater difficulties arise in relation to cases where the defendant decides to run a defence based upon ss 10(6) or 11 of the TMA 1994 or even on the basis that he thought, reasonably, that he did not need the consent of the proprietor because his rights were exhausted. Indeed our experience in this area has shown that the criminal courts are reluctant to impose a liability on a defendant where the state of the law relating to the international exhaustion of rights doctrine or the issue of implied consent is complex and unclear. We venture to suggest that legal opinion as to the effects of cases such as *Silhouette International Schmied GmbH & Co KG v Hartlauer Handelsgesellschaft mbH*[1] and *Sebago Inc v GB-Unic SA*[2] on the one hand and *Zino Davidoff SA v A & G Imports Ltd*[3] on the other make the question very vexed indeed and the opinions of practitioners are polarised on the point. Thus the defendant's state of mind might turn on which lawyer he approaches and it could hardly be said to be unreasonable for him to rely upon the advice of his lawyers.

1 Case C-355/96.
2 Case C-173/98, [1999] All ER (EC) 575, A-G's opinion, 25 March 1999; judgment of ECJ, 1 July 1999.
3 [1999] RPC 631.

20.104 As far as s 10(6) is concerned this makes it not an infringement for a registered trade mark to be used if it is in order to identify the goods of the proprietor or his licensee. This sub-section was described by Laddie J. in *Barclays Bank plc v RBS Advanta*[1] as being 'home grown'[2] in the sense that it did not derive from the Directive, or me properly, that it was optional. We shall refer to the first half of the sub-section as the primary provision and the second half as the proviso. It is necessary, however, for one of the parties to prove (in the case of the burden of proof being on the defence) that he is within the proviso, that his use was in accordance with honest practices in industrial or commercial matters and that such use did not take unfair advantage of or was not detrimental to the distinctive character of the trade mark. In the case of the burden of proof being on the prosecution, it must be shown that the defendant's use was not in accordance with honest practices in industrial or commercial matters and that such use did take unfair advantage of, or was detrimental to, the distinctive character of the trade mark. The question is who has to prove what? In civil cases, such as in the case of *Barclays Bank*[3] Laddie J accepted a concession as rightly made that the onus was on the proprietor of the trade mark to show that the defendant fell outside the proviso. Does the same rule or reasoning apply to criminal prosecutions? We start by observing that the onus would still be on the prosecutor to prove that the defendant fell outside the proviso if parliament had decided to put the entire question of trade mark infringement on a criminal footing. Secondly, the proviso is not a proviso which the defendant needs to rely upon to get him home so no apparent question arises under s 101 Magistrates' Court Act 1980 ('MCA 1980') and similarly it must apply to trials upon indictment by reason of what the House of Lords said in *R v Hunt*.[3] Accordingly we submit that consistent with the civil cases it is necessary for the prosecution to prove that the proviso applies and therefore there is a presumption that it does not.

1 [1996] RPC 307, 313, line 32.
2 Interestingly on line 22 of the same page Laddie J described the sub-section as 'a mess'!
3 [1987] AC 352.

20.105 Then there is the question of honesty in the sense of 'honest practices in industrial or commercial, matters'. In a criminal context, honesty is a matter for the jury or tribunal of fact[1] however, that is honesty in the sense as understood by the criminal law generally and relates to crimes which are crimes as such, ie honesty is part of the crime as expressed by statute or by the common law. In this regard there must be a distinction between 'honest practices' on the one hand and honesty on the other. Further, the meanings can be no different as between the civil and criminal law. The word 'honesty' as appears in the proviso is qualified to a degree which involves an element of objectivity, indeed the use of the expression 'honest practices' would tend to make it entirely objective, which means two things. Firstly that no subjective attribution of honesty insofar as the defendant is concerned can be taken account of as part of the primary facts, (though the defendant's belief that he was dishonest would entitle the jury to draw the inference that his practices were not honest and therefore he fell outside the benefit of the proviso) and secondly, honesty is not a matter for the jury or tribunal of fact to decide in the absence of direction as to what, on the evidence, the parties respective cases were in relation to 'honest practices', for instance the degree of puff that parties (or others in the same field of business) apply to their own goods or hyperbole when speaking of their competitors.[2]

1 *R v Ghosh* [1982] QB 1053.
2 See the remarks of Jacob J in *Vodafone Group plc v Orange Personal Communications Services Ltd* [1997] FSR 34, 38.

20.106   As far as s 11 of the TMA 1994 is concerned, the position is somewhat different, though it is to be observed that in relation to the section, the defendant in civil proceedings can only avail himself of it if it is shown that such use is in accordance with honest practices in industrial or commercial matters. We have already discussed, proviso to s 11 of the TMA 1994 in relation to s 10(6) of the TMA 1994 above and repeat our observations here. Each case will turn on its own facts.

Section 92(6) of the Trade Marks Act 1994 – sentencing

20.107   A person convicted of an offence under s 92 of the TMA 1994 falls to be sentenced on summary conviction to a custodial sentence of six months' imprisonment or a fine not exceeding the statutory maximum, or both [1] and upon conviction on indictment to a fine or imprisonment for a term not exceeding ten years or both.[2] The statutory maximum, for summary offences at the time of writing,[3] is set by s 37 of the Criminal Justice Act 1982 ('CJA 1982') as amended by s 17(1) of the Criminal Justice Act 1991 ('CJA 1991') to be £5,000. In relation to indictable offences, that is offences which are dealt with by the crown court (whether by reason of the defendant being convicted or pleading guilty there or by reason of the magistrates in a summary offence having insufficient powers to deal with the gravity of the offence under s 38 of the MCA 1980) the maximum fine is unlimited

1 TMA 1994, s 92(6)(a).
2 TMA 1994, s 96(2)(b).
3 With effect from 1 October 1992.

20.108   As well as fines and custody, the courts may impose a variety of other sentences such as absolute and conditional discharges, probation orders, community service orders, director's disqualification and a whole host of other orders designed to deal with offenders and to assist victims.

20.109   The overriding basis upon which sentencing is carried out is in accordance with the principle of seriousness,[1] ie does a particular sentencing option meet the seriousness of the crime committed and within that option does the severity of how that option is used (eg the length of a custodial sentence or a community service order) meet the seriousness of the crime committed. The seriousness is taken to mean that the degree of retribution which society expects to extract from a given offender, the other elements of sentencing such as deterrence, protection and rehabilitation being either impossible to achieve or irrelevant to trade mark type offences.

1 See CJA 1991 (as amended), ss 1 (custodial sentences), 2 (length of custodial sentences), 6 (community sentences), 18 (fines).

20.110   Seriousness indicators would tend to be based upon knowledge, extent of profit, the extent of dealing, concerted action, combination, danger to the proprietor and degree of deception of (though this is not so clear) and danger to the public whereas the crime is probably less serious where the defendant has acted on impulse, it is a one-off crime, the public are not deceived, and the defendant himself was duped and indeed we venture to suggest that it would be a harsh court indeed that would impose a heavy financial or even custodial sentence on this last class of offender, conditional discharges being more appropriate.

20.111   There is little case law on the subject save for the reported cases of *R v Kelly*;[1] *R v Yanko*;[2] *R v Adam*[3] and *R v Bahd*[4] and some unreported ones.

1 [1996] 1 Cr App Rep (S) 61.
2 [1996] 1 Cr App Rep (S) 217.
3 [1998] 2 Cr App Rep (S) 403.
4 [1999] S Cr App Rep (S) 139.

20.112   In *R* v *Kelly*[1] the defendant pleaded guilty under the TMA 1938 offence of fraudulent use of a trade mark. It was observed by Laws J that the defendant had a persistent string of convictions for dishonesty and that taken in combination with the fact that he pleaded guilty to four counts which would attract a sentence of three months' imprisonment tended to aggravate matters. This case is, however to be regarded with care since a major part of the Court of Appeal's reasoning related to the defendant's previous convictions.

In *R* v *Kelly* the Court of Appeal suggested that a starting point of 4.5 years' imprisonment was appropriate in the case of counterfeiting pharmaceuticals, and it was the fact that the pharmaceuticals could have been very dangerous to the public since they were not made in accordance with a licence under the Medicines Act 1968 which figured to a great extent in the reasoning of the court. It is submitted that *R* v *Kelly* is not an appropriate guidance case at all save that a term of imprisonment is a very real option for a person convicted under s 92 of the TMA 1994.

In *R* v *Adam*,[2] the appellant was sentenced to four months' imprisonment where his profit was minimal and his level of sales was very small. There was no evidence of combination although it was accepted that the offence was serious enough to warrant custody. Aggravating features were identified by the court as being 'scale' and 'persistence'. The attitude of the court in relation to market traders is that of deterrence especially where the appellant had been given a warning as to his conduct but had nevertheless persisted in his behaviour. The sentence was described as severe but not manifestly excessive.

In *R* v *Bahd*[3] in the Court of Appeal, the appellant, an embroiderer was charged with trade mark offences relating to a small number of garments bearing marks such as Polo and Reebock. The Lord Chief Justice (Lord Bingham of Cornhill) said:

> '... [W]e recognise the damage done to the conduct of legitimate trade by the production and marketing of fake products. The owners of trade marks have a commercial asset which is entitled to legal protection. Deliberately using someone else's trade mark is in effect to steal their commercial goodwill. This is properly a criminal offence and a penalty must follow on conviction. It is, however, true in our judgment that all these counts arise out of the same incident which, so far as the counts go, points towards a small-scale operation. This is a very long way away from the sort of case where a warehouse full of fake products is discovered. Nor on the evidence before the court is it fair to approach this case on the basis that the appellant was conducting a dishonest business. It was, in truth, an honest business built up through hard work and we must regard this incident as an isolated lapse. It appears to us highly questionable whether the custody threshold was in truth crossed, but we accept the submission that it is anomalous to impose a custodial sentence on the less serious Trade Descriptions Act offences while visiting a financial penalty on the more serious Trade Marks Act offences. Accordingly we shall allow the appeal, quash the sentences imposed on the four Trade Descriptions Act offences and on those counts impose no separate penalty. To that extent and for those reasons this appeal is allowed.'

which is self explanatory.

1 [1996] 1 Cr App Rep (S) 61.
2 [1998] 2 Cr App Rep (S) 403.
3 [1999] 2 Cr App Rep (S) 139 at 141.

20.113 Apart from the reported cases there have been a number of unreported decisions of the Court of Appeal which have provided some assistance.

20.114 In *R v Goodwin and Unstead*[1] the Court of Appeal, in a case involving a conspiracy, held that joint action and measures to conceal the unlawful activity concerned with a resulting loss of £750,000 to the exchequer, would justify a custodial sentence of four years.

In *R v Swallow*[2] the Court of Appeal, in a case involving about 300 items of clothing falsely bearing trade marks such as Calvin Klein, Kickers, Ralph Lauren, Adidas, Chanel and Gucci which had a street value of £18,000, held that the quantity of goods was a factor to be taken into consideration as was the fact that the appellant was storing and selling the goods concerned. Section 92 of the TMA 1994 was aimed at protecting legitimate traders (which tends to suggest that s 92 of the TMA 1994 is not a consumer protection measure) and the courts will take a serious view of the offence for that reason since it can affect economic stability. The sentence of six months' imprisonment was upheld, though there was quite considerable mitigation.

In *R v Titus*[3] the Court of Appeal held that a fine of £5,000 and three years' disqualification as a director was not appropriate in relation to two counts relating to the false application of trade marks where the proprietor stood to lose approximately £2,300 from the appellant's activities (though it did not in fact do so since he was caught red-handed). That made a fine an appropriate penalty – if the appellant could pay it, which he could not and so a conditional discharge was substituted for the fine, though the disqualification was left to stand. There was, in this case, substantial mitigation in that the appellant had suffered huge financial loss as a result of his enterprise, not all of which was unlawful.

In *R v Flynn*,[4] a video pirate, prosecuted under s 92 of the TMA 1994 was sentenced to 12 months' imprisonment although his operation was a small-scale operation, he was the prime mover. The sentence was upheld.

In *R v Ansari, Horner, Ling and Ansari*[5] the Court of Appeal observed that this was a case where reputable companies were being undermined, that the operation was professional and that profit was being made.

Finally in *R v Birt*,[6] a case involving the re-marking of memory modules, the court observed that the use of a trade mark on defective or poor quality material may have greater significance in relation to matters of health and public safety (which was said to be the reason why ten years akin to theft was the maximum penalty for trade mark related crimes whereas it was only two years for copyright related crimes). In this case, the loss to the proprietor was unquantifiable, the danger to the public was uncertain. However the mitigation was good and a sentence of two years' imprisonment was substituted for a five-year term.

1 [1997] STC 22.
2 (14 October 1997 unreported) CA.
3 (20 January 1998, unreported) CA.
4 (11 March 1999, unreported) CA.
5 (11 May 1999, unreported) CA.
6 (8 June 1999, unreported) CA.

Procedure

20.115 The offences under s 92 of the TMA 1994 are triable either way, that is they may be tried pursuant to the summary jurisdiction of the Magistrates' or pursuant to the jurisdiction of the crown court. However all proceedings however they are to be tried start their lives in the Magistrates' Court although in fraud-type cases which are brought at the instance of the crown there is a streamlined procedure in operation which avoids the necessity of certain hearings in the Magistrates' Court.

Starting the ball rolling

20.116 Although the vast majority of prosecutions are conducted by agents for the crown, being the Crown Prosecution Service ('CPS'), in the area of trade marks, many prosecutions are brought by local authorities through their trading standards department, though conducted by the legal department (at least in some cases). In this sense, the prosecutions are private, though that makes no difference to the procedure at all save that the DPP has a discretion under s 6(2) of the Prosecution of Offences Act 1985 to take over and conduct, withdraw or discontinue any private prosecution. Where proceedings are withdrawn by a private party, and therefore not resulting in a recorded verdict of not guilty, the court is under a duty to send copies of the papers to the DPP so that he may ascertain whether the prosecution ought to be resurrected in the public interest.[1]

Where it is sought to commence proceedings, they can be commenced in one of two ways being by charge or by summons.

1 Prosecution of Offences Act 1985, s 7(4).

The charge

20.117 Most trade mark type offences are not commenced by charge since the power to charge is vested in the police only and most investigations of this type are carried out by local authorities or, exceptionally, trade mark owners. However, the police have the right to investigate trade mark offences and they can, after making their enquiries, charge the accused at any police station. The charge is carried out by a relevant police officer reading the allegation to the accused and then recording any comments he has to make. Thereafter the accused is handed a charge sheet which contains information as to when the matter shall be heard by the court, which is usually the next court day or the one after. Between charge and appearance the accused is usually on police bail, subject to such conditions as the custody sergeant may impose. Sometimes, however if the custody sergeant is of the view that (1) further offences may be committed whilst on bail, (2) prosecution witnesses might be interfered with or (3) the accused might not surrender to the court, then he may place the accused in custody until such time as the court hearing commences.

The summons

20.118 The more usual method of commencing a criminal prosecution in relation to trade marks is by way of summons and this indeed is the only way that private prosecutions may be commenced. The summons is obtained by a prosecutor by 'laying' information before the justices or the clerk to the justices whose court covers the commission area where the offence is alleged to have taken place. The justices or their clerk will consider the information, which will usually be a draft summons, and will issue the summons if they think fit to do so. The issuing of a summons is a judicial act and the decision to issue must be conducted judicially.[1] Although the decision process is reviewable, the Divisional Court will not intervene unless the discretion has been exercised as a result of a legal misdirection or if it is exercised unreasonably[2] in the legally accepted sense of the expression.[3] The same applies to the justices' clerk if it is he who is being asked to issue the summons[4] and in either case the Justice of the Peace or his clerk may hear representations from the proposed defendant,[5] though this is rare. The resultant summons has the effect of compelling the defendant (ie the person to who, the summons is addressed) to attend to answer the summons.

1 *R v Adamson* (1875) 1 QBD 201; 45 LJMC 46; *R v Byrde and Pontypool Gas Co, ex p Williams* (1890) 60 LJMC 17; 63 LT 645; *R v Bros* ; 66 JP 54;(1901) 85 LT 581 *R v Kennedy* (1902) 86 LT 753; 50 WR 633; *R v Mead, ex p National Health Insurance Comrs* (1916) 85 LJKB 1065; 114 LT 1172; *R v Brentford Justices, ex p Catlin* [1975] QB 455; 2 All ER 201 and *R v Manchester Stipendiary Magistrate, ex p Hill* [1983] 1 AC 328, 343; [1982] 2 All ER 963, 971.
2 *R v Chief Metropolitan Stipendiary Magistrate, ex p Choudhury* [1991] 1 QB 429; [1991] 1 All ER 306, 311.
3 Ie being a decision which no reasonable person could possibly come to.
4 *R v Manchester Stipendiary Magistrate, ex p Hill* [1983] 1 AC 328, [1982] 2 All ER 963.
5 *R v West London Justices, ex p Klahn* [1979] 2 All ER 221, [1979] 1 WLR 933.

20.119   Once the summons is issued it will state upon its face a time for the defendant to appear to answer the summons. The defendant must then be served with the summons to attend the first hearing. There is nothing in the rules or statutes which govern Magistrates' Courts procedure which states that the first hearing, at least insofar as the summary jurisdiction is concerned, shall not be the trial though usually the first hearing is a pre-trial hearing though its form will depend upon a variety of factors which are discussed below.

The first hearing at the Magistrates' Court

20.120   Whichever court is ultimately to try the defendant, the magistrates must decide if the case is one over which they wish to exercise jurisdiction or is one which the crown court should exercise jurisdiction. It is only if the magistrates and the defendant agree that the agistrates ought to have jurisdiction that jurisdiction is ceded to them if there is no agreement then the crown court automatically has jurisdiction.[1] In order to do that, the defendant must be placed in a position such that he may make representations as to the exercise of that jurisdiction and the prosecution must provide information which is sufficient to enable the defendant to make such representations, usually in the form of witness statements or summaries of the evidence. Such information if referred to as advance information and is governed by the Magistrates' Courts (Advance Information) Rules 1985[2] which set out the procedure which the prosecutor must follow. The prosecutor, before any hearing as to the mode of trial (ie whether the matter should be heard pursuant to the magistrates' summary jurisdiction or in the crown court), must serve a notice on the defendant informing him of his right to advance information and giving him details of where such a request may be made.[3] Usually such a request is made at the first hearing, necessitating an adjournment whilst the papers are awaited or considered by the defence. Once the papers have been considered by the defence then the magistrates' will consider the question. In *Practice Note (Mode of Trial: Guidelines)*[4] (as amended by the National Mode of Trial Guidelines) certain general points should be considered, being (a) the court should never make its decision on the grounds of convenience or expedition; (b) the court should assume for the purpose of the deciding mode of trial that the prosecution version of the facts is correct; (c) the fact that the offences are alleged to be specimens is a relevant consideration though the fact that the defendant will be asking for other offences to be taken into consideration, if convicted, is not; (d) where cases involve complex questions of fact or difficult questions of law, the court should consider transfer for trial; (e) where two or more defendants are jointly charged with an offence each has an individual right to elect his mode of trial; (f) in general, except where otherwise stated, either-way offences should be tried summarily; (g) the court should also consider its powers to commit an offender for sentence, under s 38 of the MCA 1980, as amended by s 25 of the CJA 1991, if information emerges during the course of the hearing which leads them to conclude that the offence is so serious, or the offender such a risk to the public, that their powers to sentence him are inadequate. This amendment means that committal for sentence is no longer determined by reference to the character or antecedents of the defendant. If the justices come to the decision that the gravity of the offence is such that they either do not have the powers to deal with it or the ability to do so then they sit as examining justices in order to test the evidence to see whether there is sufficient evidence to commit the defendant for trial at the crown court. However, if the defendant and the magistrates agree that the matter can be tried summarily then the justices can then hear the trial, though they will usually adjourn the matter until a more convenient time.

1 MCA 1980, s 19(3)(b).
2 (SI 1985/691).
3 Magistrates' Courts (Advance Information) Rules 1985, r 3.
4 [1990] 1 WLR 1439.

Committal

20.121   Committal is now a paper procedure although when s 51 of the Crime and Disorder Act 1998 (thought to be spring 2000) comes into force there will be no committal proceedings available for indictable only offences which will affect cases of conspiracy to defraud. There are two types of committal, that with consideration of the evidence, commonly known as a 'read through' and that without consideration of the evidence which was commonly known as a 'paper committal'. Both procedures are governed by s 6 of the MCA 1980 and specific reference should be made to that section and ss 5–5F of the MCA 1980 for the manner and method of preparing evidence. The evidence is examined (upon request that it be so examined or if the accused is not legally represented) and if an essential element in the offence is missing the examining justices must decline to commit the accused for trial. However it ought to be borne in mind that declining to commit (and dismissing the summons) for trial is not the same as a finding that the accused is not guilty and the effect may be that the prosecution starts all over again but get its evidence right on the subsequent occasion. Obviously if the prosecution tries too many times then this might amount to an abuse of process.

The trial

20.122 The trial takes the usual form which is that the prosecution opens its case, followed by its evidence the defence cross-examines the witnesses and the prosecution are entitled to re-examine. The justices are the tribunal of fact and of law though in relation to matters of law they are advised by their clerk. In some cases the justices may be replaced by a stipendiary magistrate who is usually a trained lawyer. After the close of the prosecution case the defence will make submissions relating to the insufficiency of the prosecution evidence and make submissions of no case to answer.

20.123 Thereafter the defence will call its witnesses, calling the defendant first, followed by other witnesses and at the close of the defence case, the prosecution can make a final speech which is followed by the defence, closing submission. Then the justices retire and consider their verdicts.

20.124 Interestingly because the justices are the arbiters of both law and fact they have to decide questions of admissibility of evidence which may involve them hearing inadmissible evidence to evaluate its admissibility. No real point has ever been taken on this though it is submitted that evidence which is particularly prejudicial would probably necessitate a re-trial.

20.125 If the proceedings are conducted before a crown court then the procedure is much the same save that the judge is the custodian of the law whereas the jury is the tribunal of fact and a determination of no case to answer is made by the Judge.

20.126 The time for taking points on the admissibility of evidence is as it is about to be adduced, although in certain circumstances the parties are obliged to forewarn their opponents on questions of admissibility.

Fraud

20.127 The CPS has taken the view in the past that trade mark offences or offences of deception involving trade marks can amount to serious or complex fraud. In such cases, the scheme envisaged by the Criminal Justice Act 1987 ('CJA 1987') relating to serious or complex fraud comes into being. This scheme is detailed and in-depth consideration of it is dealt with by a number of other standards texts and is outside the scope of this chapter. However, in summary, the procedure involves cutting the Magistrates' Courts out of the picture insofar as relates to consideration of any evidence. The entire proceedings are transferred to the crown court, upon the prosecutor (which is restricted to crown or crown-type prosecutors) applying to transfer the matter and serving a notice of transfer on the accused and the Magistrates' Court where the summons was issued. The effect is to bring a large number of complex procedural rules into play but also its effect is to transfer the committal process to the crown court, though the defendant must apply to dismiss the transferred charges[1] as opposed to the prosecution having to satisfy the court that there is a case to answer.

1 CJA 1987, s 6.

20.128   In a transferred case, the court may order the parties to supply each other with statements of case setting out their respective factual and legal contentions. If either party then departs from that statement or fails to make a statement in default then the court may at a later stage in the trial allow the other party to comment on the failure to the jury.

Gathering of Evidence

20.129   The normal rules of criminal evidence apply to cases involving trade marks as they relate to any other criminal trial. In the normal course the prosecution evidence will comprise a person giving evidence of the purchase of any goods from the defendant, followed by evidence of the existence of any trade mark and evidence that the defendant was not licenced. Such evidence is usually not contested by the defence though there are cases where it has been.

However since most prosecutions are brought by local authorities, that is, the local authority which is the local Weights and Measures Authority[1] it is important to look at some of the evidence gathering powers of those local authorities. This is governed by s 93(2) of the TMA 1994 which incorporates the provisions ss 27–29 and 33 of the TDA 1968 into the enforcement powers of the local authority under s 92 of the TMA 1994.

1 See the TMA 1994, s 93(1), which cedes authority to the local weights and measures authority the right to enforce within their area the provisions of s 92 of that Act and for the definition of what is a local weights and measures authority see the Weights and Measures Act 1985 (WMA 1985), (as amended) s 69(1), which reads:

'69.–(1) In England, the local weights and measures authority shall be–
      (a) for each non-metropolitan county, metropolitan district and London borough, the council of that county, district or borough,
      (b) for the City of London and the Inner and Middle Temples, the Common Council of the City of London, and
      (c) for the Isles of Scilly, the Council of the Isles of Scilly.
(2) In Wales, the local weights and measures authority for each county shall be the county council *and for each county borough shall be the county borough council.*
  …
Italicised words inserted by the Local Government (Wales) Act 1994, s 66(6), Sch 16, para 75 having force from the 3 April 1995 by the Operation of art 9 of the Local Government (Wales) Act 1994 (Commencement No 4) Order 1995.

20.130   Sections 27–29 and 33 of the TDA 1968 give the local authority the power to make test purchases and the power to enter premises and inspect and seize goods and documents. Further offences are created of obstructing an officer of a local authority exercising his powers and provision is made for compensation where goods are seized and no conviction results, though this is subject to arbitration.[1]

1 See TDA 1968, s 33.

20.131   By far the most powerful provision is set out in s 28(1) of the TDA 1968, which states:

'28.–(1) A duly authorised officer of a local weights and measures authority or of a Government department may, at all reasonable hours and on production, if required, of his credentials, exercise the following powers, that is to say,–

(a) he may, for the purpose of ascertaining whether any offence under this Act has been committed, inspect any goods and enter any premises other than premises used only as a dwelling;

(b) if he has reasonable cause to suspect that an offence under this Act has been committed, he may, for the purpose of ascertaining whether it has been committed, require any person carrying on a trade or business or employed in connection with a trade or business to produce any books or documents relating to the trade or business and may take copies of, or of any entry in, any such book or document;

(c) if he has reasonable cause to believe that an offence under this Act has been committed, he may seize and detain any goods for the purpose of ascertaining, by testing or otherwise, whether the offence has been committed;

(d) he may seize and detain any goods or documents which he has reason to believe may be required as evidence in proceedings for an offence under this Act;

(e) he may, for the purpose of exercising his powers under this subsection to seize goods, but only if and to the extent that it is reasonably necessary in order to secure that the provisions of this Act and of any order made thereunder are duly observed, require any person having authority to do so to break open any container or open any vending machine and, if that person does not comply with the requirement, he may do so himself.'

20.132 Thus, as can be seen the powers are extensive and complex. What is more is that they can be exercised in the absence of a search warrant and any person who obstructs a trading standards officer (or TSO as they are known) is liable to be prosecuted.[1] In many ways the powers of trading standards officers are more extensive then those of the police, who would usually have to rely upon the provisions of the Police and Criminal Evidence Act 1984 (PACE) to get a search warrant to search premises.[2] However there are safeguards in place such as the necessity for the powers to be exercised during reasonable hours and that such powers can be exercised only in the course of the enforcement of s 92 of the TMA 1994 within the geographical area concerned.[3]

1 See TDA 1968, s 29.
2 Though there are cases where the police do not need a search warrant such as when the accused is under arrest and where special authorisation has been given by a senior police officer. See PACE, s 18.
3 Which would appear to preclude, say Borsetshire Council, from investigating offences committed in Worcestershire.

20.133 In exercising the powers afforded by s 28(1) of the TDA 1968, a duly authorised officer must either pursue certain objectives or have developed the requisite state of mind based on 'suspicion' or 'belief', thus one of two elements must be present: either a permitted objective or a permitted state of mind. Purporting to act in the public interest or for some other reason (however well intentioned) will not do. Thus paras (a) and (e) of s 28 of the TDA 1968 speak of the objective of *ascertaining* and doing that which is *necessary* whereas paras (b)–(d) speak of the states of mind of *suspicion, reasonable cause to believe,* and *reason to believe.*

20.134 If the duly authorised officer cannot show that he had the relevant objectives or states of mind then his actions will be reviewable and his actions could be struck down as ultra vires. In the case of investigations relating to trade marks this has more relevance than one would think since it is lamentably the case that the trade marks register is a most neglected Government document, at least insofar as its consultants are concerned and *R v Torbay Council, ex p Singh*[1] is illustrative of this point. Though a mere assertion by a trade mark owner might be regarded as being enough, since he must be supposed to know what rights he has, the absence of such assertion or consultation may give grounds for a right of review of the relevant duly authorised officer.

1 (1999) Times, 5 July.

20.135 What type of officers may exercise the functions bestowed by s 28 of the TDA 1968 is unclear. It must be borne in mind that a weights and measures authority and a local authority as are set out in s 69 of the WMA 1985 are different things. So the officer concerned must be an officer of the weights and measures authority and must (a) have been duly appointed to that position and (b) must be authorised to carry out the investigation under s 28 of the TDA 1968 either specifically or generally.

20.136 The only power that the local weights and measures authority has as derived from the WMA 1985 to appoint officers is contained in s 72 of that Act, being a power to appoint inspectors to carry out functions under the WMA 1985 (and *not* the TDA 1968). However the general power of a local authority to appoint officers under s 112(1) of the Local Government Act 1972 in the discharge of its functions or the functions of another authority (such as a weights and measures authority) would appear to deal with any possible lacuna in this area. Usually the power to act is derived from a meeting of the local authority and is devolved generally. No known case has ever succeeded on the issue of want of authority.

20.137 Two common questions arise for consideration in relation to the exercise of powers under s 28 of the TDA 1968 being whether the duly empowered officer is obliged to develop his state of mind at the scene of inspection or before he enters it and if not, whether he is allowed to fish for evidence.

20.138 It is quite clear that mere fishing is never going to be tolerated or allowed. However since the general function of the local weights and measures authority is to enforce s 92 of the TMA 1994 it must be entitled to make spot checks and inspections of its local markets since to deny the local weights and measures authority of such a right would be to denude it of any effective power of enforcement at all – counterfeiters who know they are going to be investigated are known to run very fast indeed and can cover their tracks (if they make them at all) extremely effectively and this is, we submit, the purpose and effect of s 28(1)(a) of the TDA 1968 which allows inspection of goods and entry to any premises[1] to *see* (ie ascertain) whether an offence has been committed. However the power to enter such premises or inspect such goods can only be exercised if the intention of inspection or entry is to see if an offence has been committed. If such has already been ascertained then, it is submitted there is no right of entry under this paragraph.

1 Save for solely domestic premises.

20.139 Section 28(1)(b) of the TDA 1968 requires not only a state of mind (reasonable cause to suspect that an offence has been committed), but also a permitted objective, for the purpose of ascertaining that it has been committed. The power thereby given is to require access to books or documents relating to the trade or business in question. That access may be required in any way whatsoever, even a request by post will suffice, although usually it is exercised whilst the relevant officers are on the relevant premises anyway.

20.140   Section 28(1)(c) of the TDA 1968 enables the seizure and detention of goods where there is reasonable cause to believe that an offence has been committed and it has to be ascertained by reference to those goods whether an offence *has* actually been committed. The precise ambit of this paragraph is unclear. Would it, for instance, allow an officer to remove blank t-shirts which were about to be illegally stamped? We submit not.

20.141   Section 28(1)(d) of the TDA 1968 is, however much wider in effect than s 28(1)(c) since it enables things to be taken where there is reason to believe that those things may be required in evidence. This may well include blank t-shirts, especially where it is sought to establish that the defendant is acting in the course of a business (and therefore with a view to profit). This does not apply to privileged communications.[1]

1 TDA 1968, s 28(7).

20.142   Section 28(1)(e) of the TDA 1968 relates to the searching and breaking open of vending machines and containers but such must be for the purposes of exercising other powers under s 28(1) of the TDA 1968 and then may only be done so if it is reasonably necessary to do so.

20.143   Section 28(2) of the TDA 1968 states:

> '(2) An officer seizing any goods or documents in the exercise of his powers under this section shall inform the person from whom they are seized and, in the case of goods seized from a vending machine, the person whose name and address are stated on the machine as being the proprietor's or, if no name and address are so stated, the occupier of the premises on which the machine stands or to which it is affixed.'

Inform such persons of what?

20.144   As can be seen there are a number of quite wide-ranging powers, the most invasive of which is the right of entry for ascertaining whether an offence has been committed. It is to be noted that these powers may only be exercised by the relevant authorised officer (ie not the police) and are not, in the first instance, the subject of judicial supervision. However circumstances may rise where a raid by the weights and measures authority would have the effect of frustrating any investigation or rights of seizure and inspection under s 28(1)(a)–(e) of the TDA 1968 either because the occupier of the premises would hide or destroy evidence or because it is not possible to attain entry (for whatever reason) then the officer concerned may apply for an entry warrant, that is a warrant allowing the officer to enter the premises (and to use force if necessary), though once on the premises he may exercise no more rights than he had under s 28(1)(a)–(e) of the TDA 1968.

20.145   An entry warrant as opposed to a search warrant may be obtained from a Justice of the Peace[1] provided that he is satisfied that there are reasonable grounds, based upon sworn written evidence[2] that there are in existence goods, books or documents which an officer would have power to inspect under s 28(1)(a)–(e) of the TDA 1968 which are on *any* premises[3] *and* that their inspection is likely to disclose evidence of the commission of an offence under s 92 of the TMA 1994.[4]

Alternatively, if the Justice of the Peace is satisfied (on the same grounds and in the same way as previously) that an offence under s 92 of the TMA 1994 has been, is being, or is about to be committed, then an entry warrant may also be issued.[5]

1 TDA 1968, s 28(3).
2 TDA 1968, s 28(3)(a).
3 Which would seem to include domestic premises even though there is no power to enter domestic premises – see TDA 1968, s 28(1)(a).
4 TDA 1968, s 28(3)(a)(i).
5 TDA 1968, s 28(3)(a)(ii).

20.146 It is a condition precedent (in addition to the matters previously raised) that either admission to enter the premises has been, or is likely to be, refused and that the occupier of the premises has been given notice of an intention to apply for an entry warrant[1] or that asking to be admitted to such premises or the giving of notice will frustrate the purposes of the entry or that the occupier is temporarily absent or that the premises are unoccupied.[2] It is only once those rigorous conditions are satisfied that an entry warrant can be obtained and even then it only lasts a month.

1 TDA 1968, s 28(3)(b)(i).
2 TDA 1968, s 28(3)(b)(ii).

20.147 When an officer enters onto premises (whether by reason of an entry warrant or by reason of his other statutory powers to do so) he may take such equipment with him as he needs and may also take any other person with him, though he must, upon leaving, secure the premises against trespass as he found them.[1]

1 TDA 1968, s 28(4).

20.148 Confidential information or indeed any information obtained in pursuance of the powers exercised under s 28(1) of the TDA 1968 must not be disclosed (unless done pursuant to enforcement of s 92 of the TMA 1994) and any person doing so is guilty of an offence.[1]

1 TDA 1968, s 28(5).

20.149 Thus the evidence-gathering powers of TSOs are powerful and can be carried out with the use of some force, there is little case law on the extent of these powers. There is little evidence of their abuse.

Evidence – generally

20.150 Most evidence is tendered by way of prosecution witness statement of business documents which are produced under s 9 of the CJA 1967 and ss 23 and 24 of the CJA 1988.

20.151 Section 9 of the CJA 1967 enables a statement of evidence to be admitted as first-hand hearsay where the parties agree to such, though the tenderee is deemed to agree if no objection is made within seven days and the court does not otherwise order. What s 9 of the CJA 1967 does not do is to make that admissible which would be inadmissible if it came from the mouth of the witness himself, giving evidence in the witness box. In other words, the modest purpose of s 9 of the CJA 1967 is to be the mouthpiece of the witness but does not otherwise expand the rule (which is strict, in comparison to civil proceedings) against hearsay.

20.152 On the other hand, ss 23 and 24 of the CJA 1988 perform slightly different functions, though they have the effect of admitting evidence which would otherwise be hearsay. Section 23 of the CJA 1988 has the effect of admitting hearsay (to the same extent and to the same degree as s 9 of the CJA 1967) where the maker of the statement, which must be made in a document, is either deceased,[1] is ill,[2] cannot, despite reasonable diligence, be found[3] or is beyond the seas[4] and it is not practicable to secure attendance.[5] Statements are also admissible if made to a police officer (or person, broadly speaking in a like position)[6] and it is desirable to keep the maker of the statement out of the way.[7] Section 23 of the CJA 1988 is of limited effect, though of great value in the correct circumstances. Its effects may be ameliorated by s 25 of the CJA 1988 which gives the crown court a discretion to refuse to admit such a statement if, in essence, it would be unfair *to the accused* to admit it,[8] though there is nothing to stop the accused from relying upon the evidential provisions of the CJA 1988 and it would appear that the prosecution is thereby disabled in the number of objections which it can make to evidence tendered under s 23 of the CJA 1988.

1 CJA 1988, s 23(1)(c)(i) and (2)(a).
2 See n 1, above.
3 CJA 1988, s 23(1)(c)(i) and (2)(c).
4 CJA 1988, s 23(1)(c)(i) and (2)(b)(i).
5 CJA 1988, s 23(1)(c)(i) and (2)(b)(ii).
6 CJA 1988, s 23(1)(c)(ii) and (3)(a).
7 CJA 1988, s 23(1)(c)(ii) and (3)(b).
8 CJA 1988, s 25(1) and (2).

20.153 Section 24 of the CJA 1988 is of far more utility (though it is also subject to s 25 of the CJA 1988) since it enables business documents to be put in evidence without further proof, though subject to certain conditions and subject to the first-hand hearsay rule, though in a much watered down form. The main condition for admissibility is that the maker of the statement must be reasonably supposed to have first hand knowledge of the matters concerned[1] and that the statement was committed to a document or received by a person in the course of his trade, profession or as an officer holder.[2] Following on from *R v Foxley*[3] the court is entitled to look at the document itself and glean from it the necessary details which enable the court to arrive at the view as to whether the document satisfies the necessary criteria of s 24 of the CJA 1988.

1 CJA 1988, s 24(1)(c)(ii).
2 CJA 1988, s 24(1)(c)(i).
3 [1995] 2 Cr App Rep 523. Though not strictly speaking a hearsay case since in fact no reliance was placed on the truth of the documents concerned.

Evidence of registration

20.154 The trade marks register is the most convenient place to get evidence of registration and indeed it is necessary to prove that the sign used by the defendant is indeed identical to or likely to be mistaken for a registered trade mark. In certain cases expert evidence of this will be allowed, where for instance a person who is well acquainted with the trade mark in question (and its scope)[1] has examined goods in question and has expressed the view that they fall foul of s 92 of the TMA 1994.[2]

1 Such as an investigations manager for a well known, high-class clothing manufacturer.
2 See *Akhtar v Grout* (1998) 162 JP 714.

20.155   The trade marks register is a pubic document, ie it is a document made by a public office, The Comptroller-General of patents, designs and trade marks so that the public might refer to the document.[1] In the case of registered trade marks the purpose of the register, or one important purpose is that traders may see what the forbidden territory is. Usually originals of the register or public document do not have to be produced, on the grounds of (in)convenience and indeed in the case of the trade marks register this would be impossible or near on impossible since it is kept on computer.[2] However there is nothing in the TMA 1994 or the Trade Marks Rules 1994 (as amended) which provides for the admissibility of the register in evidence. Accordingly s 14 of the Evidence Act 1851 states that whenever any book or other document is of such a public nature as to be admissible in evidence on its mere production from the proper custody and no statute exists which renders its contents provable by means of a copy, an examined or certified copy is admissible.

1 *Sturla v Freccia* (1880) 5 App Cas 623, 643, per Lord Blackburn.
2 See TMA 1994, s 53(3) and Trade Marks Rules 1994 (SI 1998/2583), r 32.

20.156   The question is then whether the register is indeed 'of such a public nature as to be admissible in evidence'. This is a matter of common law since there is no supervening statutory provision, though the common law is unclear since it is not invoked very often.

20.157   In *Sturla v Freccia*[1] a public document was defined by Lord Blackburn thus:

'I understand a public document there to mean a document that is made for the purpose of the public making use of it, and being able to refer to it. It is meant to be where there is a judicial, or quasi-judicial, duty to inquire, as might be said to be the case with the bishop acting under the writs issued by the Crown. That may be said to be quasi-judicial. He is acting for the public when that is done; but I think the very object of it must be that it should be made for the purpose of being kept public, so that the persons concerned in it may have access to it afterwards.

'In many cases, entries in the parish register, of births, marriages, and deaths, and other entries of that kind, before there were any statutes relating to them, were admissible, and they were 'public' then, because the Common Law of England making it an express duty to keep the register, made it a public document in that sense kept by a public officer for the purpose of a register, and so made it admissible. I think as far as my recollection goes, although I will not pledge myself to its accuracy, and so far as I have ever heard anything cited, it will be found that, in every case in which a public document of that sort has been admitted, it has been made originally with the intent that it should be retained and kept, as a register to be referred to, ever after.'

Thus the conditions for admissibility must be:

(1)   That the document is one to which the public have access:[2] *Lilley v Pettit*.[3]
(2)   That the document is intended to last for ever:[4] *Mercer v Denne*.[5]
(3)   The entry must be made promptly after the event which it purports record.[6]
(4)   The person making the entry must be under a duty to enquire in order to satisfy himself of the veracity of the recorded facts:[7] *Doe' d France v Andrews*,[8] though as was suggested by Geoffrey Lane LJ in *R v Halpin*:[9]

'The common law should move with the times and should recognise that the official charged with recording matters of public import can no longer in this highly complicated world, as like as not, have personal knowledge of their accuracy.'

Which would suggest that the duty to enquire can be shared between the person making the entry and the person declaring it to the registrar. In *R v Halpin* the Court of Appeal held that the company's register was proof of its contents even though the duty to enquire was shared between the registrar and the declarant. However an important feature of the companies' legislation at the time was that there was a duty incumbent upon the declarant to truthfully declare the recorded matters, in other words someone, somewhere must know of the truth of the matter. As we have said in the Trade Marks Registry the practice is extremely unclear and there appears t be no obligation upon the declarant to make a truthful declaration (as there was upon the company director in *R v Halpin*).

1 (1880) 5 App Cas 623, 643, 644.
2 Which they do, see the Trade Mark rules 1994 (SI 1998/2583), r 36.
3 [1946] KB 401.
4 Which it must be, though it is implicit.
5 [1905] 2 Ch 538.
6 The trade mark registry practice on this is uncertain though in *R v Halpin* [1975] QB 907, 913, Geoffrey Lane LJ suggested that this went to weight rather then admissibility.
7 Again, it is unclear what the practice of the practice of the trade mark registry is in this regard.
8 (1850) 15 QB 756, 759.
9 [1975] QB 907, 915.

20.158   The foregoing coupled with the uncertainty of trade mark registry practice would tend to suggest that proof of extracts in the register are not admissible as public documents.

20.159   It is possible that such a document is or may be admissible under s 24 of the CJA 1988 since the document would be created by a person as a holder of a paid office, the registrar, though it is unclear whether the information which he would be supplied with is information which the maker of the statement might reasonably be expected to know the truth of. Again we come up against the uncertainty of trade mark registry practice.

Evidence and procedure – disclosure

20.160   In *R v Ward*[1] the Court of Appeal expressed the view that it was incumbent upon the prosecution to make disclosure of all relevant information and that in cases of doubt it was for the court and not the prosecution to decide whether something ought to be disclosed. That is obviously subject to the proviso that disclosure should not happen if such disclosure was not in the public interest, though that would also be a matter for the court to decide.

1 [1993] 1 WLR 519.

20.161   Generally the position has been regulated by the Criminal Procedure and Investigations Act 1996 (CPIA 1996) but since many elements are preserved by the CPIA 1996 it is important to consider the pre-act position, since it is still relevant in many respects.

20.162   The rule is this: documents which the prosecution hold and the disclosure of which is in the public interest, *must* be disclosed and it is not for the prosecution to say what the public interest is. Further there is a strong public interest in a defendant being able to conduct his case without his hands being tied behind his back.

20.163 Where the prosecution seeks to withhold material documents, it should not be entitled to do so without at least telling the defence, though it was accepted in *R v Davis, Johnson and Rowe*[1] that circumstances might arise where the prosecution might not even wish to disclose the very existence of certain documents . As a result the prosecutor has to do a number of things.

1 (1993) 97 Cr App R 110, 114 CA.

20.164 Firstly, the prosecutor must disclose his entire hand, all the documents upon which the prosecution relies or which damn it, or, presumably, documents leading to relevant enquiries being made. That first point is ameliorated by the fact that the prosecutor need not disclose anything which it is not in the public interest to disclose. At that juncture the prosecution has, in some way or another, to bring the matter before the court for the court to decide whether the contention of the prosecutor is correct.

20.165 The information in which immunity is sought will fall into two classes being, information, the *existence* of which the prosecution needs to protect and information, the *detail* of which the prosecution needs to protect. An example of information falling into the former class would be something akin to the fact that an undercover surveillance operation had been conducted nearby and, though it had nothing to do with the current defendant, the surveyors might have seen something. An example of the latter class would be something akin to the name of an informant (as opposed to the fact that there was one, though such a fact might not be disclosed if the result was to enable identification of the informant in question).

20.166 In relation to information which falls into the former class the prosecution is obliged to make an ex parte application to see the judge, though the defence must be notified, save in exceptional circumstances (which have never been known to arise), that the hearing is to take place. The court may rule on the ex parte application or may rule that the inter partes procedure is to be followed. The inter partes procedure is to be followed where the type of information is disclosed to the defence but not the detail and the defence is entitled to make representations but not to see the information concerned until a ruling is made in its favour. At that point if disclosure is not made then the prosecution will have to abandon its case – this does not infrequently happen in relation to informants, whose identity may be disclosed because they might also have been a witness and one which could assist the defence.

20.167 The foregoing principles were set out by Lord Taylor of Gosforth CJ in the case of *R v Davis*[1] and he went on to say:

> 'We should add that where the court, on application by the Crown, rules in favour of non-disclosure before the hearing of a case begins, that ruling is not necessarily final. In the course of the hearing, the situation may change. Issues may emerge so that the public interest in non-disclosure may be eclipsed by the need to disclose in the interests of securing fairness to the defendant. If that were to occur, the court would have to indicate to the Crown its change of view. The Crown would then have to decide whether to disclose or offer no further evidence.'

1 [1993] 1 WLR 613.

20.168 The court must balance the public interests between disclosure and non-disclosure, always bearing in mind that if the material under consideration may establish the innocence of the accused, or prevent a miscarriage of justice, then the balance is overwhelmingly in favour of disclosure.

20.169 Accordingly, the police are required to make available to the prosecution all material which may be relevant to an investigation. It is then left to the prosecution to decide which material is to be disclosed to the defence.

20.170 At common law, the prosecution had a duty to disclose matter in its possession to the defence, which, in its opinion, was sufficiently material to issues at trial. The definition of 'materiality' was set out by Lord Taylor of Gosforth CJ *R Keane*[1] and created three heads of disclosable matter, namely, that which can be seen on a sensible appraisal by the prosecution:

(1)   to be relevant, or possibly relevant, to an issue in the case;
(2)   to raise, or possibly raise, a new issue whose existence is not apparent from the evidence the prosecution proposes to use;
(3)   to hold out a real (as opposed to fanciful) prospect of providing a lead on evidence which goes to (1) and (2).

For the purpose of determining what matter might be material, the issue of whether the particular matter might be helpful to the defence was to be disregarded, but if the matter did not fall within the above three heads, the prosecution had no obligation to disclose it.

1   [1994] 2 All ER 478.

20.171 With the introduction of the CPIA 1996 the criteria as set out in *R v Keane*[1] has been replaced by statutory regime pursuant to ss 3 and 7 thereof (which relates to primary and secondary disclosure by prosecution). However, what is important to note is that the principle of disclosure has not been diluted by the CPIA 1996 – merely the form or practice. Thus it is the question of public interest immunity which forms the most common basis for objection to disclosure, though this is by no means the only ground of objection. In other words, the prosecution now may only effectively seek to withhold matters (which otherwise would be disclosable) on the ground of public interest immunity and it has been said that other rules of common law disclosure of material by the prosecution no longer apply. But if this were ever true then one is in essence regulating the main stricture of the principle of disclosure which is: disclose if relevant or if not offending some principle of the public interest.

1   1994 2 All ER 478.

20.172 Under the CPIA 1996 the prosecution must engage in an act known as primary disclosure. This is covered by s 3 of the CPIA 1996. The prosecutor must disclose any prosecution material (not previously disclosed) which (in the prosecutor's opinion) undermines the prosecution case.[1] The prosecution must also certify the completeness of his disclosure.[2] The time for doing this may be set by the Government,[3] which at the time of writing has not been done. Accordingly the CPIA 1996 stipulates[4] that primary disclosure takes place as soon as is reasonably practicable[5] after the accused pleads not guilty,[6] or is committed for trial,[7] where the matter is transferred (as being a serious or complex fraud[8]), the count is included in the indictment[9] or the bill of indictment is preferred.[10] There are certain codes of practice which the prosecutor is bound to observe. The code[11] regulates the manner in which the information is listed and dealt with. There is a specific statutory exception where the prosecutor is not obliged to make disclosure of material where it is not in the public interest to make such disclosure.[12] At present the code provides[13] that information should not be disclosed if it falls within the following list:

— material relating to national security;
— material received from the intelligence and security agencies;
— material relating to intelligence from foreign sources which reveals sensitive intelligence gathering methods;
— material given in confidence;
— material which relates to the use of a telephone system and which is supplied to an investigator for intelligence purposes only;
— material relating to the identity or activities of informants, or undercover police officers, or other persons supplying information to the police who may he in danger if their identities are revealed;
— material revealing the location of any premises or other place used for police surveillance, or the identity of any person allowing a police officer to use them for surveillance;
— material revealing, either directly or indirectly, techniques and methods relied upon by a police officer in the course of a criminal investigation, for example covert surveillance techniques, or other methods of detecting crime;
— material whose disclosure might facilitate the commission of other offences of hinder the prevention and detection of crime;
— internal police communications such as management minutes;
— material upon the strength of which search warrants were obtained;
— material containing details of persons taking part in identification parades;
— material supplied to an investigator during a criminal investigation which has been generated by an official of a body concerned with the regulation or supervision of bodies corporate or of persons engaged in financial activities, or which has been generated by a person retained by such a body;
— material supplied to an investigator during a criminal investigation which relates to a child or young person and which has been generated by a local authority social services department, an Area Child Protection Committee or other party contacted by an investigator during the investigation.

1 CPIA 1996, s 3(1)(a).
2 CPIA 1996, s 3(1)(b).
3 CPIA 1996, s 12.
4 CPIA 1996, s 13.
5 CPIA 1996, ss 13(1) and s 3(8).
6 CPIA 1996, ss 13(1) and s 3(8)(a).
7 CPIA 1996, ss 13(1) and s 3(8)(b).
8 CPIA 1996, ss 13(1) and s 3(8)(c).
9 CPIA 1996, ss 13(1) and s 3(8)(d).
10 CPIA 1996, ss 13(1) and s 3(8)(e).
11 CPIA 1996, s 23(1).
12 CPIA 1996, s 3(6).
13 Paragraph 6.12.

20.173 Exceptionally, material may be so sensitive that it has to be disclosed to the prosecutor separately so that an appropriate ex parte application needs to be made.[1] Thereafter the applications to the prosecutor in relation to primary disclosure are governed by statutory instrument, so far as the crown court is concerned[2] – if there is ever sensitive material then there will have to be an application.

20.174   Thereafter the obligations pass to the accused to carry out two types of disclosure. The first is compulsory disclosure, which takes place where primary disclosure has happened. Compulsory disclosure is the disclosure of a defence statement of case[1] which must consist of particulars of alibi.[2] Further the accused must give his statement within the prescribed time[3] which is, this time set out in a statutory instrument[4] which must be within the period of 14 days of the giving (or purporting to give) primary disclosure.[5] Such disclosure is only compulsory in the crown court.

1 CPIA 1996, s 5(6).
2 CPIA 1996, s 5(7).
3 CPIA 1996, s 5(9).
4 The Criminal Procedure and Investigations Act 1996 (Defence Disclosure Time Limits) Regulations 1997 (SI 1997/684).
5 Regulation 2 of The Criminal Procedure and Investigations Act 1996 (Defence Disclosure Time Limits) Regulations 1997 (SI 1997/684).

20.175   The defence may give a defence statement to the prosecution if it is not otherwise obliged to do so (ie in the Magistrates' Court) which would be in the same form as the compulsory disclosure. The time limit is also 14 days from primary disclosure.

20.176   After primary disclosure and compulsory or voluntary disclosure the prosecution must disclose to the accused any prosecution material which has not previously been disclosed to the accused and which might be reasonably expected to assist the accused's defence as disclosed by the defence statement whether given compulsorily or voluntarily[1] and give to the accused a written statement that there is no material of a description aforementioned.[2]

1 CPIA 1996, s 7(2)(a).
2 CPIA 1996, s 7(2)(b).

20.177   Section 8 of the CPIA 1996 governs the position where the accused gives a defence statement and the prosecutor complies, purports or fails to comply with secondary disclosure[1] the (and only then) can the accused apply for disclosure of undisclosed material if the accused believes (reasonably) that would assist him[2] and the material had not been disclosed to him.[3]

1 CPIA 1996, s 8(1).
2 CPIA 1996, s 8(2)(a).
3 CPIA 1996, s 8(2)(b).

20.178   The prosecutor is under a continuing duty to disclose throughout[1] up to the end of the trial – this is, it is submitted, wrong since the prosecutor might come across information which would exonerate the accused upon or after conviction and yet be under no obligation to disclose it.

1 CPIA 1996, s 9.

20.179   If the prosecutor fails to observe time limits, that of itself will not be regarded as an abuse of process[1] unless it causes the accused to be denied a fair trial.[2]

However, where the accused is in default or puts forward a case which is inconsistent with his statement, adverse inferences may be drawn[3] though those inferences shall not be the sole cause of conviction.[4]

1 CPIA 1996, s 10(2).
2 CPIA 1996, s 10(3).
3 CPIA 1996, s 11(3) and (4).
4 CPIA 1996, s 11(5).

20.180   Where an investigation has begun after 15 April 1997, the CPIA 1996 applies otherwise the common law rules apply where the defence is under no obligation to make compulsory or voluntary disclosure.

Part VI

International treaties

Chapter 21

International registration under the Madrid Protocol

1 History of the Madrid Protocol

21.1 The Madrid Protocol, as stated in s 53 of the TMA 1994, is the Protocol relating to the Madrid Agreement concerning the International Registration of Marks,[1] adopted at Madrid on 27 June 1989. The International Bureau (ie the International Bureau of the World Intellectual Property Organisation), maintains the International Register, on which international registrations, obtained under the Madrid Agreement, are entered. A number of important countries have not become parties to the Madrid Agreement; these include the USA and Japan, and (in the EU) the UK, Ireland, Greece and Denmark. The aim of the Protocol, which was ratified by the UK on 9 April 1995, is to bring such countries into the system for international registration. It will enable applications to be made, through one filing, for an 'international registration' on the International Register, having the effect of national registrations of trade marks in a number of countries. The actual number of countries in which registration may be applied for will be determined by the number of countries which ratify the Madrid Protocol.[2] The Protocol came into effect on 1 April 1996. The system will, like the Madrid Agreement, operate through the International Bureau, and international registrations obtained under the Protocol will be entered in the International Register. In the TMA 1994 'international trade mark (UK)' means a trade mark entitled to protection in the UK under the Protocol.

1 14 April 1894, as revised on a number of occasions.
2 As at 15 January 1999 the following countries had ratified the Protocol: Albania, Algeria, Armenia, Austria, Azerbaijan, Belarus, Belgium, Bosnia and Herzegovina, Bulgaria, China, Croatia, Cuba, Czech Republic, Democratic People's Republic of Korea, Denmark, Egypt, Estonia, Finland, France, Georgia, Germany, Hungary, Iceland, Italy, Kenya, Kazakhstan, Kyrgyzstan, Latvia, Lesotho, Liberia, Liechtenstein, Lithuania, Luxembourg, Monaco, Mongolia, Morocco, Mozambique, the Netherlands, Norway, Poland, Portugal, Republic of Moldova, Romania, Russian Federation, San Marino. Sierra Leone, Slovakia, Slovenia, Spain, Sudan, Swaziland, Sweden, Switzerland, Tajikistan, The Former Yugoslav Republic of Macedonia, Turkey, Ukraine, UK, Uzbekistan, Viet Nam, Yugoslavia. See Appendix 6.

21.2 Before considering the Protocol in any detail, something needs to be said about the Madrid Agreement, the reasons why some countries, including in particular the UK, did not become members, and how the Protocol seeks to remedy the position.

Main provisions of the the Madrid Agreement

21.3 The purpose of the Madrid Agreement was to provide a relatively quick and inexpensive means of obtaining protection of trade marks in a number of countries through a single filing. The countries to which the Agreement applies are referred to as a 'Special Union for the International registration of marks'.[1] In order to use the Agreement it is necessary[2] to have an existing registration of the trade mark in the applicant's 'country of origin': that is the country of the Special Union where the applicant has a real and effective industrial or commercial establishment; if he has no such establishment, the country of the Special Union where he has his domicile; if he has no such domicile, the country of the Special Union of which he is a national.[3] The filing is effected at the International Bureau through the intermediary of the office of the country of origin. The Agreement[4] lays down the procedural requirements for filing, including the specific mentioning of requests for extension of protection of the mark in countries which require such a request. The International Bureau registers the mark and must notify the registration without delay, to the national offices concerned. Under art 4, from the date of registration at the International Bureau, the protection of the mark in each of the contracting countries concerned is the same as if the mark had been filed directly in those countries; contracting countries are free to determine the scope of protection of the mark given by registration, as regards goods and services. Article 5 provides for refusal of protection by national offices of contracting countries. Grounds of refusal must be those which would apply under the Paris Convention, in respect of applications for national registration, and notice of refusal, with a statement of all grounds, must be given to the International Bureau within one year from the date of the international registration or the request for extension of protection to the country concerned. Copies of the notification of refusal have to be sent to the office of the country of origin and to the proprietor, who has the same remedies as if he had filed direct in the country where protection is refused. The grounds for refusal are to be communicated to an interested party who may so request.

1 Article 1.
2 Article 1(2) and (3).
3 See also art 2, which applies to nationals of countries which were not parties to the Agreement but satisfied the conditions of art 3 of the Paris Convention.
4 Articles 3, 3bis and 3ter.

21.4 Registration of a mark with the International Bureau is for 20 years, with renewal for further periods of 20 years.[1] Article 6(3) introduces the principle of 'central attack'. Under art 6(2), after five years from the date of the international registration it becomes independent of the registration in the country of origin. If within this period of five years the mark in the country of origin ceases to enjoy, in whole or in part, legal protection in that country, then the protection resulting from the international registration may no longer be invoked. This also applies if the legal protection in the country of origin ceases as a result of action commenced during the five-year period. The fees payable to the office of the country of origin and to other national offices are determined by art 8 and the Common Regulations. Article 9bis makes provision for cases where an international registration is transferred to a proprietor in another country, and prohibits recordal of any transfer to a person who is not entitled to file an international registration.

1 Articles 6 and 7.

21.5 The system thus established was not acceptable to the UK, or to a number of other countries, for several reasons. In particular the insistence on an actual registration in the country of origin placed applicants in the UK, and in other countries where registration was comparatively difficult to obtain, at a serious disadvantage. Furthermore in countries like the UK, which had systems providing for official examination of applications and powers of refusal, and for oppositions, the time of one year for giving notice of refusal of protection was considered far too short. Also the possibility of losing the entire international registration within the first five years, through central attack, was a cause for concern. Among other difficulties was the fact that French was the sole language used in the International Bureau, and the scale of the official fees provided for was considered too low for some countries.

2   The Protocol

21.6   The Protocol goes a considerable way towards meeting the concerns which prevented the Madrid Agreement from gaining universal acceptance, although in many respects it is essentially the same system. The first important change is that it is no longer necessary to have a registration in the country of origin; an application will suffice.[1] There are similar provisions for the applications and the information to be given on the form and for registration and its effects,[2] for territorial effect and for territorial extension.[3] Article 5 deals with refusal of protection by the offices of contracting parties, and retains the same period of a year for this purpose, but allows any contracting party to declare that, for international registrations made under the Protocol, this period is replaced by a period of 18 months.[4] Such declaration[5] may also specify that, where a refusal of protection may result from an opposition, such refusal may be notified after the 18-month period. This can only be done where, before the expiry of that time limit, the office has informed the International Bureau of the possibility that oppositions may be filed after the expiry of the 18-month time limit. Furthermore, by art 5(2)(c)(ii), the notification of refusal based on opposition must be made within not more than seven months from the beginning of the opposition period and, if the opposition period expires before the seven-month time limit, the notification must be made within a month from the expiry of the opposition period. So far as the UK is concerned, this means that the notice of refusal must be given within one month from the end of the period prescribed by the 1994 Rules for opposing an application, ie within four months from the advertisement in the Trade Marks Journal.[6] A declaration under art 5(2)(b) and (c) was made by the UK on 9 April 1995, at the same time as it ratified the Protocol. The possibility of increasing the period for refusal is important for countries, like the UK, whose laws provide for examination of applications on absolute and relative grounds, and which have opposition systems. Under arts 6 and 7, international registration under the Protocol has effect for 10 years with the possibility of renewal for succeeding periods of 10 years. Article 6 of the Protocol retains the principle of central attack; after five years the international registration becomes independent of the basic application or the resulting registration in the country of origin, but if, within the five-year period, in respect of all or any of the goods or services listed in the international registration, the basic application or resulting registration has been withdrawn or has lapsed, or has for any other reason ceased to have effect, then the protection resulting from the international registration may no longer be invoked. The same applies if the basic application or registration ceases to have effect in respect of all or some of the goods or services, as a result of an appeal, action or opposition begun before the end of the five-year period. This may seem to raise the same potential difficulty as the principle of central attack was considered to do under the Madrid Agreement. However under secondary UK legislation[7] the difficulty is mitigated, so far as an international registration designating the UK is concerned, by the possibility of 'transformation'. In the case of an international registration based on a filing at the UK office as office of origin, any such difficulty should be significantly reduced in practice so long as the hope of easier registration under the TMA 1994 is fulfilled. Other changes introduced under the Protocol, which have made international registration more acceptable to the UK and other countries, are the introduction of English as a second language, and improvements regarding the fees payable to national offices.

1 Article 2.
2 Articles 3 and 4.
3 Articles 3[bis] and 3[ter].
4 Article 5(2)(b).
5 Which, under art 5(2)(d), may be made when signing or ratifying the Protocol, or subsequently.
6 Under r 13(1) the period is three months, which is non extendable—see r 62(1) and (3).
7 Article 19 of the Trade Marks (International Registration) Order 1996, SI 1996/714, made under the TMA 1994, s 54—see para **21.34** below.

21.7   In order to understand the way in which the Protocol will work in the UK, it is necessary to refer to the provisions made under the powers of subordinate legislation given by the TMA 1994 for the purposes of operating under the Protocol. Section 54(1) of the Act empowers the Secretary of State by order[1] to make such provision as he thinks fit for giving effect in the UK to the provisions of the Protocol. As is the case for regulations concerning the CTM,[2] the power is granted in very general terms, but (without detracting from such power) sub-ss (2) and (3) specify particular matters for which provision may be made.

1 Under sub-s (4), by statutory instrument subject to annulment in pursuance of a resolution of either House of Parliament.
2 See ch 22 below.

21.8   Under sub-s (2), provision may in particular be made with respect to:

(a) the making of applications for international registrations by way of the Patent Office as office of origin;

(b) the procedures to be followed where the basic UK application or registration fails or ceases to be in force;

(c) the procedures to be followed where the Patent Office receives from the International Bureau a request for extension of protection to the UK;

(d) the effects of a successful request for extension of protection to the UK;

(e) the transformation of an application for an international registration, or an international registration, into a national application for registration;

(f) the communication of information to the International Bureau;

(g) the payment of fees and amounts prescribed in respect of applications for international registrations, extensions of protection and renewals.

21.9   Under sub-s (3) provision may be made by regulations[1] applying provisions of the TMA 1994 to an international trade mark (UK). As with the CTM,[2] these provisions are s 21 (groundless threats), ss 89 to 91 (importation of infringing goods, material or articles) and ss 92, 93, 95 and 96 (offences).

1 Also by statutory instrument under sub-s (4).
2 See ch 22 below.

Provisions under the Act for giving effect to the Protocol

21.10   There are two statutory instruments which have been made under s 54, the Trade Marks (International Registration) Order 1996 ('the Order') and the Trade Marks (International Registration) (Fees) Rules 1996,[1] both of which came into force on 1 April 1996. The Fees Rules need no further discussion here.

1 SIs 1996/714 and 1996/715.

21.11   The Order is divided into six sections. After a preliminary section dealing with formal matters and interpretation (arts 1 and 2), the main section (arts 3–18) makes provisions for international registrations designating the UK. This is followed by transformation of an international registration into a national application (arts 19–20), concurrent registrations (art 21) and international applications originating in the UK (arts 22–23). The final section contains miscellaneous and general provisions (arts 24–32).

Preliminary

21.12   Under art 1 the Order came into force on 1 April 1996 and applies to England and Wales, Scotland, Northern Ireland and the Isle of Man. The Channel Islands are not included. Article 2 contains a list of definitions, many of which, including 'International Bureau', 'International Register' and 'international registration' are taken from the Protocol. An 'international registration designating the UK' is an international registration in relation to which a request has been made for extension of protection to the UK under art $3^{ter}(1)$ or (2) of the Protocol. A 'supplementary register' is established[1] for the purpose of recording, in relation to international trade marks (UK), disclaimers and limitations, and notifiable transactions.[2] As with the main UK register, the supplementary register need not be kept in documentary form. 'The Rules' are the Trade Marks Rules 1994[3] and references to a rule are to be construed accordingly unless the context otherwise requires. By art 32 the Rules apply, with the necessary modifications, in relation to an international registration designating the UK (including a protected international trade mark (UK)) as in relation to a registered trade mark or application under the TMA 1994, except as otherwise provided or where their application would be inconsistent with the provisions of the Order. In such application the Rules are to be treated in all respects as rules under the Act, and rules relating to costs and security for costs and to evidence before the registrar are enforceable in relation to proceedings under the Order in the same way as in relation to proceedings relating to a registered trade mark or application.

1 Article 24, which provides that the supplementary register is subject to rr 34–39.
2 Defined in art 6.
3 The Rules have now been amended by the Trade Marks (Amendment) Rules 1998, SI 1998/925. It is understood that the registry applies the amended Rules in relation to applications under the Protocol.

21.13   Reference should also be made here to the Common Regulations, adopted under art 10 of the Protocol with effect from 1 April 1996, and which also apply to the Madrid Agreement. The Common Regulations govern the procedures of the International Bureau including fees. They are set out in Appendix 6.

International Registrations designating the UK

21.14   Where an international registration is filed designating the UK, art 3 provides that it is entitled to become protected subject to arts 9–12 where, if the particulars of the international registration were comprised in an application made under the TMA 1994, it would satisfy the requirements for registration, including any requirements imposed by the Rules. For this purpose the provisions of ss 32–34 of the Act (covering the application for registration and its contents, the filing date and classification), and of rr 10 and 11 (deficiencies in and publication of the application) are to be disregarded. The reason for excluding the application of these provisions is that, generally speaking, the matters covered by them are dealt with by the Protocol or the Common Regulations. However one point should be noted. Section 32(3) requires the application to include a statement that the trade mark is being used (ie in the UK) by the applicant or with his consent in relation to the goods or services specified, or that he has a *bona fide* intention that it should be so used. The position of the UK registrar is that an untrue statement in this respect may provide a basis for a finding that the application was made in bad faith, within s 3(6),[1] which could be a ground for refusal or registration, or for invalidation under s 47(1). There is no requirement for such a statement in an application under the Protocol. In practice however this probably makes no difference. Where the mark applied for has been the subject of genuine use in the country of origin it may be very difficult to establish bad faith in regard to the UK, at least so long as the specification of goods or services is not too broad. In each case the question whether there is bad faith will be a question of fact, to be determined according to the whole of the circumstances of the case, not only those existing in the UK. This might be thought to support a view which has been expressed, that there is little point in requiring the UK application form to include a statement as to intention to use. Before considering the detailed provisions of art 4, which sets out the effects of a protected international trade mark (UK), and arts 5–7 dealing with the international trade mark (UK) as an object of property, notification of transactions and licensing, it is necessary to make reference to arts 8–12. These contain detailed provisions regarding priority, examination of international registrations designating the United Kingdom, publication, opposition proceedings and observations, notices of refusal and date of protection.

1 See ch 5, paras **5.118–5.121** above.

Claiming priority

21.15   So far as priority is concerned, the effect of art 8(1) is that, subject to para (2), the provisions of s 35 of the TMA 1994 (claim to priority of a Convention application) apply so as to confer a right to priority in relation to protection of an international registration designating the UK as they apply in relation to registering a trade mark under the Act. Paragraph (2) excludes the rule-making power of s 35(5), and provides that the manner of claiming priority is to be determined in accordance with the Protocol[1] and the Common Regulations.[2]

1 See art 4(2).
2 See r 9(4)(a)(iv).

Examination

21.16   When the registrar receives notification, from the International Bureau, of an international registration designating the UK, art 9 requires him to examine whether it satisfies the requirements of art 3, which includes in particular the need to satisfy the requirements of the TMA 1994 and Rules for registration. The examination includes a search, to such extent as the registrar considers necessary, of earlier trade marks. If any of the requirements are not met, or are met only in relation to some of the goods or services, the registrar will give notice of refusal to the International Bureau, specifying a period within which the holder of the international registration may make representations.[1] A holder making representations must file an address for service in the UK.[2] By art 11(1) any such notice of refusal must be given before the expiry of 18 months from the date on which notification of the request for extension was sent to the UK. A notice of refusal must[3] set out the matters required by art 5 of the Protocol and rule 17 of the Common Regulations. Under art 11(4) the registrar must inform the International Bureau if the holder makes representations in response to a notice of refusal under art 9(3), or if he makes no representations within the specified period or informs the registrar that he does not intend to make any representations. Article 11(5) requires the registrar to inform the International Bureau of any final decision made in relation to the refusal following representations on behalf of the holder. For this purpose a decision is final where the registrar, or the person appointed or the court on appeal or further appeal, decides whether the refusal shall be upheld, in whole or in relation to only some of the goods or services, once any right of appeal against the decision expires or is exhausted, where any representations are withdrawn, or where the proceedings relating to the refusal are discontinued or abandoned.[4]

1   Article 9(3) and (4).
2   On Form TM33, see art 9(5).
3   By art 11(3).
4   Article 11(6).

3   Publication, opposition proceedings and observations

21.17   In cases where it appears to the registrar that the requirements for registration are met in relation to some or all of the goods or services for which protection is sought, art 10(1) provides for publication by the registrar of a notice containing particulars of the international registration and specifying the goods or services for which protection will be conferred. Within three months of the date of publication any person may give notice of opposition to the conferring of protection. The contents of the notice are as prescribed by rule 13 and the period of three months is not extendable.[1] In accordance with art 5(2)(c)(i) of the Protocol, art 11(2) requires the registrar to inform the International Bureau of the possibility that oppositions may be filed after the expiry of the 18-month period referred to above[2] unless, at least four months before the expiry of that period, he has published the notice referred to in art 10(1). In the latter event, of course, the notice of opposition must have been filed at least a month before the expiry of the 18-month period and the registrar can therefore give notice of refusal within that period. Under art 10(3) the registrar must, within four months at the latest from the date of publication under art 10(1), give notice of refusal to the International Bureau stating the matters required to be included in the notice of opposition. Article 10(4) allows the holder three months, from the date on which notice of refusal is given to the International Bureau, in which to file a counterstatement. This period also is non-extendable.[3] In view of the fact that the notice of refusal based on opposition has to be sent by the registrar to the International Bureau, which in turn sends it to the holder,[4] the holder may have rather less than three months in which to file a counter-statement. In the event that any delay is such that the holder is unable to file a counter-statement within the three-month period, presumably rule 60 (correction of irregularities of procedure) could be applied by virtue of art 34(1), to cover irregularities in or before the International Bureau as well as the Office. In cases of refusal based on opposition art 11(3)–(6) makes similar provision, to the provisions discussed above in relation to notices under art 9(3). Thus the International Bureau must be informed of the filing of a counter-statement or the failure to do so, and of any final decision in the matter.

1 Rule 62(1)/(3).
2 Paragraph **21.6.**
3 This is the effect of r 62(1)/(3), by virtue of art 34(1) of the Order.
4 Article 5(3) of the Protocol and rule 17(5) of the Common Regulations.

21.18   Article 10(6) contains a provision, which is analogous to s 38(3) of the Act, allowing any person to make observations in writing to the registrar as to whether the trade mark should be protected. This may be done at any time after publication of the notice under art 10(1) before the trade mark has become protected in accordance with art 12. Such person does not thereby become a party to the proceedings in relation to the request for protection. It is to be noted that, unlike s 38(3) of the Act, art 10(6) does not expressly require the registrar to inform the applicant (holder) of the observations. However it is submitted that the rules of natural justice would require the holder to be informed. In any event, it would seem that the registrar is precluded by art 11(1) from giving notice of refusal based on the observations once the 18-month period has expired.

Protection

21.19   Article 12 makes provisions specifying when a trade mark becomes protected in the UK in various different situations which may occur. The 18-month period referred to is the period of 18 months following the date on which the notification of the request for extension was sent to the UK. The trade mark which is the subject of the request for protection becomes protected as a protected international trade mark (UK) either in full or as regards goods and services in respect of there has been no refusal, following examination and publication pursuant to arts 9 and 10, in the following circumstances:

   (i) the 18-month period has not expired, but the period for giving notice of refusal based on an opposition expires without notice of refusal having been given;
   (ii) the 18-month period has expired and the three-month period from publication, for giving notice of opposition, expires without notice of opposition having been given;
   (iii) notice of refusal has been given in respect of some only of the goods or services for which protection in the UK has been requested and the registrar informs the International Bureau, in accordance with art 11(4) that

the holder has made no representations or, as the case may be has filed no counter-statement within the periods specified in art 9(4) and 10(4) respectively, or has informed the registrar that he does not intend to make such representations or file such a counterstatement;

(iv) notice of refusal has been given in respect of all or some of the goods or services in respect of which protection in the UK has been requested, and the registrar notifies the International Bureau in accordance with art 11(5) that a final decision has been made that the refusal is withdrawn in respect of some or all of the goods or services.

21.20   Where the 18-month period expires without any notice of refusal having been given, and without the International Bureau having been informed that oppositions may be filed after the expiry of that period,[1] then the trade mark becomes a protected international trade mark (UK). The effect of this is, once 14 months have elapsed from the date on which notification of the request for extension was sent to the UK, if the registrar has neither given notice of refusal nor informed the International Bureau that oppositions may be filed after the expiry of the 18-month period, the mark cannot be prevented from becoming protected at the end of that period. This is subject to the possibility of the protection being declared invalid, or subsequently being revoked.[2]

1 Under art 11(2).
2 Article 13; see para **21.28** below.

21.21   Under art 12(3), when a trade mark becomes protected under the above-mentioned provisions, the registrar must publish particulars of the international registration specifying the date on which, and the goods or services in respect of which, protection is conferred. Under art 12(2), when a trade mark becomes protected it is treated as being registered under the TMA 1994 as of the date of the international registration, where the request for extension is mentioned in the international application or is made on or prior to the date of the international registration. Where the request for extension to the UK is made subsequently, the trade mark is treated as registered as of the date on which the request for extension is recorded on the International Register. These provisions are subject to art 21, which is discussed below and is concerned with the effects of an international registration where the trade mark is also registered under the TMA 1994.

Effects of Protected International Trade Mark (UK)

21.22   Essentially, the proprietor of a protected international trade mark (UK) has the same rights and remedies as are given by or under ss 9–12 and 14–20 of the TMA 1994 to the proprietor of a registered trade mark, subject to the limitations of s 11 and the provisions of s 12 relating to exhaustion of rights.[1] Under art 4(3) the trade mark is treated as being registered in respect of the goods or services for which the protected international trade mark (UK) confers protection in the UK. The effective date of protection is determined by art 4(2). The rights of the proprietor have effect as of the date on which the trade mark is to be treated as registered pursuant to art 12 or 21. The protected international trade mark (UK) is treated as being in fact registered when it becomes protected pursuant to art 12.

1 See ch 12 above.

4 Disclaimers and territorial limitations

21.23 As with applications for registration under the TMA 1994, there is no pro-vision empowering the registrar to insist on any disclaimer or territorial limitation, although an applicant or proprietor may voluntarily make a disclaimer or agree a territorial limitation, under s 13.[1] Article 4(4) makes a similar provision for an international trade mark (UK), and the registrar is required to enter the disclaimer or limitation in the supplementary register and to publish it. Under art 4(5) the rights conferred on the trade mark under the Act are restricted accordingly.

1 See ch 12, para **12.49** above as to the effect of a disclaimer.

Groundless threats of infringement proceedings

21.24 Under art 4(6) the remedy for groundless threats of infringement proceedings, given by s 21 of the TMA 1994,[1] is applied in relation to a protected international trade mark (UK) as in relation to a trade mark registered under the Act. Where s 21(3) of the Act provides that a plaintiff in a threats action is entitled to relief if the registration is invalid or liable to be revoked in a material respect, the reference to registration is treated as a reference to protection of a protected inter-national trade mark (UK). Where s 21(4) refers to notification that a trade mark is registered, or that an application for registration has been made, the reference is to be treated as a reference to notification that a trade mark is a protected international trade mark (UK), or is the subject of an international application or international registration designating the UK.

1 See ch 13.

International trade mark (UK) as an object of property

21.25 As would be expected, the provisions of the TMA 1994 relating to a regis-tered trade mark as an object of property are applied to a protected international trade mark (UK). Article 5 applies s 22, which provides that a registered trade mark is personal property (incorporeal moveable property in Scotland), s 23 (co-owner-ship of registered trade mark), s 24 (assignment, etc) except sub-s (2)(b) which concerns an assignment limited to apply in relation to use in a 'particular locality', and s 26 (trusts and equities). These provisions, which apply, with the necessary modifications, in relation to an international trade mark (UK) as in relation to a reg-istered trade mark, are discussed in detail above.[1] It is to be noted that s 27 of the Act, under which an application for registration is treated as an object of property, is not applied to an international application designating the UK.

1 Chapter 11.

Licensing

21.26 Article 7 applies all the provisions of the TMA 1994 relating to licensing, ie ss 28–31, with the necessary modifications, to licences to use a protected international trade mark (UK). The reference in s 28(1) to goods or services for which a trade mark is registered is to be treated as a reference to goods or services in respect of which the trade mark is protected in the UK.

Notification of transactions

21.27 Transactions affecting international trade marks are not treated in exactly the same way as transactions affecting trade marks registered or applied for under the TMA 1994. Instead of applying for entry of particulars of 'registrable transactions' in the register, art 6 provides for entry, in the *supplementary register* established and maintained under art 24,[1] of particulars of 'relevant transactions', which include 'notifiable transactions'. Presumably this separate procedure has been devised because of the restrictions imposed by the Protocol, in particular as to who may own an international registration.[2] Under art 6(1), 'notifiable transactions' are (a) the grant of a licence under a protected international trade mark (UK) and (b) the grant of any security interest (whether fixed or floating) over an international trade mark (UK) or any right in or under it. Under art 6(3) 'relevant transactions' are notifiable transactions, an assignment of, or the making by personal representatives of a vesting assent in relation to, an international trade mark (UK) or any right in it, and an order of a court or other competent authority transferring such a trade mark or any right in or under it. Under art 6(2), on application to the registrar by a person claiming to be entitled to an interest in or under an international trade mark (UK) by virtue of a notifiable transaction, or any other person claiming to be affected by such a transaction, the prescribed particulars[3] are to be entered into the supplementary register. There is no provision for entry of the particulars of other relevant transactions (assignments, etc), these being provided for under the Protocol and the Common Regulations,[4] and a request for recordal in the International Register is required. Article 6 contains similar provisions, to those in s 25(3) and (4) of the TMA 1994, as to the effectiveness of relevant transactions and the availability of damages or an account of profits where no application is made for registration of the prescribed particulars of a notifiable transaction or, in the case of any other relevant transaction, no request is made for recordal in the International Register. The sanctions are the same as under s 25 of the Act.[5] Until such application or request is made the transaction is of no effect as against a person acquiring an interest in or under the international trade mark (UK) in ignorance of it and persons claiming to be licensees by virtue of the transaction do not have the protection of s 30 or 31 (rights and remedies of licensee in relation to infringement). Failure to make the application or request before the end of a six-month period from the date of the transaction affects a new proprietor's or a licensee's rights to damages or an account of profits in the same way as provided for by s 25(4) of the Act.

1 See para **21.12** above.
2 Articles 2 and 9.
3 Ie the particulars prescribed by r 34—see art 6(6).
4 See para **21.13** above.
5 See ch 11, para **11.21–11.22** above.

4 Revocation and invalidity

21.28 Generally speaking, under art 13 an international trade mark (UK) may be revoked or declared invalid on any of the grounds set out in ss 46 and 47 of the TMA 1994. These are fully discussed in Chapter 7. So far as revocation is concerned, the reference in s 46(1) to the date of completion of the registration procedure is to be treated as a reference to the date of the international trade mark (UK) becoming protected, and the references in s 46(2) to the form in which a trade mark was registered is construed as a reference to the form in which the trade mark is protected. The references in s 46(5) and (6), to goods or services for which the trade mark is registered are to be construed as references to goods or services for which the trade mark is protected. In non-use cases, art 29 places the burden of proving use on the 'holder'.[1] In accordance with art 13(3) it is the *protection* of an international trade mark (UK), rather than the registration, which is revoked or declared invalid. In proceedings in the registry for revocation or invalidation, art 6(4) applies rule 31, with necessary modifications. Article 6(5) requires the registrar to notify the International Bureau whenever the protection of a protected international trade mark (UK) is revoked or declared invalid; in the former case the rights of the proprietor will be deemed to have ceased, to the extent that protection is revoked, from the date of recordal of the revocation in the International Register, but in the latter case the trade mark will, to the extent of the declaration, be deemed never to have been a protected international trade mark (UK). There is a proviso, as under s 46(6), that transactions past and closed as at the date of recordal of the invalidity, are not affected.

1 Cf TMA 1994, s 100, which uses the word 'proprietor'.

Effect of acquiescence

21.29 Article 14 applies to protected trade marks (UK) the acquiescence provisions of s 48 of the TMA 1994. The reference to a registered trade mark is to be construed as including a protected international trade mark (UK) and reference to registration as including references to protection.

Proceedings relating to invalidity and revocation of protection

21.30 Article 15(1) applies the provisions of s 73 of the TMA 1994, for certificates of validity of contested registrations, to court proceedings in which the validity of the protection of a protected international trade mark (UK) is contested. Article 15(2) applies s 74, relating to the registrar's appearance in court proceedings involving him, to proceedings involving[1] an application for revocation or a declaration of invalidity of the protection of a protected international trade mark (UK), or an application for the rectification of the supplementary register. In the last mentioned instance there does not at present appear to be any provision for applying to the court for rectification of the supplementary register.[2]

1 This includes involvement by way of counterclaim.
2 TMA 1994, s 74, refers to 'rectification of the register', which may be applied for under s 64. But s 64 does not apply to the supplementary register and is not so applied by the Order.

Importation of infringing goods, materials or articles

21.31 Under art 16 the provisions of s 89 of the TMA 1994 (relating to treatment of infringing goods, materials or articles as prohibited goods), ss 90 and 91 of the Act (power of the Commissioners of Customs & Excise to disclose information) apply to 'goods which are, in relation to a protected international trade mark (UK), infringing goods, materials or articles'. Presumably this should be read as if the word 'goods' at the start of the quoted passage was followed by 'material or articles'. Again for the purpose of this provision references to a registered trade mark are treated as references to a protected international trade mark (UK). The Trade Marks (Customs) Regulations 1994[1] are applied to notices given under s 89 of the Act in accordance with art 16.

1 SI 1994/2625.

5 Offences and forfeiture

21.32 Under art 17 the provisions of s 92 of the TMA 1994, which are intended to deal with the problem of counterfeiting of registered trade marks on goods, are applied to unauthorised use of protected international trade marks (UK), as are the provisions of ss 97 and 98, respectively relating to forfeiture in England and Wales, and Scotland. References in all these provisions, to goods in respect of which a trade mark is registered are treated as references to goods in respect of which the protected international trade mark (UK) confers protection in the UK. For an offence to be committed under s 92, art 17(3) requires that the registrar shall have published, pursuant to art 12(3), particulars of the date on which, and the goods in respect of which, protection is conferred. The criminal provisions of the TMA 1994 are discussed in Chapter 20.

Falsely representing trade mark as a protected international trade mark (UK)

21.33 Article 18 creates a separate offence, not dependent on the provisions of s 95 of the TMA 1994, of falsely representing a trade mark as a protected international trade mark (UK) or making a false representation as to the goods or services for which such a trade mark confers protection, knowing or having reason to believe that the representation is false. Nothing is said as to any particular manner in which such a representation may be made; in the absence of any accepted symbol denoting an international registration, the most likely way in which the offence might be committed is in a letter from a proprietor, his solicitor or agent. In such circumstances it will not normally be difficult to show that the defendant either knew or had reason to believe that the representation was false. The penalty (on summary conviction) is a fine not exceeding level 3 on the standard scale.

Transformation of an international registration into a national application

21.34 Articles 19 and 20 deal with the matter of transforming an international registration into a national application. Under art 19(1) this possibility arises where an international registration designating the UK is cancelled at the request of the office of origin under art 6(4) of the Protocol in respect of all or some of the goods or services listed in the registration, which can happen at any time up to five years from the date of the international registration under the rule of 'central attack'.[1] Within three months[2] of the date of such cancellation, a 'transformation application' must be made, by the person who was the holder of the international registration immediately before the cancellation, for registration in the UK of a mark identical to the international mark, in respect of some or all of the goods or services in respect of which the international registration was cancelled. The application is made on Form TM3 and must state that it is made by way of transformation. Under art 19(3) a trade mark registered pursuant to a transformation application is treated as if it was being registered as of the date of the international registration[3] or, if the request for extension to the UK was made after that date, on the date of recordal of that request.[4] Such date is deemed to be the date of registration of the trade mark, for the purposes of the Act.

1 See para **21.6** above.
2 By virtue of art 32 this time may, in appropriate circumstances, be extendable under r 62 of the Rules. However, given the possible consequences for third parties the registrar may well require good reasons to be given for failure to file the transformation within the three-month period.
3 According to art 3(4) of the Protocol.
4 According to art 3*ter* of the Protocol.

21.35 The procedure for transformation applications is laid down by art 20 and depends upon the date on which the international trade mark (UK) became protected pursuant to art 12.[1] If the mark became protected on or before the date of the transformation application, then (because the processes of examination and possible opposition will have been completed) the trade mark is registered under the TMA 1994 without further formality. If by that date the mark has not become protected, but a notice has been published by the registrar under art 10(1) in respect of the trade mark,[2] the publication of that notice is treated as publication of the transformation application under s 38(2) of the Act, any opposition being treated as opposition under s 38(2). If no notice under art 10(1) has been published at the date of the transformation application then, under art 20(3), if the registrar has issued a notice of refusal under art 9(3), that notice is treated as having been issued under s 37(3) of the Act, for the purposes of the application. An important provision of art 20(3), in view of the complexity of the procedure, is the requirement that the registrar inform the applicant of the nature of the response required (ie to the notice of refusal) and further specify the period within which the applicant must respond to the registrar. It appears that where there has been no notice under art 10(1) and no notice of refusal, the transformation application proceeds as an ordinary application under the Act and Rules.

1 See para **21.19** above.
2 See para **21.17** above.

Concurrent registrations

21.36 Article 21 of the Order is concerned with the situation in which there is an international registration of a trade mark which is also registered under the Act. The provisions only apply where the registered trade mark is also a protected international trade mark (UK), its proprietor is the holder of the international mark, all the goods and services covered by the registration are protected under the international mark, and the date of registration of the registered trade mark is earlier than the date specified in art 12(2)[1] in relation to the international mark. The provisions are without prejudice to the rights and remedies conferred in respect of a registered trade mark under the Act. Under art 21(2) the international trade mark (UK) is treated, for the purposes of application by the Order of the provisions of the Act, as being registered under the Act as of the date of registration of the registered trade mark as regards all the goods and services covered by the latter. Accordingly art 21(3) provides that in determining whether the international trade mark (UK) is an 'earlier trade mark',[2] it is to be treated as having the application date of the registered trade mark as regards all the goods and services for which the latter is registered, taking account of any priorities claimed in respect of the registered trade mark. Under art 21(4) these provisions continue to apply even if the registered trade mark lapses or is surrendered, but ceases to apply if it is revoked or declared invalid. Provision is made by art 21(5) and (6) for the holder of the international registration to apply to the registrar (on Form TM28), for the international registration to be noted in the register against the registered mark.

1 See para **21.21** above.
2 Within the TMA 1994, s 6.

21.37 An advantage of these provisions from the point of view of the holder of the international registration is that the earlier registered trade mark can be surrendered or allowed to lapse, without loss of rights, so long as the international mark is protected in the UK. It may be inadvisable to do this until the five-year period for central attack has expired; after that there would appear to be no risk involved. However this would not be so as regards goods or services covered by the registered trade mark but not covered by the international trade mark (UK). It should be emphasised that the marks must be identical and that the proprietor of the registered mark and the holder of the international mark must be the same; the provisions will not apply where the proprietor and the holder are different, even if they are in the same group of companies.

International applications originating in the UK

21.38 Articles 22 and 23 make provisions for international applications based on an application or registration under the TMA 1994. By art 22(6) the application is called the 'basic application' and the term 'basic registration' means a trade mark registered in the UK in respect of which application is made for international registration. Article 22 provides for an applicant for registration of a trade mark or the proprietor of a registered trade mark to apply through the registrar for the international registration of the mark. In order to comply with art 2(1) of the Protocol the applicant must be: a British citizen, a British dependent territories citizen, a British overseas citizen, a British subject or a British protected person; a body or a corporation sole constituted under the law of a part of the UK; a person domiciled in the UK; or a person who has a real and effective industrial or commercial establishment in the UK. If requested by the registrar the applicant must provide such evidence as may be necessary to satisfy him that the applicant is eligible to make the application in accordance with these provisions. The particulars in the application must correspond with the particulars appearing at the time in the basic application or registration. If the application complies with all these requirements, the registrar is required to submit it to the International Bureau.

21.39   Article 23 sets out certain 'events' affecting the subsistence of the basic application or registration, the occurrence of which must be notified by the registrar to the International Bureau, with a request to cancel the international registration as regards the goods or services concerned, in any case where the registrar has submitted an application for international registration. These events correspond to those specified in art 6(3) of the Protocol[1] as giving rise to the loss of an international registration under the central attack principle. In order to give rise to the obligation on the registrar to notify the International Bureau, the event must occur before the expiry of five years from the date of the international registration and the relevant decision must have become final, although this need not occur during the five-year period. Article 23(3) provides that a 'final' decision is regarded as having been made where any right of appeal against it expires or is exhausted or where proceedings relating to a application or registration are discontinued or abandoned, and that reference to an application being withdrawn include its being deemed to be withdrawn, or abandoned, or deemed never to have been made. The events specified are as follows:

(a) refusal by the registrar of the basic application as regards some or all of the goods or services covered by the international registration or, after accepting the application, refusal to register as regards some or all of such goods or services, having regard to matters coming to his attention since acceptance;

(b) opposition proceedings resulting in refusal of the basic application, in respect of all or some of such goods or services;

(c) a request by the applicant (including a request made after the five-year period at a time when the basic application was subject to an appeal against refusal or to opposition proceedings begun in either case within the five-year period) resulting in withdrawal of the basic application, or restriction as regards goods or services covered by the international registration;

(d) expiry of the registration resulting from the basic application, or of the basic registration, and its removal from the register, if either no request for its restoration is made within the time specified by r 30 (six months from the date of removal) or such a request is made and a final decision is made refusing the request;

(e) proceedings for revocation or a declaration of invalidity resulting in a final decision to revoke the registration resulting from the basic application, or the basic registration, or to declare such registration invalid;

(f) a request by the proprietor (including a request made after the five-year period at a time when (i) the basic application was subject to an appeal against refusal or to opposition proceedings begun in either case within the five year period or (ii) the registration resulting from the basic application, or the basic registration, was subject to proceedings for revocation or invalidation begun within the five year period) resulting in surrender of the registration resulting from the basic application, or the basic registration.

1 See para **21.6** above.

6   Miscellaneous and general provisions

21.40   Articles 24–31 contain miscellaneous and general provisions. Reference has already been made to arts 24 and 32,[1] and 29[2] and they need no further mention here. Like those provisions, arts 25–28 are intended generally to apply provisions of the TMA 1994 to international registrations designating the UK. Article 25 is concerned with disclosure of information by the registrar. Before publication of notice under art 10(1) in relation to an international registration designating the UK, the registrar may not publish or communicate to any person any documents or information relating to such registration other than as provided in para (2), which requires the registrar, on request, to make available for inspection by the public all information within his possession which is recorded in the International Register concerning any such registration, and also the particulars contained in any application for registration of a notifiable transaction (under art 6) and any entry in the supplementary register resulting from such an application. On the other hand under art 25(3), after publication of notice under art 10(1) in relation to an international registration designating the UK, as under s 67 of the Act in the case of published applications for registration, the registrar has a general obligation to provide any person with information requested. A request for information must be made on Form TM31M, and rr 44(2)–(5) and r 45 apply to the right of inspection given by art 25(3). Article 25(6) follows s 67(3) of the Act by providing for the registrar to permit inspection under para 25(3), before publication of a notice under art 10(1), where a person is notified that an international registration designates the UK and that the proprietor will, if the registration becomes a protected international trade mark (UK), bring proceedings against him in respect of acts done after publication of notice under art 10(1). Article 26 makes provision, corresponding to s 70 of the Act, protecting the registrar and any officer of his from liability in respect of any examination required or authorised by the Order, or any report or other proceedings consequent upon such examination. Article 27(1) corresponds to s 72 of the Act, and provides that in all legal proceedings (which by art 27(6) includes proceedings before the registrar) relating to an international trade mark (UK) the registration of a person as holder shall be prima facie evidence of the validity of the original international registration and of any subsequent assignment or transmission of it. Article 26(2) requires judicial notice to be taken of the Madrid Protocol and the Common Regulations, and also of copies issued by the International Bureau in the International Register and copies of the periodical gazette published by the International Bureau. The last two mentioned categories of document are, by para (3), admissible as evidence of any instrument or other act thereby communicated of the International Bureau. Paragraph (4) provides that evidence of any instrument issued by the International Bureau or any entry in or extract from such a document may be given in any legal proceedings by production of a copy; and any document purporting to be such a copy shall be received in evidence. In these matters the evidence is only admissible, not conclusive, and accordingly other evidence may be adduced in contradiction. Under art 28, the acts of agents are recognised in connection with a request for protection of an international registration as a protected international trade mark (UK) or procedure relating to such a mark, in the same way as the acts of agents are recognised under s 82 of the Act.

1   Para **21.12** above.
2   Para **21.28** above.

21.41 Article 30 protects the registrar in communicating information to the International Bureau. Notwithstanding s 67(2) of the TMA 1994, which limits the information which the registrar may publish or communicate before an application for registration is published, or any other enactment or rule of law, the registrar is at liberty to communicate to the International Bureau any information which the UK is required to communicate by virtue of the Order or pursuant to the Protocol or the Common Regulations. Lastly, mention should be made of art 31, which gives the registrar powers to accept fees for transmission to the International Bureau.

Chapter 22

The Paris Convention and the TRIPS Agreement

International co-operation in the protection of intellectual property rights

22.1 For many years, the Paris Convention for the Protection of Industrial Property ('the Paris Convention') has been an important feature of the international co-operation in the protection of certain rights which are included among what are now known as intellectual property rights. The Paris Convention was concluded at Paris on 20 March 1883. It has been the subject of a number of revisions since then. It was revised at Brussels on 14 December 1900, at Washington on 2 June 1911, at the Hague on 6 November 1925, at London on 2 June 1934, at Lisbon on 31 October 1958, and at Stockholm on 14 July 1967. There were also amendments made on 2 October 1979. The official English text has been established under art 29(1)(b) and is reproduced (without certain parts which relate exclusively to matters other than trade marks), in Appendix 4. The UK has ratified the Stockholm Agreement.

22.2 A more recent initiative in international co-operation is the TRIPS Agreement (Agreement on the Trade-related Aspects of Intellectual Property Rights). The TRIPS Agreement is Annex 1C of the Marrakesch Agreement Establishing the World Trade Organisation ('the WTO Agreement'), concluded on 15 April 1994, and binds all members of the WTO. The Agreement covers a broad range of intellectual property rights, including copyright which is not covered by the Paris Convention.

The Paris Convention

22.3 The provisions of the Paris Convention are not, as such, part of the law of England, or any other part of the UK. They are of no effect in the UK unless and until they have been implemented by legislation. Therefore, although the Convention binds the Crown, it cannot be relied upon directly by individual companies or persons, whether as litigants in the courts, as applicants for registration of trade marks, or by any other parties to proceedings in the courts or in the registry.[1] However in some cases, provisions of the Convention may be referred to, as part of the background against which particular legislation was enacted. This may be helpful where provisions in a statute are expressly included for the purpose of implementing a provision of the Convention. In addition to the provisions of art 4 of the Convention, relating to priority[2] and implemented in previous legislation, certain other provisions of the Convention are now specifically implemented in the TMA 1994. These include art 6[bis] relating to well-known trade marks[3] and art 6[septies], which is concerned with unauthorised registration of a trade mark by an agent or representative of the proprietor.[4] Also covered by specific provisions, and implemented in earlier legislation by provisions with similar effect, is art 6[ter] which requires protection to be given to official signs, such as state emblems and emblems of intergovernmental organisations.[5]

1 See for example the case of *Canadel Trade Mark* [1980] RPC 535.
2 1994 Act, ss 35 and 36, discussed in ch 8, paras **8.4–8.8**.
3 1994 Act, s 56, and ch 12, paras **12.52–12.56**.
4 1994 Act, s 60, ch 7, para 7.34 and ch 9, paras **9.2** and **9.15–9.16**.
5 1994 Act, ss 3(4), 4, 57 and 58, discussed in ch 5, at paras **5.108–5.117**.

22.4   There is still debate as to whether the UK yet complies with some provisions of the Convention. This aspect is discussed further below,[1] in respect of one of the provisions concerned. But it is of interest to note that the TRIPS Agreement, which is considered below,[2] contains a provision[3] which re-affirms obligations of participating States under a number of the provisions of the Paris Convention, namely arts 1–12, and 19. Because of the mechanisms for implementation and enforcement of the TRIPS Agreement, some of these provisions of the Paris Convention could possibly be of particular interest in the future.

1 See para **22.31–22.33**.
2 See para **22.38** et seq.
3 Article 2(1).

The provisions of the Paris Convention

22.5   Reference should be made to some of the provisions of the Convention which apply to trade marks. The implementation of some of these are discussed elsewhere in this book[1] with reference to specific provisions of the TMA 1994 which implement them.

1 See in paticular paras **5.111** et seq, **7.34** et seq, **8.4** et seq, **12.53** et seq.

General provisions

22.6   Article 1 states the purpose of the Convention in broad and general terms. Under para (1) the countries to which the Convention applies constitute 'a Union for the protection of industrial property'. Paragraph (2) describes the protection of industrial property as having as its object: 'patents, utility models, industrial designs, trademarks, service marks, trade names, indications of source or appellations of origin, and the repression of unfair competition'. Paragraph (3) provides that industrial property shall be understood in the broadest sense, and 'shall apply not only to industry and commerce proper, but likewise to agricultural and extractive industries and to all manufactured or natural products', a non-exhaustive list being added.

22.7   Articles 2 and 3 set out some basic principles which are to apply throughout the Union. Under art 2(1), nationals of any country of the Union shall, as regards the protection of industrial property, enjoy in all the other countries of the Union the advantages that their respective laws now grant, to nationals. This is all without prejudice to the rights specially provided for by the Convention. This requirement of equal treatment, which includes the right to the same legal remedy against infringement of rights, subject to complying with the conditions and formalities imposed on nationals of the country concerned, is a cornerstone of the Union. Paragraph (2) reinforces this with a prohibition against the imposition of any requirement as to domicile or establishment in the country where protection is claimed, upon nationals of countries of the Union for the enjoyment of any industrial property rights. Paragraph (3) expressly reserves provisions of national laws relating to judicial and administrative procedure and to jurisdiction, and to the designation or an address for service or the appointment of an agent. Article 3 extends the benefit of art 2 to nationals of countries outside the Union who are domiciled or who have real and effective industrial or commercial establishments in the territory of one of the countries of the Union. They are to be treated in the same way as nationals of the countries of the Union.

Priority

22.8   Article 4 deals comprehensively with priority. So far as trade marks (both trade marks for goods and also 'service marks', although they are not expressly provided for by art 4) are concerned, the requirements of art 4 are now implemented by s 35 of the TMA 1994, which is discussed in Chapter 8.[1]

1 See paras 8.4–8.7.

User requirements

22.9   Section C of art 5 contains some provisions concerning requirements as to use of trade marks. Paragraph (1) provides that if, in any country, use of the registered mark is compulsory, the registration may be cancelled only after a reasonable period, and then only if the person concerned does not justify his action. The period of five years provided for in s 46(1)(a) and (b) of the TMA 1994[1] is now universally regarded as reasonable, and the possibility for the proprietor to avoid revocation by showing that there are proper reasons for non-use is clearly a compliance with para (1). Paragraph (2) imposes a further requirement, which is met by s 46(2), that use of the trade mark in a form differing in elements which do not alter the distinctive character of the mark in the form in which it was registered, shall not entail invalidation of the registration and shall not diminish the protection granted to the mark. Paragraph (3) concerns concurrent use of the same mark for identical or similar goods, by persons considered as co-proprietors, under the law of the country where protection is claimed, and provides that registration is not to be prevented, or the protection granted to be diminished, in any country of the Union, provided that the use does not result in misleading the public and is not contrary to the public interest.

1 See ch 7, paras 7.5–7.17.

22.10   Section D of art 5, which applies to registrations of trade marks, as well as other specified industrial property rights, precludes countries of the Union from imposing a requirement of an indication or mention of the registration as a condition of recognition or the right to protection. There is no such requirement imposed by the TMA 1994.

Conditions for filing and registration

22.11 Article 6 is concerned with conditions for filing and registration of trade marks. Under para (1) these are to be determined in each country of the Union by its domestic legislation. Paragraph (2) precludes any country of the Union from making an application for registration, or the validity of a registration, conditional upon the effecting of filing, renewal or registration in the country of origin of an applicant or proprietor who is a national of a country of the Union. The effect of art 3 is that this applies to an applicant or proprietor who is domiciled, or has a real and effective industrial or commercial establishment, in a country of the Union. Paragraph (3) adds another important safeguard, providing that a mark duly registered in a country of the Union is to be regarded as independent of marks registered in the other countries, including the country of origin. Accordingly the cancellation of a registration, or its non-renewal, in one country of the Union may not lead to the loss of rights in another country of the Union.

Well-known marks and specially-protected emblems

22.12 Articles 6[bis] and 6[ter] of the Convention have already been mentioned,[1] and require no further consideration here.

1 See para **22.3** below.

Assignments of trade marks

22.13 Article 6[quater] is concerned with assignment of marks, and is intended to mitigate the effect of the rule, in countries where such a rule still exists, that an assignment is only valid if it takes place at the same time as the transfer of the business or goodwill to which the trade mark belongs. Sub-paragraph (1) provides that it shall suffice for the recognition of the validity of the assignment that the portion of the business or goodwill located in such a country be transferred to the assignee, together with the exclusive right to manufacture in such country, or to sell therein, the goods bearing the assigned mark. This provision became academic, under the TMA 1938[1] in the case of registered trade marks and unregistered trade marks used in the same business as a registered mark assigned at the same time. It is similarly academic under the TMA 1994, so far as registered marks are concerned,[2] but might still have some relevance where an unregistered mark was to be assigned. Under sub-para (2), nothing in the previous provision is to impose on the countries of the Union 'any obligation to regard as valid the assignment of any mark the use of which by the assignee would, in fact, be of such a nature as to mislead the public, particularly as regards the origin, nature, or essential qualities, of the goods to which the mark is applied'. This provision recognises the principles embodied in arts 3.1(g) and 12.2(b) of the EC Directive[3] and in corresponding provisions of the CTM Regulation. It is to be noted that this provision makes no reference to service marks.[4]

1 Section 22.
2 See s 24 and ch 11, paras **11.4–11.5**.
3 Implemented by the TMA 1994, ss 3(3)(b) and 46(1)(d) .
4 But see para **22.23** below.

Effect of registration in other countries of the Union

22.14 Article 6^{quinquies}, entitled 'Marks: Protection of Marks registered in One Country of the Union in the Other Countries of the Union'(sometimes called the 'telle quelle' provision, has from time to time been used as the basis for arguments to the effect that if a trade mark is registered in its 'country of origin', and that country is a country of the Union, then the mark must be accepted for registration in other countries of the Union. This argument has never been accepted in the UK, and misunderstands the provisions of art 6^{quinquies}. Apart from the fact that the Convention, as such, has not been enacted as part of the UK law, the reservations indicated may justify refusal of protection. Paragraph A(1) provides:

> 'Every trademark duly registered in the country of origin shall be accepted for filing and protected as is in the other countries of the Union, subject to the reservations indicated in this Article. Such countries may, before proceeding to final registration, require the production of a certificate of registration in the country of origin, issued by the competent authority. No authentication shall be required for this certificate.'

22.15 The term 'country of origin' is defined in para A(2). If the applicant has a 'real and effective industrial or commercial establishment' in a country of the Union, that country is the country of origin. If he has no such establishment in the Union, then the country of the Union in which he has his domicile is the country of origin, or if he has no domicile within the Union but is a national of a country of the Union, then it is that country.

22.16 The 'reservations' referred to in para A(1) are set out in para B, which provides that trademarks covered by the article may be neither denied registration nor invalidated, except in three cases. The first case is where the trademark is of such a nature as to infringe rights acquired by parties in the country where protection is claimed. 'Infringe' is probably not used here in its technical sense, and is to be understood as including infringement of rights acquired through use. This case thus, in a broad sense, allows the refusal of registration on 'relative grounds', such as are provided for in the EC Directive and the TMA 1994.

22.17 The second case, under para B.2, is in very familiar terms. This allows refusal or invalidation of registration of trademarks where they are 'devoid of any distinctive character, or consist exclusively of signs or indications which may serve, in trade, to designate the kind, quality, quantity, intended purpose, value, place of origin, of the goods, or the time of production, or have become customary in the current language or in the bona fide and established practices of the trade of the country where protection is claimed'. This is for practical purposes, so far as goods are concerned, identical to art 3.1(b), (c) and (d) of the Directive, from which s 3(1)(b), (c) and (d) of the TMA 1994 are derived.

22.18 The third case is where the mark is contrary to morality or public order and, in particular, is of such a nature as to deceive the public. Paragraph B.3 states that it is understood that a mark may not be considered contrary to public order for the sole reason that it does not conform to a provision of the legislation on marks, except if such provision itself relates to public order. Although not identical, the reservation is expressed in very similar terms to those of art 3.1(f) and (g) of the Directive, from which the provisions of s 3(3) of the TMA 1994 are derived.

22.19   It is to be noted that no mention is made of objections to 'shape' marks, covered by s 3(2) of the TMA 1994, to marks which may be refused under s 3(4) on the ground that their use is prohibited, to 'specially protected emblems' excluded by s 3(5), or to refusal of applications made in bad faith, under s 3(6). As for the kinds of shapes excluded by s 3(2), which is based upon art 3(1)(e) of the Directive, these probably would not have been regarded as 'trademarks' for the purposes of the Convention. 'Specially protected emblems' are themselves covered by Article 6ter, which has already been mentioned. The provisions of s 3(5) and (6), which are permitted by art 3.2(a) and (d) of the Directive, would appear to be covered by the 'public order' reservation.

22.20   Paragraph B concludes with an express provision that it is subject to the application of art 10bis, which requires countries of the Union to provide effective protection against unfair competition. This appears to confirm that rights acquired by use of a trade mark, such as are recognised under the law of passing off, may be the basis of refusal or invalidation of a registration.

22.21   Although not mentioned in the 'reservations' it is clear that marks are to be accepted, even though an objection under para B.2 is applicable, if they have acquired sufficient distinctive character through use. Paragraph C(1) provides that in determining whether a mark is eligible for protection, all the factual circumstances must be taken into consideration, particularly the length of time the mark has been in use. This clearly means use in the country where registration is sought. Under para C(2), no trademark is to be refused in the other countries of the Union for the sole reason that it differs from the mark protected in the country of origin only in respect of elements that do not alter its distinctive character and do not affect its identity in the form in which it has been registered in the country of origin.

22.22   Emphasising a point which is implicit in para A, para D provides that no person may benefit from the article if the mark for which he claims protection is not registered in the country of origin. However, under para E, in no case is the renewal of the registration in the country of origin to involve an obligation to renew the registration in the other countries of the Union in which the mark has been registered. This does not seem very significant; normally the obligation to renew, if continued protection is desired, is imposed by the country concerned. Finally, para F preserves the benefit of any priority under art 4, even if registration in the country of origin is effected after the expiry of the period for claiming priority.

Service marks

22.23   Under the Convention, service marks were treated differently from trade marks for goods. Under art 6^{sexies}, the countries of the Union only undertook to protect service marks, but were not required to provide for the registration of such marks. However the availability of registration for service marks has gradually increased in recent years, and the provisions of the TRIPS Agreement do not distinguish between a trade mark for goods and a service mark; they are both 'trade marks'.

Unauthorised registration in the name of agent or representative

22.24   Article 6[septies], which is mentioned above,[1] requires the provision of protection for the proprietor of a trade mark in a country of the Union, whose agent or representative registers his trade mark in another country of the Union without the proprietor's consent. The previous law, in particular the provisions of the TMA 1938 relating to opposition and rectification of the register, probably complied with this provision. It has now been implemented by s 60 of the TMA 1994,[2] and requires no further discussion here.

1 See para **22.3**.
2 See para **22.3**, n 4.

Nature of the goods to which the mark is applied

22.25   Article 7 provides that the nature of the goods to which a trade mark is to be applied shall in no case form an obstacle to the registration of the mark. This is probably of little practical significance now. It should however be noted that it is unlikely to be regarded as overriding an objection on the ground that a mark is contrary to morality or public order, even if such objection does arise because of the nature of the goods.

Collective marks

22.26   By art 7[bis](1) the countries of the Union undertook to accept for filing and to protect collective marks belonging to associations the existence of which was not contrary to the law of the country of origin, even if such associations did not possess an industrial or commercial establishment. It was clear from para (3) that this included a reference to an establishment in the country where protection was sought. Under para (2), each country was to be the judge of the particular conditions under which a collective mark was to be protected, and might refuse protection if the trade mark was contrary to the public interest. The old law in the UK did not provide for registration of collective marks as such, although some such marks probably qualified for registration as certification marks, and the law of passing off provides some protection, in certain circumstances, for what are in effect unregistered collective marks. Collective marks are now capable of registration under s 49 of the TMA 1994,[1] and the new law appears to comply with art 7[bis].

1 See ch 10.

Trade names

22.27   Article 8 requires a trade name to be protected in all the countries of the Union without the obligation of filing or regulation, whether or not it forms part of a trade mark. This does not give rise to any difficulty. Trade names are given adequate protection, in proper cases, under the law of passing off.

Goods unlawfully bearing a mark or trade name

22.28 Article 9 contains provisions intended to give protection against trade in counterfeit goods. Paragraph (1) provides that all goods 'unlawfully bearing a trademark or trade name' shall be seized on importation into those countries of the Union where such mark or trade name is entitled to legal protection. Under para (2) seizure is likewise to be effected in the country where the unlawful affixation occurred or in the country into which the goods were imported. Paragraph (3) provides that seizure shall take place at the request of the public prosecutor, or any other competent authority, or any interested party, whether a natural person or a legal entity, in conformity with the domestic legislation of each country. By virtue of para (4) the authorities are not bound to effect seizure of goods in transit. Paragraph (5) provides authorities with an alternative, where the legislation of a country does not permit seizure on importation, of replacing seizure by prohibition of importation or by seizure inside the country. If none of these measures is permitted by the legislation of a country, then para (6) requires the country, until such time as the legislation is modified accordingly, to replace the measures by 'the actions and remedies available in such cases to nationals under the law of such country'. In practice these will be the civil actions and remedies available for infringement and passing off or other acts of unfair competition.

22.29 Questions may arise in some instances as to the meaning of 'unlawfully bearing', for example in cases of parallel imports. If a mark is applied to the goods by the proprietor or with his consent in one country, it would seem clear that the mark is not 'unlawfully affixed' there, but there may be issues, in the country of importation, as to whether the goods 'unlawfully bear' the mark. These matters have to be determined in accordance with the proper interpretation of the measures introduced for the purpose of dealing with trade in counterfeit goods. The problems of counterfeiting of goods have for many years been the subject of continuing international co-operation and discussion, resulting in a range of improved measures. These include, in the UK, a number of regulations allowing intervention by customs, which may include the seizure of goods. The TMA 1994 provides, in s 92, sanctions against unauthorised use of registered trade marks, which are backed by provisions for forfeiture of the goods. In addition there are provisions in the Trade Descriptions Act 1968, which may be invoked in some cases. These measures are discussed in detail in Chapter 20.

Goods bearing false indications as to source or identity of producer

22.30 Article 10(1) applies the provisions of art 9 to cases of direct or indirect use of a false indication of the source of goods or the identity of the producer, manufacturer or merchant. Under para (2) any producer, manufacturer or merchant, whether a natural person or a legal entity, engaged in the production and manufacture of or trade in such goods and established either in the locality falsely indicated as the source, or in the region where such locality is situated, or in the country falsely indicated, or in the country where the false indication of source is used, is in any case to be deemed to be an interested party. Some of the measures mentioned above, with regard to art 9, also permit the appropriate authorities to take action in cases falling within the scope of art 10.

Unfair competition

22.31 Article 10bis has been the subject of a considerable amount of discussion, in particular as to whether the UK complies with the obligations imposed by the provision. Paragraph (1) obliges the countries of the Union 'to assure to nationals of such countries effective protection against unfair competition'. By para (2), any 'act of competition contrary to honest practices in industrial or commercial matters constitutes an act of unfair competition'. These words are becoming more familiar in the UK because of their use in s 11(2) of the 1994 Act, derived from art 6.1 of the Directive, and in s 10(6).[1]

1 See ch 12 and paras **12.17, 12.21** and **12.25** et seq.

22.32 Paragraph (3) specifies three categories of acts of unfair competition, requiring that they in particular be prohibited. These are:

1. All acts of such nature as to create confusion by any means whatever with the establishment, the goods, or the industrial or commercial activities, of a competitor.
2. False allegations in the course of trade of such a nature as to discredit the establishment, the goods, or the industrial or commercial activities, of a competitor.
3. Indications or allegations the use of which in the course of trade is liable to mislead the public as to the nature, the manufacturing process, the characteristics, the suitability for their purpose, or the quantity, of the goods.

22.33 The UK's position as regards art 10bis is that the requirements are met by a combination of the laws of passing off, malicious falsehood and trade libel, and certain consumer protection laws such as the Trade Descriptions Act 1968. While it appears that the law of passing off broadly covers para (3)1 and some aspects of para (3)3, and that the laws of malicious falsehood and trade libel meet the requirements of para (3)2, it should be noted that the definition in para (3) is not intended to be an exhaustive definition of 'unfair competition', but simply sets out three examples of the kind of conduct which comes within para (2). A further point is that the provision of criminal sanctions under consumer protection laws, under which a party affected will not usually have a civil remedy, may not be sufficient, because it seems fairly clear from art 10ter, considered below, that civil remedies are required. Most of the Member States of the European Union, and a number of other countries, have specific laws against unfair competition, although there is some divergence in their application and effect. It would seem that there is a case for arguing that the UK needs to do more to meet its obligations under art 10bis, and this may be an appropriate field in which the European Commission should be considering the idea of a Directive for the harmonisation of national laws.

Remedies and right to sue

22.34 Article 10ter makes provision for remedies and the right to sue in respect of acts referred to in arts 9, 10 and 10bis. By para (1) the countries of the Union undertake to assure to nationals of the other countries of the Union appropriate legal remedies effectively to repress all the acts referred to in these articles. Under para (2) they undertake, further, to provide measures to permit federations and associations representing interested industrialists, producers, or merchants, provided that the existence of such federations is not contrary to the laws of their countries, to take action in the courts or before the administrative authorities, with a view to repression of the acts referred to. This undertaking applies in so far as the law of the country in which protection is claimed allows such action by federations and associations of that country.[1] As indicated above, the terms of this provision are such as to suggest strongly that the countries of the Union are obliged to assure civil remedies to nationals of the other countries, and that provision of criminal sanctions is not in itself sufficient.

1 For this reason, the denial to a trade association, of the right to sue, in the *Chocosuisse* case [1998] RPC 117, Laddie J at first instance, 25 February 1999, CA, does not represent a non-compliance with this provision.

Temporary protection at certain international exhibitions

22.35 Article 11 requires the countries of the Union, in conformity with their domestic legislation, to grant temporary protection, which is not to extend the priority periods provided by art 4, to industrial property rights including trademarks, in respect of goods exhibited at official or officially recognised international exhibitions held in their territory. There is no specific provision in the UK for exhibition priority, although there is a provision for such priority in the CTM Regulation.[1] Given the need for searches in any event, before using a new trade mark, and the ease of filing applications in the UK, the absence of a national exhibition priority provision does not appear to be significant.

1 Article 33—see ch 25, para **25.6** et seq.

Special national industrial property services

22.36 Article 12 of the Convention requires each country of the Union to establish a special industrial property service and a central office for the 'communication to the public of patents, utility models, industrial designs, and trade marks', and to publish an official periodical journal. These functions are all carried out by the Patent Office.

22.37 The remaining provisions of the Convention do not require discussion here. They relate to administrative matters, and to other matters not affecting trade mark law.

The TRIPS Agreement

22.38 The TRIPS Agreement, as already mentioned, is an Annex of the WTO Agreement. It binds all the members of the WTO. The text, excluding provisions which relate exclusively to intellectual property rights other than trade marks, is at Appendix 4. In addition to the member countries, the European Union is also a signatory of the WTO Agreement, and this has certain consequences as to the effect and the manner of implementation of the TRIPS Agreement. These matters were the subject of a decision of the Patent Office in proceedings under the Copyright, Designs and Patents Act 1988 relating to copyright and design rights, in the case of

Azrak-Hamway International Inc's Licence of Right (Design Right and Copyright) Application.[1] The respondent, who was the owner of the rights, claimed that the TRIPS Agreement was directly applicable in the UK and that the licence of right provisions of the 1988 Act, on the basis of which the application was made, was incompatible with TRIPS and therefore void and of no effect. Although the respondent accepted that the TRIPS Agreement was not, as a matter of UK domestic law, capable of direct implementation without Parliamentary legislation, it was contended that the Agreement was part of Community law and thus directly applicable through the operation of the ECA 1972. The basis for this contention was that the European Commission, for the Community, had signed the WTO Agreement, as had the individual Member States, and that the TRIPS Agreement was accordingly a Community Treaty within the meaning of art 228 of the Treaty of Rome. The Hearing Officer's conclusions as to the effect of the TRIPS provisions, or rather their lack of effect, on the licence of right provisions of the 1988 Act do no require discussion here. However he said that even if he were wrong on that aspect, he did not believe that there was a basis for thinking that the relevant TRIPS provisions could be invoked directly in national law before the Comptroller.

1 [1997] RPC 134 (Mr SN Dennehey).

22.39   In the *Azrak-Hamway*[1] case, it was accepted that the TRIPS Agreement fell within Article 228 of the Treaty of Rome. Furthermore, the WTO Agreement was declared a Community Treaty as defined by s 1(2) of the ECA 1972.[2] Accordingly the implementing of certain provisions of the TRIPS Agreement has been effected by statutory instrument,[3] through the mechanism provided by s 2(2) of the ECA 1972. This includes provisions amending the TMA 1994.

1 See para **22.38**, n 1.
2 See SI 1995/265.
3 The Patents and Trade Marks (World Trade Organisation) Regulations 1999 (SI 1999/1899), which came into effect on 29 July 1999.

Amendments of the 1994 Act

22.40   As indicated in the Explanatory Note to the Regulations, an important purpose of the amendments to the TMA 1994 is to permit any country which becomes a member of the WTO to be treated automatically as a Convention country. The amendments are set out in reg 13[1] and are noted at the appropriate places in this book. Essentially, their effect is to treat the WTO Agreement as an extension of the Paris Convention, so that, for example, priority may be claimed on the basis of an application in a country which is a party to the WTO Agreement and a trade mark which is well-known in such a country is entitled to protection under s 56 of the TMA 1994 and to be treated as an earlier trade mark within s 6. Transitional provisions, in reg 14,[2] provide that the amendment of s 56 does not affect the position of a trader who commenced use of a mark in good faith prior to 1 January 1996.

1 SI 1999/1899.
2 SI 1999/1899.

General provisions and basic principles

22.41   Part 1 of the TRIPS Agreement, comprising arts 1–8, contains general provisions setting out the basic principles of the Agreement. Article 1 makes it clear that while members are required to give effect to the provisions of the Agreement, they may provide more extensive protection so long as this does not contravene the provisions of the Agreement. Members are free to determine the appropriate method of implementing the provisions of the Agreement. Members are required to accord the treatment provided for in the Agreement to the nationals of other members.

22.42   Article 2 is concerned with confirmation of obligations under existing Conventions and Treaties. In respect of Parts II, III and IV of the Agreement, which relate respectively to standards concerning the availability, scope and use of intellectual property rights, enforcement of such rights and their acquisition and maintenance, para (1) requires members to comply with arts 1–12 and art 19, of the Paris Convention. These provisions have been considered above. In addition, para (2) provides that nothing in Parts I to IV shall derogate from existing obligations that members may have to each other under the Paris Convention, the Berne Copyright Convention, the Rome Convention (for protection of Performers, etc) And the Treaty on Intellectual Property in respect of Integrated Circuits.

22.43   Article 3 ('National Treatment') requires each member to accord to the nationals of other members treatment no less favourable than it accords to its own nationals with regard to the protection of intellectual property, subject to the exceptions already provided in the Conventions and the Treaty referred to in art 2. Article 4 ('Most-Favoured Nation Treatment') provides that, with regard to the protection of intellectual property, any advantage, favour, privilege or immunity granted by a member to the nationals of any other country shall be accorded immediately and unconditionally to the nationals of all other members. This general principle is subject to certain limited exceptions, which are set out. By way of further exception, art 5 provides that the obligations under arts 3 and 4 do not apply to procedures provided in multilateral agreements concluded under the auspices of WIPO relating to the acquisition or maintenance of intellectual property rights.

22.44   Article 6 concerns exhaustion of rights. For the purpose of dispute settlement under the Agreement, subject to the provisions of arts 3 and 4, nothing in the Agreement is to be used to address the issue of the exhaustion of intellectual property rights.

Specific trade mark provisions

22.45   Section 2 of Part II of the Agreement contains provisions specifically relating to trade mark matters. Article 15 defines 'protectable subject matter' in terms which are consistent with the definitions of a trade mark and absolute grounds for refusal, contained in the EC Directive. There is an overriding requirement that grounds of objection must not derogate from the provisions of the Paris Convention. Although registrability may be made to depend upon use, actual use may not be a condition for filing an application to register. Provision is made for publication and opposition (which is optional), and for cancellation. Article 16, defines the rights conferred by registration; these are essentially the same as the rights conferred in accordance with the Directive, as regards identical or similar goods and services. Article 16.2 provides that art 6bis of the Paris Convention shall apply, mutatis mutandis, to services; this is already the case under s 56 of the 1994 Act. By art 16(3), art 6bis is to be applied, mutatis mutandis, to goods or services which are not similar to those for which a trade mark is registered. Although s 56 does not do this, the terms of the provision are such that there is effective compliance through s 10(3) of the TMA 1994, implementing a corresponding provision of the Directive.

22.46 Article 17 provides for exceptions to the rights conferred by a trade mark. Members are permitted to provide 'limited exceptions', such as fair use of descriptive terms, 'provided that such exceptions take account of the legitimate interests of the owner of the trade mark and of third parties'. There is no indication as to what is meant by 'limited'. Clearly the interests of the owner and of third parties have to be balanced against each other. Rights, such as are provided by s 11(2) of the TMA 1994, permitting use of a trader's own name and of descriptive matter, and by s 10(6), permitting fair comparative advertising, fall within the exception. But exceptions which prejudice the basic exclusive right to the trade mark, granted by registration, should, it is thought, be outside the limited exceptions envisaged. One example might be compulsory licensing, which is expressly prohibited by art 21.

22.47 Article 18 sets the term of protection at an initial minimum term of seven years, and the registration of a trade mark is renewable indefinitely. Under the TMA 1994 the initial period is ten years, with renewal for further ten-year periods. Article 19 deals with requirements as to use, and overlaps to some extent with art 5C of the Paris Convention.[1] The minimum period of non-use, before a registration may be cancelled, is set at three years, and the owner must be allowed the possibility of establishing valid reasons for the non-use. Circumstances arising independently of the will of the owner, constituting an obstacle to the use of the trade mark, such as import restrictions on or other government requirements for goods or services protected by the trade mark, are to be recognised as valid reasons. Paragraph (2) requires use subject to the control of the owner, to be recognised as use of the trade mark. All these matters are fully covered by the Directive and the non-use provisions in s 46 of the 1994 Act.

1 See para **22.9** above.

22.48 Article 20 prohibits the unjustifiable encumbering of the use of a trade mark by special requirements. Examples are given of requirements which are regarded as unjustified and as justifiable. No difficulty appears to arise, in this respect, from any provision of the TMA 1994. Finally, art 21, which deals with licensing and assignment, leaves it to members to determine the conditions for licensing and assignment of trade marks, save for the prohibition on compulsory licensing and of any restriction on the right to assign without the transfer of the business to which the trade mark belongs.

Geographical indications

22.49 Section 3 of Part 2 contains, in arts 22–24, special and detailed provisions regarding the protection of geographical indications generally, with some specific provisions for wines and spirits. The laws of the UK contain no provisions exclusively directed to the protection of geographical indications, although some protection is provided by consumer protection laws such as the Trade Descriptions Act 1968 and the law of passing off has been used successfully in some cases.[1] There are also Community Regulations which govern the use of designations of wines and spirits, and a Regulation[2] dealing specifically with geographical indications for foodstuffs. It is expected that there will be further developments in the area of protection of geographical indications.

1 See for example the recent decision of the Court of Appeal in the *Chocosuisse* case. See para **22.34**, n 1 above.
2 Regulation 2081/92. The applicability of this regulation in the UK is in some doubt, following the decision of the Court of Appeal in *Consorzio del Prosciutto di Parma v Asda Foodstores Ltd* [1999] ETMR 319.

Enforcement of intellectual property rights

22.50 Part III of the Agreement is concerned with enforcement of intellectual property rights generally. Article 41 lays down general obligations as to the provision of effective enforcement procedures and as to decisions and appeals. It is not thought that there is any deficiency in the procedural rules in the UK. The same applies to the provisions, in arts 42–47, regarding fair and equitable procedures and remedies, evidence, injunctions, damages, other remedies, and right of information, respectively. Article 48 ('Indemnification of the Defendant') covers the question of damages suffered by defendants, and their costs, in certain cases of abuse of enforcement procedures. Generally speaking, the cross-undertaking in damages, which the courts require from claimants in most cases where a preliminary remedy such as an injunction is granted, more than adequately meets the requirements of art 48. Article 49, a general provision on administrative procedures, needs no comment here.

22.51 Section 3 of Part III comprises art 50, which lays down detailed rules regarding provisional measures. The requirements appear to be fully met in the UK. Section 4 (arts 51–60) relates to 'Special Requirements Related to Border Measures', which reinforce the requirements of arts 9 and 10 of the Paris Convention. The measures available are discussed in detail in Chapters 18 and 19 . Section 5, comprising a single art 61, requires the provision of criminal procedures in member countries, at least in cases of wilful counterfeiting. The provisions of the TMA 1994, which are discussed in Chapter 20, are rather broader than art 61 requires.

Acquisition and maintenance of intellectual property rights

22.52 Part IV ('Acquisition and Maintenance of Intellectual Property Rights and Related *Inter Partes* Procedures') comprises art 62. This recognises the right of members to impose reasonable procedures and formalities for obtaining intellectual property rights, and applies art 4 of the Paris Convention (Priority) to service marks. Article 62 also imposes general requirements as to availability of opposition, revocation and cancellation procedures, and of appeals.

Dispute prevention and settlement

22.53 Part V of the Agreement contains detailed provisions, in art 63 ('Transparency') as to publication of information about laws and regulations, and final judicial decisions and administrative rulings of general application and the notification of them to the TRIPS Council,[1] which has obligations to monitor the operation of the Agreement and members' compliance with their obligations under it. Article 64 applies certain provisions of GATT 1994, regarding settlement of disputes, to the settlement of disputes under the Agreement, with certain specified exceptions.

1 See Part VII ('Institutional Arrangements; Final Provisions'), arts 68–73.

22.54 Part VI makes transitional arrangements, which include the setting of a minimum period of one year, from the date of entry into force of the WTO Agreement, in which to apply the provisions of the TRIPS Agreement, and a further period for developing countries. Article 66 makes further exceptions for 'Least-Developed Country Members', and art 66 makes provision for Technical Co-operation.

Institutional arrangements; final provisions

22.55 The final part of the Agreement, Part VII, contains provisions concerning the TRIPS Council (art 68), International Co-operation (art 69), Review and Amendment (art 71) and Security Exceptions (art 73). Article 70 ('Protection of Existing Subject Matter') should be noted. Paragraph 1 provides that the Agreement does not give rise to obligations in respect of acts which occurred before the date of application of the Agreement for the member in question. The following paragraphs contain more specific provisions on various aspects, mostly relating to rights other than trade marks. Only para 7 need be mentioned; this concerns applications for protection pending at the date of application of the Agreement for the member in question, and permits certain amendments. However it is unlikely to be of any practical significance for trade marks, and no amendment has been made to the TMA 1994 in respect of it.

Conclusions

22.56 There are no obvious respects in which the TMA 1994 or other laws, or the enforcement procedures in the UK, would appear to need amendment as a result of the TRIPS Agreement. Questions may arise from time to time, as happened in the *Azrak-Hamway* case,[1] and will have to be considered by the courts, and if necessary by the ECJ. Issues as to whether the UK complies with provisions of the Paris Convention do not arise from the TRIPS Agreement itself, although it has reaffirmed the obligations under some of those provisions.

1 See para **22.38**, n 1.

Part VII

The Community trade mark

Chapter 23

The Community Trade Mark Regulation and its implementation in the UK

Introduction

23.1 As stated in s 51 of the TMA 1994, 'the Community Trade Mark Regulation' is Council Regulation 40/94/EC of 23 December 1993 on the Community trade mark. It is referred to here as the 'CTM Regulation'. The CTM Regulation, made under art 235 of the Treaty of Rome, is directly applicable in all the Member States of the EU. The Office for the Harmonisation in the Internal Market ('OHIM'),[1] situated in Alicante, Spain, is responsible for the administration of the Community trade mark. Under art 143(1) the CTM Regulation entered into force on the 60th day following that of its publication in the Official Journal of the European Communities.[2] Article 143(2) allowed three years for Member States to take the necessary measures for implementing arts 91 and 110, relating respectively to the establishment of 'Community trade mark courts' and formal requirements for converting CTM's and CTM applications into national applications.[3] In accordance with art 143.3. OHIM fixed 1 April 1996 as the date from which applications for CTMs might be filed; under art 143(4) applications were received in the three months before that date, being deemed to have been filed then. As s 51 of the 1994 Act also states, a 'Community trade mark' is defined by art 1.1 of the CTM Regulation, which is as follows:

1. A trade mark for goods or services which is registered in accordance with the conditions contained in this Regulation and in the manner herein provided is hereinafter referred to as a 'Community trade mark'.

1 Established by art 2 of the Regulation.
2 14 January 1994.
3 See para **23.16** below.

23.2 The purpose of the CTM Regulation is to provide for protection of trade marks in all the countries of the European Union by means of a single filing resulting in a single registration. Article 1(2) of the CTM Regulation is as follows:

2. A Community trade mark shall have a unitary character. It shall have equal effect throughout the Community: it shall not be registered, transferred or surrendered or be the subject of a decision revoking the rights of the proprietor or declaring it invalid, nor shall its use be prohibited, save in respect of the whole Community. This principle shall apply unless otherwise provided in this Regulation.

The scheme of the CTM system and the administration of OHIM

23.3 The scheme laid down for the registration of a CTM by the CTM Regulation incorporates the main features of the system operated by the UK Patent Office, but with some differences. An application is made and examined, with powers to refuse registration on absolute grounds, but not on relative grounds. After an application is accepted, it is advertised for opposition purposes. Opposition can only be on relative grounds, although a third party may raise absolute grounds in written observations under art 41.[1] After registration, a CTM may be revoked on a number of grounds, similar to those provided by national laws, or declared invalid on absolute or relative grounds. An important difference from the TMA 1994 is that under the CTM Regulation, relative grounds for refusal or invalidity may only be raised by the owners of the earlier rights relied upon or licensees.

1 See ch 26, paras **26.14–26.15** below.

23.4 The provisions governing the status and administration of OHIM are set out in Title XII of the CTM Regulation. Article 111 provides that OHIM is a body of the Community. It is represented by its President and has legal personality, enjoying in each of the Member States the most extensive legal capacity accorded to legal persons under their laws. It has rights to acquire and dispose of movable and immovable property and may be a party to legal proceedings. Article 112 makes provisions regarding the staff of OHIM. Article 113 applies the Protocol on the Privileges and Immunities of the European Communities to OHIM. Article 114 contains provisions relating to OHIM's contractual and other liability and to the personal liability of its servants towards OHIM. Article 118 provides for control by the Commission over the legality of acts of the President. None of these provisions requires further consideration here.

Languages

23.5 Article 115 makes detailed provisions regarding the languages to be used in OHIM and proceedings before it. An application for a CTM must be filed in one of the official languages of the Community. The 'languages of the Office' are just four: English, French, German and Spanish. When making an application, an applicant must indicate one of the languages of the Office as a second language, the use of which he accepts as a possible language of proceedings for opposition, revocation or invalidity. Where the application is filed in a language which is not a language of the Office, OHIM has to arrange for its translation into the language indicated by the applicant. So long as the applicant is the only party, as for example at the examination stage, the language of the proceedings is the language used for filing, but where that language is not one of the languages of the Office, OHIM may send written communications to the applicant in the second language indicated by him. When any other parties are involved, the matter becomes more complicated. A notice of opposition and an application for revocation or invalidity must be filed in one of the languages of the Office. If this is the language of the original application or the second language indicated by the applicant, than that language is the language of the proceedings. But if it is neither, the opposing party or the applicant for revocation or invalidity must, at his own expense, produce a translation of his application into either the language of the original application, provided that it is a language of the Office, or into the second language which was indicated when the application was filed. The language of the translation becomes the language of the proceedings. These provisions are all subject to art 115.7, which allows the parties to agree that a different official language of the EU is to be the language of the proceedings.

23.6   A few examples will demonstrate how these provisions for choice of language may operate.

Application for registration	Second language	Language of opposition or application for revocation or invalidity	Language of proceedings
English	Spanish	–	English
Finnish	German	–	Finnish
Dutch	English	English	English
Dutch	English	French	English
Spanish	English	French	Spanish or English
Spanish	English	Spanish	Spanish
Spanish	English	English	English
English	French	German	English or French

23.7   Article 116 requires publication of applications, and of other information required to be published, to be in all the official languages of the Community. The same applies to entries in the register of CTMs. In any cases of doubt, the authentic text is that in the language of the application for registration, if that is one of the languages of the Office; if it is not, the text in the second language is the authentic text. Article 117 provides for translation services for OHIM.

Organisation of OHIM

23.8   Most of the provisions relating to the organisation of OHIM do not require detailed comment here. The powers of the President and the appointment of senior officials are the subject of arts 119 and 120 respectively. In s 3 of Title XII, arts 121 to 124 provide for the creation of an administrative board, composed of one representative of each Member State and one representative of the Commission, and for the chairmanship and meetings of the Board. Article 25 provides that for taking decisions in connection with the procedures laid down in the CTM Regulation, Examiners, Opposition Divisions, an Administration of Trade Marks and Legal Division, Cancellation Divisions, and Boards of Appeal, are competent. Articles 126, 127 and 129 specify the responsibilities of Examiners, Opposition Divisions and Cancellation Divisions respectively. Their areas of responsibility are clear. Any other matters are the responsibility of the Administration of Trade Marks and Legal Division, under art 128. These include, in particular, decisions in respect of entries in the register and the keeping of the list of professional representatives under art 89. Appeals from decisions of Examiners and the three divisions are the responsibility of the Boards of Appeal (arts 130 and 131). Article 132 makes provisions for the exclusion of Examiners and members of divisions, and Boards of Appeal, from proceedings in which they have an interest or have had previous involvement, and for objections by parties to the participation of any of these people for any such reasons. Finally, arts 133–139 lay down detailed provisions in respect of budget and financial control.

Implementing provisions

23.9   Article 140 provides for an Implementing Regulation, in which rules for implementing the CTM Regulation are to be adopted, and contains further provisions regarding the charging of fees in specified instances. Article 141 establishes a committee and procedure for the adoption of implementing regulations. The Implementing Regulation[1] is set out in Appendix 5. The provisions of this regulation are referred to in the following chapters as 'Rules'. Fees are dealt with by the Commission Regulation 2869/95/EC of the same date. The Fees Regulations, which do not affect substantive law or procedure, are not included here. A further regulation, Commission Regulation 216/96/EC of 5 February 1996, reproduced in Appendix 5, lays down the rules of procedure for the Boards of Appeal.

1 Commission Regulation 2868/95/EC of 13 December 1995 implementing Council Regulation 40/94/EC on the Community trade mark.

Other measures adopted by the Commission and OHIM

23.10   In addition to the CTM Regulation and the other regulations mentioned in the last paragraph, there are a number of other measures which have been adopted for the purposes of operating the Community trade mark system. In particular, there are a number of 'decisions' of the President of OHIM. Of particular importance are Decision EX-96–2 to adopt the Examination Guidelines, Decision EX-96–3,[1] dealing with evidence to be provided on claiming priority or seniority of Community trade mark applications, and Decision EX-98–1 to adopt Guidelines concerning proceedings before the Office.

1 See Appendix 5.

Regulations under the TMA 1994

23.11   Although the CTM Regulation is directly applicable in the UK and the TMA 1994 contains some specific references to a 'Community trade mark',[1] the regulation itself[2] required certain further action to be taken by Member States, and it was recognised that other matters needed to be covered in secondary legislation, for the purposes of operating the Community system alongside the national system in the UK. Section 52(1) of the TMA 1994 gives the Secretary of State powers to make, by regulations,[3] such provision as he considers appropriate, in connection with the operation of the CTM Regulation. These are general powers, but sub-ss (2) and (3) give specific powers to make provision for particular matters. Sub-section (2) sets out four particular matters with respect to which provision may be made:

(a)   the making of applications for Community trade marks by way of the Patent Office;

(b)   the procedures for determining a posteriori the invalidity, or liability to revocation, of the registration of a trade mark from which a Community trade mark claims seniority;

(c)   the conversion of a Community trade mark, or an application for a Community trade mark, into an application for registration under the Act; and

(d) the designation of courts in the United Kingdom having jurisdiction over proceedings arising out of the Regulation.

1 See s 5(3) and definition of 'earlier trade mark' in s 6, ch 7 above.
2 See para **23.1** above.
3 By statutory instrument subject to annulment in pursuance of a resolution of either House of Parliament—sub-s (4).

23.12 Sub-section (3) is concerned with the application of certain provisions of the TMA 1994 to CTMs. Under sub-s (3)(a), regulations may be made applying, in relation to a CTM, the provisions of s 21 (groundless threats), ss 89–91 (importation of infringing goods, material or articles), and ss 92, 93, 95 and 96 (offences). Under sub-s (3)(b), provision may be made in relation to the list of professional representatives maintained under art 89 of the regulation, and persons on that list, corresponding to the provision made or capable of being made under ss 84–88 (relating to the register of trade mark agents and registered trade mark agents).

23.13 As at 1 April 1996, when the CTM Regulation came into force, no regulations had been made under the TMA 1994. It appears that there was insufficient time to deal with the matter before that date, and the delay has not been of significance. On 23 July 1996, there were made the Community Trade Mark Regulations 1996[1] ('the 1996 Regulations'), which came into force on 14 August 1996 and cover most of the matters provided for in s 52(2) and (3) of the Act.

1 SI 1996/1908. Appendix 2.

The 1996 Regulations

23.14 The 1996 Regulations contain no provision (see s 52 (2)(a) of the TMA 1994) with respect to the making of applications for CTMs by way of the Patent Office. Presumably this is because the CTM Regulation is directly applicable, and art 25(1)(b) provides for filing at the central industrial property office of a Member State, which includes the Patent Office, or the Benelux Office. The applicant has a choice between any such office and OHIM, and an application filed as provided by art 25(1)(b) has effect as if it had been filed on the same date at OHIM. A fee is payable under the Community Trade Mark (Fees) Regulations 1995.[1]

1 SI 1995/3175.

Determination a posteriori of invalidity and liability to revocation

23.15 Regulation 3 is concerned with the situation which can arise where a CTM claims seniority, under arts 34 and 35 of the CTM Regulation, over a UK national registration, which is subsequently removed from the UK register for failure to renew, under s 43 of the TMA 1994, or is surrendered under s 45. A party affected by the CTM may wish to rely upon art 34(3) of the CTM Regulation, in order to defeat the claim to seniority, by having the national mark (from which seniority is claimed) declared to have been revoked or to be invalid. Regulation 3(1) accordingly allows a third party to apply to the registrar or the court for a declaration that, if the registered trade mark had not been removed or surrendered, it would have been liable to be revoked under s 46 or declared invalid under s 47. Regulation 3(2) applies this provision to the case where a registered mark is only surrendered for some of the goods or services for which it was registered. Regulation 3(3) applies ss 46 and 47 of the TMA 1994, which set out the circumstances in which registered trade marks may be revoked or declared invalid,[1] and ss 72 (registration prima facie evidence of validity) and ss 74 and 76, which relate respectively to appearance of the registrar in proceedings involving the register and appeals from the registrar, to any application under para (1). Regulation 3(4) applies the provisions of r 31,[2] with the necessary modifications, to the procedure on applications under reg 3(1). This seems to be unnecessary, having regard to the very general provision of reg 11.[3]

1 See ch 11 above.
2 Of 'the Rules', ie the Trade Mark Rules 1994 (SI 1994/2583)—see reg 2. These Rules have been amended by the Trade Mark (Amendment) Rules 1998 (SI 1998/925) (see Appendix 2). It is understood that in dealing with matters relating to CTMs, the registry is applying the Rules as amended.
3 See **23.23** below.

Conversion of a CTM, or an application for a CTM, into an application under the Act

23.16 Under s 52(2)(c) of the TMA 1994, reg 10 deals with the case in which a proprietor of a CTM, which is revoked or invalidated, or an applicant for a CTM, which is refused (including refusal as a result of opposition), wishes to take advantage of arts 108–110 of the CTM Regulation and convert the registration or application into one or more national applications. Regulation 10 simply provides that where the registrar decides that a request for a conversion application is admissible pursuant to art 108, it shall be treated as an application under the TMA 1994 and that a decision of the registrar in relation to a conversion application is to be treated as a decision of the registrar under the TMA 1994. The procedures for conversion, which commence at OHIM, are discussed below.[1] The provisions of art 110 ('Formal requirements for conversion') should be noted. Article 110 provides that a CTM application or CTM transmitted to a national office in accordance with art 109 shall not be subjected to formal requirements of national law which are different from, or additional to, those provided for in the CTM Regulation or the Implementing Regulation. The important word here is 'formal', and the provision does not appear to exclude the refusal of the application on relative grounds or opposition on absolute grounds, although these are not available under the CTM Regulation.

1 Chapter 24, paras **24.24–24.25**.

Designation of CTM courts

23.17 Article 91 of the CTM Regulation requires Member States to designate 'CTM courts' of first and second instance to perform the functions assigned to such courts by the Regulation. For this purpose, reg 9 of the 1996 Regulations designates the High Court in England and Wales and Northern Ireland, and the Court of Session in Scotland. The Court of Appeal is not specifically designed as a CTM court of second instance, but can act as such under art 91(5).

Groundless threats of infringement proceedings

23.18   Regulation 4 applies s 21 of the TMA 1994 in relation to a CTM as in relation to a registered trade mark. This provision is fully discussed in Chapter 13 above. It would appear that, in order to be actionable, the threats must have been made within the jurisdiction of the court in some part of the UK.

Importation of infringing goods, material or articles

23.19   Section 89[1] of the TMA 1994 makes provision for infringing goods, material or articles to be treated by the Commissioners of Customs and Excise as 'prohibited goods' on the request of the proprietor or a licensee of the registered trade mark concerned. Sections 90 and 91 respectively provide for the making of regulations by the Commissioners for purposes connected with s 89, and empower the Commissioners to disclose certain information for the purpose of facilitating the investigation or prosecution of offences under s 92 or under the TDA 1968. Under reg 6, all these provisions are applied in relation to goods which are, in relation to a CTM, infringing goods, material or articles, references to a 'registered trade mark' being construed as including a CTM, and the Trade Marks (Customs) Regulations 1994[2] are applicable to notices given under s 89 in respect of a CTM. The CTM Regulation contains no definition of infringing goods, material or articles, but these terms must clearly be understood, in relation to a CTM for the purposes of reg 6, in the same sense as the definition for a national registration, under s 17 of the Act.

1 See ch 18.
2 SI 1994/2625 – see Appendix 2.

Offences under the TMA 1994

23.20   Section 92[1] of the TMA 1994 which, although broadly entitled 'unauthorised use of trade mark, etc, in relation to goods' is particularly intended for use against the counterfeiting of goods and dealings in counterfeit goods. Under reg 7 its provisions, together with those of s 93 (enforcement function of local weights and measures authority) and ss 97 and 98 (forfeiture), are applied to a CTM in the same way as they apply to a registered trade mark, references to goods in which a trade mark is registered being construed as including goods in respect of which a CTM is registered. Regulation 7(2) provides that no offence under s 92 can be committed, in relation to a CTM, by anything done before the date of publication of registration of the CTM.[2]

1 See ch 20.
2 Under r 23(5) of the Implementing Regulation.

23.21   Section 95 of the TMA 1994, under which it is an offence to falsely represent that a mark is a registered trade mark or to make a false representation as to the goods or services for which a trade mark is registered, is not applied as such to CTMs. Regulation 8(1) makes it an offence to falsely represent that a mark is a CTM, or to make a false representation as to the goods or services for which a CTM is registered, in either case knowing or having reason to believe that the representation is false. Under para (2), as under s 95(3), a person guilty of an offence under this provision is liable on summary conviction to a fine not exceeding level 3 on the standard scale. Although the nature of the offence is the same as under s 95,[1] there is the necessary difference that there is no provision corresponding to s 95(2), as to the effect of use of the word 'registered' or 'any other word or symbol import-ing a reference (express or implied) to registration. Normally, therefore, an offence under reg 8 will only be committed by the use of terms involving the words 'Community' and 'trade mark'. It may be that, since the term 'Community trade mark' itself implies actual registration,[2] the use of that term will suffice for an offence to be committed if the mark is not registered as a CTM, unless there is a qualification such as 'pending' or 'applied for'. In due course, there may be a sym-bol, perhaps the initials 'CTM', which becomes generally accepted as indicating registration as a Community trade mark.

1 See ch 20.
2 See art 1(1).

Privilege for communications with professional representatives

23.22 Regulation 5 extends the professional privilege conferred, by s 87 of the TMA 1994, on communications between a person and his trade mark agent, to communications between a person and a representative who is on the list of profes-sional representatives maintained in pursuance of art 89 of the CTM Regulation. For that purpose, the definition of 'trade mark agent' in s 87(2) of the TMA 1994 includes professional representatives. It is to be noted that the 1996 Regulations make no reference to ss 84–86 and 88 of the Act; although these are mentioned in the enabling provision of s 52(3)(b), they are not really apt in the case of 'profes-sional representatives' on the list maintained under art 89.

Application of the Trade Mark Rules 1994

23.23 Regulation 11 applies the Rules generally, with the necessary modifica-tions, to the Regulations, except as otherwise provided by the Regulations or where their application would be inconsistent with the provisions of the Regulations. In practice, this provision will only be relevant to applications under reg 3, for deter-mination a posteriori of invalidity and liability to revocation, and to conversion applications under reg 10. As mentioned above,[1] the Rules were amended in 1998.

1 See para **23.15**, n 2.

Interpretation of the CTM Regulation

23.24 In infringement proceedings in the UK, the provisions of the CTM Regulation, being directly applicable, will be interpreted by the CTM courts desig-nated by reg 9. Applicable provisions will include the definition of infringement and the provisions regarding revocation and invalidity. In such interpretation, guidance may be derived from several sources. Apart from those courts' own deci-sions, there will be decisions from the ECJ on questions referred to it by the courts of any of the Member States, under art 177 of the Treaty of Rome. In some instances, because the wording of certain provisions of the Regulation is identical or very similar to the wording of the Directive, decisions of the ECJ on references raising questions of interpretation of the Directive will also be relevant. In addition on some points, decisions of the CFI on appeal from the Boards of Appeal at OHIM, for example in cases involving refusal of registration on absolute grounds, in opposition proceedings, and in applications for revocation or invalidation, may be referred to. Yet another source may be found in decisions of national courts in other Member States interpreting provisions of the CTM Regulation or similar provisions of the Directive. For some time, it is likely that there will be differences of opinion between the national courts in different Member States, and it remains to be seen whether the courts in the UK will be willing to apply such decisions.

23.25 Another matter to consider in relation to the interpretation of the provisions of the CTM Regulation is the applicability of the so-called 'statements', that is the 'statements for entry in the minutes of the Council meeting at which the regulation is adopted'. Similar statements exist in relation to the Directive, and are discussed above.[1] Like these, the statements relating to the CTM Regulation have now been published by OHIM,[2] but not in the Official Journal of the European Communities. They are mentioned individually below, where appropriate, in relation to the provisions of the CTM Regulation to which they purport to be applicable, although it must now be doubted whether they have any relevance or effect.

1 See ch 1, where they are referred to as the Annex to the Directive and the Annex to the Regulation.
2 See Official Journal of OHIM, 5/96, pp 607 and 613.

Arrangement of the provisions of the CTM Regulation

23.26 The CTM is arranged in a series of sections called 'Titles'. Certain provisions of the Regulation[1] were almost immediately amended, by Council Regulation 3288/94/EC of 22 December 1994 for the implementation of the agreements[2] concluded in the framework of the Uruguay Round; these amendments are discussed under the Titles affected. In Title I ('General Provisions'), art 1 has already been mentioned; it defines the term 'Community trade mark' and its unitary character. Article 2 simply provides for the establishment of the Office (OHIM). Article 3, entitled 'Capacity to act' is quite straightforward. It provides that for the purposes of implementing the CTM Regulation, companies or firms and other legal bodies are to be regarded as legal persons if, under the terms of the law governing them, they have the capacity in their own name to have rights and obligations of all kinds, to make contracts or accomplish other legal acts and to sue and be sued. It is unlikely that this will give rise to any serious disputes.

1 Articles 5 and 7 in Title II, and art 29 in Title III.
2 In particular the Agreement on Trade-Related Aspects of Intellectual Property Rights (the 'TRIPS Agreement'), set out in Appendix 4.

23.27 The basic provisions setting out the requirements for registration of CTMs, the effects of registration, the requirements for their use, and the rules governing dealings in them, are contained in Title II, 'The law relating to trade marks'. They are considered in detail in Chapter 24. Titles III and IV, considered in Chapters 25 and 26, deal with the procedures for obtaining registration of a CTM. Chapter 27 covers Title V, 'Duration, renewal and alteration of Community Trade Marks' and Title VI, 'Surrender, Revocation and Invalidity'. Chapter 28 covers the general provisions of Title IX ('Procedure'), relating to a number of different aspects of proceedings before the Office. These encompass all kinds of proceedings, including applications for registration, oppositions, and revocation and invalidity proceedings. Appeals, against decisions of all divisions of OHIM, are governed by Title VII, discussed in Chapter 29. Community collective marks, treated separately in Title VIII, are covered in Chapter 30.

23.28 Title X (Jurisdiction and procedure in legal actions relating to Community Trade marks') is discussed in Chapter 31. Also included in this chapter is Title XI ('Effects on the laws of the Member States'). Title X includes provisions concerning the jurisdiction of CTM courts and remedies for infringement, the hearing of counterclaims for revocation and for declarations of invalidity, and rules for 'related actions' in CTM courts and OHIM. Title XI is concerned with certain aspects of the relationship between CTM's and national trade marks and other rights under the national laws of Member States. Title XII ('The Office'), and Title XIII ('Final Provisions'), have already been mentioned.[1] In due course, it is expected that there will be a new Title XIII, containing provisions relating to the links between the CTM and international registration under the Madrid Protocol, in which event the present Title XIII will become Title XIV.

1 See paras **23.4–23.9** above.

Chapter 24

The Community Trade Mark Regulation: the law relating to trade marks

Definition of a CTM and obtaining a CTM

24.1　Section 1 of Title II is concerned with the definition of a CTM and obtaining a CTM, laying down the rules as to who can be proprietors and the grounds for refusal of registration of a CTM.

Definition of a Community trade mark

24.2　Article 4 of the Regulation ('Signs of which a Community trade may consist') is as follows:

> 'A Community trade mark may consist of any signs capable of being represented graphically, particularly words, including personal names, designs, letters, numerals, the shape of goods or their packaging, provided that such signs are capable of distinguishing the goods or services of one undertaking from those of other undertakings.'

The form of this definition is almost identical to art 2 of the Directive, from which s 1(1) of the TMA 1994 is derived. Although the latter provision is not precisely the same, the differences do not appear material and it is thought that the effect is the same. For the time being at least, reference may be made to decisions on s 1 of the TMA 1994 and to Chapter 5 of this book.

24.3　It is to be noted that para 4 of the Annex to the Regulation says that the Council and the Commission consider that art 4 does not rule out the possibility of registering as a CTM a combination of colours or a single colour, or registering in the future sounds as CTMs, provided that they are capable of distinguishing the goods or services of one undertaking from those of other undertakings; further that the word 'shape' is also intended to cover the three-dimensional form of goods. The possibility of registering a colour or a combination of colours hardly needs stating, and the requirement of capability of distinguishing is in art 4 itself. The possibility of registering sounds seems to have been accepted; the real issue in many cases is likely to be whether the mark is capable of graphical representation.[1] As for the statement about the shape of goods, this again does not need to be said. Therefore it is not expected that in this respect the Annex will be the subject of any contention.

1 See ch 4, paras **4.4** et seq.

24.4 Another statement in the Annex, which is rather more controversial, is that relating to art 1(1).[1] This asserts, as the view of the Council and the Commission, that 'the activity of retail trading in goods is not as such a service for which a Community trade mark may be registered ...'. No such statement appears in the Annex to the Directive. This question is discussed in Chapter 4 above.[2] It may well be that OHIM will follow the Annex, and that the matter will have to be resolved by the ECJ.

1 See **22.1** above.
2 Chapter 4, para **4.14**.

Who can be proprietors of CTMs?

24.5 Article 5 sets out in detail the natural or legal persons, which include authorities established under public law, who may be proprietors of CTMs. Such persons are:

(a) nationals of Member States;
(b) nationals of other states which are parties to the Paris Convention; also[1] parties to the Agreement[2] establishing the World Trade Organisation;
(c) nationals of other States who are domiciled in, or have real and effective industrial or commercial establishments within the Community or a State which is party to the Paris Convention;
(d) nationals of any State, not being party to the Paris Convention or the Agreement establishing the World Trade Organisation which, according to published findings, accords to nationals of all the Member States the same protection for trade marks as it accords to its own nationals. An additional requirement, where any such State requires nationals of the Member States to prove registration in the country of origin, is that the State recognises the registration if CTMs as such proof.

1 As a result of the amending Regulation of 22 December 1994.
2 To which the TRIPS Agreement is annexed. See ch 22 above.

24.6 For the purposes of these rules, art 5(2) provides that 'stateless persons', as defined therein, are treated as nationals of the country in which they have their habitual residence. Under art 5(3), persons who are nationals of a state covered by para (d) above must prove that the trade mark sought to be registered as a CTM is registered in the state of origin unless, according to published findings, such state will register their trade marks without proof of prior registration as a CTM or as a national trade mark in a Member State.

24.7 It can be seen that the provisions of art 5 are, taken as a whole, very broad. It does not appear likely that there will be many cases in which an applicant fails to qualify as a person who can be a proprietor of a CTM. Article 6 provides that a CTM shall be obtained by registration.

Grounds for refusal

24.8 The CTM Regulation uses the same terms, 'absolute grounds for refusal' and 'relative grounds for refusal' as are found in the Directive and thus in the TMA 1994.

In many respects the grounds themselves are very similar. There are, however, some important differences arising from the nature of the CTM as a unitary trade mark extending to the whole of the EU. Even where the grounds appear to be in practically identical terms, they will not necessarily be applied in the same way by OHIM as they are currently being applied by the UK registry. It is hoped that gradually, with guidance from the ECJ, a degree of harmonisation will develop, although this will inevitably take some time.

Absolute grounds for refusal

24.9 The first point that needs to be emphasised is that, in considering whether any of the absolute grounds for refusal of a CTM, set out in art 7(1), apply, the matter must not be judged only in relation to the UK. The same applies to a counterclaim in an action for infringement of a CTM, in which it is alleged that the CTM is invalid by reason of one of the absolute grounds.[1] Article 7(2) seems to make the position clear, although the application of the provision will not necessarily be straightforward in every case:

> 'Paragraph 1 shall apply notwithstanding that the grounds of non-registrability obtain in only part of the Community.'

1 Under art 51.

24.10 No doubt the approach of OHIM will become clearer as applications are examined and objections are considered by the Boards of Appeal and by the ECJ in due course. It may well be found in practice that Examiners will not have sufficient command of all the languages used in the EU to be in a position to raise all objections which might apply in each Member State. OHIM may be alerted to some possible objections by written observations made by third parties,[1] but in many cases some objections will be left to be raised, if at all, in applications for declarations of invalidity.

1 Under art 41.

24.11 The first seven grounds, set out in art 7, are almost identical to corresponding grounds laid down in the Directive. Subject to the observations in the last paragraph, reference may be made to the discussion of s 3(1)–(3) of the 1994 Act, in Chapter 5. Article 7(1)(a)–(g) provides:

> 'The following shall not be registered—
> (a) signs which do not satisfy the requirements of Article 4;
> (b) trade marks which are devoid of any distinctive character;
> (c) trade marks which consist exclusively of signs or indications which may serve, in trade, to designate the kind, quality, quantity, intended purpose, value, geographical origin, the time of production of goods or of rendering the service, or other characteristics of goods or services;
> (d) trade marks which consist exclusively of signs or indications which have become customary in the current language or in the bona fide and established practices of the trade;
> (e) signs which consist exclusively of:
>   (i) the shape which results from the nature of the goods themselves;
>   (ii) the shape of goods which is necessary to obtain a technical result;
>   (iii) the shape which gives substantial value to the goods;

(f) trade marks which are contrary to public policy or to accepted principles of morality;

(g) trade marks which are of such a nature as to deceive the public, for instance as to the nature, quality or geographical origin of the goods or service;'

24.12 The first of these grounds, that the sign sought to be registered does not fall within the definition of a CTM, corresponds to s 3(1)(a) of the TMA 1994. If the ground is valid, then it may not be possible to overcome it by evidence of use, unless such evidence demonstrates that the sign does, in fact, serve the function specified in the definition. The next three grounds, corresponding to s 3(1)(b), (c) and (d), are capable of being overcome by evidence of distinctiveness acquired through use. Article 7(3), corresponding to the proviso in s 3(1), is as follows:

'Paragraph 1(b), (c) and (d) shall not apply if the trade mark has become distinctive in relation to the goods or services for which registration is requested in consequence of the use which has been made of it.'

24.13 Questions will frequently arise, where objections are raised under art 7, as to the extent of use which must be proved to overcome the objection. Will substantial use in just one or two Member States suffice, or must such use be established in most, or even all, of the Member States? The matter must depend upon the nature of the objection and the area in which it is applicable. Where the objection obtains in only one Member State, it should only be necessary to prove acquired distinctive character in that Member State. But where the objection is valid in a number of Member States, the position is not so straightforward. In theory, where an objection obtains in several or all of the Member States, art 7(2) might seem to point to a requirement to show acquired distinctiveness in all those Member States. However, OHIM may adopt a more practical approach, and be prepared to accept use in a substantial part of the area in which the objection applies.

24.14 Article 7(1) contains no provision corresponding to art 3(2) of the Directive,[1] under which registration may be refused 'where and to the extent that the use of the trade mark may be prohibited pursuant to provisions of law other than trade mark law of the Member State concerned or of the Community'. However, reference should be made here to art 7(1)(j), which contains specific provisions concerning one kind of sign which might be refused registration under art 3.2 of the Directive. This was introduced by amendment[2] for the purpose of complying with the TRIPS provisions of the GATT, and reads as follows:

'trade marks for wines which contain or consist of a geographical indication identifying wines or for spirits which contain or consist of a geographical indication identifying spirits with respect to such wines or spirits not having that origin.'

1 On which the TMA 1994, s 3(4) is based.
2 By Council Regulation 3288/94/EC of 22 December 1994 amending the Regulation on the Community Trade Mark for the implementation of the agreements concluded in the framework of the Uruguay round.

24.15 Article 7(1)(h) and (i) cover grounds of objection which are also provided for by arts 3(1)(h) and 3(2)(c) of the Directive, and are similar to some of the grounds set out in s 3(5)[1] of the TMA 1994, which provides that 'a trade mark shall not be registered in the cases specified, or referred to, in s 4, (specially protected emblems)'. The trade marks which may be refused on these grounds are as follows:

'(h) trade marks which have not been authorized by the competent authorities and are to be refused pursuant to Article 6*ter* of the Paris Convention;
(i) trade marks which include badges, emblems or escutcheons other than those covered by Article 6*ter* of the Paris Convention and which are of particular public interest, unless the consent of the appropriate authorities to their registration has been given.'

1 See ch 6, paras **6.108** et seq.

24.16   Article 7(1)(h) corresponds to s 4(3) of the TMA 1994, which refers to ss 57 and 58, giving effect to art 6*ter* of the Paris Convention. Article 7(1)(i) has no counterpart in the TMA 1994, although s 4(1), (2) and (4) are similarly founded on considerations of public interest. Similar grounds of refusal may apply under these provisions of the CTM Regulation.

Relative grounds for refusal

24.17   The relative grounds for refusal of a CTM application, which are set out in art 8, are very similar to those provided by art 4 of the Directive, on which the provisions of s 10(1)–(4) of the 1994 Act are based. However, they are not identical and merit consideration in some detail.

24.18   Articles 8(1) and 8(5) provide for refusal based on 'earlier trade marks', which are defined in art 8(2). For these purposes, 'earlier trade marks' are CTMs, national registrations in a Member State or at the Benelux office and international registrations having effect in a Member State, and applications for any of these; also trade marks which, at the date of the CTM application (or its priority date), are well known in a Member State within the meaning of art 6*bis* of the Paris Convention. The registration or application must have an earlier date (taking account of any priorities claimed) than the CTM application under consideration, and in the case of an application the objection is subject to the mark being registered. Thus 'earlier trade marks', for the purposes of relative grounds for refusal of a CTM application, are generally the same as under s 6 of the 1994 Act. It should be noted that there is one difference of wording, in that where the trade mark relied upon as a basis for refusal is a CTM, no reference is made to any claim to seniority, derived from a national or a Benelux registration under art 34. However, this could only possibly be material where the senior mark is surrendered or allowed to lapse, but in such event the effect of art 34(2) appears to be that the mark is to be treated as an 'earlier trade mark' for the purposes of art 8(2).

24.19   Article 8(1), which applies where the goods or services for which the CTM is applied for are identical with or similar to goods or services for which the earlier trade mark is protected, is for practical purposes the same as s 5(1) and (2) of the TMA 1994.[1] For the time being at least, reference may be made to Chapter 7 and the decisions under the TMA 1994. The Annex to the Regulation contains an identical statement to that found in the Annex to the Directive, which was considered in the *Wagamama* case,[2] linking the idea of 'likelihood of association' with a doctrine said to have been developed by Benelux case-law. Although not referring to the matter, the ECJ, in *Sabel BV v Puma AG*,[3] clearly rejected the Benelux approach and must be taken to have considered that the statement has no relevance.

1 Based on art 4.1 of the Directive.
2 [1995] FSR 713. See ch 7, paras **7.33** et seq.
3 Case C-251/95, [1998] RPC 199.

24.20   Article 8(5) is concerned with oppositions by the proprietors of earlier trade marks which have a reputation, where the goods or services covered by the application are not similar to goods or services for which the earlier trade mark is protected. It is similar to s 5(3) of the TMA 1994, based upon arts 4(3) and 4(4)(a) of the Directive, and the effect appears to be the same. Where the earlier trade mark is a national trade mark, it need only have a reputation in the Member State where it has effect. If it is a CTM, the reputation must be in the 'Community'. The CTM Regulation gives no indication as to what is meant by a reputation in the Community. It is unlikely that OHIM will require proof of a reputation in all Member States. The unitary character of the CTM would seem to suggest that a sufficient reputation within a substantial area of the Community, even one Member State or possibly only a part of a Member State, should suffice.[1] The other require-ment of art 8(5), that the use of the trade mark applied for, without due cause, 'would take unfair advantage of, or be detrimental to, the distinctive character or the repute of the earlier trade mark', is the same as under s 5(3) of the TMA 1994 . On this aspect, and on the extent of reputation required generally, reference may be made to Chapter 6.[2]

1 In an Opinion of Advocate General Francis Jacobs QC, in *General Motors Corpn v Yplon SA*, Case 375/97, [1999] ETMR 122, he indicated that, for the purposes of art 5(2) of the Directive, a reputation in even one Member State may suffice. This has been confirmed by the decision of the ECJ, 14 September 1999 (unreported).
2 Paragraphs **6.59–6.71**.

24.21   Article 8(3) covers the case, separately dealt with in s 60 of the TMA 1994,[1] of the agent or representative of the proprietor of a trade mark, who applies for registration of the mark in his own name without the proprietor's consent. Where the proprietor opposes the application, the trade mark will not be registered unless the agent or representative justifies his action. It is likely that this provision will be applied in much the same circumstances as s 60. What amounts to a justifi-cation of the action of the agent or representative will generally be governed by the contractual or other relationship with the proprietor. Article 11 should also be mentioned here. It would appear from this that the proprietor of the trade mark can take proceedings to prevent use of the mark without opposing the application for registration or applying for a declaration of invalidity.[2]

1 Giving effect to art 6*septies* of the Paris Convention.
2 Under art 52.1(b).

24.22   The provisions of art 8(4), for opposition by proprietors of non-registered trade marks and other signs used in the course of trade, are in some respects similar to s 5(4)(a) of the TMA 1994,[1] but not identical. Section 5(4)(a) enables any appli-cation to be successfully opposed if the mark applied for is liable to be prevented under the law of passing off, as an instance of a law protecting an unregistered mark or other sign used in the course of trade. Article 8(4) similarly provides for opposition on the basis of rights acquired, prior to the date of application for the CTM (or the priority date claimed), which confer the right to prohibit the use of a subsequent trade mark. The non-registered trade mark or other sign must be of 'more than mere local significance'. This will, it seems, exclude many owners of small businesses from opposing CTM applications for trade marks which are in conflict with their rights acquired through use. The position of proprietors of earlier rights which are only of local significance, *vis-à-vis* CTMs, is discussed further below.[2]

1 Based on art 4(4)(b) of the Directive.
2 See paras **24.32** and **24.37**.

24.23 It is to be noted that art 8 contains no provision for opposition on the ground of conflict with other earlier rights, such as copyright and designs, corresponding to s 5(4)(b) of the TMA 1994.[1] Such grounds are only available as grounds for seeking a declaration of invalidity, under art 52(2) of the CTM Regulation.

1 See art 4(c) of the Directive.

Conversion to national procedures under art 108

24.24 Provisions of the Regulation which are of potentially great importance are arts 108–110, under which an applicant for or a proprietor of a CTM may convert his CTM application or CTM into a national trade mark application (a) to the extent that the CTM application is refused, withdrawn or deemed to be withdrawn or (b) to the extent that the CTM ceases to have effect. The right of conversion is given by, and is subject to, the provisions of art 108. Articles 109 and 110 contain procedural requirements which apply at the initial stages, before the national office becomes involved,[1] and rr 44–47 of the Implementing Regulation lay down further procedural provisions. Conversion is possible to a series of national applications within the Community, save to the extent that this is prevented by art 108(2). This provides that conversion shall not take place (a) where the rights of the proprietor of the CTM have been revoked on the ground of non-use, unless in the Member State for which conversion is requested the CTM has been put to use which would be considered to be genuine use under the laws of that Member State, or (b) for the purpose of protection in a Member State in which, in accordance with the decision of the Office or the national court, ground for refusal of registration or grounds for revocation or invalidity apply to the CTM application or the CTM. Thus, for example, if the mark was refused or held invalid on account of a prior right in Member State 'A', or because of an absolute ground applying in that State, or if it was revoked because it had become misleading or generic in the State, then the applicant or proprietor would not be allowed to convert to an application in Member State 'A'. Under art 108(3), where conversion takes place, the resulting national applications have the same filing date or priority date as the original CTM application and, where appropriate, enjoy the seniority of a trade mark in the Member State concerned, claimed under art 34 or 35. Under art 108(4), the Office, when notifying the applicant or proprietor of the refusal or deemed withdrawal of an application or that the CTM has ceased to have effect as a result of a decision of the Office or surrender, only three months from the date of the communication will be allowed in which to file a request for conversion. Where the CTM is withdrawn or the CTM ceases to have effect because of non-renewal, art 108(5) provides that the request for conversion must be filed within three months from the date of withdrawal or the expiry of the CTM. Under art 108(6) where the CTM ceases to have effect as a result of the decision of a national court, the three-month period runs from the date on which the decision became final. Under art 108(7), if a request is not filed in due time, the original CTM application ceases to be available as a regular national filing for the purpose of a claim to priority, under art 32.

1 See ch 23, para **23.16**.

24.25 It is not necessary to discuss the procedural requirements of arts 109 and 110, and rr 44–46 in detail here. They are fairly straightforward. Rule 44 sets out all the details which must be contained in the request. The conversion fee must be paid within the three-month period for filing the request and the Office also checks whether conversion may properly be requested and that the request has been filed within the time limit, before rejecting it under r 45 if the basic formalities as to time and payment of fees are not complied with or, if they are complied with, transmitting it to the appropriate national offices, giving any further information requested by a national office to enable it to decide as to the admissibility of the request. If the CTM application has been published, then art 109(2) requires receipt of the request to be recorded in the register and publication of the request; r 46 lays down detailed requirements for such publication.

Effects of CTMs

24.26 The effects of CTMs, including the rights obtained by registering a CTM, are set out in s 2 of Title II. Most of the provisions are virtually identical to the provisions of arts 5–7 of the Directive, on which ss 9–12 of the TMA 1994 are based. However, there are some differences, which will be considered first.

Use in dictionaries

24.27 Of particular interest is art 10 of the CTM Regulation, which introduces a means for dealing with the problem which sometimes occurs, of trade marks being used in dictionaries in a generic sense. If the reproduction of a CTM, in a dictionary, encyclopaedia or similar reference work, gives the impression that it constitutes the generic name of the goods or services for which the trade mark is registered, the publisher of the work must, at the request of the proprietor of the CTM, ensure that the reproduction of the trade mark, in the next edition of the publication, is accompanied by an indication that it is a registered trade mark. There is no equivalent provision in the Directive or the TMA 1994. Article 10 should be of some assistance to proprietors in protecting some trade marks against misuse. Nevertheless, the existence of provisions in the CTM Regulation for revocation of CTMs which are allowed to fall into generic use, particularly art 50(1)(b),[1] may well force proprietors to take action against publishers of dictionaries. Failure to do so could provide evidence that the generic use was the result of 'inactivity' on the part of the proprietor for the purposes of art 50(1)(b).

1 See also art 12.2(a) of the Directive and the TMA 1994, s 46(1)(c).

24.28 It is not clear from the CTM Regulation how and where the rights given by art 10 may be enforced. CTM courts are given jurisdiction[1] in respects of acts of infringement. Article 10 does not use the word 'infringement', but neither for that matter does art 9, which is the main provision defining the rights conferred by a CTM. It is plain that art 10 creates rights in a CTM which are intended to be enforceable in the courts, and it is thought that incorrect use in a dictionary could be treated as a species of infringement. Alternatively, an appropriate national court would, it is suggested, have jurisdiction in accordance with art 102.[2]

1 See arts 91 and 92.
2 See ch 31, para **31.10**..

Rights conferred by a CTM

24.29 The rights conferred by a CTM are defined in arts 9(1) and 9(2). Under art 9(1), the CTM confers on the proprietor exclusive rights therein and the proprietor is entitled to prevent all third parties not having his consent from using in the course of trade any 'sign' as specified in sub-paras (a)–(c). The rights are defined, according to whether the sign is identical or similar to the CTM, and whether the goods or services concerned are identical, similar or dissimilar to those for which the CTM is registered, in terms which are in effect identical to art 5(1) and 5(2) of the Directive, on which the provisions of s 10(1)–(3) of the TMA 1994 are based. Furthermore, the kinds of 'use' of a sign, which may be prohibited under art 9(1), are defined in precisely the same terms as in art 5(3) of the Directive and s 10(4) of the TMA 1994. Therefore, for the purpose of interpreting and applying these provisions, reference may be made to Chapter 12.

24.30 Some differences from the TMA 1994 are to be found in art 9(3). This provides that the rights conferred by a CTM shall prevail against third parties from the *date of publication of registration of the trade mark*. This is subject to a provision that reasonable compensation may be claimed in respect of matters arising after the date of publication of the CTM application, which matters would, after publication of the registration, be prohibited, although the court seized of the case may not decide upon the merits of the case until after the registration has been published. By implication, this suggests that art 9(3) permits infringement proceedings to be issued as soon as the application is published. It may also be that at that stage an interlocutory injunction could be granted[1] in appropriate circumstances. Furthermore art 99(1) of the Regulation, under which 'provisional and protective measures' are made available, expressly refers to a 'Community trade mark application', and thus clearly envisages the possibility of infringement proceedings being commenced before the mark is registered.[2] In these respects, the provision is to be contrasted with s 9 of the TMA 1994, which makes it plain that the rights conferred by a UK registration date back (after registration) to the date of the application for registration, but that until the mark is actually on the register, proceedings cannot even be issued.

1 In accordance with art 99.
2 The remedy under art 99.1 is only available if it would be available under the law of the State concerned, in respect of a national trade mark, which is not the case under the TMA 1994.

Limitation of the effects of a Community trade mark and exhaustion of rights

24.31 Article 12 of the CTM Regulation, which excludes from the scope of protection, given by registration, the use of a person's own name or address, descriptions of characteristics of goods and services, and indications of the intended purpose of goods or services, for example for use as accessories as spare parts, is in identical terms to art 6(1) of the Directive, on which s 11(2) of the TMA 1994 is based. As with those provisions there is a requirement of use in accordance with honest practices in industrial or commercial matters. Again, reference may be made to Chapter 12.

24.32 Another possible limitation on the effect of a CTM is in relation to earlier rights which are not of 'more than mere local significance' which cannot be the basis of opposition to a CTM application.[1] There is no provision in the CTM

Regulation corresponding exactly to s 11(3) of the TMA 1994[2] protecting owners of earlier rights applying in a 'particular locality' against claims for infringement of a later UK registration. Consequently, cases might arise in which CTM proprietors could claim to be entitled to prevent small businesses from using trade marks which have been used in a small area for many years. However art 107(1) of the Regulation does recognise the right of the proprietor of an earlier right, which only applies to a particular locality, to oppose the use of a conflicting CTM in the territory where his right is protected, in so far as the law of the Member State concerned so permits. Under art 107(2), this right is defeasible by acquiescence in use of the CTM in the territory concerned for five years, of which the proprietor of the earlier right was aware, unless the CTM was applied for in bad faith. It would seem to be implicit in art 107 that the proprietor of the earlier right is entitled to continue use of his mark; otherwise there would be no point in recognising his right. In any event, the courts are likely to be unsympathetic to CTM proprietors in such cases. It is to be hoped that national courts and OHIM and, if necessary, the ECJ, will give a narrow scope to the words 'of mere local significance', so as to allow for opposition and invalidation if otherwise a CTM would prevail against the use of an earlier local right.

1 See para **24.22** above.
2 See art 6.2 of the Directive.

24.33   Article 13 of the CTM Regulation, which makes provision for exhaustion of the rights conferred by a CTM, is identical to art 7 of the Directive. Section 12 of the TMA 1994 is based on that provision, but (as required by the EEA Agreement) extends the effect of exhaustion to goods coming from any country within the EEA. It would seem that the effect of art 13 of the CTM is likewise extended, by virtue of the EEA Agreement. An important difference between the position as regards a CTM and that of a national trade mark is that in the case of the CTM, there is no possibility of complication by considerations of any principle of 'international exhaustion' in respect of goods coming from outside the EU/EEA.[1] So far as the CTM Regulation is concerned, there is no room for the application of any principle of international exhaustion as such.[2]

1 As for example arose in *Silhouette International Schmied GmbH & Co KG v Hartlauer Handelsgesellschaft mbH*, Case C-355/96, [1999] Ch 77.
2 However the decision of Laddie J in a case of an application for summary judgment, *Zino Davidoff SA v A & G Imports Ltd* [1999] RPC 631 should be noted. The judge held, on the evidence, that the defendant had consented to the marketing of the parallel imported goods in the UK. If this approach is correct, a similar conclusion could be reached in the case of a CTM, on the basis that art 9 requires infringing use to be without the consent of the proprietor. The case has been referred to the ECJ.

24.34   Although it is not part of the section of the Regulation entitled 'Effects of Community Trade Marks', art 38(2) allows the Office to impose disclaimers in certain circumstances.[1] These plainly have to be taken into account by a court determining the scope of a CTM in infringement proceedings.

1 See ch 26, para **26.4**.

24.35   Another provision which may be relevant to the effects of a CTM is art 53, entitled 'Limitation in consequence of acquiescence'. This is considered in Chapter 27, because it limits the right to bring proceedings for a declaration of invalidity on relative grounds, and appears in Title VI of the Regulation ('Surrender, Revocation and Invalidity').[1] There is no provision in the CTM Regulation, or indeed the Directive, corresponding to s 11(1) of the TMA 1994, under which it is a defence to a claim for infringement that the mark used by the defendant is a registered trade mark, and the UK implementing legislation[2] does not apply s 11(1) in a case of a claim for infringement of a CTM. However, if a trade mark becomes registered as a CTM, and the proprietor of an earlier CTM acquiesces in the use of that mark for a period of five years, being aware of the use, he is precluded from objecting to the use of the later CTM, unless the later CTM was applied for in bad faith. Article 53(3) also provides, as might be thought to be obvious, that the later CTM proprietor is not entitled to object to the use of the earlier CTM.

1 See paras **27.25–27.27**.
2 The Community Trade Mark Regulations 1996 (SI 1996/1908), considered in ch 23.

Complementary application of national law relating to infringement.

24.36 Article 14(1) of the CTM Regulation states clearly that the effects of a CTM are to be governed solely by the provisions of the Regulation. However, in other respects, infringement of a CTM is governed by the national law relating to infringement of a national trade mark, in accordance with Title X.[1] Article 14(2) provides that the Regulation shall not prevent actions concerning a CTM being brought under the law of Member States, relating in particular to civil liability and unfair competition. Thus it would appear that the fact that a mark is registered as a CTM does not prevent a third party from taking action to prevent its use on the ground of passing off. The situation in this respect may be compared with the position arising under s 2(2) of the 1994 Act. So far as rules of procedure are concerned, art 14(3) provides that these are to be determined in accordance with the provisions of Title X. Article 97(3) expressly provides that, unless otherwise provided in the Regulation, a CTM court shall apply the rules of procedure governing the same type of action relating to a national trade mark in the Member State where it has its seat.

1 See art 97 (Applicable law) and art 98 (Sanctions).

Restrictions on use of CTMs

24.37 There are some circumstances in which, under the Regulation, registration of a CTM clearly does not confer a right of use as against the proprietors of other rights. As already mentioned,[1] s 11(1) of the TMA 1994, which protects a proprietor of a valid UK registration against a claim of infringement in respect of his use of the registered mark, is not applied by the Community Trade Mark Regulations[2] to CTMs. Article 106 of the CTM Regulation makes it clear that the proprietor of an earlier right, within art 8 or art 52(2) can enforce it to prevent the use of a later CTM, unless he is barred by acquiescence in the use of the CTM under art 53. Article 106(2) likewise makes it clear that the proprietor of a CTM is, unless the Regulation provides otherwise, subject to the civil, administrative and criminal laws of Member States and to other provisions of Community law. Such laws, which include the laws of passing off, malicious falsehood and unfair competition, and consumer protection laws such as the TDA 1968 (as amended), as well as Community regulations regarding wine labelling and geographical indications, are applicable to a CTM to the same extent that the use of a national trade mark may be prohibited under such laws. A further restriction on the use of a CTM is provided by art 107, in favour of the proprietor of an earlier right which only applies to a particular locality, unless he is barred by acquiescence.[3]

1 Paragraph **24.35** above.
2 SI 1996/1908, discussed in ch 22.
3 See para **24.32** above.

Use of CTMs

24.38 As under the TMA 1994 and most other national laws, the CTM Regulation makes provision for the revocation of a CTM on grounds of non-use. The sanctions are provided in art 50. Article 15(1) applies these sanctions if within a period of five years following registration, the proprietor has not put the CTM to genuine use in the Community, or if such use has been suspended during an uninterrupted period of five years. For the purposes of art 15, use of the CTM with the consent of the proprietor is deemed to constitute use by the proprietor. These provisions are essentially the same as s 46(1)(a) and (b) of the TMA 1994, based upon arts 10 and 12(1) of the Directive. As under s 46(2) of the 1994 Act, use of the CTM in a form differing in elements which do not alter the distinctive character of the mark in the form in which it was registered, and the affixing of the CTM to goods or their packaging solely for export purposes, is sufficient use for the purposes of art 15(1).

24.39 Having regard to the similarity of the provisions, the principles applicable to non-use cases ought to be much the same for a CTM as for marks registered under the TMA 1994, and for both it will be necessary for OHIM and national courts to apply decisions of the ECJ. Reference may be made to Chapter 17 , but the words 'genuine use *in the Community*' merit further consideration. Clearly, as under the Directive[1] and the TMA 1994,[2] 'genuine use' involves use which is proper commercial use, that is use which has a commercial aim in itself, and use merely effected for purposes of trade mark protection will not suffice. But, assuming that the use is genuine use, how much use is necessary and to how great a part of the Community must the use extend? As a matter of principle, it is suggested, the unitary character of the CTM requires that genuine use in one Member State, or even in a very small part of one Member State, should be sufficient to maintain a CTM. However, suggestions have been made that whether use is to be regarded as genuine use may depend upon the CTM proprietor having a sufficient share of the market in the products concerned, and that use in just one Member State will not be enough.

1 Article 12
2 See ch 17.

24.40 In making such suggestions, reliance has been placed on the provisions of art 108, for conversion of a CTM application or registration into national trade mark applications. Article 108(1) provides for such conversion (inter alia) 'to the extent that the CTM ceases to have effect'. Paragraph (a) of art 108(2) provides that conversion shall not take place 'where the rights of the proprietor have been revoked on the grounds of non-use, unless in the Member State for which conversion is requested the Community trade mark has been put to use which would be considered to be genuine use under the laws of that Member State'. The argument put forward is that if a CTM could not be revoked for non-use if it had been the subject of genuine use, during the relevant period, in only one Member State, then art 108(2)(a) would not have been necessary and is superfluous.

24.41 It is not, however, clear that art 108(2)(a) would be superfluous in such circumstances. It is, for example, possible that a CTM might be revoked on the ground of non-use, when in fact there had been genuine use in some Member State, of which no evidence had been previously adduced. Or there could have been genuine use in a Member State, or perhaps several Member States, which commenced after the expiry of the relevant five-year period but which might be regarded as use which could be relied upon for the purposes of art 108(2)(a). Moreover the argument put forward presupposes that those responsible for framing art 108 ever thought about its effect on art 15(1)[1] at all. It is submitted that the purpose of art 108(2) was to make it absolutely clear that a proprietor of a CTM could not secure protection by conversion, in a Member State in which plainly he ought not to have it. On the face of it, art 108(2) achieves this. What should be of paramount importance is that the CTM should be available to all businesses, from the very large to the very small. Purely arbitrary considerations, as of size of market share, or of area of use, should have no place in the unitary CTM system. Article 108(2), properly understood, does not require that it should be otherwise. At a meeting in 1975, attended (among others) by a representative of the Commission and the late John Burrell QC,[2] Mr Burrell, mentioned a requirement for use 'in a substantial part of the Common Market'. Following representations on the very point here being considered,[3] the wording was changed. The draft published in 1981[4] contained the words 'serious use in the Community'. No doubt there were further representations. The result is that the Regulation adopted the term 'genuine use in the Community'.

1 And art 50(1)(a).
2 One of the three authors of the Memorandum on the Community Trade Mark, discussed in ch 1, at paras **1.12–1.15.**.
3 See the note in ECTA Newsletter, October 1996, p 27.
4 [1981] CMLR 365.

24.42 For these reasons, it is submitted that the most important factor in non-use cases is the character of the use, not its amount or extent. While these are no doubt relevant matters to be considered, they should never be conclusive, and all the circumstances must be considered.[1] If the use relied upon is found to be genuine use in a commercial sense, then the proprietor should retain his rights to his CTM, even if the use is only in a very small area within the Community.

1 Compare the approach under the Trade Marks Act 1938, eg by Whitford J in the *Bon Matin* case [1989] RPC 537.

24.43 One matter not specifically dealt with in the CTM Regulation is the question of burden of proof in non-use cases. As already mentioned,[1] s 100 of the TMA 1994 expressly provides that the person asserting use must prove it, thus reversing the practice adopted under s 26 of the TMA 1938. This was done because of the obvious difficulty for a third party in having to prove non-use. When the information is within the possession of the proprietor, it was considered right that he should produce it if he wishes to retain his rights. It is to be noted that, under art 43(2) and 43(3), and art 56(2) and 56(3), where a proprietor of an 'earlier trade mark' opposes a CTM application or seeks a declaration that a CTM is invalid, he may be called upon to provide proof of genuine use. It is hoped that OHIM and the Boards of Appeal, as well as national CTM courts, will adopt the approach now expressly provided for in the 1994 Act, when dealing with non-use cases under the Regulation.

1 Chapter 11, para **11.6**.

CTMs as objects of property

24.44 Although the CTM, like a trade mark registered under the TMA 1994, is a property right, the approach of the Regulation to dealings in a CTM is in some respects rather different. To some extent, the differences arise from the fact that the CTM covers 15 Member States (with 13 distinct trade mark systems). There being no single system of property ownership in Community law, it is necessary, for purposes of dealings such as licences and assignments, for the CTM to be treated as if it were a national trade mark.

24.45 Article 16 lays down rules for determining what national law shall govern dealings in a CTM. In accordance with the unitary character of the CTM, unless arts 17–24 provide otherwise, a CTM as an object of property must be dealt with in its entirety and for the whole area of the Community, as a national trade mark registered in the Member State in which, *according to the register of CTMs:*

(a) the proprietor has his seat or his domicile on the relevant date; or
(b) where subparagraph (a) does not apply, the proprietor has an establishment on the relevant date.

24.46 Under art 16(2), in cases not provided for by para 1, the CTM will be treated as a national trade mark registered in Spain, being the Member State in which the seat of the Office is situated. Article 16(3) provides for the case where there are two or more persons mentioned in the register as joint proprietors; para 1 applies to the first mentioned. Failing this, that is where the first-named proprietor does not have his seat or domicile, or any establishment, in a Member State, para 1 applies in order to the other joint proprietors in the order in which they are mentioned on the register. If para 1 does not apply to any of the joint proprietors, then para 2 applies and the CTM is treated as a national trade mark registered in Spain.

24.47 The purpose of these provisions is to ensure that, as an object of property, the CTM and transactions affecting it must be subject to the law of one Member State, and only one. They, and in particular the words from art 16(1) quoted in italics at para **24.45** above, serve to emphasise the fact that, in making any CTM application some attention should be given to what details of proprietors will appear on the Register, especially when applicants from outside the Community are involved. There may well be tax considerations which depend on which Member State's law is to govern dealings with the CTM.

24.48 If the proprietor of the CTM is based in the EU, then usually there will be no difficulty in determining where his seat (in the case of a company) or his domicile (in the case of an individual) is located. However, if there are two or more proprietors, and their seats or domiciles are different, art 16(3) requires that the applicants should take care to name first, in order, the proprietor whose seat or domicile is in the Member State where they want the CTM to be regarded as being located. In the case of a proprietor or proprietors from outside the EU, there will be no difficulty if they have only one 'establishment' in the EU. The effect of art 16(2) is that, where there are establishments in more than one Member State, the applicant should ensure that the preferred Member State is named in the register, or at least named first. If the proprietor has no seat, domicile or establishment in the EU, then the CTM will be treated as being located in Spain, by virtue of art 16(2). In such a situation, a person contemplating an application might have to consider whether there were any disadvantages under Spanish law; if there might be, then it might be necessary to incorporate a subsidiary in a preferred Member State and make the application in the name of that subsidiary.

24.49 Under art 24, an application for a CTM is treated as an object of property in the same way as a registered CTM, and arts 16–23 are applied accordingly. Consequently, in all those provisions the word 'proprietor' may include an assignee of a pending application. Once an assignee's title is entered on the register the national law affecting dealings with the CTM may change, according to the rules laid down by art 16.

Transfer of a CTM

24.50 In accordance with art 16, a CTM cannot be divided territorially, and any transfer must be for the whole of the EU. However, art 17 makes an exception to the general requirement of art 16, that a CTM must be dealt with in its entirety, by permitting a transfer in respect of some only of the goods or services covered by the registration, although this is subject to para 4, which requires the Office to refuse to register the transfer where 'it is clear from the transfer documents that because of the transfer the Community trade mark is likely to mislead the public concerning the nature, quality or geographical origin of the goods or services in respect of which it is registered', unless the successor (ie the transferee) agrees to limit registration of the CTM to goods or services in respect of which it is not likely to mislead. This prohibition, which follows the wording of art 50(1)(c), and art 12(2)(b) of the Directive providing grounds for revocation, is of interest because neither the Directive nor the TMA 1994 contains any provision requiring refusal of a duly executed transfer of a trade mark.

24.51 Article 17(1) also permits a CTM to be transferred separately from the 'undertaking'; this means that an assignment is allowed without any part of the goodwill in the assignor's business, and is in line with s 24 of the TMA 1994. Article 17(2) provides that a transfer of the whole of the undertaking shall include the transfer of the CTM, except where, in accordance with the law governing the transfer, there is an agreement to the contrary or the circumstances clearly dictate otherwise. This provision applies to the 'contractual obligation to transfer the undertaking'. This would all seem to be the same, in effect, as the common law rules which apply in the UK. The matter is to be determined under the law of a Member State in accordance with art 16. Under art 17(3), unless the CTM is transferred with the business under art 17(2), an assignment of a CTM must, unless it is the result of a judgment, be made in writing and it must also be signed by both the parties. If not so signed, it will be void. This is different from the position under the 1994 Act, which only requires signature by or on behalf of the assignor.[1]

1 Section 24(3).

24.52 Under art 17(5), on request of one of the parties a transfer of a CTM must be entered in the register and published. This is, of course, subject to the possibility of refusal under para 4. Paragraph 6 provides that, as long as the transfer has not been entered in the register, the transferee cannot invoke the rights arising from the registration of the CTM. This appears to refer not only to infringement proceedings, but to opposition or cancellation proceedings in which the CTM, or a pending application, is relied upon as an 'earlier trade mark'. The detailed requirements for registration of a transfer of a CTM are set out in rr 31–32 of the Implementing Regulation.[1]

1 Commission Regulation 268/95/EC. Appendix 5.

24.53 Article 17(6) is concerned with time limits to be observed *vis-a-vis* the office, which applied to a proprietor before a request to register a transfer was received by the Office. The successor in title, ie the transferee, 'may make the corresponding statements to the Office once the request for registration of the transfer has been received by the Office'. It is not clear what the word 'statements' covers. Presumably these include any step involving the filing of any document, required to be taken by the proprietor in proceedings concerning the CTM before the Office, including (for instance) observations to be made in revocation and invalidation proceedings, and proof of use of an earlier trade mark under art 56. Once a transferee is registered as proprietor of a CTM, art 17(8) requires all documents, which require notification to the proprietor under art 77, to be addressed to the transferee.

24.54 Article 18 makes special provision for the case of a CTM registered in the name of the agent or representative of a person who is the proprietor of the trade mark, without such person's authorisation. This provision is separate from the right of the proprietor to oppose registration under art 8(3). Therefore, because art 24 applies the provisions of arts 16–23 to applications for CTMs, it would seem that the proprietor need not oppose a pending CTM application, but may instead rely upon the right given to him by art 18. The proprietor is entitled to demand an assignment in his favour unless the agent or representative justifies his action in registering the mark. This is an example of a case in which no written assignment by the parties is required by art 17(3); a judgment should suffice.

Rights in rem, levy of execution and bankruptcy proceedings

24.55 Articles 19–21 are concerned with other aspects of the CTM as an object of property. Under art 19 a CTM may, independently of the undertaking, ie the business which owns and uses it, be given as security or be the subject of rights in rem. How such security or rights enforced will be determined, in accordance with art 16, by the national law to which dealings with the CTM are subject. Article 20(1) provides that a CTM may be levied in execution; this would follow, at least under English law, from the general provisions of art 16. Under art 20(2), the procedure for levy of execution is within the exclusive jurisdiction of the courts and the authorities of the Member State whose laws govern dealings with the CTM in accordance with art 16.

24.56 Article 21, relating to bankruptcy or like proceedings, which include receivership and winding-up of companies, is not so straightforward. It envisages the time that common rules for the Member States are adopted for bankruptcy proceedings, and these will become applicable when they come into force. Before then, exclusive jurisdiction is given to the Member State in which the proceedings are 'first brought', within the meaning of national law or of applicable conventions. If a CTM is involved in any such proceedings then, on request of the competent national authority, an entry to that effect must be made in the register and published. The wording of art 21 leaves open the possibility for bankruptcy proceedings, affecting a CTM, being brought in a non-Member State. Such a situation could arise where the proprietor has his seat or domicile outside the EU, whether or not he has, according to the register, an establishment in a Member State. The general principles of conflict of laws will be applicable. Detailed provisions for the registration of the rights in rem in a CTM, and rights arising from levy of execution or in bankruptcy, and for cancellation of such registrations, are laid down in rr 33 and 35 of the Implementing Regulation.[1]

1 See para **24.27**, n1 above.

Licensing

24.57 Under art 22(1), a CTM may be licensed for some or all of the goods and services for which it is registered. In a further exception to the general provision of art 16, it may be licensed for the whole or part of the Community. A licence of a CTM may be exclusive or non-exclusive, the latter of course including a sole licence. Sub-licensing of a CTM is also permitted.[1] Article 22(2) preserves the right of the proprietor to take infringement proceedings against a licensee in respect of certain acts which contravene a provision in the licensing contract, with regard to its duration, the form covered by the registration in which the mark may be used, the scope of the goods or services for which the licence is granted, the territory in which the trade mark may be affixed, or the quality of the goods manufactured or the services provided by the licensee. It would appear that this provision is only intended to cover the rights of a proprietor against a licensee as such. Thus it does not exclude the right of any proprietor of an intellectual property right to take proceedings for infringement in respect of unlicensed use of the right. Accordingly a licensee could be sued for infringement if he used the licensed mark for goods or services which were not covered by his licence, although there would be no any breach of any express provision of the licensing contract. Under art 22(5), on request of either party the grant or transfer of a licence in respect of a CTM must be entered on the register and published.

1 This is clear from the Implementing Regulation, r 34.

24.58 The right of a licensee to bring proceedings for infringement depends upon whether the licence is exclusive or non-exclusive. Under art 22(3), a non-exclusive licensee may bring such proceedings only if the proprietor consents. But this is expressed to be without prejudice to the provisions of the licensing contract. If the contract provides that no consent is needed, then it may be that this overrides art 22(3). On the other hand, even if the contract provides that the licensee may not bring infringement proceedings at all, the giving of consent by the proprietor should override the contract. Where the licence is exclusive, the licensee may bring proceedings without the consent of the proprietor, if the proprietor, after formal notice, does not himself bring infringement proceedings within an appropriate period. What is an 'appropriate period' is not specified; this might be interpreted as meaning a period which is reasonable in all the circumstances. It may also be open to national courts or legislatures to prescribe a period in their own procedural rules. No rules are laid down as to making the proprietor a party to the proceedings, such as exist under the TMA 1994.[1] Again these may have to be laid down by national courts or legislatures. Article 22(4) entitles a licensee to intervene in infringement proceedings brought by the proprietor, for the purpose of obtaining compensation for damage suffered by him. Here also national procedural rules may be required. The procedures for registration of licences, and for the cancellation or modification of such registration, are set out in rr 33–35 of the Implementing Regulation.

1 Sections 30(4) and 31(4).

Effects of transactions vis-a-vis third parties

24.59   As might be expected, under art 23(1) transfers of CTMs, security interests and rights in rem, and licences of CTMs can only be effective against third parties in all the Member States after entry in the register. However, such acts may have effect against third parties before entry in the register, if such parties acquired rights in the trade mark after the act in question, having knowledge of such act. By para 2, art 23(1) does not apply in the case of a person who acquires a CTM or a right concerning the CTM by way of transfer of a whole business undertaking or by any other universal succession. So far as levy of execution is concerned, under para 3 the effects *vis-a-vis* third parties are governed by the law of the Member State determined in accordance with art 16. Paragraph 4 makes provision for bankruptcy proceedings in the same terms as art 21(1).[1]

1 See para **24.56** above.

Chapter 25

Applications for Community trade marks

Filing of applications

25.1 The CTM Regulation itself contains the basic rules for the filing of applications. Further detailed rules are laid down by the Implementing Regulation.[1] Under art 25(1), an applicant has a choice. He may file the application at the Office; alternatively, he may file it at the central industrial property office of a Member State or at the Benelux Trade Mark Office. An application filed in this way has the same effect as if it had been filed at the same date at the Office. Where an application is filed at the central industrial property office of a Member State or the Benelux Trade Mark Office, art 25(2) specifically requires such office to take all steps to forward the application to the office within two weeks after filing, and may charge a fee not exceeding the administrative costs of receiving and forwarding the application. Although these rules are intended to ensure that an applicant using the local route for filing receives the benefit of the national or Benelux Office filing date, this is not guaranteed; the matter depends upon the local office and the means of forwarding. Article 25(3) provides that such applications which reach the office more than one month after filing shall be deemed withdrawn. There is not even the possibility of being given a later filing date when the application reaches the office. Consequently it may be advisable for applicants or their agents, where a receipt for an application is not received from OHIM[2] within about three weeks from the local filing date, to make inquiries as to whether the application has been forwarded to OHIM. In case problems should arise with the existing system of filing CTM applications, art 25(4) provides for a report, ten years after the CTM came into force, on the operation of the system, together with any proposals for modifying the system.

1 Appendix 4.
2 As required by r 5(1) of the Implementing Regulation.

Conditions with which applications must comply

25.2 The basic conditions, with which a CTM application must comply, are set out in art 26. Under para 1, an application must contain (a) a request for the registration of a CTM, (b) information identifying the applicant, (c) a list of the goods or services in respect of which the registration is requested, and (d) a representation of the trade mark. These requirements are obvious essentials. Under para 2, the application is subject to the payment of the application fee and, where appropriate, one or more class fees, which are payable if registration is sought in more than three classes.[1] Paragraph 3 specifically provides that an application must also comply with the Implementing Regulation. Rule 1 of the Implementing Regulation amplifies the filing requirements. For example, the applicant must identify the state in which he is domiciled or has his seat or an establishment. As explained in Chapter 24, this is important for determining the national law which will govern dealings with the CTM. Other requirements include the provision of details of claims to priority or seniority, and specifying the languages for the application.[2]

1 Fees Regulation, Regulation 2869/95/EC, art 2.
2 In accordance with art 115(3) of the Regulation.

25.3 Under art 28, the goods and services must be classified in conformity with the system specified in the Implementing Regulation, r 2(1) of which specifies the common classification referred to in the Nice Agreement Concerning the International Classification of Goods and Services for the Purposes of the Registration of Marks, of 15 June 1957, as revised and amended. Rule 2 contains further requirements for the list of goods and services, which are to be classified according to the Nice Classification, which is also used under the TMA 1994. Rule 2(2) is important, providing that the list of goods and services 'shall be worded in such a way as to indicate clearly the nature of the goods and services and to allow each item to be classified in only one class of the Nice Classification'. It is understood that OHIM has adopted the position that a list specifying 'All goods/services in Class X' does not comply with the rules, that an application listing goods or services in this manner is ineffective and that the defect cannot be cured by amending to specify the goods and services. Rule 2(3) provides that the goods and services 'shall, in principle, be grouped according to the classes of the Nice Classification, each group being preceded by the number of the class ... and presented in the order of the classes under that Classification'. Rule 2(4) makes it clear that the classification is for administrative purposes and does not in any way determine whether goods or services are similar to or dissimilar from each other; this is the same as the position in the UK under the TMA 1994. Rule 3 contains detailed requirements for representation of the mark applied for, including limits on the size of the representation. The requirement for filing a representation is fundamental, and it should be emphasised that a mere description of the sign sought to be registered does not constitute a representation. Thus, for example, where the mark applied for was simply described: 'The trade mark consists in the vacuum packing of an article of clothing in an envelope of plastics', the Second Board of Appeal upheld the decision of the Examiner refusing to accord a filing date to the application, on the basis that no representation of the trade mark had been filed as required by art 26.[1] Similarly, where a colour per se is sought to be registered, it is insufficient, as a 'representation', merely to describe the colour; an actual representation of the colour is required.[2]

1 Case R 4/97–2. See the Official Journal of OHIM 3/98, p 181.
2 See decision of the Third Board of Appeal in Case R 7/97–3, Official Journal of OHIM 5/98, p 641.

The date of filing

25.4 Under art 27, the date of filing of a CTM application is the date on which documents containing the information required by art 26(1) are filed at the Office or, as the case may be, at the national or Benelux Office under art 25(1)(b). If the basic requirements of art 26(1) are not met, or the basic application fee is not paid within a month of filing, r 9(1) provides for notification of the applicant by the office that a filing date cannot be accorded in view of the deficiencies. Rule 9(2) allows a period of two months from the notification, for compliance, and the filing date is determined by the date at which the deficiencies are remedied. If the deficiencies are not remedied within the two-month period, then the application cannot be dealt with as a CTM application,[1] but fees paid are to be refunded. It seems clear that, in order to obtain a filing date, the additional detailed information required by the Regulation and the Implementing Regulation need not be given at the time of filing, although it often will be; neither need class fees be paid at that stage. If the applicant does not provide all the required information at filing, ie he does not comply with all the requirements of rr 1–3 and of the provisions of rr 6, 7 and 8 applying to claims of priority and seniority, and pay all the class fees in full, in accordance with r 9(3) of the Implementing Regulation the Office will invite the applicant to remedy the deficiencies within such period as it may specify.[2] If the deficiencies referred to in r 9(3)(a),[3] are not remedied by the end of the specified period (after any extension), then the application will be rejected under r 9(4). Class fees are not specifically required to be paid with the basic fee, but they are covered by r 9(3)(b), and under r 9(5) if they are not paid within the required period the application is deemed to be withdrawn, unless it is clear which class or classes the amount paid is intended to cover. If there are no other criteria to determine which classes are intended to be covered, the Office will take the classes in order of the classification. The application is deemed to be withdrawn in respect of the classes for which the class fees have not been paid, or have not been paid in full. If the deficiences in question relate to priority or seniority, as specified respectively in r 9(3)(c) and (d), then under r 9(6) and (7) the right of priority or seniority for the application,[4] as the case may be, is lost. Under r 9(8), if the deficiences referred to in r 9(3) relate only to some of the goods and services covered by the application, then refusal of the application, or loss of priority or seniority, is only in respect of those goods and services. These matters all have to be considered under art 36, as part of the examination requirements.[5]

1 It appears that conversion under art 108 of the Regulation, into national applications, is still possible. It should be noted that the two-month period under r 9(1) is not extendable under r 71, because the rule does not 'provide for a period to be specified by the Office'. See ch 28, paras **28.2–28.3**.
2 As mentioned below (paras **28.2** et seq), under r 71 the period may vary, from a minimum of one month (or two months if the applicant's domicile or its principal place of business is outside the EU and it does not have an establishment within the EU) to a maximum of six months, and the period may be extended. However, unlike the position under the TMA 1994 and Rules, the extension must be requested before the period expires.
3 Relating to the requirements of rr 1, 2 and 3 or the other formal requirements laid down in the Regulation or the Rules.
4 Seniority might still be claimed after registration, under art 35 — see para **25.15** below.
5 See ch 26.

Priority

25.5 The CTM Regulation makes provision for two kinds of priority, namely priority based on a previous application, similar to convention priority claimed under s 35 of the TMA 1994, and 'Exhibition priority'. These will be considered separately.

Priority under arts 29–32

25.6   Article 29 of the CTM Regulation provides for the claiming of priority for a CTM application, on the basis of a prior application filed by the applicant or his predecessor in title. The CTM applicant must be the same as the prior applicant; it is not sufficient for the two applicants to be companies in the same group. The provision is similar in effect to the provisions of s 35 of the TMA 1994. Originally, (subject to art 29(5)), art 29 restricted the available basis for a right of priority to a prior filing in a state which is party to the Paris Convention, but was later amended[1] to allow, as a basis for claiming priority, an application filed in a state which is party to the Agreement establishing the World Trade Organisation.[2] Under art 29(5), the first filing may serve as a basis for a claim of priority, even if the state where it was filed is not a party to the Paris Convention or the Agreement establishing the World Trade Organisation, in so far as the state, according to published findings, grants a right of priority having equivalent effect, on the basis of a first filing made at OHIM and subject to conditions equivalent to those laid down in the CTM Regulation. Effectively, this requires reciprocity of treatment.

1 By Council Regulation 40/94/EC of 20 December 1993.
2 Of which the TRIPS provisions are a part.

25.7   In order to claim priority, the CTM application must be made during a period of six months following the date of filing of the prior application, and the goods and services for which registration of the CTM is sought must be identical to, or contained within, the specification of the prior application. In order for an application to be recognised as giving rise to a right of priority, there must be a filing which is equivalent to a 'regular national filing' under the law of the state where it was made or under bilateral or multilateral agreements.[1] To be 'regular' for this purpose, art 29(3) requires the filing to be sufficient to establish the date on which it was filed, whatever the outcome of the application. Thus, for example, it seems that the application may serve as a basis for claiming priority, provided that the specification of goods and services was the same as, or broader than, the specification of the CTM application, even if the specification of the prior application is subsequently reduced so that it is narrower than that of the CTM application.

1 Such as the Benelux Trade Mark Treaty. It might be suggested that for this purpose the CTM Regulation may be regarded as a 'multilateral agreement', making it possible to claim 'internal priority' on the basis of a previously filed CTM application. A similar claim under the TMA 1994, s 35, to priority on the basis of an earlier UK application, is not possible. However it is submitted that the CTM Regulation, adopted under art 235 of the Treaty of Rome, cannot properly be described as an 'agreement'.

25.8   Article 29(4) makes provision for the case where there is more than one application in the state concerned. Where there is a subsequent application for a trade mark which was the subject of a previous first application in respect of the same goods and which is filed in the same state, the subsequent application may be treated as the 'first application' for the purposes of determining priority. In such event, the previous application may not thereafter serve as a basis for claiming a right of priority. But this can only be done if, at the date of filing the subsequent application, the previous application had been withdrawn, abandoned or refused, without having been open to public inspection and without leaving any rights outstanding. Furthermore the previous application must not have served as a basis for a priority claim. It should be emphasised that there is no possibility for an applicant to keep the previous application alive while he prosecutes the later application.

What is not clear is whether the words 'same goods or services' mean that the specifications of the previous and subsequent applications must be identical It is suggested that the matter should be considered from the point of view of the CTM application for which priority is claimed. In principle it should be sufficient that the specification of the subsequent application (within which the CTM specification must be included, because of art 29(1) falls within that of the previous application.

Procedure for claiming priority

25.9 The basic provision is art 30, which requires an applicant desiring to take advantage of the priority of a previous application to file a declaration of priority and a copy of the previous application. Further requirements are laid down by rr 1(1)(f) and 6 of the Implementing Regulation. A claim to priority may be made in the CTM application or subsequently. As appears from r 6(1), priority may be claimed on the basis of more than one previous application. For example, where the CTM application covers more than one class of goods/services, the applicant may claim separate rights of priority based upon previous applications in different classes. Under art 30, if any previous application is not in one of the languages of the Office,[1] then a translation into one of those languages must be filed. The period for doing this will be specified by the Office, under r 6(3), and will be not less than three months.[2] Under r 1(1)(f) of the Implementing Regulation the application must contain a declaration stating the date on which and the country in or for which the previous application was filed. Rule 6(1) requires the applicant to indicate the file number of the previous application and file a copy of it within three months of the filing date.[3] The copy must be certified to be an exact copy of the previous application by the authority which received that application, and be accompanied by a certificate issued by that authority, stating the date of filing of the application. Rule 6(2) applies where the claim of priority is claimed subsequently to the filing of the CTM application. The declaration of priority must be filed within two months of the filing date of the CTM application. The other material specified in r 6(1) must be submitted to the Office within three months from receipt of the declaration of priority. Again these periods would seem to be non-extendable.[4] As regards the evidence to be provided by the applicant under r 6(1),[5] where any of this is available from other sources, such as national registers, under r 6(4) the President of the Office may determine that such evidence need not be provided by the applicant.

1 English, French, German, Italian and Spanish—see art 115.
2 This period is extendable under r 71—see paras **28.2–28.3** below.
3 This period is not extendable—see paras **28.2–28.3** below.
4 See n 2 above.
5 And thus also under r 6(2).

The effect of the priority right

25.10 Article 31 states the effect of the right of priority, which is that the 'date of priority' shall count as the date of the CTM application for the purpose of establishing which rights take precedence. This is relevant for the purposes of the provisions for refusal or invalidity on 'relative grounds' on the basis of earlier rights.[1] A question may arise as to whether the date of priority may itself be affected by a claim of priority made in respect of the national filing on the basis of which the claim of priority is made for the CTM application. For example, if the first application is a UK application, which in turn claims priority, in accordance with s 35 of the TMA 1994, from a French application made within the six months prior to the UK application, can the CTM claim the date of the French application? It is submitted that this is not permissible. Under s 35(2)(a) of the TMA 1994, the priority claim determines the precedence of rights. The date of the UK application, which is set by s 40(3) as the date of the registration obtained, is not affected. In any case, whatever the national law governing the first application, it seems clear from art 29(3) and r 1(1)(f) that the date of priority for the CTM application is the date of filing of the first application.

1 Under arts 8 and 52.

25.11   Article 32 is concerned with the status of a CTM application for the purposes of priority claims in Member States. A CTM application, which has been accorded a date of filing, is to be treated, in the Member States, as equivalent to a regular national filing, where appropriate with the priority claimed for the CTM application.

Exhibition priority

25.12   Article 33 of the CTM Regulation applies where an applicant for a CTM has displayed goods or services under the mark applied for, at an official or officially recognised exhibition falling within the terms of the Convention on International Exhibitions.[1] If the application is filed within six months from the date of the first display of the goods or services under the mark, the applicant may claim a right of priority from that date, within the meaning of art 31. Article 33(2) requires the applicant to file evidence of the display of the goods or services under the mark, and refers to the conditions laid down in the Implementing Regulations which are to be observed. Under r 1(1)(g), the application must contain a declaration that exhibition priority is claimed, and state the name of the exhibition and the date of the first display of the goods or services. Rule 7(1) specifies in more detail the evidence to be filed. Within three months of the filing date,[2] the applicant must file at the Office a certificate issued at the exhibition by the authority responsible for the protection of industrial property at the exhibition. This must be issued at the exhibition, not subsequently. The certificate must declare that the mark was in fact used for the goods or services; it must also state the opening date of the exhibition, and if the first public use of the mark was not on the opening date, the date of the first public use must be stated. The certificate must be accompanied by an identification of the actual use of the trade mark, duly certified by the same authority. Where exhibition priority is claimed after the filing the CTM application, r 7(2) requires the declaration of priority, indicating the name of the exhibition and the date of first display, to be submitted within two months of the filing date, and the evidence required by r 7(1) must be filed within three months of receipt of the declaration by the Office.[3] Article 33(3) makes it clear that a claim of exhibition priority cannot extend the period of priority laid down in art 29. It should be noted that the facility of claiming exhibition priority is not available under the TMA 1994. It is not thought that claims for such priority will be a very frequent or significant feature of the CTM system.

1 Signed at Paris on 22 November 1928 and last revised on 30 November 1972.
2 As to non-extendability, see paras **28.2–28.3** below.
3 As to non-extendability of these two periods, see paras **28.2–28.3** below.

Claiming the seniority of a national trade mark

25.13 Articles 34 and 35 of the Regulation lay down provisions enabling an applicant for registration of a CTM to claim 'seniority' for the application on the basis of earlier national or Benelux registrations of the same trade mark owned by him. The mark applied for must, according to art 34(1), be 'identical' to the mark from which seniority is to be claimed. However, the Office will in practice accept a claim to seniority if any difference are insignificant. The provisions do not allow for claiming seniority where the proprietor of the earlier registration is different from the proprietor of the CTM, even where they are companies in the same group. It will be seen that a claim of seniority for a CTM is of limited effect. The purpose of the provisions is to try to encourage CTM proprietors to rely on their rights under the Regulation and to dispense in due course with national registrations, although it is likely to be a considerable time before this happens to any significant respect.

25.14 Under art 34, the basis for a claim of seniority may be an earlier trade mark, ie a trade mark with an earlier priority date, registered in a Member State or in the Benelux countries or under international arrangements having effect in a Member State. Thus registrations under the Madrid Arrangement and Protocol are included. Registration must have been obtained before seniority can be claimed. In order to provide for cases in which an application for registration, on the basis of which a claim to seniority might be made, is pending at the date of the CTM application, art 35 contains similar provisions for claiming such seniority after registration of the CTM. The goods or services covered by the CTM application must be identical with, or contained within, those for which the earlier trade mark has been registered. Seniority may only be claimed in respect of the Member State for which the earlier trade mark is registered, although in the case of the Benelux registrations all three countries will of course be covered, and seniority may be claimed in respect of more than one Member State, on the basis of separate registrations in each of them.

25.15 Further procedural provisions for claiming seniority are contained in rr 1(1)(h) and 8 of the Implementing Regulation. Where seniority is claimed under art 34, r 1(1)(h) requires the application to contain a declaration of the claim, stating the Member State or Member States in or for which the earlier mark is registered, the date from which each relevant registration was effective, and the goods and services for which the mark is registered. Under r 8(1), where seniority of any earlier registered trade mark is claimed in a CTM application, the applicant must, within three months of the filing date,[1] submit a copy of the relevant registration, certified by the competent authority to be an exact copy of the relevant registration. In the case of a claim to seniority made after the filing of the CTM application, the declaration of seniority, indicating the same matters as those required by r 1(1)(h), has to be submitted within two months from the date of filing, and the evidence required by r 8(1) must be submitted within three months from the receipt of the declaration.[2] Under r 6(3), the Office must inform the national or regional offices concerned—ie the central industrial property offices of the Member States or the

Benelux Trade Mark Office—of the effective claiming of seniority. As under r 7(3), r 8(4) allows the President of the Office to relax the extent of the requirements of r 8(1) for submitting evidence, provided that this is available to the Office from other sources. There are no specific provisions in the Implementing Regulation for the claiming of seniority of the CTM after registration, under art 35. Presumably the Office will apply analogous requirements to those of r 8, with a period of two months, from the date of the claim to seniority and a further three months for the evidence.

1 As to non-extendability, see paras **28.2–28.3** below.
2 As to non-extendability, see paras **28.2–28.3** below.

The effect of a claim to seniority

25.16 The provisions of art 34(2) and (3), which by art 35(2) are applied to claims made after registration of the CTM, state the effect of a valid claim to seniority. There is no effect at all unless and until the proprietor surrenders the earlier registration or allows it to lapse. In such event the proprietor will be deemed to continue to have the same rights as he would have had if the earlier trade mark had continued to be registered. This means that he will retain the national rights, including the priority date of the earlier registration. However the seniority claimed will lapse, in accordance with art 34(3), where the earlier trade mark is revoked or declared invalid or if it is surrendered prior to the registration of the CTM. In the UK this aspect is provided for by reg 3 of the 1996 Regulations,[1] allowing for determination a posteriori of invalidity and liability to revocation.

1 See ch 23, para **23.15** above.

Chapter 26

Registration procedure

Registration procedure

26.1   The procedure, from the filing of the application and compliance with the formalities discussed above, and up to registration, is governed by arts 36–45, contained in Title IV of the CTM Regulation. These provisions cover: examination of the application; search; publication of the application; observations by third parties and opposition; withdrawal, restriction and amendment of the application; and registration. Further detailed procedural provisions are made in the Implementing Regulation. At the outset some mention should be made of the provisions regarding extensions of time. In particular, r 71, which is discussed in further detail in Chapter 28, should be noted here. According to r 71(1), where the Regulation or Rules provide for a period to be specified by the Office, the period specified must be not less than one month (or two months where the party concerned is not domiciled, and has no principal place of business or establishment within the Community) and not more than six months. Where appropriate, this period may be extended if, and only if, the request for extension is submitted before the original period expired. It should be noted that r 71(1) does not apply where the period is actually specified in the Regulation or the Rules. Rule 71(2) provides that where there are two or more parties, which obviously includes any opposition, 'the Office may extend a period subject to the agreement of the other parties'. Although at first sight this wording might seem to imply that no extension is permitted unless the other party agrees, as explained in Chapter 28 it is probable that the purpose of r 71(2) is to permit extension, if all parties agree, beyond what is allowed under r 71(1). It would be surprising if those who framed the Rules had intended it to be impossible in any circumstances to extend a time for one party unless all other parties agreed.

Examination of applications

26.2   Reference has already been made, in paras 25.1–25.4 above, to the provisions relating to the conditions of filing. Article 36 specifically requires the Office to examine whether the CTM application satisfies the requirements for the accordance of a filing date (art 27), that the application complies with the conditions laid down in the Implementing Regulation, and that appropriate class fees have been paid within the prescribed period. Where the application does not satisfy these requirements, art 36(2) requires the Office to request the applicant to remedy the deficiencies or the default within the prescribed period. Failure to remedy these matters has varying consequences, which are set out in art 36(3)–36(7) and substantially repeated, with some additions, in r 9, the terms of which have already been considered.[1] If the deficiencies in meeting the requirements for the accordance of a date of filing under art 27[2] are not remedied within the period prescribed, ie two months of notification then according to art 36(3) the application will not be dealt with as a CTM application; if they are remedied within such period, then the application is accorded as the date of filing the date on which the deficiencies or default were remedied. If on the other hand the deficiencies relate to the conditions laid down in the Implementing Regulation, art 36(4) requires the Office to refuse the application if they are not remedied within the prescribed period, which is specified in the invitation to remedy the defects. In the case of default in payment of class fees, art 36(5) provides for the application to be deemed withdrawn unless it is clear which categories of goods or services the amount paid is intended to cover. The situation which can arise where an applicant's representative has simply miscalculated the fees due, is covered by r 9(4) which, as previously mentioned, contains a further provision under which the Office applies any money available in the order of the classification, the application only being deemed withdrawn in respect of any classes not covered by the payment received. Under art 36(6) and 36(7), the right of priority or seniority claimed for the application is lost if the deficiencies in respect of the requirements for such claims,are not remedied within the period specified.[3]

1 See ch 25, para **25.4** above.
2 These include the payment of the basic application fee within one month of the filing. See also r 9(1)(b).
3 Rule 9(6) and 9(7), mentioned above, para **25.4** ,merely repeats these provisions. Under r 9(5) the right is only lost for the goods or services to which the deficiency relates.

26.3 Article 37 requires refusal of the application where the applicant is not entitled, under art 5 of the Regulation, to be the proprietor of a CTM.[1] However, the application may not be refused before the applicant has been given the opportunity to withdraw his application or submit his observations. It is not clear whether the opportunity to withdraw gives the applicant any advantage over having the application refused. In either case he has the right to convert the application into national applications under art 108 of the Regulation. Possibly an actual refusal might be disadvantageous in some Member States where a similar objection could arise. The procedure is laid down in r 10, under which the applicant must be notified of any objection and the Office must specify a period, which is extendable under r 71(1), in which the applicant may withdraw the application or submit his observations. Such 'observations' could include evidence relating to the objection. It seems that there is no right to an oral hearing, although the Office would have the power to allow one under art 75. The general procedural rules, rr 52–99 include provisions for oral hearings.

1 See paras **24.5–24.7** above.

26.4 Article 38 is concerned with absolute grounds for refusal, under art 7,[1] and requires the Office to refuse an application to the extent that the trade mark is ineligible for registration under art 7 in respect of any of the goods or services covered by the application. Article 38(2) gives the Office a power which has been taken away from the UK registrar under the TMA 1994. Where the trade mark applied for contains an element which is not distinctive, and *where inclusion of said element in the trade mark could give rise to doubts as to the scope of protection of the trade mark,* the Office may request, as a condition of registration, that the applicant disclaims any exclusive right to such element. The disclaimer is required to be published with the application or the registration of the CTM, depending upon the stage at which the disclaimer is requested. This power to impose a disclaimer is to be contrasted with the position under the TMA 1994,[2] which, while still making disclaimers possible, gives the registrar no power to insist on a disclaimer. The need for disclaimers may be greater with the CTM because of the large territory covered. For example, the provision could be particularly useful when the element is a word in a language which is unfamiliar in some parts of the Community, although it is not confined to such cases, and might also be useful in cases where a word or device is non-distinctive but is given prominence in the mark as a whole and might otherwise be the subject of an unwarranted claim to exclusivity. Article 38(3) provides that the application shall not be refused before the applicant has been allowed the opportunity of withdrawing or amending the application or of submitting his observations. Rule 11 lays down the procedure to be followed under art 38. The Office must notify the applicant of the grounds of refusal and will specify a time for the withdrawal or amendment of the application or the submission of observations. Such period is governed by r 71 and is extendable. 'Observations' will include, where appropriate, evidence of acquired distinctiveness. In cases in which a disclaimer is requested under art 38(2), r 11(2) requires the applicant to be invited to submit the form of statement of disclaimer. Under r 11(3) the application will be refused to the extent that any objection under art 7 is not overcome, or where the applicant does not accept the proposal of a disclaimer. As with art 37, there appears to be no right to an oral hearing, although again this may be allowable under art 75 and is provided for in the general procedural rules, rr 52–99.

1 Paragraphs **24.9–24.16** above.
2 See ch 5, para **5.73** and ch 12, para **12.49** above.

26.5   There have been many decisions of the Examination Division of the Office, refusing applications on absolute grounds. They are too numerous to discuss here, and for the most part do not lay down general principles. Of more significance are decisions of the Boards of Appeal, a few of which have been published in the Official Journal. Again most of these do not seem to offer any general guidance. Of greater importance will be decisions of the CFI on appeal from decisions of the Boards of Appeal, when these occur, and also decisions of the ECJ on corresponding provisions of the Directive. Any relevant decisions to date are discussed in Chapter 5 of this book.

26.6   One matter which has been the subject of several decisions of the Boards of Appeal is the extent to which OHIM will take notice of registration of the mark applied for in other countries. In a decision of the Third Board of Appeal,[1] in which reliance was placed on a registration in the United States of America and some Member States. it was observed:

> 'The Board considers that the existence of registrations in non-member countries may be taken into account by the examiner, provided there is some evidence that similar standards of registrability obtain in the countries concerned. The existence of registrations in Member States is, however, of much greater relevance in view of the harmonisation of the provisions on absolute grounds of refusal effected by the CTMR and Council Directive ... and, in particular, those in Member States in which the language is the same as the one used for the word part of the Community trade mark application.'

Similar remarks have been made in other decisions, but it is that clear OHIM does not consider registration in other countries to be binding on Examiners, who must make their own assessment.[2] It is clear from these, decisions, and others, that if reliance is to be placed on any registrations in other countries, particularly in non-Member States, representatives should submit evidence of the standards of registrability in such countries.

1 In *'Poly Pads' Trade Mark*, Case R 68/1998–3, Official Journal of OHIM, 10/98, p 1079.
2 See eg a further decision of the Third Board of Appeal in *'Enamelize' Trade Mark*, Case R 29/1998–3 Official Journal of OHIM 10/98, p 1070, and a decision of the First Board of Appeal in *'XTRA' Trade Mark*, Case R 20/97, Official Journal of OHIM 10/98, p 1045.

Search

26.7   Although the CTM Regulation makes no provision for refusal of an application by the Office on relative grounds, art 39 requires certain searches to be made by the Office and enables national trade mark offices to make their own searches. Under art 39(1), once the Office has accorded a filing date for the application and has established that the applicant satisfies the requirements of art 5, as to qualification for proprietorship, it must draw up a Community search report citing any earlier CTM registrations or applications discovered, which may be invoked under art 8, as founding a relative ground for refusal. It is understood that, because of the unexpectedly high numbers of CTM applications made since the Office started to receive them, the Office has not in fact made any such searches. This appears to be in clear breach of the requirement of art 39(1), but it does not seem that a third party, who has been prejudiced by the failure to make a search, has any remedy.

26.8   Once a CTM application has been accorded a filing date, but without waiting for the examination under art 37 (as to eligibility for proprietorship of a CTM, under art 5), art 39(2) requires the Office to transmit a copy of the application to the central industrial property office of each Member State which has informed the Office of its decision to operate a search of its own national register of trade marks in respect of CTM applications. Apart (it is understood) from France, Germany and Italy, all the Member States have indicated their decision to make such searches. Within three months from receiving the CTM application the offices of these Member States must, pursuant to art 39(3), communicate to the Office a search report citing any earlier national trade marks or applications discovered which may be invoked under art 8 against the application, or state that the search has revealed no such rights. Article 39.4 provides for an amount to be paid to each office for each search report provided by that office. This amount is fixed by the Budget Committee.

26.9   In the case of both the Office's own CTM search under art 39(1) and of the national reports received in the time provided by art 39(3), under art 39(5) the Office must without delay transmit these to the applicant. It would seem that this obligation does not extend to national reports received after the three-month period. Furthermore, in the case of the Office's CTM search report, art 39(6) requires the Office, upon publication of the CTM application, inform the proprietors of earlier CTM registrations or applications revealed by the search, of the publication of the application. It should be noted that this provision does not apply to the national search reports. This is an example of the advantages conferred on CTM proprietors and applicants, over proprietors of national rights, and emphasises the importance of national proprietors maintaining an effective watch on CTM applications and registrations. The publication of the application, and the informing of the proprietors of such earlier rights, must not take place before the expiry of one month from the transmission of the search reports to the CTM applicant.

26.10 Article 39(7) provides for a review of the system of searching for earlier rights, five years after the opening of the Office for the filing of applications. The Commission is required to submit to the Council a report on the operation of the system of searching under art 39, including the payments to Member States under art 39(4), and, if necessary, submit proposals for amending the CTM Regulation 'with a view to adapting the system of searching on the basis of the experence gained and bearing in mind developments in searching techniques'. It does not appear that art 39(7) allows the abolition of the searches referred to. Indeed the wording of the provision suggests that the scope of searches could even be broadened, if improved technologies make this more effective.

Publication of the application

26.11 Article 40(1) provides for publication of the application once the conditions which the CTM application must satisfy have been fulfilled,[1] and the one-month period referred to in art 39(6), following the transmission of the search reports to the applicant, has expired. Publication is required to the extent that the application has not been refused pursuant to arts 37 and 38. Rule 12 specifies the information which the publication must contain. The information required is really obvious and needs little comment. It includes, of course, the applicant's name and address, particulars of any representative, the reproduction of the mark, the specification of goods and services, the date of filing and the file number, and the language of filing and the second language indicated. In addition, particulars of priority and seniority claims, and of any disclaimer, must be given and, where applicable, a statement that the mark has become distinctive through use, and a statement that the application is for a collective mark. Under art 40(2), in cases in which the application is refused after publication, under arts 37 and 38, the decision to refuse must be published upon becoming final. The CTM Regulation contains no express provision for refusal after publication on any of the grounds on which arts 37 and 38 provide for refusal, that is non-entitlement to be a proprietor of a CTM (art 5) and the absolute grounds set out in art 7. Neither is there any such provision in the Implementing Regulation. However it is implicit, from the provisions of art 41 regarding observations by third parties, discussed below, that refusal after publication is possible, at least on absolute grounds under art 7. Were this not the case the permitting of written observations would be ineffective.

1 If they are not fulfilled, and the applicant does not wish to appeal, the procedure for conversion to national applications under art 108 may be used. See ch 24, paras **24.24–24.25**.

Withdrawal, restriction and amendment of the application

26.12 Article 44(1) allows a CTM applicant to withdraw his application, or restrict the list of goods or services, at any time, whether before or after publication. If this occurs after publication, the withdrawal or restriction must also be published. So far as other amendments of a CTM application are concerned, the possibilities are very limited indeed. Under art 44(2) amendment is only permitted, on request of the applicant, by correcting the name and address of the applicant, errors of wording or copying, or obvious mistakes, but this is subject to the proviso that the correction must not substantially change the trade mark or extend the list of goods or services. Where the amendments affect the representation of the trade mark or the list of goods or services, and are made after publication, the application must be published as amended. Rule 13 sets out details of what an application for amendment must contain. Apart from the file number of the application, the name and address of the applicant and of his representative if any, the application must contain an indication of the element of the CTM application to be corrected or amended and that element in its corrected or amended version; if the amendment relates to the representation of the mark, there must be included a representation of the mark as amended, in accordance with r 3. Under r 13(2) where the application for amendment is subject to the payment of a fee, the application is not deemed to have been filed until the necessary fee has been paid. The Office must inform the applicant if the fee has not been paid, or has not been paid in full. If the Office takes the view that the requirements of art 44, for amendment, are not fulfilled, rule 13(3) requires it to communicate the deficiency to the applicant. If the deficiency is not remedied within a period specified by the Office,[1] the application for amendment is to be rejected. Under r 13(4), where there is publication of an amendment under art 44(2), rr 15 to 22, which lay down the opposition procedures, apply mutatis mutandis.[2] It is made clear by art 42.2 would seem that upon such publication there is a further period for filing notice of opposition, where the amendment affects the representation of the mark or the specification of goods or services. Rule 13(5) allows a single application for amendment of the same element in two or more CTM applications of the same applicant, but if a fee is required for the amendment it must be paid in respect of each CTM application to be amended. Under r 13(6), paras (1)–(5) apply mutatis mutandis to applications to correct the business address of a representative appointed by the applicant. Such applications are not subject to payment of a fee.

1 The period is extendable in appropriate circumstances. See r 71 and ch 28, paras **28.2–28.3** below.
2 See paras **26.16** et seq below.

26.13 Rule 14 makes provision for correction of mistakes and errors in publications. If a mistake or error is attributable to the Office, the Office must correct the mistake, of its own motion or at the applicant's request. By para (2), r 13 applies, mutatis mutandis, to a request by the applicant for correction under r 14(1); the request is not subject to payment of a fee. By r 14(3) the corrections effected must be published. Under r 14(4), where the correction concerns the list of goods or services or the representation of the mark, the conditions of art 44.2, and rr 15–22, apply mutatis mutandis; accordingly a fresh period for opposition commences.

Observations by third parties and opposition

Observations by third parties

26.14 Article 41 provides that, following the publication of the CTM application, any natural or legal person, and any group or body representing manufacturers, producers, suppliers of services, traders or consumers may submit to the Office written observations, explaining on which grounds, under s 7 in particular, the trade mark shall not be registered ex officio. There is no requirement as to the language in which observations are to be submitted, or as to translation. Presumably they must at least be in one of the languages of the Community. The objections are probably not confined to the absolute grounds; the words 'in particular' indicate that other objections may be raised. Thus an objection that the applicant does not qualify for proprietorship under art 5 might be raised. On the other hand, it is clear that grounds on which an application cannot be refused ex officio, such as relative grounds, cannot be invoked. The third parties who may submit written observations under this provision clearly include trade associations and bodies such as the Consumers Association. However professional bodies and, it would seem, associations of trade mark owners, will probably not qualify. It would seem that a person may submit observations even if he would be precluded, by art 5, from filing a CTM application himself. The third party does not become a party to the proceedings before the Office. Article 41(2) requires the Office to communicate the observations to the applicant, who is entitled to comment upon them.

26.15 It is to be noted that art 41 only allows the submission of observations after publication of the application. It has sometimes happened in the UK, under the TMA 1938,[1] that third parties have made observations to the registrar prior to publication of applications in the Trade Marks Journal. As with the TMA 1994, the Office has no express power to act on observations made prior to publication. Of course, if such an observation draws the Office's attention to an obvious omission, then it may be unreasonable to expect the Office not to act on it. But it is submitted that this should not happen except in a clear case. Unless the matter is beyond doubt, it is suggested that the proper course is to invite the third party concerned to submit the observations again if and when the application is published. In any event, if any observations made before publication are to be acted upon, then the rules of natural justice would require that, as is expressly required by art 41(2), the observations be communicated to the applicant, in order that he may comment upon them.

1 See ch 8, para **8.10** above.

Opposition

26.16 Opposition proceedings under the CTM Regulation are governed by arts 42 and 43, and rr 15–22 lay down the procedural requirements. In contrast to the position under the TMA 1994, opposition is only possible on the relative grounds, under art 8 of the Regulation.

26.17 The order of events following the giving of a notice of opposition should be mentioned briefly. There is no specific requirement in the Regulation or rules for the applicant to be served with a copy of the notice at the outset, and it appears that this is not intended to happen. At the first stage the Office considers, in accordance with r 18, whether the notice is 'inadmissible', and if it is not, must reject the notice. If the notice is not thus rejected, then the opposition proceedings 'commence', as provided in r 19. Following commencement the opposition is 'examined' and finally the Office gives its ruling. It is at the examination stage that the applicant may raise the question of use of any earlier trade marks relied upon in the notice, under art 43(2) and 43(3) of the Regulation.

26.18 As under the TMA 1994 and Rules, art 42(1) provides for a three-month period, following publication of a CTM application, for giving notice of opposition, and the period is non-extendable.[1] Unlike the position in the UK, the right to oppose is not open to all. Article 42(1) restricts opposition to: the proprietors of earlier trade marks[2] and, in some cases[3] their licensees; the proprietors of marks applied for by an agent or representative without consent;[4] and proprietors of earlier marks or signs protected through use,[5] and persons authorised under the relevant national law to exercise such rights. Article 42(2) confirms the right of persons referred to in para (1), to oppose in the event of a CTM application being amended and published in accordance with art 44(2), that is in cases of restriction and amendment of the application. Article 42(3) requires the notice of opposition to be in writing and to specify the grounds. It should be emphasised that the notice of opposition itself must contain the grounds relied upon. A decision of the Opposition Division,[6] in a case in which the grounds were submitted at a later date, outside the opposition period, makes it clear that this is a fundamental requirement and held the opposition to be admissible.

1 Rule 71(1) does not apply, since the period is set by the Regulation. See paras **28.2–28.3** below.
2 As referred to in art 8(2).
3 Under art 8(1) and (5).
4 Article 8(3).
5 Article 8(4).
6 In Opposition No B 2875 *(Instra-Lube Trade Mark)*, Official Journal of OHIM 6/98, p 711.

26.19 Further details of the requirements for opposition are set out in r 15. As well as identifying the opposed application the notice of opposition must indicate the goods and services, listed in the application, against which the opposition is entered, full details of the earlier marks and other rights relied upon, as set out in r 15(2)(b), and full particulars of the opposing party as set out in r 15(2)(c). By virtue of art 42(3), the opposition will not be treated as duly entered until the opposition fee has been paid.

26.20 Also under art 42(3), the opponent will be given a period, fixed by the Office,[1] in which to submit 'facts, evidence and arguments' in support of his case. Further information as to what this involves is to be found in r 16. It is clear from r 16 itself (see below) that the facts, evidence and arguments may be contained in the notice of opposition. It is also clear from art 42(3) that, so long as the requirements of r 15(2), as to the contents of the notice of opposition, are met, there is no *obligation* to include other facts, evidence or argument, or supporting documents, with the notice. In confirmation, r 16(3) provides that if the particulars of the facts, evidence and arguments, and other supporting documents, as referred to in para (1), and the evidence referred to in para (2), are not submitted with the notice of opposition or subsequently, these may be submitted within such period after commencement[2] of the opposition proceedings as the Office may specify pursuant to r 20(2).[3] No proper distinction is drawn between 'facts', 'evidence' and 'arguments" and there appears to be no requirement for 'evidence' to be sworn or to comply with any other formalities. In some respects r 16 is rather vague and imprecise, and it needs to be considered in some detail.

1 The period is extendable. See r 71(1) and paras **28.2–28.3** below.
2 See r 19, below.
3 See para **26.31–26.32** below.

26.21 Rule 16(1) provides that every notice of opposition 'may contain' particulars of the facts, evidence and arguments presented in support of the opposition, accompanied by the relevant supporting documents. Rule 16(2), which deals with some kinds of supporting material, seems to cover some of the same ground as para (1). It reads as follows:

'If the opposition is based on an earlier trade mark which is not a Community trade mark, the notice of opposition shall preferably be accompanied by evidence of the registration or filing of that earlier mark, such as a certificate of registration. If the opposition is based on a well-known mark as referred to in Article 8(2)(c) of the Regulation or on a mark having a reputation as referred to in Article 8(5) of the Regulation, the notice of opposition shall in principle be accompanied by evidence attesting that it is well-known or that it has a reputation. If the opposition is entered on the basis of any other earlier right, the notice of opposition shall in principle be accompanied by appropriate evidence on the acquisition and scope of protection of that right.'

26.22   The use of the words 'preferably' and 'in principle', in r 16(2) are slightly confusing. They seem to suggest that the material specified should be provided, if at all possible, in or with the notice of opposition. However, as already explained, there is no obligation to do so. On the other hand it may expedite the determination of the opposition (if that is what the opponent wants) if all the material to be relied upon, whether it consist of facts, evidence or arguments, if filed at the earliest possible stage. Where the material is not submitted with the notice of opposition, r 20(2), which is considered below,[1] provides for the Office to specify a period for submitting it.[2]

1 See **26.31–26.32** below.
2 The period is extendable. See para **26.1** above and paras **28.2–28.3** below.

Use of languages in opposition proceedings

26.23   Rule 17 makes provision for the language to be used in opposition proceedings. The notice of opposition may be filed in any official language of the Community. However r 17(1) provides that, if the language used is not that of the application for registration of the CTM, where that is one of the languages of the Office, or the second language indicated when the application was filed, the opponent must file a translation of the notice in one of those two languages within a period of one month[1] from the expiry of the opposition period. Although the wording of this provision is not clear, it appears that, in order to avoid the need for a translation, it is not sufficient that the notice is in the language of the application *unless* that language is also one of the languages of the Office. The purpose of the rule is that the language of the opposition proceedings should be one of the languages of the Office. Therefore, if only the second language indicated is a language of the Office, the opponent must choose that language for the notice of opposition or file a translation into it. If both the language of the application and the second language are languages of the Office, the opponent can choose either for the notice of opposition or the translation. Rule 17(1) having set the language of the opposition proceedings, para (2) deals with the question of any translation of the evidence filed in support of the opposition, under r 16(1) and (2). If this is not in the language of the opposition, the opponent must provide a translation, within a month of the expiry of the opposition period or within the period specified by the Office under r 16(3). Under art 115(7) it is possible for the parties to agree upon a different language, which must be one of the official languages of the Community, for the opposition. Although r 17(3) is not completely explicit on the point, it appears that the intention is that the Office must be informed, either by the opponent or the applicant, of any such agreement prior to the date on which the opposition proceedings are deemed to commence pursuant to r 19(1).[2] Since, as already mentioned, the rules do not specifically require that the notice of opposition be served on the applicant until the commencement stage, then if notice of the agreement as to language has to be given prior to that, para (3) assumes that the applicant has at least been informed, possibly by the opponent, that notice of opposition has been given. Paragraph (3) also requires the opponent, if the notice of opposition was not filed in the agreed language, to file a translation of the notice of opposition into that language within one month of the date of commencement.

1 This is non-extendable. See paras **28.2–28.3** below, and the decision of the Opposition Division in Opposition No B 2784 (*Profil Trade Mark*), Official Journal of OHIM 5/98, p 653.
2 See para **26.25** below.

Admissibility and examination of the opposition

26.24   When a notice of opposition is filed, the Office first considers whether it is 'admissible'. In particular the Office also examines the opposition for compliance with art 42. This, and other matters, is dealt with by r 18. Paragraph (1) is concerned with deficiencies which can only be rectified within the opposition period. If the Office finds that the notice of opposition does not comply with the provisions of art 42, then the Office is required to reject the notice as inadmissible unless the deficiencies have been remedied before the opposition period expires. This would apply, for example, if the opponent was not the proprietor of any of the earlier marks or rights relied upon and, in the case of earlier marks or rights coming under art 8(2), (4) or (5), was not a licensee of the mark or a person authorised to exercise the earlier rights. Under r 18(1) the notice is also required to be rejected as inadmissible where it does not clearly identify the application against which the opposition is entered or the earlier mark or the earlier right on the basis of which the opposition is being entered, unless the deficiencies are remedied before expiry of the opposition period. Failure to pay the opposition fee within the opposition period leads to a similar result: the notice of opposition is deemed not to have been entered. If the fee is paid after expiry of the opposition period, then r 18(1) requires it to be returned to the opponent. Paragraph (2) makes provision for cases in which the notice of opposition is found not to comply with other provisions of the Regulation or the Rules. The Office is required to inform the opponent accordingly and call upon him to remedy the deficiencies noted within a period of two months. If the deficiencies are not remedied within that time, then the Office must reject the opposition as inadmissible. It should be noted that the two-month period is not extendable under r 71(1), although it appears that, if the applicant agreed, the period could be extended under r 71(2).[1] It would seem, from the decision of the Opposition Division referred to above,[2] that failure to file a translation of the notice of opposition, in accordance with r 17(1), is not a 'deficiency' in compliance with 'other provisions of the Regulation or these Rules' falling within the scope of r 18(2), in respect of which the Office must give two months' notice to remedy. Rule 18(3) requires any decision to reject a notice of opposition as inadmissible under paras (1) or (2) to be communicated to the applicant. There is no express requirement for communication to the opponent, although obviously this must be implied into paras (1) and (2). What is clear from these provisions is that it is highly important to ensure, in the first place, both that the notice of opposition is correct[3] and that the fee is paid. In practice, particularly if the notice is not filed until near the end of the opposition period, there may be little or no possibility of remedying the position where para (1) applies.

1 See ch 28, paras **28.2–28.3** below.
2 See para **26.23**, n 1.
3 As demonstrated n the decision mentioned in para **26.18** above – see n 6.

26.25 Until any question as to admissibility of the notice of opposition has been determined, the opposition proceedings are not regarded as having 'commenced'. Commencement is dealt with under r 19. Under para (1), if the Office does not reject the opposition in accordance with r 18, it is required to communicate the opposition to the applicant and invite him to file his observations within such period as it may specify.[1] The Office must draw the applicant's attention to the fact that the opposition proceedings shall be deemed to commence two months after receipt of the communication, unless the applicant informs the Office within that period[2] that he withdraws his application or restricts it to goods or services against which the opposition is not directed. This provision has relevance to liability to pay costs, under art 81 of the Regulation, which is considered in Chapter 29. If the applicant withdraws or restricts his application, so that the opposition comes to an end, para (3) requires the Office to inform the opponent and to refund the opposition fee.

1 The period is extendable in accordance with r 71. See paras **28.2–28.3** below.
2 Paragraph (2) provides that the Office may, in accordance with r 71, extend this period where the request is presented jointly be the applicant and the opposing party. Since this period is not one to be specified by the Office, the relevant paragraph of r 71 is (2). See generally paras **28.2** et seq below.

26.26 Unless the applicant takes advantage of r 19(1) the opposition commences and the Office proceeds with the examination as provided by art 43. The procedures are further detailed in r 20. Under art 43(1) the Office, in such examination, is required to invite the parties, 'as often as necessary', to file observations, within a period set them by the Office, on communications from the other parties or issued by itself. This is a general procedural provision to ensure, among other things, that the parties are given the opportunity to respond to any observations by another party.

26.27 Article 43(2) and 43(3) relate respectively to oppositions based upon earlier Community trade marks and earlier national trade marks as referred to in art 8(2)(a). If the applicant for registration of the CTM so requests, the proprietor[1] of such an earlier mark must furnish proof that the trade mark has been put to genuine use, in the Community or in the Member State in which the national trade mark is protected, as the case may be, during the period of five years preceding publication of the CTM application, in connection with the goods or services for which the trade mark is registered and which are cited as justification for the opposition, or that there are proper reasons for non-use. However this only applies if the earlier trade mark has been registered for not less than five years. If such proof is not furnished, then the opposition must be rejected.

1 The provision does not appear to apply to a licensee, permitted to oppose under art 42(1). Cf the corresponding provision for an application for declaration of invalidity, art 56(2), considered at para **27.49** below.

26.28 As to the time for furnishing the proof, under r 22(1) the Office is to invite the opponent to provide the proof within such period as it shall specify, and to reject the opposition if the proof is not provided within that period.[1] Rule 22(2), (3) and (4) are concerned with the nature of the 'proof' required. Paragraph (2) provides that the 'indications and evidence for the furnishing of proof of use shall consist of indications concerning the place, time, extent and nature of use of the opposing trade mark for the goods and services in respect of which it is registered and on which the opposition is based, and evidence in support of these indications in accordance with paragraph 3'. Paragraph (3) seems to be intended to set some limit on the amount of evidence required. It provides that the evidence 'shall, in principle, be confined to the submission of supporting documents and items such as packages, labels, price lists, catalogues, invoices, photographs, newspaper advertisements, and statements in writing as referred to in art 76(1)(f) of the Regulation'. Such statements are 'statements in writing sworn or affirmed or having a similar effect under the law of the State in which the statement is drawn up'. For parties based in the UK the statement would be either an affidavit or a statutory declaration. The amount of evidence actually required will depend upon the circumstances of each case. Sometimes comparatively little evidence may be needed, because it may be very clear, even perhaps from a single transaction, that there has been genuine use. However a decision of the Opposition Division[2] demonstrates the importance of filing sufficient evidence of use. In that case, the opponent, who relied upon an earlier Spanish registration, only filed a photocopy of packaging and instructions for use of two products, without giving any indication of the period of use of the trade mark, or any information as to the extent or the nature of the use of the mark. It was held that the evidence was insufficient to establish genuine use during the relevant five-year period, and the opposition was accordingly rejected. Normally therefore, it will be advisable to set out, in the statement, details of sales and advertising under the mark during the relevant period, and to exhibit examples of the supporting documents and materials referred to in r 22(3). Under r 22(4), if the evidence supplied is not in the language of the opposition proceedings, the Office may require the opponent to submit a translation into that language, within a period specified by the Office. Whether this is required will again depend upon the circumstances; if it is quite obvious from the material provided that there has been genuine use in the relevant period in the territory concerned, there may be no useful purpose in requiring a translation.

1 This period is extendable under r 71(1). See ch 28, paras **28.2–28.3** below.
2 In Opposition No B 1810 (*Dermanorm Trade Mark*), Official Journal of OHIM 12/98, p 1393.

26.29 If the earlier trade mark has been used in relation to part only of the goods or services for which it is registered, then for the purposes of the opposition the trade mark is deemed only to be registered for the goods or services for which it has been used. It is to be noted that the requirement to furnish proof of genuine use, or of proper reasons for non-use, only applies to the goods and services on which the opponent relies as justification for the opposition. This is confirmed by r 22(2). Therefore a party contemplating opposition on the basis of an earlier trade mark which is not in use for all the goods and services for which it is registered will be well advised to consider carefully whether he needs to rely upon all such goods and services and, if he does not, to make it clear, in the notice of opposition, which are the goods and services that are the basis for the opposition. It seems that art 43(2) and (3) should be read subject to art 15(2) and (3), so that use of the mark in a form differing in elements which do not alter the distinctive character of the mark as registered, and use for export, as well as use with the proprietor's consent, are sufficient for maintaining the opposition.[1]

1 This appears to be confirmed by the decision referred to in para **26.28**, n 2 above.

26.30 The Office then proceeds with the examination of the opposition, in accordance with r 20. Before referring to r 20, art 43(4) of the Regulation should be mentioned. This provides that the Office may, if it thinks fit, invite the parties to make a friendly settlement. There is no express restriction as to the stage at which the Office may do this. There does not seem to be any point in inviting the parties to settle, as a matter of course, in every case. In order to use this power effectively, the Office must have some idea of the case and be in a position to form some kind of a preliminary view on the merits. Possibly, when considering the question of admissibility, the Office might take a view that, while properly founded, the opposition could be met by a simple amendment to the specification of goods or services. Or the evidence of use provided by the opponent in response to a request under art 43(2) or 43(3) may expose a weakness in the whole or part of the opponent's case; alternatively the evidence might reinforce the opponent's case. In such circumstances it might be appropriate for the Office to invite the parties to consider settlement. But it is considered that, except in very clear cases, the Office should be somewhat cautious in attempting to force the parties to settle on the basis of its own preliminary assessment of the prospects of success of the opposition.

26.31 Rule 20(1) confirms that, if the applicant does not withdraw or restrict the application under r 19, he must file his observations within the period specified by the Office under r 19(1). Rule 20(2) continues by making provision for the case in which the notice of opposition does not contain particulars of the 'facts, evidence and arguments' as referred to in r 16(1) and 16(2), requiring the Office to call on the opponent to submit such particulars within a period specified by the Office. This period again is extendable under r 71, but at this stage the question may arise of extending the time for the applicant to file his observations. At this stage also it is necessary to consider whether the applicant should file any evidence. It would seem sensible in most cases that the applicant should not have to file such observations until he knows what the opponent's case is. It may well be that the Office will extend the period under para (1) until an appropriate time after the opponent has complied with a direction under para (2). If the applicant files no observations, then para (3) empowers the Office to give a ruling on the opposition, ie to decide it, on the evidence before it. Despite the use of the word 'may', the Office would then normally decide the opposition. If the applicant files observations, these are to be communicated to the opponent, under para (4), who must then be called upon by the Office, if it considers it necessary to do so, to reply within a period specified by the Office. It is expected that, apart from cases in which the applicant's observations clearly do not effectively refute the opposition, the opponent will be invited to reply. Rule 20(4) deals with the case in which the applicant restricts his specification of goods and services, under art 44(1) of the Regulation. In such event the Office is required to inform the opponent and call upon him, within such period as it may specify, to submit observations stating whether he maintains the opposition, and if so, against which of the remaining goods and services. Finally, para (6) allows the Office to suspend an opposition if it is based on pending applications for registration, under art 8(2)(b) of the Regulation, until a final decision is taken in that proceeding. The Office may also suspend an opposition where other circumstances are such that this is appropriate. When the examination is complete, if it reveals that the trade mark may not be registered in respect of some or all of the goods or services covered by the application, then the application will be rejected in accordance with art 43(5) of the Regulation. Otherwise the opposition will be rejected. Article 43(6) provides for the decision to be published when it becomes final.

26.32 A number of opposition cases have now been decided by the Office, and some of the decisions are published in the Official Journal. None of these appear to lay down any matters of principle and no comment on any of them is required here. Each case will, as usual, be determined on their own facts. In due course, some guidance will be received from the Boards of Appeal and, on appeal, from the CFI. In the meantime, decisions of the ECJ have been handed down, interpreting provisions of the Directive to which provisions of the CTM Regulation correspond. These decisions, which are plainly relevant, for instance, to oppositions on relative grounds and are referred to in some of the decisions of the Opposition Division, are discussed in Chapter 6 of this book.

Multiple oppositions

26.33 Rule 21 lays down rules for dealing with multiple oppositions. Where a number of oppositions have been entered in respect of the same CTM application, para (1) empowers the Office to deal with them in one set of proceedings, and subsequently to decide no longer to deal with them together. This provision recognises the fact that, while it may often be convenient to deal with oppositions to the same application together, there may be reasons why this is not possible or practicable. For example, if there is an interruption of one opposition, as provided for under r 73, or one opponent enters into settlement negotiations with the applicant, it might not be right to delay the other oppositions. Paragraph (2) provides another example. If a preliminary examination of one or more oppositions reveals that the CTM applied for is 'possibly not eligible for registration in respect of some or all of the goods or services for which registration is sought', the Office may suspend the other opposition proceedings. The Office is required to inform the remaining opponents of any decisions taken during the proceedings which are continued. This provision is rather vague, and it remains to be seen how it is applied in practice. It may be appropriate for the Office to invoke it when one (or more) of several oppositions seem very likely to succeed, but it is submitted that this should only happen in fairly clear cases, when disposal of the one or more oppositions seems likely to have the effect of making it unnecessary to continue with the other oppositions. But it may be that the delay in disposing of the remaining oppositions will be prejudicial to the interests of the opposing parties involved. This is more likely where an outstanding opposition attacks the application in respect of a broader range of goods and services than those in which the continuing oppositions are thought to be likely to succeed. Paragraph (3) continues by providing that once a decision rejecting the application has become final, the oppositions on which a decision was deferred shall be deemed to have been disposed of and the opposing parties in those proceedings are to be informed accordingly. In such event the disposition is considered to be a case which has not proceeded to judgment within the meaning of art 81(4) of the Regulation, which means that the costs are at the discretion of the Opposition Division. Under r 21(4) the Office must refund half of the opposition fee to any opposing party, whose opposition is deemed to have been disposed of under paras (1)–(3). However if the opposition was justified it is suggested that it might be appropriate for the Office to order the unsuccessful applicant to pay the other half of the opposing party's costs.

Conversion to national procedure

26.34 If the application is refused as a result of observations by third parties, or following an opposition, the applicant may, if he does not wish to appeal, use the procedure available under art 108 to convert the application to national applications.[1]

1 See ch 24, paras **24.24–24.25**.

Registration

26.35 Article 45 provides for the trade mark to become registered where the application meets the requirements of the Regulation and where there is no notice of opposition within the three-month period specified by art 42(1) or where any opposition has been rejected by a definitive decision. It is also a requirement that the registration fee shall have been paid within the period prescribed; if it is not so paid, then the application is deemed to be withdrawn. Further provision concerning the registration procedure is contained in rr 23 and 24. Under rule 23 the fee consists of a basic fee and a class fee, for each class exceeding three in respect of which the mark is to be registered. Paragraph (2) prescribes a period of two months, within which the applicant must pay these fees once the trade mark becomes eligible for registration in accordance with art 45. Although this period is not extendable under r 71(1), para (3) permits the registration fee to be validly paid within two months of notification of a communication pointing out the failure to observe the time limit, provided that the additional fee specified in the Fees Regulations is paid. Under para (4), on receipt of the registration fee (which of course includes any such additional fee due), the trade mark and the particulars referred to in art 84(2) are recorded in the Register of Community trade marks, and under para (5) the registration is published in the CTM Bulletin. In the event that the trade mark is not registered, para (6) requires the registration fee to be refunded. Rule 24 provides for the issue of a certificate of registration, containing the particulars which are required to be entered in the register, and also enables the proprietor to request certified or uncertified copies to be supplied on payment of a fee.

Chapter 27

Maintenance of the Community trade mark and cessation or loss of rights

Duration, renewal and alteration of CTMs

Duration and renewal of registration

27.1   Article 46 of the Regulation provides that CTMs (CTMs) shall be registered for a period of ten years from the date of filing of the application. Renewal, in accordance with art 47, is for further periods of ten years. This is in line with the UK and other Member States. Under art 47, renewal may be at the request of the proprietor or any person expressly authorised by him. The fee must of course be paid. In order to assist the proprietor of a CTM, art 47(2) requires the Office to inform him, and anyone else having a registered right in respect of the CTM,[1] of the expiry of the registration, 'in good time'[2] before the expiry. However failure to give this information does not involve the responsibility of the Office. Presumably this slightly indirect statement means that the Office is not to be legally liable for such failure. Rule 29 provides expressly that failure to give notification does not affect the expiry. Under art 47(3) the request for renewal is to be submitted within six months 'ending on the last day of the month in which protection ends', and the fees must be paid within this period. Failing this, the request may be submitted and the fees paid within a further six months period, but in this event an additional fee must also be paid within the further period. Paragraph (4) provides that if the request is submitted or the fees are paid only in respect of some of the goods or services covered by the registration, renewal is only for those goods or services. The effect of art 47(3) seems to be that the renewal may be effected up to just under a month after the expiry date, depending upon the day of the month on which this falls, without attracting the additional fee. Thus, if the term of protection of a registration expires on the 1 April, the six-month period runs to the 30 April and the second six-month period expires on 30 October. In any event, under art 47(5) the renewal is effective from the day following the expiry date of the existing registration.

1 Under r 29 this includes a licensee, registered under art 22(5). It appears that owners of rights in rem, registered under art 19(2), and owners of rights arising from levy of execution or bankruptcy, registered under art 20(3) or art 21(2), must also be notified.
2 Under r 29 this is a minimum of six months before the expiry date.

27.2   Rule 30 lays down detailed requirements for the contents of an application of a renewal of a CTM registration. These include a requirement to indicate if renewal is requested for all the goods and services covered by the registration, and if not, to specify the goods and services for which renewal is required. Provision is also made, by r 30(2), for the payment of a basic fee, covering up to three classes, and for payment of class fees for further classes; also an additional fee in cases of delayed renewal. The amounts of these fees are set out in the Fees Regulation. Under r 30(3), where an application for renewal is filed within the time periods provided for in art 47(3), but other conditions of art 47 or the Rules are not satisfied, the Office is required to inform the applicant of the deficiencies found; a copy of the notification is also to be sent to any person, who filed the application with the express authorisation of the proprietor. It must be emphasised that, particularly where an application for renewal is filed at a late stage, any such notification may in fact be received not long before the expiry of the second six months period, leaving little time for remedying any deficiencies. Where, because of some deficiency in a request for renewal made during the first six-month period, the applicant runs into the second six-month period, the additional fee must also be paid before the end of the latter period. It is thus very important to ensure that the request for renewal is correct at the outset. The effect of r 30(4) is that if all the fees have not been paid, and any deficiencies in the application for renewal have not been remedied, within the second six-month period provided for in art 47(3) at the latest, the office will determine that the registration of the CTM has expired. If the deficiency is only in respect of the amount of fees paid, such determination will not be made if it is made clear which class or classes of goods or services are to be covered; otherwise the office will take the classes into account in the order of classification. Once a determination as to expiry has become final, the office is required, by para (5), to cancel the mark from the register, and the cancellation takes effect from the day following that on which the existing registration expired. In the event of non-renewal, para (6) provides for any fees paid to be refunded.

Alteration of a CTM registration

27.3   As a general rule a CTM cannot be altered in the register, during the period of registration or on renewal. This is expressly provided by art 48(1). Nevertheless, under para (2), where a CTM includes the name and address of the proprietor, an alteration thereof is permitted if it does not substantially affect the identity of the trade mark as originally registered. At present there are no decisions on what might, or might not, substantially affect the identity of the mark. The matter must be one of impression. If the name and address are not such as to give the mark its distinctive character, as when they appear in small print in a corner of a label, the alteration is likely to be acceptable. If on the other hand the name or address is a central feature of the mark, then an alteration would probably be refused.

27.4   The procedure for altering a registration is laid down in r 25, which specifies the requirements for the contents of the application. Under para (5) one application can be made in respect of the same element in two or more registrations of the same proprietor, but a fee must be paid in respect of each registration. It would appear that the marks to be altered need not be identical; it is sufficient that both or all of them contain the same element which is to be altered. An application is deemed not to have been made until the fee has been paid. In the event that the fee is not paid, or is not paid in full, or if there is some other deficiency in the application, r 25(2) and (3) provide for the applicant to be informed. Under para (3) any deficiency must be remedied within a period to be specified by the office;[1] otherwise the application is to be rejected. The possibility of remedying a 'deficiency' under para (3) does not extend to a failure in respect of payment of the fee. Since under para (2) an application unaccompanied by the full fee is deemed not to have been filed, it only becomes a filed application, to which para (3) can apply, once the whole fee has been paid. If the office accepts an application for alteration of a registration, the altered mark must be published by the office in accordance with art 48(3), and third parties whose rights may be affected by the alteration may challenge the registration of the altered mark within three months following the publication. This period is non extendable under r 71(1). In the event of a challenge, then under r 25(4) the provisions on opposition in the Regulation and Rules[2] are to apply *mutatis mutandis*.

1 This is extendable under r 71(1), although there seems to be no reason why the office should be expected to be particularly generous in this kind of application.
2 Rules 15–22 – see ch 26, paras **26.16** et seq.

Other changes in the register

27.5 The Rules make further provision for changes in the register, which do not involve altering the mark itself. Under r 26(1), as would be expected, it is permissible to change the name or address of the proprietor of a CTM in the register, and under para (6) the same applies to the name or address of the registered representative of the proprietor. Under para (7) these provisions also apply to applications for registration of a CTM. The contents of an application for such a change are set out in r 26(2), and no fee is required. Under para (4) a single application may cover any number of registrations of the same proprietor. Under para (5), if the requirements governing the recording of a change are not fulfilled, the office must communicate the deficiency to the applicant, and must reject the application if the deficiency is not remedied within a period to be specified by the Office.[1]

1 This period is extendable under r 71(1).

27.6 Rule 27 makes provision for the correction of mistakes and errors in the register or the publication of the registration. In accordance with para (1) these must be attributable to the office. In such cases the office is required to correct the error or mistake of its own motion or at the request of the proprietor. Under para (2), r 26 applies, *mutatis mutandis*, where the request is made by the proprietor, and no fee is payable. Paragraph (3) requires publication of the corrections made.

Claiming seniority after registration of the CTM

27.7 Another procedure, which involves an alteration of the register, arises under art 35, which allows a claim for a CTM under art 34, of seniority of an earlier national trade mark, to be claimed after registration. This procedure is laid down in r 28, para (1) of which specifies what the application must contain; the requirements are similar to those of r 8, which applies to claims of seniority made before registration.[1] Where any of the information is available to the office from other sources, the President of the Office may, under para (4), determine that details of the relevant registration of an earlier mark may be less than is required under para (1)(f), which otherwise requires provision of a certified copy of the registration of the trade mark from which seniority is claimed. Where the requirements for claiming seniority are not fulfilled, para (2) provides for the Office to communicate the deficiency to the applicant; if the deficiency is not remedied within a period specified by the Office,[2] the Office must reject the application. As with seniority claims made before registration, para (3) requires the office to inform the Benelux office or the national Office of other Member States concerned, of the effective claiming of seniority.

1 See ch 25, paras **25.13** et seq.
2 Again, this is extendable under r 71(1).

Surrender, revocation and invalidity

Surrender

27.8   Article 49 of the Regulation provides for surrender of a CTM. The procedure is laid down in r 36. Under art 49(1) surrender may be effected in respect of some or all of the goods or services for which the CTM is registered. According to art 49(2) the surrender must be declared to the Office in writing by the proprietor, and it does not have effect until it has been entered in the register. Article 49(3) gives protection to parties having other rights entered in register in respect of the CTM, which may include rights of licensees, rights in rem, and rights arising from levy of execution or bankruptcy.[1] Surrender may be entered only with the agreement of the proprietor of such a right. Specifically in the case of a CTM in respect of which a licence has been registered, the proprietor will not be allowed to surrender his registration unless he proves that he has informed the licensee of his intention to surrender. In view of the general provision requiring *agreement*, presumably merely notifying a licensee is not enough, unless his agreement can be inferred from his lack of response after being informed of the proprietor's intention to surrender. This view is consistent with the provisions of r 36.

1 Under arts 19–22 of the Regulation. See ch 24, paras **24.55–24.58**.

27.9   Rule 36(1) sets out details of the required contents of a declaration of surrender. Where the rights of another party, which are entered in the register, are involved, r 36(2) provides that it shall be sufficient proof of his agreement to the surrender that a declaration of consent to the surrender is signed by the proprietor of the right or his representative. In the case of a registered licence, surrender is to be registered three months after the date on which the proprietor of the CTM satisfies the Office that he has informed the licensee of his intention to surrender it. This means three months after the Office is satisfied, not three months after the licensee was informed. The time period is effectively reduced if the proprietor proves at an earlier date that the licensee has given his consent. In that event the surrender is to be registered forthwith. Paragraph (3) provides that if the requirements governing surrender are not fulfilled, the Office shall communicate the deficiencies to the declarant (ie the proprietor), and that if the deficiencies are not remedied within a period to be specified by the Office,[1] the Office shall reject the entry of the surrender in the register.

1 Which is extendable under r 71(1).

Revocation and invalidity

27.10   Articles 50–56 are concerned with applications to revoke or to invalidate a CTM registration. As under the Directive and the TMA 1994, the difference between revocation and invalidity is that the former is concerned primarily with the effect of events occurring after the registration of the mark, while the latter relates to defects in the registration itself.

Revocation

27.11 Article 50 provides four possible grounds for revocation of a CTM The first three of these correspond generally to the provisions for revocation which are found in the Directive and in s 46(1) of the TMA 1994. These grounds are non-use, the mark becoming generic, and the mark becoming misleading. A fourth ground is that the proprietor of the mark no longer satisfies the conditions laid down by art 5 of the Regulation, which lays down the requirements for a person to be the proprietor of a CTM.[1] Revocation may be ordered on application to the Office or on the basis of a counterclaim in infringement proceedings.[2] Article 50.2 provides that where the grounds for revocation exist in respect of only some of the goods or services for which the CTM is registered, the rights of the proprietor shall be declared to be revoked in respect of those goods or services only.

1 See ch 24, paras **24.5–24.7** above.
2 See ch 31 below.

27.12 The first three grounds do not need much further comment, as the main principles have been covered in the discussion of the corresponding provisions of the TMA 1994.[1]

1 See ch 7 above.

Non-use

27.13 Article 50.(1)(a) of the Regulation provides for the sanctions referred to in art 15.[1] The main difference, between art 50.1(a) and the provisions in s 46(1) of the TMA 1994 is that the former has a single provision, applying in cases where there has been non-use of the mark for a continuous period of five years, whereas the latter makes separate provision for non-use for five years following registration, and non-use for a five-year period at a later time in the life of the registration. Of course another difference is that art 50(1)(a) is concerned with non-use in the whole Community, whereas s 46(1) is, naturally, only concerned with non-use in the UK. The basic requirement of art 50(1)(a) is a lack of genuine use in the Community for a period of five years. As with s 46(1) of the TMA 1994, revocation is avoidable if the proprietor can show that there are 'proper reasons' for the non-use. Moreover, as art 50(1)(a) makes clear, it is open to the proprietor to start or resume genuine use of his mark, and thereby to defeat an application for revocation, at any time before revocation is sought. However in a case in which use is commenced or resumed within a period of three months preceding the application or counterclaim, which period commenced not earlier than the end of the period of five years' non-use, the use is to be disregarded where preparations for its commencement or resumption occurred only after the proprietor became aware that the application or counterclaim might be filed. Although the provisions are not identically worded to the provisions of the 1994 Act, the effect is essentially the same. Whether the proprietor is 'aware' that the registration might be attacked is a question of fact, to be determined on the evidence. It will normally be sufficient, for this purpose, that the third party applying or counterclaiming for revocation had approached the proprietor with requests as to the use of the mark, or even seeking consent to registration of a mark which might conflict with the CTM.

1 See ch 24, paras **24.33–24.38** above, in particular as to the extent of use required for a CTM.

27.14   For a discussion of the meaning of 'genuine use' reference should be made to Chapter 24. Whether use is 'genuine' will depend upon all the circumstances, but what is required, it is submitted, is real use with a proper commercial purpose in mind. If that is so, then even a very small amount of use may well be genuine, and this should be so for a CTM under the Regulation, just as much as for a national trade mark under the law of one Member State. The other question, which may arise under art 50.1(a), is the meaning of the words 'in the Community'. This has already been discussed above.[1]

1 See para **24.38** et seq.

27.15   Another issue which may arise, is whether there is any discretion not to revoke a CTM where there has been no genuine use of the mark for the relevant five-year period, and there are no proper reasons. On this point the Regulation seems clear. Article 15 uses the words '*shall* be subject to the sanctions provided'; if that were not enough, art 50(1) provides that the rights of the proprietor of the CTM '*shall* be declared to be revoked ...' in the circumstances set out. Accordingly, it is submitted, there can be no residual discretion.

The mark has become generic

27.16   Under art 50(1)(b) a CTM is to be revoked 'if, in consequence of acts or inactivity of the proprietor, the trade mark has become the common name in the trade for a product or service in respect of which it is registered'. These words are identical to the words of art 12(2)(a) of the Directive, and thus their effect is for practical purposes the same as s 46(1)(c) of the TMA 1994. Reference may therefore be made to Chapter 7.[1] As with non-use, it seems clear from the words of art 50 itself that there is no discretion to refuse revocation if this ground is established.

1 Paragraphs **7.18–7.19**.

The mark has become misleading

27.17   The third ground for revocation, provided by art 50.(1)(c) applies 'if, in consequence of the use made of it by the proprietor of the trade mark or with his consent in respect of the goods or services for which is registered, the trade mark is liable to mislead the public, particularly as to the nature, quality or geographical origin of those goods or services'. Again, there is an identical provision in the Directive,[1] on which s 46(1)(d) of the TMA 1994 is based, and reference may be made to Chapter 11,[2] for a discussion of the points involved.

1 Article 12.2(b).
2 Paragraphs **7.20–7.22**.

The proprietor is no longer qualified

27.18 Article 50.1(d) provides for revocation 'if the proprietor no longer satisfies the conditions laid down by art 5'. The requirements of art 5 have already been discussed, in chapter 24,[1] to which reference may be made. Cases for revocation on this ground are unlikely to arise very often, in view of the very broad provisions of art 5 itself. They would normally only arise following an assignment of the CTM, although exceptionally this ground could apply where a country withdrew from the Paris Convention or the WTO, or changed its law in such a way that it no longer gave sufficient protection to trade marks of nationals of Members States.[2]

1 Paragraphs **24.5–24.7**.
2 See art 5.1(d).

Invalidity

27.19 As with national trade mark registrations, under the Directive and the TMA 1994, a CTM may be declared invalid on either absolute or relative grounds. Applications for declarations of invalidity may be rather more frequent with CTM's because of the restriction of the office's powers of refusal and of the grounds available for opposition. As already explained, a third party cannot oppose a CTM application on absolute grounds,[1] and the office has no power to refuse an application on relative grounds.

1 He can only submit written observations under art 41.

Absolute grounds for invalidity

27.20 In accordance with art 51, a CTM is to be declared invalid on application to the Office or on the basis of a counterclaim in infringement proceedings, where it was registered in breach of the provisions of art 5 or s 7, or the applicant was acting in bad faith when he filed the application for the trade mark. The provision of art 5, which sets out the qualifications for a person to be the proprietor of a CTM, and of art 7, which contains the main 'absolute grounds' for refusal, have already been discussed,[1] and need no further consideration here. It should however be noted that, as with the Directive[2] and s 47(1) of the TMA 1994, it is provided by art 51.2 of the Regulation that, where a CTM has been registered in breach of the provisions of art 7.1(b),(c) or (d), it may nevertheless not be declared invalid 'if, in consequence of the use which has been made of it, it has after registration acquired a distinctive character in relation to the goods or services for which it is registered'. This aspect is discussed in Chapter 5.

1 In ch 24, paras **24.5–24.7**, and **24.9–24.16**.
2 Article 3.3.

27.21 As to the ground that the application for a CTM was made in bad faith, it should be noted that the Regulation does not contain a specific provision for refusal of registration on the ground that the application was made in bad faith, although such a provision is included in the Directive as one of four optional absolute grounds for refusal.[1] In the absence of any decisions from the Office, or of guidance from the CFI of the ECJ,[2] or from the ECJ on a reference for interpretation of art 3(2)(d) of the Directive, the meaning of the term 'bad faith' in article 51.1(b) of the Regulation should be regarded as not finally settled. It may be of assistance to compare art 51.1(b) with s 3(6) of the TMA 1994, derived from art 3(2)(d) of the Directive, which includes bad faith, in the making of an application for registration, as an absolute ground for refusal. The fact that the ground comes under 'absolute grounds' for refusal could suggest that the term 'bad faith' might not extend to at least some grounds which are in the nature of relative grounds, in that the applicant has acted in bad faith because of rights of a third party. Mere knowledge of earlier rights of another trader should not of itself necessarily provide a basis for an allegation of bad faith, if there was no actual dishonesty involved. There have been a number of decisions of the UK registry and English courts on the issue of bad faith for the purposes of s 3(6), and the matter is discussed in Chapter 6,[3] to which reference may be made. The position under art 51.1(b) is not necessarily the same as the position adopted in the UK, although in principle it ought to be, since the term 'bad faith' must have been intended to have the same meaning in the Directive and the Regulation.

1 Article 3(2)(d).
2 On appeals under art 63.
3 Chapter 5, paras **5.118–5.121**.

27.22 Article 51(3) provides that where the ground for invalidity exists only in respect of some of the goods or services for which the CTM is registered, the trade mark shall be declared invalid as regards those goods or services only.

Relative grounds for invalidity

27.23 The relative grounds for refusal of a CTM, which may not be raised by the office but can be invoked in opposition proceedings, and are available under art 52 of the Regulation, have been discussed in chapter 24[1] above. Under art 52(1) a CTM can be declared invalid on any of those grounds. In addition, art 52(2) introduces further relative grounds, on which a CTM may be declared invalid, based on a right to a name, a right of personal portrayal, a copyright and an industrial property right. These correspond to the provision of art 4(4)(c) of the Directive, on which s 5(4)(b) of the TMA 1994 is based.[2] Under art 52(3), none of the relative grounds for invalidity may be a basis for a declaration of invalidity where the proprietor of the earlier trade mark or right has, prior to the submission of the application for declaration, or the counterclaim, consented expressly to the registration of the CTM.

1 Chapter 24, paras **24.17–24.22**.
2 See ch 6 for discussion of all the relative grounds available under the Directive and included in the provisions of the TMA 1994.

27.24 Article 52(4) imposes an important restriction on subsequent applications for declarations of invalidity on relative grounds. Where the proprietor of one of the rights mentioned in art 52(1) or 52(2) has previously applied for a declaration that a CTM is invalid or made a counterclaim in infringement proceedings, he may not submit a new application for a declaration of invalidity or lodge a counterclaim on the basis of another of such rights, which he could have invoked in support of the first application or counterclaim. Presumably the first application must have been determined, for example by a decision or by withdrawal. This provision obviously does not apply where, under art 96 of the Regulation, a counterclaim has been made but is stayed while the defendant submits an application to the office at the request of the CTM court seized of the case. The provision, the effect of which is much the same as rules of estoppel or res judicata developed by the English courts,[1] only extends to invalidity on relative grounds. Thus, if the first or the subsequent application or counterclaim was based only on absolute grounds, art 52.4 would not apply. The restriction does not apply where a previous application or counterclaim was for revocation, as opposed to a declaration of invalidity. Curiously, the restriction is not expressly applied to a licensee or authorised user of any earlier trade marks or other rights, who is entitled to apply for a declaration of invalidity.[2] Whether the Office or the ECJ will hold that art 52(4) applies, by implication, to such persons, remains to be seen.

1 See eg *Henderson v Henderson* [1843] 3 Hare 100, and other cases cited in *Hodgkinson ana Corby Ltd v Wards Mobility Services Ltd* [1994] 1 WLR 1564 (Neuberger J), subsequently reversed by the Court of Appeal.
2 See para **27.37** below.

27.25 Article 52.5 applies art 51.3. Thus the rule, that where a ground for invalidity exists in respect of some only of the goods or services for which the CTM is registered, the trade mark will only be declared invalid, on relative grounds, for those goods or services. The position is essentially the same as under s 47(5) of the TMA 1994.

Acquiescence

27.26 Article 53, which is similar to art 9 of the Directive,[1] places restrictions on the making of applications for declarations of invalidity where there has been acquiescence by the owner of prior rights, in the use of a later CTM. There are also similar restrictions on the prevention of use of the later CTM. Article 53.1 covers the case where the earlier right is also a CTM, and applies where the proprietor of the earlier CTM has acquiesced in the use of the later CTM in the Community, for a period of five successive years, while being aware of such use. The requirement of awareness is particularly important because the use of the CTM may be only in one Member State, and may not readily come to the attention of the proprietor of the earlier CTM, if he is based in another Member State, possibly far away. The provision does not apply where the later CTM was applied for in bad faith. The term 'bad faith' has been discussed at para **27.21** above, and probably has the same meaning in art 53 as in art 51.1(b). If a trader was to be regarded as having made an application in bad faith simply because he had been aware of the earlier right, the provisions of art 53 could prove ineffective in many cases where there had been long acquiescence. Finally it should be noted that, although art 53.1 prohibits an application 'for a declaration that the later trade mark is invalid', it may be that it does not preclude such an application on absolute grounds. These are based on public policy, and on the principle that there are some signs which no one trader ought to be able to monopolise, to the detriment of other traders. Moreover, art 53 is only directed against those who fail to exercise rights which provide relative grounds for refusal.

1 See also TMA 1994, s 48, discussed at ch 16, paras **16.57–16.58**

27.27 Article 53.2 contains a similar provision, directed to proprietors of earlier national trade marks or of rights in earlier rights in unregistered trade marks, as referred to in arts 8.2 and 8.4 respectively. Again the period for acquiescence is five successive years, and the proprietor must be aware of the use. The difference, as would be expected, is that what is relevant is the use of the later CTM in the Member State in which the earlier trade mark or sign is protected. Use in a different Member State is not relevant. Again, bad faith on the part of the proprietor of the later CTM, when he applied for registration, will defeat a plea of acquiescence under this provision.

27.28 Article 53(3) deals with the position of the owner of the later CTM in the situations covered by paras 1 and 2. It states clearly that such owners are not entitled to oppose the use of the earlier right, even though the owner of the earlier right may no longer invoke it against the later CTM. This provision corresponds to art 9(3) of the Directive and s 48(2) of the TMA 1994, which is derived from it.

Consequences of revocation and invalidity

27.29 Where a claim for revocation of a CTM is successful, art 54(1) provides that the CTM shall be deemed not to have had the effects provided for in the Regulation, to the extent that the rights of the proprietor are revoked, as from the date of the application for revocation or of the counterclaim. This is the general rule, but art 54(1) further provides that an earlier date, on which one of the grounds for revocation occurred, may be fixed in the decision at the request of one of the parties. There is no further guidance as to the application of this provision. In view of the terms of art 50, which sets out the grounds for revocation, the idea of one of those grounds 'occurring' at an earlier date seems a little strange, except in a case falling within art 50.1(d) (the proprietor no longer satisfying the conditions of art 5). Section 46(6) of the TMA 1994 uses the word 'existed', which is clearer.[1] Possibly an earlier date, than either the application or the counterclaim, might be found in a non-use case, when a five-year period of non-use first expired. However this could not, it is submitted, override the provisions in art 50.1(a) as to the effect of resumption of use between the expiry of the five-year period and the application or the counterclaim. If that is so, then an earlier date for the effect of the revocation can only be set where there is no intervening resumption of use, unless the resumption is within the three months before the application or counterclaim, at a time when the proprietor was aware that the application or counterclaim might be filed. But in the cases covered by art 50.1(b) and (c), where the trade mark has become the common name of a product or service for which it is registered, or has become misleading, it would usually be very difficult to identify a date at which the ground for revocation 'occurred'. It is likely that in most of such cases the effective date will be that of the application or counterclaim, although perhaps, as part of a settlement of a dispute, the parties could agree upon an earlier date and request the office to fix it accordingly.

1 See ch 7, paras **7.2** and **7.22** above.

27.30 The approach to invalidity is different. Under art 54.2, to the extent that a CTM is declared invalid, it is invalid *ab initio*. It is deemed not to have had the effects specified in the Regulation, as from the outset. This is the same as the position under s 47(6) of the TMA 1994.

27.31   Article 54(3) contains provisions intended to save the effects of decisions as to infringement, and contracts concluded, prior to a decision revoking a CTM or declaring it invalid. In general, the retroactive effect of revocation or invalidity will not affect any decision on infringement which has acquired the authority of a final decision and been enforced prior to the revocation or invalidity decision, or any contract concluded prior to such decision, in so far as it has been performed prior to the decision. In the case of a contract, however, repayment may be claimed on grounds of equity, 'to an extent justified by the circumstances, of sums paid under the relevant contract'. These provisions are expressly subject 'to the national provisions relating either to claims for compensation for damage caused by negligence or lack of good faith on the part of the proprietor of the trade mark, or to unjust enrichment'.

27.32   Whether a decision on infringement has 'acquired the authority of a final decision' will depend upon the position under the rules applying in the Member State of the CTM court giving the decision. If it has not both acquired such authority and also been enforced, the clear inference of the provision is that the order for revocation or the declaration is to override any decision on infringement, in favour of the proprietor of a CTM. The word 'enforced' needs some consideration. If an English court finds infringement, an injunction against further infringement would normally be granted. There would also be ancillary remedies, such as delivery up or destruction on oath and an order for payment of costs, and an inquiry as to damages or an account of profits will often be ordered. However, in many infringement actions in England, very little actually happens after the decision on infringement, unless there is an appeal. Frequently the defendant simply obeys the injunction and the other orders, and pays the costs; damages or profits may be agreed or not sought. It is not clear what constitutes 'enforcement'. Perhaps the drawing up and the service of the court order is enough, subject to any outstanding appeal. In a case in which a decision has acquired the authority of a final decision and has been enforced, it will be for the defendant to invoke the provisions of the applicable national laws referred to in art 54.3. In an English court, it is possible to have a judgment set aside on the ground that it was obtained by fraud. However it is doubtful whether a judgment in England could be impugned where there was only negligence, or 'unjust enrichment'.

27.33   As regards contracts concluded before the revocation or invalidity decision, art 54(3)(b) is clearly capable of applying to contracts involving non-parties to the revocation or invalidity proceedings. Arguments could arise, for example, as to royalties already paid to the proprietor under a licence of the CTM. The matter would probably depend primarily on the terms of the licence. In the absence of any special provisions, in most cases it is considered unlikely that an English court would order repayment of any royalties paid before the CTM was revoked or declared invalid.

27.34   One matter which may not be absolutely clear is whether, in the case of a decision on infringement, 'the national provisions' referred to in art 54(3) are the provisions of the laws of the Member State of the Community trade mark court giving the decision. A claim to compensation, on grounds of negligence, lack of good faith, or unjust enrichment, could arise under some other national law, not necessarily only of another EU Member State. Since a contract, as referred to in art 54(3)(b), can be a contract subject to the law of any country, it is thought that the term 'national provisions' should not be given a restricted meaning for the purposes of art 54(3)(a).

Proceedings in the office in relation to revocation or invalidity.

27.35 Articles 55 and 56 of the Regulation deal with applications in the office for revocation, or for a declaration of invalidity, in respect of a CTM. Further procedural provisions are to be found in rr 37–41. In accordance with arts 51 and 52, applications may also be made by counterclaim in infringement proceedings; such proceedings are governed by the provisions of Title X of the Regulation, which are considered in Chapter 31 below.

27.36 Article 55 makes provision as to who may apply to the Office for revocation of the rights of the proprietor of a CTM, or for a declaration that the trade mark is invalid. In cases of revocation, and invalidity on absolute grounds, an application may be made by any natural or legal person, and also by any group or body set up for the purpose of representing the interests of manufacturers, producers, suppliers of services, traders or consumers, which under the terms of the law governing it has the capacity in its own name to sue and be sued. Thus many trade associations will be entitled to make an application; also included may be trading standards authorities and bodies such as the Consumers Association and the Royal Warrant Holders Association.

27.37 For declarations of invalidity on relative grounds, under art 52, the right to apply is more restricted. Where art 52(1) applies, that is in the case of grounds which are also possible grounds for opposition, only the persons who would have been entitled to oppose the original application, referred to in art 42(1), may make the application. They are: owners of earlier trade marks and other rights which provide the basis for opposition under art 8.1–5; where earlier trade marks (as defined in art 8(2)) provide the basis of objection under art 8.1, licensees authorised by the proprietors of such trade marks; and, where the objection is founded on rights in unregistered marks acquired through use, persons authorised under the relevant national law to exercise the rights. For the purposes of applications under art 52(2), which provides further grounds of invalidity based on other earlier national rights, (ie a right to a name, a right of personal portrayal, a copyright, or an industrial property right) the applicant must be the owner of the rights relied upon, or a person entitled under the law of the Member State concerned to exercise the right in question.

27.38 Under art 55.2 the application must be filed in a written reasoned statement, and will not be deemed to have been filed until the fee has been paid. Article 55(3) provides that an application shall be inadmissible if an application relating to the same subject matter and cause of action, and involving the same parties, has been adjudicated on by a court in a Member State and has acquired the authority of a final decision. In cases of alleged invalidity on relative grounds, this provision overlaps with art 52.4, mentioned in para 27.24 above, although it only seems to apply where the previous grounds of objection were the same. However, unlike art 52(4), art 55(3) is clearly capable of application where the party concerned is a licensee or authorised user, as well as where he is the proprietor, of the earlier trade mark or other right in question. Article 55(3) also applies to cases of revocation and of invalidity on absolute grounds, for which there is no provision corresponding to art 52(4).

27.39 Rule 37 lays down requirements as to the contents of an application for revocation or for a declaration of invalidity under art 55. As regards the registration which is attacked, r 37(a) provides that the application must contain the registration number, the name and address of the proprietor, and a statement of the goods and services covered by the registration, in respect of which revocation or a declaration of invalidity is sought. Rule 37(b) relates to the grounds on which the application is based. In the case of an application for revocation or for a declaration of invalidity on absolute grounds, r 37(b)(i) requires a statement of the grounds. In cases of relative grounds for invalidity, the requirements are slightly different for those under art 52(1), which could have been grounds for opposition, and those under art 52(2), based on other rights not available for opposition. In the former case, r 37(b)(ii) requires particulars to be provided of the right on which the application is based, and 'if necessary particulars showing that the applicant is entitled to adduce the earlier right as grounds for invalidity'. In the latter case, what are required are particulars of the right on which the application is based, and 'particulars showing that the applicant is the proprietor of an earlier right as referred to in Article 52(2) ... or that he is entitled under the national law applicable to lay claim to that right'. The words 'entitled ... to lay claim to that right' are not the same as the words of art 55(1)(c), specifying who may make the application ('entitled ... to exercise the rights in question') but must presumably be taken to have the same meaning. In all cases of applications for revocation or declarations of invalidity, r 37(b)(iv) requires the application to include 'an indication of the facts, evidence and arguments presented in support of those grounds'. Finally, under r 37(c) the applicant must give his name and address in accordance with r 1(1)(b) and, if he has appointed a representative, the name and business address of the representative, in accordance with r 1(1)(e).

27.40 The purpose of r 37(b)(i), (ii) and (iii) is to ensure that an applicant provides a sufficiently clear statement as to what the grounds for the application are, and as to the applicant's standing to make it. Rule 37(b)(iv) is rather uncertain as to what is actually required. Just what is to be regarded as 'an indication' of the matters referred to will no doubt be made clearer as the Office begins to deal with individual cases. It is necessary that the indication be sufficient to inform the Office and the proprietor of the CTM what the applicant's case is. The concept of an 'indication' of evidence is not easily understandable; perhaps it simply means that the evidence must accompany the application, since there is no other provision for the filing of actual evidence in support of the application. No sworn evidence seems to be required, which in itself is an unsatisfactory feature of the procedure, particularly because it may well be found, in many cases, that the facts, evidence, and arguments are all mixed up with each other.

27.41 Rule 38 lays down requirements as to the languages to be used in revocation or invalidity proceedings. Before considering r 38, reference should be made to some of the provisions of art 115 of the Regulation, which lays down the basic rules regarding languages in the office.[1] Article 115(3) requires an applicant for a CTM to indicate 'a second language which shall be a language of the Office the use of which he accepts as a possible language of proceedings for opposition, revocation or invalidity proceedings'. Article 115(5) requires an application for revocation or invalidity to be filed in one of the languages of the office. Article 115(6) makes further provision, in terms which foreshadow r 38(1). The first sub-para of art 115(6) is as follows:

> 'If the language chosen, in accordance with paragraph 5, for the ... application for revocation or invalidity is the language of the application for a trade mark or the

second language indicated when the application was filed, that language shall be the language of the proceedings.'

Article 115.6 continues:

'If the language chosen, in accordance with paragraph 5, for the ... application for revocation or invalidity is neither the language of the application for a trade mark nor the second language indicated when the application was filed, the opposing party or the party seeking revocation or invalidity shall be required to produce, at his own expense, a translation of his application either into the language of the application for a trade mark, provided that it is a language of the Office, or into the second language indicated when the application was filed. The translation shall be produced within the period prescribed in the implementing regulation. The language into which the application has been translated shall then become the language of the proceedings.'

27.42 The effect of these provisions is that an applicant for revocation or for a declaration of invalidity is not only in practice restricted to using one of the four languages of the Office, in accordance with art 115(5). The language of the proceedings must be a language which was indicated in the application to register the CTM in the first place. The applicant for revocation or a declaration of invalidity may thus have a choice of two languages, but if the CTM application was in a language which was not a language of the office, the language of the proceedings will be the second language indicated in accordance with art 115.3. Although the applicant for revocation, or a declaration of invalidity, may use a language of the Office which is not one of the languages indicated by the CTM applicant, he will have to provide a translation of his application into one of those languages. The only exception is provided by art 115(7), which allows the parties to agree that a different language, being an official language of the Community, is to be the language of the proceedings.

27.43 Rule 38(1) follows aĪrt 115(6), providing that where the application for revocation or for a declaration of invalidity is not filed in the language of the application for the registration of the CTM, if that language is one of the languages of the Office, or in the second language indicated[1] when the application was filed, the applicant for revocation or for a declaration of invalidity must file a translation into one of those two languages within one month of filing the application.[2] Apart from providing the period for filing the translation, it is not clear, having regard to the provisions of art 115 of the Regulation referred to above, why r 38(1) was thought to be necessary. Although not expressly stated in r 38(1), it seems clear from art 115(6) of the Regulation that the requirement for translation into one of the languages of the office is not avoided, even if the application is filed in the language of the application for registration of the CTM, if that language is not one of the languages of the office. One matter not specified in r 38(1) is the requirement, in art 115(6) of the Regulation, that any translation must be provided at the applicant's own expense. Presumably this requirement of the Regulation prevails.

1 Under art 115.3 of the Regulation.
2 This period is not extendable under r 71(1) – see ch 28 paras 28.2–28.3 – although an applicant would gain some more time if he delayed paying the fee required under art 55(2).

27.44 Rule 38(2) deals with the language to be used for evidence. This aspect is not expressly covered by art 115 of the Regulation. If the evidence in support of the application is not filed in the language of the revocation or invalidity proceedings, the applicant must file a translation of the evidence into that language within a period of two months from the filing of the evidence.[1]

27.45 Rule 38(3) deals with the exception provided by art 115(7) of the Regulation. Under r 38(3), where the applicant for revocation or invalidity informs the Office, before the expiry of a period of two months from the date at which the CTM owner receives the communication under r 40(1), that the application is not rejected under r 39 as inadmissible, that a different language has been agreed upon, the applicant is required to file a translation of the application into that language within one month from the expiry of the two-month period. Nothing is said about the filing of a translation of evidence, which may itself have already been filed. Presumably this must also be translated, although the period of two months set by r 38(3) cannot be applicable if the evidence was filed with the application.

27.46 Rule 39 makes provision for an application to be rejected as inadmissible if the requirements of art 55 of the Regulation or r 37, or any other provisions of the Regulation or rules,[1] are not complied with. In case of any non-compliance, r 39(1) requires the Office to inform the applicant and to call upon him to remedy the deficiencies found within such period as the office may specify.[2] Subject to any extension, if the deficiencies are not remedied within the specified period, the application will be rejected as inadmissible. Of course, where a time specified in the Rules is non-extendable, as for example the period set under r 38(1) and (2) for filing translations, the deficiency will not be remediable and the application will be rejected. Rule 39(2) is concerned with non-payment of fees. If they have not been paid, the Office must inform the applicant, and inform him that if the required fees are not paid within a period specified by the Office[3] the application will be deemed not to have been filed. If the fees are paid after the expiry of the specified period, they are to be refunded. In accordance with art 55(2) the effective date of the application will be the date on which the fees were actually paid. This may have some significance in non-use cases if the proprietor resumes use. Rule 39(3) requires the applicant to be notified of any decision to reject the application under r 39(1), or to treat the application as not having been filed, under r 39(2).

1 This will include the language requirement of r 38.
2 This period is extendable by the Office under r 71(1).
3 Again, extendable under r 71(1).

27.47 Once the application has passed the hurdle of admissibility, it is examined by the Office. The examination of the application is governed by art 56 of the Regulation and r 40. Article 56(1) contains a general provision, that in the examination of an application for revocation or for a declaration of invalidity, the Office shall invite the parties, as often as necessary, to file observations, within a period to be fixed by the Office, on communications from the other parties or issued by itself. First of all, as required by r 40(1), if the office does not reject the application under r 39, as being inadmissible, it must communicate the application to the proprietor of the CTM and request him to file his observations within such period as it may specify. Under r 40(2), if the proprietor of the CTM files no observations, the Office may decide on the matter on the basis of the evidence before it. By r 40(3), any observations filed by the proprietor are to be communicated to the applicant, who will be requested by the Office, if it sees fit, to reply within a period specified by the office. To facilitate the application of art 56(1) and the rules just referred to, r 40(5) requires all communications under art 56(1) and all observations filed, to be sent to the parties concerned.

27.48   The words 'as often as necessary' in art 56(1) and 'if it sees fit' in r 40(3) merit some comment. Clearly the Office must send the application and the evidence and other matter filed under r 39(b) to the proprietor of the CTM. There is however a suggestion that in the case of the proprietor's observations there is some kind of option. Nevertheless, if such observations are considered possibly to have any effect on the decision of the Office, it is submitted that the applicant ought to be sent a copy and given the opportunity to respond. Thus any such option must be governed by the words 'shall invite the parties, as often as necessary ...' in art 56(1).

27.49   Paragraphs 2 and 3 of art 56 are similar to art 43(2) and 43(3), which apply in oppositions based on earlier registered marks. If the proprietor of the CTM sought to be invalidated so requests, the proprietor of an earlier trade mark relied upon, being a party to the proceedings, must furnish proof of genuine use, in the Community or the Member State(s) concerned, as the case may be, during the period of five years preceding the date of the application for a declaration of invalidity, in relation to the goods or services covered by the registration which are cited as justification for the application, or that there are proper reasons for non-use. The requirements for use contained in art 43(2) must also be shown satisfied as at the date of the publication of the CTM application, if the earlier mark had at that date been registered for not less than five years. If the earlier mark has been used in relation to part only of the goods or services for which it is registered, for the purposes of the examination of the application it will be deemed to be registered only for those goods or services. It appears that a licensee seeking a declaration of invalidity cannot be called upon to furnish evidence of use. By r 40(5), the provisions of r 22, which govern the furnishing of proof of genuine use or of proper reasons for non-use in opposition proceedings,[1] apply *mutatis mutandis*. Rule 41 makes provision for multiple applications relating to the same CTM. The office may deal with them in one set of proceedings, but may subsequently decide no longer to deal with them in this way. The provisions of r 21(2)(3) and (4), which govern multiple oppositions,[2] are applied *mutatis mutandis*. In practice, the office will inform the parties concerned of its intentions, and invite observations from them as required by the general provision of art 56.1, when considering the exercise of its powers under r 41.

1 See paras **26.27–26.29** above.
2 See para **26.33** above.

27.50   Article 56(4) should be noted; this permits the office, if it thinks fit, to invite the parties to make a friendly settlement.[1] If the application proceeds, art 56(5), consistently with art 52(3) and 52(50), provides that if the examination of the application reveals that the trade mark should not have been registered in respect of some or all of the goods or services for which it is registered, the rights of the proprietor of the CTM shall be revoked, or it shall be declared invalid, for those goods or services. Otherwise the application will be rejected. The words 'should not have been registered' are not really apt for revocation cases, and should presumably be understood in the sense 'should not remain on the register'. Article 56(6) requires the decision revoking the rights of the proprietor of the CTM, or declaring it invalid, to be entered in the register on becoming final.

1 See remarks on the corresponding provision for oppositions, art 43(4), at para **26.30** above.

Conversion to national procedure

27.51 If the office upholds an application for revocation or for a declaration of invalidity, in whole or in part, the applicant may, if he does not wish to appeal, request conversion to national applications in accordance with art 108.[1]

1 See ch 23, paras **24.24–24.25**.

Chapter 28

Procedure before the Office

Introduction

28.1 Title IX of the Regulation, comprising arts 73–89, contains a number of procedural provisions governing various aspects of proceedings before the Office. Further procedural provisions are to be found in rr 52–99 of the Implementing Regulation ('the Rules'). A number of these provisions have been mentioned in earlier chapters, in relation to specific aspects of proceedings before the office. Many of the provisions are comparatively straightforward and do not require detailed consideration here. There are however some points which are sufficiently important to merit some attention.

Time limits and extensions of time

28.2 Mention should be made at the outset of some of the detailed provisions in the Rules regarding time limits and extensions of time. Generally speaking the approach of the CTM Regulation and the Rules is different from that of the UK TMA 1994 and Rules. Under the latter, periods of time set for doing various acts are for the most part extendable in appropriate circumstances, the number of exceptions, which are clearly specified, being quite limited. Under the CTM Regulation and Rules there are rather more periods of time which are not extendable. Some these are identified in earlier chapters. The matter seems to depend primarily upon whether the period of time in question is actually specified in the Regulation or in the Rules, or whether it is left to the office to specify the period. Rules 70–73 are concerned with time limits. Rule 71 contains an important provision affecting time limits, and is as follows:

> '(1) Where the Regulation or these Rules provide for a period to be specified by the Office, such period shall, when the party concerned has its domicile or its principal place of business or an establishment within the Community, be not less than one month, or, when those conditions are not fulfilled, not less than two months, and no more than six months. The Office may, when this is appropriate under the circumstances, grant an extension of a period specified if such extension is requested by the party concerned and the request is submitted before the original period expired.
>
> (2) Where there are two or more parties, the Office may extend a period subject to the agreement of the other parties.'

28.3   There are two important points about r 71(1). The first is that a time appears not to be extendable under this rule if it is specified in the Regulation or the Rules; it is only extendable if the Regulation or Rules provide for a period to be specified by the Office. Secondly, an application for an extension has to be submitted before the expiry of the period to be extended. In the case of proceedings, such as oppositions, where there are two or more parties, r 71(2) at first sight seems to imply that extension is not permitted unless the other parties agree. However, it would make nonsense of r 71(1) if a party's refusal to agree to an extension were treated as final. It is submitted that the purpose of r 71(2) is not to restrict the application of r 71(1), by limiting the power of the Office to grant extensions where justice requires, in proceedings where there are two or more parties, but rather to give a broader discretionary power to the Office to extend time in such proceedings, if all the parties agree. However, it cannot be said that the wording is satisfactory or the position entirely clear.[1]

1 See also para **26.1** above.

28.4   The Rules say nothing about the basis on which extensions of time, where allowable, will be granted. It is thought that the Office will not readily give extensions, particularly in proceedings involving two or more parties. Any request for an extension must be accompanied by reasons to justify an extension. The Office is understood to be quite strict even where the parties themselves request the extension. A particular instance in which an extension will normally be granted is where the parties are negotiating with a view to a settlement.

28.5   Rule 70 lays down detailed provisions for determining when a time limit actually expires. Under para (1), periods are to be laid down in terms of full years, months, weeks or days. Under para (2), calculations are made by reference to 'relevant events'. An event is a procedural step or the expiry of another period; where the procedural step is a notification, the event is the receipt of the document notified, unless otherwise provided. Calculation of any period starts on the day following the day on which the relevant event occurred. In accordance with para (3), where a period is expressed as a year or a certain number of years, the period expires in the relevant subsequent year in the month having the same name and on the day having the same number as the month and the day on which the event occurred. If the relevant month has no day with the same number, the period expires on the last day of the month. Thus, where the event occurred on 31 January 1997, a period of one year expired on 31 January 1998. Where the event occurred on 29 February 1996 a period of one year would have expired on 28 February 1997. Months are dealt with similarly under para (4). In general, a period expressed as month or a certain number of months expires in the relevant subsequent month on the day having the same number as the day of the relevant event. However, where that day was the last day of a month, or where the relevant subsequent month has no day with the same number, the period expires on the last day of that month. Thus, a period of one month from 31 July 1998 expired on 31 August 1998; but three months from 30 April 1998 expired on 31 July 1998, and one month from 31 January 1998 expired on 28 February 1998. Under para (5), in the case of a period expressed as one week or a certain number of weeks, expiry is on the day in the subsequent week having the same name as the date on which the relevant event occurred.

28.6 Rule 72 provides for certain exceptions for 'expiry of time limits in special cases'. Rule 72(1) applies where a time limit expires on a day on which the Office is not open for receipt of documents or on which, for reasons other than those referred to in para (2), ordinary mail is not delivered in the locality in which the Office is located; in such cases the time limit is extended to the first day thereafter on which the Office is open for the receipt of documents and on which ordinary mail is delivered. The days on which the Office is not open for receipt of documents are determined by the President before the beginning of each calendar year. These are published in the Official Journal of OHIM. Paragraph (2) applies where a time limit expires on a day on which there is a 'general interruption or subsequent dislocation in the delivery of mail in a Member State or between a Member State and the Office'. In these cases, for parties whose residence or registered Office is in the state concerned, or who have appointed representatives with a place of business in that state, the time expires on the next day following the end of the period of interruption or dislocation. If the state concerned is Spain,[1] then the provision applies to all parties. The duration of the period of interruption or dislocation is determined by the President of the Office. The most obvious kind of situation covered by para (2) would be that created by strike action, or perhaps a natural disaster. It is not clear what 'other reasons', which might exist for non-delivery of mail, in the locality in which the Office is situated, are contemplated by the first sentence of para (1). Under r 72(3) the provisions of paras (1) and (2) apply *mutatis mutandis* to the time limits provided for in the Regulation or Rules in the case of transactions to be carried out with the competent authority within the meaning of art 25(1)(b) of the Regulation.[2] Paragraph (4) is concerned not with events affecting acts to be done by a party within a time limit, but with cases in which some communication from the Office to parties, concerning the expiry of a time limit, is delayed, due to any 'exceptional occurrence such as a natural disaster[3] or strike', which 'interrupts or dislocates the proper functioning of the Office'. It seems clear that there may be other 'exceptional occurrence' covered by para (4), apart from natural disasters or strikes. For example, the provision might perhaps also apply in the event of a delivery van being stolen or the destruction of mail in an accident involving a delivery van. In all cases covered by para (4), acts to be completed within the time limit may be validly completed within one month after the notification of the delayed communication. The date of commencement and ending of the interruption or dislocation is determined by the President of the Office.

1 Because the Office is located there.
2 Ie national industrial property Offices or the Benelux Trade Mark Office.
3 An example of a case in which the period for filing opposition was extended because of natural disaster is Opposition No B 2875 ('*Instra-Lube*'), Official Journal of the OHIM 6/98, p 711.

Interruption of proceedings

28.7 Rule 73 deals with interruption of proceedings before the Office in certain circumstances. Paragraph (1) provides for interruption of proceedings in three situations. The first is the death or legal incapacity of the applicant for or the proprietor of a CTM or of the person authorised by national law to act on his behalf. However to the extent that such event does not affect the authorisation of a representative appointed under art 89 of the Regulation, the proceedings are interrupted only on the application of the representative. In cases of death or legal incapacitation of an applicant or proprietor or his legal representative, a representative appointed under art 89 should take immediate steps to ascertain whether under national law his authorisation is affected, and, if it is not, to make the necessary application for the proceedings to be interrupted. The second situation is that in which the applicant or proprietor, as a result of some action taken against his property, is prevented for legal reasons from continuing the proceedings before the Office. This might arise as a result of bankruptcy or winding up proceedings, or perhaps the grant of an injunction. The third situation is that of the death or legal incapacity of the representative of an applicant or proprietor, or his being prevented, for legal reasons resulting from action taken against his property, from continuing the proceedings before the Office. In either of the first two situations, para (2) provides that, when the Office has been informed of the identity of the person authorised to continue the proceedings before the Office, the Office shall communicate to the person concerned, and to any interested third parties, that the proceedings shall be resumed as from a date to be fixed by the Office. Such person might, for example, be a receiver or liquidator, or a personal representative. In the third kind of situation, under para (3) the proceedings are resumed when the Office has been informed of the appointment of a new representative of the applicant, or when the Office has notified to the other parties the communication of the appointment of a new representative of the proprietor. Where, three months after the beginning of the interruption of the proceedings, the Office has not been informed of the appointment of a new representative, the Office is required to inform the applicant for or proprietor of the CTM: (a) where art 88(2) of the Regulation[1] applies, that the CTM application will be deemed to be withdrawn if the information is not submitted within two months after this communication is notified; or (b) where art 88(2) is not applicable, that the proceedings will be resumed with the applicant or proprietor as from the date on which the communication is notified. As for time limits in force as regards the applicant or CTM proprietor at the date of interruption of the proceedings, apart from the time limit for paying renewal fees, r 73(4) provides that these begin again as from the date on which the proceedings are resumed.

1 Concerned with parties not having their domicile or principal place of business, or a real and effective commercial establishment, within the EU, who are generally required to appoint a representative in any proceedings, other than in filing a CTM application.

28.8   It is to be noted that r 73 says nothing about cases of death or legal incapacity of other parties, such as opponents or applicants for revocation or a declaration of invalidity, or of their representatives. Presumably in these proceedings such situations can be dealt with by granting appropriate extensions of times under r 71.

Procedure generally

28.9   Section 1 of Title IX and rr 52–69 contain general provisions relating to procedure before the Office, several of which merit consideration. The provisions relate to decisions (art 73 and rr 52–55), examination of facts (art 74), oral proceedings (art 75 and rr 56–60), evidence (art 76), notification (art 77 and rr 61–69), restitutio in integrum (art 78), reference to general principles (art 79) and termination of financial obligations (art 80).

Decisions

28.10 As would be expected, art 73 requires decisions of the Office to state the reasons on which they are based. They are to be based only on reasons or evidence on which the parties concerned have had an opportunity to present their comments. Rule 52 contains provisions as to the form of decisions, and allows an oral decision at oral proceedings, the written decision to be notified to the parties subsequently. Decisions which are open to appeal must be accompanied by a written communication that notice of appeal must be filed in writing within two months of the date of notification of the decision. Rule 53 provides for correction of errors in decisions, correctable errors being limited to linguistic errors, errors of transcription and obvious mistakes. Where the Office finds that loss of rights results from the Regulation or Rules without any decision having been taken, r 54(1) requires this to be communicated to the person concerned in accordance with art 77, drawing attention to the substance of para (2). If the person concerned considers that the finding is inaccurate, under para (2) he may, within two months after the notification, apply for a decision on the matter by the Office. A decision need only be given if the Office disagrees with the person requesting it; otherwise the Office will amend its finding and notify the person concerned. Rule 55 lays down requirements as to signature, sealing etc, of decisions, communications and notices from the Office.

Examination of facts by the Office of its own motion

28.11 Article 74(1) requires the Office, in proceedings before it, to examine the facts of its own motion. However in proceedings relating to relative grounds for refusal, the Office is restricted in its examination to the facts, evidence and arguments provided by the parties and the relief sought. Under art 74(2) the Office may disregard facts or evidence which are not submitted in due time by the parties concerned. The word 'may' suggests that the Office has a discretion, although there would need to be good reasons for taking late filed evidence into account.

28.12 The restriction in art 74(1) does not apply to absolute grounds for refusal, where clearly the Office has to make its own inquiries into relevant facts, although the applicant will obviously be entitled to be informed of any material relied upon by the Office. The Rules are silent as to examination of facts in applications for revocation or for declarations of invalidity. In such a situation, art 79 ('reference to general principles) might be applicable.[1] Presumably, on principles of natural justice, the second part of art 74(1) could be applied by analogy.

1 See para **28.32** below.

Oral proceedings and the taking of evidence

28.13 Under art 75, the Office may propose oral proceedings, or such proceedings may be requested by a party. Oral proceedings may be held only if the Office considers that they would be expedient. It is expected that the number of occasions on which the Office considers that oral proceedings are expedient will be limited. This provision appears to apply to Boards of Appeal, as well as to the Examiners, the Opposition Divisions and the Cancellation Divisions. It may be that in due course the CFI will give further guidance as and when an appellant complains of not being granted an oral hearing. Article 76 sets out the principal means for giving evidence in proceedings before the Office. Rules 56–60 contain detailed provisions as to the summons to oral proceedings, the taking of evidence by the Office, the commissioning of experts, the costs of the taking of evidence and minutes of oral proceedings and of evidence. These do not require detailed consideration here, save that it should be noted that under r 58 the Office may itself appoint an expert, subject to the parties' right to object under para (4), on grounds of incompetence or on the same grounds as those on which objection may be made to an examiner, or to a member of a Division or a Board of Appeal, under art 132(1) and 132(3) of the Regulation.

Notifications

28.14 Of crucial importance to those involved in the prosecution of proceedings before the Office, and to the working of the Office itself, are the provisions in art 77 of the Regulation and in the Implementing Regulation regarding notifications by the Office. Article 77 requires the Office, as a matter of course, to notify those concerned of decisions and summonses and of any notice or communication from which a time limit is reckoned, or of which those concerned must be notified under other provisions of the Regulation or of the Implementing Regulation, or of which notification has been ordered by the President of the Office. The detailed provisions are contained in rr 61–69.

28.15 By r 61(1), in proceedings before the Office, any notifications to be made by the Office must take the form of the original document, or a copy of it, certified by, or bearing the seal[1] of, the Office, or of a computer print-out bearing such seal. Copies of documents emanating from the parties themselves do not require such certification.

1 See also r 55.

28.16 Rule 61(2) specifies five different means of notification, each in accordance with one of rr 62–66. They are: (a) by post (r 62); (b) by hand delivery (r 63); deposit in a post box at the Office (r 64); by telecopier and other technical means (r 65); and by public notification (r 66).

28.17 Rule 62 distinguishes between certain categories of notification which must be made by registered letter and those which may be made by ordinary mail. Under para (1), decisions subject to a time limit for appeal, summonses, and other documents as determined by the President of the Office, must be notified by registered letter with advice of delivery. Decisions and communications subject to some other time limit must be notified by registered letter, unless the President determines otherwise. All other communications are to be made by ordinary mail.

28.18 Rule 62(2) is concerned with notifications in respect of addressees having neither their domicile nor their principal place of business nor an establishment in the Community and who have not appointed a representative in accordance with art 88(2) of the Regulation, and provides that these shall be effected by posting the document requiring notification by ordinary mail to the last address of the addressee known to the Office. Notification is deemed to have been effected when the posting has taken place.

28.19   Rule 62(3) makes further provision in respect of notifications effected by registered letter, whether or not with advice of delivery. This is deemed to be delivered to the addressee on the 10th day following that of its posting, unless the letter has failed to reach the addressee or has reached him at a later date. By para (4), such a notification is deemed to have been effected even if the addressee refuses to accept delivery. An important part of this provision is that, in the event of any dispute, it is for the Office to establish that the letter has reached its destination or to establish the date on which it was delivered to the addressee, as the case may be.

28.20   It is to be noted that para (3) does not apply to cases of delivery by ordinary mail. In the case of delivery by this means under para (1), it appears that the situation may governed by the applicable local law. Paragraph (5) provides that to the extent that notification by post is not covered by paras (1)–(4), the law of the state on the territory of which notification is made shall apply. On the other hand where delivery is by ordinary mail under para (2), since the notification will be deemed to have been effected when the posting has taken place, there is no room for the application of para (5). In these cases the addressee does not have the benefit of the provision requiring the Office to establish delivery or the date of delivery. This serves to emphasise the importance of appointing a representative in accordance with art 88(2) of the Regulation.

28.21   Rule 63, which is clearly an alternative to r 62, allows for notification to be effected on the premises of the Office by hand delivery of the document to the addressee, who is required to acknowledge its receipt on delivery.

28.22   Another alternative means of notification is provided by r 64, where an addressee has been provided with a post box at the Office. Notification is effected by depositing the document in the post box. A written notification of the deposit must be inserted in the file and the date of the deposit recorded on the document. In order to allow time for collection by the addressee, notification is deemed to have taken place on the fifth day following the deposit of the document in the post box.

28.23   Under r 65(1), notification by telecopier is required to be effected by transmitting either the original or a copy, as provided for in r 61(1), of the document to be notified. The details of such transmission are to be determined by the President of the Office. Paragraph (2) relates to notification by other technical means, which will include e-mail. Again the details of such notification are to be determined by the President of the Office.

28.24   The provisions for public notification, which is in effect a kind of substituted service, are contained in r 66. Under para (1), if the address of the addressee cannot be established, or if notification in accordance with r 62(1) has proved to be impossible even after a second attempt by the Office, then notification shall be by public notice, which must be published at least in the CTMs Bulletin. Rule 66(2) provides for the President of the Office to determine how the public notice is to be given, and to fix the beginning of the one-month period on the expiry of which the document will be deemed to have been notified.

28.25 Rule 67 contains provisions for the situation which will arise in many cases, ie those in which parties have representatives acting for them. If a representative has been appointed, or in cases in which the applicant first named in a common application is considered to be the common representative pursuant to r 75(1), notifications are to be addressed to that appointed or common representative. Where several representatives have been appointed for a single interested party, r 67(2) provides that notification to any one of them shall be sufficient, unless a specific address for service has been indicated in accordance with r 1(1)(e). Under r 67(3), if several interested parties have appointed a common representative, notification of a single document to the common representative is sufficient.

28.26 Rule 68 covers cases of irregularities in notification, where the Office cannot prove that a document has been duly notified, or if provisions regarding notification have not been observed. In such cases, if the document has in fact reached the addressee, it is deemed to have been notified on the date established by the Office as the date of receipt. Finally, r 69 lays down requirements for notifying documents, emanating from parties and containing substantive proposals or a declaration of withdrawal of a substantive proposal, to other parties to proceedings, as a matter of course.

Restitutio in integrum

28.27 Article 78 contains a special provision which is of considerable practical importance in some situations in which a time limit is missed in spite of all due care having been taken. It is available to an applicant for, or proprietor of a CTM and to any other party to proceedings before the Office who has been unable to observe a time limit *vis-à-vis* the Office, in spite of all due care required by the circumstances having been taken. Under para (1) such a person may, upon application, have his rights re-established if the non-observance has the direct consequence, by virtue of the provisions of the Regulation, of causing the loss of any right or means of redress. An example of the application of art 78 is provided by a case in which an applicant, in opposition proceedings, failed to meet a deadline for submitting observations in reply to the opposition because of a mistake on the part of a well-known and reputable international courier service company.[1] The application for re-establishing of the applicant's rights, so as to enable it to defend the opposition, was granted by the Opposition Division.

1 Opposition No B 1471 (*'Birthday Bear'*), Official Journal of the OHIM 10/98, p 1093.

28.28 Paragraphs (2) and (3) lay down the procedural requirements for an application for re-establishment of rights. The application must be filed in writing, stating the grounds on which it is based, within two months from the removal of the cause for non-compliance with the time limit, and the omitted act must be completed within the same period. The application will only be admissible within the year immediately following the expiry of the unobserved time limit. In a case arising from a failure to renew registration of a CTM or to pay the renewal fee, the further period of six months provided under art 47(3) is deducted from the period of one year. The applicable fee must be paid within the two month period. These periods are non-extendable. Under para (4) the application is decided upon by the department competent to decide on the omitted act.

28.29 It is important to note that the provisions of art 78 are not applicable to the time limits set by para (2). Nor are they applicable to the six-month period for filing an application claiming priority under art 29(1) or to the three-month period for opposition, under art 42(1).

28.30 Paragraphs (6) and (7) provide safeguards to protect the position of third parties in certain circumstances. Where an applicant for a CTM or a CTM proprietor has his rights re-established, he may not invoke his rights against a third party who, in good faith, has put goods on the market or provided services under a sign which identical or similar to the CTM during the period between the loss of rights in the application or CTM and publication of the mention of re-establishment of the rights. In addition, such a third party has a period of two months from the publication of the mention of re-establishment, in which to bring proceedings to challenge the decision re-establishing the rights.

28.31 The provisions of art 78 only apply to non-observance of time limits *vis-à-vis* the Office. Therefore para (8) provides that nothing in art 78 shall limit the right of a Member State to grant restitution in integrum in respect of time limits provided for in the Regulation and to be observed *vis-à-vis* the authorities of such state.

Reference to general principles

28.32 Article 79 is intended to cover the position where there are no applicable provisions in the Regulation, the Implementing Regulation, the fees regulations or the Rules of Procedure of the Boards of Appeal. In such a situation the Office will take into account the principles of procedural law generally recognised in the Member States. Whether there are in fact any such generally recognised principles may be debatable. However the provision would no doubt enable the Office to adopt a fair procedure in the circumstances.

Financial obligations and costs

28.33 Article 30 sets a four-year limitation on claims of fees or refunds due to or from the Office, but the period is interrupted by a request in writing from the Office or reasoned claim in writing submitted to the Office. The maximum period, taking such interruptions into account, is six years from the end of the first year in which the period originally began, unless judicial proceedings to enforce the right have begun in the meantime. In that case the period ends, at the earliest, one year after the judgment becomes final. Rule 74 allows the President of the Office to waive any sums due if they are minimal or where recovery is too uncertain.

28.34 General principles in awarding costs in proceedings before the Office are set out in art 81. In opposition proceedings and in proceedings for revocation or a declaration of invalidity, and in appeal proceedings, the general rule is that the losing party must pay the costs. Certain limits on the amount of costs recoverable, and other procedural matters, are covered in detail in r 94 of the Implementing Regulation. Where each party succeeds on some heads and fails on others, or if reasons of equity so dictate, the Division or the Board of Appeal concerned will decide a different apportionment of costs. Under art 81.3 a party who terminates proceedings, whether by withdrawing a CTM application, by withdrawing an opposition, an application for revocation or a declaration of invalidity or an appeal, or by not renewing or by surrendering a CTM, will bear the costs of the other party. If a case does not proceed to judgment, art 81.4 provides that the costs are to be at the discretion of the Division or the Board of Appeal concerned. It is open to parties to make their own agreement as to costs, and if the costs payable under an order of the Office cannot be agreed, the Division or Board can be requested to fix the amount of the costs. Under para (6) such amount may be reviewed by the Division or Board concerned on a request filed within the prescribed period, which is set by r 84(4) at one month from the notification of the award.

Information of the public and official authorities of the Member States

28.35   Articles 83–87, and rr 84–93 lay down detailed provisions under which the public and the official authorities of Member States are informed about CTMs and various matters relating to them. The provisions cover the register of CTMs (art 83 and r 84), inspection of files (art 84 and rr 88–91), periodical publications, namely the CTM Bulletin and the Official Journal (art 85 and rr 85–86), administrative co-operation (art 86 and rr 92–93), and exchange of publications between the Office and national industrial property Offices of Member States, free of charge (art 87). Most of these need little comment here.

Inspection of files

28.36   The provisions for inspection of files merit some mention. The general rule, under art 84(1), is that files relating to CTM applications which have not yet been published, are not to be made available for inspection without the consent of the applicant. Article 84(2) provides an exception to this where a person can prove that the applicant for a CTM has stated that after the trade mark has been registered he will invoke the rights under it against him, he may obtain inspection without the applicant's consent. It would appear that the statement need not be made directly in a letter to the person concerned, but might take the form of a public statement. Under art 84(3), after a CTM application has been published the files relating to it and the resulting trade mark may be inspected on request. However in all cases certain documents may be withheld from inspection in accordance with the provisions of the Implementing Regulation. Documents excluded from inspection, under r 88, are documents relating to exclusion or objection (of examiners and members of the Divisions and the Boards of Appeal) under art 132, draft decisions and opinions and other internal documents used for their preparation, and parts of the file which the party concerned showed a special interest in keeping confidential before the application for inspection of the files was made. However this last provision does not apply if inspection of such part of the file is justified by overriding legitimate interests of the party seeking inspection. This is an important provision, which should ensure that a party cannot use the cloak of confidence to prevent another party from seeing material which he requires for the proper preparation and presentation of his case.

28.37 Procedures for the inspection of files are laid down by r 89, which provides for inspection at the premises of the Office and also makes provision for inspection by the issue of copies of documents. Fees are payable for inspection. Where a file is very voluminous, r 90 gives the Office the option to obtain inspection of the file itself if appropriate. Rule 91 requires files to be kept for at least five years after an application is rejected or withdrawn, or deemed to be withdrawn, the registration of the CTM expires completely or the complete surrender of it is registered, or the CTM is completely removed from the register as a result of an application for revocation or a declaration of invalidity.

Periodical publications

28.38 Under art 85 the Bulletin contains entries made in the register of CTMs as well as other particulars the publication of which is prescribed by the Regulation or the Implementing Regulation. The Official Journal contains notices and information of a general character issued by the President of the Office, as well as any other information relevant to the Regulation or its implementation. Such other information includes relevant Community Regulations and Directives, other relevant instruments including treaties, for example the TRIPS Agreement, decisions of the ECJ and decisions of the Examining, Opposition and Cancellation Divisions and of the Boards of Appeal, and information about accession of countries to the Madrid Protocol and other Treaties and additions or alterations to the list of professional representatives. Rules 85 and 86 make further provisions as to the form and content of the Bulletin and the Official Journal respectively.

The data bank

28.39 Rule 87 requires the Office to maintain an electronic data bank with the particulars of applications for registration and entries in the register. The contents of the data bank may be made available on CD-ROM or in any other machine readable form. The terms on which it is made available, including charges, are determined by the President of the Office.

Administrative co-operation

28.40 Article 86 provides for the Office and the courts or authorities of the Member States on request, unless otherwise provided in the Regulation or in national laws, to give assistance to each other by communicating information or opening files for inspection. Rule 92 makes further provisions regarding the exchange of information and communications between the Office and the authorities of Member States about filing of applications for CTMs and national marks and proceedings relating to such applications and marks registered as a result thereof. These communications are not subject to any of the restrictions laid down in art 84. Where the Office lays files open to inspection by courts, Public Prosecutors' Offices or central industrial property Offices – as is done by r 93 – again the inspection is not subject to the restrictions laid down in art 84.

Representation at the Office

28.41   Under art 88(1), but subject to para (2), no person can be compelled to be represented before the Office. Paragraph makes an important exception in the case of natural or legal persons not having either their domicile or their principal place of business or a real and effective commercial establishment in the Community. Such persons must be represented before the Office in accordance with art 89 in all proceedings established by the Regulation, save that they may file a CTM application without representation. The Implementing Regulation may make other exceptions but none are made in the current Implementing Regulation. Under para (3) other natural or legal persons may be represented before the Office by an employee, who must file with the Office a signed authorisation for insertion on the files; the details of this are set out in the Implementing Regulation, r 76. An employee of a legal person to whom this provision applies may also represent other legal persons which have economic connections with the first legal person, ie related companies, even of they have neither their domicile nor their principal place of business nor a real and effective industrial or commercial establishment within the Community. Rule 75 covers cases of joint applications for registration and joint opponents or applicants for revocation or a declaration of invalidity, and cases where an application is transferred to more than one person, setting requirements for the appointment of a common representative if one is not named.

28.42   Article 89 defines the categories of persons who may undertake representation of natural or legal persons before the Office. They are (a) any legal practitioner qualified in one of the Member States and having his place of business within the Community, to the extent that he is entitled, within such state, to act as a representative in trade mark matters, and (b) professional representatives whose names appear on the list maintained by the Office for that purpose. Representatives appearing before the Office must file with it a signed authorisation for insertion on the files; again the details are in r 76 of the Implementing Regulation. The requirements for entry on the list of representatives are set out in para (2). In order to be entered on the list, a natural person must (a) be a national of a Member State, (b) have his place of business or employment in the Community and (c) be entitled to represent natural or legal persons in trade mark matters before the central Office of industrial property of the Member State where he has his place of business or employment. Where in such state the entitlement is not conditional upon the requirement of special professional qualifications, a person applying for entry on the list must have habitually practised before such Office for at least five years. This requirement does not apply to persons whose professional qualification is officially recognised in accordance with the a regulations of the Member State concerned. Under para (3) entry is effected on request, accompanied by the appropriate certificate from the central industrial property Office of the Member State. Paragraph (4) allows the President of the Office to grant exemption from the requirement of (2)(c) if the applicant proves that he has acquired the requisite qualification in some other way, and from the nationality requirement of (2)(a) in special circumstances. Paragraph (5) provides for the conditions for removal of a person from the list of professional representatives to be laid down in the Implementing Regulation, and this is done by r 78. This applies at the representatives request, and generally in circumstances in which a representative no longer fulfills the requirements of art 89. For this purpose the national Offices must inform the Office of relevant events.

28.43   Rule 77 states the effect of professional representation. Any notification or communication addressed by the Office to a duly authorised representative has the same effect as if addressed to the represented person. Any communication addressed to the Office by the duly authorised representative has the same effect as if it originated from the represented person.

Communications and forms

28.44   Rules 79–82 lay down detailed rules as to the means by which communications may be made with the Office, which include post, personal delivery, telecopier, telex or telegram and electronic means. Rule 83 sets out in detail the various forms which the Office is required to make available, free of charge, for the purposes specified.

Languages

28.45   The matter of languages for use in the Office has already been discussed in chapter 22[1] and in other chapters dealing with different kinds of proceedings before the Office. The main provisions are in art 115 of the Regulation. Without prejudice to those provisions, rr 95–99 make still further provisions relating to use of languages in proceedings, covering in addition other matters such as certificates and legal authenticity of translations and interpretation at hearings. Particular matters to note include the possibility, under r 97(1) for a party to oral proceedings to use one of the official languages of the Community, even if this is not the language of the proceedings, if he makes provision for interpretation into the language of the proceedings, and under r 97(4) for the use of any official language of the Community if the parties and the Office so agree.

1 Paragraphs **23.5–23.7**.

Chapter 29

Appeals

1   Appeals from decisions in the Office

29.1   Appeals from decisions in the Office are governed by arts 57–63 of the Regulation. Article 57 contains a general provision for appeals against decisions of the Office, which are to the Boards of Appeal established within the Office itself. Article 63 provides for a further appeal in certain cases, to the ECJ. The organisation of the Office, including the establishment of the various Divisions and the Boards of Appeal, and their constitution, is the subject of arts 125–132 of the Regulation.[1] Further provisions concerning appeals are contained in rr 48–51. In addition, there is a separate Regulation governing procedure of the Boards of Appeal[2] (the 'Appeal Rules'). Many of the Appeal Rules relate to matters of organisation and composition of the Boards for hearing appeals, and formalities such as communications to the parties and deliberations preceding decisions, and are not discussed here.

1 See para **23.8** above.
2 Commission Regulation **216/96** (EC) of 5 February 1996 laying down the rules of procedure of the Boards of Appeal of the Office for Harmonisation in the Internal Market (Trade Marks and Designs) – OJ L28, 6.2.1996, p 11, set out in Appendix 4.

Decisions subject to appeal

29.2   Article 57(1) of the Regulation provides that an appeal shall lie from decisions of the examiners, Opposition Divisions, Administration of Trade Marks and Legal Division and Cancellation Divisions, and shall have suspensive effect. Although this means that any decision in the Office is subject to appeal, there is a restriction as to when a decision which does not determine the whole matter before the Office, such as an interlocutory decision, may be appealed. Under art 57(2), if a decision does not terminate proceedings as regards one of the parties, there can only be an appeal together with an appeal against the final decision, unless the decision in question allows a separate appeal. No guidance is given as to when a separate appeal might be allowed. This might be appropriate, for example, in a case where the effect of a decision against one party might be that he could not realistically continue with the proceedings. If this is likely to be the case, it might be advisable for the party concerned to request in advance that the decision, if adverse, should allow for a separate appeal.

Formalities

29.3   Article 58 provides that any party to proceedings adversely affected by a decision may appeal, and that any other parties to the proceedings shall be parties to the appeal proceedings as of right. This excludes for example, third parties who submit observations as to absolute grounds for refusal, under art 41(1). Article 59 imposes a time limit of two months, from the date of notification of the decision, in which to file a notice of appeal, which must be in writing. With this in mind, r 52(2) provides that decisions of the Office which are open to appeal shall be accompanied by a written communication indicating that notice of appeal must be filed in writing at the Office within two months of the date of notification of the decision. The communication must also draw attention to the provisions of arts 57, 58 and 59 of the Regulation. The notice is to be deemed to have been filed only when the fee for appeal[1] has been paid. Emphasising this, r 49(3) provides that where the fee is paid after expiry of the two-month period, the appeal shall be deemed not to have been filed and the fee shall be refunded. Within four months of the date of notification of the decision, a written statement setting out the grounds of the appeal must be filed. Since these times of two and four months are specified in the Regulation, they are not extendable under r 71(1).[2] The requirements as to the content of the notice of appeal are set out in r 48(1). The notice must contain the name and address of the appellant in accordance with r 1(1)(b),[3] the name and address of the appellant's representative if one has been appointed, in accordance with r 1(1)(e), and a statement identifying the contested decision and the extent to which amendment or cancellation of the decision is requested. Rule 48(2) requires the notice to be filed in the language of the proceedings in which the appealed decision was taken.

1 See art 59.
2 See ch 28.6, paras **28.2–28.3**.
3 This may possibly also import a requirement to state the nationality, which r 1(1)(b) requires.

Non-compliance with formalities – inadmissibility of the appeal

29.4   If all the formalities are not complied with, the appeal may then be subject to rejection as inadmissible, under r 49. If the appeal does not comply with arts 57, 58 and 59 of the Regulation, and with r 48(1)(c) and (2) relating respectively to the identification of the contested decision and the extent to which it is contested, and the language of the notice, the Board of Appeal must reject it as inadmissible, unless each deficiency has been remedied before the relevant time limit laid down in art 59 has expired. Since art 59 lays down two separate time limits, ie two months for the notice of appeal and four for the written grounds, it seems that it may be contemplated that examination for inadmissibility will not take place until the grounds of appeal are filed. Even if that is not so, r 49(1) underlines the importance of compliance with the requirements and the advisability of not leaving the filing of the notice to the last possible moment. The only possible non-compliance with art 57 would arise under para (2), where the decision was not final and the decision did not allow a separate appeal. As for art 58, the only possibility, in practice, of non-compliance capable of being remedied would be the incorrect naming of a party to the proceedings. There might be non-compliance on the basis that the appellant was not adversely affected by the decision, but it is difficult to see how this could be remedied. Under art 59, a failure to file the notice or the grounds of appeal within the periods set will be incapable of remedy. Failure to pay the fee would have to be remedied before the two-month period for appealing had expired.

Likewise non-compliance with r 48(1)(c) and (2) can only be remedied within the same two-month period.

29.5 By contrast with r 48(1), r 48(2) allows for some defects to be remedied within such period as it may specify. This period, which by r 71(1) must be a minimum of one or two months, depending on whether the appellant has his domicile, his principal place of business or an establishment within or outside the Community, and may not be more than six months, is extendable. Rule 49(2) applies to 'other requirements of the Regulation or other provisions of these Rules, in particular r 48(1)(a) and (b)'. However there do not appear to be any other relevant provisions of the Regulation or the Rules, save for r 48(1)(a) and (b), which relate to the names and addresses of the appellant and his representative, that could be the subject of non-compliance. The Board notifies the appellant of the deficiencies and requests him to remedy them within the time specified. Rule 49(2) continues by providing that if the appeal is not corrected in good time, the Board of Appeal shall reject it as inadmissible. 'In good time' must presumably mean within the time specified or any extension of such time as may have been allowed, and is perhaps to be taken as an indication that extensions of time will not readily be granted.

Joinder of appeals

29.6 Article 7 of the Appeal Rules makes provision for cases where there is more than one appeal against the same decision. For instance in opposition proceedings, or proceedings for revocation or invalidation of a CTM, more than one party may be dissatisfied with some aspect of the decision. The appeals are all to be considered in the same proceedings. Under art 7(2), where appeals are filed against separate decisions and all the appeals are designated to be examined by one Board having the same composition, that Board may deal with those appeals in joined proceedings with the consent of the parties. Although not specified, the intention seems to be that this provision should apply where the decisions appealed from are at different stages of the same matter or are in proceedings raising common issues.

Remission to the department of first instance

29.7 Article 3 of the Appeal Rules enables a Board of Appeal to deal with the position where the proceedings of the department of first instance whose decision is the subject of an appeal are vitiated by fundamental deficiencies. In such a case the Board may set aside the decision and, unless there are reasons for not doing so, remit the case to that instance or decide the matter itself. Thus if there is a fatal deficiency in the proceedings below, the Board need not reach a substantive conclusion but can send it back for proper examination. However the possibility of deciding the appeal is retained, which may be appropriate where the 'fundamental deficiency' did not actually cause any prejudice to the party appealing.

Interlocutory revision

29.8 Article 60 introduces the concept of 'interlocutory revision', enabling the department whose decision is contested to rectify its decision without going through the procedure of examination of the appeal. This may happen where the department considers the appeal to be admissible and well founded. The provision does not apply where the appellant is opposed by another party to the proceedings. This does not exclude its application in appeals from Opposition and Cancellation Divisions, for example when a party such as an applicant or a CTM proprietor does not attempt to contest an opposition or an application for revocation or invalidation. Interlocutory revision will take place within a month from receipt of the statement of grounds. Under art 60.2, if the decision is not rectified within that period, the appeal must be remitted to the Board of Appeal without delay, and without comment as to its merit. It is not clear what happens if the department concerned considers the appeal to be well founded only in some respects. Presumably there is no reason why a department should not concede some issues, leaving the others to be determined by the Board of Appeal.

Comments on questions of general interest

29.9 Article 11 of the Appeal Rules introduces a special procedure which may be adopted where an appeal raises a question that is of general interest. In such a case the Board may, on its own initiative or at the written, reasoned request of the President of the Office, invite him to comment orally or in writing on such a question which arises in the course of proceedings pending before the Board. The parties are entitled to submit their observations on the President's comments. In the case of a request from the President, the requirement that it be 'reasoned' is important. He cannot simply ask to be invited to comment on any issue. The provision is silent as to whether the parties are to be informed of such a request from the President, or of a proposal from the Board to invite comments from the President. Since the form in which any question is put may be crucial to the appeal, it would seem appropriate that the parties should be informed.

Examination of appeals

29.10 Once any questions of inadmissibility and interlocutory revision have been disposed of, and the appeal has been found to be admissible, art 61.1 requires the Board of Appeal to examine whether the appeal is allowable. Rule 50(1) states that, unless otherwise provided, the provisions relating to proceedings before the department which has made the decision appealed from shall be applicable to appeal proceedings mutatis mutandis. These provisions are not specified, but are presumably intended to include the general provisions of rr 56–100 governing all aspects of proceedings in the Office. They might also include art 43 of the Regulation (and the applicable Rules, such as rules 20), relating to oppositions, and art 56 (with r 40) relating to applications for revocation and invalidity, although it is difficult to see how in practice these would be applied to appeals, apart from the provisions for the Office to invite the parties to make a friendly settlement.[1] Article 61(2) provides that, in the examination of the appeal, the Board of Appeal shall invite the parties, as often as necessary, to file observations, within a period to be fixed by the Board of Appeal,[2] on communications from the other parties or issued by itself. This provision is similar to arts 43(1) and 56(1). Clearly the Board of Appeal, under art 61(2), will invite the other parties to respond to the appellant's statement of grounds, and the appellant can expect to be invited to reply; the Office may, if appropriate, allow further rounds of observations from the parties.

29.11   Article 9 of the Appeal Rules concerns oral proceedings, if they are to take place. There appears to be is no absolute right to an oral hearing, and such a hearing will presumably only be directed where it is considered necessary for fairly disposing of the appeal. Article 9(1) lays down certain necessary procedural requirements, so as to ensure that all relevant material is before the Board before the hearing and that the case is ready for decision at the conclusion of the oral proceedings, unless there are special reasons to the contrary. Article 9(2) enables the Board, when issuing the summons to attend oral proceedings, to add a communication drawing attention to matters which seem to be of special significance, or to the fact that certain questions appear no longer to be contentious, or containing other observations that 'may help to concentrate on essentials during the oral proceedings'. There are no specific provisions for the conduct of oral hearings of appeals. However rr 52–99 of the Implementing Regulation which, as observed above, appear to apply to appeals, by virtue of r 50(1), contain a number of provisions relating to oral proceedings, which can be applied to hearings of appeals, where appropriate.

Decisions in respect of appeals

29.12   The provisions concerning decisions in respect of appeals are contained in art 62 of the Regulation and r 50. Under art 62(1) the Board of Appeal must decide on the appeal following the examination as to its allowability. This examination, as already seen, comprises consideration of the statement of grounds and any observations from the parties, including anything said at any oral hearing, where this takes place. The Board of Appeal may either exercise any power within the competence of the department responsible for the decision appealed, or remit the case to that department for further prosecution. If the latter course is adopted, under art 62(2) the department concerned is bound by the ratio decidendi of the Board of Appeal, *in so far as the facts are the same.* The effect of the italicised words is not clear. If the Board of Appeal does not make different findings of fact the question does not arise. But if the Board reaches different findings of fact, then it must be intended that the department concerned should have to accept them. Perhaps the words were added to cover the case where further evidence is received by the department after remission of the case to it by the Board of Appeal.

29.13   Article 62 and r 50 say nothing expressly about the decisions being in writing, but r 52 requires decisions of the Office to be in writing (save where there are oral proceedings, in which case the decision may be given orally, although the decision in writing must be notified subsequently). The effect of r 50(1) must be that the same applies to decisions of the Board of Appeal.

29.14   Rule 50(2) lays down what the Board of Appeal's decision must contain. The most important of these are, the names of the parties and their representatives, a statement of the issues to be decided, a summary of the facts, the reasons, and the order of the Board of Appeal, including, where necessary, a decision on costs. The other matters are essentially formal, being a statement that the decision is given by the Board, the date when the decision was taken, the names of the Chairman and the other members of the Board taking part, and the name of the competent employee of the registry. Under r 50(3) the decision must be signed by the Chairman, the other members of the Board and by the employee of the registry. Article 62(3) of the Regulation provides that the decisions of the Boards of Appeal are to take effect only as from the date of expiration of the period of two months from the date of notification of the decision of the Board of Appeal, referred to in art 63(5), being the period within which an action must be brought before the Court of Justice against a decision of the Board of Appeal, or, if an action has been brought before the Court of Justice within that period, as from the date of rejection of that action.

Reimbursement of appeal fees

29.15 Rule 51 makes provision for reimbursement of appeal fees in some circumstances. Where there is an interlocutory revision of a decision under art 60 of the Regulation, or where the Board of Appeal deems an appeal to be allowable, the reimbursement of appeal fees shall be ordered if such reimbursement is equitable by reason of a substantial procedural violation. This provision is only dealing with appeal fees, not costs generally, which are governed by arts 81 and 82 of the Regulation and r 94. A 'substantial procedural violation' is probably to be understood as a material error of procedure on the part of the department concerned. In the event of interlocutory revision the reimbursement is to be ordered by the department concerned; in other cases it will be ordered by the Board of Appeal.

Actions before the Court of Justice

29.16 In accordance with art 63.1 of the Regulation, actions may be brought before the ECJ against decisions of the Boards of Appeal on appeals. Article 63.2 specifies the circumstances in which such action can be brought. The grounds are lack of competence, infringement of an essential procedural requirement, infringement of the Treaty, of the Regulation, or of any rule of law relating to their application, or misuse of power. To some extent this may be a limitation of the scope for bring a case before the ECJ, but the provision is very broadly drawn and appears to cover most cases in which it is wished to say that a decision of a Board of Appeal was wrong. While clearly the ECJ can and should deal with any question as to interpretation or application of a provision of the Treaty or Regulation, it may be doubted whether it would re-consider findings of fact by a Board of Appeal or the department responsible for the original decision. Article 63.3 gives the ECJ jurisdiction to annul or to alter the contested decision. Under art 63.4 an action before the Court of Justice may be taken by any party to the proceedings before the Board of Appeal adversely affected by its decision. Article 63.5 requires that the action be brought before the ECJ within two months of the date of notification of the decision of the Board of Appeal. Under the rules of the ECJ, the CFI is responsible for dealing with the matter. Article 63.6 provides that the Office shall be required to take the necessary measures to comply with the judgment of the ECJ.

Chapter 30

Community collective marks

Community collective marks

30.1 Title VIII of the Regulation, comprising arts 64–72, contains separate provisions for Community collective marks. The applicable rules are rr 42 and 43.[1] As is clear from the provisions considered below, the Community collective mark is a mark of the same type as the collective mark which is now protectable by registration in the UK.[2]

1 Of the Implementing Regulation.
2 TMA 1994, s. 49 and Sch 1, discussed in ch 10.

Definition of a Community collective mark

30.2 In general, as provided by art 64.3, Community collective marks are subject to the provisions of the Regulation in the same way as ordinary CTMs, unless arts 65–72 provide otherwise. Article 64(1) states that a Community collective mark shall be a Community trade mark which is described as such when the mark is applied for and is capable of distinguishing the goods or services of the members of the association which is the proprietor of the mark from those of other undertakings. The similarity to the wording at the end of art 4 will be noted. The kinds of signs which may be Community collective marks are the same as those described in art 4.

30.3 Article 64.1 continues with a definition of the kinds or organisations which may apply for Community collective marks. They are associations of manufacturers, producers, suppliers of services, or traders which, under the terms of the law governing them, have the capacity in their own name to have rights and obligations of all kinds, to make contracts or accomplish other legal acts and to sue and be sued, as well as legal persons governed by public law. Thus the proprietor of a Community collective may either be an 'association' of the kind indicated, or a 'legal person' governed by public law, such as a specially-constituted public corporation. It is to be noted that there is no separate provision in the Regulation for certification or guarantee marks. However in some cases at least, what would be registered as certification marks in the UK[1] may well be capable of protection under the Regulation as Community collective marks.

1 TMA 1994, s 50 and Sch. 2, discussed in ch 10.

Absolute grounds for refusal

30.4   Article 64.2 makes a special provision for Community collective marks in respect of one of the absolute grounds for refusal of registration under art 7 of the Regulation, which otherwise apply generally by virtue of art 64.3. In derogation from art 7.1(c), signs or indications which may serve, in trade, to designate the geographical origin of the goods or services may constitute Community collective marks. The wording here is perhaps slightly misleading. It is not of course the case that such signs and indications can never constitute ordinary CTMs under the Regulation; the difficulty is in establishing registrability. Although some objections to registration of geographical names may be very hard to overcome, art 7.3 provides that such an objection shall not apply where the trade mark has become distinctive, in relation to the goods or services for which registration is requested, in consequence of the use which has been made of it. The effect of art 64.2 is that an applicant for a Community collective mark does not have to overcome this hurdle. However safeguards are provided for third parties. The proprietor of a Community collective mark is not entitled to prohibit a third party from using such geographical signs or indications in the course of trade, provided he uses them in accordance with honest practices in industrial or commercial matters; in particular, art 64.2 continues, 'a Community collective mark may not be invoked against a third party who is entitled to use a geographical name'. There is a very similar provision in Sch 1 to the TMA 1994.[1] No guidance is given as to when anyone might be 'entitled' to use a geographical name. No doubt persons carrying on business in a particular area might be regarded as entitled to use the name. Indeed, art 65.2 compels the association making the application to provide, in the regulations filed at the Office, that anyone may join the association if his goods or services originate in the area concerned.[2] The overriding requirement is that of honest practices. The provision would probably not permit use of the name as a trade mark other than as a certification mark in accordance with the regulations.

1 Paragraph **3**. See ch 10, para **10.12**.
2 See paragraph **30.6** below.

Regulations governing use of the mark

30.5   As with collective marks under the TMA 1994, regulations governing the use of a Community collective mark must be filed. An applicant is required, by art 65(1) of the Regulation, to submit regulations governing the use of the Community collective mark, within the period prescribed. Under r 43(1), if the regulations are not contained in the application for registration of the Community collective mark, they must be submitted to the Office within a period of two months after the date of filing. It appears that this period is extendable under r 71 since r 71(1) applies only where 'the Regulation or these Rules provide for a period to be specified by the Office'.[1]

1 See ch 28, paras **28.2–28.3**.

30.6   Under art 65(2) the regulations governing use must specify the persons authorised to use the mark, the conditions of membership of the association and, where they exist, the conditions of use of the mark including sanctions. In the case of a mark referred to in art 64(2), ie a geographical sign or indication, the regulations must authorise any person whose goods or services originate in the geographical area concerned to become a member of the association which is the proprietor of the mark. Rule 43(2) sets out further matters which must be specified in the regulations governing Community collective marks. In addition to the matters expressly covered in art 65.2 of the Regulation, which are repeated in r 43(2)(d)–(f), paras (a)–(c) require the regulations to specify the name of the applicant and his Office address, the object of the association or the object for which the legal person governed by public law is constituted, and the bodies authorised to represent the association or legal person.

Refusal of the application

30.7 Article 66 of the Regulation provides for further grounds for refusal of a Community collective mark, in addition to those on which an application for a CTM may be refused under arts 36 and 38. These are that the provisions of arts 64 and 65 are not satisfied, and a further general ground, that the regulations governing use are contrary to public policy or to accepted principles or morality. It is to be noted that this last objection echoes the words of the absolute ground for refusal set out in art 7.1(f). Presumably the intention is to apply the same rules to the regulations governing use of Community collective marks. Article 66(2) provides for yet another ground for refusal, that the public is liable to be confused as regards the character or the significance of the mark, in particular if it is likely to be taken to be something other than a collective mark. It may be noted that, under the TMA 1994 [1] such an objection may be met by requiring the mark to include an indication that it is a collective mark. This does not appear to be possible under the CTM Regulation, since such an alteration of the mark would not be within art 44(2). However under art 66(3), objections under paras 1 and 2 may be met by appropriate amendments to the regulations governing use, and an objection under art 66(2) might perhaps be met by an amendment to the regulations so as to require authorised users of the mark to include an indication that the mark is a collective mark. This would not involve altering the mark itself as registered. Article 67 extends the possibilities, for observations by third parties under art 41, regarding absolute grounds for refusal, to observations based on the particular grounds referred to in art 66.

1 TMA1994, Sch 1, paras 4(1) and (2).

Use of Community collective marks

30.8 In view of the special nature of a Community collective mark, provision is necessary as to what is regarded as use of the mark. Under art 68 the general conditions imposed by the Regulation, as to use of a CTM, apply; subject to these, use of the mark by any person who has authority to use it will satisfy the requirements of the Regulation.

Amendment of the regulations governing use of the mark

30.9 Article 69(1), read with art 69(4), makes it clear that any amended regulations, governing the use of a Community collective mark, must be submitted to the Office, and may not take effect before they have been mentioned in the register. Article 69(2) requires the amended regulations to satisfy the requirements of art 65 (and by implication, r 43(2)), and not to involve one of the grounds of refusal under art 66, before they can be mentioned in the register. Under art 69(3) observations may be made by third parties, in accordance with art 67, in respect of the amended regulations.

Persons who are entitled to bring an action for infringement

30.10   As to be expected, special provisions are required as to who may take action to prevent infringement of a Community collective mark. These are found in art 70 of the Regulation. Any person, who has authority to use a Community collective mark is placed in the same position as a licensee of a CTM. Article 70.1 refers back to art 22(3) and 22(4) of the Regulation.[1] Under art 22.3 a licensee may bring proceedings for infringement only if the proprietor consents, although this is without prejudice to the provisions of the licensing contract. For these purposes the regulations governing the use of a Community collective mark are presumably the 'licensing contract', which may include consent for the licensee to bring infringement proceeding, or preclude him from doing so. Although art 22.3 also allows an exclusive licensee to bring proceedings if the proprietor, after formal notice, does not himself bring infringement proceedings within an appropriate period, this does not seem to have any practical significance for collective marks. In accordance with art 22(4) an authorised user of a Community collective mark will be entitled to intervene in proceedings brought by the proprietor, for the purpose of claiming compensation for damage suffered. Under art 70(2), the proprietor of a Community collective mark may claim compensation on behalf of persons who have authority to use the mark, where they have sustained damage through unauthorised use of the mark. Presumably this provision extends to infringements generally, even if the infringing mark is not identical to the Community collective mark.

1 See ch 24, paras **24.57–24.58**.

Grounds for revocation

30.11   Article 71 of the Regulation adds further grounds for revocation of a Community collective mark, in addition to those available for revocation of a CTM under art 50. The first ground is that the proprietor does not take reasonable steps to prevent the mark being used in a manner incompatible with the conditions of use, where these exist, laid down in the regulations governing use (including any amendments mentioned in the register). A Community collective mark may be revoked under art 71(b) if the manner in which it has been used by the proprietor has caused it to become liable to mislead the public as to the character or significance of the mark, contrary to art 66(2). The third ground, under art 71(c), is that an amendment to the regulations governing use has been mentioned in the register in breach of art 69(2), ie if the amended regulations do not satisfy art 65 or involve one of the grounds for refusal under art 66, unless the proprietor complies with art 69(2) by further amendments.

Grounds for invalidity

30.12   Similarly, art 72 adds a further ground for invalidity, to those available under art 51 and 52. This ground is that the Community collective mark was registered in breach of art 66, unless the proprietor complies with the requirements of those provisions by amending the regulations governing use.

Chapter 31

Proceedings for infringement

General

31.1   Title X of the CTM Regulation, comprising arts 90–104, is concerned with 'Jurisdiction and Procedure in Legal Actions relating to CTMs'. These provisions cover all aspects of enforcement of CTMs, including jurisdiction over validity as well as infringement. Also indicated in this chapter is the question of overlapping actions based on national trade marks, covered by art 105 in Title XI ('Effects on the Laws of Member States').

The Convention on jurisdiction and enforcement

31.2   Article 90 of the Regulation relates to the application of the Convention on jurisdiction and the enforcement of judgments in civil and commercial matters, signed at Brussels on 27 September 1968, as amended by the Conventions on the accession to that Convention of the states acceding to the European Communities, together referred to in the Regulation as the 'Convention on Jurisdiction and Enforcement', and referred to in this chapter as the 'Brussels Convention'. Unless otherwise specified in the Regulation, the Brussels Convention is applied to proceedings relating to CTMs and applications for CTMs, as well as to proceedings relating to simultaneous and successive actions on the basis of CTMs and national trade marks. Article 90.2 deals specifically with actions and claims relating to CTMs, as referred to in art 92, ie actions for infringement and for declarations of non-infringement, actions under art 9.3 relating to compensation for infringing acts committed after publication and before registration, and counterclaims for revocation or for a declaration of invalidity pursuant to art 96. Article 90.2(a) excludes the application of arts 2, 4, 5(1), 5(3)–(5) and 24 of the Brussels Convention. Articles 17 and 18 of the Convention are applied by paragraph (b), subject to the limitations in art 93.4 of the Regulation. Under para (c) the provisions of Title II of the Brussels Convention which are applicable to persons domiciled in a Member State are also applicable to persons who do not have a domicile in any Member State but have an establishment therein.

Disputes concerning the infringement and validity of CTMs

31.3   Section 2 of Title X (arts 91–101) govern infringement disputes and (despite the title of the section) disputes regarding revocation as well as the validity of

611

CTMs. For this purpose art 91 requires the establishment of CTM courts, of first and second instance, in all the Member States. The deadline, under art 91.2, for Member States to communicate to the Commission a list of such courts, indicating their names and territorial jurisdiction, was three years from the entry into force of the Regulation, ie by 14 March1997. The UK has designated as the CTM courts in England and Wales and Northern Ireland, the High Court and in Scotland the Court of Session.[1] It is understood that Germany and Sweden have also designated their CTM courts. Under para (3) subsequent changes of the list, in the number, names or territorial jurisdiction of the courts must be notified to the Commission without delay. Paragraph (4) provides for the information relating to CTM courts to be published in the Official Journal of the European Communities. In default of designation of CTM courts in any Member State, para (5) provides that jurisdiction for any proceedings covered by art 92 and for which the courts of such State have jurisdiction under art 93, shall lie with that court of the State in question which would have jurisdiction ratione loci and rationae materiae in the case of proceedings relating to a national trade mark registered in that state.

1 See the CTM Regulations 1996 (SI 1996 1908), which came into force on 14 August 1996.

31.4 Under art 92 the CTM courts have exclusive jurisdiction in respect of all the proceedings listed. In addition to actions for infringement of CTMs, there are included actions in respect of threatened infringement and for declaration on non-infringement, if they are permitted under national law.[1] Also included, as already mentioned, are actions brought as a result of acts referred to in the second sentence of art 9.3, under which compensation is recoverable for acts committed between publication of a CTM application and registration, and counterclaims for revocation or for a declaration of invalidity of a CTM pursuant to art 96.

1 Both such actions are permitted under the TMA 1994. Regulation 4 of the CTM Regulations applies TMA 1994, s 21 to CTMs and declarations of non-infringement fall within the normal jurisdiction of the courts.

The forum for the proceedings

31.5 Article 93 lays down detailed rules for determining the Member States whose courts are to have jurisdiction in respect of the proceedings referred to in art 92. With the exception of an action for a declaration of non-infringement, by virtue of art 93.5 any proceedings in respect of actions or claims referred to in art 92 may be brought in the courts of the Member State in which the act of infringement has been committed or threatened, or in which an act complained of within art 9(3) (second sentence) has been committed. This does not of course apply to revocation or declarations of invalidity, where there is no 'act' on which to found the proceedings; here the only proceeding in a court is by way of counterclaim. As will be seen, the court's jurisdiction in cases in which it is invoked under art 93(5) is limited. If a claimant wishes to obtain an order from the court which has effect in all Member States, then he must follow the rules laid down by art 93(1)–(4).

31.6 Under para (1), subject to the provisions of the Regulation and to applicable provisions of the Brussels Convention, proceedings in respect of the actions and claims referred to in art 92 are to be brought in the courts of the Member State in which the defendant is domiciled or, if he is not domiciled in any of the Member States, in which he has an establishment. Therefore if the defendant is domiciled within the EU, the proceedings should be brought in the courts of the Member State of his domicile, and it matters not that he has an establishment in another Member State. Within the UK, the domicile may be in England and Wales, in Scotland or in Northern Ireland. If the defendant is domiciled outside the EU, then it is necessary to consider whether he has an establishment in any Member State. For these purposes 'establishment' must mean a place at or from which a business is carried on. It does not appear to be necessary that the acts complained of should be committed or threatened there. Whether a proposed defendant has an establishment in a particular place is a question of fact, and it is possible that he may have more than one establishment within the EU, perhaps in different Member States. To this extent a claimant may have a choice of forum.

31.7 Where the defendant is not domiciled within the EU and has no establishment in any Member State, art 93.2 provides that if the claimant is domiciled in a Member State, the proceedings are to be brought in the courts of that Member State. If he is domiciled outside the EU, then if he has an establishment in a Member State the proceedings should be brought in the courts of that Member State. Here again there may be a choice if the claimant has more than one establishment within the EU.

31.8 Article 93.3 covers cases where neither the defendant nor the claimant is domiciled, or has any establishment, in any Member State. In such cases the proceedings should be brought in the Spanish courts, since the seat of the Office is in Spain.

31.9 Article 93(4) provides for exceptions to the general rules laid down by paras (1)–(3). These are (a) that art 17 of the Brussels Convention shall apply if the parties agree that a different CTM court shall have jurisdiction and (b) that art 18 of that Convention shall apply if the defendant enters an appearance before a different CTM court. Article 17 applies where the parties, one or more of whom is domiciled in a Contracting State, have agreed that a court or the courts of a Contracting State are to have jurisdiction to settle any disputes which have arisen or which may arise in connection with a particular legal relationship. This is unlikely to arise in a normal infringement proceeding, but could arise, for example, under an agreement entered into for the purpose of settling a dispute. So far as entering an appearance is concerned, under the new Civil Procedure Rules of the courts this is not necessary in all cases.[1] It is possible that taking some other step, such as serving a defence, will be treated as having the same effect. Article 18 does not apply[2] where appearance was entered solely to contest the jurisdiction.[3]

1 See Parts 8 and 10 of the CPR 1998.
2 Neither does it apply where another court has exclusive jurisdiction by virtue of art 16, although this has no importance in the case of a CTM.
3 Under Part 11 of the CPR 1998.

31.10 Article 102 of the Regulation contains supplementary provisions on the jurisdiction of national courts, other than CTM courts, in respect of actions other than those referred to in art 92. Under para (1) jurisdiction in respect of such actions is given to the courts of a Member State having jurisdiction under art 90.1, ie in accordance with the applicable provisions of the Brussels Convention, which would have jurisdiction ratione loci and ratione materiae in the case of actions relating to a national trade mark registered in that State. Paragraph (2) provides that where no court has jurisdiction over such actions under art 90(1), jurisdiction is given to the Spanish courts, where the seat of the Office is located.

Extent of jurisdiction

31.11   Under art 94.1, where the jurisdiction of a CTM court is based on any of the provisions of art 93(1)–(4), the court has jurisdiction in respect of acts of infringement committed or threatened, and all acts within art 9(3) (second sentence) committed, within the territory of any of the Member States. This appears to confer jurisdiction to grant the appropriate remedies, including injunctions and damages, which are available in the jurisdiction, in respect of all such acts in any Member State. Remedies are the subject of arts 98 and 99, which are considered below. In a case in which the jurisdiction of the court is based on art 93(5), there is jurisdiction only in respect of acts committed or threatened within the territory of the Member State in which the court is situated.

Validity of the CTM

31.12   Article 95.1 provides that the CTM courts shall treat the CTM as valid unless its validity is put in issue by the defendant with a counterclaim for revocation or for a declaration of invalidity. Clearly in this part of the Regulation the word 'validity' is used in a broader sense, to cover validity against an attack by way of application for revocation, as well as by an application for a declaration of invalidity. Article 95.1 notwithstanding, under para (3), in an action for infringement or threats, or for compensation under art 9.3, a plea relating to revocation or invalidity submitted otherwise than by way of counterclaim is admissible in so far as the defendant claims that the rights of the CTM proprietor could be revoked for lack of use or that the CTM could be declared invalid on account of an earlier right of the defendant. Usually, however, it would be preferable for the defendant to submit the plea by way of a counterclaim, particularly if non-use was relied upon and there was a risk that the CTM proprietor might commence or re-commence use of his mark. Article 95.2 provides that the validity of a CTM may not be put in issue in an action for a declaration of non-infringement. The position would be the same in the UK – a claimant seeking a declaration of non-infringement would have to make a specific claim for revocation or a declaration of invalidity if he wished to put validity in issue.

Counterclaims

31.13   Under art 96.1 a counterclaim for revocation or for a declaration of invalidity may only be based on the grounds mentioned in the Regulation. In order to prevent unsuccessful attacks on a CTM from being raised again, art 96(2) provides that a CTM court shall reject a counterclaim if a decision of the Office relating to the same subject matter and cause of action and involving the same parties has already become final. This would probably not prevent a fresh application for revocation, on the ground of non-use, since it can be argued that a new five-year period commences every day. This might be important, for example, where an earlier application had been rejected because the period of non-use proved was less than five years.

31.14   Since infringement proceedings may, under art 22, be brought by a licensee, art 96.3 provides that if the counterclaim is brought in a legal action to which the proprietor of the trade mark is not a party, the proprietor shall be informed of the counterclaim and may be joined as a party to the action in accordance with the conditions set out in national law. In the UK, such conditions might include those applied by ss 30 and 31 of the TMA 1994, under which a proprietor is normally required to be joined as a party, either as claimant or defendant; also included will be the relevant provisions of the CPR 1998. Under Article 96(4) the Office must be informed of the date on which any counterclaim, for revocation or for a declaration of invalidity of a CTM, was filed, and the Office must record the fact in the CTM register. Neither paragraph (3) nor (4) says who is to inform the proprietor or the Office, as the case may be. Presumably this is the obligation of the party filing the counterclaim, unless the national procedural rules provide otherwise.

31.15 Article 96.5 provides that 'Article 56(3), (4), (5) and (6) shall apply'. The effect of this is not entirely clear. Those provisions are concerned with examination by OHIM of applications for revocation or a declaration of invalidity,[1] including requests by proprietors for proof of use of earlier marks relied upon in an application for a declaration of invalidity. Apart from the requirements, of para (5) as to partial cancellation and para (6), to enter a decision to revoke a CTM or to declare it invalid in the register upon becoming final, which is repeated in effect by art 96.6[2], they do not seem obviously applicable to a counterclaim made and proceeding in a national court. Perhaps under paragraph (4) OHIM can invite the parties to make a friendly settlement even if the counterclaim is being dealt with in the Community Trade Mark court.

1 See ch 27, paras **27.46–27.48**.
2 Under r 84(3)(r) and (m) respectively of the Implementing Regulation, the date of submission of an application under art 55 of the CTM Regulation or the filing of a counterclaim pursuant to art 96 4), and the date and content of a decision on the application or counterclaim pursuant to artcle 56(6) or art 96(6) of the CTM Regulation, must be entered in the register.

31.16 Article 96.7 introduces an important procedural possibility where a counterclaim for revocation or for a declaration of invalidity of a CTM is before a CTM court. On application by the proprietor of the CTM–not, it should be noted, the defendant or a licensee who is a claimant, the court may stay the proceedings, and after hearing the other parties may request the defendant to submit an application for revocation or for a declaration of invalidity to the Office within a time limit which the court shall determine. If such application is not made within the time limit, the proceedings continue and the counterclaim is to be deemed withdrawn. Article 100(3) is applied, so that in the event that the court does stay the proceedings it may order provisional and protective measures for the duration of the stay; the courts in the UK can probably order such measures under their own rules. It is likely that a CTM proprietor will only seek to invoke the court's powers under art 96(7) if it feels that the national court may be more likely to revoke the CTM or declare it invalid than would the Office. Clearly the court has a discretion in the matter, and in many cases may well feel that the issues are closely related to the issue of infringement and that it is able to determine the counterclaim itself.

Applicable law

31.17 Article 97(1) requires the CTM courts to apply the provisions of the Regulation, which of course has direct effect in Member States in any event. Under art 97(2), on all matters not covered by the Regulation, a CTM court must apply its national law, including its private international law. For example, if any questions arise under a contract, such as a licence, which is not covered in the Regulation, or under the law of trusts on a question of ownership of a CTM, an English court would apply the relevant English law. Procedural matters are dealt with by art 97(3); unless otherwise provided in the Regulation, a CTM court is required to apply the same rules of procedure governing the same type of action relating to a national trade in the Member State of the court concerned. Thus, before an English court, the section of Part 49 of the CPR 1998 relating to trade marks, and any other applicable provisions of those Rules, will be applied to actions and claims relating to CTMs.

Sanctions, and provisional and protective measures

31.18 Article 98.1, which above all demonstrates the real advantage obtained by registering a trade mark as a CTM, provides that where a CTM court finds that the defendant has infringed or threatened to infringe a CTM, it shall, unless there are special reasons for not doing so, issue an order prohibiting the defendant from proceeding with the acts which infringed or would infringe the CTM, and shall also take such measures in accordance with its national law as are aimed at ensuring that this prohibition is complied with. This requires the court, in the absence of special reasons, to grant an injunction prohibiting the defendant from using the infringing mark for the goods or services in question, in any Member State. Although not specified, the terms of arts 94 and 99(2) indicate that EU wide injunction is not required, or appropriate, where jurisdiction is based on the locality of the act complained of. The other measures for ensuring that the prohibition is complied with would include not only contempt proceedings in cases of breach of an order, but also ancillary orders such as orders for erasure of infringing marks and for delivery up. Under art 98.2, in all other respects–which covers damages and profits, and some ancillary orders–the CTM court is to apply the law of the Member State to which the acts of infringement or threatened infringement were committed, including the private international law. It is not clear how this provision will be applied as regards pecuniary remedies in respect of infringements in other Member States, but local rules of private international laws would probably enable the CTM court to assess and award damages or profits on all infringements within the EU.

31.19 Article 99 concerns 'provisional and protective measures'. These are not defined, but it is clear from the words used that 'protective' measures are one instance of 'preliminary' measures. Such measures will include interlocutory injunctions and other orders, formerly called 'Anton Piller' and 'Mareva' orders, for searching for and seizing infringing materials and preservation of assets. Article 99(1) provides that application may be made to the courts of a Member State, including CTM courts, for such provisional, including protective, measures in respect of a CTM or CTM application as may be available under the law of that state in respect of a national trade mark, even if, under the Regulation, a CTM court of another Member State has jurisdiction as to the substance of the matter. It is important to note the reference to a 'CTM application'. The effect of this is that, in spite of the fact that art 9(3) does not expressly provide for any infringement claim being made prior to publication of an application, a claim can be brought, and an application for provisional measures made under art 99(1), at any time from the application date, provided that the national court concerned could entertain such an application in respect of a national mark. Under art 99(1), a court whose jurisdiction is invoked under art 93(5) may grant such measures, even if proceedings are pending before another CTM court which has jurisdiction under art 93(1)–(4). However, in accordance with art 99(2), a court having jurisdiction only under art 93(5) cannot grant provisional or protective measures which have effect outside its own Member State. In the case of courts having jurisdiction under the other provisions of art 93, the measures may, subject to any necessary procedure for recognition and enforcement pursuant to Title III of the Brussels Convention, be applicable throughout the EU.

31.20 Enforcement of orders outside the territorial jurisdiction of the court hearing the case is not the subject of any provision of the Regulation. So far as enforcement in the UK of judgments of other Member States is concerned, this is dealt with under the Brussels Convention. As regards orders for payment of costs, costs awarded by OHIM are covered by the European Communities (Enforcement of Community Judgments) (Amendment) Order 1998,[1] amending the European Communities (Enforcement of Community Judgments) Order 1972.[2] The 1998 Order came into force on 22 June 1998. The 1972 Order provided for the registration and enforcement in the UK of certain decisions, judgments and orders of Community institutions. The 1998 Order extends the provisions to awards of costs made by OHIM.

1 SI 1998/1259.
2 SI 1972/1590.

Further appeals

31.21 Article 101(1) provides that an appeal to the CTM courts of second instance shall lie from judgments of the CTM courts of first instance in respect of proceedings arising from the actions and claims referred to in art 92. However an appeal does not necessarily lie as of right. Under para (2) the conditions under which an appeal may be lodged with a CTM court of second instance are to be determined by the national law of the Member States in which that court is located. In England and Wales, for example, in almost all cases it will be necessary to obtain the permission of the court of first instance, or the Court of Appeal, before an appeal can be lodged. Similar observations apply to further appeals from the Court of Appeal to the House of Lords. Paragraph (3) applies the national rules to such further appeals.

Related actions

31.22 The Regulation contains several provisions which are intended to avoid duplication of validity proceedings between different Member States or between Member States and OHIM, and of infringement proceedings between the same parties based on the same trade marks.

31.23 Article 100(1) requires a CTM court hearing an action referred to in art 92, other than an action for a declaration of non-infringement, of its own motion after hearing the parties or at the request of one of the parties and after hearing the other parties, and unless there are special grounds for continuing the hearing, to stay the proceedings where the validity of the CTM is in issue before another CTM court on account of a counterclaim or where an application for revocation or for a declaration of invalidity has already been filed at the Office. If the court does stay the proceedings, art 100(3) empowers it to order provisional and protective measures for the duration of the stay.

31.24 The question whether there are special grounds for continuing the 'hearing' —which in its context is not confined to the trial but must extend generally to proceeding with the matter—is essentially for the national court to determine. Prima facie it seems that there should be a stay in the circumstances described. A party should not, it is submitted, be able to proceed merely because there might be some advantage to him in having the matter determined by the court, as opposed to the earlier CTM court or the Office. The provision presupposes that the claimant may have brought proceedings for infringement of the CTM is more than one Member State, which could be possible where there is a choice of forum under art 93(1) or 2 or whether an action is brought under art 93(5) as well as under one of the other provisions. Generally speaking a claimant ought to be held to proceeding in the court in which he chose to proceed first.

31.25 Article 100(2) applies where the Office is seized of an application for revocation or for a declaration of invalidity and the validity of the CTM is already in issue in account of a counterclaim before a CTM court. The Office must, of its own motion after hearing the parties or at the request of one of the parties and after hearing the others, stay the proceedings unless there are special grounds for continuing the hearing. However if one of the parties to the court proceedings so requests the court may, after hearing the other parties, stay those proceedings. If this happens, the Office shall continue the proceedings before it. It is difficult to see what might be 'special reasons' for the Office continuing the hearing. It most instances it should be for one of the parties to raise the matter before the CTM court. If the matter is one in which, had there been no proceedings pending before the Office, the court would have stayed the proceedings under art 96(7) and directed the defendant to make an application before the Office, then it would seem appropriate for the court to make an order for a stay under art 100(2). Again, if a stay is ordered by the court, it can grant provisional and protective measures under para (3).

31.26 Article 105 deals with some different situations, where there are or have been simultaneous or successive actions on the basis of CTMs and national trade marks. The precise effect of these provisions is unclear. They have presumably been included not only to avoid situations in which defendants may be put in 'double jeopardy' but also to encourage proprietors to use the CTM system in preference to the national systems. However laudable these aims, there are some grounds for believing that the provisions could produce an unjust result in some circumstances.

31.27 Article 105(1) applies where actions for infringement involving the same cause of action and between the same parties are brought in the courts of different Member States, one seized on the basis of a CTM and the other seized on the basis of a national trade mark. What is to happen depends upon whether the trade marks concerned, and the goods or services concerned, are identical or only similar. The provisions do not apply where the actions are both proceeding in the same Member State, although in such a situation art 105(2) or (3) could become applicable.

31.28 Where the trade marks concerned are identical and valid for identical goods or services, under para (1)(a) the court which is not the court first seized must of its own motion decline jurisdiction in favour of the court first seized, unless the jurisdiction of that court is contested, in which case the court may stay the proceedings. It would seem to follow that if the challenge to the jurisdiction of the court first seized is unsuccessful, then the second court will be required to decline jurisdiction; if it succeeds, then the stay would be removed and the action would proceed.

31.29 Where the trade marks concerned are identical and valid for similar goods or services, or where the trade marks concerned are similar and valid for identical or similar goods or services, then the second court is not obliged to decline jurisdiction in favour of the court first seized, but under para (1)(b) has a discretion to stay the proceedings.

31.30 Before commenting on these provisions, it is helpful to consider art 105(2) and (30, which cover cases which may overlap with there may be overlap with art 105910(a). Under para (2), where a court is hearing an action for infringement on the basis of a CTM, it must reject the action if a final judgment on the merits has been given on the same cause of action and between the same parties on the basis of an identical national trade mark valid for identical goods or services. Article (3) deals with the reverse situation, where the first action is based upon a CTM and the second action is based upon a national trade mark. If the final judgment in the first action was on the same cause of action and the trade marks are identical and valid for identical goods or services, then the second action must be rejected. It will be noted that these provisions apply whether the two actions are brought in the same Member State or in different Member States. They apply not only to cases in which the claimant succeeded in the first action, but to some cases in which the first action was dismissed. They apply where the first action was dismissed on the ground that the defendant's mark was not similar to the registered mark, or because there was no likelihood of confusion, or even where the defendant's goods or services were dissimilar to those covered by the registration and the requirements of art 9.1(c), as to reputation, etc, were not met. On the other hand they do not apply where the trade mark in the first action is held invalid, which might be important where the first action was founded on a CTM which was revoked or held invalid on grounds which did not apply in the Member State in which the subsequent action was brought for infringement of a national trade mark.

31.31 The last mentioned situation does not seem to cause any real problem in practice. Moreover it would seem reasonable that a claimant, who has already succeeded in a claim founded on a CTM where the judgment is effective throughout the Community, should not be free to bring a further action against the same party for infringement of an identical national trade mark registered for the same goods or services. On the other hand a proprietor of a national trade mark, who has obtained judgment against a defendant for infringement, appears to be prevented from proceeding against the same defendant in order to obtain a Community-wide injunction on the basis of a CTM, even if the CTM was not registered when the original judgment was obtained and possibly even if the defendant starts to use a different infringing mark, or to use the infringing mark for different goods or services which were not the subject of the earlier judgment. A source of some of the potential difficulties lies in the fact that the provisions focus on the claimant's trade mark and the goods or services for which it is registered, and ignore in particular the nature of the defendant's mark and his goods or services.

31.32 Similar comments may be made regarding art 105(1)(a). Some of the possibly unfair consequences may be avoided if the provision is interpreted as only applying where both actions are still pending, so that it is open to the claimant in an earlier national trade mark infringement action to discontinue the action in order to bring an action for infringement of a CTM. Article 105(1)(b) is likely to cause less difficulty because the court seized of the second action has a discretion as to whether to stay the proceedings. Attention should also be drawn to the provisions of art 105(4), under which paras 1, 2 and 3 do not apply in respect of provisional, including protective, measures. This might at first sight seem to mitigate the effects of those paragraphs. However it is difficult to see how any provisional measures can really assist if the court seized of the second action is required to decline jurisdiction, as art 105(1)(a) requires, or to reject the action, as required by art 105(2) and 3. The other way in which courts will have some possibility of avoiding unreasonable and, it is submitted, unintended results is by giving a strict interpretation to the terms 'same cause of action', 'same parties', and 'identical' as applied to a trade mark or to goods or services. Thus, for example, a parent of a group of companies holding a CTM would not be the 'same party' as a subsidiary which held a national trade mark that was the subject of an earlier action or judgment. And an action brought in respect of the use of a mark 'A' for goods or services 'X' might not be regarded as being 'on the same cause of action' as a later action brought in respect of the use of a different mark 'B' for goods or services 'X', or of mark 'A' for different goods or services 'Y'.

31.33 It is clear of course that the provisions of art 105 only apply to proceedings for infringement. They therefore do not apply where the earlier action was brought on the basis of other laws, such as passing off or unfair competition and do not have the effect of precluding a subsequent action against the same parties founded on such laws.

Contents

Appendix 1　　　　　**United Kingdom statutes**

The Trade Marks Act 1994　625
The Trade Marks Act 1938 (as amended): For 'goods' marks　687
　　　　　　　　　　　　　　　　　　　'service' marks　731
The Import, Export and Customs Powers (Defence) Act 1939, ss 3, 8 and 9　764
The Trading with the Enemy Act 1939, ss 2, 7, 15 and 17　766
The Trade Descriptions Act 1968, ss 1-6 , 24, 26-28, 33, 34, 39 and 43　769
The Customs and Excise Management Act 1979, ss 1 (in part), 40, 139-144 and
　　Sch 3　776
The Copyright, Designs and Patents Act 1988, ss 274-286 and 306　787
The Olympic Symbol etc (Protection) Act 1995　793

Appendix 2　　　　　**Secondary legislation**

The Patent Agents (Non recognition of certain agents by comptroller) Rules 1990,
　　SI 1990/1454　803
The Register of Trade Mark Agents Rules 1990, SI 1990/1458　804
The Registered Trade Mark Agents (Mixed Partnerships and Bodies Corporate)
　　Rules 1994, SI 1994/363　810
The Partnerships (Unrestricted Size) No 11 Regulations 1994, SI 1994/644　810
The Trade Marks Act 1994 (Commencement) Order 1994, SI 1994/2550　811
The Trade Marks Rules 1994 (as amended), SI 1994/2583　814
The Trade Marks (Customs) Regulations 1994, SI 1994/2625　841
The Trade Marks (Claims to Priority from Relevant Countries) Order 1994 (as
　　amended), SI 1994/2803　844
The Olympic Symbol etc (Protection) Act 1995 (Commencement) Order 1995,
　　SI 1995/2472　846
The Olympics Association Right (Appointment of Proprietor) Order 1995,
　　SI 1995/2473　846
The Community Trade Mark (Fees) Regulations 1995, SI 1995/3175　846
The Olympics Association Right (Infringement Proceedings) Regulations 1995,
　　SI 1995/3325　847

The Trade Marks (International Registration) Order 1996, SI 1996/714   849
The Trade Marks Act 1994 (Isle of Man) Order 1996, SI 1996/729   862
The Community Trade Mark Regulations 1996, SI 1996/1908   865
The Partnerships (Unrestricted Size) No 12 Regulations 1997, SI 1997/1937   867
The Trade Marks (Fees) Rules 1998, SI 1998/1776   867
The Goods Infringing Intellectual Property Rights (Customs) Regulations 1999,
    SI 1999/1601   870
The Goods Infringing Intellectual Property Rights (Consequential Provisions)
    Regulations 1999, SI 1999/1618   872
The Patents and Trade Marks (World Trade Organisation) Regulations 1999 (Pts I
    and IV and Explanatory Note), SI 1999/1899   875
The Patent Office (Address) (Revocation) Rules 1999, SI 1999/1993   877

Appendix 3   Rules of Court

Civil Procedure Rules, Pt 49   879
Civil Procedure Rules Practice Direction, Pt 49E 21.1 25.3   879

Appendix 4   International conventions

Relevant articles of the Paris Convention   895
Relevant provisions of GATT/TRIPS, articles 315-24 & 41-61   915

Appendix 5   European material

Treaty of Rome provisions (Including Articles 28-30, 81, 82, 94, 234 & 308)
    (re-numbered)   937
Provisions of EEA Agreement   939
The First Council Directive 89/104/EEC of 21 December 1988 to approximate
    the laws of the Member States relating to trade marks and Decision of
    19 December 1991 92/10/EEC   955
The Community Trade Mark Regulation (Council Regulation 40/94/EC
    (incorporating 1995 amendment)   964
Commission Regulation 2868/95/EC of 13 December 1995 implementing
    Council Regulation 40/94/EC on the Community Trade Mark   1014
Commission Regulation 216/96/EC of 5 February 1996 laying down the rules of
    procedure for the Boards of Appeal   1059
Decision EX-96-3 on evidence to be provided on claiming priority or seniority of
    Community Trade Mark applications   1063
The Guidelines for Opposition proceedings   1064
Council Regulation 3295/94/EC of 22 December 1994 laying down measures to
prohibit the release for free circulation, export, re-export or entry for a
suspensive procedure of counterfeit and pirated goods as amended by Council
Regulation 241/99/EC of 25 January 1999 amending Regulation
    3295/94/EC laying down measures to prohibit the release for free circulation,
    export, re-export or entry for a suspensive procedure of counterfeit and pirated
    goods   1095
Commission Regulation 1367/95/EC of 16 June 1995 laying down provisions for

the implementation of Council Regulation 3295/94/EC laying down measures
to prohibit the release for free circulation, export, re-export or entry for a
suspensive procedure of counterfeit and pirated goods   1105
Council Regulation 2081/92/EEC of 14 July 1992 on the protection of
geographical indications and designations of origin for agricultural products
and foodstuffs   1107

Appendix 6   International registration

The Madrid Agreement   1119
The Madrid Protocol   1121
The Common Regulations   1136

Appendix 7   Miscellaneous registry material

Trade Marks Registry Guide to the Cross Searching of Trade Marks in the UK
1189
The Trade Marks Forms   1201
The International Classification of Goods and Services   1254

Appendix 1

United Kingdom statutes

TRADE MARKS ACT 1994
(c 26)

General Note
As amended by the Olympic Symbol etc (Protection) Act 1995, the Criminal Procedure (Consequential Provisions) (Scotland) Act 1995, the Trade Marks (EC Measures Relating to Counterfeit Goods) Regulations 1995, SI 1995/1444, the Plant Varieties Act 1997, the Northern Ireland Act 1998, the Transfer of Functions (Lord Advocate and Secretary of State) Order 1999, SI 1999/678, and the Patents and Trade Marks (World Trade Organisation) Regulations 1999, SI 1999/1899.

ARRANGEMENT OF SECTIONS

PART I
REGISTERED TRADE MARKS

Introductory
1 Trade marks
2 Registered trade marks

Grounds for refusal of registration
3 Absolute grounds for refusal of registration
4 Specially protected emblems
5 Relative grounds for refusal of registration
6 Meaning of 'earlier trade mark'
7 Raising of relative grounds in case of honest concurrent use
8 Power to require that relative grounds be raised in opposition proceedings

Effects of registered trade mark
9 Rights conferred by registered trade mark
10 Infringement of registered trade mark
11 Limits on effect of registered trade mark
12 Exhaustion of rights conferred by registered trade mark
13 Registration subject to disclaimer or limitation

Infringement proceedings
14 Action for infringement
15 Order for erasure, &c of offending sign
16 Order for delivery up of infringing goods, material or articles
17 Meaning of 'infringing goods, material or articles'
18 Period after which remedy of delivery up not available
19 Order as to disposal of infringing goods, material or articles
20 Jurisdiction of sheriff court or county court in Northern Ireland
21 Remedy for groundless threats of infringement proceedings

Appendix 1

Registered trade mark as object of property
22 Nature of registered trade mark
23 Co-ownership of registered trade mark
24 Assignment, &c of registered trade mark
25 Registration of transactions affecting registered trade mark
26 Trusts and equities
27 Application for registration of trade mark as an object of property

Licensing
28 Licensing of registered trade mark
29 Exclusive licences
30 General provisions as to rights of licensees in case of infringement
31 Exclusive licensee having rights and remedies of assignee

Application for registered trade mark
32 Application for registration
33 Date of filing
34 Classification of trade marks

Priority
35 Claim to priority of Convention application
36 Claim to priority from other relevant overseas application

Registration procedure
37 Examination of application
38 Publication, opposition proceedings and observations
39 Withdrawal, restriction or amendment of application
40 Registration
41 Registration: supplementary provisions

Duration, renewal and alteration of registered trade mark
42 Duration of registration
43 Renewal of registration
44 Alteration of registered trade mark

Surrender, revocation and invalidity
45 Surrender of registered trade mark
46 Revocation of registration
47 Grounds for invalidity of registration
48 Effect of acquiescence

Collective marks
49 Collective marks

Certification marks
50 Certification marks

PART II
COMMUNITY TRADE MARKS AND INTERNATIONAL MATTERS

Community trade marks
51 Meaning of 'Community trade mark'
52 Power to make provision in connection with Community Trade Mark Regulation

The Madrid Protocol: international registration
53 The Madrid Protocol
54 Power to make provision giving effect to Madrid Protocol

The Paris Convention: supplementary provisions
55 The Paris Convention
56 Protection of well-known trade marks: Article 6*bis*
57 National emblems, &c of Convention countries: Article 6*ter*

58 Emblems, &c of certain international organisations: Article 6*ter*
59 Notification under Article 6*ter* of the Convention
60 Acts of agent or representative: Article 6*septies*

Miscellaneous
61 Stamp duty

PART III
ADMINISTRATIVE AND OTHER SUPPLEMENTARY PROVISIONS

The registrar
62 The registrar

The register
63 The register
64 Rectification or correction of the register
65 Adaptation of entries to new classification

Powers and duties of the registrar
66 Power to require use of forms
67 Information about applications and registered trade marks
68 Costs and security for costs
69 Evidence before registrar
70 Exclusion of liability in respect of official acts
71 Registrar's annual report

Legal proceedings and appeals
72 Registration to be prima facie evidence of validity
73 Certificate of validity of contested registration
74 Registrar's appearance in proceedings involving the register
75 The court
76 Appeals from the registrar
77 Persons appointed to hear and determine appeals

Rules, fees, hours of business, &c
78 Power of Secretary of State to make rules
79 Fees
80 Hours of business and business days
81 The trade marks journal

Trade mark agents, &c
82 Recognition of agents
83 The register of trade mark agents
84 Unregistered persons not to be described as registered trade mark agents
85 Power to prescribe conditions, &c for mixed partnerships and bodies corporate
86 Use of the term 'trade mark attorney'
87 Privilege for communications with registered trade mark agents
88 Power of registrar to refuse to deal with certain agents

Importation of infringing goods, material or articles
89 Infringing goods, material or articles may be treated as prohibited goods
90 Power of Commissioners of Customs and Excise to make regulations
91 Power of Commissioners of Customs and Excise to disclose information

Offences
92 Unauthorised use of trade mark, &c in relation to goods
93 Enforcement function of local weights and measures authority
94 Falsification of register, &c
95 Falsely representing trade mark as registered
96 Supplementary provisions as to summary proceedings in Scotland

Forfeiture of counterfeit goods, &c
97 Forfeiture: England and Wales or Northern Ireland

627

98 Forfeiture: Scotland

PART IV
MISCELLANEOUS AND GENERAL PROVISIONS

Miscellaneous
  99 Unauthorised use of Royal arms, &c
 100 Burden of proving use of trade mark
 101 Offences committed by partnerships and bodies corporate

Interpretation
 102 Adaptation of expressions for Scotland
 103 Minor definitions
 104 Index of defined expressions

Other general provisions
 105 Transitional provisions
 106 Consequential amendments and repeals
 107 Territorial waters and the continental shelf
 108 Extent
 109 Commencement
 110 Short title

SCHEDULES:
  Schedule 1–Collective marks
  Schedule 2–Certification marks
  Schedule 3–Transitional provisions
  Schedule 4–Consequential amendments
  Schedule 5–Repeals and revocations

An Act to make new provision for registered trade marks, implementing Council Directive No 89/104/EEC of 21st December 1988 to approximate the laws of the Member States relating to trade marks; to make provision in connection with Council Regulation (EC) No 40/94 of 20th December 1993 on the Community trade mark; to give effect to the Madrid Protocol Relating to the International Registration of Marks of 27th June 1989, and to certain provisions of the Paris Convention for the Protection of Industrial Property of 20th March 1883, as revised and amended; and for connected purposes

[21st July 1994]

BE IT ENACTED by the Queen's most Excellent Majesty, by and with the advice and consent of the Lords Spiritual and Temporal, and Commons, in this present Parliament assembled, and by the authority of the same, as follows–

PART I
REGISTERED TRADE MARKS

Introductory

1. Trade Marks
(1) In this Act a 'trade mark' means any sign capable of being represented graphically which is capable of distinguishing goods or services of one undertaking from those of other undertakings.

A trade mark may, in particular, consist of words (including personal names), designs, letters, numerals or the shape of goods or their packaging.
(2) References in this Act to a trade mark include, unless the context otherwise

requires, references to a collective mark (see section 49) or certification mark (see section 50).

2. Registered trade marks

(1) A registered trade mark is a property right obtained by the registration of the trade mark under this Act and the proprietor of a registered trade mark has the rights and remedies provided by this Act.

(2) No proceedings lie to prevent or recover damages for the infringement of an unregistered trade mark as such; but nothing in this Act affects the law relating to passing off.

Grounds for refusal of registration

3. Absolute grounds for refusal of registration

(1) The following shall not be registered—

    (a) signs which do not satisfy the requirements of section 1(1),

    (b) trade marks which are devoid of any distinctive character,

    (c) trade marks which consist exclusively of signs or indications which may serve, in trade, to designate the kind, quality, quantity, intended purpose, value, geographical origin, the time of production of goods or of rendering of services, or other characteristics of goods or services,

    (d) trade marks which consist exclusively of signs or indications which have become customary in the current language or in the bona fide and established practices of the trade:

Provided that, a trade mark shall not be refused registration by virtue of paragraph (b), (c) or (d) above if, before the date of application for registration, it has in fact acquired a distinctive character as a result of the use made of it.

(2) A sign shall not be registered as a trade mark if it consists exclusively of—

    (a) the shape which results from the nature of the goods themselves,

    (b) the shape of goods which is necessary to obtain a technical result, or

    (c) the shape which gives substantial value to the goods.

(3) A trade mark shall not be registered if it is—

    (a) contrary to public policy or to accepted principles of morality, or

    (b) of such a nature as to deceive the public (for instance as to the nature, quality or geographical origin of the goods or service).

(4) A trade mark shall not be registered if or to the extent that its use is prohibited in the United Kingdom by any enactment or rule of law or by any provision of Community law.

(5) A trade mark shall not be registered in the cases specified, or referred to, in section 4 (specially protected emblems).

(6) A trade mark shall not be registered if or to the extent that the application is made in bad faith.

4. Specially protected emblems

(1) A trade mark which consists of or contains—

    (a) the Royal arms, or any of the principal armorial bearings of the Royal arms, or any insignia or device so nearly resembling the Royal arms or any such armorial bearing as to be likely to be mistaken for them or it,

(b) a representation of the Royal crown or any of the Royal flags,

(c) a representation of Her Majesty or any member of the Royal family, or any colourable imitation thereof, or

(d) words, letters or devices likely to lead persons to think that the applicant either has or recently has had Royal patronage or authorisation,

shall not be registered unless it appears to the registrar that consent has been given by or on behalf of Her Majesty or, as the case may be, the relevant member of the Royal family.

(2) A trade mark which consists of or contains a representation of—

(a) the national flag of the United Kingdom (commonly known as the Union Jack), or

(b) the flag of England, Wales, Scotland, Northern Ireland or the Isle of Man,

shall not be registered if it appears to the registrar that the use of the trade mark would be misleading or grossly offensive.

Provision may be made by rules identifying the flags to which paragraph (b) applies.

(3) A trade mark shall not be registered in the cases specified in—

section 57 (national emblems, &c of Convention countries), or
section 58 (emblems, &c of certain international organisations).

(4) Provision may be made by rules prohibiting in such cases as may be prescribed the registration of a trade mark which consists of or contains—

(a) arms to which a person is entitled by virtue of a grant of arms by the Crown, or

(b) insignia so nearly resembling such arms as to be likely to be mistaken for them,

unless it appears to the registrar that consent has been given by or on behalf of that person.

Where such a mark is registered, nothing in this Act shall be construed as authorising its use in any way contrary to the laws of arms.

[(5) A trade mark which consists of or contains a controlled representation within the meaning of the Olympic Symbol etc (Protection) Act 1995 shall not be registered unless it appears to the registrar

(a) that the application is made by the person for the time being appointed under section 1(2) of the Olympic Symbol etc (Protection) Act 1995 (power of Secretary of State to appoint a person as the proprietor of the Olympics association right), or

(b) that consent has been given by or on behalf of the person mentioned in paragraph (a) above.]

General note
Sub-s (5) was inserted, in relation to applications for registration made on or after 20th September 1995, by the Olympic Symbol etc (Protection) Act 1995, s 13(2), (3).

Subordinate legislation
The Trade Marks Rules 1994, SI 1994/2583, as amended by SI 1998/925.

5. Relative grounds for refusal of registration

(1) A trade mark shall not be registered if it is identical with an earlier trade mark and the goods or services for which the trade mark is applied for are identical with the goods or services for which the earlier trade mark is protected.

(2) A trade mark shall not be registered if because—

(a) it is identical with an earlier trade mark and is to be registered for goods or services similar to those for which the earlier trade mark is protected, or

(b) it is similar to an earlier trade mark and is to be registered for goods or services identical with or similar to those for which the earlier trade mark is protected,

there exists a likelihood of confusion on the part of the public, which includes the likelihood of association with the earlier trade mark.

(3) A trade mark which—

(a) is identical with or similar to an earlier trade mark, and

(b) is to be registered for goods or services which are not similar to those for which the earlier trade mark is protected,

shall not be registered if, or to the extent that, the earlier trade mark has a reputation in the United Kingdom (or, in the case of a Community trade mark, in the European Community) and the use of the later mark without due cause would take unfair advantage of, or be detrimental to, the distinctive character or the repute of the earlier trade mark.

(4) A trade mark shall not be registered if, or to the extent that, its use in the United Kingdom is liable to be prevented—

(a) by virtue of any rule of law (in particular, the law of passing off) protecting an unregistered trade mark or other sign used in the course of trade, or

(b) by virtue of an earlier right other than those referred to in subsections (1) to (3) or paragraph (a) above, in particular by virtue of the law of copyright, design right or registered designs.

A person thus entitled to prevent the use of a trade mark is referred to in this Act as the proprietor of an 'earlier right' in relation to the trade mark.

(5) Nothing in this section prevents the registration of a trade mark where the proprietor of the earlier trade mark or other earlier right consents to the registration.

6. Meaning of 'earlier trade mark'

(1) In this Act an 'earlier trade mark' means–

(a) a registered trade mark, international trade mark (UK) or Community trade mark which has a date of application for registration earlier than that of the trade mark in question, taking account (where appropriate) of the priorities claimed in respect of the trade marks,

(b) a Community trade mark which has a valid claim to seniority from an earlier registered trade mark or international trade mark (UK), or

(c) a trade mark which, at the date of application for registration of the trade mark in question or (where appropriate) of the priority claimed in respect of the application, was entitled to protection under the Paris Convention [or the WTO agreement] as a well known trade mark.

(2) References in this Act to an earlier trade mark include a trade mark in respect of which an application for registration has been made and which, if registered,

would be an earlier trade mark by virtue of subsection 1(a) or (b), subject to its being so registered.

(3) A trade mark within subsection (1)(a) or (b) whose registration expires shall continue to be taken into account in determining the registrability of a later mark for a period of one year after the expiry unless the registrar is satisfied that there was no *bona fide* use of the mark during the two years immediately preceding the expiry.

General note
In sub-s (1), the words in square brackets in para (c) were inserted by the Patents and Trade Marks (World Trade Organisation) Regulations 1999, SI 1999/1899, reg 13(1).

7. Raising of relative grounds in case of honest concurrent use

(1) This section applies where on an application for the registration of a trade mark it appears to the registrar—

   (a) that there is an earlier trade mark in relation to which the conditions set out in section 5(1), (2) or (3) obtain, or
   (b) that there is an earlier right in relation to which the condition set out in section 5(4) is satisfied,

but the applicant shows to the satisfaction of the registrar that there has been honest concurrent use of the trade mark for which registration is sought.

(2) In that case the registrar shall not refuse the application by reason of the earlier trade mark or other earlier right unless objection on that ground is raised in opposition proceedings by the proprietor of that earlier trade mark or other earlier right.

(3) For the purposes of this section 'honest concurrent use' means such use in the United Kingdom, by the applicant or with his consent, as would formerly have amounted to honest concurrent use for the purposes of section 12(2) of the Trade Marks Act 1938.

(4) Nothing in this section affects—

   (a) the refusal of registration on the grounds mentioned in section 3 (absolute grounds for refusal), or
   (b) the making of an application for a declaration of invalidity under section 47(2) (application on relative grounds where no consent to registration).

(5) This section does not apply when there is an order in force under section 8 below.

8. Power to require that relative grounds be raised in opposition proceedings

(1) The Secretary of State may by order provide that in any case a trade mark shall not be refused registration on a ground mentioned in section 5 (relative grounds for refusal) unless objection on that ground is raised in opposition proceedings by the proprietor of the earlier trade mark or other earlier right.

(2) The order may make such consequential provision as appears to the Secretary of State appropriate—

   (a) with respect to the carrying out by the registrar of searches of earlier trade marks, and
   (b) as to the persons by whom an application for a declaration of invalidity may be made on the grounds specified in section 47(2) (relative grounds).

(3) An order making such provision as is mentioned in subsection (2)(a) may direct that so much of section 37 (examination of application) as requires a search to be carried out shall cease to have effect.

(4) An order making such provision as is mentioned in subsection (2)(b) may provide that so much of section 47(3) as provides that any person may make an application for a declaration of invalidity shall have effect subject to the provisions of the order.

(5) An order under this section shall be made by statutory instrument, and no order shall be made unless a draft of it has been laid before and approved by a resolution of each House of Parliament.

No such draft of an order making such provision as is mentioned in subsection (1) shall be laid before Parliament until after the end of the period of ten years beginning with the day on which applications for Community trade marks may first be filed in pursuance of the Community Trade Mark Regulation.

(6) An order under this section may contain such transitional provisions as appear to the Secretary of State to be appropriate.

Effects of registered trade mark

9. Rights conferred by registered trade mark

(1) The proprietor of a registered trade mark has exclusive rights in the trade mark which are infringed by use of the trade mark in the United Kingdom without his consent.

The acts amounting to infringement, if done without the consent of the proprietor, are specified in section 10.

(2) References in this Act to the infringement of a registered trade mark are to any such infringement of the rights of the proprietor.

(3) The rights of the proprietor have effect from the date of registration (which in accordance with section 40(3) is the date of filing of the application for registration):

Provided that—

   (a) no infringement proceedings may be begun before the date on which the trade mark is in fact registered; and
   (b) no offence under section 92 (unauthorised use of trade mark, &c in relation to goods) is committed by anything done before the date of publication of the registration.

10. Infringement of registered trade mark

(1) A person infringes a registered trade mark if he uses in the course of trade a sign which is identical with the trade mark in relation to goods or services which are identical with those for which it is registered.

(2) A person infringes a registered trade mark if he uses in the course of trade a sign where because—

   (a) the sign is identical with the trade mark and is used in relation to goods or services similar to those for which the trade mark is registered, or
   (b) the sign is similar to the trade mark and is used in relation to goods or services identical with or similar to those for which the trade mark is registered,

there exists a likelihood of confusion on the part of the public, which includes the likelihood of association with the trade mark.

(3) A person infringes a registered trade mark if he uses in the course of trade a sign which—

(a) is identical with or similar to the trade mark, and

(b) is used in relation to goods or services which are not similar to those for which the trade mark is registered,

where the trade mark has a reputation in the United Kingdom and the use of the sign, being without due cause, takes unfair advantage of, or is detrimental to, the distinctive character or the repute of the trade mark.

(4) For the purposes of this section a person uses a sign if, in particular, he—

(a) affixes it to goods or the packaging thereof;

(b) offers or exposes goods for sale, puts them on the market or stocks them for those purposes under the sign, or offers or supplies services under the sign;

(c) imports or exports goods under the sign; or

(d) uses the sign on business papers or in advertising.

(5) A person who applies a registered trade mark to material intended to be used for labelling or packaging goods, as a business paper, or for advertising goods or services, shall be treated as a party to any use of the material which infringes the registered trade mark if when he applied the mark he knew or had reason to believe that the application of the mark was not duly authorised by the proprietor or a licensee.

(6) Nothing in the preceding provisions of this section shall be construed as preventing the use of a registered trade mark by any person for the purpose of identifying goods or services as those of the proprietor or a licensee.

But any such use otherwise than in accordance with honest practices in industrial or commercial matters shall be treated as infringing the registered trade mark if the use without due cause takes unfair advantage of, or is detrimental to, the distinctive character or repute of the trade mark.

11. Limits on effect of registered trade mark

(1) A registered trade mark is not infringed by the use of another registered trade mark in relation to goods or services for which the latter is registered (but see section 47(6) (effect of declaration of invalidity of registration)).

(2) A registered trade mark is not infringed by—

(a) the use by a person of his own name or address,

(b) the use of indications concerning the kind, quality, quantity, intended purpose, value, geographical origin, the time of production of goods or of rendering of services, or other characteristics of goods or services, or

(c) the use of the trade mark where it is necessary to indicate the intended purpose of a product or service (in particular, as accessories or spare parts),

provided the use is in accordance with honest practices in industrial or commercial matters.

(3) A registered trade mark is not infringed by the use in the course of trade in a particular locality of an earlier right which applies only in that locality.

For this purpose an 'earlier right' means an unregistered trade mark or other sign continuously used in relation to goods or services by a person or a predecessor in title of his from a date prior to whichever is the earlier of—

(a) the use of the first-mentioned trade mark in relation to those goods or services by the proprietor or a predecessor in title of his, or

(b) the registration of the first-mentioned trade mark in respect of those goods or services in the name of the proprietor or a predecessor in title of his;

and an earlier right shall be regarded as applying in a locality if, or to the extent that, its use in that locality is protected by virtue of any rule of law (in particular, the law of passing off).

12. Exhaustion of rights conferred by registered trade mark

(1) A registered trade mark is not infringed by the use of the trade mark in relation to goods which have been put on the market in the European Economic Area under that trade mark by the proprietor or with his consent.

(2) Subsection (1) does not apply where there exist legitimate reasons for the proprietor to oppose further dealings in the goods (in particular, where the condition of the goods has been changed or impaired after they have been put on the market).

13. Registration subject to disclaimer or limitation

(1) An applicant for registration of a trade mark, or the proprietor of a registered trade mark, may—

    (a) disclaim any right to the exclusive use of any specified element of the trade mark, or

    (b) agree that the rights conferred by the registration shall be subject to a specified territorial or other limitation;

and where the registration of a trade mark is subject to a disclaimer or limitation, the rights conferred by section 9 (rights conferred by registered trade mark) are restricted accordingly.

(2) Provision shall be made by rules as to the publication and entry in the register of a disclaimer or limitation.

Subordinate legislation
The Trade Marks Rules 1994, SI 1994/2583, as amended by SI 1998/925.

Infringement proceedings

14. Action for infringement

(1) An infringement of a registered trade mark is actionable by the proprietor of the trade mark.

(2) In an action for infringement all such relief by way of damages, injunctions, accounts or otherwise is available to him as is available in respect of the infringement of any other property right.

15. Order for erasure, &c of offending sign

(1) Where a person is found to have infringed a registered trade mark, the court may make an order requiring him—

    (a) to cause the offending sign to be erased, removed or obliterated from any infringing goods, material or articles in his possession, custody or control, or

    (b) if it is not reasonably practicable for the offending sign to be erased, removed or obliterated, to secure the destruction of the infringing goods, material or articles in question.

(2) If an order under subsection (1) is not complied with, or it appears to the court likely that such an order would not be complied with, the court may order that

the infringing goods, material or articles be delivered to such person as the court may direct for erasure, removal or obliteration of the sign, or for destruction, as the case may be.

16. Order for delivery up of infringing goods, material or articles
(1) The proprietor of a registered trade mark may apply to the court for an order for the delivery up to him, or such other person as the court may direct, of any infringing goods, material or articles which a person has in his possession, custody or control in the course of a business.

(2) An application shall not be made after the end of the period specified in section 18 (period after which remedy of delivery up not available); and no order shall be made unless the court also makes, or it appears to the court that there are grounds for making, an order under section 19 (order as to disposal of infringing goods, &c).

(3) A person to whom any infringing goods, material or articles are delivered up in pursuance of an order under this section shall, if an order under section 19 is not made, retain them pending the making of an order, or the decision not to make an order, under that section.

(4) Nothing in this section affects any other power of the court.

17. Meaning of 'infringing goods, material or articles'
(1) In this Act the expressions 'infringing goods', 'infringing material' and 'infringing articles' shall be construed as follows.

(2) Goods are 'infringing goods', in relation to a registered trade mark, if they or their packaging bear a sign identical or similar to that mark and—

> (a) the application of the sign to the goods or their packaging was an infringement of the registered trade mark, or
>
> (b) the goods are proposed to be imported into the United Kingdom and the application of the sign in the United Kingdom to them or their packaging would be an infringement of the registered trade mark, or
>
> (c) the sign has otherwise been used in relation to the goods in such a way as to infringe the registered trade mark.

(3) Nothing in subsection (2) shall be construed as affecting the importation of goods which may lawfully be imported into the United Kingdom by virtue of an enforceable Community right.

(4) Material is 'infringing material', in relation to a registered trade mark if it bears a sign identical or similar to that mark and either—

> (a) it is used for labelling or packaging goods, as a business paper, or for advertising goods or services, in such a way as to infringe the registered trade mark, or
>
> (b) it is intended to be so used and such use would infringe the registered trade mark.

(5) 'Infringing articles', in relation to a registered trade mark, means articles—

> (a) which are specifically designed or adapted for making copies of a sign identical or similar to that mark, and
>
> (b) which a person has in his possession, custody or control, knowing or having reason to believe that they have been or are to be used to produce infringing goods or material.

18. Period after which remedy of delivery up not available
(1) An application for an order under section 16 (order for delivery up of infringing goods, material or articles) may not be made after the end of the period of six years from—

(a) in the case of infringing goods, the date on which the trade mark was applied to the goods or their packaging,

(b) in the case of infringing material, the date on which the trade mark was applied to the material, or

(c) in the case of infringing articles, the date on which they were made,

except as mentioned in the following provisions.

(2) If during the whole or part of that period the proprietor of the registered trade mark—

(a) is under a disability, or

(b) is prevented by fraud or concealment from discovering the facts entitling him to apply for an order,

an application may be made at any time before the end of the period of six years from the date on which he ceased to be under a disability or, as the case may be, could with reasonable diligence have discovered those facts.

(3) In subsection (2) 'disability'—

(a) in England and Wales, has the same meaning as in the Limitation Act 1980;

(b) in Scotland, means legal disability within the meaning of the Prescription and Limitation (Scotland) Act 1973;

(c) in Northern Ireland, has the same meaning as in the Limitation (Northern Ireland) Order 1989.

19. Order as to disposal of infringing goods, material or articles
(1) Where infringing goods, material or articles have been delivered up in pursuance of an order under section 16, an application may be made to the court—

(a) for an order that they be destroyed or forfeited to such person as the court may think fit, or

(b) for a decision that no such order should be made.

(2) In considering what order (if any) should be made, the court shall consider whether other remedies available in an action for infringement of the registered trade mark would be adequate to compensate the proprietor and any licensee and protect their interests.

(3) Provision shall be made by rules of court as to the service of notice on persons having an interest in the goods, material or articles, and any such person is entitled—

(a) to appear in proceedings for an order under this section, whether or not he was served with notice, and

(b) to appeal against any order made, whether or not he appeared;

and an order shall not take effect until the end of the period within which notice of an appeal may be given or, if before the end of that period notice of appeal is duly given, until the final determination or abandonment of the proceedings on the appeal.

(4) Where there is more than one person interested in the goods, material or arti-

cles, the court shall make such order as it thinks just.

(5) If the court decides that no order should be made under this section, the person in whose possession, custody or control the goods, material or articles were before being delivered up is entitled to their return.

(6) References in this section to a person having an interest in goods, material or articles include any person in whose favour an order could be made under this section or under section 114, 204 or 231 of the Copyright, Designs and Patents Act 1988 (which make similar provision in relation to infringement of copyright, rights in performances and design right).

20. Jurisdiction of sheriff court or county court in Northern Ireland
Proceedings for an order under section 16 (order for delivery up of infringing goods, material or articles) or section 19 (order as to disposal of infringing goods, &c) may be brought—

   (a) in the sheriff court in Scotland, or
   (b) in a county court in Northern Ireland.

This does not affect the jurisdiction of the Court of Session or the High Court in Northern Ireland.

21. Remedy for groundless threats of infringement proceedings
(1) Where a person threatens another with proceedings for infringement of a registered trade mark other than—

   (a) the application of the mark to goods or their packaging,
   (b) the importation of goods to which, or to the packaging of which, the mark has been applied, or
   (c) the supply of services under the mark,

any person aggrieved may bring proceedings for relief under this section.

(2) The relief which may be applied for is any of the following—

   (a) a declaration that the threats are unjustifiable,
   (b) an injunction against the continuance of the threats,
   (c) damages in respect of any loss he has sustained by the threats;

and the plaintiff is entitled to such relief unless the defendant shows that the acts in respect of which proceedings were threatened constitute (or if done would constitute) an infringement of the registered trade mark concerned.

(3) If that is shown by the defendant, the plaintiff is nevertheless entitled to relief if he shows that the registration of the trade mark is invalid or liable to be revoked in a relevant respect.

(4) The mere notification that a trade mark is registered, or that an application for registration has been made, does not constitute a threat of proceedings for the purposes of this section.

Registered trade mark as object of property

22. Nature of registered trade mark
A registered trade mark is personal property (in Scotland, incorporeal moveable property).

23. Co-ownership of registered trade mark

(1) Where a registered trade mark is granted to two or more persons jointly each of them is entitled, subject to any agreement to the contrary, to an equal undivided share in the registered trade mark.

(2) The following provisions apply where two or more persons are co-proprietors of a registered trade mark, by virtue of subsection (1) or otherwise.

(3) Subject to any agreement to the contrary, each co-proprietor is entitled, by himself or his agents, to do for his own benefit and without the consent of or the need to account to the other or others, any act which would otherwise amount to an infringement of the registered trade mark.

(4) One co-proprietor may not without the consent of the other or others —

    (a) grant a licence to use the registered trade mark, or

    (b) assign or charge his share in the registered trade mark (or, in Scotland, cause or permit security to be granted over it).

(5) Infringement proceedings may be brought by any co-proprietor, but he may not, without the leave of the court, proceed with the action unless the other, or each of the others, is either joined as a plaintiff or added as a defendant.

A co-proprietor who is thus added as a defendant shall not be made liable for any costs in the action unless he takes part in the proceedings.

Nothing in this subsection affects the granting of interlocutory relief on the application of a single co-proprietor.

(6) Nothing in this section affects the mutual rights and obligations of trustees or personal representatives, or their rights and obligations as such.

24. Assignment, &c of registered trade mark

(1) A registered trade mark is transmissible by assignment, testamentary disposition or operation of law in the same way as other personal or moveable property.

It is so transmissible either in connection with the goodwill of a business or independently.

(2) An assignment or other transmission of a registered trade mark may be partial, that is, limited so as to apply —

    (a) in relation to some but not all of the goods or services for which the trade mark is registered, or

    (b) in relation to use of the trade mark in a particular manner or a particular locality.

(3) An assignment of a registered trade mark, or an assent relating to a registered trade mark, is not effective unless it is in writing signed by or on behalf of the assignor or, as the case may be, a personal representative.

Except in Scotland, this requirement may be satisfied in a case where the assignor or personal representative is a body corporate by the affixing of its seal.

(4) The above provisions apply to assignment by way of security as in relation to any other assignment.

(5) A registered trade mark may be the subject of a charge (in Scotland, security) in the same way as other personal or moveable property.

(6) Nothing in this Act shall be construed as affecting the assignment or other transmission of an unregistered trade mark as part of the goodwill of a business.

25. Registration of transactions affecting registered trade mark

(1) On application being made to the registrar by —

(a) a person claiming to be entitled to an interest in or under a registered trade mark by virtue of a registrable transaction, or

(b) any other person claiming to be affected by such a transaction,

the prescribed particulars of the transaction shall be entered in the register.

(2) The following are registrable transactions—

(a) an assignment of a registered trade mark or any right in it;

(b) the grant of a licence under a registered trade mark;

(c) the granting of any security interest (whether fixed or floating) over a registered trade mark or any right in or under it;

(d) the making by personal representatives of an assent in relation to a registered trade mark or any right in or under it;

(e) an order of a court or other competent authority transferring a registered trade mark or any right in or under it.

(3) Until an application has been made for registration of the prescribed particulars of a registrable transaction—

(a) the transaction is ineffective as against a person acquiring a conflicting interest in or under the registered trade mark in ignorance of it, and

(b) a person claiming to be a licensee by virtue of the transaction does not have the protection of section 30 or 31 (rights and remedies of licensee in relation to infringement).

(4) Where a person becomes the proprietor or a licensee of a registered trade mark by virtue of a registrable transaction, then unless—

(a) an application for registration of the prescribed particulars of the transaction is made before the end of the period of six months beginning with its date, or

(b) the court is satisfied that it was not practicable for such an application to be made before the end of that period and that an application was made as soon as practicable thereafter,

he is not entitled to damages or an account of profits in respect of any infringement of the registered trade mark occurring after the date of the transaction and before the prescribed particulars of the transaction are registered.

(5) Provision may be made by rules as to—

(a) the amendment of registered particulars relating to a licence so as to reflect any alteration of the terms of the licence, and

(b) the removal of such particulars from the register—

(i) where it appears from the registered particulars that the licence was granted for a fixed period and that period has expired, or

(ii) where no such period is indicated and, after such period as may be prescribed, the registrar has notified the parties of his intention to remove the particulars from the register.

(6) Provision may also be made by rules as to the amendment or removal from the register of particulars relating to a security interest on the application of, or with the consent of, the person entitled to the benefit of that interest.

Subordinate legislation
The Trade Marks Rules 1994, SI 1994/2583, as amended by SI 1998/925.

26. Trusts and equities

(1) No notice of any trust (express, implied or constructive) shall be entered in the register; and the registrar shall not be affected by any such notice.

(2) Subject to the provisions of this Act, equities (in Scotland, rights) in respect of a registered trade mark may be enforced in like manner as in respect of other personal or moveable property.

27. Application for registration of trade mark as an object of property

(1) The provisions of sections 22 to 26 (which relate to a registered trade mark as an object of property) apply, with the necessary modifications, in relation to an application for the registration of a trade mark as in relation to a registered trade mark.

(2) In section 23 (co-ownership of registered trade mark) as it applies in relation to an application for registration the reference in subsection (1) to the granting of the registration shall be construed as a reference to the making of the application.

(3) In section 25 (registration of transactions affecting registered trade marks) as it applies in relation to a transaction affecting an application for the registration of a trade mark, the references to the entry of particulars in the register, and to the making of an application to register particulars, shall be construed as references to the giving of notice to the registrar of those particulars.

Licensing

28. Licensing of registered trade mark

(1) A licence to use a registered trade mark may be general or limited.

A limited licence may, in particular, apply—

   (a) in relation to some but not all of the goods or services for which the trade mark is registered, or

   (b) in relation to use of the trade mark in a particular manner or a particular locality.

(2) A licence is not effective unless it is in writing signed by or on behalf of the grantor.

Except in Scotland, this requirement may be satisfied in a case where the grantor is a body corporate by the affixing of its seal.

(3) Unless the licence provides otherwise, it is binding on a successor in title to the grantor's interest.

References in this Act to doing anything with, or without, the consent of the proprietor of a registered trade mark shall be construed accordingly.

(4) Where the licence so provides, a sub-licence may be granted by the licensee; and references in this Act to a licence or licensee include a sub-licence or sub-licensee.

29. Exclusive licences

(1) In this Act an 'exclusive licence' means a licence (whether general or limited) authorising the licensee to the exclusion of all other persons, including the person granting the licence, to use a registered trade mark in the manner authorised by the licence.

The expression 'exclusive licensee' shall be construed accordingly.

(2) An exclusive licensee has the same rights against a successor in title who is bound by the licence as he has against the person granting the licence.

30. General provisions as to rights of licensees in case of infringement

(1) This section has effect with respect to the rights of a licensee in relation to infringement of a registered trade mark.

The provisions of this section do not apply where or to the extent that, by virtue of section 31(1) below (exclusive licensee having rights and remedies of assignee), the licensee has a right to bring proceedings in his own name.

(2) A licensee is entitled, unless his licence, or any licence through which his interest is derived, provides otherwise, to call on the proprietor of the registered trade mark to take infringement proceedings in respect of any matter which affects his interests.

(3) If the proprietor—

(a) refuses to do so, or
(b) fails to do so within two months after being called upon,

the licensee may bring the proceedings in his own name as if he were the proprietor.

(4) Where infringement proceedings are brought by a licensee by virtue of this section, the licensee may not, without the leave of the court, proceed with the action unless the proprietor is either joined as a plaintiff or added as a defendant.

This does not affect the granting of interlocutory relief on an application by a licensee alone.

(5) A proprietor who is added as a defendant as mentioned in subsection (4) shall not be made liable for any costs in the action unless he takes part in the proceedings.

(6) In infringement proceedings brought by the proprietor of a registered trade mark any loss suffered or likely to be suffered by licensees shall be taken into account; and the court may give such directions as it thinks fit as to the extent to which the plaintiff is to hold the proceeds of any pecuniary remedy on behalf of licensees.

(7) The provisions of this section apply in relation to an exclusive licensee if or to the extent that he has, by virtue of section 31(1), the rights and remedies of an assignee as if he were the proprietor of the registered trade mark.

31. Exclusive licensee having rights and remedies of assignee

(1) An exclusive licence may provide that the licensee shall have, to such extent as may be provided by the licence, the same rights and remedies in respect of matters occurring after the grant of the licence as if the licence had been an assignment.

Where or to the extent that such provision is made, the licensee is entitled, subject to the provisions of the licence and to the following provisions of this section, to bring infringement proceedings, against any person other than the proprietor, in his own name.

(2) Any such rights and remedies of an exclusive licensee are concurrent with those of the proprietor of the registered trade mark; and references to the proprietor of a registered trade mark in the provisions of this Act relating to infringement shall be construed accordingly.

(3) In an action brought by an exclusive licensee by virtue of this section a defendant may avail himself of any defence which would have been available to him if the action had been brought by the proprietor of the registered trade mark.

(4) Where proceedings for infringement of a registered trade mark brought by the proprietor or an exclusive licensee relate wholly or partly to an infringement in respect of which they have concurrent rights of action, the proprietor or, as the case

may be, the exclusive licensee may not, without the leave of the court, proceed with the action unless the other is either joined as a plaintiff or added as a defendant.

This does not affect the granting of interlocutory relief on an application by a proprietor or exclusive licensee alone.

(5) A person who is added as a defendant as mentioned in subsection (4) shall not be made liable for any costs in the action unless he takes part in the proceedings.

(6) Where an action for infringement of a registered trade mark is brought which relates wholly or partly to an infringement in respect of which the proprietor and an exclusive licensee have or had concurrent rights of action—

(a) the court shall in assessing damages take into account—

   (i) the terms of the licence, and
   (ii) any pecuniary remedy already awarded or available to either of them in respect of the infringement;

(b) no account of profits shall be directed if an award of damages has been made, or an account of profits has been directed, in favour of the other of them in respect of the infringement; and

(c) the court shall if an account of profits is directed apportion the profits between them as the court considers just, subject to any agreement between them.

The provisions of this subsection apply whether or not the proprietor and the exclusive licensee are both parties to the action; and if they are not both parties the court may give such directions as it thinks fit as to the extent to which the party to the proceedings is to hold the proceeds of any pecuniary remedy on behalf of the other.

(7) The proprietor of a registered trade mark shall notify any exclusive licensee who has a concurrent right of action before applying for an order under section 16 (order for delivery up); and the court may on the application of the licensee make such order under that section as it thinks fit having regard to the terms of the licence.

(8) The provisions of subsections (4) to (7) above have effect subject to any agreement to the contrary between the exclusive licensee and the proprietor.

Application for registered trade mark

32. Application for registration

(1) An application for registration of a trade mark shall be made to the registrar.

(2) The application shall contain—

(a) a request for registration of a trade mark,
(b) the name and address of the applicant,
(c) a statement of the goods or services in relation to which it is sought to register the trade mark, and
(d) a representation of the trade mark.

(3) The application shall state that the trade mark is being used, by the applicant or with his consent, in relation to those goods or services, or that he has a *bona fide* intention that it should be so used.

(4) The application shall be subject to the payment of the application fee and such class fees as may be appropriate.

33. Date of filing

(1) The date of filing of an application for registration of a trade mark is the date on which documents containing everything required by section 32(2) are furnished to the registrar by the applicant.

If the documents are furnished on different days, the date of filing is the last of those days.

(2) References in this Act to the date of application for registration are to the date of filing of the application.

34. Classification of trade marks

(1) Goods and services shall be classified for the purposes of the registration of trade marks according to a prescribed system of classification.

(2) Any question arising as to the class within which any goods or services fall shall be determined by the registrar, whose decision shall be final.

Subordinate legislation
The Trade Marks Rules 1994, SI 1994/2583, as amended by SI 1998/925.

Priority

35. Claim to priority of Convention application

(1) A person who has duly filed an application for protection of a trade mark in a Convention country (a 'Convention application'), or his successor in title, has a right to priority, for the purposes of registering the same trade mark under this Act for some or all of the same goods or services, for a period of six months from the date of filing of the first such application.

(2) If the application for registration under this Act is made within that six-month period—

    (a) the relevant date for the purposes of establishing which rights take precedence shall be the date of filing of the first Convention application, and

    (b) the registrability of the trade mark shall not be affected by any use of the mark in the United Kingdom in the period between that date and the date of the application under this Act.

(3) Any filing which in a Convention country is equivalent to a regular national filing, under its domestic legislation or an international agreement, shall be treated as giving rise to the right of priority.

A 'regular national filing' means a filing which is adequate to establish the date on which the application was filed in that country, whatever may be the subsequent fate of the application.

(4) A subsequent application concerning the same subject as the first Convention application, filed in the same Convention country, shall be considered the first Convention application (of which the filing date is the starting date of the period of priority), if at the time of the subsequent application—

    (a) the previous application has been withdrawn, abandoned or refused, without having been laid open to public inspection and without leaving any rights outstanding, and

    (b) it has not yet served as a basis for claiming a right of priority.

The previous application may not thereafter serve as a basis for claiming a right of priority.

(5) Provision may be made by rules as to the manner of claiming a right to prior-

ity on the basis of a Convention application.

(6) A right to priority arising as a result of a Convention application may be assigned or otherwise transmitted, either with the application or independently.

The reference in subsection (1) to the applicant's successor in title shall be construed accordingly.

Subordinate legislation
The Trade Marks Rules 1994, SI 1994/2583, as amended by SI 1998/925.

36. Claim to priority from other relevant overseas application

(1) Her Majesty may by Order in Council make provision for conferring on a person who has duly filed an application for protection of a trade mark in—

(a) any of the Channel Islands or a colony, or

(b) a country or territory in relation to which Her Majesty's Government in the United Kingdom have entered into a treaty, convention, arrangement or engagement for the reciprocal protection of trade marks,

a right to priority, for the purpose of registering the same trade mark under this Act for some or all of the same goods or services, for a specified period from the date of filing of that application.

(2) An Order in Council under this section may make provision corresponding to that made by section 35 in relation to Convention countries or such other provision as appears to Her Majesty to be appropriate.

(3) A statutory instrument containing an Order in Council under this section shall be subject to annulment in pursuance of a resolution of either House of Parliament.

Subordinate legislation
The Trade Marks (Claims to Priority from Relevant Countries) Order 1994, SI 1994/2803, as amended by SI 1995/2997

Registration procedure

37. Examination of application

(1) The registrar shall examine whether an application for registration of a trade mark satisfies the requirements of this Act (including any requirements imposed by rules).

(2) For that purpose he shall carry out a search, to such extent as he considers necessary, of earlier trade marks.

(3) If it appears to the registrar that the requirements for registration are not met, he shall inform the applicant and give him an opportunity, within such period as the registrar may specify, to make representations or to amend the application.

(4) If the applicant fails to satisfy the registrar that those requirements are met, or to amend the application so as to meet them, or fails to respond before the end of the specified period, the registrar shall refuse to accept the application.

(5) If it appears to the registrar that the requirements for registration are met, he shall accept the application.

38. Publication, opposition proceedings and observations

(1) When an application for registration has been accepted, the registrar shall cause the application to be published in the prescribed manner.

(2) Any person may, within the prescribed time from the date of the publication

of the application, give notice to the registrar of opposition to the registration.

The notice shall be given in writing in the prescribed manner, and shall include a statement of the grounds of opposition.

(3) Where an application has been published, any person may, at any time before the registration of the trade mark, make observations in writing to the registrar as to whether the trade mark should be registered; and the registrar shall inform the applicant of any such observations.

A person who makes observations does not thereby become a party to the proceedings on the application.

Subordinate legislation
The Trade Marks Rules 1994, SI 1994/2583, as amended by SI 1998/925.

39. Withdrawal, restriction or amendment of application

(1) The applicant may at any time withdraw his application or restrict the goods or services covered by the application.

If the application has been published, the withdrawal or restriction shall also be published.

(2) In other respects, an application may be amended, at the request of the applicant, only by correcting—

(a) the name or address of the applicant,
(b) errors of wording or of copying, or
(c) obvious mistakes,

and then only where the correction does not substantially affect the identity of the trade mark or extend the goods or services covered by the application.

(3) Provision shall be made by rules for the publication of any amendment which affects the representation of the trade mark, or the goods or services covered by the application, and for the making of objections by any person claiming to be affected by it.

Subordinate legislation
The Trade Marks Rules 1994, SI 1994/2583, as amended by SI 1998/925.

40. Registration

(1) Where an application has been accepted and—

(a) no notice of opposition is given within the period referred to in section 38(2), or
(b) all opposition proceedings are withdrawn or decided in favour of the applicant,

the registrar shall register the trade mark, unless it appears to him having regard to matters coming to his notice since he accepted the application that it was accepted in error.

(2) A trade mark shall not be registered unless any fee prescribed for the registration is paid within the prescribed period.

If the fee is not paid within that period, the application shall be deemed to be withdrawn.

(3) A trade mark when registered shall be registered as of the date of filing of the application for registration; and that date shall be deemed for the purposes of this Act to be the date of registration.

(4) On the registration of a trade mark the registrar shall publish the registration

in the prescribed manner and issue to the applicant a certificate of registration.

Subordinate legislation
The Trade Marks Rules 1994, SI 1994/2583, as amended by SI 1998/925.

41. Registration: supplementary provisions

(1) Provision may be made by rules as to—

(a) the division of an application for the registration of a trade mark into several applications;
(b) the merging of separate applications or registrations;
(c) the registration of a series of trade marks.

(2) A series of trade marks means a number of trade marks which resemble each other as to their material particulars and differ only as to matters of a non-distinctive character not substantially affecting the identity of the trade mark.

(3) Rules under this section may include provision as to—

(a) the circumstances in which, and conditions subject to which, division, merger or registration of a series is permitted, and
(b) the purposes for which an application to which the rules apply is to be treated as a single application and those for which it is to be treated as a number of separate applications.

Subordinate legislation
The Trade Marks Rules 1994, SI 1994/2583, as amended by SI 1998/925.

Duration, renewal and alteration of registered trade mark

42

Duration of registration

(1) A trade mark shall be registered for a period of ten years from the date of registration.

(2) Registration may be renewed in accordance with section 43 for further periods of ten years.

43. Renewal of registration

(1) The registration of a trade mark may be renewed at the request of the proprietor, subject to payment of a renewal fee.

(2) Provision shall be made by rules for the registrar to inform the proprietor of a registered trade mark, before the expiry of the registration, of the date of expiry and the manner in which the registration may be renewed.

(3) A request for renewal must be made, and the renewal fee paid, before the expiry of the registration.

Failing this, the request may be made and the fee paid within such further period (of not less than six months) as may be prescribed, in which case an additional renewal fee must also be paid within that period.

(4) Renewal shall take effect from the expiry of the previous registration.

(5) If the registration is not renewed in accordance with the above provisions, the registrar shall remove the trade mark from the register.

Provision may be made by rules for the restoration of the registration of a trade mark which has been removed from the register, subject to such conditions (if any) as may be prescribed.

(6) The renewal or restoration of the registration of a trade mark shall be published in the prescribed manner.

Subordinate legislation
The Trade Marks Rules 1994, SI 1994/2583, as amended by SI 1998/925.

44. Alteration of registered trade mark

(1) A registered trade mark shall not be altered in the register, during the period of registration or on renewal.

(2) Nevertheless, the registrar may, at the request of the proprietor, allow the alteration of a registered trade mark where the mark includes the proprietor's name or address and the alteration is limited to alteration of that name or address and does not substantially affect the identity of the mark.

(3) Provision shall be made by rules for the publication of any such alteration and the making of objections by any person claiming to be affected by it.

Subordinate legislation
The Trade Marks Rules 1994, SI 1994/2583, as amended by SI 1998/925.

Surrender, revocation and invalidity

45. Surrender of registered trade mark

(1) A registered trade mark may be surrendered by the proprietor in respect of some or all of the goods or services for which it is registered.

(2) Provision may be made by rules—

(a) as to the manner and effect of a surrender, and
(b) for protecting the interests of other persons having a right in the registered trade mark.

Subordinate legislation
The Trade Marks Rules 1994, SI 1994/2583, as amended by SI 1998/925.

46. Revocation of registration

(1) The registration of a trade mark may be revoked on any of the following grounds—

(a) that within the period of five years following the date of completion of the registration procedure it has not been put to genuine use in the United Kingdom, by the proprietor or with his consent, in relation to the goods or services for which it is registered, and there are no proper reasons for non-use;
(b) that such use has been suspended for an uninterrupted period of five years, and there are no proper reasons for non-use;
(c) that, in consequence of acts or inactivity of the proprietor, it has become the common name in the trade for a product or service for which it is registered;
(d) that in consequence of the use made of it by the proprietor or with his consent in relation to the goods or services for which it is registered, it is liable to mislead the public, particularly as to the nature, quality or geographical origin of those goods or services.

(2) For the purposes of subsection (1) use of a trade mark includes use in a form differing in elements which do not alter the distinctive character of the mark in the form in which it was registered, and use in the United Kingdom includes affixing the trade mark to goods or to the packaging of goods in the United Kingdom solely for export purposes.

(3) The registration of a trade mark shall not be revoked on the ground mentioned in subsection (1)(a) or (b) if such use as is referred to in that paragraph is commenced or resumed after the expiry of the five year period and before the application for revocation is made:

Provided that, any such commencement or resumption of use after the expiry of the five year period but within the period of three months before the making of the application shall be disregarded unless preparations for the commencement or resumption began before the proprietor became aware that the application might be made.

(4) An application for revocation may be made by any person, and may be made either to the registrar or to the court, except that—

    (a) if proceedings concerning the trade mark in question are pending in the court, the application must be made to the court; and

    (b) if in any other case the application is made to the registrar, he may at any stage of the proceedings refer the application to the court.

(5) Where grounds for revocation exist in respect of only some of the goods or services for which the trade mark is registered, revocation shall relate to those goods or services only.

(6) Where the registration of a trade mark is revoked to any extent, the rights of the proprietor shall be deemed to have ceased to that extent as from—

    (a) the date of the application for revocation, or

    (b) if the registrar or court is satisfied that the grounds for revocation existed at an earlier date, that date.

47. Grounds for invalidity of registration

(1) The registration of a trade mark may be declared invalid on he ground that the trade mark was registered in breach of section 3 or any of the provisions referred to in that section (absolute grounds for refusal of registration).

Where the trade mark was registered in breach of subsection (1)(b), (c) or (d) of that section, it shall not be declared invalid if, in consequence of the use which has been made of it, it has after registration acquired a distinctive character in relation to the goods or services for which it is registered.

(2) The registration of a trade mark may be declared invalid on the ground—

    (a) that there is an earlier trade mark in relation to which the conditions set out in section 5(1), (2) or (3) obtain, or

    (b) that there is an earlier right in relation to which the condition set out in section 5(4) is satisfied,

unless the proprietor of that earlier trade mark or other earlier right has consented to the registration.

(3) An application for a declaration of invalidity may be made by any person, and may be made either to the registrar or to the court, except that—

    (a) if proceedings concerning the trade mark in question are pending in the court, the application must be made to the court; and

    (b) if in any other case the application is made to the registrar, he may at any stage of the proceedings refer the application to the court.

(4) In the case of bad faith in the registration of a trade mark, the registrar himself may apply to the court for a declaration of the invalidity of the registration.

(5) Where the grounds of invalidity exist in respect of only some of the goods or services for which the trade mark is registered, the trade mark shall be declared invalid as regards those goods or services only.

(6) Where the registration of a trade mark is declared invalid to any extent, the registration shall to that extent be deemed never to have been made:

Provided that this shall not affect transactions past and closed.

48. Effect of acquiescence

(1) Where the proprietor of an earlier trade mark or other earlier right has acquiesced for a continuous period of five years in the use of a registered trade mark in the United Kingdom, being aware of that use, there shall cease to be any entitlement on the basis of that earlier trade mark or other right—

(a) to apply for a declaration that the registration of the later trade mark is invalid, or
(b) to oppose the use of the later trade mark in relation to the goods or services in relation to which it has been so used,

unless the registration of the later trade mark was applied for in bad faith.

(2) Where subsection (1) applies, the proprietor of the later trade mark is not entitled to oppose the use of the earlier trade mark or, as the case may be, the exploitation of the earlier right, notwithstanding that the earlier trade mark or right may no longer be invoked against his later trade mark.

Collective marks

49. Collective marks

(1) A collective mark is a mark distinguishing the goods or services of members of the association which is the proprietor of the mark from those of other undertakings.

(2) The provisions of this Act apply to collective marks subject to the provisions of Schedule 1.

Certification marks

50. Certification marks

(1) A certification mark is a mark indicating that the goods or services in connection with which it is used are certified by the proprietor of the mark in respect of origin, material, mode of manufacture of goods or performance of services, quality, accuracy or other characteristics.

(2) The provisions of this Act apply to certification marks subject to the provisions of Schedule 2.

PART II
COMMUNITY TRADE MARKS AND INTERNATIONAL MATTERS

Community trade marks

51. Meaning of 'Community trade mark'

In this Act—

'Community trade mark' has the meaning given by Article 1(1) of the Community Trade Mark Regulation; and

'the Community Trade Mark Regulation' means Council Regulation 40/94/EC of 20th December 1993 on the Community trade mark.

52. Power to make provision in connection with Community Trade Mark Regulation

(1) The Secretary of State may by regulations make such provision as he considers appropriate in connection with the operation of the Community Trade Mark Regulation.

(2) Provision may, in particular, be made with respect to—

(a) the making of applications for Community trade marks by way of the Patent Office;

(b) the procedures for determining *a posteriori* the invalidity, or liability to revocation, of the registration of a trade mark from which a Community trade mark claims seniority;

(c) the conversion of a Community trade mark, or an application for a Community trade mark, into an application for registration under this Act;

(d) the designation of courts in the United Kingdom having jurisdiction over proceedings arising out of the Community Trade Mark Regulation.

(3) Without prejudice to the generality of subsection (1), provision may be made by regulations under this section—

(a) applying in relation to a Community trade mark the provisions of—

(i) section 21 (remedy for groundless threats of infringement proceedings);

(ii) sections 89 to 91 (importation of infringing goods, material or articles); and

(iii) sections 92, 93, 95 and 96 (offences); and

(b) making in relation to the list of professional representatives maintained in pursuance of Article 89 of the Community Trade Mark Regulation, and persons on that list, provision corresponding to that made by, or capable of being made under, sections 84 to 88 in relation to the register of trade mark agents and registered trade mark agents.

(4) Regulations under this section shall be made by statutory instrument which shall be subject to annulment in pursuance of a resolution of either House of Parliament.

Subordinate legislation
The Community Trade Mark (Fees) Regulations 1995, SI 1995/3175; the Community Trade Mark Regulations 1996, SI 1996/1908.

The Madrid Protocol: international registration

53. The Madrid Protocol

In this Act—

'the Madrid Protocol' means the Protocol relating to the Madrid Agreement concerning the International Registration of Marks, adopted at Madrid on 27th June 1989;

'the International Bureau' has the meaning given by Article 2(1) of that Protocol; and

'international trade mark (UK)' means a trade mark which is entitled to protection in the United Kingdom under that Protocol.

54. Power to make provision giving effect to Madrid Protocol

(1) The Secretary of State may by order make such provision as he thinks fit for giving effect in the United Kingdom to the provisions of the Madrid Protocol.

(2) Provision may, in particular, be made with respect to—

(a) the making of applications for international registrations by way of the Patent Office as office of origin;

(b) the procedures to be followed where the basic United Kingdom application or registration fails or ceases to be in force;

(c) the procedures to be followed where the Patent Office receives from the International Bureau a request for extension of protection to the United Kingdom;

(d) the effects of a successful request for extension of protection to the United Kingdom;

(e) the transformation of an application for an international registration, or an international registration, into a national application for registration;

(f) the communication of information to the International Bureau;

(g) the payment of fees and amounts prescribed in respect of applications for international registrations, extensions of protection and renewals.

(3) Without prejudice to the generality of subsection (1), provision may be made by regulations under this section applying in relation to an international trade mark (UK) the provisions of—

(a) section 21 (remedy for groundless threats of infringement proceedings);

(b) sections 89 to 91 (importation of infringing goods, material or articles); and

(c) sections 92, 93, 95 and 96 (offences).

(4) An order under this section shall be made by statutory instrument which shall be subject to annulment in pursuance of a resolution of either House of Parliament.

Subordinate legislation
The Trade Marks (International Registration) Order 1996, SI 1996/714; the Trade Marks (Fees) Rules 1998, SI 1998/1776.

The Paris Convention: supplementary provisions

55. The Paris Convention

(1) In this Act—

(a)   'the Paris Convention' means the Paris Convention for the Protection of Industrial Property of March 20th 1883, as revised or amended from time to time, . . .

[(aa) 'the WTO agreement' means the Agreement establishing the World Trade

Organisation signed at Marrakesh on 15th April 1994, and]
(b)   a 'Convention country' means a country, other than the United Kingdom, which is a party to that Convention.

(2) The Secretary of State may by order make such amendments of this Act, and rules made under this Act, as appear to him appropriate in consequence of any revision or amendment of the Paris Convention [or the WTO agreement] after the passing of this Act.

(3) Any such order shall be made by statutory instrument which shall be subject to annulment in pursuance of a resolution of either House of Parliament.

General note
In sub-s (1), the word omitted was repealed and para (aa) was inserted and in sub-s (2), the words in square brackets were inserted by the Patents and Trade Marks (World Trade Organisation) Regulations 1999, SI 1999/1899, reg 13(2), (3).

56.   Protection of well-known trade marks: Article 6bis

(1) References in this Act to a trade mark which is entitled to protection under the Paris Convention [or the WTO agreement] as a well known trade mark are to a mark which is well-known in the United Kingdom as being the mark of a person who—

(a) is a national of a Convention country, or
(b) is domiciled in, or has a real and effective industrial or commercial establishment in, a Convention country,

whether or not that person carries on business, or has any goodwill, in the United Kingdom.

References to the proprietor of such a mark shall be construed accordingly.

(2) The proprietor of a trade mark which is entitled to protection under the Paris Convention [or the WTO agreement] as a well known trade mark is entitled to restrain by injunction the use in the United Kingdom of a trade mark which, or the essential part of which, is identical or similar to his mark, in relation to identical or similar goods or services, where the use is likely to cause confusion.

This right is subject to section 48 (effect of acquiescence by proprietor of earlier trade mark).

(3) Nothing in subsection (2) affects the continuation of any *bona fide* use of a trade mark begun before the commencement of this section.

General note
In sub-ss (1), (2), the words in square brackets were inserted by the Patents and Trade Marks (World Trade Organisation) Regulations 1999, SI 1999/1899, reg 13(4), subject to transitional provisions in reg 14 thereof.

57.   National emblems, &c of Convention countries: Article 6ter

(1) A trade mark which consists of or contains the flag of a Convention country shall not be registered without the authorisation of the competent authorities of that country, unless it appears to the registrar that use of the flag in the manner proposed is permitted without such authorisation.

(2) A trade mark which consists of or contains the armorial bearings or any other state emblem of a Convention country which is protected under the Paris Convention [or the WTO agreement] shall not be registered without the authorisation of the competent authorities of that country.

(3) A trade mark which consists of or contains an official sign or hallmark adopted by a Convention country and indicating control and warranty shall not,

where the sign or hallmark is protected under the Paris Convention [or the WTO agreement], be registered in relation to goods or services of the same, or a similar kind, as those in relation to which it indicates control and warranty, without the authorisation of the competent authorities of the country concerned.

(4) The provisions of this section as to national flags and other state emblems, and official signs or hallmarks, apply equally to anything which from a heraldic point of view imitates any such flag or other emblem, or sign or hallmark.

(5) Nothing in this section prevents the registration of a trade mark on the application of a national of a country who is authorised to make use of a state emblem, or official sign or hallmark, of that country, notwithstanding that it is similar to that of another country.

(6) Where by virtue of this section the authorisation of the competent authorities of a Convention country is or would be required for the registration of a trade mark, those authorities are entitled to restrain by injunction any use of the mark in the United Kingdom without their authorisation.

General note
In sub-ss (2), (3), the words in square brackets were inserted by the Patents and Trade Marks (World Trade Organisation) Regulations 1999, SI 1999/1899, reg 13(5).

58. Emblems, &c of certain international organisations: Article 6ter

(1) This section applies to—

(a) the armorial bearings, flags or other emblems, and
(b) the abbreviations and names,

of international intergovernmental organisations of which one or more Convention countries are members.

(2) A trade mark which consists of or contains any such emblem, abbreviation or name which is protected under the Paris Convention [or the WTO agreement] shall not be registered without the authorisation of the international organisation concerned, unless it appears to the registrar that the use of the emblem, abbreviation or name in the manner proposed—

(a) is not such as to suggest to the public that a connection exists between the organisation and the trade mark, or
(b) is not likely to mislead the public as to the existence of a connection between the user and the organisation.

(3) The provisions of this section as to emblems of an international organisation apply equally to anything which from a heraldic point of view imitates any such emblem.

(4) Where by virtue of this section the authorisation of an international organisation is or would be required for the registration of a trade mark, that organisation is entitled to restrain by injunction any use of the mark in the United Kingdom without its authorisation.

(5) Nothing in this section affects the rights of a person whose *bona fide* use of the trade mark in question began before 4th January 1962 (when the relevant provisions of the Paris Convention entered into force in relation to the United Kingdom).

General note
In sub-s (2), the words in square brackets were inserted by the Patents and Trade Marks (World Trade Organisation) Regulations 1999, SI 1999/1899, reg 13(6), subject to transitional provisions in reg 14 thereof.

59. Notification under Article 6ter of the Convention

(1) For the purposes of section 57 state emblems of a Convention country (other than the national flag), and official signs or hallmarks, shall be regarded as protected under the Paris Convention only if, or to the extent that—

(a) the country in question has notified the United Kingdom in accordance with Article 6*ter*(3) of the Convention that it desires to protect that emblem, sign or hallmark,

(b) the notification remains in force, and

(c) the United Kingdom has not objected to it in accordance with Article 6*ter*(4) or any such objection has been withdrawn.

(2) For the purposes of section 58 the emblems, abbreviations and names of an international organisation shall be regarded as protected under the Paris Convention only if, or to the extent that—

(a) the organisation in question has notified the United Kingdom in accordance with Article 6*ter*(3) of the Convention that it desires to protect that emblem, abbreviation or name,

(b) the notification remains in force, and

(c) the United Kingdom gas not objected to it in accordance with Article 6*ter*(4) or any such objection has been withdrawn.

(3) Notification under Article 6*ter*(3) of the Paris Convention shall have effect only in relation to applications for registration made more than two months after the receipt of the notification.

(4) The registrar shall keep and make available for public inspection by any person, at all reasonable hours and free of charge, a list of—

(a) the state emblems and official signs or hallmarks, and

(b) the emblems, abbreviations and names of international organisations.

which are for the time being protected under the Paris Convention by virtue of notification under Article 6*ter*(3).

[(5) Any reference in this section to Article 6ter of the Paris Convention shall be construed as including a reference to that Article as applied by the WTO agreement.]

General note

Sub-s (5) was added by the Patents and Trade Marks (World Trade Organisation) Regulations 1999, SI 1999/1899, reg 13(7).

60. Acts of agent or representative: Article 6septies

(1) The following provisions apply where an application for registration of a trade mark is made by a person who is an agent or representative of a person who is the proprietor of the mark in a Convention country.

(2) If the proprietor opposes the application, registration shall be refused.

(3) If the application (not being so opposed) is granted, the proprietor may—

(a) apply for a declaration of the invalidity of the registration, or

(b) apply for the rectification of the register so as to substitute his name as the proprietor of the registered trade mark.

(4) The proprietor may (notwithstanding the rights conferred by this Act in relation to a registered trade mark) by injunction restrain any use of the trade mark in

the United Kingdom which is not authorised by him.

(5) Subsections (2), (3) and (4) do not apply if, or to the extent that, the agent or representative justifies his action.

(6) An application under subsection (3)(a) or (b) must be made within three years of the proprietor becoming aware of the registration; and no injunction shall be granted under subsection (4) in respect of a use in which the proprietor has acquiesced for a continuous period of three years or more.

Miscellaneous

61. Stamp duty

Stamp duty shall not be chargeable on an instrument relating to a Community trade mark or an international trade mark (UK), or an application for any such mark, by reason only of the fact that such a mark has legal effect in the United Kingdom.

PART III
ADMINISTRATIVE AND OTHER SUPPLEMENTARY PROVISIONS

The registrar

62. The registrar

In this Act 'the registrar' means the Comptroller-General of Patents, Designs and Trade Marks.

The register

63. The register

(1) The registrar shall maintain a register of trade marks.

References in this Act to 'the register' are to that register; and references to registration (in particular, in the expression 'registered trade mark') are, unless the context otherwise requires, to registration in that register.

(2) There shall be entered in the register in accordance with this Act—

(a) registered trade marks,
(b) such particulars as may be prescribed of registrable transactions affecting a registered trade mark, and
(c) such other matters relating to registered trade marks as may be prescribed.

(3) The register shall be kept in such manner as may be prescribed, and provision shall in particular be made for—

(a) public inspection of the register, and
(b) the supply of certified or uncertified copies, or extracts, of entries in the register.

Subordinate legislation
The Trade Marks Rules 1994, SI 1994/2583, as amended by SI 1998/925.

64. Rectification or correction of the register

(1) Any person having a sufficient interest may apply for the rectification of an error or omission in the register:

Provided that an application for rectification may not be made in respect of a matter affecting the validity of the registration of a trade mark.

(2) An application for rectification may be made either to the registrar or to the court, except that—

(a) if proceedings concerning the trade mark in question are pending in the court, the application must be made to the court; and

(b) if in any other case the application is made to the registrar, he may at any stage of the proceedings refer the application to the court.

(3) Except where the registrar or the court directs otherwise the effect of rectification of the register is that the error or omission in question shall be deemed never to have been made.

(4) The registrar may, on request made in the prescribed manner by the proprietor of a registered trade mark, or a licensee, enter any change in his name or address as recorded in the register.

(5) The registrar may remove from the register matter appearing to him to have ceased to have effect.

Subordinate legislation
The Trade Marks Rules 1994, SI 1994/2583, as amended by SI 1998/925.

65. Adaptation of entries to new classification

(1) Provision may be made by rules empowering the registrar to do such things as he considers necessary to implement any amended or substituted classification of goods or services for the purposes of the registration of trade marks.

(2) Provision may in particular be made for the amendment of existing entries on the register so as to accord with the new classification.

(3) Any such power of amendment shall not be exercised so as to extend the rights conferred by the registration, except where it appears to the registrar that compliance with this requirement would involve undue complexity and that any extension would not be substantial and would not adversely affect the rights of any person.

(4) The rules may empower the registrar—

(a) to require the proprietor of a registered trade mark, within such time as may be prescribed, to file a proposal for amendment of the register, and

(b) to cancel or refuse to renew the registration of the trade mark in the event of his failing to do so.

(5) Any such proposal shall be advertised, and may be opposed, in such manner as may be prescribed.

Subordinate legislation
The Trade Marks Rules 1994, SI 1994/2583, as amended by SI 1998/925.

Powers and duties of the registrar

66. Power to require use of forms

(1) The registrar may require the use of such forms as he may direct for any purpose relating to the registration of a trade mark or any other proceeding before him under this Act.

(2) The forms, and any directions of the registrar with respect to their use, shall be published in the prescribed manner.

Subordinate legislation
The Trade Marks Rules 1994, SI 1994/2583, as amended by SI 1998/925.

67. Information about applications and registered trade marks

(1) After publication of an application for registration of a trade mark, the registrar shall on request provide a person with such information and permit him to inspect such documents relating to the application, or to any registered trade mark resulting from it, as may be specified in the request, subject, however, to any prescribed restrictions.

Any request must be made in the prescribed manner and be accompanied by the appropriate fee (if any).

(2) Before publication of an application for registration of a trade mark, documents or information constituting or relating to the application shall not be published by the registrar or communicated by him to any person except—

    (a) in such cases and to such extent as may be prescribed, or
    (b) with the consent of the applicant;

but subject as follows.

(3) Where a person has been notified that an application for registration of a trade mark has been made, and that the applicant will if the application is granted bring proceedings against him in respect of acts done after publication of the application, he may make a request under subsection (1) notwithstanding that the application has not been published and that subsection shall apply accordingly.

Subordinate legislation
The Trade Marks Rules 1994, SI 1994/2583, as amended by SI 1998/925.

68. Costs and security for costs

(1) Provision may be made by rules empowering the registrar, in any proceedings before him under this Act—

    (a) to award any party such costs as he may consider reasonable, and
    (b) to direct how and by what parties they are to be paid.

(2) Any such order of the registrar may be enforced—

    (a) in England and Wales or Northern Ireland, in the same way as an order of the High Court;
    (b) in Scotland, in the same way as a decree for expenses granted by the Court of Session.

(3) Provision may be made by rules empowering the registrar, in such cases as may be prescribed, to require a party to proceedings before him to give security for costs, in relation to those proceedings or to proceedings on appeal, and as to the consequences if security is not given.

Subordinate legislation
The Trade Marks Rules 1994, SI 1994/2583, as amended by SI 1998/925.

69. Evidence before registrar

Provision may be made by rules—

    (a) as to the giving of evidence in proceedings before the registrar under this Act by affidavit or statutory declaration;
    (b) conferring on the registrar the powers of an official referee of the Supreme

Court as regards the examination of witnesses on oath and the discovery and production of documents; and

(c) applying in relation to the attendance of witnesses in proceedings before the registrar the rules applicable to the attendance of witnesses before such a referee.

Subordinate legislation
The Trade Marks Rules 1994, SI 1994/2583, as amended by SI 1998/925.

70. Exclusion of liability in respect of official acts

(1) The registrar shall not be taken to warrant the validity of the registration of a trade mark under this Act or under any treaty, convention, arrangement or engagement to which the United Kingdom is a party.

(2) The registrar is not subject to any liability by reason of, or in connection with, any examination required or authorised by this Act, or any such treaty, convention, arrangement or engagement, or any report or other proceedings consequent on such examination.

(3) No proceedings lie against an officer of the registrar in respect of any matter for which, by virtue of this section, the registrar is not liable.

71. Registrar's annual report

(1) The Comptroller-General of Patents, Designs and Trade Marks shall in his annual report under section 121 of the Patents Act 1977, include a report on the execution of this Act, including the discharge of his functions under the Madrid Protocol.

(2) The report shall include an account of all money received and paid by him under or by virtue of this Act.

Legal proceedings and appeals

72. Registration to be prima facie evidence of validity

In all legal proceedings relating to a registered trade mark (including proceedings for rectification of the register) the registration of a person as proprietor of a trade mark shall be prima facie evidence of the validity of the original registration and of any subsequent assignment or other transmission of it.

73. Certificate of validity of contested registration

(1) If in proceedings before the court the validity of the registration of a trade mark is contested and it is found by the court that the trade mark is validly registered, the court may give a certificate to that effect.

(2) If the court gives such a certificate and in subsequent proceedings—

(a) the validity of the registration is again questioned, and
(b) the proprietor obtains a final order or judgment in his favour,

he is entitled to his costs as between solicitor and client unless the court directs otherwise.

This subsection does not extend to the costs of an appeal in any such proceedings.

74. Registrar's appearance in proceedings involving the register

(1) In proceedings before the court involving an application for—

(a) the revocation of the registration of a trade mark,
(b) a declaration of the invalidity of the registration of a trade mark, or

659

(c) the rectification of the register,

the registrar is entitled to appear and be heard, and shall appear if so directed by the court.

(2) Unless otherwise directed by the court, the registrar may instead of appearing submit to the court a statement in writing signed by him, giving particulars of—

(a) any proceedings before him in relation to the matter in issue,
(b) the grounds of any decision given by him affecting it,
(c) the practice of the Patent Office in like cases, or
(d) such matters relevant to the issues and within his knowledge as registrar as he thinks fit;

and the statement shall be deemed to form part of the evidence in the proceedings.

(3) Anything which the registrar is or may be authorised or required to do under this section may be done on his behalf by a duly authorised officer.

75.   The court

In this Act, unless the context otherwise requires, 'the court' means—

(a) in England and Wales and Northern Ireland, the High Court, and
(b) in Scotland, the Court of Session.

76.   Appeals from the registrar

(1) An appeal lies from any decision of the registrar under this Act, except as otherwise expressly provided by rules.

For this purpose 'decision' includes any act of the registrar in exercise of a discretion vested in him by or under this Act.

(2) Any such appeal may be brought either to an appointed person or to the court.

(3) Where an appeal is made to an appointed person, he may refer the appeal to the court if—

(a) it appears to him that a point of general legal importance is involved,
(b) the registrar requests that it be so referred, or
(c) such a request is made by any party to the proceedings before the registrar in which the decision appealed against was made.

Before doing so the appointed person shall give the appellant and any other party to the appeal an opportunity to make representations as to whether the appeal should be referred to the court.

(4) Where an appeal is made to an appointed person and he does not refer it to the court, he shall hear and determine the appeal and his decision shall be final.

(5) The provisions of sections 68 and 69 (costs and security for costs; evidence) apply in relation to proceedings before an appointed person as in relation to proceedings before the registrar.

Subordinate legislation
The Trade Marks Rules 1994, SI 1994/2583, as amended by SI 1998/925.

77.   Persons appointed to hear and determine appeals

(1) For the purposes of section 76 an 'appointed person' means a person appointed by the Lord Chancellor to hear and decide appeals under this Act.

(2) A person is not eligible for such appointment unless—

    (a) he has a 7 year general qualification, within the meaning of section 71 of the Courts and Legal Services Act 1990;

    (b) he is an advocate or solicitor in Scotland of at least 7 years' standing;

    (c) he is a member of the Bar of Northern Ireland or solicitor of the Supreme Court of Northern Ireland of at least 7 years' standing; or

    (d) he has held judicial office.

(3) An appointed person shall hold and vacate office in accordance with his terms of appointment, subject to the following provisions—

    (a) there shall be paid to him such remuneration (whether by way of salary or fees), and such allowances, as the Secretary of State with the approval of the Treasury may determine;

    (b) he may resign his office by notice in writing to the Lord Chancellor;

    (c) the Lord Chancellor may by notice in writing remove him from office if—

        (i) he has become bankrupt or made an arrangement with his creditors or, in Scotland, his estate has been sequestrated or he has executed a trust deed for his creditors or entered into a composition contract, or

        (ii) he is incapacitated by physical or mental illness,

or if he is in the opinion of the Lord Chancellor otherwise unable or unfit to perform his duties as an appointed person.

(4) The Lord Chancellor shall consult the [Secretary of State] before exercising his powers under this section.

General note
In sub-s (4), the words in square brackets were substituted by virtue of the Transfer of Functions (Lord Advocate and Secretary of State) Order 1999, SI 1999/678, art 2(1), Schedule.

Rules, fees, hours of business, &c

78. Power of Secretary of State to make rules

(1) The Secretary of State may make rules—

    (a) for the purposes of any provision of this Act authorising the making of rules with respect to any matter, and

    (b) for prescribing anything authorised or required by any provision of this Act to be prescribed,

and generally for regulating practice and procedure under this Act.

(2) Provision may, in particular, be made—

    (a) as to the manner of filing of applications and other documents;

    (b) requiring and regulating the translation of documents and the filing and authentication of any translation;

    (c) as to the service of documents;

    (d) authorising the rectification of irregularities of procedure;

    (e) prescribing time limits for anything required to be done in connection with any proceeding under this Act;

    (f) providing for the extension of any time limit so prescribed, or specified by the registrar, whether or not it has already expired.

(3) Rules under this Act shall be made by statutory instrument which shall be subject to annulment in pursuance of a resolution of either House of Parliament.

Subordinate legislation
The Trade Marks Rules 1994, SI 1994/2583, as amended by SI 1998/925; the Register of Patent Agents and the Register of Trade Mark Agents (Amendment) Rules 1999, SI 1999/983; the Patent Office (Address) (Revocation) Rules 1999, SI 1999/1993.

79.   Fees

(1) There shall be paid in respect of applications and registration and other matters under this Act such fees as may be prescribed.

(2) Provision may be made by rules as to—

(a) the payment of a single fee in respect of two or more matters, and

(b) the circumstances (if any) in which a fee may be repaid or remitted.

Subordinate legislation
The Trade Marks (Fees) Rules 1998, SI 1998/1776.

80.   Hours of business and business days

(1) The registrar may give directions specifying the hours of business of the Patent Office for the purpose of the transaction by the public of business under this Act, and the days which are business days for that purpose.

(2) Business done on any day after the specified hours of business, or on a day which is not a business day, shall be deemed to have been done on the next business day; and where the time for doing anything under this Act expires on a day which is not a business day, that time shall be extended to the next business day.

(3) Directions under this section may make different provision for different classes of business and shall be published in the prescribed manner.

Subordinate legislation
The Trade Marks Rules 1994, SI 1994/2583, as amended by SI 1998/925.

81.   The trade marks journal

Provision shall be made by rules for the publication by the registrar of a journal containing particulars of any application for the registration of a trade mark (including a representation of the mark) and such other information relating to trade marks as the registrar thinks fit.

Subordinate legislation
The Trade Marks Rules 1994, SI 1994/2583, as amended by SI 1998/925.

Trade mark agents, &c

82.   Recognition of agents

Except as otherwise provided by rules, any act required or authorised by this Act to be done by or to a person in connection with the registration of a trade mark, or any procedure relating to a registered trade mark, may be done by or to an agent authorised by that person orally or in writing.

Subordinate legislation
The Trade Marks Rules 1994, SI 1994/2583, as amended by SI 1998/925.

83.   The register of trade mark agents

(1) The Secretary of State may make rules requiring the keeping of a register of persons who act as agent for others for the purpose of applying for or obtaining the registration of trade marks; and in this Act a registered trade mark agent means a person whose name is entered in the register kept under this section.

(2) The rules may contain such provision as the Secretary of State thinks it regulating the registration of persons, and may in particular—

(a) require the payment of such fees as may be prescribed, and
(b) authorise in prescribed cases the erasure from the register of the name of any person registered in it, or the suspension of a person's registration.

(3) The rules may delegate the keeping of the register to another person, and may confer on that person—

(a) power to make regulations—

(i) with respect to the payment of fees, in the cases and subject to the limits prescribed by the rules, and
(ii) with respect to any other matter which could be regulated by the rules, and

(b) such other functions, including disciplinary functions, as may be prescribed by the rules.

Subordinate legislation
The Register of Trade Mark Agents Rules 1990, SI 1990/1458, as amended by SI 1999/983.

84. Unregistered persons not to be described as registered trade mark agents

(1) An individual who is not a registered trade mark agent shall not—

(a) carry on a business (otherwise than in partnership) under any name or other description which contains the words 'registered trade mark agent'; or
(b) in the course of a business otherwise describe or hold himself out, or permit himself to be described or held out, as a registered trade mark agent.

(2) A partnership shall not—

(a) carry on a business under any name or other description which contains the words 'registered trade mark agent'; or
(b) in the course of a business otherwise describe or hold itself out, or permit itself to be described or held out, as a firm of registered trade mark agents,

unless all the partners are registered trade mark agents or the partnership satisfies such conditions as may be prescribed for the purposes of this section.

(3) A body corporate shall not—

(a) carry on a business (otherwise than in partnership) under any name or other description which contains the words 'registered trade mark agent'; or
(b) in the course of a business otherwise describe or hold itself out, or permit itself to be described or held out, as a registered trade mark agent,

unless all the directors of the body corporate are registered trade mark agents or the body satisfies such conditions as may be prescribed for the purposes of this section.

(4) A person who contravenes this section commits an offence and is liable on summary conviction to a fine not exceeding level 5 on the standard scale; and proceedings for such an offence may be begun at any time within a year from the date of the offence.

85. Power to prescribe conditions, &c for mixed partnerships and bodies corporate

(1) The Secretary of State may make rules prescribing the conditions to be satisfied

for the purposes of section 84 (persons entitled to be described as registered trade mark agents)—

> (a) in relation to a partnership where not all the partners are qualified persons, or
> (b) in relation to a body corporate where not all the directors are qualified persons,

and imposing requirements to be complied with by such partnerships or bodies corporate.

(2) The rules may, in particular—

> (a) prescribe conditions as to the number or proportion of partners or directors who must be qualified persons;
> (b) impose requirements as to—
>> (i) the identification of qualified and unqualified persons in professional advertisements, circulars or letters issued by or with the consent of the partnership or body corporate and which relate to its business, and
>> (ii) the manner in which a partnership or body corporate is to organise its affairs so as to secure that qualified persons exercise a sufficient degree of control over the activities of unqualified persons.

(3) Contravention of a requirement imposed by the rules is an offence for which a person is liable on summary conviction to a fine not exceeding level 5 on the standard scale.

(4) In this section *qualified person* means a registered trade mark agent.

Subordinate legislation
The Registered Trade Mark Agents (Mixed Partnerships and Bodies Corporate) Rules 1994, SI 1994/363.

86. Use of the term 'trade mark attorney'

(1) No offence is committed under the enactments restricting the use of certain expressions in reference to persons not qualified to act as solicitors by the use of the term 'trade mark attorney' in reference to a registered trade mark agent.

(2) The enactments referred to in subsection (1) are section 21 of the Solicitors Act 1974, section 31 of the Solicitors (Scotland) Act 1980 and Article 22 of the Solicitors (Northern Ireland) Order 1976.

87. Privilege for communications with registered trade mark agents

(1) This section applies to communications as to any matter relating to the protection of any design or trade mark, or as to any matter involving passing off.

(2) Any such communication—

> (a) between a person and his trade mark agent, or
> (b) for the purpose of obtaining, or in response to a request for, information which a person is seeking for the purpose of instructing his trade mark agent,

is privileged from, or in Scotland protected against, disclosure in legal proceedings in the same way as a communication between a person and his solicitor or, as the case may be, a communication for the purpose of obtaining, or in response to a request for, information which a person is seeking for the purpose of instructing his solicitor.

(3) In subsection (2) 'trade mark agent' means—

(a) a registered trade mark agent, or

(b) a partnership entitled to describe itself as a firm of registered trade mark agents, or

(c) a body corporate entitled to describe itself as a registered trade mark agent.

88. Power of registrar to refuse to deal with certain agents

(1) The Secretary of State may make rules authorising the registrar to refuse to recognise as agent in respect of any business under this Act—

(a) a person who has been convicted of an offence under section 84 (unregistered persons describing themselves as registered trade mark agents);

(b) an individual whose name has been erased from and not restored to, or who is suspended from, the register of trade mark agents on the ground of misconduct;

(c) a person who is found by the Secretary of State to have been guilty of such conduct as would, in the case of an individual registered in the register of trade mark agents, render him liable to have his name erased from the register on the ground of misconduct;

(d) a partnership or body corporate of which one of the partners or directors is a person whom the registrar could refuse to recognise under paragraph (a), (b) or (c) above.

(2) The rules may contain such incidental and supplementary provisions as appear to the Secretary of State to be appropriate and may, in particular, prescribe circumstances in which a person is or is not to be taken to have been guilty of misconduct.

Subordinate legislation
The Trade Marks Rules 1994, SI 1994/2583, as amended by SI 1998/925.

Importation of infringing goods, material or articles

89. Infringing goods, material or articles may be treated as prohibited goods

(1) The proprietor of a registered trade mark, or a licensee, may give notice in writing to the Commissioners of Customs and Excise—

(a) that he is the proprietor or, as the case may be, a licensee of the registered trade mark,

(b) that, at a time and place specified in the notice, goods which are, in relation to that registered trade mark, infringing goods, material or articles are expected to arrive in the United Kingdom—

(i) from outside the European Economic Area, or

(ii) from within that Area but not having been entered for free circulation, and

(c) that he requests the Commissioners to treat them as prohibited goods.

(2) When a notice is in force under this section the importation of the goods to which the notice relates, otherwise than by a person for his private and domestic use, is prohibited; but a person is not by reason of the prohibition liable to any penalty other than forfeiture of the goods.

[(3) This section does not apply to goods entered, or expected to be entered, for free circulation, export, re-export or for a suspensive procedure in respect of which an application may be made under Article 3(1) of Council Regulation 3295/94/EC laying down measures to prohibit the release for free circulation, export, re-export or entry for a suspensive procedure of counterfeit and pirated goods.]

General note
Sub-s (3) was substituted by the Trade Marks (EC Measures Relating to Counterfeit Goods) Regulations 1995, SI 1995/1444, reg 2.

90. Power of Commissioners of Customs and Excise to make regulations

(1) The Commissioners of Customs and Excise may make regulations prescribing the form in which notice is to be given under section 89 and requiring a person giving notice—

(a) to furnish the Commissioners with such evidence as may be specified in the regulations, either on giving notice or when the goods are imported, or at both those times, and

(b) to comply with such other conditions as may be specified in the regulations.

(2) The regulations may, in particular, require a person giving such a notice—

(a) to pay such fees in respect of the notice as may be specified by the regulations;

(b) to give such security as may be so specified in respect of any liability or expense which the Commissioners may incur in consequence of the notice by reason of the detention of any goods or anything done to goods detained;

(c) to indemnify the Commissioners against any such liability or expense, whether security has been given or not.

(3) The regulations may make different provision as respects different classes of case to which they apply and may include such incidental and supplementary provisions as the Commissioners consider expedient.

(4) Regulations under this section shall be made by statutory instrument which shall be subject to annulment in pursuance of a resolution of either House of Parliament.

(5) Section 17 of the Customs and Excise Management Act 1979 (general provisions as to Commissioners receipts) applies to fees paid in pursuance of regulations under this section as to receipts under the enactments relating to customs and excise.

Subordinate legislation
The Trade Marks (Customs) Regulations 1994, SI 1994/2625.

91. Power of Commissioners of Customs and Excise to disclose information

Where information relating to infringing goods, material or articles has been obtained by the Commissioners of Customs and Excise for the purposes of, or in connection with, the exercise of their functions in relation to imported goods, the Commissioners may authorise the disclosure of that information for the purpose of facilitating the exercise by any person of any function in connection with the investigation or prosecution of an offence under section 92 below (unauthorised use of trade mark, &c in relation to goods) or under the Trade Descriptions Act 1968.

Offences

92. Unauthorised use of trade mark, &c in relation to goods

(1) A person commits an offence who with a view to gain for himself or another, or with intent to cause loss to another, and without the consent of the proprietor—

    (a) applies to goods or their packaging a sign identical to, or likely to be mistaken for, a registered trade mark, or

    (b) sells or lets for hire, offers or exposes for sale or hire or distributes goods which bear, or the packaging of which bears, such a sign, or

    (c) has in his possession, custody or control in the course of a business any such goods with a view to the doing of anything, by himself or another, which would be an offence under paragraph (b).

(2) A person commits an offence who with a view to gain for himself or another, or with intent to cause loss to another, and without the consent of the proprietor—

    (a) applies a sign identical to, or likely to be mistaken for, a registered trade mark to material intended to be used—

        (i) for labelling or packaging goods,

        (ii) as a business paper in relation to goods, or

        (iii) for advertising goods, or

    (b) uses in the course of a business material bearing such a sign for labelling or packaging goods, as a business paper in relation to goods, or for advertising goods, or

    (c) has in his possession, custody or control in the course of a business any such material with a view to the doing of anything, by himself or another, which would be an offence under paragraph (b).

(3) A person commits an offence who with a view to gain for himself or another, or with intent to cause loss to another, and without the consent of the proprietor—

    (a) makes an article specifically designed or adapted for making copies of a sign identical to, or likely to be mistaken for, a registered trade mark, or

    (b) has such an article in his possession, custody or control in the course of a business,

knowing or having reason to believe that it has been, or is to be, used to produce goods, or material for labelling or packaging goods, as a business paper in relation to goods, or for advertising goods.

(4) A person does not commit an offence under this section unless—

    (a) the goods are goods in respect of which the trade mark is registered, or

    (b) the trade mark has a reputation in the United Kingdom and the use of the sign takes or would take unfair advantage of, or is or would be detrimental to, the distinctive character or the repute of the trade mark.

(5) It is a defence for a person charged with an offence under this section to show that he believed on reasonable grounds that the use of the sign in the manner in which it was used, or was to be used, was not an infringement of the registered trade mark.

(6) A person guilty of an offence under this section is liable—

    (a) on summary conviction to imprisonment for a term not exceeding six months or a fine not exceeding the statutory maximum, or both;

(b) on conviction on indictment to a fine or imprisonment for a term not exceeding ten years, or both.

93. Enforcement function of local weights and measures authority

(1) It is the duty of every local weights and measures authority to enforce within their area the provisions of section 92 (unauthorised use of trade mark, &c in relation to goods).

(2) The following provisions of the Trade Descriptions Act 1968 apply in relation to the enforcement of that section as in relation to the enforcement of that Act—

section 27 (power to make test purchases),
section 28 (power to enter premises and inspect and seize goods and documents),
section 29 (obstruction of authorised officers), and
section 33 (compensation for loss, &c of goods seized).

(3) Subsection (1) above does not apply in relation to the enforcement of section 92 in Northern Ireland, but it is the duty of the Department of Economic Development to enforce that section in Northern Ireland.

For that purpose the provisions of the Trade Descriptions Act 1968 specified in subsection (2) apply as if for the references to a local weights and measures authority and any officer of such an authority there were substituted references to that Department and any of its officers.

(4) Any enactment which authorises the disclosure of information for the purpose of facilitating the enforcement of the Trade Descriptions Act 1968 shall apply as if section 92 above were contained in that Act and as if the functions of any person in relation to the enforcement of that section were functions under that Act.

(5) Nothing in this section shall be construed as authorising a local weights and measures authority to bring proceedings in Scotland for an offence.

94. Falsification of register, &c

(1) It is an offence for a person to make, or cause to be made, a false entry in the register of trade marks, knowing or having reason to believe that it is false.

(2) It is an offence for a person—

(a) to make or cause to be made anything falsely purporting to be a copy of an entry in the register, or
(b) to produce or tender or cause to be produced or tendered in evidence any such thing,

knowing or having reason to believe that it is false.

(3) A person guilty of an offence under this section is liable—

(a) on conviction on indictment, to imprisonment for a term not exceeding two years or a fine, or both;
(b) on summary conviction, to imprisonment for a term not exceeding six months or a fine not exceeding the statutory maximum, or both.

95. Falsely representing trade mark as registered

(1) It is an offence for a person—

(a) falsely to represent that a mark is a registered trade mark, or
(b) to make a false representation as to the goods or services for which a trade

mark is registered

knowing or having reason to believe that the representation is false.

(2) For the purposes of this section, the use in the United Kingdom in relation to a trade mark—

(a) of the word registered, or
(b) of any other word or symbol importing a reference (express or implied) to registration,

shall be deemed to be a representation as to registration under this Act unless it is shown that the reference is to registration elsewhere than in the United Kingdom and that the trade mark is in fact so registered for the goods or services in question.

(3) A person guilty of an offence under this section is liable on summary conviction to a fine not exceeding level 3 on the standard scale.

96. Supplementary provisions as to summary proceedings in Scotland

(1) Notwithstanding anything in [section 136 of the Criminal Procedure (Scotland) Act 1995], summary proceedings in Scotland for an offence under this Act may be begun at any time within six months after the date on which evidence sufficient in the Lord Advocate's opinion to justify the proceedings came to his knowledge.

For this purpose a certificate of the Lord Advocate as to the date on which such evidence came to his knowledge is conclusive evidence.

(2) For the purposes of subsection (1) and of any other provision of this Act as to the time within which summary proceedings for an offence may be brought, proceedings in Scotland shall be deemed to be begun on the date on which a warrant to apprehend or to cite the accused is granted, if such warrant is executed without undue delay.

General note
In sub-s (1), the words in square brackets were substituted by the Criminal Procedure (Consequential Provisions) (Scotland) Act 1995, s 5, Sch 4, para 92(2).

Forfeiture of counterfeit goods, &c

97. Forfeiture: England and Wales or Northern Ireland

(1) In England and Wales or Northern Ireland where there has come into the possession of any person in connection with the investigation or prosecution of a relevant offence—

(a) goods which, or the packaging of which, bears a sign identical to or likely to be mistaken for a registered trade mark,
(b) material bearing such a sign and intended to be used for labelling or packaging goods, as a business paper in relation to goods, or for advertising goods, or
(c) articles specifically designed or adapted for making copies of such a sign,

that person may apply under this section for an order for the forfeiture of the goods, material or articles.

(2) An application under this section may be made—

(a) where proceedings have been brought in any court for a relevant offence relating to some or all of the goods, material or articles, to that court;
(b) where no application for the forfeiture of the goods, material or articles has

been made under paragraph (a), by way of complaint to a magistrates' court.

(3) On an application under this section the court shall make an order for the forfeiture of any goods, material or articles only if it is satisfied that a relevant offence has been committed in relation to the goods, material or articles.

(4) A court may infer for the purposes of this section that such an offence has been committed in relation to any goods, material or articles if it is satisfied that such an offence has been committed in relation to goods, material or articles which are representative of them (whether by reason of being of the same design or part of the same consignment or batch or otherwise).

(5) Any person aggrieved by an order made under this section by a magistrates' court, or by a decision of such a court not to make such an order, may appeal against that order or decision—

(a) in England and Wales, to the Crown Court;
(b) in Northern Ireland, to the county court;

and an order so made may contain such provision as appears to the court to be appropriate for delaying the coming into force of the order pending the making and determination of any appeal (including any application under section 111 of the Magistrates' Courts Act 1980 or Article 146 of the Magistrates' Courts (Northern Ireland) Order 1981 (statement of case)).

(6) Subject to subsection (7), where any goods, material or articles are forfeited under this section they shall be destroyed in accordance with such directions as the court may give.

(7) On making an order under this section the court may, if it considers it appropriate to do so, direct that the goods, material or articles to which the order relates shall (instead of being destroyed) be released, to such person as the court may specify, on condition that that person—

(a) causes the offending sign to be erased, removed or obliterated and
(b) complies with any order to pay costs which has been made against him in the proceedings for the order for forfeiture.

(8) For the purposes of this section a 'relevant offence' means an offence under section 92 above (unauthorised use of trade mark, &c in relation to goods) or under the Trade Descriptions Act 1968 or any offence involving dishonesty or deception.

General note
This section is modified, in relation to representations of the Olympic symbol, motto or protected word, by the Olympic Symbol etc (Protection) Act 1995, s 11.

98. Forfeiture: Scotland

(1) In Scotland the court may make an order for the forfeiture of any—

(a) goods which bear, or the packaging of which bears, a sign identical to or likely to be mistaken for a registered trade mark,
(b) material bearing such a sign and intended to be used for labelling or packaging goods, as a business paper in relation to goods, or for advertising goods, or
(c) articles specifically designed or adapted for making copies of such a sign.

(2) An order under this section may be made—

(a) on an application by the procurator-fiscal made in the manner specified in [section 134 of the Criminal Procedure (Scotland) Act 1995], or

(b) where a person is convicted of a relevant offence, in addition to any other penalty which the court may impose.

(3) On an application under subsection (2)(a), the court shall make an order for the forfeiture of any goods, material or articles only if it is satisfied that a relevant offence has been committed in relation to the goods, material or articles.

(4) The court may infer for the purposes of this section that such an offence has been committed in relation to any goods, material or articles if it is satisfied that such an offence has been committed in relation to goods, material or articles which are representative of them (whether by reason of being of the same design or part of the same consignment or batch or otherwise).

(5) The procurator-fiscal making the application under subsection (2)(a) shall serve on any person appearing to him to be the owner of, or otherwise to have an interest in, the goods, material or articles to which the application relates a copy of the application, together with a notice giving him the opportunity to appear at the hearing of the application to show cause why the goods, material or articles should not be forfeited.

(6) Service under subsection (5) shall be carried out, and such service may be proved, in the manner specified for citation of an accused in summary proceedings under the [Criminal Procedure (Scotland) Act 1995].

(7) Any person upon whom notice is served under subsection (5) and any other person claiming to be the owner of, or otherwise to have an interest in, goods, material or articles to which an application under this section relates shall be entitled to appear at the hearing of the application to show cause why the goods, material or articles should not be forfeited.

(8) The court shall not make an order following an application under subsection (2)(a)—

(a) if any person on whom notice is served under subsection (5) does not appear, unless service of the notice on that person is proved; or

(b) if no notice under subsection (5) has been served, unless the court is satisfied that in the circumstances it was reasonable not to serve such notice.

(9) Where an order for the forfeiture of any goods, material or articles is made following an application under subsection (2)(a), any person who appeared, or was entitled to appear, to show cause why goods, material or articles should not be forfeited may, within 21 days of the making of the order, appeal to the High Court by Bill of Suspension; and [section 182(5)(a) to (e) of the Criminal Procedure (Scotland) Act 1995] shall apply to an appeal under this subsection as it applies to a stated case under Part II of that Act.

(10) An order following an application under subsection (2)(a) shall not take effect—

(a) until the end of the period of 21 days beginning with the day after the day on which the order is made; or

(b) if an appeal is made under subsection (9) above within that period, until the appeal is determined or abandoned.

(11) An order under subsection (2)(b) shall not take effect—

(a) until the end of the period within which an appeal against the order could be brought under the [Criminal Procedure (Scotland) Act 1995]; or

(b) if an appeal is made within that period, until the appeal is determined or abandoned.

(12) Subject to subsection (13), goods, material or articles forfeited under this section shall be destroyed in accordance with such directions as the court may give.

(13) On making an order under this section the court may if it considers it appropriate to do so, direct that the goods, material or articles to which the order relates shall (instead of being destroyed) be released, to such person as the court may specify, on condition that that person causes the offending sign to be erased, removed or obliterated.

(14) For the purposes of this section—

'relevant offence' means an offence under section 92 (unauthorised use of trade mark, &c in relation to goods) or under the Trade Descriptions Act 1968 or any offence involving dishonesty or deception,

'the court' means—

(a) in relation to an order made on an application under subsection (2)(a), the sheriff, and

(b) in relation to an order made under subsection (2)(b), the court which imposed the penalty.

General note

In sub-ss (2), (6), (9), (11), the words in square brackets were substituted by the Criminal Procedure (Consequential Provisions) (Scotland) Act 1995, s 5, Sch 4, para 92(3).

This section is modified, in relation to representations of the Olympic symbol, motto or protected word, by the Olympic Symbol etc (Protection) Act 1995, s 12.

PART IV
MISCELLANEOUS AND GENERAL PROVISIONS

Miscellaneous

99.   Unauthorised use of Royal arms, &c

(1) A person shall not without the authority of Her Majesty use in connection with any business the Royal arms (or arms so closely resembling the Royal arms as to be calculated to deceive) in such manner as to be calculated to lead to the belief that he is duly authorised to use the Royal arms.

(2) A person shall not without the authority of Her Majesty or of a member of the Royal family use in connection with any business any device, emblem or title in such a manner as to be calculated to lead to the belief that he is employed by, or supplies goods or services to, Her Majesty or that member of the Royal family.

(3) A person who contravenes subsection (1) commits an offence and is liable on summary conviction to a fine not exceeding level 2 on the standard scale.

(4) Contravention of subsection (1) or (2) may be restrained by injunction in proceedings brought by—

(a) any person who is authorised to use the arms, device, emblem or title in question, or

(b) any person authorised by the Lord Chamberlain to take such proceedings.

(5) Nothing in this section affects any right of the proprietor of a trade mark containing any such arms, device, emblem or title to use that trade mark.

100.   Burden of proving use of trade mark

If in any civil proceedings under this Act a question arises as to the use to which a registered trade mark has been put, it is for the proprietor to show what use has been made of it.

101.   Offences committed by partnerships and bodies corporate

(1) Proceedings for an offence under this Act alleged to have been committed by a partnership shall be brought against the partnership in the name of the firm and not in that of the partners; but without prejudice to any liability of the partners under subsection (4) below.

(2) The following provisions apply for the purposes of such proceedings as in relation to a body corporate—

    (a) any rules of court relating to the service of documents;

    (b) in England and Wales or Northern Ireland, Schedule 3 to the Magistrates' Courts Act 1980 or Schedule 4 to the Magistrates' Courts (Northern Ireland) Order 1981 (procedure on charge of offence).

(3) A fine imposed on a partnership on its conviction in such proceedings shall be paid out of the partnership assets.

(4) Where a partnership is guilty of an offence under this Act, every partner, other than a partner who is proved to have been ignorant of or to have attempted to prevent the commission of the offence, is also guilty of the offence and liable to be proceeded against and punished accordingly.

(5) Where an offence under this Act committed by a body corporate is proved to have been committed with the consent or connivance of a director, manager, secretary or other similar officer of the body, or a person purporting to act in any such capacity, he as well as the body corporate is guilty of the offence and liable to be proceeded against and punished accordingly.

Interpretation

102.   Adaptation of expressions for Scotland

In the application of this Act to Scotland—

    'account of profits' means accounting and payment of profits;
    'accounts' means count, reckoning and payment;
    'assignment' means assignation;
    'costs' means expenses;
    'declaration' means declarator;
    'defendant' means defender;
    'delivery up' means delivery;
    'injunction' means interdict;
    'interlocutory relief' means interim remedy; and
    'plaintiff' means pursuer.

103.   Minor definitions

(1) In this Act—

    'business' includes a trade or profession;
    'director', in relation to a body corporate whose affairs are managed by its members, means any member of the body;
    'infringement proceedings', in relation to a registered trade mark, includes proceedings under section 16 (order for delivery up of infringing goods, &c);
    'publish' means make available to the public, and references to publication—

(a) in relation to an application for registration, are to publication under section 38(1), and

(b) in relation to registration, are to publication under section 40(4);

'statutory provisions' includes provisions of subordinate legislation within the meaning of the Interpretation Act 1978;

'trade' includes any business or profession.

(2) References in this Act to use (or any particular description of use) of a trade mark, or of a sign identical with, similar to, or likely to be mistaken for a trade mark, include use (or that description of use) otherwise than by means of a graphic representation.

(3) References in this Act to a Community instrument include references to any instrument amending or replacing that instrument.

104. Index of defined expressions

In this Act the expressions listed below are defined by or otherwise fall to be construed in accordance with the provisions indicated—

Account of profits and accounts (in Scotland)	section 102
appointed person (for purposes of section 76)	section 77
assignment (in Scotland)	section 102
business	section 103(1)
certification mark	section 50(1)
collective mark	section 49(1)
commencement (of this Act)	section 109(2)
Community trade mark	section 51
Community Trade Mark Regulation	section 51
Convention country	section 55(1)(b)
costs (in Scotland)	section 102
the court	section 75
date of application	section 33(2)
date of filing	section 33(1)
date of registration	section 40(3)
defendant (in Scotland)	section 102
delivery up (in Scotland)	section 102
director	section 103(1)
earlier right	section 5(4)
earlier trade mark	section 6
exclusive licence and licensee	section 29(1)
infringement (of registered trade mark)	sections 9(1) and (2) and 10
infringement proceedings	section 103(1)
infringing articles	section 17
infringing goods	section 17
infringing material	section 17
injunction (in Scotland)	section 102
interlocutory relief (in Scotland)	section 102
the International Bureau	section 53
international trade mark (UK)	section 53
Madrid Protocol section 53 Paris Convention	section 55(1)(a)
plaintiff (in Scotland)	section 102
prescribed	section 78(1)(b)
protected under the Paris Convention	

—well-known trade marks	section 56(1)
—state emblems and official signs or hallmarks	section 57(1)
—emblems, &c of international organisations	section 58(2)
publish and references to publication	section 103(1)
register, registered (and related expressions)	section 63(1)
registered trade mark agent	section 83(1)
registrable transaction	section 25(2)
the registrar	section 62
rules	section 78
statutory provisions	section 103(1)
trade	section 103(1)
trade mark	
—generally	section 1(1)
—includes collective mark or certification mark	section 1(2)
United Kingdom (references include Isle of Man)	section 108(2)
use (of trade mark or sign)	section 103(2)
well-known trade mark (under Paris Convention)	section 56(1)

Other general provisions

105. Transitional provisions

The provisions of Schedule 3 have effect with respect to transitional matters, including the treatment of marks registered under the Trade Marks Act 1938, and applications for registration and other proceedings pending under that Act, on the commencement of this Act.

106. Consequential amendments and repeals

(1) The enactments specified in Schedule 4 are amended in accordance with that Schedule, the amendments being consequential on the provisions of this Act.

(2) The enactments specified in Schedule 5 are repealed to the extent specified.

107. Territorial waters and the continental shelf

(1) For the purposes of this Act the territorial waters of the United Kingdom shall be treated as part of the United Kingdom.

(2) This Act applies to things done in the United Kingdom sector of the continental shelf on a structure or vessel which is present there for purposes directly connected with the exploration of the sea bed or subsoil or the exploitation of their natural resources as it applies to things done in the United Kingdom.

(3) The United Kingdom sector of the continental shelf means the areas designated by order under section 1(7) of the Continental Shelf Act 1964.

108. Extent

(1) This Act extends to England and Wales, Scotland and Northern Ireland.

(2) This Act also extends to the Isle of Man, subject to such exceptions and modifications as Her Majesty may specify by Order in Council; and subject to any such Order references in this Act to the United Kingdom shall be construed as including the Isle of Man.

Subordinate legislation
The Trade Marks Act 1994 (Isle of Man) Order 1996, SI 1996/729.

109.   Commencement

(1) The provisions of this Act come into force on such day as the Secretary of State may appoint by order made by statutory instrument.

Different days may be appointed for different provisions and different purposes.

(2) The references to the commencement of this Act in Schedules 3 and 4 (transitional provisions and consequential amendments) are to the commencement of the main substantive provisions of Parts I and III of this Act and the consequential repeal of the Trade Marks Act 1938.

Provision may be made by order under this section identifying the date of that commencement.

Subordinate legislation
The Trade Marks Act 1994 (Commencement) Order 1994, SI 1994/2550.

110.   Short title

This Act may be cited as the Trade Marks Act 1994.

SCHEDULES

SCHEDULE 1
COLLECTIVE MARKS

Section 49

General
1.—The provisions of this Act apply to collective marks subject to the following provisions.

Signs of which a collective mark may consist
2.—In relation to a collective mark the reference in section 1(1) (signs of which a trade mark may consist) to distinguishing goods or services of one undertaking from those of other undertakings shall be construed as a reference to distinguishing goods or services of members of the association which is the proprietor of the mark from those of other undertakings.

Indication of geographical origin
3.—(1) Notwithstanding section 3(1)(c), a collective mark may be registered which consists of signs or indications which may serve, in trade, to designate the geographical origin of the goods or services.

(2) However, the proprietor of such a mark is not entitled to prohibit the use of the signs or indications in accordance with honest practices in industrial or commercial matters (in particular, by a person who is entitled to use a geographical name).

Mark not to be misleading as to character or significance
4.—(1) A collective mark shall not be registered if the public is liable to be misled as regards the character or significance of the mark, in particular if it is likely to be taken to be something other than a collective mark.

(2) The registrar may accordingly require that a mark in respect of which application is made for registration include some indication that it is a collective mark.

Notwithstanding section 39(2), an application may be amended so as to comply with any such requirement.

Regulations governing use of collective mark
5.—(1) An applicant for registration of a collective mark must file with the registrar regulations governing the use of the mark.

(2) The regulations must specify the persons authorised to use the mark, the conditions of membership of the association and, where they exist, the conditions of use of the mark, including any sanctions against misuse.

Further requirements with which the regulations have to comply may be imposed by rules.

Approval of regulations by registrar
6.—(1) A collective mark shall not be registered unless the regulations governing the use of the mark—

   (a) comply with paragraph 5(2) and any further requirements imposed by rules, and

   (b) are not contrary to public policy or to accepted principles of morality.

(2) Before the end of the prescribed period after the date of the application for registration of a collective mark, the applicant must file the regulations with the registrar and pay the prescribed fee.

If he does not do so, the application shall be deemed to be withdrawn.

7.—(1) The registrar shall consider whether the requirements mentioned in paragraph 6(1) are met.

(2) If it appears to the registrar that those requirements are not met, he shall inform the applicant and give him an opportunity, within such period as the registrar may specify, to make representations or to file amended regulations.

(3) If the applicant fails to satisfy the registrar that those requirements are met, or to file regulations amended so as to meet them, or fails to respond before the end of the specified period, the registrar shall refuse the application.

(4) If it appears to the registrar that those requirements, and the other requirements for registration, are met, he shall accept the application and shall proceed in accordance with section 38 (publication, opposition proceedings and observations).

8.—The regulations shall be published and notice of opposition may be given, and observations may be made, relating to the matters mentioned in paragraph 6(1).

This is in addition to any other grounds on which the application may be opposed or observations made.

Regulations to be open to inspection
9.—The regulations governing the use of a registered collective mark shall be open to public inspection in the same way as the register.

Amendment of regulations
10.—(1) An amendment of the regulations governing the use of a registered collective mark is not effective unless and until the amended regulations are filed with the registrar and accepted by him.

(2) Before accepting any amended regulations the registrar may in any case where it appears to him expedient to do so cause them to be published.

(3) If he does so, notice of opposition may be given, and observations may be made, relating to the matters mentioned in paragraph 6(1).

Infringement: rights of authorised users
11.—The following provisions apply in relation to an authorised user of a registered collective mark as in relation to a licensee of a trade mark—

   (a) section 10(5) (definition of infringement: unauthorised application of mark to certain material);

   (b) section 19(2) (order as to disposal of infringing goods, material or articles: adequacy of other remedies);

   (c) section 89 (prohibition of importation of infringing goods, material or articles: request to Commissioners of Customs and Excise).

12.—(1) The following provisions (which correspond to the provisions of section 30 (general provisions as to rights of licensees in case of infringement)) have effect as regards the rights of an authorised user in relation to infringement of a registered collective mark.

(2) An authorised user is entitled, subject to any agreement to the contrary between him and the proprietor, to call on the proprietor to take infringement proceedings in respect of any matter which affects his interests.

(3) If the proprietor—

   (a) refuses to do so, or

   (b) fails to do so within two months after being called upon,

the authorised user may bring the proceedings in his own name as if he were the proprietor.

(4) Where infringement proceedings are brought by virtue of this paragraph, the authorised user may not, without the leave of the court, proceed with the action unless the proprietor is either joined as a plaintiff or added as a defendant.

This does not affect the granting of interlocutory relief on an application by an authorised user alone.

(5) A proprietor who is added as a defendant as mentioned in sub-paragraph (4) shall not be made liable for any costs in the action unless he takes part in the proceedings.

(6) In infringement proceedings brought by the proprietor of a registered collective mark any loss suffered or likely to be suffered by authorised users shall be taken into account; and the court may give such directions as it thinks fit as to the extent to which the plaintiff is to hold the proceeds of any pecu-

niary remedy on behalf of such users.

Grounds for revocation of registration
13.—Apart from the grounds of revocation provided for in section 46, the registration of a collective mark may be revoked on the ground—

   (a) that the manner in which the mark has been used by the proprietor has caused it to become liable to mislead the public in the manner referred to in paragraph 4(1), or
   (b) that the proprietor has failed to observe, or to secure the observance of, the regulations governing the use of the mark, or
   (c) that an amendment of the regulations has been made so that the regulations—

      (i) no longer comply with paragraph 5(2) and any further conditions imposed by rules, or
      (ii) are contrary to public policy or to accepted principles of morality.

Grounds for invalidity of registration
14.—Apart from the grounds of invalidity provided for in section 47, the registration of a collective mark may be declared invalid on the ground that the mark was registered in breach of the provisions of paragraph 4(1) or 6(1).

Subordinate legislation
The Trade Marks Rules 1994, SI 1994/2583, as amended by SI 1998/925.

SCHEDULE 2
CERTIFICATION MARKS

Section 50

General
1.—The provisions of this Act apply to certification marks subject to the following provisions.

Signs of which a certification mark may consist
2.—In relation to a certification mark the reference in section 1(1) (signs of which a trade mark may consist) to distinguishing goods or services of one undertaking from those of other undertakings shall be construed as a reference to distinguishing goods or services which are certified from those which are not.

Indication of geographical origin
3.—(1) Notwithstanding section 3(1)(c), a certification mark may be registered which consists of signs or indications which may serve, in trade, to designate the geographical origin of the goods or services.

   (2) However, the proprietor of such a mark is not entitled to prohibit the use of the signs or indications in accordance with honest practices in industrial or commercial matters (in particular, by a person who is entitled to use a geographical name).

Nature of proprietor's business
4.—A certification mark shall not be registered if the proprietor carries on a business involving the supply of goods or services of the kind certified.

Mark not to be misleading as to character or significance
5.—(1) A certification mark shall not be registered if the public is liable to be misled as regards the character or significance of the mark, in particular if it is likely to be taken to be something other than a certification mark.

   (2) The registrar may accordingly require that a mark in respect of which application is made for registration include some indication that it is a certification mark.

   Notwithstanding section 39(2), an application may be amended so as to comply with any such requirement.

Regulations governing use of certification mark
6.—(1) An applicant for registration of a certification mark must file with the registrar regulations governing the use of the mark.

   (2) The regulations must indicate who is authorised to use the mark, the characteristics to be certified by the mark, how the certifying body is to test those characteristics and to supervise the use of the mark,

the fees (if any) to be paid in connection with the operation of the mark and the procedures for resolving disputes.

Further requirements with which the regulations have to comply may be imposed by rules.

Approval of regulations, &c

7.—(1) A certification mark shall not be registered unless—

(a) the regulations governing the use of the mark—

(i) comply with paragraph 6(2) and any further requirements imposed by rules, and

(ii) are not contrary to public policy or to accepted principles of morality, and

(b) the applicant is competent to certify the goods or services for which the mark is to be registered.

(2) Before the end of the prescribed period after the date of the application for registration of a certification mark, the applicant must file the regulations with the registrar and pay the prescribed fee.

If he does not do so, the application shall be deemed to be withdrawn.

8.—(1) The registrar shall consider whether the requirements mentioned in paragraph 7(1) are met.

(2) If it appears to the registrar that those requirements are not met, he shall inform the applicant and give him an opportunity, within such period as the registrar may specify, to make representations or to file amended regulations.

(3) If the applicant fails to satisfy the registrar that those requirements are met, or to file regulations amended so as to meet them, or fails to respond before the end of the specified period, the registrar shall refuse the application.

(4) If it appears to the registrar that those requirements, and the other requirements for registration, are met, he shall accept the application and shall proceed in accordance with section 38 (publication, opposition proceedings and observations).

9.—The regulations shall be published and notice of opposition may be given, and observations may be made, relating to the matters mentioned in paragraph 7(1).

This is in addition to any other grounds on which the application may be opposed or observations made.

Regulations to be open to inspection

10.—The regulations governing the use of a registered certification mark shall be open to public inspection in the same way as the register.

Amendment of regulations

11.—(1) An amendment of the regulations governing the use of a registered certification mark is not effective unless and until the amended regulations are filed with the registrar and accepted by him.

(2) Before accepting any amended regulations the registrar may in any case where it appears to him expedient to do so cause them to be published.

(3) If he does so, notice of opposition may be given, and observations may be made, relating to the matters mentioned in paragraph 7(1).

Consent to assignment of registered certification mark

12.—The assignment or other transmission of a registered certification mark is not effective without the consent of the registrar.

Infringement: rights of authorised users

13.—The following provisions apply in relation to an authorised user of a registered certification mark as in relation to a licensee of a trade mark—

(a) section 10(5) (definition of infringement: unauthorised application of mark to certain material);

(b) section 19(2) (order as to disposal of infringing goods, material or articles: adequacy of other remedies);

(c) section 89 (prohibition of importation of infringing goods, material or articles: request to Commissioners of Customs and Excise).

14.—In infringement proceedings brought by the proprietor of a registered certification mark any loss suffered or likely to be suffered by authorised users shall be taken into account; and the court may give such directions as it thinks fit as to the extent to which the plaintiff is to hold the proceeds of any pecuniary remedy on behalf of such users.

Grounds for revocation of registration

15.—Apart from the grounds of revocation provided for in section 46, the registration of a certification mark may be revoked on the ground—

(a) that the proprietor has begun to carry on such a business as is mentioned in paragraph 4,

(b) that the manner in which the mark has been used by the proprietor has caused it to become liable to mislead the public in the manner referred to in paragraph 5(1),

(c) that the proprietor has failed to observe, or to secure the observance of, the regulations governing the use of the mark,

(d) that an amendment of the regulations has been made so that the regulations—

(i) no longer comply with paragraph 6(2) and any further conditions imposed by rules, or

(ii) are contrary to public policy or to accepted principles of morality, or

(e) that the proprietor is no longer competent to certify the goods or services for which the mark is registered.

Grounds for invalidity of registration

16.—Apart from the grounds of invalidity provided for in section 47, the registration of a certification mark may be declared invalid on the ground that the mark was registered in breach of the provisions of paragraph 4, 5(1) or 7(1).

Subordinate legislation

The Trade Marks Rules 1994, SI 1994/2583, as amended by SI 1998/925.

SCHEDULE 3
TRANSITIONAL PROVISIONS

Section 105

Introductory

1.—(1) In this Schedule—

'existing registered mark' means a trade mark, certification trade mark or service mark registered under the 1938 Act immediately before the commencement of this Act;

'the 1938 Act' means the Trade Marks Act 1938; and

'the old law' means that Act and any other enactment or rule of law applying to existing registered marks immediately before the commencement of this Act.

(2) For the purposes of this Schedule—

(a) an application shall be treated as pending on the commencement of this Act if it was made but not finally determined before commencement, and

(b) the date on which it was made shall be taken to be the date of filing under the 1938 Act.

Existing registered marks

2.—(1) Existing registered marks (whether registered in Part A or B of the register kept under the 1938 Act) shall be transferred on the commencement of this Act to the register kept under this Act and have effect, subject to the provisions of this Schedule, as if registered under this Act.

(2) Existing registered marks registered as a series under section 21(2) of the 1938 Act shall be similarly registered in the new register.

Provision may be made by rules for putting such entries in the same form as is required for entries under this Act.

(3) In any other case notes indicating that existing registered marks are associated with other marks shall cease to have effect on the commencement of this Act.

3.—(1) A condition entered on the former register in relation to an existing registered mark immediately before the commencement of this Act shall cease to have effect on commencement.

Proceedings under section 33 of the 1938 Act (application to expunge or vary registration for breach of condition) which are pending on the commencement of this Act shall be dealt with under the old law and any necessary alteration made to the new register.

(2) A disclaimer or limitation entered on the former register in relation to an existing registered mark immediately before the commencement of this Act shall be transferred to the new register and have effect as if entered on the register in pursuance of section 13 of this Act.

Effects of registration: infringement

4.—(1) Sections 9 to 12 of this Act (effects of registration) apply in relation to an existing registered mark as from the commencement of this Act and section 14 of this Act (action for infringement) applies in relation to infringement of an existing registered mark committed after the commencement of this Act, subject to sub-paragraph (2) below.

The old law continues to apply in relation to infringements committed before commencement.

(2) It is not an infringement of—

    (a) an existing registered mark, or

    (b) a registered trade mark of which the distinctive elements are the same or substantially the same as those of an existing registered mark and which is registered for the same goods or services,

to continue after commencement any use which did not amount to infringement of the existing registered mark under the old law.

Infringing goods, material or articles

5.—Section 16 of this Act (order for delivery up of infringing goods, material or articles) applies to infringing goods, material or articles whether made before or after the commencement of this Act.

Rights and remedies of licensee or authorised user

6.—(1) Section 30 (general provisions as to rights of licensees in case of infringement) of this Act applies to licences granted before the commencement of this Act, but only in relation to infringements committed after commencement.

(2) Paragraph 14 of Schedule 2 of this Act (court to take into account loss suffered by authorised users, &c) applies only in relation to infringements committed after commencement.

Co-ownership of registered mark

7.—The provisions of section 23 of this Act (co-ownership of registered mark) apply as from the commencement of this Act to an existing registered mark of which two or more persons were immediately before commencement registered as joint proprietors.

But so long as the relations between the joint proprietors remain such as are described in section 63 of the 1938 Act (joint ownership) there shall be taken to be an agreement to exclude the operation of sub-sections (1) and (3) of section 23 of this Act (ownership in undivided shares and right of co-proprietor to make separate use of the mark).

Assignment, &c of registered mark

8.—(1) Section 24 of this Act (assignment or other transmission of registered mark) applies to transactions and events occurring after the commencement of this Act in relation to an existing registered mark; and the old law continues to apply in relation to transactions and events occurring before commencement.

(2) Existing entries under section 25 of the 1938 Act (registration of assignments and transmissions) shall be transferred on the commencement of this Act to the register kept under this Act and have effect as if made under section 25 of this Act.

Provision may be made by rules for putting such entries in the same form as is required for entries made under this Act.

(3) An application for registration under section 25 of the 1938 Act which is pending before the registrar on the commencement of this Act shall be treated as an application for registration under section 25 of this Act and shall proceed accordingly.

The registrar may require the applicant to amend his application so as to conform with the requirements of this Act.

(4) An application for registration under section 25 of the 1938 Act which has been determined by the registrar but not finally determined before the commencement of this Act shall be dealt with under the old law; and sub-paragraph (2) above shall apply in relation to any resulting entry in the register.

(5) Where before the commencement of this Act a person has become entitled by assignment or transmission to an existing registered mark but has not registered his title, any application for registration after commencement shall be made under section 25 of this Act.

(6) In cases to which sub-paragraph (3) or (5) applies section 25(3) of the 1938 Act continues to apply (and section 25(3) and (4) of this Act do not apply) as regards the consequences of failing to register.

Licensing of registered mark

9.—(1) Sections 28 and 29(2) of this Act (licensing of registered trade mark; rights of exclusive licensee against grantor's successor in title) apply only in relation to licences granted after the commencement of this Act; and the old law continues to apply in relation to licences granted before commencement.

(2) Existing entries under section 28 of the 1938 Act (registered users) shall be transferred on the commencement of this Act to the register kept under this Act and have effect as if made under section 25 of this Act.

Provision may be made by rules for putting such entries in the same form as is required for entries made under this Act.

(3) An application for registration as a registered user which is pending before the registrar on the commencement of this Act shall be treated as an application for registration of a licence under section 25(1) of this Act and shall proceed accordingly.

The registrar may require the applicant to amend his application so as to conform with the requirements of this Act.

(4) An application for registration as a registered user which has been determined by the registrar but not finally determined before the commencement of this Act shall be dealt with under the old law; and sub-paragraph (2) above shall apply in relation to any resulting entry in the register.

(5) Any proceedings pending on the commencement of this Act under section 28(8) or (10) of the 1938 Act (variation or cancellation of registration of registered user) shall be dealt with under the old law and any necessary alteration made to the new register.

Pending applications for registration
10.—(1) An application for registration of a mark under the 1938 Act which is pending on the commencement of this Act shall be dealt with under the old law, subject as mentioned below, and if registered the mark shall be treated for the purposes of this Schedule as an existing registered mark.

(2) The power of the Secretary of State under section 78 of this Act to make rules regulating practice and procedure, and as to the matters mentioned in subsection (2) of that section, is exercisable in relation to such an application; and different provision may be made for such applications from that made for other applications.

(3) Section 23 of the 1938 Act (provisions as to associated trade marks) shall be disregarded in dealing after the commencement of this Act with an application for registration.

Conversion of pending application
11.—(1) In the case of a pending application for registration which has not been advertised under section 18 of the 1938 Act before the commencement of this Act, the applicant may give notice to the registrar claiming to have the registrability of the mark determined in accordance with the provisions of this Act.

(2) The notice must be in the prescribed form, be accompanied by the appropriate fee and be given no later than six months after the commencement of this Act.

(3) Notice duly given is irrevocable and has the effect that the application shall be treated as if made immediately after the commencement of this Act.

Trade marks registered according to old classification
12.—The registrar may exercise the powers conferred by rules under section 65 of this Act (adaptation of entries to new classification) to secure that any existing registered marks which do not conform to the system of classification prescribed under section 34 of this Act are brought to conformity with that system.

This applies, in particular, to existing registered marks classified according to the pre-1938 classification set out in Schedule 3 to the Trade Marks Rules 1986.

Claim to priority from overseas application
13.—Section 35 of this Act (claim to priority of Convention application) applies to an application for registration under this Act made after the commencement of this Act notwithstanding that the Convention application was made before commencement.

14.—(1) Where before the commencement of this Act a person has duly filed an application for protection of a trade mark in a relevant country within the meaning of section 39A of the 1938 Act which is not a Convention country (a 'relevant overseas application'), he, or his successor in title, has a right to priority, for the purposes of registering the same trade mark under this Act for some or all of the same goods or services, for a period of six months from the date of filing of the relevant overseas application.

(2) If the application for registration under this Act is made within that six-month period—

(a) the relevant date for the purposes of establishing which rights take precedence shall be the date of filing of the relevant overseas application, and

(b) the registrability of the trade mark shall not be affected by any use of the mark in the United Kingdom in the period between that date and the date of the application under this Act.

(3) Any filing which in a relevant country is equivalent to a regular national filing, under its domestic legislation or an international agreement, shall be treated as giving rise to the right of priority.

A 'regular national filing' means a filing which is adequate to establish the date on which the application was filed in that country, whatever may be the subsequent fate of the application.

(4) A subsequent application concerning the same subject as the relevant overseas application, filed in the same country, shall be considered the relevant overseas application (of which the filing date is the starting date of the period of priority), if at the time of the subsequent application—

(a) the previous application has been withdrawn, abandoned or refused, without having been laid open to public inspection and without leaving any rights outstanding, and

(b) it has not yet served as a basis for claiming a right of priority.

The previous application may not thereafter serve as a basis for claiming a right of priority.

(5) Provision may be made by rules as to the manner of claiming a right to priority on the basis of a relevant overseas application.

(6) A right to priority arising as a result of a relevant overseas application may be assigned or otherwise transmitted, either with the application or independently.

The reference in sub-paragraph (1) to the applicant's 'successor in title' shall be construed accordingly.

(7) Nothing in this paragraph affects proceedings on an application for registration under the 1938 Act made before the commencement of this Act (see paragraph 10 above).

Duration and renewal of registration

15.—(1) Section 42(1) of this Act (duration of original period of registration) applies in relation to the registration of a mark in pursuance of an application made after the commencement of this Act; and the old law applies in any other case.

(2) Sections 42(2) and 43 of this Act (renewal) apply where the renewal falls due on or after the commencement of this Act; and the old law continues to apply in any other case.

(3) In either case it is immaterial when the fee is paid.

Pending application for alteration of registered mark

16.—An application under section 35 of the 1938 Act (alteration of registered trade mark) which is pending on the commencement of this Act shall be dealt with under the old law and any necessary alteration made to the new register.

Revocation for non-use

17.—(1) An application under section 26 of the 1938 Act (removal from register or imposition of limitation on ground of non-use) which is pending on the commencement of this Act shall be dealt with under the old law and any necessary alteration made to the new register.

(2) An application under section 46(1)(a) or (b) of this Act (revocation for non-use) may be made in relation to an existing registered mark at any time after the commencement of this Act.

Provided that no such application for the revocation of the registration of an existing registered mark registered by virtue of section 27 of the 1938 Act (defensive registration of well-known trade marks) may be made until more than five years after the commencement of this Act.

Application for rectification, &c

18.—(1) An application under section 32 or 34 of the 1938 Act (rectification or correction of the register) which is pending on the commencement of this Act shall be dealt with under the old law and any necessary alteration made to the new register.

(2) For the purposes of proceedings under section 47 of this Act (grounds for invalidity of registration) as it applies in relation to an existing registered mark, the provisions of this Act shall be deemed to have been in force at all material times.

Provided that no objection to the validity of the registration of an existing registered mark may be taken on the ground specified in subsection (3) of section 5 of this Act (relative grounds for refusal of registration: conflict with earlier mark registered for different goods or services).

Regulations as to use of certification mark

19.—(1) Regulations governing the use of an existing registered certification mark deposited at the Patent Office in pursuance of section 37 of the 1938 Act shall be treated after the commencement of this Act as if filed under paragraph 6 of Schedule 2 to this Act.

(2) Any request for amendment of the regulations which was pending on the commencement of this

Act shall be dealt with under the old law.

Sheffield marks
20.—(1) For the purposes of this Schedule the Sheffield register kept under Schedule 2 to the 1938 Act shall be treated as part of the register of trade marks kept under that Act.

(2) Applications made to the Cutlers' Company in accordance with that Schedule which are pending on the commencement of this Act shall proceed after commencement as if they had been made to the registrar.

Certificate of validity of contested registration
21.—A certificate given before the commencement of this Act under section 47 of the 1938 Act (certificate of validity of contested registration) shall have effect as if given under section 73(1) of this Act.

STrade mark agents
22.—(1) Rules in force immediately before the commencement of this Act under section 282 or 283 of the Copyright, Designs and Patents Act 1988 (register of trade mark agents; persons entitled to described themselves as registered) shall continue in force and have effect as if made under section 83 or 85 of this Act.

(2) Rules in force immediately before the commencement of this Act under section 40 of the 1938 Act as to the persons whom the registrar may refuse to recognise as agents for the purposes of business under that Act shall continue in force and have effect as if made under section 88 of this Act.

(3) Rules continued in force under this paragraph may be varied or revoked by further rules made under the relevant provisions of this Act.

Subordinate legislation
The Trade Marks Rules 1994, SI 1994/2583, as amended by SI 1998/925.

SCHEDULE 4
CONSEQUENTIAL AMENDMENTS

Section 106(1)

General adaptation of existing references

1.—(1) References in statutory provisions passed or made before the commencement of this Act to trade marks or registered trade marks within the meaning of the Trade Marks Act 1938 shall, unless the context otherwise requires, be construed after the commencement of this Act as references to trade marks or registered trade marks within the meaning of this Act.

(2) Sub-paragraph (1) applies, in particular, to the references in the following provisions—

Industrial Organisation and Development Act 1947	Schedule 1, paragraph 7
Crown Proceedings Act 1947	section 3(1)(b)
Horticulture Act 1960	section 15(1)(b)
Printer's Imprint Act 1961	section 1(1)(b)
Northern Ireland Constitution Act 1973	*Schedule 3, paragraph 17*
Patents Act 1977	section 19(2)
	section 27(4)
	section 123(7)
Unfair Contract Terms Act 1977	Schedule 1, paragraph 1(c)
Judicature (Northern Ireland) Act 1978	section 94A(5)
State Immunity Act 1978	section 7(a) and (b)
Supreme Court Act 1981	section 72(5)
	Schedule 1, paragraph 1(i)
Civil Jurisdiction and Judgments Act 1982	Schedule 5, paragraph 2
	Schedule 8, paragraph 2(14) and 4(2)
Value Added Tax Act 1983	Schedule 3, paragraph 1
Companies Act 1985	section 396(3A)(a) or (as substituted by the Companies Act 1989) section 396(2)(d)(i)
	section 410(4)(c)(v)
	Schedule 4, Part I, Balance Sheet Formats 1 and 2 and Note (2)

	Schedule 9, Part I, paragraphs 5(2)'(d) and 10(2)
Law Reform (Miscellaneous Provisions) (Scotland) Act 1985	section 15(5)
Atomic Energy Authority Act 1986	section 8(2)
Northern Ireland Constitution Act 1973	*Schedule 3, paragraph 17*
Companies (Northern Ireland) Order 1986	article 403(3A)(a) or (as substituted by the Companies (No 2) (Northern Ireland) Order 1990) article 403(2)(d)(i) Schedule 4, Part I, Balance Sheet Formats 1 and 2 and Note (2) Schedule 9, Part I, paragraphs 5(2)'(d) and 10(2)
Consumer Protection Act 1987	section 2(2)(b)
Consumer Protection (Northern Ireland) Order 1987	article 5(2)(b)
Income and Corporation Taxes Act 1988	section 83(a)
Taxation of Chargeable Gains Act 1992	section 275(h)
Tribunals and Inquiries Act 1992	Schedule 1, paragraph 34.

Patents and Designs Act 1907 (c 29)

2.—(1)–
    (3) . . .
    (4) The repeal by the Patents Act 1949 and the Registered Designs Act 1949 of the whole of the 1907 Act, except certain provisions, shall be deemed not to have extended to the long title, date of enactment or enacting words or to so much of section 99 as provides the Act with its short title.

3–9

. . .

General note
In para 1(2) the entry 'Plant Varieties and Seeds Act 1964' was repealed by the Plant Varieties Act 1997, s 52, Sch 4.
In para 1(2) the entry relating to the 'Northern Ireland Constitution Act 1973' is repealed by the Northern Ireland Act 1998, s 100(2), Sch 15, as from a day to be appointed.
Para 2(1)–(3) amend the Patents and Designs Act 1907, ss 62, 63.
Paras 3–9 amend the Patents, Designs, Copyright and Trade Marks (Emergency) Act 1939, ss 4(1)(c), 6(1), 7(1)(a), 10(1), the Trade Descriptions Act 1968, s 34, the Solicitors Act 1974, s 22(2), (3A), the House of Commons Disqualification Act 1975, Sch 1, Pt III, the Copyright, Designs and Patents Act 1988, ss 114(6), 204(6), 231(6), 280(1) and the Tribunals and Inquiries Act 1992, Sch 1, Pt I, and substitute the Patents, Designs, Copyright and Trade Marks (Emergency) Act 1939, s 3, and the Restrictive Trade Practices Act 1976, Sch 3, para 4.

SCHEDULE 5
REPEALS AND REVOCATIONS

Section 106(2)

Chapter or number	**Short title**	**Extent of repeal or revocation**
1891 c 50	Commissioners for Oaths Act 1891	In section 1, the words 'or the Patents, Designs and Trade Marks Acts, 1883 to 1888'
1907 c 29	Patents and Designs Act 1907	In section 63(2), the words from 'and those salaries' to the end
1938 c 22	Trade Marks Act 1938	The whole Act
1947 c 44	Crown Proceedings Act 1947	In section 3(1)(b), the words 'or registered service mark'

Chapter or number	Short title	Extent of repeal or revocation
1949 c 87	Patents Act 1949	Section 92(2)
1964 c 14	Plant Varieties and Seeds Act 1964	In section 5A(4), the words 'under the Trade Marks Act 1938'
1967 c 80	Criminal Justice Act 1967	In Schedule 3, in Parts I and IV, the entries relating to the Trade Marks Act 1938
1978 c 23	Judicature (Northern Ireland) Act 1978	In Schedule 5, in Part II, the paragraphs amending the Trade Marks Act 1938
1984 c 19	Trade Marks (Amendment) Act 1984	The whole Act 1985 c 6 Companies Act 1985 In section 396— (a) in subsection (3A)(a), and (b) in subsection (2)(d)(i) as inserted by the Companies Act 1989, the words 'service mark,'
1986 c 12	Statute Law (Repeals) Act 1986	In Schedule 2, paragraph 2
1986 c 39	Patents, Designs and Marks Act 1986	Section 2 Section 4(4) In Schedule 1, paragraphs 1 and 2 Schedule 2 SI 1986/1032 (NI 6) Companies (Northern Ireland) Order 1986 In article 403— (a) in paragraph (3A)(a), and (b) in paragraph (2)(d)(i) as inserted by the Companies (No 2) (Northern Ireland) Order 1990, the words 'service mark,'
1987 c 43	Consumer Protection Act 1987	In section 45— (a) in subsection (1), the definition of 'mark' and 'trade mark'; (b) subsection (4)
SI 1987/2049	Consumer Protection (Northern Ireland) Order 1987	In article 2— (a) in paragraph (2), the definitions of 'mark' and 'trade mark'; (b) paragraph (3)
1988 c 1	Income and Corporation Taxes Act 1988	In section 83, the words from 'References in this section' to the end
1988 c 48	Copyright, Designs and Patents Act 1988	Sections 282 to 284 In section 286, the definition of 'registered trade mark agent' Section 300
1992 c 12	Taxation of Chargeable Gains Act 1992	In section 275(h), the words 'service marks' and 'service mark'

686

TRADE MARKS ACT 1938
(1938 c 22)

(As amended by the Statute Law Revision Act 1950, the Industrial Expansion Act 1968, the Trade Descriptions Act 1968, the Courts Act 1971, the Judicature (Northern Ireland) Act 1978, the Customs and Excise Management Act 1979, the Trade Marks (Amendment) Act 1984, the Patents, Designs and Marks Act 1986, the Statute Law (Repeals) Act 1986, the Copyright, Designs and Patents Act 1988 and the High Court and County Courts Jurisdiction Order 1991, SI 1991/724, and by virtue of the Criminal Justice Act 1982.)

ARRANGEMENT OF SECTIONS

REGISTRATION, INFRINGEMENT AND OTHER SUBSTANTIVE PROVISIONS

The Register
  1 The Register of trade marks etc

Effect of registration and the action for infringement
  2 No action for infringement of unregistered trade mark
  3 Registration to be in respect of particular goods
  4 Right given by registration in Part A, and infringement thereof
  5 Right given by registration in Part B, and infringement thereof
  6 Infringement by breach of certain restrictions
  7 Saving for vested interests
  8 Saving for use of name, address, or description of goods

Registrability and validity of registration
  9 Distinctiveness requisite for registration in Part A
  10 Capability of distinguishing requisite for registration in Part B
  11 Prohibition of registration of deceptive, etc, matter
  12 Prohibition of registration of identical and resembling trade marks
  13 Registration in Part A to be conclusive as to validity after seven years
  14 Registration subject to disclaimer
  15 Words used as name or description of an article or substance
  16 Effect of limitation as to colour, and of absence thereof

Procedure for, and duration of, registration
  17 Application for registration
  18 Opposition to registration
  19 Registration
  20 Duration and renewal of registration
  21 Registration of parts of trade marks and of trade marks as a series

Assignment and transmission
  22 Powers of, and restrictions on, assignment and transmission
  23 Certain trade marks to be associated so as to be assignable and transmissible as a whole only
  24 Power of registered proprietor to assign and give receipts
  25 Registration of assignments and transmissions

Use and non-use
  26 Removal from register and imposition of limitations on ground of non-use
  27 Defensive registration of well known trade marks
  28 Registered users
  29 Proposed use of trade mark by corporation to be constituted, etc
  30 Use of one of associated or substantially identical trade marks equivalent to use of another
  31 Use of trade mark for export trade

Rectification and correction of the register
  32 General power to rectify entries in register
  33 Power to expunge or vary registration for breach of condition
  34 Correction of register

35 Alteration of registered trade mark
36 Adaptation of entries in register to amended or substituted classification of goods

Certification trade marks
37 Certification trade marks

Sheffield marks
38 Sheffield marks

Manchester Branch
39 Trade marks for textile goods
39A Registration of trade mark following overseas application

GENERAL AND MISCELLANEOUS

Rules and fees
40 Power of Board of Trade to make rules
40A Hours of business and excluded days
41 Fees

Powers and duties of Registrar
42 Preliminary advice by Registrar as to distinctiveness
43 Hearing before exercise of Registrar's discretion
44 Power of Registrar to award costs
45 Annual reports of Registrar

Legal proceedings and appeals
46 Registration to be prima facie evidence of validity
47 Certificate of validity
48 Costs of Registrar in proceedings before Court, and payment of costs by Registrar
49   Trade usage, etc to be considered
50 Registrar's appearance in proceedings involving rectification
51 Court's power to review Registrar's decision
52 Discretion of Court in appeals
53 Procedure on appeal to Board of Trade
54 Procedure in cases of option to apply to Court or Registrar

Evidence
55 Mode of giving evidence
56 Evidence of orders, etc of Board of Trade

Offences and restraint of use of Royal Arms
58A Fraudulent application or use of trade mark an offence
58B Delivery up of offending goods and materials
58C Order as to disposal of offending goods or material
58D Enforcement of section 58A
59 Falsification of entries in register a misdemeanour
60 Fine for falsely representing a trade mark as registered
61 Restraint of use of Royal Arms, etc

Miscellaneous
62 Change of form of trade connection not to be deemed to cause deception
63   Jointly owned trade marks
64 Trusts and equities
64A Restriction on importation of goods bearing infringing trade marks
65 Recognition of agents
66 Saving for jurisdiction of courts in Scotland, Northern Ireland and Isle of Man

Supplemental
68 Interpretation
69 Transitional provisions
70 Repeal and savings
71 Short title, commencement and extent

SCHEDULES:
First Schedule—Certification Trade Marks
Second Schedule—Sheffield Marks
Third Schedule—Transitional Provisions

An Act to consolidate the Trade Marks Act 1905, the Trade Marks Act 1919, and the Trade Marks (Amendment) Act 1937

[13 April 1938]

General note

This Act has been repealed by the Trade Marks Act 1994, s 106(2), Sch 5, and is printed below as amended immediately prior to its repeal on 31 October 1994. The 1938 Act was amended, to make provision for marks for services, by the Trade Marks (Amendment) Act 1984; this was itself amended by the Patents, Designs and Marks Act 1986, which also amended the 1938 Act in some respects. These changes came into effect on 1 October 1986. By virtue of the Trade Marks (Amendment) Act 1984, s 1(1) as amended (also repealed), the 1938 Act had effect with respect to service marks (as defined in s 1(7) of the 1984 Act) as it had effect with respect to trade marks, references to goods having effect as references to services; as so applied, the 1938 Act had effect in relation to service marks subject to the modifications in Sch 1 to the 1984 Act. As a result of the amendments it became necessary to reproduce the amended 1938 Act in two versions, one applying to trade marks for goods and the other to service marks. The 1938 Act, as modified for service marks, is printed immediately following the version set out below, which applied to trade marks for goods.

REGISTRATION, INFRINGEMENT AND OTHER SUBSTANTIVE PROVISIONS

The register

[1. The Register of trade marks etc

(1) The Comptroller-General of Patents, Designs and Trade Marks (in this Act referred to as 'the Registrar') shall maintain the register of trade marks, in which shall be entered—

(a) all registered trade marks with the names and addresses of their proprietors;
(b) notifications of assignments and transmissions;
(c) the names and addresses of all registered users;
(d) disclaimers, conditions and limitations; and
(e) such other matters relating to registered trade marks as may be prescribed.

(2) The register shall continue to be divided into two parts called respectively Part A and Part B.

(3) The register need not be kept in documentary form.

(4) Subject to any rules under this Act, the public shall have a right to inspect the register at the Patent Office at all convenient times.

(5) Any person who applies for a certified copy of an entry in the register or a certified extract from the register shall be entitled to obtain such a copy or extract on payment of a fee prescribed in relation to certified copies and extracts; and the rules may provide that any person who applies for an uncertified copy or extract shall be entitled to such a copy or extract on payment of a fee prescribed in relation to uncertified copies and extracts.

(6) Application under subsection (5) above or rules made by virtue of that subsection shall be made in such manner as may be prescribed.

(7) In relation to any portion of the register kept otherwise than in documentary form—

(a) the right of inspection conferred by subsection (4) above is a right to inspect the material on the register; and

(b) the right to a copy or extract conferred by subsection (5) above or the rules is a right to a copy or extract in a form in which it can be taken away and in which it is visible and legible.

(8) A certificate purporting to be signed by the Registrar and certifying that any entry which he is authorised by this Act or rules to make has or has not been made, or that any other thing which he is so authorised to do has or has not been done, shall be prima facie evidence, and in Scotland shall be sufficient evidence, of the matters so certified.

(9) A copy of an entry in the register or an extract from the register which is supplied under subsection (5) above and purports to be a certified copy or certified extract shall, subject to subsection (10) below, be admitted in evidence without further proof and without production of any original; and in Scotland such evidence shall be sufficient evidence.

(10) In the application of this section to England and Wales nothing in it shall be taken as detracting from section 69 or 70 of the Police and Criminal Evidence Act 1984 or any provision made by virtue of either of them.

(11) In this section 'certified copy' and 'certified extract' mean a copy and extract certified by the Registrar and sealed with the seal of the Patent Office.]

General note
This section was substituted by the Patents, Designs and Marks Act 1986, s 1 and Sch 1, para 1.

Effect of registration and the action for infringement

2.   No action for infringement of unregistered trade mark
No person shall be entitled to institute any proceeding to prevent, or to recover damages for, the infringement of an unregistered trade mark, but nothing in this Act shall be deemed to affect rights of action against any person for passing off … or the remedies in respect thereof.

General note
The words omitted were repealed by the Trade Marks (Amendment) Act 1984, s 1(5)(a).

3.   Registration to be in respect of particular goods
A trade mark must be registered in respect of particular goods or classes of goods, and any question arising as to the class within which any goods fall shall be determined by the Registrar, whose decision shall be final.

4.   Right given by registration in Part A, and infringement thereof
(1) Subject to the provisions of this section, and of sections seven and eight of this Act, the registration (whether before or after the commencement of this Act) of a person in Part A of the register as proprietor of a trade mark (other than a certification trade mark) in respect of any goods shall, if valid, give or be deemed to have given to that person the exclusive right to the use of the trade mark in relation to those goods and, without prejudice to the generality of the foregoing words, that right shall be deemed to be infringed by any person who, not being the proprietor of the trade mark or a registered user thereof using by way of the permitted use, uses [in the course of trade a mark identical with or nearly resembling it], in relation to any goods in respect of which it is registered, and in such manner as to render the use of the mark likely to be taken either—

(a) as being use as a trade mark; or

(b) in a case in which the use is use upon the goods or in physical relation thereto or in an advertising circular or other advertisement issued to the public, as importing a reference to some person having the right either as proprietor or as registered user to use the trade mark or to goods with which such a person as aforesaid is connected in the course of trade.

(2) The right to the use of a trade mark given by registration as aforesaid shall be subject to any conditions or limitations entered on the register, and shall not be deemed to be infringed by the use of any such mark as aforesaid in any mode, in relation to goods to be sold or otherwise traded in in any place, in relation to goods to be exported to any market, or in any other circumstances, to which, having regard to any such limitations, the registration does not extend.

(3) The right to the use of a trade mark given by registration as aforesaid shall not be deemed to be infringed by the use of any such mark as aforesaid by any person—

(a) in relation to goods connected in the course of trade with the proprietor or a registered user of the trade mark if, as to those goods or a bulk of which they form part, the proprietor or the registered user conforming to the permitted use has applied the trade mark and has not subsequently removed or obliterated it, or has at any time expressly or impliedly consented to the use of the trade mark; or

(b) in relation to goods adapted to form part of, or to be accessory to, other goods in relation to which the trade mark has been used without infringement of the right given as aforesaid or might for the time being be so used, if the use of the mark is reasonably necessary in order to indicate that the goods are so adapted and neither the purpose nor the effect of the use of the mark is to indicate otherwise than in accordance with the fact a connection in the course of trade between any person and the goods.

(4) The use of a registered trade mark, being one of two or more registered trade marks that are identical or nearly resemble each other, in exercise of the right to the use of that trade mark given by registration as aforesaid, shall not be deemed to be an infringement of the right so given to the use of any other of those trade marks.

General note
In sub-s (1), the words in square brackets were substituted by the Trade Marks (Amendment) Act 1984, s 1(4) and Sch 2, para 1.

5. Right given by registration in Part B, and infringement thereof

(1) Except as provided by subsection (2) of this section, the registration (whether before or after the commencement of this Act) of a person in Part B of the register as proprietor of a trade mark in respect of any goods shall, if valid, give or be deemed to have given to that person the like right in relation to those goods as if the registration had been in Part A of the register, and the provisions of the last foregoing section shall have effect in like manner in relation to a trade mark registered in Part B of the register as they have effect in relation to a trade mark registered in Part A of the register.

(2) In any action for infringement of the right to the use of a trade mark given by registration as aforesaid in Part B of the register, otherwise than by an act that is deemed to be an infringement by virtue of the next succeeding section, no injunction or other relief shall be granted to the plaintiff if the defendant establishes to the satisfaction of the court that the use of which the plaintiff complains is not likely to

deceive or cause confusion or to be taken as indicating a connection in the course of trade between the goods and some person having the right either as proprietor or as registered user to use the trade mark.

6. Infringement by breach of certain restrictions

(1) Where, by a contract in writing made with the proprietor or a registered user of a registered trade mark, a purchaser or owner of goods enters into an obligation to the effect that he will not do, in relation to the goods, an act to which this section applies, any person who, being the owner for the time being of the goods and having notice of the obligation, does that act, or authorises it to be done, in relation to the goods, in the course of trade or with a view to any dealing therewith in the course of trade, shall be deemed thereby to infringe the right to the use of the trade mark given by the registration thereof, unless that person became the owner of the goods by purchase for money or money's worth in good faith before receiving notice of the obligation or by virtue of a title derived through another who so became the owner thereof.

(2) The acts to which this section applies are—

(a) the application of the trade mark upon the goods after they have suffered alteration in any manner specified in the contract as respects their state or condition, get-up or packing;

(b) in a case in which the trade mark is upon the goods, the alteration, part removal or part obliteration thereof;

(c) in a case in which the trade mark is upon the goods, and there is also thereon other matter, being matter indicating a connection in the course of trade between the proprietor or registered user and the goods, the removal or obliteration, whether wholly or partly, of the trade mark unless that other matter is wholly removed or obliterated;

(d) in a case in which the trade mark is upon the goods, the application of any other trade mark to the goods;

(e) in a case in which the trade mark is upon the goods, the addition to the goods of any other matter in writing that is likely to injure the reputation of the trade mark.

(3) In this section references in relation to any goods to the proprietor, to a registered user, and to the registration, of a trade mark shall be construed, respectively, as references to the proprietor in whose name the trade mark is registered, to a registered user who is registered, and to the registration of the trade mark, in respect of those goods, and the expression 'upon' includes in relation to any goods a reference to physical relation thereto.

7. Saving for vested rights

Nothing in this Act shall entitle the proprietor or a registered user of a registered trade mark to interfere with or restrain the use by any person of a trade mark identical with or nearly resembling it in relation to goods in relation to which that person or a predecessor in title of his has continuously used that trade mark from a date anterior—

(a) to the use of the first-mentioned trade mark in relation to those goods by the proprietor or a predecessor in title of his; or

(b) to the registration of the first-mentioned trade mark in respect of those goods in the name of the proprietor or a predecessor in title of his;

whichever is the earlier, or to object (on such use being proved) to that person being put on the register for that identical or nearly resembling trade mark in respect of those goods under subsection (2) of section twelve of this Act.

8.   Saving for use of name, address, or description of goods
No registration of a trade mark shall interfere with—

(a) any bona fide use by a person of his own name or of the name of his place of business, or of the name, or of the name of the place of business, of any of his predecessors in business; or

(b) the use by any person of any bona fide description of the character or quality of his goods, not being a description that would be likely to be taken as importing any such reference as is mentioned in paragraph (b) of subsection (1) of section four, or in paragraph (b) of subsection (3) of section thirty-seven, of this Act.

Registrability and validity of registration

9.   Distinctiveness requisite for registration in Part A
(1) In order for a trade mark (other than a certification trade mark) to be registrable in Part A of the register, it must contain or consist of at least one of the following essential particulars:—

(a) the name of a company, individual, or firm, represented in a special or particular manner;

(b) the signature of the applicant for registration or some predecessor in his business;

(c) an invented word or invented words;

(d) a word or words having no direct reference to the character or quality of the goods, and not being according to its ordinary signification a geographical name or a surname;

(e) any other distinctive mark, but a name, signature, or word or words, other than such as fall within the descriptions in the foregoing paragraphs (a), (b), (c) and (d), shall not be registrable under the provisions of this paragraph except upon evidence of its distinctiveness.

(2) For the purposes of this section 'distinctive' means adapted, in relation to the goods in respect of which a trade mark is registered or proposed to be registered, to distinguish goods with which the proprietor of the trade mark is or may be connected in the course of trade from goods in the case of which no such connection subsists, either generally or, where the trade mark is registered or proposed to be registered subject to limitations, in relation to use within the extent of the registration.

(3) In determining whether a trade mark is adapted to distinguish as aforesaid the tribunal may have regard to the extent to which—

(a) the trade mark is inherently adapted to distinguish as aforesaid; and

(b) by reason of the use of the trade mark or of any other circumstances, the trade mark is in fact adapted to distinguish as aforesaid.

10.   Capability of distinguishing requisite for registration in Part B
(1) In order for a trade mark to be registrable in Part B of the register it must be capable, in relation to the goods in respect of which it is registered or proposed to be registered, of distinguishing goods with which the proprietor of the trade mark is or may be connected in the course of trade from goods in the case of which no such

693

connection subsists, either generally or, where the trademark is registered or proposed to be registered subject to limitations, in relation to use within the extent of the registration.

(2) In determining whether a trade mark is capable of distinguishing as aforesaid the tribunal may have regard to the extent which—

(a) the trade mark is inherently capable of distinguishing as aforesaid; and
(b) by reason of the use of the trade mark or of any other circumstances, the trade mark is in fact capable of distinguishing as aforesaid.

(3) A trade mark may be registered in Part B notwithstanding any registration in Part A in the name of the same proprietor of the same trade mark or any part or parts thereof.

11. Prohibition of registration of deceptive, etc, matter

It shall not be lawful to register as a trade mark or part of a trade mark any matter the use of which would, by reason of its being likely to deceive or cause confusion or otherwise, be disentitled to protection in a court of justice, or would be contrary to law or morality, or any scandalous design.

12. Prohibition of registration of identical and resembling trade marks

(1) Subject to the provisions of subsection (2) of this section, no trade mark shall be registered in respect of any goods or description of goods that is identical with [or nearly resembles a mark belonging to a different proprietor and already on the register in respect of—

(a) the same goods,
(b) the same description of goods, or
(c) services or a description of services which are associated with those goods or goods of that description.]

(2) In case of honest concurrent use, or of other special circumstances which in the opinion of the Court or the Registrar make it proper so to do, the Court or the Registrar may permit the registration [by more than one proprietor, in respect of—

(a) the same goods,
(b) the same description of goods, or
(c) goods and services or descriptions of goods and services which are associated with each other,

of marks that are identical or nearly resemble each other,] subject to such conditions and limitations, if any, as the Court or the Registrar, as the case may be, may think it right to impose.

(3) Where separate applications are made by different persons to be registered as proprietors respectively of [marks that are identical or nearly resemble each other, in respect of—

(a) the same goods,
(b) the same description of goods, or
(c) goods and services or descriptions of goods and services which are associated with each other,]

the Registrar may refuse to register any of them until their rights have been determined by the Court, or have been settled by agreement in a manner approved by him or on an appeal (which may be brought either to the Board of Trade or to the Court at the option of the appellant) by the Board or the Court, as the case may be.

General note
The words in square brackets in sub-ss (1), (2), (3) were substituted by the Trade Marks (Amendment) Act 1984, s 1(4) and Sch 2, para 2.

13. Registration in Part A to be conclusive as to validity after seven years

(1) In all legal proceedings relating to a trade mark registered in Part A of the register (including applications under section thirty-two of this Act) the original registration in Part A of the register of the trade mark shall, after the expiration of seven years from the date of that registration, be taken to be valid in all respects, unless—

(a) that registration was obtained by fraud, or
(b) the trade mark offends against the provisions of section eleven of this Act.

(2) Nothing in subsection (1) of section five of this Act shall be construed as making applicable to a trade mark, as being a trade mark registered in Part B of the register, the foregoing provisions of this section relating to a trade mark registered in Part A of the register.

14. Registration subject to disclaimer

If a trade mark—

(a) contains any part not separately registered by the proprietor as a trade mark; or
(b) contains matter common to the trade or otherwise of a non-distinctive character;

the Registrar or the Board of Trade or the Court, in deciding whether the trade mark shall be entered or shall remain on the register, may require, as a condition of its being on the register,—

(i) that the proprietor shall disclaim any right to the exclusive use of any part of the trade mark, or to the exclusive use of all or any portion of any such matter as aforesaid, to the exclusive use of which the tribunal holds him not to be entitled; or

(ii) that the proprietor shall make such other disclaimer as the tribunal may consider necessary for the purpose of defining his rights under the registration:

Provided that no disclaimer on the register shall affect any rights of the proprietor of a trade mark except such as arise out of the registration of the trade mark in respect of which the disclaimer is made.

15. Words used as name or description of an article or substance

(1) The registration of a trade mark shall not be deemed to have become invalid by reason only of any use, after the date of the registration, of a word or words which the trade mark contains, or of which it consists, as the name or description of an article or substance:
Provided that, if it is proved either—

(a) that there is a well-known and established use of the word or words as the name or description of the article or substance by a person or persons carrying on a trade therein, not being use in relation to goods connected in the course of trade with the proprietor or a registered user of the trade mark or (in the case of a certification trade mark) goods certified by the proprietor; or

(b) that the article or substance was formerly manufactured under a patent (being a patent in force on, or granted after, the twenty-third day of December nineteen hundred and nineteen), that a period of two years or more after the cesser of the patent has elapsed, and that the word or words is or are the only practicable name or description of the article or substance;

the provisions of the next succeeding subsection shall have effect.

(2) Where the facts mentioned in paragraph (a) or (b) of the proviso to the foregoing subsection are proved with respect to any word or words, then—

(a) if the trade mark consists solely of that word or those words, the registration of the trade mark, so far as regards registration in respect of the article or substance in question or of any goods of the same description, shall be deemed for the purposes of section thirty-two of this Act to be an entry wrongly remaining on the register;

(b) if the trade mark contains that word or those words and other matter, the Court or the Registrar, in deciding whether the trade mark shall remain on the register, so far as regards registration in respect of the article or substance in question and of any goods of the same description, may in case of a decision in favour of its remaining on the register require as a condition thereof that the proprietor shall disclaim any right to the exclusive use in relation to that article or substance and any goods of the same description of that word or those words, so, however, that no disclaimer on the register shall affect any rights of the proprietor of a trade mark except such as arise out of the registration of the trade mark in respect of which the disclaimer is made; and

(c) for the purposes of any other legal proceedings relating to the trade mark,—

(i) if the trade mark consists solely of that word or those words, all rights of the proprietor, whether under the common law or by registration, to the exclusive use of the trade mark in relation to the article or substance in question or to any goods of the same description, or

(ii) if the trade mark contains that word or those words and other matter, all such rights of the proprietor to the exclusive use of that word or those words in such relation as aforesaid,

shall be deemed to have ceased on the date at which the use mentioned in paragraph (a) of the proviso to the foregoing subsection first became well known and established, or at the expiration of the period of two years mentioned in paragraph (b) of that proviso.

(3) No word which is the commonly used and accepted name of any single chemical element or single chemical compound, as distinguished from a mixture, shall be registered as a trade mark in respect of a chemical substance or preparation, and any such registration in force at the commencement of this Act or thereafter shall, notwithstanding anything in section thirteen of this Act, be deemed for the purposes of section thirty-two of this Act to be an entry made in the register without sufficient cause, or an entry wrongly remaining on the register, as the circumstances may require:

Provided that the foregoing provisions of this subsection shall not have effect in relation to a word which is used to denote only a brand or make of the element or compound as made by the proprietor or a registered user of the trade mark, as distinguished from the element or compound as made by others, and in association with a suitable name or description open to the public use.

16. Effect of limitation as to colour, and of absence thereof

A trade mark may be limited in whole or in part to one or more specified colours, and in any such case the fact that it is so limited shall be taken into consideration by any tribunal having to decide on the distinctive character of the trade mark.

If and so far as a trade mark is registered without limitation of colour, it shall be deemed to be registered for all colours.

Procedure for, and duration of, registration

17. Application for registration

(1) Any person claiming to be the proprietor of a trade mark used or proposed to be used by him who is desirous of registering it must apply in writing to the Registrar in the prescribed manner for registration either in Part A or in Part B of the register.

(2) Subject to the provisions of this Act, the Registrar may refuse the application, or may accept it absolutely or subject to such amendments, modifications, conditions or limitations, if any, as he may think right.

(3) In the case of an application for registration of a trade mark (other than a certification trade mark) in Part A of the register, the Registrar may, if the applicant is willing, instead of refusing the application, treat it as an application for registration in Part B and deal with the application accordingly.

(4) In the case of a refusal or conditional acceptance, the Registrar shall, if required by the applicant, state in writing the grounds of his decision and the materials used by him in arriving thereat, and the decision shall be subject to appeal to the Board of Trade or to the Court at the option of the applicant.

(5) An appeal under this section shall be made in the prescribed manner, and on the appeal the tribunal shall, if required, hear the applicant and the Registrar, and shall make an order determining whether, and subject to what amendments, modifications, conditions or limitations, if any, the application is to be accepted.

(6) Appeals under this section shall be heard on the materials stated as aforesaid by the Registrar, and no further grounds of objection to the acceptance of the application shall be allowed to be taken by the Registrar, other than those so stated as aforesaid by him, except by leave of the tribunal hearing the appeal. Where any further grounds of objection are taken, the applicant shall be entitled to withdraw his application without payment of costs on giving notice as prescribed.

(7) The Registrar or the Board of Trade or the Court, as the case may be, may at any time, whether before or after acceptance, correct any error in or in connection with the application, or may permit the applicant to amend his application upon such terms as the Registrar or the Board of Trade or the Court, as the case may be, may think fit.

18. Opposition to registration

(1) When an application for registration of a trade mark has been accepted, whether absolutely or subject to conditions or limitations, the Registrar shall, as soon as may be after acceptance, cause the application as accepted to be advertised in the prescribed manner, and the advertisement shall set forth all conditions and limitations subject to which the application has been accepted:

Provided that the Registrar may cause an application to be advertised before acceptance if it is made under paragraph (e) of subsection (1) of section nine of this Act, or in any other case where it appears to him that it is expedient by reason of any exceptional circumstances so to do, and where an application has been so advertised the Registrar may, if he thinks fit, advertise it again when it has been accepted but shall not be bound so to do.

(2) Any person may, within the prescribed time from the date of the advertisement of an application, give notice to the Registrar of opposition to the registration.

(3) The notice shall be given in writing in the prescribed manner, and shall include a statement of the grounds of opposition.

(4) The Registrar shall send a copy of the notice to the applicant, and within the prescribed time after receipt thereof the applicant shall send to the Registrar, in the prescribed manner, a counter-statement of the grounds on which he relies or his application, and, if he does not do so, he shall be deemed to have abandoned his application.

(5) If the applicant sends such a counter-statement as aforesaid, the Registrar shall furnish a copy thereof to the persons giving notice of opposition, and shall, after hearing the parties, if so required, and considering the evidence, decide whether, and subject to what conditions or limitations, if any, registration is to be permitted.

(6) The decision of the Registrar shall be subject to appeal to the Court.

(7) An appeal under this section shall be made in the prescribed manner, and on the appeal the Court shall, if required, hear the parties and the Registrar, and shall make an order determining whether, and subject to what conditions or limitations, if any, registration is to be permitted.

(8) On the hearing of an appeal under this section any party may, either in the manner prescribed or by special leave of the Court, bring forward further material for the consideration of the Court.

(9) On an appeal under this section no further grounds of objection to the registration of a trade mark shall be allowed to be taken by the opponent or the Registrar, other than those so stated as aforesaid by the opponent, except by leave of the Court. Where any further grounds of objection are taken, the applicant shall be entitled to withdraw his application without payment of the costs of the opponent on giving notice as prescribed.

(10) On an appeal under this section the Court may, after hearing the Registrar, permit the trade mark proposed to be registered to be modified in any manner not substantially affecting the identity thereof, but in any such case the trade mark as so modified shall be advertised in the prescribed manner before being registered.

(11) If a person giving notice of opposition or an applicant sending a counter-statement after receipt of a copy of such a notice, or an appellant, neither resides nor carries on business in the United Kingdom, the tribunal may require him to give security for costs of the proceedings before the tribunal relative to the opposition or to the appeal, as the case may be, and in default of such security being duly given may treat the opposition or application, or the appeal, as the case may be, as abandoned.

19. Registration

(1) When an application for registration of a trade mark in Part A or in Part B of the register has been accepted, and either—

(a) the application has not been opposed and the time for notice of opposition has expired, or

(b) the application has been opposed and the opposition has been decided in favour of the applicant,

the Registrar shall, unless the application has been accepted in error or unless the Board of Trade otherwise direct, register the trade mark in Part A or Part B, as the case may be, and the trade mark, when registered, shall be registered[, subject to section 39A(2) below,] as of the date of the application for registration, and that date shall be deemed for the purposes of this Act to be the date of registration:

...

(2) On the registration of a trade mark the Registrar shall issue to the applicant a certificate in the prescribed form of the registration thereof sealed with the seal of the Patent Office.

(3) Where registration of a trade mark is not completed within twelve months from the date of the application by reason of default on the part of the applicant, the Registrar may, after giving notice of the non-completion to the applicant in writing in the prescribed manner, treat the application as abandoned unless it is completed within the time specified in that behalf in the notice.

General note
The words in square brackets in sub-s (1) were inserted and the words omitted repealed by the Patents, Designs and Marks Act 1986, ss 2(3), 3(2) and Sch 2, para 3, Sch 3, Pt II.

20. Duration and renewal of registration

(1) The registration of a trade mark shall be for a period of seven years, but may be renewed from time to time in accordance with the provisions of this section:
Provided that, in relation to a registration as of a date before the appointed day, this subsection shall have effect with the substitution of a period of fourteen years for the said period of seven years.

(2) The Registrar shall, on application made by the registered proprietor of a trade mark in the prescribed manner and within the prescribed period, renew the registration of the trade mark for a period of fourteen years from the date of expiration of the original registration or of the last renewal of registration, as the case may be, which date is in this section referred to as 'the expiration of the last registration.'

(3) At the prescribed time before the expiration of the last registration of a trade mark, the Registrar shall send notice in the prescribed manner to the registered proprietor of the date of expiration and the conditions as to payment of fees and otherwise upon which a renewal of registration may be obtained, and, if at the expiration of the time prescribed in that behalf those conditions have not been duly complied with, the Registrar may remove the trade mark from the register, subject to such conditions, if any, as to its restoration to the register as may be prescribed.

(4) Where a trade mark has been removed from the register for non-payment of the fee for renewal, it shall, nevertheless, for the purpose of any application for the registration of a mark during one year next after the date of the removal, be deemed to be a trade mark that is already on the register:
Provided that the foregoing provisions of this subsection shall not have effect where the tribunal is satisfied either—

(a) that there has been no bona fide trade use of the trade mark that has been removed during the two years immediately preceding its removal; or

(b) that no deception or confusion would be likely to arise from the use of the mark that is the subject of the application for registration by reason of any previous use of the trade mark that has been removed.

21. Registration of parts of trade marks and of trade marks as a series

(1) Where the proprietor of a trade mark claims to be entitled to the exclusive use of any part thereof separately, he may apply to register the whole and any such part as separate trade marks.
Each such separate trade mark must satisfy all the conditions of an independent trade mark and shall, subject to the provisions of subsection (3) of section twenty-three and subsection (2) of section thirty of this Act, have all the incidents of an independent trade mark.

(2) Where a person claiming to be the proprietor of several trade marks, in respect of the same goods or description of goods, which, while resembling each other in the material particulars thereof, yet differ in respect of—

(a) statements of the goods in relation to which they are respectively used or proposed to be used; or
(b) statements of number, price, quality or names of places; or
(c) other matter of a non-distinctive character which does not substantially affect the identity of the trade mark; or
(d) colour;

seeks to register those trade marks, they may be registered as a series in one registration.

Assignment and transmission

22. Powers of, and restrictions on, assignment and transmission

(1) Notwithstanding any rule of law or equity to the contrary, a registered trade mark shall be, and shall be deemed always to have been, assignable and transmissible either in connection with the goodwill of a business or not.

(2) A registered trade mark shall be, and shall be deemed always to have been, assignable and transmissible in respect either of all the goods in respect of which it is registered, or was registered, as the case may be, or of some (but not all) of those goods.

(3) The provisions of the two foregoing subsections shall have effect in the case of an unregistered trade mark used in relation to any goods as they have effect in the case of a registered trade mark registered in respect of any goods, if at the time of the assignment or transmission of the unregistered trade mark it is or was used in the same business as a registered trade mark, and if it is or was assigned or transmitted at the same time and to the same person as that registered trade mark and in respect of goods all of which are goods in relation to which the unregistered trade mark is or was used in that business and in respect of which that registered trade mark is or was assigned or transmitted.

(4) Notwithstanding anything in the foregoing subsections, a trade mark shall not be, or be deemed to having been assignable or transmissible in a case in which as a result of an assignment or transmission there would in the circumstances subsist, or have subsisted, whether under the common law or by registration, exclusive rights in more than one of the persons concerned to the use, in relation to

(a) the same goods,
(b) the same description of goods, or
(c) goods and services or descriptions of goods and services which are associated with each other]

of marks nearly resembling each other or of identical marks, if, having regard to the similarity of the goods [or the association of the goods and services or description of goods and services and to the similarity of the marks], the use of the marks in exercise of those rights would be, or have been, likely to deceive or cause confusion:

Provided that, where a trade mark is, or has been, assigned or transmitted in such a case as aforesaid, the assignment or transmission shall not be deemed to be, or to have been, invalid under this subsection if the exclusive rights subsisting as a result thereof in the persons concerned respectively are, or were, having regard to limitations imposed thereon, such as not to be exercisable by two or more of those persons in relation to goods to be sold, or otherwise traded in, within the United

Kingdom (otherwise than for export therefrom) or in relation to goods to be exported to the same market outside the United Kingdom.

(5) The proprietor of a registered trade mark who proposes to assign it in respect of any goods in respect of which it is registered may submit to the Registrar in the prescribed manner a statement of case setting out the circumstances, and the Registrar may issue to him a certificate stating whether, having regard to the similarity of [the goods or the association of the goods and services or descriptions of goods and services and to the similarity] of the marks referred to in the case, the proposed assignment of the first-mentioned trade mark would or would not be invalid under the last foregoing subsection, and a certificate so issued shall, subject to the provisions of this section as to appeal and unless it is shown that the certificate was obtained by fraud or misrepresentation, be conclusive as to the validity or invalidity under the last foregoing subsection of the assignment in so far as such validity or invalidity depends upon the facts set out in the case, but, as regards a certificate in favour of validity, only if application for the registration under section twenty-five of this Act of the title of the person becoming entitled is made within six months from the date on which the certificate is issued.

(6) Notwithstanding anything in subsections (1) to (3) of this section, a trade mark shall not, on or after the appointed day, be assignable or transmissible in a case in which as a result of an assignment or transmission thereof there would in the circumstances subsist, whether under the common law or by registration,

(a) an exclusive right in one of the persons concerned to the use of the mark limited to use in relation to goods to be sold, or otherwise traded in, in a place or places in the United Kingdom; and
(b) an exclusive right in another of the persons concerned to the use of a mark identical with or nearly resembling the mark referred to in paragraph (a) above in relation to—

   (i) the same goods,
   (ii) the same description of goods or
   (iii) services which are associated with those goods or goods of that description,

limited to use in relation to goods to be sold, or otherwise traded in, or services for use or available for acceptance, in another place or places in the United Kingdom;]

Provided that, on application in the prescribed manner by the proprietor of a trade mark who proposes to assign it, or of a person who claims that a trade mark has been transmitted to him or to a predecessor in title of his on or after the appointed day, in any such case, the Registrar, if he is satisfied that in all the circumstances the use of the marks in exercise of the said rights would not be contrary to the public interest, may approve the assignment or transmission, and an assignment or transmission so approved shall not be deemed to be, or to have been, invalid under this subsection or under subsection (4) of this section, so, however, that in the case of a registered trade mark this provision shall not have effect unless application for the registration under section twenty-five of this Act of the title of the person becoming entitled is made within six months from the date on which the approval is given or, in the case of a transmission, was made before that date.

(7) Where an assignment in respect of any goods of a trade mark that is at the time of the assignment used in a business in those goods is made, on or after the appointed day, otherwise than in connection with the goodwill of that business, the assignment shall not take effect until the following requirements have been satis-

fied, that is to say, the assignee must, not later than the expiration of six months from the date on which the assignment is made or within such extended period, if any, as the Registrar may allow, apply to him for directions with respect to the advertisement of the assignment, and must advertise it in such form and manner and within such period as the Registrar may direct.

(8) Any decision of the Registrar under this section shall be subject to appeal to the Court.

General note
The words in square brackets in sub-ss (4), (5), (6) were substituted by the Trade Marks (Amendment) Act 1984, s 1(4) and Sch 2, para 3.

23. Certain trade marks to be associated so as to be assignable and transmissible as a whole only

(1) Trade marks that are registered as, or that are deemed by virtue of this Act to be, associated trade marks shall be assignable and transmissible only as a whole and not separately, but they shall for all other purposes be deemed to have been registered as separate trade marks.

(2) Where a trade mark that is registered, or is the subject of an application for registration, in respect of any goods is identical with another trade mark that is registered, or is the subject of an application for registration, in the name of the same proprietor in respect of the same goods or description of goods, or so nearly resembles it as to be likely to deceive or cause confusion if used by a person other than the proprietor, the Registrar may at any time require that the trade marks shall be entered on the register as associated trade marks.
Any decision of the Registrar under this subsection shall be subject to appeal to the Board of Trade, or to the Court, at the option of the appellant.

[(2A) Where there is an identicality or near resemblance of marks that are registered, or are the subject of applications for registration, in the name of the same proprietor in respect of goods and in respect of services which are associated with those goods or goods of that description, subsection (2) applies as it applies where there is an identicality or near resemblance of marks that are registered, or are the subject of applications for registration, in the name of the same proprietor in respect of the same goods or description of goods.]

(3) Where a trade mark and any part or parts thereof are, by virtue of subsection (1) of section twenty-one of this Act, registered as separate trade marks in the name of the same proprietor, they shall be deemed to be, and shall be registered as, associated trade marks.

(4) All trade marks that are, by virtue of subsection (2) of section twenty-one of this Act, registered as a series in one registration shall be deemed to be, and shall be registered as, associated trade marks.

(5) On application made in the prescribed manner by the registered proprietor of two or more marks registered as associated marks, the Registrar may dissolve the association as respects any of them if he is satisfied that there would be no likelihood of deception or confusion being caused if that mark were used by another person in relation to any of the [goods] [services] in respect of which it is registered, and may amend the register accordingly.

Any decision of the Registrar under this subsection shall be subject to appeal to the Board of Trade, or to the Court, at the option of the appellant.

General note
Sub-s (2A) was inserted by the Trade Marks (Amendment) Act 1984, s 1(4) and Sch 2, para 4.

24. Power of registered proprietor to assign and give receipts

Subject to the provisions of this Act, the person for the time being entered in the register as proprietor of a trade mark shall, subject to any rights appearing from the register to be vested in any other person, have power to assign the trade mark, and to give effectual receipts for any consideration for an assignment thereof.

25. Registration of assignments and transmissions

(1) Where a person becomes entitled by assignment or transmission to a registered trade mark, he shall make application to the Registrar to register his title, and the Registrar shall, on receipt of the application and on proof of title to his satisfaction, register him as the proprietor of the trade mark in respect of the goods in respect of which the assignment or transmission has effect, and shall cause particulars of the assignment or transmission to be entered on the register.

(2) Any decision of the Registrar under this section shall be subject to appeal to the Court.

(3) Except for the purposes of an appeal under this section or of an application under section thirty-two of this Act, a document or instrument in respect of which no entry has been made in the register in accordance with the provisions of subsection (1) of this section shall not be admitted in evidence in any court in proof of the title to a trade mark unless the court otherwise directs.

Use and non-use

26. Removal from register and imposition of limitations on ground of non-use

(1) Subject to the provisions of the next succeeding section, a registered trade mark may be taken off the register in respect of any of the goods in respect of which it is registered on application by any person aggrieved to the Court or, at the option of the applicant and subject to the provisions of section fifty-four of this Act, to the Registrar, on the ground either—

  (a) that the trade mark was registered without any bona fide intention on the part of the applicant for registration that it should be used in relation to those goods by him, and that there has in fact been no bona fide use of the trade mark in relation to those goods by any proprietor thereof for the time being up to the date one month before the date of the application; or

  (b) that up to the date one month before the date of the application a continuous period of five years or longer elapsed during which the trade mark was a registered trade mark and during which there was no bona fide use thereof in relation to those goods by any proprietor thereof for the time being:

Provided that (except where the applicant has been permitted under subsection (2) of section twelve of this Act to register an identical or nearly resembling trade mark in respect of the goods in question or where the tribunal is of opinion that he might properly be permitted so to register such a trade mark) the tribunal may refuse an application made under paragraph (a) or (b) of this subsection in relation to any goods, if it is shown that there has been, before the relevant date or during the relevant period, as the case may be, bona fide use [of the mark by the proprietor thereof for the time being in relation to—

  (i) goods of the same description; or

  (ii) services associated with those goods or goods of that description, being goods or, as the case may be, services in respect of which the mark is registered.]

(2) Where in relation to any goods in respect of which a trade mark is registered—

  (a) the matters referred to in paragraph (b) of the foregoing subsection are shown so far as regards non-use of the trade mark in relation to goods to be sold, or otherwise traded in, in a particular place in the United Kingdom (otherwise than for export from the United Kingdom), or in relation to goods to be exported to a particular market outside the United Kingdom; and

  (b) a person has been permitted under subsection (2) of section twelve of this Act to register an identical or nearly resembling trade mark in respect of those goods under a registration extending to use in relation to goods to be sold, or otherwise traded in, in that place (otherwise than for export from the United Kingdom), or in relation to goods to be exported to that market, or the tribunal is of opinion that he might properly be permitted so to register such a trade mark;

on application by that person to the Court or, at the option of the applicant and subject to the provisions of section fifty-four of this Act, to the Registrar the tribunal may impose on the registration of the first-mentioned trade mark such limitations as the tribunal thinks proper for securing that that registration shall cease to extend to such use as last aforesaid.

(3) An applicant shall not be entitled to rely for the purposes of paragraph (b) of subsection (1), or for the purposes of subsection (2), of this section on any non-use of a trade mark that is shown to have been due to special circumstances in the trade and not to any intention not to use or to abandon the trade mark in relation to the goods to which the application relates.

General note

In sub-s (1) the words in square brackets were substituted by the Patents, Designs and Marks Act 1986, s 2(3) and Sch 2, para 4.

27.   Defensive registration of well known trade marks

(1) Where a trade mark consisting of an invented word or invented words has become so well known as respects any goods in respect of which it is registered and in relation to which it has been used that the use thereof in relation to other goods would be likely to be taken as indicating a connection in the course of trade between those goods and a person entitled to use the trade mark in relation to the first-mentioned goods, then, notwithstanding that the proprietor registered in respect of the first-mentioned goods does not use or propose to use the trade mark in relation to those other goods and notwithstanding anything in the last foregoing section, the trade mark may, on the application in the prescribed manner of the proprietor registered in respect of the first-mentioned goods, be registered in his name in respect of those other goods as a defensive trade mark and, while so registered, shall not be liable to be taken off the register in respect of those goods under the last foregoing section.

(2) The registered proprietor of a trade mark may apply for the registration thereof in respect of any goods as a defensive trade mark notwithstanding that it is already registered in his name in respect of those goods otherwise than as a defensive trade mark, or may apply for the registration thereof in respect of any goods otherwise than as a defensive trade mark notwithstanding that it is already

registered in his name in respect of those goods as a defensive trade mark, in lieu in each case of the existing registration.

(3) A trade mark registered as a defensive trade mark and that trade mark as otherwise registered in the name of the same proprietor shall, notwithstanding that the respective registrations are in respect of different goods, be deemed to be, and shall be registered as, associated trade marks.

(4) On application by any person aggrieved to the Court or, at the option of the applicant and subject to the provisions of section fifty-four of this Act, to the Registrar, the registration of a trade mark as a defensive trade mark may be cancelled on the ground that the requirements of subsection (1) of this section are no longer satisfied in respect of any goods in respect of which the trade mark is registered in the name of the same proprietor otherwise than as a defensive trade mark, or may be cancelled as respects any goods in respect of which it is registered as a defensive trade mark on the ground that there is no longer any likelihood that the use of the trade mark in relation to those goods would be taken as giving the indication mentioned in subsection (1) of this section.

(5) The Registrar may at any time cancel the registration as a defensive trade mark of a trade mark of which there is no longer any registration in the name of the same proprietor otherwise than as a defensive trade mark.

(6) Except as otherwise expressly provided in this section, the provisions of this Act shall apply in respect of the registration of trade marks as defensive trade marks and of trade marks so registered as they apply in other cases.

28. Registered users

(1) Subject to the provisions of this section, a person other than the proprietor of a trade mark may be registered as a registered user thereof in respect of all or any of the goods in respect of which it is registered (otherwise than as a defensive trade mark) and either with or without conditions or restrictions.

The use of a trade mark by a registered user thereof in relation to goods with which he is connected in the course of trade and in respect of which for the time being the trade mark remains registered and he is registered as a registered user, being use such as to comply with any conditions or restrictions to which his registration is subject, is in this Act referred to as the 'permitted use' thereof.

(2) The permitted use of a trade mark shall be deemed to be use by the proprietor thereof, and shall be deemed not to be use by a person other than the proprietor, for the purposes of section twenty-six of this Act and for any other purpose for which such use is material under this Act or at common law.

(3) Subject to any agreement subsisting between the parties, a registered user of a trade mark shall be entitled to call upon the proprietor thereof to take proceedings to prevent infringement thereof, and, if the proprietor refuses or neglects to do so within two months after being so called upon, the registered user may institute proceedings for infringement in his own name as if he were the proprietor, making the proprietor a defendant.

A proprietor so added as defendant shall not be liable for any costs unless he enters an appearance and takes part in the proceedings.

(4) Where it is proposed that a person should be registered as a registered user of a trade mark, the proprietor and the proposed registered user must apply in writing to the Registrar in the prescribed manner and must furnish him with a statutory declaration made by the proprietor, or by some person authorised to act on his behalf and approved by the Registrar,—

    (a) giving particulars of the relationship, existing or proposed, between the proprietor and the proposed registered user, including particulars showing the degree of control by the proprietor over the permitted use which their relationship will confer and whether it is a term of their relationship that the proposed registered user shall be the sole registered user or that there shall be any other restriction as to persons for whose registration as registered users application may be made;

(b) stating the goods in respect of which registration is proposed;

(c) stating any conditions or restrictions proposed with respect to the characteristics of the goods, to the mode or place of permitted use, or to any other matter; and

(d) stating whether the permitted use is to be for a period or without limit of period, and, if for a period, the duration thereof;

and with such further documents, information or evidence as may be required under the rules or by the Registrar.

(5) When the requirements of the last foregoing subsection have been complied with, if the Registrar, after considering the information furnished to him under that subsection, is satisfied that in all the circumstances the use of the trade mark in relation to the proposed goods or any of them by the proposed registered user subject to any conditions or restrictions which the Registrar thinks proper would not be contrary to the public interest, the Registrar may register the proposed registered user as a registered user in respect of the goods as to which he is so satisfied subject as aforesaid.

(6) The Registrar shall refuse an application under the foregoing provisions of this section if it appears to him that the grant thereof would tend to facilitate trafficking in a trade mark.

(7) The Registrar shall, if so required by an applicant, take steps for securing that information given for the purposes of an application under the foregoing provisions of this section (other than matter entered in the register) is not disclosed to rivals in trade.

(8) Without prejudice to the provisions of section thirty-two of this Act, the registration of a person as a registered user—

(a) may be varied by the Registrar as regards the goods in respect of which, or any conditions or restrictions subject to which, it has effect, on the application in writing in the prescribed manner of the registered proprietor of the trade mark to which the registration relates;

(b) may be cancelled by the Registrar on the application in writing in the prescribed manner of the registered proprietor or of the registered user or of any other registered user of the trade mark; or

(c) may be cancelled by the Registrar on the application in writing in the prescribed manner of any person on any of the following grounds, that is to say,—

(i) that the registered user has used the trade mark otherwise than by way of the permitted use, or in such a way as to cause, or to be likely to cause, deception or confusion;

(ii) that the proprietor or the registered user misrepresented, or failed to disclose, some fact material to the application for the registration, or that the circumstances have materially changed since the date of the registration;

(iii) that the registration ought not to have been effected having regard to rights vested in the applicant by virtue of a contract in the performance of which he is interested.

(9) Provision shall be made by the rules for the notification of the registration of a person as a registered user to any other registered user of the trade mark, and for the notification of an application under the last foregoing subsection to the registered proprietor and each registered user (not being the applicant) of the trade mark, and for giving to the applicant on such an application, and to all persons to whom such an application is notified and who intervene in the proceedings in accordance with the rules, an opportunity of being heard.

(10) The Registrar may at any time cancel the registration of a person as a registered user of a trade mark in respect of any goods in respect of which the trade mark is no longer registered.

(11) Any decision of the Registrar under the foregoing provisions of this section shall be subject to appeal to the Court.

(12) Nothing in this section shall confer on a registered user of a trade mark any assignable or transmissible right to the use thereof.

29. Proposed use of trade mark by corporation to be constituted, etc

(1) No application for the registration of a trade mark in respect of any goods shall be refused, nor shall permission for such registration be withheld, on the ground only that it appears that the applicant does not use or propose to use the trade mark,—

(a) if the tribunal is satisfied that a body corporate is about to be constituted, and that the applicant intends to assign the trade mark to the corporation with a view to the use thereof in relation to those goods by the corporation; or

(b) if the application is accompanied by an application for the registration of a person as a registered user of the trade mark, and the tribunal is satisfied that the proprietor intends it to be used by that person in relation to those goods and the tribunal is also satisfied that that person will be registered as a registered user thereof immediately after the registration of the trade mark.

(2) The provisions of section twenty-six of this Act shall have effect, in relation to a trade mark registered under the power conferred by the foregoing subsection, as if for the reference, in paragraph (a) of subsection (1) of that section, to intention on the part of an applicant for registration that a trade mark should be used by him there were substituted a reference to intention on his part that it should be used by the corporation or registered user concerned.

(3) The tribunal may, as a condition of the exercise of the power conferred by subsection (1) of this section in favour of an applicant who relies on intention to assign to a corporation as aforesaid, require him to give security for the costs of any proceedings before the tribunal relative to any opposition or appeal, and in default of such security being duly given may treat the application as abandoned.

(4) Where a trade mark is registered in respect of any goods under the power conferred by subsection (1) of this section in the name of an applicant who relies on intention to assign to a corporation as aforesaid, then, unless within such period as may be prescribed, or within such further period not exceeding six months as the Registrar may on application being made to him in the prescribed manner allow, the corporation has been registered as the proprietor of the trade mark in respect of those goods, the registration shall cease to have effect in respect thereof at the expiration of that period, and the Registrar shall amend the register accordingly.

707

30. Use of one of associated or substantially identical trade marks equivalent to use of another

(1) Where under the provisions of this Act use of a registered trade mark is required to be proved for any purpose, the tribunal may, if and so far as the tribunal thinks right, accept use of an associated registered trade mark, or of the trade mark with additions or alterations not substantially affecting its identity, as an equivalent for the use required to be proved.

(2) The use of the whole of a registered trade mark shall for the purposes of this Act be deemed to be also a use of any registered trade mark, being a part thereof, registered in the name of the same proprietor by virtue of subsection (1) of section twenty-one of this Act.

31. Use of trade mark for export trade

The application in the United Kingdom of a trade mark to goods to be exported from the United Kingdom, and any other act done in the United Kingdom in relation to goods to be so exported which, if done in relation to goods to be sold or otherwise traded in within the United Kingdom, would constitute use of a trade mark therein, shall be deemed to constitute use of the trade mark in relation to those goods for any purpose for which such use is material under this Act or at common law.

Rectification and correction of the register

32. General power to rectify entries in register

(1) Any person aggrieved by the non-insertion in or omission from the register of any entry, or by any entry made in the register without sufficient cause, or by any entry wrongly remaining on the register, or by any error or defect in any entry in the register, may apply in the prescribed manner to the Court or, at the option of the applicant and subject to the provisions of section fifty-four o this Act, to the Registrar, and the tribunal may make such order for making, expunging or varying the entry as the tribunal may think fit.

(2) The tribunal may in any proceeding under this section decide any question that it may be necessary or expedient to decide in connection with the rectification of the register.

(3) In case of fraud in the registration, assignment or transmission of a registered trade mark, the Registrar may himself apply to the Court under the provisions of this section.

(4) Any order of the Court rectifying the register shall direct that notice of the rectification shall be served in the prescribed manner on the Registrar, and the Registrar shall on receipt of the notice rectify the register accordingly.

(5) The power to rectify the register conferred by this section shall include power to remove a registration in Part A of the register to Part B.

33. Power to expunge or vary registration for breach of condition

On application by any person aggrieved to the Court, or, at the option of the applicant and subject to the provisions of section fifty-four of this Act, to the Registrar, or on application by the Registrar to the Court, the tribunal may make such order as the tribunal may think fit for expunging or varying the registration of a trade mark on the ground of any contravention of, or failure to observe, a condition entered on the register in relation thereto.

34. Correction of register

(1) The Registrar may, on request made in the prescribed manner by the registered proprietor, —

    (a) correct any error in the [name or address] of the registered proprietor of a trade mark;

    (b) enter any change in the [name or address] of the person who is registered as proprietor of a trade mark;

    (c) cancel the entry of a trade mark on the register;

    (d) strike out any goods or classes of goods from those in respect of which a trade mark is registered; or

    (e) enter a disclaimer or memorandum relating to a trade mark which does not in any way extend the rights given by the existing registration of the trade mark.

(2) The Registrar may, on request made in the prescribed manner by a registered user of a trade mark, correct any error, or enter any change, in the [name or address] of the registered user.

(3) Any decision of the Registrar under this section shall be subject to appeal to the Board of Trade, or to the Court, at the option of the appellant.

General note
The words in square brackets in sub-ss (1), (2) were substituted by the Patents, Designs and Marks Act 1986, s 1 and Sch 1, para 2.

35. Alteration of registered trade mark

(1) The registered proprietor of a trade mark may apply in the prescribed manner to the Registrar for leave to add to or alter the trade mark in any manner not substantially affecting the identity thereof, and the Registrar may refuse leave or may grant it on such terms and subject to such limitations as he may think fit.

(2) The Registrar may cause an application under this section to be advertised in the prescribed manner in any case where it appears to him that it is expedient so to do, and where he does so, if within the prescribed time from the date of the advertisement any person gives notice to the Registrar in the prescribed manner of opposition to the application, the Registrar shall, after hearing the parties if so required, decide the matter.

(3) Any decision of the Registrar under this section shall be subject to appeal to the Board of Trade, or to the Court, at the option of the appellant.

(4) Where leave as aforesaid is granted, the trade mark as altered shall be advertised in the prescribed manner, unless it has already been advertised, in the form to which it has been altered, in an advertisement under subsection (2) of this section.

36. Adaptation of entries in register to amended or substituted classification of goods

(1) The Board of Trade may from time to time make such rules, prescribe such forms and generally do such things as they think expedient, for empowering the Registrar to amend the register, whether by making or expunging or varying entries therein, so far as may be requisite for the purpose of adapting the designation therein of the goods or classes of goods in respect of which trade marks are registered to any amended or substituted classification that may be prescribed.

(2) The Registrar shall not, in exercise of any power conferred on him for the purpose aforesaid, make any amendment of the register that would have the effect of adding any goods or classes of goods to those in respect of which a trade mark is

registered (whether in one or more classes) immediately before the amendment is to be made, or of antedating the registration of a trade mark in respect of any goods:

Provided that this subsection shall not have effect in relation to goods as to which the Registrar is satisfied that compliance with this subsection in relation thereto would involve undue complexity and that the addition or antedating, as the case may be, would not affect any substantial quantity of goods and would not substantially prejudice the rights of any person.

(3) A proposal for the amendment of the register for the purpose aforesaid shall be notified to the registered proprietor of the trade mark affected, shall be subject to appeal by the registered proprietor to the Board of Trade, or at his option to the Court, shall be advertised with any modifications, and may be opposed before the Registrar by any person aggrieved on the ground that the proposed amendment contravenes the provisions of the last foregoing subsection, and the decision of the Registrar on any such opposition shall be subject to appeal to the Court.

Certification trade marks

37.   Certification trade marks

(1) A mark adapted in relation to any goods to distinguish in the course of trade goods certified by any person in respect of origin, material, mode of manufacture, quality, accuracy or other characteristic, from goods not so certified shall be registrable as a certification trade mark in Part A of the register in respect of those goods in the name, as proprietor thereof, of that person:
Provided that a mark shall not be so registrable in the name of a person who carries on a trade in goods of the kind certified.

(2) In determining whether a mark is adapted to distinguish as aforesaid, the tribunal may have regard to the extent to which—

(a) the mark is inherently adapted to distinguish as aforesaid in relation to the goods in question; and
(b) by reason of the use of the mark or of any other circumstances, the mark is in fact adapted to distinguish as aforesaid in relation to the goods in question.

(3) Subject to the provisions of subsections (4) to (6) of this section, and of sections seven and eight of this Act, the registration of a person as proprietor of a certification trade mark in respect of any goods shall, if valid, give to that person the exclusive right to the use of the trade mark in relation to those goods, and, without prejudice to the generality of the foregoing words that right shall be deemed to be infringed by any person who, not being the proprietor of the trade mark or a person authorised by him under the regulations in that behalf using it in accordance therewith, uses a mark identical with it or so nearly resembling it as to be likely to deceive or cause confusion, in the course of trade, in relation to any goods in respect of which, it is registered, and in such manner as to render the use of the mark likely to be taken either—

(a) as being use as a trade mark; or
(b) in a case in which the use is use upon the goods or in physical relation thereto or in an advertising circular or other advertisement issued to the public, as importing a reference to some person having the right either as proprietor or by his authorisation under the relevant regulations to use the trade mark or to goods certified by the proprietor.

(4) The right to the use of a certification trade mark given by registration as aforesaid shall be subject to any conditions or limitations entered on the register and shall not be deemed to be infringed by the use of any such mark as aforesaid in any mode, in relation to goods to be sold or otherwise traded in in any place, in relation to goods to be exported to any market, or in any other circumstances, to which, having regard to any such limitations, the registration does not extend.

(5) The right to the use of a certification trade mark given by registration as aforesaid shall not be deemed to be infringed by the use of any such mark as aforesaid by any person—

(a) in relation to goods certified by the proprietor of the trade mark if, as to those goods or a bulk of which they form part, the proprietor or another in accordance with his authorisation under the relevant regulations has applied the trade mark and has not subsequently removed or obliterated it, or the proprietor has at any time expressly or impliedly consented to the use of the trade mark; or

(b) in relation to goods adapted to form part of, or to be accessory to, other goods in relation to which the trade mark has been used without infringement of the right given as aforesaid or might for the time being be so used, if the use of the mark is reasonably necessary in order to indicate that the goods are so adapted and neither the purpose nor the effect of the use of the mark is to indicate otherwise than in accordance with the fact that the goods are certified by the proprietor:

Provided that paragraph (a) of this subsection shall not have effect in the case of use consisting of the application of any such mark as aforesaid to any goods, notwithstanding that they are such goods as are mentioned in that paragraph, if such application is contrary to the relevant regulations.

(6) Where a certification trade mark is one of two or more registered trade marks that are identical or nearly resemble each other, the use of any of those trade marks in exercise of the right to the use of that trade mark given by registration shall not be deemed to be an infringement of the right so given to the use of any other of those trade marks.

(7) There shall be deposited at the Patent Office in respect of every trade mark registered under this section regulations approved by the Board of Trade for governing the use thereof, which shall include provisions as to the cases in which the proprietor is to certify goods and to authorise the use of the trade mark, and may contain any other provisions that the Board of Trade may require or permit to be inserted therein (including provisions conferring a right of appeal to the Registrar against any refusal of the proprietor to certify goods or to authorise the use of the trade mark in accordance with the regulations). Regulations so deposited shall be open to inspection in like manner as the register.

(8) A certification mark shall not be assignable or transmissible otherwise than with the consent of the Board of Trade.

(9) The provisions of the First Schedule to this Act shall have effect with respect to the registration of a mark under this section and to marks so registered.

Sheffield marks

38. Sheffield marks

The provisions of the Second Schedule to this Act shall have effect with respect to the master, wardens, searchers, assistants, and commonalty of the Company of Cutlers in Hallamshire, in the County of York (in this Act called 'the Cutlers'

Company'), and the marks or devices assigned or registered by the master, wardens, searchers and assistants of that Company.

Manchester Branch

39. Trade marks for textile goods

(1) The Manchester Branch of the Trade Marks Registry of the Patent Office (in this section referred to as 'the Manchester Branch') shall be continued under a chief officer, who shall be styled 'the Keeper of the Manchester Branch' and shall act under the direction of the Registrar.

(2) The rules shall specify certain of the classes for the time being established for the purposes of the registration of trade marks (being such of those classes as consist of, or appear to the Board of Trade to relate materially to, any of the following goods, that is to say, goods included immediately before the appointed day in any of the classes numbered twenty-three to thirty-five and thirty-eight respectively and similar goods made from artificial silk or from other artificial fibres) as being classes to which this section applies.

In this section the expression 'textile goods' means goods of any of the classes for the time being so specified other than goods of a kind as to which it may be provided by the rules that this section is not to apply thereto.

(3) The rules for prescribing the manner in which applications for the registration of trade marks are to be made shall make provision for the sending of an application for the registration of a trade mark in respect of textile goods to the Registrar either at the Patent Office or at the Manchester Branch, at the option of the applicant.

(4) The Keeper of the Manchester Branch shall furnish the Registrar with a report on every application for the registration of a trade mark sent to the Manchester Branch, and, before deciding under subsection (2) of section seventeen of this Act on any such application, the Registrar shall consider the report.

(5) In respect of textile goods being piece goods—

   (a) no mark consisting of a line heading alone shall be registrable as a trade mark;
   (b) a line heading shall not be deemed to be adapted to distinguish or capable of distinguishing;
   (c) the registration of a trade mark shall not give any exclusive right to the use of a line heading.

(6) There shall be kept at the Manchester Branch for the purposes of this Act a record called the Manchester Record wherein shall be entered copies of all entries in the register relating to trade marks registered in respect of textile goods on or after the appointed day and, as soon as may be, copies of all entries relating to trade marks so registered before the appointed day and for the time being subsisting, and the Manchester Record shall at all convenient times be open to the inspection of the public, subject to such regulations as may be prescribed.

(7) The right of inspection conferred by the last foregoing subsection shall extend to and include the right to inspect all applications whatsoever for registration that were made to the Manchester Branch, between the passing of the Trade Marks Registration Act 1875 and the appointed day, in respect of cotton goods, whether registered, refused, lapsed, expired, withdrawn, abandoned, cancelled or pending.

(8) Refused marks which, immediately before the appointed day, were included in the collection of refused marks kept under rules one hundred and twelve to one hundred and sixteen of the Trade Marks Rules 1920 and are at the time of the

application for the registration of a trade mark included in that collection under the rules shall be treated for the purposes of subsections (1) and (2) of section twelve of this Act, but for no other purpose, as if they had been registered trade marks.

(9) Before making any rule, or prescribing any form, that is to deal specially with trade marks registered or proposed to be registered in respect of textile goods other than clothing, the Board of Trade shall send a draft thereof to the Trade and Merchandise Marks Committee of the Manchester Chamber of Commerce, and shall, if the said committee so request, give them an opportunity of being heard.

(10) The Registrar, or the Keeper of the Manchester Branch, may consult the said committee where it appears to him to be expedient so to do with respect to any circumstances peculiar to the cotton trade arising on an application to register a trade mark in respect of textile goods other than clothing.

(11) A certificate purporting to be under the hand of the Keeper of the Manchester Branch as to any copy entered in the Manchester Record of an entry in the register shall be prima facie evidence of the entry having been made in the register and of the contents thereof.

(12) ...

General note
Sub-s (12) was repealed by the Courts Act 1971, s 56(4), Sch 11, Pt II.

[39A. Registration of trade mark following overseas application

(1) Any person who has applied for protection for any trade mark in a relevant country or his legal representative or assignee shall be entitled on an application for registration made within six months of the application for protection in the relevant country to registration of his mark under this Act in priority to other applicants.

(2) A mark registered on an application made under this section shall be registered as of the date of the application in the relevant country and that date shall be deemed for the purposes of this Act to be the date of registration.

(3) Nothing in this section shall entitle the proprietor of the mark to recover damages for infringements happening prior to the date of the application for registration under this Act.

(4) The registration of a mark under this section shall not be invalidated by reason only of the use of the mark in the United Kingdom during the period of 6 months within which the application may be made.

(5) The application for the registration of a mark under this section must be made in the same manner as an ordinary application under this Act.

(6) Where a person has applied for protection for any mark by an application which—

   (a) in accordance with the terms of a treaty subsisting between any two or more relevant countries, is equivalent to an application duly made in any one of those countries; or
   (b) in accordance with the law of any relevant country, is equivalent to an application duly made in that country,

he shall be deemed for the purposes of this section to have applied in that country.

(7) Subject to subsection (8) below, Her Majesty may by Order in Council direct that this section shall apply to a country specified in the Order.

(8) If a country is not a dependent territory, an Order in Council under this section may only be made in relation to it with a view to the fulfilment of a treaty, convention, arrangement or engagement.

(9) An Order in Council under this section shall be subject to annulment in pursuance of a resolution of either House of Parliament and may be varied or revoked by a subsequent Order.

(10) In this section—
'country' includes any territory;
'dependent territory' means any of the Channel Islands or a colony;
'relevant country' means a country which was specified in an Order in Council under this section at the time of the application under this section or such other time as may be specified in the Order in Council.]

General note
This section was inserted by the Patents, Designs and Marks Act 1986, s 2(3) and Sch 2, para 5.

GENERAL AND MISCELLANEOUS

Rules and fees

40. Power of Board of Trade to make rules

(1) The Board of Trade may from time to time make such rules, prescribe such forms and generally do such things as they think expedient—

(a) for regulating the practice under this Act, including the service of documents;
(b) for classifying goods for the purposes of registration of trade marks;
(c) for making or requiring duplicates of trade marks and other documents;
(d) for securing and regulating the publishing and selling or distributing, in such manner as the Board of Trade think fit, of copies of trade marks and other documents;
(e) generally for regulating the business of the Patent Office in relation to trade marks and all things by this Act placed under the direction or control of the Registrar or of the Board of Trade.

(2) ...

(3) Before making any rules under this Act, the Board of Trade shall publish notice of their intention to make the rules and of the place where copies of the draft rules may be obtained, in such manner as the Board consider most expedient so as to enable persons affected to make representations to the Board before the rules are finally settled.

(4) Any rules so made shall be forthwith advertised twice in the Trade Marks Journal, and shall be laid before both Houses of Parliament, ...

(5) If either House of Parliament, within the next forty days after any rules have been so laid before it, resolves that the rules or any of them ought to be annulled, the rule or rules shall thenceforth be of no effect, but without prejudice to the validity of anything previously done thereunder or to the making of any new rule or rules.

General note
Sub-s (2) and the words omitted from sub-s (4) were repealed by the Statute Law (Repeals) Act 1986.

[40A. Hours of business and excluded days

(1) Rules under section 40 of this Act may specify the hour at which the Patent Office shall be deemed to be closed on any day for purposes of the transaction by the public of business under this Act or of any class of such business, and may specify days as excluded days for any such purposes.

(2) Any business done under this Act on any day after the hour specified as aforesaid in relation to business of that class, or on a day which is an excluded day in relation to business of that class, shall be deemed to have been done on the next following day not being an excluded day; and where the time for doing anything under this Act expires on an excluded day, that time shall be extended to the next following day not being an excluded day.]

General note
This section was inserted by the Statute Law (Repeals) Act 1986, s 1(2) and Sch 2, para 2.

41. Fees
There shall be paid in respect of applications and registration and other matters under this Act such fees as may be, with the sanction of the Treasury, prescribed by the Board of Trade.

Powers and duties of Registrar

42. Preliminary advice by Registrar as to distinctiveness
(1) The power to give to a person who proposes to apply for the registration of a trade mark in Part A or Part B of the register advice as to whether the trade mark appears to the Registrar prima facie to be inherently adapted to distinguish, or capable of distinguishing, as the case may be, shall be a function of the Registrar under this Act.

(2) Any such person who is desirous of obtaining such advice must make application to the Registrar therefor in the prescribed manner.

(3) If on application for the registration of a trade mark as to which the Registrar has given advice as aforesaid in the affirmative, made within three months after the advice is given, the Registrar, after further investigation or consideration, gives notice to the applicant of objection on the ground that the trade mark is not adapted to distinguish, or capable of distinguishing, as the case may be, the applicant shall be entitled, on giving notice of withdrawal of the application within the prescribed period, to have repaid to him any fee paid on the filing of the application.

43. Hearing before exercise of Registrar's discretion
Where any discretionary or other power is given to the Registrar by this Act or the rules, he shall not exercise that power adversely to the applicant for registration or the registered proprietor of the trade mark in question without (if duly required so to do within the prescribed time) giving to the applicant or registered proprietor an opportunity of being heard.

44. Power of Registrar to award costs
In all proceedings before the Registrar under this Act, the Registrar shall have power to award to any party such costs as he may consider reasonable, and to direct how and by what parties they are to be paid, and any such order may, by leave of the Court or a judge thereof, be enforced in the same manner as a judgment or order of the Court to the same effect.

45. Annual reports of Registrar
The Comptroller-General of Patents, Designs and Trade Marks shall, in his annual report on the execution by or under him of the Patents and Designs Act 1907 and Acts amending that Act, include a report respecting the execution by or under him of this Act as if it formed a part of or was included in those Acts.

Legal proceedings and appeals

46. Registration to be prima facie evidence of validity
In all legal proceedings relating to a registered trade mark (including applications under section thirty-two of this Act) the fact that a person is registered as proprietor of the trade mark shall be prima facie evidence of the validity of the original registration of the trade mark and of all subsequent assignments and transmissions thereof.

47. Certificate of validity
In any legal proceeding in which the validity of the registration of a registered trade mark comes into question and is decided in favour of the proprietor of the trade mark, the Court may certify to that effect, and if it so certifies then in any subsequent legal proceeding in which the validity of the registration comes into question the proprietor of the trade mark on obtaining a final order or judgment in his favour shall have his full costs, charges and expenses as between solicitor and client, unless in the subsequent proceeding the Court certifies that he ought not to have them.

48. Costs of Registrar in proceedings before Court, and payment of costs by Registrar
(1) In all proceedings before the Court under this Act the costs of the Registrar shall be in the discretion of the Court, but, in any proceedings in England or Northern Ireland, the Registrar shall not, except in accordance with the provisions of subsection (2) of this section in a case in which he has appeared in the proceedings, be ordered to pay the costs of any other of the parties.

(2) Where the Registrar appears in any proceedings before the Court in England or Northern Ireland under this Act, section seven of the Administration of Justice (Miscellaneous Provisions) Act 1933, or any corresponding enactment which may be passed by the Parliament of Northern Ireland, as the case may be, shall have effect as it has effect in relation to other proceedings to which the Crown is a party in a court having the power to award costs in cases between subjects.

49. Trade usage, etc to be considered
In any action or proceeding relating to a trade mark or trade name, the tribunal shall admit evidence of the usages of the trade concerned and of any relevant trade mark or trade name or get-up legitimately used by other persons.

50. Registrar's appearance in proceedings involving rectification
(1) In any legal proceeding in which the relief sought includes alteration or rectification of the register, the Registrar shall have the right to appear and be heard, and shall appear if so directed by the Court.

(2) Unless otherwise directed by the Court, the Registrar in lieu of appearing and being heard may submit to the Court a statement in writing signed by him, giving particulars of the proceedings before him in relation to the matter in issue or of the grounds of any decision given by him affecting it or of the practice of the Patent Office in like cases or of such other matters relevant to the issues, and within his knowledge as Registrar, as he thinks fit, and the statement shall be deemed to form part of the evidence in the proceeding.

51. Court's power to review Registrar's decision
The Court, in dealing with any question of the rectification of the register (including all applications under the provisions of section thirty-two of this Act), shall

have power to review any decision of the Registrar relating to the entry in question or the correction sought to be made.

52. Discretion of Court in appeals

In any appeal from a decision of the Registrar to the Court under this Act, the Court shall have and exercise the same discretionary powers as under this Act are conferred upon the Registrar.

53. Procedure on appeal to Board of Trade

Where under this Act an appeal is made to the Board of Trade, the Board of Trade may, if they think fit, refer the appeal to the Court in lieu of hearing and deciding it themselves, but, unless the Board so refer the appeal, it shall be heard and decided by the Board, and the decision of the Board shall be final.

54. Procedure in cases of option to apply to Court or Registrar

Where under any of the foregoing provisions of this Act an applicant has an option to make an application either to the Court or to the Registrar—

(a) if an action concerning the trade mark in question is pending, the application must be made to the Court;

(b) if in any other case the application is made to the Registrar, he may, at any stage of the proceedings, refer the application to the Court, or he may, after hearing the parties, determine the question between them, subject to appeal to the Court.

Evidence

55. Mode of giving evidence

In any proceeding under this Act before the Board of Trade or the Registrar, the evidence shall be given by statutory declaration in the absence of directions to the contrary, but, in any case in which the tribunal thinks it right so to do, the tribunal may take evidence viva voce in lieu of or in addition to evidence by declaration. Any such statutory declaration may in the case of appeal be used before the Court in lieu of evidence by affidavit, but if so used shall have all the incidents and consequences of evidence by affidavit.

In case any part of the evidence is taken viva voce, the Board of Trade or the Registrar shall, in respect of requiring the attendance of witnesses and taking evidence on oath, be in the same position in all respects as an official referee of the Supreme Court.

56. Evidence of orders, etc of Board of Trade

(1) All documents purporting to be orders made by the Board of Trade and to be sealed with the seal of the Board, or to be signed by a secretary or an undersecretary or an assistant secretary of the Board, or by any person authorised in that behalf by the President of the Board, shall be received in evidence, and shall be deemed to be such orders without further proof, unless the contrary is shown.

(2) A certificate, signed by the President of the Board of Trade, that any order made or act done is the order or act of the Board, shall be conclusive evidence of the fact so certified.

Offences and restraint of use of Royal Arms

57, 58

...

General note
These sections were repealed by the Patents, Designs and Marks Act 1986, s 3(1) and Sch 3, Pt I.

[58A. Fraudulent application or use of trade mark an offence

(1) It is an offence, subject to subsection (3) below, for a person—

(a) to apply a mark identical to or nearly resembling a registered trade mark to goods, or to material used or intended to be used for labelling, packaging or advertising goods, or

(b) to sell, let for hire, or offer or expose for sale or hire or distribute—

(i) goods bearing such a mark, or
(ii) material bearing such a mark which is used or intended to be used for labelling, packaging or advertising goods, or

(c) to use material bearing such a mark in the course of a business for labelling, packaging or advertising goods, or

(d) to possess in the course of a business goods or material bearing such a mark with a view to doing any of the things mentioned in paragraphs (a) to (c),

when he is not entitled to use the mark in relation to the goods in question and the goods are not connected in the course of trade with a person who is so entitled.

(2) It is also an offence, subject to subsection (3) below, for a person to possess in the course of a business goods or material bearing a mark identical to or nearly resembling a registered trade mark with a view to enabling or assisting another person to do any of the things mentioned in subsection (1)(a) to (c), knowing or having reason to believe that the other person is not entitled to use the mark in relation to the goods in question and that the goods are not connected in the course of trade with a person who is so entitled.

(3) A person commits an offence under subsection (1) or (2) only if—

(a) he acts with a view to gain for himself or another, or with intent to cause loss to another, and

(b) he intends that the goods in question should be accepted as connected in the course of trade with a person entitled to use the mark in question;

and it is a defence for a person charged with an offence under subsection (1) to show that he believed on reasonable grounds that he was entitled to use the mark in relation to the goods in question.

(4) A person guilty of an offence under this section is liable—

(a) on summary conviction to imprisonment for a term not exceeding six months or a fine not exceeding the statutory maximum, or both;

(b) on conviction on indictment to a fine or imprisonment for a term not exceeding ten years, or both.

(5) Where an offence under this section committed by a body corporate is proved to have been committed with the consent or connivance of a director, manager, secretary or other similar officer of the body, or a person purporting to act in any such capacity, he as well as the body corporate is guilty of the offence and liable to be proceeded against and punished accordingly.

In relation to a body corporate whose affairs are managed by its members 'director' means a member of the body corporate.

(6) In this section 'business' includes a trade or profession.]

General note
This section was inserted by the Copyright, Designs and Patents Act 1988, s 300.

[58B. Delivery up of offending goods and materials

(1) The court by which a person is convicted of an offence under section 58A may, if satisfied that at the time of his arrest or charge he had in his possession, custody or control—

(a) goods or material in respect of which the offence was committed, or
(b) goods of the same description as those in respect of which the offence was committed, or material similar to that in respect of which the offence was committed, bearing a mark identical to or nearly resembling that in relation to which the offence was committed,

order that the goods or material be delivered up to such person as the court may direct.

(2) For this purpose a person shall be treated as charged with an offence—

(a) in England, Wales and Northern Ireland, when he is orally charged or is served with a summons or indictment;
(b) in Scotland, when he is cautioned, charged or served with a complaint or indictment.

(3) An order may be made by the court of its own motion or on the application of the prosecutor (or, in Scotland, the Lord Advocate or procurator-fiscal), but shall not be made if it appears to the court unlikely that any order will be made under section 58C (order as to disposal of offending goods or material).

(4) An appeal lies from an order made under this section by a magistrates' court—

(a) in England and Wales, to the Crown Court, and
(b) in Northern Ireland, to the county court;

and in Scotland, where an order has been made under this section, the person from whose possession, custody or control the goods or material have been removed may, without prejudice to any other form of appeal under any rule of law, appeal against that order in the same manner as against sentence.

(5) A person to whom goods or material are delivered up in pursuance of an order under this section shall retain it pending the making of an order under section 58C.

(6) Nothing in this section affects the powers of the court under section 43 of the Powers of Criminal Courts Act 1973, [Part II of the Proceeds of Crime (Scotland) Act 1995] or Article 7 of the Criminal Justice (Northern Ireland) Order 1980 (general provisions as to forfeiture in criminal proceedings).]

General note
This section was inserted by the Copyright, Designs and Patents Act 1988, s 300.

The words in square brackets in sub-s (6) were substituted by the Criminal Procedure (Consequential Provisions) (Scotland) Act 1995, s 5 and Sch 4, para 4 (notwithstanding the repeal of this Act on 31 October 1994).

[58C. Order as to disposal of offending goods or material

(1) Where goods or material have been delivered up in pursuance of an order under

section 58B, an application may be made to the court for an order that they be destroyed or forfeited to such person as the court may think fit.

(2) Provision shall be made by rules of court as to the service of notice on persons having an interest in the goods or material, and any such person is entitled—

(a) to appear in proceedings for an order under this section, whether or not he was served with notice, and
(b) to appeal against any order made, whether or not he appeared;

and an order shall not take effect until the end of the period within which notice of an appeal may be given or, if before the end of that period notice of appeal is duly given, until the final determination or abandonment of the proceedings on the appeal.

(3) Where there is more than one person interested in goods or material, the court shall make such order as it thinks just.

(4) References in this section to a person having an interest in goods or material include any person in whose favour an order could be made under this section or under sections 114, 204 or 231 of the Copyright, Designs and Patents Act 1988 (which make similar provision in relation to infringement of copyright, rights in performances and design right).

(5) Proceedings for an order under this section may be brought—

(a) in a county court in England, Wales and Northern Ireland, [save that in Northern Ireland such proceedings may be brought in a county court only where] the value of the goods or material in question does not exceed the county court limit for actions in tort, and
(b) in a sheriff court in Scotland;

but this shall not be construed as affecting the jurisdiction of the High Court or, in Scotland, the Court of Session.]

General note
This section was inserted by the Copyright, Designs and Patents Act 1988, s 300.
The words in square brackets in sub-s (5) were substituted by the High Court and County Courts Jurisdiction Order 1991, SI 1991/724, art 2(1)(b), (8), Schedule, Pt I.

[58D. Enforcement of section 58A

(1) The functions of a local weights and measures authority include the enforcement in their area of section 58A.

(2) The following provisions of the Trade Descriptions Act 1968 apply in relation to the enforcement of that section as in relation to the enforcement of that Act—

section 27 (power to make test purchases),
section 28 (power to enter premises and inspect and seize goods and documents),
section 29 (obstruction of authorised officers), and
section 33 (compensation for loss, &c of goods seized under s 28).

(3) Subsection (1) above does not apply in relation to the enforcement of section 58A in Northern Ireland, but the functions of the Department of Economic Development include the enforcement of that section in Northern Ireland.

For that purpose the provisions of the Trade Descriptions Act 1968 specified in subsection (2) apply as if for the references to a local weights and measures authority and any officer of such an authority there were substituted references to that Department and any of its officers.

(4) Any enactment which authorises the disclosure of information for the purpose of facilitating the enforcement of the Trade Descriptions Act 1968 shall apply as if section 58A above were contained in that Act and as if the functions of any person in relation to the enforcement of that section were functions under that Act.]

General note
This section was inserted by the Copyright, Designs and Patents Act 1988, s 300.

59. Falsification of entries in register a misdemeanour
(1) If any person makes or causes to be made a false entry in the register, or a writing falsely purporting to be a copy of an entry in the register, or produces or tenders or causes to be produced or tendered in evidence any such writing, knowing the entry or writing to be false, he shall be guilty of a misdemeanour.

(2) In the Isle of Man the punishment for an offence under this section shall be imprisonment for any term not exceeding two years, with or without hard labour and with or without a fine not exceeding one hundred pounds, at the discretion of the court.

60. Fine for falsely representing a trade mark as registered
(1) Any person who makes a representation—

    (a) with respect to a mark not being a registered trade mark, to the effect that it is a registered trade mark; or

    (b) with respect to a part of a registered trade mark not being a part separately registered as a trade mark, to the effect that it is so registered; or

    (c) to the effect that a registered trade mark is registered in respect of any goods in respect of which it is not registered; or

    (d) to the effect that the registration of a trade mark gives an exclusive right to the use thereof in any circumstances in which, having regard to limitations entered on the register, the registration does not give that right;

shall be liable on summary conviction to a fine not exceeding [level 3 on the standard scale].

(2) For the purposes of this section, the use in the United Kingdom in relation to a trade mark of the word 'registered', or of any other word referring whether expressly or impliedly to registration, shall be deemed to import a reference to registration in the register, except—

    (a) where that word is used in physical association with other words delineated in characters at least as large as those in which that word is delineated and indicating that the reference is to registration as a trade mark under the law of a country outside the United Kingdom, being a country under the law of which the registration referred to is in fact in force;

    (b) where that word (being a word other than the word 'registered') is of itself such as to indicate that the reference is to such registration as last aforesaid; or

    (c) where that word is used in relation to a mark registered as a trade mark under the law of a country outside the United Kingdom and in relation to goods to be exported to that country.

(3) Any offence under this section committed in the Isle of Man may be prosecuted, and any fine in respect thereof recovered, at the instance an person aggrieved, in the manner in which offences punishable on summary conviction may for the time being be prosecuted.

General note
The reference to level 3 on the standard scale in sub-s (1) is substituted by virtue of the Criminal Justice
Act 1982, ss 37, 38, 46.

61. Restraint of use of Royal Arms, etc

If any person, without the authority of His Majesty, uses, in connection with any
trade, business, calling or profession, the Royal Arms (or arms so closely resembling
the same as to be calculated to deceive) in such manner as to be calculated to lead to
the belief that he is duly authorised so to use the Royal Arms, or if any person, without the authority of His Majesty or of a member of the Royal Family, uses, in connection with any trade, business, calling or profession, any device, emblem or title in
such manner as to be calculated to lead to the belief that he is employed by, [supplies
goods to or provides services for], His Majesty or such member of the Royal Family,
he may, at the suit of any person who is authorised to use such arms or such device,
emblem or title, or is authorised by the Lord Chamberlain to take proceedings in that
behalf, be restrained by injunction from continuing so to use the same:

Provided that nothing in this section shall be construed as affecting the right, if
any, of the proprietor of a trade mark containing any such arms, device, emblem or
title to continue to use such trade mark.

General note
The words in square brackets were substituted by the Patents, Designs and Marks Act 1986, s 2(3) and
Sch 2, para 6.

Miscellaneous

62. Change of form of trade connection not to be deemed to cause deception

The use of a registered trade mark in relation to goods between which and the person using it any form of connection in the course of trade subsists shall not be
deemed to be likely to cause deception or confusion on the ground only that the
trade mark has been, or is, used in relation to goods between which and that person
or a predecessor in title of his a different form of connection in the course of trade
subsisted or subsists.

63. Jointly owned trade marks

Where the relations between two or more persons interested in a trade mark are
such that no one of them is entitled as between himself and the other or others of
them to use it except—

   (a) on behalf of both or all of them, or
   (b) in relation to an article with which both or all of them are connected in the
       course of trade,

those persons may be registered as joint proprietors of the trade mark, and this Act
shall have effect in relation to any rights to the use of the trade mark vested in those
persons as if those rights had been vested in a single person.

Subject as aforesaid, nothing in this Act shall authorise the registration of two or
more persons who use a trade mark independently, or propose so to use it, as joint
proprietors thereof.

64. Trusts and equities

(1) There shall not be entered in the register any notice of any trust express,
implied or constructive, nor shall any such notice be receivable by the Registrar.

(2) Subject to the provisions of this Act, equities in respect of a trade mark may be enforced in like manner as in respect of any other personal property.

[64A. Restriction on importation of goods bearing infringing trade marks

(1) The person who is registered as the proprietor or registered user of a trade mark in respect of any goods may give notice in writing to the Commissioners of Customs and Excise (in this section referred to as the Commissioners)—

(a) that he is the proprietor or registered user of that trade mark, and
(b) that such goods bearing the trade mark are expected to arrive in the United Kingdom at a time and place and by a consignment specified in the notice, and
(c) that the use within the United Kingdom of the trade mark in relation to the goods would infringe the proprietor's exclusive right to that use, and
(d) that he requests the Commissioners to treat the goods as prohibited goods.

(2) Where a notice has been given under this section in respect of any goods bearing a trade mark and has not been withdrawn and the requirements of any regulations made under this section are complied with, then, subject to the following provisions of this section, the importation into the United Kingdom of the goods shall, if the condition of paragraph (c) of the preceding subsection is satisfied, be deemed to be prohibited unless the importation is for the private and domestic use of the person importing the goods.

(3) The Commissioners may make regulations prescribing the form in which notices are to be given under this section, and requiring a person giving such a notice, either at the time of giving the notice or at the time when the goods in question are imported, or at both those times, to furnish the Commissioners with such evidence, and to comply with such other conditions (if any), as may be specified in the regulations, and any such regulations may include such incidental and supplementary provisions as the Commissioners consider expedient for the purposes of this section.

(4) Without prejudice to the generality of the preceding subsection, regulations made under that subsection may include provision for requiring a person who has given a notice under subsection (1) of this section, or a notice purporting to be a notice under that subsection,—

(a) to pay such fees in respect of the notice as may be prescribed by the regulations;
(b) to give to the Commissioners such security as may be so prescribed, in respect of any liability or expense which they may incur in consequence of the detention of any goods to which the notice relates, or in consequence of anything done in relation to goods so detained;
(c) whether any such security is given or not, to keep the Commissioners indemnified against any such liability or expense as is mentioned in the preceding paragraph.

(5) For the purposes of [section 17 of the Customs and Excise Management Act 1979] (which relates to the disposal of duties) any fees paid in pursuance of regulations made under this section shall be treated as money collected on account of [duties (whether of customs or excise) charged on imported goods].

(6) Regulations under subsection (3) of this section shall be made by statutory instrument, which shall be subject to annulment in pursuance of a resolution of either House of Parliament.]

General note
This section was inserted by the Trade Descriptions Act 1968, s 17.
The words in square brackets in sub-s (5) were substituted by the Customs and Excise Management Act
1979, s 177(1) and Sch 4, para 12, Table, Pt I.

65. Recognition of agents

Where by this Act any act has to be done by or to any person in connection with a
trade mark or proposed trade mark or any procedure relating thereto, the act may
under and in accordance with the rules, or in particular cases by special leave of the
Board of Trade, be done by or to an agent of that person duly authorised in the prescribed manner.

66. Saving for jurisdiction of courts in Scotland, Northern Ireland and Isle of Man

(1) The provisions of this Act conferring a special jurisdiction on the Court as
defined by this Act shall not, except so far as the jurisdiction extends, affect the
jurisdiction of any court in Scotland or Northern Ireland in any proceedings relating
to trade marks; and with reference to any such proceedings in Scotland the expression 'the Court' means the Court of Session; and with reference to any such proceedings in Northern Ireland the expression 'the Court' means the High Court of
Justice in Northern Ireland.

(2) Nothing in this Act shall affect the jurisdiction of the courts in the Isle of
Man in proceedings for infringement or in any action or proceeding respecting a
trade mark competent to those courts.

67

...

General note
This section was repealed by the Industrial Expansion Act 1968, s 18 and Sch 4.

Supplemental

68. Interpretation

(1) In this Act, unless the context otherwise requires, the following expressions
have the meanings hereby assigned to them respectively, that is to say:—

> 'the appointed day' has the meaning assigned to it by section seventy-one of
> this Act;
> 'assignment' means assignment by act of the parties concerned;
> 'the Court' means (subject to provisions relating to Scotland, Northern Ireland
> or the Isle of Man) His Majesty's High Court of Justice in England;
> 'limitations' means any limitation of the exclusive right to the use of a trade
> mark given by the registration of a person as proprietor thereof, including
> limitations of that right as to mode of use, as to use in relation to goods to
> be sold, or otherwise traded in, in any place within the United Kingdom, or
> as to use in relation to goods to be exported to any market outside the
> United Kingdom;
> 'mark' includes a device, brand, heading, label, ticket, name, signature, word,
> letter, numeral, or any combination thereof;
> 'permitted use' has the meaning assigned to it by subsection (1) of section
> twenty-eight of this Act;
> 'prescribed' means [(subject to provisions relating to Northern Ireland)], in

relation to proceedings before the Court, prescribed by rules of court, and, in other cases, prescribed by this Act or the rules;

'the register' means the register of trade marks kept under this Act;

'registered trade mark' means a trade mark that is actually on the register;

'registered user' means a person who is for the time being registered as such under section twenty-eight of this Act;

'the Registrar' means the Comptroller-General of Patents, Designs and Trade Marks;

'the rules' means rules made by the Board of Trade under section thirty-six or section forty of this Act;

'trade mark' means, except in relation to a certification trade mark, a mark used or proposed to be used in relation to goods for the purpose of indicating, or so as to indicate, a connection in the course of trade between the goods and some person having the right either as proprietor or as registered user to use the mark, whether with or without any indication of the identity of that person, and means, in relation to a certification trade mark, a mark registered or deemed to have been registered under section thirty-seven of this Act;

'transmission' means transmission by operation of law, devolution on the personal representative of a deceased person, and any other mode of transfer not being assignment;

'United Kingdom' includes the Isle of Man.

(2) References in this Act to the use of a mark shall be construed as references to the use of a printed or other visual representation of the mark, and references therein to the use of a mark in relation to goods shall be construed as references to the use thereof upon, or in physical or other relation to, goods.

[(2A) For the purposes of this Act goods and services are associated with each other if it is likely that those goods might be sold or otherwise traded in and those services might be provided by the same business, and so with descriptions of goods and descriptions of services.

(2B) References in this Act to a near resemblance of marks are references to a resemblance so near as to be likely to deceive or cause confusion.]

(3) In the application of this Act to Scotland, the expressions 'injunction', 'plaintiff' and 'defendant' mean respectively 'interdict', 'pursuer' and 'defender'.

General note
The words in square brackets in the definition 'prescribed' in sub-s (1) were inserted by the Judicature (Northern Ireland) Act 1978, s 122(1) and Sch 5, Pt II.
Sub-ss (2A), (2B) were inserted by the Trade Marks (Amendment) Act 1984, s 1(5).

69. Transitional provisions
The transitional provisions set out in the Third Schedule to this Act shall have effect with respect to the matters therein mentioned respectively.

70. Repeal and savings
(1) ...

(2) Nothing in this Act shall affect any order, rule, regulation or requirement made, table of fees or certificate issued, notice, decision, determination, direction or approval given, application made, or thing done, under any enactment repealed by this Act; and every such order, rule, regulation, requirement, table of fees, certificate, notice, decision, determination, direction, approval, application or thing shall, if in force at the commencement of this Act, continue in force and shall, so far as it

could have been made, issued, given or done under this Act, have effect as if made, issued, given or done under the corresponding enactment of this Act.

(3) Any document referring to any enactment repealed by this Act shall be construed as referring to the corresponding enactment of this Act.

(4) Nothing in this section shall be taken to prejudice the provisions of section thirty-eight of the Interpretation Act 1889.

General note

Sub-s (1) was repealed by the Statute Law Revision Act 1950.

71. Short title, commencement and extent

(1) This Act may be cited as the Trade Marks Act 1938.

(2) ...

(3) It is hereby declared that this Act extends to Northern Ireland.

(4) This Act shall extend to the Isle of Man.

General note

Sub-s (2) was repealed by the Statute Law Revision Act 1950.

SCHEDULES
FIRST SCHEDULE

CERTIFICATION TRADE MARKS

Section 37

1.   (1) An application for the registration of a mark under section thirty-seven of this Act must be made to the Registrar in writing in the prescribed manner by the person proposed to be registered as the proprietor thereof.

(2) The provisions of subsection (2) and of subsections (4) to (7) of section seventeen of this Act shall have effect in relation to an application under the said section thirty-seven as they have effect in relation to an application under subsection (1) of the said section seventeen, except that for references therein to acceptance of an application there shall be substituted references to authorisation to proceed with the application.

(3) In dealing under the said provisions with an application under the said section thirty-seven the tribunal shall have regard to the like considerations, so far as relevant, as if the application were an application under section seventeen of this Act and to any other considerations (not being matters within the competence of the Board of Trade under subparagraph (5) of this paragraph) relevant to applications under the said section thirty-seven, including the desirability of securing that a certification trade mark shall comprise some indication that it is such a trade mark.

(4) An applicant for the registration of a mark under the said section thirty-seven shall transmit to the Registrar draft regulations for governing the use thereof at such time before the decision of the Registrar on the application as he may require in order to enable him to consider the draft, and the Registrar shall report thereon to the Board of Trade.

(5) When authorisation to proceed with an application has been given, the Board of Trade shall consider the application with regard to the following matters, that is to say: —

(a) whether the applicant is competent to certify the goods in respect of which the mark is to be registered;

(b) whether the draft regulations are satisfactory; and

(c) whether in all the circumstances the registration applied for would be to the public advantage;

and may either—

(i) direct that the application shall not be accepted; or

(ii) direct the Registrar to accept the application, and approve the regulations, either without modification and unconditionally or subject to any conditions or limitations or to any amendments or modifications of the application or of the regulations, which they think requisite having regard to any of the matters aforesaid;

but, except in the case of a direction for acceptance and approval without modification and unconditionally, the Board shall not decide the matter without giving to the applicant an opportunity of being heard:

Provided that the Board may, at the request of the applicant made with the concurrence of the Registrar, consider the application with regard to any of the matters aforesaid before authorisation to proceed with the application has been given, so however that the Board shall be at liberty to reconsider any matter on which they have given a decision under this proviso if any amendment or modification is thereafter made in the application or in the draft regulations.

2. (1) When an application has been accepted, the Registrar shall, as soon as may be after such acceptance, cause the application as accepted to be advertised in the prescribed manner, and the provisions of subsections (2) to (11) of section eighteen of this Act shall have effect in relation to the registration of the mark as if the application had been an application under section seventeen of this Act:

Provided that, in deciding under the said provisions, the tribunal shall have regard only to the considerations referred to in subparagraph (3) of the last foregoing paragraph, and a decision under the said provisions in favour of the applicant shall be conditional on the determination in his favour by the Board of Trade under subparagraph (2) of this paragraph of any opposition relating to any of the matters referred to in subparagraph (5) of the last foregoing paragraph.

(2) When notice of opposition is given relating to any of the matters referred to in subparagraph (5) of the last foregoing paragraph, the Board of Trade shall, after hearing the parties, if so required, and considering any evidence, decide whether, and subject to what conditions or limitations, or amendments or modifications of the application or of the regulations, if any, registration is, having regard to those matters, to be permitted.

3. (1) The regulations deposited in respect of a certification trade mark may, on the application of the registered proprietor, be altered by the Registrar, with the consent of the Board of Trade.

(2) The Board of Trade may cause an application for their consent to be advertised in any case where it appears to the Board that it is expedient so to do, and, where the Board cause an application to be advertised, if within the prescribed time from the date of the advertisement any person gives notice to the Board of opposition to the application, the Board shall not decide the matter without giving the parties an opportunity of being heard.

4. (1) The Board of Trade may, on the application in the prescribed manner of any person aggrieved, or on the application of the Registrar, make such order as they think fit for expunging or varying any entry in the register relating to a certification trade mark, or for varying the deposited regulations, on the ground—

(a) that the proprietor is no longer competent, in the case of any of the goods in respect of which the trade mark is registered, to certify those goods;

(b) that the proprietor has failed to observe a provision of the deposited regulations to be observed on his part;

(c) that it is no longer to the public advantage that the trade mark should be registered; or

(d) that it is requisite for the public advantage that, if the trade mark remains registered, the regulations should be varied;

and neither the Court nor the Registrar shall have any jurisdiction to make an order under section thirty-two of this Act on any of those grounds.

(2) The Registrar shall rectify the register and the deposited regulations in such manner as may be requisite for giving effect to an order made under the foregoing subparagraph.

5. Notwithstanding anything in section forty-four of this Act, the Registrar shall not have any jurisdiction to award costs to or against any party on an appeal to him against a refusal of the proprietor of a certification trade mark to certify goods or to authorise the use of the trade mark.

6. The following provisions of this Act shall not have effect in relation to a certification trade mark, that is to say, section four, section six, section nine, sections seventeen and eighteen (except as expressly applied by this Schedule), subsections (4) to (8) of section twenty-two, sections twenty-six to twenty-nine, section sixty-two, and any provisions the operation of which is limited by the terms thereof to registration in Part B of the Register.

SECOND SCHEDULE

SHEFFIELD MARKS

Section 38

1. The Cutlers' Company shall continue to keep at Sheffield the register of trade marks (in this Schedule called 'the Sheffield register') kept by them immediately before the appointed day, and, save as otherwise provided by this Schedule, the Sheffield register shall for all purposes form part of the register.

2 An application by a person carrying on business in Hallamshire, or within six miles thereof, for the registration of a trade mark in respect of metal goods may be made either to the Registrar or to the Cutlers' Company, at the option of the applicant.

3. An application for the registration of a trade mark made to the Cutlers' Company shall be notified to the Registrar in the prescribed manner, and the Cutlers' Company shall not proceed with such an application until authorised so to do by the Registrar.

4.   The Registrar shall consider an application notified to him as aforesaid and shall either authorise the Cutlers' Company to proceed therewith or, if it appears to him that there is any objection to the application, shall give notice of his objection to the Cutlers' Company, who shall communicate it to the applicant.

5.   Within the prescribed time after receipt of a notice of objection under the last foregoing paragraph, the applicant may submit to the Cutlers' Company either orally or in writing arguments against, or proposals for meeting, the objection, and the Cutlers' Company shall notify to the Registrar any arguments or proposals so submitted to them together with any observations that they may desire to make thereon.

6.   The Registrar shall consider any arguments, proposals or observations notified to him as aforesaid and shall, if so required by an applicant who has submitted arguments or proposals as aforesaid, give the applicant an opportunity of being heard by him, and may refuse authorisation to proceed with the application or may authorise the Cutlers' Company to proceed therewith either without modification and unconditionally or subject to such conditions, amendments or modifications, or to such limitations, if any, as he may think right.

7.   Where the Registrar refuses authorisation to proceed with an application, or authorises the Cutlers' Company to proceed therewith subject as aforesaid, the provisions of subsection (4) to (6) of section seventeen of this Act shall have effect in relation to the refusal or conditional authorisation as they have effect in relation to a refusal to accept, or a conditional acceptance of, an application, except that for references therein to acceptance of the application there shall be substituted references to authorisation to the Cutlers' Company to proceed with the application.

8.   Upon the registration of a trade mark in the Sheffield register, the Cutlers' Company shall give notice thereof to the Registrar, who shall thereupon enter the trade mark in the register, and such registration shall bear date as of the day of the application to the Cutlers' Company and have the same effect as if the application had been made to the Registrar on that day.

9.   The provisions of this Act and of the rules with respect to the registration of trade marks, and all matters relating thereto, shall, subject to the provisions of this Schedule (and notwithstanding anything in any Act relating to the Cutlers' Company), apply to the registration of trade marks in respect of metal goods by the Cutlers' Company and to all matters relating thereto, and this Act and the rules shall, so far as applicable, be construed accordingly with the substitution of the Cutlers' Company, the office of the Cutlers' Company, and the Sheffield register, for the Registrar, the Patent Office, and the register respectively, and notice of every entry, cancellation, or correction made in the Sheffield register shall be given to the Registrar by the Cutlers' Company:

Provided that anything that by virtue of this Schedule is required or authorised to be done by, before or in relation to the Cutlers' Company or at their office may, with the consent of the party or parties concerned, be done by, before or in relation to the Registrar or at the Patent Office, as the case may be.

10.   When the Registrar receives an application for the registration of a trade mark in respect of metal goods, he shall in the prescribed manner notify the application and proceedings thereon to the Cutlers' Company.

11.   Any person aggrieved by a decision of the Cutlers' Company in respect of anything done or omitted under this Act may, in the prescribed manner, appeal to the Court or, in a case in which, if the decision had been a decision of the Registrar, the person aggrieved would have had an option under this Act of appealing to the Board of Trade, to the Court or the Board at the option of the appellant.

12.   (1) For the purposes of this Schedule the expression 'metal goods' means all metals, whether wrought, unwrought, or partly wrought, and all goods which are comprised in any of such classes as may be prescribed as being classes which refer predominantly to metal goods, and are goods composed wholly or principally of any metal; and for the purpose of determining whether any goods are goods principally of any metal regard shall be had to the importance and nature of the metal part or parts of the goods having regard to the purposes for which the goods are adapted.

(2) Any question arising in connection with an application made to the Cutlers' Company for the registration of a trade mark, as to whether the goods in respect of which the trade mark is proposed to be registered are metal goods, shall be referred to and determined by the Registrar, whose decision shall be final.

(3) The validity of the registration by the Cutlers' Company of a trade mark shall not be questioned on the ground only that the goods in respect of which it is so registered are not metal goods.

13.   A certificate purporting to be under the hand of the master of the Cutlers' Company as to any entry, matter or thing that the Cutlers' Company are authorised by this Schedule or the rules to make or do shall be prima facie evidence of the entry having been made and of the contents thereof and of the matter or thing having been done or not done.

THIRD SCHEDULE

TRANSITIONAL PROVISIONS

Section 69

Validity of registrations under previous Act
1. (1) Subject to the provisions of this paragraph and of section thirteen of this Act, the validity of the original entry of a trade mark on the register of trade marks existing at the commencement of the Trade Marks Act 1905, or on any of the registers of trade marks kept under previous Acts that were deemed part of the same record as the last-mentioned register, shall be determined in accordance with the Acts in force at the date of such entry, and any such trade mark shall retain its original date, but for all other purposes it shall be deemed to have been registered under the Trade Marks Act 1905.

(2) No trade mark which was on the register at the commencement of the Trade Marks Act 1905 and which under that Act was then a registrable trade mark, shall be removed from the register on the ground that it was not registrable under the Acts in force at the date of its registration.

(3) No trade mark which was on the register at the commencement of the Trade Marks (Amendment) Act 1937 and which, having regard to any amendment by that Act of the Trade Marks Act 1905, or of the Trade Marks Act 1919, whether as respects limitations that might be imposed on registration or as respects any other matter, was then a registrable trade mark under the Trade Marks Acts 1905 to 1937, shall be removed from the register on the ground that it was not registrable under the Acts in force at the date of its registration.

(4) Nothing in the Trade Marks (Amendment) Act 1937 shall be taken to have invalidated the original registration of a trade mark that immediately before the commencement of that Act was validly on the register.

(5) Nothing in section thirty-six of the Trade Marks Act 1905 or in the Trade Marks (Amendment) Act 1937 shall be construed as having subjected any person to any liability in respect of any act or thing done before the commencement of those Acts respectively to which he would not have been subject under the Acts then in force.

Assignments and transmissions (before appointed day) giving exclusive rights in different places in the United Kingdom
2. (1) The validity of an assignment or transmission of a trade mark effected or claimed to have been effected before the appointed day, in any such case as is mentioned in subsection (6) of section twenty-two of this Act, shall be determined as if the provisions contained in subsections (1) to (5) of that section had not been enacted:
Provided that, on application made in the prescribed manner within two years from the commencement of this Act, by a person who claims that an assignment or transmission of a registered trade mark to him or to a predecessor in title of his has been so effected, the Registrar shall have the like jurisdiction as under the proviso to subsection (6) of section twenty-two of this Act, and an assignment or transmission approved by him shall not be deemed to have been invalid on the ground of the subsistence of such rights as are mentioned in the said subsection (6) or on the ground that the assignment or transmission was effected otherwise than in connection with the goodwill of a business or was effected in respect of some (but not all) of the goods in respect of which the trade mark was registered, if application for the registration under section twenty-five of this Act of the title of the person becoming entitled is made within six months from the date on which the approval is given, or was made before that date.

(2) Any decision of the Registrar under this paragraph shall be subject to appeal to the Court.
Saving as to retrospective provisions relating to assignments and transmissions
3. The retrospective provisions contained in section twenty-two of this Act, and in the last foregoing paragraph, shall have effect without prejudice to any determination of a competent tribunal that was made before the appointed day, or to the determination of any appeal from a determination so made, or to any title acquired for valuable consideration before the appointed day.

Association of trade marks assignable or transmissible as a whole only under the Trade Marks Act 1919
4. Where immediately before the appointed day a trade mark was registered in Part B of the register subject to a condition rendering it assignable or transmissible only as a whole with another trade mark registered in the name of the same proprietor or with two or more other trade marks so registered, and not separately, the trade marks shall be deemed to be associated trade marks, and the entries in the register relating thereto may be amended accordingly.

Previous use of a trade mark by person becoming registered user on application made within one year of appointed day
5. Where a person is registered as a registered user of a trade mark on an application made within one year from the commencement of this Act, subsection (2) of section twenty-eight of this Act shall have

effect in relation to any previous use (whether before or after the commencement of this Act) of the trade mark by that person, being use in relation to the goods in respect of which he is registered and, where he is registered subject to conditions or restrictions, being use such as to comply substantially therewith, as if such previous use had been permitted use.

Use of trade mark for export trade before appointed day
6.   Section thirty-one of this Act shall be deemed to have had effect in relation to an act done before the appointed day as it has effect in relation to an act done after the commencement of this Act, without prejudice, however, to any determination of a competent tribunal which was made before the appointed day, or to the determination of any appeal from a determination so made.

Trade marks registered under section sixty-two of the Trade Marks Act 1905 to be deemed to have been registered under section thirty-seven of this Act
7.   Section thirty-seven of this Act shall have effect, in relation to a trade mark that immediately before the appointed day was on the register by virtue of section sixty-two of the Trade Marks Act 1905, as if the said section thirty-seven had been in force at the date of the registration of the trade mark and it had been registered under that section, subject however to the following modifications, that is to say: —

(a) the proviso to subsection (1) of the said section thirty-seven shall not apply;
(b) in a case in which regulations for governing the use of the trade mark are deposited at the Patent Office at the commencement of this Act, those regulations shall be deemed to have been deposited under the said section thirty-seven;
(c) in a case in which no such regulations are deposited at the commencement of this Act, the proprietor shall be at liberty, or may be required by the Board of Trade as a condition of the continuance of the registration, to deposit at any time thereafter such regulations as the Board may permit or require; and
(d) in a case in which no such regulations are for the time being deposited, the said section thirty-seven shall have effect as if references therein, and in the First Schedule to this Act to the regulations had been omitted.

Cotton marks registered before appointed day
8.   No registration as of a date before the appointed day of a cotton mark as defined in section sixty-four of the Trade Marks Act 1905 in respect of cotton piece goods or cotton yarn shall give any exclusive right to the use of any letter, numeral, line heading, or any combination thereof.

FOURTH SCHEDULE

ENACTMENTS REPEALED

. . .

General note
This Schedule was repealed by the Statute Law Revision Act 1950.

TRADE MARKS ACT 1938
(1938 c 22)

(As amended and modified by the Statute Law Revision Act 1950, the Judicature (Northern Ireland) Act 1978, the Trade Marks (Amendment) Act 1984, the Patents, Designs and Marks Act 1986 and the Statute Law (Repeals) Act 1986 and by virtue of the Criminal Justice Act 1982.)

ARRANGEMENT OF SECTIONS

REGISTRATION, INFRINGEMENT AND OTHER SUBSTANTIVE PROVISIONS

The Register
  1 The Register of trade marks etc

Effect of registration and the action for infringement
  2 No action for infringement of unregistered service mark
  3 Registration to be in respect of particular services
  4 Right given by registration in Part A, and infringement thereof
  5 Right given by registration in Part B, and infringement thereof
  7 Saving for vested interests
  8 Saving for use of name, address, or description of services

Registrability and validity of registration
  9 Distinctiveness requisite for registration in Part A
 10 Capability of distinguishing requisite for registration in Part B
 11 Prohibition of registration of deceptive, etc, matter
 12 Prohibition of registration of identical and resembling marks
 13 Registration in Part A to be conclusive as to validity after seven years
 14 Registration subject to disclaimer
 15 Words used as name or description of some activity
 16 Effect of limitation as to colour, and of absence thereof

Procedure for, and duration of, registration
 17 Application for registration
 18 Opposition to registration
 19 Registration
 20 Duration and renewal of registration
 21 Registration of parts of service marks and of service marks as a series

Assignment and transmission
 22 Powers of, and restrictions on, assignment and transmission
 23 Certain service marks to be associated so as to be assignable and transmissible as a whole only
 24 Power of registered proprietor to assign and give receipts
 25 Registration of assignments and transmissions

Use and non-use
 26 Removal from register and imposition of limitations on ground of non-use
 28 Registered users
 29 Proposed use of service mark by corporation to be constituted, etc
 30 Use of one of associated or substantially identical service marks equivalent to use of another
 31 Use of service mark for export trade

Rectification and correction of the register
 32 General power to rectify entries in register
 33 Power to expunge or vary registration for breach of condition
 34 Correction of register
 35 Alteration of registered service mark
 36 Adaptation of entries in register to amended or substituted classification of services
39A Registration of service mark following overseas application

GENERAL AND MISCELLANEOUS

Rules and fees
40 Power of Board of Trade to make rules
40A Hours of business and excluded days
41 Fees

Powers and duties of Registrar
42 Preliminary advice by Registrar as to distinctiveness
43 Hearing before exercise of Registrar's discretion
44 Power of Registrar to award costs
45 Annual reports of Registrar

Legal proceedings and appeals
46 Registration to be prima facie evidence of validity
47 Certificate of validity
48 Costs of Registrar in proceedings before Court, and payment of costs by Registrar
49 Trade usage, etc to be considered
50 Registrar's appearance in proceedings involving rectification
51 Court's power to review Registrar's decision
52 Discretion of Court in appeals
53 Procedure on appeal to Board of Trade
54 Procedure in cases of option to apply to Court or Registrar

Evidence
55 Mode of giving evidence
56 Evidence of orders, etc of Board of Trade

Offences and restraint of use of Royal Arms
59 Falsification of entries in register a misdemeanour
60 Fine for falsely representing a service mark as registered
61 Restraint of use of Royal Arms, etc

Miscellaneous
62 Change of form of trade connection not to be deemed to cause deception
63 Jointly owned service marks
64 Trusts and equities
65 Recognition of agents
66 Saving for jurisdiction of courts in Scotland, Northern Ireland and Isle of Man

Supplemental
68 Interpretation
70 Repeal and savings
71 Short title, commencement and extent

An Act to consolidate the Trade Marks Act 1905, the Trade Marks Act 1919, and the Trade Marks (Amendment) Act 1937

[13 April 1938]

General note

This Act has been repealed by the Trade Marks Act 1994, s 106(2), Sch 5, and is printed below as amended immediately prior to its repeal on 31 October 1994. The 1938 Act was amended, to make provision for marks for services, by the Trade Marks (Amendment) Act 1984; this was itself amended by the Patent's Designs and Marks Act 1986, which also amended the 1938 Act in some respects. These changes came into effect on 1 October 1986. By virtue of the Trade Marks (Amendment) Act 1984, s 1(1) (also repealed), the 1938 Act had effect with respect to service marks (as defined in s 1(7) of the 1984 Act; see below) as it had effect with respect to trade marks, references to goods having effect as references to services; as so applied, this Act had effect in relation to service marks subject to the modifications set out in Sch 1 to the 1984 Act. As a result of the amendments, it became necessary to reproduce the amended 1938 Act in two versions, one applying to trade marks for goods and the other for service marks. The 1938 Act, as modified for service marks, is printed below, references to 'trade marks' accordingly being replaced by references to 'service marks' or (where any indication may be to trade marks or service marks), to 'marks', as appropriate.

'Service mark' was defined in the Trade Marks (Amendment) Act 1984, s 1(7), as substituted by the Patents, Designs and Marks Act 1986, s 2(1) (repealed) as follows: ''Service mark' means a mark (including a device, name, signature, word, letter, numeral, or any combination thereof) used or proposed to be used in relation to services for the purpose of indicating, or so as to indicate, that a particular person is connected, in the course of business, with the provision of those services, whether with or without any indication of the identity of that person'.

REGISTRATION, INFRINGEMENT AND OTHER SUBSTANTIVE PROVISIONS

The register

[1. The Register of trade marks etc

(1) The Comptroller-General of Patents, Designs and Trade Marks (in this Act referred to as 'the Registrar') shall maintain the register of trade marks, in which shall be entered—

(a) all registered service marks with the names and addresses of their proprietors;

(b) notifications of assignments and transmissions;

(c) the names and addresses of all registered users;

(d) disclaimers, conditions and limitations; and

(e) such other matters relating to registered service marks as may be prescribed.

(2) The register shall continue to be divided into two parts called respectively Part A and Part B.

(3) The register need not be kept in documentary form.

(4) Subject to any rules under this Act, the public shall have a right to inspect the register at the Patent Office at all convenient times.

(5) Any person who applies for a certified copy of an entry in the register or a certified extract from the register shall be entitled to obtain such a copy or extract on payment of a fee prescribed in relation to certified copies and extracts; and the rules may provide that any person who applies for an uncertified copy or extract shall be entitled to such a copy or extract on payment of a fee prescribed in relation to uncertified copies and extracts.

(6) Application under subsection (5) above or rules made by virtue of that subsection shall be made in such manner as may be prescribed.

(7) In relation to any portion of the register kept otherwise than in documentary form—

(a) the right of inspection conferred by subsection (4) above is a right to inspect the material on the register; and

(b) the right to a copy or extract conferred by subsection (5) above or the rules is a right to a copy or extract in a form in which it can be taken away and in which it is visible and legible.

(8) A certificate purporting to be signed by the Registrar and certifying that any entry which he is authorised by this Act or rules to make has or has not been made, or that any other thing which he is so authorised to do has or has not been done, shall be prima facie evidence, and in Scotland shall be sufficient evidence, of the matters so certified.

(9) A copy of an entry in the register or an extract from the register which is supplied under subsection (5) above and purports to be a certified copy or certified extract shall, subject to subsection (10) below, be admitted in evidence without

further proof and without production of any original; and in Scotland such evidence shall be sufficient evidence.

(10) In the application of this section to England and Wales nothing in it shall be taken as detracting from section 69 or 70 of the Police and Criminal Evidence Act 1984 or any provision made by virtue of either of them.

(11) In this section 'certified copy' and 'certified extract' mean a copy and extract certified by the Registrar and sealed with the seal of the Patent Office.]

General note
This section was substituted by the Patents, Designs and Marks Act 1986, s 1 and Sch 1, para 1.

Effect of registration and the action for infringement

2. No action for infringement of unregistered service mark

No person shall be entitled to institute any proceeding to prevent, or to recover damages for, the infringement of an unregistered service mark, but nothing in this Act shall be deemed to affect rights of action against any person for passing off ... or the remedies in respect thereof.

General note
The words omitted were repealed by the Trade Marks (Amendment) Act 1984, s 1(5)(a).

3. Registration to be in respect of particular services

A service mark must be registered in respect of particular services or classes of services, and any question arising as to the class within which any services fall shall be determined by the Registrar, whose decision shall be final.

4. Right given by registration in Part A, and infringement thereof

(1) Subject to the provisions of this section, and of sections seven and eight of this Act, the registration [after the coming into force of the Trade Marks (Amendment) Act 1984] of a person in Part A of the register as proprietor of a service mark in respect of any services shall, if valid, give to that person the exclusive right to the use of the service mark in relation to those services and, without prejudice to the generality of the foregoing words, that right shall be deemed to be infringed by any person who, not being the proprietor of the service mark or a registered user thereof using by way of the permitted use, uses [in connection with the provision of any services a mark identical with or nearly resembling it], in relation to any services in respect of which it is registered, and in such manner as to render the use of the mark likely to be taken either—

    (a) as being use as a service mark; or
    (b) in a case in which the use is use at or near the place where the services are available for acceptance or performed or in an advertising circular or other advertisement issued to the public, as importing a reference to some person having the right either as proprietor or as registered user to use the service mark or to services with the provision of which such a person as aforesaid is connected in the course of business.]

(2) The right to the use of a service mark given by registration as aforesaid shall be subject to any conditions or limitations entered on the register, and shall not be deemed to be infringed by the use of any such mark as aforesaid in any mode, in relation to [services for use or available for acceptance in any place, country or territory], or in any other circumstances, to which, having regard to any such limitations, the registration does not extend.

(3) The right to the use of a service mark given by registration as aforesaid shall not be deemed to be infringed by the use of any such mark as aforesaid by any person—

(a) in relation to services to which the proprietor of the service mark or a registered user conforming to the permitted use has applied the service mark, where the purpose and effect of the use of the mark is to indicate, in accordance with the fact, that those services have been performed by the proprietor or a registered user of the service mark; or

(b) in relation to services the provision of which is connected in the course of business with the proprietor or a registered user of the service mark, where the proprietor or registered user has at any time expressly or impliedly consented to the use of the service mark; or

in relation to services available for use with other services in relation to which the mark has been used without infringement of the right given by registration or might for the time being be so used, if—

the use of the mark is reasonably necessary in order to indicate that the services are available for such use, and

neither the purpose nor the effect of the use of the mark is to indicate otherwise than in accordance with the fact a connection in the course of business between any person and the provision of those services.]

(4) The use of a registered service mark, being one of two or more registered service marks that are identical or nearly resemble each other, in exercise of the right to the use of that service mark given by registration as aforesaid, shall not be deemed to be an infringement of the right so given to the use of any other of those service marks.

General note
The words in square brackets in sub-ss (1), (2) were substituted and the words omitted from those subsections were removed by the Trade Marks (Amendment) Act 1984, s 1(2) and Sch 1, para 3.

5. Right given by registration in Part B, and infringement thereof

(1) Except as provided by subsection (2) of this section, the registration [after the commencement of the Trade Marks (Amendment) Act 1984] of a person in Part B of the register as proprietor of a service mark in respect of any services shall, if valid, give to that person the like right in relation to those services as if the registration had been in Part A of the register, and the provisions of the last foregoing section shall have effect in like manner in relation to a service mark registered in Part B of the register as they have effect in relation to a service mark registered in Part A of the register.

(2) In any action for infringement of the right to the use of a service mark given by registration as aforesaid in Part B of the register, no injunction or other relief shall be granted to the plaintiff if the defendant establishes to the satisfaction of the court that the use of which the plaintiff complains is not likely to deceive or cause confusion or to be taken as indicating [that a person having the right either as proprietor or as registered user to use the service mark is connected in the course of business with the provision of the services].

General note
The words in square brackets in sub-ss (1), (2) were substituted and the words omitted from those subsections were removed by the Trade Marks (Amendment) Act 1984, s 1(2) and Sch 1, para 3.

6. ...

General note
By virtue of the Trade Marks (Amendment) Act 1984, s 1(2) and Sch 1, para 4, this section was omitted, not being applicable to service marks.

7. Saving for vested rights

Nothing in this Act shall entitle the proprietor or a registered user of a registered service mark to interfere with or restrain the use by any person of a service mark identical with or nearly resembling it in relation to services in relation to which that person or a predecessor in title of his has continuously used that mark from a date anterior—

(a) to the use of the first-mentioned service mark in relation to those services by the proprietor or a predecessor in title of his; or
(b) to the registration of the first-mentioned service mark in respect of those services in the name of the proprietor or a predecessor in title of his;

whichever is the earlier, or to object (on such use being proved) to that person being put on the register for that identical or nearly resembling service mark in respect of those services under subsection (2) of section twelve of this Act.

General note
In the application by virtue of the Trade Marks (Amendment) Act 1984, s 1(1) of this section, the references to the use of the mark by a person's predecessors in title are, as respects use before the 1984 Act came into force, to be construed as references to use by any predecessor of his in business; see s 1(6) of the 1984 Act.

8. Saving for use of name, address, or description of services

No registration of a service mark shall interfere with—

(a) any bona fide use by a person of his own name or of the name of his place of business, or of the name, or of the name of the place of business, of any of his predecessors in business; or
(b) the use by any person of any bona fide description of the character or quality of his services, not being a description that would be likely to be taken as importing any such reference as is mentioned in paragraph (b) of subsection (1) of section four, ... , of this Act.

General note
The words omitted from para (b) were removed by the Trade Marks (Amendment) Act 1984, s 1(2) and Sch 1, para 5.

Registrability and validity of registration

9. Distinctiveness requisite for registration in Part A

(1) In order for a service mark ... to be registrable in Part A of the register, it must contain or consist of at least one of the following essential particulars:—

(a) the name of a company, individual, or firm, represented in a special or particular manner;
(b) the signature of the applicant for registration or some predecessor in his business;
(c) an invented word or invented words;

(d) a word or words having no direct reference to the character or quality of the services, and not being according to its ordinary signification a geographical name or a surname;

(e) any other distinctive mark, but a name, signature, or word or words, other than such as fall within the descriptions in the foregoing paragraphs (a), (b), (c) and (d), shall not be registrable under the provisions of this paragraph except upon evidence of its distinctiveness.

(2) For the purposes of this section 'distinctive' means adapted, in relation to the services in respect of which a service mark is registered or proposed to be registered, to [distinguish services with the provision of which the proprietor is or may be connected, in the course of business, from services with the provision of which he is not so connected], either generally or, where the service mark is registered or proposed to be registered subject to limitations, in relation to use within the extent of the registration.

(3) In determining whether a service mark is adapted to distinguish as aforesaid the tribunal may have regard to the extent to which—

(a) the service mark is inherently adapted to distinguish as aforesaid; and

(b) by reason of the use of the service mark or of any other circumstances, the service mark is in fact adapted to distinguish as aforesaid.

General note
The words omitted from sub-s (1) were removed and the words in square brackets in sub-s (2) were substituted by the Trade Marks (Amendment) Act 1984, s 1(2) and Sch 1, para 6.

10. Capability of distinguishing requisite for registration in Part B

(1) In order for a service mark to be registrable in Part B of the register it must be capable, in relation to the services in respect of which it is registered or proposed to be registered, of [distinguishing services with the provision of which the proprietor of the service mark is or may be connected in the course of business from services with the provision of which he is not so connected], either generally or, where the service mark is registered or proposed to be registered subject to limitations, in relation to use within the extent of the registration.

(2) In determining whether a service mark is capable of distinguishing as aforesaid the tribunal may have regard to the extent which—

(a) the service mark is inherently capable of distinguishing as aforesaid; and

(b) by reason of the use of the service mark or of any other circumstances, the service mark is in fact capable of distinguishing as aforesaid.

(3) A service mark may be registered in Part B notwithstanding any registration in Part A in the name of the same proprietor of the same service mark or any part or parts thereof.

General note
The words in square brackets in sub-s (1) were substituted by the Trade Marks (Amendment) Act 1984, s 1(2) and Sch 1, para 7.

11. Prohibition of registration of deceptive, etc, matter

It shall not be lawful to register as a service mark or part of a service mark any matter the use of which would, by reason of its being likely to deceive or cause confusion or otherwise, be disentitled to protection in a court of justice, or would be contrary to law or morality, or any scandalous design.

12. Prohibition of registration of identical and resembling marks

(1) Subject to the provisions of subsection (2) of this section, no service mark shall be registered in respect of any services or description of services that is identical with [or nearly resembles a mark belonging to a different proprietor and already on the register in respect of the same services, the same description of services, or goods or a description of goods which are associated with those services or services of that description.]

(2) In case of honest concurrent use, or of other special circumstances which in the opinion of the Court or the Registrar make it proper so to do, the Court or the Registrar may permit the registration [by more than one proprietor, in respect of—

    (a) the same services,
    (b) the same description of services, or
    (c) services and goods or descriptions of services and goods which are associated with each other,

of marks that are identical or nearly resemble each other] subject to such conditions and limitations, if any, as the Court or the Registrar, as the case may be, may think it right to impose.

(3) Where separate applications are made by different persons to be registered as proprietors respectively of [marks that are identical or nearly resemble each other, in respect of—

    (a) the same services,
    (b) the same description of services, or
    (c) services and goods or descriptions of services and goods which are associated with each other,]

the Registrar may refuse to register any of them until their rights have been determined by the Court, or have been settled by agreement in a manner approved by him or on an appeal (which may be brought either to the Board of Trade or to the Court at the option of the appellant) by the Board or the Court, as the case may be.

General note
The words in square brackets in sub-ss (1), (2), (3) were substituted by the Trade Marks (Amendment) Act 1984, s 1(2) and Sch 1, para 8.

13. Registration in Part A to be conclusive as to validity after seven years

(1) In all legal proceedings relating to a service mark registered in Part A of the register (including applications under section thirty-two of this Act) the original registration in Part A of the register of the service mark shall, after the expiration of seven years from the date of that registration, be taken to be valid in all respects, unless—

    (a) that registration was obtained by fraud, or
    (b) the service mark offends against the provisions of section eleven of this Act.

(2) Nothing in subsection (1) of section five of this Act shall be construed as making applicable to a service mark, as being a service mark registered in Part B of the register, the foregoing provisions of this section relating to a service mark registered in Part A of the register.

14. Registration subject to disclaimer
If a service mark—

(a) contains any part not separately registered by the proprietor as a service mark; or

(b) contains matter common to [the provision of services of that description] or otherwise of a non-distinctive character;

the Registrar or the Board of Trade or the Court, in deciding whether the service mark shall be entered or shall remain on the register, may require, as a condition of its being on the register, —

    (i) that the proprietor shall disclaim any right to the exclusive use of any part of the service mark, or to the exclusive use of all or any portion of any such matter as aforesaid, to the exclusive use of which the tribunal holds him not to be entitled; or

    (ii) that the proprietor shall make such other disclaimer as the tribunal may consider necessary for the purpose of defining his rights under the registration:

Provided that no disclaimer on the register shall affect any rights of the proprietor of a service mark except such as arise out of the registration of the service mark in respect of which the disclaimer is made.

General note
The words in square brackets in para (b) were substituted by the Trade Marks (Amendment) Act 1984, s 1(2) and Sch 1, para 9.

15. Words used as name or description of an article or substance

(1) The registration of a service mark shall not be deemed to have become invalid by reason only of any use, after the date of the registration, of a word or words which the service mark contains, or of which it consists, as the name or description of [some activity]:
[Provided that, if it is proved that there is a well-known and established use of the word or words as the name or description of some activity by a person or persons providing services which include that activity, not being use in relation to services with the provision of which the proprietor or a registered user of the service mark is connected in the course of business, the provisions of subsection (2) below shall have effect.]

    (2) Where the facts mentioned in ... the proviso to the foregoing subsection are proved with respect to any word or words, then—

(a) if the service mark consists solely of that word or those words, the registration of the service mark, so far as regards registration in respect of the [activity in question], shall be deemed for the purposes of section thirty-two of this Act to be an entry wrongly remaining on the register;

(b) if the service mark contains that word or those words and other matter, the Court or the Registrar, in deciding whether the service mark shall remain on the register, so far as regards registration in respect of the [activity in question], may in case of a decision in favour of its remaining on the register require as a condition thereof that the proprietor shall disclaim any right to the exclusive use in relation to [that activity] of that word or those words, so, however, that no disclaimer on the register shall affect any rights of the proprietor of a service mark except such as arise out of the registration of the service mark in respect of which the disclaimer is made; and

(c) for the purposes of any other legal proceedings relating to the service mark,—

(i) if the service mark consists solely of that word or those words, all rights of the proprietor, whether under the common law or by registration, to the exclusive use of the service mark in relation to the [activity in question], or

(ii) if the service mark contains that word or those words and other matter, all such rights of the proprietor to the exclusive use of that word or those words in such relation as aforesaid,

shall be deemed to have ceased on the date at which the use mentioned in ... the proviso to the foregoing subsection first became well known and established ...

(3) ...

General note
The words in square brackets in sub-ss (1), (2) were substituted and the words omitted from sub-s (2), and the whole of sub-s (3), were removed by the Trade Marks (Amendment) Act 1984, s 1(2) and Sch 1, para 10.

16. Effect of limitation as to colour, and of absence thereof

A service mark may be limited in whole or in part to one or more specified colours, and in any such case the fact that it is so limited shall be taken into consideration by any tribunal having to decide on the distinctive character of the service mark.

If and so far as a service mark is registered without limitation of colour, it shall be deemed to be registered for all colours.

Procedure for, and duration of, registration

17. Application for registration

(1) Any person claiming to be the proprietor of a service mark used or proposed to be used by him who is desirous of registering it must apply in writing to the Registrar in the prescribed manner for registration either in Part A or in Part B of the register.

(2) Subject to the provisions of this Act, the Registrar may refuse the application, or may accept it absolutely or subject to such amendments, modifications, conditions or limitations, if any, as he may think right.

(3) In the case of an application for registration of a service mark *(other than a certification trade mark)* in Part A of the register, the Registrar may, if the applicant is willing, instead of refusing the application, treat it as an application for registration in Part B and deal with the application accordingly.

(4) In the case of a refusal or conditional acceptance, the Registrar shall, if required by the applicant, state in writing the grounds of his decision and the materials used by him in arriving thereat, and the decision shall be subject to appeal to the Board of Trade or to the Court at the option of the applicant.

(5) An appeal under this section shall be made in the prescribed manner, and on the appeal the tribunal shall, if required, hear the applicant and the Registrar, and shall make an order determining whether, and subject to what amendments, modifications, conditions or limitations, if any, the application is to be accepted.

(6) Appeals under this section shall be heard on the materials stated as aforesaid by the Registrar, and no further grounds of objection to the acceptance of the application shall be allowed to be taken by the Registrar, other than those so stated as aforesaid by him, except by leave of the tribunal hearing the appeal. Where any further grounds of objection are taken, the applicant shall be entitled to withdraw his application without payment of costs on giving notice as prescribed.

(7) The Registrar or the Board of Trade or the Court, as the case may be, may at any time, whether before or after acceptance, correct any error in or in connection with the application, or may permit the applicant to amend his application upon such terms as the Registrar or the Board of Trade or the Court, as the case may be, may think fit.

General note
Note that the reference to a certification trade mark in sub-s (3), although of no relevance to service marks, was not repealed by the Trade Marks (Amendment) Act 1984, s 1(2), Sch 1, unlike the other references to certification marks.

18. Opposition to registration

(1) When an application for registration of a service mark has been accepted, whether absolutely or subject to conditions or limitations, the Registrar shall, as soon as may be after acceptance, cause the application as accepted to be advertised in the prescribed manner, and the advertisement shall set forth all conditions and limitations subject to which the application has been accepted:
Provided that the Registrar may cause an application to be advertised before acceptance if it is made under paragraph (e) of subsection (1) of section nine of this Act, or in any other case where it appears to him that it is expedient by reason of any exceptional circumstances so to do, and where an application has been so advertised the Registrar may, if he thinks fit, advertise it again when it has been accepted but shall not be bound so to do.

(2) Any person may, within the prescribed time from the date of the advertisement of an application, give notice to the Registrar of opposition to the registration.

(3) The notice shall be given in writing in the prescribed manner, and shall include a statement of the grounds of opposition.

(4) The Registrar shall send a copy of the notice to the applicant, and within the prescribed time after receipt thereof the applicant shall send to the Registrar, in the prescribed manner, a counter-statement of the grounds on which he relies or his application, and, if he does not do so, he shall be deemed to have abandoned his application.

(5) If the applicant sends such a counter-statement as aforesaid, the Registrar shall furnish a copy thereof to the persons giving notice of opposition, and shall, after hearing the parties, if so required, and considering the evidence, decide whether, and subject to what conditions or limitations, if any, registration is to be permitted.

(6) The decision of the Registrar shall be subject to appeal to the Court.

(7) An appeal under this section shall be made in the prescribed manner, and on the appeal the Court shall, if required, hear the parties and the Registrar, and shall make an order determining whether, and subject to what conditions or limitations, if any, registration is to be permitted.

(8) On the hearing of an appeal under this section any party may, either in the manner prescribed or by special leave of the Court, bring forward further material for the consideration of the Court.

(9) On an appeal under this section no further grounds of objection to the registration of a service mark shall be allowed to be taken by the opponent or the Registrar, other than those so stated as aforesaid by the opponent, except by leave of the Court. Where any further grounds of objection are taken, the applicant shall be entitled to withdraw his application without payment of the costs of the opponent on giving notice as prescribed.

(10) On an appeal under this section the Court may, after hearing the Registrar, permit the service mark proposed to be registered to be modified in any manner not

substantially affecting the identity thereof, but in any such case the service mark as so modified shall be advertised in the prescribed manner before being registered.

(11) If a person giving notice of opposition or an applicant sending a counter-statement after receipt of a copy of such a notice, or an appellant, neither resides nor carries on business in the United Kingdom, the tribunal may require him to give security for costs of the proceedings before the tribunal relative to the opposition or to the appeal, as the case may be, and in default of such security being duly given may treat the opposition or application, or the appeal, as the case may be, as abandoned.

19. Registration

(1) When an application for registration of a service mark in Part A or in Part B of the register has been accepted, and either—

(a) the application has not been opposed and the time for notice of opposition has expired, or
(b) the application has been opposed and the opposition has been decided in favour of the applicant,

the Registrar shall, unless the application has been accepted in error or unless the Board of Trade otherwise direct, register the service mark in Part A or Part B, as the case may be, and the service mark, when registered, shall be registered[, subject to section 39A(2) below,] as of the date of the application for registration, and that date shall be deemed for the purposes of this Act to be the date of registration:

...

(2) On the registration of a service mark the Registrar shall issue to the applicant a certificate in the prescribed form of the registration thereof sealed with the seal of the Patent Office.

(3) Where registration of a service mark is not completed within twelve months from the date of the application by reason of default on the part of the applicant, the Registrar may, after giving notice of the non-completion to the applicant in writing in the prescribed manner, treat the application as abandoned unless it is completed within the time specified in that behalf in the notice.

General note
The words in square brackets in sub-s (1) were inserted and the words omitted removed by the Patents, Designs and Marks Act 1986, ss 2(3), 3(2) and Sch 2, para 3, Sch 3, Pt II.

20. Duration and renewal of registration

(1) The registration of a service mark shall be for a period of seven years, but may be renewed from time to time in accordance with the provisions of this section:

...

(2) The Registrar shall, on application made by the registered proprietor of a service mark in the prescribed manner and within the prescribed period, renew the registration of the service mark for a period of fourteen years from the date of expiration of the original registration or of the last renewal of registration, as the case may be, which date is in this section referred to as 'the expiration of the last registration.'

(3) At the prescribed time before the expiration of the last registration of a service mark, the Registrar shall send notice in the prescribed manner to the registered proprietor of the date of expiration and the conditions as to payment of fees and otherwise upon which a renewal of registration may be obtained, and, if at the expiration of the time prescribed in that behalf those conditions have not been duly

complied with, the Registrar may remove the service mark from the register, subject to such conditions, if any, as to its restoration to the register as may be prescribed.

(4) Where a service mark has been removed from the register for non-payment of the fee for renewal, it shall, nevertheless, for the purpose of any application for the registration of a mark during one year next after the date of the removal, be deemed to be a service mark that is already on the register:
Provided that the foregoing provisions of this subsection shall not have effect where the tribunal is satisfied either—

> (a) that there has been no bona fide [business use] of the service mark that has been removed during the two years immediately preceding its removal; or
> (b) that no deception or confusion would be likely to arise from the use of the mark that is the subject of the application for registration by reason of any previous use of the service mark that has been removed.

General note
The words omitted from sub-s (1) were omitted and the words in square brackets in sub-s (4) were substituted by the Trade Marks (Amendment) Act 1984, s 1(2) and Sch 1, para 11.

21.   Registration of parts of service marks and of service marks as a series
(1) Where the proprietor of a service mark claims to be entitled to the exclusive use of any part thereof separately, he may apply to register the whole and any such part as separate service marks.
Each such separate service mark must satisfy all the conditions of an independent service mark and shall, subject to the provisions of subsection (3) of section twenty-three and subsection (2) of section thirty of this Act, have all the incidents of an independent service mark.

(2) Where a person claiming to be the proprietor of several service marks, in respect of the same services or description of services, which, while resembling each other in the material particulars thereof, yet differ in respect of—

> (a) statements of the services in relation to which they are respectively used or proposed to be used; or
> (b) statements of number, price, quality or names of places; or
> (c) other matter of a non-distinctive character which does not substantially affect the identity of the service mark; or
> (d) colour;

seeks to register those service marks, they may be registered as a series in one registration.

Assignment and transmission

22.   Powers of, and restrictions on, assignment and transmission
(1) ... , a registered service mark shall be, ... , assignable and transmissible either in connection with the goodwill of a business or not.

(2) A registered service mark shall be, ... , assignable and transmissible in respect either of all the services in respect of which it is registered, ... , or of some (but not all) of those services.

(3) The provisions of the two foregoing subsections shall have effect in the case of an unregistered service mark used in relation to any services as they have effect in the case of a registered service mark registered in respect of any services, if at

the time of the assignment or transmission of the unregistered service mark it is … used in the same business as a registered service mark, and if it is … assigned or transmitted at the same time and to the same person as that registered service mark and in respect of services all of which are services in relation to which the unregistered service mark is … used in that business and in respect of which that registered service mark is … assigned or transmitted.

[(4) Notwithstanding anything in subsections (1) to (3) of this section a service mark shall not be assignable or transmissible in a case in which as a result of an assignment or transmission there would in the circumstances subsist, whether under the common law or by registration, exclusive rights in more than one of the persons concerned to the use, in relation to—

(a) the same services,
(b) the same description of services, or
(c) services and goods or descriptions of services and goods which are associated with each other,

of marks nearly resembling each other or of identical marks, if, having regard to the similarity of the services or the association of the goods and services or description of goods and services, and to the similarity of the marks, the use of the marks in exercise of those rights would be likely to deceive or cause confusion:

Provided that, where a service mark is assigned or transmitted in such a case, the assignment or transmission shall not be deemed to be invalid under this subsection if the exclusive rights subsisting as a result thereof in the persons concerned respectively are, having regard to limitations imposed thereon, such as not to be exercisable by two or more of those persons in relation to services for use in the United Kingdom, in relation to services for use in the same country or territory outside the United Kingdom or in relation to services available for acceptance in the United Kingdom (wherever they are to be used).]

(5) The proprietor of a registered service mark who proposes to assign it in respect of any services in respect of which it is registered may submit to the Registrar in the prescribed manner a statement of case setting out the circumstances, and the Registrar may issue to him a certificate stating whether, having regard to the similarity of [the services or the association of the services and goods or descriptions of services and goods and to the similarity] of the marks referred to in the case, the proposed assignment of the first-mentioned service mark would or would not be invalid under the last foregoing subsection, and a certificate so issued shall, subject to the provisions of this section as to appeal and unless it is shown that the certificate was obtained by fraud or misrepresentation, be conclusive as to the validity or invalidity under the last foregoing subsection of the assignment in so far as such validity or invalidity depends upon the facts set out in the case, but, as regards a certificate in favour of validity, only if application for the registration under section twenty-five of this Act of the title of the person becoming entitled is made within six months from the date on which the certificate is issued.

(6) Notwithstanding anything in subsections (1) to (3) of this section, a service mark shall not, … , be assignable or transmissible in a case in which as a result of an assignment or transmission thereof there would in the circumstances subsist, whether under the common law or by registration,

[(a) an exclusive right in one of the persons concerned to the use of the service mark limited to use in relation to services for use or services available for acceptance in a place or places in the United Kingdom; and

(b) an exclusive right in another of the persons concerned to the use of a mark identical with or nearly resembling the service mark referred to in paragraph (a) above in relation to—

(i) the same services,

(ii) the same description of services, or

(iii) goods which are associated with those services or service of that description,

limited to use in relation to services for use, services available for acceptance or goods to be sold or otherwise traded in, in another place or places in the United Kingdom.]

Provided that, on application in the prescribed manner by the proprietor of a service mark who proposes to assign it, or of a person who claims that a service mark has been transmitted to him or to a predecessor in title of his … , in any such case, the Registrar, if he is satisfied that in all the circumstances the use of the marks in exercise of the said rights would not be contrary to the public interest, may approve the assignment or transmission, and an assignment or transmission so approved shall not be deemed to be, or to have been, invalid under this subsection or under subsection (4) of this section, so, however, that in the case of a registered service mark this provision shall not have effect unless application for the registration under section twenty-five of this Act of the title of the person becoming entitled is made within six months from the date on which the approval is given or, in the case of a transmission, was made before that date.

(7) Where an assignment in respect of any services of a service mark that is at the time of the assignment used in a business [of providing those services is made], otherwise than in connection with the goodwill of that business, the assignment shall not take effect until the following requirements have been satisfied, that is to say, the assignee must, not later than the expiration of six months from the date on which the assignment is made or within such extended period, if any, as the Registrar may allow, apply to him for directions with respect to the advertisement of the assignment, and must advertise it in such form and manner and within such period as the Registrar may direct.

(8) Any decision of the Registrar under this section shall be subject to appeal to the Court.

General note

The words omitted from sub-ss (1), (2), (3), (6) were removed and sub-s (4) and the words in square brackets in sub-ss (5), (6), (7) were substituted by the Trade Marks (Amendment) Act 1984, s 1(2) and Sch 1, para 12.

23. Certain service marks to be associated so as to be assignable and transmissible as a whole only

(1) Service marks that are registered as, or that are deemed by virtue of this Act to be, associated service marks shall be assignable and transmissible only as a whole and not separately, but they shall for all other purposes be deemed to have been registered as separate service marks.

(2) Where a service mark that is registered, or is the subject of an application for registration, in respect of any services is identical with another service mark that is registered, or is the subject of an application for registration, in the name of the same proprietor in respect of the same services or description of services, or so nearly resembles it as to be likely to deceive or cause confusion if used by a person other than the proprietor, the Registrar may at any time

745

require that the service marks shall be entered on the register as associated service marks.

Any decision of the Registrar under this subsection shall be subject to appeal to the Board of Trade, or to the Court, at the option of the appellant.

[(2A) Where there is an identicality or near resemblance of marks that are registered, or are the subject of applications for registration, in the name of the same proprietor in respect of services and in respect of goods which are associated with those services or services of that description, subsection (2) above applies as it applies where there is an identicality or near resemblance of service marks that are registered, or are the subject of applications for registration, in the name of the same proprietor in respect of the same services or description of services.]

(3) Where a service mark and any part or parts thereof are, by virtue of subsection (1) of section twenty-one of this Act, registered as separate service marks in the name of the same proprietor, they shall be deemed to be, and shall be registered as, associated service marks.

(4) All service marks that are, by virtue of subsection (2) of section twenty-one of this Act, registered as a series in one registration shall be deemed to be, and shall be registered as, associated service marks.

(5) On application made in the prescribed manner by the registered proprietor of two or more marks registered as associated marks, the Registrar may dissolve the association as respects any of them if he is satisfied that there would be no likelihood of deception or confusion being caused if that mark were used by another person in relation to any of the [services] [goods] in respect of which it is registered, and may amend the register accordingly.

Any decision of the Registrar under this subsection shall be subject to appeal to the Board of Trade, or to the Court, at the option of the appellant.

General note
Sub-s (2A) was inserted by the Trade Marks (Amendment) Act 1984, s 1(2) and Sch 1, para 13.

24. Power of registered proprietor to assign and give receipts
Subject to the provisions of this Act, the person for the time being entered in the register as proprietor of a service mark shall, subject to any rights appearing from the register to be vested in any other person, have power to assign the service mark, and to give effectual receipts for any consideration for an assignment thereof.

25. Registration of assignments and transmissions
(1) Where a person becomes entitled by assignment or transmission to a registered service mark, he shall make application to the Registrar to register his title, and the Registrar shall, on receipt of the application and on proof of title to his satisfaction, register him as the proprietor of the service mark in respect of the services in respect of which the assignment or transmission has effect, and shall cause particulars of the assignment or transmission to be entered on the register.

(2) Any decision of the Registrar under this section shall be subject to appeal to the Court.

(3) Except for the purposes of an appeal under this section or of an application under section thirty-two of this Act, a document or instrument in respect of which no entry has been made in the register in accordance with the provisions of subsection (1) of this section shall not be admitted in evidence in any court in proof of the title to a service mark unless the court otherwise directs.

Use and non-use

26. Removal from register and imposition of limitations on ground of non-use

(1) ... , a registered service mark may be taken off the register in respect of any of the services in respect of which it is registered on application by any person aggrieved to the Court or, at the option of the applicant and subject to the provisions of section fifty-four of this Act, to the Registrar, on the ground either—

(a) that the service mark was registered without any bona fide intention on the part of the applicant for registration that it should be used in relation to those services by him, and that there has in fact been no bona fide use of the service mark in relation to those services by any proprietor thereof for the time being up to the date one month before the date of the application; or

(b) that up to the date one month before the date of the application a continuous period of five years or longer elapsed during which the service mark was a registered service mark and during which there was no bona fide use thereof in relation to those services by any proprietor thereof for the time being:

Provided that (except where the applicant has been permitted under subsection (2) of section twelve of this Act to register an identical or nearly resembling service mark in respect of the services in question or where the tribunal is of opinion that he might properly be permitted so to register such a service mark) the tribunal may refuse an application made under paragraph (a) or (b) of this subsection in relation to any services, if it is shown that there has been, before the relevant date or during the relevant period, as the case may be, bona fide use [of the mark by the proprietor thereof for the time being in relation to—

[(i) services of the same description; or
(ii) goods associated with those services or services of that description,

being services or, as the case may be, goods in respect of which the mark is registered.]]

[(2) Where in relation to any services in respect of which a service mark is registered—

(a) the matters referred to in paragraph (b) of subsection (1) above are shown so far as regards non-use of the service mark in relation to services for use or available for acceptance in a particular place in the United Kingdom, or for use in a country or territory outside the United Kingdom; and

(b) a person has been permitted under subsection (2) of section 12 of this Act to register an identical or nearly-resembling service mark in respect of those services under a registration extending to use in relation to services for use or available for acceptance in that place or for use or available for acceptance in that place or for use in that country or territory, or the tribunal is of opinion that he might properly be permitted so to register such a service mark;]

on application by that person to the Court or, at the option of the applicant and subject to the provisions of section fifty-four of this Act, to the Registrar the tribunal may impose on the registration of the first-mentioned service mark such limitations as the tribunal thinks proper for securing that that registration shall cease to extend to such use as last aforesaid.

(3) An applicant shall not be entitled to rely for the purposes of paragraph (b) of subsection (1), or for the purposes of subsection (2), of this section on any non-use of a service mark [in relation to particular services that is shown to have been due to special circumstances affecting the provision of those services] and not to any intention not to use or to abandon the service mark in relation to the services to which the application relates.

General note
In sub-s (1) the words in the first (outer) pair of square brackets were substituted by the Patents, Designs and Marks Act 1986, s 2(3), Sch 2, para 4, and the words in the second (inner) pair of square brackets in that subsection were substituted by the Trade Marks (Amendment) Act 1984, s 1(2) and Sch 1, para 14(1), (2), as amended by s 2(3) of, and Sch 2, para 10 to, the 1986 Act.
The words in square brackets in sub-ss (2), (3) were substituted by the Trade Marks (Amendment) Act 1984, s 1(2) and Sch 1, para 14(1), (3), (4).

27. ...

General note
By virtue of the Trade Marks (Amendment) Act 1984, s 1(2) and Sch 1, para 15, this section was omitted, as being inapplicable to service marks.

28. Registered users
(1) Subject to the provisions of this section, a person other than the proprietor of a service mark may be registered as a registered user thereof in respect of all or any of the services in respect of which it is registered ... and either with or without conditions or restrictions.

The use of a service mark by a registered user thereof in relation to [services with the provision of which he is connected in the course of business] and in respect of which for the time being the service mark remains registered and he is registered as a registered user, being use such as to comply with any conditions or restrictions to which his registration is subject, is in this Act referred to as the 'permitted use' thereof.

(2) The permitted use of a service mark shall be deemed to be use by the proprietor thereof, and shall be deemed not to be use by a person other than the proprietor, for the purposes of section twenty-six of this Act and for any other purpose for which such use is material under this Act or at common law.

(3) Subject to any agreement subsisting between the parties, a registered user of a service mark shall be entitled to call upon the proprietor thereof to take proceedings to prevent infringement thereof, and, if the proprietor refuses or neglects to do so within two months after being so called upon, the registered user may institute proceedings for infringement in his own name as if he were the proprietor, making the proprietor a defendant.

A proprietor so added as defendant shall not be liable for any costs unless he enters an appearance and takes part in the proceedings.

(4) Where it is proposed that a person should be registered as a registered user of a service mark, the proprietor and the proposed registered user must apply in writing to the Registrar in the prescribed manner and must furnish him with a statutory declaration made by the proprietor, or by some person authorised to act on his behalf and approved by the Registrar,—

(a) giving particulars of the relationship, existing or proposed, between the proprietor and the proposed registered user, including particulars showing the degree of control by the proprietor over the permitted use which their relationship will confer and whether it is a term of their relationship that the proposed registered user shall be the sole registered user or that there shall be any other restriction as to persons for whose registration as registered users application may be made;

(b) stating the services in respect of which registration is proposed;

(c) stating any conditions or restrictions proposed with respect to the characteristics of the services, to the mode or place of permitted use, or to any other matter; and

(d) stating whether the permitted use is to be for a period or without limit of period, and, if for a period, the duration thereof;

and with such further documents, information or evidence as may be required under the rules or by the Registrar.

(5) When the requirements of the last foregoing subsection have been complied with, if the Registrar, after considering the information furnished to him under that subsection, is satisfied that in all the circumstances the use of the service mark in relation to the proposed services or any of them by the proposed registered user subject to any conditions or restrictions which the Registrar thinks proper would not be contrary to the public interest, the Registrar may register the proposed registered user as a registered user in respect of the services as to which he is so satisfied subject as aforesaid.

(6) The Registrar shall refuse an application under the foregoing provisions of this section if it appears to him that the grant thereof would tend to facilitate trafficking in a service mark.

(7) The Registrar shall, if so required by an applicant, take steps for securing that information given for the purposes of an application under the foregoing provisions of this section (other than matter entered in the register) is not disclosed to rivals in [business].

(8) Without prejudice to the provisions of section thirty-two of this Act, the registration of a person as a registered user—

(a) may be varied by the Registrar as regards the services in respect of which, or any conditions or restrictions subject to which, it has effect, on the application in writing in the prescribed manner of the registered proprietor of the service mark to which the registration relates;

(b) may be cancelled by the Registrar on the application in writing in the prescribed manner of the registered proprietor or of the registered user or of any other registered user of the service mark; or

(c) may be cancelled by the Registrar on the application in writing in the prescribed manner of any person on any of the following grounds, that is to say,—

(i) that the registered user has used the service mark otherwise than by way of the permitted use, or in such a way as to cause, or to be likely to cause, deception or confusion;

(ii) that the proprietor or the registered user misrepresented, or failed to disclose, some fact material to the application for the registration, or that the circumstances have materially changed since the date of the registration;

(iii) that the registration ought not to have been effected having regard to rights vested in the applicant by virtue of a contract in the performance of which he is interested.

(9) Provision shall be made by the rules for the notification of the registration of a person as a registered user to any other registered user of the service mark, and for the notification of an application under the last foregoing subsection to the

registered proprietor and each registered user (not being the applicant) of the service mark, and for giving to the applicant on such an application, and to all persons to whom such an application is notified and who intervene in the proceedings in accordance with the rules, an opportunity of being heard.

(10) The Registrar may at any time cancel the registration of a person as a registered user of a service mark in respect of any services in respect of which the service mark is no longer registered.

(11) Any decision of the Registrar under the foregoing provisions of this section shall be subject to appeal to the Court.

(12) Nothing in this section shall confer on a registered user of a service mark any assignable or transmissible right to the use thereof.

General note
The words omitted from sub-s (1) were removed and the words in square brackets in sub-ss (1), (7) were substituted by the Trade Marks (Amendment) Act 1984, s 1(2) and Sch 1, para 16.

29. Proposed use of service mark by corporation to be constituted, etc

(1) No application for the registration of a service mark in respect of any services shall be refused, nor shall permission for such registration be withheld, on the ground only that it appears that the applicant does not use or propose to use the service mark, —

(a) if the tribunal is satisfied that a body corporate is about to be constituted, and that the applicant intends to assign the service mark to the corporation with a view to the use thereof in relation to those services by the corporation; or

(b) if the application is accompanied by an application for the registration of a person as a registered user of the service mark, and the tribunal is satisfied that the proprietor intends it to be used by that person in relation to those services and the tribunal is also satisfied that that person will be registered as a registered user thereof immediately after the registration of the service mark.

(2) The provisions of section twenty-six of this Act shall have effect, in relation to a service mark registered under the power conferred by the foregoing subsection, as if for the reference, in paragraph (a) of subsection (1) of that section, to intention on the part of an applicant for registration that a service mark should be used by him there were substituted a reference to intention on his part that it should be used by the corporation or registered user concerned.

(3) The tribunal may, as a condition of the exercise of the power conferred by subsection (1) of this section in favour of an applicant who relies on intention to assign to a corporation as aforesaid, require him to give security for the costs of any proceedings before the tribunal relative to any opposition or appeal, and in default of such security being duly given may treat the application as abandoned.

(4) Where a service mark is registered in respect of any services under the power conferred by subsection (1) of this section in the name of an applicant who relies on intention to assign to a corporation as aforesaid, then, unless within such period as may be prescribed, or within such further period not exceeding six months as the Registrar may on application being made to him in the prescribed manner allow, the corporation has been registered as the proprietor of the service mark in respect of those services, the registration shall cease to have effect in respect thereof at the expiration of that period, and the Registrar shall amend the register accordingly.

30. Use of one of associated or substantially identical service marks equivalent to use of another

(1) Where under the provisions of this Act use of a registered service mark is required to be proved for any purpose, the tribunal may, if and so far as the tribunal thinks right, accept use of an associated registered service mark, or of the service mark with additions or alterations not substantially affecting its identity, as an equivalent for the use required to be proved.

(2) The use of the whole of a registered service mark shall for the purposes of this Act be deemed to be also a use of any registered service mark, being a part thereof, registered in the name of the same proprietor by virtue of subsection (1) of section twenty-one of this Act.

31. Use of service mark for export trade

[Any act done in the United Kingdom in relation to services for use outside the United Kingdom which, if done in relation to services provided within the United Kingdom for use there, would constitute use of a service mark in the United Kingdom, shall be deemed to constitute use of the service mark in relation to those services for any purpose for which such use is material under this Act or at common law.]

General note
This section was substituted by the Trade Marks (Amendment) Act 1984, s 1(2) and Sch 1, para 17.

Rectification and correction of the register

32. General power to rectify entries in register

(1) Any person aggrieved by the non-insertion in or omission from the register of any entry, or by any entry made in the register without sufficient cause, or by any entry wrongly remaining on the register, or by any error or defect in any entry in the register, may apply in the prescribed manner to the Court or, at the option of the applicant and subject to the provisions of section fifty-four o this Act, to the Registrar, and the tribunal may make such order for making, expunging or varying the entry as the tribunal may think fit.

(2) The tribunal may in any proceeding under this section decide any question that it may be necessary or expedient to decide in connection with the rectification of the register.

(3) In case of fraud in the registration, assignment or transmission of a registered mark, the Registrar may himself apply to the Court under the provisions of this section.

(4) Any order of the Court rectifying the register shall direct that notice of the rectification shall be served in the prescribed manner on the Registrar, and the Registrar shall on receipt of the notice rectify the register accordingly.

(5) The power to rectify the register conferred by this section shall include power to remove a registration in Part A of the register to Part B.

33. Power to expunge or vary registration for breach of condition

On application by any person aggrieved to the Court, or, at the option of the applicant and subject to the provisions of section fifty-four of this Act, to the Registrar, or on application by the Registrar to the Court, the tribunal may make such order as the tribunal may think fit for expunging or varying the registration of a service mark on the ground of any contravention of, or failure to observe, a condition entered on the register in relation thereto.

34. Correction of register

(1) The Registrar may, on request made in the prescribed manner by the registered proprietor, —

(a) correct any error in the [name or address] of the registered proprietor of a service mark;

(b) enter any change in the [name or address] of the person who is registered as proprietor of a service mark;

(c) cancel the entry of a service mark on the register;

(d) strike out any services or classes of services from those in respect of which a service mark is registered; or

(e) enter a disclaimer or memorandum relating to a service mark which does not in any way extend the rights given by the existing registration of the service mark.

(2) The Registrar may, on request made in the prescribed manner by a registered user of a service mark, correct any error, or enter any change, in the [name or address] of the registered user.

(3) Any decision of the Registrar under this section shall be subject to appeal to the Board of Trade, or to the Court, at the option of the appellant.

General note
The words in square brackets in sub-ss (1), (2) were substituted by the Patents, Designs and Marks Act 1986, s 1 and Sch 1, para 2.

35. Alteration of registered service mark

(1) The registered proprietor of a service mark may apply in the prescribed manner to the Registrar for leave to add to or alter the service mark in any manner not substantially affecting the identity thereof, and the Registrar may refuse leave or may grant it on such terms and subject to such limitations as he may think fit.

(2) The Registrar may cause an application under this section to be advertised in the prescribed manner in any case where it appears to him that it is expedient so to do, and where he does so, if within the prescribed time from the date of the advertisement any person gives notice to the Registrar in the prescribed manner of opposition to the application, the Registrar shall, after hearing the parties if so required, decide the matter.

(3) Any decision of the Registrar under this section shall be subject to appeal to the Board of Trade, or to the Court, at the option of the appellant.

(4) Where leave as aforesaid is granted, the service mark as altered shall be advertised in the prescribed manner, unless it has already been advertised, in the form to which it has been altered, in an advertisement under subsection (2) of this section.

36. Adaptation of entries in register to amended or substituted classification of services

(1) The Board of Trade may from time to time make such rules, prescribe such forms and generally do such things as they think expedient, for empowering the Registrar to amend the register, whether by making or expunging or varying entries therein, so far as may be requisite for the purpose of adapting the designation therein of the services or classes of services in respect of which service marks are registered to any amended or substituted classification that may be prescribed.

(2) The Registrar shall not, in exercise of any power conferred on him for the purpose aforesaid, make any amendment of the register that would have the effect of adding any services or classes of services to those in respect of which a service

mark is registered (whether in one or more classes) immediately before the amendment is to be made, or of antedating the registration of a service mark in respect of any services:

Provided that this subsection shall not have effect in relation to services as to which the Registrar is satisfied that compliance with this subsection in relation thereto would involve undue complexity and that the addition or antedating, as the case may be, would not affect any substantial quantity of services and would not substantially prejudice the rights of any person.

(3) A proposal for the amendment of the register for the purpose aforesaid shall be notified to the registered proprietor of the service mark affected, shall be subject to appeal by the registered proprietor to the Board of Trade, or at his option to the Court, shall be advertised with any modifications, and may be opposed before the Registrar by any person aggrieved on the ground that the proposed amendment contravenes the provisions of the last foregoing subsection, and the decision of the Registrar on any such opposition shall be subject to appeal to the Court.

37. ...

General note
By virtue of the Trade Marks (Amendment) Act 1984, s 1(2) and Sch 1, para 18, this section was omitted because no provision was made for registration of certification marks for services.

38. ...

General note
This section was repealed by the Trade Marks (Amendment) Act 1984, s 1(2) and Sch 1, para 18A, as inserted by the Patents, Designs and Marks Act 1986, s 2(3) and Sch 2, para 11.

39. ...

General note
This section was repealed by the Trade Marks (Amendment) Act 1984, s 1(2) and Sch 1, para 18B, as inserted by the Patents, Designs and Marks Act 1986, s 2(3) and Sch 2, para 11.

[39A. Registration of service mark following overseas application
(1) Any person who has applied for protection for any service mark in a relevant country or his legal representative or assignee shall be entitled on an application for registration made within six months of the application for protection in the relevant country to registration of his service mark under this Act in priority to other applicants.

(2) [Subject to subsection (2A) below, a] service mark registered on an application made under this section shall be registered as of the date of the application in the relevant country and that date shall be deemed for the purposes of this Act to be the date of registration.

[(2A)   Where an application for protection for a service mark was made in a relevant country before the date on which the Trade Marks (Amendment) Act 1984 came into force, a service mark registered on an application under this section shall be registered as of that date.]

(3) Nothing in this section shall entitle the proprietor of the service mark to recover damages for infringements happening prior to the date of the application for registration under this Act.

(4) The registration of a service mark under this section shall not be invalidated by reason only of the use of the mark in the United Kingdom during the period of 6 months within which the application may be made.

(5) The application for the registration of a service mark under this section must be made in the same manner as an ordinary application under this Act.

(6) Where a person has applied for protection for any service mark by an application which—

(a) in accordance with the terms of a treaty subsisting between any two or more relevant countries, is equivalent to an application duly made in any one of those countries; or

(b) in accordance with the law of any relevant country, is equivalent to an application duly made in that country,

he shall be deemed for the purposes of this section to have applied in that country.

(7) Subject to subsection (8) below, Her Majesty may by Order in Council direct that this section shall apply to a country specified in the Order.

[(8) If a country is not a dependent territory, an Order in Council under this section may only be made in relation to it—

with a view to the fulfilment of a treaty, convention, arrangement or engagement; or

if Her Majesty is satisfied that provision has been or will be made under the laws of that country whereby priority for the protection of service marks in respect of which application for registration under this Act has been made will be given on a basis comparable to that for which provision is made by this section in relation to applications for registration made in a relevant country.]

(9) An Order in Council under this section shall be subject to annulment in pursuance of a resolution of either House of Parliament and may be varied or revoked by a subsequent Order.

(10) In this section—

'country' includes any territory;

'dependent territory' means any of the Channel Islands or a colony;

'relevant country' means a country which was specified in an Order in Council under this section at the time of the application under this section or such other time as may be specified in the Order in Council.]

General note
This section was inserted by the Patents, Designs and Marks Act 1986, s 2(3)and Sch 2, para 5.

The words in square brackets in sub-s (2) and the whole of sub-s (8) were substituted and sub-s (2A) were inserted by the Trade Marks (Amendment) Act 1984, s 1(2) and Sch 1, para 18C, as inserted by the Patents, Designs and Marks Act 1986, s 2(3) and Sch 2, para 11.

GENERAL AND MISCELLANEOUS

Rules and fees

40. Power of Board of Trade to make rules

(1) The Board of Trade may from time to time make such rules, prescribe such forms and generally do such things as they think expedient—

(a) for regulating the practice under this Act, including the service of documents;

(b) for classifying services for the purposes of registration of service marks;

(c) for making or requiring duplicates of service marks and other documents;

(d) for securing and regulating the publishing and selling or distributing, in such manner as the Board of Trade think fit, of copies of service marks and other documents;

    (e) generally for regulating the business of the Patent Office in relation to service marks and all things by this Act placed under the direction or control of the Registrar or of the Board of Trade.

(2) ...

(3) Before making any rules under this Act, the Board of Trade shall publish notice of their intention to make the rules and of the place where copies of the draft rules may be obtained, in such manner as the Board consider most expedient so as to enable persons affected to make representations to the Board before the rules are finally settled.

(4) Any rules so made shall be forthwith advertised twice in the Trade Marks Journal, and shall be laid before both Houses of Parliament, ...

(5) If either House of Parliament, within the next forty days after any rules have been so laid before it, resolves that the rules or any of them ought to be annulled, the rule or rules shall thenceforth be of no effect, but without prejudice to the validity of anything previously done thereunder or to the making of any new rule or rules.

General note
Sub-s (2) and the words omitted from sub-s (4) were repealed by the Statute Law (Repeals) Act 1986.

[40A. Hours of business and excluded days

(1) Rules under section 40 of this Act may specify the hour at which the Patent Office shall be deemed to be closed on any day for purposes of the transaction by the public of business under this Act or of any class of such business, and may specify days as excluded days for any such purposes.

(2) Any business done under this Act on any day after the hour specified as aforesaid in relation to business of that class, or on a day which is an excluded day in relation to business of that class, shall be deemed to have been done on the next following day not being an excluded day; and where the time for doing anything under this Act expires on an excluded day, that time shall be extended to the next following day not being an excluded day.]

General note
This section was inserted by the Statute Law (Repeals) Act 1986, s 1(2) and Sch 2, para 2.

41. Fees

There shall be paid in respect of applications and registration and other matters under this Act such fees as may be, with the sanction of the Treasury, prescribed by the Board of Trade.

Powers and duties of Registrar

42. Preliminary advice by Registrar as to distinctiveness

(1) The power to give to a person who proposes to apply for the registration of a service mark in Part A or Part B of the register advice as to whether the service mark appears to the Registrar prima facie to be inherently adapted to distinguish, or capable of distinguishing, as the case may be, shall be a function of the Registrar under this Act.

(2) Any such person who is desirous of obtaining such advice must make application to the Registrar therefor in the prescribed manner.

(3) If on application for the registration of a service mark as to which the

Registrar has given advice as aforesaid in the affirmative, made within three months after the advice is given, the Registrar, after further investigation or consideration, gives notice to the applicant of objection on the ground that the service mark is not adapted to distinguish, or capable of distinguishing, as the case may be, the applicant shall be entitled, on giving notice of withdrawal of the application within the prescribed period, to have repaid to him any fee paid on the filing of the application.

43. Hearing before exercise of Registrar's discretion

Where any discretionary or other power is given to the Registrar by this Act or the rules, he shall not exercise that power adversely to the applicant for registration or the registered proprietor of the service mark in question without (if duly required so to do within the prescribed time) giving to the applicant or registered proprietor an opportunity of being heard.

44. Power of Registrar to award costs

In all proceedings before the Registrar under this Act, the Registrar shall have power to award to any party such costs as he may consider reasonable, and to direct how and by what parties they are to be paid, and any such order may, by leave of the Court or a judge thereof, be enforced in the same manner as a judgment or order of the Court to the same effect.

45. Annual reports of Registrar

The Comptroller-General of Patents, Designs and Trade Marks shall, in his annual report on the execution by or under him of the Patents and Designs Act 1907 and Acts amending that Act, include a report respecting the execution by or under him of this Act as if it formed a part of or was included in those Acts.

Legal proceedings and appeals

46. Registration to be prima facie evidence of validity

In all legal proceedings relating to a registered service mark (including applications under section thirty-two of this Act) the fact that a person is registered as proprietor of the service mark shall be prima facie evidence of the validity of the original registration of the service mark and of all subsequent assignments and transmissions thereof.

47. Certificate of validity

In any legal proceeding in which the validity of the registration of a registered service mark comes into question and is decided in favour of the proprietor of the service mark, the Court may certify to that effect, and if it so certifies then in any subsequent legal proceeding in which the validity of the registration comes into question the proprietor of the service mark on obtaining a final order or judgment in his favour shall have his full costs, charges and expenses as between solicitor and client, unless in the subsequent proceeding the Court certifies that he ought not to have them.

48. Costs of Registrar in proceedings before Court, and payment of costs by Registrar

(1) In all proceedings before the Court under this Act the costs of the Registrar shall be in the discretion of the Court, but, in any proceedings in England or

Northern Ireland, the Registrar shall not, except in accordance with the provisions of subsection (2) of this section in a case in which he has appeared in the proceedings, be ordered to pay the costs of any other of the parties.

(2) Where the Registrar appears in any proceedings before the Court in England or Northern Ireland under this Act, section seven of the Administration of Justice (Miscellaneous Provisions) Act 1933, or any corresponding enactment which may be passed by the Parliament of Northern Ireland, as the case may be, shall have effect as it has effect in relation to other proceedings to which the Crown is a party in a court having the power to award costs in cases between subjects.

49. Trade usage, etc to be considered
In any action or proceeding relating to a service mark or [business name], the tribunal shall admit evidence of [business usages in the provision of the services in question] and of any relevant service mark or [business name] or get-up legitimately used by other persons.

General note
The words in square brackets were substituted by the Trade Marks (Amendment) Act 1984, s 1(2) and Sch 1, para 19.

50. Registrar's appearance in proceedings involving rectification
(1) In any legal proceeding in which the relief sought includes alteration or rectification of the register, the Registrar shall have the right to appear and be heard, and shall appear if so directed by the Court.

(2) Unless otherwise directed by the Court, the Registrar in lieu of appearing and being heard may submit to the Court a statement in writing signed by him, giving particulars of the proceedings before him in relation to the matter in issue or of the grounds of any decision given by him affecting it or of the practice of the Patent Office in like cases or of such other matters relevant to the issues, and within his knowledge as Registrar, as he thinks fit, and the statement shall be deemed to form part of the evidence in the proceeding.

51. Court's power to review Registrar's decision
The Court, in dealing with any question of the rectification of the register (including all applications under the provisions of section thirty-two of this Act), shall have power to review any decision of the Registrar relating to the entry in question or the correction sought to be made.

52. Discretion of Court in appeals
In any appeal from a decision of the Registrar to the Court under this Act, the Court shall have and exercise the same discretionary powers as under this Act are conferred upon the Registrar.

53. Procedure on appeal to Board of Trade
Where under this Act an appeal is made to the Board of Trade, the Board of Trade may, if they think fit, refer the appeal to the Court in lieu of hearing and deciding it themselves, but, unless the Board so refer the appeal, it shall be heard and decided by the Board, and the decision of the Board shall be final.

54. Procedure in cases of option to apply to Court or Registrar
Where under any of the foregoing provisions of this Act an applicant has an option to make an application either to the Court or to the Registrar—

(a) if an action concerning the service mark in question is pending, the application must be made to the Court;

(b) if in any other case the application is made to the Registrar, he may, at any stage of the proceedings, refer the application to the Court, or he may, after hearing the parties, determine the question between them, subject to appeal to the Court.

Evidence

55. Mode of giving evidence

In any proceeding under this Act before the Board of Trade or the Registrar, the evidence shall be given by statutory declaration in the absence of directions to the contrary, but, in any case in which the tribunal thinks it right so to do, the tribunal may take evidence viva voce in lieu of or in addition to evidence by declaration. Any such statutory declaration may in the case of appeal be used before the Court in lieu of evidence by affidavit, but if so used shall have all the incidents and consequences of evidence by affidavit.

In case any part of the evidence is taken viva voce, the Board of Trade or the Registrar shall, in respect of requiring the attendance of witnesses and taking evidence on oath, be in the same position in all respects as an official referee of the Supreme Court.

56. Evidence of orders, etc of Board of Trade

1) All documents purporting to be orders made by the Board of Trade and to be sealed with the seal of the Board, or to be signed by a secretary or an undersecretary or an assistant secretary of the Board, or by any person authorised in that behalf by the President of the Board, shall be received in evidence, and shall be deemed to be such orders without further proof, unless the contrary is shown.

(2) A certificate, signed by the President of the Board of Trade, that any order made or act done is the order or act of the Board, shall be conclusive evidence of the fact so certified.

Offences and restraint of use of Royal Arms

57, 58. ...

General note
These sections were repealed by the Patents, Designs and Marks Act 1986, s 3(1) and Sch 3, Pt I.

59. Falsification of entries in register a misdemeanour

(1) If any person makes or causes to be made a false entry in the register, or a writing falsely purporting to be a copy of an entry in the register, or produces or tenders or causes to be produced or tendered in evidence any such writing, knowing the entry or writing to be false, he shall be guilty of a misdemeanour.

(2) In the Isle of Man the punishment for an offence under this section shall be imprisonment for any term not exceeding two years, with or without hard labour and with or without a fine not exceeding one hundred pounds, at the discretion of the court.

60. Fine for falsely representing a service mark as registered

(1) Any person who makes a representation—

(a) with respect to a service mark not being a registered service mark, to the effect that it is a registered service mark; or

   (b) with respect to a part of a registered service mark not being a part separately registered as a service mark, to the effect that it is so registered; or

   (c) to the effect that a registered service mark is registered in respect of any
services in respect of which it is not registered; or

   (d) to the effect that the registration of a service mark gives an exclusive right
to the use thereof in any circumstances in which, having regard to limitations entered on the register, the registration does not give that right;

shall be liable on summary conviction to a fine not exceeding [level 3 on the standard scale].

(2) For the purposes of this section, the use in the United Kingdom in relation to
a service mark of the word 'registered', or of any other word referring whether
expressly or impliedly to registration, shall be deemed to import a reference to registration in the register, except—

   (a) where that word is used in physical association with other words delineated
in characters at least as large as those in which that word is delineated and
indicating that the reference is to registration as a service mark under the
law of a country outside the United Kingdom, being a country under the
law of which the registration referred to is in fact in force;

   (b) where that word (being a word other than the word 'registered') is of itself
such as to indicate that the reference is to such registration as last aforesaid, or

   (c) where that word is used in relation to a service mark registered as a service
mark under the law of a country outside the United Kingdom and in relation to [services for use in that country].

(3) Any offence under this section committed in the Isle of Man may be prosecuted, and any fine in respect thereof recovered, at the instance an person
aggrieved, in the manner in which offences punishable on summary conviction may
for the time being be prosecuted.

General note
The reference to level 3 on the standard scale in sub-s (1) is substituted by virtue of the Criminal Justice
Act 1982, ss 37, 38, 46.
The words in square brackets in sub-s (2)(c) were substituted by the Trade Marks (Amendment) Act
1984, s 1(2) and Sch 1, para 20.

61.   Restraint of use of Royal Arms, etc

If any person, without the authority of His Majesty, uses, in connection with any
trade, business, calling or profession, the Royal Arms (or arms so closely resembling the same as to be calculated to deceive) in such manner as to be calculated to
lead to the belief that he is duly authorised so to use the Royal Arms, or if any person, without the authority of His Majesty or of a member of the Royal Family, uses,
in connection with any trade, business, calling or profession, any device, emblem
or title in such manner as to be calculated to lead to the belief that he is employed
by, [supplies goods to or provides services for], His Majesty or such member of the
Royal Family, he may, at the suit of any person who is authorised to use such arms
or such device, emblem or title, or is authorised by the Lord Chamberlain to take
proceedings in that behalf, be restrained by injunction from continuing so to use the
same:

   Provided that nothing in this section shall be construed as affecting the right, if
any, of the proprietor of a service mark containing any such arms, device, emblem
or title to continue to use such service mark.

General note
The words in square brackets were substituted by the Patents, Designs and Marks Act 1986, s 2(3) and Sch 2, para 6.

Miscellaneous

62. Change of form of trade connection not to be deemed to cause deception

The use of a registered service mark in relation to [services between the provision of] which and the person using it any form of connection in the course of [business] subsists shall not be deemed to be likely to cause deception or confusion on the ground only that the service mark has been, or is, used in relation to [services between the provision of] which and that person or a predecessor in title of his a different form of connection in the course of [business] subsisted or subsists.

General note
The words in square brackets were substituted by the Trade Marks (Amendment) Act 1984, s 1(2) and Sch 1, para 22.

63. Jointly owned service marks

Where the relations between two or more persons interested in a service mark are such that no one of them is entitled as between himself and the other or others of them to use it except—

(a) on behalf of both or all of them, or
[(b) in relation to services with the provision of which both or all of them are connected in the course of business,]

those persons may be registered as joint proprietors of the service mark, and this Act shall have effect in relation to any rights to the use of the service mark vested in those persons as if those rights had been vested in a single person.

Subject as aforesaid, nothing in this Act shall authorise the registration of two or more persons who use a service mark independently, or propose so to use it, as joint proprietors thereof.

General note
Para (b) was substituted by the Trade Marks (Amendment) Act 1984, s 1(2) and Sch 1, para 23.

64. Trusts and equities

(1) There shall not be entered in the register any notice of any trust express, implied or constructive, nor shall any such notice be receivable by the Registrar.

(2) Subject to the provisions of this Act, equities in respect of a service mark may be enforced in like manner as in respect of any other personal property.

[64A] ...

General note
This section, which was inserted by the Trade Descriptions Act 1968, s 17, was repealed by the Trade Marks (Amendment) Act 1984, s 1(2) and Sch 1, para 24.

65. Recognition of agents

Where by this Act any act has to be done by or to any person in connection with a service mark or proposed service mark or any procedure relating thereto, the act may under and in accordance with the rules, or in particular cases by special leave of the Board of Trade, be done by or to an agent of that person duly authorised in the prescribed manner.

66. Saving for jurisdiction of courts in Scotland, Northern Ireland and Isle of Man

(1) The provisions of this Act conferring a special jurisdiction on the Court as defined by this Act shall not, except so far as the jurisdiction extends, affect the jurisdiction of any court in Scotland or Northern Ireland in any proceedings relating to service marks; and with reference to any such proceedings in Scotland the expression 'the Court' means the Court of Session; and with reference to any such proceedings in Northern Ireland the expression 'the Court' means the High Court of Justice in Northern Ireland.

(2) Nothing in this Act shall affect the jurisdiction of the courts in the Isle of Man in proceedings for infringement or in any action or proceeding respecting a service mark competent to those courts.

67. ...

General note
This section was repealed by the Industrial Expansion Act 1968, s 18, Sch 4.

Supplemental

68. Interpretation

(1) In this Act, unless the context otherwise requires, the following expressions have the meanings hereby assigned to them respectively, that is to say:—

'the appointed day' has the meaning assigned to it by section seventy-one of this Act;

'assignment' means assignment by act of the parties concerned;

'the Court' means (subject to provisions relating to Scotland, Northern Ireland or the Isle of Man) His Majesty's High Court of Justice in England;

'limitations' means any limitation of the exclusive right to the use of a service mark given by the registration of a person as proprietor thereof, including limitations of that right as to mode of use, as to use in relation to [services for use or available for acceptance in any place within the United Kingdom or in relation to services for use in any place outside the United Kingdom];

'mark' includes a device, ... , name, signature, word, letter, numeral, or any combination thereof;

'permitted use' has the meaning assigned to it by subsection (1) of section twenty-eight of this Act;

'prescribed' means [(subject to provisions relating to Northern Ireland)], in relation to proceedings before the Court, prescribed by rules of court, and, in other cases, prescribed by this Act or the rules;

['provision', in relation to services, means their provision for money or money's worth;]

'the register' means the register of trade marks kept under this Act;

'registered service mark' means a service mark that is actually on the register;

'registered user' means a person who is for the time being registered as such under section twenty-eight of this Act;

'the Registrar' means the Comptroller-General of Patents, Designs and Trade Marks;

'the rules' means rules made by the Board of Trade under section thirty-six or section forty of this Act;

...

'transmission' means transmission by operation of law, devolution on the personal representative of a deceased person, and any other mode of transfer not being assignment;

'United Kingdom' includes the Isle of Man.

(2) References in this Act to the use of a mark shall be construed as references to the use of a printed or other visual representation of the mark, and references therein to the use of a mark in relation to [services shall be construed as references to the use of the mark as or as part of any statement about the availability or performance of services or otherwise in relation to services].

[(2A) For the purposes of this Act goods and services are associated with each other if it is likely that those goods might be sold or otherwise traded in and those services might be provided by the same business, and so with descriptions of goods and descriptions of services.

(2B) References in this Act to a near resemblance of marks are references to a resemblance so near as to be likely to deceive or cause confusion.]

(3) In the application of this Act to Scotland, the expressions 'injunction', 'plaintiff' and 'defendant' mean respectively 'interdict', 'pursuer' and 'defender'.

General note

The definition 'trade mark' in sub-s (1) has been omitted as being otiose in this Act as modified in relation to service marks. Note that 'service mark' is defined in the Trade Marks (Amendment) Act 1984, s 1(7); that definition is printed in the General note at the beginning of this Act.

The words in square brackets in the definition 'limitations' in sub-s (1) and in sub-s (2) were substituted, the words omitted from the definition 'mark' in sub-s (1) were removed and the definition 'provision' was inserted in sub-s (1) by the Trade Marks (Amendment) Act 1984, s 1(2) and Sch 1, para 25, as amended by the Patents, Designs and Marks Act 1986, s 2(3) and Sch 2, para 12.

The words in square brackets in the definition 'prescribed' in sub-s (1) were inserted by the Judicature (Northern Ireland) Act 1978, s 112 and Sch 5, Pt II.

Sub-ss (2A), (2B) were inserted by the Trade Marks (Amendment) Act 1984, s 1(5)(b).

69.   ...

General note

This section was repealed by the Trade Marks (Amendment) Act 1984, s 1(2) and Sch 1, para 26.

70.   Repeal and savings

(1)   ...

(2) Nothing in this Act shall affect any order, rule, regulation or requirement made, table of fees or certificate issued, notice, decision, determination, direction or approval given, application made, or thing done, under any enactment repealed by this Act; and every such order, rule, regulation, requirement, table of fees, certificate, notice, decision, determination, direction, approval, application or thing shall, if in force at the commencement of this Act, continue in force and shall, so far as it could have been made, issued, given or done under this Act, have effect as if made, issued, given or done under the corresponding enactment of this Act.

(3) Any document referring to any enactment repealed by this Act shall be construed as referring to the corresponding enactment of this Act.

(4) Nothing in this section shall be taken to prejudice the provisions of section thirty-eight of the Interpretation Act 1889.

General note

Sub-s (1) was repealed by the Statute Law Revision Act 1950.

71.   Short title, commencement and extent
(1) This Act may be cited as the Trade Marks Act 1938.

(2) ...

(3) It is hereby declared that this Act extends to Northern Ireland.

(4) This Act shall extend to the Isle of Man.

General note
Sub-s (2) was repealed by the Statute Law Revision Act 1950.

SCHEDULES

FIRST SCHEDULE

...

General note
This Schedule was repealed by the Trade Marks (Amendment) Act 1984, s 1(2) and Sch 1, para 18.

SECOND SCHEDULE

...

General note
This Schedule was repealed by the Trade Marks (Amendment) Act 1984, s 1(2) and Sch 1, para 18A, as inserted by the Patents, Designs and Marks Act 1986, s 2(3) and Sch 2, para 11.

THIRD SCHEDULE

...

General note
This Schedule was repealed by the Trade Marks (Amendment) Act 1984, s 1(2) and Sch 1, para 26.

FOURTH SCHEDULE

...

General note
This Schedule was repealed by the Statute Law Revision Act 1950.

IMPORT, EXPORT AND CUSTOMS POWERS (DEFENCE) ACT 1939
(c 69)

General note

As amended by the Customs and Excise Act 1952, the Emergency Laws (Miscellaneous Provisions) Act 1953, the Industrial Expansion Act 1968, the Customs and Excise Management Act 197 and the Import and Export Control Act 1990, and by virtue of the Criminal Justice Act 1982.

An Act to provide for controlling the importation, exportation and carriage coastwise of goods and the shipment of goods as ships' stores; to provide for facilitating the enforcement of the law relating to the matters aforesaid and the law relating to trading with the enemy; and to provide for purposes connected with the matters aforesaid.

[1st September 1939]

3. Application and extension of law as to prohibited goods

(1) If any goods —

  (a) are imported, exported, carried coastwise or shipped as ships' stores in contravention either of an order under this Act or of the law relating to trading with the enemy, or

  (b) are brought to any quay or other place, or waterborne, for the purpose of being exported or of being so carried or shipped in contravention either of an order under this Act or of the law relating to trading with the enemy,

those goods shall be deemed to be prohibited goods and shall be forfeited; and the exporter of the goods or his agent, or the shipper of the goods, shall be liable, in addition to any other penalty under the [enactments for the time being in force relating to customs or excise], to a customs penalty [not exceeding level 5 on the standard scale].

(2) If any such order as aforesaid prohibits the exportation of any goods unless consigned to a particular place or person, and such goods so consigned are delivered otherwise than to that place or person, as the case may be, the vessel in which the goods were exported shall be deemed to have been used in the conveyance of prohibited goods.

(3) If any goods are imported, exported, carried coastwise or shipped as ships' stores, or are brought to any quay or other place, or waterbourne, for the purpose of being exported or of being so carried or shipped, an officer of Customs and Excise may require any person possessing or having control of the goods to furnish proof that the importation, exportation or carriage coastwise of the goods or the shipment of the goods as ships' stores, as the case may be, is not unlawful by virtue either of an order under this Act or of the law relating to trading with the enemy; and if such proof is not furnished to the satisfaction of the Commissioners of Customs and Excise, [then, unless the contrary is proved, the goods shall be deemed to be prohibited goods and be forfeited].

. . .

General note

In sub-s (1), the words in the first pair of square brackets were substituted by the Customs and Excise Management Act 1979, s 177(1), Sch 4, para 12, Table, Pt I, and the words in the second pair of square brackets are substituted by virtue of the Customs and Excise Management Act 1979, s 156, and the Criminal Justice Act 1982, ss 38, 46.

In sub-s (3), the words in square brackets were substituted by the Emergency Laws (Miscellaneous Provisions) Act 1953, ss 1, 13, Sch 1, para 5(1), and the words omitted were repealed by the Customs and Excise Act 1952, s 320, Sch 12, Pt I.

8. Interpretation, etc

(1) For the purposes of this Act–

(a) the Isle of Man shall be deemed to form part of the United Kingdom;
(b) the expression 'enemy' means—

(i) any State, or Sovereign of a State, at war with His Majesty;
(ii) any individual resident in enemy territory;
(iii) any body of persons (whether corporate or unincorporate) carrying on business in any place, if and so long as the body is controlled by a person who, under this subsection, is an enemy;
(iv) any body of persons constituted or incorporated in, or under the laws of, a State at war with His Majesty; or
(v) any other person, who for the purposes of any Act relating to trading with the enemy is to be deemed to be an enemy;

but does not include any person by reason only that he is an enemy subject;
(c) the expression 'enemy subject' means—

(i) an individual who, not being either a British subject or a British protected person, possesses the nationality of a State at war with His Majesty, or
(ii) a body of persons constituted or incorporated in, or under the laws of, any such State; and

(d) the expression 'enemy territory' means any area which is under the sovereignty of, or in the occupation of, a Power with whom His Majesty is at war, not being an area in the occupation of His Majesty or of a Power allied with His Majesty.

(2) A certificate of a Secretary of State that any area is or was under the sovereignty of, or in the occupation of, any Power, or as to the time at which any area became or ceased to be under such sovereignty or in such occupation shall, for the purposes of any proceedings taken by virtue of this Act, be conclusive evidence of the facts stated in the certificate.

(3) . . .

General note
Sub-s (3) was repealed by the Industrial Expansion Act 1968, s 18(2), Sch 4.

9. Short title, construction and duration of Act

(1) This Act may be cited as the Import, Export and Customs Powers (Defence) Act 1939.

(2) This Act shall be construed as one with the [Customs and Excise Management Act 1979].

(3) . . .

General note
In sub-s (2), the words in square brackets were substituted by the Customs and Excise Management Act 1979, s 177(1), Sch 4, para 12, Table, Pt I.
Sub-s (3) was repealed by the Import and Export Control Act 1990, s 1.

TRADING WITH THE ENEMY ACT 1939
(c 89)

General note
As amended by the Emergency Laws (Miscellaneous Provisions) Act 1953 and the Statute Law (Repeals) Act 1995, and by virtue of the Criminal Justice Act 1982.

An Act to impose penalties for trading with the enemy, to make provision as respects the property of enemies and enemy subjects, and for purposes connected with the matters aforesaid

[5th September 1939]

Trading with the Enemy and matters relating thereto

2. Definition of enemy
(1) Subject to the provisions of this section, the expression 'enemy' for the purposes of this Act means—

 (a) any State, or Sovereign of a State, at war with His Majesty,
 (b) any individual resident in enemy territory,
 (c) any body of persons (whether corporate or unincorporate) carrying on business in any place, if and so long as the body is controlled by a person who, under this section, is an enemy . . .
 (d) any body of persons constituted or incorporated in, or under the laws of, a State at war with His Majesty; [and
 (e) as respects any business carried on in enemy territory, any individual or body of persons (whether corporate or unincorporate) carrying on that business]

but [does not include any individual by reason only that he is an enemy subject].

(2) The Board of Trade may by order direct that any person specified in the order shall, for the purposes of this Act, be deemed to be, while so specified, an enemy.

General note
In sub-s (1), the words in square brackets were substituted or inserted, and the words omitted were repealed, by the Emergency Laws (Miscellaneous Provisions) Act 1953, s 2, Sch 2, para 3.

Property of Enemies and Enemy Subjects

7. Collection of enemy debts and custody of enemy property
(1) With a view to preventing the payment of money to enemies and of preserving enemy property in contemplation of arrangements to be made at the conclusion of peace, the Board of Trade may appoint custodians of enemy property for England, Scotland and Northern Ireland respectively, and may by order—

 (a) require the payment to the prescribed custodian of money which would, but for the existence of a state of war, be payable to or for the benefit of a person who is an enemy, or which would, but for the provisions of section four or section five of this Act, be payable to any other person;
 (b) vest in the prescribed custodian such enemy property as may be prescribed, or provide for, and regulate, the vesting in that custodian of such enemy property as may be prescribed;
 (c) vest in the prescribed custodian the right to transfer such other enemy

property as may be prescribed, being enemy property which has not been, and is not required by the order to be, vested in the custodian;

(d) confer and impose on the custodians and on any other person such rights, powers, duties and liabilities as may be prescribed as respects—

(i) property which has been, or is required to be, vested in a custodian by or under the order,

(ii) property of which the right of transfer has been, or is required to be, so vested,

(iii) any other enemy property which has not been, and is not required to be, so vested, or

(iv) money which has been, or is by the order required to be, paid to a custodian;

(e) require the payment of the prescribed fees to the custodians in respect of such matters as may be prescribed and regulate the collection of an accounting for such fees;

(f) require any person to furnish to the custodian such returns, accounts and other information and to produce such documents, as the custodian considers necessary for the discharge of his functions under the order;

and any such order may contain such incidental and supplementary provisions as appear to the Board of Trade to be necessary or expedient for the purposes of the order.

(2) Where any requirement or direction with respect to any money or property is addressed to any person by a custodian and accompanied by a certificate of the custodian that the money or property is money or property to which an order under this section applies, the certificate shall be evidence of the facts stated therein, and if that person complies with the requirement or direction, he shall not be liable to any action or other legal proceeding by reason only of such compliance.

(3) Where, in pursuance of an order made under this section,—

(a) any money is paid to a custodian,

(b) any property, or the right to transfer any property, is vested in a custodian, or

(c) a direction is given to any person by a custodian in relation to any property which appears to the custodian to be property to which the order applies,

neither the payment, vesting or direction nor any proceedings in consequence thereof shall be invalidated or affected by reason only that a material time—

(i) some person who was or might have been interested in the money or property, and who was an enemy or an enemy subject, had died or had ceased to be an enemy or an enemy subject, or

(ii) some person who was so interested, and who was believed by the custodian to be an enemy subject, was not an enemy or an enemy subject.

(4) Any order under this section shall have effect notwithstanding anything in any Act passed before this Act.

(5) If any person pays any debt, or deals with any property, to which any order under this section applies, otherwise than in accordance with the provisions of the order, he shall be liable on summary conviction to imprisonment for a term not exceeding six months or to a fine not exceeding [level 3 on the standard scale] or to both such imprisonment and such fine; and the payment or dealing shall be void.

(6) If any person, without reasonable cause, fails to produce or furnish in accordance with the requirements of an order under this section, any document or information which he is required under the order to produce or furnish, he shall be liable on summary conviction to a fine not exceeding ten pounds for every day on which the default continues.

(7) All fees received by any custodian by virtue of an order under this section shall be paid into the Exchequer of the United Kingdom.

(8) In this section—

(a) the expression 'enemy property' means any property for the time being belonging to or held or managed on behalf of an enemy or an enemy subject;

(b) the expression 'property' means real or personal property, and includes any estate or interest in real or personal property, any negotiable instrument, debt or other chose in action, and any other right or interest, whether in possession or not; and

(c) the expression 'prescribed' means prescribed by an order made under this section.

General note
In sub-s (5), the words in square brackets are substituted by virtue of the Criminal Justice Act 1982, ss 38, 46.

General and Supplementary Provisions

15. Interpretation

(1) In this Act the following expressions have the meanings hereby respectively assigned to them:—

'enemy subject' means—
(a) an individual who, not being either a British subject or a British protected person, possesses the nationality of a State at war with His Majesty, or
(b) a body of persons constituted or incorporated in, or under the laws of, any such State; and
'enemy territory' means any area which is under the sovereignty of, or in the occupation of, a Power with whom His Majesty is at war, not being an area in the occupation of His Majesty or of a Power allied with His Majesty.

[(1A) The Board of Trade may by order direct that the provisions of this Act shall apply in relation to any area specified in the order as they apply in relation to enemy territory, and the said provisions shall apply accordingly.]

(2) A certificate of a Secretary of State that any area is or was under the sovereignty of, or in the occupation of any Power, or as to the time at which any area became or ceased to be under such sovereignty or in such occupation shall, for the purposes of any proceedings under or arising out of this Act, be conclusive evidence of the facts stated in the certificate.,

(3) In considering for the purposes of any of the provisions of this Act whether any person has been an enemy or an enemy subject, no account shall be taken of any state of affairs existing before the commencement of this Act.,

(4) For the purposes of this Act, a person shall be deemed to be a director of a body corporate if he occupies in relation thereto the position of a director, by whatever name called; and, for the purposes of the provisions of this Act relating to offences by bodies corporate, a person shall be deemed to be a director of a body

corporate if he is a person in accordance with whose directions or instructions the directors of that body act:

Provided that a person shall not, by reason only that the directors of a body corporate act on advice given by him in a professional capacity, be taken to be a person in accordance with whose directions or instructions those directors act.

(5) Any power conferred by the preceding provisions of this Act to make an Order in Council or an order shall be construed as including a power, exercisable in the like manner, to vary or revoke the Order in Council or order.

General note
Sub-s (1A) was inserted by the Emergency Laws (Miscellaneous Provisions) Act 1953, s 2, Sch 2, para 8.

17. Short title and commencement
(1) This Act may be cited as the Trading with the Enemy Act 1939.
(2), (3) . . .

General note
Sub-ss (2), (3) were repealed by the Statute Law (Repeals) Act 1995.

TRADE DESCRIPTIONS ACT 1968
(c 29)

General note
As amended by the Medicines Act 1968, the Agriculture Act 1970, the European Communities Act 1972, the Consumer Credit Act 1974, the Local Government, Planning and Land Act 1980, the Weights and Measures Act 1985, the Consumer Safety Act 1987, the Consumer Protection Act 1987, the Broadcasting Act 1990, the Food Safety Act 1990, the Food Safety (Northern Ireland) Order 1991, SI 1991/762, the Trade Marks Act 1994 and the Plant Varieties Act 1997.

An Act to replace the Merchandise Marks Acts 1887 to 1953 by fresh provisions prohibiting misdescriptions of goods, services, accommodation and facilities provided in the course of trade; to prohibit false or misleading indications as to the price of goods; to confer power to require information or instructions relating to goods to be marked on or to accompany the goods or to be included in advertisements; to prohibit the unauthorised use of devices or emblems signifying royal awards; to enable the Parliament of Northern Ireland to make laws relating to merchandise marks; and for purposes connected with those matters

[30th May 1968]

Prohibition of false trade descriptions

1. Prohibition of false trade descriptions
(1) Any person who, in the course of a trade or business,—

    (a) applies a false trade description to any goods; or
    (b) supplies or offers to supply any goods to which a false trade description is applied;

shall, subject to the provisions of this Act, be guilty of an offence.

(2) Sections 2 to 6 of this Act shall have effect for the purposes of this section and for the interpretation of expressions used in this section, wherever they occur in this Act.

2. Trade description

(1) A trade description is an indication, direct or indirect, and by whatever means given of any of the following matters with respect to any goods or parts of goods, that is to say—

    (a) quantity, size or gauge;
    (b) method of manufacture, production, processing or reconditioning;
    (c) composition;
    (d) fitness for purpose, strength, performance, behaviour or accuracy;
    (e) any physical characteristics not included in the preceding paragraphs;
    (f) testing by any person and results thereof;
    (g) approval by any person or conformity with a type approved by any person;
    (h) place or date of manufacture, production, processing or reconditioning;
    (i) person by whom manufactured, produced, processed or reconditioned;
    (j) other history, including previous ownership or use.

(2) The matters specified in subsection (1) of this section shall be taken—

    (a) in relation to any animal, to include sex, breed or cross, fertility and soundness;
    (b) in relation to any semen, to include the identity and characteristics of the animal from which it was taken and measure of dilution.

(3) In this section 'quantity' includes length, width, height, area, volume, capacity, weight and number.

(4) Notwithstanding anything in the preceding provisions of this section, the following shall be deemed not to be trade descriptions, that is to say, any description or mark applied in pursuance of—

    (a) . . . ;
    (b) section 2 of the Agricultural Produce (Grading and Marking) Act 1928 (as amended by the Agricultural Produce (Grading and Marking) Amendment Act 1931) or any corresponding enactment of the Parliament of Northern Ireland;
    (c) the Plant Varieties and Seeds Act 1964;
    (d) the Agriculture and Horticulture Act 1964 [or any Community grading rules within the meaning of Part III of that Act];
    (e) the Seeds Act (Northern Ireland) 1965;
    (f) the Horticulture Act (Northern Ireland) 1966;
    [(g) the Consumer Protection Act 1987;]
    [(h) the Plant Varieties Act 1997;]

[any statement made in respect of, or mark applied to, any material in pursuance of Part IV of the Agriculture Act 1970, any name or expression to which a meaning has been assigned under section 70 of that Act when applied to any material in the circumstances specified in that section] . . . any mark prescribed by a system of classification compiled under section 5 of the Agriculture Act 1967 [and any designation, mark or description applied in pursuance of a scheme brought into force under section 6(1) or an order made under section 25(1) of the Agriculture Act 1970].

(5) Notwithstanding anything in the preceding provisions of this section,

    [(a)] where provision is made under [the Food Safety Act 1990] or the [Food Safety (Northern Ireland) Order 1991] [or the Consumer Protection Act 1987] prohibiting the application of a description except to goods in the case of which the requirements specified in that provision are complied with, that description, when applied to such goods, shall be deemed not to be a trade description.

[(b) where by virtue of any provision made under Part V of the Medicines Act 1968 (or made under any provisions of the said Part V as applied by an order made under section 104 or section 105 of that Act) anything which, in accordance with this Act, constitutes the application of a trade description to goods is subject to any requirements or restrictions imposed by that provision, any particular description specified in that provision, when applied to goods in circumstances to which those requirements or restrictions are applicable, shall be deemed not to be a trade description]

General note

In sub-s (4), para (a) was repealed by the European Communities Act 1972, s 4, Sch 3, Pt II, Sch 4, para 4(2), in para (d) the words in square brackets were inserted by the European Communities Act 1972, s 4, Sch 3, Pt II, Sch 4, para 4(2), para (g) was inserted by the Consumer Safety Act 1987, s 7(8) and substituted by the Consumer Protection Act 1987, s 48, Sch 4, para 2, para (h) was inserted by the Plant Varieties Act 1997, s 51(4), the words from 'any statement' to 'in that section' in square brackets were substituted by the Agriculture Act 1970, s 87(3), the words omitted in the second place were repealed and the words from 'and any' to 'Agriculture Act 1970' in square brackets were inserted by the Agriculture Act 1970, ss 6(4), 113(3), Sch 5, Pt V.

In sub-s (5), para '(a)' was numbered as such and para (b) was inserted by the Medicines Act 1968, s 135(1), Sch 5, para 16, in para (a), the words in the first pair of square brackets were substituted by the Food Safety Act 1990, s 59(1), Sch 3, para 6, the words in the second pair of square brackets were substituted by the Food Safety (Northern Ireland) Order 1991, SI 1991/762, art 51(1), Sch 2, para 3, and the words in the final pair of square brackets were substituted by the Consumer Protection Act 1987, s 48, Sch 4, para 2.

The Northern Ireland Act 1998 makes new provision for the government of Northern Ireland for the purpose of implementing the Belfast Agreement (the agreement reached at multi-party talks on Northern Ireland and set out in Command Paper 3883). As a consequence of that Act, any reference in this section to the Parliament of Northern Ireland or the Assembly established under the Northern Ireland Assembly Act 1973, s 1, certain office-holders and Ministers, and any legislative act and certain financial dealings thereof, shall, for the period specified, be construed in accordance with Sch 12, paras 1–11 to the 1998 Act.

3. False trade description

(1) A false trade description is a trade description which is false to a material degree.

(2) A trade description which, though not false, is misleading, that is to say, likely to be taken for such an indication of any of the matters specified in section 2 of this Act as would be false to a material degree, shall be deemed to be a false trade description.

(3) Anything which, though not a trade description, is likely to be taken for an indication of any of those matters and, as such an indication, would be false to a material degree, shall be deemed to be a false trade description.

(4) A false indication, or anything likely to be taken as an indication which would be false, that any goods comply with a standard specified or recognised by any person or implied by the approval of any person shall be deemed to be a false trade description, if there is no such person or no standard so specified, recognised or implied.

4. Applying a trade description to goods

(1) A person applies a trade description to goods if he—

(a) affixes or annexes it to or in any manner marks it on or incorporates it with—

    (i) the goods themselves, or

    (ii) anything in, on or with which the goods are supplied; or

(b) places the goods in, on or with anything which the trade description has been affixed or annexed to, marked on or incorporated with, or places any such thing with the goods; or

(c) uses the trade description in any manner likely to be taken as referring to the goods.

(2) An oral statement may amount to the use of a trade description.

(3) Where goods are supplied in pursuance of a request in which a trade description is used and circumstances are such as to make it reasonable to infer that the goods are supplied as goods corresponding to that trade description, the person supplying the goods shall be deemed to have applied that trade description to the goods.

5. Trade descriptions used in advertisements

(1) The following provisions of this section shall have effect where in an advertisement a trade description is used in relation to any class of goods.

(2) The trade description shall be taken as referring to all goods of the class, whether or not in existence at the time the advertisement is published —

(a) for the purpose of determining whether an offence has been committed under paragraph (a) of section 1(1) of this Act; and

(b) where goods of the class are supplied or offered to be supplied by a person publishing or displaying the advertisement, also for the purpose of determining whether an offence has been committed under paragraph (b) of the said section 1(1).

(3) In determining for the purposes of this section whether any goods are of a class to which a trade description used in an advertisement relates regard shall be had not only to the form and content of the advertisement but also to the time, place, manner and frequency of its publication and all other matters making it likely or unlikely that a person to whom the goods are supplied would think of the goods as belonging to the class in relation to which the trade description is used in the advertisement.

6. Offer to supply

A person exposing goods for supply or having goods in his possession for supply shall be deemed to offer to supply them.

Defences

24. Defence of mistake, accident, etc

(1) In any proceedings for an offence under this Act it shall, subject to subsection (2) of this section, be a defence for the person charged to prove —

(a) that the commission of the offence was due to a mistake or to reliance on information supplied to him or to the act or default of another person, an accident or some other cause beyond his control; and

(b) that he took all reasonable precautions and exercised all due diligence to avoid the commission of such an offence by himself or any person under his control.

(2) If in any case the defence provided by the last foregoing subsection involves the allegation that the commission of the offence was due to the act or default of

another person or to reliance on information supplied by another person, the person charged shall not, without leave of the court, be entitled to rely on that defence unless, within a period ending seven clear days before the hearing, he has served on the prosecutor a notice in writing giving such information identifying or assisting in the identification of that other person as was then in his possession.

(3) In any proceedings for an offence under this Act of supplying or offering to supply goods to which a false trade description is applied it shall be a defence for the person charged to prove that he did not know, and could not with reasonable diligence have ascertained, that the goods did not conform to the description or that the description had been applied to the goods.

Enforcement

26. Enforcing authorities
(1) It shall be the duty of every local weights and measures authority to enforce within their area the provisions of this Act and of any order made under this Act; . . .

(2) Every local weights and measures authority shall, whenever the Board of Trade so direct, make to the Board a report on the exercise of their functions under this Act in such form and containing such particulars as the Board may direct.

(3)–(5) . . .

General note
In sub-s (1), the words omitted were repealed with savings by the Weights and Measures Act 1985, ss 96(1), 98(1), Sch 11, para 18(2), Sch 13, Pt I.
Sub-ss (3), (4) were repealed by the Local Government, Planning and Land Act 1980, ss 1(4), 194, Sch 4, para 10, Sch 34, Pt IV.
Sub-s (5) applies to Scotland only.

27. Power to make test purchases
A local weights and measures authority shall have power to make, or to authorise any of their officers to make on their behalf, such purchases of goods, and to authorise any of their officers to secure the provision of such services, accommodation or facilities, as may appear expedient for the purpose of determining whether or not the provisions of this Act and any order made thereunder are being complied with.

28. Power to enter premises and inspect and seize goods and documents
(1) A duly authorised officer of a local weights and measures authority or of a Government department may, at all reasonable hours and on production, if required, of his credentials, exercise the following powers, that is to say,—

(a) he may, for the purpose of ascertaining whether any offence under this Act has been committed, inspect any goods and enter any premises other than premises used only as a dwelling;
(b) if he has reasonable cause to suspect that an offence under this Act has been committed, he may, for the purpose of ascertaining whether it has been committed, require any person carrying on a trade or business or employed in connection with a trade or business to produce any books or documents relating to the trade or business and may take copies of, or of any entry in, any such book or document;
(c) if he has reasonable cause to believe that an offence under this Act has been committed, he may seize and detain any goods for the purpose of ascertaining, by testing or otherwise, whether the offence has been committed;

(d) he may seize and detain any goods or documents which he has reason to believe may be required as evidence in proceedings for an offence under this Act;

(e) he may, for the purpose of exercising his powers under this subsection to seize goods, but only if and to the extent that it is reasonably necessary in order to secure that the provisions of this Act and of any order made thereunder are duly observed, require any person having authority to do so to break open any container or open any vending machine and, if that person does not comply with the requirement, he may do so himself.

(2) An officer seizing any goods or documents in the exercise of his powers under this section shall inform the person from whom they are seized and, in the case of goods seized from a vending machine, the person whose name and address are stated on the machine as being the proprietor's or, if no name and address are so stated, the occupier of the premises on which the machine stands or to which it is affixed.

(3) If a justice of the peace, on sworn information in writing—

(a) is satisfied that there is reasonable ground to believe either—

(i) that any goods, books or documents which a duly authorised officer has power under this section to inspect are on any premises and that their inspection is likely to disclose evidence of the commission of an offence under this Act; or

(ii) that any offence under this Act has been, is being or is about to be committed on any premises; and

(b) is also satisfied either—

(i) that admission to the premises has been or is likely to be refused and that notice of intention to apply for a warrant under this subsection has been given to the occupier; or

(ii) that an application for admission, or the giving of such a notice, would defeat the object of the entry or that the premises are unoccupied or that the occupier is temporarily absent and it might defeat the object of the entry to await his return,

the justice may by warrant under his hand, which shall continue in force for a period of one month, authorise an officer of a local weights and measures authority or of a Government department to enter the premises, if need be by force.

. . .

(4) An officer entering any premises by virtue of this section may take with him such other persons and such equipment as may appear to him necessary; and on leaving any premises which he has entered by virtue of a warrant under the preceding subsection he shall, if the premises are unoccupied or the occupier is temporarily absent, leave them as effectively secured against trespassers as he found them.

(5) If any person discloses to any person—

(a) any information with respect to any manufacturing process or trade secret obtained by him in premises which he has entered by virtue of this section; or

(b) any information obtained by him in pursuance of this Act;

he shall be guilty of an offence unless the disclosure was made in or for the purpose of the performance by him or any other person of functions under this Act.

[(5A) Subsection (5) of this section does not apply to disclosure for a purpose specified in [section 38(2)(a), (b) or (c) of the Consumer Protection Act 1987].]

(6) If any person who is not a duly authorised officer of a local weights and measures authority or of a Government department purports to act as such under this section he shall be guilty of an offence.

(7) Nothing in this section shall be taken to compel the production by a solicitor of a document containing a privileged communication made by or to him in that capacity or to authorise the taking of possession of any such document which is in his possession.

General note
In sub-s (3), the words omitted apply to Scotland only.
Sub-s (5A) was inserted by the Consumer Credit Act 1974, s 192(3)(a), Sch 4, Pt I, para 28, and the words in square brackets were substituted by the Consumer Protection Act 1987, s 48, Sch 4, para 2.

Miscellaneous and supplemental

33. Compensation for loss, etc of goods seized under s 28
(1) Where, in the exercise of his powers under section 28 of this Act, an officer of a local weights and measures authority or of a Government department seizes and detains any goods and their owner suffers loss by reason thereof or by reason that the goods, during the detention, are lost or damaged or deteriorate, then, unless the owner is convicted of an offence under this Act committed in relation to the goods, the authority or department shall be liable to compensate him for the loss so suffered.

(2) Any disputed question as to the right to or the amount of any compensation payable under this section shall be determined by arbitration and, in Scotland, by a single arbiter appointed, failing agreement between the parties, by the sheriff

34. Trade marks containing trade descriptions
The fact that a trade description is a trade mark, or part of a trade mark, . . . does not prevent it from being a false trade description when applied to any goods, except where the following conditions are satisfied, that is to say —

(a) that it could have been lawfully applied to the goods if this Act had not been passed; and
(b) that on the day this Act is passed the trade mark either is registered under the Trade Marks Act 1938 or is in use to indicate a connection in the course of trade between such goods and the proprietor of the trade mark; and
(c) that the trade mark as applied is used to indicate such a connection between the goods and the proprietor of the trade mark or[, in the case of a registered trade mark, a person licensed to use it]; and
(d) that the person who is the proprietor of the trade mark is the same person as, or a successor in title of, the proprietor on the day this Act is passed.

General note
The words omitted were repealed, and the words in square brackets were substituted, by the Trade Marks Act 1994, s 106(1), Sch 4, para 4.
References to trade marks or registered trade marks within the meaning of the Trade Marks Act 1938 shall, unless the context otherwise requires, be construed as references to trade marks or registered trade marks within the meaning of the Trade Marks Act 1994; see the Trade Marks Act 1994, Sch 4, para 1.

39. Interpretation
(1) The following provisions shall have effect, in addition to sections 2 to 6 of this Act, for the interpretation in this Act of expressions used therein, that is to say, —

'advertisement' includes a catalogue, a circular and a price list;
'goods' includes ships and aircraft, things attached to land and growing crops;
'premises' includes any place and any stall, vehicle, ship or aircraft; and
'ship' includes any boat and any other description of vessel used in navigation.

(2) For the purposes of this Act, a trade description or statement published in any newspaper, book or periodical or in any film or sound or television broadcast [or in any programme included in any programme service (within the meaning of the Broadcasting Act 1990) other than a sound or television broadcasting service] shall not be deemed to be a trade description applied or statement made in the course of a trade or business unless it is or forms part of an advertisement.

General note
In sub-s (2), the words in square brackets were substituted by the Broadcasting Act 1990, s 203(1), Sch 20, para 11.

43. Short title and commencement
(1) This Act may be cited as the Trade Descriptions Act 1968.
(2) This Act shall come into force on the expiration of the period of six months beginning with the day on which it is passed.

CUSTOMS AND EXCISE MANAGEMENT ACT 1979
(c 2)

General note
As amended by the Alcoholic Liquors(Amendment of Enactments Relating to Strength and to Units of Measurement) Order 1979, SI 1979/241, the Isle of Man Act 1979, the Betting and Gaming Duties Act 1981, the Finance Act 1981, the Police and Criminal Evidence Act 1984, the Territorial Sea Act 1987, the Finance Act 1991, the Finance (No 2) Act 1992, the Finance Act 1993, the Merchant Shipping Act 1995, the Finance Act 1997, the Police (Northern Ireland) Act 1998, the Reserve Forces Act 1996 (Consequential Provisions etc) Regulations 1998, SI 1998/3086, and the Scotland Act 1998 (Consequential Modifications) (No 1) Order 1999, SI 1999/1042, and by virtue of the Criminal Justice Act 1982.

An Act to consolidate the enactments relating to the collection and management of the revenues of customs and excise and in some cases to other matters in relation to which the Commissioners of Customs and Excise for the time being perform functions, with amendments to give effect to recommendations of the Law Commission and the Scottish Law Commission

[22nd March 1979]

BE IT ENACTED by the Queen's most Excellent Majesty, by and with the advice and consent of the Lords Spiritual and Temporal, and Commons, in this present Parliament assembled, and by the authority of the same, as follows—

PART I
PRELIMINARY

1. Interpretation
(1) In this Act, unless the context otherwise requires—

'armed forces' means the Royal Navy, the Royal Marines, the regular army and the regular air force, and any reserve or auxiliary force of any of those services which has been called out on permanent service, . . ., or embodied;

'British ship' means a British ship within the meaning of the [Merchant Shipping Act 1995];

'claimant', in relation to proceedings for the condemnation of any thing as being forfeited, means a person claiming that the thing is not liable to forfeiture;

'commander', in relation to an aircraft, includes any person having or taking the charge or command of the aircraft;

'the Commissioners' means the Commissioners of Customs and Excise;

'container' includes any bundle or package and any box, cask or other receptacle whatsoever;

'the customs and excise Acts' means the Customs and Excise Acts 1979 and any other enactment for the time being in force relating to customs or excise;

'the Customs and Excise Acts 1979' means—

> this Act,
> the Customs and Excise Duties (General Reliefs) Act 1979,
> the Alcoholic Liquor Duties Act 1979,
> the Hydrocarbon Oil Duties Act 1979,
> . . ., and
> the Tobacco Products Duty Act 1979;

'dutiable goods', except in the expression 'dutiable or restricted goods', means goods of a class or description subject to any duty of customs or excise, whether or not those goods are in fact chargeable with that duty, and whether or not that duty has been paid thereon;

'goods' includes stores and baggage;

'hovercraft' means a hovercraft within the meaning of the Hovercraft Act 1968;

'importer', in relation to any goods at any time between their importation and the time when they are delivered out of charge, includes any owner or other person for the time being possessed of or beneficially interested in the goods and, in relation to goods imported by means of a pipe-line, includes the owner of the pipe-line;

'law officer of the Crown' means the Attorney General or [for the purpose of criminal proceedings in Scotland, the Lord Advocate or, for the purpose of civil proceedings in Scotland, the appropriate Law Officer within the meaning of section 4A of the Crown Suits (Scotland) Act 1857] or in Northern Ireland the Attorney General for Northern Ireland;

'master', in relation to a ship, includes any person having or taking the charge or command of the ship;

'officer' means, subject to section 8(2) below, a person commissioned by the Commissioners;

'owner', in relation to an aircraft, includes the operator of the aircraft;

'port' means a port appointed by the Commissioners under section 19 below;

'proper', in relation to the person by, with or to whom, or the place at which, anything is to be done, means the person or place appointed or authorised in that behalf by the Commissioners;

'Queen's warehouse' means any place provided by the Crown or appointed by the Commissioners for the deposit of goods for security thereof and of the duties chargeable thereon;

'the revenue trade provisions of the customs and excise Acts' means—

(a) the provisions of the customs and excise Acts relating to the protection, security, collection or management of the revenues derived from the duties of excise on goods produced or manufactured in the United Kingdom;

(b) the provisions of the customs and excise Acts relating to any activity or facility for the carrying on or provision of which an excise licence is required; . . .

(c) the provisions of [the Betting and Gaming Duties Act 1981] (so far as not included in paragraph (b) above); [. . .

(d) the provisions of Chapter II of Part I of the Finance Act 1993;]

[(e) the provisions of sections 10 to 15 of, and Schedule 1 to, the Finance Act 1997;]

'revenue trader' means

[(a)] any person carrying on a trade or business subject to any of the revenue trade provisions of the customs and excise Acts [or which consists of or includes —

(i) the buying, selling, importation, exportation, dealing in or handling of any goods of a class or description which is subject to a duty of excise (whether or not duty is chargeable on the goods);

. . .

[(ia) the buying, selling, importation, exportation, dealing in or handling of tickets or chances on the taking of which lottery duty is or will be chargeable; . . .]

[(ib) being (within the meaning of sections 10 to 15 of the Finance Act 1997) the provider of any premises for gaming;

(ic) the organisation, management or promotion of any gaming (within the meaning of the Gaming Act 1968 or the Betting, Gaming, Lotteries and Amusements (Northern Ireland) Order 1985); or]

(ii) the financing or facilitation of any such transactions or activities [as are mentioned in sub-paragraph (i)[, (ia), (ib) or (ic)] above],]

whether or not that trade or business is an excise licence trade[; and

(b) any person who is a wholesaler or an occupier of an excise warehouse (so far as not included in paragraph (a) above),

and includes a registered club];

'ship' and 'vessel' include any boat or other vessel whatsoever (and, to the extent provided in section 2 below, any hovercraft);

'tons register' means the tons of a ship's net tonnage as ascertained and registered according to the tonnage regulations of the [Merchant Shipping Act 1995] or, in the case of a ship which is not registered under that Act, ascertained in like manner as if it were to be so registered;

['United Kingdom waters' means any waters (including inland waters) within the seaward limits of the territorial sea of the United Kingdom;]

'vehicle' includes a railway vehicle;

(2) This Act and the other Acts included in the Customs and Excise Acts 1979 shall be construed as one Act but where a provision of this Act refers to this Act that reference is not to be construed as including a reference to any of the others.

(3) Any expression used in this Act or in any instrument made under this Act to which a meaning is given by any other Act included in the Customs and Excise

Acts 1979 has, except where the context otherwise requires, the same meaning in this Act or any such instrument as in that Act; and for ease of reference the Table below indicates the expressions used in this Act to which a meaning is given by any other such Act—

Alcoholic Liquor Duties Act 1979

'spirits'

(6) In computing for the purposes of this Act any period expressed therein as a period of clear days no account shall be taken of the day of the event from which the period is computed or of any Sunday or holiday.

General note
Only the provisions of this section which are relevant to the provisions of this Act which are printed are reproduced.

In sub-s (1), in the definition 'armed forces' the words omitted were repealed by the Reserve Forces Act 1996 (Consequential Provisions etc) Regulations 1998, SI 1998/3086, reg 10(3), in the definitions 'British ship' and 'tons register' the words in square brackets were substituted by the Merchant Shipping Act 1995, s 314(2), Sch 13, para 53(2), in the definition 'Customs and Excise Acts 1979' the words omitted were repealed by the Finance (No 2) Act 1992, s 82, Sch 18, Pt II, in the definition 'law officer of the Crown' the words in square brackets were substituted by the Scotland Act 1998 (Consequential Modifications) (No 1) Order 1999, SI 1999/1042, art 4, Sch 2, para 6, in the definition 'the revenue trade provisions of the customs and excise acts' in para (c) the words in square brackets were substituted by the Betting and Gaming Duties Act 1981, s 34(1), Sch 5, para 5(a), the word omitted from the end of para (b) was repealed and para (d) was inserted by the Finance Act 1993, ss 30(2), 213, Sch 23, Pt I, the word omitted from the end of para (c) was repealed and para (e) was inserted by the Finance Act 1997, ss 13, 113, Sch 2, para 2(2), (4), Sch 18, Pt II, in relation to any gaming on or after 1 October 1997, in the definition 'revenue trader' para (a) was numbered as such and the words in the final pair of square brackets were inserted by the Finance Act 1981, s 11(1), Sch 8, Pt I, para 1(1), the words in the first pair of square brackets were inserted by the Finance Act 1991, s 11(2), the word omitted from the end of sub-para (i) was repealed, sub-para (ia) was inserted, and in sub-para (ii) the words in the first pair of square brackets were inserted, by the Finance Act 1993, ss 30(3), 213, Sch 23, Pt I, the word omitted from the end of sub-para (ia) was repealed, sub-paras (ib), (ic) were inserted, and in sub-para (ii) the words ', (ia), (ib) or (ic)' were substituted, by the Finance Act 1997, ss 13, 113, Sch 2, para 2(3), (4), Sch 18, Pt II, in relation to any gaming on or after 1 October 1997, and the definition 'United Kingdom waters' was inserted by the Territorial Sea Act 1987, s 3, Sch 1, para 4.

PART IV
CONTROL OF IMPORTATION

Inward entry and clearance

40. Removal of uncleared goods to Queen's warehouse
(1) Where in the case of any imported goods—

(a) entry has not been made thereof by the expiration of the relevant period; or

[(b) at the expiration of 21 clear days from the date when they were presented at the proper office of customs and excise they have not been produced for examination and clearance and the failure to produce them is attributable to an act or omission for which the importer is responsible; or]

(c) being goods imported by sea and not being in large quantity, they are at any time after the arrival of the importing ship at the port at which they are to be unloaded the only goods remaining to be unloaded from that ship at that port,

the proper officer may cause the goods to be deposited in a Queen's warehouse.

(2) Where any small package or consignment of goods is imported, the proper officer may at any time after the relevant date cause that package or consignment to be deposited in a Queen's warehouse to await entry.

(3) Without prejudice to section 99(3) below, if any goods deposited in a Queen's warehouse by the proper officer under this section are not cleared by the importer thereof—

    (a) in the case of goods which are in the opinion of the Commissioners of a perishable nature, forthwith; or

    (b) in any other case, within 3 months after they have been so deposited or such longer time as the Commissioners may in any case allow,

the Commissioners may sell them.

(4) In this section—

    (a) 'the relevant period' means a period of, in the case of goods imported by air, 7 or, in any other case, 14 clear days from the relevant date; and

    (b) 'the relevant date' means, subject to subsection (5) below, the date when report was made of the importing ship, aircraft or vehicle or of the goods under section 35 above, or, where no such report was made, the date when it should properly have been made.

(5) Where any restriction is placed upon the unloading of goods from any ship or aircraft by virtue of any enactment relating to the prevention of epidemic and infectious diseases, then, in relation to that ship or aircraft, 'the relevant date' in this section means the date of the removal of the restriction.

General note

In sub-s (1), para (b) was substituted by the Finance Act 1981, s 10(1), Sch 6, para 5.

This section is modified by the Postal Packets (Customs and Excise) Regulations 1986, SI 1986/260, regs 5, 14, and, in relation to references to an entry on the importation of goods, by the Customs and Excise (Single Market etc) Regulations 1992, SI 1992/3095, reg 10(1), Sch 1, para 1.

PART XI
[ARREST] OF PERSONS, FORFEITURE AND LEGAL PROCEEDINGS

General note

The word in square brackets was substituted by the Police and Criminal Evidence Act 1984, s 114(1).

Forfeiture

139. Provisions as to detention, seizure and condemnation of goods, etc

(1) Any thing liable to forfeiture under the customs and excise Acts may be seized or detained by any officer or constable or any member of Her Majesty's armed forces or coastguard.

(2) Where any thing is seized or detained as liable to forfeiture under the customs and excise Acts by a person other than an officer, that person shall, subject to subsection (3) below, either—

    (a) deliver that thing to the nearest convenient office of customs and excise; or

    (b) if such delivery is not practicable, give to the Commissioners at the nearest convenient office of customs and excise notice in writing of the seizure or detention with full particulars of the thing seized or detained.

(3) Where the person seizing or detaining any thing as liable to forfeiture under the customs and excise Acts is a constable and that thing is or may be required for

use in connection with any proceedings to be brought otherwise than under those Acts it may, subject to subsection (4) below, be retained in the custody of the police until either those proceedings are completed or it is decided that no such proceedings shall be brought.

(4) The following provisions apply in relation to things retained in the custody of the police by virtue of subsection (3) above, that is to say —

(a) notice in writing of the seizure or detention and of the intention to retain the thing in question in the custody of the police, together with full particulars as to that thing, shall be given to the Commissioners at the nearest convenient office of customs and excise;

(b) any officer shall be permitted to examine that thing and take account thereof at any time while it remains in the custody of the police;

(c) nothing in the Police (Property) Act 1897 shall apply in relation to that thing.

(5) Subject to subsections (3) and (4) above and to Schedule 3 to this Act, any thing seized or detained under the customs and excise Acts shall, pending the determination as to its forfeiture or disposal, be dealt with, and, if condemned or deemed to have been condemned or forfeited, shall be disposed of in such manner as the Commissioners may direct.

(6) Schedule 3 to this Act shall have effect for the purpose of forfeitures, and of proceedings for the condemnation of any thing as being forfeited, under the customs and excise Acts.

(7) If any person, not being an officer, by whom any thing is seized or detained or who has custody thereof after its seizure or detention, fails to comply with any requirement of this section or with any direction of the Commissioners given thereunder, he shall be liable on summary conviction to a penalty of [level 2 on the standard scale].

(8) Subsections (2) to (7) above shall apply in relation to any dutiable goods seized or detained by any person other than an officer notwithstanding that they were not so seized as liable to forfeiture under the customs and excise Acts.

General note
In sub-s (4), in para (c) the words 'section 31 of the Police (Northern Ireland) Act 1998' are substituted for the words 'the Police (Property) Act 1897' in relation to Northern Ireland by the Police (Northern Ireland) Act 1998, s 74, Sch 4, para 14, as from a day to be appointed.
In sub-s (7), the reference to level 2 on the standard scale is substituted by virtue of the Criminal Justice Act 1982, ss 37, 46.

140. Forfeiture of spirits

Where, by any provision of, or of any instrument made under, the Customs and Excise Acts 1979, any spirits become liable to forfeiture by reason of some offence committed by a revenue trader, then —

(a) where that provision specifies the quantity of those spirits but does not specify the spirits so liable, the Commissioners may seize the equivalent of that quantity . . . from any spirits in the stock of that trader; and

(b) where that provision specifies the spirits so liable the Commissioners may, if they think fit, seize instead of the spirits so specified an equivalent quantity . . . of any other spirits in the stock of that trader.

General note
The words omitted were repealed by the Alcoholic Liquors(Amendment of Enactments Relating to Strength and to Units of Measurement) Order 1979, SI 1979/241.

141. Forfeiture of ships, etc used in connection with goods liable to forfeiture

(1) Without prejudice to any other provision of the Customs and Excise Acts 1979, where any thing has become liable to forfeiture under the customs and excise Acts—

   (a) any ship, aircraft, vehicle, animal, container (including any article of passengers' baggage) or other thing whatsoever which has been used for the carriage, handling, deposit or concealment of the thing so liable to forfeiture, either at a time when it was so liable or for the purposes of the commission of the offence for which it later became so liable; and
   (b) any other thing mixed, packed or found with the thing so liable,

shall also be liable to forfeiture.

(2) Where any ship, aircraft, vehicle or animal has become liable to forfeiture under the customs and excise Acts, whether by virtue of subsection (1) above or otherwise, all tackle, apparel or furniture thereof shall also be liable to forfeiture.

(3) Where any of the following, that is to say—

   (a) any ship not exceeding 100 tons register;
   (b) any aircraft; or
   (c) any hovercraft,

becomes liable to forfeiture under this section by reason of having been used in the importation, exportation or carriage of goods contrary to or for the purpose of contravening any prohibition or restriction for the time being in force with respect to those goods, or without payment having been made of, or security given for, any duty payable thereon, the owner and the master or commander shall each be liable on summary conviction to a penalty equal to the value of the ship, aircraft or hovercraft or [level 5 on the standard scale], whichever is the less.

General note
In sub-s (3), the reference to level 5 on the standard scale is substituted by virtue of the Criminal Justice Act 1982, ss 37, 38, 46.
This section is modified by the Channel Tunnel (Customs and Excise) Order 1990, SI 1990/2167, art 4, Schedule, para 21.

142. Special provision as to forfeiture of larger ships

(1) Notwithstanding any other provision of the Customs and Excise Acts 1979, a ship of 250 or more tons register shall not be liable to forfeiture under or by virtue of any provision of the Customs and Excise Acts 1979, except under section 88 above, unless the offence in respect of or in connection with which the forfeiture is claimed—

   (a) was substantially the object of the voyage during which the offence was committed; or
   (b) was committed while the ship was under chase by a vessel in the service of Her Majesty after failing to bring to when properly summoned to do so by that vessel.

(2) For the purposes of this section, a ship shall be deemed to have been properly summoned to bring to—

   (a) if the vessel making the summons did so by means of an international signal code or other recognised means and while flying her proper ensign; and
   (b) in the case of a ship which is not a British ship, if at the time when the summons was made the ship was [in United Kingdom waters].

(3) For the purposes of this section, all hovercraft (of whatever size) shall be treated as ships of less than 250 tons register.

(4) The exemption from forfeiture of any ship under this section shall not affect any liability to forfeiture of goods carried therein.

General note
In sub-s (2), the words in square brackets were substituted by the Territorial Sea Act 1987, s 3, Sch 1, para 4.

143. Penalty in lieu of forfeiture of larger ship where responsible officer implicated in offence

(1) Where any ship of 250 or more tons register would, but for section 142 above, be liable to forfeiture for or in connection with any offence under the customs and excise Acts and, in the opinion of the Commissioners, a responsible officer of the ship is implicated either by his own act or by neglect in that offence, the Commissioners may fine that ship such sum not exceeding £50 as they see fit.

(2) For the purposes of this section, all hovercraft (of whatever size) shall be treated as ships of less than 250 tons register.

(3) Where any ship is liable to a fine under subsection (1) above but the Commissioners consider that fine an inadequate penalty for the offence, they may take proceedings in accordance with Schedule 3 to this Act, in like manner as they might but for section 142 above have taken proceedings for the condemnation of the ship if notice of claim had been given in respect thereof, for the condemnation of the ship in such sum not exceeding £500 as the court may see fit.

(4) Where any fine is to be imposed or any proceedings are to be taken under this section, the Commissioners may require such sum as they see fit, not exceeding £50 or, as the case may be, £500, to be deposited with them to await their final decision or, as the case may be, the decision of the court, and may detain the ship until that sum has been so deposited.

(5) No claim shall lie against the Commissioners for damages in respect of the payment of any deposit or the detention of any ship under this section.

(6) For the purposes of this section—

    (a) 'responsible officer', in relation to any ship, means the master, a mate or an engineer of the ship and, in the case of a ship carrying a passenger certificate, the purser or chief steward and, in the case of a ship manned wholly or partly by Asiatic seamen, the serang or other leading Asiatic officer of the ship;

    (b) without prejudice to any other grounds upon which a responsible officer of any ship may be held to be implicated by neglect, he may be so held if goods not owned to by any member of the crew are discovered in a place under that officer's supervision in which they could not reasonably have been put if he had exercised proper care at the time of the loading of the ship or subsequently.

144. Protection of officers, etc in relation to seizure and detention of goods, etc

(1) Where, in any proceedings for the condemnation of any thing seized as liable to forfeiture under the customs and excise Acts, judgment is given for the claimant, the court may, if it sees fit, certify that there were reasonable grounds for the seizure.

(2) Where any proceedings, whether civil or criminal, are brought against the Commissioners, a law officer of the Crown or any person authorised by or under

the Customs and Excise Acts 1979 to seize or detain any thing liable to forfeiture under the customs and excise Acts on account of the seizure or detention of any thing, and judgment is given for the plaintiff or prosecutor, then if either—

    (a) a certificate relating to the seizure has been granted under subsection (1) above; or

    (b) the court is satisfied that there were reasonable grounds for seizing or detaining that thing under the customs and excise Acts,

the plaintiff or prosecutor shall not be entitled to recover any damages or costs and the defendant shall not be liable to any punishment.

(3) Nothing in subsection (2) above shall affect any right of any person to the return of the thing seized or detained or to compensation in respect of any damage to the thing or in respect of the destruction thereof.

(4) Any certificate under subsection (1) above may be proved by the production of either the original certificate or a certified copy thereof purporting to be signed by an officer of the court by which it was granted.

PART XII
GENERAL AND MISCELLANEOUS

Miscellaneous

178.   Citation and commencement
(1) This Act may be cited as the Customs and Excise Management Act 1979.

(2) This Act, the Customs and Excise Duties (General Reliefs) Act 1979, the Alcoholic Liquor Duties Act 1979, the Hydrocarbon Oil Duties Act 1979, . . . and the Tobacco Products Duty Act 1979 may be cited together as the Customs and Excise Acts 1979.

(3) This Act shall come into operation on 1st April 1979.

General note
In sub-s (2), the words omitted were repealed by the Finance (No 2) Act 1992, s 82, Sch 18, Pt II.

SCHEDULE 3

PROVISIONS RELATING TO FORFEITURE

Sections 139, 143, 145

Notice of seizure
1.—(1) The Commissioners shall, except as provided in sub-paragraph (2) below, give notice of the seizure of any thing as liable to forfeiture and of the grounds therefor to any person who to their knowledge was at the time of the seizure the owner or one of the owners thereof.

    (2) Notice need not be given under this paragraph if the seizure was made in the presence of—

    (a) the person whose offence or suspected offence occasioned the seizure; or
    (b) the owner or any of the owners of the thing seized or any servant or agent of his; or
    (c) in the case of anything seized in any ship or aircraft, the master or commander.

2.—Notice under paragraph 1 above shall be given in writing and shall be deemed to have been duly served on the person concerned—

    (a) if delivered to him personally; or
    (b) if addressed to him and left or forwarded by post to him at his usual or last known place of abode or business or, in the case of a body corporate, at their registered or principal office; or
    (c) where he has no address within the United Kingdom [or the Isle of Man], or his address is unknown, by publication of notice of the seizure in the London, Edinburgh or Belfast Gazette.

Notice of claim

3.—Any person claiming that any thing seized as liable to forfeiture is not so liable shall, within one month of the date of the notice of seizure or, where no such notice has been served on him, within one month of the date of the seizure, give notice of his claim in writing to the Commissioners at any office of customs and excise.

4.—(1) Any notice under paragraph 3 above shall specify the name and address of the claimant and, in the case of a claimant who is outside the United Kingdom [and the Isle of Man], shall specify the name and address of a solicitor in the United Kingdom who is authorised to accept service of process and to act on behalf of the claimant.

(2) Service of process upon a solicitor so specified shall be deemed to be proper service upon the claimant.

Condemnation

5.—If on the expiration of the relevant period under paragraph 3 above for the giving of notice of claim in respect of any thing no such notice has been given to the Commissioners, or if, in the case of any such notice given, any requirement of paragraph 4 above is not complied with, the thing in question shall be deemed to have been duly condemned as forfeited.

6.—Where notice of claim in respect of any thing is duly given in accordance with paragraphs 3 and 4 above, the Commissioners shall take proceedings for the condemnation of that thing by the court. and if the court finds that the thing was at the time of seizure liable to forfeiture the court shall condemn it as forfeited.

7.—Where any thing is in accordance with either of paragraphs 5 or 6 above condemned or deemed to have been condemned as forfeited, then, without prejudice to any delivery up or sale of the thing by the Commissioners under paragraph 16 below, the forfeiture shall have effect as from the date when the liability to forfeiture arose.

Proceedings for condemnation by court

8.—Proceedings for condemnation shall be civil proceedings and may be instituted—

    (a) in England or Wales either in the High Court or in a magistrates' court;
    (b) . . .
    (c) in Northern Ireland either in the High Court or in a court of summary jurisdiction.

9.—Proceedings for the condemnation of any thing instituted in a magistrates' court in England or Wales, in the sheriff court in Scotland or in a court of summary jurisdiction in Northern Ireland may be so instituted—

    (a) in any such court having jurisdiction in the place where any offence in connection with that thing was committed or where any proceedings for such an offence are instituted; or
    (b) in any such court having jurisdiction in the place where the claimant resides or, if the claimant has specified a solicitor under paragraph 4 above, in the place where that solicitor has his office; or
    (c) in any such court having jurisdiction in the place where that thing was found, detained or seized or to which it is first brought after being found, detained or seized.

10.—(1) In any proceedings for condemnation instituted in England, Wales or Northern Ireland, the claimant or his solicitor shall make oath that the thing seized was, or was to the best of his knowledge and belief, the property of the claimant at the time of the seizure.

(2) In any such proceedings instituted in the High Court, the claimant shall give such security for the costs of the proceedings as may be determined by the Court.

(3) If any requirement of this paragraph is not complied with, the court shall give judgment for the Commissioners.

11.—(1) In the case of any proceedings for condemnation instituted in a magistrates' court in England or Wales, without prejudice to any right to require the statement of a case for the opinion of the High Court, either party may appeal against the decision of that court to the Crown Court.

(2) In the case of any proceedings for condemnation instituted in a court of summary jurisdiction in Northern Ireland, without prejudice to any right to require the statement of a case for the opinion of the High Court, either party may appeal against the decision of that court to the county court.

12.—Where an appeal, including an appeal by way of case stated, has been made against the decision of the court in any proceedings for the condemnation of any thing, that thing shall, pending the final determination of the matter, be left with the Commissioners or at any convenient office of customs and excise.

Provisions as to proof

13.—In any proceedings arising out of the seizure of any thing, the fact, form and manner of the seizure shall be taken to have been as set forth in the process without any further evidence thereof, unless the contrary is proved.

14.—In any proceedings, the condemnation by a court of any thing as forfeited may be proved by the production either of the order or certificate of condemnation or of a certified copy thereof purporting to be signed by an officer of the court by which the order or certificate was made or granted.

Special provisions as to certain claimants

15.—For the purposes of any claim to, or proceedings for the condemnation of, any thing, where that thing is at the time of seizure the property of a body corporate, of two or more partners or of any number of persons exceeding five, the oath required by paragraph 10 above to be taken and any other thing required by this Schedule or by any rules of the court to be done by, or by any person authorised by, the claimant or owner may be taken or done by, or by any other person authorised by, the following persons respectively, that is to say—

    (a) where the owner is a body corporate, the secretary or some duly authorised officer of that body;

    (b) where the owners are in partnership, any one of those owners;

    (c) where the owners are any number of persons exceeding five not being in partnership, any two of those persons on behalf of themselves and their co-owners.

Power to deal with seizures before condemnation, etc.

16.—Where any thing has been seized as liable to forfeiture the Commissioners may at any time if they see fit and notwithstanding that the thing has not yet been condemned, or is not yet deemed to have been condemned, as forfeited—

    (a) deliver it up to any claimant upon his paying to the Commissioners such sum as they think proper, being a sum not exceeding that which in their opinion represents the value of the thing, including any duty or tax chargeable thereon which has not been paid;

    (b) if the thing seized is a living creature or is in the opinion of the Commissioners of a perishable nature, sell or destroy it.

17.—(1) If, where any thing is delivered up, sold or destroyed under paragraph 16 above, it is held in proceedings taken under this Schedule that the thing was not liable to forfeiture at the time of its seizure, the Commissioners shall, subject to any deduction allowed under sub-paragraph (2) below, on demand by the claimant tender to him—

    (a) an amount equal to any sum paid by him under sub-paragraph (a) of that paragraph; or

    (b) where they have sold the thing, an amount equal to the proceeds of sale; or

    (c) where they have destroyed the thing, an amount equal to the market value of the thing at the time of its seizure.

(2) Where the amount to be tendered under sub-paragraph (1)(a), (b) or (c) above includes any sum on account of any duty or tax chargeable on the thing which had not been paid before its seizure the Commissioners may deduct so much of that amount as represents that duty or tax.

(3) If the claimant accepts any amount tendered to him under sub-paragraph (1) above, he shall not be entitled to maintain any action on account of the seizure, detention, sale or destruction of the thing.

(4) For the purposes of sub-paragraph (1)(c) above, the market value of any thing at the time of its seizure shall be taken to be such amount as the Commissioners and the claimant may agree or, in default of agreement, as may be determined by a referee appointed by the Lord Chancellor (not being an official of any government department), whose decision shall be final and conclusive; and the procedure on any reference to a referee shall be such as may be determined by the referee.

General note

In paras 2, 4, the words in square brackets were inserted by the Isle of Man Act 1979, s 13, Sch 1, paras 23, 24.

In para 8, the words omitted apply to Scotland only.

This Schedule is modified by the Postal Packets (Customs and Excise) Regulations 1986, SI 1986/260, reg 5, and references to solicitors etc are modified to include references to bodies recognised under the Administration of Justice Act 1985, s 9, by the Solicitors' Incorporated Practices Order 1991, SI 1991/2684, arts 4, 5, Sch 1.

COPYRIGHT DESIGNS AND PATENTS ACT 1988
(c 48)

General note
As amended by the Trade Marks Act 1994.

An Act to restate the law of copyright, with amendments; to make fresh provision as to the rights of performers and others in performances; to confer a design right in original designs; to amend the Registered Designs Act 1949; to make provision with respect to patent agents and trade mark agents; to confer patents and designs jurisdiction on certain county courts; to amend the law of patents; to make provision with respect to devices designed to circumvent copy-protection of works in electronic form; to make fresh provision penalising the fraudulent reception of transmissions; to make the fraudulent application or use of a trade mark an offence; to make provision for the benefit of the Hospital for Sick Children, Great Ormond Street, London; to enable financial assistance to be given to certain international bodies; and for connected purposes

[15th November 1988]

BE IT ENACTED by the Queen's most Excellent Majesty, by and with the advice and consent of the Lords Spiritual and Temporal, and Commons, in this present Parliament assembled, and by the authority of the same, as follows–

PART V
PATENT AGENTS AND TRADE MARK AGENTS

Patent agents

274. Persons permitted to carry on business of a patent agent
(1) Any individual, partnership or body corporate may, subject to the following provisions of this Part, carry on the business of acting as agent for others for the purpose of—

(a) applying for or obtaining patents, in the United Kingdom or elsewhere, or
(b) conducting proceedings before the comptroller relating to applications for, or otherwise in connection with, patents.

(2) This does not affect any restriction under the European Patent Convention as to who may act on behalf of another for any purpose relating to European patents.

275. The register of patent agents
(1) The Secretary of State may make rules requiring the keeping of a register of persons who act as agent for others for the purposes of applying for or obtaining patents; and in this Part a 'registered patent agent' means a person whose name is entered in the register kept under this section.

(2) The rules may contain such provision as the Secretary of State thinks fit regulating the registration of persons, and may in particular—

(a) require the payment of such fees as may be prescribed, and
(b) authorise in prescribed cases the erasure from the register of the name of any person registered in it, or the suspension of a person's registration.

(3) The rules may delegate the keeping of the register to another person, and may confer on that person—

    (a) power to make regulations—

        (i) with respect to the payment of fees, in the cases and subject to the limits prescribed by rules, and

        (ii) with respect to any other matter which could be regulated by rules, and

    (b) such other functions, including disciplinary functions, as may be prescribed by rules.

    (4) Rules under this section shall be made by statutory instrument which shall be subject to annulment in pursuance of a resolution of either House of Parliament.

Subordinate legislation
The Register of Patent Agents Rules 1990, SI 1990/1457, as amended by SI 1999/983.

276. Persons entitled to describe themselves as patent agents

(1) An individual who is not a registered patent agent shall not—

    (a) carry on a business (otherwise than in partnership) under any name or other description which contains the words 'patent agent' or 'patent attorney'; or

    (b) in the course of a business otherwise describe himself, or permit himself to be described, as a 'patent agent' or 'patent attorney'.

    (2) A partnership shall not—

    (a) carry on a business under any name or other description which contains the words 'patent agent' or 'patent attorney'; or

    (b) in the course of a business otherwise describe itself, or permit itself to be described as, a firm of 'patent agents' or 'patent attorneys',

unless all the partners are registered patent agents or the partnership satisfies such conditions as may be prescribed for the purposes of this section.

    (3) A body corporate shall not—

    (a) carry on a business (otherwise than in partnership) under any name or other description which contains the words 'patent agent' or 'patent attorney'; or

    (b) in the course of a business otherwise describe itself, or permit itself to be described as, a 'patent agent' or 'patent attorney',

unless all the directors of the body corporate are registered patent agents or the body satisfies such conditions as may be prescribed for the purposes of this section.

    (4) Subsection (3) does not apply to a company which began to carry on business as a patent agent before 17th November 1917 if the name of a director or the manager of the company who is a registered patent agent is mentioned as being so registered in all professional advertisements, circulars or letters issued by or with the company's consent on which its name appears.

    (5) Where this section would be contravened by the use of the words 'patent agent' or 'patent attorney' in reference to an individual, partnership or body corporate, it is equally contravened by the use of other expressions in reference to that person, or his business or place of business, which are likely to be understood as indicating that he is entitled to be described as a 'patent agent' or 'patent attorney'.

    (6) A person who contravenes this section commits an offence and is liable on summary conviction to a fine not exceeding level 5 on the standard scale; and proceedings for such an offence may be begun at any time within a year from the date of the offence.

    (7) This section has effect subject to—

(a) section 277 (persons entitled to describe themselves as European patent attorneys, &c), and

(b) section 278(1) (use of term 'patent attorney' in reference to solicitors).

General note
References to solicitors etc are modified to include references to bodies recognised under the Administration of Justice Act 1985, s 9, by the Solicitors' Incorporated Practices Order 1991, SI 1991/2684, arts 4, 5, Sch 1.

277. Persons entitled to describe themselves as European patent attorneys, &c

(1) The term 'European patent attorney' or 'European patent agent' may be used in the following cases without any contravention of section 276.

(2) An individual who is on the European list may—

(a) carry on business under a name or other description which contains the words 'European patent attorney' or 'European patent agent', or

(b) otherwise describe himself, or permit himself to be described, as a 'European patent attorney' or 'European patent agent'.

(3) A partnership of which not less than the prescribed number or proportion of partners is on the European list may—

(a) carry on a business under a name or other description which contains the words 'European patent attorneys' or 'European patent agents', or

(b) otherwise describe itself, or permit itself to be described, as a firm which carries on the business of a 'European patent attorney' or 'European patent agent'.

(4) A body corporate of which not less than the prescribed number or proportion of directors is on the European list may—

(a) carry on a business under a name or other description which contains the words 'European patent attorney' or 'European patent agent', or

(b) otherwise describe itself, or permit itself to be described as, a company which carries on the business of a 'European patent attorney' or 'European patent agent'.

(5) Where the term 'European patent attorney' or 'European patent agent' may, in accordance with this section, be used in reference to an individual, partnership or body corporate, it is equally permissible to use other expressions in reference to that person, or to his business or place of business, which are likely to be understood as indicating that he is entitled to be described as a 'European patent attorney' or 'European patent agent.'

278. Use of the term 'patent attorney': supplementary provisions

(1) The term 'patent attorney' may be used in reference to a solicitor, and a firm of solicitors may be described as a firm of 'patent attorneys', without any contravention of section 276.

(2) No offence is committed under the enactments restricting the use of certain expressions in reference to persons not qualified to act as solicitors—

(a) by the use of the term 'patent attorney' in reference to a registered patent agent, or

(b) by the use of the term 'European patent attorney' in reference to a person on the European list.

(3) The enactments referred to in subsection (2) are section 21 of the Solicitors Act 1974, section 31 of the Solicitors (Scotland) Act 1980 and Article 22 of the Solicitors (Northern Ireland) Order 1976.

General note
References to solicitors etc are modified to include references to bodies recognised under the Administration of Justice Act 1985, s 9, by the Solicitors' Incorporated Practices Order 1991, SI 1991/2684, arts 4, 5, Sch 1.

279. Power to prescribe conditions, &c for mixed partnerships and bodies corporate

(1) The Secretary of State may make rules—

   (a) prescribing the conditions to be satisfied for the purposes of section 276 (persons entitled to describe themselves as patent agents) in relation to a partnership where not all the partners are qualified persons or a body corporate where not all the directors are qualified persons, and
   (b) imposing requirements to be complied with by such partnerships and bodies corporate.

(2) The rules may, in particular—

   (a) prescribe conditions as to the number or proportion of partners or directors who must be qualified persons;
   (b) impose requirements as to—

      (i) the identification of qualified and unqualified persons in professional advertisements, circulars or letters issued by or with the consent of the partnership or body corporate and which relate to it or to its business; and
      (ii) the manner in which a partnership or body corporate is to organise its affairs so as to secure that qualified persons exercise a sufficient degree of control over the activities of unqualified persons.

(3) Contravention of a requirement imposed by the rules is an offence for which a person is liable on summary conviction to a fine not exceeding level 5 on the standard scale.

(4) The Secretary of State may make rules prescribing for the purposes of section 277 the number or proportion of partners of a partnership or directors of a body corporate who must be qualified persons in order for the partnership or body to take advantage of that section.

(5) In this section 'qualified person'—

   (a) in subsections (1) and (2), means a person who is a registered patent agent, and
   (b) in subsection (4), means a person who is on the European list.

(6) Rules under this section shall be made by statutory instrument which shall be subject to annulment in pursuance of a resolution of either House of Parliament.

Subordinate legislation
The Patent Agents (Mixed Partnerships and Bodies Corporate) Rules 1994, SI 1994/362.

280. Privilege for communications with patent agents

(1) This section applies to communications as to any matter relating to the protection of any invention, design, technical information, [or trade mark], or as to any matter involving passing off.

(2) Any such communication—

(a) between a person and his patent agent, or

(b) for the purpose of obtaining, or in response to a request for, information which a person is seeking for the purpose of instructing his patent agent,

is privileged from disclosure in legal proceedings in England, Wales or Northern Ireland in the same way as a communication between a person and his solicitor or, as the case may be, a communication for the purpose of obtaining, or in response to a request for, information which a person seeks for the purpose of instructing his solicitor.

(3) In subsection (2) 'patent agent' means—

(a) a registered patent agent or a person who is on the European list,

(b) a partnership entitled to describe itself as a firm of patent agents or as a firm carrying on the business of a European patent attorney, or

(c) a body corporate entitled to describe itself as a patent agent or as a company carrying on the business of a European patent attorney.

(4) It is hereby declared that in Scotland the rules of law which confer privilege from disclosure in legal proceedings in respect of communications extend to such communications as are mentioned in this section.

General note
In sub-s (1), the words in square brackets were substituted by the Trade Marks Act 1994, s 106(1), Sch 4, para 8(3).

References to trade marks or registered trade marks within the meaning of the Trade Marks Act 1938 shall, unless the context otherwise requires, be construed as references to trade marks or registered trade marks within the meaning of the Trade Marks Act 1994; see the Trade Marks Act 1994, Sch 4, para 1.

281. Power of comptroller to refuse to deal with certain agents

(1) This section applies to business under the Patents Act 1949, the Registered Designs Act 1949 or the Patents Act 1977.

(2) The Secretary of State may make rules authorising the comptroller to refuse to recognise as agent in respect of any business to which this section applies—

(a) a person who has been convicted of an offence under section 88 of the Patents Act 1949, section 114 of the Patents Act 1977 or section 276 of this Act;

(b) an individual whose name has been erased from and not restored to, or who is suspended from, the register of patent agents on the ground of misconduct;

(c) a person who is found by the Secretary of State to have been guilty of such conduct as would, in the case of an individual registered in the register of patent agents, render him liable to have his name erased from the register on the ground of misconduct;

(d) a partnership or body corporate of which one of the partners or directors is a person whom the comptroller could refuse to recognise under paragraph (a), (b) or (c) above.

(3) The rules may contain such incidental and supplementary provisions as appear to the Secretary of State to be appropriate and may, in particular, prescribe circumstances in which a person is or is not to be taken to have been guilty of misconduct.

(4) Rules made under this section shall be made by statutory instrument which shall be subject to annulment in pursuance of a resolution of either House of Parliament.

(5) The comptroller shall refuse to recognise as agent in respect of any business to which this section applies a person who neither resides nor has a place of

business in the United Kingdom, the Isle of Man or another member State of the European Economic Community.

Subordinate legislation
The Patent Agents (Non-recognition of Certain Agents by Comptroller) Rules 1990, SI 1990/1454.

Supplementary

285. Offences committed by partnerships and bodies corporate
(1) Proceedings for an offence under this Part alleged to have been committed by a partnership shall be brought in the name of the partnership and not in that of the partners; but without prejudice to any liability of theirs under subsection (4) below.

(2) The following provisions apply for the purposes of such proceedings as in relation to a body corporate—

(a) any rules of court relating to the service of documents;
(b) in England, Wales or Northern Ireland, Schedule 3 to the Magistrates' Courts Act 1980 or Schedule 4 to the Magistrates' Courts (Northern Ireland) Order 1981 (procedure on charge of offence).

(3) A fine imposed on a partnership on its conviction in such proceedings shall be paid out of the partnership assets.

(4) Where a partnership is guilty of an offence under this Part, every partner, other than a partner who is proved to have been ignorant of or to have attempted to prevent the commission of the offence, is also guilty of the offence and liable to be proceeded against and punished accordingly.

(5) Where an offence under this Part committed by a body corporate is proved to have been committed with the consent or connivance of a director, manager, secretary or other similar officer of the body, or a person purporting to act in any such capacity, he as well as the body corporate is guilty of the offence and liable to be proceeded against and punished accordingly.

286. Interpretation
In this Part—
'the comptroller' means the Comptroller-General of Patents, Designs and Trade Marks;
'director', in relation to a body corporate whose affairs are managed by its members, means any member of the body corporate;
'the European list' means the list of professional representatives maintained by the European Patent Office in pursuance of the European Patent Convention;
'registered patent agent' has the meaning given by section 275(1);
. . . .

General note
The definition omitted was repealed by the Trade Marks Act 1994, s 106(2), Sch 5.

PART VII
MISCELLANEOUS AND GENERAL

General

306. Short title
This Act may be cited as the Copyright, Designs and Patents Act 1988.

OLYMPIC SYMBOL ETC (PROTECTION) ACT 1995
(c 32)

General note
As amended by the Northern Ireland Act 1998 and the Scotland Act 1998 (Consequential Modifications)
(No 1) Order 1999, SI 1999/1042.

An Act to make provision about the use for commercial purposes of the Olympic symbol and certain words associated with the Olympic games; and for connected purposes

[19th July 1995]

BE IT ENACTED by the Queen's most Excellent Majesty, by and with the advice and consent of the Lords Spiritual and Temporal, and Commons, in this present Parliament assembled, and by the authority of the same, as follows—

The Olympics association right

1. Creation

(1) There shall be a right, to be known as the Olympics association right.

(2) The right shall carry with it the rights and remedies provided by this Act, which shall be exercisable by such person as the Secretary of State may by order made by statutory instrument appoint for the purposes of this subsection.

(3) An order under subsection (2) above which revokes a previous order under that subsection may contain such supplementary and transitional provision as the Secretary of State thinks fit.

(4) A statutory instrument containing an order under subsection (2) above shall be subject to annulment in pursuance of a resolution of either House of Parliament.

Subordinate legislation
The Olympics Association Right (Appointment of Proprietor) Order 1995, SI 1995/2473.

2. Rights conferred

(1) The Olympics association right shall confer exclusive rights in relation to the use of the Olympic symbol, the Olympic motto and the protected words.

(2) Subject to sections 4 and 5 below, the rights conferred by subsection (1) above shall be infringed by any act done in the United Kingdom which—

(a) constitutes infringement under section 3 below, and
(b) is done without the consent of the person for the time being appointed under section 1(2) above (in this Act referred to as 'the proprietor').

(3) The proprietor may exploit the rights conferred by subsection (1) above for gain, but may not make any disposition of or of any interest in or over, them.

(4) This section shall not have effect to permit the doing of anything which would otherwise be liable to be prevented by virtue of a right

(a) subsisting immediately before the day on which this Act comes into force, or
(b) created by—

(i) the registration of a design under the Registered Designs Act 1949 on or after the day on which this Act comes into force, or
(ii) the registration of a trade mark under the Trade Marks Act 1994 on or after that day.

(5) Consent given for the purposes of subsection (2)(b) above by a person appointed under section 1(2) above shall, subject to its terms, be binding on any person subsequently appointed under that provision; and references in this Act to doing anything with, or without, the consent of the proprietor shall be construed accordingly.

3. Infringement

(1) A person infringes the Olympics association right if in the course of trade he uses—

   (a) a representation of the Olympic symbol, the Olympic motto or a protected word, or
   (b) a representation of something so similar to the Olympic symbol or the Olympic motto as to be likely to create in the public mind an association with it,

(in this Act referred to as 'a controlled representation').

(2) For the purposes of this section, a person uses a controlled representation if, in particular, he—

   (a) affixes it to goods or the packaging thereof,
   (b) incorporates it in a flag or banner,
   (c) offers or exposes for sale, puts on the market or stocks for those purposes goods which bear it or whose packaging bears it,
   (d) imports or exports goods which bear it or whose packaging bears it,
   (e) offers or supplies services under a sign which consists of or contains it, or
   (f) uses it on business papers or in advertising.

4. Limits on effect

(1) The Olympics association right is not infringed by use of a controlled representation where—

   (a) the use consists of use in a work of any of the descriptions mentioned in subsection (3) below, and
   (b) the person using the representation does not intend the work to be used in relation to goods or services in circumstances which would involve an infringement of the Olympics association right,

provided the use is in accordance with honest practices in industrial or commercial matters.

(2) The Olympics association right is not infringed by use of a controlled representation where—

   (a) the use consists of use of a work of any of the descriptions mentioned in subsection (3) below, and
   (b) the use of the work is not in relation to goods or services,

provided the use of the representation is in accordance with honest practices in industrial or commercial matters.

(3) The descriptions of work referred to in subsections (1)(a) and (2)(a) above are a literary work, a dramatic work, a musical work, an artistic work, a sound recording, a film, a broadcast and a cable programme, in each case within the meaning of Part I of the Copyright, Designs and Patents Act 1988.

(4) For the purposes of subsection (2)(b) above, there shall be disregarded any use in relation to a work which—

(a) is of any of the descriptions mentioned in subsection (3) above, and

(b) is to any extent about the Olympic games or the Olympic movement.

(5) For the purposes of subsection (2)(b) above, use of a work in relation to goods shall be disregarded where—

(a) the work is to any extent about the Olympic games or the Olympic movement, and

(b) the person using the work does not do so with a view to gain for himself or another or with the intent to cause loss to another.

(6) In the case of a representation of a protected word, the Olympics association right is not infringed by use which is not such as ordinarily to create an association with—

(a) the Olympic games or the Olympic movement, or

(b) a quality ordinarily associated with the Olympic games or the Olympic movement.

(7) In the case of a representation of a protected word, the Olympics association right is not infringed by use which creates an association between the Olympic games or the Olympic movement and any person or thing where the association fairly represents a connection between the two, provided the use is in accordance with honest practices in industrial or commercial matters.

(8) The Olympics association right is not infringed by use of a controlled representation where—

(a) the use is in relation to goods which bear, or whose packaging bears, the representation,

(b) the goods are not infringing goods by virtue of paragraph (a) or (b) of section 7(2) below, and

(c) the use involves doing any of the things mentioned in section 3(2)(c) or (d) above.

(9)   The Olympics association right is not infringed by use of a controlled representation where—

(a) the use is in relation to goods,

(b) the goods have been put on the market in the European Economic Area by the proprietor or with his consent, and

(c) the representation was used in relation to the goods when they were so put on the market.

(10) Subsection (9) above shall not apply where there exist legitimate reasons for the proprietor to oppose further dealings in the goods (in particular, where the condition of the goods has been changed or impaired after they have been put on the market).

(11) The Olympics association right is not infringed by use of a controlled representation where—

(a) the use is for the purposes of an undertaking, and

(b) the way in which the representation is used for the purposes of the undertaking is a way in which it has been continuously used for those purposes since a date prior to the commencement of this Act.

(12) In the case of a representation of a protected word, the Olympics association right is not infringed by use as part of—

(a) the name of a company, being a name which was the company's corporate name immediately before the day on which this Act comes into force, or

(b) the name under which a business is carried on, being a business which was carried on under that name immediately before the day on which this Act comes into force.

(13) The Olympics association right is not infringed by use of a controlled representation where the use—

(a) takes place under a right subsisting immediately before the day on which this Act comes into force, or

(b) is liable to be prevented by virtue of such a right.

(14) The Olympics association right is not infringed by use of a controlled representation where the use—

(a) takes place under a right created by—

(i) the registration of a design under the Registered Designs Act 1949 on or after the day on which this Act comes into force, or

(ii) the registration of a trade mark under the Trade Marks Act 1994 on or after that day, or

(b) is liable to be prevented by virtue of such a right.

(15) The Olympics association right is not infringed by use of a controlled representation for the purposes of—

(a) judicial or parliamentary proceedings, or

(b) a Royal Commission or statutory inquiry.

(16) In subsection (15) above—

'judicial proceedings' includes proceedings before any court, tribunal or person having authority to decide any matter affecting a person's legal rights or liabilities;

'parliamentary proceedings' includes proceedings [of the Scottish Parliament,] of the Northern Ireland Assembly or of the European Parliament;

'Royal Commission' includes a Commission appointed for Northern Ireland *by the Secretary of State in pursuance of the prerogative powers of Her Majesty delegated to him under section 7(2) of the Northern Ireland Constitution Act 1973* **[by a Minister, within the meaning of the Northern Ireland Act 1998, or Northern Ireland department in pursuance of the prerogative powers of Her Majesty exercisable by the Minister or department under section 23 of that Act]**; and

'statutory inquiry' means an inquiry held or investigation conducted in pursuance of a duty imposed or power conferred by or under an enactment.

(17) In this section, references to use of a work in relation to goods include use of a work on goods.

General note

In sub-s (16), in the definition 'parliamentary proceedings' the words in square brackets were inserted by the Scotland Act 1998 (Consequential Modifications) (No 1) Order 1999, SI 1999/1042, art 3, Sch 1, para 12, and in the definition 'Royal Commission' the words in bold type are substituted for the words in italics by the Northern Ireland Act 1998, s 99, Sch 13, para 15, as from a day to be appointed.

The Northern Ireland Act 1998 makes new provision for the government of Northern Ireland for the purpose of implementing the Belfast Agreement (the agreement reached at multi-party talks on Northern Ireland and set out in Command Paper 3883). As a consequence of that Act, any reference in this section to the Parliament of Northern Ireland or the Assembly established under the Northern Ireland Assembly Act 1973, s 1, certain office-holders and Ministers, and any legislative act and certain financial dealings thereof, shall, for the period specified, be construed in accordance with Sch 12, paras 1–11 to the 1998 Act.

5. Power to prescribe further limits on effect
(1) The Secretary of State may by order made by statutory instrument specify additional cases in which the Olympics association right is not infringed.

(2) Without prejudice to the generality of subsection (1) above, the matters by reference to which a case may be specified under that subsection include—

    (a) the description of controlled representation used, and

    (b) the description of persons by whom a controlled representation is used.

(3) An order under this section may contain such supplementary and transitional provision and savings as the Secretary of State thinks fit.

Remedies in relation to infringement

6. Action for infringement
(1) An infringement of the Olympics association right shall be actionable by the proprietor.

(2) In an action for infringement, all such relief by way of damages, injunctions, accounts or otherwise shall be available to the proprietor as is available in respect of the infringement of a property right.

7. Orders in relation to infringing goods, material or articles
(1) The Secretary of State may by regulations make, in relation to infringing goods, material and articles, provision corresponding to that made by the following provisions of the Trade Marks Act 1994 in relation to goods, material and articles which are infringing goods, material and articles for the purposes of that Act—

    section 15 (order for erasure etc of offending sign),
    section 16 (order for delivery up of infringing goods, material or articles),
    section 18 (period after which remedy of delivery up not available),
    section 19 (order as to disposal of infringing goods, material or articles), and
    section 20 (jurisdiction in Scotland and Northern Ireland in relation to proceedings for an order under section 16 or 19).

(2) Goods are 'infringing goods' for the purposes of this Act if they or their packaging bear a controlled representation and—

    (a) the application of the representation to the goods or their packaging was an infringement of the Olympics association right,

    (b) the goods are proposed to be imported into the United Kingdom and the application of the representation in the United Kingdom to them or their packaging would be an infringement of that right, or

    (c) the representation has otherwise been used in relation to the goods in such a way as to infringe that right.

(3) Material is 'infringing material' for the purposes of this Act if it bears a controlled representation and either—

    (a) it is used for labelling or packaging goods, as a business paper, or for advertising goods or services, in such a way as to infringe the Olympics association right, or

(b) it is intended to be so used and such use would infringe that right.

(4) Articles are 'infringing articles' for the purposes of this Act if they are articles—

(a) which are specifically designed or adapted for making copies of a controlled representation, and
(b) which a person has in his possession, custody or control, knowing or having reason to believe that they have been or are to be used to produce infringing goods or material.

(5) The power conferred by subsection (1) above shall be exercisable by statutory instrument which shall be subject to annulment in pursuance of a resolution of either House of Parliament.

(6) Nothing in subsection (2) above shall be construed as affecting the importation of goods which may lawfully be imported into the United Kingdom by virtue of an enforceable Community right.

Subordinate legislation
The Olympics Association Right (Infringement Proceedings) Regulations 1995, SI 1995/3325.

Criminal sanctions

8. Offences in relation to goods

(1) A person shall be guilty of an offence if with a view to gain for himself or another, or with intent to cause loss to another, and without the consent of the proprietor, he—

(a) applies a controlled representation to goods or their packaging,
(b) sells or lets for hire, offers or exposes for sale or hire or distributes goods which bear, or the packaging of which bears, such a representation, or
(c) has in his possession, custody or control in the course of a business any such goods with a view to the doing of anything, by himself or another, which would be an offence under paragraph (b) above.

(2) A person shall be guilty of an offence if with a view to gain for himself or another, or with intent to cause loss to another, and without the consent of the proprietor, he—

(a) applies a controlled representation to material intended to be used—

(i) for labelling or packaging goods,
(ii) as a business paper in relation to goods, or
(iii) for advertising goods,

(b) uses in the course of a business material bearing such a representation for labelling or packaging goods, as a business paper in relation to goods, or for advertising goods, or
(c) has in his possession, custody or control in the course of a business any such material with a view to the doing of anything, by himself or another, which would be an offence under paragraph (b) above.

(3) A person shall be guilty of an offence if with a view to gain for himself or another, or with intent to cause loss to another, and without the consent of the proprietor, he—

(a) makes an article specifically designed or adapted for making copies of a controlled representation, or

(b) has such an article in his possession, custody or control in the course of a business,

knowing or having reason to believe that it has been, or is to be, used to produce goods, or material for labelling or packaging goods, as a business paper in relation to goods, or for advertising goods.

(4) It shall be a defence for a person charged with an offence under this section to show that he believed on reasonable grounds that the use of the representation in the manner in which it was used, or was to be used, was not an infringement of the Olympics association right.

(5) A person guilty of an offence under this section shall be liable—

(a) on summary conviction, to a fine not exceeding the statutory maximum, and

(b) on conviction on indictment, to a fine.

9. Supplementary provisions as to summary proceedings in Scotland

(1) Notwithstanding anything in section 331 of the Criminal Procedure (Scotland) Act 1975, summary proceedings in Scotland for an offence under this Act may be begun at any time within six months after the date on which evidence sufficient in the Lord Advocate's opinion to justify the proceedings came to his knowledge.

(2) For the purposes of subsection (1) above—

(a) a certificate of the Lord Advocate as to the date mentioned in that subsection shall be conclusive evidence, and

(b) proceedings in Scotland shall be deemed to be begun on the date on which a warrant to apprehend or to cite the accused is granted, if such warrant is executed without undue delay.

10. Partnerships and bodies corporate

Section 101 of the Trade Marks Act 1994 (offences committed by partnerships and bodies corporate) shall apply in relation to an offence under this Act as it applies in relation to an offence under that Act.

Forfeiture of counterfeit goods, etc

11. Forfeiture: England and Wales or Northern Ireland

(1) Section 97 of the Trade Marks Act 1994 (which makes provision about the forfeiture of certain goods, material or articles which come into the possession of any person in connection with the investigation or prosecution of a relevant offence) shall also have effect with the following modifications.

(2) In subsection (1) (which describes the goods, material or articles concerned)—

(a) in paragraph (a), for sign identical to or likely to be mistaken for a registered trade mark there shall be substituted representation within paragraph (a) or (b) of section 3(1) of the Olympic Symbol etc (Protection) Act 1995, and

(b) paragraphs (b) and (c), for sign there shall be substituted representation.

(3) In subsection (7)(a) (power of court to direct release instead of destruction on condition that offending sign erased etc) for sign there shall be substituted representation.

799

(4) In subsection (8) (which defines relevant offence) for section 92 above (unauthorised use of trade mark etc in relation to goods) there shall be substituted section 8 of the Olympic Symbol etc (Protection) Act 1995.

12. Forfeiture: Scotland

(1) Section 98 of the Trade Marks Act 1994 (which makes provision about the forfeiture of certain goods, material or articles on application by the procurator-fiscal or where a person is convicted of a relevant offence) shall also have effect with the following modifications.

(2) In subsection (1) (which describes the goods, material or articles concerned)—

  (a) in paragraph (a), for 'sign identical to or likely to be mistaken for a registered trade mark' there shall be substituted 'representation within paragraph (a) or (b) of section 3(1) of the Olympic Symbol etc (Protection) Act 1995', and

  (b) in paragraphs (b) and (c), for 'sign' there shall be substituted 'representation'.

(3) In subsection (13) (power of court to direct release instead of destruction on condition that offending sign erased etc) for 'sign' there shall be substituted 'representation'.

(4) In subsection (14), in the definition of 'relevant offence', for 'section 92 (unauthorised use of trade mark, &c in relation to goods)' there shall be substituted 'section 8 of the Olympic Symbol etc (Protection) Act 1995'.

Restrictions on acquisition of competing rights

13. Registration of designs and trade marks

(1), (2) . . .

(3) This section has effect in relation to applications for registration made on or after the day on which this Act comes into force.

General note
Sub-ss (1), (2) insert the Registered Designs Act 1949, s 1(6), and the Trade Marks Act 1994, s 4(5).

14. Acquisition of design right

(1) . . .

(2) Subsection (1) above has effect in relation to designs created on or after the day on which this Act comes into force.

(3) For the purposes of subsection (2) above, a design is created on the first day on which—

  (a) it is recorded in a design document, or

  (b) an article is made to it.

General note
Sub-s (1) inserts the Copyright, Designs and Patents Act 1988, s 213(5A).

Miscellaneous

15. Power to give directions to proprietor

(1) The proprietor shall comply with any directions given by the Secretary of State with respect to the exercise of the rights conferred by section 2(1) above.

(2) Directions under this section may be of a general or particular character and may be varied or revoked by subsequent directions.

(3) A transaction between any person and the proprietor in his capacity as such shall not be void by reason only that the transaction was carried out in contravention of a direction given under this section; and a person dealing with the proprietor shall not be concerned to see or enquire whether a direction under this section has been given or complied with.

16. Remedy for groundless threats of infringement proceedings

(1) Where the proprietor threatens another with proceedings for infringement of the Olympics association right other than—

(a) the application to goods or their packaging of a controlled representation,
(b) the importation of goods to which, or to the packaging of which, such a representation has been applied, or
(c) the supply of services under a sign which consists of or contains such a representation,

any person aggrieved may bring proceedings for relief under this section.

(2) The relief which may be applied for is any of the following—

(a) a declaration that the threats are unjustifiable,
(b) an injunction against the continuance of the threats, and
(c) damages in respect of any loss he has sustained by the threats;

(3) A plaintiff under this section shall be entitled to the relief applied for unless the defendant shows that the acts in respect of which proceedings were threatened constitute (or if done would constitute) an infringement of the Olympics association right.

(4) The mere notification of the rights conferred by this Act shall not constitute a threat of proceedings for the purposes of this section.

17. Burden of proof

(1) Subject to subsection (2) below, if in any civil proceedings under this Act a question arises as to the use to which a controlled representation has been put, it shall be for the proprietor to show what use was made of it.

(2) If in any civil proceedings under this Act a question arises as to the application of any of subsections (1), (2) and (6) to (15) of section 4 above or any case specified under section 5 above, it shall be for the person who alleges that the subsection or case applies to show that it does.

General

18. Interpretation

(1) In this Act—

'business includes' a trade or profession;
'controlled representation' has the meaning given by section 3(1) above;
'infringing articles' has the meaning given by section 7(4) above;
'infringing goods' has the meaning given by section 7(2) above;
'infringing material' has the meaning given by section 7(3) above;
'Olympic motto' means the motto of the International Olympic Committee, 'Citius, altius, fortius';
'Olympic symbol' means the symbol of the International Olympic Committee, consisting of five interlocking rings;

'proprietor' has the meaning given by section 2(2) above; and
'trade' includes a business or profession.

(2) For the purposes of this Act each of the following is a protected word, namely, 'Olympiad', 'Olympiads', 'Olympian', 'Olympians', 'Olympic' and 'Olympics'.

(3) In this Act, references to the Olympic motto or a protected word include the motto or word in translation into any language.

(4) In the application of this Act to Scotland—

'accounts' means count, reckoning and payment;
'declaration' means declarator;
'defendant' means defender;
'injunction' means interdict; and
'plaintiff' means pursuer.

19.   Short title, commencement and extent

(1) This Act may be cited as the Olympic Symbol etc (Protection) Act 1995.

(2) This Act shall come into force on such day as the Secretary of State may by order made by statutory instrument appoint.

(3) This Act extends to Northern Ireland.

Subordinate legislation
The Olympic Symbol etc (Protection) Act 1995 (Commencement) Order 1995, SI 1995/2472.

Appendix 2

Secondary legislation

PATENT AGENTS (NON-RECOGNITION OF CERTAIN AGENTS BY COMP-
TROLLER) RULES 1990
(SI 1990/1454)
Made 18th July 1990

1 These Rules may be cited as the Patent Agents (Non-recognition of Certain Agents by Comptroller) Rules 1990 and shall come into force on 13th August 1990.

2 In these Rules—

'the Act' means the Copyright, Designs and Patents Act 1988;
'the Comptroller' means the Comptroller-General of Patents, Designs and Trade Marks;
'the register' means the register of patent agents required to be kept pursuant to rules made under section 275 of the Act.

3 The Comptroller is hereby authorised to refuse to recognise as agent in respect of any business under the Patents Act 1949, the Registered Designs Act 1949 or the Patents Act 1977—

(a) a person who has been convicted of an offence under section 83 of the Patents Act 1949, section 114 of the Patents Act 1977 or section 276 of the Act;

(b) an individual whose name has been erased from and not restored to the register on the ground of misconduct;

(c) a person who is found by the Secretary of State to have been guilty of such conduct as would, in the case of an individual registered in the register, render him liable to have his name erased from the register on the ground of misconduct;

(d) a partnership or body corporate of which one of the partners or directors is a person whom the Comptroller could refuse to recognise under paragraph (a), (b) or (c) above.

[REGISTER OF TRADE MARK AGENTS RULES 1990
(SI 1990/1458)

(As amended by the Register of Patent Agents and the Register of Trade Mark Agents (Amendment) Rules 1999 (SI 1999/983))
Made 18th July 1990

General note
Authority: following the repeal of the Copyright, Designs and Patents Act 1988, s 282, these Rules have effect as if made under the Trade Marks Act 1994, s 83, by virtue of Sch 3, para 22 thereof.

1 Citation and commencement
These Rules may be cited as the Register of Trade Mark Agents Rules 1990 and shall come into force on 1st October 1990.

2 Interpretation
In these Rules, unless the context otherwise requires—

'the Comptroller' means the Comptroller-General of Patents, Designs and Trade Marks;

['the Institute' means the Institute of Trade Mark Attorneys];

'the register' means the register of trade mark agents required to be kept under these Rules, and 'registered trade mark agent' means a trade mark agent whose name is entered in the register;

'the Registrar' means the person appointed in accordance with rule 7 below to maintain the register;

'trade mark agency work' means work done in the course of carrying on the business of acting as agent for others for the purpose of applying for or obtaining the registration of trade marks in the United Kingdom or of conducting proceedings before the Comptroller relating to applications for or otherwise in connection with the registration of trade marks;

'the United Kingdom' includes the Isle of Man.

General note
The definition 'the Institute' was substituted by SI 1999/983, r 3.
References to trade marks or registered trade marks within the meaning of the Trade Marks Act 1938 shall, unless the context otherwise requires, be construed as references to trade marks or registered trade marks within the meaning of the Trade Marks Act 1994; see the Trade Marks Act 1994, Sch 4, para 1.

3 The register
There shall be kept by the Institute a register, to be known as the register of trade mark agents, in which shall be entered the name of each person who is entitled to be registered pursuant to rule 10 below, together with his business address, the date of his registration, his qualifications, and such other particulars as the Registrar may, at the request of that person, think fit to include.

4 Special record
There shall also be kept by the Institute a special record and the Registrar shall transfer thereto the name and particulars of any person whose name has been erased under rule 12 or 13 or pursuant to a direction under rule 14 below and he shall enter therein, against such name, the reason for the erasure.

5 Inspection of register and special record
The register and the special record or, if they are kept otherwise than in documen-

tary form, entries therein made available in documentary form, shall be open to public inspection at such times and in such manner as the Registrar may, subject to any general directions of the Comptroller under rule 21 below, direct.

6 Publication of list of registered trade mark agents
Not later than 1st April in each year the Institute shall cause to be printed, published and placed on sale a copy of the entries in the register (with the names arranged alphabetically) as at the end of the preceding calendar year.

7 The Registrar
(1) There shall be a Registrar who shall be charged with the duty of maintaining the register and the special record in accordance with these Rules and who shall, subject thereto and to any general directions of the Comptroller under rule 21 below, be under the directions of the Institute.
(2) The Registrar shall be appointed by the Institute for a period of one year and shall on ceasing to hold office be eligible for reappointment. He shall hold and vacate his office in accordance with such terms and conditions as the Institute may, after consultation with the Comptroller, determine.

8 Qualifying examinations
(1) The Institute may, by regulations made by it after consultation with the Chartered Institute of Patent Agents and with the approval of the Comptroller, make provision for such educational qualifications, training and qualifying examinations (which examinations shall be offered at least once in every year) as it considers appropriate for the registration of persons under these Rules and shall, subject to any such regulations and any general directions of the Comptroller under rule 21 below, have the entire management and control of such examinations.
(2) Any such regulations may make transitional provision for candidates who have, before the coming into force of the regulations, entered for any examinations held or to be held by the Institute for the purpose of admission to ordinary membership of the Institute to complete or take the same or part or parts thereof or such other examinations in lieu thereof within such time and subject to such conditions as may be specified.

9 Qualifications for registration
(1) Subject to paragraph (2) below, each of the following persons shall qualify for registration under these Rules—

   (a) a person who has passed the qualifying examinations of the Institute and who has completed—
      (i) not less than two years' full-time practice in the field of intellectual property, including substantial experience in trade mark agency work, under the supervision of either a registered trade mark agent or of a registered patent agent, barrister, solicitor or, in Scotland or the Isle of Man, an advocate, being a registered patent agent, barrister, solicitor or advocate who is engaged in or has substantial experience of trade mark agency work in the United Kingdom, or
      (ii) not less than four years' full-time practice in the field of intellectual property, including substantial experience in trade mark agency work in the United Kingdom;
   (b) a Fellow or an ordinary member of the Institute;
   (c) a person, being a registered patent agent, or barrister, solicitor, or in

Scotland or the Isle of Man, an advocate, who has in the period of eight years immediately preceding the date he seeks to have his name entered in the register under rule 10 below completed a total of three years' practice in trade mark agency work;

(d) a person who has in the period of eleven years immediately preceding the date he seeks to have his name entered in the register under rule 10 below completed a total of eight years of full-time practice in trade mark agency work; and

(e) a person who passed in March 1990 the examination paper, entitled 'Advanced Trade Marks Practice (T3)', set by the Chartered Institute of Patents Agents, and—
  (i) becomes a registered patent agent before 31 December 1992, or
  (ii) passes before 31 December 1991 a special advanced trade mark examination paper set by the Institute pursuant to any regulations made by it under rule 8 above.

(2) A person mentioned in sub-paragraph (b), (c) or (d) above shall not be entitled, by virtue of his qualification for registration thereunder, to have his name entered in the register under rule 10 below after the expiration of—

(a) in the case of the person mentioned in sub-paragraph (b) above, the period of three years commencing from the operative date;

(b) in the case of the person mentioned in sub-paragraph (c) above, the period of four years commencing from the operative date; and

(c) in the case of the person mentioned in sub-paragraph (d) above, the period of two years commencing from the operative date.

(3) In this rule—

'the operative date' means the date of the coming into force of this rule; and
'registered patent agent' means a person whose name is entered in the register kept under rules made under section 275 of the Copyright, Designs and Patents Act 1988.

10 Entitlement to registration

(1) Unless a direction under paragraph (3) below in relation to him is in force, a person who qualifies for registration under rule 9 above shall be entitled to have his name entered in the register on production to the Registrar of evidence that he qualifies for registration under that rule and on the payment of the fee prescribed by regulations under rule 20 below.

(2) The Registrar may, for the purpose of satisfying himself that a person has completed the requisite number of years of practice, require that person to submit to him a statutory declaration attesting to that fact and may require such further particulars of that practice as he may consider necessary.

(3) The Secretary of State may, upon being satisfied after due inquiry in accordance with rule 15 below that a person (who would otherwise be entitled to be registered) has been guilty of misconduct, direct that the name of that person shall not be registered, and upon such direction the Registrar shall not, except with the prior consent of the Secretary of State, register the name of that person.

11 Amendment of the register

A registered trade mark agent shall give notice to the Registrar of any change in the particulars relating to him entered in the register and the Registrar shall, on payment of the fee (if any) prescribed by regulations made under rule 20 below, amend the register accordingly.

12 Erasure of registration for failure to pay fee
(1) If any registered trade mark agent fails to pay any annual practice fee that may be prescribed by regulations made under rule 20 below within one month from the day on which it becomes payable, the Registrar shall send to him at his business address (as shown in the register) a notice requiring him to pay the fee on or before a day specified in the notice, and if that person fails to pay the fee on or before that date the Registrar may erase his name from the register.
(2) The name of a person erased from the register under this rule may be restored to it by direction of the Institute on payment by him of the fee or fees due from him, together with such further sum not exceeding the amount prescribed for the annual practice fee as the Institute may in each particular case direct.

13 Correction of entries in register
(1) The Registrar may, upon being satisfied in accordance with paragraph (2) below that any entry in the register has been made in error or that any entry is incorrect, erase or correct the same.
(2) No erasure or correction of any entry in the Register shall be made under paragraph (1) above unless the Registrar has first served notice of the proposed erasure or correction on the person appearing to him to be affected, has afforded that person the opportunity to make written representations regarding the same and has taken into account any such representations.

14 Erasure of registration after due inquiry into misconduct
Where the Secretary of State is satisfied, after due inquiry in accordance with rule 15 below, that a person has been guilty of misconduct, that is to say, conduct discreditable to a registered trade mark agent, he may at his discretion, having regard to the circumstances of the misconduct, direct that the name of that person be erased from the register, and he may further direct that the name shall remain erased during such period as he may specify; and upon a direction under this rule the Registrar shall erase the name and particulars of that person from the register accordingly.

15 Inquiry by Secretary of State
(1) Where it appears to the Secretary of State under rule 10(3) or rule 14 above that a person may have been guilty of misconduct he shall serve on that person (hereinafter referred to as the person affected) a notice—

    (a) informing him of the grounds on which it so appears to the Secretary of State and the substance of any allegations of misconduct made against him, and

    (b) inviting him to submit to the Secretary of State, within such period (being not less than 21 days) as may be specified in the notice, his representations in writing and requiring him to serve notice, if he wishes, of his intention to make oral representations.

(2) A copy of the notice served on the person affected under paragraph (1) above and a copy of any written representations submitted by him to the Secretary of State shall be served by the Secretary of State on the Institute.
(3) Where the person affected has served notice under paragraph (1)(b) above of his intentions to make oral representations, the Secretary of State shall give him not less than 21 days notice, or such shorter notice as the person affected may request or consent to accept, of the date, time and place at which his representations will be

heard.

(4) If the Secretary of State considers that he should proceed with his inquiry but for a reason which differs or on grounds which differ from those set out in the notice served under paragraph (1) above he shall give a further notice under that paragraph.

16 Hearing of representations

(1) At the hearing of oral representations held pursuant to rule 15(3) above the Secretary of State shall, at the request of the person affected, permit any other person (in addition to the person affected) to make representations on his behalf or to give evidence or to introduce documents for him.

(2) The Secretary of State shall not refuse to admit evidence solely on the grounds that it would not be admissible in a court of law.

(3) The hearing may be adjourned at the discretion of the Secretary of State and if adjourned he shall give the person affected reasonable notice of the date, time and place at which the hearing is to be resumed.

(4) The Secretary of State shall inform the Institute of the date, time and place appointed for any hearing and the Institute shall be entitled to be represented at the hearing and to make submissions touching on the matters in issue.

17 Decision

The Secretary of State shall, in deciding whether to issue a direction, take into account any written or oral representations made in accordance with rules 15 and 16 above and shall —

(a) if he decides not to issue a direction, give notice of that decision to the person affected, the Institute and, where the decision relates to any allegations of misconduct made by any person against the person affected, to that person (if known), but nothing in this rule shall require the Secretary of State to state the reasons for that decision;

(b) if he decides to issue a direction, give notice of his decision, the terms thereof and his reasons for the decision to the person affected, the Institute and, where the decision relates to any allegations of misconduct made by any person against the person affected, to that person (if known).

18 Restoration of name to register

(1) On an application made to him by a person whose name has been erased from the register under rule 14 above, the Secretary of State may, if he thinks fit, direct that the name of that person shall be restored to the register, and he may further direct that such restoration shall be made either without fee or on payment of such fee as he may fix not exceeding the fee prescribed by regulations made under rule 20 below for the registration of a name.

(2) The Registrar shall, upon a direction for the restoration of the name of a person under this rule, restore the name and particulars of that person to the register and shall, in the case of a person whose name has been erased for a specified period and in respect of whom no direction has been issued under this rule, restore his name and particulars upon the expiration of that period and upon payment of the fee prescribed by regulations made under rule 20 below for the registration of a name.

19 Appeal to Comptroller from decision of the Institute or Registrar

(1) A person aggrieved by any decision of the Institute or the Registrar under these Rules may appeal to the Comptroller by serving on the Comptroller, within one

month from the date of the decision, a notice of appeal, stating the grounds of appeal with a statement of his case in support thereof. A copy of the notice with a copy of the statement of case shall, at the same time, be served by that person (the appellant) on the Institute or the Registrar, as appropriate.

(2) The Comptroller shall, on receipt of the notice of appeal, give such directions as he thinks fit for the purpose of hearing the appeal and shall give the appellant and the Institute or the Registrar, as the case may be, not less than 14 days notice, or such shorter notice as the appellant and the Institute or Registrar may consent to accept, of the date, time and place appointed for the hearing of the appeal.

(3) At the hearing the Comptroller shall, at the request of any party, permit any other person (in addition to that party) to appear on his behalf.

(4) The Comptroller shall give his decision on the appeal in writing with a statement of his reasons and shall serve a copy thereof on the appellant and the Institute or Registrar.

(5) The Comptroller's decision on the appeal shall be final and for the purposes of giving effect to it he may give such directions to the Institute or Registrar as he thinks fit.

20 Fees

(1) The Institute may, by regulations made by it with the approval of the Comptroller, prescribe the fees to be paid by—

(a) every candidate for any examinations (or part or parts thereof) held in accordance with regulations made under rule 8 above,

(b) every person for the registration of his name,

(c) every registered trade mark agent as an annual practice fee,

(d) a registered trade mark agent requesting an amendment of the register under rule 11 above,

and any such regulations may provide for the remission or refund of any fees in such circumstances as may be prescribed thereunder.

(2) When prescribing any fees for the purposes of paragraph (1)(a) above the Institute shall, as far as practicable, secure that the income therefrom does not exceed the expenditure properly incurred in administering any examinations, taking one year with another.

21 Directions by Comptroller

The Comptroller may from time to time give general directions to the Institute as to any matters relating to the register and in respect of such matters as in his opinion will be conducive to the better regulation of any examinations held by the Institute.

22 Report of the Institute

The Institute shall before 30th April in each year send to the Comptroller a report stating—

(a) the number of applications for registration which were made in the preceding year and the number of registrations effected in that year;

(b) the examinations which were held in that year and the results thereof;

(c) the amount of the fees received by the Institute in that year; and

(d) that rule 20(2) above has been complied with and showing, by reference to income and expenditure, its compliance with that rule;

and shall include in the report a statement on such other matters in relation to the provisions of these Rules (including any regulations made by the Institute pursuant thereto) as the Comptroller may from time to time require.

REGISTERED TRADE MARK AGENTS (MIXED PARTNERSHIPS AND BODIES CORPORATE) RULES 1994
(SI 1994/363)
Made 17th February 1994

General note
Authority: following the repeal of the Copyright, Designs and Patents Act 1988, s 283, these Rules have effect as if made under the Trade Marks Act 1994, s 85(1), (2), by virtue of Sch 3, para 22 thereof.

1 These Rules may be cited as the Registered Trade Mark Agents (Mixed Partnerships and Bodies Corporate) Rules 1994 and shall come into force on 24th March 1994.

2 In these Rules—

'the Act' means the Copyright, Designs and Patents Act 1988;
'registered trade mark agent' means a person whose name is entered in the register kept pursuant to rules made under section 282 of the Act.

3 For the purposes of section 283 of the Act (persons entitled to describe themselves as registered trade mark agents) the conditions to be satisfied, in the case of a partnership where not all the partners are registered trade mark agents or in the case of a body corporate where not all the directors are registered trade mark agents, are—

(a) that each partner or, as the case may be, director shall be a person whose name is entered in at least one of the registers kept pursuant to rules made under sections 275 and 282 of the Act; and
(b) that at least one-quarter of the partners or, as the case may be, the directors shall be registered trade mark agents.

PARTNERSHIPS (UNRESTRICTED SIZE) NO 11 REGULATIONS 1994
(SI 1994/644)
Made 7th March 1994

1 These Regulations may be cited as the Partnerships (Unrestricted Size) No 11 Regulations 1994, and shall come into force on 29th March 1994.

2
(1)   Section 716(1) of the Companies Act 1985 does not prohibit the formation of partnerships consisting of more than 20 persons—

(a) for the purpose of carrying on business as patent agents, where each such person is a patent agent,
(b) for the purpose of carrying on business as registered trade mark agents, where each such person is a registered trade mark agent, or
(c) for the purpose of carrying on business as either patent agents or registered trade mark agents, or as both patent agents and registered trade mark agents, where the partnership concerned satisfies the conditions prescribed by paragraphs (a) and (b) of Rule 3 of the Patent Agents (Mixed Partnerships and Bodies Corporate) Rules 1994 [SI 1994/362] or Rule 3 of the Registered Trade Mark Agents (Mixed Partnerships and Bodies

Corporate) Rules 1994 [SI 1994/363].

(2) In these Regulations,
- (a) 'patent agent' means a person whose name is entered in the register kept pursuant to rules made under section 275 of the Copyright, Designs and Patents Act 1988, and
- (b) 'registered trade mark agent' means a person whose name is entered in the register kept pursuant to rules made under section 282 of that Act.

3

. . .

General note
This regulation revokes the Partnerships (Unrestricted Size) No 1 Regulations 1968, SI 1968/1222, reg 1(a).

TRADE MARKS ACT 1994 (COMMENCEMENT) ORDER 1994
(SI 1994/2550)
Made 29th September 1994

1
This Order may be cited as the Trade Marks Act 1994 (Commencement) Order 1994.

2
All the provisions of the Trade Marks Act 1994 ('the Act') shall come into force on 31st October 1994; and, accordingly, for the purposes of subsection (2) of the said section 109, that date shall be the date of commencement in respect of the references to commencement of the Act in Schedules 3 and 4 to the Act (transitional provisions and consequential amendments).

3
(1) The provisions of the Act specified in the Schedule to this Order shall come into force forthwith for the purpose only of enabling the making of subordinate legislation thereunder, by the authority shown in relation to those provisions, expressed to come into force on 31st October 1994.
(2) Section 66(1) (power of registrar to require use of forms and give directions as to their use) and section 80(1) and (3) (power of the registrar to give directions as to the hours of business and business days) of the Act shall come into force forthwith for the purpose of enabling the registrar to exercise his powers thereunder, the same being effective on 31st October 1994.

SCHEDULE

Article 3(1)

Provision and Authority Subject-matter
Rules by the Secretary of State under the following provisions, as read with
(except in the case of items (u) and (cc)(i) and (iv) below) paragraph (a) or (b), or
both, as appropriate, of subsection (1) of section 78—

(a)   section 4(4)
Prohibiting the registration of a trade mark which consists of arms to which a person is entitled by virtue of a grant of arms by the Crown

(b)   section 13(2)

Providing for the publication and entry in the register of a disclaimer or limitation with respect to the registration of a trade mark

(c)   section 25(1), (5) and (6)

Prescribing the particulars of transactions affecting registered trade marks to be entered in the register; providing for amendments to, or removal of registered particulars relating to licences or to a security interest

(d)   section 34(1)

Prescribing the system of classification of trade marks

(e)   section 35(5)

Providing for the manner of claiming a right to priority on the basis of a Convention application

(f)   section 38(1) and (2)

Prescribing the manner of publication of an application for registration, the time within which, and the manner in which, notice of opposition to the registration must be given

(g)   section 39(3)

Providing for the publication of amendments of applications for registration

(h)   section 40(4)

Prescribing the manner of publication of the registration of a trade mark

(i)   section 41(I) and (3)

Providing as to division or merging of an application for registration and the registration of a series of trade marks

(j)   section 43(2), (3), (5) and (6)

Providing for informing the proprietor of the date of expiry of the registration; prescribing the period for the payment of the renewal fee; providing for the restoration of a trade mark to the register and the manner of publication of the renewal or restoration of the registration

(k)   section 44(3)

Providing for the publication of any alteration of a registered trade mark and for the making of objections thereto by persons affected

(l)   section 45(2)

Providing for the manner of surrender of a registered trade mark and for protecting interests of other persons having a right therein

(m)   section 63(2) and (3)

Prescribing the particulars of registrable transactions to be entered in the register and the manner in which the register shall be kept; providing for public inspection of the register and the supply of copies of entries therein

(n)   section 64(4)

Prescribing the manner in which a request may be made for a change in the name or address of the proprietor as recorded in the register

(o)   section 65(1), (3), (4) and (5)

Providing for the adaptation of entries to new classification; prescribing the time within which a proposal for amendment may be filed and the manner in which such proposal shall be advertised and opposed

(p)   section 66(2)

Prescribing the manner of publication of the forms required by the registrar and his directions as to their use

(q)   section 67(1) and (2)

Prescribing restrictions with regard to information about applications and the manner of requesting information

(r)   section 68(1) and (3)

Providing for the registrar to award costs and direct how and by what parties they are to be paid and for him to require a party to give security for costs

(s)   section 69

Providing for the giving of evidence by affidavit or statutory declaration in proceedings before the registrar, conferring on him the powers of an official referee of the Supreme Court and applying the rules applicable to the attendance of witnesses

(t)   section 76(1)

Providing for decisions of the registrar from which no appeal lies

(u)   section 78

Providing for rules for the purposes of any provision of the Act authorising rules or for prescribing anything required to be prescribed by any provision of the Act, and generally for regulating practice and procedure and for other matters

(v)   section 79

Prescribing fees in respect of applications and registration and other matters; providing for the payment of a single fee in respect of two or more matters and the circumstances in which a fee may be repaid or remitted

(w)   section 80(3)

Prescribing the manner of publication of the registrar's directions on hours of business and business days of the Office

(x)   section 81

Providing for the publication of a journal

(y)   section 82

Providing for the recognition of persons authorised to act as agents

(z)   section 88

Providing for the registrar to refuse to deal with certain agents

(aa)   Schedule 1, paragraph 6(2)

Prescribing the period during which the applicant for a collective mark must file the regulations

(bb)   Schedule 2, paragraph 7(2)

Prescribing the period during which the applicant for a certification mark must file the regulations

(cc)   Schedule 3—

(i)   paragraph 10(2)

In relation to an application for registration pending on the commencement of the Act, the exercise of powers under section 78 of the Act

(ii)   paragraph 11(2)

Prescribing the form of the notice claiming to have the registrability of the mark determined in accordance with the provisions of the Act

(iii)   paragraph 12

Providing for the exercise by the registrar of his powers under section 65 of the Act (adaptation of entries to new classification)

(iv)   paragraph 14(5)
Providing as to the manner of claiming a right to priority on the basis of a relevant
overseas application under section 39A of the Trade Marks Act 1938
Regulations by the Commissioners of Customs and Excise under section 90
Prescribing the form in which notice is to be given under section 89 of the Act and
requiring security or indemnity from a person giving such a notice

TRADE MARKS RULES 1994
(SI 1994/2583)
(As amended by the Trade Marks (Amendment) Rules 1998 (SI 1998/925))
Made 5th October 1994
Preliminary

1 Citation and commencement
These Rules may be cited as the Trade Marks Rules 1994 and shall come into force
on 31st October 1994.

2 Interpretation
(1) In these Rules, unless the context otherwise requires—

'the Act' means the Trade Marks Act 1994;
'the Journal' means the Trade Marks Journal published in accordance with rule
       65 below;
'the Office' means the Patent Office;
'old law' means the Trade Marks Act 1938 (as amended) and any rules made
       thereunder existing immediately before the commencement of the Act;
'proprietor' means the person registered as the proprietor of the trade mark;
'publish' means publish in the Journal;
'send' includes give;
'specification' means the statement of goods or services in respect of which a
       trade mark is registered or proposed to be registered;
'United Kingdom' includes the Isle of Man.

(2) In these Rules, except where otherwise indicated, a reference to a section is a
reference to that section in the Act, a reference to a rule is a reference to that rule in
these Rules, a reference to a Schedule is a reference to that Schedule to these Rules
and a reference to a form is a reference to that form as published by the registrar
under rule 3 below.
(3) In these Rules references to the filing of any application, notice or other document are to be construed as references to its being sent or delivered to the registrar
at the Office.

3 Forms and directions of the registrar under s 66
(1) Any forms required by the registrar to be used for the purpose of registration of
a trade mark or any other proceedings before him under the Act pursuant to section
66 and any directions with respect to their use shall be published and any amendment or modification of a form or of the directions with respect to its use shall be
published.
(2)   A requirement under this rule to use a form as published is satisfied by the
use either of a replica of that form or of a form which is acceptable to the registrar
and contains the information required by the form as published and complies with
any directions as to the use of such a form.

4 Requirement as to fees

(1) The fees to be paid in respect of any application, registration or any other matter under the Act and these Rules shall be those (if any) prescribed in relation to such matter by rules under section 79 (fees).

(2) Any form required to be filed with the registrar in respect of any specified matter shall be subject to the payment of the fee (if any) prescribed in respect of that matter by those rules.

Application for registration

5 *Applications for registration; s 32 (Form TM 3)]*
An application for the registration of a trade mark shall be filed on Form TM3 and shall be subject to the payment of the application fee and such class fees as may be appropriate.

5 Applications for registration; s 32 (Form TM 3)
(1) An application for the registration of a trade mark shall be filed on Form TM3 and shall be subject to the payment of the application fee and such class fees as may be appropriate.

(2) An application for registration of a three-dimensional mark shall not be treated as such unless the application contains a statement to that effect.

(3) Where colour is claimed as an element of the trade mark, it shall not be treated as such unless the application contains a statement to that effect and specifies the colour.

(4) An application to register a trade mark which is a word shall be treated as an application to register that word in the graphical form shown in the application, unless the applicant includes a statement that the application is for registration of the word without regard to its graphical form.

General note
The rule in bold type was substituted for the rule in italics by SI 1998/925, r 4.

6 Claim to priority; ss 35 & 36

(1) Where a right to priority is claimed by reason of an application for protection of a trade mark duly filed in a Convention country under section 35 or in another country or territory in respect of which provision corresponding to that made by section 35 is made under section 36, particulars of that claim shall be included in the application for registration under rule 5 above and, where no certificate as is referred to in paragraph (2) below is filed with the application, such particulars shall include the country or countries and the date or dates of filing.

(2) Unless it has been filed at the time of the filing of the application for registration, there shall be filed, within three months of the filing of the application under rule 5, a certificate by the registering or other competent authority of that country certifying, or verifying to the satisfaction of the registrar, the date of the filing of the application, the country or registering or competent authority, the representation of the mark, and the goods or services covered by the application.

7 Classification of goods and services; s 34

(1) For the purposes of trade mark registrations in respect of goods dated before 27th July 1938, goods are classified in accordance with Schedule 3 to these Rules, except where a specification has been converted, whether under the old law or under rule 40 below, to Schedule 4.

(2) For the purposes of trade mark registrations in respect of goods dated on or after 27th July 1938 and for the purposes of any registrations dated before that date

in respect of which the specifications were converted under the old law, and for the purposes of trade mark registrations in respect of services, goods and services are classified in accordance with Schedule 4, which sets out the current version of the classes of the International Classification of Goods and Services.

8 Application may relate to more than one class and shall specify the class (Form TM3A)

(1)   An application may be made for registration in more than one class of Schedule 4.

(2) Every application shall specify the class in Schedule 4 to which it relates; and if the application relates to more than one class in that Schedule the specification contained in it shall set out the classes in consecutive numerical order and list under each class the goods or services appropriate to that class.

(3) If the specification contained in the application lists items by reference to a class in Schedule 4 in which they do not fall, the applicant may request, by filing Form TM3A, that his application be amended to include the appropriate class for those items, and upon the payment of such class fee as may be appropriate the registrar shall amend his application accordingly.

9 Prohibition on registration of mark consisting of arms; s 4

Where a representation of any arms or insignia as is referred to in section 4(4) appears on a mark, the registrar shall refuse to accept an application for the registration of the mark unless satisfied that the consent of the person entitled to the arms has been obtained.

10 Address for service (Form TM33)

(1) For the purposes of any proceedings before the registrar under these Rules or any appeal from a decision of the registrar under the Act or these Rules, an address for service in the United Kingdom shall be filed by—

    (a) every applicant for the registration of a trade mark;

    (b) every person opposing an application for registration of a trade mark;

    (c) every applicant applying to the registrar under section 46 for the revocation of the registration of a trade mark, under section 47 for the invalidation of the registration of a trade mark, or under section 64 for the rectification of the register;

    (d) every person granted leave to intervene under rule 31(5) (the intervener); and

    (e) every proprietor of a registered trade mark which is the subject of an application to the registrar for the revocation, invalidation or rectification of the registration of the mark.

(2) The address for service of an applicant for registration of a trade mark shall upon registration of the mark be deemed to be the address for service of the registered proprietor, subject to any filing to the contrary under paragraph (1) above or rule 38(2) below.

(3) In any case in which an address for service is filed at the same time as the filing of a form required by the registrar under rule 3 which requires the furnishing of an address for service, the address shall be filed on that form and in any other case it shall be filed on Form TM33.

(4) Anything sent to any applicant, opponent, intervener or registered proprietor at his address for service shall be deemed to be properly sent; and the registrar may,

where no address for service is filed, treat as the address for service of the person concerned his trade or business address in the United Kingdom, if any.

(5) An address for service in the United Kingdom may be filed at any time by the proprietor of a registered trade mark and by any person having an interest in or charge on a registered trade mark which has been registered under rule 34.

(6) Where an address for service is not filed as required by paragraph (1) above, the registrar shall send the person concerned notice to file an address for service within two months of the date of the notice and if that person fails to do so—

(a) in the case of an applicant as is referred to in sub-paragraph (a) or (c), the application shall be treated as abandoned;

(b) in the case of a person as is referred to in sub-paragraph (b) or (d), he shall be deemed to have withdrawn from the proceedings; and

(c) in the case of the proprietor referred to in sub-paragraph (e), he shall not be permitted to take part in any proceedings.

11 Deficiencies in application; s 32

Where an application for registration of a trade mark does not satisfy the requirements of section 32(2), (3) or (4) or *rule 5 or 8(2)* **rule 5(1) or 8(2)**, the registrar shall send notice thereof to the applicant to remedy the deficiencies or, in the case of section 32(4), the default of payment and if within two months of the date of the notice the applicant—

(a) fails to remedy any deficiency notified to him in respect of section 32(2), the application shall be deemed never to have been made; or

(b) fails to remedy any deficiency notified to him in respect of section 32(3) or rule 5 or 8(2) or fails to make payment as required by section 32(4), the application shall be treated as abandoned.

General note
The words in bold type were substituted for the words in italics by SI 1998/925, r 5.

Publication, observations, oppositions and registration

12 Publication of application for registration; s 38(1)

An application which has been accepted for registration shall be published.

13 Opposition proceedings; s 38(2) (Forms TM7 & TM8)]

(1) Notice of opposition to the registration of a trade mark shall be sent to the registrar on Form TM7 within three months of the date on which the application was published under rule 12, and shall include a statement of the grounds of opposition; the registrar shall send a copy of the notice and the statement to the applicant.

(2) Within three months of the date on which a copy of the statement is sent by the registrar to the applicant the applicant may file, in conjunction with notice of the same on Form TM8, a counter-statement; the registrar shall send a copy of the Form TM8 and the counter-statement to the person opposing the application.

(3) Within three months of the date on which a copy of the counter-statement is sent by the registrar to the person opposing the registration, that person shall file such evidence by way of statutory declaration or affidavit as he may consider necessary to adduce in support of his opposition and shall send a copy thereof to the applicant.

(4) If the person opposing the registration files no evidence under paragraph (3) above, he shall, unless the registrar otherwise directs, be deemed to have abandoned his opposition.

(5) If the person opposing the registration files evidence under paragraph (3) above or the registrar otherwise directs under paragraph (4) above, the applicant shall, within three months of the date on which either a copy of the evidence or a copy of the direction is sent to the applicant, file such evidence by way of statutory declaration or affidavit as he may consider necessary to adduce in support of his application, and shall send a copy thereof to the person opposing the application.

(6) Within three months of the date on which a copy of the applicant's evidence is sent to him, the person opposing the application may file evidence in reply by statutory declaration or affidavit which shall be confined to matters strictly in reply to the applicant's evidence, and shall send a copy thereof to the applicant.

(7) No further evidence may be filed, except that, in relation to any proceedings before him, the registrar may at any time if he thinks fit give leave to either party to file evidence upon such terms as he may think fit.

(8) Upon completion of the evidence the registrar shall, if a hearing is requested by any party to the proceedings, send to the parties notice of a date for the hearing.

13 Opposition proceedings; s 38(2) (Forms TM7 & TM8)

(1) Notice of opposition to the registration of a trade mark shall be filed on Form TM7 within three months of the date on which the application was published under rule 12, and shall include a statement of the grounds of opposition; the registrar shall send a copy of the notice and the statement to the applicant.

(2) Within three months of the date on which a copy of the notice and statement is sent by the registrar to the applicant, the applicant may file a counter-statement, in conjunction with a notice of the same, on Form TM8; where such a notice and counter-statement are filed within the prescribed period, the registrar shall send a copy of the Form TM8 and the counter-statement to the person opposing the application.

(3) Where a notice and counter-statement are not filed by the applicant within the period prescribed by paragraph (2), he shall be deemed to have withdrawn his application for registration.

(4) Within three months of the date upon which a copy of the counter-statement is sent by the registrar to the person opposing the registration, that person may file such evidence by way of statutory declaration or affidavit as he may consider necessary to adduce in support of his opposition and shall send a copy thereof to the applicant.

(5) If the person opposing the registration files no evidence under paragraph (4) above in support of his opposition, he shall, unless the registrar otherwise directs, be deemed to have withdrawn his opposition.

(6) If the person opposing the registration files evidence under paragraph (4) above or the registrar otherwise directs under paragraph (5) above, the applicant who has filed a notice and counter-statement under paragraph (2) above may, within three months of the date on which either a copy of the evidence or a copy of the direction is sent to him, file such evidence by way of statutory declaration or affidavit as he may consider necessary to adduce in support of his application for registration and shall send a copy thereof to the person opposing the application.

(7) Within three months of the date upon which a copy of the applicant's evidence is sent to him under paragraph (6) above, the person opposing the application may file evidence in reply by statutory declaration or affidavit which shall be confined to matters strictly in reply to the applicant's evidence, and shall send a copy thereof to the applicant.

(8) No further evidence may be filed, except that, in relation to any proceedings before him, the registrar may at any time if he thinks fit give leave to either party to file such evidence upon such terms as he may think fit.

(9) Upon completion of the evidence the registrar shall request the parties to state by notice to him in writing whether they wish to be heard; if any party requests to be heard the registrar shall send to the parties notice of a date for the hearing.

General note
The rule in bold type was substituted for the rule in italics by SI 1998/925, r 6.

14 Decision of registrar in opposition proceedings

(1) When the registrar has made a decision on the acceptability of an application for registration following the procedure under rule 13, he shall send the applicant and the person opposing the application written notice of it, stating the reasons for his decision.

(2) For the purpose of any appeal against the registrar's decision the date of the decision shall be the date when notice of the decision is sent under paragraph (1) above.

15 Observations on application to be sent to applicant; s 38(3)

The registrar shall send to the applicant a copy of any documents containing observations made under section 38(3).

16 Publication of registration; s 40

On the registration of the trade mark the registrar shall publish the registration, specifying the date upon which the trade mark was entered in the register.

Amendment of application

17 Amendment of application; s 39 (Form TM21)

A request for an amendment of an application to correct an error or to change the name or address of the applicant or in respect of any amendment requested after publication of the application shall be made on Form TM21.

18 Amendment of application after publication; s 39

(1) Where, pursuant to section 39, a request is made for amendment of an application which has been published and the amendment affects the representation of the trade mark or the goods or services covered by the application, the amendment or a statement of the effect of the amendment shall also be published.

(2) Notice of opposition to the amendment shall be *sent to the registrar* **filed** on Form TM7 within one month of the date on which the application as amended was published under paragraph (1) above, and shall include a statement of the grounds of objection and, in particular, how the amendments would be contrary to section 39(2).

(3) The provisions of rule 13 shall apply to proceedings relating to the opposition to the amendment of the application as they apply to proceedings relating to opposition to the registration of a trade mark.

General note
The word in bold type in para (2) was substituted for the words in italics by SI 1998/925, r 7.

Division, merger and series of marks

19 Division of application; s 41 (Form TM12)

(1) At any time before registration an applicant may send to the registrar a request on Form TM12 for a division of his application for registration (the original application) into two or more separate applications (divisional applications), indicating for each division the specification of goods or services; each divisional application shall be treated as a separate application for registration with the same filing date as the original application.

(2) Where the request to divide an application is sent after publication of the application, any objections in respect of, or opposition to, the original application shall be taken to apply to each divisional application and shall be proceeded with accordingly.

(3) Upon division of an original application in respect of which notice has been given to the registrar of particulars relating to the grant of a licence, or a security interest or any right in or under it, the notice and the particulars shall be deemed to apply in relation to each of the applications into which the original application has been divided.

20 Merger of separate applications or registrations; s 41 (Form TM17)

(1) An applicant who has made separate applications for registration of a mark may, at any time before preparations for the publication of any of the applications have been completed by the Office, request the registrar on Form TM17 to merge the separate applications into a single application.

(2) The registrar shall, if satisfied that all the applications which are the subject of the request for merger—

    (a) are in respect of the same trade mark,

    (b) bear the same date of application, and

    (c) are, at the time of the request, in the name of the same person,

merge them into a single application.

(3) The proprietor of two or more registrations of a trade mark may request the registrar on Form TM17 to merge them into a single registration; and the registrar shall, if satisfied that the registrations are in respect of the same trade mark, merge them into a single registration.

(4) Where any registration of a trade mark to be merged under paragraph (3) above is subject to a disclaimer or limitation, the merged registration shall also be restricted accordingly.

(5) Where any registration of a trade mark to be merged under paragraph (3) above has had registered in relation to it particulars relating to the grant of a licence or a security interest or any right in or under it, or of any memorandum or statement of the effect of a memorandum, the registrar shall enter in the register the same particulars in relation to the merged registration.

(6) The date of registration of the merged registration shall, where the separate registrations *bear different dates* **bear different dates of registration**, be the latest of those dates.

General note
The words in bold type in para (6) were substituted for the words in italics by SI 1998/925, r 8.

21 Registration of a series of trade marks; s 41 (Form TM12)

(1) The proprietor of a series of trade marks may apply to the registrar on Form

TM3 for their registration as a series in a single registration and there shall be included in such application a representation of each mark claimed to be in the series; and the registrar shall, if satisfied that the marks constitute a series, accept the application.

(2) At any time before preparations of publication of the application have been completed by the Office, the applicant under paragraph (1) above may request on Form TM12 the division of the application into separate applications in respect of one or more marks in that series and the registrar shall, if he is satisfied that the division requested conforms with section 41(2), divide the application accordingly.

(3) At any time the applicant for registration of a series of trade marks or the proprietor of a registered series of trade marks may request the deletion of a mark in that series, and the registrar shall delete the mark accordingly.

(4) The division of an application into one or more applications under paragraph (2) above shall be subject to the payment of a divisional fee and such application and class fees as are appropriate.

Collective and certification marks

22 Filing of regulations for collective and certification marks; Schs 1 & 2 (Form TM35)

Within nine months of the date of the application for the registration of a collective or certification mark, the applicant shall file Form TM35 accompanied by a copy of the regulations governing the use of the mark.

23 Amendment of regulations of collective and certification marks; Sch 1 para 10 and Sch 2 para 11 (Forms TM36 & TM7)

(1) An application for the amendment of the regulations governing the use of a registered collective or certification mark shall be filed on Form TM36.

(2) Where it appears expedient to the registrar that the amended regulations should be made available to the public he shall publish a notice indicating where copies of the amended regulations may be inspected.

(3) Any person may, within three months of the date of publication of the notice under paragraph (2) above, make observations to the registrar on the amendments relating to the matters referred to in paragraph 6(1) of Schedule 1 in relation to a collective mark, or, paragraph 7(1) of Schedule 2 in relation to a certification mark; the registrar shall send a copy thereof to the proprietor.

(4) Any person may, within three months of the date of publication of the notice, file notice on Form TM7 to the registrar of opposition to the amendment, accompanied by a statement of the grounds of opposition, indicating why the amended regulations do not comply with the requirements of paragraph 6(1) of Schedule 1 or, as the case may be, paragraph 7(1) of Schedule 2.

(5) The registrar shall send a copy of the notice and the statement to the proprietor and thereafter the procedure in *rule 13(2)–(8)* **paragraphs (2) and (4)–(9) of rule 13** shall apply to the proceedings as they apply to proceedings relating to opposition to an application for registration.

General note
The words in bold type in para (5) were substituted for the words in italics by SI 1998/925, r 9.

Disclaimers, limitations and alteration or surrender of registered trade mark

24 Registration subject to disclaimer or limitation; s 13

Where the applicant for registration of a trade mark or the proprietor by notice in writing sent to the registrar—

(a) disclaims any right to the exclusive use of any specified element of the trade mark, or

(b) agrees that the rights conferred by the registration shall be subject to a specified territorial or other limitation,

the registrar shall make the appropriate entry in the register and publish such disclaimer or limitation.

25 Alteration of registered trade marks; s 44 (Forms TM25 & TM7)

(1) The proprietor may request the registrar on Form TM25 for such alteration of his registered mark as is permitted under section 44; and the registrar may require such evidence by statutory declaration or otherwise as to the circumstances in which the application is made.

(2) Where, upon the request of the proprietor, the registrar proposes to allow such alteration, he shall publish the mark as altered.

(3) Any person claiming to be affected by the alteration may within three months of the date of publication of the alteration under paragraph (2) send a notice on Form TM7 to the registrar of opposition to the alteration and shall include a statement of the grounds of opposition; the registrar shall send a copy of the notice and the statement to the proprietor and thereafter the procedure in *rule 13(2)–(8)* **paragraphs (2) and (4)–(9) of rule 13** shall apply to the proceedings as they apply to proceedings relating to opposition to an application for registration.

General note
The words in bold type in para (3) were substituted for the words in italics by SI 1998/925, r 9.

26 Surrender of registered trade mark; s 45 (Forms TM22 & TM23)

(1) Subject to paragraph (2) below, the proprietor may surrender a registered trade mark, by sending notice to the registrar—

(a) on Form TM22 in respect of all the goods or services for which it is registered; or

(b) on Form TM23, in respect only of those goods or services specified by him in the notice.

(2) A notice under paragraph (1) above shall be of no effect unless the proprietor in that notice—

(a) gives the name and address of any person having a registered interest in the mark, and

(b) certifies that any such person—

(i) has been sent not less than three months' notice of the proprietor's intention to surrender the mark, or

(ii) is not affected or if affected consents thereto.

(3) The registrar shall, upon the surrender taking effect, make the appropriate entry in the register and publish the same.

Renewal and restoration

27 Reminder of renewal of registration; s 43

At any time not earlier than six months nor later than one month before the expiration of the last registration of a trade mark, the registrar shall (except where renewal has already been effected under rule 28 below) send to the registered

proprietor notice of the approaching expiration and inform him at the same time
that the registration may be renewed in the manner described in rule 28 below.

27 Reminder of renewal of registration; s 43

(1) Subject to paragraph (2) below, at any time not earlier than six months nor later
than one month before the expiration of the last registration of a trade mark, the
registrar shall (except where renewal has already been effected under rule 28
below) send to the registered proprietor notice of the approaching expiration and
inform him at the same time that the registration may be renewed in the manner
described in rule 28 below.

(2) If it appears to the registrar that a trade mark may be registered under section
40 at any time within six months before or after the date on which renewal would
be due (by reference to the date of application for registration), the registrar shall be
taken to have complied with paragraph (1) if he sends to the applicant notice
thereof within one month following the date of actual registration.

General note
The rule in bold type was substituted for the rule in italics by SI 1998/925, r 10.

28 Renewal of registration; s 43 (Form TM11)

Renewal of registration shall be effected by filing a request for renewal on Form
TM11 at any time within the period of six months ending on the date of the expiration of the registration.

29 Delayed renewal and removal of registration; s 43 (Form TM11)

(1) If on the expiration of the last registration of a trade mark, the renewal fee has
not been paid, the registrar shall publish that fact; and if, within six months from
the date of the expiration of the last registration, the request for renewal is filed on
Form TM11 accompanied by the appropriate renewal fee and additional renewal
fee, the registrar shall renew the registration without removing the mark from the
register.

(2) Where no request for renewal is filed as aforesaid, the registrar shall, subject to
rule 30 below, remove the mark from the register.

(3) Where, in the case of a mark the registration of which (by reference to the date
of application for registration) becomes due for renewal, the mark is registered at
any time within six months before the date on which renewal is due, the registration
may be renewed by the payment of—

    (a) the renewal fee within six months after the actual date of registration; or
    (b) the renewal fee and additional renewal fee within the period commencing
    on the date six months after the actual date of registration (that is to say, at
    the end of the period referred to in paragraph (a)) and ending on the date
    six months after the due date of renewal;

and, where the fees referred to in paragraph (b) are not paid within the period
specified in that paragraph the registrar shall, subject to rule 30 below, remove the
mark from the register.

    (4) Where, in the case of a mark the registration of which (by reference to the
    date of application for registration) becomes due for renewal, the mark is
    registered after the date of renewal, the registration may be renewed by the
    payment of the renewal fee within six months of the actual date of registra-
    tion; and where the renewal fee is not paid within that period the registrar
    shall, subject to rule 30 below, remove the mark from the register.

(5) The removal of the registration of a trade mark shall be published.

(3) Where a mark is due to be registered after the date on which it is due for renewal (by reference to the date of application for registration), the request for renewal shall be filed together with the renewal fee and additional renewal fee within six months after the date of actual registration.
(4) The removal of the registration of a trade mark shall be published.

General note
Paras (3), (4) in bold type were substituted for paras (3)–(5) as originally enacted (in italics) by SI 1998/925, r 11.

30 Restoration of registration; s 43 (Form TM13)
(1) Where the registrar has removed the mark from the register for failure to renew its registration in accordance with rule 29 above, he may, upon a request filed on Form TM13 within six months of the date of the removal of the mark accompanied by the appropriate renewal fee and appropriate restoration fee, restore the mark to the register and renew its registration if, having regard to the circumstances of the failure to renew, he is satisfied that it is just to do so.
(2) The restoration of the registration shall be published, with the date of restoration shown.

Revocation, invalidation and rectification

31 Procedure on application for revocation, declaration of invalidity and rectification of the register; ss 46, 47 & 64 (Forms TM26 & TM27)
(1) An application to the registrar for revocation under section 46 or declaration of invalidity under section 47 of the registration of a trade mark or for the rectification of an error or omission in the register under section 64 shall be made on Form TM26 together with a statement of the grounds on which the application is made.
(2) Where any application is made under paragraph (1) by a person other than the proprietor of the registered trade mark, the registrar shall send a copy of the application and the statement to the proprietor.
(3) Within three months of the date on which the registrar sends a copy of the application and the statement to the proprietor, the proprietor may file a counter-statement together with Form TM8 and the registrar shall send a copy thereof to the applicant:
   Provided that where an application for revocation is based on the ground of non-use under section 46(1)(a) or (b), the proprietor shall file (within the period allowed for the filing of any counter-statement) evidence of the use by him of the mark; and if he fails so to file evidence the registrar may treat his opposition to the application as having been withdrawn.
(4) Subject to paragraph (2) above and paragraphs (6) and (7) below, the provisions of rule 13 shall apply to proceedings relating to the application as they apply to opposition proceedings for the registration of a trade mark, save that, in the case of an application for revocation on the grounds of non-use under section 46(1)(a) or (b), the application shall be granted where no counter-statement is filed.
(5) Any person, other than the registered proprietor, claiming to have an interest in proceedings on an application under this rule may file an application to the registrar on From TM27 for leave to intervene, stating the nature of his interest and the registrar may, after hearing the parties concerned if so required, refuse such leave or grant leave upon such terms or conditions (including any undertaking as to costs) as he thinks fit.
(6) Any person granted leave to intervene (the intervener) shall, subject to the terms and conditions imposed in respect of the intervention, be treated as a party

for the purposes of the application of the provisions of rule 13 to the proceedings on an application under this rule.

(7) When the registrar has made a decision on the application following any opposition, intervention or proceedings held in accordance with this rule, he shall send the applicant, the person opposing the application and the intervener (if any) written notice of it, stating the reasons for his decision; and for the purposes of any appeal against the registrar's decision the date when the notice of the decision is sent shall be taken to be the date of the decision.

The register

32 Form of register; s 63(1)
The register required to be maintained by the registrar under section 63(1) need not be kept in documentary form.

33 Entry in register of particulars of registered trade marks; s 63(2) (Form TM24)
In addition to the entries in the register of registered trade marks required to be made by section 63(2)(a), there shall be entered in the register in respect of each trade mark registered therein the following particulars—

(a) the date of registration as determined in accordance with section 40(3) (that is to say, the date of the filing of the application for registration);

(b) the actual date of registration (that is to say, the date of the entry in the register);

(c) the priority date (if any) to be accorded pursuant to a claim to a right to priority made under section 35 or 36;

(d) the name and address of the proprietor;

(e) the address for service (if any) as furnished pursuant to rule 10 above;

(f) any disclaimer or limitation of rights under section 13(1)(a) or (b);

(g) any memorandum or statement of the effect of any memorandum relating to a trade mark of which the registrar has been notified on Form TM24;

(h) the goods or services in respect of which the mark is registered;

(i) where the mark is a collective or certification mark, that fact; *and*

(j) *where the mark is registered pursuant to section 5(5) with the consent of the proprietor of an earlier trade mark or other earlier right, that fact.*

(j) where the mark is registered pursuant to section 5(5) with the consent of the proprietor of an earlier trade mark or other earlier right, that fact;

(k) where the mark is registered pursuant to a transformation application, the number of the international registration and either:
(i) the date accorded to the international registration under Article 3(4), or
(ii) the date of recordal of the request for extension to the United Kingdom of the international registration under Article 3ter,
as the case may be, of the Madrid Protocol;

(l) where the mark arises from the conversion of a Community trade mark or an application for a Community trade mark, the number of any other registered trade mark from which the Community trade mark or the application for a Community trade mark claimed seniority and the earliest seniority date.

General note
The word in italics at the end of para (i) was revoked and paras (j)–(l) in bold type were substituted for para (j) as originally enacted (in italics) by SI 1998/925, r 12.

34 Entry in register of particulars of registrable transactions; s 25

Upon application made to the registrar by such person as is mentioned in section 25(1)(a) or (b) there shall be entered in the register the following particulars of registrable transactions, that is to say—

    (a) in the case of an assignment of a registered trade mark or any right in it—
        (i) the name and address of the assignee,
        (ii) the date of the assignment, and
        (iii)where the assignment is in respect of any right in the mark, a description of the right assigned;

    (b) in the case of the grant of a licence under a registered trade mark—
        (i) the name and address of the licensee,
        (ii) where the licence is an exclusive licence, that fact,
        (iii)where the licence is limited, a description of the limitation, and
        (iv)the duration of the licence if the same is or is ascertainable as a definite period;

    (c) in the case of the grant of any security interest over a registered trade mark or any right in or under it—
        (i) the name and address of the grantee,
        (ii) the nature of the interest (whether fixed or floating), and
        (iii)the extent of the security and the right in or under the mark secured;

    (d) in the case of the making by personal representatives of an assent in relation to a registered trade mark or any right in or under it—
        (i) the name and address of the person in whom the mark or any right in or under it vests by virtue of the assent, and
        (ii) the date of the assent; and

    (e) in the case of a court or other competent authority transferring a registered trade mark or any right in or under it—
        (i) the name and address of the transferee,
        (ii) the date of the order, and
        (iii)where the transfer is in respect of a right in the mark, a description of the right transferred;

and, in each case, there shall be entered the date on which the entry is made.

35 Application to register or give notice of transaction; ss 25 & 27(3) (Forms TM16, TM24, TM50 & TM51)

(1) An application to register particulars of a transaction to which section 25 applies or to give notice to the registrar of particulars of a transaction to which section 27(3) applies shall be made, subject to paragraph (2) below,

    (a) relating to an assignment or transaction other than a transaction referred to in sub-paragraphs (b) to (d) below, on form TM16;
    (b) relating to a grant of a licence, on form TM50;
    (c) relating to an amendment to, or termination of a licence, on form TM51;
    (d) relating to the grant, amendment or termination of any security interest, on form TM24; and
    (e) relating to the making by personal representatives of an assent or to an order of a court or other competent authority, on form TM24.

(2) An application under paragraph (1) above shall—

    (a) where the transaction is an assignment, be signed by or on behalf of the parties to the assignment;
    (b) where the transaction falls within sub-paragraphs (b), (c) or (d) of para-

graph (1) above, be signed by or on behalf of the grantor of the licence or security interest;

or be accompanied by such documentary evidence as suffices to establish the transaction.

(3) Where the transaction is effected by an instrument chargeable with duty, the application shall be subject to the registrar being satisfied that the instrument has been duly stamped.

(4) Where an application to give notice to the registrar has been made of particulars relating to an application for registration of a trade mark, upon registration of the trade mark, the registrar shall enter those particulars in the register.

36 Public inspection of register; s 63(3)

(1) The register shall be open for public inspection at the Office during the hours of business of the Office as published in accordance with rule 64 below.

(2) Where any portion of the register is kept otherwise than in documentary form, the right of inspection is a right to inspect the material on the register.

37 Supply of certified copies etc; s 63(3) (Form TM31R)

The registrar shall supply a certified copy or extract or uncertified copy or extract, as requested on Form TM31R, of any entry in the register.

38 Request for change of name or address in register; s 64(4) (Forms TM21 & TM33)

(1) The registrar shall, on a request made on Form TM21 by the proprietor of a registered trade mark or a licensee or any person having an interest in or charge on a registered trade mark which has been registered under rule 34, enter any change in his name or address as recorded in the register.

(2) The registrar may at any time, on a request made on Form TM33 by any person who has furnished an address for service under rule 10 above, if the address is recorded in the register, change it.

39 Removal of matter from register; s 64(5) (Form TM7)

(1) Where it appears to the registrar that any matter in the register has ceased to have effect, before removing it from the register—

    (a) he may, where he considers it appropriate, publish his intention to remove that matter, and

    (b) where any person appears to him to be affected by the removal, he shall send notice of his intention to that person.

(2) Within three months of the date on which his intention to remove the matter is published, or notice of his intention is sent, as the case may be—

    (a) any person may file notice of opposition to the removal on form TM7; and

    (b) the person to whom a notice is sent under paragraph (1)(b) above may file, in writing—

        (i) his objections, if any, to the removal, or

        (ii) a request to have his objections heard orally;

and where such opposition or objections are made, *rule 47* **rule 48** shall apply.

(3) If the registrar is satisfied after considering any objections or opposition to the removal that the matter has not ceased to have effect, he shall not remove it.

(4) Where there has been no response to the registrar's notice he may remove the matter; where representations objecting to the removal of the entry have been made

(whether in writing or orally) the registrar may, if he is of the view after considering the objections that the entry or any part thereof has ceased to have effect, remove it or, as appropriate, the part thereof.

General note
The words in bold type in para (2) were substituted for the words in italics by SI 1998/925, r 13.

Change of classification

40 Change of classification; ss 65(2) & 76(1)

(1) Subject to section 65(3), the registrar may—

(a) in order to reclassify the specification of a registered trade mark founded on Schedule 3 to one founded on Schedule 4, or
(b) consequent upon an amendment of the International Classification of Goods and Services referred to in rule 7(2) above,

make such amendments to entries on the register as he considers necessary for the purposes of reclassifying the specification of the registered trade mark.

(2) Before making any amendment to the register under paragraph (1) above the registrar shall give the proprietor of the mark written notice of his proposals for amendment and shall at the same time advise him that—

(a) he may make written objections to the proposals, within three months of the date of the notice, stating the grounds of his objections, and
(b) if no written objections are received within the period specified the registrar will publish the proposals and he will not be entitled to make any objections thereto upon such publication.

(3) If the proprietor makes no written objections within the period specified in paragraph (2)(a) above or at any time before the expiration of that period gives the registrar written notice of his intention not to make any objections, the registrar shall as soon as practicable after the expiration of that period or upon receipt of the notice publish the proposals.

(4) Where the proprietor makes written objections within the period specified in paragraph (2)(a) above, the registrar shall, as soon as practicable after he has considered the objections, publish the proposals or, where he has amended the proposals, publish the proposals as amended; and his decision shall be final and not subject to appeal.

41 Opposition to proposals; ss 65(3) & 76(1)

(1) Notice of any opposition shall be filed on Form TM7 within three months of the date of publication of the proposals under rule 40 above and there shall be stated in the notice the grounds of opposition and, in particular, how the proposed amendments would be contrary to section 65(3).

(2) The registrar may require or admit evidence directed to the questions in issue and if so requested by any person opposing the proposal give that person the opportunity to be heard thereon before deciding the matter.

(3) If no notice of opposition under paragraph (1) above is filed within the time specified, or where any opposition has been determined, the registrar shall make the amendments as proposed and shall enter in the register the date when they were made; and his decision shall be final and not subject to appeal.

Request for information, inspection of documents and confidentiality

42 Request for information; s 67(1) (Form TM31C)

A request for information relating to an application for registration or to a registered trade mark shall be made on Form TM31C.

43 Information available before publication; s 67(2)

Before publication of an application for registration the registrar shall make available for inspection by the public the application and any amendments made to it and any particulars contained in a notice given to the registrar under rule 35.

44 Inspection of documents; ss 67 & 76(1)

(1) Subject to paragraphs (2) and (3) below, the registrar shall permit all documents filed or kept at the Office in relation to a registered mark or, where an application for the registration of a trade mark has been published, in relation to that application, to be inspected.

(2) The registrar shall not be obliged to permit the inspection of any such document as is mentioned in paragraph (1) above until he has completed any procedure, or the stage in the procedure which is relevant to the document in question, which he is required or permitted to carry out under the Act or these Rules.

(3) The right of inspection under paragraph (1) above does not apply to—

(a) any document until fourteen days after it has been filed at the Office;

(b) any document prepared in the Office solely for use therein;

(c) any document sent to the Office, whether at its request or otherwise, for inspection and subsequent return to the sender;

(d) any request for information under rule 42 above;

(e) any document issued by the Office which the registrar considers should be treated as confidential;

(f) any document in respect of which the registrar issues directions under rule 45 below that it be treated as confidential.

(4) Nothing in paragraph (1) shall be construed as imposing on the registrar any duty of making available for public inspection—

(a) any document or part of a document which in his opinion disparages any person in a way likely to damage him; or

(b) any document filed with or sent to the Office before 31st October 1994.

(b) **any document or information filed at or sent to or by the Office before 31st October 1994, or**

(c) **any document or information filed at or sent to or by the Office after 31st October 1994 relating to an application for registration of a trade mark under the Trade Marks Act 1938.**

(5) No appeal shall lie from a decision of the registrar under paragraph (4) above not to make any document or part of a document available for public inspection.

General note

Para (4)(b), (c) in bold type were substituted for para (4)(b) as originally enacted (in italics) by SI 1998/925, r 14.

45 Confidential documents

(1) Where a document other than a form required by the registrar and published in accordance with rule 3 above is filed at the Office and the person filing it requests, at the time of filing or within fourteen days of the filing, that it or a specified part of it be treated as confidential, giving his reasons, the registrar may direct that it or part of it, as the case may be, be treated as confidential, and the document shall not be open to public inspection while the matter is being determined by the registrar.

(2) Where such direction has been given and not withdrawn, nothing in this rule

shall be taken to authorise or require any person to be allowed to inspect the document or part of it to which the direction relates except by leave of the registrar.

(3) The registrar shall not withdraw any direction given under this rule without prior consultation with the person at whose request the direction was given, unless the registrar is satisfied that such prior consultation is not reasonably practical.

(4) The registrar may where he considers that any document issued by the Office should be treated as confidential so direct, and upon such direction that document shall not be open to public inspection except by leave of the registrar.

(5) Where a direction is given under this rule for a document to be treated as confidential a record of the fact shall be filed with the document.

Agents

46 Proof of authorisation of agent may be required; s 82 (Form TM33)

(1) Where an agent has been authorised under section 82, the registrar may in any particular case require the personal signature or presence of the agent or the person authorising him to act as agent.

(2) Where after a person has become a party to proceedings before the registrar, he appoints an agent for the first time or appoints one agent in substitution for another, the newly appointed agent shall file Form TM33, and any act required or authorised by the Act in connection with the registration of a trade mark or any procedure relating to a trade mark may not be done by or to the newly appointed agent until on or after the date on which he files that form.

(3) The registrar may by notice in writing sent to an agent require him to produce evidence of his authority.

47 Registrar may refuse to deal with certain agents; s 88

The registrar may refuse to recognise as agent in respect of any business under the Act—

- (a) a person who has been convicted of an offence under section 84;
- (b) an individual whose name has been erased from and not restored to, or who is suspended from, the register of trade mark agents on the ground of misconduct;
- (c) a person who is found by the Secretary of State to have been guilty of such conduct as would, in the case of an individual registered in that register, render him liable to have his name erased from it on the ground of misconduct;
- (d) a partnership or body corporate of which one of the partners or directors is a person whom the registrar could refuse to recognise under paragraph (a), (b) or (c) above.

Decision of registrar, evidence and costs

48 Decisions of registrar to be taken after hearing

(1) Without prejudice to any provisions of the Act or these Rules requiring the registrar to hear any party to proceedings under the Act or these Rules, or to give such party an opportunity to be heard, the registrar shall, before taking any decision on any matter under the Act or these Rules which is or may be adverse to any party to any proceedings before him, give that party an opportunity to be heard.

(2) The registrar shall give that party at least fourteen days' notice of the time when he may be heard unless that party consents to shorter notice.

49 Evidence in proceedings before registrar; s 69

(1) Where under these Rules evidence may be admitted by the registrar in any proceedings before him, it shall be by the filing of a statutory declaration or affidavit.

(2) The registrar may in any particular case take oral evidence in lieu of or in addition to such evidence and shall, unless he otherwise directs, allow any witness to be cross-examined on his statutory declaration, affidavit or oral evidence.

50 Making and subscription of statutory declaration or affidavit

(1) Any statutory declaration or affidavit filed under the Act or these Rules shall be made and subscribed as follows—

    (a) in the United Kingdom, before any justice of the peace or any commissioner or other officer authorised by law in any part of the United Kingdom to administer an oath for the purpose of any legal proceedings;

    (b) in any other part of Her Majesty's dominions or in the Republic of Ireland, before any court, judge, justice of the peace or any officer authorised by law to administer an oath there for the purpose of any legal proceedings; and

    (c) elsewhere, before a commissioner for oaths, notary public, judge or magistrate.

(2) Any document purporting to have affixed, impressed or subscribed thereto or thereon the seal or signature of any person authorised by paragraph (1) above to take a declaration may be admitted by the registrar without proof of the genuineness of the seal or signature, or of the official character of the person or his authority to take the declaration.

51 Registrar's power to require documents, information or evidence

At any stage of any proceedings before the registrar, he may direct that such documents, information or evidence as he may reasonably require shall be filed within such period as he may specify.

52 Registrar to have power of an official referee; s 69

(1) The registrar shall in relation to the examination of witnesses on oath and the discovery and production of documents have all the powers of an official referee of the Supreme Court.

(2) The rules applicable to the attendance of witnesses before such a referee shall apply in relation to the attendance of witnesses in proceedings before the registrar.

53 Hearings before registrar to be in public

(1) The hearing before the registrar of any dispute between two or more parties relating to any matter in connection with an application for the registration of a mark or a registered mark shall be in public unless the registrar, after consultation with those parties who appear in person or are represented at the hearing, otherwise directs.

(2) Nothing in this rule shall prevent a member of the Council on Tribunals or of its Scottish Committee from attending a hearing in his capacity as such.

54 Costs of proceedings; s 68

The registrar may, in any proceedings before him under the Act or these Rules, by order award to any party such costs as he may consider reasonable, and direct how and by what parties they are to be paid.

55 Security for costs; s 68

(1) The registrar may require any person who is a party in any proceedings before him under the Act or these Rules to give security for costs in relation to those proceedings; and he may require security for the costs of any appeal from his decision.
(2) In default of such security being given, the registrar, in the case of the proceedings before him, or, in the case of an appeal, the person appointed under section 76 may treat the party in default as having withdrawn his application, opposition, objection or intervention, as the case may be.

56 Decision of registrar (Form TM5)

(1) When, in any proceedings before him, the registrar has made a decision following a hearing or, if a hearing has not been requested, after considering any submission in writing, he shall send notice of his decision in writing to each party to the proceedings, and for the purpose of any appeal against the registrar's decision, subject to paragraph (2) below, the date of the decision shall be the date when the notice is sent.

(1) When, in any proceedings before him, the registrar has made a decision, he shall send to each party to the proceedings written notice of it, and for the purposes of any appeal against that decision, subject to paragraph (2) below, the date on which the notice is sent shall be taken to be the date of the decision.
(2) Where a statement of the reasons for the decision is not included in the notice sent under paragraph (1) above, any party may, within one month of the date on which the notice was sent to him, request the registrar on form TM5 to send him a statement of the reasons for the decision and upon such request the registrar shall send such a statement; and the date on which that statement is sent shall be deemed to be the date of the registrar's decision for the purpose of any appeal against it.

General note
Para (1) in bold type was substituted for para (1) in italics by SI 1998/925, r 15.

Appeals

57 Appeal to person appointed; s 76

(1) Notice of appeal to the person appointed under section 76 shall be sent to the registrar within one month of the date of the registrar's decision which is the subject of the appeal accompanied by a statement in writing of the appellant's grounds of appeal and of his case in support of the appeal.
(2) The registrar shall send the notice and the statement to the person appointed.
(3) Where any person other than the appellant was a party to the proceedings before the registrar in which the decision appealed against was made, the registrar shall send to that person a copy of the notice and the statement.

58 Determination whether appeal should be referred to court; s 76(3)

(1) Within one month of the date on which the notice of appeal is sent by the registrar under rule 57(3) above;

(a) the registrar, or
(b) any person who was a party to the proceedings in which the decision appealed against was made,

may request that the person appointed refer the appeal to the court.
(2) Where the registrar requests that the appeal be referred to the court, he shall send a copy of the request to each party to the proceedings.
(3) A request under paragraph (1)(b) above shall be sent to the registrar; the regis-

trar shall send it to the person appointed and shall send a copy of the request to any other party to the proceedings.

(4) Within one month of the date on which a copy of a request is sent by the registrar under paragraph (2) or (3) above, the person to whom it is sent may make representations as to whether the appeal should be referred to the court.

(5) In any case where it appears to the person appointed that a point of general legal importance is involved in the appeal, he shall send to the registrar and to every party to the proceedings in which the decision appealed against was made, notice thereof.

(6) Within one month of the date on which a notice is sent under paragraph (5) above, the person to whom it was sent may make representations as to whether the appeal should be referred to the court.

59 Hearing of appeal; s 76(4)

(1) Where the person appointed does not refer the appeal to the court, he shall send notice of the time and place appointed for the hearing of the appeal—

(a) where no person other than the appellant was a party to the proceedings in which the decision appealed against was made, to the registrar and to the appellant, and

(b) in any other case, to the registrar and to each person who was a party to those proceedings.

(2) The provisions of rule 48(2) and rules 49 to 55 shall apply to the person appointed and to proceedings before the person appointed as they apply to the registrar and to proceedings before the registrar.

(3) The person appointed shall send a copy of his decision, with a statement of his reasons therefor, to the registrar and to each person who was a party to the proceedings before him.

Correction of irregularities, calculation and extension of time

60 Correction of irregularities of procedure

(1) Any irregularity in procedure in or before the Office or the registrar may be rectified, subject to paragraph (2) below, on such terms as he may direct.

(2) In the case of an irregularity or prospective irregularity—

(a) which consists of a failure to comply with any limitation as to times or periods specified in the Act, these Rules or the old law as that law continues to apply and which has occurred or appears to the registrar as likely to occur in the absence of a direction under this rule, and

(b) which is attributable wholly or in part to an error, default or omission on the part of the Office or the registrar and which it appears to him should be rectified,

he may direct that the time or period in question shall be altered in such manner as he may specify.

(3) Paragraph (2) above is without prejudice to the registrar's power to extend any time or periods under rule 62 below.

60 Correction of irregularities of procedure

Subject to rule 62 below, any irregularity in procedure in or before the Office or the registrar, may be rectified on such terms as the registrar may direct.

General note
The rule in bold type was substituted for the rule in italics by SI 1998/925, r 16.

61 Calculation of times and periods

(1) Where, on any day, there is—

  (a) a general interruption or subsequent dislocation in the postal services of the United Kingdom, or
  (b) an event or circumstances causing an interruption in the normal operation of the Office,

the registrar may certify the day as being one on which there is an 'interruption' and, where any period of time specified in the Act or these Rules for the giving, making or filing of any notice, application or other document expires on a day so certified the period shall be extended to the first day next following (not being an excluded day) which is not so certified.

(2) Any certificate of the registrar given pursuant to this rule shall be posted in the Office.

(3) If in any particular case the registrar is satisfied that the failure to give, make or file any notice, application or other document within any period of time specified in the Act or these Rules for such giving, making or filing was wholly or mainly attributable to a failure or undue delay in the postal services in the United Kingdom, the registrar may, if he thinks fit, extend the period so that it ends on the day of the receipt by the addressee of the notice, application or other document (or, if the day of such receipt is an excluded day, on the first following day which is not an excluded day), upon such notice to other parties and upon such terms as he may direct.

(4) In this rule 'excluded day' means a day which is not a business day of the Office under the registrar's direction pursuant to section 80, as published in accordance with rule 64 below.

62 Alteration of time limits (Form TM9)

(1) The time or periods—

  (a) prescribed by these Rules, other than the times or periods prescribed by the rules mentioned in paragraph (3) below, or
  (b) specified by the registrar for doing any act or taking any proceedings,

may, at the request of the person or party concerned, be extended by the registrar as he thinks fit, upon such notice to any other person or party affected and upon such terms as he may direct. **subject to paragraph (2) below, may, at the written request of the person or party concerned, be extended by the registrar as he thinks fit and upon such terms as he may direct.**

(2) A request for the extension of a period prescribed by these Rules which is filed after the application has been published under rule 12 above shall be on Form TM9 and shall in any other case be on that form if the registrar so directs.

(2) Where a request for the extension of a time or periods prescribed by these Rules—

  (a) is sought in respect of a time or periods prescribed by rules 13, 18, 23, or 25, the party seeking the extension shall send a copy of the request to each person party to the proceedings;
  (b) is filed after the application has been published under rule 12 above, the request shall be on Form TM9 and shall in any other case be on

that form if the registrar so directs.

(3) The rules excepted from paragraph (1) above are rule 10(6) (failure to file address for service), rule 11 (deficiencies in application), rule 13(1) (time for filing opposition), rule 13(2) (time for filing counter-statement), rule 29 (delayed renewal) and rule 30 (restoration of registration).

(3) The rules excepted from paragraph (1) above are rule 10(6) (failure to file address for service), rule 11 (deficiencies in application), rule 13(1) (time for filing opposition), rule 13(2) (time for filing counter-statement), rule 23(4) (time for filing opposition), rule 25(3) (time for filing opposition), rule 29 (delayed renewal), rule 30 (restoration of registration), and rule 41 (time for filing opposition).

(4) Subject to paragraph (5) below, a request for extension under paragraph (1) above shall be made before the time or period in question has expired.

(5) Where the request for extension is made after the time or period has expired, the registrar may, at his discretion, extend the period or time if he is satisfied with the explanation for the delay in requesting the extension *and it appears to him that any extension would not disadvantage any other person or party affected by it* **and it appears to him to be just and equitable to do so.**

(6) Where the period within which any party to any proceedings before the registrar may file evidence under these Rules is to begin upon the expiry of any period in which any other party may file evidence and that other party notifies the registrar that he does not wish to file any, or any further, evidence the registrar may direct that the period within which the first mentioned party may file evidence shall begin on such date as may be specified in the direction and shall notify all parties to the dispute of that date.

(7) Without prejudice to the above, in the case of any irregularity or prospective irregularity in or before the Office or the registrar which—

(a) consists of a failure to comply with any limitation as to times or periods specified in the Act, these Rules or the old law as that law continues to apply and which has occurred or appears to the registrar as likely to occur in the absence of a direction under this rule, and

(b) is attributable wholly or in part to an error, default or omission on the part of the Office or the registrar and which it appears to him should be rectified,

he may direct that the time or period in question shall be altered in such manner as he may specify upon such terms as he may direct.

General note
The words in bold type were substituted for the words in italics in paras (1) and (5), paras (2) and (3) in bold type were substituted for paras (2) and (3) in italics and para (7) in bold type was added by SI 1998/925, r 17.

Filing of documents, hours of business, Trade Marks Journal and translations

63 Filing of documents by electronic means
The registrar may, at his discretion, permit as an alternative to the sending by post or delivery of the application, notice or other document in legible form the filing of the application, notice or other document by electronic means subject to such terms or conditions as he may specify either generally by published notice or in any particular case by written notice to the person desiring to file any such documents by such means.

64 Directions on hours of business; s 80
Any directions given by the registrar under section 80 specifying the hours of busi-

ness of the Office and business days of the Office shall be published and posted in the Office.

65 Trade Marks Journal; s 81

The registrar shall publish a journal, entitled 'The Trade Marks Journal', containing particulars of any application for the registration of a trade mark (including a representation of the mark), such information as is required to be published under these Rules and such other information as the registrar thinks fit.

66 Translations

(1) Where any document or part thereof which is in a language other than English is filed or sent to the registrar in pursuance of the Act or these Rules, the registrar may require that there be furnished a translation into English of the document or that part, verified to the satisfaction of the registrar as corresponding to the original text.

(2) The registrar may refuse to accept any translation which is in his opinion inaccurate and thereupon another translation of the document in question verified as aforesaid shall be furnished.

Transitional provisions and revocations

67 Pending applications for registration; Sch 3, para 10(2)

Where an application for registration of a mark made under the old law is advertised on or after 31st October 1994, the period within which notice of opposition may be filed shall be three months from the date of advertisement, and such period shall not be extendible.

68 Form for conversions of pending application; Sch 3, para 11(2)

A notice to the registrar under paragraph 11(2) of Schedule 3 to the Act, claiming to have the registrability of the mark determined in accordance with the provisions of the Act, shall be in the form set out in Schedule 2 to these Rules.

General note
This rule was revoked by SI 1998/925, r 18.

69 Revocation of previous Rules

(1) The rules specified in Schedule 1 are hereby revoked.

(2) Except as provided by rule 67 above, where—

    (a) immediately before these Rules come into force, any time or period prescribed by the Rules hereby revoked has effect in relation to any act or proceeding and has not expired, and

    (b) the corresponding time or period prescribed by these Rules would have expired or would expire earlier,

the time or period prescribed by those Rules and not by these Rules shall apply to that act or proceeding.

SCHEDULE 1
Revocations

Rule 69

Rules revoked   **Reference**

The Trade Marks and Service Marks Rules 1986   SI 1986/1319

The Trade Marks and Service Marks (Amendment) Rules 1988	SI 1988/1112
The Trade Marks and Service Marks (Amendment) Rules 1989	SI 1989/1117
The Trade Marks and Service Marks (Amendment) Rules 1990	SI 1990/1459
The Trade Marks and Service Marks (Amendment) (No 2) Rules 1990	SI 1990/1799
The Trade Marks and Service Marks (Amendment) Rules 1991	SI 1991/1431
The Trade Marks and Service Marks (Amendment) Rules 1994	SI 1994/2549

Schedule 2

Rule 68

Form TM15
Notice under Schedule 3, paragraph 11 of the Act: Claim to have registrability of a mark applied for before 31st October 1994 determined under the Act (Conversion of application)

1
Your reference

2
Give details of the application you made under the Trade Marks Act 1938
Number   Class

3
Full name, address and postcode of the applicant
Trade Marks ADP number (if you know it)

4
Name of agent (if appropriate) address for service in the United Kingdom which all correspondence should be sent to (including postcode)
Trade Marks ADP number (if you know it)
I claim to have the registrability of the mark determined in accordance with the provisions of the Trade Marks Act 1994. I acknowledge that this notice is irrevocable.
Signature
Name (block capitals)
Date
Name and daytime telephone number of person we should contact
State the number of any sheets attached to this form
Reminder
You cannot amend a mark under the 1994 Act. If you want to amend the mark you must file form TM21 before or with this form.
The new filing date of your converted application will be the 31st October 1994, which is the commencement date of the 1994 Act.

Form TM15

General note
This Schedule was revoked by SI 1998/925, r 18.

SCHEDULE 3
Classification of Goods (Pre-1938)

Rule 7(1)

Class 1 Chemical substances used in manufactures, photography, or philosophical research, and anti-corrosives.

Class 2 Chemical substances used for agricultural, horticultural, veterinary and sanitary purposes.

Class 3 Chemical substances prepared for use in medicine and pharmacy.

Class 4 Raw, or partly prepared, vegetable, animal, and mineral substances used in manufactures, not included in other Classes.

Class 5 Unwrought and partly wrought metals used in manufacture.

Class 6 Machinery of all kinds, and parts of machinery, except agricultural and horticultural machines and their parts included in Class 7.

Class 7 Agricultural and horticultural machinery, and parts of such machinery.

Class 8 Philosophical instruments, scientific instruments, and apparatus for useful purposes; instruments and apparatus for teaching.

Class 9 Musical instruments.

Class 10 Horological instruments.

Class 11 Instruments, apparatus, and contrivances, not medicated, for surgical or curative purposes, or in relation to the health of men or animals.

Class 12 Cutlery and edge tools.

Class 13 Metal goods, not included in other Classes.

Class 14 Goods of precious metals and jewellery, and imitations of such goods and jewellery.

Class 15 Glass.

Class 16 Porcelain and earthenware.

Class 17 Manufactures from mineral and other substances for building or decoration.

Class 18 Engineering, architectural, and building contrivances.

Class 19 Arms, ammunition, and stores, not included in Class 20.

Class 20 Explosive substances.

Class 21 Naval architectural contrivances and naval equipments not included in other Classes.

Class 22 Carriages.

Class 23 (a) Cotton yarn; (b) Sewing cotton.

Class 24 Cotton piece goods.

Class 25 Cotton goods not included in other Classes.

Class 26 Linen and hemp yarn and thread.

Class 27 Linen and hemp piece goods.

Class 28 Linen and hemp goods not included in other Classes.

Class 29 Jute yarns and tissues, and other articles made of jute, not included in other Classes.

Class 30 Silk, spun, thrown, or sewing.

Class 31 Silk piece goods.

Class 32 Silk goods not included in other Classes.

Class 33 Yarns of wool, worsted, or hair.

Class 34 Cloths and stuffs of wool, worsted, or hair.

Class 35 Woollen and worsted and hair goods, not included in other Classes.

Class 36 Carpets, floor-cloth, and oil-cloth.

Class 37 Leather, skins unwrought and wrought, and articles made of leather not included in other Classes.

Class 38 Articles of clothing.

Class 39 Paper (except paper hangings), stationery, and bookbinding.

Class 40 Goods manufactured from india-rubber and gutta-percha not included in other Classes.

Class 41 Furniture and upholstery.

Class 42 Substances used as food or as ingredients in food.

Class 43 Fermented liquors and spirits.

Class 44 Mineral and aerated waters, natural and artificial, including ginger beer.

Class 45 Tobacco, whether manufactured or unmanufactured.

Class 46 Seeds for agricultural and horticultural purposes.

Class 47 Candles, common soap, detergents; illuminating, heating, or lubricating oils; matches; and starch, blue, and other preparations for laundry purposes.

Class 48 Perfumery (including toilet articles, preparations for the teeth and hair, and perfumed soap).

Class 49 Games of all kinds and sporting articles not included in other Classes.

Class 50 Miscellaneous:—

    (1) Goods manufactured from ivory, bone or wood, not included in other Classes.

    (2) Goods manufactured from straw or grass, not included in other Classes.

    (3) Goods manufactured from animal and vegetable substances, not included in other Classes.

    (4) Tobacco pipes.

    (5) Umbrellas, walking sticks, brushes and combs for the hair.

    (6) Furniture cream, plate powder.

    (7) Tarpaulins, tents, rick-cloths, rope (jute or hemp), twine.

    (8) Buttons of all kinds other than of precious metal or imitations thereof.

    (9) Packing and hose.

    (10) Other goods not included in the foregoing Classes.

SCHEDULE 4
Classification of Goods and Services

Rule 7(2)

Goods

Class 1 Chemicals used in industry, science and photography, as well as in agriculture, horticulture and forestry; unprocessed artificial resins, unprocessed plastics; manures; fire extinguishing compositions; tempering and soldering preparations; chemical substances for preserving foodstuffs; tanning substances; adhesives used in industry.

Class 2 Paints, varnishes, lacquers; preservatives against rust and against deterioration of wood; colorants; mordants; raw natural resins; metals in foil and powder form for painters, decorators, printers and artists.

Class 3 Bleaching preparations and other substances for laundry use; cleaning, polishing, scouring and abrasive preparations; soaps; perfumery, essential oils, cosmetics, hair lotions; dentifrices.

Class 4 Industrial oils and greases; lubricants; dust absorbing, wetting and binding compositions; fuels (including motor spirit) and illuminants; candles, wicks.

Class 5 Pharmaceutical, veterinary and sanitary preparations; dietetic substances adapted for medical use, food for babies; plasters, materials for dressings; material for stopping teeth, dental wax; disinfectants; preparations for destroying vermin; fungicides, herbicides.

Class 6 Common metals and their alloys; metal building materials; transportable buildings of metal; materials of metal for railway tracks; non-electric cables and wires of common metal; ironmongery, small items of metal hardware; pipes and tubes of metal; safes; goods of common metal not included in other classes; ores.

Class 7 Machines and machine tools; motors and engines (except for land vehi-

cles); machine coupling and transmission components (except for land vehicles); agricultural implements; incubators for eggs.

Class 7 Machines and machine tools; motors and engines (except for land vehicles); machine coupling and transmission components (except for land vehicles); agricultural implements (other than hand operated); incubators for eggs;

Class 8 Hand tools and implements (hand operated); cutlery; side arms; razors.

Class 9 Scientific, nautical, surveying, electric, photographic, cinematographic, optical, weighing, measuring, signalling, checking (supervision), life-saving and teaching apparatus and instruments; apparatus for recording, transmission or reproduction of sound or images; magnetic data carriers, recording discs; automatic vending machines and mechanisms for coin-operated apparatus; cash registers, calculating machines, data processing equipment and computers; fire-extinguishing apparatus.

Class 10 Surgical, medical, dental and veterinary apparatus and instruments, artificial limbs, eyes and teeth; orthopaedic articles; suture materials.

Class 11 Apparatus for lighting, heating, steam generating, cooking, refrigerating, drying, ventilating, water supply and sanitary purposes.

Class 12 Vehicles; apparatus for locomotion by land, air or water.

Class 13 Firearms; ammunition and projectiles; explosives; fireworks.

Class 14 Precious metals and their alloys and goods in precious metals or coated therewith, not included in other classes; jewellery, precious stones; horological and chronometric instruments.

Class 15 Musical instruments.

Class 16 Paper, cardboard and goods made from these materials, not included in other classes; printed matter; bookbinding material; photographs; stationery; adhesives for stationery or household purposes; artists' materials; paint brushes; typewriters and office requisites (except furniture); instructional and teaching material (except apparatus); plastic materials for packaging (not included in other classes); playing cards; printers' type; printing blocks.

Class 17 Rubber, gutta-percha, gum, asbestos, mica and goods made from these materials and not included in other classes; plastics in extruded form for use in manufacture; packing, stopping and insulating materials; flexible pipes, not of metal.

Class 18 Leather and imitations of leather, and goods made of these materials and not included in other classes; animal skins, hides; trunks and travelling bags; umbrellas, parasols and walking sticks; whips, harness and saddlery.

Class 19 Building materials (non-metallic); non-metallic rigid pipes for building; asphalt, pitch and bitumen; non-metallic transportable buildings; monuments, not of metal.

Class 20 Furniture, mirrors, picture frames; goods (not included in other classes) of wood, cork, reed, cane, wicker, horn, bone, ivory, whalebone, shell, amber, mother-of-pearl, meerschaum and substitutes for all these materials, or of plastics.

Class 21 Household or kitchen utensils and containers (not of precious metal or coated therewith); combs and sponges; brushes (except paint brushes); brush-making materials; articles for cleaning purposes; steelwool; unworked or semi-worked glass (except glass used in building); glassware, porcelain and earthenware not included in other classes.

Class 22 Ropes, string, nets, tents, awnings, tarpaulins, sails, sacks and bags (not included in other classes); padding and stuffing materials (except of rubber or plastics); raw fibrous textile materials.

Class 23 Yarns and threads, for textile use.

Class 24 Textiles and textile goods, not included in other classes; bed and table covers.

Class 25 Clothing, footwear, headgear.

Class 26 Lace and embroidery, ribbons and braid; buttons, hooks and eyes, pins and needles; artificial flowers.

Class 27 Carpets, rugs, mats and matting, linoleum and other materials for covering existing floors; wall hangings (non-textile).

Class 28 Games and playthings; gymnastic and sporting articles not included in other classes; decorations for Christmas trees.

Class 29 Meat, fish, poultry and game; meat extracts; preserved, dried and cooked fruits and vegetables; jellies, jams, fruit sauces; eggs, milk and milk products; edible oils and fats.

Class 30 Coffee, tea, cocoa, sugar, rice, tapioca, sago, artificial coffee; flour and preparations made from cereals, bread, pastry and confectionery, ices; honey, treacle; yeast, baking-powder; salt, mustard; vinegar, sauces (condiments); spices; ice.

Class 31 Agricultural, horticultural and forestry products and grains not included in other classes; live animals; fresh fruits and vegetables; seeds, natural plants and flowers; foodstuffs for animals, malt.

Class 32 Beers; mineral and aerated waters and other non-alcoholic drinks; fruit drinks and fruit juices; syrups and other preparations for making beverages.

Class 33 Alcoholic beverages (except beers).

Class 34 Tobacco; smokers' articles; matches.

Services

Class 35 Advertising; business management; business administration; office functions.

Class 36 Insurance; financial affairs; monetary affairs; real estate affairs.

Class 37 Building construction; repair; installation services.

Class 38 Telecommunications.

Class 39 Transport; packaging and storage of goods; travel arrangement.

Class 40 Treatment of materials.

Class 41 Education; providing of training; entertainment; sporting and cultural activities.

Class 42 Providing of food and drink; temporary accommodation; medical, hygienic and beauty care; veterinary and agricultural services; legal services; scientific and industrial research; computer programming; services that cannot be placed in other classes.

General note
Class 7 in bold type was substituted for Class 7 in italics by SI 1998/925, r 19.

TRADE MARKS (CUSTOMS) REGULATIONS 1994
(SI 1994/2625)
Made 11th October 1994

1 These Regulations may be cited as the Trade Marks (Customs) Regulations 1994 and shall come into force on 31st October 1994.

2 If notice is given under section 89(1) of The Trade Marks Act 1994 by the proprietor or licensee of a registered trade mark in respect of certain goods it shall be in the form set out in the Schedule to these Regulations or a form to the like effect approved by the Commissioners; and separate notices shall be given in respect of each arrival of such goods.

3 A fee of £30 (plus value added tax) in respect of each notice shall be paid to the Commissioners at the time it is given.

4 The person giving the notice shall give to the Commissioners such security or further security within such time and in such manner, whether by deposit of a sum of money or guarantee, as the Commissioners may require, in respect of any liability or expense which they may incur in consequence of the notice by reason of the detention of any goods or anything done to goods so detained: and if such security or further security is not given within the time specified by the Commissioners, then (but without prejudice to the operation of regulation 5 below) the notice shall have no effect.

5 In every case, whether any security or further security is given or not, the person who has given the notice shall keep the Commissioners indemnified against all such liability and expense as is mentioned in regulation 4 above.

6 (1)   The person giving the notice shall, either on giving notice or when the goods are imported, furnish the Commissioners with the certificate of registration (or a copy of it) issued by the Registrar of Trade Marks on the registration of the trade mark specified in the notice, together with evidence that such registration was duly renewed at all such times as it may have expired.
(2) If such a certificate or copy and, where applicable, evidence of renewal is not furnished in accordance with paragraph (1) above then the goods shall not be detained, or, if detained, shall be released, and (but without prejudice to the operation of regulation 5 above) any notice given in respect of them shall have no effect.

7 . . .

General note
This regulation revokes the Trade Marks (Customs) Regulations 1970, SI 1970/212.

SCHEDULE
Notice Under Section 89 Trade Marks Act 1994 Requesting Infringing Goods, Material or Articles to be Treated as Prohibited Goods

Regulation 2
Please read these notes before completing this notice

1 This notice may only be given by the proprietor of a registered trade mark, or a licensee. A separate notice must be given in respect of each consignment.

2 Please note that in Part 3 it is not mandatory to provide details other than the time and place of expected arrival of infringing goods but it will greatly increase the prospect of intercepting the consignment concerned if all the details requested are given.

3 A fee of £30 (plus VAT) is payable for each notice given. Please enclose a cheque for the required amount, made payable to 'Commissioners of Customs and Excise'.

4 A copy of the certificate of registration for the trade mark, as well as the certificate of renewal (where applicable), is to be enclosed with the notice, **or** submitted when the goods are imported.

5 The person who has given notice shall keep the Commissioners of Customs and Excise indemnified against any liability or expense which they may incur in consequence of the notice by reason of the detention of any goods or anything done to goods detained. The person giving the notice may be required to provide a security to cover this indemnity.

1   Person giving notice

I/We (delete as necessary)..

Full name of signatory in BLOCK LETTERS

give notice to the Commissioners of Customs and Excise that

....

Name and address of proprietor or licensee in BLOCK LETTERS

....

is the proprietor/licensee (delete as necessary) of a trade mark registered in the United Kingdom and that infringing goods, material or articles are expected to arrive in the United Kingdom, and I/we (delete as necessary) request that they be treated as prohibited goods.

2   Details of infringing goods, material or articles

Trade mark...

Infringing goods, material or articles ....

Quantity ....

Commodity...

Code(s) ....

3   Details of expected importation

Place of importation ....

Method of importation ....

Please include details of ship, aircraft or vehicle, where known

Expected dateof arrival...

Country oforigin ....

Country of

consignment ....

Importer's

details ....

Please include VAT number, if known

Consignor's

details ....

4 Declaration

I declare that the information given by me in this notice is true.

Signature ....

(Sole Proprietor/Partner/Director/Company Secretary/Duly Authorised Person
(delete as necessary))

Date ....

5 Submission of notice
Please send the completed notice, fee and copies of relevant certificates to:
HM Customs and Excise
CD3A
New King's Beam House
22 Upper Ground
London SE1 9PJ

TRADE MARKS (CLAIMS TO PRIORITY FROM RELEVANT COUNTRIES)
ORDER 1994
(SI 1994/2803)
(As amended by the Trade Marks (Claims to Priority from Relevant Countries) (Amendment) Order 1995 (SI 1995/2997))
Made 2nd November 1994‡

This Order may be cited as the Trade Marks (Claims to Priority from Relevant Countries) Order 1994 and shall come into force on 5th December 1994.

2 In this Order—
'the Act' means the Trade Marks Act 1994;
'duly filed' means a filing which is adequate to establish the date on which the application was filed in the relevant country in question, whatever may be the subsequent fate of the application; and
'relevant country' means any country or territory specified in the Schedule to this Order.

3 A person who has duly filed an application for the protection of a trade mark in a relevant country shall have a right to priority, for the purpose of registering the same trade mark under the Act for some or all of the same goods or services, for a period of six months from the date of filing of the application in that country.

4 Where the application for registration under the Act is made within the aforesaid period of six months—
(a) the relevant date for the purpose of establishing which rights take precedence shall be the date of the filing of the application in the relevant country, and
(b) the registrability of the trade mark shall not be affected by any use of the mark in the United Kingdom in the period between that date and the date of the application under the Act.

5 A subsequent application concerning the same subject as the first application, duly filed in the same relevant country, shall be considered the first application to be filed in that country (of which the filing date shall be the starting date of the period of priority) if at the time of the subsequent application—

    (a) the previous application has been withdrawn, abandoned or refused, without having been laid open to public inspection and without leaving any rights outstanding, and

    (b) it has not yet served as a basis for claiming a right of priority.

6 A previous application may not serve as a basis for claiming a right of priority where a subsequent application is considered, in accordance with article 5 above, as the first application to be duly filed.

7 A right to priority conferred by this Order—

    (a) shall (unless otherwise stated in the application) vest in the person filing the application or his successor in title; and

    (b) may be assigned or otherwise transmitted, either with the application or independently.

8 (1)   Where a right to priority is claimed by reason of an application to which this Order relates, particulars of that claim shall be included in the application for registration filed under the Act and, unless a certificate as is referred to in paragraph (2) below is filed with the application, such particulars shall include the relevant country and the date of filing.

(2) There shall be filed within three months of the filing of the application for registration under the Act a certificate by the registering or other competent authority of the relevant country certifying, or verifying to the satisfaction of the registrar—

    (a) the date of the filing of the application,

    (b) the relevant country or registering or competent authority,

    (c) the representation of the mark, and

    (d) the goods or services covered by the application.

[SCHEDULE
Relevant Countries

Article 2
Antigua and Barbuda
Bahrain
Belize
Bolivia
Botswana
Brunei Darussalam
Colombia
Djibouti
Dominica
Ecuador
Guatemala
Hong Kong
India
Jamaica
Kuwait
Macau
Maldives
Mozambique
Myanmar
Namibia

Nicaragua
Pakistan
Sierra Leone
Thailand]

General note
The Schedule was substituted by SI 1995/2997, art 2, Schedule.

OLYMPIC SYMBOL ETC (PROTECTION) ACT 1995 (COMMENCEMENT) ORDER 1995
(SI 1995/2472)
Made 19th September 1995
The Secretary of State in exercise of the powers conferred on her by section 19(2) of the Olympic Symbol etc (Protection) Act 1995 and of all other powers enabling her in that behalf hereby makes the following Order: —

1 This Order may be cited as The Olympic Symbol etc (Protection) Act 1995 (Commencement) Order 1995.

2 The Olympic Symbol etc (Protection) Act 1995 shall come into force on 20th September 1995.

[OLYMPICS ASSOCIATION RIGHT (APPOINTMENT OF PROPRIETOR) ORDER 1995
(SI 1995/2473)
Made 20th September 1995
The Secretary of State in exercise of the powers conferred on her by section 1(2) of the Olympic Symbol etc (Protection) Act 1995 and of all other powers enabling her in that behalf hereby makes the following Order: —

1 Citation and commencement
This Order may be cited as The Olympics Association Right (Appointment of Proprietor) Order 1995 and shall come into force on 18th October 1995.

2 Appointment of the proprietor of the Olympics association right
The Secretary of State hereby appoints The British Olympic Association (a company limited by guarantee) whose registered office is at 1 Wandsworth Plain, Wandsworth, London SW18 for the purposes of section 1(2) of the Olympic Symbol etc (Protection) Act 1995.

COMMUNITY TRADE MARK (FEES) REGULATIONS 1995
(SI 1995/3175)
Made 5th December 1995
The Secretary of State, in exercise of the powers conferred by section 52 of the Trade Marks Act 1994, of the power conferred on him by the Department of Trade and Industry (Fees) Order 1988, and of all other powers enabling him in that behalf, hereby makes the following Regulations: —

1 These Regulations may be cited as the Community Trade Mark (Fees) Regulations 1995 and shall come into force on 1st January 1996.

2 Where, pursuant to Article 25 of the Community Trade Mark Regulation, an application for a Community trade mark is filed at the Patent Office, the fee to be paid shall be £15.00.

OLYMPICS ASSOCIATION RIGHT (INFRINGEMENT PROCEEDINGS) REGULATIONS 1995
(SI 1995/3325)
Made 20th December 1995
The Secretary of State for National Heritage as respects England, Wales and Northern Ireland and the Secretary of State for Scotland as respects Scotland, in exercise of the powers conferred on them by section 7(1) of the Olympic Symbol etc (Protection) Act 1995 and of all other powers enabling them in that behalf, hereby make the following Regulations:—

1 Citation, commencement and interpretation
(1) These Regulations may be cited as The Olympics Association Right (Infringement Proceedings) Regulations 1995 and shall come into force on 12th January 1996.
(2) In these Regulations the expression 'the court' shall, unless the context otherwise requires, mean—
    (a) in England and Wales and Northern Ireland, the High Court, and
    (b) in Scotland, the Court of Session.

2 Order for erasure &c of controlled representations
(1) Where a person is found to have infringed the Olympics association right the court may make an order requiring him—
    (a) to cause the offending controlled representation to be erased, removed or obliterated from any infringing goods, material or articles in his possession, custody or control, or
    (b) if it is not reasonably practicable for the offending controlled representation to be erased, removed or obliterated, to secure the destruction of the infringing goods, material or articles in question.
(2) If an order under paragraph (1) above is not complied with, or it appears to the court likely that such an order would not be complied with, the court may order that the infringing goods, material or articles be delivered to such person as the court may direct for erasure, removal or obliteration of the offending controlled representation or for destruction, as the case may be.

3 Order for delivery up of infringing goods, material or articles
(1) The proprietor of the Olympics association right may apply to the court for an order for the delivery up to him, or such other person as the court may direct, of any infringing goods, material or articles which a person has in his possession, custody or control in the course of a business.
(2) An application shall not be made after the end of the period specified in regulation 4 (period after which remedy of delivery up is not available); and no order shall be made unless the court also makes, or it appears to the court that there are grounds for making, an order under regulation 5 (order as to disposal of infringing goods, etc).
(3) A person to whom any infringing goods, material or articles are delivered up in pursuance of an order under this Regulation shall, if an order under regulation 5 is not made, retain them pending the making of an order, or the decision not to make

847

an order, under that regulation.

(4) Nothing in this Regulation affects any other power of the court.

4 Period after which remedy of delivery up is not available

(1) An application for an order under regulation 3 (order for the delivery up of infringing goods, material or articles) may not be made after the end of the period of six years from—

    (a) in the case of infringing goods, the date on which the controlled representation was applied to the goods or their packaging,

    (b) in the case of infringing material, the date on which the controlled representation was applied to the material, or

    (c) in the case of infringing articles, the date on which they were made,

except as mentioned in the following provision.

(2) If during the whole or part of the relevant period in paragraph (1) above the proprietor of the Olympics association right—

    (a) is under a disability, or

    (b) is prevented by fraud or concealment from discovering the facts entitling him to apply for an order,

an application may be made at any time before the end of the period of six years from the date on which he ceased to be under a disability or, as the case may be, could with reasonable diligence have discovered those facts.

(3) In paragraph (2) 'disability'—

    (a) in England and Wales, has the same meaning as in the Limitation Act 1980,

    (b) in Scotland, means legal disability within the meaning of the Prescription and Limitation (Scotland) Act 1973,

    (c) in Northern Ireland, has the same meaning as in the Limitation (Northern Ireland) Order 1989.

5 Order as to the disposal of infringing goods, material or articles etc

(1) Where infringing goods, material or articles have been delivered up in pursuance of an order under regulation 3, an application may be made to the court—

    (a) for an order that they be destroyed or forfeited to such person as the court may think fit, or

    (b) for a decision that no such order should be made.

(2) In considering what order (if any) should be made, the court shall consider whether other remedies available in an action for infringement of the Olympics association right would be adequate to compensate the proprietor and any licensee and protect their interests.

(3) Provision shall be made by rules of court as to the service of notice on persons having an interest in the goods, material or articles, and any such person is entitled—

    (a) to appear in proceedings for an order under this regulation, whether or not he was served with notice, and

    (b) to appeal against any order made, whether or not he appeared,

and an order shall not take effect until the end of the period within which notice of an appeal may be given or, if before the end of that period notice of appeal is duly given, until the final determination or abandonment of the proceedings on the appeal.

(4) Where there is more than one person interested in the goods, material or arti-

cles, the court shall make such order as it thinks just.

(5) If the court decides that no order should be made under this Regulation, the person in whose possession, custody or control the goods, material or articles were before being delivered up is entitled to their return.

(6) References in this Regulation to a person having interest in goods, material or articles include any person in whose favour an order could be made under this Regulation or under section 114, 204 or 231 of the Copyright, Designs and Patents Act 1988 (which make similar provision in relation to infringement of copyright, rights in performances and design right).

6 Jurisdiction of sheriff court or county court in Northern Ireland

Proceedings for an order under regulation 3 (order for delivery up of infringing goods, material or articles) or regulation 5 (order as to disposal of infringing goods, etc) may be brought—

    (a) in the sheriff court in Scotland, or
    (b) in a county court in Northern Ireland.

This does not affect the jurisdiction of the Court of Session or the High Court in Northern Ireland.

TRADE MARKS (INTERNATIONAL REGISTRATION) ORDER 1996
(SI 1996/714)
Made 11th March 1996
The Secretary of State, in exercise of the powers conferred on him by section 54 of the Trade Marks Act 1994 thereby makes the following Order:—

PRELIMINARY

1 Citation commencement and extent

(1) This Order may be cited as the Trade Marks (International Registration) Order 1996 and comes into force on 1st April 1996.

(2) This Order extends to England and Wales, Scotland, Northern Ireland and the Isle of Man.

2 Interpretation

In this Order—
    'the Act' means the Trade Marks Act 1994, and references to a section are, unless the context otherwise requires, to sections of that Act;
    'basic application' and 'basic registration' have the respective meanings given by article 22;
    'Common Regulations' means the regulations adopted under article 10 of the Madrid Protocol with effect from 1 April 1996;
    'international application' means an application to the International Bureau for registration of a trade mark in the International Register;
    'International Bureau' means the International Bureau of the World Intellectual Property Organisation;
    'International Register' means the register of trade marks maintained by the International Bureau for the purposes of the Madrid Protocol;
    'international registration' means the registration of a trade mark in the International Register;
    'international registration designating the United Kingdom' means an international registration in relation to which a request has been made (either in

the relevant international application or subsequently) for extension of protection to the United Kingdom under Article 3ter (1) or (2) of the Madrid Protocol;

'notifiable transaction' has the meaning given by article 6;

'protected international trade mark (UK)' has the meaning given by article 12, and references to 'protection' and 'protected' shall be construed accordingly;

'the Rules' means the Trade Marks Rules 1994 [SI 1994/2583], and references to a rule shall, unless the context otherwise requires, be construed accordingly;

'supplementary register' has the meaning given by article 24;

'transformation application' has the meaning given by article 19;

'United Kingdom' includes the Isle of Man.

INTERNATIONAL REGISTRATIONS DESIGNATING THE UNITED KINGDOM

3 Entitlement to protection

(1) An international registration designating the United Kingdom shall be entitled to become protected subject to the provisions of articles 9 to 12 where, if the particulars of the international registration were comprised in an application for registration of a trade mark under the Act, such an application would satisfy the requirements for registration (including any imposed by the Rules).

(2) For that purpose, sections 32 to 34, rules 5 to 8 and rules 10 and 11 shall be disregarded.

4 Effects of Protected International Trade Mark (UK)

(1) The proprietor of a protected international trade mark (UK) has, subject to the provisions of this Order, the same rights and remedies as are given by or under sections 9 to 12 and 14 to 20 to the proprietor of a registered trade mark, subject to the limits on effect and to the provisions relating to exhaustion which are applicable to a registered trade mark by virtue of section 11 and section 12 respectively.

(2) For the purposes of section 9 (rights conferred by registered trade mark)—

(a) the rights of the proprietor shall have effect as of the date on which it is to be treated as registered pursuant to article 12 or article 21;

(b) a protected international trade mark (UK) shall be treated as being in fact registered when it becomes protected pursuant to article 12.

(3) References in sections 10 and 11 to goods or services in respect of which a trade mark is registered are to goods or services in respect of which a protected international trade mark (UK) confers protection in the United Kingdom.

(4) Where the holder of an international registration designating the United Kingdom by notice in writing sent to the registrar—

(a) disclaims any right to the exclusive use of any specified element of the trade mark, or

(b) agrees that the rights conferred in the United Kingdom by the international registration shall be subject to a specified territorial or other limitation,

the registrar shall enter the disclaimer or limitation in the supplementary register and shall publish the disclaimer or limitation.

(5) Where a protected international trade mark (UK) is subject to a disclaimer or limitation, the rights conferred in relation to it by the application of section 9 are

restricted accordingly.

(6) The remedy for groundless threats of infringement proceedings given by section 21 applies in relation to a protected international trade mark (UK) as in relation to a registered trade mark; and for this purpose—

(a) the reference in section 21(3) to the registration of the trade mark shall be treated as a reference to protection of a protected international trade mark (UK); and

(b) the reference in section 21(4) to notification that a trade mark is registered, or that an application for registration has been made, shall be treated as a reference to notification that a trade mark is a protected international trade mark (UK) or is the subject of an international application or international registration designating the United Kingdom.

5 International Trade mark (UK) as an object of property

The provisions of sections 22, 23, 24 (except subsection (2)(b)) and 26 (which relate to a registered trade mark as an object of property) apply, with the necessary modifications, in relation to an international trade mark (UK) as in relation to a registered trade mark.

6 Notification of transactions

(1) The following are notifiable transactions for the purposes of this article—

(a) the grant of a licence under a protected international trade mark (UK);

(b) the granting of any security interest (whether fixed or floating) over an international trade mark (UK) or any right in or under it.

(2) On application being made to the registrar by—

(a) a person claiming to be entitled to an interest in or under an international trade mark (UK) by virtue of a notifiable transaction, or

(b) any other person claiming to be affected by such a transaction,

the prescribed particulars of the transaction shall be entered in the supplementary register.

(3) The following are relevant transactions for the purposes of this article—

(a) a notifiable transaction;

(b) an assignment of an international trade mark (UK) or any right in it;

(c) the making by personal representatives of an assent in relation to an international trade mark (UK) or any right in or under it;

(d) an order of a court or other competent authority transferring an international trade mark (UK) or any right in or under it.

(4) Until (in the case of a notifiable transaction) an application has been made for registration of the prescribed particulars or (in the case of any other relevant transaction) the transaction has been recorded in the International Register—

(a) the transaction is ineffective as against a person acquiring an interest in or under the international trade mark (UK) in ignorance of it, and

(b) a person claiming to be a licensee by virtue of the transaction does not have the protection of section 30 or 31 (rights and remedies of licensee in relation to infringement).

(5) Where a person becomes the proprietor or a licensee of an international trade mark (UK) by virtue of a relevant transaction, then unless—

(a) an application for registration of the transaction (in the case of a notifiable transaction) is made, or (in the case of any other relevant transaction) a request for recordal in the International Register is made, before the end of a period of six months beginning with its date, or

(b) the court is satisfied that it was not practicable for such an application or request for recordal to be made before the end of that period and that an application or request for recordal (as the case may be) was made as soon as practicable thereafter,

he is not entitled to damages or an account of profits in respect of any infringement of the international trade mark (UK) occurring after the date of the transaction and before (in the case of a notifiable transaction) the prescribed particulars of the transaction are registered or (in the case of any other relevant transaction) the transaction is recorded in the International Register.

(6) 'Prescribed particulars' means the particulars prescribed by rule 34.

7 Licensing

(1) The provisions of sections 28 to 31 apply, with the necessary modifications, in relation to licences to use a protected international trade mark (UK).

(2) The reference in section 28(1) to goods or services for which a trade mark is registered shall be treated as a reference to goods or services in respect of which the trade mark is protected in the United Kingdom.

8 Priority

(1) The provisions of section 35 (claim to priority of Convention application) apply, subject as mentioned below, so as to confer a right to priority in relation to protection of an international registration designating the United Kingdom as they apply in relation to registering a trade mark under the Act.

(2) Subsection (5) of that section does not apply and the manner of claiming priority shall be determined in accordance with the Madrid Protocol and the Common Regulations.

9 Examination

(1) Upon receiving from the International Bureau notification of an international registration designating the United Kingdom, the registrar shall examine whether it satisfies the requirements of article 3.

(2) For that purpose, he shall carry out a search, to such extent as he considers necessary, of earlier trade marks.

(3) If it appears to the registrar that the requirements referred to in paragraph (1) above are not met, or are met only in relation to some of the goods or services in respect of which protection in the United Kingdom has been requested, he shall give notice of refusal to the International Bureau.

(4) Notice of refusal shall specify a period within which the holder may make representations.

(5) A holder making representations shall file an address for service in the United Kingdom on Form TM33.

10 Publication, opposition proceedings and observations

(1) Where following examination pursuant to article 9 it appears to the registrar that the requirements of article 3 are met in relation to all or some of the goods or services comprised in the international registration, the registrar shall publish a notice specifying particulars of the international registration and specifying the goods or services for which protection will be conferred.

(2) Any person may, within three months of the date of publication pursuant to paragraph (1) above, give notice to the registrar of opposition to the conferring of protection.

The notice shall be given in writing in the manner prescribed by rule 13, shall include a statement of the grounds of opposition and shall where opposition is based on an earlier trade mark indicate the goods or services on which the opposition is based.

(3) The registrar shall, upon notice of opposition being given, and in any event within four months of publication pursuant to paragraph (1) above, give notice of refusal to the International Bureau stating the matters relating to the opposition referred to in paragraph (2) above.

(4) Within three months of the date on which notice of refusal based on opposition is given to the International Bureau, the holder may file a counter-statement, in conjunction with notice of the same on Form TM8 and an address for service in the United Kingdom.

(5) Subject to the provisions of this article, rules 13 and 14 shall apply in relation to opposition proceedings, with the substitution of the holder for the applicant.

(6) Where a notice has been published pursuant to paragraph (1) above, any person may, at any time before the trade mark has become protected in accordance with article 12, make observations in writing to the registrar as to whether the trade mark should be protected.

A person who makes observations does not thereby become a party to proceedings in relation to the request for protection.

11 Notices of refusal

(1) Except where refusal is based on an opposition, notice of refusal shall not be given after the expiry of 18 months from the date on which the notification of the request for extension was sent to the United Kingdom.

(2) The registrar shall inform the International Bureau that oppositions may be filed after the expiry of the period of 18 months referred to in paragraph (1) above unless, at least four months before the expiry of the said period, he has published the notice referred to in article 10(1).

(3) Notices of refusal shall set out the matters required by Article 5 of the Madrid Protocol and Rule 17 of the Common Regulations.

(4) Where—

    (a) notice of refusal has been given pursuant to article 9(3), and

        (i) the holder makes representations within the period specified under article 9(4), or

        (ii) the holder makes no representations within that period, or informs the registrar that he does not intend to make any representations; or

    (b) notice of refusal based on an opposition has been given pursuant to article 10(3) and

        (i) the holder files a counter-statement within the period specified in article 10(4), or

        (ii) the holder files no counter-statement within that period or informs the registrar that he does not intend to file a counter-statement,

the registrar shall inform the International Bureau of that fact.

(5) Where—

    (a) after notice of refusal has been given pursuant to article 9(3), the holder makes representations within the period specified under article 9(4); or

(b) after notice of refusal based on an opposition, the holder files a counter-statement within the period specified in article 10(4),

the registrar shall, upon a final decision being made in relation to the refusal, notify the International Bureau of that decision.

(6) For the purposes of paragraph (5) above, a final decision shall be regarded as being made where—

(a) the registrar, or the appointed person or the court on appeal or further appeal from the registrar, decides whether the refusal shall be upheld, in whole or in relation to some only of the goods or services in relation to which protection in the United Kingdom is requested, and any right of appeal against that decision expires or is exhausted;
(b) the representations or counter-statement are withdrawn; or
(c) the proceedings relating to the refusal are discontinued or abandoned.

12 Protection

(1) Where—

(a) following examination and publication pursuant to articles 9 and 10—
  (i) the period of 18 months from the date on which the notification of the request for extension was sent to the United Kingdom has not expired, but the period for giving notice of refusal based on an opposition in accordance with article 10(3) expires without notice of refusal (whether based on opposition or otherwise) having been given,
  (ii) the period of 18 months from the date on which the notification of the request for extension was sent to the United Kingdom has expired, and the period for giving notice of opposition in accordance with article 10(2) expires without notice of opposition having been given,
  (iii) notice of refusal has been given in respect of some only of the goods or services in respect of which protection in the United Kingdom has been requested and the registrar informs the International Bureau in accordance with article 11(4) that the holder has made no representations within the period specified in article 9(4) or has filed no counter-statement within the period specified in article 10(4) (as the case may be) or that the holder has informed the registrar that he does not intend to make such representations or file such a counter-statement, or
  (iv) notice of refusal has been given in respect of all or some of the goods or services in respect of which protection in the United Kingdom has been requested and the registrar notifies the International Bureau in accordance with article 11(5) that a final decision has been made that the refusal is withdrawn, or is withdrawn in respect of some of the goods or services in respect of which protection in the United Kingdom has been requested; or
(b) the period of 18 months from the date on which the notification of the request for extension was sent to the United Kingdom expires without any notice of refusal having been given and without the International Bureau having been informed that oppositions may be filed after the expiry of that period,

the trade mark which is the subject of the request for protection shall thereupon be protected as a protected international trade mark (UK); and in a case where a refusal subsists in respect of some of the goods or services in respect of which protection in the United Kingdom has been requested, protection shall apply only as regards the remaining goods or services.

(2) For the purposes of application by this Order of provisions of the Act, subject to article 21, a trade mark so protected shall be treated as being registered under the Act as of the following date: —

(a) where the request for extension of protection to the United Kingdom is mentioned in the international application, or is made subsequently, but on or before the date of the international registration, the date of that international registration;

(b) where the request for such extension is made subsequently to the international registration, the date on which the request is recorded in the International Register.

(3) When a trade mark becomes protected pursuant to this article, the registrar shall publish particulars of the international registration specifying the date on which, and the goods or services in respect of which, protection is conferred.

13 Revocation and Invalidity

(1) The provisions of section 46 (revocation of registration) and section 47 (grounds for invalidity of registration) shall apply, subject to the adaptations set out below, so as to permit the protection of a protected international trade mark (UK) to be revoked, or declared invalid.

(2) The reference in section 46(1) to the date of completion of the registration procedure shall be construed as a reference to the date of the protected international trade mark (UK) becoming protected; the reference in section 46(2) to the form in which a trade mark was registered shall be construed as reference to the form in which it is protected; and the references in section 46(5) and section 47(5) to goods or services for which the trade mark is registered shall be construed as references to those in respect of which it is protected.

(3) The references in section 46 to the registration of a trade mark being revoked and the references in section 47 to the registration of a trade mark being declared invalid shall be construed as references to the protection of a protected international trade mark (UK) being revoked or declared invalid, as the case may be.

(4) The provisions of rule 31, with necessary modifications, apply in relation to the procedure on application for revocation and declaration of invalidity of protection of a protected international trade mark (UK).

(5) Where the protection of a protected international trade mark (UK) is revoked or declared invalid to any extent, the registrar shall notify the International Bureau, and

(a) in the case of a revocation, the rights of the proprietor shall be deemed to have ceased to exist to that extent as from the date on which the revocation is recorded in the International Register;

(b) in the case of a declaration of invalidity, the trade mark shall to that extent be deemed never to have been a protected international trade mark (UK):

Provided that this shall not affect transactions past and closed as at the date when the invalidity is recorded in the International Register.

14 Effect of acquiescence

Section 48 (effect of acquiescence) applies where the proprietor of an earlier trade mark has acquiesced for a continuous period of five years in the use of a protected international trade mark (UK); and for that purpose—

(a) the reference to a registered trade mark shall be construed as including a protected international trade mark (UK);

(b) the references to registration shall include references to protection of a protected international trade mark (UK).

15 Proceedings relating to invalidity and revocation of protection

(1) The provisions of section 73 (certificate of validity of contested registration) apply, with the necessary modifications, in relation to proceedings before the court in which the validity of the protection of a protected international trade mark (UK) is contested.

(2) The provisions of section 74 (registrar's appearance in proceedings involving the registrar) apply, with the necessary modifications, in relation to proceedings before the court involving an application for—

(a) the revocation of the protection of a protected international trade mark (UK);

(b) a declaration of the invalidity of the protection of a protected international trade mark (UK);

(c) the rectification of the supplementary register.

16 Importation of infringing goods, materials or articles

The provisions of section 89 (infringing goods, material or articles may be treated as prohibited goods) section 90 and section 91 of the Act (power of Commissioners of Customs and Excise to disclose information) apply in relation to goods which are, in relation to a protected international trade mark (UK), infringing goods, materials or articles, and for the purposes of those provisions—

(a) references to a registered trade mark shall be to a protected international trade mark (UK);

(b) the Trade Marks (Customs) Regulations 1994 [SI 1994/2625] shall apply in relation to notices given under the provisions of section 89.

17 Offences and forfeiture

(1) The provisions of section 92 (unauthorised use of trade mark, etc, in relation to goods), section 93 (enforcement function of local weights and measures authority), section 97 (forfeiture: England and Wales) and section 98 (forfeiture: Scotland) apply in relation to a protected international trade mark (UK).

(2) For the purposes of the provisions referred to in paragraph (1) above—

(a) references to a registered trade mark shall be treated as references to a protected international trade mark (UK);

(b) references to goods in respect of which a trade mark is registered shall be treated as references to goods in respect of which a protected international trade mark (UK) confers protection in the United Kingdom.

(3) No offence under section 92 in relation to a protected international trade mark is committed by anything done before the date of publication pursuant to article 12(3).

18 Falsely representing trade mark as a protected international trade mark (UK)

(1) It is an offence for a person—

(a) falsely to represent that a mark is a protected international trade mark (UK), or

(b) to make a false representation as to the goods or services for which a protected international trade mark (UK) confers protection in the United Kingdom

knowing or having reason to believe that the representation is false.

(2) A person guilty of an offence under this article is liable on summary conviction

to a fine not exceeding level 3 on the standard scale.

TRANSFORMATION OF AN INTERNATIONAL REGISTRATION INTO A NATIONAL APPLICATION

19 Transformation applications

(1) The provisions of this article apply where—

    (a) an international registration designating the United Kingdom is cancelled at the request of the Office of origin under Article 6(4) of the Madrid Protocol in respect of all or some of the goods or services listed in the registration;

    (b) an application (a 'transformation application') is made to the registrar, within three months of the date on which the international registration was cancelled, for registration in the United Kingdom of a trade mark identical to that comprised in the international registration in respect of some or all of the goods or services in respect of which the international registration was cancelled; and

    (c) the application is made by the person who was the holder of the international registration immediately before its cancellation.

(2) A transformation application shall be made on Form TM3 and shall state that it is made by way of transformation.

(3) A trade mark registered pursuant to a transformation application shall be treated as if it were registered as of the date of the international registration according to Article 3(4) of the Madrid Protocol or, where the request for extension to the United Kingdom was made subsequently to the international registration, on the date of recordal of that request according to Article 3ter of the Madrid Protocol, and that date shall be deemed for the purposes of the Act to be the date of registration.

20 Procedure on transformation application

(1) Where the international trade mark (UK) has become protected pursuant to article 12 on or before the actual date on which the transformation application is made ('the transformation date') the trade mark shall be registered under the Act.

(2) Where the international registration designating the United Kingdom has not become protected under article 12 at the transformation date and a notice has been published pursuant to article 10(1) in respect of the trade mark, the registrar shall treat the publication of such notice as being the publication of the transformation application under section 38(1) and shall publish a notice that it is being so treated. Any opposition shall be treated as opposition under section 38(2).

(3) Where a notice has not yet been published pursuant to article 10(1) at the transformation date and the registrar has issued a notice of refusal pursuant to article 9(3), the registrar shall for the purposes of the transformation application treat the notice of refusal as if it had been issued under section 37(3).

The registrar shall in that event inform the applicant of the nature of the response required of him in respect of his transformation application and shall further specify the period within which the applicant must respond to the registrar.

CONCURRENT REGISTRATIONS

21 Effects of international registration where trade mark is also registered under the Act

(1) The provisions of this article apply, without prejudice to the rights and remedies conferred in respect of a trade mark registered under the Act, where —

    (a) the registered trade mark is also a protected international trade mark (UK);

    (b) the proprietor of the registered trade mark is the holder of the international trade mark (UK);

    (c) all the goods or services in respect of which the registered trade mark is registered are protected under the protected international trade mark (UK);

    (d) the date of registration of the registered trade mark is earlier than the date specified in article 12(2) in relation to the international trade mark (UK).

(2) For the purposes of application by this Order of the provisions of the Act, the protected international trade mark (UK) shall be treated, notwithstanding the provisions of article 12(2), as being registered under the Act as of the date of registration of the registered trade mark as regards all the goods or services in respect of which the registered trade mark was registered.

(3) For the purpose of determining whether the international trade mark (UK) is an earlier trade mark, it shall be treated as having the date of application of the registered trade mark as regards all the goods or services in respect of which the registered trade mark was registered, taking account (where appropriate) of the priorities claimed in respect of the registered trade mark.

(4) Where the conditions specified in paragraph (1) above are satisfied in relation to a trade mark, the provisions of paragraphs (2) and (3) above shall continue to apply in respect of the relevant international trade mark (UK) notwithstanding that the relevant registered trade mark lapses or is surrendered, but shall cease to apply if it is revoked or declared invalid.

(5) On the application of the holder of the protected international trade mark (UK), the registrar shall note the international registration in the register against the registered trade mark.

(6) For the purposes of paragraph (5) above, the holder of the protected international trade mark (UK) shall make an application to the registrar using Form TM28.

INTERNATIONAL APPLICATIONS ORIGINATING IN THE UNITED KINGDOM

22 Application for international registration

(1) An applicant for the registration of a trade mark, or the proprietor of a registered trade mark, may, subject to the provisions of this article, apply through the registrar for the international registration of the trade mark.

(2) An application for international registration may be made only where the applicant for such registration is —

    (a) a British citizen, a British dependent territories citizen, a British overseas citizen, a British subject or a British protected person;

    (b) a body or a corporation sole incorporated or constituted under the law of any part of the United Kingdom;

    (c) a person domiciled in the United Kingdom; or

    (d) a person who has a real and effective industrial or commercial establishment in the United Kingdom.

(3) The particulars appearing in the application shall correspond with the particulars appearing at that time in the basic application or basic registration as the case may be.

(4) The applicant for international registration shall provide at the request of the registrar such evidence as may be necessary to satisfy him that the applicant is eli-

gible to make the application in accordance with paragraph (2) above.

(5) If an international application complies with the requirements set out in this article, the registrar shall submit the international application to the International Bureau.

(6) In this Order—

(a) 'basic application' means an application for registration of a trade mark in the United Kingdom in respect of which application is made for international registration;

(b) 'basic registration' means a trade mark registered in the United Kingdom in respect of which application is made for international registration.

23 Notification to International Bureau

(1) Where the registrar has submitted an application for international registration, he shall notify the International Bureau of the occurrence of any of the events specified in paragraph (2) below and shall request the International Bureau to cancel the international registration as regards those goods or services covered by the international application in respect of which the basic application or basic registration has ceased to subsist by reason of that event.

(2) The following events are specified for the purposes of paragraph (1) above:

(a) before the expiry of five years from the date of the international registration, the registrar refuses to accept the basic application as regards some or all of the goods or services covered by the international registration or, after accepting the application, refuses to register the trade mark as regards some or all of those goods or services, having regard to matters coming to his notice since he accepted the application, and in either case that decision becomes a final decision, whether before or after the expiry of that period of five years;

(b) opposition proceedings begun before the expiry of five years from the date of the international registration result in a final decision not to register the trade mark as regards some or all of the goods or services covered by the international registration;

(c) the basic application is withdrawn, or is restricted as regards goods or services covered by the international registration, as a result of a request by the applicant made before the expiry of five years from the date of the international registration, or made subsequently when the basic application was at the time of the request subject to an appeal against refusal of registration or to opposition proceedings begun in either case before the expiry of that five year period;

(d) the registration resulting from the basic application or the basic registration expires without renewal and is removed from the register before the expiry of five years from the date of the international registration and no request for its restoration is made within the time specified in rule 30 or such a request is made and a final decision is made to refuse the request;

(e) a final decision is made to revoke or declare invalid the registration resulting from the basic application or the basic registration, as a result of proceedings begun before the expiry of five years from the date of the international registration;

(f) the registration resulting from the basic application, or the basic registration, is surrendered as a result of a request by the proprietor made before the expiry of five years from the date of the international registration, or made subsequently where at the time of the request—

(i) the basic application was subject to an appeal against refusal of registration or to opposition proceedings; or

(ii) the registration resulting from the basic application, or the basic registration, was subject to proceedings for revocation or invalidation;

and such appeal or proceedings were begun before the expiry of five years from the date of the international registration.

(3) For the purposes of this article:—

   (a) a final decision shall be regarded as made where—

      (i) any right of appeal against the decision expires or is exhausted, or

      (ii) proceedings relating to an application or registration are discontinued or abandoned;

   (b) reference to an application being withdrawn includes its being deemed to be withdrawn, or abandoned, or deemed never to have been made.

MISCELLANEOUS AND GENERAL PROVISIONS

24 Supplementary Register

(1) The registrar shall maintain a register ('the supplementary register') for the purpose of recording, in relation to international trade marks (UK)—

   (a) disclaimers and limitations;

   (b) notifiable transactions.

(2) The supplementary register need not be kept in documentary form.

(3) Rules 34 to 39 apply, with the necessary modifications, in relation to the supplementary register.

25 Disclosure of Information

(1) Before publication of notice under article 10(1) in relation to an international registration designating the United Kingdom, the registrar shall not publish or communicate to any person documents or information relating to the international registration other than as provided in paragraph (2) below.

(2) In relation to an international registration designating the United Kingdom, the registrar shall on request make available for inspection by the public all information in his possession which is recorded in the International Register concerning that registration, the particulars contained in any application for registration of a notifiable transaction and any entry in the supplementary register resulting from such an application.

(3) Subject to paragraph (5) below, after publication of notice under article 10(1) in relation to an international registration designating the United Kingdom, the registrar shall on request provide a person with such information and permit him to inspect such documents, relating to the international registration as may be specified in the request.

(4) A request for information relating to an international registration designating the United Kingdom shall be made on Form TM31M.

(5) Paragraphs (2) to (5) of rule 44, and rule 45, apply in relation to the right of inspection conferred by paragraph (3) above.

(6) Where a person has been notified that an international registration designates the United Kingdom and that the proprietor will, if the registration becomes a protected international trade mark (UK), bring proceedings against him in respect of acts done after publication of notice under article 10(1), the registrar shall on request permit inspection under paragraph (3) above notwithstanding that such

notice has not been published and that paragraph shall apply accordingly.

26 Exclusion of Liability

(1) The registrar is not subject to any liability by reason of, or in connection with, any examination required or authorised by this Order, or in any report or other proceedings consequent on such examination.

(2) No proceedings lie against an officer of the registrar in respect of any matter for which, by virtue of this article, the registrar is not liable.

27 Evidence of certain matters relating to an international registration

(1) In all legal proceedings relating to an international trade mark (UK), the registration of a person as holder of an international trade mark (UK) shall be prima facie evidence of the validity of the original international registration and of any subsequent assignment or other transmission of it.

(2) Judicial notice shall be taken of the following—

    (a) the Madrid Protocol and the Common Regulations;

    (b) copies issued by the International Bureau of entries in the International Register;

    (c) copies of the periodical gazette published by the International Bureau.

(3) Any document mentioned in paragraph (2)(b) or (c) above shall be admissible as evidence of any instrument or other act thereby communicated of the International Bureau.

(4) Evidence of any instrument issued by the International Bureau or any entry in or extract from such a document may be given in any legal proceedings by production of a copy; and any document purporting to be such a copy shall be received in evidence.

(5) In any legal proceedings in Scotland, evidence of any matter given in any manner authorised by this article shall be sufficient evidence of it.

(6) In this article, 'legal proceedings' includes proceedings before the registrar.

28 Agents

Any act required or authorised by this Order to be done by or to a person in connection with a request for protection of an international registration as a protected international trade mark (UK) or any procedure relating to a protected international trade mark (UK) may be done by or to an agent authorised by that person orally or in writing.

29 Burden of proving use of international trade mark (UK)

If in any civil proceedings pursuant to this Order a question arises as to the use to which an international trade mark (UK) has been put, it is for the holder to show what use has been made of it.

30 Communication of information to the International Bureau

Notwithstanding section 67(2) or any other enactment or rule of law, the registrar may communicate to the International Bureau any information which the United Kingdom is required to communicate by virtue of this Order or pursuant to the Madrid Protocol or the Common Regulations.

31 Transmission of fees to the International Bureau

The registrar may accept for transmission to the International Bureau fees payable to the International Bureau in respect of an application for international registration originating in the United Kingdom or a renewal of such an international registration, subject to such terms and conditions as he may specify, either generally by published notice, or in any particular case by written notice to the applicant desiring to make payment by such means.

32 Application of Trade Marks Rules 1994

(1) Except as otherwise provided, or where their application would be inconsistent with the provisions of this Order, the Rules shall apply, with the necessary modifications, in relation to an international registration designating the United Kingdom, (including a protected international trade mark (UK)) as in relation to a registered trade mark or application.

(2) In their application to an international registration designating the United Kingdom, the Rules shall be treated in all respects as rules made under the Act and, in particular, rules relating to costs and security for costs and to evidence before the registrar shall be enforceable in relation to proceedings under this Order in the same manner as in relation to proceedings relating to a registered trade mark or application.

TRADE MARKS ACT 1994 (ISLE OF MAN) ORDER 1996
(SI 1996/729)
Made 13th March 1996
Her Majesty, in pursuance of section 108(2) of the Trade Marks Act 1994, is pleased, by and with the advice of Her Privy Council, to order, and it is hereby ordered, as follows:—

1 This Order may be cited as the Trade Marks Act 1994 (Isle of Man) Order 1996 and shall come into force on 1st April 1996.

2 The Trade Marks Act 1994 in its extension to the Isle of Man shall have effect subject to the exceptions and modifications specified in the Schedule to this Order.

SCHEDULE

Exceptions and Modifications Subject to which the Trade Marks Act 1994 Extends to the Isle of Man

Article 2

1 (1) Any reference to an Act of Parliament (including the Trade Marks Act 1994) or to a provision of such an Act shall be construed, unless the contrary intention appears, as a reference to that Act or provision as it has effect in the Isle of Man.
(2) Any reference to an Act of Tynwald shall be construed, unless the contrary intention appears, as a reference to it as amended or replaced by or under any other such enactment.

2 In section 18, for subsection (3) there shall be substituted—
'(3) In subsection (2) 'disability' has the same meaning as in the Limitation Act 1984 (an Act of Tynwald).'.

3 In Section 19(6), for the words from 'section 114,' to the end there shall be substituted the words 'section 113 of the Copyright Act 1991 (an Act of Tynwald) or section 19 of the Design Right Act 1991 (an Act of Tynwald) (which make similar provision in relation to infringement of copyright and design right).'.

4 Section 20 shall be omitted.

5 Sections 51 and 52 shall be omitted.

6 In section 68, for subsection (2) there shall be substituted—
'(2) Any such order of the registrar may be enforced in the Isle of Man in the same way as an order of the High Court of Justice of the Isle of Man.'.

7 In section 75, after paragraph (a) there shall be inserted—
    '(aa)in the Isle of Man, the High Court of Justice of the Isle of Man, and'.

8 In section 77(2), after paragraph (b) there shall be inserted—

    '(ba)   he is an advocate in the Isle of Man of at least 7 years' standing;'.

9 For section 86 there shall be substituted—

'**86**   No offence is committed under section 1 of the Legal Practitioners Registration Act 1986 (an Act of Tynwald) (which restricts the use of certain words including 'advocate' and 'attorney') by the use of the term 'trade mark attorney' in reference to a registered trade mark agent.'.

10 (1)   In sections 89, 90 and 91, for the words 'Commissioners of Customs and Excise' and 'Commissioners' wherever they appear there shall be substituted the word 'Treasury'.
(2) In section 89(1)(b), for the words 'United Kingdom' there shall be substituted the words 'Isle of Man'.
(3) In section 89, for subsection (3) there shall be substituted—
'(3) This section does not apply to goods entered, or expected to be entered, for free circulation, export, re-export or for a suspensive procedure in respect of which an application may be made under Article 3(1) of Council Regulation (EC) No 3295/94 laying down measures to prohibit the release for free circulation, export, re-export or for a suspensive procedure of counterfeit and pirated goods.
(4) In this section and sections 90 and 91, 'the Treasury' means the Department of that name established under the Government Departments Act 1987 (an Act of Tynwald).'.
(4) In section 90, for subsections (4) and (5) there shall be substituted the following subsection:
'(4) Regulations under this section shall not have effect unless they are approved by Tynwald.'.
(5) In section 91, for the words 'Trade Descriptions Act 1968' there shall be substituted the words 'Consumer Protection (Trade Descriptions) Act 1970 (an Act of Tynwald)'.

11 In sections 92(6)(b) and 94(3)(a), for the words 'indictment' there shall be substituted the word 'information'.

12 Sections 93, 96 and 98 shall be omitted.

13 (1)   In section 97(1), for the words 'England and Wales or Northern Ireland' there shall be substituted the words 'the Isle of Man'.
(2) In section 97(2)(b) and (5), for the words 'magistrates' court' there shall be substituted the words 'court of summary jurisdiction'.
(3) In section 97(5)—

(a) for paragraphs (a) and (b) there shall be substituted the words 'in the Isle of Man, to the High Court of Justice of the Isle of Man;'; and

(b) for the words from 'section 111' to '1981' there shall be substituted the words 'section 109 of the Summary Jurisdiction Act 1989 (an Act of Tynwald)'.

(4) In section 97(8), for the words 'Trade Descriptions Act 1968' there shall be substituted the words 'Consumer Protection (Trade Descriptions) Act 1970 (an Act of Tynwald)'.

14 In section 101(2)(b), for the words from 'in England' to '1981' there shall be substituted the words 'in the Isle of Man, section 32 of the Summary Jurisdiction Act 1989 (an Act of Tynwald)'.

15 Section 102 shall be omitted.

16 In the table in section 104, at the appropriate place there shall be inserted—
'the Treasury   section 89(4)'.

17 (1) Section 106 and Schedules 4 and 5 shall have effect in relation only to statutory provisions which extend to the Isle of Man.

(2) In Schedule 4, at the appropriate places there shall be inserted the following paragraphs—

'Consumer Protection (Trade Descriptions) Act 1970 (an Act of Tynwald)

4 In the Consumer Protection (Trade Descriptions) Act 1970 (an Act of Tynwald), in section 34 (exemption of trade description contained in pre-1970 trade mark)—

(a) in the opening words, omit 'within the meaning of the Trade Marks Act 1938 (an Act of Parliament as extended to the Isle of Man by section 71(4) thereof),';

(b) in paragraph (c), for 'a person registered under section 28 of the said Trade Marks Act 1938 as a registered user of the trade mark' substitute ', in the case of a registered trade mark, a person licensed to use it'.

Copyright Act 1991 (an Act of Tynwald)

8A In section 113(6), for 'section 58C of the Trade Marks Act 1938' substitute 'section 19 of the Trade Marks Act 1994'.

Design Right Act 1991 (an Act of Tynwald)

8B In section 19(6), for 'section 58C of the Trade Marks Act 1938' substitute 'section 19 of the Trade Marks Act 1994'.

Consumer Protection Act 1991 (an Act of Tynwald)

8C (1) In section 58(1), for 'section 58A (fraudulent application or use of trade mark) of the Trade Marks Act 1938' substitute 'section 92 (unauthorised use of trade mark &c in relation to goods) of the Trade Marks Act 1994'.

(2) In section 58(3), for '58A' substitute '92'.'.

(3) In Schedule 5, at the appropriate places in chronological order there shall be inserted the following entries—

'XXI p 482   Consumer Protection (Trade

	Descriptions) Act 1970 (an Act o Tynwald)	Section 17.
1980 c18 (IOM)	Misrepresentation and Unfair Contract Terms Act 1980 (an Act of Tynwald)	In Schedule 1, words from 'The reference' onwards.
1989 c6 (IOM)	Statute Law Revision Act 1989 (an Act of Tynwald).'	In Schedule 1, paragraph 32.

COMMUNITY TRADE MARK REGULATIONS 1996
(SI 1996/1908)
Made 23rd July 1996
The Secretary of State, in exercise of powers conferred by section 52 of the Trade Marks Act 1994 hereby makes the following Regulations:—

1 (1) These Regulations may be cited as the Community Trade Mark Regulations 1996 and come into force on 14th August 1996.
(2) These Regulations extend to England and Wales, Scotland and Northern Ireland.

2 Interpretation
In these Regulations—
    'the Act' means the Trade Marks Act 1994, and references to a section are, unless the context otherwise requires, to sections of that Act;
    'the Community Trade Mark Regulation' means Council Regulation (EC) No 40/94 of 20th December 1993 on the Community trade mark;
    'the Rules' means the Trade Marks Rules 1994 [SI 1994/2583] and references to a rule shall, unless the context otherwise requires, be construed accordingly.

3 Determination *a posteriori* of invalidity and liability to revocation
(1) Where the proprietor of a Community trade mark claims the seniority of a registered trade mark which has been removed from the register under section 43 or has been surrendered under section 45, application may be made to the registrar or to the court by any person for a declaration that, if the registered trade mark had not been so removed or surrendered, it would have been liable to be revoked under section 46 or declared invalid under section 47.
(2) Where a registered trade mark has been surrendered in respect of some only of the goods or services for which it is registered, paragraph (1) above shall apply in relation to those goods or services.
(3) The provisions of section 46 or 47 (as the case may be), sections 72, 74 and 76, with necessary modifications, apply in relation to an application under paragraph (1) above.
(4) The provisions of rule 31, with necessary modifications, apply in relation to the procedure on applications made under paragraph (1) above.

4 Groundless threats of infringement proceedings
The provisions of section 21 apply in relation to a Community trade mark as in relation to a registered trade mark.

5 Privilege for communications with professional representatives
The provisions of section 87 (privilege for communications between a person and his registered trade mark agent) apply in relation to persons on the list of professional representatives maintained in pursuance of Article 89 of the Community Trade Mark Regulation ('professional representatives') and for this purpose the definition of 'trade mark agent' in subsection (3) of that section includes professional representatives.

6 Importation of infringing goods, material or articles
The provisions of section 89 (infringing goods, material or articles may be treated as prohibited goods) section 90 and section 91 of the Act (power of Commissioners of Customs and Excise to disclose information) apply in relation to goods which are, in relation to a Community trade mark, infringing goods, material or articles, and for the purposes of those provisions —

  (a) references to a registered trade mark shall include a Community trade mark;
  (b) the Trade Marks (Customs) Regulations 1994 [SI 1994/2625] shall apply in relation to notices given under the provisions of section 89.

7 Offences and forfeiture
The provisions of section 92 (unauthorised use of trade mark, etc, in relation to goods), section 93 (enforcement function of local weights and measures authority), section 97 (forfeiture: England and Wales) and section 98 (forfeiture: Scotland) apply in relation to a Community trade mark and for the purposes of those provisions —

  (a) references to a registered trade mark shall include a Community trade mark;
  (b) references to goods in respect of which a trade mark is registered shall include goods in respect of which a Community trade mark is registered.

8 Falsely representing trade mark as a Community trade mark
(1) It is an offence for a person —

  (a) falsely to represent that a mark is a Community trade mark, or
  (b) to make a false representation as to the goods or services for which a Community trade mark is registered,

knowing or having reason to believe that the representation is false.
(2) A person guilty of an offence under this regulation is liable on summary conviction to a fine not exceeding level 3 on the standard scale.

9 Designation of Community Trade Mark courts
For the purposes of Article 91 of the Community Trade Mark Regulation, the following courts are designated as Community trade mark courts —

  (a) in England and Wales and Northern Ireland, the High Court, and
  (b) in Scotland, the Court of Session.

10 Conversion
(1) The provisions of this Regulation apply where the applicant for or the propri-

etor of a Community trade mark requests the conversion of his Community trade mark application or Community trade mark into an application for registration of a trade mark under the Act ('conversion application') pursuant to Article 108 of the Community Trade Mark Regulation.

(2) Where the registrar decides that a request for a conversion application is admissible pursuant to Article 108, it shall be treated as an application for registration of a trade mark under the Act.

(3) A decision of the registrar in relation to a conversion application shall be treated as a decision of the registrar under the Act.

11 Application of Trade Marks Rules 1994

Except as otherwise provided, or where their application would be inconsistent with the provisions of these Regulations, the Rules shall apply, with the necessary modifications, to these Regulations.

PARTNERSHIPS (UNRESTRICTED SIZE) NO 12 REGULATIONS 1997
(SI 1997/1937)
Made 31st July 1997
The Secretary of State, in exercise of the power conferred on her by sections 716(2)(d) and 744 of the Companies Act 1985, hereby makes the following Regulations:—

1 These Regulations may be cited as the Partnerships (Unrestricted Size) No 12 Regulations 1997 and shall come into force on 1st September 1997.

2 Section 716(1) of the Companies Act 1985 does not prohibit the formation, for the purpose of carrying on practice in relation to matters connected with the European Patent Convention, of a partnership consisting of persons the majority of whom are members of the Institute of Professional Representatives before the European Patent Office.

3 For the purposes of these Regulations the European Patent Convention is the Convention on the Grant of European Patents signed in Munich on 5th October 1973 as from time to time amended.

TRADE MARKS (FEES) RULES 1998
(SI 1998/1776)
Made 9th July 1998
The Secretary of State, in exercise of the powers conferred by sections 54 and 79 of the Trade Marks Act 1994 ('the Act'), of the power conferred on her by the Department of Trade and Industry (Fees) Order 1988, and of all other powers enabling her in that behalf, hereby makes the following Rules:—

1 These Rules may be cited as the Trade Marks (Fees) Rules 1998 and shall come into force on 1st October 1998.

2 These Rules shall be construed as one with the Trade Marks Rules 1994 [SI 1994/2583] and the Trade Marks (International Registration) Order 1996 [SI 1996/714].

3 The fees to be paid in respect of any matters arising under the Act, the Trade

Marks Rules 1994 and the Trade Marks (International Registration) Order 1996 shall be those specified in the Schedule to these Rules; and in any case where a form specified in the Schedule as the corresponding form in relation to any matter is specified in the Trade Marks Rules 1994 or the Trade Marks (International Registration) Order 1996 that form shall be accompanied by the fee, if any, specified in respect of that matter (unless the Rules or the Order otherwise provide).

4 Where a fee has been paid in error, the registrar shall repay the same; and where a fee is paid in excess of the amount specified hereunder, the registrar shall remit the amount paid in excess.

5 The Trade Mark (Fees) Rules 1996 [SI 1996/1942], except as provided for by rule 5(2), are hereby revoked.

SCHEDULE
Fees Payable

Rule 3

(In this Schedule, references to a rule are references to that rule in the Trade Marks Rules 1994 [SI 1994/2583] and references to an article are references to that article in the Trade Marks (International Registration) Order 1996 [SI 1996/714].)

Number of Item corresponding form		Amount £
TM3	Application for registration of a trade mark (rule 5) or a series of trade marks (rule 21)	200
	Class fee (rule 5), for each class over one	50
	Transformation application (articles 19–20)	—
TM3A	Application for additional classes following examination of a mark (rule 8(3)), for each additional class	50
TM5	Request to the registrar for a statement of the reasons for his decision (rule 56(2))	100
TM7	Notice of opposition to the registration of a mark (rule 13(1)), to the amendment of an application (rule 18(2)), or to the amendment of the regulations relating to a certification or collective trade mark (rule 23(4)), to the alteration of a registered trade mark (rule 25(3)), to the removal of matter from the register (rule 39(2)(a)), to the reclassification of a mark from Schedule 3 to Schedule 4 (rule 41(1))	200
	Notice of opposition on the conferring of protection to the international registration (article 10)	200
TM9	Request for extension of time (rule 62(2))	50
TM11	Renewal of registration (rule 28)	200
	Class fee for each class over one	50
	Delayed renewal of registration (rule 29(1))	50
TM12	Request for division of an application (rule 19(1))	100

TM13	Request for the restoration and renewal of a registration removed from the register for failure to renew (rule 30(1))	100
TM16	Request to enter details of an assignment (rule 35(1)(a))	50
TM17	Request to merge either applications or registrations (rule 20(1))	—
TM23	Request by the registered proprietor for the partial surrender of a registered trade mark (rule 26(1)(b))	—

Number of Item corresponding form		*Amount £*
TM24	Application to record or cancel a registrable transaction other than an assignment or licence (rule 35(1)(d))	—
	Application to record or cancel a notifiable transaction (article 6)	—
TM26	Request for the revocation or invalidation of a registration (rule 31(1))	200
	Request for the rectification of a registration (rule 31(1))	—
	Request for the revocation or invalidation of a protected international trade mark (UK) (article 13)	200
	Request for the rectification of the supplementary register (article 15)	—
TM28	Recordal of concurrent registration (article 21)	—
TM31C	Request for information about applications and registered trade marks (rule 42)	20
TM31M	Request for information in relation to an international trade mark (UK) (article 25)	20
TM31R	Request for certified copy of an entry on the register (rule 37), per certificate	20
TM35	Filing of regulations governing the use of a certification or collective mark (rule 22)	200
TM36	Request to amend regulations governing the use of a certification or collective mark (rule 23(1))	100
TM50	Application for the registration of a licence under registered trade mark (rule 35(1)(b))	—
	Submission fee for an application for international registration to the International Bureau by the Patent Office (article 22)	40
	Handling fee for the transmission by the Patent Office of monies payable to the International Bureau for renewal of an international registration (article 31)	20

GOODS INFRINGING INTELLECTUAL PROPERTY RIGHTS (CUSTOMS)
REGULATIONS 1999
(SI 1999/1601)
Made 9th June 1999
The Commissioners of Customs and Excise, being a Department designated for the
purposes of section 2(2) of the European Communities Act 1972 in relation to measures relating to counterfeit and pirated goods, goods infringing a patent and goods
infringing a supplementary protection certificate, in exercise of the powers conferred upon them by the said section 2(2) and of all other powers enabling them in
that behalf, hereby make the following Regulations:—

1 These Regulations may be cited as the Goods Infringing Intellectual Property
Rights (Customs) Regulations 1999 and shall come into force on 1st July 1999.

2 In these Regulations—
'application' means an application under Article 3(1) of the Council
Regulation, and 'applicant' shall be construed accordingly;
'business day' has the meaning given in section 92 of the Bills of Exchange Act
1882;
'the Commissioners' means the Commissioners of Customs and Excise;
'Community trademark' means a trade mark as defined in Council Regulation
(EC) No 40/94;
'the Council Regulation' means Council Regulation (EC) No 3295/94, as
amended by Council Regulation (EC) No 241/1999, laying down measures
concerning the entry into the Community and the export and re-export
from the Community of goods infringing certain intellectual property
rights;
'decision' means a decision granting an application in accordance with Article
3(5) of the Council Regulation;
'goods infringing an intellectual property right' has the meaning given by
Article 1(2)(a) of the Council Regulation (counterfeit goods, pirated goods
and goods infringing a patent or supplementary protection certificate), and
'intellectual property right' shall be construed accordingly.

3 Except where it specifies a Community trademark which the applicant holds or is
authorised to use and seeks action by the customs authorities of another member
State, an application made to the Commissioners shall be in the form set out in the
Schedule to these Regulations, or a form to the like effect approved by the
Commissioners, containing full particulars of the matters specified therein.

4 (1)   The applicant shall give to the Commissioners such security or further
security, within such time and in such manner, whether by deposit of a sum of
money or guarantee, as the Commissioners may require, against the matters mentioned in paragraph (2) below.
(2) The matters against which security or further security shall be given are all
actions, proceedings, claims and demands whatsoever which may be taken or made
against, or costs and expenses which may be incurred by, the Commissioners in
consequence of the detention of, or anything done in relation to, any goods to
which the application or decision relates.

5 In every case, whether any security or further security is given or not, the applicant shall keep the Commissioners indemnified against all such liability and
expense as is mentioned in regulation 4(2) above and in particular shall repay to

them all expense which may be incurred by them in consequence of the detention of, or anything done in relation to, any goods to which the application or decision relates.

6 (1)   Where a decision is given, the applicant shall pay the Commissioners a fee of the relevant amount in relation to each of the following—
    (a) the period specified in the decision; and
    (b) any period by which that period is extended.
(2) The fee mentioned in paragraph (1) above shall be payable notwithstanding that the application is not made to the Commissioners but—

    (a) the application specifies a Community trademark which the applicant holds or is authorised to use;
    (b) the application has been made to the customs authorities of another member State;
    (c) the application seeks action by the Commissioners; and
    (d) a decision granting the application has been forwarded to the Commissioners in accordance with Article 5(2) of the Council Regulation.
(3) For the purposes of this regulation the relevant amount is—
    (a) for a period not exceeding one month, £200 plus VAT;
    (b) for a period not exceeding three months, £400 plus VAT;
    (c) for a period not exceeding six months, £700 plus VAT;
    (d) for a period not exceeding twelve months, £1,200 plus VAT; or
    (e) for a period of or exceeding twelve months—
        (i) £1,200 plus VAT for each complete period of twelve months, and
        (ii) an amount calculated in accordance with sub-paragraphs (a) to (d) above for any additional period.

7 In the event that the Commissioners require the applicant to examine a sample of detained goods which appear to them both to correspond to the description of goods contained in a decision and to be goods infringing an intellectual property right the applicant shall, within 10 business days from the date of the request by the Commissioners, or within such further time, not exceeding 10 business days, as the Commissioners may allow, provide such information as the Commissioners may require in order to be satisfied that the sample is comprised of goods infringing an intellectual property right.

8 A decision shall have no effect or no further effect where—

    (a) the applicant has failed to comply with any of the requirements of these Regulations;
    (b) any change, following the making of the application, which takes place in the ownership or authorised use of the intellectual property right specified in the application, is not communicated in writing to the Commissioners; or
    (c) the intellectual property right specified in the application expires.

9 The Counterfeit and Pirated Goods (Customs) Regulations 1995 [SI 1995/1430] are hereby revoked.

SCHEDULE

Regulation 3

(The full text of this form is currently unavailable. Please see the original.)

GOODS INFRINGING INTELLECTUAL PROPERTY RIGHTS (CONSEQUEN-
TIAL PROVISIONS) REGULATIONS 1999
(SI 1999/1618)
Made 9th June 1999
The Secretary of State, being designated for the purposes of section 2(2) of the
European Communities Act 1972 in relation to measures relating to counterfeit and
pirated goods, goods infringing a patent and goods infringing a supplementary pro-
tection certificate, in exercise of powers conferred on him by the said section 2(2),
and of all other enabling powers, hereby makes the following Regulations: —

1 These Regulations may be cited as the Goods Infringing Intellectual Property
Rights (Consequential Provisions) Regulations 1999 and shall come into force on
1st July 1999.

2 (1) In these Regulations:
'the 1979 Act' means the Customs and Excise Management Act 1979;
'application' means an application under Article 3(1) of the Council
Regulation;
'business day' has the meaning given by section 92 of the Bills of Exchange
Act 1882;
'the Commissioners' means the Commissioners of Customs and Excise;
'the Council Regulation' means Council Regulation (EC) No 3295/94 as
amended by Council Regulation (EC) No 241/1999, laying down measures
concerning the entry into the Community and the export and re-export
from the Community of goods infringing certain intellectual property
rights;
'counterfeit goods' has the meaning given by Article 1(2)(a) of the Council
Regulation;
'decision' means a decision granting an application in accordance with Article
3(5) of the Council Regulation;
'design right' has the meaning given by section 213(1) of Part III of the
Copyright, Designs and Patents Act 1988;
'goods infringing an intellectual property right' has the meaning given by
Article 1(2)(a) of the Council Regulation (counterfeit goods, pirated goods
and goods infringing a patent or supplementary protection certificate), and
related expressions shall be construed accordingly;
'goods infringing a patent' has the same meaning as in the Council Regulation;
'goods infringing a supplementary protection certificate' has the same meaning
as in the Council Regulation;
'holder of a right' has the meaning given by Article 1(2)(b) of the Council
Regulation;
'pirated goods' has the meaning given by Article 1(2)(a) of the Council
Regulation;
'registered design' shall be construed in accordance with the Registered
Designs Act 1949.
(2) For the purposes of the Council Regulation, any reference in it to 'copyright, or
neighbouring rights' is to be construed as a reference to 'copyright, or rights in performances'.
(3) These Regulations shall apply to goods which fall to be treated by virtue of

Article 1(3) of the Council Regulation as being goods within paragraph (2)(a) of that Article as they apply to any goods within that paragraph; but these Regulations shall not apply to any goods in relation to which the Council Regulation does not apply by virtue of Article 1(4) thereof.

3 Subject to paragraph (2) of regulation 4 below, goods infringing an intellectual property right which correspond to the description of goods contained in a decision shall be liable to forfeiture if any of the conditions mentioned in Article 1(1)(a) of the Council Regulation applies during the period specified in the decision.

4 (1) If, in the course of checks carried out in relation to goods as regards which any of the conditions mentioned in Article 1(1)(a) of the Council Regulation applies and before an application is made in respect of those goods, or, if made, before a decision is given, it appears to the Commissioners that the goods are goods infringing an intellectual property right, the Commissioners may, in accordance with Article 4 of the Council Regulation—

 (a) notify a holder of a right of the possible infringement of the right;
 (b) suspend the release of, or detain, those goods; and
 (c) if they do so suspend or detain, invite the holder of a right, in the absence of an existing application, to make an application within three business days of the date of suspension or detention.

(2) If at any time during the period of suspension or detention under paragraph (1) above a decision is given in respect of the goods, the condition mentioned in Article 1(1)(a) of the Council Regulation shall be taken to have applied during the period specified in the decision for the purposes of regulation 3 above.

(3) Where no application in respect of the goods is or has been made by any holder of a right within three business days of the date of suspension or detention, the suspension or detention shall cease.

5 (1) Subject to regulation 6 below, section 139 of, and Schedule 3 to, the 1979 Act (provisions as to detention, seizure and condemnation of goods, etc; forfeiture) shall apply in respect of any goods liable to forfeiture by virtue of regulation 3 above as they apply in respect of goods liable to forfeiture under the customs and excise Acts; and, accordingly:—

 (a) section 144 of the 1979 Act (protection of officers, etc in relation to seizure and detention of goods etc) shall apply in respect of seizure or detention effected by virtue of this regulation; and
 (b) sections 145, 146 and 152 to 155 of the 1979 Act (general provisions as to legal proceedings) shall apply in respect of condemnation proceedings brought by virtue of this regulation.

(2) Where in any condemnation proceedings brought by virtue of paragraph (1) above any question arises as to whether or not any goods are or were liable to forfeiture under regulation 3 above, the burden of proof shall lie upon the party alleging that they are not or were not so liable.

6 (1) Regulation 5 above shall not apply in relation to goods as regards which the decision specifies as subsisting in those goods any one or more of the following intellectual property rights (whether or not they also appear to infringe any other intellectual property right):

 (a) a patent;

    (b) a supplementary protection certificate;

    (c) a registered design;

    (d) design right.

(2) A holder of a right may, within 10 business days of his having been notified by the Commissioners of the suspension of release of the goods or of the goods having been detained, give notice in writing to the Commissioners waiving, for the purpose of both the Council Regulation and of these Regulations, any intellectual property right of his in the goods, being a right mentioned in sub-paragraphs (a) to (d) in paragraph (1) above.

(3) Where notice has been given in accordance with paragraph (2) above —

    (a) any right so waived shall be disregarded, as regards that holder of a right, in determining whether the goods fall within paragraph (1) above; and

    (b) the goods shall accordingly be treated for the purposes of the Council Regulation and these Regulations as if that person did not have the right concerned in those goods.

(4) The following provisions of the 1979 Act shall apply to any goods falling within paragraph (1) above as they apply in respect of goods liable to forfeiture under the customs and excise Acts:

    (a) section 139, except subsections (5) and (6) (things seized or detained to be dealt with or disposed of as Commissioners direct; Schedule 3 to have effect);

    (b) section 144.

(5) Any thing seized or detained by virtue of this regulation shall be dealt with in such manner as the Commissioners may direct; but this paragraph shall apply subject to section 139(3) and (4) of the 1979 Act (detention or seizure by a constable; things retained in the custody of the police) in the cases there mentioned.

7 (1) In the case of goods falling within paragraph (1) of regulation 6 above, the commencement of the proceedings described in paragraph (2) below, and only such proceedings, shall constitute a referral to the authority competent to take a substantive decision for the purposes of the Council Regulation.

(2) The proceedings mentioned in paragraph (1) above are proceedings commenced in the relevant court by a holder of a right alleging that the goods infringe an intellectual property right of his and seeking relief which that court has the power to grant after a finding of such infringement.

(3) Without prejudice to any provision of the Council Regulation, if at any time the Commissioners —

    (a) are not satisfied, or cease to be satisfied, that the proceedings described in paragraph (2) above have been commenced; or

    (b) are satisfied that such proceedings have been withdrawn or otherwise terminated without other such proceedings having been commenced,

the suspension of the release of the goods or their detention shall cease.

(4) For the purposes of this regulation proceedings shall not be taken to have been commenced before —

    (a) an originating process has been issued or, in the case of the Court of Session, signeted by the relevant court;

    (b) that process has been served on the other party or, if more than one, all the other parties to the proceedings, in accordance with the rules of the court concerned.

(5) In paragraph (4) above, the reference to an originating process is a reference

to—
(a) in England and Wales, a claim form;
(b) in Scotland, a summons; or
(c) in Northern Ireland, a writ.
(6) For the purposes of this regulation the relevant court is—
(a) in England and Wales, the High Court or any patents county court having jurisdiction by virtue of an order under section 287 of the Copyright, Designs and Patents Act 1988;
(b) in Scotland, the Court of Session; or
(c) in Northern Ireland, the High Court.

8 Nothing in these Regulations shall be taken to affect—

(a) any power of the Commissioners conferred otherwise than by any provision of these Regulations to suspend the release of, or detain, any goods; or
(b) the power of any court to grant any relief, including any power to make an order by way of interim relief.

9 The Counterfeit and Pirated Goods (Consequential Provisions) Regulations 1995 [SI 1995/1447] are hereby revoked.

PATENTS AND TRADE MARKS (WORLD TRADE ORGANISATION) REGULATIONS 1999
(SI 1999/1899)
Made 1st July 1999
The Secretary of State, being a Minister designated for the purposes of section 2(2) of the European Communities Act 1972 in relation to measures relating to patents and trade marks, in exercise of powers conferred by section 2(2) of the said Act of 1972, hereby makes the following Regulations:—

Part I
Introductory Provisions

1 Citation and commencement
(1) These Regulations may be cited as the Patents and Trade Marks (World Trade Organisation) Regulations 1999.
(2) These Regulations come into force on 29th July 1999.

2 Interpretation
In these Regulations—
    'the 1977 Act' means the Patents Act 1977;
    'the 1994 Act' means the Trade Marks Act 1994;
    'the 1995 rules' means the Patent Rules 1995.

Part IV
Amendments of the Trade Marks Act 1994

13 Amendments of 1994 Act
(1) In subsection (1)(c) of section 6 of the 1994 Act (meaning of 'earlier trade mark'), after the words 'protection under the Paris Convention' insert the words 'or the WTO agreement'.
(2) In subsection (1) of section 55 of the 1994 Act (Paris Convention: supplemen-

tary provisions), omit the word 'and' at the end of paragraph (a) and after that paragraph insert—

> '(aa)'the WTO agreement' means the Agreement establishing the World Trade Organisation signed at Marrakesh on 15th April 1994, and'.

(3) In subsection (2) of that section, after the words 'the Paris Convention' there shall be inserted the words 'or the WTO agreement'.

(4) In subsections (1) and (2) of section 56 of that Act (protection of well-known trade marks), after the words 'the Paris Convention' insert the words 'or the WTO agreement'.

(5) In subsections (2) and (3) of section 57 of that Act (national emblems etc of Convention countries), after the words 'the Paris Convention' insert the words 'or the WTO agreement'.

(6) In subsection (2) of section 58 of that Act (emblems etc of certain international organisations), after the words 'the Paris Convention' insert the words 'or the WTO agreement'.

(7) After subsection (4) of section 59 of that Act (notification under Article 6ter of Convention) insert—

> '(5) Any reference in this section to Article 6ter of the Paris Convention shall be construed as including a reference to that Article as applied by the WTO agreement'.

14 Part IV: transitional provisions

(1) The amendment of section 56(2) of the 1994 Act made by regulation 13(4) shall not affect the continuation of any bona fide use of a trade mark begun before the 1st January 1996.

(2) The amendment made by regulation 13(6) shall not affect the rights of a person whose bona fide use of the trade mark in question began before that date.

EXPLANATORY NOTE

(This note is not part of the Regulations)
These Regulations modify the Patents Act 1977, the Patents Rules 1995 (SI 1995/2093) and the Trade Marks Act 1994 in pursuance of the United Kingdom's obligations under the Agreement establishing the World Trade Organisation signed at Marrakesh on 15th April 1994 and the Agreement on Trade-Related Aspects of Intellectual Property Rights which is an integral part of the WTO Agreement.

The principal amendments are to those provisions of—
    (a) the Patents Act 1977 (regulations 3 to 8), and
    (b) the Patents Rules 1995 (regulations 9 to 12),

which concern the application for and the grant of compulsory licences. Where the proprietor of the patent in respect of which such an application is made is a national of, or is domiciled or has a real and effective industrial or commercial establishment in, a country which is a member of the World Trade Organisation, the grounds upon which a compulsory licence may be granted are more restricted than the grounds which would otherwise be available to an applicant (regulation 4).

Amendments are also made to the Patents Act 1977 and to the Trade Marks Act 1994 to permit any country which becomes a member of the World Trade Organisation to be treated automatically as a Convention country (regulations 7(1) and 13).

A Regulatory Impact Assessment is not required for this Instrument.

PATENT OFFICE (ADDRESS) (REVOCATION) RULES 1999
(SI 1999/1993)
Made 13th July 1999

The Secretary of State, in exercise of the powers conferred upon him by section 78(1) of the Trade Marks Act 1994, section 36(1) of the Registered Designs Act 1949, and section 123(1) of, and paragraph 14 of Schedule 4 to, the Patents Act 1977, hereby makes the following Rules:—

1 These Rules may be cited as the Patent Office (Address) (Revocation) Rules 1999 and shall come into force on 10th August 1999.

2 The Patent Office (Address) Rules 1991 [SI 1991/675] are hereby revoked.

Appendix 3

Rules of Court

Civil Procedure Rules 1998

PART 49
SPECIALIST PROCEEDINGS

49 (1)   These Rules shall apply to the proceedings listed in paragraph (2) subject to the provisions of the relevant practice direction which applies to those proceedings.

(2)   The proceedings referred to in paragraph (1) are—
   (a) admiralty proceedings;
   (b) arbitration proceedings;
   (c) commercial and mercantile actions;
   (d) Patents Court business (as defined by the relevant practice direction) and proceedings under—
      (i) the Copyright, Designs and Patents Act 1988;
      (ii) the Trade Marks Act 1994; and
      (iii)the Olympic Symbol etc Protection Act 1995 and Olympic Association Right (Infringement Proceeding) Regulations 1995);
   (e) Technology and Construction Court Business (as defined by the relevant practice direction);
   (f) proceedings under the Companies Act 1985 and the Companies Act 1989; and
   (g) contentious probate proceedings.

NOTES
The Practice Directions currently made and in force in relation to specialist proceedings are as follows:
A   Contentious Probate Proceedings;
B   Applications under the Companies Act 1985.
C   Technology and Construction Court;
D   Commercial Court (and see also The Commercial Court Guide);
E   Patents etc;
F   Admiralty
G   Arbitrations.
H   Mercantile Courts and Business Lists.

PRACTICE DIRECTION—PATENTS ETC

THIS PRACTICE DIRECTION SUPPLEMENTS CPR PART 49 AND
REPLACES, WITH MODIFICATIONS, RSC ORDER 104, ORDER 100 AND
ORDER 93, RULE 24 AND CCR ORDER 48A AND ORDER 49 RULE 4A

GENERAL
1.1   This practice direction applies to the business of the Patents Court and

proceedings under the Copyright, Designs and Patents Act 1988, the Trade Marks Acts 1938 and 1994 and the Olympic Symbol etc Protection Act 1995 and Olympic Association Right (infringement Proceedings) Regulations 1995.

1.2   The Civil Procedure Rules apply to Patents Court business and proceedings under the Copyright, Designs and Patents Act 1988, the Trade Marks Acts 1938 and 1994 and the Olympic Symbol etc Protection Act 1995 and Olympic Association Right (Infringement Proceedings) Regulations 1995 subject to the provisions of this and any other Patents Court practice direction.

1.3   Definitions

In this Practice Direction—

'the 1949 Act' means the Patents Act 1949;

'the 1977 Act' means the Patents Act 1977;

'the Comptroller' means the Comptroller-General of Patents, Designs and Trade Marks;

'the Court,' means the Patents Court;

'existing patent' means a patent mentioned in section 127(2)(a) or (c) of the 1977 Act;

'the journal' means the journal published pursuant to rules made under section 123(6) of the 1977 Act;

'1977 Act patent' means a patent under the 1977 Act;

'patent' means an existing patent or a 1977 Act patent and includes any application for a patent, supplementary protection certificate granted pursuant to the Patents (Supplementary Protection Certificates) Rules 1997, the Patents (Supplementary Protection Certificate for Medicinal Products) Regulations 1992 and the Patents (Supplementary Protection Certificate for Plant Protection Products) Regulations 1996.

'Patents Court' includes the Patents Court of the High Court and the Patents County Court.

'Patents Court business' includes:

(a) any claim under the Patents Acts 1949 to 1961 and 1977;

(b) any claim under the Registered Designs Acts 1949 to 1961;

(c) any claim under the Defence Contracts Act 1958, and

(d) all proceedings for the determination of a question or the making of a declaration relating to a patent (or an application for a patent) under the inherent jurisdiction of the High Court.

'the CPR' means the Civil Procedure Rules.

ALLOCATION OF PATENTS COURT BUSINESS

2.1   Patents Court business may be dealt with either in the High Court or the Patents county court.

2.2   Before the issue of a claim form relating to Patents Court business, the claim form, whether it is to be issued in the High Court or the county court, should be marked in the top right hand corner 'Patents Court' and the claim will then be allocated to the Patents Court.

2.3   The Patents Court is a specialist list for the purposes of Part 30 of the CPR but no order for the transfer of proceedings to or from the Patents Court shall be made unless the parties have either:

(a) had an opportunity of being heard on the issue, or

(b) consented to the order.

2.4   Every claim in the Patents Court will be allocated to the Multi-track and the CPR relating to allocation questionnaires and track allocation will not apply.

2.5

(1) Where a claim has been allocated to the Patents Court either on issue (ie. in every case in which the claim form has been marked Patents Court) or by transfer to the Patents Court, an application for directions (including an application for a fixed date of hearing) shall be made by the claimant within 14 days of the filing by the defendant of an acknowledgement of service or of a defence (whichever is the earlier) or, as the case may be, within 14 days of the date of the order of transfer.

(2) If the claimant does not make an application in accordance with paragraph 2.5, any other party may do so or may apply for the claim of the claimant in default to be struck out or dismissed.

(3) Any application under this paragraph must be made to a judge of the Patents Court unless a judge of the Patents Court otherwise directs.

(4) On the hearing of the application for directions under paragraph 2.5(1) the judge shall give directions for any further directions hearing and direct the time by which the hearing of any further application for directions is to take place.

2.6   Except where inconsistent with the provisions of this Practice Direction, CPR Part 29 and the Multi-track Practice Direction apply to Patents Court business.

2.7   This practice direction shall apply with any necessary modifications to proceedings in respect of Registered Designs.

SERVICE OF DOCUMENTS

3.1   This rule applies to the service of any document on a party until such time as that party has provided an address for service in accordance with CPR rule 6.5.

3.2   Subject to sub-paragraph (3) below, for the purposes of any proceedings relating to a patent or a registered design (including proceedings for revocation, declaration as to non-infringement or groundless threats of infringement proceedings or any other proceedings of a kind mentioned in this Practice Direction) where any document is served in the manner authorised by CPR Part 6 at an address for service given in the register kept under section 32 of the 1977 Act or, as the case may be, section 17 of the Registered Designs Act 1949—

(1) service shall be deemed to have been effected on the registered proprietor of the patent or registered design on the date on which the document was served at the said address;

(2) the party on whom service is deemed to have been effected under subparagraph (a) shall be treated, for the purposes of any provision of these rules which specifies a time-limit for responding to the document so served (whether by filing or serving an admission, filing a defence, acknowledging service, or otherwise), as having been served on the seventh day after the date on which the document was served at the said address.

3.3   Nothing in paragraph 3.2 shall prevent service being effected on the proprietor in accordance with the provisions of Part 6 of the CPR.

APPLICATION IN PROCEEDINGS BEFORE THE COURT FOR PERMISSION TO AMEND A PATENT SPECIFICATION UNDER S.30 OF THE 1949 ACT OR S.75 OF THE 1977 ACT

4.1   A patentee or the proprietor of a patent intending to apply in proceedings before the Court under section 30 of the 1949 Act or under section 75 of the 1977 Act for permission to amend his specification must give notice of his intention to the Comptroller accompanied by a copy of an advertisement—

(1) identifying the proceedings pending before the Court in which it is

intended to apply for such permission;

(2) giving particulars of the amendment sought;

(3) stating the applicant's address for service within the United Kingdom;

(4) stating that a Statement of Reasons is available from that address; and

(5) stating that any person intending to oppose the amendment must within 28 days after the appearance of the advertisement give written notice of his intention to the applicant; such notice to be accompanied by a Statement of Opposition

and the Comptroller shall insert the advertisement once in the journal. A person who gives notice in accordance with the advertisement shall be entitled to be heard on the application subject to any direction of the Court as to costs.

4.2   The applicant must at the same time as giving notice to the Comptroller serve a copy of the Statement of Reasons together with a copy of the patent as proposed to be amended on all parties to the proceedings.

4.3   The Statement of Reasons referred to in paragraph 4.1(4) shall contain full particulars of the amendment sought, of the reasons therefor and of the reasons why the applicant contends that in the exercise of discretion the amendment should be allowed. In particular the Statement should contain

(1) A statement whether the amendment is by way of deletion of claims or rewriting of claims.

(2) Insofar as it involve re-writing claims, details as to why the proposed amendment is in accordance with the statutory requirements of an amendment.

(3) Insofar as the amendment is sought to distinguish (more clearly) over prior art, an indication of the prior art.

4.4   The Statement of Opposition shall contain full particulars of all grounds of opposition to the application to amend.

4.5   As soon as may be after the expiration of 35 days from the appearance of the advertisement the applicant must make his application under the said section 30 or 75, as the case may be, by an application notice in the proceedings before the Court; and the application notice, together with a copy of the specification certified by the Comptroller and showing in coloured ink the amendment sought, must be served on the Comptroller, the parties to the proceedings and any person who has given notice of his intention to oppose the amendment.

4.6   Not less than two days before the date fixed for the hearing of the application, the applicant, the Comptroller, the parties to the proceedings and any other opponent should serve on all other parties and on the Court a Statement of Directions being the directions which that party seeks for the further conduct of the proceedings. Any of the foregoing not serving a Statement of Directions shall take no further part in the proceedings without permission of the Court and shall not be liable for the costs thereof.

4.7   On the hearing of the amendment application the Court shall give such directions for its further conduct as it thinks necessary or expedient and, in particular, directions—

(1) determining whether the application shall be heard forthwith or with the other proceedings relating to the patent in question or separately and, if separately, fixing the date of hearing thereof;

(2) as to whether any evidence is necessary, and, if so, as to the manner in which the that evidence shall be given and, if written evidence is to be given, fixing the times within which the affidavits or witness statements

must be filed;

    (3) as to whether any disclosure is necessary, and, if so, as to the extent of disclosure and the manner and time within which the same is to be given.

4.8   Where the Court allows a specification to be amended, the applicant must forthwith file with the Comptroller an office copy of the order made in the Court and, if so required by the Court or Comptroller, leave at the Patent Office a new specification and drawings as amended, prepared in compliance with the 1949 or 1977 Act, whichever is applicable, and the rules made under those Acts respectively.

4.9   The Comptroller shall cause a copy of the order to be inserted at least once in the journal.

APPLICATION FOR REVOCATION

5.1   An application under section 72 of the 1977 Act for the revocation of a patent shall be commenced by the issue of a claim form. This direction does not apply to an application made in existing proceedings. An application in existing proceedings shall be made by way of a counterclaim or other Part 20 claim (as defined in CPR rule 20.2(1)).

CLAIM FOR INFRINGEMENT

6.1   The claimant in a claim for infringement must serve with his claim form particulars of the infringement relied on, showing which of the claims in the specification of the patent are alleged to be infringed and giving at least one instance of each type of infringement alleged.

6.2   If a defendant in such a claim alleges, as a defence to the claim, that at the time of the infringement there was in force a contract or licence relating to the patent made by or with the consent of the claimant and containing a condition or term void by virtue of section 44 of the 1977 Act, he must serve on the claimant particulars of the date of, and parties to, each such contract or licence and particulars of each such condition or term.

OBJECTIONS TO VALIDITY

7.1   A person who presents a claim for the revocation of a patent must serve with his claim form particulars of the objections to the validity of the patent on which he relies.

7.2   A party to a claim concerning a patent who either challenges the validity of the patent or applies by counterclaim or other Part 20 claim for revocation of the patent must, serve his defence, counterclaim or other Part 20 claim (as the case may be), together with particulars of the objections to the validity of the patent on which he relies, within 42 days after service upon him of the claim form.

7.3   Particulars given pursuant to paragraph 7.1 or 7.2 must state every ground on which the validity of the patent is challenged and must include such particulars as will clearly define every issue (including any challenge to any claimed priority date) which it is intended to raise.

7.4   If the grounds stated in the particulars of objections include want of novelty or want of any inventive step, the particulars must state the manner, time and place of every prior publication or user relied upon and, if prior user is alleged, must:

    (1) specify the name of every person alleged to have made such user,

    (2) state whether such user is alleged to have continued until the priority date

of the claim in question or of the invention, as may be appropriate, and, if not, the earliest and latest date on which such user is alleged to have taken place,

(3) contain a description accompanied by drawings, if necessary, sufficient to identify such user, and

(4) if such user relates to machinery or apparatus, state whether the machinery or apparatus is in existence and where it can be inspected.

7.5   I   f either (a) in the case of an existing patent one of the grounds stated in the particulars of objections is that the invention, so far as claimed in any claim of the complete specification, is not useful, or, (b) in the case of a patent one of the grounds stated in the particulars of objections is that the specification of the patent does not disclose the invention clearly enough and completely enough for the invention to be performed and it is intended, in connection with either of such grounds, to rely on the fact that an example of the invention which is the subject of any claim cannot be made to work, either at all or as described in the specification, the particulars must state that fact and identify each such claim and must include particulars of each such example, specifying the respects in which it is alleged that it does not work or does not work as described.

7.6   In any proceedings relating to a patent in which the validity of the patent has been put in issue on the ground of obviousness a party who wishes to rely on the commercial success of the patent must state in his pleadings the grounds upon which he so relies.

ADMISSIONS

8.1   Where a party desires any other party to admit any facts, he shall, within 21 days after service of a reply or after the expiration of the period fixed for the service thereof, serve on that other party a notice requiring him to admit for the purpose of the claim the facts specified in the notice.

8.2   A party upon whom a notice under paragraph 8.1 is served shall within 21 days after service thereof serve upon the party making the request a notice stating in respect of each fact specified in the notice whether or not he admits it.

DISCLOSURE AND INSPECTION

9.1   CPR Part 31 shall apply in a claim for infringement of a patent or a declaration of non-infringement of a patent or any proceedings where the validity of a patent is in issue.

9.2   Standard disclosure does not require the disclosure of documents in the following exempt classes: —

(1) documents relating to the infringement of a patent by a product or process if, before serving a list of documents, the party against whom the allegation of infringement is made has served on the other parties full particulars of the product or process alleged to infringe, including if necessary drawings or other illustrations;

(2) documents relating to any ground on which the validity of a patent is put in issue, except documents which came into existence within the period beginning two years before the earliest claimed priority date and ending two years after that date; and

(3) documents relating to the issue of commercial success.

9.3   Where the issue of commercial success arises in any proceedings specified in paragraph 9.1, the patentee shall, within such time limit as the Court may direct, serve a schedule containing the following details—

(1) where the commercial success relates to an article or product—

    (a) an identification of the article or product (for example by product code number) which the patentee asserts has been made in accordance with the claims of the patent;

    (b) a summary by convenient periods of sales of any such article or product;

    (c) a summary for the equivalent periods of sales, if any, of any equivalent prior article or product marketed before the article or product mentioned in sub-paragraph (a); and

    (d) a summary by convenient periods of any expenditure on advertising and promotion which supported the marketing of the articles or products mentioned in sub-paragraphs (a) and (c),

(2) where the commercial success relates to the use of a process—

    (a) an identification of the process the patentee asserts has been used in accordance with the claims of the patent;

    (b) a summary by convenient periods of the revenues received from the use of such process;

    (c) a summary for the equivalent periods of the revenues, if any, received from the use of any equivalent prior art process; and

    (d) a summary by convenient periods of any expenditure which supported the use of the process mentioned in sub-paragraphs (a) and (c).

EXPERIMENTS

10.1 Where a party desires to establish any fact by experimental proof he must, at least 21 days before the service of the application notice for directions under paragraph 10.3 or within such other time as the Court may direct at a hearing for further directions pursuant to paragraph 2.5(4), serve on the other party a notice stating the facts which he desires to establish and giving full particulars of the experiments proposed to establish them.

10.2 A party upon whom a notice under paragraph 10.1 is served shall, within 21 days after service thereof, serve upon the other party a notice stating in respect of each fact whether or not he admits it.

10.3 Where any fact which a party desires to establish by experimental proof is not admitted he shall apply to the Court for directions in respect of such experiments.

APPLICATION FOR FURTHER DIRECTIONS

11.1

(1) The parties must comply with any directions given by the judge pursuant to paragraph 2.5(4) in respect of any hearing for further directions.

(2) If the claimant does not serve an application notice for further directions in accordance with this paragraph, the defendant may do so.

(3) The application notice must be accompanied by minutes of the order proposed, and such other documents as will be necessary for the hearing of the application.

11.2 At a further directions hearing under this paragraph the judge may give such directions relating to:

(1) the service of further pleadings or of further information pursuant to Part 18 of the CPR;

(2) disclosure and inspection of documents;

(3) requests for or the making of admissions pursuant to paragraphs 8.1 and 8.2 above and Part 14 of the CPR;

(4) the obtaining of written evidence relating to matters requiring expert knowledge, and for the filing of affidavits or witness statements and the service of copies thereof on the other parties;

(5) the holding of a meeting of such experts as the judge may specify, for the purpose of producing a joint report on the state of the relevant art;

(6) the exchanging of experts' reports, in respect of those matters on which they are not agreed;

(7) the making of experiments, tests, inspections or reports;

(8) the determination, as a preliminary issue, of any question that may arise (including any questions as to the construction of the specification or other documents)

and otherwise as the judge thinks necessary or expedient for the purpose of giving effect to the overriding objective. Where evidence is directed to be given by affidavit or witness statement, the witnesses must attend at the trial for cross-examination unless, with the concurrence of the Court, the parties otherwise agree.

11.3 On the hearing of an application under this paragraph the judge shall consider, if necessary of his own initiative, whether:

(a) the parties' advisers should be required to meet for the purpose of agreeing which documents will be required at the trial and of paginating such documents;

(b) an independent scientific adviser should be appointed to assist the Court, whether as an assessor under CPR rule 35.15 or otherwise.

RESTRICTIONS ON ADMISSION OF EVIDENCE

12.1 Except with the permission of the judge hearing any claim or other proceedings relating to a patent, no evidence shall be admissible in proof of any alleged infringement, or of any objection to the validity, of the patent, if the infringement or objection was not raised in the particulars of infringements or objections, as the case may be.

12.2 In any claim or other proceedings relating to a patent, evidence which is not in accordance with a statement contained in particulars of objections to the validity of the patent shall not be admissible in support of such an objection unless the judge hearing the proceeding allows the evidence to be admitted.

12.3 If any machinery or apparatus alleged to have been used before the priority date mentioned in paragraph 7.4(2) is in existence at the date of service of the particulars of objections, no evidence of its user before that date shall be admissible unless it is proved that the party relying on such user offered, where the machinery or apparatus is in his possession, inspection of it to the other parties to the proceedings or, where it is not, used all reasonable endeavours to obtain inspection of it for those parties.

DETERMINATION OF QUESTION OR APPLICATION WHERE COMPTROLLER DECLINES TO DEAL WITH IT.

13. Where the Comptroller—

(1) declines to deal with a question under section 8(7), 12(2), 37(8) or 61(5) of the 1977 Act;

(2) declines to deal with an application under section 40(5) of that Act; or

(3) certifies under section 72(7)(b) of that Act that the question whether a

patent should be revoked is one which would more properly be determined by the court,

any person entitled to do so may, within 28 days after the Comptroller's decision apply to the Court to determine the question or application.

APPLICATION BY EMPLOYEE FOR COMPENSATION UNDER SECTION 40 OF THE 1977 ACT

14.1   An application by an employee for compensation under section 40(1) or (2) of the 1977 Act shall be begun by the issue of a claim form within the period which begins when the relevant patent is granted and which expires one year after it has ceased to have effect.

Provided that, where a patent has ceased to have effect by reason of a failure to pay any renewal fee within the period prescribed for the payment thereof and an application for restoration is made to the Comptroller under section 28 of the said Act, the said period shall—

(1) if restoration is ordered, continue as if the patent had remained continuously in effect, or

(2) if restoration is refused, be treated as expiring one year after the patent ceased to have effect or six months after the refusal, whichever is the later.

14.2   Either at the hearing of an application for directions under paragraph 2.5(1) or at a hearing of an application for further directions under paragraphs 11.1–11.3, the Court must give directions as to the manner in which the evidence (including any accounts of expenditure and receipts relating to the claim) shall be given at the hearing of the claim and, if written evidence is to be given, specify the period within which witness statements or affidavits must be filed.

14.3   The Court must also give directions as to the provision by the defendant to the claimant, or a person deputed by him for the purpose, of reasonable facilities for inspecting and taking extracts from the books of account by which the defendant proposes to verify the accounts mentioned in paragraph 14.2 or from which those accounts have been derived.

PROCEDURE FOR THE DETERMINATION OF CERTAIN DISPUTES

15.1   The following proceedings must be begun by the issue of a claim form, that is to say—

(1) proceedings for the determination of any dispute referred to the court under—

(a) section 48 of the 1949 Act or section 58 of the 1977 Act;

(b) paragraph 3 of Schedule 1 to the Registered Designs Act 1949;

(c) section 4 of the Defence Contracts Act 1958; or

(d) section 252 of the Copyright, Designs and Patent Act 1988;

(2) any application under section 45(3) of the 1977 Act.

APPEALS FROM THE COMPTROLLER

16.1   in this paragraph 'the Court' means the Patents Court of the High Court.

16.2   An appeal to the Court from a decision of the Comptroller in any case in which a right of appeal is given by the 1949 or 1977 Act must be brought by issuing a Notice of Appeal. The parties are, in this paragraph, referred to as 'appellant' and 'respondent' respectively.

16.3   The Notice of Appeal shall be issued:

(1) in the case of a decision on a matter of procedure, within 14 days after the date of the decision; and

(2) in any other case, within six weeks after the date of the decision.

16.4   The Comptroller may determine whether any decision is on a matter of procedure and any such determination shall itself be a decision on a matter of procedure.

16.5   Except with permission of the Court, no appeal shall be entertained unless the Notice of Appeal has been issued within the period specified in paragraph 16.3 or within such further time as the Comptroller may allow upon request made to him prior to the expiry of that period.

16.6   The Notice of Appeal may be given in respect of the whole or any specific part of the decision of the Comptroller and must specify the grounds of the appeal and the relief which the appellant seeks.

16.7   Except with the permission of the Court the appellant shall not be entitled on the hearing of the appeal to rely on any ground of appeal or to apply for any relief not specified in the Notice of Appeal.

16.8   The appellant shall, within 21 days of issuing the Notice of Appeal, serve a copy thereof on the Comptroller and any other party to the proceedings before the Comptroller.

16.9   After receiving the Notice of Appeal the Comptroller shall lodge with the Clerk or other person in charge of the Patents Court list all papers relating to the matter which is subject of the appeal.

16.10   A respondent who, not having appealed from the decision of the Comptroller, desires to contend on the appeal that the decision should be varied, either in any event or in the event of the appeal being allowed in whole or in part, must give notice to that effect, specifying the grounds of that contention and the relief which he seeks from the Court.

16.11   A respondent who desires to contend on the appeal that the decision of the Comptroller should be affirmed on grounds other than those set out in the decision must give notice to that effect, specifying the grounds of that contention.

16.12   A respondent's notice shall be served on the Comptroller and on the appellant and every other party to the proceedings before the Comptroller within 14 days after service of the Notice of Appeal by the respondent, or within such further time as the Court may direct.

16.13   A party by whom a respondent's notice is given must within 5 days after service of the notice on the appellant, furnish 2 copies of the notice to the Clerk or other person in charge of the Patents List.

16.14   The Clerk or other person in charge of the Patents list shall give to the Comptroller and to the appellant and every other party to the proceedings before the Comptroller not less than seven days' notice of the date appointed for the hearing of the appeal, unless the Court directs shorter notice to be given.

16.15   An appeal shall be by way of rehearing and the evidence used on appeal shall be the same as that used before the Comptroller and, except with the permission of the Court, no further evidence shall be given.

16.16   Any notice given in proceedings under this rule may be signed by or served on any patent agent, or member of the Bar of England and Wales not in actual practice, who is acting for the person giving the notice or, as the case may be, the person on whom the notice is to be served, as if the patent agent or member of the Bar were a solicitor.

16.17   The Notice of Appeal shall be in the form annexed hereto or in such other form as may be approved by the Court.

COMMUNICATION OF INFORMATION TO THE EUROPEAN PATENT OFFICE

17.1   The Court may authorise the communication to the European Patent Office or the competent authority of any country which is a party to the European Patent Convention of any such information in the files of the court as the Court thinks fit.

17.2   Before complying with a request for the disclosure of information under paragraph 17.1 the Court shall afford to any party appearing to be affected by the request the opportunity of making representations, in writing or otherwise, on the question whether the information should be disclosed.

CLAIM FOR RECTIFICATION OF REGISTER OF PATENTS OR DESIGNS

18.1   Where a claim is made for the rectification of the register of patents, the claimant shall at the same time as serving the other party serve a copy of the claim form and the accompanying documents on the Comptroller, who shall be entitled to appear and to be heard on the application.

OTHER INTELLECTUAL PROPERTY MATTERS INCLUDED IN THIS PRACTICE DIRECTION

A. COPYRIGHT MATTERS

ADDITIONAL DAMAGES UNDER SECTION 97(2) OF THE COPYRIGHT, DESIGNS AND PATENTS ACT 1988.

19.1   Where a claimant seeks to recover additional damages under section 97(2) of the Copyright, Designs and Patents Act 1988, he must so state in his claim form and the particulars of claim must set out the grounds relied upon in support.

APPLICATIONS FOR DELIVERY UP AND FORFEITURE UNDER SECTIONS 99, 114, 195, 204, 230 OR 231 OF THE COPYRIGHT DESIGNS AND PATENTS ACT 1988

20.1   An application under Sections 99, 114, 195, 204, 230 or 231 of the Copyright, Designs and Patents Act 1988 ('CDPA') shall be made by the issue of a claim form or, if made in existing proceedings, an application notice in those proceedings.

20.2   Where such an application is made the applicant shall serve the claim form or application notice on all persons having an interest in the goods, material or articles within the meaning of sections 114, 204 or 231 of the CDPA insofar as such persons are reasonably ascertainable.

B. TRADEMARK MATTERS

DEFINITIONS

21.1   In this section of this practice direction—

'the 1938 Act' means the Trade Marks Act 1938 as amended by the Trade Marks (Amendment) Act 1984 and the Patents, Designs and Marks Act 1986;

'the 1994 Act' means the Trade Marks Act 1994;

'the Olympic Symbol Act' means the Olympic Symbol etc. (Protection) Act 1995;

'the Olympic Symbol Regulations' means the Olympic Association Right (Infringement Proceedings) Regulations 1995;

'the Registrar' means the Comptroller-General of Patents, Designs and Trade Marks;

'the register' means the register of trade marks maintained by the Registrar pursuant to section 63 of the 1994 Act;

'appointed person' means a person appointed by the Lord Chancellor to hear and decide appeals under the 1994 Act.

ASSIGNMENT TO THE CHANCERY DIVISION

22.1   Proceedings in the High Court under the 1938 Act, the 1994 Act or the Olympic Symbol Act and Regulations shall be dealt with in the Chancery Division.

APPEALS AND APPLICATIONS UNDER THE 1938 ACT, THE 1994 ACT AND THE OLYMPIC SYMBOL ACT AND THE OLYMPIC SYMBOL REGULATIONS

23.1   Every appeal to the High Court under the 1938 Act or the 1994 Act shall be heard and determined by a single judge.

23.2   Such appeals shall be brought by a Notice of Appeal in such form as may be approved by the court.

23.3   The Notice of Appeal must be issued within 28 days of the decision appealed from.

23.4   Within 21 days of issue the Notice of Appeal must be served on the Registrar and any Respondents and lodged with the Clerk or other person in charge of the Chancery List.

23.5   Every other application to the High Court under the said Acts and the Olympic Symbol Regulations must be begun by the issue of a claim form under CPR Part 8 or, if made in existing proceedings, an application notice in those proceedings.

23.6   Notices of Appeal, claim forms or application notices by which any such application is begun must be served on the Registrar.

23.7   Where —

(1) the Registrar refers to the High Court an application made to him under the 1938 Act or the 1994 Act;

(2) the Board of Trade under the 1938 Act or an appointed person under section 76 of the 1994 Act refers to that Court an appeal,

then unless within one month after receiving notification of the decision to refer, the applicant or the appellant, as the case may be, makes to that Court the application or appeal referred, he shall be deemed to have abandoned it.

23.8   The period prescribed above in relation to an appeal to which paragraph 23.1 applies or the period prescribed by paragraph 23.7 in relation to an application or appeal to which that paragraph applies, may be extended by the Registrar on the application of any party interested and may be so extended although the application is not made until after the expiration of that period, but the foregoing provision shall not be taken to affect the power of the Court to extend that period.

23.9   Where under subsection (6) of section 17 or subsection (9) of section 18 of the 1938 Act an appellant becomes entitled and intends to withdraw the application which is the subject-matter of the appeal, he must give notice of his intention to the Registrar and to any other party to the appeal within one month after the Court has given permission under the said subsection (6) or the said subsection (9), as the case may be, for further grounds of objection to be taken.

23.10   Where an application is made under section 19 of the 1994 Act or under regulation 5 of the Olympic Symbol Regulations the applicant shall serve the claim form or application notice on all persons having an interest in the goods, material or articles within the meaning of section 19 of the 1994 Act or Regulation 5 of the Olympic Symbol Regulations as the case may be insofar as such persons are reasonably ascertainable.

PROCEEDINGS FOR INFRINGEMENT OF REGISTERED TRADE MARK; VALIDITY OF REGISTRATION DISPUTED OR REVOCATION OR RECTIFICATION SOUGHT

24.1 Where in any proceedings a claim is made for relief for infringement of the rights conferred on the proprietor of a registered trade mark by section 9 of the 1994 Act, the party against whom the claim is made may in his defence put in issue the validity of the registration of that trade mark or may apply by counterclaim or other Part 20 claim for an order for revocation of the registration or for a declaration of invalidity of the registration or for rectification of the register, or may do any or all of those things.

24.2 A party to any such proceedings who in his pleading (whether a defence or counterclaim or other Part 20 claim) disputes the validity of the registration of a registered trade mark or seeks a declaration of invalidity or an order for revocation of the registration, or rectification of the register, must serve with his pleading particulars of the objections to the validity of the registration or of any grounds for revocation or rectification, on which he relies.

24.3 A party to any such proceedings who applies for an order for revocation of the registration or for a declaration of invalidity of the registration or for rectification of the register must serve on the Registrar a copy of his counterclaim or other Part 20 claim together with a copy of the particulars mentioned in paragraph 24.2 and the Registrar shall be entitled to take such part in the proceedings as he may think fit but need not serve a defence or other statement of case unless ordered to do so by the Court.

SERVICE OF DOCUMENTS

25.1 This rule applies to the service of any document on a party until such time as that party has provided an address for service in accordance CPR rule 6.5.

25.2 Subject to paragraph 25.3 for the purposes of any proceedings relating to a registered trade mark (including proceedings for revocation, declaration of invalidity or non-infringement or groundless threats of infringement proceedings or any other proceedings under the 1938 Act or the 1994 Act), where any document is served in the manner authorised by Part 6 of the CPR at an address for service given in the register kept under section 63 of the 1994 Act—

(1) service shall be deemed to have been effected on the registered proprietor of the trade mark on the date on which the document was served at the said address;

(2) the party on whom service is deemed to have been effected under subparagraph (1), shall be treated, for the purposes of any provision which specifies a time-limit for responding to the document so served (whether by acknowledging service, giving notice of intention to defend or otherwise), as having been served on the seventh day after the date on which the document was served at the said address.

25.3 Nothing in paragraph 25.2 shall prevent service being effected on the proprietor in accordance with the provisions of CPR Part 6.

SERVICE OF ORDERS ON THE REGISTRAR

Where an order is made by the Court in any case under the 1938 Act or the 1994 Act, the person in whose favour the order is made (if there is more than one, such one of them as the Court shall direct) shall serve an office copy of the order on the

Registrar.

IN THE HIGH COURT OF JUSTICE CHANCERY DIVISION
PATENTS COURT
NOTICE OF APPEAL

(a) Here insert the nature of the application or proceedings, the name of the Patentee or Applicant the number of the Patent or Application for Letters Patent followed by the name of the Opponent
(if any)

(b) Patent Agent or Applicant in person

(c) Here insert name(s) and full address(es) of Appellant(s)

(d) Here insert 'the decision 'or' that part of the decision' as the case may be

(e) Here insert 'Comptroller General' or 'Officer acting for the Comptroller General' as the case may be

(f) Summarise the decision appealed against   **IN THE MATTER(a)**

(e.g. of an Application by ....
          and
          an Opposition by ....

TAKE NOTICE that the HIGH COURT OF JUSTICE, CHANCERY DIVISION, PATENTS COURT, will be moved before a Judge of the Patents Court at a time to be set by the Patents Court not less than twenty-four days after service of this notice, or so soon thereafter as Counsel(b) can be heard by Counsel(b), on behalf of(c)

....

by the way of appeal from(d) ....

of the(e) ....

dated the .... day of .... 19......

whereby he(f) ....

....
....
....

(g)   Here set out the grounds of appeal
The grounds of appeal are as follows: —(g)

(h)   Here set out the relief which the Appellant
seeks   I/WE ask the Patents Court to grant the relief
set out below: —(h)

                                       DATE
....

(i)   To be signed by the
SIGNATURE ....(i)

Appellant personally or by his duly authorised representative   ADDRESS

....

....

....

(j)   To be addressed to the other side and to their authorised representative
and to the Comptroller-General at the Patent Office.   TO

....(j)

....

....

                           NOTE: Two copies of this Notice of Appeal
must be sent to the Chancery Chambers (Room 307), Thomas More Building,
Royal Courts of Justice, Strand, London WC2A 2LL. They must be accompanied
with the remittance for the prescribed fee. The remittance must if sent by post be
*paid by Bankers Draft or **postal order made payable to H.M. Paymaster General***
***and crossed**. A copy of the notice must be sent to the Comptroller-General at the*
Patent Office, Room GR15, Concept House, Cardiff Road, Gwent NP10 1RH and
to any party entitled to appear before the Patents Court within the period pre-
*scribed by paragraph 16 of **the Patents Practice Direction***

Appendix 4

International conventions

PARIS CONVENTION FOR THE PROTECTION OF INDUSTRIAL
PROPERTY of March 20, 1883,

as revised at BRUSSELS on December 14, 1900,
at WASHINGTON on June 2, 1911,
at THE HAGUE on November 6, 1925,
at LONDON on June 2, 1934,
at LISBON on October 31, 1958,
and at STOCKHOLM on, July 14, 1967,
and as amended on October 2, 1979

Article 1
Establishment of the Union; Scope of Industrial Property
Articles have been given titles to facilitate their identification. There are no titles in the signed (French) text.

(1) The countries to which this Convention applies constitute a Union for the protection of industrial property.
(2) The protection of industrial property has as its object patents, utility models, industrial designs, trademarks, service marks, trade names, indications of source or appellations of origin, and the repression of unfair competition.
(3) Industrial property shall be understood in the broadest sense and shall apply not only to industry and commerce proper, but likewise to agricultural and extractive industries and to all manufactured or natural products, for example, wines, grain, tobacco leaf, fruit, cattle, minerals, mineral waters, beer, flowers, and flour.
(4) Patents shall include the various kinds of industrial patents recognized by the laws of the countries of the Union, such as patents of importation, patents of improvement, patents and certificates of addition, etc.

Article 2
National Treatment for Nationals of Countries of the Union

(1) Nationals of any country of the Union shall, as regards the protection of industrial property, enjoy in all the other countries of the Union the advantages that their respective laws now grant, or may hereafter grant, to nationals; all without preju-

895

dice to the rights specially provided for by this Convention. Consequently, they shall have the same protection as the latter, and the same legal remedy against any infringement of their rights, provided that the conditions and formalities imposed upon nationals are complied with.

(2) However, no requirement as to domicile or establishment in the country where protection is claimed may be imposed upon nationals of countries of the Union for the enjoyment of any industrial property rights.

(3) The provisions of the laws of each of the countries of the Union relating to judicial and administrative procedure and to jurisdiction, and to the designation of an address for service or the appointment of an agent, which may be required by the laws on industrial property are expressly reserved.

Article 3
Same Treatment for Certain Categories of Persons as for Nationals of Countries of the Union

Nationals of countries outside the Union who are domiciled or who have real and effective industrial or commercial establishments in the territory of one of the countries of the Union shall be treated in the same manner as nationals of the countries of the Union.

Article 4
A to I: Patents, Utility Models, Industrial Designs, Marks, Inventors' Certificates: Right of Priority.
G: Patents: Division of the Application

A.

(1) Any person who has duly filed an application for a patent, or for the registration of a utility model, or of an industrial design, or of a trademark, in one of the countries of the Union, or his successor in title, shall enjoy, for the purpose of filing in the other countries, a right of priority during the periods hereinafter fixed.

(2) Any filing that is equivalent to a regular national filing under the domestic legislation of any country of the Union or under bilateral or multilateral treaties concluded between countries of the Union shall be recognized as giving rise to the right of priority.

(3) By a regular national filing is meant any filing that is adequate to establish the date on which the application was filed in the country concerned, whatever may be the subsequent fate of the application.

B.

Consequently, any subsequent filing in any of the other countries of the Union before the expiration of the periods referred to above shall not be invalidated by reason of any acts accomplished in the interval, in particular, another filing, the publication or exploitation of the invention, the putting on sale of copies of the design, or the use of the mark, and such acts cannot give rise to any third-party right or any right of personal possession. Rights acquired by third parties before the date of the first application that serves as the basis for the right of priority are reserved in accordance with the domestic legislation of each country of the Union

C.

(1) The periods of priority referred to above shall be twelve months for patents and utility models, and six months for industrial designs and trademarks.

(2) These periods shall start from the date of filing of the first application; the day of filing shall not be included in the period.

(3) If the last day of the period is an official holiday, or a day when the Office is not open for the filing of applications in the country where protection is claimed, the period shall be extended until the first following working day.

(4) A subsequent application concerning the same subject as a previous first application within the meaning of paragraph (2), above, filed in the same country of the Union. shall be considered as the first application, of which the filing date shall be the starting point of the period of priority, if, at the time of filing the subsequent application, the said previous application has been withdrawn, abandoned, or refused, without having been laid open to public inspection and without leaving any rights outstanding, and if it has not yet served as a basis for claiming a right of priority. The previous application may not thereafter serve as a basis for claiming a right of priority

D.

(1) Any person desiring to take advantage of the priority of a previous filing shall be required to make a declaration indicating the date of such filing and the country in which it was made. Each country shall determine the latest date on which such declaration must be made.

(2) These particulars shall be mentioned in the publications issued by the competent authority, and in particular in the patents and the specifications relating thereto.

(3) The countries of the Union may require any person making a declaration of priority to produce a copy of the application (description, drawings, etc.) previously filed. The copy, certified as correct by the authority which received such application, shall not require any authentication, and may in any case be filed, without fee, at any time within three months of the filing of the subsequent application. They may require it to be accompanied by a certificate from the same authority showing the date of filing, and by a translation.

(4) No other formalities may be required for the declaration of priority at the time of filing the application. Each country of the Union shall determine the consequences of failure to comply with the formalities prescribed by this Article, but such consequences shall in no case go beyond the loss of the right of priority.

(5) Subsequently, further proof may be required. Any person who avails himself of the priority of a previous application shall be required to specify the number of that application; this number shall be published as provided for by paragraph (2), above.

Article 5

A. *Patents: Importation of Articles; Failure to Work or Insufficient Working; Compulsory Licenses.*

B. *Industrial Designs: Failure to Work; Importation of Articles.*

C. *Marks: Failure to Use; Different Forms; Use by Co-proprietors.*

D. *Patents, Utility Models, Marks, Industrial Designs: Marking*

C.

(1) If, in any country, use of the registered mark is compulsory, the registration

may be cancelled only after a reasonable period, and then only if the person concerned does not justify his inaction.

(2) Use of a trademark by the proprietor in a form differing in elements which do not alter the distinctive character of the mark in the form in which it was registered in one of the countries of the Union shall not entail invalidation of the registration and shall not diminish the protection granted to the mark.

(3) Concurrent use of the same mark on identical or similar goods by industrial or commercial establishments considered as co-proprietors of the mark according to the provisions of the domestic law of the country where protection is claimed shall not prevent registration or diminish in any way the protection granted to the said mark in any country of the Union, provided that such use does not result in misleading the public and is not contrary to the public interest.

D.

No indication or mention of the patent, of the utility model, of the registration of the trademark, or of the deposit of the industrial design, shall be required upon the goods as a condition of recognition of the right to protection.

Article 6

Marks: Conditions of Registration; Independence of Protection of Same Mark in Different Countries

(1) The conditions for the filing and registration of trademarks shall be determined in each country of the Union by its domestic legislation.

(2) However, an application for the registration of a mark filed by a national of a country of the Union in any country of the Union may not be refused, nor may a registration be invalidated, on the ground that filing, registration, or renewal, has not been effected in the country of origin.

(3) A mark duly registered in a country of the Union shall be regarded as independent of marks registered in the other countries of the Union, including the country of origin.

Article 6bis

Marks: Well-Known Marks

(1) The countries of the Union undertake, ex officio if their legislation so permits, or at the request of an interested party, to refuse or to cancel the registration, and to prohibit the use, of a trademark which constitutes a reproduction, an imitation, or a translation, liable to create confusion, of a mark considered by the competent authority of the country of registration or use to be well known in that country as being already the mark of a person entitled to the benefits of this Convention and used for identical or similar goods. These provisions shall also apply when the essential part of the mark constitutes a reproduction of any such well-known mark or an imitation liable to create confusion therewith.

(2) A period of at least five years from the date of registration shall be allowed for requesting the cancellation of such a mark. The countries of the Union may provide for a period within which the prohibition of use must be requested.

(3) No time limit shall be fixed for requesting the cancellation or the prohibition of the use of marks registered or used in bad faith.

Article 6ter

Marks: Prohibitions concerning State Emblems, Official Hallmarks, and Emblems of Intergovernmental Organizations

(1)

    (a) The countries of the Union agree to refuse or to invalidate the registration, and to prohibit by appropriate measures the use, without authorization by the competent authorities, either as trademarks or as elements of trademarks, of armorial bearings, flags, and other State emblems, of the countries of the Union, official signs and hallmarks indicating control and warranty adopted by them, and any imitation from a heraldic point of view.

    (b) The provisions of subparagraph (a), above, shall apply equally to armorial bearings, flags, other emblems, abbreviations, and names, of international intergovernmental organizations of which one or more countries of the Union are members, with the exception of armorial bearings, flags, other emblems, abbreviations, and names, that are already the subject of international agreements in force, intended to ensure their protection.

    (c) No country of the Union shall be required to apply the provisions of subparagraph (b), above, to the prejudice of the owners of rights acquired in good faith before the entry into force, in that country, of this Convention. The countries of the Union shall not be required to apply the said provisions when the use or registration referred to in subparagraph (a), above, is not of such a nature as to suggest to the public that a connection exists between the organization concerned and the armorial bearings, flags, emblems, abbreviations, and names, or if such use or registration is probably not of such a nature as to mislead the public as to the existence of a connection between the user and the organization.

(2) Prohibition of the use of official signs and hallmarks indicating control and warranty shall apply solely in cases where the marks in which they are incorporated are intended to be used on goods of the same or a similar kind.

(3)

    (a) For the application of these provisions, the countries of the Union agree to communicate reciprocally, through the intermediary of the International Bureau, the list of State emblems, and official signs and hallmarks indicating control and warranty, which they desire, or may hereafter desire, to place wholly or within certain limits under the protection of this Article, and all subsequent modifications of such list. Each country of the Union shall in due course make available to the public the lists so communicated. Nevertheless such communication is not obligatory in respect of flags of States.

    (b) The provisions of paragraph (1)(b) of this Article shall apply only to such armorial bearings, flags, other emblems, abbreviations, and names, of international intergovernmental organizations as the latter have communicated to the countries of the Union through the intermediary of the International Bureau.

(4) Any country of the Union may, within a period of twelve months from the receipt of the notification, transmit its objections, if any, through the intermediary of the International Bureau, to the country or international intergovernmental organization concerned.

(5) In the case of State flags, the measures prescribed by paragraph (1), above, shall apply solely to marks registered after November 6, 1925.

(6) In the case of State emblems other than flags, and of official signs and hallmarks of the countries of the Union, and in the case of armorial bearings, flags, other emblems. abbreviations. and names, of international intergovernmental organizations, these provisions shall apply only to marks registered more than two months after receipt of the communication provided for in paragraph (3), above.

(7) In cases of bad faith, the countries shall have the right to cancel even those marks incorporating State emblems, signs, and hallmarks, which were registered before November 6, 1925.

(8) Nationals of any country who are authorized to make use of the State emblems, signs, and hallmarks, of their country may use them even if they are similar to those of another country.

(9) The countries of the Union undertake to prohibit the unauthorized use in trade of the State armorial bearings of the other countries of the Union, when the use is of such a nature as to be misleading as to the origin of the goods.

(10) The above provisions shall not prevent the countries from exercising the right given in Article 6quinquies(B)(3), to refuse or to invalidate the registration of marks incorporating, without authorization, armorial bearings, flags, other State emblems, or official signs and hallmarks adopted by a country of the Union, as well as the distinctive signs of international intergovernmental organizations referred to in paragraph (1), above.

Article 6quater
Marks: Assignment of Marks
(1) When, in accordance with the law of a country of the Union, the assignment of a mark is valid only if it takes place at the same time as the transfer of the business or goodwill to which the mark belongs, it shall suffice for the recognition of such validity that the portion of the business or goodwill located in that country be transferred to the assignee, together with the exclusive right to manufacture in the said country, or to sell therein, the goods bearing the mark assigned.

(2) The foregoing provision does not impose upon the countries of the Union any obligation to regard as valid the assignment of any mark the use of which by the assignee would, in fact, be of such a nature as to mislead the public, particularly as regards the origin, nature, or essential qualities, of the goods to which the mark is applied.

Article 6quinquies
Marks: Protection of Marks Registered in One Country of the Union in the Other Countries of the Union
A.
(1) Every trademark duly registered in the country of origin shall be accepted for filing and protected as is in the other countries of the Union, subject to the reservations indicated in this Article. Such countries may, before proceeding to final registration, require the production of a certificate of registration in the country of origin, issued by the competent authority. No authentication shall be required for this certificate.

(2) Shall be considered the country of origin the country of the Union where the

applicant has a real and effective industrial or commercial establishment, or, if he has no such establishment within the Union, the country of the Union where he has his domicile, or. if he has no domicile within the Union but is a national of a country of the Union, the country of which he is a national.

B.

Trademarks covered by this Article may be neither denied registration nor invalidated except in the following cases:

1. when they are of such a nature as to infringe rights acquired by third parties in the country where protection is claimed;

2. when they are devoid of any distinctive character, or consist exclusively of signs or indications which may serve, in trade, to designate the kind, quality, quantity, intended purpose, value, place of origin, of the goods, or the time of production, or have become customary in the current language or in the bona fide and established practices of the trade of the country where protection is claimed;

3. when they are contrary to morality or public order and, in particular, of such a nature as to deceive the public. It is understood that a mark may not be considered contrary to public order for the sole reason that it does not conform to a provision of the legislation on marks, except if such provision itself relates to public order. This provision is subject, however, to the application of Article 10bis.

C.

(1) In determining whether a mark is eligible for protection, all the factual circumstances must be taken into consideration, particularly the length of time the mark has been in use.

(2) No trademark shall be refused in the other countries of the Union for the sole reason that it differs from the mark protected in the country of origin only in respect of elements that do not alter its distinctive character and do not affect its identity in the form in which it has been registered in the said country of origin.

D.

No person may benefit from the provisions of this Article if the mark for which he claims protection is not registered in the country of origin.

E.

However, in no case shall the renewal of the registration of the mark in the country of origin involve an obligation to renew the registration in the other countries of the Union in which the mark has been registered.

F.

The benefit of priority shall remain unaffected for applications for the registration of marks filed within the period fixed by Article 4, even if registration in the country of origin is effected after the expiration of such period.

Article 6sexies
Marks: Service Marks

The countries of the Union undertake to protect service marks. They shall not be required to provide for the registration of such marks.

Article 6septies
Marks: Registration in the Name of the Agent or Representative of the Proprietor Without the Latter's Authorization

(1) If the agent or representative of the person who is the proprietor of a mark in

901

one of the countries of the Union applies, without such proprietor's authorization, for the registration of the mark in his own name, in one or more countries of the Union, the proprietor shall be entitled to oppose the registration applied for or demand its cancellation or, if the law of the country so allows, the assignment in his favour of the said registration, unless such agent or representative justifies his action.

(2) The proprietor of the mark shall, subject to the provisions of paragraph (1), above, be entitled to oppose the use of his mark by his agent or representative if he has not authorized such use.

(3) Domestic legislation may provide an equitable time limit within which the proprietor of a mark must exercise the rights provided for in this Article.

Article 7
Marks: Nature of the Goods to which the Mark is Applied
The nature of the goods to which a trademark is to be applied shall in no case form an obstacle to the registration of the mark.

Article 7bis
Marks: Collective Marks
(1) The countries of the Union undertake to accept for filing and to protect collective marks belonging to associations the existence of which is not contrary to the law of the country of origin, even if such associations do not possess an industrial or commercial establishment.

(2) Each country shall be the judge of the particular conditions under which a collective mark shall be protected and may refuse protection if the mark is contrary to the public interest.

(3) Nevertheless, the protection of these marks shall not be refused to any association the existence of which is not contrary to the law of the country of origin, on the ground that such association is not established in the country where protection is sought or is not constituted according to the law of the latter country.

Article 8
Trade Names
A trade name shall be protected in all the countries of the Union without the obligation of filing or registration, whether or not it forms part of a trademark.

Article 9
Marks, Trade Names: Seizure, on Importation, etc., of Goods Unlawfully Bearing a Mark or Trade Name
(1) All goods unlawfully bearing a trademark or trade name shall be seized on importation into those countries of the Union where such mark or trade name is entitled to legal protection.

(2) Seizure shall likewise be effected in the country where the unlawful affixation occurred or in the country into which the goods were imported.

(3) Seizure shall take place at the request of the public prosecutor, or any other competent authority, or any interested party, whether a natural person or a legal entity, in conformity with the domestic legislation of each country.

(4) The authorities shall not be bound to effect seizure of goods in transit.

(5) If the legislation of a country does not permit seizure on importation, seizure shall be replaced by prohibition of importation or by seizure inside the country.

(6) If the legislation of a country permits neither seizure on importation nor prohibition of importation nor seizure inside the country, then, until such time as the legislation is modified accordingly, these measures shall be replaced by the actions and remedies available in such cases to nationals under the law of such country.

Article 10

False Indications: Seizure, on Importation, etc., of Goods Bearing False Indications as to their Source or the Identity of the Producer

(1) The provisions of the preceding Article shall apply in cases of direct or indirect use of a false indication of the source of the good or the identity of the producer, manufacturer, or merchant.

(2) Any producer, manufacturer, or merchant, whether a natural person or a legal entity, engaged in the production or manufacture of or trade in such goods and established either in the locality falsely indicated as the source, or in the region where such locality is situated, or in the country falsely indicated, or in the country where the false indication of source is used, shall in any case he deemed an interested party.

Article 10bis

Unfair Competition

(1) The countries of the Union are bound to assure to nationals of such countries effective protection against unfair competition.

(2) Any act of competition contrary to honest practices in industrial or commercial matters constitutes an act of unfair competition.

(3) The following in particular shall be prohibited:

1. all acts of such a nature as to create confusion by any means whatever with the establishment, the goods, or the industrial or commercial activities, of a competitor;
2. false allegations in the course of trade of such a nature as to discredit the establishment, the goods, or the industrial or commercial activities, of a competitor;
3. indications or allegations the use of which in the course of trade is liable to mislead the public as to the nature, the manufacturing process, the characteristics, the suitability for their purpose, or the quantity, of the goods.

Article 10ter

Marks, Trade Names, False Indications, Unfair Competition: Remedies, Right to Sue

(1) The countries of the Union undertake to assure to nationals of the other countries of the Union appropriate legal remedies effectively to repress all the acts referred to in Articles 9, 10, and 10bis.

(2) They undertake, further, to provide measures to permit federations and associations representing interested industrialists, producers, or merchants, provided that the existence of such federations and associations is not contrary to the laws of their countries, to take action in the courts or before the administrative authorities, with a view to the repression of the acts referred to in Articles 9, 10, and 10bis, in

so far as the law of the country in which protection is claimed allows such action by federations and associations of that country.

Article 11

Inventions, Utility Models, Industrial Designs, Marks: Temporary Protection at Certain International Exhibitions

(1) The countries of the Union shall, in conformity with their domestic legislation, grant temporary protection to patentable inventions, utility models, industrial designs, and trademarks, in respect of goods exhibited at official or officially recognized international exhibitions held in the territory of any of them.

(2) Such temporary protection shall not extend the periods provided by Article 4. If, later, the right of priority is invoked, the authorities of any country may provide that the period shall start from the date of introduction of the goods into the exhibition.

(3) Each country may require, as proof of the identity of the article exhibited and of the date of its introduction, such documentary evidence as it considers necessary.

Article 12

Special National Industrial Property Services

(1) Each country of the Union undertakes to establish a special industrial property service and a central office for the communication to the public of patents, utility models, industrial designs, and trademarks.

(2) This service shall publish an official periodical journal. It shall publish regularly:

    (a) the names of the proprietors of patents granted, with a brief designation of the inventions patented;

    (b) the reproductions of registered trademarks.

Article 13

Assembly of the Union

(1)

    (a) The Union shall have an Assembly consisting of those countries of the Union which are bound by Articles 13 to 17.

    (b) The Government of each country shall be represented by one delegate, who may be assisted by alternate delegates, advisors, and experts.

    (c) The expenses of each delegation shall be borne by the Government which has appointed it.

(2)

    (a) The Assembly shall:

        (i) deal with all matters concerning the maintenance and development of the Union and the implementation of this Convention;

        (ii) give directions concerning the preparation for conferences of revision to the International Bureau of Intellectual Property (hereinafter designated as "the International Bureau") referred to in the Convention establishing the World Intellectual Property Organization (hereinafter designated as "the Organization"), due account being taken of any comments made by those countries of the Union which are not hound by Articles 13 to 17;

        (iii) review and approve the reports and activities of the Director General of the Organization concerning the Union, and give him all necessary instructions concerning matters within the competence of the Union;

(iv) elect the members of the Executive Committee of the Assembly;

(v) review and approve the reports and activities of its Executive Committee, and give instructions to such Committee;

(vi) determine the program and adopt the biennial budget of the Union, and approve its final accounts;

(vii) adopt the financial regulations of the Union;

(viii) establish such committees of experts and working groups as it deems appropriate to achieve the objectives of the Union;

(ix) determine which countries not members of the Union and which intergovernmental and international nongovernmental organizations shall be admitted to its meetings as observers;

(x) adopt amendments to Articles 13 to 17;

(xi) take any other appropriate action designed to further the objectives of the Union;

(xii) perform such other functions as are appropriate under this Convention;

(xiii) subject to its acceptance, exercise such rights as are given to it in the Convention establishing the Organization.

(b) with respect to matters which are of interest also to other Unions administered by the Organization, the Assembly shall make its decisions after having heard the advice of the Coordination Committee of the Organization.

(3)

(a) Subject to the provisions of subparagraph (b), a delegate may represent one country only.

(b) Countries of the Union grouped under the terms of a special agreement in a common office possessing for each of them the character of a special national service of industrial property as referred to in Article 12 may be jointly represented during discussions by one of their number.

(4)

(a) Each country member of the Assembly shall have one vote.

(b) One-half of the countries members of the Assembly shall constitute a quorum.

(c) Notwithstanding the provisions of subparagraph (b), if, in any session, the number of countries represented is less than one-half but equal to or more than one-third of the countries members of the Assembly, the Assembly may make decisions but, with the exception of decisions concerning its own procedure, all such decisions shall take effect only if the conditions, set forth hereinafter are fufilled. The International Bureau shall communicate the said decisions to the countries members of the Assembly which were not represented and shall invite them to express in writing their vote or abstention within a period of three months from the date of the communication. If, at the expiration of this period, the number of countries having thus expressed their vote or abstention attains the number of countries which was lacking for attaining the quorum in the session itself, such decisions shall take effect provided that at the same time the required majority still obtains.

(d) Subject to the provisions of Article 17(2), the decisions of the Assembly shall require two-thirds of the votes cast.

(e) Abstentions shall not be considered as votes.

(5)

    (a) Subject to the provisions of subparagraph (b), a delegate may vote in the name of one country only.

    (b) The countries of the Union referred to in paragraph (3)(b) shall, as a general rule, endeavor to send their own delegations to the sessions of the Assembly. If, however, for exceptional reasons, any such country cannot send its own delegation, it may give to the delegation of another such country the power to vote in its name, provided that each delegation may vote by proxy for one country only. Such power to vote shall be granted in a document signed by the Head of State or the competent Minister.

(6) Countries of the Union not members of the Assembly shall be admitted to the meetings of the latter as observers.

(7)

    (a) The Assembly shall meet once in every second calendar year in ordinary session upon convocation by the Director General and, in the absence of exceptional circumstances, during the same period and at the same place as the General Assembly of the Organization.

    (b) The Assembly shall meet in extraordinary session upon convocation by the Director General, at the request of the Executive Committee or at the request of one-fourth of the countries members of the Assembly.

(8) The Assembly shall adopt its own rules of procedure.

Article 14

Executive Committee

(1) The Assembly shall have an Executive Committee.

(2)

    (a) The Executive Committee shall consist of countries elected by the Assembly from among countries members of the Assembly. Furthermore, the country on whose territory the Organization has its headquarters shall, subject to the provisions of Article 16(7)(b), have an ex officio seat on the Committee.

    (b) The Government of each country member of the Executive Committee shall be represented by one delegate, who may be assisted by alternate delegates, advisors, and experts.

    (c) The expenses of each delegation shall be borne by the Government which has appointed it.

(3) The number of countries members of the Executive Committee shall correspond to one-fourth of the number of countries members of the Assembly. In establishing the number of seats to be filled, remainders after division by four shall be disregarded.

(4) In electing the members of the Executive Committee, the Assembly shall have due regard to an equitable geographical distribution and to the need for countries party to the Special Agreements established in relation with the Union to be among the countries constituting the Executive Committee.

(5)

   (a) Each member of the Executive Committee shall serve from the close of the session of the Assembly which elected it to the close of the next ordinary session of the Assembly.

   (b) Members of the Executive Committee may be re-elected, but only up to a maximum of two-thirds of such members.

   (c) The Assembly shall establish the details of the rules governing the election and possible re-election of the members of the Executive Committee.

(6)

   (a) The Executive Committee shall:

      (i) prepare the draft agenda of the Assembly;

      (ii) submit proposals to the Assembly in respect of the draft program and biennial budget of the Union prepared by the Director General;

      (iii) deleted

      (iv) submit, with appropriate comments, to the Assembly the periodical reports of the Director General and the yearly audit reports on the accounts;

      (v) take all necessary measures to ensure the execution of the program of the Union by the Director General, in accordance with the decisions of the Assembly and having regard to circumstances arising between two ordinary sessions of the Assembly;

      (vi) perform such other functions as are allocated to it tinder this Convention.

(b) With respect to matters which are of interest also to other Unions administered by the Organization, the Executive Committee shall make its decisions after having heard the advice of the Coordination Committee of the Organization.

(7)

(a) The Executive Committee shall meet once a year in ordinary session upon convocation by the Director General, preferably during the same period and at the same place as the Coordination Committee of the Organization.

(b) The Executive Committee shall meet in extraordinary session upon convocation by the Director General, either on his own initiative, or at the request of its Chairman or one fourth of its members.

(8)

   (a) Each country member of the Executive Committee shall have one vote.

   (b) One-half of the members of the Executive Committee shall constitute a quorum.

   (c) Decisions shall be made by a simple majority of the votes cast.

   (d) Abstentions shall not be considered as votes.

   (e) A delegate may represent, and vote in the name of, one country only.

(9) Countries of the Union not members of the Executive Committee shall be admitted to its meetings as observers.

(10) The Executive Committee shall adopt its own rules of procedure.

Article 15
International Bureau

(1)

   (a) Administrative tasks concerning the Union shall be performed by the International Bureau, which is a continuation of the Bureau of the Union united with the Bureau of the Union established by the International Convention for the Protection of Literary and Artistic Works.

(b) In particular, the International Bureau shall provide the secretariat of the various organs of the Union.

(c) The Director General of the Organization shall be the chief executive of the Union and shall represent the Union.

(2) The International Bureau shall assemble and publish information concerning the protection of industrial property. Each country of the Union shall promptly communicate to the International Bureau all new laws and official texts concerning the protection of industrial property. Furthermore, it shall furnish the International Bureau with all the publications of its industrial property service of direct concern to the protection of industrial property which the International Bureau may find useful in its work.

(3) The International Bureau shall publish a monthly periodical.

(4) The International Bureau shall, on request, furnish any country of the Union with information on matters concerning the protection of industrial property.

(5) The International Bureau shall conduct Studies, and shall provide services, designed to facilitate the protection of industrial property.

(6) The Director General and any staff member designated by him shall participate, without the right to vote, in all meetings of the Assembly, the Executive Committee, and any other committee of experts or working group. The Director General, or a staff member designated by him, shall be ex officio secretary of these bodies.

(7)

(a) The International Bureau shall, in accordance with the directions of the Assembly and in cooperation with the Executive Committee, make the preparations for the conferences of revision of the provisions of the Convention other than Articles 13 to 17.

(b) The International Bureau may consult with intergovernmental and international non-governmental organizations concerning preparations for conferences of revision.

(c) The Director General and persons designated by him shall take part, without the right to vote, in the discussions at these conferences.

(8) The International Bureau shall carry out any other tasks assigned to it.

Article 16
Finances

(1)

(a) The Union shall have a budget.

(b) The budget of the Union shall include the income and expenses proper to the Union, its contribution to the budget of expenses common to the Unions, and, where applicable, the sum made available to the budget of the Conference of the Organization.

(c) Expenses not attributable exclusively to the Union but also to one or more other Unions administered by the Organization shall be considered as expenses common to the Unions. The share of the Union in such common expenses shall be in proportion to the interest the Union has in them.

(2) The budget of the Union shall be established with due regard to the require-

ments of coordination with the budgets of the other Unions administered by the Organization.

(3) The budget of the Union shall be financed from the following sources:

    (i) contributions of the countries of the Union;

    (ii) fees and charges due for services rendered by the International Bureau in relation to the Union;

    (iii) sale of, or royalties on, the publications of the International Bureau concerning the Union;

    (iv) gifts, bequests, and subventions;

    (v) rents, interests, and other miscellaneous income.

(4)

    (a) For the purpose of establishing its contribution towards the budget, each country of the Union shall belong to a class, and shall pay its annual contributions on the basis of a number of units fixed as follows:

Class I 25
Class II 20
Class III 15
Class IV 10
Class V 5
Class VI 3
Class VII 1

    (b) Unless it has already done so, each country shall indicate, concurrently with depositing its instrument of ratification or accession, the class to which it wishes to belong. Any country may change class. If it chooses a lower class, the country must announce such change to the Assembly at one of its ordinary sessions. Any such change shall take effect at the beginning of the calendar year following the said session.

    (c) The annual contribution of each country shall be an amount in the same proportion to the total sum to be contributed to the budget of the Union by all countries as the number of its units is to the total of the units of all contributing countries.

    (d) Contributions shall become due on the first of January of each year.

    (e) A country which is in arrears in the payment of its contributions may not exercise its right to vote in any of the organs of the Union of which it is a member if the amount of its arrears equals or exceeds the amount of the contributions due from it for the preceding two full years. However, any organ of the Union may allow such a country to continue to exercise its right to vote in that organ if, and as long as, it is satisfied that the delay in payment is due to exceptional and unavoidable circumstances.

    (f) If the budget is not adopted before the beginning of a new financial period, it shall be at the same level as the budget of the previous year, as provided in the financial regulations

(5) The amount of the fees and charges due for services rendered by the International Bureau in relation to the Union shall be established, and shall be reported to the Assembly and the Executive Committee, by the Director General.

(6)

    (a) The Union shall have a working capital fund which shall be constituted by a single payment made by each country of the Union. If the fund becomes insufficient, the Assembly shall decide to increase it.

    (b) The amount of the initial payment of each country to the said fund or of its participation in the increase thereof shall be a proportion of the contribution of that country for the year in which the fund is established or the decision to increase it is made.

(c) The proportion and the terms of payment shall be fixed by the Assembly on the proposal of the Director General and after it has heard the advice of the Coordination Committee of the Organization.

(7)

(a) In the headquarters agreement concluded with the country on the territory of which the Organization has its headquarters, it shall be provided that, whenever the working capital fund is insufficient, such country shall grant advances. The amount of these advances and the conditions on which they are granted shall be the subject of separate agreements, in each case, between such country and the Organization. As long as it remains under the obligation to grant advances, such country shall have an ex officio seat on the Executive Committee.

(b) The country referred to in subparagraph (a) and the Organization shall each have the right to denounce the obligation to grant advances, by written notification. Denunciation shall take effect three years after the end of the year in which it has been notified.

(8) The auditing of the accounts shall be effected by one or more of the countries of the Union or by external auditors, as provided in the financial regulations. They shall be designated, with their agreement, by the Assembly.

Article 17
Amendment of Articles 13 to 17

(1) Proposals for the amendment of Articles 13, 14, 15, 16, and the present Article, may be initiated by any country member of the Assembly, by the Executive Committee, or by the Director General. Such proposals shall be communicated by the Director General to the member countries of the Assembly at least six months in advance of their consideration by the Assembly.

(2) Amendments to the Articles referred to in paragraph (1) shall be adopted by the Assembly. Adoption shall require three-fourths of the votes cast, provided that any amendment to Article 13, and to the present paragraph, shall require four-fifths of the votes cast.

(3) Any amendment to the Articles referred to in paragraph (1) shall enter into force one month after written notifications of acceptance, effected in accordance with their respective constitutional processes, have been received by the Director General from three-fourths of the countries members of the Assembly at the time it adopted the amendment. Any amendment to the said Articles thus accepted shall bind all the countries which are members of the Assembly at the time the amendment enters into force, or which become members thereof at a subsequent date, provided that any amendment increasing the financial obligations of countries of the Union shall bind only those countries which have notified their acceptance of such amendment.

Article 18
Revision of Articles 1 to 12 and 18 to 30

(1) This Convention shall be submitted to revision with a view to the introduction

of amendments designed to improve the system of the Union.

(2) For that purpose, conferences shall be held successively in one of the countries of the Union among the delegates of the said countries.

(3) Amendments to Articles 13 to 17 are governed by the provisions of Article 17.

Article 19

Special Agreements

It is understood that the countries of the Union reserve the right to make separately between themselves special agreements for the protection of industrial property, in so far as these agreements do not contravene the provisions of this Convention.

Article 20

Ratification or Accession by Countries of the Union; Entry Into Force

(1)

    (a) Any country of the Union which has signed this Act may ratify it, and, if it has not signed it, may accede to it. Instruments of ratification and accession shall be deposited with the Director General.

    (b) Any country of the Union may declare in its instrument of ratification or accession that its ratification or accession shall not apply:
    (i) to Articles 1 to 12, or
    (ii) to Articles 13 to 17.

    (c) Any country of the Union which, in accordance with subparagraph (b), has excluded from the effects of its ratification or accession one of the two groups of Articles referred to in that subparagraph may at any later time declare that it extends the effects of its ratification or accession to that group of Articles. Such declaration shall be deposited with the Director General.

(2)

    (a) Articles 1 to 12 shall enter into force, with respect to the first ten countries of the Union which have deposited instruments of ratification or accession without making the declaration permitted under paragraph (1)(b)(i), three months after the deposit of the tenth such instrument of ratification or accession.

    (b) Articles 13 to 17 shall enter into force, with respect to the first ten countries of the Union which have deposited instruments of ratification or accession without making the declaration permitted under paragraph (1)(b)(ii), three months after the deposit of the tenth such instrument of ratification or accession.

    (c) Subject to the initial entry into force, pursuant to the provisions of subparagraphs (a) and (b), of each of the two groups of Articles referred to in paragraph (1)(b)(i) and (1)(b)(ii), and subject to the provisions of paragraph (1)(b), Articles 1 to 17 shall, with respect to any country of the Union, other than those referred to in subparagraphs (a) and (b), which deposits an instrument of ratification or accession or any country of the Union which deposits a declaration pursuant to paragraph (1)(c), enter into force three months after the date of notification by the Director General of such deposit, unless a subsequent date has been indicated in the instrument or declaration deposited. In the latter case, this Act shall enter into force with respect to that country on the date thus indicated.

(3) With respect to any country of the Union which deposits an instrument of ratification or accession, Articles 18 to 30 shall enter into force on the earlier of the dates on which any of the groups of Articles referred to in paragraph (1)(b) enters into force with respect to that country pursuant to paragraph (2)(a), (2)(b), or (2)(c).

Article 21

Accession by Countries Outside the Union; Entry Into Force

(1) Any country outside the Union may accede to this Act and thereby become a member of the Union. Instruments of accession shall be deposited with the Director General.

(2)

    (a) With respect to any country outside the Union which deposits its instrument of accession one month or more before the date of entry into force of any provisions of the present Act, this Act shall enter into force, unless a subsequent date has been indicated in the instrument of accession, on the date upon which provisions first enter into force pursuant to Article 20(2)(a) or 20(2)(b); provided that:

        (i) if Articles 1 to 12 do not enter into force on that date, such country shall, during the interim period before the entry into force of such provisions, and in substitution therefor, be bound by Articles 1 to 12 of the Lisbon Act.

        (ii) if Articles 13 to 17 do not enter into force on that date, such country shall, during the interim period before the entry into force of such provisions, and in substitution therefor, be bound by Articles 13 and 14(3), 14(4), and 14(5), of the Lisbon Act. If a country indicates a subsequent date in its instrument of accession, this Act shall enter into force with respect to that country on the date thus indicated.

    (b) With respect to any country outside the Union which deposits its instrument of accession on a date which is subsequent to, or precedes by less than one month, the entry into force of one group of Articles of the present Act, this Act shall, subject to the proviso of subparagraph (a), enter into force three months after the date on which its accession has been notified by the Director General, unless a subsequent date has been indicated in the instrument of accession. In the latter case, this Act shall enter into force with respect to that country on the date thus indicated.

(3) With respect to any country outside the Union which deposits its instrument of accession after the date of entry into force of the present Act in its entirety, or less than one month before such date, this Act shall enter into force three months after the date on which its accession has been notified by the Director General, unless a subsequent date has been indicated in the instrument of accession. In the latter case, this Act shall enter into force with respect to that country on the date thus indicated.

Article 22

Consequences of Ratification or Accession

Subject to the possibilities of exceptions provided for in Articles 20(1)(b) and 28(2), ratification or accession shall automatically entail acceptance of all the clauses and admission to all the advantages of this Act.

Article 23
Accession to Earlier Acts
After the entry into force of this Act in its entirety, a country may not accede to earlier Acts of this Convention.

Article 24
Territories
(1) Any country may declare in its instrument of ratification or accession, or may inform the Director General by written notification any time thereafter, that this Convention shall be applicable to all or part of those territories, designated in the declaration or notification, for the external relations of which it is responsible.
(2) Any country which has made such a declaration or given such a notification may, at any time, notify the Director General that this Convention shall cease to be applicable to all or part of such territories.
(3)

    (a) Any declaration made under paragraph (1) shall take effect on the same date as the ratification or accession in the instrument of which it was included, and any notification given under such paragraph shall take effect three months after its notification by the Director General.
    (b) Any notification given tinder paragraph (2) shall take effect twelve months after its receipt by the Director General.

Article 25
Implementation of the Convention on the Domestic Level
(1) Any country party to this Convention undertakes to adopt, in accordance with its constitution, the measures necessary to ensure the application of this Convention.
(2) It is understood that, at the time a country deposits its instrument of ratification or accession, it will be in a position under its domestic law to give effect to the provisions of this Convention.

Article 26
Denunciation
(1) This Convention shall remain in force without limitation as to time.
(2) Any country may denounce this Act by notification addressed to the Director General. Such denunciation shall constitute also denunciation of all earlier Acts and shall affect only the country making it, the Convention remaining in full force and effect as regards the other countries of the Union.
(3) Denunciation shall take effect one year after the day on which the Director General has received the notification.
(4) The right of denunciation provided by this Article shall not be exercised by any country before the expiration of five years from the date upon which it becomes a member of the Union.

Article 27
Application of Earlier Acts
(1) The present Act shall, as regards the relations between the countries to which it applies, and to the extent that it applies, replace the Convention of Paris of March

20, 1883 and the subsequent Acts of revision.

(2)

    (a) As regards the countries to which the present Act does not apply, or does not apply in its entirety, but to which the Lisbon Act of October 31, 1958, applies, the latter shall remain in force in its entirety or to the extent that the present Act does not replace it by virtue of paragraph (1).

    (b) Similarly, as regards the countries to which neither the present Act, nor portions thereof, nor the Lisbon Act applies, the London Act of June 2, 1934, shall remain in force in its entirety or to the extent that the present Act does not replace it by virtue of paragraph (1).

    (c) Similarly, as regards the countries to which neither the present Act, nor portions thereof, nor the Lisbon Act, nor the London Act applies, the Hague Act of November 6, 1925, shall remain in force in its entirety or to the extent that the present Act does not replace it by virtue of paragraph (1).

(3) Countries outside the Union which become party to this Act shall apply it with respect to any country of the Union not party to this Act or which, although party to this Act, has made a declaration pursuant to Article 20(1)(b)(i). Such countries recognize that the said country of the Union may apply, in its relations with them, the provisions of the most recent Act to which it is party.

Article 28

Disputes

(1) Any dispute between two or more countries of the Union concerning the interpretation or application of this Convention, not settled by negotiation, may, by any one of the countries concerned, he brought before the International Court of Justice by application in conformity with the Statute of the Court, unless the countries concerned agree on some other method of settlement. The country bringing the dispute before the Court shall inform the International Bureau; the International Bureau shall bring the matter to the attention of the other countries of the Union.

(2) Each country may, at the time it signs this Act or deposits its instrument of ratification or accession, declare that it does not consider itself hound by the provisions of paragraph (1). With regard to any dispute between such country and any other country of the Union, the provisions of paragraph (1) shall not apply.

(3) Any country having made a declaration in accordance with the provisions of paragraph (2) may, at any time, withdraw its declaration by notification addressed to the Director General.

Article 29

Signature, Languages, Depositary Functions

(1)

    (a) This Act shall be signed in a single copy in the French language and shall be deposited with the Government of Sweden.

    (b) Official texts shall be established by the Director General, after consultation with the interested Governments, in the English, German, Italian, Portuguese, Russian and Spanish languages, and such other languages as the Assembly may designate.

    (c) In case of differences of opinion on the interpretation of the various texts, the French text shall prevail.

(2) This Act shall remain open for signature at Stockholm until January 13, 1968.

(3) The Director General shall transmit two copies, certified by the Government of Sweden, of the signed text of this Act to the Governments of all countries of the Union and, on request, to the Government of any other country.

(4) The Director General shall register this Act with the Secretariat of the United Nations.

(5) The Director General shall notify the Governments of all countries of the Union of signatures, deposits of instruments of ratification or accession and any declarations included in such instruments or made pursuant to Article 20(1)(c), entry into force of any provisions of this Act, notifications of denunciation, and notifications pursuant to Article 24.

Article 30
Transitional Provisions

(1) Until the first Director General assumes office, references in this Act to the International Bureau of the Organization or to the Director General shall be deemed to be references to the Bureau of the Union or its Director, respectively.

(2) Countries of the Union not hound by Articles 13 to 17 may, until five years after the entry into force of the Convention establishing the Organization, exercise, if they so desire. The rights provided under Articles 13 to 17 of this Act as if they were hound by those Articles. Any country desiring to exercise such rights shall give written notification to that effect to the Director General; such notification shall be effective from the date of its receipt. Such countries shall be deemed to be members of the Assembly until the expiration of the said period.

(3) As long as all the countries of the Union have not become Members of the Organization, the International Bureau of the Organization shall also function as the Bureau of the Union, and the Director General as the Director of the said Bureau.

(4) Once all the countries of the Union have become Members of the Organization, the rights, obligations, and property, of the Bureau of the Union shall devolve on the International Bureau of the Organization.

Reproduced with the kind permission of WIPO.

Relevant provisions of GATT/TRIPS, articles 315-24 and 41-61

AGREEMENT ON TRADE-RELATED ASPECTS OF INTELLECTUAL PROPERTY RIGHTS

Members,

Desiring to reduce distortions and impediments to international trade, and taking into account the need to promote effective and adequate protection of intellectual property rights, and to ensure that measures and procedures to enforce intellectual property rights do not themselves become barriers to legitimate trade;

Recognizing, to this end, the need for new rules and disciplines concerning:

    (a) the applicability of the basic principles of GATT 1994 and of relevant international intellectual property agreements or conventions;

    (b) the provision of adequate standards and principles concerning the availabil-

ity, scope and use of trade-related intellectual property rights;
(c) the provision of effective and appropriate means for the enforcement of trade-related intellectual property rights, taking into account differences in national legal systems;
(d) the provision of effective and expeditious procedures for the multilateral prevention and settlement of disputes between governments; and
(e) transitional arrangements aiming at the fullest participation in the results of the negotiations;

Recognizing the need for a multilateral framework of principles, rules and disciplines dealing with international trade in counterfeit goods;

Recognizing that intellectual property rights are private rights;

Recognizing the underlying public policy objectives of national systems for the protection of intellectual property, including developmental and technological objectives;

Recognizing also the special needs of the least-developed country Members in respect of maximum flexibility in the domestic implementation of laws and regulations in order to enable them to create a sound and viable technological base;

Emphasizing the importance of reducing tensions by reaching strengthened commitments to resolve disputes on trade-related intellectual property issues through multilateral procedures;

Desiring to establish a mutually supportive relationship between the WTO and the World Intellectual Property Organization (referred to in this Agreement as 'WIPO') as well as other relevant international organizations;

Hereby agree as follows:

PART I
GENERAL PROVISIONS AND BASIC PRINCIPLES

Article 1

Nature and Scope of Obligations

1. Members shall give effect to the provisions of this Agreement. Members may, but shall not be obliged to, implement in their law more extensive protection than is required by this Agreement, provided that such protection does not contravene the provisions of this Agreement. Members shall be free to determine the appropriate method of implementing the provisions of this Agreement within their own legal system and practice.

2. For the purposes of this Agreement, the term 'intellectual property' refers to all categories of intellectual property that are the subject of Sections 1 through 7 of Part II.

3. Members shall accord the treatment provided for in this Agreement to the nationals of other Members. In respect of the relevant intellectual property right, the nationals of other Members shall be understood as those natural or legal persons that would meet the criteria for eligibility for protection provided for in the Paris Convention (1967), the Berne Convention (1971), the Rome Convention and the Treaty on Intellectual Property in Respect of Integrated Circuits, were all Members of the WTO members of those conventions. Any Member availing itself of the possibilities provided in paragraph 3 of Article 5 or paragraph 2 of Article 6 of the

Rome Convention shall make a notification as foreseen in those provisions to the Council for Trade-Related Aspects of Intellectual Property Rights (the 'Counci. for TRIPS').

Article 2

Intellectual Property Conventions

1. In respect of Parts II, III and IV of this Agreement, Members shall comply with Articles 1 through 12, and Article 19, of the Paris Convention (1967).

2. Nothing in Parts I to IV of this Agreement shall derogate from existing obligations that Members may have to each other under the Paris Convention, the Berne Convention, the Rome Convention and the Treaty on Intellectual Property in Respect of Integrated Circuits.

Article 3

National Treatment

1. Each Member shall accord to the nationals of other Members treatment no less favourable than that it accords to its own nationals with regard to the protection of intellectual property, subject to the exceptions already provided in, respectively, the Paris Convention (1967), the Berne Convention (1971), the Rome Convention or the Treaty on Intellectual Property in Respect of Integrated Circuits. In respect of performers, producers of phonograms and broadcasting organizations, this obligation only applies in respect of the rights provided under this Agreement. Any Member availing itself of the possibilities provided in Article 6 of the Berne Convention (1971) or paragraph 1(b) of Article 16 of the Rome Convention shall make a notification as foreseen in those provisions to the Council for TRIPS.

2. Members may avail themselves of the exceptions permitted under paragraph 1 in relation to judicial and administrative procedures, including the designation of an address for service or the appointment of an agent within the jurisdiction of a Member, only where such exceptions are necessary to secure compliance with laws and regulations which are not inconsistent with the provisions of this Agreement and where such practices are not applied in a manner which would constitute a disguised restriction on trade.

Article 4

Most-Favoured-Nation Treatment

With regard to the protection of intellectual property, any advantage, favour, privilege or immunity granted by a Member to the nationals of any other country shall be accorded immediately and unconditionally to the nationals of all other Members. Exempted from this obligation are any advantage, favour, privilege or immunity accorded by a Member:

(a) deriving from international agreements on judicial assistance or law enforcement of a general nature and not particularly confined to the protection of intellectual property;

(b) granted in accordance with the provisions of the Berne Convention (1971) or the Rome Convention authorizing that the treatment accorded be a function not of national treatment but of the treatment accorded in another country;

(c) in respect of the rights of performers, producers of phonograms and broadcasting organizations not provided under this Agreement;

(d) deriving from international agreements related to the protection of intellectual property which entered into force prior to the entry into force of the WTO Agreement, provided that such agreements are notified to the Council for TRIPS and do not constitute an arbitrary or unjustifiable discrimination against nationals of other Members.

Article 5

Multilateral Agreements on Acquisition or Maintenance of Protection

The obligations under Articles 3 and 4 do not apply to procedures provided in multilateral agreements concluded under the auspices of WIPO relating to the acquisition or maintenance of intellectual property rights.

Article 6

Exhaustion

For the purposes of dispute settlement under this Agreement, subject to the provisions of Articles 3 and 4 nothing in this Agreement shall be used to address the issue of the exhaustion of intellectual property rights.

Article 7

Objectives

The protection and enforcement of intellectual property rights should contribute to the promotion of technological innovation and to the transfer and dissemination of technology, to the mutual advantage of producers and users of technological knowledge and in a manner conducive to social and economic welfare, and to a balance of rights and obligations.

Article 8

Principles

1. Members may, in formulating or amending their laws and regulations, adopt measures necessary to protect public health and nutrition, and to promote the public interest in sectors of vital importance to their socio-economic and technological development, provided that such measures are consistent with the provisions of this Agreement.

2. Appropriate measures, provided that they are consistent with the provisions of this Agreement, may be needed to prevent the abuse of intellectual property rights by right holders or the resort to practices which unreasonably restrain trade or adversely affect the international transfer of technology.

Section 2: Trademarks

Article 15

Protectable Subject Matter

1. Any sign, or any combination of signs, capable of distinguishing the goods or

services of one undertaking from those of other undertakings, shall be capable of constituting a trademark. Such signs, in particular words including personal names, letters, numerals, figurative elements and combinations of colours as well as any combination of such signs, shall be eligible for registration as trademarks. Where signs are not inherently capable of distinguishing the relevant goods or services, Members may make registrability depend on distinctiveness acquired through use. Members may require, as a condition of registration, that signs be visually perceptible.

2. Paragraph 1 shall not be understood to prevent a Member from denying registration of a trademark on other grounds, provided that they do not derogate from the provisions of the Paris Convention (1967).

3. Members may make registrability depend on use. However, actual use of a trademark shall not be a condition for filing an application for registration. An application shall not be refused solely on the ground that intended use has not taken place before the expiry of a period of three years from the date of application.

4. The nature of the goods or services to which a trademark is to be applied shall in no case form an obstacle to registration of the trademark.

5. Members shall publish each trademark either before it is registered or promptly after it is registered and shall afford a reasonable opportunity for petitions to cancel the registration. In addition, Members may afford an opportunity for the registration of a trademark to be opposed.

Article 16

Rights Conferred

1. The owner of a registered trademark shall have the exclusive right to prevent all third parties not having the owner's consent from using in the course of trade identical or similar signs for goods or services which are identical or similar to those in respect of which the trademark is registered where such use would result in a likelihood of confusion. In case of the use of an identical sign for identical goods or services, a likelihood of confusion shall be presumed. The rights described above shall not prejudice any existing prior rights, nor shall they affect the possibility of Members making rights available on the basis of use.

2. Article 6bis of the Paris Convention (1967) shall apply, mutatis mutandis, to services. In determining whether a trademark is well-known, Members shall take account of the knowledge of the trademark in the relevant sector of the public, including knowledge in the Member concerned which has been obtained as a result of the promotion of the trademark.

3. Article 6bis of the Paris Convention (1967) shall apply, mutatis mutandis, to goods or services which are not similar to those in respect of which a trademark is registered, provided that use of that trademark in relation to those goods or services would indicate a connection between those goods or services and the owner of the registered trademark and provided that the interests of the owner of the registered trademark are likely to be damaged by such use.

Article 17

Exceptions

Members may provide limited exceptions to the rights conferred by a trademark, such as fair use of descriptive terms, provided that such exceptions take account of the legitimate interests of the owner of the trademark and of third parties.

Article 18

Term of Protection
Initial registration, and each renewal of registration, of a trademark shall be for a term of no less than seven years. The registration of a trademark shall be renewable indefinitely.

Article 19

Requirement of Use
1. If use is required to maintain a registration, the registration may be cancelled only after an uninterrupted period of at least three years of non-use, unless valid reasons based on the existence of obstacles to such use are shown by the trademark owner. Circumstances arising independently of the will of the owner of the trademark which constitute an obstacle to the use of the trademark, such as import restrictions on or other government requirements for goods or services protected by the trademark, shall be recognized as valid reasons for non-use.
2. When subject to the control of its owner, use of a trademark by another person shall be recognized as use of the trademark for the purpose of maintaining the registration.

Article 20

Other Requirements
The use of a trademark in the course of trade shall not be unjustifiably encumbered by special requirements, such as use with another trademark, use in a special form or use in a manner detrimental to its capability to distinguish the goods or services of one undertaking from those of other undertakings. This will not preclude a requirement prescribing the use of the trademark identifying the undertaking producing the goods or services along with, but without linking it to, the trademark distinguishing the specific goods or services in question of that undertaking.

Article 21

Licensing and Assignment
Members may determine conditions on the licensing and assignment of trademarks, it being understood that the compulsory licensing of trademarks shall not be permitted and that the owner of a registered trademark shall have the right to assign the trademark with or without the transfer of the business to which the trademark belongs.

Section 3: Geographical Indications

Article 22

Protection of Geographical Indications
1. Geographical indications are, for the purposes of this Agreement, indications

which identify a good as originating in the territory of a Member, or a region or locality in that territory, where a given quality, reputation or other characteristic of the good is essentially attributable to its geographical origin.

2. In respect of geographical indications, Members shall provide the legal means for interested parties to prevent:

(a) the use of any means in the designation or presentation of a good that indicates or suggests that the good in question originates in a geographical area other than the true place of origin in a manner which misleads the public as to the geographical origin of the good;

(b) any use which constitutes an act of unfair competition within the meaning of Article 10bis of the Paris Convention (1967).

3. A Member shall, ex officio if its legislation so permits or at the request of an interested party, refuse or invalidate the registration of a trademark which contains or consists of a geographical indication with respect to goods not originating in the territory indicated, if use of the indication in the trademark for such goods in that Member is of such a nature as to mislead the public as to the true place of origin.

4. The protection under paragraphs 1, 2 and 3 shall be applicable against a geographical indication which, although literally true as to the territory, region or locality in which the goods originate, falsely represents to the public that the goods originate in another territory.

Article 23

Additional Protection for Geographical Indications for Wines and Spirits

1. Each Member shall provide the legal means for interested parties to prevent use of a geographical indication identifying wines for wines not originating in the place indicated by the geographical indication in question or identifying spirits for spirits not originating in the place indicated by the geographical indication in question, even where the true origin of the goods is indicated or the geographical indication is used in translation or accompanied by expressions such as 'kind', 'type', 'style', 'imitation' or the like.

2. The registration of a trademark for wines which contains or consists of a geographical indication identifying wines or for spirits which contains or consists of a geographical indication identifying spirits shall be refused or invalidated, ex officio if a Member's legislation so permits or at the request of an interested party, with respect to such wines or spirits not having this origin.

3. In the case of homonymous geographical indications for wines, protection shall be accorded to each indication, subject to the provisions of paragraph 4 of Article 22. Each Member shall determine the practical conditions under which the homonymous indications in question will be differentiated from each other, taking into account the need to ensure equitable treatment of the producers concerned and that consumers are not misled.

4. In order to facilitate the protection of geographical indications for wines, negotiations shall be undertaken in the Council for TRIPS concerning the establishment of a multilateral system of notification and registration of geographical indications for wines eligible for protection in those Members participating in the system.

Article 24

International Negotiations; Exceptions

1. Members agree to enter into negotiations aimed at increasing the protection of individual geographical indications under Article 23. The provisions of paragraphs 4 through 8 below shall not be used by a Member to refuse to conduct negotiations or to conclude bilateral or multilateral agreements. In the context of such negotiations, Members shall be willing to consider the continued applicability of these provisions to individual geographical indications whose use was the subject of such negotiations.

2. The Council for TRIPS shall keep under review the application of the provisions of this Section; the first such review shall take place within two years of the entry into force of the WTO Agreement. Any matter affecting the compliance with the obligations under these provisions may be drawn to the attention of the Council, which, at the request of a Member, shall consult with any Member or Members in respect of such matter in respect of which it has not been possible to find a satisfactory solution through bilateral or plurilateral consultations between the Members concerned. The Council shall take such action as may be agreed to facilitate the operation and further the objectives of this Section.

3. In implementing this Section, a Member shall not diminish the protection of geographical indications that existed in that Member immediately prior to the date of entry into force of the WTO Agreement.

4. Nothing in this Section shall require a Member to prevent continued and similar use of a particular geographical indication of another Member identifying wines or spirits in connection with goods or services by any of its nationals or domiciliaries who have used that geographical indication in a continuous manner with regard to the same or related goods or services in the territory of that Member either (*a*) for at least 10 years preceding 15 April 1994 or (*b*) in good faith preceding that date.

5. Where a trademark has been applied for or registered in good faith, or where rights to a trademark have been acquired through use in good faith either:
(a) before the date of application of these provisions in that Member as defined in Part VI; or
(b) before the geographical indication is protected in its country of origin;
measures adopted to implement this Section shall not prejudice eligibility for or the validity of the registration of a trademark, or the right to use a trademark, on the basis that such a trademark is identical with, or similar to, a geographical indication.

6. Nothing in this Section shall require a Member to apply its provisions in respect of a geographical indication of any other Member with respect to goods or services for which the relevant indication is identical with the term customary in common language as the common name for such goods or services in the territory of that Member. Nothing in this Section shall require a Member to apply its provisions in respect of a geographical indication of any other Member with respect to products of the vine for which the relevant indication is identical with the customary name of a grape variety existing in the territory of that Member as of the date of entry into force of the WTO Agreement.

7. A Member may provide that any request made under this Section in connection with the use or registration of a trademark must be presented within five years after

the adverse use of the protected indication has become generally known in that Member or after the date of registration of the trademark in that Member provided that the trademark has been published by that date, if such date is earlier than the date on which the adverse use became generally known in that Member, provided that the geographical indication is not used or registered in bad faith.

8. The provisions of this Section shall in no way prejudice the right of any person to use, in the course of trade, that person's name or the name of that person's prede-cessor in business, except where such name is used in such a manner as to mislead the public.

9. There shall be no obligation under this Agreement to protect geographical indica-tions which are not or cease to be protected in their country of origin, or which have fallen into disuse in that country.

PART III

ENFORCEMENT OF INTELLECTUAL PROPERTY RIGHTS

Section 1: General obligations

Article 41
1. Members shall ensure that enforcement procedures as specified in this Part are available under their law so as to permit effective action against any act of infringe-ment of intellectual property rights covered by this Agreement, including expedi-tious remedies to prevent infringements and remedies which constitute a deterrent to further infringements. These procedures shall be applied in such a manner as to avoid the creation of barriers to legitimate trade and to provide for safeguards against their abuse.

2. Procedures concerning the enforcement of intellectual property rights shall be fair and equitable. They shall not be unnecessarily complicated or costly, or entail unreasonable time-limits or unwarranted delays.

3. Decisions on the merits of a case shall preferably be in writing and reasoned. They shall be made available at least to the parties to the proceeding without undue delay. Decisions on the merits of a case shall be based only on evidence in respect of which parties were offered the opportunity to be heard.

4. Parties to a proceeding shall have an opportunity for review by a judicial author-ity of final administrative decisions and, subject to jurisdictional provisions in a Member's law concerning the importance of a case, of at least the legal aspects of initial judicial decisions on the merits of a case. However, there shall be no obliga-tion to provide an opportunity for review of acquittals in criminal cases.

5. It is understood that this Part does not create any obligation to put in place a judi-cial system for the enforcement of intellectual property rights distinct from that for the enforcement of law in general, nor does it affect the capacity of Members to enforce their law in general. Nothing in this Part creates any obligation with respect to the distribution of resources as between enforcement of intellectual property rights and the enforcement of law in general.

Section 2: Civil and administrative procedures and remedies

Article 42

Fair and Equitable Procedures

Members shall make available to right holders civil judicial procedures concerning the enforcement of any intellectual property right covered by this Agreement. Defendants shall have the right to written notice which is timely and contains sufficient detail, including the basis of the claims. Parties shall be allowed to be represented by independent legal counsel, and procedures shall not impose overly burdensome requirements concerning mandatory personal appearances. All parties to such procedures shall be duly entitled to substantiate their claims and to present all relevant evidence. The procedure shall provide a means to identify and protect confidential information, unless this would be contrary to existing constitutional requirements.

Article 43

Evidence

1. The judicial authorities shall have the authority, where a party has presented reasonably available evidence sufficient to support its claims and has specified evidence relevant to substantiation of its claims which lies in the control of the opposing party, to order that this evidence be produced by the opposing party, subject in appropriate cases to conditions which ensure the protection of confidential information.
2. In cases in which a party to a proceeding voluntarily and without good reason refuses access to, or otherwise does not provide necessary information within a reasonable period, or significantly impedes a procedure relating to an enforcement action, a Member may accord judicial authorities the authority to make preliminary and final determinations, affirmative or negative, on the basis of the information presented to them, including the complaint or the allegation presented by the party adversely affected by the denial of access to information, subject to providing the parties an opportunity to be heard on the allegations or evidence.

Article 44

Injunctions

1. The judicial authorities shall have the authority to order a party to desist from an infringement, *inter alia* to prevent the entry into the channels of commerce in their jurisdiction of imported goods that involve the infringement of an intellectual property right, immediately after customs clearance of such goods. Members are not obliged to accord such authority in respect of protected subject matter acquired or ordered by a person prior to knowing or having reasonable grounds to know that dealing in such subject matter would entail the infringement of an intellectual property right.
2. Notwithstanding the other provisions of this Part and provided that the provisions of Part II specifically addressing use by governments, or by third parties authorized by a government, without the authorization of the right holder are com-

plied with, Members may limit the remedies available against such use to payment of remuneration in accordance with subparagraph (h) of Article 31. In other cases, the remedies under this Part shall apply or, where these remedies are inconsistent with a Member's law, declaratory judgments and adequate compensation shall be available.

Article 45

Damages

1. The judicial authorities shall have the authority to order the infringer to pay the right holder damages adequate to compensate for the injury the right holder has suffered because of an infringement of that person's intellectual property right by an infringer who knowingly, or with reasonable grounds to know, engaged in infringing activity.

2. The judicial authorities shall also have the authority to order the infringer to pay the right holder expenses, which may include appropriate attorney's fees. In appropriate cases, Members may authorize the judicial authorities to order recovery of profits and/or payment of pre-established damages even where the infringer did not knowingly, or with reasonable grounds to know, engage in infringing activity.

Article 46

Other Remedies

In order to create an effective deterrent to infringement, the judicial authorities shall have the authority to order that goods that they have found to be infringing be, without compensation of any sort, disposed of outside the channels of commerce in such a manner as to avoid any harm caused to the right holder, or, unless this would be contrary to existing constitutional requirements, destroyed. The judicial authorities shall also have the authority to order that materials and implements the predominant use of which has been in the creation of the infringing goods be, without compensation of any sort, disposed of outside the channels of commerce in such a manner as to minimize the risks of further infringements. In considering such requests, the need for proportionality between the seriousness of the infringement and the remedies ordered as well as the interests of third parties shall be taken into account. In regard to counterfeit trademark goods, the simple removal of the trademark unlawfully affixed shall not be sufficient, other than in exceptional cases, to permit release of the goods into the channels of commerce.

Article 47

Right of Information

Members may provide that the judicial authorities shall have the authority, unless this would be out of proportion to the seriousness of the infringement, to order the infringer to inform the right holder of the identity of third persons involved in the production and distribution of the infringing goods or services and of their channels of distribution.

Article 48

Indemnification of the Defendant

1. The judicial authorities shall have the authority to order a party at whose request measures were taken and who has abused enforcement procedures to provide to a party wrongfully enjoined or restrained adequate compensation for the injury suffered because of such abuse. The judicial authorities shall also have the authority to order the applicant to pay the defendant expenses, which may include appropriate attorney's fees.

2. In respect of the administration of any law pertaining to the protection or enforcement of intellectual property rights, Members shall only exempt both public authorities and officials from liability to appropriate remedial measures where actions are taken or intended in good faith in the course of the administration of that law.

Article 49

Administrative Procedures

To the extent that any civil remedy can be ordered as a result of administrative procedures on the merits of a case, such procedures shall conform to principles equivalent in substance to those set forth in this Section.

Secion 3: Provisional measures

Article 50

1. The judicial authorities shall have the authority to order prompt and effective provisional measures:
(a) to prevent an infringement of any intellectual property right from occurring, and in particular to prevent the entry into the channels of commerce in their jurisdiction of goods, including imported goods immediately after customs clearance;
(b) to preserve relevant evidence in regard to the alleged infringement.

2. The judicial authorities shall have the authority to adopt provisional measures inaudita altera parte where appropriate, in particular where any delay is likely to cause irreparable harm to the right holder, or where there is a demonstrable risk of evidence being destroyed.

3. The judicial authorities shall have the authority to require the applicant to provide any reasonably available evidence in order to satisfy themselves with a sufficient degree of certainty that the applicant is the right holder and that the applicant's right is being infringed or that such infringement is imminent, and to order the applicant to provide a security or equivalent assurance sufficient to protect the defendant and to prevent abuse.

4. Where provisional measures have been adopted inaudita altera parte, the parties affected shall be given notice, without delay after the execution of the measures at the latest. A review, including a right to be heard, shall take place upon request of the defendant with a view to deciding, within a reasonable period after the notification of the measures, whether these measures shall be modified, revoked or confirmed.

5. The applicant may be required to supply other information necessary for the

identification of the goods concerned by the authority that will execute the provisional measures.

6. Without prejudice to paragraph 4, provisional measures taken on the basis of paragraphs 1 and 2 shall, upon request by the defendant, be revoked or otherwise cease to have effect, if proceedings leading to a decision on the merits of the case are not initiated within a reasonable period, to be determined by the judicial authority ordering the measures where a Member's law so permits or, in the absence of such a determination, not to exceed 20 working days or 31 calendar days, whichever is the longer.

7. Where the provisional measures are revoked or where they lapse due to any act or omission by the applicant, or where it is subsequently found that there has been no infringement or threat of infringement of an intellectual property right, the judicial authorities shall have the authority to order the applicant, upon request of the defendant, to provide the defendant appropriate compensation for any injury caused by these measures.

8. To the extent that any provisional measure can be ordered as a result of administrative procedures, such procedures shall conform to principles equivalent in substance to those set forth in this Section.

Section 4: Special requirements related to border measures

Article 51

Suspension of Release by Customs Authorities
Members shall, in conformity with the provisions set out below, adopt procedures to enable a right holder, who has valid grounds for suspecting that the importation of counterfeit trademark or pirated copyright goods may take place, to lodge an application in writing with competent authorities, administrative or judicial, for the suspension by the customs authorities of the release into free circulation of such goods. Members may enable such an application to be made in respect of goods which involve other infringements of intellectual property rights, provided that the requirements of this Section are met. Members may also provide for corresponding procedures concerning the suspension by the customs authorities of the release of infringing goods destined for exportation from their territories.

Article 52

Application
Any right holder initiating the procedures under Article 51 shall be required to provide adequate evidence to satisfy the competent authorities that, under the laws of the country of importation, there is prima facie an infringement of the right holder's intellectual property right and to supply a sufficiently detailed description of the goods to make them readily recognizable by the customs authorities. The competent authorities shall inform the applicant within a reasonable period whether they have accepted the application and, where determined by the competent authorities, the period for which the customs authorities will take action.

Article 53

Security or Equivalent Assurance
1. The competent authorities shall have the authority to require an applicant to provide a security or equivalent assurance sufficient to protect the defendant and the competent authorities and to prevent abuse. Such security or equivalent assurance shall not unreasonably deter recourse to these procedures.
2. Where pursuant to an application under this Section the release of goods involving industrial designs, patents, layout-designs or undisclosed information into free circulation has been suspended by customs authorities on the basis of a decision other than by a judicial or other independent authority, and the period provided for in Article 55 has expired without the granting of provisional relief by the duly empowered authority, and provided that all other conditions for importation have been complied with, the owner, importer, or consignee of such goods shall be entitled to their release on the posting of a security in an amount sufficient to protect the right holder for any infringement. Payment of such security shall not prejudice any other remedy available to the right holder, it being understood that the security shall be released if the right holder fails to pursue the right of action within a reasonable period of time.

Article 54

Notice of Suspension
The importer and the applicant shall be promptly notified of the suspension of the release of goods according to Article 51.

Article 55

Duration of Suspension
If, within a period not exceeding 10 working days after the applicant has been served notice of the suspension, the customs authorities have not been informed that proceedings leading to a decision on the merits of the case have been initiated by a party other than the defendant, or that the duly empowered authority has taken provisional measures prolonging the suspension of the release of the goods, the goods shall be released, provided that all other conditions for importation or exportation have been complied with; in appropriate cases, this time-limit may be extended by another 10 working days. If proceedings leading to a decision on the merits of the case have been initiated, a review, including a right to be heard, shall take place upon request of the defendant with a view to deciding, within a reasonable period, whether these measures shall be modified, revoked or confirmed. Notwithstanding the above, where the suspension of the release of goods is carried out or continued in accordance with a provisional judicial measure, the provisions of paragraph 6 of Article 50 shall apply.

Article 56

Indemnification of the Importer and of the Owner of the Goods
Relevant authorities shall have the authority to order the applicant to pay the

importer, the consignee and the owner of the goods appropriate compensation for any injury caused to them through the wrongful detention of goods or through the detention of goods released pursuant to Article 55.

Article 57

Right of Inspection and Information

Without prejudice to the protection of confidential information, Members shall provide the competent authorities the authority to give the right holder sufficient opportunity to have any goods detained by the customs authorities inspected in order to substantiate the right holder's claims. The competent authorities shall also have authority to give the importer an equivalent opportunity to have any such goods inspected. Where a positive determination has been made on the merits of a case, Members may provide the competent authorities the authority to inform the right holder of the names and addresses of the consignor, the importer and the consignee and of the quantity of the goods in question.

Article 58

Ex Officio Action

Where Members require competent authorities to act upon their own initiative and to suspend the release of goods in respect of which they have acquired prima facie evidence that an intellectual property right is being infringed:

(a) the competent authorities may at any time seek from the right holder any information that may assist them to exercise these powers;

(b) the importer and the right holder shall be promptly notified of the suspension. Where the importer has lodged an appeal against the suspension with the competent authorities, the suspension shall be subject to the conditions, *mutatis mutandis*, set out at Article 55;

(c) Members shall only exempt both public authorities and officials from liability to appropriate remedial measures where actions are taken or intended in good faith.

Article 59

Remedies

Without prejudice to other rights of action open to the right holder and subject to the right of the defendant to seek review by a judicial authority, competent authorities shall have the authority to order the destruction or disposal of infringing goods in accordance with the principles set out in Article 46. In regard to counterfeit trademark goods, the authorities shall not allow the re-exportation of the infringing goods in an unaltered state or subject them to a different customs procedure, other than in exceptional circumstances.

Article 60

De Minimis Imports

Members may exclude from the application of the above provisions small quantities of goods of a non-commercial nature contained in travellers' personal luggage or sent in small consignments.

Section 5: Criminal procedures

Article 61
Members shall provide for criminal procedures and penalties to be applied at least in cases of wilful trademark counterfeiting or copyright piracy on a commercial scale. Remedies available shall include imprisonment and/or monetary fines sufficient to provide a deterrent, consistently with the level of penalties applied for crimes of a corresponding gravity. In appropriate cases, remedies available shall also include the seizure, forfeiture and destruction of the infringing goods and of any materials and implements the predominant use of which has been in the commission of the offence. Members may provide for criminal procedures and penalties to be applied in other cases of infringement of intellectual property rights, in particular where they are committed wilfully and on a commercial scale.

PART IV

ACQUISITION AND MAINTENANCE OF INTELLECTUAL PROPERTY

RIGHTS AND RELATED INTER-PARTES PROCEDURES

Article 62
1. Members may require, as a condition of the acquisition or maintenance of the intellectual property rights provided for under Sections 2 through 6 of Part II, compliance with reasonable procedures and formalities. Such procedures and formalities shall be consistent with the provisions of this Agreement.
2. Where the acquisition of an intellectual property right is subject to the right being granted or registered, Members shall ensure that the procedures for grant or registration, subject to compliance with the substantive conditions for acquisition of the right, permit the granting or registration of the right within a reasonable period of time so as to avoid unwarranted curtailment of the period of protection.
3. Article 4 of the Paris Convention (1967) shall apply *mutatis mutandis* to service marks.
4. Procedures concerning the acquisition or maintenance of intellectual property rights and, where a Member's law provides for such procedures, administrative revocation and inter partes procedures such as opposition, revocation and cancellation, shall be governed by the general principles set out in paragraphs 2 and 3 of Article 41.
5. Final administrative decisions in any of the procedures referred to under paragraph 4 shall be subject to review by a judicial or quasi-judicial authority. However, there shall be no obligation to provide an opportunity for such review of decisions in cases of unsuccessful opposition or administrative revocation, provided that the grounds for such procedures can be the subject of invalidation procedures.

PART V

DISPUTE PREVENTION AND SETTLEMENT

Article 63

Transparency

1. Laws and regulations, and final judicial decisions and administrative rulings of general application, made effective by a Member pertaining to the subject matter of this Agreement (the availability, scope, acquisition, enforcement and prevention of the abuse of intellectual property rights) shall be published, or where such publication is not practicable made publicly available, in a national language, in such a manner as to enable governments and right holders to become acquainted with them. Agreements concerning the subject matter of this Agreement which are in force between the government or a governmental agency of a Member and the government or a governmental agency of another Member shall also be published.

2. Members shall notify the laws and regulations referred to in paragraph 1 to the Council for TRIPS in order to assist that Council in its review of the operation of this Agreement. The Council shall attempt to minimize the burden on Members in carrying out this obligation and may decide to waive the obligation to notify such laws and regulations directly to the Council if consultations with WIPO on the establishment of a common register containing these laws and regulations are successful. The Council shall also consider in this connection any action required regarding notifications pursuant to the obligations under this Agreement stemming from the provisions of Article 6ter of the Paris Convention (1967).

3. Each Member shall be prepared to supply, in response to a written request from another Member, information of the sort referred to in paragraph 1. A Member, having reason to believe that a specific judicial decision or administrative ruling or bilateral agreement in the area of intellectual property rights affects its rights under this Agreement, may also request in writing to be given access to or be informed in sufficient detail of such specific judicial decisions or administrative rulings or bilateral agreements.

4. Nothing in paragraphs 1, 2 and 3 shall require Members to disclose confidential information which would impede law enforcement or otherwise be contrary to the public interest or would prejudice the legitimate commercial interests of particular enterprises, public or private.

Article 64

Dispute Settlement

1. The provisions of Articles XXII and XXIII of GATT 1994 as elaborated and applied by the Dispute Settlement Understanding shall apply to consultations and the settlement of disputes under this Agreement except as otherwise specifically provided herein.

2. Subparagraphs 1(b) and 1(c) of Article XXIII of GATT 1994 shall not apply to the settlement of disputes under this Agreement for a period of five years from the

date of entry into force of the WTO Agreement.

3. During the time period referred to in paragraph 2, the Council for TRIPS shall examine the scope and modalities for complaints of the type provided for under subparagraphs 1(b) and 1(c) of Article XXIII of GATT 1994 made pursuant to this Agreement, and submit its recommendations to the Ministerial Conference for approval. Any decision of the Ministerial Conference to approve such recommendations or to extend the period in paragraph 2 shall be made only by consensus, and approved recommendations shall be effective for all Members without further formal acceptance process.

PART VI

TRANSITIONAL ARRANGEMENTS

Article 65

Transitional Arrangements

1. Subject to the provisions of paragraphs 2, 3 and 4, no Member shall be obliged to apply the provisions of this Agreement before the expiry of a general period of one year following the date of entry into force of the WTO Agreement.

2. A developing country Member is entitled to delay for a further period of four years the date of application, as defined in paragraph 1, of the provisions of this Agreement other than Articles 3, 4 and 5.

3. Any other Member which is in the process of transformation from a centrally-planned into a market, free-enterprise economy and which is undertaking structural reform of its intellectual property system and facing special problems in the preparation and implementation of intellectual property laws and regulations, may also benefit from a period of delay as foreseen in paragraph 2.

4. To the extent that a developing country Member is obliged by this Agreement to extend product patent protection to areas of technology not so protectable in its territory on the general date of application of this Agreement for that Member, as defined in paragraph 2, it may delay the application of the provisions on product patents of Section 5 of Part II to such areas of technology for an additional period of five years.

5. A Member availing itself of a transitional period under paragraphs 1, 2, 3 or 4 shall ensure that any changes in its laws, regulations and practice made during that period do not result in a lesser degree of consistency with the provisions of this Agreement.

Article 66

Least-Developed Country Members

1. In view of the special needs and requirements of least-developed country Members, their economic, financial and administrative constraints, and their need for flexibility to create a viable technological base, such Members shall not be required to apply the provisions of this Agreement, other than Articles 3, 4 and 5, for a period of 10 years from the date of application as defined under paragraph 1 of

Article 65. The Council for TRIPS shall, upon duly motivated request by a least-developed country Member, accord extensions of this period.

2. Developed country Members shall provide incentives to enterprises and institutions in their territories for the purpose of promoting and encouraging technology transfer to least-developed country Members in order to enable them to create a sound and viable technological base.

Article 67

Technical Cooperation

In order to facilitate the implementation of this Agreement, developed country Members shall provide, on request and on mutually agreed terms and conditions, technical and financial cooperation in favour of developing and least-developed country Members. Such cooperation shall include assistance in the preparation of laws and regulations on the protection and enforcement of intellectual property rights as well as on the prevention of their abuse, and shall include support regarding the establishment or reinforcement of domestic offices and agencies relevant to these matters, including the training of personnel.

PART VII

INSTITUTIONAL ARRANGEMENTS; FINAL PROVISIONS

Article 68

Council for Trade-Related Aspects of Intellectual Property Rights

The Council for TRIPS shall monitor the operation of this Agreement and, in particular, Members' compliance with their obligations hereunder, and shall afford Members the opportunity of consulting on matters relating to the trade-related aspects of intellectual property rights. It shall carry out such other responsibilities as assigned to it by the Members, and it shall, in particular, provide any assistance requested by them in the context of dispute settlement procedures. In carrying out its functions, the Council for TRIPS may consult with and seek information from any source it deems appropriate. In consultation with WIPO, the Council shall seek to establish, within one year of its first meeting, appropriate arrangements for cooperation with bodies of that Organization.

Article 69

International Cooperation

Members agree to cooperate with each other with a view to eliminating international trade in goods infringing intellectual property rights. For this purpose, they shall establish and notify contact points in their administrations and be ready to exchange information on trade in infringing goods. They shall, in particular, promote the exchange of information and cooperation between customs authorities with regard to trade in counterfeit trademark goods and pirated copyright goods.

Article 70

Protection of Existing Subject Matter

1. This Agreement does not give rise to obligations in respect of acts which occurred before the date of application of the Agreement for the Member in question.

2. Except as otherwise provided for in this Agreement, this Agreement gives rise to obligations in respect of all subject matter existing at the date of application of this Agreement for the Member in question, and which is protected in that Member on the said date, or which meets or comes subsequently to meet the criteria for protection under the terms of this Agreement. In respect of this paragraph and paragraphs 3 and 4, copyright obligations with respect to existing works shall be solely determined under Article 18 of the Berne Convention (1971), and obligations with respect to the rights of producers of phonograms and performers in existing phonograms shall be determined solely under Article 18 of the Berne Convention (1971) as made applicable under paragraph 6 of Article 14 of this Agreement.

3. There shall be no obligation to restore protection to subject matter which on the date of application of this Agreement for the Member in question has fallen into the public domain.

4. In respect of any acts in respect of specific objects embodying protected subject matter which become infringing under the terms of legislation in conformity with this Agreement, and which were commenced, or in respect of which a significant investment was made, before the date of acceptance of the WTO Agreement by that Member, any Member may provide for a limitation of the remedies available to the right holder as to the continued performance of such acts after the date of application of this Agreement for that Member. In such cases the Member shall, however, at least provide for the payment of equitable remuneration.

5. A Member is not obliged to apply the provisions of Article 11 and of paragraph 4 of Article 14 with respect to originals or copies purchased prior to the date of application of this Agreement for that Member.

6. Members shall not be required to apply Article 31, or the requirement in paragraph 1 of Article 27 that patent rights shall be enjoyable without discrimination as to the field of technology, to use without the authorization of the right holder where authorization for such use was granted by the government before the date this Agreement became known.

7. In the case of intellectual property rights for which protection is conditional upon registration, applications for protection which are pending on the date of application of this Agreement for the Member in question shall be permitted to be amended to claim any enhanced protection provided under the provisions of this Agreement. Such amendments shall not include new matter.

8. Where a Member does not make available as of the date of entry into force of the WTO Agreement patent protection for pharmaceutical and agricultural chemical products commensurate with its obligations under Article 27, that Member shall:

(a) notwithstanding the provisions of Part VI, provide as from the date of entry into force of the WTO Agreement a means by which applications for patents for such inventions can be filed;

(b) apply to these applications, as of the date of application of this Agreement, the criteria for patentability as laid down in this Agreement as if those criteria were being applied on the date of filing in that Member or, where priority is available and claimed, the priority date of the application; and

(c) provide patent protection in accordance with this Agreement as from the grant of the patent and for the remainder of the patent term, counted from the filing date in accordance with Article 33 of this Agreement, for those of these applications that meet the criteria for protection referred to in subparagraph (b).

9. Where a product is the subject of a patent application in a Member in accordance with paragraph 8(a), exclusive marketing rights shall be granted, notwithstanding the provisions of Part VI, for a period of five years after obtaining marketing approval in that Member or until a product patent is granted or rejected in that Member, whichever period is shorter, provided that, subsequent to the entry into force of the WTO Agreement, a patent application has been filed and a patent granted for that product in another Member and marketing approval obtained in such other Member.

Article 71

Review and Amendment

1. The Council for TRIPS shall review the implementation of this Agreement after the expiration of the transitional period referred to in paragraph 2 of Article 65. The Council shall, having regard to the experience gained in its implementation, review it two years after that date, and at identical intervals thereafter. The Council may also undertake reviews in the light of any relevant new developments which might warrant modification or amendment of this Agreement.

2. Amendments merely serving the purpose of adjusting to higher levels of protection of intellectual property rights achieved, and in force, in other multilateral agreements and accepted under those agreements by all Members of the WTO may be referred to the Ministerial Conference for action in accordance with paragraph 6 of Article X of the WTO Agreement on the basis of a consensus proposal from the Council for TRIPS.

Article 72

Reservations

Reservations may not be entered in respect of any of the provisions of this Agreement without the consent of the other Members.

Article 73

Security Exceptions

Nothing in this Agreement shall be construed:

(a) to require a Member to furnish any information the disclosure of which it considers contrary to its essential security interests; or

(b) to prevent a Member from taking any action which it considers necessary for the protection of its essential security interests;

    (i) relating to fissionable materials or the materials from which they are derived;

    (ii) relating to the traffic in arms, ammunition and implements of war and to such traffic in other goods and materials as is carried on directly or indirectly for the purpose of supplying a military establishment;

(iii) taken in time of war or other emergency in international relations; or
(c) to prevent a Member from taking any action in pursuance of its obligations under the United Nations Charter for the maintenance of international peace and security.

Appendix 5

European materials

TREATY OF AMSTERDAM

Notes

Treaty of Amsterdam amending the Treaty on European Union, the Treaties establishing the European Communities and certain related acts, signed at Amsterdam, 2 October 1997.

PART THREE–COMMUNITY POLICIES

TITLE I–FREE MOVEMENT OF GOODS

CHAPTER 2 *Prohibition of quantitative restrictions between member states*

Article 28 (ex Article 30)

Quantitative restrictions on imports and all measures having equivalent effect shall be prohibited between Member States.

Article 29 (ex Article 34)

Quantitative restrictions on exports, and all measures having equivalent effect, shall be prohibited between Member States.

Article 30 (ex Article 36)

The provisions of Articles 28 and 29 shall not preclude prohibitions or restrictions on imports, exports or goods in transit justified on grounds of public morality, public policy or public security; the protection of health and life of humans, animals or plants; the protection of national treasures possessing artistic, historic or archaeological value; or the protection of industrial and commercial property. Such prohibitions or restrictions shall not, however, constitute a means of arbitrary discrimination or a disguised restriction on trade between Member States.

TITLE VI (ex Title V)–COMMON RULES ON COMPETITION, TAXATION AND APPROXIMATION OF LAWS

CHAPTER 1 *Rules on competition*

Section 1

Article 81 (ex Article 85)

Rules applying to undertakings

1. The following shall be prohibited as incompatible with the common market: all

agreements between undertakings, decisions by associations of undertakings and concerted practices which may affect trade between Member States and which have as their object or effect the prevention, restriction or distortion of competition within the common market, and in particular those which:

    (a) directly or indirectly fix purchase or selling prices or any other trading conditions;

    (b) limit or control production, markets, technical development, or investment;

    (c) share markets or sources of supply;

    (d) apply dissimilar conditions to equivalent transactions with other trading parties, thereby placing them at a competitive disadvantage;

    (e) make the conclusion of contracts subject to acceptance by the other parties of supplementary obligations which, by their nature or according to commercial usage, have no connection with the subject of such contracts.

2. Any agreements or decisions prohibited pursuant to this Article shall be automatically void.

3. The provisions of paragraph 1 may, however, be declared inapplicable in the case of:

    –any agreement or category of agreements between undertakings;

    –any decision or category of decisions by associations of undertakings;

    –any concerted practice or category of concerted practices,

which contributes to improving the production or distribution of goods or to promoting technical or economic progress, while allowing consumers a fair share of the resulting benefit, and which does not:

    (a) impose on the undertakings concerned restrictions which are not indispensable to the attainment of these objectives;

    (b) afford such undertakings the possibility of eliminating competition in respect of a substantial part of the products in question.

Article 82 (ex Article 86)

Any abuse by one or more undertakings of a dominant position within the common market or in a substantial part of it shall be prohibited as incompatible with the common market insofar as it may affect trade between Member States.

Such abuse may, in particular, consist in:

    (a) directly or indirectly imposing unfair purchase or selling prices or other unfair trading conditions;

    (b) limiting production, markets or technical development to the prejudice of consumers;

    (c) applying dissimilar conditions to equivalent transactions with other trading parties, thereby placing them at a competitive disadvantage;

    (d) making the conclusion of contracts subject to acceptance by the other parties of supplementary obligations which, by their nature or according to commercial usage, have no connection with the subject of such contracts.

CHAPTER 3

Article 94 (ex Article 100)

Approximation of laws

The Council shall, acting unanimously on a proposal from the Commission and after consulting the European Parliament and the Economic and Social Committee, issue directives for the approximation of such laws, regulations or administrative provisions of the Member States as directly affect the establishment or functioning of the common market.

Article 234 (ex Article 177)

The Court of Justice shall have jurisdiction to give preliminary rulings concerning:

- (a) the interpretation of this Treaty;
- (b) the validity and interpretation of acts of the institutions of the Community and of the ECB;
- (c) the interpretation of the statutes of bodies established by an act of the Council, where those statutes so provide.

Where such a question is raised before any court or tribunal of a Member State, that court or tribunal may, if it considers that a decision on the question is necessary to enable it to give judgment, request the Court of Justice to give a ruling thereon.

Where any such question is raised in a case pending before a court or tribunal of a Member State against whose decisions there is no judicial remedy under national law, that court or tribunal shall bring the matter before the Court of Justice.

Article 308 (ex Article 235)

If action by the Community should prove necessary to attain, in the course of the operation of the common market, one of the objectives of the Community and this Treaty has not provided the necessary powers, the Council shall, acting unanimously on a proposal from the Commission and after consulting the European Parliament, take the appropriate measures.

AGREEMENT ON THE EUROPEAN ECONOMIC AREA - FINAL ACT -
JOINT DECLARATIONS - DECLARATIONS BY THE GOVERNMENTS OF
THE MEMBER STATES OF THE COMMUNITY AND THE EFTA STATES -
ARRANGEMENTS - AGREED MINUTES - DECLARATIONS BY ONE OR
SEVERAL OF THE CONTRACTING PARTIES OF THE AGREEMENT ON
THE EUROPEAN ECONOMIC AREA

Official Journal L 1, 3/1/1994, pp3-36

PART I OBJECTIVES AND PRINCIPLES

Article 1

1. The aim of this Agreement of association is to promote a continuous and balanced strengthening of trade and economic relations between the Contracting Parties with equal conditions of competition, and the respect of the same rules, with a view to creating a homogeneous European Economic Area, hereinafter referred to as the EEA.

2. In order to attain the objectives set out in paragraph 1, the association shall entail, in accordance with the provisions of this Agreement:

- (a) the free movement of goods;
- (b) the free movement of persons;
- (c) the free movement of services;
- (d) the free movement of capital;
- (e) the setting up of a system ensuring that competition is not distorted and that the rules thereon are equally respected; as well as
- (f) closer cooperation in other fields, such as research and development, the environment, education and social policy.

Article 2

For the purposes of this Agreement:

(a) the term 'Agreement' means the main Agreement, its Protocols and Annexes as well as the acts referred to therein;

(b) the term 'EFTA States' means the Contracting Parties, which are members of the European Free Trade Association;

(c) the term 'Contracting Parties' means, concerning the Community and the EC Member States, the Community and the EC Member States, or the Community, or the EC Member States. The meaning to be attributed to this expression in each case is to be deduced from the relevant provisions of this Agreement and from the respective competences of the Community and the EC Member States as they follow from the Treaty establishing the European Economic Community and the Treaty establishing the European Coal and Steel Community.

Article 3

The Contracting Parties shall take all appropriate measures, whether general or particular, to ensure fulfilment of the obligations arising out of this Agreement.

They shall abstain from any measure which could jeopardize the attainment of the objectives of this Agreement.

Moreover, they shall facilitate cooperation within the framework of this Agreement.

Article 4

Within the scope of application of this Agreement, and without prejudice to any special provisions contained therein, any discrimination on grounds of nationality shall be prohibited.

Article 5

A Contracting Party may at any time raise a matter of concern at the level of the EEA Joint Committee or the EEA Council according to the modalities laid down in Articles 92(2) and 89(2), respectively.

Article 6

Without prejudice to future developments of case-law, the provisions of this Agreement, in so far as they are identical in substance to corresponding rules of the Treaty establishing the European Economic Community and the Treaty establishing the European Coal and Steel Community and to acts adopted in application of these two Treaties, shall, in their implementation and application, be interpreted in conformity with the relevant rulings of the Court of Justice of the European Communities given prior to the date of signature of this Agreement.

Article 7

Acts referred to or contained in the Annexes to this Agreement or in decisions of the EEA Joint Committee shall be binding upon the Contracting Parties and be, or be made, part of their internal legal order as follows:

(a) an act corresponding to an EEC regulation shall as such be made part of the internal legal order of the Contracting Parties;

(b) an act corresponding to an EEC directive shall leave to the authorities of the Contracting Parties the choice of form and method of implementation.

PART II FREE MOVEMENT OF GOODS

CHAPTER 1 BASIC PRINCIPLES

Article 8
1. Free movement of goods between the Contracting Parties shall be established in conformity with the provisions of this Agreement.
2. Unless otherwise specified, Articles 10 to 15, 19, 20 and 25 to 27 shall apply only to products originating in the Contracting Parties.
3. Unless otherwise specified, the provisions of this Agreement shall apply only to:

(a) products falling within Chapters 25 to 97 of the Harmonized Commodity Description and Coding System, excluding the products listed in Protocol 2;

(b) products specified in Protocol 3, subject to the specific arrangements set out in that Protocol.

Article 9
1. The rules of origin are set out in Protocol 4. They are without prejudice to any international obligations which have been, or may be, subscribed to by the Contracting Parties under the General Agreement on Tariffs and Trade.
2. With a view to developing the results achieved in this Agreement, the Contracting Parties will continue their efforts in order further to improve and simplify all aspects of rules of origin and to increase cooperation in customs matters.
3. A first review will take place before the end of 1993. Subsequent reviews will take place at two-yearly intervals. On the basis of these reviews, the Contracting Parties undertake to decide on the appropriate measures to be included in this Agreement.

Article 10
Customs duties on imports and exports, and any charges having equivalent effect, shall be prohibited between the Contracting Parties. Without prejudice to the arrangements set out in Protocol 5, this shall also apply to customs duties of a fiscal nature.

Article 11
Quantitative restrictions on imports and all measures having equivalent effect shall be prohibited between the Contracting Parties.

Article 12
Quantitative restrictions on exports and all measures having equivalent effect shall be prohibited between the Contracting Parties.

Article 13
The provisions of Articles 11 and 12 shall not preclude prohibitions or restrictions on imports, exports or goods in transit justified on grounds of public morality, public policy or public security; the protection of health and life of humans, animals or plants; the protection of national treasures possessing artistic, historic or archaeological value; or the protection of industrial and commercial property. Such prohibitions or restrictions shall not, however, constitute a means of arbitrary discrimination or a disguised restriction on trade between the Contracting Parties.

Article 14
No Contracting Party shall impose, directly or indirectly, on the products of other Contracting Parties any internal taxation of any kind in excess of that imposed directly or indirectly on similar domestic products.

Furthermore, no Contracting Party shall impose on the products of other Contracting Parties any internal taxation of such a nature as to afford indirect protection to other products.

Article 15
Where products are exported to the territory of any Contracting Party, any repayment of internal taxation shall not exceed the internal taxation imposed on them whether directly or indirectly.

Article 16
1. The Contracting Parties shall ensure that any State monopoly of a commercial character be adjusted so that no discrimination regarding the conditions under which goods are procured and marketed will exist between nationals of EC Member States and EFTA States.
2. The provisions of this Article shall apply to any body through which the competent authorities of the Contracting Parties, in law or in fact, either directly or indirectly supervise, determine or appreciably influence imports or exports between Contracting Parties. These provisions shall likewise apply to monopolies delegated by the State to others.

CHAPTER 2 AGRICULTURAL AND FISHERY PRODUCTS

Article 17
Annex I contains specific provisions and arrangements concerning veterinary and phytosanitary matters.

Article 18
Without prejudice to the specific arrangements governing trade in agricultural products, the Contracting Parties shall ensure that the arrangements provided for in Articles 17 and 23 (a) and (b), as they apply to products other than those covered by Article 8(3), are not compromised by other technical barriers to trade. Article 13 shall apply.

Article 19
1. The Contracting Parties shall examine any difficulties that might arise in their trade in agricultural products and shall endeavour to seek appropriate solutions.
2. The Contracting Parties undertake to continue their efforts with a view to achieving progressive liberalization of agricultural trade.
3. To this end, the Contracting Parties will carry out, before the end of 1993 and subsequently at two-yearly intervals, reviews of the conditions of trade in agricultural products.
4. In the light of the results of these reviews, within the framework of their respective agricultural policies and taking into account the results of the Uruguay Round, the Contracting Parties will decide, within the framework of this Agreement, on a preferential, bilateral or multilateral, reciprocal and mutually beneficial basis, on further reductions of any type of barriers to trade in the agricultural sector, including those resulting from State monopolies of a commercial character in the agricultural field.

Article 20
Provisions and arrangements that apply to fish and other marine products are set out in Protocol 9.

CHAPTER 3 COOPERATION IN CUSTOMS-RELATED MATTERS AND TRADE FACILITATION

Article 21

1. In order to facilitate trade between them, the Contracting Parties shall simplify border controls and formalities. Arrangements for this purpose are set out in Protocol 10.

2. The Contracting Parties shall assist each other in customs matters in order to ensure that customs legislation is correctly applied. Arrangements for this purpose are set out in Protocol 11.

3. The Contracting Parties shall strengthen and broaden cooperation with the aim of simplifying the procedures for trade in goods, in particular in the context of Community programmes, projects and actions aimed at trade facilitation, in accordance with the rules set out in Part VI.

4. Notwithstanding Article 8(3), this Article shall apply to all products.

Article 22

A Contracting Party which is considering the reduction of the effective level of its duties or charges having equivalent effect applicable to third countries benefiting from most-favoured-nation treatment, or which is considering the suspension of their application, shall, as far as may be practicable, notify the EEA Joint Committee not later than 30 days before such reduction or suspension comes into effect. It shall take note of any representations by other Contracting Parties regarding any distortions which might result therefrom.

CHAPTER 4 OTHER RULES RELATING TO THE FREE MOVEMENT OF GOODS

Article 23

Specific provisions and arrangements are laid down in:

   (a) Protocol 12 and Annex II in relation to technical regulations, standards, testing and certification;

   (b) Protocol 47 in relation to the abolition of technical barriers to trade in wine;

   (c) Annex III in relation to product liability.

They shall apply to all products unless otherwise specified.

Article 24

Annex IV contains specific provisions and arrangements concerning energy.

Article 25

Where compliance with the provisions of Articles 10 and 12 leads to:

   (a) re-export towards a third country against which the exporting Contracting Party maintains, for the product concerned, quantitative export restrictions, export duties or measures or charges having equivalent effect; or

   (b) a serious shortage, or threat thereof, of a product essential to the exporting Contracting Party;

and where the situations referred to above give rise, or are likely to give rise, to major difficulties for the exporting Contracting Party, that Contracting Party may take appropriate measures in accordance with the procedures set out in Article 113.

Article 26

Anti-dumping measures, countervailing duties and measures against illicit commercial practices attributable to third countries shall not be applied in relations between the Contracting Parties, unless otherwise specified in this Agreement.

CHAPTER 5 COAL AND STEEL PRODUCTS

Article 27
Provisions and arrangements concerning coal and steel products are set out in Protocols 14 and 25.

PART III FREE MOVEMENT OF PERSONS, SERVICES AND CAPITAL
CHAPTER 1 WORKERS AND SELF-EMPLOYED PERSONS

PART IV COMPETITION AND OTHER COMMON RULES CHAPTER 1 RULES APPLICABLE TO UNDERTAKINGS

PART V HORIZONTAL PROVISIONS RELEVANT TO THE FOUR FREE-DOMS CHAPTER 1 SOCIAL POLICY

PART VI COOPERATION OUTSIDE THE FOUR FREEDOMS

PART VII INSTITUTIONAL PROVISIONS

CHAPTER 1 THE STRUCTURE OF THE ASSOCIATION

Section 1 The EEA Council

Article 89
1. An EEA Council is hereby established. It shall, in particular, be responsible for giving the political impetus in the implementation of this Agreement and laying down the general guidelines for the EEA Joint Committee.
To this end, the EEA Council shall assess the overall functioning and the development of the Agreement. It shall take the political decisions leading to amendments of the Agreement.
2. The Contracting Parties, as to the Community and the EC Member States in their respective fields of competence, may, after having discussed it in the EEA Joint Committee, or directly in exceptionally urgent cases, raise in the EEA Council any issue giving rise to a difficulty.
3. The EEA Council shall by decision adopt its rules of procedure.

Article 90
1. The EEA Council shall consist of the members of the Council of the European Communities and members of the EC Commission, and of one member of the Government of each of the EFTA States.
Members of the EEA Council may be represented in accordance with the conditions to be laid down in its rules of procedure.
2. Decisions by the EEA Council shall be taken by agreement between the Community, on the one hand, and the EFTA States, on the other.

Article 91
1. The office of President of the EEA Council shall be held alternately, for a period of six months, by a member of the Council of the European Communities and a member of the Government of an EFTA State.
2. The EEA Council shall be convened twice a year by its President. The EEA Council shall also meet whenever circumstances so require, in accordance with its rules of procedure.

Section 2 The EEA Joint Committee

Article 92

1. An EEA Joint Committee is hereby established. It shall ensure the effective implementation and operation of this Agreement. To this end, it shall carry out exchanges of views and information and take decisions in the cases provided for in this Agreement.

2. The Contracting Parties, as to the Community and the EC Member States in their respective fields of competence, shall hold consultations in the EEA Joint Committee on any point of relevance to the Agreement giving rise to a difficulty and raised by one of them.

3. The EEA Joint Committee shall by decision adopt its rules of procedure.

Article 93

1. The EEA Joint Committee shall consist of representatives of the Contracting Parties.

2. The EEA Joint Committee shall take decisions by agreement between the Community, on the one hand, and the EFTA States speaking with one voice, on the other.

Article 94

1. The office of President of the EEA Joint Committee shall be held alternately, for a period of six months, by the representative of the Community, i.e. the EC Commission, and the representative of one of the EFTA States.

2. In order to fulfil its functions, the EEA Joint Committee shall meet, in principle, at least once a month. It shall also meet on the initiative of its President or at the request of one of the Contracting Parties in accordance with its rules of procedure.

3. The EEA Joint Committee may decide to establish any subcommittee or working group to assist it in carrying out its tasks. The EEA Joint Committee shall in its rules of procedure lay down the composition and mode of operation of such subcommittees and working groups. Their tasks shall be determined by the EEA Joint Committee in each individual case.

4. The EEA Joint Committee shall issue an annual report on the functioning and the development of this Agreement.

Section 3 Parliamentary cooperation

Article 95

1. An EEA Joint Parliamentary Committee is hereby established. It shall be composed of equal numbers of, on the one hand, members of the European Parliament and, on the other, members of Parliaments of the EFTA States. The total number of members of the Committee is laid down in the Statute in Protocol 36.

2. The EEA Joint Parliamentary Committee shall alternately hold sessions in the Community and in an EFTA State in accordance with the provisions laid down in Protocol 36.

3. The EEA Joint Parliamentary Committee shall contribute, through dialogue and debate, to a better understanding between the Community and the EFTA States in the fields covered by this Agreement.

4. The EEA Joint Parliamentary Committee may express its views in the form of reports or resolutions, as appropriate. It shall, in particular, examine the annual report of the EEA Joint Committee, issued in accordance with Article 94(4), on the functioning and the development of this Agreement.

5. The President of the EEA Council may appear before the EEA Joint Parliamentary Committee in order to be heard by it.

6. The EEA Joint Parliamentary Committee shall adopt its rules of procedure.

Section 4 Cooperation between economic and social partners

Article 96

1. Members of the Economic and Social Committee and other bodies representing the social partners in the Community and the corresponding bodies in the EFTA States shall work to strengthen contacts between them and to cooperate in an organized and regular manner in order to enhance the awareness of the economic and social aspects of the growing interdependence of the economies of the Contracting Parties and of their interests within the context of the EEA.

2. To this end, an EEA Consultative Committee is hereby established. It shall be composed of equal numbers of, on the one hand, members of the Economic and Social Committee of the Community and, on the other, members of the EFTA Consultative Committee. The EEA Consultative Committee may express its views in the form of reports or resolutions, as appropriate.

3. The EEA Consultative Committee shall adopt its rules of procedure.

CHAPTER 2 THE DECISION-MAKING PROCEDURE

Article 97

This Agreement does not prejudge the right for each Contracting Party to amend, without prejudice to the principle of non-discrimination and after having informed the other Contracting Parties, its internal legislation in the areas covered by this Agreement:

— if the EEA Joint Committee concludes that the legislation as amended does not affect the good functioning of this Agreement; or

— if the procedures referred to in Article 98 have been completed.

Article 98

The Annexes to this Agreement and Protocols 1 to 7, 9 to 11, 19 to 27, 30 to 32, 37, 39, 41 and 47, as appropriate, may be amended by a decision of the EEA Joint Committee in accordance with Articles 93(2), 99, 100, 102 and 103.

Article 99

1. As soon as new legislation is being drawn up by the EC Commission in a field which is governed by this Agreement, the EC Commission shall informally seek advice from experts of the EFTA States in the same way as it seeks advice from experts of the EC Member States for the elaboration of its proposals.

2. When transmitting its proposal to the Council of the European Communities, the EC Commission shall transmit copies thereof to the EFTA States.

At the request of one of the Contracting Parties, a preliminary exchange of views takes place in the EEA Joint Committee.

3. During the phase preceding the decision of the Council of the European Communities, in a continuous information and consultation process, the Contracting Parties consult each other again in the EEA Joint Committee at the significant moments at the request of one of them.

4. The Contracting Parties shall cooperate in good faith during the information and consultation phase with a view to facilitating, at the end of the process, the decision-taking in the EEA Joint Committee.

Article 100

The EC Commission shall ensure experts of the EFTA States as wide a participation as possible according to the areas concerned, in the preparatory stage of draft measures to be submitted subsequently to the committees which assist the EC Commission in the exercise of its executive powers. In this regard, when drawing up draft measures the EC Commission shall refer to experts of the EFTA States on the same basis as it refers to experts of the EC Member States.

In the cases where the Council of the European Communities is seized in accordance with the procedure applicable to the type of committee involved, the EC Commission shall transmit to the Council of the European Communities the views of the experts of the EFTA States.

Article 101

1. In respect of committees which are covered neither by Article 81 nor by Article 100 experts from EFTA States shall be associated with the work when this is called for by the good functioning of this Agreement.

These committees are listed in Protocol 37. The modalities of such an association are set out in the relevant sectoral Protocols and Annexes dealing with the matter concerned.

2. If it appears to the Contracting Parties that such an association should be extended to other committees which present similar characteristics, the EEA Joint Committee may amend Protocol 37.

Article 102

1. In order to guarantee the legal security and the homogeneity of the EEA, the EEA Joint Committee shall take a decision concerning an amendment of an Annex to this Agreement as closely as possible to the adoption by the Community of the corresponding new Community legislation with a view to permitting a simultaneous application of the latter as well as of the amendments of the Annexes to the Agreement. To this end, the Community shall, whenever adopting a legislative act on an issue which is governed by this Agreement, as soon as possible inform the other Contracting Parties in the EEA Joint Committee.

2. The part of an Annex to this Agreement which would be directly affected by the new legislation is assessed in the EEA Joint Committee.

3. The Contracting Parties shall make all efforts to arrive at an agreement on matters relevant to this Agreement.

The EEA Joint Committee shall, in particular, make every effort to find a mutually acceptable solution where a serious problem arises in any area which, in the EFTA States, falls within the competence of the legislator.

4. If, notwithstanding the application of the preceding paragraph, an agreement on an amendment of an Annex to this Agreement cannot be reached, the EEA Joint Committee shall examine all further possibilities to maintain the good functioning of this Agreement and take any decision necessary to this effect, including the possibility to take notice of the equivalence of legislation. Such a decision shall be taken at the latest at the expiry of a period of six months from the date of referral to the EEA Joint Committee or, if that date is later, on the date of entry into force of the corresponding Community legislation.

5. If, at the end of the time-limit set out in paragraph 4, the EEA Joint Committee has not taken a decision on an amendment of an Annex to this Agreement, the affected part thereof, as determined in accordance with paragraph 2, is regarded as provisionally suspended, subject to a decision to the contrary by the EEA Joint Committee. Such a suspension shall take effect six months after the end of the period referred to in paragraph 4, but in no event earlier than the date on which the corresponding EC act is implemented in the Community. The EEA Joint Committee shall pursue its efforts to agree on a mutually acceptable solution in order for the suspension to be terminated as soon as possible.

6. The practical consequences of the suspension referred to in paragraph 5 shall be discussed in the EEA Joint Committee. The rights and obligations which individuals and economic operators have already acquired under this Agreement shall remain. The Contracting Parties shall, as appropriate, decide on the adjustments necessary due to the suspension.

Article 103

1. If a decision of the EEA Joint Committee can be binding on a Contracting Party only after the fulfilment of constitutional requirements, the decision shall, if a date is contained therein, enter into force on that date, provided that the Contracting Party concerned has notified the other Contracting Parties by that date that the constitutional requirements have been fulfilled.

In the absence of such a notification by that date, the decision shall enter into force on the first day of the second month following the last notification.

2. If upon the expiry of a period of six months after the decision of the EEA Joint Committee such a notification has not taken place, the decision of the EEA Joint Committee shall be applied provisionally pending the fulfilment of the constitutional requirements unless a Contracting Party notifies that such a provisional application cannot take place. In the latter case, or if a Contracting Party notifies the non-ratification of a decision of the EEA Joint Committee, the suspension provided for in Article 102(5) shall take effect one month after such a notification but in no event earlier than the date on which the corresponding EC act is implemented in the Community.

Article 104

Decisions taken by the EEA Joint Committee in the cases provided for in this Agreement shall, unless otherwise provided for therein, upon their entry into force be binding on the Contracting Parties which shall take the necessary steps to ensure their implementation and application.

CHAPTER 3 HOMOGENEITY, SURVEILLANCE PROCEDURE AND SETTLEMENT OF DISPUTES

Section 1 Homogeneity

Article 105

1. In order to achieve the objective of the Contracting Parties to arrive at as uniform an interpretation as possible of the provisions of the Agreement and those provisions of Community legislation which are substantially reproduced in the Agreement, the EEA Joint Committee shall act in accordance with this Article.

2. The EEA Joint Committee shall keep under constant review the development of the case-law of the Court of Justice of the European Communities and the EFTA Court. To this end judgments of these Courts shall be transmitted to the EEA Joint Committee which shall act so as to preserve the homogeneous interpretation of the Agreement.

3. If the EEA Joint Committee within two months after a difference in the case-law of the two Courts has been brought before it, has not succeeded to preserve the homogeneous interpretation of the Agreement, the procedures laid down in Article 111 may be applied.

Article 106

In order to ensure as uniform an interpretation as possible of this Agreement, in full deference to the independence of courts, a system of exchange of information concerning judgments by the EFTA Court, the Court of Justice of the European

Communities and the Court of First Instance of the European Communities and the Courts of last instance of the EFTA States shall be set up by the EEA Joint Committee. This system shall comprise:

(a) transmission to the Registrar of the Court of Justice of the European Communities of judgments delivered by such courts on the interpretation and application of, on the one hand, this Agreement or, on the other hand, the Treaty establishing the European Economic Community and the Treaty establishing the European Coal and Steel Community, as amended or supplemented, as well as the acts adopted in pursuance thereof in so far as they concern provisions which are identical in substance to those of this Agreement;

(b) classification of these judgments by the Registrar of the Court of Justice of the European Communities including, as far as necessary, the drawing up and publication of translations and abstracts;

(c) communications by the Registrar of the Court of Justice of the European Communities of the relevant documents to the competent national authorities, to be designated by each Contracting Party.

Article 107

Provisions on the possibility for an EFTA State to allow a court or tribunal to ask the Court of Justice of the European Communities to decide on the interpretation of an EEA rule are laid down in Protocol 34.

Section 2 Surveillance procedure

Article 108

1. The EFTA States shall establish an independent surveillance authority (EFTA Surveillance Authority) as well as procedures similar to those existing in the Community including procedures for ensuring the fulfilment of obligations under this Agreement and for control of the legality of acts of the EFTA Surveillance Authority regarding competition.

2. The EFTA States shall establish a court of justice (EFTA Court).

The EFTA Court shall, in accordance with a separate agreement between the EFTA States, with regard to the application of this Agreement be competent, in particular, for:

(a) actions concerning the surveillance procedure regarding the EFTA States;

(b) appeals concerning decisions in the field of competition taken by the EFTA Surveillance Authority;

(c) the settlement of disputes between two or more EFTA States.

Article 109

1. The fulfilment of the obligations under this Agreement shall be monitored by, on the one hand, the EFTA Surveillance Authority and, on the other, the EC Commission acting in conformity with the Treaty establishing the European Economic Community, the Treaty establishing the European Coal and Steel Community and this Agreement.

2. In order to ensure a uniform surveillance throughout the EEA, the EFTA Surveillance Authority and the EC Commission shall cooperate, exchange information and consult each other on surveillance policy issues and individual cases.

3. The EC Commission and the EFTA Surveillance Authority shall receive any complaints concerning the application of this Agreement. They shall inform each other of complaints received.

4. Each of these bodies shall examine all complaints falling within its competence and shall pass to the other body any complaints which fall within the competence of that body.

5. In case of disagreement between these two bodies with regard to the action to be taken in relation to a complaint or with regard to the result of the examination, either of the bodies may refer the matter to the EEA Joint Committee which shall deal with it in accordance with Article 111.

Article 110

Decisions under this Agreement by the EFTA Surveillance Authority and the EC Commission which impose a pecuniary obligation on persons other than States, shall be enforceable. The same shall apply to such judgments under this Agreement by the Court of Justice of the European Communities, the Court of First Instance of the European Communities and the EFTA Court.

Enforcement shall be governed by the rules of civil procedure in force in the State in the territory of which it is carried out. The order for its enforcement shall be appended to the decision, without other formality than verification of the authenticity of the decision, by the authority which each Contracting Party shall designate for this purpose and shall make known to the other Contracting Parties, the EFTA Surveillance Authority, the EC Commission, the Court of Justice of the European Communities, the Court of First Instance of the European Communities and the EFTA Court.

When these formalities have been completed on application by the party concerned, the latter may proceed to enforcement, in accordance with the law of the State in the territory of which enforcement is to be carried out, by bringing the matter directly before the competent authority.

Enforcement may be suspended only by a decision of the Court of Justice of the European Communities, as far as decisions by the EC Commission, the Court of First Instance of the European Communities or the Court of Justice of the European Communities are concerned, or by a decision of the EFTA Court as far as decisions by the EFTA Surveillance Authority or the EFTA Court are concerned. However, the courts of the States concerned shall have jurisdiction over complaints that enforcement is being carried out in an irregular manner.

Section 3 Settlement of disputes

Article 111

1. The Community or an EFTA State may bring a matter under dispute which concerns the interpretation or application of this Agreement before the EEA Joint Committee in accordance with the following provisions.

2. The EEA Joint Committee may settle the dispute. It shall be provided with all information which might be of use in making possible an in-depth examination of the situation, with a view to finding an acceptable solution. To this end, the EEA Joint Committee shall examine all possibilities to maintain the good functioning of the Agreement.

3. If a dispute concerns the interpretation of provisions of this Agreement, which are identical in substance to corresponding rules of the Treaty establishing the European Economic Community and the Treaty establishing the European Coal and Steel Community and to acts adopted in application of these two Treaties and if the dispute has not been settled within three months after it has been brought before the EEA Joint Committee, the Contracting Parties to the dispute may agree to request the Court of Justice of the European Communities to give a ruling on the interpretation of the relevant rules.

If the EEA Joint Committee in such a dispute has not reached an agreement on a solution within six months from the date on which this procedure was initiated or if, by then, the Contracting Parties to the dispute have not decided to ask for a ruling by the Court of Justice of the European Communities, a Contracting Party may, in order to remedy possible imbalances,

— either take a safeguard measure in accordance with Article 112(2) and following the procedure of Article 113;
— or apply Article 102 mutatis mutandis.

4. If a dispute concerns the scope or duration of safeguard measures taken in accordance with Article 111(3) or Article 112, or the proportionality of rebalancing measures taken in accordance with Article 114, and if the EEA Joint Committee after three months from the date when the matter has been brought before it has not succeeded to resolve the dispute, any Contracting Party may refer the dispute to arbitration under the procedures laid down in Protocol 33. No question of interpretation of the provisions of this Agreement referred to in paragraph 3 may be dealt with in such procedures. The arbitration award shall be binding on the parties to the dispute.

CHAPTER 4 SAFEGUARD MEASURES

Article 112
1. If serious economic, societal or environmental difficulties of a sectorial or regional nature liable to persist are arising, a Contracting Party may unilaterally take appropriate measures under the conditions and procedures laid down in Article 113.
2. Such safeguard measures shall be restricted with regard to their scope and duration to what is strictly necessary in order to remedy the situation. Priority shall be given to such measures as will least disturb the functioning of this Agreement.
3. The safeguard measures shall apply with regard to all Contracting Parties.

Article 113
1. A Contracting Party which is considering taking safeguard measures under Article 112 shall, without delay, notify the other Contracting Parties through the EEA Joint Committee and shall provide all relevant information.
2. The Contracting Parties shall immediately enter into consultations in the EEA Joint Committee with a view to finding a commonly acceptable solution.
3. The Contracting Party concerned may not take safeguard measures until one month has elapsed after the date of notification under paragraph 1, unless the consultation procedure under paragraph 2 has been concluded before the expiration of the stated time-limit. When exceptional circumstances requiring immediate action exclude prior examination, the Contracting Party concerned may apply forthwith the protective measures strictly necessary to remedy the situation.
For the Community, the safeguard measures shall be taken by the EC Commission.
4. The Contracting Party concerned shall, without delay, notify the measures taken to the EEA Joint Committee and shall provide all relevant information.
5. The safeguard measures taken shall be the subject of consultations in the EEA Joint Committee every three months from the date of their adoption with a view to their abolition before the date of expiry envisaged, or to the limitation of their scope of application.
Each Contracting Party may at any time request the EEA Joint Committee to review such measures.

Article 114

1. If a safeguard measure taken by a Contracting Party creates an imbalance between the rights and obligations under this Agreement, any other Contracting Party may towards that Contracting Party take such proportionate rebalancing measures as are strictly necessary to remedy the imbalance. Priority shall be given to such measures as will least disturb the functioning of the EEA.

2. The procedure under Article 113 shall apply.

PART VIII FINANCIAL MECHANISM

Article 115

With a view to promoting a continuous and balanced strengthening of trade and economic relations between the Contracting Parties, as provided for in Article 1, the Contracting Parties agree on the need to reduce the economic and social disparities between their regions. They note in this regard the relevant provisions set out elsewhere in this Agreement and its related Protocols, including certain of the arrangements regarding agriculture and fisheries.

Article 116

A Financial Mechanism shall be established by the EFTA States to contribute, in the context of the EEA and in addition to the efforts already deployed by the Community in this regard, to the objectives laid down in Article 115.

Article 117

Provisions governing the Financial Mechanism are set out in Protocol 38.

PART IX GENERAL AND FINAL PROVISIONS

Article 118

1. Where a Contracting Party considers that it would be useful in the interests of all the Contracting Parties to develop the relations established by this Agreement by extending them to fields not covered thereby, it shall submit a reasoned request to the other Contracting Parties within the EEA Council. The latter may instruct the EEA Joint Committee to examine all the aspects of this request and to issue a report.

The EEA Council may, where appropriate, take the political decisions with a view to opening negotiations between the Contracting Parties.

2. The agreements resulting from the negotiations referred to in paragraph 1 will be subject to ratification or approval by the Contracting Parties in accordance with their own procedures.

Article 119

The Annexes and the acts referred to therein as adapted for the purposes of this Agreement as well as the Protocols shall form an integral part of this Agreement.

Article 120

Unless otherwise provided in this Agreement and in particular in Protocols 41, 43 and 44, the application of the provisions of this Agreement shall prevail over provisions in existing bilateral or multilateral agreements binding the European Economic Community, on the one hand, and one or more EFTA States, on the other, to the extent that the same subject matter is governed by this Agreement.

Article 121

The provisions of this Agreement shall not preclude cooperation:

(a) within the framework of the Nordic cooperation to the extent that such cooperation does not impair the good functioning of this Agreement;

(b) within the framework of the regional union between Switzerland and Liechtenstein to the extent that the objectives of this union are not attained by the application of this Agreement and the good functioning of this Agreement is not impaired;

(c) within the framework of cooperation between Austria and Italy concerning Tyrol, Vorarlberg and Trentino-South Tyrol/Alto Adige, to the extent that such cooperation does not impair the good functioning of this Agreement.

Article 122

The representatives, delegates and experts of the Contracting Parties, as well as officials and other servants acting under this Agreement shall be required, even after their duties have ceased, not to disclose information of the kind covered by the obligation of professional secrecy, in particular information about undertakings, their business relations or their cost components.

Article 123

Nothing in this Agreement shall prevent a Contracting Party from taking any measures:

(a) which it considers necessary to prevent the disclosure of information contrary to its essential security interests;

(b) which relate to the production of, or trade in, arms, munitions and war materials or other products indispensable for defence purposes or to research, development or production indispensable for defence purposes, provided that such measures do not impair the conditions of competition in respect of products not intended for specifically military purposes;

(c) which it considers essential to its own security in the event of serious internal disturbances affecting the maintenance of law and order, in time of war or serious international tension constituting threat of war or in order to carry out obligations it has accepted for the purpose of maintaining peace and international security.

Article 124

The Contracting Parties shall accord nationals of EC Member States and EFTA States the same treatment as their own nationals as regards participation in the capital of companies or firms within the meaning of Article 34, without prejudice to the application of the other provisions of this Agreement.

Article 125

This Agreement shall in no way prejudice the rules of the Contracting Parties governing the system of property ownership.

Article 126

1. The Agreement shall apply to the territories to which the Treaty establishing the European Economic Community and the Treaty establishing the European Coal and Steel Community is applied and under the conditions laid down in those Treaties, and to the territories of the Republic of Austria, the Republic of Finland, the Republic of Iceland, the Principality of Liechtenstein, the Kingdom of Norway, the Kingdom of Sweden and the Swiss Confederation.

2. Notwithstanding paragraph 1, this Agreement shall not apply to the Åland Islands. The Government of Finland may, however, give notice, by a declaration deposited when ratifying this Agreement with the Depositary, which shall transmit a certified copy thereof to the Contracting Parties, that the Agreement shall apply to those Islands under the same conditions as it applies to other parts of Finland sub-

ject to the following provisions:

    (a) The provisions of this Agreement shall not preclude the application of the provisions in force at any given time on the Åland Islands on:
        (i) restrictions on the right for natural persons who do not enjoy regional citizenship in Åland, and for legal persons, to acquire and hold real property on the Åland Islands without permission by the competent authorities of the Islands;
        (ii) restrictions on the right of establishment and the right to provide services by natural persons who do not enjoy regional citizenship in Åland, or by any legal person, without permission by the competent authorities of the Åland Islands.
    (b) The rights enjoyed by Ålanders in Finland shall not be affected by this Agreement.
    (c) The authorities of the Åland Islands shall apply the same treatment to all natural and legal persons of the Contracting Parties.

Article 127

Each Contracting Party may withdraw from this Agreement provided it gives at least 12 months' notice in writing to the other Contracting Parties.

Immediately after the notification of the intended withdrawal, the other Contracting Parties shall convene a diplomatic conference in order to envisage the necessary modifications to bring to the Agreement.

Article 128

1. Any European State becoming a member of the Community shall, or becoming a member of EFTA may, apply to become a Party to this Agreement. It shall address its application to the EEA Council.

2. The terms and conditions for such participation shall be the subject of an agreement between the Contracting Parties and the applicant State. That agreement shall be submitted for ratification or approval by all Contracting Parties in accordance with their own procedures.

Article 129

1. This Agreement is drawn up in a single original in the Danish, Dutch, English, Finnish, French, German, Greek, Icelandic, Italian, Norwegian, Portuguese, Spanish and Swedish languages, each of these texts being equally authentic.

The texts of the acts referred to in the Annexes are equally authentic in Danish, Dutch, English, French, German, Greek, Italian, Portuguese and Spanish as published in the Official Journal of the European Communities and shall for the authentication thereof be drawn up in the Finnish, Icelandic, Norwegian and Swedish languages.

2. This Agreement shall be ratified or approved by the Contracting Parties in accordance with their respective constitutional requirements.

It shall be deposited with the General Secretariat of the Council of the European Communities by which certified copies shall be transmitted to all other Contracting Parties.

The instruments of ratification or approval shall be deposited with the General Secretariat of the Council of the European Communities which shall notify all other Contracting Parties.

3. This Agreement shall enter into force on 1 January 1993, provided that all Contracting Parties have deposited their instruments of ratification or approval before that date. After that date this Agreement shall enter into force on the first day

of the second month following the last notification. The final date for such a notification shall be 30 June 1993. After that date the Contracting Parties shall convene a diplomatic conference to appreciate the situation.

FIRST COUNCIL DIRECTIVE

of 21 December 1998

to approximate the laws of the Member States relating to trade marks

(89/104/EEC)

THE COUNCIL OF THE EUROPEAN COMMUNITIES

Having regard to the Treaty establishing the European Economic Community, and in particular Article 100a thereof,

Having regard to the proposal from the Commission,

In co-operation with the European Parliament,

Having regard to the opinion of the Economic and Social Committee,

Whereas the trade mark laws at present applicable in the Member States contain disparities which may impede the free movement of goods and freedom to provide services and may distort competition within the common market; whereas it is therefore necessary, in view of the establishment and functioning of the internal market, to approximate the laws of Member States;

Whereas it is important not to disregard the solutions and advantages which the Community trade mark system may afford to undertakings wishing to acquire trade marks;

Whereas it does not appear to be necessary at present to undertake full-scale approximation cf the trade mark laws of the Member States and it will be sufficient if approximation is limited to those national provisions of law which most directly affect the functioning of the internal market;

Whereas the Directive does not deprive the Member States of the right to continue to protect trade marks acquired through use but takes them into account only in regard to the relationship between them and trade marks acquired by registration;

Whereas Member States also remain free to fix the provisions of procedure concerning the registration, the revocation and the invalidity of trade marks acquired by registration; whereas they can, for example, determine the form of trade mark registration and invalidity procedures, decide whether earlier rights should be invoked either in the registration procedure or in the invalidity procedure or in both and, if they allow earlier rights to be invoked in the registration procedure, have an opposition procedure or an ex officio examination procedure or both; whereas Member States remain free to determine the effects of revocation or invalidity of trade marks;

Whereas this Directive does not exclude the application to trade marks of provisions of law of the Member States other than trade mark law, such as the provisions relating to unfair competition, civil liability or consumer protection;

Whereas attainment of the objectives at which this approximation of laws is aiming requires that the conditions for obtaining and continuing to hold a registered trade mark are, in general, identical in all Member States; whereas, to this end, it is necessary to list examples of signs which may constitute a trade mark, provided that such signs are capable of distinguishing the goods or services of one undertaking from those of other undertakings; whereas the grounds for refusal or invalidity concerning the trade mark itself for example, the absence of any distinctive character, or concerning conflicts between the trade mark and earlier rights, are to be listed in an exhaustive manner, even if some of these grounds are listed as an option for the Member States which will therefore be able to maintain or introduce those grounds in their legislation; whereas Member States will be able to maintain or introduce into their legislation grounds of refusal or invalidity linked to conditions for obtaining and continuing to hold a trade mark for which there is no provision of approximation, concerning, for example, the eligibility for the grant of a trade mark, the renewal of the trade mark or rules on fees, or related to the non-compliance with procedural rules;

Whereas in order to reduce the total number of trade marks registered and protected in the Community and, consequently, the number of conflicts which arise between them, it is essential to require that registered trade marks must actually be used or, if not used, be subject to revocation; whereas it is necessary to provide that a trade mark cannot be invalidated on the basis of the existence of a non-used earlier trade mark, while the Member States remain free to apply the same principle in respect of the registration of a trade mark or to provide that a trade mark may not be successfully invoked in infringement proceedings if it is established as a result of a plea that the trade mark could be revoked; whereas in all these cases it is up to the Member States to establish the applicable rules of procedure;

Whereas it is fundamental, in order to facilitate the free circulation of goods and services, to ensure that henceforth registered trade marks enjoy the same protection under the legal systems of all the Member States; whereas this should however not prevent the Member States from granting at their option extensive protection to those trade marks which have a reputation;

Whereas the protection afforded by the registered trade mark, the function of which is in particular to guarantee the trade mark as an indication of origin, is absolute in the case of identity between the mark and the sign and goods or services; whereas the protection applies also in case of similarity between the mark and the sign and the goods or services; whereas it is indispensable to give an interpretation of the concept of similarity in relation to the likelihood of confusion; whereas the likelihood of confusion, the appreciation of which depends on numerous elements and, in particular, on the recognition of the trade mark on the market, of the association which can be made with the used or registered sign, of the degree of similarity between the trade mark and the sign and between the goods or services identified, constitutes the specific condition for such protection; whereas the ways in which likelihood of confusion may be established, and in particular the onus of proof, are a matter for national procedural rules which are not prejudiced by the Directive;

Whereas it is important, for reasons of legal certainty and without inequitably prejudicing the interests of a proprietor of an earlier trade mark, to provide that the latter may no longer request a declaration of invalidity nor may he oppose the use of a trade mark subsequent to his own of which he has knowingly tolerated the use for a substantial length of time, unless the application for the subsequent trade mark was made in bad faith;

Whereas all Member States of the Community are bound by the Paris Convention for the Protection of Industrial Property; whereas it is necessary that the provisions of this Directive are entirely consistent with those of the Paris Convention; whereas the obligations of the Member States resulting from this Convention are not affected by this Directive; whereas, where appropriate, the second subparagraph of Article 234 of the Treaty is applicable.

HAS ADOPTED THIS DIRECTIVE:

Article 1

Scope

This Directive shall apply to every trade mark in respect of goods or services which is the subject of registration or of an application in a Member State for registration as an individual trade mark, a collective mark or a guarantee or certification mark, or which is the subject of a registration or an application for registration in the Benelux Trade Mark Office or of an international registration having effect in a Member State.

Article 2

Signs of which a trade mark may consist

A trade mark may consist of any sign capable of being represented graphically, particularly words, including personal names, designs, letters, numerals, the shape of goods or of their packaging, provided that such signs are capable of distinguishing the goods or services of one undertaking from those of other undertakings.

Article 3

Grounds for refusal or invalidity

1. The following shall not be registered or if registered shall be liable to be declared invalid—

   (a) signs which cannot constitute a trade mark;
   (b) trade marks which are devoid of any distinctive character;
   (c) trade marks which consist exclusively of signs or indications which may serve, in trade, to designate the kind, quality, quantity, intended purpose, value, geographical origin, or the time of production of the goods or of rendering of the service, or other characteristics of the goods or service;
   (d) trade marks which consist exclusively of signs or indications which have become customary in the current language or in the bona fide and established practices of the trade;
   (e) signs which consist exclusively of—
      —the shape which results from the nature of the goods themselves, or
      —the shape of goods which is necessary to obtain a technical result, or
      —the shape which gives substantial value to the goods;
   (f) trade marks which are contrary to public policy or to accepted principles of morality;
   (g) trade marks which are of such a nature as to deceive the public, for instance as to the nature, quality or geographical origin of the goods or service;
   (h) trade marks which have not been authorised by the competent authorities and are to be refused or invalidated pursuant to Article 6ter of the Paris Convention for the Protection of Industrial Property, hereinafter referred to as the 'Paris Convention'.

2. Any Member State may provide that a trade mark shall not be registered or, if registered, shall be liable to be declared invalid where and to the extent that—

   (a) the use of that trade mark may be prohibited pursuant to provisions of law other than trade mark law of the Member State concerned or of the Community;
   (b) the trade mark covers a sign of high symbolic value, in particular a religious symbol;
   (c) the trade mark includes badges, emblems and escutcheons other than those

957

covered by Article 6ter of the Paris Convention and which are of public interest, unless the consent of the appropriate authorities to its registration has been given in conformity with the legislation of the Member State;

(d) the application for registration of the trade mark was made in bad faith by the applicant.

3. A trade mark shall not be refused registration or be declared invalid in accordance with paragraph 1(b), (c) or (d) if, before the date of application for registration and following the use which has been made of it, it has acquired a distinctive character. Any Member State may in addition provide that this provision shall also apply where the distinctive character was acquired after the date of application for registration or after the date of registration.

4. Any Member State may provide that, by derogation from the preceding paragraphs, the grounds of refusal of registration or invalidity in force in that State prior to the date on which the provisions necessary to comply with this Directive enter into force, shall apply to trade marks for which application has been made prior to that date.

Article 4

Further grounds for refusal or invalidity concerning conflicts with earlier rights

1. A trade mark shall not be registered or, if registered, shall be liable to be declared invalid—

(a) if it is identical with an earlier trade mark, and the goods or services for which the trade mark is applied for or is registered are identical with the goods or services for which the earlier trade mark is protected;

(b) if because of its identity with, or similarity to, the earlier trade mark and the identity or similarity of the goods or services covered by the trade marks, there exists a likelihood of confusion on the part of the public, which includes the likelihood of association with the earlier trade mark.

2. 'Earlier trade marks' within the meaning of paragraph 1 means—

(a) trade marks of the following kinds with a date of application for registration which is earlier than the date of application for registration of the trade mark, taking account, where appropriate, of the priorities claimed in respect of those trade marks—
   (i) Community trade marks;
   (ii) trade marks registered in the Member State or, in the case of Belgium, Luxembourg or the Netherlands, at the Benelux Trade Mark Office;
   (iii) trade marks registered under international arrangements which have effect in the Member State;

(b) Community trade marks which validly claim seniority, in accordance with the Regulation on the Community trade mark, from a trade mark referred to in (a) (ii) and (iii), even when the latter trade mark has been surrendered or allowed to lapse;

(c) applications for the trade marks referred to in (a) and (b), subject to their registration;

(d) trade marks which, on the date of application for registration of the trade mark, or, where appropriate, of the priority claimed in respect of the application for registration of the trade mark, are well known in a Member State, in the sense in which the words 'well known' are used in Article 6bis of the Paris Convention;

3. A trade mark shall furthermore not be registered or, if registered, shall be liable to be declared invalid if it is identical with, or similar to, an earlier Community trade mark within the meaning of paragraph 2 and is to be, or has been, registered for goods or services which are not similar to those for which the earlier Community trade mark is registered, where the earlier Community trade mark has a reputation in the Community and where the use of the later trade mark without due cause would take unfair advantage of, or be detrimental to, the distinctive character or the repute of the earlier Community trade mark.

4. Any Member State may furthermore provide that a trade mark shall not be registered or, if registered, shall be liable to be declared invalid where, and to the extent that—

(a) the trade mark is identical with, or similar to, an earlier national trade mark within the meaning of paragraph 2 and is to be, or has been, registered for goods or services which are not similar to those for which the earlier trade mark is registered, where the earlier trade mark has a reputation in the Member State concerned and where the use of the later trade mark without due cause would take unfair advantage of, or be detrimental to, the distinctive character or the repute of the earlier trade mark;

(b) rights to a non-registered trade mark or to another sign used in the course of trade were acquired prior to the date of application for registration of the subsequent trade mark, or the date of the priority claimed for the application for registration of the subsequent trade mark and that non-registered trade mark or other sign confers on its proprietor the right to prohibit the use of a subsequent trade mark;

(c) the use of the trade mark may be prohibited by virtue of an earlier right other than the rights referred to in paragraphs 2 and 4(b) and in particular—

   (i) a right to a name;
   (ii) a right of personal portrayal;
   (iii) a copyright;
   (iv) an industrial property right;

(d) the trade mark is identical with, or similar to, an earlier collective trade mark conferring a right which expired within a period of a maximum of three years preceding application;

(e) the trade mark is identical with, or similar to, an earlier guarantee or certification mark conferring a right which expired within a period preceding application the length of which is fixed by the Member State;

(f) the trade mark is identical with, or similar to, an earlier trade mark which was registered for identical or similar goods or services and conferred on them a right which has expired for failure to renew within a period of a maximum of two years preceding application, unless the proprietor of the earlier trade mark gave his agreement for the registration of the later mark or did not use his trade mark;

(g) the trade mark is liable to be confused with a mark which was in use abroad on the filing date of the application and which is still in use there, provided that at the date of the application the applicant was acting in bad faith.

5. The Member States may permit that in appropriate circumstances registration need not be refused or the trade mark need not be declared invalid where the proprietor of the earlier trade mark or other earlier right consents to the registration of the later trade mark.

959

6. Any Member State may provide that, by derogation from paragraphs 1 to 5, the grounds for refusal of registration or invalidity in force in that State prior to the date on which the provisions necessary to comply with this Directive enter into force, shall apply to trade marks for which application has been made prior to that date.

Article 5

Rights conferred by a trade mark

1. The registered trade mark shall confer on the proprietor exclusive rights therein. The proprietor shall be entitled to prevent all third parties not having his consent from using in the course of trade—

    (a) any sign which is identical with the trade mark in relation to goods or services which are identical with those for which the trade mark is registered;

    (b) any sign where, because of its identity with, or similarity to, the trade mark and the identity or similarity of the goods or services covered by the trade mark and the sign, there exists a likelihood of confusion on the part of the public, which includes the likelihood of association between the sign and the trade mark.

2. Any Member State may also provide that the proprietor shall be entitled to prevent all third parties not having his consent from using in the course of trade any sign which is identical with, or similar to, the trade mark in relation to goods or services which are not similar to those for which the trade mark is registered, where the latter has a reputation in the Member State and where use of that sign without due cause takes unfair advantage of, or is detrimental to, the distinctive character or the repute of the trade mark.

3. The following, inter alia, may be prohibited under paragraphs 1 and 2—

    (a) affixing the sign to the goods or to the packaging thereof;

    (b) offering the goods, or putting them on the market or stocking them for these purposes under that sign, or offering or supplying services thereunder;

    (c) importing or exporting the goods under the sign;

    (d) using the sign on business papers and in advertising.

4. Where, under the law of the Member State, the use of a sign under the conditions referred to in 1(b) or 2 could not be prohibited before the date on which the provisions necessary to comply with this Directive entered into force in the Member State concerned, the rights conferred by the trade mark may not be relied on to prevent the continued use of the sign.

5. Paragraphs 1 to 4 shall not affect provisions in any Member State relating to the protection against the use of a sign other than for the purposes of distinguishing goods or services, where use of that sign without due cause takes unfair advantage of, or is detrimental to, the distinctive character or the repute of the trade mark.

Article 6

Limitation of the effects of a trade mark

1. The trade mark shall not entitle the proprietor to prohibit a third party from using, in the course of trade—

    (a) his own name or address;

    (b) indications concerning the kind, quality, quantity, intended purpose, value, geographical origin, the time of production of goods or of rendering of the

service, or other characteristics of goods or services;
(c) the trade mark where it is necessary to indicate the intended purpose of a product or service, in particular as accessories or spare parts;

provided he uses them in accordance with honest practices in industrial or commercial matters.

2. The trade mark shall not entitle the proprietor to prohibit a third party from using, in the course of trade, an earlier right which only applies in a particular locality if that right is recognised by the laws of the Member State in question and within the limits of the territory in which it is recognised.

Article 7

Exhaustion of the rights conferred by a trade mark

1. The trade mark shall not entitle the proprietor to prohibit its use in relation to goods which have been put on the market in the Community under that trade mark by the proprietor or with his consent.

2. Paragraph 1 shall not apply where there exist legitimate reasons for the proprietor to oppose further commercialisation of the goods, especially where the condition of the goods is changed or impaired after they have been put on the market.

Article 8

Licensing

1. A trade mark may be licensed for some or all of the goods or services for which it is registered and for the whole or part of the Member State concerned. A license may be exclusive or non-exclusive.

2. The proprietor of a trade mark may invoke the rights conferred by that trade mark against a licensee who contravenes any provision in his licensing contract with regard to its duration, the form covered by the registration in which the trade mark may be used, the scope of the goods or services for which the licence is granted, the territory in which the trade mark may be affixed, or the quality of the goods manufactured or of the services provided by the licensee.

Article 9

Limitation in consequence of acquiescence

1. Where, in a Member State, the proprietor of an earlier trade mark as referred to in Article 4(2) has acquiesced, for a period of five successive years, in the use of a later trade mark registered in that Member State while being aware of such use, he shall no longer be entitled on the basis of the earlier trade mark either to apply for a declaration that the later trade mark is invalid or to oppose the use of the later trade mark in respect of the goods or services for which the later trade mark has been used, unless registration of the later trade mark was applied for in bad faith.

2. Any Member State may provide that paragraph 1 shall apply mutatis mutandis to the proprietor of an earlier trade mark referred to in Article 4(4)(a) or an other earlier right referred to in Article 4(4)(b) or (c).

3. In the cases referred to in paragraphs 1 and 2, the proprietor of a later registered trade mark shall not be entitled to oppose the use of the earlier right, even though that right may no longer be invoked against the later trade mark.

Article 10

Use of trade marks

1. If, within a period of five years following the date of the completion of the registration procedure, the proprietor has not put the trade mark to genuine use in the

Member State in connection with the goods or services in respect of which it is registered, or if such use has been suspended during an uninterrupted period of five years, the trade mark shall be subject to the sanctions provided for in this Directive, unless there are proper reasons for non-use.

2. The following shall also constitute use within the meaning of paragraph 1—

  (a) use of the trade mark in a form differing in elements which do not alter the distinctive character of the mark in the form in which it was registered;
  (b) affixing of the trade mark to goods or to the packaging thereof in the Member State concerned solely for export purposes.

3. Use of the trade mark with the consent of the proprietor or by any person who has authority to use a collective mark or a guarantee or certification mark shall be deemed to constitute use by the proprietor.

4. In relation to trade marks registered before the date on which the provisions necessary to comply with this Directive enter into force in the Member State concerned—

  (a) where a provision in force prior to that date attaches sanctions to non-use of a trade mark during an uninterrupted period, the relevant period of five years mentioned in paragraph 1 shall be deemed to have begun to run at the same time as any period of non-use which is already running at that date;
  (b) where there is no use provision in force prior to that date, the periods of five years mentioned in paragraph 1 shall be deemed to run from that date at the earliest.

Article 11

Sanctions for non use of a trade mark in legal or administrative proceedings

1. A trade mark may not be declared invalid on the ground that there is an earlier conflicting trade mark if the latter does not fulfil the requirements of use set out in Article 10(1), (2) and (3) or in Article 10(4), as the case may be.

2. Any Member State may provide that registration of a trade mark may not be refused on the ground that there is an earlier conflicting trade mark if the latter does not fulfil the requirements of use set out in Article 10(1), (2) and (3) or in Article 10(4), as the case may be.

3. Without prejudice to the application of Article 12, where a counter-claim for revocation is made, any Member State may provide that a trade mark may not be successfully invoked in infringement proceedings if it is established as a result of a plea that the trade mark could be revoked pursuant to Article 12(1).

4. If the earlier trade mark has been used in relation to part only of the goods or services for which it is registered, it shall, for purposes of applying paragraphs 1, 2 and 3, be deemed to be registered in respect only of that part of the goods or services.

Article 12

Grounds for revocation

1. A trade mark shall be liable to revocation if, within a continuous period of five years, it has not been put to genuine use in the Member State in connection with the goods or services in respect of which it is registered, and there are no proper reasons for non-use; however, no person may claim that the proprietor's rights in a trade mark should be revoked where, during the interval between expiry of the five-year period and filing of the application for revocation, genuine use of the trade mark has been started or resumed; the commencement or resumption of use within

a period of three months preceding the filing of the application for revocation which began at the earliest on expiry of the continuous period of five years of non-use, shall, however, be disregarded where preparations for the commencement or resumption occur only after the proprietor becomes aware that the application for revocation may be filed.

2. A trade mark shall also be liable to revocation if, after the date on which it was registered—

(a) in consequence of acts or inactivity of the proprietor, it has become the common name in the trade for a product or service in respect of which it is registered;

(b) in consequence of the use made of it by the proprietor of the trade mark or with his consent in respect of the goods or services for which it is registered, it is liable to mislead the public, particularly as to the nature, quality or geographical origin of those goods or services.

Article 13

Grounds for refusal or revocation or invalidity relating to only some of the goods or services

Where grounds for refusal of registration or for revocation or invalidity of a trade mark exist in respect of only some of the goods or services for which that trade mark has been applied for or registered, refusal of registration or revocation or invalidity shall cover those goods or services only.

Article 14

Establishment a posteriori of invalidity or revocation of a trade mark

Where the seniority of an earlier trade mark which has been surrendered or allowed to lapse, is claimed for a Community trade mark, the invalidity or revocation of the earlier trade mark may be established a posteriori.

Article 15

Special provisions in respect of collective marks, guarantee marks and certification marks

1. Without prejudice to Article 4, Member States whose laws authorise the registration of collective marks or of guarantee or certification marks may provide that such marks shall not be registered, or shall be revoked or declared invalid, on grounds additional to those specified in Articles 3 and 12 where the function of those marks so requires.

2. By way of derogation from Article 3(1)(c), Member States may provide that signs or indications which may serve, in trade, to designate the geographical origin of the goods or services may constitute collective, guarantee or certification marks. Such a mark does not entitle the proprietor to prohibit a third party from using in the course of trade such signs or indications, provided he uses them in accordance with honest practices in industrial or commercial matters; in particular, such a mark may not be invoked against a third party who is entitled to use a geographical name.

Article 16

National provisions to be adopted pursuant to this Directive

1. The Member States shall bring into force the laws, regulations and administrative provisions necessary to comply with this Directive not later than [31 December

1992]. They shall immediately inform the Commission thereof.

2. Acting on a proposal from the Commission, the Council, acting by qualified majority, may defer the date referred to in paragraph 1 until 31 December 1992 at the latest.

3. Member States shall communicate to the Commission the text of the main provisions of national law which they adopt in the field governed by this Directive.

NOTES
Para 1: words in square brackets substituted by Council Decision 92/10/EEC, Art 1.

Article 17

Addressees
This Directive is addressed to the Member States.

COUNCIL REGULATION

of 20 December 1993

on the Community trade mark

(40/94/EEC)

NOTES
Date of publication in OJ: OJ L11, 14.1.94, p 1.

THE COUNCIL OF THE EUROPEAN UNION,
Having regard to the Treaty establishing the European Community, and in particular Article 235 thereof,
Having regard to the proposal from the Commission,
Having regard to the opinion of the European Parliament,
Having regard to the opinion of the Economic and Social Committee,
Whereas it is desirable to promote throughout the Community a harmonious development of economic activities and a continuous and balanced expansion by completing an internal market which functions properly and offers conditions which are similar to those obtaining in a national market; whereas in order to create a market of this kind and make it increasingly a single market, not only must be barriers to free movement of goods and services be removed and arrangements be instituted which ensure that competition is not distorted, but, in addition, legal conditions must be created which enable undertakings to adapt their activities to the scale of the Community, whether in manufacturing and distributing goods or in providing services; whereas for those purposes, trade marks enabling the products and services of undertakings to be distinguished by identical means throughout the entire Community, regardless of frontiers, should feature amongst the legal instruments which undertakings have at their disposal;
Whereas action by the Community would appear to be necessary for the purpose of attaining the Community's said objectives; whereas such action involves the creation of Community arrangements for trade marks whereby undertakings can by means of one procedural system obtain Community trade marks to which uniform protection is given and which produce their effects throughout the entire area of the Community; whereas the principle of the unitary character of the Community trade mark thus stated will apply unless otherwise provided for in this Regulation;
Whereas the barrier of territoriality of the rights conferred on proprietors of trade marks by the laws of the Member States cannot be removed by approximation of

laws; whereas in order to open up unrestricted economic activity in the whole of the common market for the benefit of undertakings, trade marks need to be created which are governed by a uniform Community law directly applicable in all Member States;

Whereas since the Treaty has not provided the specific powers to establish such a legal instrument, Article 235 of the Treaty should be applied;

Whereas the Community law relating to trade marks nevertheless does not replace the laws of the Member States on trade marks; whereas it would not in fact appear to be justified to require undertakings to apply for registration of their trade marks as Community trade marks; whereas national trade marks continue to be necessary for those undertakings which do not want protection of their trade marks at Community level;

Whereas the rights in a Community trade mark may not be obtained otherwise than by registration, and registration is to be refused in particular if the trade mark is not distinctive, if it is unlawful or if it conflicts with earlier rights;

Whereas the protection afforded by a Community trade mark, the function of which is in particular to guarantee the trade mark as an indication of origin, is absolute in the case of identity between the mark and the sign and the goods or services; whereas the protection applies also in cases of similarity between the mark and the sign and the goods or services; whereas an interpretation should be given of the concept of similarity in relation to the likelihood of confusion; whereas the likelihood of confusion, the appreciation of which depends on numerous elements and, in particular, on the recognition of the trade mark on the market, the association which can be made with the used or registered sign, the degree of similarity between the trade mark and the sign and between the goods or services identified, constitutes the specific condition for such protection;

Whereas it follows from the principle of free flow of goods that the proprietor of a Community trade mark must not be entitled to prohibit its use by a third party in relation to goods which have been put into circulation in the Community, under the trade mark, by him or with his consent, save where there exist legitimate reasons for the proprietor to oppose further commercialisation of the goods;

Whereas there is no justification for protecting Community trade marks or, as against them, any trade mark which has been registered before them, except where the trade marks are actually used;

Whereas a Community trade mark is to be regarded as an object of property which exists separately from the undertakings whose goods or services are designated by it; whereas accordingly, it must be capable of being transferred, subject to the overriding need to prevent the public being misled as a result of the transfer. It must also be capable of being charged as security in favour of a third party and of being the subject matter of licences;

Whereas administrative measures are necessary at Community level for implementing in relation to every trade mark the trade mark law created by this Regulation; whereas it is therefore essential, while retaining the Community's existing institutional structure and balance of powers, to establish an Office for Harmonisation in the Internal Market (trade marks and designs) which is independent in relation to technical matters and has legal, administrative and financial autonomy; whereas to this end it is necessary and appropriate that it should be a body of the Community having legal personality and exercising the implementing powers which are conferred on it by this Regulation, and that it should operate within the framework of Community law without detracting from the competencies exercised by the Community institutions;

Whereas it is necessary to ensure that parties who are affected by decisions made by the Office are protected by the law in a manner which is suited to the special character of trade mark law; whereas to that end provision is made for an appeal to lie from decisions of the examiners and of the various divisions of the Office; whereas if the department whose decision is contested does not rectify its decision it is to remit the appeal to a Board of Appeal of the Office, which is to decide on it; whereas decisions of the Boards of Appeal are, in turn, amenable to actions before the Court of Justice of the European Communities, which has jurisdiction to annul or to alter the contested decision;

Whereas under Council Decision 88/591/ECSC, EEC, Euratom of 24 October 1988 establishing a Court of First Instance of the European Communities, as amended by Decision 93/350/Euratom, ECSC, EEC of 8 June 1993, that Court shall exercise at the first instance the jurisdiction conferred on the Court of Justice by the Treaties establishing the Communities—with particular regard to appeals lodged under the second subparagraph of Article 173 of the EC Treaty—and by the acts adopted in implementation thereof, save as otherwise provided in an act setting up a body governed by Community law; whereas the jurisdiction which this Regulation confers on the Court of Justice to cancel and reform decisions of the appeal courts shall accordingly be exercised at the first instance by the Court in accordance with the above Decision;

Whereas in order to strengthen the protection of Community trade marks the Member States should designate, having regard to their own national system, as limited a number as possible of national courts of first and second instance having jurisdiction in matters of infringement and validity of Community trade marks;

Whereas decisions regarding the validity and infringement of Community trade marks must have effect and cover the entire area of the Community, as this is the only way of preventing inconsistent decisions on the part of the courts and the Office and of ensuring that the unitary character of Community trade marks is not undermined; whereas the rules contained in the Brussels Convention of Jurisdiction and the Enforcement of Judgments in Civil and Commercial Matters will apply to all actions at law relating to Community trade marks, save where this Regulation derogates from those rules;

Whereas contradictory judgments should be avoided in actions which involve the same acts and the same parties and which are brought on the basis of a Community trade mark and parallel national trade marks; whereas for this purpose, when the actions are brought in the same Member State, the way in which this is to be achieved is a matter for national procedural rules, which are not prejudiced by this Regulation, whilst when the actions are brought in different Member States, provisions modelled on the rules on lis pendens and related actions of the abovementioned Brussels Convention appear appropriate;

Whereas in order to guarantee the full autonomy and independence of the Office, it is considered necessary to grant it an autonomous budget whose revenue comes principally from fees paid by the users of the system; whereas however, the Community budgetary procedure remains applicable as far as any subsidies chargeable to general budget of the European Communities are concerned; whereas moreover, the auditing of accounts should be undertaken by the Court of Auditors;

Whereas implementing measures are required for the Regulation's application, particularly as regards the adoption and amendment of fees regulations and an Implementing Regulation; whereas such measures should be adopted by the Commission, assisted by a Committee composed of representatives of the Member States, in accordance with the procedural rules laid down in Article 2, procedure III(b), of Council Decision 87/373/EEC of 13 July 1987 laying down the procedures for the exercise of implementing powers conferred on the Commission,

HAS ADOPTED THIS REGULATION—

TITLE I

GENERAL PROVISIONS

Article 1

Community trade mark

1. A trade mark for goods or services which is registered in accordance with the conditions contained in this Regulation and in the manner herein provided is hereinafter referred to as a 'Community trade mark'.

2. A Community trade mark shall have a unitary character. It shall have equal effect throughout the Community: it shall not be registered, transferred or surrendered or be the subject of a decision revoking the rights of the proprietor or declaring it invalid, nor shall its use be prohibited, save in respect of the whole Community. This principle shall apply unless otherwise provided in this Regulation.

Article 2

Office

An Office for Harmonisation in the Internal Market (trade marks and designs), hereinafter referred to as 'the Office', is hereby established.

Article 3

Capacity to act

For the purpose of implementing this Regulation, companies or firms and other legal bodies shall be regarded as legal persons if, under the terms of the law governing them, they have the capacity in their own name to have rights and obligations of all kinds, to make contracts or accomplish other legal acts and to sue and be sued.

TITLE II

THE LAW RELATING TO TRADE MARKS

SECTION 1
DEFINITION OF A COMMUNITY TRADE MARK OBTAINING A COMMUNITY TRADE MARK

Article 4

Signs of which a Community trade mark may consist

A Community trade mark may consist of any signs capable of being represented graphically, particularly words, including personal names, designs, letters, numerals, the shape of goods or of their packaging, provided that such signs are capable of distinguishing the goods or services of one undertaking from those of other undertakings.

Article 5

Persons who can be proprietors of Community trade marks

1. The following natural or legal persons, including authorities established under public law, may be proprietors of Community trade marks—

(a) nationals of the Member States; or

[(b) nationals of other States which are parties to the Paris Convention for the protection of industrial property, hereinafter referred to as 'the Paris Convention', or to the Agreement establishing the World Trade Organization;] or

(c) nationals of States which are not parties to the Paris Convention who are domiciled or have their seat or who have real and effective industrial or commercial establishments within the territory of the Community or of a State which is party to the Paris Convention; or

[(d) nationals, other than those referred to under subparagraph (c), of any State which is not party to the Paris Convention or to the Agreement establishing the World Trade Organization and which, according to published findings, accords to nationals of all the Member States the same protection for trade marks as it accords to its own nationals and, if nationals of the Member States are required to prove registration in the country of origin, recognizes the registration of Community trade marks as such proof.]

2. With respect to the application of paragraph 1, stateless persons as defined by Article 1 of the Convention relating to the Status of Stateless Persons signed at New York on 28 September 1954, and refugees as defined by Article 1 of the Convention relating to the Status of Refugees signed at Geneva on 28 July 1951 and modified by the Protocol relating to the Status of Refugees signed at New York on 31 January 1967, shall be regarded as nationals of the country in which they have their habitual residence.

3. Persons who are nationals of a State covered by paragraph 1(d) must prove that the trade mark for which an application for a Community trade mark has been submitted is registered in the State of origin, unless, according to published findings, the trade marks of nationals of the Member States are registered in the State of origin in question without proof of prior registration as a Community trade mark or as a national trade mark in a Member State.

NOTES
Para 1: sub-paras (b), (d) substituted by Council Regulation 3288/94/EC, Art 1(1), (2).

Article 6

Means whereby a Community trade mark is obtained
A Community trade mark shall be obtained by registration.

Article 7

Absolute grounds for refusal
1. The following shall not be registered—
   (a) signs which do not conform to the requirements of Article 4;
   (b) trade marks which are devoid of any distinctive character;
   (c) trade marks which consist exclusively of signs or indications which may serve, in trade, to designate the kind, quality, quantity, intended purpose, value, geographical origin or the time of production of the goods or of rendering of the service, or other characteristics of the goods or service;
   (d) trade marks which consist exclusively of signs or indications which have become customary in the current language or in the bona fide and established practices of the trade;
   (e) signs which consist exclusively of—
      (i) the shape which results from the nature of the goods themselves; or

(ii) the shape of goods which is necessary to obtain a technical result; or

(iii) the shape which gives substantial value to the goods;

(f) trade marks which are contrary to public policy or to accepted principles of morality;

(g) trade marks which are of such a nature as to deceive the public, for instance as to the nature, quality or geographical origin of the goods or service;

(h) trade marks which have not been authorised by the competent authorities and are to be refused pursuant to Article 6ter of the Paris Convention;

(i) trade marks which include badges, emblems or escutcheons other than those covered by Article 6ter of the Paris Convention and which are of particular public interest, unless the consent of the appropriate authorities to their registration has been given;

[(j) trade marks for wines which contain or consist of a geographical indication identifying wines or for spirits which contain or consist of a geographical indication identifying spirits with respect to such wines or spirits not having that origin.]

2. Paragraph 1 shall apply notwithstanding that the grounds of non-registrability obtain in only part of the Community.

3. Paragraph 1(b), (c) and (d) shall not apply if the trade mark has become distinctive in relation to the goods or services for which registration is requested in consequence of the use which has been made of it.

NOTES
Para 1: sub-para (j) added by Council Regulation 3288/94/EC, Art 1(3).

Article 8

Relative grounds for refusal

1. Upon opposition by the proprietor of an earlier trade mark, the trade mark applied for shall not be registered—

(a) if it is identical with the earlier trade mark and the goods or services for which registration is applied for are identical with the goods or services for which the earlier trade mark is protected;

(b) if because of its identity with or similarity to the earlier trade mark and the identity or similarity of the goods or services covered by the trade marks there exists a likelihood of confusion on the part of the public in the territory in which the earlier trade mark is protected; the likelihood of confusion includes the likelihood of association with the earlier trade mark.

2. For the purposes of paragraph 1, 'Earlier trade marks' means—

(a) trade marks of the following kinds with a date of application for registration which is earlier than the date of application for registration of the Community trade mark, taking account, where appropriate, of the priorities claimed in respect of those trade marks—

(i) Community trade marks;

(ii) trade marks registered in a Member State, or, in the case of Belgium, the Netherlands or Luxembourg, at the Benelux Trade Mark Office;

(iii) trade marks registered under international arrangements which have effect in a Member State;

(b) applications for the trade marks referred to in subparagraph (a), subject to their registration;

(c) trade marks which, on the date of application for registration of the Community trade mark, or, where appropriate, of the priority claimed in respect of the application for registration of the Community trade mark, are well known in a Member State, in the sense in which the words 'well known' are used in Article 6bis of the Paris Convention.

3. Upon opposition by the proprietor of the trade mark, a trade mark shall not be registered where an agent or representative of the proprietor of the trade mark applies for registration thereof in his own name without the proprietor's consent, unless the agent or representative justifies his action.

4. Upon opposition by the proprietor of a non-registered trade mark or of another sign used in the course of trade of more than mere local significance, the trade mark applied for shall not be registered where and to the extent that, pursuant to the law of the Member State governing that sign,

    (a) rights to that sign were acquired prior to the date of application for registration of the Community trade mark, or the date of the priority claimed for the application for registration of the Community trade mark;

    (b) that sign confers on its proprietor the right to prohibit the use of a subsequent trade mark.

5. Furthermore, upon opposition by the proprietor of an earlier trade mark within the meaning of paragraph 2, the trade mark applied for shall not be registered where it is identical with or similar to the earlier trade mark and is to be registered for goods or services which are not similar to those for which the earlier trade mark is registered, where in the case of an earlier Community trade mark the trade mark has a reputation in the Community and, in the case of an earlier national trade mark, the trade mark has a reputation in the Member State concerned and where the use without due cause of the trade mark applied for would take unfair advantage of, or be detrimental to, the distinctive character or the repute of the earlier trade mark.

SECTION 2
EFFECTS OF COMMUNITY TRADE MARKS

Article 9

Rights conferred by a Community trade mark

1. A Community trade mark shall confer on the proprietor exclusive rights therein. The proprietor shall be entitled to prevent all third parties not having his consent from using in the course of trade —

    (a) any sign which is identical with the Community trade mark in relation to goods or services which are identical with those for which the Community trade mark is registered;

    (b) any sign where, because of its identity with or similarity to the Community trade mark and the identity or similarity of the goods or services covered by the Community trade mark and the sign, there exists a likelihood of confusion on the part of the public; the likelihood of confusion includes the likelihood of association between the sign and the trade mark;

    (c) any sign which is identical with or similar to the Community trade mark in relation to goods or services which are not similar to those for which the Community trade mark is registered, where the latter has a reputation in the Community and where use of that sign without due cause takes unfair advantage of, or is detrimental to, the distinctive character or the repute of the Community trade mark.

2. The following, inter alia, may be prohibited under paragraph 1 —

    (a) affixing the sign to the goods or to the packaging thereof;

    (b) offering the goods, putting them on the market or stocking them for these purposes under that sign, or offering or supplying services thereunder;

(c) importing or exporting the goods under that sign;

(d) using the sign on business papers and in advertising.

3. The rights conferred by a Community trade mark shall prevail against third parties from the date of publication of registration of the trade mark. Reasonable compensation may, however, be claimed in respect of matters arising after the date of publication of a Community trade mark application, which matters would, after publication of the registration of the trade mark, be prohibited by virtue of that publication. The court seized of the case may not decide upon the merits of the case until the registration has been published.

Article 10

Reproduction of Community trade marks in dictionaries

If the reproduction of a Community trade mark in a dictionary, encyclopaedia or similar reference work gives the impression that it constitutes the generic name of the goods or services for which the trade mark is registered, the publisher of the work shall, at the request of the proprietor of the Community trade mark, ensure that the reproduction of the trade mark at the latest in the next edition of the publication is accompanied by an indication that it is a registered trade mark.

Article 11

Prohibition on the use of a Community trade mark registered in the name of an agent or representative

Where a Community trade mark is registered in the name of the agent or representative of a person who is the proprietor of that trade mark, without the proprietor's authorisation, the latter shall be entitled to oppose the use of his mark by his agent or representative if he has not authorised such use, unless the agent or representative justifies his action.

Article 12

Limitation of the effects of a Community trade mark

A Community trade mark shall not entitle the proprietor to prohibit a third party from using in the course of trade—

(a) his own name or address;

(b) indications concerning the kind, quality, quantity, intended purpose, value, geographical origin, the time of production of the goods or of rendering of the service, or other characteristics of the goods or service;

(c) the trade mark where it is necessary to indicate the intended purpose of a product or service, in particular as accessories or spare parts,

provided he uses them in accordance with honest practices in industrial or commercial matters.

Article 13

Exhaustion of the rights conferred by a Community trade mark

1. A Community trade mark shall not entitle the proprietor to prohibit its use in relation to goods which have been put on the market in the Community under that trade mark by the proprietor or with his consent.

2. Paragraph 1 shall not apply where there exist legitimate reasons for the proprietor to oppose further commercialisation of the goods, especially where the condition of the goods is changed or impaired after they have been put on the market.

Article 14

Complementary application of national law relating to infringement
1. The effects of Community trade marks shall be governed solely by the provisions of this Regulation. In other respects, infringement of a Community trade mark shall be governed by the national law relating to infringement of a national trade mark in accordance with the provisions of Title X.
2. This Regulation shall not prevent actions concerning a Community trade mark being brought under the law of Member States relating in particular to civil liability and unfair competition.
3. The rules of procedure to be applied shall be determined in accordance with the provisions of Title X.

SECTION 3
USE OF COMMUNITY TRADE MARKS

Article 15

Use of Community trade marks
1. If, within a period of five years following registration, the proprietor has not put the Community trade mark to genuine use in the Community in connection with the goods or services in respect of which it is registered, or if such use has been suspended during an uninterrupted period of five years, the Community trade mark shall be subject to the sanctions provided for in this Regulation, unless there are proper reasons for non-use.
2. The following shall also constitute use within the meaning of paragraph 1 —
   (a) use of the Community trade mark in a form differing in elements which do not alter the distinctive character of the mark in the form in which it was registered;
   (b) affixing of the Community trade mark to goods or to the packaging thereof in the Community solely for export purposes.
3. Use of the Community trade mark with the consent of the proprietor shall be deemed to constitute use by the proprietor.

SECTION 4
COMMUNITY TRADE MARKS AS OBJECTS OF PROPERTY

Article 16

Dealing with Community trade marks as national trade marks
1. Unless Articles 17 to 24 provide otherwise, a Community trade mark as an object of property shall be dealt with in its entirety, and for the whole area of the Community, as a national trade mark registered in the Member State in which, according to the Register of Community trade marks,
   (a) the proprietor has his seat or his domicile on the relevant date; or
   (b) where subparagraph (a) does not apply, the proprietor has an establishment on the relevant date.
2. In cases which are not provided for by paragraph 1, the Member State referred to in that paragraph shall be the Member State in which the seat of the Office is situated.
3. If two or more persons are mentioned in the Register of Community trade marks as joint proprietors, paragraph 1 shall apply to the joint proprietor first mentioned; failing this, it shall apply to the subsequent joint proprietors in the order in which

they are mentioned. Where paragraph 1 does not apply to any of the joint proprietors, paragraph 2 shall apply.

Article 17

Transfer
1. A Community trade mark may be transferred, separately from any transfer of the undertaking in respect of some or all of the goods or services for which it is registered.
2. A transfer of the whole of the undertaking shall include the transfer of the Community trade mark except where, in accordance with the law governing the transfer, there is agreement to the contrary or circumstances clearly dictate otherwise. This provision shall apply to the contractual obligation to transfer the undertaking.
3. Without prejudice to paragraph 2, an assignment of the Community trade mark shall be made in writing and shall require the signature of the parties to the contract, except when it is a result of a judgment; otherwise it shall be void.
4. Where it is clear from the transfer documents that because of the transfer the Community trade mark is likely to mislead the public concerning the nature, quality or geographical origin of the goods or services in respect of which it is registered, the Office shall not register the transfer unless the successor agrees to limit registration of the Community trade mark to goods or services in respect of which it is not likely to mislead.
5. On request of one of the parties a transfer shall be entered in the Register and published.
6. As long as the transfer has not been entered in the Register, the successor in title may not invoke the rights arising from the registration of the Community trade mark.
7. Where there are time limits to be observed vis-à-vis the Office, the successor in title may make the corresponding statements to the Office once the request for registration of the transfer has been received by the Office.
8. All documents which require notification to the proprietor of the Community trade mark in accordance with Article 77 shall be addressed to the person registered as proprietor.

Article 18

Transfer of a trade mark registered in the name of an agent
Where a Community trade mark is registered in the name of the agent or representative of a person who is the proprietor of that trade mark, without the proprietor's authorisation, the latter shall be entitled to demand the assignment in his favour of the said registration, unless such agent or representative justifies his action.

Article 19

Rights in rem
1. A Community trade mark may, independently of the undertaking, be given as security or be the subject of rights in rem.
2. On request of one of the parties, rights mentioned in paragraph 1 shall be entered in the Register and published.

Article 20

Levy of execution
1. A Community trade mark may be levied in execution.
2. As regards the procedure for levy of execution in respect of a Community trade mark, the courts and authorities of the Member States determined in accordance with Article 16 shall have exclusive jurisdiction.
3. On request of one the parties, levy of execution shall be entered in the Register and published.

Article 21

Bankruptcy or like proceedings
1. Until such time as common rules for the Member States in this field enter into force, the only Member State in which a Community trade mark may be involved in bankruptcy or like proceedings shall be that in which such proceedings are first brought within the meaning of national law or of conventions applicable in this field.
2. Where a Community trade mark is involved in bankruptcy or like proceedings, on request of the competent national authority an entry to this effect shall be made in the Register and published.

Article 22

Licensing
1. A Community trade mark may be licensed for some or all of the goods or services for which it is registered and for the whole or part of the Community. A licence may be exclusive or non-exclusive.
2. The proprietor of a Community trade mark may invoke the rights conferred by that trade mark against a licensee who contravenes any provision in his licensing contract with regard to its duration, the form covered by the registration in which the trade mark may be used, the scope of the goods or services for which the licence is granted, the territory in which the trade mark may be affixed, or the quality of the goods manufactured or of the services provided by the licensee.
3. Without prejudice to the provisions of the licensing contract, the licensee may bring proceedings for infringement of a Community trade mark only if its proprietor consents thereto. However, the holder of an exclusive licence may bring such proceedings if the proprietor of the trade mark, after formal notice, does not himself bring infringement proceedings within an appropriate period.
4. A licensee shall, for the purpose of obtaining compensation for damage suffered by him, be entitled to intervene in infringement proceedings brought by the proprietor of the Community trade mark.
5. On request of one of the parties the grant or transfer of a licence in respect of a Community trade mark shall be entered in the Register and published.

Article 23

Effects vis-à-vis third parties
1. Legal acts referred to in Article 17, 19 and 22 concerning a Community trade mark shall only have effects vis-à-vis third parties in all the Member States after entry in the Register. Nevertheless, such an act, before it is so entered, shall have effect vis-à-vis third parties who have acquired rights in the trade mark after the date of that act but who knew of the act at the date on which the rights were acquired.

2. Paragraph 1 shall not apply in the case of a person who acquires the Community trade mark or a right concerning the Community trade mark by way of transfer of the whole of the undertaking or by any other universal succession.

3. The effects vis-à-vis third parties of the legal acts referred to in Article 20 shall be governed by the law of the Member State determined in accordance with Article 16.

4. Until such time as common rules for the Member States in the field of bankruptcy enter into force, the effects vis-à-vis third parties of bankruptcy or like proceedings shall be governed by the law of the Member State in which such proceedings are first brought within the meaning of national law or of conventions applicable in this field.

Article 24

The application for a Community trade mark as an object of property
Articles 16 to 23 shall apply to applications for Community trade marks.

TITLE III

APPLICATION FOR COMMUNITY TRADE MARKS

SECTION 1
FILING OF APPLICATIONS AND THE CONDITIONS WHICH GOVERN THEM

Article 25

Filing of applications
1. An application for a Community trade mark shall be filed, at the choice of the applicant,
  (a) at the Office; or
  (b) at the central industrial property office of a Member State or at the Benelux Trade Mark Office. An application filed in this way shall have the same effect as if it had been filed on the same date at the Office.

2. Where the application is filed at the central industrial property office of a Member State or at the Benelux Trade Mark Office, that office shall take all steps to forward the application to the Office within two weeks after filing. It may charge the applicant a fee which shall not exceed the administrative costs of receiving and forwarding the application.

3. Applications referred to in paragraph 2 which reach the Office more than one month after filing shall be deemed withdrawn.

4. Ten years after the entry into force of this Regulation, the Commission shall draw up a report on the operation of the system of filing applications for Community trade marks, together with any proposals for modifying this system.

Article 26

Conditions with which applications must comply
1. An application for a Community trade mark shall contain —
  (a) a request for the registration of a Community trade mark;
  (b) information identifying the applicant;
  (c) a list of the goods or services in respect of which the registration is requested;
  (d) a representation of the trade mark.

2. The application for a Community trade mark shall be subject to the payment of the application fee and, when appropriate, of one or more class fees.

3. An application for a Community trade mark must comply with the conditions laid down in the implementing Regulation referred to in Article 140.

Article 27

Date of filing
The date of filing of a Community trade mark application shall be the date on which documents containing the information specified in Article 26(1) are filed with the Office by the applicant or, if the application has been filed with the central office of a Member State or with the Benelux Trade Mark Office, with that office, subject to payment of the application fee within a period of one month of filing the abovementioned documents.

Article 28

Classification
Goods and services in respect of which Community trade marks are applied for shall be classified in conformity with the system of classification specified in the Implementing Regulation.

SECTION 2
PRIORITY

Article 29

Right of priority
[1. A person who has duly filed an application for a trade mark in or for any State party to the Paris Convention or to the Agreement establishing the World Trade Organization, or his successors in title, shall enjoy, for the purpose of filing a Community trade mark application for the same trade mark in respect of goods or services which are identical with or contained within those for which the application has been filed, a right or priority during a period of six months from the date of filing of the first application.]

2. Every filing that is equivalent to a regular national filing under the national law of the State where it was made or under bilateral or multilateral agreements shall be recognised as giving rise to a right of priority.

3. By a regular national filing is meant any filing that is sufficient to establish the date on which the application was filed, whatever may be the outcome of the application.

4. A subsequent application for a trade mark which was the subject of a previous first application in respect of the same goods or services, and which is filed in or in respect of the same State shall be considered as the first application for the purposes of determining priority, provided that, at the date of filing of the subsequent application, the previous application has been withdrawn, abandoned or refused, without being open to public inspection and without leaving any rights outstanding, and has not served as a basis for claiming a right of priority. The previous application may not thereafter serve as a basis for claiming a right of priority.

[5. If the first filing has been made in a State which is not a party to the Paris Convention or to the Agreement establishing the World Trade Organization, paragraphs 1 to 4 shall apply only in so far as that State, according to published findings, grants, on the basis of the first filing made at the Office and subject to conditions equivalent to those laid down in this Regulation, a right of priority having equivalent effect.]

NOTES
Para 1: substituted by Council Regulation 3288/94/EC, Art 1(4).
Para 5: substituted by Council Regulation 3288/94/EC, Art 1(5).

Article 30

Claiming priority

An applicant desiring to take advantage of the priority of a previous application shall file a declaration of priority and a copy of the previous application. If the language of the latter is not one of the languages of the Office, the applicant shall file a translation of the previous application in one of those languages.

Article 31

Effect of priority right

The right of priority shall have the effect that the date of priority shall count as the date of filing of the Community trade mark application for the purposes of establishing which rights take precedence.

Article 32

Equivalence of Community filing with national filing

A Community trade mark application which has been accorded a date of filing shall, in the Member States, be equivalent to a regular national filing, where appropriate with the priority claimed for the Community trade mark application.

SECTION 3
EXHIBITION PRIORITY

Article 33

Exhibition priority

1. If an applicant for a Community trade mark has displayed goods or services under the mark applied for, at an official or officially recognised international exhibition falling within the terms of the Convention on International Exhibitions signed at Paris on 22 November 1928 and last revised on 30 November 1972, he may, if he files the application within a period of six months from the date of the first display of the goods or services under the mark applied for, claim a right of priority from that date within the meaning of Article 31.
2. An applicant who wishes to claim priority pursuant to paragraph 1 must file evidence of the display of goods or services under the mark applied for under the conditions laid down in the Implementing Regulation.
3. An exhibition priority granted in a Member State or in a third country does not extend the period of priority laid down in Article 29.

SECTION 4
CLAIMING THE SENIORITY OF A NATIONAL TRADE MARK

Article 34

Claiming the seniority of a national trade mark

1. The proprietor of an earlier trade mark registered in a Member State, including a trade mark registered in the Benelux countries, or registered under international arrangements having effect in a Member State, who applies for an identical trade

mark for registration as a Community trade mark for goods or services which are identical with or contained within those for which the earlier trade mark has been registered, may claim for the Community trade mark the seniority of the earlier trade mark in respect of the Member State in or for which it is registered.

2. Seniority shall have the sole effect under this Regulation that, where the proprietor of the Community trade mark surrenders the earlier trade mark or allows it to lapse, he shall be deemed to continue to have the same rights as he would have had if the earlier trade mark had continued to be registered.

3. The seniority claimed for the Community trade mark shall lapse if the earlier trade mark the seniority of which is claimed is declared to have been revoked or to be invalid or if it is surrendered prior to the registration of the Community trade mark.

Article 35

Claiming seniority after registration of the Community trade mark

1. The proprietor of a Community trade mark who is the proprietor of an earlier identical trade mark registered in a Member State, including a trade mark registered in the Benelux countries, or of a trade mark registered under international arrangements having effect in a Member State, for identical goods or services, may claim the seniority of the earlier trade mark in respect of the Member State in or for which it is registered.

2. Article 34(2) and (3) shall apply.

TITLE IV
REGISTRATION PROCEDURE

SECTION 1
EXAMINATION OF APPLICATIONS

Article 36

Examination of the conditions of filing

1. The Office shall examine whether—
    (a) the Community trade mark application satisfies the requirements for the accordance of a date of filing in accordance with Article 27;
    (b) the Community trade mark application complies with the conditions laid down in the Implementing Regulation;
    (c) where appropriate, the class fees have been paid within the prescribed period.

2. Where the Community trade mark application does not satisfy the requirements referred to in paragraph 1, the Office shall request the applicant to remedy the deficiencies or the default on payment within the prescribed period.

3. If the deficiencies or the default on payment established pursuant to paragraph 1(a) are not remedied within this period, the application shall not be dealt with as a Community trade mark application. If the applicant complies with the Office's request, the Office shall accord as the date of filing of the application the date on which the deficiencies or the default on payment established are remedied.

4. If the deficiencies established pursuant to paragraph 1(b) are not remedied within the prescribed period, the Office shall refuse the application.

5. If the default on payment established pursuant to paragraph 1(c) is not remedied within the prescribed period, the application shall be deemed to be withdrawn unless it is clear which categories of goods or services the amount paid is intended

to cover.

6. Failure to satisfy the requirements concerning the claim to priority shall result in loss of the right of priority for the application.

7. Failure to satisfy the requirements concerning the claiming of seniority of a national trade mark shall result in loss of that right for the application.

Article 37

Examination of the conditions relating to the entitlement of the proprietor

1. Where, pursuant to Article 5, the applicant may not be the proprietor of a Community trade mark, the application shall be refused.

2. The application may not be refused before the applicant has been given the opportunity to withdraw his application or submit his observations.

Article 38

Examination as to absolute grounds for refusal

1. Where, under Article 7, a trade mark is ineligible for registration in respect of some or all of the goods or services covered by the Community trade mark application, the application shall be refused as regards those goods or services.

2. Where the trade mark contains an element which is not distinctive, and where the inclusion of said element in the trade mark could give rise to doubts as to the scope of protection of the trade mark, the Office may request, as a condition for registration of said trade mark, that the applicant state that he disclaims any exclusive right to such element. Any disclaimer shall be published together with the application or the registration of the Community trade mark, as the case may be.

3. The application shall not be refused before the applicant has been allowed the opportunity of withdrawing or amending the application or of submitting his observations.

SECTION 2

SEARCH

Article 39

Search

1. Once the Office has accorded a date of filing to a Community trade mark application and has established that the applicant satisfies the conditions referred to in Article 5, it shall draw up a Community search report citing those earlier Community trade marks or Community trade mark applications discovered which may be invoked under Article 8 against the registration of the Community trade mark applied for.

2. As soon as a Community trade mark application has been accorded a date of filing, the Office shall transmit a copy thereof to the central industrial property office of each Member State which has informed the Office of its decision to operate a search in its own register of trade marks in respect of Community trade mark applications.

3. Each of the central industrial property offices referred to in paragraph 2 shall communicate to the Office within three months as from the date on which it received the Community trade mark application a search report which shall either cite those earlier national trade marks or trade mark applications discovered which may be invoked under Article 8 against the registration of the Community trade mark applied for, or state that the search has revealed no such rights.

4. An amount shall be paid by the Office to each central industrial property office

for each search report provided by that office in accordance with paragraph 3. The amount, which shall be the same for each office, shall be fixed by the Budget Committee by means of a decision adopted by a majority of three-quarters of the representatives of the Member States.

5. The Office shall transmit without delay to the applicant for the Community trade mark the Community search report and the national search reports received within the time limit laid down in paragraph 3.

6. Upon publication of the Community trade mark application, which may not take place before the expiry of a period of one month as from the date on which the Office transmits the search reports to the applicant, the Office shall inform the proprietors of any earlier Community trade marks or Community trade mark applications cited in the Community search report of the publication of the Community trade mark application.

7. The Commission shall, five years after the opening of the Office for the filing of applications, submit to the Council a report on the operation of the system of searching resulting from this Article, including the payments made to Member States under paragraph 4, and, if necessary, appropriate proposals for amending this Regulation with a view to adapting the system of searching on the basis of the experience gained and bearing in mind developments in searching techniques.

SECTION 3
PUBLICATION OF THE APPLICATION

Article 40

Publication of the application
1. If the conditions which the application for a Community trade mark must satisfy have been fulfilled and if the period referred to in Article 39(6) has expired, the application shall be published to the extent that it has not been refused pursuant to Articles 37 and 38.
2. Where, after publication, the application is refused under Articles 37 and 38, the decision that it has been refused shall be published upon becoming final.

SECTION 4
OBSERVATIONS BY THIRD PARTIES AND OPPOSITION

Article 41

Observations by third parties
1. Following the publication of the Community trade mark application, any natural or legal person and any group or body representing manufacturers, producers, suppliers of services, traders or consumers may submit to the Office written observations, explaining on which grounds under Article 7, in particular, the trade mark shall not be registered em officio. They shall not be parties to the proceedings before the Office.
2. The observations referred to in paragraph 1 shall be communicated to the applicant who may comment on them.

Article 42

Opposition
1. Within a period of three months following the publication of a Community trade mark application, notice of opposition to registration of the trade mark may be given on the grounds that it may not be registered under Article 8—

(a) by the proprietors of earlier trade marks referred to in Article 8(2) as well as licensees authorised by the proprietors of those trade marks, in respect of Article 8(1) and (5);

(b) by the proprietors of trade marks referred to it Article 8(3);

(c) by the proprietors of earlier marks or signs referred to in Article 8(4) and by persons authorised under the relevant national law to exercise these rights.

2. Notice of opposition to registration of the trade mark may also be given, subject to the conditions laid down in paragraph 1, in the event of the publication of an amended application in accordance with the second sentence of Article 44(2).

3. Opposition must be expressed in writing and must specify the grounds on which it is made. It shall not be treated as duly entered until the opposition fee has been paid. Within a period fixed by the Office, the opponent may submit in support of his case facts, evidence and arguments.

Article 43

Examination of opposition

1. In the examination of the opposition the Office shall invite the parties, as often as necessary, to file observations, within a period set them by the Office, on communications from the other parties or issued by itself.

2. If the applicant so requests, the proprietor of an earlier Community trade mark who has given notice of opposition shall furnish proof that, during the period of five years preceding the date of publication of the Community trade mark application, the earlier Community trade mark has been put to genuine use in the Community in connection with the goods or services in respect of which it is registered and which he cites as justification for his opposition, or that there are proper reasons for non-use, provided the earlier Community trade mark has at that date been registered for not less than five years. In the absence of proof to this effect, the opposition shall be rejected. If the earlier Community trade mark has been used in relation to part only of the goods or services for which it is registered it shall, for the purposes of the examination of the opposition, be deemed to be registered in respect only of that part of the goods or services.

3. Paragraph 2 shall apply to earlier national trade marks referred to in Article 8(2) (a), by substituting use in the Member State in which the earlier national trade mark is protected for use in the Community.

4. The Office may, if it thinks fit, invite the parties to make a friendly settlement.

5. If examination of the opposition reveals that the trade mark may not be registered in respect of some or all of the goods or services for which the Community trade mark application has been made, the application shall be refused in respect of those goods or services. Otherwise the opposition shall be rejected.

6. The decision refusing the application shall be published upon becoming final.

SECTION 5

WITHDRAWAL, RESTRICTION AND AMENDMENT OF THE APPLICATION

Article 44

Withdrawal, restriction and amendment of the application

1. The applicant may at any time withdraw his Community trade mark application or restrict the list of goods or services contained therein. Where the application has already been published, the withdrawal or restriction shall also be published.

2. In other respects, a Community trade mark application may be amended, upon

request of the applicant, only by correcting the name and address of the applicant, errors of wording or of copying, or obvious mistakes, provided that such correction does not substantially change the trade mark or extend the list of goods or services. Where the amendments affect the representation of the trade mark or the list of goods or services and are made after publication of the application, the trade mark application shall be published as amended.

SECTION 6
REGISTRATION

Article 45

Registration

Where an application meets the requirements of this Regulation and where no notice of opposition has been given within the period referred to in Article 42(1) or where opposition has been rejected by a definitive decision, the trade mark shall be registered as a Community trade mark, provided that the registration fee has been paid within the period prescribed. If the fee is not paid within this period the application shall be deemed to be withdrawn.

TITLE V

DURATION, RENEWAL AND ALTERATION OF COMMUNITY TRADE
MARKS

Article 46

Duration of registration

Community trade marks shall be registered for a period of ten years from the date of filing of the application. Registration may be renewed in accordance with Article 47 for further periods of ten years.

Article 47

Renewal

1. Registration of the Community trade mark shall be renewed at the request of the proprietor of the trade mark or any person expressly authorised by him, provided that the fees have been paid.
2. The Office shall inform the proprietor of the Community trade mark, and any person having a registered right in respect of the Community trade mark, of the expire of the registration in good time before the said expiry. Failure to give such information shall not involve the responsibility of the Office.
3. The request for renewal shall be submitted within a period of six months ending on the last day of the month in which protection ends. The fees shall also be paid within this period. Failing this, the request may be submitted and the fees paid within a further period of six months following the day referred to in the first sentence, provided that an additional fee is paid within this further period.
4. Where the request is submitted or the fees paid in respect of only some of the goods or services for which the Community trade mark is registered, registration shall be renewed for those goods or services only.
5. Renewal shall take effect from the day following the date on which the existing registration expires. The renewal shall be registered.

Article 48

Alteration

1. The Community trade mark shall not be altered in the register during the period of registration or on renewal thereof.

2. Nevertheless, where the Community trade mark includes the name and address of the proprietor, any alteration thereof not substantially affecting the identity of the trade mark as originally registered may be registered at the request of the proprietor.

3. The publication of the registration of the alteration shall contain a representation of the Community trade mark as altered. Third parties whose rights may be affected by the alteration may challenge the registration thereof within a period of three months following publication.

TITLE VI

SURRENDER, REVOCATION AND INVALIDITY

SECTION 1
SURRENDER

Article 49

Surrender

1. A Community trade mark may be surrendered in respect of some or all of the goods or services for which it is registered.

2. The surrender shall be declared to the Office in writing by the proprietor of the trade mark. It shall not have effect until it has been entered in the Register.

3. Surrender shall be entered only with the agreement of the proprietor of a right entered in the Register. If a licence has been registered, surrender shall only be entered in the Register if the proprietor of the trade mark proves that he has informed the licensee of his intention to surrender; this entry shall be made on expiry of the period prescribed by the Implementing Regulation.

SECTION 2
GROUNDS FOR REVOCATION

Article 50

Grounds for revocation

1. The rights of the proprietor of the Community trade mark shall be declared to be revoked on application to the Office or on the basis of a counterclaim infringement proceedings—

   (a) if, within a continuous period of five years, the trade mark has not been put to genuine use in the Community in connection with the goods or services in respect of which it is registered, and there are no proper reasons for non-use; however, no person may claim that the proprietor's rights in a Community trade mark should be revoked where, during the interval between expiry of the five-year period and filing of the application or counterclaim, genuine use of the trade mark has been started or resumed; the commencement or resumption of use within a period of three months preceding the filing of the application or counterclaim which began at the earliest on expiry of the continuous period of five years of non-use shall, however, be disregarded where preparations for the commencement or resumption occur only after the proprietor becomes aware that the application or counterclaim may be filed;

   (b) if, in consequence of acts or inactivity of the proprietor, the trade mark has become the common name in the trade for a product or service in respect of which it is registered;

   (c) if, in consequence of the use made of it by the proprietor of the trade mark or with his consent in respect of the goods or services for which it is registered, the trade mark is liable to mislead the public, particularly as to the nature, quality or geographical origin of those goods or services;

   (d) if the proprietor of the trade mark no longer satisfies the conditions laid down by Article 5.

2. Where the grounds for revocation of rights exist in respect of only some of the goods or services for which the Community trade mark is registered, the rights of the proprietor shall be declared to be revoked in respect of those goods or services only.

SECTION 3
GROUNDS FOR INVALIDITY

Article 51

Absolute grounds for invalidity

1. A Community trade mark shall be declared invalid on application to the Office or on the basis of a counterclaim in infringement proceedings,

   (a) where the Community trade mark has been registered in breach of the provisions of Article 5 or of Article 7;

   (b) where the applicant was acting in bad faith when he filed the application for the trade mark.

2. Where the Community trade mark has been registered in breach of the provisions of Article 7(1) (b), (c) or (d), it may nevertheless not be declared invalid if, in consequence of the use which has been made of it, it has after registration acquired a distinctive character in relation to the goods or services for which it is registered.

3. Where the ground for invalidity exists in respect of only some of the goods or services for which the Community trade mark is registered, the trade mark shall be declared invalid as regards those goods or services only.

Article 52

Relative grounds for invalidity

1. A Community trade mark shall be declared invalid on application to the Office or on the basis of a counterclaim in infringement proceedings —

   (a) where there is an earlier trade mark as referred to in Article 8(2) and the conditions set out in paragraph 1 or paragraph 5 of that Article are fulfilled;

   (b) where there is a trade mark as referred to in Article 8(3) and the conditions set out in that paragraph are fulfilled;

   (c) where there is an earlier right as referred to in Article 8(4) and the conditions set out in that paragraph are fulfilled.

2. A Community trade mark shall also be declared invalid on application to the Office or on the basis of a counterclaim in infringement proceedings where the use of such trade mark may be prohibited pursuant to the national law governing the protection of any other earlier right and in particular—

   (a) a right to a name;

(b) a right of personal portrayal;

(c) a copyright;

(d) an industrial property right.

3. A Community trade mark may not be declared invalid where the proprietor of a right referred to in paragraphs 1 or 2 consents expressly to the registration of the Community trade mark before submission of the application for a declaration of invalidity or the counterclaim.

4. Where the proprietor of one of the rights referred to in paragraphs 1 or 2 has previously applied for a declaration that a Community trade mark is invalid or made a counterclaim in infringement proceedings, he may not submit a new application for a declaration of invalidity or lodge a counterclaim on the basis of another of the said rights which he could have invoked in support of his first application or counterclaim.

5. Article 51(3) shall apply.

Article 53

Limitation in consequence of acquiescence

1. Where the proprietor of a Community trade mark has acquiesced, for a period of five successive years, in the use of a later Community trade mark in the Community while being aware of such use, he shall no longer be entitled on the basis of the earlier trade mark either to apply for a declaration that the later trade mark is invalid or to oppose the use of the later trade mark in respect of the goods or services for which the later trade mark has been used, unless registration of the later Community trade mark was applied for in bad faith.

2. Where the proprietor of an earlier national trade mark as referred to in Article 8(2) or of another earlier sign referred to in Article 8(4) has acquiesced, for a period of five successive years, in the use of a later Community trade mark in the Member State in which the earlier trade mark or the other earlier sign is protected while being aware of such use, he shall no longer be entitled on the basis of the earlier trade mark or of the other earlier sign either to apply for a declaration that the later trade mark is invalid or to oppose the use of the later trade mark in respect of the goods or services for which the later trade mark has been used, unless registration of the later Community trade mark was applied for in bad faith.

3. In the cases referred to in paragraphs 1 and 2, the proprietor of a later Community trade mark shall not be entitled to oppose the use of the earlier right, even though that right may no longer be invoked against the later Community trade mark.

SECTION 4
CONSEQUENCES OF REVOCATION AND INVALIDITY

Article 54

Consequences of revocation and invalidity

1. The Community trade mark shall be deemed not to have had, as from the date of the application for revocation or of the counterclaim, the effects specified in this Regulation, to the extent that the rights of the proprietor have been revoked. An earlier date, on which one of the grounds for revocation occurred, may be fixed in the decision at the request of one of the parties.

2. The Community trade mark shall be deemed not to have had, as from the outset, the effects specified in this Regulation, to the extent that the trade mark has been declared invalid.

3. Subject to the national provisions relating either to claims for compensation for damage caused by negligence or lack of good faith on the part of the proprietor of the trade mark, or to unjust enrichment, the retroactive effect of revocation or invalidity of the trade mark shall not affect—

    (a) any decision on infringement which has acquired the authority of a final decision and been enforced prior to the revocation or invalidity decision;

    (b) any contract concluded prior to the revocation or invalidity decision, in so far as it has been performed before that decision; however, repayment, to an extent justified by the circumstances, of sums paid under the relevant contract, may be claimed on grounds of equity.

SECTION 5
PROCEEDINGS IN THE OFFICE IN RELATION TO REVOCATION OR INVALIDITY

Article 55

Application for revocation or for a declaration of invalidity

1. An application for revocation of the rights of the proprietor of a Community trade mark or for a declaration that the trade mark is invalid may be submitted to the Office—

    (a) where Articles 50 and 51 apply, by any natural or legal person and any group or body set up for the purpose of representing the interests of manufacturers, producers, suppliers of services, traders or consumers, which under the terms of the law governing it has the capacity in its own name to sue and be sued;

    (b) where Article 52(1) applies, by the persons referred to in Article 42(1);

    (c) where Article 52(2) applies, by the owners of the earlier rights referred to in that provision or by the persons who are entitled under the law of the Member State concerned to exercise the rights in question.

2. The application shall be filed in a written reasoned statement. It shall not be deemed to have been filed until the fee has been paid.

3. An application for revocation or for a declaration of invalidity shall be inadmissible if an application relating to the same subject matter and cause of action, and involving the same parties, has been adjudicated on by a court in a Member State and has acquired the authority of a final decision.

Article 56

Examination of the application

1. In the examination of the application for revocation of rights or for a declaration of invalidity, the Office shall invite the parties, as often as necessary, to file observations, within a period to be fixed by the Office, on communications from the other parties or issued by itself.

2. If the proprietor of the Community trade mark so requests, the proprietor of an earlier Community trade mark, being a party to the invalidity proceedings, shall furnish proof that, during the period of five years preceding the date of the application for a declaration of invalidity, the earlier Community trade mark has been put to genuine use in the Community in connection with the goods or services in respect of which it is registered and which he cites as justification for his application, or that there are proper reasons for non-use, provided the earlier Community trade mark has at that date been registered for non-use, provided the earlier Community trade mark has at that date been registered for not less than five years.

If, at the date on which the Community trade mark application was published, the earlier Community trade mark had been registered for not less than five years, the proprietor of the earlier Community trade mark shall furnish proof that, in addition, the conditions contained in Article 43(2) were satisfied at that date. In the absence of proof to this effect the application for a declaration of invalidity shall be rejected. If the earlier Community trade mark has been used in relation to part only of the goods or services for which it is registered it shall, for the purpose of the examination of the application for a declaration of invalidity, be deemed to be registered in respect only of that part of the goods or services.

3. Paragraph 2 shall apply to earlier national trade marks referred to in Article 8(2)(a), by substituting use in the Member State in which the earlier national trade mark is protected for use in the Community.

4. The Office may, if it thinks fit, invite the parties to make a friendly settlement.

5. If the examination of the application for revocation of rights or for a declaration of invalidity reveals that the trade mark should not have been registered in respect of some or all of the goods or services for which it is registered, the rights of the proprietor of the Community trade mark shall be revoked or it shall be declared invalid in respect of those goods or services. Otherwise the application for revocation of rights or for a declaration of invalidity shall be rejected.

6. The decision revoking the rights of the proprietor of the Community trade mark or declaring it invalid shall be entered in the Register upon becoming final.

TITLE VII

APPEALS

Article 57

Decisions subject to appeal

1. An appeal shall lie from decisions of the examiners, Opposition Divisions, Administration of Trade Marks and Legal Division and Cancellation Divisions. It shall have suspensive effect.

2. A decision which does not terminate proceedings as regards one of the parties can only be appealed together with the final decision, unless the decision allows separate appeal.

Article 58

Persons entitled to appeal and to be parties to appeal proceeding

Any party to proceedings adversely affected by a decision may appeal. Any other parties to the proceedings shall be parties to the appeal proceedings as of right.

Article 59

Time limit and form of appeal

Notice of appeal must be filed in writing at the Office within two months after the date of notification of the decision appealed from. The notice shall be deemed to have been filed only when the fee for appeal has been paid. Within four months after the date of notification of the decision, a written statement setting out the grounds of appeal must be filed.

Article 60

Interlocutory revision

1. If the department whose decision is contested considers the appeal to be admissi-

ble and well founded, it shall rectify its decision. This shall not apply where the appellant is opposed by another party to the proceedings.

2. If the decision is not rectified within one month after receipt of the statement of grounds, the appeal shall be remitted to the Board of Appeal without delay, and without comment as to its merit.

Article 61

Examination of appeals

1. If the appeal is admissible, the Board of Appeal shall examine whether the appeal is allowable.

2. In the examination of the appeal, the Board of Appeal shall invite the parties, as often as necessary, to file observations, within a period to be fixed by the Board of Appeal, on communications from the other parties or issued by itself.

Article 62

Decisions in respect of appeals

1. Following the examination as to the allowability of the appeal, the Board of Appeal shall decide on the appeal. The Board of Appeal may either exercise any power within the competence of the department which was responsible for the decision appealed or remit the case to that department for further prosecution.

2. If the Board of Appeal remits the case for further prosecution to the department whose decision was appealed, that department shall be bound by the ratio decidendi of the Board of Appeal, in so far as the facts are the same.

3. The decisions of the Boards of Appeal shall take effect only as from the date of expiration of the period referred to in Article 63(5) or, if an action has been brought before the Court of Justice within that period, as from the date of rejection of such action.

Article 63

Actions before the Court of Justice

1. Actions may be brought before the Court of Justice against decisions of the Boards of Appeal on appeals.

2. The action may be brought on grounds of lack of competence, infringement of an essential procedural requirement, infringement of the Treaty, of this Regulation or of any rule of law relating to their application or misuse of power.

3. The Court of Justice has jurisdiction to annul or to alter the contested decision.

4. The action shall be open to any party to proceedings before the Board of Appeal adversely affected by its decision.

5. The action shall be brought before the Court of Justice within two months of the date of notification of the decision of the Board of Appeal.

6. The Office shall be required to take the necessary measures to comply with the judgment of the Court of Justice.

TITLE VIII

COMMUNITY COLLECTIVE MARKS

Article 64

Community collective marks

1. A Community collective mark shall be a Community trade mark which is

described as such when the mark is applied for and is capable of distinguishing the goods or services of the members of the association which is the proprietor of the mark from those of other undertakings. Associations of manufacturers, producers, suppliers of services, or traders which, under the terms of the law governing them, have the capacity in their own name to have rights and obligations of all kinds, to make contracts or accomplish other legal acts and to sue and be sued, as well as legal persons governed by public law, may apply for Community collective marks.

2. In derogation from Article 7(1)(c), signs or indications which may serve, in trade, to designate the geographical origin of the goods or services may constitute Community collective marks within the meaning of paragraph 1. A collective mark shall not entitle the proprietor to prohibit a third party from using in the course of trade such signs or indications, provided he uses them in accordance with honest practices in industrial or commercial matters; in particular, such a mark may not be invoked against a third party who is entitled to use a geographical name.

3. The provisions of this Regulation shall apply to Community collective marks, unless Articles 65 to 72 provide otherwise.

Article 65

Regulations governing use of the mark

1. An applicant for a Community collective mark must submit regulations governing its use within the period prescribed.

2. The regulations governing use shall specify the persons authorised to use the mark, the conditions of membership of the association and, where they exist, the conditions of use of the mark including sanctions. The regulations governing use of a mark referred to in Article 64(2) must authorise any person whose goods or services originate in the geographical area concerned to become a member of the association which is the proprietor of the mark.

Article 66

Refusal of the application

1. In addition to the grounds for refusal of a Community trade mark application provided for in Articles 36 and 38, an application for a Community collective mark shall be refused where the provisions of Article 64 or 65 are not satisfied, or where the regulations governing use are contrary to public policy or to awaited principles of morality.

2. An application for a Community collective mark shall also be refused if the public is liable to be misled as regards the character or the significance of the mark, in particular if it is likely to be taken to be something other than a collective mark.

3. An application shall not be refused if the applicant, as a result of amendment of the regulations governing use, meets the requirements of paragraphs 1 and 2.

Article 67

Observations by third parties

Apart from the cases mentioned in Article 41, any person, group or body referred to in that Article may submit to the Office written observations based on the particular grounds on which the application for a Community collective mark should be refused under the terms of Article 66.

Article 68

Use of marks
Use of a Community collective mark by any person who has authority to use it shall satisfy the requirements of this Regulation, provided that the other conditions which this Regulation imposes with regard to the use of Community trade marks are fulfilled.

Article 69

Amendment of the regulations governing use of the mark
1. The proprietor of a Community collective mark must submit to the Office any amended regulations governing use.
2. The amendment shall not be mentioned in the Register if the amended regulations do not satisfy the requirements of Article 65 or involve one of the grounds for refusal referred to in Article 66.
3. Article 67 shall apply to amended regulations governing use.
4. For the purposes of applying this Regulation, amendments to the regulations governing use shall take effect only from the date of entry of the mention of the amendment in the Register.

Article 70

Persons who are entitled to bring an action for infringement
1. The provisions of Article 22(3) and (4) concerning the rights of licensees shall apply to every person who has authority to use a Community collective mark.
2. The proprietor of a Community collective mark shall be entitled to claim compensation on behalf of persons who have authority to use the mark where they have sustained damage in consequence of unauthorised use of the mark.

Article 71

Grounds for revocation
Apart from the grounds for revocation provided for in Article 50, the rights of the proprietor of a Community collective mark shall be revoked on application to the Office or on the basis of a counterclaim in infringement proceedings, if—
  (a) the proprietor does not take reasonable steps to prevent the mark being used in a manner incompatible with the conditions of use, where these exist, laid down in the regulations governing use, amendments to which have, where appropriate, been mentioned in the Register;
  (b) the manner in which the mark has been used by the proprietor has caused it to become liable to mislead the public in the manner referred to in Article 66(2);
  (c) an amendment to the regulations governing use of the mark has been mentioned in the Register in breach of the provisions of Article 69(2), unless the proprietor of the mark, by further amending the regulations governing use, complies with the requirements of those provisions.

Article 72

Grounds for invalidity
Apart from the grounds for invalidity provided for in Articles 51 and 52, a Community collective mark which is registered in breach of the provisions of Article 66 shall be declared invalid on application to the Office or on the basis of a

counterclaim in infringement proceedings, unless the proprietor of the mark, by amending the regulations governing use, complies with the requirements of those provisions.

TITLE IX

PROCEDURE

SECTION 1
GENERAL PROVISIONS

Article 73

Statement of reasons on which decisions are based
Decisions of the Office shall state the reasons on which they are based. They shall be based only on reasons or evidence on which the parties concerned have had on opportunity to present their comments.

Article 74

Examination of the facts by the Office of its own motion
1. In proceedings before it the Office shall examine the facts of its own motion; however, in proceedings relating to relative grounds for refusal of registration, the Office shall be restricted in this examination to the facts, evidence and arguments provided by the parties and the relief sought.
2. The Office may disregard facts or evidence which are not submitted in due time by the parties concerned.

Article 75

Oral proceedings
1. If the Office considers that oral proceedings would be expedient they shall be held either at the instance of the Office or at the request of any party to the proceedings.
2. Oral proceedings before the examiners, the Opposition Division and the Administration of Trade Marks and Legal Division shall not be public.
3. Oral proceedings, including delivery of the decision, shall be public before the Cancellation Division and the Boards of Appeal, in so far as the department before which the proceedings are taking place does not decide otherwise in cases where admission of the public could have serious and unjustified disadvantages, in particular for a party to the proceedings.

Article 76

Taking of evidence
1. In any proceedings before the Office, the means of giving or obtaining evidence shall include the following—
   (a) hearing the parties;
   (b) requests for information;
   (c) the production of documents and items of evidence;
   (d) hearing witnesses;
   (e) opinions by experts;
   (f) statements in writing sworn or affirmed or having a similar effect under the law of the State in which the statement is drawn up.

2. The relevant department may commission one of its members to examine the evidence adduced.

3. If the Office considers it necessary for a party, witness or expert to give evidence orally, it shall issue a summons to the person concerned to appear before it.

4. The parties shall be informed of the hearing of a witness or expert before the Office. They shall have the right to be present and to put questions to the witness or expert.

Article 77

Notification

The Office shall, as a matter of course, notify those concerned of decisions and summonses and of any notice or other communication from which a time limit is reckoned, or of which those concerned must be notified under other provisions of this Regulation or of the Implementing Regulation, or of which notification has been ordered by the President of the Office.

Article 78

Restitutio in integrum

1. The applicant for or proprietor of a Community trade mark or any other party to proceedings before the Office who, in spite of all due care required by the circumstances having been taken, was unable to observe a time limit vis-à-vis the Office shall, upon application, have his rights re-established if the non-observance in question has the direct consequence, by virtue of the provisions of this Regulation, of causing the loss of any right or means of redress.

2. The application must be filed in writing within two months from the removal of the cause of non-compliance with the time limit. The omitted act must be completed within this period. The application shall only be admissible within the year immediately following the expire of the unobserved time limit. In the case of non-submission of the request for renewal of registration or of non-payment of a renewal fee, the further period of six months provided in Article 47(3), third sentence, shall be deducted from the period of one year.

3. The application must state the grounds on which it is based and must set out the facts on which it relies. It shall not be deemed to be filed until the fee for re-establishment of rights has been paid.

4. The department competent to decide on the omitted act shall decide upon the application.

5. The provisions of this Article shall not be applicable to the time limits referred to in paragraph 2 of this Article, Articles 29(1) and 42(1).

6. Where the applicant for or proprietor of a Community trade mark has his rights re-established, he may not invoke his rights vis-à vis a third party who, in good faith, has put goods on the market or supplied services under a sign which is identical with or similar to the Community trade mark in the course of the period between the loss of rights in the application or in the Community trade mark and publication of the mention of re-establishment of those rights.

7. A third party who may avail himself of the provisions of paragraph 6 may bring third party proceedings against the decision re-establishing the rights of the applicant for or proprietor of a Community trade mark within a period of two months as from the date of publication of the mention of re-establishment of those rights.

8. Nothing in this Article shall limit the right of a Member State to grant restitutio in integrum in respect of time limits provided for in this Regulation and to be observed vis-à-vis the authorities of such State.

Article 79

Reference to general principles

In the absence of procedural provisions in this Regulation, the Implementing Regulation, the fees regulations or the rules of procedure of the Boards of Appeal, the Office shall take into account the principles of procedural law generally recognised in the Member States.

Article 80

Termination of financial obligations

1. Rights of the Office to the payment of a fee shall be extinguished after four years from the end of the calendar year in which the fee fell due.

2. Rights against the Office for the refunding of fees or sums of money paid in excess of a fee shall be extinguished after four years from the end of the calendar year in which the right arose.

3. The period laid down in paragraphs 1 and 2 shall be interrupted in the case covered by paragraph 1 by a request for payment of the fee and in the case covered by paragraph 2 by a reasoned claim in writing. On interruption it shall begin again immediately and shall end at the latest six years after the end of the year in which it originally began, unless, in the meantime, judicial proceedings to enforce the right have begun in this case the period shall end at the earliest one year after the judgment has acquired the authority of a final decision.

SECTION 2
COSTS

Article 81

Costs

1. The losing party in opposition proceedings, proceedings for revocation, proceedings for a declaration of invalidity or appeal proceedings shall bear the fees incurred by the other party as well as all costs, without prejudice to Article 115(6), incurred by him essential to the proceedings, including travel and subsistence and the remuneration of an agent, adviser or advocate, within the limits of the scales set for each category of costs under the conditions laid down in the Implementing Regulation.

2. However, where each party succeeds on some and fails on other heads, or if reasons of equity so dictate, the Opposition Division, Cancellation Division or Board of Appeal shall decide a different apportionment of costs.

3. The party who terminates the proceedings by withdrawing the Community trade mark application, the opposition, the application for revocation of rights, the application for a declaration of invalidity or the appeal, or by not renewing registration of the Community trade mark or by surrendering the Community trade mark, shall bear the fees and the costs incurred by the other party as stipulated in paragraphs 1 and 2.

4. Where a case does not proceed to judgment the costs shall be at the discretion of the Opposition Division, Cancellation Division or Board of Appeal.

5. Where the parties conclude before the Opposition Division, Cancellation Division or Board of Appeal a settlement of costs differing from that provided for in the preceding paragraphs, the department concerned shall take note of that agreement.

6. On request the registry of the Opposition Division or Cancellation Division or

Board of Appeal shall fix the amount of the costs to be paid pursuant to the preceding paragraphs. The amount so determined may be reviewed by a decision of the Opposition Division or Cancellation Division or Board of Appeal on a request filed within the prescribed period.

Article 82

Enforcement of decisions fixing the amount of costs

1. Any final decision of the Office fixing the amount of costs shall be enforceable.

2. Enforcement shall be governed by the rules of civil procedure in force in the State in the territory of which it is carried out. The order for its enforcement shall be appended to the decision, without other formality than verification of the authenticity of the decision, by the national authority which the Government of each Member State shall designate for this purpose and shall make known to the Office and to the Court of Justice.

3. When these formalities have been completed on application by the party concerned, the latter may proceed to enforcement in accordance with the national law, by bringing the matter directly before the competent authority.

4. Enforcement may be suspended only by a decision of the Court of Justice. However, the courts of the country concerned shall have jurisdiction over complaints that enforcement is being carried out in an irregular manner.

SECTION 3
INFORMATION OF THE PUBLIC AND OF THE OFFICIAL AUTHORITIES OF THE MEMBER STATES

Article 83

Register of Community trade marks

The Office shall keep a register to the known as the Register of Community trade marks, which shall contain those particulars the registration or inclusion of which is provided for by this Regulation or by the Implementing Regulation. The Register shall be open to public inspection.

Article 84

Inspection of files

1. The files relating to Community trade mark applications which have not yet been published shall not be made available for inspection without the consent of the applicant.

2. Any person who can prove that the applicant for a Community trade mark has stated that after the trade mark has been registered he will invoke the rights under it against him may obtain inspection of the files prior to the publication of that application and without the consent of the applicant.

3. Subsequent to the publication of the Community trade mark application, the files relating to such application and the resulting trade mark may be inspected on request.

4. However, where the files are inspected pursuant to paragraphs 2 or 3, certain documents in the file may be withheld from inspection in accordance with the provisions of the Implementing Regulation.

Article 85

Periodical publications

The Office shall periodically publish—

(a) a Community Trade Marks Bulletin containing entries made in the Register of Community trade marks as well as other particulars the publication of which is prescribed by this Regulation or by the Implementing Regulation;

(b) an Official Journal containing notices and information of a general character issued by the President of the Office, as well as any other information relevant to this Regulation or its implementation.

Article 86

Administrative co-operation

Unless otherwise provided in this Regulation or in national laws, the Office and the courts or authorities of the Member States shall on request give assistance to each other by communicating information or opening files for inspection. Where the Office lays files open to inspection by courts, Public Prosecutors' Offices or central industrial property offices, the inspection shall not be subject to the restrictions laid down in Article 84.

Article 87

Exchange of publications

1. The offices and the central industrial property offices of the Member States shall dispatch to each other on request and for their own use one or more copies of the respective publications free of charge.

2. The Office may conclude agreements relating to the exchange or supply of publications.

SECTION 4
REPRESENTATION

Article 88

General principles of representation

1. Subject to the provisions of paragraph 2, no person shall be compelled to be represented before the Office.

2. Without prejudice to paragraph 3, second sentence, natural or legal persons not having either their domicile or their principal place of business or a real and effective industrial or commercial establishment in the Community must be represented before the Office in accordance with Article 89(1) in all proceedings established by this Regulation, other than in filing an application for a Community trade mark; the Implementing Regulation may permit other exceptions.

3. Natural or legal persons having their domicile or principal place of business or a real and effective industrial or commercial establishment in the Community may be represented before the Office by an employee, who must file with it a signed authorisation for insertion on the files, the details of which are set out in the Implementing Regulation. An employee of a legal person to which this paragraph applies may also represent other legal persons which have economic connections with the first legal person, even if those other legal persons have neither their domicile nor their principal place of business nor a real and effective industrial or commercial establishment within the Community.

Article 89

Professional representatives

1. Representation of natural or legal persons before the Office may only be under-

taken by—
- (a) any legal practitioner qualified in one of the Member States and having his place of business within the Community, to the extent that he is entitled, within the said State, to act as a representative in trade mark matters; or
- (b) professional representatives whose names appear on the list maintained for this purpose by the Office.

Representatives acting before the Office must file with it a signed authorisation for insertion on the files, the details of which are set out in the Implementing Regulation.

2. Any natural person who fulfils the following conditions may be entered on the list of professional representatives—
- (a) he must be a national of one of the Member States;
- (b) he must have his place of business or employment in the Community;
- (c) he must be entitled to represent natural or legal persons in trade mark matters before the central industrial property office of the Member State in which he has his place of business or employment. Where, in that State, the entitlement is not conditional upon the requirement of special professional qualifications, persons applying to be entered on the list who act in trade mark matters before the central industrial property office of the said State must have habitually so acted for at least five years. However, persons whose professional qualification to represent natural or legal persons in trade mark matters before the central industrial property office of one of the Member States is officially recognised in accordance with the regulations laid down by such State shall not be subject to the condition of having exercised the profession.

3. Entry shall be effected upon request, accompanied by a certificate furnished by the central industrial property office of the Member State concerned, which must indicate that the conditions laid down in paragraph 2 are fulfilled.

4. The President of the Office may grant exemption from—
- (a) the requirement of paragraph 2(c), second sentence, if the applicant furnishes proof that he has acquired the requisite qualification in another way;
- (b) the requirement of paragraph 2(a) in special circumstances.

5. The conditions under which a person may be removed from the list of professional representatives shall be laid down in the Implementing Regulation.

TITLE X

JURISDICTION AND PROCEDURE IN LEGAL ACTIONS RELATING TO COMMUNITY TRADE MARKS

SECTION 1
APPLICATION OF THE CONVENTION ON JURISDICTION AND ENFORCEMENT

Article 90

Application of the Convention on Jurisdiction and Enforcement

1. Unless otherwise specified in this Regulation, the Convention on Jurisdiction and the Enforcement of Judgments in Civil and Commercial Matters, signed in Brussels on 27 September 1968, as amended by the Conventions on the Accession to that Convention of the States acceding to the European Communities, the whole of which Convention and of which Conventions of Accession are hereinafter referred

to as the 'Convention on Jurisdiction and Enforcement', shall apply to proceedings relating to Community trade marks and applications for Community trade marks, as well as to proceedings relating to simultaneous and successive actions on the basis of Community trade marks and national trade marks.

2. In the case of proceedings in respect of the actions and claims referred to in Article 92—

    (a) Articles 2, 4, 5(1), (3), (4) and (5) and Article 24 of the Convention on Jurisdiction and Enforcement shall not apply;

    (b) Articles 17 and 18 of that Convention shall apply subject to the limitations in Article 93(4) of this Regulation;

    (c) the provisions of Title II of that Convention which are applicable to persons domiciled in a Member State shall also be applicable to persons who do not have a domicile in any Member State but have an establishment therein.

SECTION 2
DISPUTES CONCERNING THE INFRINGEMENT AND VALIDITY OF COMMUNITY TRADE MARKS

Article 91

Community trade mark courts

1. The Member States shall designate in their territories as limited a number as possible of national courts and tribunals of first and second instance, hereinafter referred to as 'Community trade mark courts', which shall perform the functions assigned to them by this Regulation.

2. Each Member State shall communicate to the Commission within three years of the entry into force of this Regulation a list of Community trade mark courts indicating their names and their territorial jurisdiction.

3. Any change made after communication of the list referred to in paragraph 2 in the number, names or territorial jurisdiction of the courts shall be notified without delay by the Member State concerned to the Commission.

4. The information referred to in paragraphs 2 and 3 shall be notified by the Commission to the Member States and published in the Official Journal of the European Communities.

5. As long as a Member State has not communicated the list as stipulated in paragraph 2, jurisdiction for any proceedings resulting from an action or application covered by Article 92, and for which the courts of that State have jurisdiction under Article 93, shall lie with that court of the State in question which would have jurisdiction ratione loci and ratione materiale in the case of proceedings relating to a national trade mark registered in that State.

Article 92

Jurisdiction over infringement and validity

The Community trade mark courts shall have exclusive jurisdiction—

    (a) for all infringement actions and—if they are permitted under national law—actions in respect of threatened infringement relating to Community trade marks;

    (b) for actions for declaration of non-infringement, if they are permitted under national law;

    (c) for all actions brought as a result of acts referred to in Article 9(3), second sentence;

(d) for counterclaims for revocation or for a declaration of invalidity of the Community trade mark pursuant to Article 96.

Article 93

International jurisdiction
1. Subject to the provisions of this Regulation as well as to any provisions of the Convention on Jurisdiction and Enforcement applicable by virtue of Article 90, proceedings in respect of the actions and claims referred to in Article 92 shall be brought in the courts of the Member State in which the defendant is domiciled or, if he is not domiciled in any of the Member States, in which he has an establishment.
2. If the defendant is neither domiciled nor has an establishment in any of the Member States, such proceedings shall be brought in the courts of the Member State in which the plaintiff is domiciled or, if he is not domiciled in any of the Member States, in which he has an establishment.
3. If neither the defendant nor the plaintiff is so domiciled or has such an establishment, such proceedings shall be brought in the courts of the Member State where the Office has its seat.
4. Notwithstanding the provisions of paragraphs 1, 2 and 3—
    (a) Article 17 of the Convention on Jurisdiction and Enforcement shall apply if the parties agree that a different Community trade mark court shall have jurisdiction;
    (b) Article 18 of that Convention shall apply if the defendant enters an appearance before a different Community trade mark court.
5. Proceedings in respect of the actions and claims referred to in Article 92, with the exception of actions for a declaration of non-infringement of a Community trade mark, may also be brought in the courts of the Member State in which the act of infringement has been committed or threatened, or in which an act within the meaning of Article 9(3), second sentence, has been committed.

Article 94

Extent of jurisdiction
1. A Community trade mark court whose jurisdiction is based on Article 93(1) to (4) shall have jurisdiction in respect of—
    — acts of infringement committed or threatened within the territory of any of the Member States,
    — acts within the meaning of Article 9(3), second sentence, committed within the territory of any of the Member States.
2. A Community trade mark court whose jurisdiction is based on Article 93(5) shall have jurisdiction only in respect of acts committed or threatened within the territory of the Member State in which that court is situated.

Article 95

Presumption of validity—Defence as to the merits
1. The Community trade mark courts shall treat the Community trade mark as valid unless its validity is put in issue by the defendant with a counterclaim for revocation or for a declaration of invalidity.
2. The validity of a Community trade mark may not be put in issue in an action for a declaration of non-infringement.
3. In the actions referred to in Article 92(a) and (c) a plea relating to revocation or

invalidity of the Community trade mark submitted otherwise than by way of a counterclaim shall be admissible in so far as the defendant claims that the rights of the proprietor of the Community trade mark could be revoked for lack of use or that Community trade mark could be declared invalid on account of an earlier right of the defendant.

Article 96

Counterclaims

1. A counterclaim for revocation or for a declaration of invalidity may only be based on the grounds for revocation or invalidity mentioned in this Regulation.

2. A Community trade mark court shall reject a counterclaim for revocation or for a declaration of invalidity if a decision taken by the Office relating to the same subject matter and cause of action and involving the same parties has already become final.

3. If the counterclaim is brought in a legal action to which the proprietor of the trade mark is not already a party, he shall be informed thereof and may be joined as a party to the action in accordance with the conditions set out in national law.

4. The Community trade mark court with which a counterclaim for revocation or for a declaration of invalidity of the Community trade mark has been filed shall inform the Office of the date on which the counterclaim was filed. The latter shall record this fact in the Register of Community trade marks.

5. Article 56(3), (4), (5) and (6) shall apply.

6. Where a Community trade mark court has given a judgment which has become final on a counterclaim for revocation or for invalidity of a Community trade mark, a copy of the judgment shall be sent to the Office. Any party may request information about such transmission. The Office shall mention the judgment in the Register of Community trade marks in accordance with the provisions of the Implementing Regulation.

7. The Community trade mark court hearing a counterclaim for revocation or for a declaration of invalidity may stay the proceedings on application by the proprietor of the Community trade mark and after hearing the other parties and may request the defendant to submit an application for revocation or for a declaration of invalidity to the Office within a time limit which it shall determine. If the application is not made within the time limit, the proceedings shall continue; the counterclaim shall be deemed withdrawn. Article 100(3) shall apply.

Article 97

Applicable law

1. The Community trade mark courts shall apply the provisions of this Regulation.

2. On all matters not covered by this Regulation a Community trade mark court shall apply its national law, including its private international law.

3. Unless otherwise provided in this Regulation, a Community trade mark court shall apply the rules of procedure governing the same type of action relating to a national trade mark in the Member State where it has its seat.

Article 98

Sanctions

1. Where a Community trade mark court finds that the defendant has infringed or threatened to infringe a Community trade mark, it shall, unless there are special reasons for not doing so, issue an order prohibiting the defendant from proceeding

with the acts which infringed or would infringe the Community trade mark. It shall also take such measures in accordance with its national law as are aimed at ensuring that this prohibition is complied with.

2. In all other respects the Community trade mark court shall apply the law of the Member State to which the acts of infringement or threatened infringement were committed, including the private international law.

Article 99

Provisional and protective measures

1. Application may be made to the courts of a Member State, including Community trade mark courts, for such provisional, including protective, measures in respect of a Community trade mark or Community trade mark application as may be available under the law of that State in respect of a national trade mark, even if, under this Regulation, a Community trade mark court of another Member State has jurisdiction as to the substance of the matter.

2. A Community trade mark court whose jurisdiction is based on Article 93(1), (2), (3) or (4) shall have jurisdiction to grant provisional and protective measures which, subject to any necessary procedure for recognition and enforcement pursuant to Title III of the Convention on Jurisdiction and Enforcement, are applicable in the territory of any Member State. No other court shall have such jurisdiction.

Article 100

Specific rules on related actions

1. A Community trade mark court hearing an action referred to in Article 92, other than an action for a declaration of non-infringement shall, unless there are special grounds for continuing the hearing, of its own motion after hearing the parties or at the request of one of the parties and after hearing the other parties, stay the proceedings where the validity of the Community trade mark is already in issue before another Community trade mark court on account of a counterclaim or where an application for revocation or for a declaration of invalidity has already been filed at the Office.

2. The Office, when hearing an application for revocation or for a declaration of invalidity shall, unless there are special grounds for continuing the hearing, of its own motion after hearing the parties or at the request of one of the parties and after hearing the other parties, stay the proceedings where the validity of the Community trade mark is already in issue on account of a counterclaim before a Community trade mark court. However, if one of the parties to the proceedings before the Community trade mark court so requests, the court may, after hearing the other parties to these proceedings, stay the proceedings. The Office shall in this instance continue the proceedings pending before it.

3. Where the Community trade mark court stays the proceedings it may order provisional and protective measures for the duration of the stay.

Article 101

Jurisdiction of Community trade mark courts of second instance — Further appeal

1. An appeal to the Community trade mark courts of second instance shall lie from judgments of the Community trade mark courts of first instance in respect of proceedings arising from the actions and claims referred to in Article 92.

2. The conditions under which an appeal may be lodged with a Community trade

mark court of second instance shall be determined by the national law of the Member State in which that court is located.

3. The national rules concerning further appeal shall be applicable in respect of judgments of Community trade mark courts of second instance.

SECTION 3
OTHER DISPUTES CONCERNING COMMUNITY TRADE MARKS

Article 102

Supplementary provisions on the jurisdiction of national courts other than Community trade mark courts

1. Within the Member State whose courts have jurisdiction under Article 90(1) those courts shall have jurisdiction for actions other than those referred to in Article 92, which would have jurisdiction ratione loci and ratione materiae in the case of actions relating to a national trade mark registered in that State.

2. Actions relating to a Community trade mark, other than those referred to in Article 92, for which no court has jurisdiction under Article 90(1) and paragraph 1 of this Article may be heard before the courts of the Member State in which the Office has its seat.

Article 103

Obligation of the national court

A national court which is dealing with an action relating to a Community trade mark, other than the action referred to in Article 92, shall treat the trade mark as valid.

SECTION 4
TRANSITIONAL PROVISION

Article 104

Transitional provision relating to the application of the Convention on Jurisdiction and Enforcement

The provisions of the Convention on Jurisdiction and Enforcement which are rendered applicable by the preceding Articles shall have effect in respect of any Member State solely in the text of the Convention which is in force in respect of that State at any given time.

TITLE XI

EFFECTS ON THE LAWS OF THE MEMBER STATES

SECTION 1
CIVIL ACTIONS ON THE BASIS OF MORE THAN ONE TRADE MARK

Article 105

Simultaneous and successive civil actions on the basis of Community trade marks and national trade marks

1. Where actions for infringement involving the same cause of action and between the same parties are brought in the courts of different Member States, one seized on the basis of a Community trade mark and the other seized on the basis of a national trade mark —

(a) the court other than the court first seized shall of its own motion decline jurisdiction in favour of that court where the trade marks concerned are identical and valid for identical goods or services. The court which would be required to decline jurisdiction may stay its proceedings if the jurisdiction of the other court is contested;

(b) the court other than the court first seized may stay its proceedings where the trade marks concerned are identical and valid for similar goods or services and where the trade marks concerned are similar and valid for identical or similar goods or services.

2. The court hearing an action for infringement on the basis of a Community trade mark shall reject the action if a final judgment on the merits has been given on the same cause of action and between the same parties on the basis of an identical national trade mark valid for identical goods or services.

3. The court hearing an action for infringement on the basis of a national trade mark shall reject the action if a final judgment on the merits has been given on the same cause of action and between the same parties on the basis of an identical Community trade mark valid for identical goods or services.

4. Paragraphs 1, 2 and 3 shall not apply in respect of provisional, including protective, measures.

SECTION 2
APPLICATION OF NATIONAL LAWS FOR THE PURPOSE OF PROHIBITING THE USE OF COMMUNITY TRADE MARKS

Article 106

Prohibition of use of Community trade marks

1. This Regulation shall, unless otherwise provided for, not affect the right existing under the laws of the Member States to invoke claims for infringement of earlier rights within the meaning of Article 8 or Article 52(2) in relation to the use of a later Community trade mark. Claims for infringement of earlier rights within the meaning of Article 8(2) and (4) may, however, no longer be invoked if the proprietor of the earlier right may no longer apply for a declaration that the Community trade mark is invalid in accordance with Article 53(2).

2. This Regulation shall, unless otherwise provided for, not affect the right to bring proceedings under the civil, administrative or criminal law of a Member Sate or under provisions of Community law for the purpose of prohibiting the use of a Community trade mark to the extent that the use of a national trade mark may be prohibited under the law of that Member State or under Community law.

Article 107

Prior rights applicable to particular localities

1. The proprietor of an earlier right which only applies to a particular locality may oppose the use of the Community trade mark in the territory where his right is protected in so far as the law of the Member State concerned so permits.

2. Paragraph 1 shall cease to apply if the proprietor of the earlier right has acquiesced in the use of the Community trade mark in the territory where his right is protected for a period of five successive years, being aware of such use, unless the Community trade mark was applied for in bad faith.

3. The proprietor of the Community trade mark shall not be entitled to oppose use of the right referred to in paragraph 1 even though that right may no longer be invoked against the Community trade mark.

SECTION 3
CONVERSION INTO A NATIONAL TRADE MARK APPLICATION

Article 108

Request for the application of national procedure

1. The applicant for or proprietor of a Community trade mark may request the conversion of his Community trade mark application or Community trade mark into a national trade mark application—
   (a) to the extent that the Community trade mark application is refused, withdrawn, or deemed to be withdrawn;
   (b) to the extent that the Community trade mark ceases to have effect.
2. Conversion shall not take place—
   (a) where the rights of the proprietor of the Community trade mark have been revoked on the grounds of non-use, unless in the Member State for which conversion is requested the Community trade mark has been put to use which would be considered to be genuine use under the laws of that Member State;
   (b) for the purpose of protection in a Member State in which, in accordance with the decision of the Office or of the national court, grounds for refusal of registration or grounds for revocation or invalidity apply to the Community trade mark application or Community trade mark.
3. The national trade mark application resulting from the conversion of a Community trade mark application or a Community trade mark shall enjoy in respect of the Member State concerned the date of filing or the date of priority of that application or trade mark and, where appropriate, the seniority of a trade mark of that State claimed under Article 34 or 35.
4. Where—
   — the Community trade mark application is deemed to be withdrawn or is refused by a decision of the Office which has become final,
   — the Community trade mark ceases to have effect as a result of a decision of the Office which has become final or as a result of registration of surrender of the Community trade mark,
   the Office shall notify to the applicant or proprietor a communication fixing a period of three months from the date of that communication in which a request for conversion may be filed.
5. Where the Community trade mark application is withdrawn or the Community trade mark ceases to have effect as a result of failure to renew the registration, the request for conversion shall be filed within three months after the date on which the Community trade mark application is withdrawn or on which the registration of the Community trade mark expires.
6. Where the Community trade mark ceases to have effect as a result of a decision of a national court, the request for conversion shall be filed within three months after the date on which that decision acquired the authority of a final decision.
7. The effect referred to in Article 32 shall lapse if the request is not filed in due time.

Article 109

Submission, publication and transmission of the request for conversion

1. A request for conversion shall be filed with the Office and shall specify the Member States in which application of the procedure for registration of a national trade mark is desired. The request shall not be deemed to be filed until the conver-

sion fee has been paid.

2. If the Community trade mark application has been published, receipt of any such request shall be recorded in the Register of Community trade marks and the request for conversion shall be published.

3. The Office shall check whether conversion may be requested in accordance with Article 108(1), whether the request has been filed within the period laid down in Article 108(4), (5) or (6), as the case may be, and whether the conversion fee has been paid. If these conditions are fulfilled, the Office shall transmit the request to the central industrial property offices of the States specified therein. At the request of the central industrial property office of a State concerned, the Office shall give it any information enabling that office to decide as to the admissibility of the request.

Article 110

Formal requirements for conversion

1. Any central industrial property office to which the request is transmitted shall decide as to its admissibility.

2. A Community trade mark application or a Community trade mark transmitted in accordance with Article 109 shall not be subjected to formal requirements of national law which are different from or additional to those provided for in this Regulation or in the Implementing Regulation.

3. Any central industrial property office to which the request is transmitted may require that the applicant shall, within not less than two months—

    (a) pay the national application fee;

    (b) file a translation in one of the official languages of the State in question of the request and of the documents accompanying it;

    (c) indicate an address for service in the State in question;

    (d) supply a representation of the trade mark in the number of copies specified by the State in question.

TITLE XII

THE OFFICE

SECTION 1
GENERAL PROVISIONS

Article 111

Legal status

1. The Office shall be a body of the Community. It shall have legal personality.

2. In each of the Member States the Office shall enjoy the most extensive legal capacity accorded to legal persons under their laws; it may, in particular, acquire or dispose of movable and immovable property and may be a party to legal proceedings.

3. The Office shall be represented by its President.

Article 112

Staff

1. The Staff Regulations of officials of the European Communities, the Conditions of Employment of other servants of the European Communities, and the rules adopted by agreement between the Institutions of the European Communities for giving effect to those Staff Regulations and Conditions of Employment shall apply

to the staff of the Office, without prejudice to the application of Article 131 to the members of the Boards of Appeal.

2. Without prejudice to Article 120, the powers conferred on each Institution by the Staff Regulations and by the Conditions of Employment of other servants shall be exercised by the Office in respect of its staff.

Article 113

Privileges and immunities

The Protocol on the Privileges and Immunities of the European Communities shall apply to the Office.

Article 114

Liability

1. The contractual liability of the Office shall be governed by the law applicable to the contract in question.

2. The Court of Justice shall be competent to give judgment pursuant to any arbitration clause contained in a contract concluded by the Office.

3. In the case of non-contractual liability, the Office shall, in accordance with the general principles common to the laws of the Member States, make good any damage caused by its departments or by its servants in the performance of their duties.

4. The Court of Justice shall have jurisdiction in disputes relating to compensation for the damage referred to in paragraph 3.

5. The personal liability of its servants towards the Office shall be governed by the provisions laid down in their Staff Regulations or in the Conditions of Employment applicable to them.

Article 115

Languages

1. The application for a Community trade mark shall be filed in one of the official languages of the European Community.

2. The languages of the Office shall be English, French, German, Italian and Spanish.

3. The applicant must indicate a second language which shall be a language of the Office the use of which he accepts as a possible language of proceedings for opposition, revocation or invalidity proceedings.

If the application was filed in a language which is not one of the languages of the Office, the Office shall arrange to have the application, as described in Article 26(1), translated into the language indicated by the applicant.

4. Where the applicant for a Community trade mark is the sole party to proceedings before the Office, the language of proceedings shall be the language used for filing the application for a Community trade mark. If the application was made in a language other than the languages of the Office, the Office may send written communications to the applicant in the second language indicated by the applicant in his application.

5. The notice of opposition and an application for revocation or invalidity shall be filed in one of the languages of the Office.

6. If the language chosen, in accordance with paragraph 5, for the notice of opposition or the application for revocation or invalidity is the language of the application for a trade mark or the second language indicated when the application was filed, that language shall be the language of the proceedings.

If the language chosen, in accordance with paragraph 5, for the notice of opposition or the application for revocation or invalidity is neither the language of the application for a trade mark nor the second language indicated when the application was filed, the opposing party or the party seeking revocation or invalidity shall be required to produce, at his own expense, a translation of his application either into the language of the application for a trade mark, provided that it is a language of the Office, or into the second language indicated when the application was filed. The translation shall be produced within the period prescribed in the implementing regulation. The language into which the application has been translated shall then become the language of the proceedings.

7. Parties to opposition, revocation, invalidity or appeal proceedings may agree that a different official language of the European Community is to be the language of the proceedings.

Article 116

Publication; entries in the Register

1. An application for a Community trade mark, as described in Article 26(1), and all other information the publication of which is prescribed by this Regulation or the implementing regulation, shall be published in all the official languages of the European Community.

2. All entries in the Register of Community trade marks shall be made in all the official languages of the European Community.

3. In cases of doubt, the text in the language of the Office in which the application for the Community trade mark was filed shall be authentic. If the application was filed in an official language of the European Community other than one of the languages of the Office, the text in the second language indicated by the applicant shall be authentic.

Article 117

The translation services required for the functioning of the Office shall be provided by the Translation Centre of the Bodies of the Union once this begins operation.

Article 118

Control of legality

1. The Commission shall check the legality of those acts of the President of the Office in respect of which Community law does not provide for any check on legality by another body and of acts of the Budget Committee attached to the Office pursuant to Article 133.

2. It shall require that any unlawful acts as referred to in paragraph 1 be altered or annulled.

3. Member States and any person directly and personally involved may refer to the Commission any act as referred to in paragraph 1, whether express or implied, for the Commission to examine the legality of that act. Referral shall be made to the Commission within 15 days of the day on which the party concerned first became aware of the act in question. The Commission shall take a decision within one month. If no decision has been taken within this period, the case shall be deemed to have been dismissed.

SECTION 2

MANAGEMENT OF THE OFFICE

Article 119

Powers of the President

1. The Office shall be managed by the President.

2. To this end the President shall have in particular the following functions and powers—

    (a) he shall take all necessary steps, including the adoption of internal administrative instructions and the publication of notices, to ensure the functioning of the Office;

    (b) he may place before the Commission any proposal to amend this Regulation, the Implementing Regulation, the rules of procedure of the Boards of Appeal, the fees regulations and any other rules applying to Community trade marks after consulting the Administrative Board and, in the case of the fees regulations and the budgetary provisions of this Regulation, the Budget Committee;

    (c) he shall draw up the estimates of the revenue and expenditure of the Office and shall implement the budget;

    (d) he shall submit a management report to the Commission, the European Parliament and the Administrative Board each year;

    (e) he shall exercise in respect of the staff the powers laid down in Article 112(2);

    (f) he may delegate his powers.

3. The President shall be assisted by one or more Vice-Presidents. If the President is absent or indisposed the Vice-President or one of the Vice-Presidents shall take his place in accordance with the procedure laid down by the Administrative Board.

Article 120

Appointment of senior officials

1. The President of the Office shall be appointed by the Council from a list of at most three candidates, which shall be prepared by the Administrative Board. Power to dismiss the President shall lie with the Council, acting on a proposal from the Administrative Board.

2. The term of office of the President shall not exceed five years. This term of office shall be renewable.

3. The Vice-President or Vice-Presidents of the Office shall be appointed or dismissed as in paragraph 1, after consultation with the President.

4. The Council shall exercise disciplinary authority over the officials referred to in paragraphs 1 and 3 of this Article.

SECTION 3

ADMINISTRATIVE BOARD

Article 121

Creation and powers

1. An Administrative Board is hereby set up, attached to the Office. Without prejudice to the powers attributed to the Budget Committee in Section 5—budget and financial control—the Administrative Board shall have the powers defined below.

2. The Administrative Board shall draw up the lists of candidates provided for in

Article 120.

3. It shall fix the date for the first filing of Community trade mark applications, pursuant to Article 143(3).

4. It shall advise the President on matters for which the Office is responsible.

5. It shall be consulted before adoption of the guidelines for examination in the Office and in the other cases provided for in this Regulation.

6. It may deliver opinions and requests for information to the President and to the Commission where it considers that this is necessary.

Article 122

Composition

1. The Administrative Board shall be composed of one representative of each Member State and one representative of the Commission and their alternates.

2. The members of the Administrative Board may, subject to the provisions of its rules of procedure, be assisted by advisers or experts.

Article 123

Chairmanship

1. The Administrative Board shall elect a chairman and a deputy chairman from among its members. The deputy chairman shall ex officio replace the chairman in the event of his being prevented from attending to his duties.

2. The duration of the terms of office of the chairman and the deputy chairman shall be three years. The terms of office shall be renewable.

Article 124

Meetings

1. Meetings of the Administrative Board shall be convened by its chairman.

2. The President of the Office shall take part in the deliberations, unless the Administrative Board decides otherwise.

3. The Administrative Board shall hold an ordinary meeting once a year; in addition, it shall meet on the initiative of its chairman or at the request of the Commission or of one-third of the Member States.

4. The Administrative Board shall adopt rules of procedure.

5. The Administrative Board shall take its decisions by a simple majority of the representatives of the Member States. However, a majority of three-quarters of the representatives of the Member States shall be required for the decisions which the Administrative Board is empowered to take under Article 120(1) and (3). In both cases each Member State shall have one vote.

6. The Administrative Board may invite observers to attend its meetings.

7. The Secretariat for the Administrative Board shall be provided by the Office.

SECTION 4
IMPLEMENTATION OF PROCEDURES

Article 125

Competence

For taking decisions in connection with the procedures laid down in this Regulation, the following shall be competent—

    (a) Examiners;

    (b) Opposition Divisions;

(c) an Administration of Trade Marks and Legal Division;
(d) Cancellation Divisions;
(e) Boards of Appeal.

Article 126

Examiners

An examiner shall be responsible for taking decisions on behalf of the Office in relation to an application for registration of a Community trade mark, including the matters referred to in Articles 36, 37, 38 and 66, except in so far as an Opposition Division is responsible.

Article 127

Opposition Divisions

1. An Opposition Division shall be responsible for taking decisions on an opposition to an application to register a Community trade mark.
2. An Opposition Division shall consist of three members. At least one of the members must be legally qualified.

Article 128

Administration of Trade Marks and Legal Division

1. The Administration of Trade Marks and Legal Division shall be responsible for those decisions required by this Regulation which do not fall within the competence of an examiner, an Opposition Division or a Cancellation Division. It shall in particular be responsible for decisions in respect of entries in the Register of Community trade marks.
2. It shall also be responsible for keeping the list of professional representatives which is referred to in Article 89.
3. A decision of the Division shall be taken by one member.

Article 129

Cancellation Divisions

1. A Cancellation Division shall be responsible for taking decisions in relation to an application for the revocation or declaration of invalidity of a Community trade mark.
2. A Cancellation Division shall consist of three members. At least one of the members must be legally qualified.

Article 130

Boards of Appeal

1. The Boards of Appeal shall be responsible for deciding on appeals from decisions of the examiners, Opposition Divisions, Administration of Trade Marks and Legal Division and Cancellation Divisions.
2. A Board of Appeal shall consist of three members. At least two of the members must be legally qualified.

Article 131

Independence of the members of the Boards of Appeal

1. The members, including the chairmen, of the Boards of Appeal shall be appointed, in accordance with the procedure laid down in Article 120, for the

appointment of the President of the Office, for a term of five years. They may not be removed from office during this term, unless there are serious grounds for such removal and the Court of Justice, on application by the body which appointed them, takes a decision to this effect. Their term of office shall be renewable.

2. The members of the Boards of Appeal shall be independent. In their decisions they shall not be bound by any instructions.

3. The members of the Boards of Appeal may not be examiners or members of the Opposition Divisions, Administration of Trade Marks and Legal Division or Cancellation Divisions.

Article 132

Exclusion and objection

1. Examiners and members of the Divisions set up within the Office or of the Boards of Appeal may not take part in any proceedings if they have any personal interest therein, or if they have previously been involved as representatives of one of the parties. Two of the three members of an Opposition Division shall not have taken part in examining the application. Members of the Cancellation Divisions may not take part in any proceedings if they have participated in the final decision on the case in the proceedings for registration or opposition proceedings. Members of the Boards of Appeal may not take part in appeal proceedings if they participated in the decision under appeal.

2. If, for one of the reasons mentioned in paragraph 1 or for any other reason, a member of a Division or of a Board of Appeal considers that he should not take part in any proceedings, he shall inform the Division or Board accordingly.

3. Examiners and members of the Divisions or of a Board of Appeal may be objected to by any party for one of the reasons mentioned in paragraph 1, or if suspected of partiality. An objection shall not be admissible if, while being aware of a reason for objection, the party has taken a procedural step. No objection may be based upon the nationality of examiners or members.

4. The Divisions and the Boards of Appeal shall decide as to the action to be taken in the cases specified in paragraphs 2 and 3 without the participation of the member concerned. For the purposes of taking this decision the member who withdraws or has been objected to shall be replaced in the Division or Board of Appeal by his alternate.

SECTION 5
BUDGET AND FINANCIAL CONTROL

Article 133

Budget Committee

1. A Budget Committee is hereby set up, attached to the Office. The Budget Committee shall have the powers assigned to it in this Section and in Article 39(4).

2. Articles 121(6), 122, 123 and 124(1) to (4), (6) and (7) shall apply to the Budget Committee mutatis mutandis.

3. The Budget Committee shall take its decisions by a simple majority of the representatives of the Member States. However, a majority of three-quarters of the representatives of the Member States shall be required for the decisions which the Budget Committee is empowered to take under Articles 39(4), 135(3) and 138. In both cases each Member State shall have one vote.

Article 134

Budget

1. Estimates of all the Office's revenue and expenditure shall be prepared for each financial year and shall be shown in the Office's budget, and each financial year shall correspond with the calendar year.

2. The revenue and expenditure shown in the budget shall be in balance.

3. Revenue shall comprise, without prejudice to other types of income, total fees payable under the fees regulations, and, to the extent necessary, a subsidy entered against a specific heading of the general budget of the European Communities, Commission Section.

Article 135

Preparation of the budget

1. The President shall draw up each year an estimate of the Office's revenue and expenditure for the following year and shall send it to the Budget Committee not later than 31 March in each year, together with a list of posts.

2. Should the budget estimates provide for a Community subsidy, the Budget Committee all immediately forward the estimate to the Commission, which shall forward it to the budget authority of the Communities. The Commission may attach an opinion on the estimate along with an alternative estimate.

3. The Budget Committee shall adopt the budget, which shall include the Office's list of posts. Should the budget estimates contain a subsidy from the general budget of the Communities, the Office's budget shall, if necessary, be adjusted.

Article 136

Financial control

Control of commitment and payment of all expenditure and control of the existence and recovery of all revenue of the Office shall be carried out by the Financial Controller appointed by the Budget Committee.

Article 137

Auditing of accounts

1. Not later than 31 March in each year the President shall transmit to the Commission, the European Parliament, the Budget Committee and the Court of Auditors accounts of the Office's total revenue and expenditure for the preceding financial year. The Court of Auditors shall examine them in accordance with Article 188c of the Treaty.

2. The Budget Committee shall give a discharge to the President of the Office in respect of the implementation of the budget.

Article 138

Financial provisions

The Budget Committee shall, after consulting the Court of Auditors of the European Communities and the Commission, adopt internal financial provisions specifying, in particular, the procedure for establishing and implementing the Office's budget. As far as is compatible with the particular nature of the Office, the financial provisions shall be based on the financial regulations adopted for other bodies set up by the Community.

Article 139

Fees regulations

1. The fees regulations shall determine in particular the amounts of the fees and the ways in which they are to be paid.
2. The amounts of the fees shall be fixed at such a level as to ensure that the revenue in respect thereof is in principle sufficient for the budget of the Office to be balanced.
3. The fees regulations shall be adopted and amended in accordance with the procedure laid down in Article 141.

TITLE XIII

FINAL PROVISIONS

Article 140

Community implementing provisions

1. The rules implementing this Regulation shall be adopted in an Implementing Regulation.
2. In addition to the fees provided for in the preceding Articles, fees shall be charged, in accordance with the detailed rules of application laid down in the Implementing Regulation, in the cases listed below —
    1. alteration of the representation of a Community trade mark;
    2. late payment of the registration fee;
    3. issue of a copy of the certificate of registration;
    4. registration of the transfer of a Community trade mark;
    5. registration of a licence or another right in respect of a Community trade mark;
    6. registration of a licence or another right in respect of an application for a Community trade mark;
    7. cancellation of the registration of a licence or another right;
    8. alteration of a registered Community trade mark;
    9. issue of an extract from the Register;
    10. inspection of the files;
    11. issue of copies of file documents;
    12. issue of certified copies of the application;
    13. communication of information in a file;
    14. review of the determination of the procedural costs to be refunded.
3. The Implementing Regulation and the rules of procedure of the Boards of Appeal shall be adopted and amended in accordance with the procedure laid down in Article 141.

Article 141

Establishment of a committee and procedure for the adoption of implementing regulations

1. The Commission shall be assisted by a Committee on Fees, Implementation Rules and the Procedure of the Boards of Appeal of the Office for Harmonisation in the Internal Market (trade marks and designs), which shall be composed of representatives of the Member States and chaired by a representative of the Commission.
2. The representative of the Commission shall submit to the Committee a draft of the measures to be taken. The Committee shall deliver its opinion on the draft

within a time limit which the chairman may lay down according to the urgency of the matter. The opinion shall be delivered by the majority laid down in Article 148(2) of the Treaty in the case of decisions which the Council is required to adopt on a proposal from the Commission. The votes of the representatives of the Member States within the Committee shall be weighted in the manner set out in that Article. The chairman shall not vote.

The Commission shall adopt the measures envisaged if they are in accordance with the opinion of the Committee.

If the measures envisaged are not in accordance with the opinion of the Committee, or if no opinion is delivered, the Commission shall, without delay, submit to the Council a proposal relating to the measures to be taken. The Council shall act by a qualified majority.

If, on the expiry of a period of three months from the date of referral to the Council, the Council has not acted, the proposed measures shall be adopted by the Commission, save where the Council has decided against the measures by a simple majority.

Article 142

Compatibility with other Community legal provisions
This Regulation shall not affect Council Regulation 2081/92/EEC on the protection of geographical indications and designations of origin for agricultural products and foodstuffs of 14 July 1992, and in particular Article 14 thereof.

Article 143

Entry into force
1. This Regulation shall enter into force on the 60th day following that of its publication in the Official Journal of the European Communities.
2. The Member States shall within three years following entry into force of this Regulation take the necessary measures for the purpose of implementing Articles 91 and 110 hereof and shall forthwith inform the Commission of those measures.
3. Applications for Community trade marks may be filed at the Office from the date fixed by the Administrative Board on the recommendation of the President of the Office.
4. Applications for Community trade marks filed within three months before the date referred to in paragraph 3 shall be deemed to have been filed on that date.

This Regulation shall be binding in its entirety and directly applicable in all Member States.

    Statement by the Council and the Commission on the seat of the Office for Harmonisation in the Internal Market (trade marks and designs)1

'In adopting the Regulation on the Community Trade Mark, the Council and the Commission note—
— that the representatives of the Governments of the Member States, meeting at Head of State and Government level on 29 October 1993, decided that the Office for Harmonisation in the Internal Market (trade marks and designs) should have its seat in Spain, in a town to be determined by the Spanish Government;
— that the Spanish Government has designated Alicante as the seat of the Office.'

Notes
Date of publication in OJ: OJ L11, 14.1.94, p 36.

COMMISSION REGULATION

of 13 December 1995

implementing Council Regulation 40/94/EC on the Community trade mark

(2868/95/EC)

Notes
Date of publication in OJ: OJ L303, 15.12.95, p 1.

THE COMMISSION OF THE EUROPEAN COMMUNITIES,

Having regard to the Treaty establishing the European Community,

Having regard to Council Regulation 40/94/EC of 20 December 1993 on the Community trade mark as amended by Regulation 3288/94/EC, and in particular Article 140 thereof,

Whereas Regulation 40/94/EC (hereinafter the 'Regulation') creates a new trade mark system allowing a trade mark having effect throughout the Community to be obtained on the basis of an application to the Office for Harmonisation in the Internal Market (trade marks and designs) ('the Office');

Whereas for this purpose, the Regulation contains the necessary provisions for a procedure leading to the registration of a Community trade mark, as well as for the administration of Community trade marks, for appeals against decisions of the Office and for proceedings for the revocation or invalidation of a Community trade mark;

Whereas Article 140 of the Regulation provides that the rules implementing the Regulation shall be adopted in an implementing regulation;

Whereas the implementing regulation is to be adopted in accordance with the procedure laid down in Article 141 of the Regulation;

Whereas this implementing regulation therefore lays down the rules necessary for implementing the provisions of the Regulation on the Community trade mark;

Whereas these rules should ensure the smooth and efficient operating of trade mark proceedings before the Office;

Whereas in accordance with Article 116(1) of the Regulation, all the elements of the application for a Community trade mark specified in its Article 26(1) as well as any other information the publication of which is prescribed by this implementing regulation should be published in all the official languages of the Community;

Whereas, however, it is not appropriate for the trade mark itself, names, addresses, dates and any other similar data to be translated and published in all the official languages of the Community;

Whereas the Office should make available standard forms for proceedings before the Office in all official languages of the Community;

Whereas the measures envisaged in this Regulation are in accordance with the opinion of the Committee established under Article 141 of the Regulation,

HAS ADOPTED THIS REGULATION—

Article 1

The rules implementing the Regulation shall be as follows—

TITLE I
APPLICATION PROCEDURE

Rule 1

Content of the application

(1) The application for a Community trade mark shall contain—

(a) a request for registration of the mark as a Community trade mark,

(b) the name, address and nationality of the applicant and the State in which he is domiciled or has his seat or an establishment. Names of natural persons shall be indicated by the person's family name and given name(s). Names of legal entities, as well as bodies falling under Article 3 of the Regulation, shall be indicated by their official designation, which may be abbreviated in a customary manner; furthermore, the law of the State governing them shall be indicated. The telegraphic and teletype address, telephone as well as fax numbers and details of other data communications links may be given. Only one address shall, in principle, be indicated for each applicant; where several addresses are indicated, only the address mentioned first shall be taken into account, except where the applicant designates one of the addresses as an address for service;

(c) a list of the goods and services for which the trade mark is to be registered, in accordance with Rule 2;

(d) a representation of the mark in accordance with Rule 3;

(e) if the applicant has appointed a representative, his name and the address of his place of business in accordance with point (b); if the representative has more than one business address or if there are two or more representatives with different business addresses, the application shall indicate which address shall be used as an address for service; where such an indication is not made, only the first-mentioned address shall be taken into account as an address for service;

(f) where the priority of a previous application is claimed pursuant to Article 30 of the Regulation, a declaration to that effect, stating the date on which and the country in or for which the previous application was filed;

(g) where exhibition priority is claimed pursuant to Article 33 of the Regulation, a declaration to that effect, stating the name of the exhibition and the date of the first display of the goods or services;

(h) where the seniority of one or more earlier trade marks, registered in a Member State, including a trade mark registered in the Benelux countries or registered under international arrangements having effect in a Member State (hereinafter referred to as 'earlier registered trade marks, as referred to in Article 34 of the Regulation') is claimed pursuant to Article 34 of the Regulation, a declaration to that effect, stating the Member State or Member States in or for which the earlier mark is registered, the date from which the relevant registration was effective, the number of the relevant registration, and the goods and services for which the mark is registered;

(i) where applicable, a statement that the application is for registration of a Community collective mark pursuant to Article 64 of the Regulation;

(j) specification of the language in which the application has been filed, and of the second language pursuant to Article 115(3) of the Regulation;

(k) the signature of the applicant or his representative.

(2) The application for a Community collective mark may include the regulations governing its use.

(3) The application may include a statement by the applicant that he disclaims any exclusive right to an element of the trade mark which is not distinctive, to be specified by the applicant.

(4) If there is more than one applicant, the application may contain the appointment of one applicant or representative as common representative.

Rule 2

List of goods and services

(1) The common classification referred to in Article 1 of the Nice Agreement Concerning the International Classification of Goods and Services for the Purposes of the Registration of Marks of 15 June 1957, as revised and amended, shall be applied to the classification of the goods and services.

(2) The list of goods and services shall be worded in such a way as to indicate clearly the nature of the goods and services and to allow each item to be classified in only one class of the Nice Classification.

(3) The goods and services shall, in principle, be grouped according to the classes of the Nice classification, each group being preceded by the number of the class of that Classification to which that group of goods or services belongs and presented in the order of the classes under that Classification.

(4) The classification of goods and services shall serve exclusively administrative purposes. Therefore, goods and services may not be regarded as being similar to each other on the ground that they appear in the same class under the Nice Classification, and goods and services may not be regarded as being dissimilar from each other on the ground that they appear in different classes under the Nice Classification.

Rule 3

Representation of the mark

(1) If the applicant does not wish to claim any special graphic feature or colour, the mark shall be reproduced in normal script, as for example, by typing the letters, numerals and signs in the application. The use of small letters and capital letters shall be permitted and shall be followed accordingly in publications of the mark and in the registration by the Office.

(2) In cases other than those referred to in paragraph 1, the mark shall be reproduced on a sheet of paper separate from the sheet on which the text of the application appears. The sheet on which the mark is reproduced shall not exceed DIN A4 size (29.7 cm high, 21 cm wide) and the space used for the reproduction (type-area) shall not be larger than 26.2 cm x 17 cm. A margin of at least 2.5 cm shall be left on the left-hand side. Where it is not obvious, the correct position of the mark shall be indicated by adding the word 'top' to each reproduction. The reproduction of the mark shall be of such quality as to enable it to be reduced or enlarged to a size not more than 8 cm wide by 16 cm high for publication in the Community Trade Mark Bulletin. The separate sheet shall also indicate the name and address of the applicant. Four copies of the separate sheet carrying the reproduction shall be filed.

(3) In cases to which paragraph 2 applies, the application shall contain an indication to that effect. The application may contain a description of the mark.

(4) Where registration of a three-dimensional mark is applied for, the application shall contain an indication to that effect. The representation shall consist of a photographic reproduction or a graphic representation of the mark. The representation may contain up to six different perspectives of the mark.

(5) Where registration in colour is applied for, the application shall contain an indi-

cation to that effect. The colours making up the mark shall also be indicated. The reproduction under paragraph 2 shall consist of the colour reproduction of the mark.

(6) The President of the Office may determine that, as far as the requirements of paragraph 2 are concerned, the mark may be reproduced in the text of the application itself and not on a separate sheet of paper and that the number of copies of the reproduction of the mark may be less than four.

Rule 4

Fees for the application

The fees payable for the application shall be —
    (a) the basic fee;
    and
    (b) a class fee for each class exceeding three to which the goods or services belong according to Rule 2.

Rule 5

Filing of the application

(1) The Office shall mark the documents making up the application with the date of its receipt and the file number of the application. The Office shall issue to the applicant without delay a receipt which shall include at least the file number, a representation, description or other identification of the mark, the nature and the number of the documents and the date of their receipt.

(2) If the application is filed with the central industrial property office of a Member Sate or at the Benelux Trade Mark Office in accordance with Article 25 of the Regulation, the office of filing shall number all the pages of the application with arabic numerals. Before forwarding, the office of filing shall mark the documents making up the application with the date of receipt and the number of pages. The office of filing shall issue to the applicant without delay a receipt which shall include at least the nature and the number of the documents and the date of their receipt.

(3) If the Office receives an application forwarded by the central industrial property office of a Member State or the Benelux Trade Mark Office, it shall mark the application with the date of receipt and the file number and shall issue to the applicant without delay a receipt in accordance with the second sentence of paragraph 1, indicating the date of receipt at the Office.

Rule 6

Claiming priority

(1) Where the priority of one or more previous applications pursuant to Article 30 of the Regulation is claimed in the application, the applicant shall indicate the file number of the previous application and file a copy of it within three months from the filing date. The copy shall be certified to be an exact copy of the previous application by the authority which received the previous application, and shall be accompanied by a certificate issued by that authority stating the date of filing of the previous application.

(2) Where the applicant wishes to claim the priority of one or more previous applications pursuant to Article 30 of the Regulation subsequent to the filing of the application, the declaration of priority, stating the date on which and the country in or for which the previous application was made, shall be submitted within a period

of two months from the filing date. The indications and evidence required under paragraph 1 shall be submitted to the Office within a period of three months from receipt of the declaration of priority.

(3) If the language of the previous application is not one of the languages of the Office, the Office shall require the applicant to file, within a period specified by the Office, which shall be not less than three months, a translation of the previous application into one of these languages.

(4) The President of the Office may determine that the evidence to be provided by the applicant may consist of less than is required under paragraph 1, provided that the information required is available to the Office from other sources.

Rule 7

Exhibition priority

(1) Where the exhibition priority pursuant to Article 33 of the Regulation has been claimed in the application, the applicant shall, within three months from the filing date, file a certificate issued at the exhibition by the authority responsible for the protection of industrial property at the exhibition. This certificate shall declare that the mark was in fact used for the goods or services, and shall state the opening date of the exhibition and, where the first public use did not coincide with the opening date of the exhibition, the date of such first public use. The certificate must be accompanied by an identification of the actual use of the mark, duly certified by the abovementioned authority.

(2) Where the applicant wishes to claim an exhibition priority subsequently to the filing of the application, the declaration of priority, indicating the name of the exhibition and the date of the first display of the goods or services, shall be submitted within a period of two months from the filing date. The indications and evidence required under paragraph 1 shall be submitted to the Office within a period of three months from receipt of the declaration of priority.

Rule 8

Claiming the seniority of a national trade mark

(1) Where the seniority of one or more earlier registered trade marks, as referred to in Article 34 of the Regulation, has been claimed in the application, the applicant shall, within three months from the filing date, submit a copy of the relevant registration. The copy must be certified by the competent authority to be an exact copy of the relevant registration.

(2) Where the applicant wishes to claim the seniority of one or more earlier registered trade marks as referred to in Article 34 of the Regulation, subsequent to the filing of the application, the declaration of seniority, indicating the Member State or Member States in or for which the mark is registered, the date from which the relevant registration was effective, the number of the relevant registration, and the goods and services for which the mark is registered, shall be submitted within a period of two months from the filing date. The evidence required under paragraph 1 shall be submitted to the Office within a period of three months from receipt of the declaration of seniority.

(3) The Office shall inform the Benelux Trade Mark Office or the central industrial property office of the Member State concerned of the effective claiming of seniority.

(4) The President of the Office may determine that the evidence to be provided by the applicant may consist of less than is required under paragraph 1, provided that the information required is available to the Office from other sources.

Rule 9

Examination of requirements for a filing date and of formal requirements

(1) If the application fails to meet the requirements for according a filing date because—

    (a) the application does not contain—

        (i) a request for registration of the mark as a Community trade mark;

        (ii) information identifying the applicant;

        (iii) a list of the goods and services for which the mark is to be registered;

        (iv) a representation of the trade mark; or

    (b) the basic fee for the application has not been paid within one month of the filing of the application with the Office or, if the application has been filed with the central industrial property office of a Member State or with the Benelux Trade Mark Office, with that office,

the Office shall notify the applicant that a date of filing cannot be accorded in view of those deficiencies.

(2) If the deficiencies referred to under paragraph 1 are remedied within two months of receipt of the notification, the date on which all the deficiencies are remedied shall determine the date of filing. If the deficiencies are not remedied before the time limit expires, the application shall not be dealt with as a Community trade mark application. Any fees paid shall be refunded.

(3) Where, although a date of filing has been accorded, the examination reveals that—

    (a) the requirements of Rules 1, 2 and 3 or the other formal requirements governing applications laid down in the Regulation or in these Rules are not complied with;

    (b) the full amount of the class fees payable under Rule 4(b), read in conjunction with Commission Regulation 2869/95/EC (hereinafter 'the Fees Regulation') has not been received by the Office;

    (c) where priority has been claimed pursuant to Rules 6 and 7, either in the application itself or within two months after the date of filing, the other requirements of the said Rules are not complied with; or

    (d) where seniority has been claimed pursuant to Rule 8, either in the application itself or within two months after the date of filing, the other requirements of Rule 8 are not complied with,

the Office shall invite the applicant to remedy the deficiencies noted within such period as it may specify.

(4) If the deficiencies referred to in paragraph 3(a) are not remedied before the time limit expires, the Office shall reject the application.

(5) If the outstanding class fees are not paid before the time limit expires, the application shall be deemed to have been withdrawn, unless it is clear which class or classes the amount paid is intended to cover. In the absence of other criteria to determine which classes are intended to be covered, the Office shall take the classes in the order of the classification. The application shall be deemed to have been withdrawn with regard to those classes for which the class fees have not been paid or have not been paid in full.

(6) If the deficiencies referred to in paragraph 3 concern the claim to priority, the right of priority for the application shall be lost.

(7) If the deficiencies referred to in paragraph 3 concern the claim to seniority, the right of seniority in respect of that application shall be lost.

(8) If the deficiencies referred to in paragraph 3 concern only some of the goods and services, the Office shall refuse the application, or the right of priority or the

right of seniority shall be lost, only in so far as those goods and services are concerned.

Rule 10

Examination of the conditions relating to the entitlement to be proprietor
Where, pursuant to Article 5 of the Regulation, the applicant is not entitled to be the proprietor of a Community trade mark, the Office shall notify the applicant thereof. The Office shall specify a period within which the applicant may withdraw the application or submit his observations. Where the applicant fails to overcome the objections to registration, the Office shall refuse the application.

Rule 11

Examination as to absolute grounds for refusal
(1) Where, pursuant to Article 7 of the Regulation, the trade mark may not be registered for all or any part of the goods or services applied for, the office shall notify the applicant of the grounds for refusing registration. The Office shall specify a period within which the applicant may withdraw or amend the application or submit his observations.
(2) Where, pursuant to Article 38(2) of the Regulation, registration of the Community trade mark is subject to the applicant's stating that he disclaims any exclusive right in the non-distinctive elements in the mark, the Office shall notify the applicant thereof, stating the reasons, and shall invite him to submit the relevant statement within such period as it may specify.
(3) Where the applicant fails to overcome the ground for refusing registration or to comply with the condition laid down in paragraph 2 within the time limit, the Office shall refuse the application in whole or in part.

Rule 12

Publication of the application
The publication of the application shall contain—
    (a) the applicant's name and address;
    (b) where applicable, the name and business address of the representative appointed by the applicant other than a representative falling within the first sentence of Article 88(3) of the Regulation; if there is more than one representative with the same business address, only the name and business address of the first-named representative shall be published and it shall be followed by the words 'and others'; if there are two or more representatives with different business addresses, only the address for service determined pursuant to Rule 1(1)(e) shall be published; where an association of representatives is appointed under Rule 76(9), only the name and business address of the association shall be published;
    (c) the reproduction of the mark, together with the indications and descriptions pursuant to Rule 3; where registration in colour is applied for, the publication shall contain the indication 'in colour' and indicate the colour or colours making up the mark;
    (d) the list of goods and services, grouped according to the classes of the Nice classification, each group being preceded by the number of the class of that classification to which that group of goods or services belongs, and presented in the order of the classes of that classification;
    (e) the date of filing and the file number;

(f) where applicable, particulars of the claim of priority pursuant to Article 30 of the Regulation;

(g) where applicable, particulars of the claim of exhibition priority pursuant to Article 33 of the Regulation;

(h) where applicable, particulars of the claim of seniority pursuant to Article 34 of the Regulation;

(i) where applicable, a statement that the mark has become distinctive in consequence of the use which has been made of it, pursuant to Article 7(3) of the Regulation;

(j) where applicable, a statement that the application is for a Community collective mark;

(k) where applicable, a statement by the applicant disclaiming any exclusive right to an element of the mark pursuant to Rule 1(3) or Rule 11(2);

(l) the language in which the application was filed and the second language which the applicant has indicated pursuant to Article 115(3) of the Regulation.

Rule 13

Amendment of the application

(1) An application for amendment of the application under Article 44 of the Regulation shall contain—

(a) the file number of the application;

(b) the name and the address of the applicant in accordance with Rule 1(1)(b);

(c) where the applicant has appointed a representative, the name and the business address of the representative in accordance with Rule 1(1)(e);

(d) the indication of the element of the application to be corrected or amended, and that element in its corrected or amended version;

(e) where the amendment relates to the representation of the mark, a representation of the mark as amended, in accordance with Rule 3.

(2) Where the application for amendment is subject to the payment of a fee, the application shall not be deemed to have been filed until the required fee has been paid. If the fee has not been paid or has not been paid in full, the Office shall inform the applicant accordingly.

(3) If the requirements governing the amendment of the application are not fulfilled, the Office shall communicate the deficiency to the applicant. If the deficiency is not remedied within a period to be specified by the Office, the Office shall reject the application for amendment.

(4) Where the amendment is published pursuant to Article 44(2) of the Regulation, Rules 15 to 22 shall apply mutatis mutandis.

(5) A single application for amendment may be made for the amendment of the same element in two or more applications of the same applicant. Where the application for amendment is subject to the payment of a fee, the required fee shall be paid in respect of each application to be amended.

(6) Paragraphs 1 to 5 shall apply mutatis mutandis for applications to correct the name or the business address of a representative appointed by the applicant. Such applications shall not be subject to the payment of a fee.

Rule 14

Correction of mistakes and errors in publications

(1) Where the publication of the application contains a mistake or error attributable

to the Office, the Office shall correct the mistake or error acting of its own motion or at the request of the applicant.

(2) Where a request as referred to in paragraph 1 is made by the applicant, Rule 13 shall apply mutatis mutandis. The request shall not be subject to the payment of a fee.

(3) The corrections effected under this Rule shall be published.

(4) Article 42(2) of the Regulation and Rules 15 to 22 shall apply mutatis mutandis where the correction concerns the list of goods or services or the representation of the mark.

TITLE II
PROCEDURE FOR OPPOSITION AND PROOF OF USE

Rule 15

Contents of the notice of opposition

(1) Opposition may be entered on the basis of one or more earlier marks within the meaning of Article 8(2) of the Regulation ('earlier marks') or of one or more other earlier rights within the meaning of Article 8(4) of the Regulation ('earlier rights').

(2) The notice of opposition shall contain—
- (a) as concerns the application against which opposition is entered—
    - (i) the file number of the application against which opposition is entered;
    - (ii) an indication of the goods and services listed in the Community trade mark application against which opposition is entered;
    - (iii) the name of the applicant for the Community trade mark;
- (b) as concerns the earlier mark or the earlier right on which the opposition is based—
    - (i) where the opposition is based on an earlier mark, a statement to that effect and an indication that the earlier mark is a Community mark or an indication of the Member State or Member States including, where applicable, the Benelux, where the earlier mark has been registered or applied for, or, where the earlier mark is an internationally registered mark, an indication of the Member State or Member States including, where applicable, the Benelux, to which protection of that earlier mark has been extended;
    - (ii) where available, the file number or the registration number and the filing date, including the priority date of the earlier mark;
    - (iii) where the opposition is based on an earlier mark which is a well-known mark within the meaning of Article 8(2)(c) of the Regulation, an indication to that effect and an indication of the Member State or Member States in which the earlier mark is well-known;
    - (iv) where the opposition is based on an earlier mark having a reputation within the meaning of Article 8(5) of the Regulation, an indication to that effect, and an indication of where that earlier mark is registered or applied for in accordance with subparagraph (i);
    - (v) where the opposition is based on an earlier right, an indication to that effect, and an indication of the Member State or Member States where that earlier right exists;
    - (vi) a representation and, where appropriate, a description of the earlier mark or earlier right;
    - (vii) the goods and services in respect of which the earlier mark has been registered or applied for or in respect of which the earlier mark is

well-known within the meaning of Article 8(2)(c) of the Regulation or has a reputation within the meaning of Article 8(5) of the Regulation; the opposing party shall, when indicating all the goods and services for which the earlier mark is protected, also indicate those goods and services on which the opposition is based;

(c) as concerns the opposing party —

    (i) where the opposition is entered by the proprietor of the earlier mark or of the earlier right, his name and address in accordance with Rule 1(1)(b) and an indication that he is the proprietor of such mark or right;

    (ii) where opposition is entered by a licensee, the name of the licensee and his address in accordance with Rule 1(1)(b) and an indication that he has been authorised to enter the opposition;

    (iii) where the opposition is entered by the successor in title to the registered proprietor of a Community trade mark who has not yet been registered as new proprietor, an indication to that effect, the name and address of the opposing party in accordance with Rule 1(1)(b), and an indication of the date on which the application for registration of the new proprietor was received by the Office or, where this information is not available, was sent to the Office;

    (iv) where opposition is entered on the basis of an earlier right by a person who is not the proprietor of that right, the name of the person and his address in accordance with Rule 1(1)(b) and an indication that he is entitled under the relevant national law to exercise that right;

    (v) where the opposing party has appointed a representative, the name of the representative and his business in accordance with Rule 1(1)(e);

(d) a specification of the grounds on which the opposition is based.

(3) Paragraphs 1 and 2 shall apply mutatis mutandis to an opposition entered pursuant to Article 8(3) of the Regulation.

Rule 16

Facts, evidence and arguments presented in support of the opposition

(1) Every notice of opposition may contain particulars of the facts, evidence and arguments presented in support of the opposition, accompanied by the relevant supporting documents.

(2) If the opposition is based on an earlier mark which is not a Community trade mark, the notice of opposition shall preferably be accompanied by evidence of the registration or filing of that earlier mark, such as a certificate of registration. If the opposition is based on a well-known mark as referred to in Article 8(2)(c) of the Regulation or on a mark having a reputation as referred to in Article 8(5) of the Regulation, the notice of opposition shall in principle be accompanied by evidence, attesting that it is well-known or that it has a reputation. If the opposition is entered on the basis of any other earlier right, the notice of opposition shall in principle be accompanied by appropriate evidence on the acquisition and scope of protection of that right.

(3) The particulars of the facts, evidence and arguments and other supporting documents as referred to in paragraphs 1, and the evidence referred to in paragraph 2 may, if they are not submitted together with the notice of opposition or subsequent thereto, be submitted within such period after commencement of the opposition proceedings as the Office may specify pursuant to Rule 20(2).

Rule 17

Use of languages in opposition proceedings

(1) Where the notice of opposition is not filed in the language of the application for registration of the Community trade mark, if that language is one of the languages of the Office, or in the second language indicated when the application was filed, the opposing party shall file a translation of the notice of opposition in one of those languages within a period of one month from the expiry of the opposition period.

(2) Where the evidence in support of the opposition as provided for in Rule 16(1) and (2) is not filed in the language of the opposition proceedings, the opposing party shall file a translation of that evidence into that language within a period of one month from the expiry of the opposition period or, where applicable, within the period specified by the Office pursuant to Rule 16(3).

(3) Where the opposing party or the applicant informs the Office, before the date on which the opposition proceedings shall be deemed to commence pursuant to Rule 19(1), that the applicant and the opposing party have agreed on a different language for the opposition proceeding pursuant to Article 115(7) of the Regulation, the opposing party shall, where the notice of opposition has not been filed in that language, file a translation of the notice of opposition in that language within a period of one month from the said date.

Rule 18

Rejection of notice of opposition as inadmissible

(1) If the Office finds that the notice of opposition does not comply with the provisions of Article 42 of the Regulation, or where the notice of opposition does not clearly identify the application against which opposition is entered or the earlier mark or the earlier right on the basis of which the opposition is being entered, the Office shall reject the notice of opposition as inadmissible unless those deficiencies have been remedied before expiry of the opposition period. If the opposition fee has not been paid within the opposition period, the notice of opposition shall be deemed not to have been entered. If the opposition fee has been paid after the expiry of the opposition period, it shall be refunded to the opposing party.

(2) If the Office finds that the notice of opposition does not comply with other provisions of the Regulation or of these Rules, it shall inform the opposing party accordingly and shall call upon him to remedy the deficiencies noted within a period of two months. If the deficiencies are not remedied before the time limit expires, the Office shall reject the notice of opposition as inadmissible.

(3) Any decision to reject a notice of opposition as inadmissible under paragraphs 1 or 2 shall be communicated to the applicant.

Rule 19

Commencement of opposition proceedings

(1) If the Office does not reject the notice of opposition in accordance with Rule 18, it shall communicate the opposition to the applicant and shall invite him to file his observations within such period as it may specify. The Office shall draw the applicant's attention to the fact that the opposition proceedings shall be deemed to commence two months after receipt of the communication, unless the applicant informs the Office, before the expiry of this period, that he withdraws his application or restricts the application to goods and services against which the opposition is not directed.

(2) The Office may, pursuant to Rule 71, grant an extension of the period referred to

in the second sentence of paragraph 1 where such request is presented jointly by the applicant and the opposing party.

(3) There the application is withdrawn or restricted within the period specified in the second sentence of paragraph 1 or within any extension of that period granted under paragraph 2, the Office shall inform the opposing party accordingly and shall refund the opposition fee.

Rule 20

Examination of opposition

(1) If the application is not withdrawn or restricted pursuant to Rule 19, the applicant shall file his observations within the period specified by the Office in its communication referred to in the first sentence of Rule 19(1).

(2) Where the notice of opposition does not contain particulars of the facts, evidence and arguments as referred to in Rule 16(1) and (2), the Office shall call upon the opposing party to submit such particulars within a period specified by the Office. Any submission by the opposing party shall be communicated to the applicant who shall be given an opportunity to reply within a period specified by the Office.

(3) If the applicant files no observations, the Office may give a ruling on the opposition on the basis of the evidence before it.

(4) The observations filed by the applicant shall be communicated to the opposing party who shall be called upon by the Office, if it considers it necessary to do so, to reply within a period specified by the Office.

(5) If, pursuant to Article 44(1) of the Regulation, the applicant restricts the list of goods and services, the Office shall communicate this to the opposing party and call upon him, within such period as it may specify, to submit observations stating whether he maintains the opposition and, if so, against which of the remaining goods and services.

(6) The Office may suspend any opposition proceeding where the opposition is based on an application for registration pursuant to Article 8(2)(b) of the Regulation until a final decision is taken in that proceeding, or where other circumstances are such that such suspension is appropriate.

Rule 21

Multiple oppositions

(1) Where a number of oppositions have been entered in respect of the same application for a Community trade mark, the Office may deal with them in one set of proceedings. The Office may subsequently decide to no longer deal with them in this way.

(2) If a preliminary examination of one or more oppositions reveals that the Community trade mark for which an application for registration has been filed is possibly not eligible for registration in respect of some or all of the goods or services for which registration is sought, the Office may suspend the other opposition proceedings. The Office shall inform the remaining opposing parties of any relevant decisions taken during those proceedings which are continued.

(3) Once a decision rejecting the application has become final, the oppositions on which a decision was deferred in accordance with paragraph 2 shall be deemed to have been disposed of and the opposing parties concerned shall be informed accordingly. Such disposition shall be considered to constitute a case which has not proceeded to judgment within the meaning of Article 81(4) of the Regulation.

(4) The Office shall refund 50% of the opposition fee paid by each opposing party

whose opposition is deemed to have been disposed of in accordance with paragraphs 1, 2 and 3.

Rule 22

Proof of use
(1) Where, pursuant to Article 43(2) or (3) of the Regulation, the opposing party has to furnish proof of use or show that there are proper reasons for non-use, the Office shall invite him to provide the proof required within such period as it shall specify. If the opposing party does not provide such proof before the time limit expires, the Office shall reject the opposition.
(2) The indications and evidence for the furnishing of proof of use shall consist of indications concerning the place, time, extent and nature of use of the opposing trade mark for the goods and services in respect of which it is registered and on which the opposition is based, and evidence in support of these indications in accordance with paragraph 3.
(3) The evidence shall, in principle, be confined to the submission of supporting documents and items such as packages, labels, price lists, catalogues, invoices, photographs, newspaper advertisements, and statements in writing as referred to in Article 76(1)(f) of the Regulation.
(4) Where the evidence supplied pursuant to paragraphs 1, 2 and 3 is not in the language of the opposition proceedings, the Office may require the opposing party to submit a translation of that evidence in that language, within a period specified by the Office.

TITLE III
REGISTRATION PROCEDURE

Rule 23

Registration of the trade mark
(1) The registration fee provided for in Article 45 of the Regulation shall consist of—
    (a) a basic fee;
    and
    (b) a class fee for each class exceeding three in respect of which the mark is to be registered.
(2) Where no opposition has been entered or where any opposition entered has been finally disposed of by withdrawal, rejection or other disposition, the Office shall request the applicant to pay the registration fee within two months of receipt of the request.
(3) If the registration fee is not paid within due time, it may still be validly paid within two months of notification of a communication pointing out the failure to observe the time limit, provided that within this period the additional fee specified in the Fees Regulations is paid.
(4) On receipt of the registration fee the mark applied for and the particulars referred to in Rule 84(2) shall be recorded in the Register of Community trade marks.
(5) The registration shall be published in the Community Trade Marks Bulletin.
(6) The registration fee shall be refunded if the trade mark applied for is not registered.

Rule 24

Certificate of registration
(1) The Office shall issue to the proprietor of the trade mark a certificate of registration which shall contain the entries in the Register provided for in Rule 84(2) and a statement to the effect that those entries have been recorded in the Register.
(2) The proprietor of the trade mark may request that certified or uncertified copies of the certificate of registration be supplied to him upon payment of a fee.

Rule 25

Alteration of the registration
(1) An application for alteration of the registration pursuant to Article 48(2) of the Regulation shall contain—
    (a) the registration number,
    (b) the name and the address of the proprietor of the mark in accordance with Rule 1(1)(b);
    (c) where the proprietor has appointed a representative, the name and the business address of the representative in accordance with Rule 1(1)(e);
    (d) the indication of the element in the representation of the mark to be altered and that element in its altered version;
    (e) a representation of the mark as altered, in accordance with Rule 3.
(2) The application shall be deemed not to have been filed until the required fee has been paid. If the fee has not been paid or has not been paid in full, the Office shall inform the applicant accordingly.
(3) If the requirements governing the alteration of the registration are not fulfilled, the Office shall communicate the deficiency to the applicant. If the deficiency is not remedied within a period to be specified by the Office, the Office shall reject the application.
(4) Where the registration of the alteration is challenged pursuant to Article 48(3) of the Regulation, the provisions on opposition contained in the Regulation and in these Rules shall apply mutatis mutandis.
(5) A single application may be made for the alteration of the same element in two or more registrations of the same proprietor. The required fee shall be paid in respect of each registration to be altered.

Rule 26

Change of the name or address of the proprietor of the Community trade mark or of his registered representative
(1) A change of the name or address of the proprietor of the Community trade mark which is not an alteration of the Community trade mark pursuant to Article 48(2) of the Regulation and which is not the consequence of a whole or partial transfer of the registered mark shall, at the request of the proprietor, be recorded in the register.
(2) An application for the change of the name or address of the proprietor of the registered mark shall contain—
    (a) the registration number of the mark;
    (b) the name and the address of the proprietor of the mark as recorded in the register;
    (c) the indication of the name and address of the proprietor of the mark, as amended, in accordance with Rule 1(1)(e).
    (d) where the proprietor has appointed a representative, the name and the business address of the representative, in accordance with Rule 1(1)(e).

(3) The application shall not be subject to payment of a fee.

(4) A single application may be made for the change of the name or address in respect of two or more registrations of the same proprietor.

(5) If the requirements governing the recording of a change are not fulfilled, the Office shall communicate the deficiency to the applicant. If the deficiency is not remedied within a period to be specified by the Office, the Office shall reject the application.

(6) Paragraphs 1 to 5 shall apply mutatis mutandis to a change of the name or address of the registered representative.

(7) Paragraphs 1 to 6 shall apply mutatis mutandis to applications for Community trade marks. The change shall be recorded in the files kept by the Office on the Community trade mark application.

Rule 27

Correction of mistakes and errors in the register and in the publication of the registration

(1) Where the registration of the mark or the publication of the registration contains a mistake or error attributable to the Office, the Office shall correct the error or mistake of its own motion or at the request of the proprietor.

(2) Where such a request is made by the proprietor, Rule 26 shall apply mutatis mutandis. The request shall not be subject to payment of a fee.

(3) The Office shall publish the corrections made under this Rule.

Rule 28

Claiming seniority after registration of the Community trade mark

(1) An application pursuant to Article 35 of the Regulation to obtain the seniority of one or more earlier registered trade marks as referred to in Article 34 of the Regulation, shall contain—

    (a) the registration number of the Community trade mark;

    (b) the name and address of the proprietor of the Community trade mark in accordance with Rule 1(1)(b);

    (c) where the proprietor has appointed a representative, the name and the business address of the representative in accordance with Rule 1(1)(e);

    (d) an indication of the Member State or Member States in or for which the earlier mark is registered, the date from which the relevant registration was effective, the number of the relevant registration, and the goods and services for which the earlier mark is registered;

    (e) an indication of the goods and services in respect of which seniority is claimed;

    (f) a copy of the relevant registration; the copy must be certified as an exact copy of the relevant registration by the competent authority.

(2) If the requirements governing the claiming of seniority are nor fulfilled, the Office shall communicate the deficiency to the applicant. If the deficiency is not remedied within a period specified by the Office, the Office shall reject the application.

(3) The Office shall inform the Benelux Trade Mark Office or the central industrial property office of the Member State concerned of the effective claiming of seniority.

(4) The President of the Office may determine that the material to be provided by the applicant may consist of less than is required under paragraph 1(f), provided that the information required is available to the Office from other sources.

TITLE IV
RENEWAL

Rule 29

Notification of expiry
At least six months before expiry of the registration the Office shall inform the proprietor of the Community trade mark, and any person having a registered right, including a licence, in respect of the Community trade mark, that the registration is approaching expiry. Failure to give such notification shall not affect the expiry of the registration.

Rule 30

Renewal of registration
(1) An application for renewal shall contain—
- (a) where the application is filed by the proprietor of the trade mark, his name and address in accordance with Rule 1(1)(b);
- (b) where the application is filed by a person expressly authorised to do so by the proprietor of the mark, the name and address of that person and evidence that he is authorised to file the application;
- (c) where the applicant has appointed a representative, the name and business address of the representative in accordance with Rule 1(1)(e);
- (d) the registration number;
- (e) an indication that renewal is requested for all the goods and services covered by the registration or, if the renewal is not requested for all the goods and services for which the mark is registered, an indication of those classes or those goods and services for which renewal is requested or those classes or those goods and services for which renewal is not requested, grouped according to the classes of the Nice classification, each group being preceded by the number of the class of that classification to which that group of goods or services belongs and presented in the order of the classes of that classification.

(2) The fees payable under Article 47 of the Regulation for the renewal of a Community trade mark shall consist of—
- (a) a basic fee;
- (b) a class fee for each class exceeding three in the list of classes in respect of which renewal is applied for as shown in paragraph 1(e); and
- (c) where applicable, the additional fee for late payment of the renewal fee or late submission of the request for renewal, pursuant to Article 47(3) of the Regulation, as specified in the Fees Regulation.

(3) Where the application for renewal is filed within the time periods provided for in Article 47(3) of the Regulation, but the other conditions governing renewal provided for in Article 47 of the Regulation and these Rules are not satisfied, the Office shall inform the applicant of the deficiencies found. If the application is filed by a person whom the proprietor of the trade mark has expressly authorised to do so, the proprietor of the trade mark shall receive a copy of the notification.

(4) Where an application for renewal is not submitted or is submitted after expiry of the period provided for in the third sentence of Article 47(3) of the Regulation, or if

the fees are not paid or are paid only after the period in question has expired, or if the deficiencies are not remedied within that period, the Office shall determine that the registration has expired and shall so notify the proprietor of the Community trade mark and, where appropriate, the applicant and the person recorded in the Register as having rights in the mark. Where the fees paid are insufficient to cover all the classes of goods and services for which renewal is requested, such a determination shall not be made if it is clear which class or classes are to be covered. In the absence of other criteria, the Office shall take the classes into account in the order of classification.

(5) Where the determination made pursuant to paragraph 4 has become final, the Office shall cancel the mark from the register. The cancellation shall take effect from the day following the day on which the existing registration expired.

(6) Where the renewal fees provided for in paragraph 2 have been paid but the registration is not renewed, those fees shall be refunded.

TITLE V
TRANSFER, LICENCES AND OTHER RIGHTS, CHANGES

Rule 31

Transfer

(1) An application for registration of a transfer under Article 17 of the Regulation shall contain—
- (a) the registration number of the Community trade mark;
- (b) particulars of the new proprietor in accordance with Rule 1(1)(b);
- (c) where not all the registered goods or services are included in the transfer, particulars of the registered goods or services to which the transfer relates;
- (d) documents duly establishing the transfer in accordance with Article 17(2) and (3) of the Regulation;

(2) The application may contain, where applicable, the name and business address of the representative of the new proprietor, to be set out in accordance with Rule 1(1)(e).

(3) Transfers to any natural or legal persons who cannot be proprietors of Community trade marks pursuant to Article 5 of the Regulation shall not be registered.

(4) The application shall not be deemed to have been filed until the required fee has been paid. If the fee is not paid or is not paid in full, the Office shall so notify the applicant.

(5) It shall constitute sufficient proof of transfer under paragraph 1(d)—
- (a) that the application for registration of the transfer is signed by the registered proprietor or his representative and by the successor in title or his representative; or,
- (b) that the application, if submitted by the successor in title, is accompanied by a declaration, signed by the registered proprietor or his representative, that he agrees to the registration of the successor in title; or
- (c) that the application is accompanied by a completed transfer form or document, as specified in Rule 83(1)(d), signed by the registered proprietor or his representative and by the successor in title or his representative.

(6) Where the conditions applicable to the registration of a transfer, as laid down in Article 17(1) to (4) of the Regulation, in paragraphs 1 to 4 above, and in other applicable Rules are not fulfilled, the Office shall notify the applicant of the deficiencies. If the deficiencies are not remedied within a period specified by the

Office, it shall reject the application for registration of the transfer.

(7) A single app.ication for registration of a transfer may be submitted for two or more marks, provided that the registered proprietor and the successor in title are the same in each case.

(8) Paragraphs 1 to 7 shall apply mutatis mutandis to applications for Community trade marks. The transfer shall be recorded in the files kept by the Office concerning the Community trade mark application.

Rule 32

Partial Transfers

(1) Where the application for registration of a transfer relates only to some of the goods and services for which the mark is registered, the application shall contain an indication of the goods and services to which the partial transfer relates.

(2) The goods and services in the original registration shall be distributed between the remaining registration and the new registration so that the goods and services in the remaining registration and the new registration shall not overlap.

(3) Rule 31 shall apply mutatis mutandis to applications for registrations of a partial transfer.

(4) The Office shall establish a separate file for the new registration, which shall consist of a complete copy of the file of the original registration and the application for registration of the partial transfer; a copy of that application shall be included in the file of the remaining registration. The Office shall also assign a new registration number to the new registration.

(5) Any application made by the original proprietor pending with regard to the original registration shall be deemed to be pending with regard to the remaining registration and the new registration. Where such application is subject to the payment of fees and these fees have been paid by the original proprietor, the new proprietor shall not be liable to pay any additional fees with regard to such application.

Rule 33

Registration of licences and other rights

(1) Rule 31(1)(a), (b) and (c), (2), (4) and (7) shall apply mutatis mutandis to the registration of the grant or transfer of a licence, to registration of the creation or transfer of a right in rem in respect of a Community trade mark, and to registration of enforcement measures. However, where a Community trade mark is involved in bankruptcy or like proceedings, the request of the competent national authority for an entry in the register to this effect shall not be subject to payment of a fee.

(2) Where the Community trade mark is licensed for only part of the goods and services for which the mark is registered, or for only a part of the Community, or for a limited period of time, the application for registration shall indicate the goods and services or the part of the Community or the time period for which the licence is granted.

(3) Where the conditions applicable to registration, as laid down in Articles 19, 20 or 22 of the Regulation, in paragraphs 1 and 2 above, and the other applicable Rules are not fulfilled, the Office shall notify the applicant of the irregularity. If the irregularity is not corrected within a period specified by the Office, it shall reject the application for registration.

(4) Paragraphs 1, 2 and 3 shall apply mutatis mutandis to applications for Community trade marks. Licences, rights in rem and enforcement measures shall be recorded in the files kept by the Office concerning the Community trade mark

application.

Rule 34

Special provisions for the registration of a licence

(1) A licence in respect of a Community trade mark shall be recorded in the Register as an exclusive licence if the proprietor of the trade mark or the licencee so request.

(2) A licence in respect of a Community trade mark shall be recorded in the Register as a sub-licence where it is granted by a licensee whose licence is recorded in the Register.

(3) A licence in respect of a Community trade mark shall be recorded in the Register as a licence limited as to the goods and services or as a territorially limited licence if it is granted for only a part of the goods or services for which the mark is registered or if it is granted only for a part of the Community.

(4) A licence in respect of a Community trade mark shall be recorded in the Register as a temporary licence if it is granted for a limited period of time.

Rule 35

Cancellation or modification of the registration of licences and other rights

(1) A registration effected under Rule 33(1) shall be cancelled at the request of one of the persons concerned.

(2) The application shall contain—
    (a) the registration number of the Community trade mark; and
    (b) particulars of the right whose registration is to be cancelled.

(3) Application for cancellation of the registration of a licence or another right shall not be deemed to have been filed until the required fee has been paid. If the fee is not paid or is not paid in full, the Office shall so notify the applicant. However, the request of the competent national authority for the cancellation of an entry where a Community trade mark is involved in bankruptcy or like proceedings shall not be subject to payment of a fee.

(4) The application shall be accompanied by documents showing that the registered right no longer exists or by a statement by the licensee or the holder of another right, to the effect that he consents to cancellation of the registration.

(5) Where the requirements for cancellation of the registration are not satisfied, the Office shall notify the applicant of the irregularity. If the irregularity is not corrected within a period specified by the Office, it shall reject the application for cancellation of the registration.

(6) Paragraphs 1, 2, 4 and 5 shall apply mutatis mutandis to a request for the modification of a registration effected under Rule 33(1).

(7) Paragraphs 1 to 6 shall apply mutatis mutandis to entries made in the files pursuant to Rule 33(4).

TITLE VI

SURRENDER

Rule 36

Surrender

(1) A declaration of surrender pursuant to Article 49 of the Regulation shall contain—

(a) the registration number of the Community trade mark;

(b) the name and address of the proprietor in accordance with Rule 1(1)(b);

(c) where a representative has been appointed, the name and business address of the representative in accordance with Rule 1(1)(e);

(d) where surrender is declared only for some of the goods and services for which the mark is registered, the goods and services for which the surrender is declared or the goods and services for which the mark is to remain registered.

(2) Where a right of a third party relating to the Community trade mark is entered in the register, it shall be sufficient proof of his agreement to the surrender that a declaration of consent to the surrender is signed by the proprietor of that right or his representative. Where a licence has been registered, surrender shall be registered three months after the date on which the proprietor of the Community trade mark satisfies the Office that he has informed the licensee of his intention to surrender it. If the proprietor proves to the Office before the expiry of that period that the licensee has given his consent, the surrender shall be registered forthwith.

(3) If the requirements governing surrender are not fulfilled, the Office shall communicate the deficiencies to the declarant. If the deficiencies are not remedied within a period to be specified by the Office, the Office shall reject the entry of the surrender in the Register.

TITLE VII
REVOCATION AND INVALIDITY

Rule 37

Application for revocation or for a declaration of invalidity

An application to the Office for revocation or for a declaration of invalidity pursuant to Article 55 of the Regulation shall contain—

(a) as concerns the registration in respect of which revocation or a declaration of invalidity is sought—

(i) the registration number of the Community trade mark in respect of which revocation or a declaration of invalidity is sought;

(ii) the name and address of the proprietor of the Community trade mark in respect of which revocation or a declaration of invalidity is sought;

(iii) a statement of the registered goods and services in respect of which revocation or a declaration of invalidity is sought;

(b) as regards the grounds on which the application is based—

(i) in the case of an application pursuant to Article 50 or Article 51 of the Regulation, a statement of the grounds on which the application for revocation or a declaration of invalidity is based;

(ii) in the case of an application pursuant to Article 52(1) of the Regulation, particulars of the right on which the application for a declaration of invalidity is based and if necessary particulars showing that the applicant is entitled to adduce the earlier right as grounds for invalidity;

(iii) in the case of an application pursuant to Article 52(2) of the Regulation, particulars of the right on which the application for a declaration of invalidity is based and particulars showing that the applicant is the proprietor of an earlier right as referred to in Article 52(2) of the Regulation or that he is entitled under the national law applicable to lay claim to that right;

(iv) an indication of the facts, evidence and arguments presented in support of those grounds;
(c) as concerns the applicant—
   (i) his name and address in accordance with Rule 1(1)(b);
   (ii) if the applicant has appointed a representative, the name and the business address of the representative, in accordance with Rule 1(1)(e).

Rule 38

Languages used in revocation or invalidity proceedings

(1) Where the application for revocation or for a declaration of invalidity is not filed in the language of the application for the registration of the Community trade mark, if that language is one of the languages of the Office, or in the second language indicated when the application was filed, the applicant for revocation or for a declaration of invalidity shall file a translation of his application in one of those two languages within a period of one month from the filing of his application.

(2) Where the evidence in support of the application is not filed in the language of the revocation or invalidity proceedings, the applicant shall file a translation of that evidence into that language within a period of two months after the filing of such evidence.

(3) Where the applicant for revocation or for a declaration of invalidity or the proprietor of the Community trade mark inform the Office before the expiry of a period of two months from receipt by the Community trade mark proprietor of the communication referred to in Rule 40(1), that they have agreed on a different language of proceedings pursuant to Article 115(7) of the Regulation, the applicant shall, where the application was not filed in that language, file a translation of the application in that language within a period of one month from the said date.

Rule 39

Rejection of the application for revocation or for declaration of invalidity as inadmissible

(1) If the Office find that the application does not comply with Article 55 of the Regulation, Rule 37 or any other provision of the Regulation or these Rules, it shall inform the applicant accordingly and shall call upon him to remedy the deficiencies found within such period as it may specify. If the deficiencies are not remedied before expiry of the time limit, the Office shall reject the application as inadmissible.

(2) Where the Office finds that the required fees have not been paid, it shall inform the applicant accordingly and shall inform him that the application will be deemed not to have been filed if the required fees are not paid within a period specified by the Office. If the required fees are paid after expiry of the period specified by the Office, they shall be refunded to the applicant.

(3) Any decision to reject an application for revocation or for a declaration of invalidity under paragraph 1 shall be communicated to the applicant. Where the application is considered not to have been filed pursuant to paragraph 2, the applicant shall be informed accordingly.

Rule 40

Examination of the application for revocation or for a declaration of invalidity

(1) If the Office does not reject the application in accordance with Rule 39, it shall communicate such application to the proprietor of the Community trade mark and

shall request him to file his observations within such period as it may specify.

(2) If the proprietor of the Community trade mark files no observations, the Office may decide on the revocation or invalidity on the basis of the evidence before it.

(3) Any observations filed by the proprietor of the Community trade mark shall be communicated to the applicant, who shall be requested by the Office, if it sees fit, to reply within a period specified by the Office.

(4) All communications under Article 56(1) of the Regulation and all observations filed in this respect shall be sent to the parties concerned.

(5) If the applicant, under Article 56(2) or (3) of the Regulation, has to furnish proof of use or proof that there are proper reasons for non-use, Rule 22 shall apply mutatis mutandis.

Rule 41

Multiple applications for revocation or for a declaration of invalidity

(1) Where a number of applications for revocation or for a declaration of invalidity have been filed relating to the same Community trade mark, the Office may deal with them in one set of proceedings. The Office may subsequently decide no longer to deal with them in this way.

(2) Rule 21(2), (3) and (4) shall apply mutatis mutandis.

TITLE VIII

COMMUNITY COLLECTIVE MARKS

Rule 42

Application of provisions

The provisions of these Rules shall apply to Community collective marks, subject to Rule 43.

Rule 43

Regulation governing Community collective marks

(1) Where the application for a Community collective trade mark does not contain the regulations governing its use pursuant to Article 65 of the Regulation, those regulations shall be submitted to the Office within a period of two months after the date of filing.

(2) The regulations governing Community collective marks shall specify—

    (a) the name of the applicant and his office address;

    (b) the object of the association or the object for which the legal person governed by public law is constituted;

    (c) the bodies authorised to represent the association or the said legal person;

    (d) the conditions for membership;

    (e) the persons authorised to use the mark;

    (f) where appropriate, the conditions governing use of the mark, including sanctions;

    (g) where appropriate, the authorisation referred to in the second sentence of Article 65(2) of the Regulation.

TITLE IX
CONVERSION

Rule 44

Application for conversion

(1) An application for conversion of a Community trade mark application or a registered Community trade mark into a national trademark application pursuant to Article 108 of the Regulation shall contain—

    (a) the name and the address of the applicant for conversion in accordance with Rule 1(1)(b);

    (b) where the applicant for conversion has appointed a representative, the name and the business address of the representative in accordance with Rule 1(1)(e);

    (c) the filing number of the Community trade mark application or the registration number of the Community trade mark;

    (d) the date of filing of the Community trade mark application or the Community trade mark and, where applicable, particulars of the claim to priority for the Community trade mark application or the Community trade mark pursuant to Articles 30 and 33 of the Regulation and particulars of the claim to seniority pursuant to Articles 34 and 35 of the Regulation;

    (e) a representation of the mark as contained in the application or as registered;

    (f) the specification of the Member State or the Member States in respect of which conversion is requested;

    (g) where the request does not relate to all of the goods and services for which the application has been filed or for which the trade mark has been registered, an indication of the goods and services for which conversion is requested, and, where conversion is requested in respect of more than one Member State and the list of goods and services is not the same for all Member States, an indication of the respective goods and services for each Member State;

    (h) where conversion is requested pursuant to Article 108(4) of the Regulation, an indication to that effect;

    (i) where conversion is requested pursuant to Article 108(5) of the Regulation following a withdrawal of an application for registration, an indication to that effect, and the date on which the application for registration was withdrawn;

    (j) where conversion is requested pursuant to Article 108(5) of the Regulation following a failure to renew the registration, an indication to that effect, and the date on which the period of protection has expired, the period of three months provided for in Article 108(5) of the Regulation shall begin to run on the day following the last day on which the request for renewal can be presented pursuant to Article 47(3) of the Regulation;

    (k) where conversion is requested pursuant to Article 108(6) of the Regulation, an indication to that effect, the date on which the decision of the national court has become final, and a copy of that decision.

(2) Where a copy of a court decision pursuant to paragraph 1(k) is required, that copy may be submitted in the language in which the decision was given.

Rule 45

Examination of application for conversion

(1) Where the application for conversion does not comply with the requirements of

Article 108(1) of the Regulation or was not filed within the relevant period of three months, the Office shall reject it.

(2) Where the conversion fee has not been paid within the relevant period of three months, the Office shall inform the applicant that the application for conversion shall be deemed not to have been filed.

(3) Where the other requirements governing conversion as provided for in Rule 44 and in other Rules governing such applications are not fulfilled, the Office shall inform the applicant accordingly and invite him to remedy the deficiency within a period specified by the Office. If the deficiencies are not remedied within that period, the Office shall reject the application for conversion.

Rule 46

Publication of application for conversion
(1) Where the application for conversion relates to a Community trade mark application which has already been published in the Community Trade Mark Bulletin pursuant to Article 40 of the Regulation or where the application for conversion relates to a Community trade mark, the application for conversion shall be published in the Community Trade Marks Bulletin.
(2) The publication of the application for conversion shall contain—
  (a) the filing number or the registration number of the trade mark in respect of which conversion is requested;
  (b) a reference to the previous publication of the application or the registration in the Community Trade Marks Bulletin;
  (c) an indication of the Member State or Member States in respect of which conversion has been requested;
  (d) where the request does not relate to all of the goods and services for which the application has been filed or for which the trade mark has been registered, an indication of the goods and services for which conversion is requested;
  (e) where conversion is requested in respect of more than one Member State and the list of goods and services is not the same for all Member States, an indication of the respective goods and services for each Member State;
  (f) the date of the application for conversion.

Rule 47

Transmission to central industrial property offices of the Member States
Where the application for conversion complies with the requirements of the Regulation and these Rules, the Office shall transmit without delay the application for conversion to the central industrial property offices of the Member States specified therein, including the Benelux Trade Mark Office. The Office shall inform the applicant of the date of transmission.

TITLE X
APPEALS

Rule 48

Content of the notice of appeal
(1) The notice of appeal shall contain—
  (a) the name and address of the appellant in accordance with rule 1(1)(b);
  (b) where the appellant has appointed a representative, the name and the busi-

ness address of the representative in accordance with Rule 1(1)(e);
  (c) a statement identifying the decision which is contested and the extent to which amendment or cancellation of the decision is requested.
(2) The notice of appeal shall be filed in the language of the proceedings in which the decision subject to the appeal was taken.

Rule 49

Rejection of the appeal as inadmissible
(1) If the appeal does not comply with Articles 57, 58 and 59 of the Regulation and Rule 48(1)(c) and (2), the Board of Appeal shall reject it as inadmissible, unless each deficiency has been remedied before the relevant time limit laid down in Article 59 of the Regulation has expired.
(2) If the Board of Appeal finds that the appeal does not comply with other provisions of the Regulation or other provisions of these Rules, in particular Rule 48(1)(a) and (b), it shall inform the appellant accordingly and shall request him to remedy the deficiencies noted within such period as it may specify. If the appeal is not corrected in good time, the Board of Appeal shall reject it as inadmissible.
(3) If the fee for appeal has been paid after expiry of the period for the filing of appeal pursuant to Article 59 of the Regulation, the appeal shall be deemed not to have been filed and the appeal fee shall be refunded to the appellant.

Rule 50

Examination of appeals
(1) Unless otherwise provided, the provisions relating to proceedings before the department which has made the decision against which the appeal is brought shall be applicable to appeal proceedings before the department which has made the decision against which the appeal is brought shall be applicable to appeal proceedings mutatis mutandis.
(2) The Board of Appeal's decision shall contain—
  (a) a statement that it is delivered by the Board;
  (b) the date when the decision was taken;
  (c) the names of the Chairman and of the other members of the Board of Appeal taking part;
  (d) the name of the competent employee of the registry;
  (e) the names of the parties and of their representatives;
  (f) a statement of the issues to be decided;
  (g) a summary of the facts;
  (h) the reasons;
  (i) the order of the Board of Appeal, including, where necessary, a decision on costs.
(3) The decision shall be signed by the Chairman and the other members of the Board of Appeal and by the employee of the registry of the Board of Appeal.

Rule 51

Reimbursement of appeal fees
The reimbursement of appeal fees shall be ordered in the event of interlocutory revision or where the Board of Appeal deems an appeal to be allowable, if such reimbursement is equitable by reason of a substantial procedural violation. In the event of interlocutory revision, reimbursement shall be ordered by the department whose decision has been impugned, and in other cases by the Board of Appeal.

TITLE XI
GENERAL PROVISIONS

Part A
Decisions and communications of the Office

Rule 52

Form of decisions
(1) Decisions of the Office shall be in writing and shall state the reasons on which they are based. Where oral proceedings are held before the Office, the decision may be given orally. Subsequently, the decision in writing shall be notified to the parties.
(2) Decisions of the Office which are open to appeal shall be accompanied by a written communication indicating that notice of appeal must be filed in writing at the Office within two months of the date of notification of the decision from which appeal is to be made. The communications shall also draw the attention of the parties to the provisions laid down in Articles 57, 58 and 59 of the Regulation. The parties may not plead any failure to communicate the availability proceedings.

Rule 53

Correction of errors in decisions
In decisions of the Office, only linguistic errors, errors of transcription and obvious mistakes may be corrected. They shall be corrected by the department which took the decision, acting of its own motion or at the request of an interested party.

Rule 54

Noting of loss of rights
(1) If the Office finds that the loss of any rights results from the Regulation or these Rules without any decision having been taken, it shall communicate this to the person concerned in accordance with Article 77 of the Regulation, and shall draw his attention to the substance of paragraph 2 of this Rule.
(2) If the person concerned considers that the finding of the Office is inaccurate, he may, within two months after notification of the communication referred to in paragraph 1, apply for a decision on the matter by the Office. Such decision shall be given only if the Office disagrees with the person requesting it; otherwise the Office shall amend its finding and inform the person requesting the decision.

Rule 55

Signature, name, seal
(1) Any decision, communication or notice from the Office shall indicate the department or division of the Office as well as the name or the names of the official or officials responsible. They shall be signed by the official or officials, or, instead of a signature, carry a printed or stamped seal of the Office.
(2) The President of the Office may determine that other means of identifying the department or division of the Office and the name of the official or officials responsible or an identification other than a seal may be used where decisions, communications or notices are transmitted by telecopier or any other technical means of communication.

Part B
Oral proceedings and taking of evidence

Rule 56

Summons to oral proceedings
(1) The parties shall be summoned to oral proceedings provided for in Article 75 of the Regulation and their attention shall be drawn to paragraph 3 of this Rule. At least one month's notice of the summons shall be given unless the parties agree to a shorter period.
(2) When issuing the summons, the Office shall draw attention to the points which in its opinion need to be discussed in order for the decision to be taken.
(3) If a party who has been duly summoned to oral proceedings before the Office does not appear as summoned, the proceedings may continue without him.

Rule 57

Taking of evidence by the Office
(1) Where the Office considers it necessary to hear the oral evidence of parties, of witnesses or of experts or to carry out an inspection, it shall take a decision to that end, stating the means by which it intends to obtain evidence, the relevant facts to be proved and the date, time and place of hearing or inspection. If oral evidence of witnesses and experts is requested by a party, the decision of the Office shall determine the period of time within which the party filing the request must make known to the Office the names and addresses of the witnesses and experts whom the party wishes to be heard.
(2) The period of notice given in the summons of a party, witness or expert to give evidence shall be at least one month, unless they agree to a shorter period. The summons shall contain—
    (a) an extract from the decision mentioned in paragraph 1, indicating in particular the date, time and place of the hearing ordered and stating the facts regarding which the parties, witnesses and experts are to be heard;
    (b) the names of the parties to proceedings and particulars of the rights which the witnesses or experts may invoke under Rule 59(2) to (5).

Rule 58

Commissioning of experts
(1) The Office shall decide in what form the report made by an expert whom it appoints shall be submitted.
(2) The terms of reference of the expert shall include—
    (a) a precise description of his task;
    (b) the time limit laid down for the submission of the expert report;
    (c) the names of the patties to the proceedings;
    (d) particulars of the claims which he may invoke under Rule 59(2), (3) and (4).
(3) A copy of any written report shall be submitted to the parties.
(4) The parties may object to an expert on grounds of incompetence or on the same grounds as those on which objection may be made to an examiner or to a member of a Division or Board of Appeal pursuant to Article 132(1) and (3) of the Regulation. The department of the Office concerned shall rule on the objection.

Rule 59

Costs of taking of evidence
(1) The taking of evidence by the Office may be made conditional upon deposit with it, by the party who has requested the evidence to be taken, of a sum which shall be fixed by reference to an estimate of the costs.
(2) Witnesses and experts who are summoned by and appear before the Office shall be entitled to reimbursement of reasonable expenses for travel and subsistence. An advance for these expenses may be granted to them by the Office. The first sentence shall apply also to witnesses and experts who appear before the Office without being summoned by it and are heard as witnesses or experts.
(3) Witnesses entitled to reimbursement under paragraph 2 shall also be entitled to appropriate compensation for loss of earnings, and experts to fees for their work. These payments shall be made to the witnesses and experts after they have fulfilled their duties or tasks, where such witnesses and experts have been summoned by the Office of its own initiative.
(4) The amounts and the advances for expenses to be paid pursuant to paragraphs 1, 2 and 3 shall be determined by the President of the Office and shall be published in the Official Journal of the Office. The amounts shall be calculated on the same basis as the compensation and salaries received by officials in grades A4 to A8 as laid down in the Staff Regulations of Officials of the European Communities and Annex VII thereto.
(5) Final liability for the amounts due or paid pursuant to paragraphs 1 to 4 shall lie with—
  (a) the Office where the Office, at its own initiative, considered it necessary to hear the oral evidence of witnesses or experts;

  or
  (b) the party concerned where that party requested the giving of oral evidence by witnesses or experts, subject to the decision on apportionment and fixing of costs pursuant to Articles 81 and 82 of the Regulation and Rule 94. Such party shall reimburse the Office for any advances duly paid.

Rule 60

Minutes of oral proceedings and of evidence
(1) Minutes of oral proceedings or the taking of evidence shall be drawn up, containing the essentials of the oral proceedings or of the taking of evidence, the relevant statements made by the parties, the testimony of the parties, witnesses or experts and the result of any inspection.
(2) The minutes of the testimony of a witness, expert or party shall be read out or submitted to him so that he may examine them. it shall be noted in the minutes that this formality has been carried out and that the person who gave the testimony approved the minutes. Where his approval is not given, his objections shall be noted.
(3) The minutes shall be signed by the employee who drew them up and by the employee who conducted the oral proceedings or taking of evidence.
(4) The parties shall be provided with a copy of the minutes.
(5) Upon request, the Office shall make available to the parties transcripts of recordings of the oral proceedings, in typescript or in any other machine-readable form. The release under the first sentence of the oral proceedings shall be subject to the payment of the costs incurred by the Office in making such transcript. The amount to be charged shall be determined by the President of the Office.

Part C

Notifications

Rule 61

General provisions on notifications

(1) In proceedings before the Office, any notifications to be made by the Office shall take the form of the original document, of a copy thereof certified by, or bearing the seal of, the Office or of a computer print-out bearing such seal. Copies of documents emanating from the parties themselves shall not require such certification.

(2) Notifications shall be made—

    (a) by post in accordance with Rule 62;

    (b) by hand delivery in accordance with Rule 63;

    (c) by deposit in a post box at the Office in accordance with Rule 64;

    (d) by telecopier and other technical means in accordance with Rule 65;

    (e) by public notification in accordance with Rule 66.

Rule 62

Notification by post

(1) Decisions subject to a time limit for appeal, summonses and other documents as determined by the President of the Office shall be notified by registered letter with advice of delivery. Decisions and communications subject to some other time limit shall be notified by registered letter, unless the President of the Office determines otherwise. All other communications shall be ordinary mail.

(2) Notifications in respect of addresses having neither their domicile nor their principal place of business nor an establishment in the Community and who have not appointed a representative in accordance with Article 88(2) of the Regulation shall be effected by posting the document requiring notification by ordinary mail to the last address of the addressee known to the Office. Notification shall be deemed to have been effected when the posting has taken place.

(3) Where notification is effected by registered letter, whether or not with advice of delivery, this shall be deemed to be delivered to the addressee on the 10th day following that of its posting, unless the letter has failed to reach the addressee or has reached him at a later date. In the event of any dispute, it shall be for the Office to establish that the letter has reached its destination or to establish the date on which it was delivered to the addressee, as the case may be.

(4) Notification by registered letter, with or without advice of delivery, shall be deemed to have been effected even if the addressee refuses to accept the letter.

(5) To the extent that notification by post is not covered by paragraphs 1 to 4, the law of the State on the territory of which notification is made shall apply.

Rule 63

Notification by hand delivery

Notification may be effected on the premises of the Office by hand delivery of the document to the addressee, who shall on delivery acknowledge its receipt.

Rule 64

Notification by deposit in a post box at the Office

Notification may also be effected to addressees who have been provided with a post box at the Office, by depositing the document therein. A written notification of deposit shall be inserted in the files. The date of deposit shall be recorded on the document. Notification shall be deemed to have taken place on the fifth day following deposit of the document in the post box at the Office.

Rule 65

Notification by telecopier and other technical means
(1) Notification by telecopier shall be effected by transmitting either the original or a copy, as provided for in Rule 61(1), of the document to be notified. The details of such transmission shall be determined by the President of the Office.
(2) Details of notification by other technical means of communication shall be determined by the President of the Office.

Rule 66

Public notification
(1) If the address of the addressee cannot be established, or if notification in accordance with Rule 62(1) has proved to be impossible even after a second attempt by the Office, notification shall be effected by public notice. Such notice shall be published at least in the Community Trade Marks Bulletin.
(2) The President of the Office shall determine how the public notice is to be given and shall fix the beginning of the one-month period on the expiry of which the document shall be deemed to have been notified.

Rule 67

Notification to representatives
(1) If a representative has been appointed or where the applicant first named in a common application is considered to be the common representative pursuant to Rule 75(1), notifications shall be addressed to that appointed or common representative.
(2) If several representatives have been appointed for a single interested party, notification to any one of them shall be sufficient, unless a specific address for service has been indicated in accordance with Rule 1(1)(e).
(3) If several interested parties have appointed a common representative, notification of a single document to the common representative shall be sufficient.

Rule 68

Irregularities in notification
Where a document has reached the addressee, if the Office is unable to prove that it has been duly notified, or if provisions relating to its notification have not been observed, the document shall be deemed to have been notified on the date established by the Office as the date of receipt.

Rule 69

Notification of documents in the case of several parties
Documents emanating from parties which contain substantive proposals, or a declaration of withdrawal of a substantive proposal, shall be notified to the other parties as a matter of course. Notification may be dispensed with where the document contains no new pleadings and the matter is ready for decision.

Part D
Timelimits

Rule 70

Calculation of time limits
(1) Periods shall be laid down in terms of full years, months, weeks or days.
(2) Calculation shall start on the day following the day on which the relevant event occurred, the event being either a procedural step or the expiry of another period. Where that procedural step is a notification, the event considered shall be the receipt of the document notified, unless otherwise provided.
(3) Where a period is expressed as one year or a certain number of years, it shall expire in the relevant subsequent year in the month having the same name and on the day having the same number as the month and the day on which the said event occurred. Where the relevant month has no day with the same number the period shall expire on the last day of that month.
(4) Where a period is expressed as one month or a certain number of months, it shall expire in the relevant subsequent month on the day which has the same number as the day on which the said event occurred. Where the day on which the said event occurred was the last day of a month or where the relevant subsequent month has no day with the same number the period shall expire on the last day of that month.
(5) Where a period is expressed as one week or a certain number of weeks, it shall expire in the relevant subsequent week on the day having the same name as the day on which the said event occurred.

Rule 71

Duration of time limits
(1) Where the Regulation or these Rules provide for a period to be specified by the Office, such period shall, when the party concerned has its domicile or its principal place of business or an establishment within the Community, be not less than one month, or, when those conditions are not fulfilled, not less than two months, and no more than six months. The Office may, when this is appropriate under the circumstances, grant an extension of a period specified if such extension is requested by the party concerned and the request is submitted before the original period expired.
(2) Where there are two or more parties, the Office may extend a period subject to the agreement of the other parties.

Rule 72

Expiry of time limits in special cases
(1) If a time limit expires on a day on which the Office is not open for receipt of documents or on which, for reasons other than those referred to in paragraph 2, ordinary mail is not delivered in the locality in which the Office is located, the time limit shall extend until the first day thereafter on which the Office is open for receipt of documents and on which ordinary mail is delivered. The days referred to in the first sentence shall be as determined by the President of the Office before the commencement of each calendar year.
(2) If a time limit expires on a day on which there is a general interruption or subsequent dislocation in the delivery of mail in a Member State or between a Member State and the Office, the time limit shall extend until the first day following the end of the period of interruption or dislocation, for parties having their residence or reg-

istered office in the State concerned or who have appointed representatives with a place of business in that State. In the event of the Member State concerned being the State in which the Office is located, this provision shall apply to all parties. The duration of the abovementioned period shall be as determined by the President of the Office.

(3) Paragraphs 1 and 2 shall apply mutatis mutandis to the time limits provided for in the Regulation or these Rules in the case of transactions to be carried out with the competent authority within the meaning of Article 25(1)(b) of the Regulation.

(4) If an exceptional occurrence such as natural disaster or strike interrupts or dislocates the proper functioning of the Office so that any communication from the Office to parties concerning the expiry of a time limit is delayed, acts to be completed within such a time limit may still be validly completed within one month after the notification of the delayed communication. The date of commencement and the end of any such interruption or dislocation shall be as determined by the President of the Office.

Part E
Interruption of proceedings

Rule 73

Interruption of proceedings

(1) Proceedings before the Office shall be interrupted —

(a) in the event of the death or legal incapacity of the applicant for or proprietor of a Community trade mark or of the person authorised by national law to act on his behalf. To the extent that the above events do not affect the authorisation of a representative appointed under Article 89 of the Regulation, proceedings shall be interrupted only on application by such representative;

(b) in the event of the applicant for or proprietor of a Community trade mark, as a result of some action taken against his property, being prevented for legal reasons from continuing the proceedings before the Office;

(c) in the event of the death or legal incapacity of the representative of an applicant for or proprietor of a Community trade mark or of his being prevented for legal reasons resulting from action taken against his property from continuing the proceedings before the Office.

(2) When, in the cases referred to in paragraph 1(a) and (b), the Office has been informed of the identity of the person authorised to continue the proceedings before the Office, the Office shall communicate to such person and to any interested third parties that the proceedings shall be resumed as from a date to be fixed by the Office.

(3) In the case referred to in paragraph 1(c), the proceedings shall be resumed when the Office has been informed of the appointment of a new representative of the applicant or when the Office has notified to the other parties the communication of the appointment of a new representative of the proprietor of the Community trade mark. If, three months after the beginning of the interruption of the proceedings, the Office has not been informed of the appointment of a new representative, it shall inform the applicant for or proprietor of the Community trade mark —

(a) where Article 88(2) of the Regulation is applicable, that the Community trade mark application will be deemed to be withdrawn if the information is not submitted within two months after this communication is notified; or

(b) where Article 88(2) of the Regulation is not applicable, that the proceedings will be resumed with the applicant for or proprietor of the Community trade mark as from the date on which this communication is notified.

(4) The time limits, other than the time limit for paying the renewal fees, in force as regards the applicant for or proprietor of the Community trade mark at the date of interruption of the proceedings, shall begin again as from the day on which the proceedings are resumed.

Part F
Waiving of enforced recovery procedures

Rule 74

Waiving of enforced recovery procedures
The President of the Office may waive action for the enforced recovery of any sum due where the sum to be recovered is minimal or where such recovery is too uncertain.

Part G
Representation

Rule 75

Appointment of a common representative
(1) If there is more than one applicant and the application for a Community trade mark does not name a common representative, the applicant first named in the application shall be considered to be the common representative. However, if one of the applicants is obliged to appoint a professional representative, such representative shall he considered to be the common representative unless the applicant named first in the application has appointed a professional representative. The same shall apply mutatis mutandis to third parties acting in common in filing notice of opposition or applying for revocation or for a declaration of invalidity, and to joint proprietors of a Community trade mark.

(2) If, during the course of proceedings, transfer is made to more than one person, and such persons have not appointed a common representative, paragraph 1 shall apply. If such application is not possible, the Office shall require such persons to appoint a common representative within two months. If this request is not complied with, the Office shall appoint the common representative.

Rule 76

Authorisations
(1) Representatives acting before the Office must file with it a signed authorisation for inclusion in the files. The authorisation may cover one or more applications or one or more registered trade marks.

(2) A general authorisation enabling a representative to act in respect of all trade mark transactions of the party giving the authorisation may be filed.

(3) The authorisation may be filed in any language of the Office and in the language of the proceedings if that language is not one of the languages of the Office.

(4) Where the appointment of a representative is communicated to the Office, the necessary authorisation shall be filed within a period specified by the Office. If the authorisation is not filed in due time, proceedings shall be continued with the represented person. Any procedural steps other than the filing of the application taken by the representative shall be deemed not to have been taken if the represented person does not approve them. The application of Article 88(2) of the Regulation shall

remain unaffected.

(5) Paragraphs 1 to 3 shall apply mutatis mutandis to a document withdrawing an authorisation.

(6) Any representative who has ceased to he authorised shall continue to be regarded as the representative until the termination of his authorisation has been communicated to the Office.

(7) Subject to any provisions to the contrary contained therein, an authorisation shall not terminate vis-à-vis the Office upon the death of the person who gave it.

(8) Where several representatives are appointed by the same party, they may, notwithstanding any provisions to the contrary in their authorisations, act either jointly or singly.

(9) The authorisation of an association of representatives shall he deemed to be an authorisation of any representative who can establish that he practises within that association.

Rule 77

Representation

Any notificaticn or other communication addressed by the Office to the duly authorised representative shall have the same effect as if it had been addressed to the represented person. Any communication addressed to the Office by the duly authorised representative shall have the same effect as if it originated from the represented person.

Rule 78

Amendment of the list of professional representatives

(1) The entry of a professional representative in the list of professional representatives, as referred to in Article 89 of the Regulation, shall be deleted at his request.

(2) The entry of a professional representative shall be deleted automatically—

(a) in the event of the death or legal incapacity of the professional representative;

(b) where the professional representative is no longer a national of a Member State, unless the President of the Office has granted an exemption under Article 89(4)(b) of the Regulation;

(c) where the professional representative no longer has his place of business or employment in the Community;

(d) where the professional representative no longer possesses the entitlement referred to in the first sentence of Article 89(2)(c) of the Regulation.

(3) The entry of a professional representative shall be suspended of the Office's own motion where his entitlement to represent natural or legal persons before the central industrial property office of the Member State as referred to in the first sentence of Article 89(2)(c) has been suspended.

(4) A person whose entry has been deleted shall, upon request pursuant to Article 89(3) of the Regulation, be reinstated in the list of professional representatives if the conditions for deletion no longer exist.

(5) The Benelux Trade Mark Office and the central industrial property offices of the Member States concerned shall, where they are aware thereof, promptly inform the Office of any relevant events under paragraphs 2 and 3.

(6) The amendments of the list of professional representatives shall be published in the Official Journal of the Office.

Part H
Written communications and forms

Rule 79

Communication in writing or by other means

Applications for the registration of a Community trade mark as well as any other application provided for in the Regulation and all other communications addressed to the Office shall be submitted as follows—

    (a) by submitting a signed original of the document in question at the Office, such as by post, personal delivery, or by any other means; annexes to documents submitted need not be signed;

    (b) by transmitting a signed original by telecopier in accordance with Rule 80;

    (c) by telex or telegram in accordance with Rule 81;

    (d) by transmitting the contents of the communication by electronic means in accordance with Rule 82.

Rule 80

Communication by telecopier

(1) Where an application for registration of a trade mark is submitted to the Office by telecopier and the application contains a reproduction of the mark pursuant to Rule 3(2) which does not satisfy the requirements of that Rule, the required number of original reproductions shall be submitted to the Office in accordance with Rule 79(a). Where the reproductions are received by the Office within a period of one month from the date of the receipt of the telecopy by the Office, the application shall be deemed to have been received by the Office on the date on which the telecopy was received by the Office. Where the reproductions are received by the Office after the expiry of that period and the reproduction is necessary for the obtaining of a filing date, the application shall be deemed to have been received by the Office on the date on which the reproductions were received by the Office.

(2) Where a communication received by telecopier is incomplete or illegible, or where the Office has reasonable doubts as to the accuracy of the transmission, the Office shall inform the sender accordingly and shall invite him, within a period to be specified by the Office, to retransmit the original by telecopy or to submit the original in accordance with Rule 79(a). Where this request is complied with within the period specified, the date of the receipt of the retransmission or of the original shall be deemed to be the date of the receipt of the original communication, provided that where the deficiency concerns the granting of a filing date for an application to register a trade mark, the provisions on the filing date shall apply. Where the request is not complied with within the period specified, the communication shall be deemed not to have been received.

(3) Any communication submitted to the Office by telecopier shall be considered to be duly signed if the reproduction of the signature appears on the printout produced by the telecopier.

(4) The President of the Office may determine additional requirements of communication by telecopier, such as the equipment to be used, technical details of communication, and methods of identifying the sender.

Rule 81

Communication by telex or telegram

(1) Where an application for registration of a trade mark is submitted to the Office

by telex or by telegram and the application contains a reproduction of the mark pursuant to Rule 3(2), Rule 80(1) shall apply mutatis mutandis.

(2) Where a communication is submitted by telex or telegram, Rule 80(2) shall apply mutatis mutandis.

(3) Where a communication is submitted by telex or telegram, the indication of the name of the sender shall be deemed equivalent to the signature.

Rule 82

Communication by electronic means

(1) Where an application for registration of a trademark is submitted by electronic means and the application contains a reproduction of the mark pursuant to Rule 3(2), Rule 80(1) shall apply mutatis mutandis.

(2) Where a communication is sent by electronic means, Rule 80(2) shall apply mutatis mutandis.

(3) Where a communication is sent to the Office by electronic means, the indication of the name of the sender shall be deemed to be equivalent to the signature.

(4) The President of the Office shall determine the requirements as to communication by electronic means, such as the equipment to be used, technical details of communication, and methods of identifying the sender.

Rule 83

Forms

(1) The Office shall make available free of charge forms for the purpose of—
   (a) filing an application for a Community trade mark;
   (b) entering opposition to registration of a Community trade mark;
   (c) applying for an amendment of an application or a registration, for correction of names and addresses and of mistakes and errors;
   (d) applying for the registration of a transfer and the transfer form and transfer document provided for in Rule 31(5);
   (e) applying for the registration of a licence;
   (f) applying for renewal of the registration of a Community trade mark;
   (g) applying for revocation or for a declaration of invalidity of a Community trade mark;
   (h) applying for restitutio in integrum;
   (i) making an appeal;
   (j) authorising a representative, in the form of an individual authorisation and in the form of a general authorisation.

(2) The Office may make other forms available free of charge.

(3) The Office shall make available the forms referred to in paragraphs 1 and 2 in all the official languages of the Community.

(4) The Office shall place the forms at the disposal of the Benelux Trade Mark Office and the Member States' central industrial property offices free of charge.

(5) The Office may also make available the forms in machine-readable form.

(6) Parties to proceedings before the Office shall use the forms provided by the Office, or copies of these forms, or forms with the same content and format as these forms, such as forms generated by means of electronic data processing.

(7) Forms shall be completed in such a manner as to permit an automated input of the content into a computer, such as by character recognition or scanning.

Part I

Information of the public

Rule 84

Register of Community Trade Marks

(1) The Register of Community Trade Marks may be maintained in the form of an electronic database.

(2) The Register of Community Trade Marks shall contain the following entries—
  (a) the date of filing the application;
  (b) the file number of the application;
  (c) the date of the publication of the application;
  (d) the name, the address and the nationality of the applicant and the State in which he is domiciled or has his seat or establishment;
  (e) the name and business address of the representative, other than a representative falling within the first sentence of Article 88(3) of the Regulation; where there is more than one representative, only the name and business address of the first named representative, followed by the words and others, shall be recorded; where an association of representatives is appointed, only the name and address of the association shall be recorded;
  (f) the reproduction of the mark, with indications as to its nature, unless it is a mark falling under Rule 3(1); where the registration of the mark is in colour, the indication 'in colour' with an indication of the colour or colours making up the mark; where applicable, a description of the mark;
  (g) an indication of the goods and services by their names, grouped according to the classes of the Nice Classification; each group shall be preceded by the number of the class of that classification to which that group of goods and services belongs and shall be presented in the order of the classes of that classification;
  (h) particulars of claims of priority pursuant to Article 30 of the Regulation;
  (i) particulars of claims of exhibition priority pursuant to Article 33 of the Regulation;
  (j) particulars of claims of seniority of an earlier registered trade mark as referred to in Article 34 of the Regulation;
  (k) a statement that the mark has become distinctive in consequence of the use which has been made of it, pursuant to Article 7(3) of the Regulation;
  (l) a declaration by the applicant disclaiming any exclusive right to some element of the mark pursuant to Article 38(2) of the Regulation;
  (m) an indication that the mark is a collective mark;
  (n) the language in which the application was filed and the second language which the applicant has indicated in his application, pursuant to Article 115(3) of the Regulation;
  (o) the date of registration of the mark in the Register and the registration number.

(3) The Register of Community Trade Marks shall also contain the following entries, each accompanied by the date of recording of such entry—
  (a) changes in the name, the address or the nationality of the proprietor of a Community trade mark or in the State in which he is domiciled or has his seat or establishment;
  (b) changes in the name or business address of the representative, other than a representative falling within Article 88(3), first sentence, of the Regulation;
  (c) when a new representative is appointed, the name and business address of

that representative;

(d) alterations of the mark pursuant to Article 48 of the Regulation and corrections of mistakes and errors;

(e) notice of amendments to the regulations governing the use of the collective mark pursuant to Article 69 of the Regulation;

(f) particulars of claims of seniority of an earlier registered trade mark as referred to in Article 34 of the Regulation, pursuant to Article 35 of the Regulation;

(g) total or partial transfers pursuant to Article 17 of the Regulation;

(h) the creation or transfer of a right in rem pursuant to Article 19 of the Regulation and the nature of the right in rem;

(i) levy of execution pursuant to Article 20 of the Regulation and bankruptcy or like proceedings pursuant to Article 21 of the Regulation;

(j) the grant or transfer of a licence pursuant to Article 22 of the Regulation and, where applicable, the type of licence pursuant to Rule 34;

(k) renewal of the registration pursuant to Article 47 of the Regulation, the date from which it takes effect and any restrictions pursuant to Article 47(4) of the Regulation;

(l) a record of the determination of the expiry of the registration pursuant to Article 47 of the Regulation;

(m) a declaration of surrender by the proprietor of the mark pursuant to Article 49 of the Regulation;

(n) the date of submission of an application pursuant to Article 55 of the Regulation or of the filing of a counterclaim pursuant to Article 96(4) of the Regulation for revocation or for a declaration of invalidity;

(o) the date and content of the decision on the application or counterclaim pursuant to Article 56(6) or the third sentence of Article 96(6) of the Regulation;

(p) a record of the receipt of a request for conversion pursuant to Article 109(2) of the Regulation;

(q) the cancellation of the representative recorded pursuant to paragraph 2(e);

(r) the cancellation of the seniority of a national mark;

(s) the modification or cancellation from the Register of the items referred to in subparagraphs (h), (i) and (j).

(4) The President of the Office may determine that items other than those referred to in paragraphs 2 and 3 shall be entered in the Register.

(5) The proprietor of the trade mark shall be notified of any change in the Register.

(6) The Office shall provide certified or uncertified extracts from the Register on request, on payment of a fee.

Part J
Community Trade Marks Bulletin and Official Journal of the Office

Rule 85

Community Trade Marks Bulletin

(1) The Community Trade Marks Bulletin shall be published in periodic editions. The Office may make available to the public editions of the Bulletin on CD-ROM or in any other machine-readable form.

(2) The Community Trade Marks Bulletin shall contain publications of applications and of entries made in the Register as well as other particulars relating to applications or registrations of trade marks whose publication is prescribed by the

Regulation or by these Rules.

(3) Where particulars whose publication is prescribed in the Regulation or in these Rules are published in the Community Trade Marks Bulletin, the date of issue shown on the Bulletin shall be taken as the date of publication of the particulars.

(4) To the extent that the entries regarding the registration of a trade mark contain no changes as compared to the publication of the application, the publication of such entries shall be made by way of a reference to the particulars contained in the publication of the application.

(5) The elements of the application for a Community trade mark, as set out in Article 26(1) of the Regulation as well as any other information the publication of which is prescribed in Rule 12 shall, where appropriate, be published in all the official languages of the Community.

(6) The Office shall take into account any translation submitted by the applicant. If the language of the application is not one of the languages of the Office, the translation into the second language indicated by the applicant shall be communicated to the applicant. The applicant may propose changes to the translation within a period to be specified by the Office. If the applicant does not respond within this period or if the Office considers the proposed changes to be inappropriate, the translation proposed by the Office shall be published.

Rule 86

Official Journal of the Office
(1) The Official Journal of the Office shall be published in periodic editions. The Office may make available to the public editions of the Official Journal on CD-ROM or in any other machine-readable form.

(2) The Official Journal shall be published in the languages of the Office. The President of the Office may determine that certain items shall be published in all the official languages of the Community.

Rule 87

Data bank
(1) The Office shall maintain an electronic data bank with the particulars of applications for registration of trade marks and entries in the Register. The Office may also make available the contents of this data bank on CD-ROM or in any other machine-readable form.

(2) The President of the Office shall determine the conditions of access to the data bank and the manner in which the contents of this data bank may be made available in machine-readable form, including the charges for these acts.

Part K
Inspection of files and keeping of files

Rule 88

Parts of the file excluded from inspection
The parts of the file which shall be excluded from inspection pursuant to Article 84(4) of the Regulation shall be—
   (a) documents relating to exclusion or objection pursuant to Article 132 of the Regulation;
   (b) draft decisions and opinions, and all other internal documents used for the preparation of decisions and opinions;
   (c) parts of the file which the party concerned showed a special interest in

keeping confidential before the application for inspection of the files was made, unless inspection of such part of the file is justified by overriding legitimate interests of the party seeking inspection.

Rule 89

Procedures for the inspection of files
(1) Inspection of the files of Community trade mark applications and of registered Community trade marks shall either be of the original document, or of copies thereof, or of technical means of storage if the files are stored in this way. The means of inspection shall be determined by the President of the Office. The request for inspection of the files shall not be deemed to have been made until the required fee has been paid.
(2) Where inspection of the files of a Community trade mark application is requested, the request shall contain an indication and evidence to the effect that the applicant —
    (a) has consented to the inspection; or
    (b) has stated that after the trade mark has been registered he will invoke the rights under it against the party requesting the inspection.
(3) Inspection of the files shall take place on the premises of the Office.
(4) On request, inspection of the files shall be effected by means of issuing copies of file documents. Such copies shall incur fees.
(5) The office shall issue on request certified or uncertified copies of the application for a Community trade mark or of those file documents of which copies may be issued pursuant to paragraph 4 upon payment of a fee.

Rule 90

Communication of information contained in the files
Subject to the restrictions provided for in Article 84 of the Regulation and Rule 88, the Office may, upon request, communicate information from any file of a Community trade mark applied for or of a registered Community trade mark, subject to payment of a fee. However, the Office may require the exercise of the option to obtain inspection of the file itself should it deem this to be appropriate in view of the quantity of information to be supplied.

Rule 91

Keeping of files
(1) The Office shall keep the files relating to Community trade mark applications and registered Community trade marks for at least five years from the end of the year in which —
    (a) the application is rejected or withdrawn or is deemed to be withdrawn;
    (b) the registration of the Community trade mark expires completely pursuant to Article 47 of the Regulation;
    (c) the complete surrender of the Community trade mark is registered pursuant to Article 49 of the Regulation;
    (d) the Community trade mark is completely removed from the Register pursuant to Article 56(6) or Article 96(6) of the Regulation.
(2) The President of the Office shall determine the form in which the files shall be kept.

Part L
Administrative cooperation

Rule 92

Exchange of information and communications between the Office and the authorities of the Member States

(1) The Office and the central industrial property offices of the Member States shall, upon request, communicate to each other relevant information about the filing of applications for Community trade marks or national marks and about proceedings relating to such applications and the marks registered as a result thereof. Such communications shall not be subject to the restrictions provided for in Article 84 of the Regulation.

(2) Communications between the Office and the courts or authorities of the Member States which arise out of the application of the Regulation or these Rules shall be effected directly between these authorities. Such communication may also be effected through the central industrial property offices of the Member States.

(3) Expenditure in respect of communications under paragraphs 1 and 2 shall be chargeable to the authority making the communications, which shall be exempt from fees.

Rule 93

Inspection of files by or via courts or authorities of the Member States

(1) Inspection of files relating to Community trade marks applied for or registered Community trade marks by courts or authorities of the Member States be of the original documents or of copies thereof, otherwise Rule 89 shall not apply.

(2) Courts or Public Prosecutors' Offices of the Member States may, in the course of proceedings before them, open files or copies thereof transmitted by the Office to inspection by third parties. Such inspection shall be subject to Article 84 of the Regulation. The Office shall not charge any fee for such inspection.

(3) The Office shall, at the time of transmission of the files or copies thereof to the courts or Public Prosecutors' Offices of the Member States, indicate the restrictions to which the inspection of files relating to Community trade marks applied for or registered Community trade marks is subject pursuant to Article 84 of the Regulation and Rule 88.

Part M
Costs

Rule 94

Apportionment and fixing of costs

(1) Apportionment of costs pursuant to Article 81(1) and (2) of the Regulation shall be dealt with in the decision on the opposition, the decision on the application for revocation or for a declaration of invalidity of a Community trade mark, or the decision on the appeal.

(2) Apportionment of costs pursuant to Article 81(3) and (4) of the Regulation shall be dealt with in a decision on costs by the Opposition Division, the Cancellation Division or the Board of Appeal.

(3) A bill of costs, with supporting evidence, shall be attached to the request for the fixing of costs provided for in the first sentence of Article 81(6) of the Regulation. The request shall be admissible only if the decision in respect of which the fixing of costs is required has become final. Costs may be fixed once their credibility is

established.

(4) The request provided for in the second sentence of Article 81(6) of the Regulation for a review of the decision of the registry on the fixing of costs, stating the reasons on which it is based, must be filed at the Office within one month after the date of notification of the awarding of costs. It shall not be deemed to be filed until the fee for reviewing the amount of the costs has been paid.

(5) The Opposition Division, the Cancellation Division or the Board of Appeal, as the case may be, shall take a decision on the request referred to in paragraph 4 without oral proceedings.

(6) The fees to be borne by the losing party pursuant to Article 81(1) of the Regulation shall be limited to the fees incurred by the other party for opposition, for an application for revocation or for a declaration of invalidity of the Community trade mark and for appeal.

(7) Cost essential to the proceedings and actually incurred by the successful party shall be borne by the losing party in accordance with Article 81(1) of the Regulation on the basis of the following maximum rates—

  (a) travel expenses of one party for the outward and return journey between the place of residence or the place of business and the place where oral proceedings are held or where evidence is taken, as follows—

    (i) the cost of the first-class rail-fare including usual transport supplements where the total distance by rail does not exceed 800 km;

    (ii) the cost of the tourist-class air-fare where the total distance by rail exceeds 800 km or the route includes a sea-crossing;

  (b) subsistence expenses by one party equal to the daily subsistence allowance for officials in grades A4 to A8 as laid down in Article 13 of Annex VII to the Staff Regulations of Officials of the European Communities;

  (c) travel expenses of representatives within the meaning of Article 89(1) of the Regulation and of witnesses and of experts, at the rates provided for in subparagraph (a);

  (d) subsistence expenses of representatives within the meaning of Article 89(1) of the Regulation and of witnesses and experts, at the rates provided for in subparagraph (b);

  (e) costs entailed in the taking of evidence in the form of examination of witnesses, opinions by experts or inspection—
  up to ECU 300 per proceedings;

  (f) cost of representation, within the meaning of Article 89(1) of the Regulation—

    (i) of the opposing party in opposition proceedings—
up to ECU 250;

    (ii) of the applicant in opposition proceedings—
up to ECU 250;

    (iii) of the applicant in proceedings relating to revocation or invalidity of a Community trade mark—
up to ECU 400;

    (iv) of the proprietor of the trade mark in proceedings relating to revocation or invalidity of a Community trade mark—
up to ECU 400;

    (v) of the appellant in appeal proceedings—
up to ECU 500;

    (vi) of the defendant in appeal proceedings—
up to ECU 500;

Where the taking of evidence in any of the abovementioned proceedings involves the examination of witnesses, opinions by experts or inspection, an additional amount shall be granted for representation costs of up to ECU 600 per proceedings;

(g) where the successful party is represented by more than one representative within the meaning of Article 89(1) of the Regulation, the losing party shall bear the costs referred to in subparagraphs (c), (d) and (f) for one such person only;

(h) the losing party shall not be obliged to reimburse the successful party for any costs, expenses and fees other than those referred to in subparagraphs (a) to (g).

Part N
Languages

Rule 95

Applications and declarations
Without prejudice to Article 115(5) of the Regulation—

(a) any application or declaration relating to a Community trade mark application may be filed in the language used for filing the application for a Community trade mark or in the second language indicated by the applicant in his application;

(b) any application or declaration relating to a registered Community trade mark may be filed in one of the languages of the Office. However, when the application is filed by using any of the forms provided by the Office pursuant to Rule 83, such forms may be used in any of the official languages of the Community, provided that the form is completed in one of the languages of the Office, as far as textual elements are concerned.

Rule 96

Written proceedings
(1) Without prejudice to Article 115(4) and (7) of the Regulation, and unless otherwise provided for in these Rules, in written proceedings before the Office any party may use any language of the Office. If the language chosen is not the language of the proceedings, the party shall supply a translation into that language within one month from the date of the submission of the original document. Where the applicant for a Community trade mark is the sole party to proceedings before the Office and the language used for the filing of the application for the Community trade mark is not one of the languages of the Office, the translation may also be filed in the second language indicated by the applicant in his application.

(2) Unless otherwise provided for in these Rules, documents to be used in proceedings before the Office may be filed in any official language of the Community. Where the language of such documents is not the language of the proceedings the Office may require that a translation be supplied, within a period specified by it, in that language or, at the choice of the party to the proceeding, in any language of the Office.

Rule 97

Oral proceedings
(1) Any party to oral proceedings before the Office may, in place of the language of proceedings, use one of the other official languages of the Community, on condition that he makes provision for interpretation into the language of proceedings.

Where the oral proceedings are held in a proceeding concerning the application for registration of a trade mark, the applicant may use either the language of the application or the second language indicated by him.

(2) In oral proceedings concerning the application for registration of a trade mark, the staff of the Office may use either the language of the application or the second language indicated by the applicant. In all other oral proceedings, the staff of the Office may use, in place of the language of the proceedings, one of the other languages of the Office, on condition that the party or parties to the proceedings agree to such use.

(3) In the case of taking of evidence, any party to be heard, witness or expert who is unable to express himself adequately in the language of proceedings, may use any of the official languages of the Community. Should the taking of evidence be decided upon following a request by a party to the proceedings, parties to be heard, witnesses or experts who express themselves in languages other than the language of proceedings may be heard only if the party who made the request makes provision for interpretation into that language. In proceedings concerning the application for registration of a trade mark, in place of the language of the application, the second language indicated by the applicant may be used. In any proceedings with only one party the Office may on request of the party concerned permit derogations from the provisions in this paragraph.

(4) If the parties and Office so agree, any official language of the Community may be used in oral proceedings.

(5) The Office shall, if necessary, make provision at its own expense for interpretation into the language of proceedings, or, where appropriate, into its other languages, unless this interpretation is the responsibility of one of the parties to the proceedings.

(6) Statements by staff of the Office, by parties to the proceedings and by witnesses and experts, made in one of the languages of the Office during oral proceedings shall be entered in the minutes in the language employed. Statements made in any other language shall be entered in the language of proceedings. Amendments to the text of the application for or the registration of a Community trade mark shall be entered in the minutes in the language of proceedings.

Rule 98

Certification of translations

(1) When a translation of any document is to be filed, the Office may require the filing, within a period to be specified by it, of a certificate that the translation corresponds to the original text. Where the certificate relates to the translation of a previous application pursuant to Article 30 of the Regulation, such period shall not be less than three months after the date of filing of the application. Where the certificate is not filed within that period, the document shall be deemed not to have been received.

(2) The President of the Office may determine the manner in which translations are certified.

Rule 99

Legal authenticity of translations

In the absence of evidence to the contrary, the Office may assume that a translation corresponds to the relevant original text.

Part O
Organisation of the office

Rule 100

Allocation of duties

(1) The President of the Office shall determine the examiners and their number, the members of the Opposition Divisions and Cancellation Divisions, and the members of the Administration of Trade Marks and Legal Division. He shall allocate duties to the examiners and the Divisions.

(2) The President of the Office may provide that examiners may also be members of the Opposition Divisions, Cancellation Divisions, and the Administration of Trade Marks and Legal Division, and that members of these Divisions may also be examiners.

(3) In addition to the responsibilities vested in them under the Regulation, the President of the Office may allocate further duties to the examiners and the members of the Opposition Divisions, Cancellation Divisions and the Administration of Trade Marks and Legal Division.

(4) The President of the Office may entrust to other members of the staff of the Office who are not examiners or members of any of the Divisions mentioned in paragraph 1 the execution of individual duties falling to the examiners, Opposition Divisions, Cancellation Divisions or the Administration of Trade Marks and Legal Division and involving no special difficulties.

TITLE XII
RECIPROCITY

Rule 101

Publication of reciprocity

(1) If necessary, the President of the Office shall request the Commission to enquire whether a State which is not party to the Paris Convention or to the Agreement establishing the World Trade Organisation accords reciprocal treatment within the meaning of Article 5(1)(d), Article 5(3) and Article 29(5) of the Regulation.

(2) If the Commission determines that reciprocal treatment in accordance with paragraph 1 is accorded, it shall publish a communication to this effect in the Official Journal of the European Communities.

(3) Article 5(1)(d), Article 5(3) and Article 29(5) of the Regulation shall take effect for the nationals of the States concerned from the date of publication in the Official Journal of the European Communities of the communication referred to in paragraph 2, unless the communication states an earlier date from which it is applicable. They shall cease to be effective from the date of publication in the Official Journal of the European Communities of a communication of the Commission to the effect that reciprocal treatment is no longer accorded, unless the communication states an earlier date from which it is applicable.

(4) Communications referred to in paragraphs 2 and 3 shall also be published in the Official Journal of the Office.

Article 2

Transitional Provisions

(1) Any application for registration of a Community trade mark filed within three months prior to the date determined pursuant to Article 143(3) of the Regulation shall be marked by the Office with the filing date determined pursuant to that provi-

sion and with the actual date of receipt of the application.

(2) With regard to the application, the priority period of six months provided for in Articles 29 and 33 of the Regulation shall be calculated from the date determined pursuant to Article 143(3) of the Regulation.

(3) The Office may issue a receipt to the applicant prior to the date determined pursuant to Article 143(3) of the Regulation.

(4) The Office may examine the applications prior to the date determined pursuant to Article 143(3) of the Regulation and communicate with the applicant with a view to remedying any deficiencies prior to that date. Any decisions with regard to such applications may be taken only after that date.

(5) With regard to the application, the Office shall not carry out any search pursuant to Article 39(1) of the Regulation, regardless of whether or not a priority was claimed for such application pursuant to Articles 29 or 33 of the Regulation.

(6) Where the date of receipt of an application for the registration of a Community trade mark by the Office, by the central industrial property office of a Member State or by the Benelux Trade Mark Office is before the commencement of the three months period specified in Article 143(4) of the Regulation the application shall be deemed not to have been filed. The application shall be informed accordingly and the application shall be sent back to him.

Article 3

Entry into force

This Regulation shall enter into force on the seventh day following that of its publication in the Official Journal of the European Communities.

This Regulation shall be binding in its entirety and directly applicable in all Member States.

Done at Brussels, 13 December 1995.

COMMISSION REGULATION

of 5 February 1996

Laying down the rules of procedure of the Boards of Appeal of the Office for Harmonization in the Internal Market (Trade Marks and Designs)

216/96/EC

THE COMMISSION OF THE EUROPEAN COMMUNITIES,

Having regard to the Treaty establishing the European Community,

Having regard to Council Regulation 40/94/EC of 20 December 1994 on the Community trade mark (1), as amended by Regulation 3288/94/EC (2), and in particular Article 140 (3) thereof,

Whereas Regulation 40/94/EC (hereinafter 'the Regulation') creates a new trade mark system allowing a trade mark having effect throughout the Community to be obtained on the basis of an application to the Office for Harmonization in the Internal Market (Trade Marks and Designs) ('the Office`);

Whereas for this purpose the Regulation contains in particular the necessary provisions for a procedure leading to the registration of a Community trade marks, as well as for the administration of Community trade marks, for appeals against decisions of the Office and for proceedings in relation to revocation or invalidity of a Community trade mark;

Whereas under Article 130 of the Regulation, the Boards of Appeal are to be responsible for deciding on appeals from decisions of the examiners, the Opposition Divisions, the Administration of Trade Marks and Legal Division and the Cancellation Divisions;

Whereas Title VII of the Regulation contains basic principles regarding appeals against decisions of examiners, the Opposition Divisions, the Administration of Trade Marks and Legal Division and the Cancellation Divisions;

Whereas Title X of Commission Regulation 2868/95/EC of 13 December 1995 implementing Council Regulation 40/94/EC on the Community Trade Mark (3) contains implementing rules to Title VII of the Regulation;

Whereas this Regulation supplements those other rules, in particular as regards the organization of the Boards and the oral procedure;

Whereas before the beginning of each working year a scheme should be established for the distribution of business between the Boards of Appeal by an Authority established for that purpose; whereas to this end the said Authority should apply objective criteria such as classes of products and services or initial letters of the names of applicants;

Whereas to facilitate the handling and disposal of appeals, a rapporteur should be designated for each case, who should be responsible inter alia for preparing communications with the parties and drafting decisions;

Whereas the parties to proceedings before the Boards of Appeal may not be in a position or may not be willing to bring questions of general relevance to a pending case to the attention of the Boards of Appeal; whereas, therefore, the Boards of Appeal should have the power, of their own motion or pursuant to a request by the President, to invite the President of the Office, to submit comments on questions of general interest in relation to a case pending before the Boards of Appeal;

Whereas the measures provided for in this Regulation are in accordance with the opinion of the Committee established under Article 141 of the Regulation,

HAS ADOPTED THIS REGULATION:

Article 1

Allocation of duties and Authority competent to allocate

1. Before the beginning of each working year, duties shall be allocated to the Boards of Appeal according to objective criteria, and the members of each of the Boards and their alternates shall be designated. Any member of a Board of Appeal may be designated for several Boards of Appeal as a member or an alternate. These measures may, where necessary, be amended during the working year in question.

2. The measures referred to in paragraph 1 shall be taken by an Authority composed of the President of the Office as Chairman, the Vice-President of the Office responsible for the Boards of Appeal, the Chairmen of the Boards of Appeal and three other members of the Boards of Appeal elected by the full membership of those Boards, except the Chairmen, for the working year in question. The Authority may validly deliberate only if at least five of its members are present, including the President or the Vice-President of the Office and two Chairmen of Boards of Appeal. Decisions shall be taken by majority vote. In the event of a tie, the vote of the Chairman shall be decisive. The Authority may lay down its internal rules of procedure.

3. The Authority provided for in paragraph 2 shall decide on conflicts regarding the

allocation of duties among different Boards of Appeal.

4. Until more than three Boards of Appeal have been set up, the Authority referred to in paragraph 2 shall consist of the President of the Office, who shall act as Chairman, the Vice-President of the Office responsible for the Boards of Appeal, the Chairman or Chairmen of the Boards of Appeal which have already been set up and one other member of the Boards of Appeal elected by their full membership of the Board, except the Chairman or Chairmen, for the working year in question. The Authority may validly deliberate only if at least three of its members are present, including the President or the Vice-President of the Office.

Article 2

Replacement of members

1. Reasons for replacement by alternates shall in particular include leave, sickness, inescapable commitments and the grounds of exclusion set out in Article 132 of the Regulation.

2. Any member asking to be replaced by an alternate shall without delay inform the Chairman of the Board concerned of his unavailability.

Article 3

Exclusion and objection

1. If a Board has knowledge of a possible reason for exclusion or objection under Article 132 (3) of the Regulation which does not originate from a member himself or from any party to the proceedings, the procedure of Article 132 (4) of the Regulation shall be applied.

2. The member concerned shall be invited to present his comments as to whether there is a reason for exclusion or objection.

3. Before a decision is taken on the action to be taken pursuant to Article 132 (4) of the Regulation, there shall be no further proceedings in the case.

Article 4

Rapporteurs

1. The Chairman of each Board shall for each appeal designate a member of his Board, or himself, as rapporteur.

2. The rapporteur shall carry out a preliminary study of the appeal. He may prepare communications to the parties subject to the direction of the Chairman of the Board. Communications shall be signed by the rapporteur on behalf of the Board.

3. The rapporteur shall prepare internal meetings of the Board and the oral proceedings.

4. The rapporteur shall draft decisions.

Article 5

Registries

1. Registries shall be established for the Boards of Appeal. Registrars shall be responsible for the discharge of the functions of the Registries. One of the Registrars may be designated Senior Registrar.

2. The Authority provided for in Article 1 (2) may entrust to the Registrars the performance of functions which involve no legal or technical difficulties, particularly with regard to representation, the submission of translations, inspection of files and notifications.

3. The Registrar shall submit to the Chairman of the Board concerned a report on

the admissibility of each newly-filed appeal.

4. Minutes of oral proceedings and of the taking of evidence shall be drawn up by the Registrar or, if the President of the Office has agreed thereto, such other officer of the Office as the Chairman of the Board may designate.

Article 6

Change in the composition of a Board

1. If the composition of a Board is changed after oral proceedings, the parties to the proceedings shall be informed that, at the request of any party, fresh oral proceedings shall be held before the Board in its new composition. Fresh oral proceedings shall also be held if so requested by the new member and if the other members of the Board have given their agreement.

2. The new member shall be bound to the same extent as the other members by an interim decision which has already been taken.

3. If, when a Board has already reached a final decision, a member is unable to act, he shall not be replaced by an alternate. If the Chairman is unable to act, then the member of the Board concerned having the longer service on the Board, or where members have the same length of service, the older member, shall sign the decision on behalf of the Chairman.

Article 7

Joinder of appeal proceedings

1. If several appeals are filed against a decision, those appeals shall be considered in the same proceedings.

2. If appeals are filed against separate decisions and all the appeals are designated to be examined by one Board having the same composition, that Board may deal with those appeals in joined proceedings with the consent of the parties.

Article 8

Remission to the department of first instance

Where the proceedings of the department of first instance whose decision is the subject of an appeal are vitiated by fundamental deficiencies, the Board shall set aside the decision and, unless there are reasons for not doing so, remit the case to that instance or decide the matter itself.

Article 9

Oral proceedings

1. If oral proceedings are to take place, the Board shall ensure that the parties have provided all relevant information and documents before the hearing.

2. The Board may, when issuing the summons to attend oral proceedings, add a communication drawing attention to matters which seem to be of special significance, or to the fact that certain questions appear no longer to be contentious, or containing other observations that may help to concentrate on essentials during the oral proceedings.

3. The Board shall ensure that the case is ready for decision at the conclusion of the oral proceedings, unless there are special reasons to the contrary.

Article 10

Communications to the parties

If a Board deems it expedient to communicate with the parties regarding a possible appraisal of substantive or legal matters, such communication shall be made in such a way as not to imply that the Board is in any way bound by it.

Article 11

Comments on questions of general interest

The Board may, on its own initiative or at the written, reasoned request of the President of the Office, invite him to comment in writing or orally on questions of general interest which arise in the course of proceedings pending before it. The parties shall be entitled to submit their observations on the President's comments.

Article 12

Deliberations preceding decisions

The rapporteur shall submit to the other members of the Board a draft of the decision to be taken and shall set a reasonable time-limit within which to oppose it or to ask for changes. The Board shall meet to deliberate on the decision to be taken if it appears that the members of a Board are not all of the same opinion. Only members of the Board shall participate in the deliberations; the Chairman of the Board concerned may, however, authorize other officers such as registrars or interpreters to attend. Deliberations shall be secret.

Article 13

Order of voting

1. During the deliberations between members of a Board, the opinion of the rapporteur shall be heard first, and, if the rapporteur is not the Chairman, the Chairman last.
2. If voting is necessary, votes shall be taken in the same sequence, save that if the Chairman is also the rapporteur, be shall vote last. Abstentions shall not be permitted.

Article 14

Entry into force

This Regulation shall enter into force the third day following its publication in the Official Journal of the European Communities.
This Regulation shall be binding in its entirety and directly applicable in all Member States.

DECISION No EX-96-3 OF THE PRESIDENT OF THE OFFICE

of 5 March 1996

concerning the evidence to be provided on claiming priority or seniority

THE PRESIDENT OF THE OFFICE FOR HARMONIZATION IN THE
INTERNAL MARKET (TRADE MARKS AND DESIGNS),

Having regard to Council Regulation 40/94/EC of 20 December 1993 on the Community trade mark, in particular Article 119 (2) (a) thereof,
Having regard to Commission Regulation 2868/95/EC of 13 December 1995

implementing Council Regulation 40/94/EC on the Community trade mark (hereinafter referred to as 'the Implementing Regulation'), in particular Rules 6 (4), 8 (4) and 28 (4) thereof,

Whereas the information contained in the originals of the documents to be submitted pursuant to Rule 6 (1) of the Implementing Regulation to support a claim of priority and pursuant to Rule 8 (1) and Rule 28 (1) (f) of the Implementing Regulation to support a claim of seniority, is available to the Office from an accurate photocopy of such documents,

HAS ADOPTED THE FOLLOWING DECISION:

Article 1

Documents to support a claim of priority

Instead of filing the originals of documents in support of a priority claim issued by the authority which received the previous application as provided for in Rule 6 (1) of the Implementing Regulation, accurate photocopies of such documents may be filed. To the extent that the originals of the documents contain a representation of the mark in colour, the photocopy shall also be in colour.

Article 2

Documents to support a claim of seniority

Instead of submitting a copy of the earlier registered trade mark certified by the competent authority to be an exact copy of the registration as provided for in Rule 8 (1) and Rule 28 (1) (f) of the Implementing Regulation, an accurate photocopy of a document issued by the competent registration authority relating to the earlier registration may be submitted. Where that document contains a reproduction of the mark in colour, the photocopy shall also be in colour.

When a photocopy of an original document is submitted pursuant to paragraph 1, it shall be accompanied by a statement by the applicant or his representative that the information contained in the photocopy corresponds to the current status of the relevant registration at the time of submitting the photocopy, except when the original document has been issued not later than six months before the date on which the photocopy was submitted.

Article 3

Entry into force

This Decision shall enter into force on 7 March 1996. It shall be published in the Official Journal of the Office.

GUIDELINES CONCERNING PROCEEDINGS BEFORE THE OFFICE FOR
HARMONIZATION IN THE INTERNAL MARKET (TRADE MARKS AND
DESIGNS)

Part C: Opposition Proceedings

Introduction

Chapter 1—General rules for applying to opposition proceedings

    1. Place and methods of filing

2. Time limits specific to opposition proceedings

3. Choice of language in opposition proceedings

CHAPTER 2—ADMISSIBILITY OF THE OPPOSITION

1. Grounds for inadmissability that cannot be remedied after the opposition period

2. Grounds for inadmissability that can be remedied after the opposition period

3. Decision as to the admissability of the opposition

CHAPTER 3—EXAMINATION OF THE OPPOSITION

1. Notification of the opposition and commencement of the proceedings

2. Observations by the parties to the opposition

3. Examination of the file

4. The end of the opposition proceedings

CHAPTER 4—SPECIAL FEATURES OF THE PROCEEDINGS: SUSPENSION, JOINDER, FRIENDLY SETTLEMENT, ORAL PROCEEDINGS

1. Suspension of opposition proceedings

2. Joinder of proceedings and their separation

3. Friendly settlement

4. Oral proceedings

INTRODUCTION

Article 8 of the Community Trade Mark Regulation entitled 'Relative grounds for refusal' provides the possibility for third parties to file opposition to CTM applications on grounds of earlier rights.

Articles 42 and 43 of the Regulation establish how the opposition proceedings should be conducted.

In addition, title II of the Implementing Regulation establishes the rules of procedure for conducting opposition proceedings.

This part of the Guidelines is intended to serve as a guide to examiners, applicants and their representatives in filing, conducting and examining oppositions and consists of two parts. Firstly it is composed of procedural guidelines to which standard letters are attached in the annex and, secondly, of substantive guidelines still to be published.

The procedural part comprises four chapters:

General Rules applying to opposition proceedings.

Examination of the admissibility of the opposition.

Examination of the opposition.

Special features of the proceedings: suspension, joinder and separation of proceedings, friendly settlement and oral proceedings.

CHAPTER 1—GENERAL RULES APPLYING TO OPPOSITION PROCEEDINGS

Opposition proceedings are intended to settle a particular type of dispute that may arise during the registration of a Community trade mark. It is for this reason, to ensure in particular the fair application of the principles of the adversarial procedure, that provisions applying to such proceedings only, complementary to the general rules, are necessary. They must be respected both by the Office and by the parties involved.

1. PLACE AND METHODS OF FILING

In order to prevent the proceedings from being unnecessarily prolonged and in a concern for efficiency, a certain number of general provisions have been adapted to the needs of the opposition proceedings. These provisions relate to the place and methods of filing, time limits and the choice of the language of proceedings.

1.1. Place of filing

An opposition to a Community trade mark application of a mark may be filed only at the Office for Harmonization in the Internal Market (Trade Marks and Designs), i.e. at the seat of the Office in Alicante (Spain).

1.2. Methods of filing

CTMR 42

All oppositions must be filed in writing. It is strongly recommended to use the forms, published in the Official Journal of the Office No. 3/97 page 201 supplied free of charge by the Office. It is also possible to use a copy of the form or a form having the same format and content.

IR 83(6)

Forms are currently available only in paper form.

The notice of opposition may be submitted to the Office by fax or by other electronic means (preferred methods of the Office), by post or by personal delivery. [1]

A receipt will be issued by the Office indicating the date when the opposition was received in the Office and the number allocated to the opposition.

2. TIME LIMITS SPECIFIC TO OPPOSITION PROCEEDINGS

The basic Regulation and the Implementing Regulation provide for a certain number of time limits.

Some time limits are expressly set out in these regulations and others are specified by the Office. The general rules set out in Part A (General Part of Guidelines) are applicable to those time limits and in particular those relating to the calculation of time limits. [2]

These time limits set out in the regulations relate mainly to the 'pre-adversarial' stage of the proceedings.

The following time limits in chronological order are expressly provided for in the regulations:

CTMR	42(1),(2)
IR	17(1)
IR	17(2)
IR	18(2)

IR 17(3)

3 months following the publication of the application for entry of opposition and payment of the fee (non extendible period).

1 month from the expiry of the opposition period, for filing, where necessary, of a translation of the notice of opposition (non-extendible period).

1 month from the expiry of the opposition period, for filing, where necessary, of a translation of the evidence and supporting documents, relating either to facts or to the reputation or well-known nature of the earlier trade mark, or to the acquisition and scope of protection of earlier rights, presented in support of the opposition (non-extendible period).

2 months from the date of receipt of the notification of deficiency in order to remedy certain deficiencies noted in the notice of opposition (non-extendible period).

2 months from the date of receipt of the communication of the opposition for determining the date of commencement of the proceedings (extendible period).

1 month from the date of commencement of the opposition proceedings for submission, if the parties have agreed upon another language for the proceedings, of a translation of the notice of opposition into the language chosen (non extendible period).

The time limits to be specified by the Office, within opposition proceedings, are always expressed in months and in principle have a period of two months.

IR 19(2)

Their extension, when possible, is subject in principle to the agreement of both parties. Such agreement is a condition as regards extending the time limit establishing the date of commencement of the opposition proceedings.

All time limits (fixed by the regulations or to be fixed by the Office) which concern a rectification of the notice of opposition or of any other document, are considered exhausted once the Office has received the rectification. The Office will forward to the other party, without delay, the rectified document and the procedure will continue. However, when the notice of opposition is rectified before the expiry of the opposition period, the Office will wait until the end of this period to notify the opposition. [3]

On the other hand, time limits granted to a party in order to enable it to present or reply to observations, are considered exhausted only at the end of the fixed time limit. However, these time limits can be reduced where the party concerned by the time limit expressly states that he does not wish to use all of the time available to it. Therefore, unless a corresponding statement is filed, the Office will transmit only the observations at the end of the time limit imposed.

3.   CHOICE OF LANGUAGE IN OPPOSITION PROCEEDINGS

As the opposition proceedings may involve parties of different nationalities and languages, there are strict rules for determining the language to be used for these proceedings.

3.1.   The notice of opposition

CTMR 115(5)

Contrary to a Community trade mark application, which may be filed in any of the official languages of the European Community, the notice of opposition must always be '... filed in one of the languages of the Office', ie Spanish, German, English, French or Italian.

CTMR 115(6)
If the language chosen by the opposing party is both one of the two languages of the Community trade mark application and one of the languages of the Office, this will naturally be the language of the proceedings.

CTMR 115(6)
IR17(1)
If the opposition is filed in a language of the Office which is not one of the two languages of the application, the opposing party must submit a translation of this notice, within a time limit of one month from the expiry of the opposition period. Otherwise, the opposition will be inadmissible.
This translation must be into either the language of the application, when this is one of the languages of the Office, or into the second language indicated in the application which is necessarily a language of the Office. The language of the proceedings will therefore be the language into which the translation has been made.
A notice of opposition filed in a language of the Community which is not one of the languages of the Office is deemed inadmissible. This defect may be remedied only within the opposition period.

CTMR 115(7)
Before the date of `commencement' of the opposition proceedings [4], the parties may jointly agree that an official language of the European Community other than the language of the proceedings as defined according to the above rules is to be the language of the proceedings.

IR 17(3)
In this case, the opposing party must submit, where necessary, a translation of its notice of opposition, within a period of one month from the date of commencement of the opposition proceedings.

3.2.   *Communications submitted during the proceedings*

IR 96(1)
All communications submitted during the proceedings, such as observations in reply or the statements of the parties, may be filed either in the language of the proceedings chosen, or in one of the languages of the Office, with a translation into the language of the proceedings within one month from the date of submission of the original document.

3.3.   *Evidence, supporting documents*
As regards evidence, supporting documents, information, observations and other documents, a distinction needs to be made depending on the nature and purpose of these documents.
IR 16(1-3)
IR 17(2)
IR 20(2)
All documents that the opposing party presents in support of its opposition (particulars of facts, supporting documents or evidence relating to the nature of the earlier

mark in particular as a well-known mark or a mark having a reputation) must be produced in the language of the proceedings. Failing this, the opposing party must supply a translation thereof within one month of the expiry of the opposition period or, where appropriate, within the period specified by the Office for submitting such evidence or documents.

Since these documents form part of the notice of opposition, they are subject to the language rules applicable to the notice of opposition and must therefore be submitted in the language of the proceedings.

However, only elements that are translatable and needed for the opposition must be translated. In particular, a translation is required of the goods and services and other inscriptions having consequences for the opposition (licenses, assignments, disclaimers...). On the other hand, the administrative comments in the registration certificates do not have to be translated.

IR 76

However, the authorisation has its own language regime. It can be submitted in one of the languages of the Office independently of the language of the proceedings. If the language of the proceedings is not a language of the Office it may equally be submitted in this language.

If the opposing party makes a reference to a general authorisation already registered with the Office or to an individual authorisation sent to the Office within the registration procedure, a translation of the authorisation is not necessary for whatever language used in the authorisations.

IR 96(2)

Any other documents used in the proceedings may be presented in one of the official languages of the Community, the Office having the right to request their translation into either the language of the proceedings or, if the party chooses, into one of the languages of the Office.

IR 22(4)

When the opposing party, during the proceedings and at the request of the applicant, is required to furnish proof of use, the opposing party may furnish it in one of the official languages of the Community. If it thinks fit, the Office may require the opposing party to provide a translation into the language of the proceedings within a period to be specified.

CHAPTER 2 — ADMISSIBILITY OF THE OPPOSITION

IR 18

The admissibility of the notice of opposition is examined prior to any communication with the applicant.

The Implementing Regulation sets out two main categories of deficiencies. The first, relating mainly to the rights of the parties, may be remedied only within the opposition period. The second, relating mainly to the formal conditions of the notice, may be remedied within a period of two months, which cannot be extended, from the notification of these deficiencies.

IR 18(1)

The following deficiencies fall into the first category:

failure to comply with the provisions of Article 42 CTMR,

failure to clearly identify the application against which the opposition is entered, or the earlier mark or earlier right on the basis of which the opposition is being entered.

IR 18(2)
The following deficiencies fall into the second category:
> failure to comply with other provisions of the Community Trade Mark Regulation or the Implementing Regulation.

It is recommended that parties file their notices of opposition, and the documents relating thereto, in as complete a manner as possible in order to avoid any unnecessary prolongation of the proceedings.

1. GROUNDS FOR INADMISSIBILITY THAT CANNOT BE REMEDIED AFTER THE OPPOSITION PERIOD

IR 18(1)
Rule 18 (1) of the Implementing Regulation lists the following deficiencies:
> Failure to comply with the provisions of Article 42 of the Community Trade Mark Regulation. These relate primarily to the time limit for filing an opposition, entitlement to bring opposition, and the indication of the grounds on which the opposition is based.
>
> Failure to clearly identify the application against which the opposition is entered.
>
> Failure to clearly identify the earlier mark or the earlier sign on the basis of which the opposition is entered.

These deficiencies, which predominantly concern the rights of the parties in dispute, can be remedied only within the three-month period for entry of opposition.

Failure to comply with one or more of these conditions means that the Office will reject the opposition as inadmissible 'ex officio'.

Payment of the opposition fee

CTMR 42
Article 42 of the Community Trade Mark Regulation states that '... the opposition is not treated as duly entered until the opposition fee has been paid'. Accordingly, failure to pay the opposition fee or payment of an incomplete amount of the fee [5], within the opposition period, is not a cause of inadmissibility per se.

IR 18(1)
The notice of opposition is, in this case '... deemed not to have been entered'. Consequently, as the notice does not legally exist, the Office does not have to examine it.

IR 54
The opposing party will be notified that his opposition is deemed not to have been entered. The notification states a loss of rights. In its notification to the opposing party the Office shall draw his attention to the fact that, if he considers that the Office has taken an incorrect view, he may request a decision to this effect within a period of 2 months.

IR 18(1)
If the opposition fee has been paid after the opposition period or has been partially paid, it is refunded to the opposing party in full, since in this case the opposition has no object.

The fee is considered to have been paid when it reaches the Office in full before the expiry of the opposition period.

When steps have been taken within the opposition period but the fee does not reach the Office until after the expiry of the opposition period, the opposition will be deemed not to have been entered, except where the opponent brings forward proof showing that the payment has been made before the expiry of the opposition period. If the payment order has been given within the last ten days of the opposition period, the opponent must pay a surcharge of 10 % [6].

1.1. Oppositions entered outside the period

CTMR 42(1)
An opposition to the registration of a Community trade mark must be entered within a period of three months following the publication of the application.
IR 85(3)
IR 70(2)
The opposition period commences on the day following the date specified as date of publication of the Bulletin in which the application in question is published and ends three months after this date (example: publication date 10 June, end of opposition period 10 September 24.00 h).
Any opposition that is received or delivered prior to the expiry of this period, by the methods mentioned in Part A of this guidelines, i.e. by post, fax, personal delivery or any other electronic means, is entered within the period. [7]
Any opposition filed after the effective date of publication of an application but before the official date of publication of the Bulletin in which the application in question is published is considered to be filed on the day of the official publication.
Any opposition that is received or delivered prior to the publication of an application is treated by the Office as a simple communication. If a fee has been paid it will be refunded to the opposing party.

CTMR 78(5)
The time limit of an opposition is expressly excluded from the scope of application of Article 78 of the Community Trade Mark Regulation relating to `Restitutio in integrum'. The rights of an opposing party may not be re-established if it has been prevented in any way from entering an opposition.

1.2. Oppositions not in writing

CTMR 42(3)
Oppositions must be filed in writing [8].
An opposition that is entered orally is treated as non-existent.

1.3. Oppositions submitted by persons who are not authorised

CTMR 42(1)
In order to be admissible, the opposition must be entered either by the applicant(s) or proprietor(s) of trade marks/earlier signs; by the licensees authorised by these proprietors; or by persons authorised, under the national law applicable, to exercise the rights of earlier non-registered trade marks or earlier signs.

IR 75(1)
When an opposition is filed jointly by a number of opposing parties, all these parties must be indicated in the notice of opposition.

1.3.1. PROPRIETORS

Proprietors of earlier trade marks or signs may be the original proprietors or the new proprietors following a transfer of these rights.

CTMR 17(6)
In the case of Community trade marks, however, new proprietors may file oppositions only when transfers are entered in the Register.

CTMR 17(7)
IR 15(2)(c)(iii)
In cases in which transfers have not yet been registered, new proprietors must indicate the date of their application for registration of the transfer, which must be prior or at least identical to the date of entry of their opposition.

In the case of national trade marks, the capacity to act of a new proprietor following a transfer is determined by the applicable national law.

Reminder: Proprietors may enter opposition to the registration of a Community trade mark in the following cases:

CTMR	42(1)(a),(c)
CTMR	42(1)(b)

CTMR 42(1)(c)
> The contested application is identical or similar to the earlier trade mark invoked, for identical or similar goods or even different goods if the earlier registered trade mark has a reputation;
> The contested application has been filed in the name of the agent without the proprietor's consent;
> The contested application is prejudicial to an earlier non-registered trade mark or an earlier sign used in the course of trade which is not of mere local significance.

1.3.2. AUTHORISED LICENSEES

Authorised licensees are the second category of persons who may enter an opposition. Their authorisation to act in opposition proceedings must be stated in the notice of opposition.

CTMR 22
In the case of a licensee of a Community trade mark, the registration of the licence is not a condition for the admissibility of the capacity to act. They must prove that they are properly authorised by the proprietor to act in opposition proceedings in order to 'defend' the earlier trade mark.

In the case of national trade marks, national law governs the licensee's capacity to act and the opposability of the license itself.

Reminder: authorised licensees may enter an opposition in the following case:

CTMR 42(1)(a)
The contested application is identical or similar to the earlier trade mark invoked, for identical or similar goods or even different goods if the earlier trade mark has a reputation.

1.3.3. AUTHORISED PERSONS

Authorised persons are the last category of persons who may enter an opposition. National rights determine this category.

Reminder: persons authorised under the relevant national laws to exercise the rights of non-registered trade marks or earlier signs may enter an opposition in the following case:

CTMR 42(1)(c)
The contested application is prejudicial to an earlier non-registered trade mark or to an earlier sign used in the course of trade and not of mere local significance.

1.3.4. EXAMINATION OF THE CAPACITY TO ACT
As regards admissibility, the examination of the opposing party's capacity to act is limited to formalities.

IR 15(c)(i),(ii)
Opposing parties must provide, where necessary, an indication that they are the proprietors of the earlier trade mark or right or, if they are licensees, an indication that they are authorised to enter an opposition or, if they are not the proprietors of the earlier right in question, an indication that the relevant national law authorises them to invoke this right.

1.4. The opposition does not clearly indicate the application for registration

IR 18(1)
The opposing party must clearly indicate the application against which the opposition is entered.

IR 15(2)(a)
It will be considered sufficient to indicate the name of the applicant and the file number of the contested application. Failure to indicate the name and number will constitute grounds for inadmissibility, except where the contested application is specifically indicated in some other manner allowing the Office to identify it.
In order to be admissible, the opposition must also specify the scope of the opposition. The opposing party must therefore indicate the goods or services to be contested.
If the opposition is entered against all goods or services of the contested application, a statement to that effect is sufficient.
However, if the opposing party limits the opposition to some of the goods or services they must be specifically listed.
It is also possible to indicate merely the numbers of the classes as shown in the publication and covering the contested goods or services. The Office considers in this case that the opposition is entered against all the goods or services of the class indicated. Where no indication is given in this regard, the Office will consider the opposition as being directed against all the goods or services in the contested application.

1.5. The opposition does not clearly indicate the earlier right

1.5.1. THE EARLIER RIGHT

IR 18(1)
The opposing party must clearly indicate the earlier trade mark(s) or earlier sign(s) on the basis of which the opposition is entered. Otherwise, the opposition will be inadmissible.

CTMR 8(2)
Earlier trade marks are, for the purpose of the opposition proceedings, trade marks or trade mark applications whose date of filing is earlier than that of the contested application, taking account, where necessary, of the date of priority.
These trade marks must also belong to one of the following five categories:
Community trade marks;
trade marks registered in a Member State or at the Benelux Trade Mark Office;
international trade marks which have effect in a Member State;

well-known marks under Article 6 bis of the Paris Convention;
registered trade marks that have a reputation in the Community or in a Member State in accordance with Article 8 (5) of the Community Trade Mark Regulation.

CTMR 8(4)
Earlier signs are, for the purposes of the opposition proceedings, non-registered trade marks or signs used in the course of trade of more than mere local significance.
These signs may be invoked by the opposing party, however, only to the extent that, '... pursuant to the law of the Member State governing that sign:

rights to that sign were acquired prior to the date of' the contested 'application for registration...' and

'this sign confers on its proprietor the right to prohibit the use of a subsequent trade mark'.

IR 15(2)(b)
At this stage of the proceedings, the Office will assess admissibility on the following basis:

IR 15(2)(b)(i)
In the case of earlier trade marks, the opposing party must indicate whether the earlier trade mark is a Community trade mark, a trade mark registered in a Member State or an internationally registered trade mark.
In the latter two cases, the opposing party must indicate the Member State(s) in which the trade mark has been registered or in which it has effect.

IR 15(2)(b)(ii),(vi)
The opposing party must also supply a representation of its trade mark(s), indicate the file number or registration number of its trade mark(s) and, in cases where the opposing party invokes the benefit of a priority date, must specify this date.

IR	15(2)(b)(iii),(vi)
IR	15(2)(b)(iv),(vi)
IR	15(2)(b)(v),(vi)
CTMR	8(3)

IR15(3)
In the case of well-known marks in accordance with Article 6 bis of the Paris Convention, a statement to that effect is required together with the name(s) of the Member State(s) in which they are well-known. The opposing party must also supply a representation of its trade mark(s).
In the case of marks having a reputation, a statement to that effect is required together with the indication whether a Community trade mark or a national mark or an internationally registered mark is relied on; in the two latter cases the Member State(s) where they have been registered or have effect must be indicated. The opposing party must supply a representation of its trade mark(s). He must also indicate the registration number and date of its trade mark(s).
In the case of earlier signs, a statement to that effect is required together with the name(s) of the Member State(s) in which these rights have been acquired and with the indication of their juridical nature (trade name, company name...) and with a representation of these rights.
In the case of marks filed fraudulently in their own name by the agent or rep-

resentative, the opposing party must supply a representation of the trade mark and indicate the country of origin of its trade mark. Under Article 8 (3) of the Community Trade Mark Regulation, there are no limits in this regard. Consequently, the country where the proprietor is the owner of the mark may be any one of the Member States of the European Community as well as any third country outside the Community.

This provision applies solely to trade marks and does not therefore concern other earlier rights.

IR 15(2)(b)

In all cases, failure to comply with one of these above elements constitutes a ground for inadmissibility, except where the earlier rights are specifically indicated in some other manner allowing the Office to identify them. [9]

1.5.2. Earlier goods or services

The opposing party must indicate the goods or services of the earlier trade marks or of the earlier signs on which the opposition is based.

In the case of earlier trade marks (application or registered) and in the case of marks having a reputation, if the opposition is based on all goods or services of the earlier trade marks, a statement to that effect may be sufficient. However, if the opposing party limits the basis of its opposition to some of those goods or services, they must be specifically listed.

It is also possible to indicate merely the numbers of the classes covering the goods or services on which the opposition is based. The Office considers in this case that the opposition is based on all the goods or services of the class indicated. Where no indication is given in this regard, the Office will consider the opposition as based on all the goods or services of the earlier trade mark.

In the case of well-known marks in accordance with Article 6 bis of the Paris Convention and in the case of national non-registered marks the goods or services must be specifically listed.

In the case of earlier signs, the goods or services of the economic activity must be specifically listed.

1.6.   Oppositions not specifying grounds

CTMR 42(3)

The opposition, in order to be admissible, must specify the grounds on which it is made.

Regarding these grounds, even if specified in brief statements or limited to the essential elements, the Office considers them sufficient for the opposition to be admissible.

It is however strongly recommended to include already in the notice of opposition a full explanation of the reasons for the opposition, such as the reasons for the existence of likelihood of confusion by providing a comparison of the marks and/or the goods or services involved or any other element relied on to support the opposition.

IR 15(2)(d)

As regards the grounds on which the opposition is based, these must be clearly specified and may relate only to the relative grounds for refusal as defined in Article 8 of the Community Trade Mark Regulation. Basing an opposition solely on other grounds means, ipso facto, that it is inadmissible on lack of grounds.

2.   GROUNDS FOR INADMISSIBILITY THAT CAN BE REMEDIED
AFTER THE OPPOSITION PERIOD

IR 18(2)
Rule 18 (2) of the Implementing Regulation does not give an exhaustive list of grounds for inadmissibility. It states only that 'If the Office finds that the notice of opposition does not comply with other provisions of the Regulation or of these Rules, it shall inform the opposing party accordingly and shall call upon him to remedy the deficiencies noted within a period of two months'.

These grounds relate mainly to the formal aspects of the notice of opposition and in particular to:

the requirements relating to representation before the Office (Article 88 of the Community Trade Mark Regulation and Rule 76 of the Implementing Regulation);

the signature of the notice of opposition (Rules 79, 80 and 82 of the Implementing Regulation).

Moreover some deficiencies may relate to elements of Rule 15 of the Implementing Regulation which do not fall under cases of absolute inadmissibility.

If the notice of opposition contains any of these deficiencies, the Office notifies the opposing party thereof. If these deficiencies have not been remedied within the period of two months from the receipt of the notice, the Office will reject the opposition.

2.1.   Representation

CTMR 88(1)
In principle, no person shall be compelled to be represented before the Office [10].

CTMR 88(2),(3)
However, opposing parties that do not have either a domicile, a principal place of business or a real or effective industrial or commercial establishment in the Community, must be represented before the Office, as and from the date of submission of the opposition. If they are not represented they must, in order for the opposition to be admissible, appoint a representative within the period of two months. This representative may be an employee of a legal person with economic connections with the opposing party and which has a domicile, principal place of business or a real or effective industrial or commercial establishment in the Community.
CTMR 89(1)
CTMR 88(3)
Where a representative is appointed his name and address must be indicated. If the representative has an ID number a reference to it is sufficient.

IR 76(1)
He must also file an authorisation signed by the opposing party entitling him to represent the opposing party.

IR 76(2),(3)
The authorisation may be either a General Authorisation or an Individual Authorisation. The authorisation must clearly indicate (even if the word 'opposition' does not appear on the authorisation) that the representative is entitled to represent the opposing party during the opposition proceedings. The wording of the authorisation form drawn up by the Office includes the opposition proceedings as it

is part of the registration procedure.

IR 76(4)

If the authorisation is not filed together with the notice of opposition, the Office will request the representative to file it within a period of two months.

Failure to file the authorisation has the following consequences:

IR 76(4)

IR 76(4)

IR 54

In the case of mandatory representation, the opposition is rejected on grounds of inadmissibility.

In the case of non-mandatory representation, the proceedings are continued with the opposing party. Procedural steps taken by the representative are, however, deemed 'not to have been taken' if the opposing party does not approve them. Where the opposing party does not approve them, the Office establishes the loss of this right and informs both parties. If the opposing party considers that the findings of the Office are inaccurate, he may request a decision on the matter.

With the exception, therefore, of the case of mandatory representation, failure to file an authorisation never constitutes a ground for inadmissibility, and the proceedings continue with the party directly involved if procedural steps taken by the representative have been approved by the party.

2.2.   *Signature of the notice of opposition*

The notice of opposition, in order to be admissible, must be signed by the opposing party or the appointed representative.

The manner of supplying the signature differs depending on the type of communication used [11].

IR 79(a)

When the method chosen is by post or hand delivery, a signed original of the notice of opposition must be submitted to the Office. Annexes enclosed thereto need not be signed.

IR 79(b)

IR 80(3),(4)

If the method chosen is by fax, the requirement of the signature is fulfilled if the signature appears on the relevant printout of the said fax. Additional methods of identifying the sender may be determined by the President of the Office.

IR 82(3),(4)

Lastly, if the method chosen is by electronic means, the indication of the name of the sender is deemed to be equivalent to the signature. The Office considers computer faxes as falling into this category.

3.   DECISION AS TO THE ADMISSIBILITY OF THE OPPOSITION

IR 19(1)

If the opponent has complied with the admissibility requirements, the opposition is communicated to the applicant or his representative after the expiry of the opposition period. No formal decision on the admissibility of the opposition is required.

If the opposition does not comply with the admissibility requirements, the Office will decide that the opposition is inadmissible and will reject it. This decision must be communicated to the opposing party together with the required information regarding appeal of that decision.

IR 18(3)
This decision is always communicated to the applicant for information purposes.

IR 18(1)
If the fee has been paid, the rejection of the opposition on grounds of inadmissibility does not entail any refund, even partial, of the fee.

CHAPTER 3—EXAMINATION OF THE OPPOSITION

Once the opposition has been considered as admissible by the Office, its examination begins.
It should be borne in mind that the opposition proceedings involve two parties. It is therefore important for the Office to observe the adversarial principle throughout the examination of the case.
The Office must ensure that all the information filed is communicated to the other party and give the other party sufficient time to reply. In order to ensure that the parties receive the same treatment and to prevent the proceedings from being prolonged, the time limits specified by the Office during the written stage of the opposition proceedings are in principle two months.
Observance of the adversarial principle also means that the Office can rule only on information on which the other party has had an opportunity to comment.
In principle, opposition proceedings are, moreover, written proceedings. Although the parties can at any time request oral proceedings, it is the Office which, if it thinks fit, accepts or rejects this request. The Office may also, in cases where it thinks fit, initiate oral proceedings on its own motion (ex officio).
Chapter 3 reviews the written stage of the examination. Oral proceedings, as well as other external events that may arise during examination, such as suspension, joinder, friendly settlement, etc., are analysed in Chapter 4.

1. NOTIFICATION OF THE OPPOSITION AND COMMENCEMENT OF THE PROCEEDINGS

1.1. Notification of the opposition

IR 19(1)
At the end of the time period for filing an opposition and as soon as the Office finds that the notice of opposition complies with all the admissibility requirements, the Office communicates it to the applicant or, where appropriate, to his representative.
In its communication, the Office draws the applicant's attention to the fact that the opposition proceedings are deemed to commence only two months after receipt of this communication [12] and that this period may be extended if both parties jointly so request. The Office also informs the opposing party of the exact date of commencement of the proceedings and of the possibility of extending this period if both parties so request.
Within the technical means available, the Office also communicates information on other oppositions which have been entered against the application and where the admissibility has not yet been determined.
The time limit for response by the applicant is in principle three months. This time limit is due to the fact that the Office takes into account the period of two months prior to the commencement of the proceedings as set out in Rule 19 (1) of the Implementing Regulation. Where this period is extended, the time limit for

response will end one month after the commencement of the opposition proceedings.

If opposing parties submit, either together with, or separately from, the filing of the notice, additional documents in support of their opposition, these must also be communicated to the applicant without delay.

1.2. Date of commencement of proceedings

The notion of 'commencement of proceedings' relates to the commencement of the adversarial part of the opposition proceedings rather than the actual opposition proceedings which began previously when the notice of opposition was filed at the Office. The expression 'opposition proceedings' used below in place of the expression 'adversarial part of the opposition proceedings' is therefore no more than a simplification of language.

The opposition proceedings therefore commence in principle only two months after the receipt by the applicant of the notice of opposition. This period may be extended by the Office at the joint request of the parties.

The purpose of this two-month pre-examination period (also called 'cooling-off' period) is to allow a quick resolution of the opposition without proceeding to the adversarial stage.

IR 19(1)

Having received the opposition, the applicant may decide to withdraw his application or restrict it to goods and services against which the opposition is not directed [13].

IR 19(3)

As soon as the withdrawal or restriction to goods and services against which the opposition is not directed has been notified to the Office, the Office informs the opposing party accordingly and refunds the opposition fee, as the opposition no longer has any object.

If the restriction relates only to some of the goods and services against which the opposition is directed or if it is not clear whether the opposition is also directed against the remaining goods or services, the Office cannot automatically declare the opposition to be without object. In these situations, the Office communicates the restriction to the opposing party and his agreement to the 'closure' of the proceedings is requested. If the opposing party maintains the opposition, the opposing party will be invited to declare whether the opposition is maintained against some or all of the remaining goods or services.

The applicant may enter into negotiations with the opposing party. In order for the opposing party to benefit from the reimbursement of the opposition fee, however, these negotiations, if they are successful, must end with the withdrawal of the Community trade mark application or with the restriction of this application to goods and services against which the opposition is not directed. There is no provision for a refund of the opposition fee if the opposition is withdrawn.

If the negotiations end in such a withdrawal (of the opposition), the possible apportionment of costs are at the parties' sole charge. Article 81 (1) and (3) of the Community Trade Mark Regulation are not applicable as the proceedings have not yet commenced.

IR 71(2)
IR 19(2)

In order to facilitate their negotiations, the parties may jointly request an extension of the period of two months prior to the commencement of proceedings.

The Office may, at the request of the parties and if it thinks fit, extend this period several times. The Office therefore has to examine the grounds for these requests, which may be in the form of a brief statement, in order to avoid any unnecessary prolongation of the proceedings. If it considers that the extension is not justified, the Office may refuse a request for extension.

CTMR 115(7)

IR 17(3)

During the 'cooling-off' period the parties may jointly agree to use a language for the proceedings that differs from the from the language specified by the normal rules. This new language may be one of the official languages of the Community. The opposing party must, where necessary, file a translation of its notice of opposition within a period of one month from the date of commencement of the proceedings. [14]

1.3.   *Facts, evidence and arguments presented in support of the opposition*

CTMR 42(3)

IR 16(1)

Article 42 of the Community Trade Mark Regulation states that the opposing party may present facts, evidence and arguments in support of its opposition.

IR 16(2)

This information may relate to all aspects of earlier rights, for instance to the nature of these rights, to the fact that the prior trade mark is a national, international or Community trade mark, a well-known trade mark or a trade mark having a reputation.

If the prior trade mark is a Community trade mark, the Office already keeps the information relating to registration. The opposing party does not have to provide the information.

IR 16(2)

This information takes the form, in particular, of a copy of the certificate of registration and particulars and supporting evidence in respect of the well-known nature or reputation of a trade mark or in respect of the acquisition and scope of protection of a right.

Such information may also relate to market awareness of the trade mark, evidence of confusion, advertising expenditure etc.

In practice, when it concerns an application or an earlier mark, it is recommended that the opposing party produce a copy of the mark in its last state. In case of a non-registered mark or other earlier sign, the representation must consist of a sample of the mark or the signs as they are being used.

The copy of the registration certificate is the normal proof, but the Office also accepts a copy of all documents upon which the origin is clearly indicated by the opposing party. For example copies of extracts of registers or bulletins published in paper form or on CD-ROM are accepted. If the extracts contain codes, it is necessary for the opposing party to produce the definition of the codes.

The opposing party must also indicate that the produced copies are true copies of the original and reflect the actual registration situation.

IR   16(3)

IR 20(2)

If these particulars and supporting documents are not submitted together with the notice of opposition or subsequent thereto, the Office gives the opposing party—after the commencement of the proceedings—a time limit of two months to submit them. The Office also informs the applicant and gives him, if necessary, a new time limit for response to the opposition. This new time limit will allow the applicant to reply only once to the notice of opposition as a whole.

Where the documents which have been produced are obviously erroneous or incomplete, the Office may ask for a clarification.

IR 20(2)

On receipt, the Office communicates these particulars and supporting documents to the applicant without delay and specifies a new time limit for response.

If the opposing party submits no supporting documents, the Office rules on the opposition on the basis of the evidence before it and on the reply of the applicant.

2. OBSERVATIONS BY THE PARTIES TO THE OPPOSITION

In principle, bearing in mind that a rapid examination and resolution of the opposition is in the interest of the parties and the Office, the Office generally asks the applicant and the opposing party to submit their observations only once.

There are, however, as many exchanges as are needed in cases that raise particular difficulties with respect either to facts or evidence, in particular where the opposing party is required to provide proof of use, or with respect to complex legal arguments, or with respect to both aspects together.

CTMR 43(1)

The Office therefore assesses the number of exchanges that are required on a case by case basis. It then invites the parties to file observations both on communications from the other party or on its own communications or on its request for clarification.

Any observations received from one party are always communicated to the other party without delay. Similarly, observations reaching the Office after a given time limit are communicated to the other party by virtue of the adversarial principle. The parties are informed, however, that the Office cannot take these into account in its decision.

The analysis given below therefore reviews only the initial exchanges between the parties as practices are identical for all subsequent communications and observations.

2.1. *Observations by the applicant in response to the opposition*

IR 20(1)

Observations in response coming directly from the applicant or his representative must reach the Office within the specified period of three months or, if the 'cooling-off' period is extended, within one month after the commencement of the proceedings.

IR 20(2)

In cases in which the Office has specified a time limit for the opposing party to give facts, evidence and arguments in support of its opposition, the response period runs from the date of receipt by the applicant of this information supplementing the opposition [15].

IR 20(3)

If the applicant does not file any observations within the period specified, the Office may rule directly on the opposition on the basis of the evidence received.

Lastly, observations from the applicant that reach the Office after the end of the three-month period, although communicated to the opposing party, are not taken into account by the Office.

2.2.   *Request for proof of use*

CTMR 43(2),(3)

The applicant may invite the opposing party to furnish proof that, '... during the period of five years preceding the date of publication of the Community trade mark application...' the earlier Community or national trade mark '...has been put to genuine use...' in the Community or in the Member State concerned '...in connection with the goods or services in respect of which it is registered and which he cites as justification for his opposition, or that there are proper reasons for non-use, provided the earlier trade mark has at that date been registered for not less than five years'.

While the Regulation does not specify the stage of the proceedings at which this request may be made by the applicant, it is nevertheless strongly recommended that the applicant enter this request as early as possible in the proceedings, in particular in his observations in reply to the opposition.

CTMR 79
CTMR 74 (2)

In consideration of the principles generally accepted in this respect in the Member States, the request for proof of use, as a means of defence and in compliance with the adversarial principle, must be brought to the attention of the opposing party as soon as possible. The Office may reject a request submitted at too late a stage, particularly after the parties have had an opportunity to file all their observations and there is enough information for a decision to be taken.

IR 22(1)

The opposing party will be given a time limit within which to furnish proof of use of its trade mark or show that there are proper reasons for its non-use.

The opposing party must therefore provide proof that during the five years preceding the publication of the contested trade mark its own trade mark has been used in the European Community or in the Member State in which it is registered, and that this use has been genuine or, in the case of non-use, that there are proper reasons for non-use.

IR 22(2)

'The indications and evidence for the furnishing of proof of use shall consist of indications concerning the place, time, extent and nature of use of the opposing trade mark for the goods and services ...' on which the opposition is based.

IR 22(3)

It is recommended that proof of use is confined to two-dimensional evidence that can be readily communicated and that can be readily scanned, such as labels, price lists, catalogues, invoices, photographs, newspaper advertisements, market studies, advertising or marketing research reports, etc.

It is also recommended that two copies are sent of documents containing a large number of pages, such as catalogues, in order to facilitate their communication to

the applicant.
CTMR 76(1)(f)
IR 22(3)
The opposing party may also prove genuine use of its trade mark by furnishing documents in the form of statements in writing as specified in Article 76 (1) (f) of the Community Trade Mark Regulation. These include '... statements in writing sworn or affirmed or having a similar effect under the law of the State in which the statement is drawn up'.
If this proof is not provided within the time limit, the Office rejects the opposition.

CTMR 43(3)
If such proof is submitted in time, the Office then has the task of assessing the nature and extent of use. When the Office finds that the proof furnished is not suffi-cient to establish genuine and serious use of the goods and services, the opposition will be rejected.

CTMR 43(2),(3)
If the proof submitted shows use only for some of the goods and services on which the opposition is based, the earlier trade mark is then deemed to be registered, for the purposes of the examination of the opposition, only in respect of the goods and services for which the mark was actually used, unless the opposing party can show proper reasons for the non-use of the mark for these products and services. The opposition is then rejected in whole or in part to the extent that it is based on these goods or services.
If the opposing party brings forward proof of use or in absence of proof of use fur-nishes proof establishing proper reasons for the non-use of its trade mark, the Office rules on the opposition on the basis of the evidence presented in support of the opposition and in response thereto.

IR 22(4)
If the opposing party submits documents in a language other than that of the pro-ceedings, the Office requests a translation for its own needs only when it thinks fit or if translation is necessary for the proceedings, for instance, when a translation is necessary for the applicant.

2.3.   *Withdrawal or restriction of the application for registration*

CTMR 44(1)
IR 20(5)
The applicant may, at any stage of the proceedings, withdraw his application or restrict the lost of goods and services. A withdrawal or restriction cannot be revoked.

2.3.1.   WITHDRAWAL OF THE APPLICATION

IR 20(5)
A withdrawal automatically leads to the end of the proceedings.
The withdrawal of an application is not subject to any particular formalities. The applicant must, however, specify the number of the applications being withdrawn, together with his name and address or those of his representative.
The applicant must submit the withdrawal in writing, so that it may be communi-cated to the opposing party for information purposes. The latter's agreement to the

withdrawal is not required.

IR 19(1-3)
The main difference, depending on the date of withdrawal, lies in the financial consequences. If the withdrawal takes place before the date of commencement of the proceedings, the Office refunds the opposition fee. As the Office does not have to examine the file, it does not have to take a decision.

CTMR 81(3)
If the withdrawal takes place after the date of commencement, the opposition fee is not refunded. As the applicant is the party terminating the opposition proceedings, he must bear the fees and costs incurred by the opposing party in the course of the proceedings unless the parties agree otherwise. The Office may also, in particular for reasons of equity, apportion the costs differently.

CTMR 108(4)
Lastly, the Office informs the applicant that he may request the conversion of his application for a Community trade mark into an application for a national trade mark.

CTMR 44(1)
The withdrawal is published in the Bulletin of Community Trade Marks.

2.3.2.   RESTRICTION OF THE APPLICATION

IR 13
The request for restriction must contain the following information:
the file number of the CTM application,
the name and the address of the applicant or his representative,
a clear indication of the goods or services for which the application is withdrawn or for which it is maintained.
IR   19(3)
IR 20(5)
A restriction of the application to the goods or services against which the opposition is not directed leads automatically, like a withdrawal, to conclusion of the proceedings. However, if the Office has the slightest doubt as to the scope of the goods and services the application is restricted to, it shall not automatically end the proceedings but ask for the opinion of the opponent.

IR 20(5)
On receipt of the restriction, the Office communicates it to the opposing party who will be invited expressly to state whether or not the opposition is maintained. If no reply is received within the time limit, the Office considers the opposition to be maintained. The opposing party is notified of this in the notification communicating the restriction.
There are two main outcomes:

2.3.2.1.   THE OPPOSING PARTY MAINTAINS THE OPPOSITION

IR 20(5)
Within the time limit set by the Office, the opposing party must state whether or not the opposition is maintained and, if so, against which of the remaining goods or services. This may be the outcome when, for instance, the applicant withdraws only

some of the goods and services against which the opposition is directed.

The opposing party obviously cannot extend the basis of his opposition to goods and services that were not included in the notice of opposition.

As soon as the opposing party gives notice that he is maintaining the opposition, the Office communicates the reply to the applicant.

The Office may, together with this communication, specify a new time limit for the applicant to submit observations in reply if he has not already done so together with the restriction.

The opposing party may make the withdrawal of its opposition subject to further requirements relating to the withdrawal of other goods or services against which the opposition is directed. In this case, the Office communicates these requirements to the applicant and specifies a period for response. If the applicant satisfies the opposing party's requirements, the opposition is then deemed to be withdrawn without further consultation of the opposing party, who is simply informed thereof.

2.3.2.2. THE OPPOSING PARTY DOES NOT MAINTAIN THE OPPOSITION

IR 20(5)

If the opposing party does not maintain the opposition, the Office will terminate the proceedings.

For the opposing party, the formal withdrawal of the opposition is the clearest way of showing that it has decided not to maintain its opposition.

If the opposing party does not formally withdraw the opposition but merely declares that the opposition is not maintained, it becomes groundless. The opposition proceedings are then terminated without a decision on the merits.

CTMR 81(3)

Except in case of equity, the applicant will be required to bear the costs of the opposing party as it was the restriction of the application which led to the termination of proceedings.

CTMR 44(1)

The restriction is published in the Bulletin of Community Trade Marks when the mark is registered.

CTMR 108(4)

The Office also informs the applicant of the possibility of converting the Community trade mark application into a national trade mark application for the goods and services withdrawn.

2.4.   Observations by the opposing party

IR 20(4)

Any observations of any kind filed by the applicant are communicated to the opposing party by the Office which specifies a period for reply, in principle of two months, so that the opposing party may make its position known or, where necessary, provide proof of use.

In the same way as observations in response to the opposition, any observations received from the opposing party are communicated without delay to the applicant. Similarly, observations which reach the Office after the time limit specified, whether or not they have been preceded by other observations, are forwarded to the applicant by virtue of the adversarial principle. The parties are informed, however, that the Office cannot take them into account.

IR 20(3)
If the opposing party files no observations within the time limit specified, the Office rules directly on the opposition on the basis of the evidence before it.
CTMR 43(2),(3)
IR 22(1)
If the opposing party furnishes proof of use [16], the Office communicates it to the applicant and specifies a period for his response, in principle two months. The response is necessarily communicated to the opposing party who is given a further period of two months to make his views known.

3.   EXAMINATION OF THE FILE

CTMR 43(5)
When the Office has received, within the time limits specified, all the observations of the parties and, where necessary, proof of use of the earlier trade mark, it will decide on the opposition after examining the file.

CTMR 74(2)
There is no provision that the Office must inform the parties of a date for the `closure' of the written proceedings, after which no additional observations will be accepted. In the case of a single exchange of observations between the parties, the written proceedings are deemed to be closed on expiry of the time limit given to the opposing party to reply to the applicant's observations.
If, however, the Office considers that the file is incomplete or if the parties so request, it may extend the exchange by giving the parties a new time limit for response, after which the written proceedings will be deemed to be closed.

CTMR 74(1)
Decisions are therefore always based only on the information submitted by the parties, without taking into account other facts.

4.   THE END OF THE OPPOSITION PROCEEDINGS

CTMR 43(5)
IR 94(1)
The opposition proceedings may be brought to conclusion in several ways. First of all by a decision on the opposition, the CTM application and costs.
It may also be brought to conclusion by measures such as the withdrawal of the application or the opposition, a friendly settlement between the parties or a loss of the applicant's rights which result in a case which does not proceed to judgment. In these cases, the apportionment of costs may be different depending on whether paragraph 3 or paragraph 4 of Article 81 of the Community Trade Mark Regulation apply.

4.1.   Decisions

4.1.1.   DECISION ON THE OPPOSITION AND THE APPLICATION FOR REGISTRATION

CTMR 127(2)
The decision ruling on the opposition is taken by a panel of three members of the

Opposition Division, at least one of whom must be legally qualified.

CTMR	73
IR	55

IR 52

The decision given by the Office must respect certain formalities. It must be in writing, must state the reasons on which it is based and must be signed by the three members of the opposition division. It must also specify the time limit for, and and methods of appeal open to, the parties.

IR 61

The decision is communicated to the parties in accordance with the rules set out in Part A of these Guidelines [17].

CTMR 43(6)

The decision refusing the CTM application and upholding the opposition is published upon becoming final. The applicant also receives information on the possibility of converting his Community trade mark application into a national trade mark application.

CTMR	43(2)

IR 22(1)

In certain cases, the Office is bound as regards the outcome of the decision. It must, therefore, reject the opposition when the opposing party fails to furnish proof of use. The Office is bound in the same way when the opposing party loses its rights following a rejection of the application on which the opposition is based, following an administrative or legal action, following a failure to renew the registration of the earlier trade mark or following a surrender of the earlier trade mark.

4.1.2.   DECISION ON COSTS

CTMR 81(1)
IR 94

In principle, the losing party in opposition proceedings bears the '... fees incurred by the other party as well as, without prejudice to Article 115 (6), all costs incurred by him essential to the proceedings, including travel and subsistence and the remuneration of an agent, advisor or advocate, within the limit of the scales set for each category of costs...' as set out in Rule 94 (7) of the Implementing Regulation.

IR 94(6)

These fees and costs are limited to those actually incurred by the winning party in opposition proceedings to the extent that they were necessary.

CTMR 81(2)

However, if each of the parties to the proceedings loses, i.e., in particular, if the opposition is only partially upheld or '... if reasons of equity so dictate...', the Office may decide on a different apportionment.

IR 94(1),(2)

The Office will therefore, in its decision ruling on the opposition, also determine the apportionment of the fees and costs that may have been incurred by each of the parties.

CTMR 81(5)

If, however, '... the parties conclude before the Opposition Division ... a settlement of costs differing from that provided for pursuant to ...' the application of the regulatory texts, the Opposition Division '... shall take note of that agreement'. A decision on costs is not necessary in these circumstances.

CTMR 81(6)
The actual amount of the costs in application of the apportionment decision will be fixed upon request in a decision taken by the registry of the Opposition Division.

IR 94(3)
This request must be presented in writing and should be filed, if necessary, together with the evidence of the costs. The request is communicated to the other party by the Office which specifies a period for reply of two months so that this party may make its position known.

The decision of the registry may be reviewed by the Opposition Division in question.

IR 94(4)
A request for a review of the amount of costs must be filed by writing within one month of the date of notification of the apportionment decision. It shall not be deemed to be filed until the fee for reviewing the amount of the cost has been paid. The request will be communicated to the other party which will be given an opportunity to submit its observations within a period of two months.

IR 94(5)
The Division in question takes its decision without hearing the parties.

4.2.   Cases which do not proceed to judgment
Opposition proceedings may be brought to conclusion, at the instigation of the parties involved, prior to a decision ruling on the opposition, the application and costs being made. This may occur, for instance, upon the withdrawal of the opposition or the application, upon the restriction of the application, upon a friendly settlement between the parties or upon the suspension of the proceedings. These and other instances are explained below.

4.2.1.   WITHDRAWAL OF THE CONTESTED APPLICATION
As withdrawal was already dealt with earlier above in Section 2-3, it is mentioned here only for systematic reasons.

4.2.2.   WITHDRAWAL OF THE OPPOSITION
Only complete withdrawal of the opposition can be envisaged as a way of bringing the proceedings to conclusion. This may, in particular, be the outcome of a friendly settlement [18].

Of course, the opposing party may, during the proceedings, restrict the opposition to a smaller number of the goods or services contested or restrict the number of goods or services on which the opposition is based. This may be the case, for instance, when the applicant asks for proof of use that the opposing party cannot or does not wish to furnish.

As there are no formalities required in this regard, a simple written request from the opposing party, that is sufficiently clear, is enough to bring the proceedings to conclusion. Closure takes place automatically on receipt of the withdrawal as the proceedings no longer have a basis.

Lastly, in contrast to the withdrawal or restriction of the application, this withdrawal does not need to be published.

CTMR 81(3)
The apportionment of the fees and costs depends on the origin of the withdrawal. If the withdrawal is carried out by the opposing party, without intervention by the other party, the opposing party is liable for the costs. If the withdrawal is the result of a restriction of the application, the applicant is liable for the costs.

4.2.3. FRIENDLY SETTLEMENT

CTMR 43(4)
Friendly settlements provided for by the Community Trade Mark Regulation are examined in detail in Section 3 of Chapter 4.
The parties are free to decide on the measure that brings the opposition proceedings to conclusion. While they can decide on the withdrawal of the opposition, they can also simply ask the Office to state that the case does not proceed to judgment without giving specific reasons. It suffices to communicate the written agreement of the parties, which does not have to include a statement of grounds, to the Office for the proceedings to be 'closed' by a decision not to proceed to judgment. The Office then takes the necessary steps to close the proceedings on the basis of this agreement.

CTMR 81(3)
If the negotiations end with a withdrawal of the application or the opposition, the parties will probably, in order to avoid the financial risks connected with Article 81 (3) of the Community Trade Mark Regulation as analysed above, settle the apportionment of costs in their agreement.

CTMR 81(4)
If the negotiations end in a case that does not proceed to judgment, the apportionment of fees and costs is at the discretion of the Office, unless otherwise agreed by the parties.

4.2.4. *The loss of the applicant's rights*

4.2.4.1. MULTIPLE OPPOSITIONS

IR 21(2)
If a number of oppositions are entered in respect of the same application, the Office may, after an initial examination of these oppositions, decide to examine one or several cases and suspend the others. [19]

IR 21(3)
If examination of the initial case leads to the rejection of the application, the Office must automatically terminate proceedings in respect of the other cases, whose opposition is '... deemed to have been disposed of'. 'Such disposition shall be considered to constitute a case which has not proceeded to judgment within the meaning of Article 81 (4) of the Regulation'. This means that the apportionment of any costs that may have been incurred is settled at the discretion of the Office.

IR 21(4)

In these situations, the Office refunds 50% of the fee paid by each opposing party whose opposition has been suspended and is deemed to have been disposed of.

4.2.4.2 OBSERVATIONS BY THIRD PARTIES

CTMR 41

Third parties to the opposition proceedings may, after the publication of the application for registration of a Community trade mark submit observations based in particular on absolute grounds [20], on which grounds the trademark shall not be registered ex officio.

CTMR 81(4)

If the Office, after examining these grounds, rejects the application for registration, the opposition has no purpose and the Office rules that it is a case that does not proceed to judgment. The apportionment of the fees and costs is then at the discretion of the Office, unless otherwise agreed by the parties.

CHAPTER 4—SPECIAL FEATURES OF THE PROCEEDINGS: SUSPENSION, JOINDER, FRIENDLY SETTLEMENT, ORAL PROCEEDINGS

This chapter deals with special features of opposition proceedings, namely suspension, joinder, friendly settlements, and oral proceedings.

The parties may request, at any time, the suspension of the proceedings or may request oral proceedings before the Opposition Division.

Similarly, the Office may, on its own initiative, invite the parties to reach a friendly settlement or invite parties for oral proceedings or take any measure relating to the taking of evidence or suspend one or several oppositions entered in respect of the same application. It may also join oppositions entered in respect of the same application and subsequently decide to separate them again.

1.   SUSPENSION OF OPPOSITION PROCEEDINGS

Opposition proceedings may be suspended in three cases:

> oppositions based on an application for registration of a trade mark,
>
> multiple oppositions in respect of the same application for registration,
>
> other circumstances justifying such a suspension.

Suspension, on the initiative of the parties or the Office, may take place at any time during the proceedings, although in principle it takes place at the beginning of the proceedings. It is obvious that the proceedings must have commenced if they are to be suspended. Suspension can therefore take place only after the date of commencement of the proceedings.

IR 19(2)

Before this date, parties who wish to reach a friendly settlement and 'suspend' the proceedings must in practice jointly request an extension of the two-month period prior to the commencement of the proceedings.

Suspension is not mandatory. The Office will decide to suspend proceedings only if there are genuine and proper reasons.

If the Office receives observations during the period of suspension, they cannot be taken into account at this stage of the proceedings but may possibly be taken into account at the end of the suspension, after they have been communicated to the other party.

If the proceedings have not been terminated at the end of the suspension, they resume at the point at which they were suspended.

1.1. *Oppositions based on an application for registration*

CTMR 8(2)(b)
IR 20(6)

Subject to its registration, an opposition may be based on a Community or national trade mark application or an application filed at the Benelux Trade Mark Office. In this case, the Office is entitled to suspend the opposition proceedings until the application is registered.

Therefore, if there are genuine doubts about the validity of the application, the Office will suspend the proceedings as it can rule on the opposition only if the earlier trade mark is registered. This suspension will take place where possible at the beginning of the opposition proceedings.

The Office, nevertheless, does not suspend the proceedings when the earlier application is at the final stage of its registration proceeding and is likely to be registered before the decision ruling on the opposition.

If it appears that the two trade mark applications (that of the opposing party and that of the applicant) are not in conflict, the Office does not suspend the proceedings as the decision on substance will entail the rejection of the opposition.

In the case of a national trade mark application or an application filed at the Benelux Trade Mark Office, the Office is unable systematically to ascertain from the national offices or the Benelux Office whether or not this application is subject to proceedings based on absolute or relative grounds of refusal which are likely to entail its complete or partial rejection.

Consequently, the Office will suspend the proceedings only when it is informed that proceedings for the total or partial rejection of the application have been set in motion. In the case of final rejection, the Office rules that the opposition will be rejected [21].

1.2. *Multiple oppositions*

IR 21(2)

If several oppositions are entered in respect of the same application, the Office may, after a preliminary examination of the oppositions, decide to examine one or several oppositions and suspend the others.

Suspension is not automatic in this case either. It takes place only when an initial examination of the notices of opposition shows that the application is very likely to be rejected on the basis of one of the oppositions.

In all cases where there is doubt, the Office will therefore deal with oppositions in parallel.

IR 21(2)

When the Office suspends opposition proceedings for this reason, it must inform the opposing parties '...of any relevant decisions taken during those proceedings which are continued' and, in particular, of any events having a decisive effect on the case or bringing the opposition proceedings to conclusion. These include, in particular, decisions to reject the contested application partially or its withdrawal.

IR 21(3)

Once the contested application has been finally rejected, the suspended opposition proceedings are deemed to have been disposed of and the Office will close the proceedings as cases that do not proceed to judgment. The Office informs each opposing party thereof.

IR 21(4)
The Office refunds 50% of the fee paid by each opposing party whose opposition has been suspended and is deemed to have been disposed of.

CTMR 81(4)
Lastly, when the decision ending the suspension(s) is that the case does not proceed to judgment, the apportionment of costs is at the discretion of the Office.

1.3.   Other circumstances

IR 20(6)
The Implementing Regulation gives no specific details of the nature of these '... other circumstances ...' where '... such a suspension is appropriate'.
Some examples can, however, be given.

1.3.1.   AT THE REQUEST OF THE PARTIES
Suspension may be requested by the parties following, for instance, a friendly settlement procedure that they or the Office have set in motion.
A request for suspension on the grounds of negotiation must in principle come from both parties. If, however, the Office considers that a unilateral request is justified or that the other party's refusal is obviously improper, it may accept this request and suspend the proceedings.
As there are no specific requirements in this regard, the period of the suspension and its renewal is entirely at the discretion of the Office, taking account of both the interests of the parties and the need to avoid an unnecessary prolongation of the proceedings.
If observations are filed during the suspension, they will be communicated to the other party who will be informed that, if these observations are likely to bring the suspension to conclusion, it must notify the Office thereof as soon as possible.
The parties may jointly ask, at any time during the suspension, for the proceedings to recommence. In any case, the proceedings automatically recommence at the end of the time period fixed for the suspension, without communication by the Office.

1.3.2.   JUDICIAL OR ADMINISTRATIVE ACTION
Actions of this type are entered by one of the parties to the opposition or by a third party in respect of the trade mark on which the opposition is based.
The reasons for entering such actions may vary. They may for instance be actions for revocation of rights, invalidity, infringement, etc.
These actions must be entered either before the Office or before the Community Trade Mark Courts in the case of Community trade marks, or before the national offices, if the law of the Member State so authorises, or before the national courts for national trade marks or international trade marks having effect in one of the Member States.
The Office does not automatically suspend the opposition proceedings. The Office may rule on the opposition if it considers that the two trade marks are not in conflict and that it will reject the opposition.
In practice, the Office analyses each case individually and will suspend the proceedings only when it has serious doubts on the validity of the earlier trade mark.

The suspension is continued until the final resolution of the judicial or administrative action. The Office, as it is a third party to these proceedings, is notified thereof by the parties or by any others.

1.3.3. OBSERVATIONS BY THIRD PARTIES

CTMR 41

The Community Trade Mark Regulation states that third parties may submit, at any time after the publication of the application and before the registration of the Community trade mark, observations based on absolute grounds. These observations may therefore make it necessary for the Examination Division of the Office to 'review' the CTM application.

The opposition proceedings are suspended only when the Examination Division decides to re-examine the absolute grounds for refusal of the application. The suspension ends when the decision relating to this examination becomes final.

2. JOINDER OF PROCEEDINGS AND THEIR SEPARATION

IR 21(1)

If several oppositions are entered in respect of the same application, the Office may not only suspend a certain number of oppositions, but also decide to examine several oppositions by joining them.

Joining of oppositions may for instance be envisaged when several oppositions, each in a specific class and coming from the same opponent, are entered in respect of an application filed in several classes.

Another case that may be envisaged is when oppositions in respect of the same application come from several companies that are legally independent but belong to the same economic grouping (for instance subsidiaries of an enterprise).

The parties are informed of this joinder and the Office deals with the case in the same way as a single opposition.

Depending on the circumstances and the interest of the oppositions, the Office may at any time separate the proceedings.

3. FRIENDLY SETTLEMENT

CTMR 43(4)

'The Office may, if it thinks fit, invite the parties to make a friendly settlement'.

The Office, as well as the parties, may therefore initiate a friendly settlement procedure. The Office may also, if it thinks fit, issue proposals for friendly settlement.

As, in principle, the Office cannot (and does not wish to) replace the parties, it will take action only if a settlement between the parties appears desirable in the light of the case or if there are good reasons for considering that the proceedings can be ended by a settlement, in particular because one party has made known that it wishes to negotiate.

The Office can, moreover, if expressly requested by the parties, offer assistance with their negotiations, for instance by acting as an intermediary or by providing them with any material resources that they need. Any costs incurred are borne by the parties.

Friendly settlement may be preceded by a request for suspension.

The parties are free to decide on the measure that brings the opposition proceedings to conclusion. While they can decide on the withdrawal of the opposition, they can also simply ask the Office without giving specific reasons to rule that the case will not proceed to judgment. It suffices to communicate the written agreement of the parties, which does not have to include a statement of grounds, to the Office for the proceedings to be 'closed' by a decision not to proceed to judgment. The Office then takes the steps needed to close the proceedings on the basis of this agreement.

CTMR 81(3)

If the negotiations end with a withdrawal of the application or the opposition, the parties will probably, in order to prevent one party from having to bear the costs alone, settle the apportionment of costs in their agreement.

CTMR 81(4)

If the friendly settlement ends with an agreement between the parties, the Office 'closes' the proceedings as a case that does not proceed to judgment. If negotiations end in this way, the apportionment of costs and fees is at the discretion of the Office, unless otherwise agreed by the parties.

Parties that reach a friendly settlement before the date of commencement of the proceedings and withdraw the opposition (and not the application) are not, moreover, entitled to a refund of the opposition fee. This fee is refunded only when the application is withdrawn or restricted to goods and services against which the opposition is not directed.

4.   ORAL PROCEEDINGS

CTMR 75

During the opposition proceedings, the parties may at any time request oral proceedings. The Office may also summon the parties to an oral hearing on its own initiative.

CTMR 75(1)

As, however, the opposition proceedings are in principle written proceedings, decisions as to whether it is expedient to summon the parties to a hearing are entirely at the discretion of the Office. The Office makes use of this option only in cases of genuine need.

IR 56(2)

In its summons, the Office draws attention to the points which '... in its opinion need to be discussed in order for the decision to be taken'.

CTMR   75(2)

IR 56(1)

Oral proceedings before the Opposition Division are not public. The parties are notified of this in the summons.

The Office must also give at least one month's notice of the summons, unless the parties agree to a shorter period.

IR 56(3)

The failure of one or both parties to appear at the oral proceedings in no way prevents the proceedings from continuing.

IR 60

Minutes are drawn up for oral proceedings and are signed by the person who drew them up and by the person who conducted the oral proceedings. They contain the essentials of the oral proceedings and statements made by the parties and are submitted to the latter for approval.

IR 60(2)
If a party fails to give this approval, the Office takes note of his objections and indicates them in the final decision ruling on the opposition.

IR 60(5)
Lastly, if the parties so request, the Office may make available '... a recording or a transcript of the oral proceedings...'.
If the Office thinks fit, it may, after the end of the oral proceedings, allow the parties to file observations, comments or assessments in respect of the oral discussions. These observaticns have to be confined to the arguments put forward during the oral proceedings.

COUNCIL REGULATION

of 22 December 1994

[laying down measures concerning the entry into the Community and the export and re-export from the Community of goods infringing certain intellectual property rights]

(3295/94/EC)

Notes
Words in square brackets substituted by Council Regulation 241/1999/EC, Art 1(1).

THE COUNCIL OF THE EUROPEAN UNION,
Having regard tc the Treaty establishing the European Community, and in particular Article 113 thereof,
Having regard to the proposal from the Commission,
Having regard to the opinion of the European Parliament,
Having regard to the opinion of the Economic and Social Committee,
Whereas Council Regulation 3842/86/EEC of 1 December 1986 laying down measures to prohibit the release for free circulation of counterfeit goods has been in force since 1 January 1988; whereas conclusions should be drawn from the experience gained during the early years of its implementation with a view to improving the operation of the system it set up;
Whereas the marketing of counterfeit goods and pirated goods causes considerable injury to law-abiding manufacturers and traders and to holders of the copyright or neighbouring rights and misleads consumers; whereas such goods should as far as possible be prevented from being placed on the market and measures should be adopted to that end to deal effectively with this unlawful activity without impeding to freedom of legitimate trade; whereas this objective is also being pursued through efforts being made along the same lines at international level;
Whereas, in so far as counterfeit or pirated goods and similar products are imported from third countries, it is important to prohibit their release for free circulation in the Community or their entry for a suspensive procedure and to set up an appropriate procedure enabling the customs authorities to act to ensure that such a prohibition can be properly enforced;
Whereas action by the customs authorities to prohibit the release for free circula-

tion of counterfeit or pirated goods or their entry for a suspensive procedure should also apply to the export or re-export of such goods from the Community;

Whereas, as regards suspensive procedures and re-export subject to notification, action by the customs authorities will take place only where suspected counterfeit or pirated goods are discovered during a check;

Whereas the Community takes into account the terms of the GATT agreement on trade-related intellectual property issues, including a trade in counterfeit goods, in particular the measures to be taken at the frontier;

Whereas provision should be made that the customs authorities are empowered to take decisions on applications for action to be taken that are submitted to them;

Whereas action by the customs authorities should consist either in suspending the release for free circulation, export or re-export of goods suspected of being counterfeit or pirated or in detaining such goods when they are entered for a suspensive procedure or re-exported subject to notification for as long as is necessary to enable it to be determined whether the goods are actually counterfeit or pirated;

Whereas it is appropriate to authorise the Member States to detain the goods in question for a certain period even before an application by the right holder has been lodged or approved in order to allow him to lodge an application for action by the customs authorities;

Whereas the competent authority should decide cases submitted to it by reference to the criteria which are used to determine whether goods produced in the Member State concerned infringe intellectual property rights; whereas Member States' provisions on the competence of the judicial authorities and procedures are not affected by this Regulation;

Whereas it is necessary to determine the measures to be applied to the goods in question where it is established that they are counterfeit or pirated; whereas those measures should not only deprive those responsible for trading in such goods of the economic benefits of the transaction and penalise them but also constitute an effective deterrent to further transactions of the same kind;

Whereas in order to avoid serious disruption to the clearing of goods contained in travellers' personal luggage, it is necessary to exclude from the scope of this Regulation goods which may be counterfeit or pirated which are imported from third countries within the limits laid down by Community rules in respect of relief from customs duty;

Whereas uniform application of the common rules laid down by this Regulation must be ensured and to that end a Community procedure must be established enabling measures implementing these rules to be adopted within appropriate periods and mutual assistance between the Member States, of the one part, and between the Member States and the Commission, of the other part, to be strengthened so as to ensure greater effectiveness;

Whereas it will be appropriate to consider the possibility of increasing the number of intellectual property rights covered by this Regulation in the light, inter alia, of the experience gained in its implementation;

Whereas Regulation 3842/86/EEC should therefore be repealed,

HAS ADOPTED THIS REGULATION:

CHAPTER I

General

[Article 1

1. This Regulation lays down—
    (a) the conditions under which the customs authorities shall take action where goods suspected of being goods referred to in paragraph 2(a) are—
        – entered for free circulation, export or re-export, in accordance with Article 61 of Council Regulation 2913/92/EEC of 12 October 1992 establishing the Community Customs Code,
        – found in the course of checks on goods under customs supervision within the meaning of Article 37 of Council Regulation 2913/92/EEC, placed under a suspensive procedure within the meaning of Article 84(1)(a) of that Regulation, re-exported subject to notification or placed in a free zone or free warehouse within the meaning of Article 166 thereof;
  and
    (b) the measures which shall be taken by the competent authorities with regard to those goods where it has been established that they are indeed goods referred to in paragraph 2(a).
2. For the purposes of this Regulation—
    (a) 'goods infringing an intellectual property right' means
        - 'counterfeit goods', namely:
    - goods, including the packaging thereof, bearing without authorisation a trade mark which is identical to the trade mark validly registered in respect of the same type of goods, or which cannot be distinguished in its essential aspects from such trade mark, and which thereby infringes the rights of the holder of the trade mark in question under Community law or the law of the Member State where the application for action by the customs authorities is made,
    - any trade mark symbol (logo, label, sticker, brochure, instructions for use, guarantee document) whether presented separately or not, in the same circumstances as the goods referred to in the first indent,
    - packaging materials bearing the trade marks of counterfeit goods, presented separately in the same circumstances as the goods referred to in the first indent;
        - 'pirated goods', namely: goods which are or embody copies made without the consent of the holder of the copyright or neighbouring rights, or of the holder of a design right, whether registered under national law or not, or of a person duly authorised by the holder in the country of production, where the making of those copies infringes the right in question under Community law or the law of the Member State in which the application for action by the customs authorities is made;
        - goods infringing, in the Member State in which the application for action by the customs authorities is made, a patent under the law of that Member State or a supplementary protection certificate as provided for by Council Regulation 1768/92/EEC or Regulation 1610/96/EC of the European Parliament and of the Council;
    (b) 'holder of a right' means the holder of a trade mark, a patent or a certificate and/or one of the rights referred to in (a), or any other person authorised to use that trademark, patent, certificate and/or right, or a representative thereof;
    (c) 'Community trademark' means the trademark defined in Article 1 of Council Regulation 40/94/EC;
    (d) 'certificate' means the supplementary protection certificate provided for by Regulation 1768/92/EEC or by Regulation 1610/96/EC.
3. Any mould or matrix which is specifically designed or adapted for the manufacture of a counterfeit trade mark or of goods bearing such a trade mark, for the manufacture of goods infringing a patent or a certificate or for the manufacture of pirated goods shall be treated as goods referred to in paragraph 2(a), provided that

the use of such moulds or matrices infringes the rights of the holder of the right in question under Community law or the law of the Member State in which the application for action by the customs authorities is made.

4. This Regulation shall not apply to goods which bear a trade mark with the consent of the holder of that trade mark or which are protected by a patent or a certificate, by a copyright or neighbouring right or by a design right and which have been manufactured with the consent of the holder of the right but are placed in one of the situations referred to in paragraph 1(a) without the latter's consent.

It shall similarly not apply to goods referred to in the first subparagraph which have been manufactured or bear a trade mark under conditions other than those agreed with the holder of the rights in question.]

Notes
Substituted by Council Regulation 241/1999/EC, Art 1(2).

CHAPTER II

[Prohibition of the entry, release for free circulation, export, re-export, placing under a suspensive procedure, or placing in a free zone or free warehouse, of goods infringing certain intellectual property rights

Article 2
The entry into the Community, release for free circulation, export, re-export, placing under a suspensive procedure or placing in a free zone or free warehouse of goods found to be goods referred to in Article 1(2)(a) on completion of the procedure provided for in Article 6 shall be prohibited.]

Notes
Art 2 and the Chapter heading immediately preceding it, are substituted by Council Regulation 241/1999/EC, Art 1(3), (4).

CHAPTER III

Application for action by the customs authorities

Article 3
1. In each Member State, the holder of a right may lodge an application in writing with the competent service of the customs authority for action by the customs authorities where the goods are placed in one of the situations referred to in Article 1(1)(a).

[Where the applicant holds a Community trade mark, the application may seek action not only by the customs authorities of the Member State in which the application is lodged but by the customs authorities of one or more other Member States as well.

Where electronic data interchange systems exist, Member States may provide that the application for customs action can be made by using a data processing technique.]

2. The application referred to in paragraph 1 shall include—
   — a sufficiently detailed description of the goods to enable the customs authorities to recognise them,
   — proof that the applicant is the holder of the right for the goods in question.

The holder of the right must also provide all other pertinent information available to him to enable the competent customs service to take a decision in full knowledge of the facts without, however, that information being a condition of admissibility of the application.

[By way of indication, in the case of pirated goods or of goods infringing patents or certificates, that information shall, wherever possible, include—]

— the place where the goods are situated or the intended destination,
— particulars identifying the consignment or packages,
— the scheduled date of arrival or departure of the goods,
— the means of transport used,
— the identity of the importer, exporter or holder.

[3. Save where the second subparagraph of paragraph 1 is applied, the application must specify the length of the period during which the customs authorities are requested to take action.

Applications under the second subparagraph of paragraph 1 shall indicate the Member State or States in which the customs authorities are requested to take action.

4. The applicant may be charged a fee to cover the administrative costs incurred in dealing with the application.

The applicant or his representative may also be charged a fee in each of the Member States where the decision granting the application is effective, to cover the costs incurred in implementing the said decision.

Such fees shall not be disproportionate to the service provided.]

5. The competent customs service with which an application drawn up pursuant to paragraph 2 has been lodged shall deal with the application and shall forthwith notify the applicant in writing of its decision.

Where that service grants the application, the service shall specify the period during which the customs authorities shall take action. That period may, upon application by the holder of the right, be extended by the service which took the initial decision.

[Where an application is submitted under the second subparagraph of paragraph 1 the said period shall be set at one year, but may be extended for a further year, at the right-holder's request, by the service which took the original decision.]

Any refusal to grant an application shall give the reasons for refusal and may form the subject of an appeal.

6. Member States may require the holder of a right, where his application has been granted, or where action as referred to in Article 1(1)(a) has been taken pursuant to Article 6(1), to provide a security—

— to cover any liability on his part vis-à-vis the persons involved in one of the operations referred to in Article 1(1)(a) where the procedure initiated pursuant to Article 6(1) is discontinued owing to an act or omission by the holder of the right or where the goods in question are subsequently found not be [goods referred to in Article 1(2)(a)],
— to ensure payment of the costs incurred in accordance with this Regulation, in keeping the goods under customs control pursuant to Article 6.

[Where an application is submitted under the second subparagraph of paragraph 1, the security shall be provided in each of the Member States in which it is required and the decision granting the application is effective.]

[7. The holder of the right is required to inform the service referred to in paragraph 1 and, where appropriate, the service or services referred to in the second subparagraph of Article 5(2), if his right should happen no longer to be validly registered or to have expired.]

8. Each Member State shall designate the service within the customs authority competent to receive and deal with the applications referred to in this Article.

[9. Paragraphs 1 to 8 shall apply mutatis mutandis to the extension of the decision on the original application.]

Notes
Para 1: words in square brackets added by Council Regulation 241/1999/EC, Art 1(5)(a).
Para 2: words in square brackets substituted by Council Regulation 241/1999/EC, Art 1(5)(b).
Paras 3, 4: substituted by Council Regulation 241/1999/EC, Art 1(5)(c).
Para 5: words in square brackets inserted by Council Regulation 241/1999/EC, Art 1(5)(d).
Para 6: words in first pair of square brackets substituted and words in second pair of square brackets added by Council Regulation 241/1999/EC, Art 1(5)(e), (f).
Para 7: substituted by Council Regulation 241/1999/EC, Art 1(5)(g).
Para 9: added by Council Regulation 241/1999/EC, Art 1(5)(h).

Article 4

Where, in the course of checks made under one of the customs procedures referred to in Article 1(1)(a) and before an application by the holder of the right has been lodged or approved, it appears evident to the customs office that goods are [goods referred to in Article 1(2)(a)], the customs authority may, in accordance with the rules in force in the Member States concerned, notify the holder of the right, where known, of a possible infringement thereof. The customs authority shall be authorised to suspend release of the goods or detain them for a period of three working days to enable the holder of the right to lodge an application for action in accordance with Article 3.

Notes
Words in square brackets substituted by Council Regulation 241/1999/EC, Art 1(6).

[Article 5

1. The decision granting the application by the holder of the right shall be forwarded immediately to the customs offices of the Member State which are liable to be concerned with the goods alleged in the application to be goods referred to in Article 1(2)(a).

2. Where an application is submitted under the second subparagraph of Article 3(1), the first indent of Article 250 of Regulation 2913/92/EEC shall apply mutatis mutandis to the decision granting the said application and the decisions extending or repealing it.

When the decision granting the said application has been taken, it shall be up to the applicant to forward that decision together, where appropriate, with any other useful information and any translations to the customs-authority service referred to in the first subparagraph of Article 3(1) in the Member State or States where the applicant has requested that action be taken. However, with the agreement of the applicant, the information and translations may be forwarded directly by the customs-authority service which took the decision. The applicant shall provide additional information as deemed necessary for the execution of the decision, at the request of the customs authorities of the other Member States concerned.

The period referred to in the third subparagraph of Article 3(5) shall run from the date on which the decision granting the application was taken. The said decision shall not enter into force in the Member State or States to which it is addressed until the submission referred to in the second subparagraph has been made and, where appropriate, until the fee referred to in the second subparagraph of Article 3(4) has been paid and the security referred to in Article 3(6) has been provided. However, the period of validity of the said decision may not, in any circumstances, exceed the period of one year from the date of adoption of the decision granting the original application.

The said decision shall then be forwarded immediately to the national customs offices liable to be concerned with the alleged counterfeit goods to which it relates. This paragraph shall apply mutatis mutandis to any decision to extend the original decision.]

Notes
Substituted by Council Regulation 241/1999/EC, Art 1(7).

CHAPTER IV

Conditions governing action by the customs authorities and by the authority competent to take a substantive decision

Article 6
1. Where a customs office to which the decision granting an application by the holder of a right has been forwarded pursuant to Article 5 is satisfied, after consulting the applicant where necessary, that goods placed in one of the situations referred to in Article 1(1)(a) correspond to the description of the [goods referred to in Article 1(2)(a)] contained in that decision, it shall suspend release of the goods or detain them.

The customs office shall immediately inform the service which dealt with the application in accordance with Article 3. That service or the customs office, shall forthwith inform the declarant and the person who applied for action to be taken. In accordance with national provisions on the protection of personal data, commercial and industrial secrecy and professional and administrative confidentiality, the customs office or the service which dealt with the application shall notify the holder of the right, at his request, of the name and address of the declarant and, if known, of those of the consignee so as to enable the holder of the right to ask the competent authorities to take a substantive decision. The customs office shall afford the applicant and the persons involved in any of the operations referred to in Article 1(1)(a) the opportunity to inspect the goods whose release has been suspended or which have been detained.

When examining the goods the customs office may take samples in order to expedite the procedure.

2. The law in force in the Member State within the territory of which the goods are placed in one of the situations referred to in Article 1(1)(a) shall apply as regards —
   (a) referral to the authority competent to take a substantive decision and immediate notification of the customs service or office referred to in paragraph 1 of that referral, unless referral is effected by that service or office;
   (b) reaching the decision to be taken by that authority. In the absence of Community rules in this regard, the criteria to be used in reaching that decision shall be the same as those used to determine whether goods produced in the Member State concerned infringe the rights of the holder. Reasons shall be given for decisions adopted by the competent authority.

Notes
Para 1: words in square brackets substituted by Council Regulation 241/1999/EC, Art 1(8).

Article 7
1. If, within 10 working days of notification of suspension of release or of detention, the customs office referred to in Article 6(1) has not been informed that the matter has been referred to the authority competent to take a substantive decision on the case in accordance with Article 6(2) or that the duly empowered authority has adopted interim measures, the goods shall be released, provided that all the customs formalities have been complied with and the detention order has been

revoked.
This period may be extended by a maximum of 10 working days in appropriate cases.
[2. In the case of goods suspected of infringing patents, certificates or design rights, the owner, importer or consignee of the goods shall be able to have the goods in question released or their detention revoked against provision of a security, provided that—

(a) the customs service or office referred to in Article 6(1) has been informed, within the time limit referred to in paragraph 1 of this Article, that the matter has been referred to the authority competent to take a substantive decision referred to in the aforesaid paragraph 1;

(b) on expiry of the time limit, the authority empowered for this purpose has not imposed interim measures; and

(c) all the customs formalities have been completed.

The security must be sufficient to protect the interests of the holder of the right. Provision of the security shall be without prejudice to the other remedies open to the holder of the right. Where the matter has been referred to the authority competent to take a substantive decision other than on the initiative of the holder of the patent, certificate or design right, the security shall be released if that person does not exercise his right to institute legal proceedings within 20 working days of the date on which he is notified of the suspension of release or detention. Where the second subparagraph of paragraph 1 applies, this period may be extended to a maximum of 30 working days.]
3. The conditions governing storage of the goods during the period of suspension of release or detention shall be determined by each Member State.

Notes
Para 2: substituted by Council Regulation 241/1999/EC, Art 1(9).

CHAPTER V

[Provisions applicable to goods found to be goods infringing an intellectual property right

Article 8
1. Without prejudice to the other forms of legal recourse open to the right-holder, Member States shall adopt the measures necessary to allow the competent authorities—

(a) as a general rule, and in accordance with the relevant provisions of national law, to destroy goods found to be goods referred to in Article 1(2)(a), or dispose of them outside the channels of commerce in such a way as to preclude injury to the holder of the right, without compensation of any sort and without cost to the Exchequer;

(b) to take, in respect of such goods, any other measures having the effect of effectively depriving the persons concerned of the economic benefits of the transaction.

Save in exceptional cases, simply removing the trademarks which have been affixed to the counterfeit goods without authorisation shall not be regarded as having such effect.
2. The goods referred to in Article 1(2)(a) may be handed over to the Exchequer. In that case, paragraph 1(a) shall apply.
3. In addition to the information given pursuant to the second subparagraph of Article 6(1) and under the conditions laid down therein, the customs office or the

competent service shall inform the holder of the right, upon request, of the names and addresses of the consignor, of the importer or exporter and of the manufacturer of the goods found to be goods referred to in Article 1(2)(a) and of the quantity of the goods in question.]

Notes
Art 8 and the Chapter heading immediately preceding it are substituted by Council Regulation 241/1999/EC, Art 1(10), (11).

CHAPTER VI

Final provisions

Article 9
[1. Save as provided by the law of the Member State in which an application in accordance with Article 3(2) is lodged or, in the case of an application under the second subparagraph of Article 3(1), by the law of the Member State in which goods referred to in Article 1(2)(a) escape detection by a customs office, the acceptance of an application shall not entitle the holder of a right to compensation where such goods are not detected by a customs office and are released or no action is taken to detain them in accordance with Article 6(1).
2. Save as provided by the law of the Member State in which the application is made or, in the case of an application under the second subparagraph of Article 3(1), by the law of the Member State in which loss or damage is incurred, exercise by a customs office or by another duly empowered authority of the powers conferred on them in regard to taking measures against goods referred to in Article 1(2)(a) shall not render them liable towards the persons involved in the operations referred to in Article 1(1)(a) or Article 4, in the event of their suffering loss or damage as a result of their action.]
3. The civil liability of the holder of a right shall be governed by the law of the Member State in which the goods in question were placed in one of the situations referred to in Article 1(1)(a).

Notes
Paras (1), (2): substituted by Council Regulation 241/1999/EC, Art 1(12).

Article 10
This Regulation shall not apply to goods of a non-commercial nature contained in travellers' personal luggage within the limits laid down in respect of relief from customs duty.

Article 11
Moreover, each Member State shall introduce penalties to apply in the event of infringements of Article 2. [Such penalties shall be effective and proportionate and constitute an effective deterrent.]

Notes
Words in square brackets substituted by Council Regulation 241/1999/EC, Art 1(13).

Article 12
The provisions necessary for the application of this Regulation shall be adopted in accordance with the procedure laid down in Article 13(3) and (4).

Article 13
1. The Commission shall be assisted by the Committee set up under Article 247 of Regulation 2913/92/EEC.

2. The Committee shall examine any matter concerning implementation of this Regulation which its chairman may raise, either on his own initiative or at the request of the representative of a Member State.

3. The representative of the Commission shall submit to the Committee a draft of the measures to be taken. The Committee shall deliver its opinion on the draft within a time limit which the chairman may lay down according to the urgency of the measures to be taken. The opinion shall be delivered by the majority laid down in Article 148(2) of the Treaty in the case of decisions which the Council is required to adopt on a proposal from the Commission. The votes of the representatives of the Member States within the Committee shall be weighted in the manner set out in that Article. The chairman shall not vote.

4. The Commission shall adopt measures which shall apply immediately. However, if the measures are not in accordance with the opinion of the Committee, they shall be communicated by the Commission to the Council forthwith. In the event—

— the Commission shall defer application of the measures which it has decided for not more than three months from the date of their communication,
— the Council, acting by a qualified majority, may take a different decision within the time limit provided for in the first indent.

Article 14

Member States shall communicate all relevant information on the application of this Regulation to the Commission.

The Commission shall communicate that information to the other Member States.

For the purpose of the application of this Regulation, the provisions of Regulation 1468/81/EEC of 19 May 1981 on mutual assistance between the administrative authorities of the Member States and cooperation between the latter and the Commission to ensure the correct application of the law on customs or agricultural matters shall apply mutatis mutandis.

The details of the information procedure shall be drawn up in the framework of the implementing provisions in accordance with Article 13(2), (3) and (4).

Article 15

Within two years of the entry into force of this Regulation, the Commission shall, on the basis of the information referred to in Article 14, report to the European Parliament and the Council on the operation of the system particularly with regard to the economic and social consequences of counterfeiting and shall propose any amendments or additions required, within a period of two years from the implementation of this Regulation.

Article 16

Regulation 3842/86/EEC shall be repealed as from the date of implementation of this Regulation.

Article 17

This Regulation shall enter into force on the third day following its publication in the Official Journal of the European Communities.

It shall apply from 1 July 1995.

This Regulation shall be binding in its entirety and directly applicable in all Member States.

Done at Brussels, 22 December 1994.

COMMISSION REGULATION

of 16 June 1995

laying down provisions for the implementation of Council Regulation 3295/94/EC
laying down measures to prohibit the release for free circulation, export, re-export
or entry for a suspensive procedure of counterfeit and pirated goods

(1367/95/EC)

THE COMMISSION OF THE EUROPEAN COMMUNITIES,

Having regard to the Treaty establishing the European Community,

Having regard to Council Regulation 3295/94/EC of 22 December 1994 laying
down measures to prohibit the release for free circulation, export, re-export or entry
for a suspensive procedure of counterfeit and pirated goods, and in particular
Articles 12, 13 and 14 thereof,1

Whereas Regulation 3295/94/EC introduced common rules with a view to prohibiting the release for free circulation, export, re-export or entry for a suspensive procedure of counterfeit and pirated goods and dealing effectively with the illegal
marketing of such goods without impeding the freedom of legitimate trade;

Whereas the nature of the proof of ownership of intellectual property required by
the second indent of the first subparagraph of Article 3(2) of Regulation
3295/94/EC should be established;

Whereas Article 14 of Regulation 3295/94/EC provides that Member States are to
communicate to the Commission all relevant information for applying that
Regulation and that the Commission is to communicate that information to the
other Member States; whereas the procedure for exchanging that information
should be laid down;

Whereas Commission Regulation 3077/872/EEC should be repealed;

Whereas the measures provided for in this Regulation are in accordance with the
opinion of the Customs Code Committee,

HAS ADOPTED THIS REGULATION:

Article 1

For the purposes of Article 1(2)(c) of Regulation 3295/94/EC, hereinafter referred
to as 'the basic Regulation' the holder of a right or any other person authorised to
use the right may be represented by a natural or legal person; such a person
includes a collecting society which has as its sole or principal purpose the management or administration of copyrights or neighbouring rights.

Article 2

The proof that the applicant holds one of the rights referred to in points (a) and (b)
of Article 1(2) of the basic Regulation, which must be submitted when applying for
action in accordance with the second indent of the first subparagraph of Article 3(2)
of that Regulation, shall be as follows—
    (a) where the holder of the right applies himself—
        — in the case of a right that is registered or for which an application has
            been lodged (trademark or design right): proof of registration with the
            relevant office or lodging of the application,
        — in the case of a copyright, neighbouring rights or design right that is
            unregistered or for which an application has not been lodged: any proof

of authorship or of his status as original holder;

(b) where the application is made by any other person authorised to use one of the rights referred to in points (a) and (b) of Article 1(2) of the basic Regulation in addition to the proof required under (a) hereof: the document by virtue of which the person is authorised to use the right in question;

(c) where a representative of the holder or of any other person authorised to use one of the rights referred to in points (a) and (b) of Article 1(2) of the basic Regulation applies: in addition to the proof required under (a) and (b) hereof, proof of authorisation to act.

Article 3

The pertinent information referred to in the second subparagraph of Article 3(2) of the basic Regulation shall include particulars of the goods, notably their value and their packaging, plus any information that could help distinguish them from goods for which there is a protected right. under the terms of the second subparagraph of Article 3(2), this information should be as detailed as possible to enable the customs authorities, using risk analysis, to identify suspect consignments accurately and without excessive effort.

Article 4

If an application is lodged in accordance with Article 4 of the basic Regulation before expiry of the time-limit of three days, the time-limits referred to in Article 7 of the Regulation shall be counted from the day of receipt of the request for action.

If the customs authority suspends release of the goods or detains them in accordance with Article 4 of the basic Regulation, it shall forthwith inform the declarant.

Article 5

1. Each Member State shall, at the earliest opportunity, send the Commission details of—

(a) the laws, regulations or administrative provisions which it adopts in implementation of this Regulation. It shall likewise inform the Commission of any provisions of its national law which preclude informing the holder as provided for in the second subparagraph of Article 6(1) and in Article 8(3) of the basic Regulation;

(b) the competent customs department responsible for receiving and handling the holder's written application, referred to in Article 3(8) of the basic Regulation.

2. To enable the Commission to monitor the effective application of the procedure laid down by the basic Regulation and draw up, in due course, the report referred to in Article 15 thereof, each Member State shall send the Commission—

(a) at the end of each calendar year, a list of all the written applications under Article 3(1) of the basic Regulation, together with the name and address of the holder, a brief description of the goods and, where relevant, the trademark, and the action taken in response to the application;

(b) at the end of each quarter, a list of specific cases in which goods have been detained or their release suspended. The information provided on each case must include:

— the name and address of the holder of the right and a brief description of the goods and, where relevant, the trademark, and

— the customs situation, country of consignment or destination, description, quantity and declared value of the goods the release of which has been suspended or which have been detained, and the date of such suspension or detention.

3. The Commission shall, in an appropriate manner, communicate to all Member States such information as it receives pursuant to this Article. Details of cases provided for in point (b) of paragraph 2 shall be sent quarterly to the Member States by the Commission.

4. Details communicated pursuant to paragraphs 1, 2 and 3 may be used only for the purposes established by the basic Regulation.

Article 6

Regulation 3077/87/EEC is hereby repealed with effect from 1 July 1995.

Article 7

This Regulation shall enter into force on the third day following its publication in the Official Journal of the European Communities.

It shall apply from 1 July 1995.

This Regulation shall be binding in its entirety and directly applicable in all Member States.

Done at Brussels, 16 June 1995.

COUNCIL REGULATION

of 14 July 1992

on the protection of geographical indications and designations of origin for agricultural products and foodstuffs

(2081/92/EC)

THE COUNCIL OF THE EUROPEAN COMMUNITIES,

Having regard to the Treaty establishing the European Economic Community, and in particular Article 43,

Having regard to the proposal from the Commission,1

Having regard to the opinion of the European Parliament,2

Having regard to the opinion of the Economic and Social Committee,3

Whereas the production, manufacture and distribution of agricultural products and foodstuffs play an important role in the Community economy;

Whereas, as part of the adjustment of the common agricultural policy the diversification of agricultural production should be encouraged so as to achieve a better balance between supply and demand on the markets;

Whereas the promotion of products having certain characteristics could be of considerable benefit to the rural economy, in particular to less-favoured or remote areas, by improving the incomes of farmers and by retaining the rural population in these areas;

Whereas, moreover, it has been observed in recent years that consumers are tending to attach greater importance to the quality of foodstuffs rather than to quantity; whereas this quest for specific products generates a growing demand for agricultural products or foodstuffs with an identifiable geographical origin;

Whereas in view of the wide variety of products marketed and of the abundance of information concerning them provided, consumers must, in order to be able to make the best choice, be given clear and succinct information regarding the origin of the product;

Whereas the labelling of agricultural products and foodstuffs is subject to the general rules laid down in Council Directive 79/112/EEC of 18 December 1978 on the approximation of the laws of the Member States relating to the labelling, presentation and advertising of foodstuffs;4 whereas, in view of their specific nature, additional special provisions should be adopted for agricultural products and foodstuffs from a specified geographical area;

Whereas the desire to protect agricultural products or foodstuffs which have an identifiable geographical origin has led certain Member States to introduce 'registered designations of origin'; whereas these have proved successful with producers, who have secured higher incomes in return for a genuine effort to improve quality, and with consumers, who can purchase high quality products with guarantees as to the method of production and origin;

Whereas, however, there is diversity in the national practices for implementing registered designations or origin and geographical indications; whereas a Community approach should be envisaged; whereas a framework of Community rules on protection will permit the development of geographical indications and designations of origin since, by providing a more uniform approach, such a framework will ensure fair competition between the producers of products bearing such indications and enchance the credibility of the products in the consumers' eyes;

Whereas the planned rules should take account of existing Community legislation on wines and spirit drinks, which provide for a higher level of protection;

Whereas the scope of this Regulation is limited to certain agricultural products and foodstuffs for which a link between product or foodstuff characteristics and geographical origin exists; whereas, however, this scope could be enlarged to encompass other products or foodstuffs;

Whereas existing practices make it appropriate to define two different types of geographical description, namely protected geographical indications and protected designations of origin;

Whereas an agricultural product or foodstuff bearing such an indication must meet certain conditions set out in a specification;

Whereas to enjoy protection in every Member State geographical indications and designations of origin must be registered at Community level; whereas entry in a register should also provide information to those involved in trade and to consumers;

Whereas the registration procedure should enable any person individually and directly concerned in a Member State to exercise his rights by notifying the Commission of his opposition;

Whereas there should be procedures to permit amendment of the specification, after registration, in the light of technological progress or withdrawal from the register of the geographical indication or designation of origin of an agricultural product or foodstuff if that product or foodstuff ceases to conform to the specification on the basis of which the geographical indication or designation of origin was granted;

Whereas provision should be made for trade with third countries offering equivalent guarantees for the issue and inspection of geographical indications or designations of origin granted on their territory;

Whereas provision should be made for a procedure establishing close cooperation between the Member States and the Commission through a Regulatory Committee set up for that purpose,

HAS ADOPTED THIS REGULATION:

Article 1

1. This Regulation lays down rules on the protection of designations of origin and

geographical indications of agricultural products intended for human consumption referred to in Annex II to the Treaty and of the foodstuffs referred to in Annex I to this Regulation and agricultural products listed in Annex II to this Regulation. However, this Regulation shall not apply to wine products or to spirit drinks. [Annexes I and II may be amended in accordance with the procedure set out in Article 15.]
2. This Regulation shall apply without prejudice to other specific Community provisions.
3. Council Directive 83/189/EEC of 28 March 1983 laying down a procedure for the provision of information in the field of technical standards and regulations shall not apply to the designations of origin and geographical indications covered by this Regulation.

Notes
Para 1: words in square brackets substituted by Council Regulation 535/97/EC, Art 1(1).

Article 2
1. Community protection of designations of origin and of geographical indications of agricultural products and foodstuffs shall be obtained in accordance with this Regulation.
2. For the purposes of this Regulation—
   (a) designation of origin: means the name of a region, a specific place or, in exceptional cases, a country, used to describe an agricultural product or a foodstuff—
      — originating in that region, specific place or country, and
      — the quality or characteristics of which are essentially or exclusively due to a particular geographical environment with its inherent natural and human factors, and the production, processing and preparation of which take place in the defined geographical area;
   (b) geographical indication: means the name of a region, a specific place or, in exceptional cases, a country, used to describe an agricultural product or a foodstuff—
      — originating in that region, specific place or country, and
      — which possesses a specific quality, reputation or other characteristics attributable to that geographical origin and the production and/or processing and/or preparation of which take place in the defined geographical area.
3. Certain traditional geographical or non-geographical names designating an agricultural product or a foodstuff originating in a region or a specific place, which fulfil the conditions referred to in the second indent of paragraph 2(a) shall also be considered as designations of origin.
4. By way of derogation from Article 2(a), certain geographical designations shall be treated as designations of origin where the raw materials of the products concerned come from a geographical area larger than or different from the processing area, provided that—
   — the production area of the raw materials is limited,
   — special conditions for the production of the raw materials exist, and
   — there are inspection arrangements to ensure that those conditions are adhered to.
5. For the purposes of paragraph 4, only live animals, meat and milk may be considered as raw materials. Use of other raw materials may be authorised in accordance with the procedure laid down in Article 15.

6. In order to be eligible for the derogation provided for in paragraph 4, the designations in question may be or have already been recognised as designations of origin with national protection by the Member State concerned, or, if no such scheme exists, have a proven, traditional character and an exceptional reputation and renown.

7. In order to be eligible for the derogation provided for in paragraph 4, applications for registration must be lodged within two years of the entry into force of this Regulation.

[In the case of Austria, Finland and Sweden, the above period shall begin from the date of their accession.]

Notes
Para 7: words in square brackets added by AA4, as adjusted by Council Decision 95/1/EC, Annex I(V)(A)(III), para 1.

Article 3

1. Names that have become generic may not be registered.

For the purposes of this Regulation, a 'name that has become generic' means the name of an agricultural product or a foodstuff which, although it relates to the place or the region where this product or foodstuff was originally produced or marketed, has become the common name of an agricultural product or a foodstuff.

To establish whether or not a name has become generic, account shall be taken of all factors, in particular—

— the existing situation in the Member State in which the name originates and in areas of consumption,
— the existing situation in other Member States,
— the relevant national or Community laws.

Where, following the procedure laid down in Articles 6 and 7, an application of registration is rejected because a name has become generic, the Commission shall publish that decision in the Official Journal of the European Communities.

2. A name may not be registered as a designation of origin or a geographical indication where it conflicts with the name of a plant variety or an animal breed and as a result is likely to mislead the public as to the true origin of the product.

3. Before the entry into force of this Regulation, the Council, acting by a qualified majority on a proposal from the Commission, shall draw up and publish in the Official Journal of the European Communities a non-exhaustive, indicative list of the names of agricultural products or foodstuffs which are within the scope of this Regulation and are regarded under the terms of paragraph 1 as being generic and thus not able to be registered under this Regulation.

Article 4

1. To be eligible to use a protected designation of origin (PDO) or a protected geographical indication (PGI) an agricultural product or foodstuff must comply with a specification.

2. — The product specification shall include at least—
   (a) the name of the agricultural product or foodstuffs, including the designation of origin or the geographical indication;
   (b) a description of the agricultural product or foodstuff including the raw materials, if appropriate, and principal physical, chemical, microbiological and/or organoleptic characteristics of the product or the foodstuff;
   (c) the definition of the geographical area and, if appropriate, details indicating compliance with the requirements in Article 2(4);
   (d) evidence that the agricultural product or the foodstuff originates in the geo-

graphical area, within the meaning of Article 2(2)(a) or (b), whichever is applicable;

(e) a description of the method of obtaining the agricultural product or food-stuff and, if appropriate, the authentic and unvarying local methods;

(f) the details bearing out the link with the geographical environment or the geographical origin within the meaning of Article 2(2)(a) or (b), whichever is applicable;

(g) details of the inspection structures provided for in Article 10;

(h) the specific labelling details relating to the indication PDO or PGI, whichever is applicable, or the equivalent traditional national indications;

(i) any requirements laid down by Community and/or national provisions.

Article 5

1. Only a group or, subject to certain conditions to be laid down in accordance with the procedure provided for in Article 15, a natural or legal person, shall be entitled to apply for registration.

For the purposes of this Article, 'Group' means any association, irrespective of its legal form or composition, of producers and/or processors working with the same agricultural product or foodstuff. Other interested parties may participate in the group.

2. A group or a natural or legal person may apply for registration only in respect of agricultural products or foodstuffs which it produces or obtains within the meaning of Article 2(2)(a) or (b).

3. The application for registration shall include the product specification referred to in Article 4.

4. The application shall be sent to the Member State in which the geographical area is located.

5. The Member State shall check that the application is justified and shall forward the application, including the product specification referred to in Article 4 and other documents on which it has based its decision, to the Commission, if it considers that it satisfies the requirements of this Regulation.

[That Member State may, on a transitional basis only, grant on the national level a protection in the sense of the present Regulation to the name forwarded in the manner prescribed, and, where appropriate, an adjustment period, as from the date of such forwarding; these may also be granted transitionally subject to the same conditions in connection with an application for the amendment of the product specification.

Such transitional national protection shall cease on the date on which a decision on registration under this Regulation is taken. When that decision is taken, a period of up to five years may be allowed for adjustment, on condition that the undertakings concerned have legally marketed the products in question, using the names concerned continuously, for at least five years prior to the date of the publication provided for in Article 6(2).

The consequences of such national protection, where a name is not registered under this Regulation, shall be the sole responsibility of the Member State concerned.

The measures taken by Member States under the second subparagraph shall produce effects at national level only; they shall have no effect on intra-Community trade.]

If the application concerns a name indicating a geographical area situated in another Member State also, that Member State shall be consulted before any decision is taken.

6. Member States shall introduce the laws, regulations and administrative provi-

sions necessary to comply with this Article.

Notes
Para 5: words in square brackets inserted by Council Regulation 535/97/EC, Art 1(2).

Article 6

1. Within a period of six months the Commission shall verify, by means of a formal investigation, whether the registration application includes all the particulars provided for in Article 4.
The Commission shall inform the Member State concerned of its findings.
2. If, after taking account of paragraph 1, the Commission concludes that the name qualifies for protection, it shall publish in the Official Journal of the European Communities the name and address of the applicant, the name of the product, the main points of the application, the references to national provisions governing the preparation, production or manufacture of the product and, if necessary, the grounds for its conclusions.
3. If no statement of objections is notified to the Commission in accordance with Article 7, the name shall be entered in a register kept by the Commission entitled 'Register of protected designations of origin and protected geographical indications', which shall contain the names of the groups and the inspection bodies concerned.
4. The Commission shall publish in the Official Journal of the European Communities —
   — the names entered in the Register,
   — amendments to the Register made in accordance with Article 9 and 11.
5. If, in the light of the investigation provided for in paragraph 1, the Commission concludes that the name does not qualify for protection, it shall decide, in accordance with the procedure provided for in Article 15, not to proceed with the publication provided for in paragraph 2 of this Article.
Before publication as provided for in paragraphs 2 and 4 and registration as provided for in paragraph 3, the Commission may request the opinion of the Committee provided for in Article 15.

Article 7

1. Within six months of the date of publication in the Official Journal of the European Communities referred to in Article 6(2), any Member State may object to the registration.
2. The competent authorities of the Member States shall ensure that all persons who can demonstrate a legitimate economic interest are authorised to consult the application. In addition and in accordance with the existing situation in the Member States, the Member States may provide access to other parties with a legitimate interest.
3. Any legitimately concerned natural or legal person may object to the proposed registration by sending a duly substantiated statement to the competent authority of the Member State in which he resides or is established. The competent authority shall take the necessary measures to consider these comments or objection within the deadlines laid down.
4. A statement of objection shall be admissible only if it —
   — either shows non-compliance with the conditions referred to in Article 2,
   — [shows that the registration of the name proposed would jeopardize the existence of an entirely or partly identical name or of a mark or the existence of products which have been legally on the market for at least five

years preceding the date of the publication provided for in Article 6(2).]
— or indicates the features which demonstrate that the name whose registration is applied for is generic in nature.
[Austria, Finland and Sweden shall publish such particulars within six months of their accession.]
5. Where an objection is admissible within the meaning of paragraph 4, the Commission shall ask the Member States concerned to seek agreement among themselves in accordance with their internal procedures within three months. If—

(a) agreement is reached, the Member States in question shall communicate to the Commission all the factors which made agreement possible together with the applicant's opinion and that of the objector. Where there has been no change to the information received under Article 5, the Commission shall proceed in accordance with Article 6(4). If there has been a change, it shall again initiate the procedure laid down in Article 7;

(b) no agreement is reached, the Commission shall take a decision in accordance with the procedure laid down in Article 15, having regard to traditional fair practice and of the actual likelihood of confusion. Should it decide to proceed with registration, the Commission shall carry out publication in accordance with Article 6(4).

Notes
Para 4: words in first pair of square brackets substituted by Council Regulation 535/97/EC, Art 1(3), and words in second pair of square brackets added by AA4, as adjusted by Council Decision 95/1/EC, Annex I(V)(A)(III), para 2.

Article 8
The indications PDO, PGI or equivalent traditional national indications may appear only on agricultural products and foodstuffs that comply with this Regulation.

Article 9
The Member State concerned may request the amendment of a specification, in particular to take account of developments in scientific and technical knowledge or to redefine the geographical area.
The Article 6 procedure shall apply mutatis mutandis.
The Commission may, however, decide, under the procedure laid down in Article 15, not to apply the Article 6 procedure in the case of a minor amendment.

Article 10
1. Member States shall ensure that not later than six months after the entry into force of this Regulation inspection structures are in place, the function of which shall be to ensure that agricultural products and foodstuffs bearing a protected name meet the requirements laid down in the specifications.
2. An inspection structure may comprise one or more designated inspection authorities and/or private bodies approved for that purpose by the Member State. Member States shall send the Commission lists of the authorities and/or bodies approved and their respective powers. The Commission shall publish those particulars in the Official Journal of the European Communities.
3. Designated inspection authorities and/or approved private bodies must offer adequate guarantees of objectivity and impartiality with regard to all producers or processors subject to their control and have permanently at their disposal the qualified staff and resources necessary to carry out inspection of agricultural products and foodstuffs bearing a protected name.
If an inspection structure uses the services of another body for some inspections, that body must offer the same guarantees. In that event the designated inspection

authorities and/or approved private bodies shall, however, continue to be responsible vis-à-vis the Member State for all inspections.

As from 1 January 1998, in order to be approved by the Member States for the purpose of this Regulation, private bodies must fulfil the requirements laid down in standard EN 45011 of 26 June 1989.

4. If a designated inspection authority and/or private body in a Member State establishes that an agricultural product or a foodstuff bearing a protected name of origin in that Member State does not meet the criteria of the specification, they shall take the steps necessary to ensure that this Regulation is complied with. They shall inform the Member State of the measures taken in carrying out their inspections. The parties concerned must be notified of all decisions taken.

5. A Member State must withdraw approval from an inspection body where the criteria referred to in paragraphs 2 and 3 are no longer fulfilled. It shall inform the Commission, which shall publish in the Official Journal of the European Communities a revised list of approved bodies.

6. The Member States shall adopt the measures necessary to ensure that a producer who complies with this Regulation has access to the inspection system.

7. The costs of inspections provided for under this Regulation shall be borne by the producers using the protected name.

Article 11

1. Any Member State may submit that a condition laid down in the product specification of an agricultural product or foodstuff covered by a protected name has not been met.

2. The Member State referred to in paragraph 1 shall make its submission to the Member State concerned. The Member State concerned shall examine the complaint and inform the other Member State of its findings and of any measures taken.

3. In the event of repeated irregularities and the failure of the Member States concerned to come to an agreement, a duly substantiated application must be sent to the Commission.

4. The Commission shall examine the application by consulting the Member States concerned. Where appropriate, having consulted the committee referred to in Article 15, the Commission shall take the necessary steps. These may include cancellation of the registration.

Article 12

1. Without prejudice to international agreements, this Regulation may apply to an agricultural product or foodstuff from a third country provided that—

— the third country is able to give guarantees identical or equivalent to those referred to in Article 4,

— the third country concerned has inspection arrangements equivalent to those laid down in Article 10,

— the third country concerned is prepared to provide protection equivalent to that available in the Community to corresponding agricultural products for foodstuffs coming from the Community.

2. If a protected name of a third country is identical to a Community protected name, registration shall be granted with due regard for local and traditional usage and the practical risks of confusion.

Use of such names shall be authorised only if the country of origin of the product is clearly and visibly indicated on the label.

Article 13

1. Registered names shall be protected against—

(a) any direct or indirect commercial use of a name registered in respect of products not covered by the registration in so far as those products are comparable to the products registered under that name or insofar as using the name exploits the reputation of the protected name;

(b) any misuse, imitation or evocation, even if the true origin of the product is indicated or if the protected name is translated or accompanied by an expression such as 'style', 'type', 'method', 'as produced in', 'imitation' or similar;

(c) any other false or misleading indication as to the provenance, origin, nature or essential qualities of the product, on the inner or outer packaging, advertising material or documents relating to the product concerned, and the packing of the product in a container liable to convey a false impression as to its origin;

(d) any other practice liable to mislead the public as to the true origin of the product.

Where a registered name contains within it the name of an agricultural product or foodstuff which is considered generic, the use of that generic name on the appropriate agricultural product or foodstuff shall not be considered to be contrary to (a) or (b) in the first subparagraph.

[2. By way of derogation from paragraph 1(a) and (b), Member States may maintain national systems that permit the use of names registered under Article 17 for a period of not more than five years after the date of publication of registration, provided that—

— the products have been marketed legally using such names for at least five years before the date of publication of this Regulation,

— the undertakings have legally marketed the products concerned using those names continuously during the period referred to in the first indent,

— the labelling clearly indicates the true origin of the product.

However, this derogation may not lead to the marketing of products freely within the territory of a Member State where such names were prohibited.]

3. Protected names may not become generic.

[4. In the case of names, for which registration has been applied under Article 5, provision may be made for a transitional period of up to five years under Article 7(5)(b), solely where a statement of objection had been declared admissible on the grounds that registration of the proposed name would jeopardize the existence of an entirely or partly identical name or the existence of products which have been legally on the market for at least five years preceding the date of the publication provided for in Article 6(2).

Such transitional period may be provided for only where undertakings have legally marketed the products concerned using the names in question continuously for at least five years preceding the date of the publication provided for in Article 6(2).]

Notes
Para 2: substituted by Council Regulation 535/97/EC, Art 1(4).
Para 4: added by Council Regulation 535/97/EC, Art 1(5).

Article 14

1. Where a designation of origin or geographical indication is registered in accordance with this Regulation, the application for registration of a trade mark corresponding to one of the situations referred to in Article 13 and relating to the same type of product shall be refused, provided that the application for registration of the trade mark was submitted after the date of the publication provided for in Article 6(2).Trade marks registered in breach of the first subparagraph shall be declared

invalid.

This paragraph shall also apply where the application for registration of a trade mark was lodged before the date of publication of the application for registration provided for in Article 6(2), provided that that publication occurred before the trade mark was registered.

[In the case of Austria, Finland and Sweden the above period shall begin from the date of their accession.]

2. With due regard for Community law, use of a trade mark corresponding to one of the situations referred to in Article 13 which was registered in good faith before the date on which application for registration of a designation of origin or geographical indication was lodged may continue notwithstanding the registration of a designation of origin or geographical indication, where there are no grounds for invalidity or revocation of the trade mark as provided respectively by Article 3(1)(c) and (g) and Article 12(2)(b) of First Council Directive 89/104/EEC of 21 December 1988 to approximate the laws of the Member States relating to trade marks.1

3. A designation of origin or geographical indication shall not be registered where, in the light of a trade mark's reputation and renown and the length of time it has been used, registration is liable to mislead the consumer as to the true identity of the product.

Notes
OJ L40, 11.2.89, p 1, as amended by OJ L6, 11.1.92, p 35.
Para 1: words in square brackets added by AA4, as adjusted by Council Decision 95/1/EC, Annex I(V)(A)(III), para 2.

Article 15

The Commission shall be assisted by a committee composed of the representatives of the Member States and chaired by the representative of the Commission.

The representative of the Commission shall submit to the committee a draft of the measures to be taken. The committee shall deliver its opinion on the draft within a time limit which the chairman may lay down according to the urgency of the matter. The opinion shall be delivered by the majority laid down in Article 148(2) of the Treaty in the case of decisions which the Council is required to adopt on a proposal from the Commission. The votes of the representatives of the Member States within the committee shall be weighted in the manner set out in that Article. The chairman shall not vote.

The Commission shall adopt the measures envisaged if they are in accordance with the opinion of the committee.

If the measures envisaged are not in accordance with the opinion of the committee, or if no opinion is delivered, the Commission shall, without delay, submit to the Council a proposal relating to the measures to be taken. The Council shall act by a qualified majority.

If, on the expiry of a period of three months from the date of referral to the Council, the Council has not acted, the proposed measures shall be adopted by the Commission.

Article 16

Detailed rules for applying this Regulation shall be adopted in accordance with the procedure laid down in Article 15.

Article 17

1. Within six months of the entry into force of the Regulation, Member States shall inform the Commission which of their legally protected names or, in those Member States where there is no protection system, which of their names established by

usage they wish to register pursuant to this Regulation.

2. In accordance with the procedure laid down in Article 15, the Commission shall register the names referred to in paragraph 1 which comply with Articles 2 and 4. Article 7 shall not apply. However, generic names shall not be added.

3. Member States may maintain national protection of the names communicated in accordance with paragraph 1 until such time as a decision on registration has been taken.

Notes
Amended by AA4.

Article 18
This Regulation shall enter into force twelve months after the date of its publication in the Official Journal of the European Communities.

This Regulation shall be binding in its entirety and directly applicable in all Member States.

Done at Brussels, 14 July 1992.

ANNEX I

Foodstuffs referred to in Article 1(1)
— Beer
— Natural mineral waters and spring waters,
— Beverages made from plant extracts,
— Bread, pastry, cakes, confectionery, biscuits and other baker's wares
— Natural gums and resins.

ANNEX II

Agricultural products referred to in Article 1(1)
— Hay
— Essential oils
[— cork
— cochineal (raw product of animal origin).]

Notes
Annex II: words in square brackets added by Commission Regulation 1068/97/EC, Art 1.

Appendix 6

International registration

Madrid Agreement Concerning the International Registration of Marks
of April 14, 1891,
as revised at Brussels on December 14, 1900,
at Washington on June 2, 1911,
at The Hague on November 6, 1925,
at London on June 2, 1934,
at Nice on June 15, 1957,
and at Stockholm on July 14, 1967, *
* *English title.*

Entry into force (of the 1979 amendments): October 23, 1983.
Source: International Bureau of WIPO.

Note: Lists, updated on January 1 each year, of member States of the treaties administered by WIPO are published each year in the January issue of Industrial Property.

Article 1
[Establishment of a Special Union.
Filing of Marks at International Bureau.
Definition of Country of Origin]*

* *Articles have been given titles to facilitate their identification. There are no titles in the signed, French text.*

(1)   The countries to which this Agreement applies constitute a Special Union for the international registration of marks.

(2)   Nationals of any of the contracting countries may, in all the other countries party to this Agreement, secure protection for their marks applicable to goods or services, registered in the country of origin, by filing the said marks at the International Bureau of Intellectual Property (hereinafter designated as 'the International Bureau') referred to in the Convention Establishing the World Intellectual Property Organization (hereinafter designated as 'the Organization'), through the intermediary of the Office of the said country of origin.

(3)   Shall be considered the country of origin the country of the Special Union

where the applicant has a real and effective industrial or commercial establishment; if he has no such establishment in a country of the Special Union, the country of the Special Union where he has his domicile; if he has no domicile within the Special Union but is a national of a country of the Special Union, the country of which he is a national.

Article 2
[Reference to Article 3 of Paris Convention
(Same Treatment for Certain Categories of Persons as for Nationals of
Countries of the Union)]
Nationals of countries not having acceded to this Agreement who, within the territory of the Special Union constituted by the said Agreement, satisfy the conditions specified in Article 3 of the Paris Convention for the Protection of Industrial Property shall be treated in the same manner as nationals of the contracting countries.

Article 3
[Contents of Application for International Registration]
(1)   Every application for international registration must be presented on the form prescribed by the Regulations; the Office of the country of origin of the mark shall certify that the particulars appearing in such application correspond to the particulars in the national register, and shall mention the dates and numbers of the filing and registration of the mark in the country of origin and also the date of the application for international registration.

(2)   The applicant must indicate the goods or services in respect of which protection of the mark is claimed and also, if possible, the corresponding class or classes according to the classification established by the Nice Agreement Concerning the International Classification of Goods and Services for the Purposes of the Registration of Marks. If the applicant does not give such indication, the International Bureau shall classify the goods or services in the appropriate classes of the said Classification. The indication of classes given by the applicant shall be subject to control by the International Bureau, which shall exercise the said control in association with the national Office. In the event of disagreement between the national Office and the International Bureau, the opinion of the latter shall prevail.

(3)   If the applicant claims color as a distinctive feature of his mark, he shall be required:

1.   to state the fact, and to file with his application a notice specifying the color or the combination of colors claimed;

2.   to append to his application copies in color of the said mark, which shall be attached to the notification given by the International Bureau. The number of such copies shall be fixed by the Regulations.

(4)   The International Bureau shall register immediately the marks filed in accor-

dance with Article 1. The registration shall bear the date of the application for
international registration in the country of origin, provided that the application has
been received by the International Bureau within a period of two months from that
date. If the application has not been received within that period, the International
Bureau shall record it as at the date on which it received the said application. The
International Bureau shall notify such registration without delay to the Offices concerned. Registered marks shall be published in a periodical journal issued by the
International Bureau, on the basis of the particulars contained in the application for
registration. In the case of marks comprising a figurative element of a special form
of writing, the Regulations shall determine whether a printing block must be supplied by the applicant.

(5)   With a view to the publicity to be given in the contracting countries to registered marks, each Office shall receive from the International Bureau a number of
copies of the said publication free of charge and a number of copies at a reduced
price, in proportion to the number of units mentioned in Article 16(4)(a) of the
Paris Convention for the Protection of Industrial Property, under the conditions
fixed by the Regulations. Such publicity shall be deemed in all the contracting
countries to be sufficient, and no other publicity may be required of the applicant.

Protocol Relating to the Madrid Agreement
Concerning the International Registration of Marks*
(as signed at Madrid on June 28, 1989)

Official English title.

Entry into force: See Article 14.

Source: International Bureau of WIPO.

Article 1
Membership in the Madrid Union
The States party to this Protocol (hereinafter referred to as 'the Contracting
States'), even where they are not party to the Madrid Agreement Concerning the
International Registration of Marks as revised at Stockholm in 1967 and as
amended in 1979 (hereinafter referred to as 'the Madrid (Stockholm) Agreement'),
and the organizations referred to in Article 14(1)(b) which are party to this Protocol
(hereinafter referred to as 'the Contracting Organizations') shall be members of the
same Union of which countries party to the Madrid (Stockholm) Agreement are
members. Any reference in this Protocol to 'Contracting Parties' shall be construed
as a reference to both Contracting States and Contracting Organizations.

Article 2
Securing Protection Through International Registration
(1)   Where an application for the registration of a mark has been filed with the
Office of a Contracting Party, or where a mark has been registered in the register of

the Office of a Contracting Party, the person in whose name that application (here-inafter referred to as 'the basic application') or that registration (hereinafter referred to as 'the basic registration') stands may, subject to the provisions of this Protocol, secure protection for his mark in the territory of the Contracting Parties, by obtaining the registration of that mark in the register of the International Bureau of the World Intellectual Property Organization (hereinafter referred to as 'the international registration,' 'the International Register,' 'the International Bureau' and 'the Organization,' respectively), provided that,

(i) where the basic application has been filed with the Office of a Contracting State or where the basic registration has been made by such an Office, the person in whose name that application or registration stands is a national of that Contracting State, or is domiciled, or has a real and effective industrial or commer-cial establishment, in the said Contracting State,

(ii) where the basic application has been filed with the Office of a Contracting Organization or where the basic registration has been made by such an Office, the person in whose name that application or registration stands is a national of a State member of that Contracting Organization, or is domiciled, or has a real and effective industrial or commercial establishment, in the territory of the said Contracting Organization.

(2)   The application for international registration (hereinafter referred to as 'the international application') shall be filed with the International Bureau through the intermediary of the Office with which the basic application was filed or by which the basic registration was made (hereinafter referred to as 'the Office of origin'), as the case may be.

(3)   Any reference in this Protocol to an 'Office' or an 'Office of a Contracting Party' shall be construed as a reference to the office that is in charge, on behalf of a Contracting Party, of the registration of marks, and any reference in this Protocol to 'marks' shall be construed as a reference to trademarks and service marks.

(4)   For the purposes of this Protocol, 'territory of a Contracting Party' means, where the Contracting Party is a State, the territory of that State and, where the Contracting Party is an intergovernmental organization, the territory in which the constituting treaty of that intergovernmental organization applies.

Article 3
International Application
(1)   Every international application under this Protocol shall be presented on the form prescribed by the Regulations. The Office of origin shall certify that the par-ticulars appearing in the international application correspond to the particulars appearing, at the time of the certification, in the basic application or basic registra-tion, as the case may be. Furthermore, the said Office shall indicate,

(i) in the case of a basic application, the date and number of that application,

(ii) in the case of a basic registration, the date and number of that registration as well as the date and number of the application from which the basic registration resulted.

The Office of origin shall also indicate the date of the international application.

(2) The applicant must indicate the goods and services in respect of which protection of the mark is claimed and also, if possible, the corresponding class or classes according to the classification established by the Nice Agreement Concerning the International Classification of Goods and Services for the Purposes of the Registration of Marks. If the applicant does not give such indication, the International Bureau shall classify the goods and services in the appropriate classes of the said classification. The indication of classes given by the applicant shall be subject to control by the International Bureau, which shall exercise the said control in association with the Office of origin. In the event of disagreement between the said Office and the International Bureau, the opinion of the latter shall prevail.

(3) If the applicant claims color as a distinctive feature of his mark, he shall be required

(i) to state the fact, and to file with his international application a notice specifying the color or the combination of colors claimed;
(ii) to append to his international application copies in color of the said mark, which shall be attached to the notifications given by the International Bureau; the number of such copies shall be fixed by the Regulations.

(4) The International Bureau shall register immediately the marks filed in accordance with Article 2. The international registration shall bear the date on which the international application was received in the Office of origin, provided that the international application has been received by the International Bureau within a period of two months from that date. If the international application has not been received within that period, the international registration shall bear the date on which the said international application was received by the International Bureau. The International Bureau shall notify the international registration without delay to the Offices concerned. Marks registered in the International Register shall be published in a periodical gazette issued by the International Bureau, on the basis of the particulars contained in the international application.

(5) With a view to the publicity to be given to marks registered in the international Register, each Office shall receive from the International Bureau a number of copies of the said gazette free of charge and a number of copies at a reduced price, under the conditions fixed by the Assembly referred to in Article 10 (hereinafter referred to as 'the Assembly'). Such publicity shall be deemed to be sufficient for the purposes of all the Contracting Parties, and no other publicity may be required of the holder of the international registration.

Article 3bis
Territorial Effect

The protection resulting from the international registration shall extend to any Contracting Party only at the request of the person who files the international application or who is the holder of the international registration. However, no such request can be made with respect to the Contracting Party whose Office is the Office of origin.

Article 3ter
Request for 'Territorial Extension'

(1)　Any request for extension of the protection resulting from the international registration to any Contracting Party shall be specially mentioned in the international application.

(2)　A request for territorial extension may also be made subsequently to the international registration. Any such request shall be presented on the form prescribed by the Regulations. It shall be immediately recorded by the International Bureau, which shall notify such recordal without delay to the Office or Offices concerned. Such recordal shall be published in the periodical gazette of the International Bureau. Such territorial extension shall be effective from the date on which it has been recorded in the International Register; it shall cease to be valid on the expiry of the international registration to which it relates.

Article 4
Effects of International Registration

(1)

　　(a)　From the date of the registration or recordal effected in accordance with the provisions of Articles 3 and 3ter, the protection of the mark in each of the Contracting Parties concerned shall be the same as if the mark had been deposited direct with the Office of that Contracting Party. If no refusal has been notified to the International Bureau in accordance with Article 5(1) and 5(2) or if a refusal notified in accordance with the said Article has been withdrawn subsequently, the protection of the mark in the Contracting Party concerned shall, as from the said date, be the same as if the mark had been registered by the Office of that Contracting Party.

　　(b)　The indication of classes of goods and services provided for in Article 3 shall not bind the Contracting Parties with regard to the determination of the scope of the protection of the mark.

(2)　Every international registration shall enjoy the right of priority provided for by Article 4 of the Paris Convention for the Protection of Industrial Property, without it being necessary to comply with the formalities prescribed in Section 4.D.

Article 4bis
Replacement of a National or Regional Registration by an International Registration

(1)　Where a mark that is the subject of a national or regional registration in the

Office of a Contracting Party is also the subject of an international registration and both registrations stand in the name of the same person, the international registration is deemed to replace the national or regional registration, without prejudice to any rights acquired by virtue of the latter, provided that

(i) the protection resulting from the international registration extends to the said Contracting Party under Article 3ter(1) or 3ter(2),

(ii) all the goods and services listed in the national or regional registration are also listed in the international registration in respect of the said Contracting Party,

(iii) such extension takes effect after the date of the national or regional registration.

(2) The Office referred to in paragraph (1) shall, upon request, be required to take note in its register of the international registration.

Article 5
Refusal and Invalidation of Effects of International Registration in Respect of Certain Contracting Parties

(1) Where the applicable legislation so authorizes, any Office of a Contracting Party which has been notified by the International Bureau of an extension to that Contracting Party, under Article 3ter(1) or 3ter(2), of the protection resulting from the international registration shall have the right to declare in a notification of refusal that protection cannot be granted in the said Contracting Party to the mark which is the subject of such extension. Any such refusal can be based only on the grounds which would apply, under the Paris Convention for the Protection of Industrial Property, in the case of a mark deposited direct with the Office which notifies the refusal. However, protection may not be refused, even partially, by reason only that the applicable legislation would permit registration only in a limited number of classes or for a limited number of goods or services.

(2)

(a) Any Office wishing to exercise such right shall notify its refusal to the International Bureau, together with a statement of all grounds, within the period prescribed by the law applicable to that Office and at the latest, subject to subparagraphs (b) and (c), before the expiry of one year from the date on which the notification of the extension referred to in paragraph (1) has been sent to that Office by the International Bureau.

(b) Notwithstanding subparagraph (a), any Contracting Party may declare that, for international registrations made under this Protocol, the time limit of one year referred to in subparagraph (a) is replaced by 18 months.

(c) Such declaration may also specify that, when a refusal of protection may result from an opposition to the granting of protection, such refusal may be notified by the Office of the said Contracting Party to the International Bureau after the expiry of the 18-month time limit. Such an Office may, with respect to any given international registration, notify a refusal of protection after the expiry of the 18-month time limit, but only if

(i) it has, before the expiry of the 18-month time limit, informed the International Bureau of the possibility that oppositions may be filed after the expiry of the 18-month time limit, and

(ii) the notification of the refusal based on an opposition is made within a time limit of not more than seven months from the date on which the opposition period begins; if the opposition period expires before this time limit of seven months, the notification must be made within a time limit of one month from the expiry of the opposition period.

(d)　Any declaration under subparagraphs (b) or (c) may be made in the instruments referred to in Article 14(2), and the effective date of the declaration shall be the same as the date of entry into force of this Protocol with respect to the State or intergovernmental organization having made the declaration. Any such declaration may also be made later, in which case the declaration shall have effect three months after its receipt by the Director General of the Organization (hereinafter referred to as 'the Director General'), or at any later date indicated in the declaration, in respect of any international registration whose date is the same as or is later than the effective date of the declaration.

(e)　Upon the expiry of a period of ten years from the entry into force of this Protocol, the Assembly shall examine the operation of the system established by subparagraphs (a) to (d). Thereafter, the provisions of the said subparagraphs may be modified by a unanimous decision of the Assembly.

(3)　The International Bureau shall, without delay, transmit one of the copies of the notification of refusal to the holder of the international registration. The said holder shall have the same remedies as if the mark had been deposited by him direct with the Office which has notified its refusal. Where the International Bureau has received information under paragraph (2)(c)(i), it shall, without delay, transmit the said information to the holder of the international registration.

(4)　The grounds for refusing a mark shall be communicated by the International Bureau to any interested party who may so request.

(5)　Any Office which has not notified, with respect to a given international registration, any provisional or final refusal to the International Bureau in accordance with paragraphs (1) and (2) shall, with respect to that international registration, lose the benefit of the right provided for in paragraph (1).

(6)　Invalidation, by the competent authorities of a Contracting Party, of the effects, in the territory of that Contracting Party, of an international registration may not be pronounced without the holder of such international registration having, in good time, been afforded the opportunity of defending his rights. Invalidation shall be notified to the International Bureau.

Article 5bis

Documentary Evidence of Legitimacy of Use of Certain Elements of the Mark

Documentary evidence of the legitimacy of the use of certain elements incorporated in a mark, such as armorial bearings, escutcheons, portraits, honorary distinctions, titles, trade names, names of persons other than the name of the applicant, or other like inscriptions, which might be required by the Offices of the Contracting Parties shall be exempt from any legalization as well as from any certification other than that of the Office of origin.

Article 5ter
Copies of Entries in International Register; Searches for Anticipations; Extracts from International Register
(1)   The International Bureau shall issue to any person applying therefor, upon the payment of a fee fixed by the Regulations, a copy of the entries in the International Register concerning a specific mark.

(2)   The International Bureau may also, upon payment, undertake searches for anticipations among marks that are the subject of international registrations.

(3)   Extracts from the International Register requested with a view to their production in one of the Contracting Parties shall be exempt from any legalization.

Article 6
**Period of Validity of International Registration;
Dependence and Independence of International Registration**
(1)   Registration of a mark at the International Bureau is effected for ten years, with the possibility of renewal under the conditions specified in Article 7.

(2)   Upon expiry of a period of five years from the date of the international registration, such registration shall become independent of the basic application or the registration resulting therefrom, or of the basic registration, as the case may be, subject to the following provisions.

(3)   The protection resulting from the international registration, whether or not it has been the subject of a transfer, may no longer be invoked if, before the expiry of five years from the date of the international registration, the basic application or the registration resulting therefrom, or the basic registration, as the case may be, has been withdrawn, has lapsed, has been renounced or has been the subject of a final decision of rejection, revocation, cancellation or invalidation, in respect of all or some of the goods and services listed in the international registration. The same applies if:

(i)   an appeal against a decision refusing the effects of the basic application,
(ii)   an action requesting the withdrawal of the basic application or the revocation, cancellation or invalidation of the registration resulting from the basic application or of the basic registration,
or
(iii) an opposition to the basic application
results, after the expiry of the five-year period, in a final decision of rejection, revocation, cancellation or invalidation, or ordering the withdrawal, of the basic

application, or the registration resulting therefrom, or the basic registration, as the case may be, provided that such appeal, action or opposition had begun before the expiry of the said period. The same also applies if the basic application is withdrawn, or the registration resulting from the basic application or the basic registration is renounced, after the expiry of the five-year period, provided that, at the time of the withdrawal or renunciation, the said application or registration was the subject of a proceeding referred to in item (i), (ii) or (iii) and that such proceeding had begun before the expiry of the said period.

(4)   The Office of origin shall, as prescribed in the Regulations, notify the International Bureau of the facts and decisions relevant under paragraph (3), and the International Bureau shall, as prescribed in the Regulations, notify the interested parties and effect any publication accordingly. The Office of origin shall, where applicable, request the International Bureau to cancel, to the extent applicable, the international registration, and the International Bureau shall proceed accordingly.

Article 7
Renewal of International Registration
(1)   Any international registration may be renewed for a period of ten years from the expiry of the preceding period, by the mere payment of the basic fee and, subject to Article 8(7), of the supplementary and complementary fees provided for in Article 8(2).

(2)   Renewal may not bring about any change in the international registration in its latest form.

(3)   Six months before the expiry of the term of protection, the International Bureau shall, by sending an unofficial notice, remind the holder of the international registration and his representative, if any, of the exact date of expiry.

(4)   Subject to the payment of a surcharge fixed by the Regulations, a period of grace of six months shall be allowed for renewal of the international registration.

Article 8
Fees for International Application and Registration
(1)   The Office of origin may fix, at its own discretion, and collect, for its own benefit, a fee which it may require from the applicant for international registration or from the holder of the international registration in connection with the filing of the international application or the renewal of the international registration.

(2)   Registration of a mark at the International Bureau shall be subject to the advance payment of an international fee which shall, subject to the provisions of paragraph (7)(a), include,
        (i) a basic fee;
        (ii) a supplementary fee for each class of the International Classification, beyond three, into which the goods or services to which the mark is applied will

fall;

   (iii) a complementary fee for any request for extension of protection under Article 3ter.

(3) However, the supplementary fee specified in paragraph (2)(ii) may, without prejudice to the date of the international registration, be paid within the period fixed by the Regulations if the number of classes of goods or services has been fixed or disputed by the International Bureau. If, upon expiry of the said period, the supplementary fee has not been paid or the list of goods or services has not been reduced to the required extent by the applicant, the international application shall be deemed to have been abandoned.

(4) The annual product of the various receipts from international registration, with the exception of the receipts derived from the fees mentioned in paragraph (2)(ii) and (2)(iii), shall be divided equally among the Contracting Parties by the International Bureau, after deduction of the expenses and charges necessitated by the implementation of this Protocol.

(5) The amounts derived from the supplementary fees provided for in paragraph (2)(ii) shall be divided, at the expiry of each year, among the interested Contracting Parties in proportion to the number of marks for which protection has been applied for in each of them during that year, this number being multiplied, in the case of Contracting Parties which make an examination, by a coefficient which shall be determined by the Regulations.

(6) The amounts derived from the complementary fees provided for in paragraph (2)(iii) shall be divided according to the same rules as those provided for in paragraph (5).

(7)

   (a) Any Contracting Party may declare that, in connection with each international registration in which it is mentioned under Article 3ter, and in connection with the renewal of any such international registration, it wants to receive, instead of a share in the revenue produced by the supplementary and complementary fees, a fee (hereinafter referred to as 'the individual fee') whose amount shall be indicated in the declaration, and can be changed in further declarations, but may not be higher than the equivalent of the amount which the said Contracting Party's Office would be entitled to receive from an applicant for a ten-year registration, or from the holder of a registration for a ten-year renewal of that registration, of the mark in the register of the said Office, the said amount being diminished by the savings resulting from the international procedure. Where such an individual fee is payable,

   (i) no supplementary fees referred to in paragraph (2)(ii) shall be payable if only Contracting Parties which have made a declaration under this subparagraph are mentioned under Article 3ter, and

   (ii) no complementary fee referred to in paragraph (2)(iii) shall be payable in respect of any Contracting Party which has made a declaration under this subparagraph.

(b) Any declaration under subparagraph (a) may be made in the instruments referred to in Article 14(2), and the effective date of the declaration shall be the same as the date of entry into force of this Protocol with respect to the State or intergovernmental organization having made the declaration. Any such declaration may also be made later, in which case the declaration shall have effect three months after its receipt by the Director General, or at any later date indicated in the declaration, in respect of any international registration whose date is the same as or is later than the effective date of the declaration.

Article 9
Recordal of Change in the Ownership of an International Registration
At the request of the person in whose name the international registration stands, or at the request of an interested Office made ex officio or at the request of an interested person, the International Bureau shall record in the International Register any change in the ownership of that registration, in respect of all or some of the Contracting Parties in whose territories the said registration has effect and in respect of all or some of the goods and services listed in the registration, provided that the new holder is a person who, under Article 2(1), is entitled to file international applications.

Article 9bis
Recordal of Certain Matters Concerning an International Registration
The International Bureau shall record in the International Register

(i) any change in the name or address of the holder of the international registration,

(ii) the appointment of a representative of the holder of the international registration and any other relevant fact concerning such representative,

(iii) any limitation, in respect of all or some of the Contracting Parties, of the goods and services listed in the international registration,

(iv) any renunciation, cancellation or invalidation of the international registration in respect of all or some of the Contracting Parties,

(v) any other relevant fact, identified in the Regulations, concerning the rights in a mark that is the subject of an international registration.

Article 9ter
Fees for Certain Recordals
Any recordal under Article 9 or under Article 9bis may be subject to the payment of a fee.

Article 9quater
Common Office of Several Contracting States
(1) If several Contracting States agree to effect the unification of their domestic legislations on marks, they may notify the Director General

(i) that a common Office shall be substituted for the national Office of each of them, and

(ii) that the whole of their respective territories shall be deemed to be a single State for the purposes of the application of all or part of the provisions preceding this Article as well as the provisions of Articles 9quinquies and 9sexies.

(2)   Such notification shall not take effect until three months after the date of the communication thereof by the Director General to the other Contracting Parties.

Article 9quinquies
Transformation of an International Registration into National or Regional Applications

Where, in the event that the international registration is cancelled at the request of the Office of origin under Article 6(4), in respect of all or some of the goods and services listed in the said registration, the person who was the holder of the international registration files an application for the registration of the same mark with the Office of any of the Contracting Parties in the territory of which the international registration had effect, that application shall be treated as if it had been filed on the date of the international registration according to Article 3(4) or on the date of recordal of the territorial extension according to Article 3ter(2) and, if the international registration enjoyed priority, shall enjoy the same priority, provided that

(i)   such application is filed within three months from the date on which the international registration was cancelled,

(ii) the goods and services listed in the application are in fact covered by the list of goods and services contained in the international registration in respect of the Contracting Party concerned, and

(iii)

such application complies with all the requirements of the applicable law, including the requirements concerning fees.

Article 9sexies
Safeguard of the Madrid (Stockholm) Agreement

(1)   Where, with regard to a given international application or a given international registration, the Office of origin is the Office of a State that is party to both this Protocol and the Madrid (Stockholm) Agreement, the provisions of this Protocol shall have no effect in the territory of any other State that is also party to both this Protocol and the Madrid (Stockholm) Agreement.

(2)   The Assembly may, by a three-fourths majority, repeal paragraph (1), or restrict the scope of paragraph (1), after the expiry of a period of ten years from the entry into force of this Protocol, but not before the expiry of a period of five years from the date on which the majority of the countries party to the Madrid (Stockholm) Agreement have become party to this Protocol. In the vote of the Assembly, only those States which are party to both the said Agreement and this Protocol shall have the right to participate.

Article 10
Assembly
(1)

    (a)   The Contracting Parties shall be members of the same Assembly as the countries party to the Madrid (Stockholm) Agreement.

    (b)   Each Contracting Party shall be represented in that Assembly by one delegate, who may be assisted by alternate delegates, advisors, and experts.

    (c)   The expenses of each delegation shall be borne by the Contracting Party which has appointed it, except for the travel expenses and the subsistence allowance of one delegate for each Contracting Party, which shall be paid from the funds of the Union.

(2)   The Assembly shall, in addition to the functions which it has under the Madrid (Stockholm) Agreement, also

    (i) deal with all matters concerning the implementation of this Protocol;

    (ii) give directions to the International Bureau concerning the preparation for conferences of revision of this Protocol, due account being taken of any comments made by those countries of the Union which are not party to this Protocol;

    (iii) adopt and modify the provisions of the Regulations concerning the implementation of this Protocol;

    (iv) perform such other functions as are appropriate under this Protocol.

(3)

    (a)   Each Contracting Party shall have one vote in the Assembly. On matters concerning only countries that are party to the Madrid (Stockholm) Agreement, Contracting Parties that are not party to the said Agreement shall not have the right to vote, whereas, on matters concerning only Contracting Parties, only the latter shall have the right to vote.

    (b)   One-half of the members of the Assembly which have the right to vote on a given matter shall constitute the quorum for the purposes of the vote on that matter.

    (c)   Notwithstanding the provisions of subparagraph (b), if, in any session, the number of the members of the Assembly having the right to vote on a given matter which are represented is less than one-half but equal to or more than one-third of the members of the Assembly having the right to vote on that matter, the Assembly may make decisions but, with the exception of decisions concerning its own procedure, all such decisions shall take effect only if the conditions set forth hereinafter are fulfilled. The International Bureau shall communicate the said decisions to the members of the Assembly having the right to vote on the said matter which were not represented and shall invite them to express in writing their vote or abstention within a period of three months from the date of the communication. If, at the expiry of this period, the number of such members having thus expressed their vote or abstention attains the number of the members which was lacking for attaining the quorum in the session itself, such decisions shall take effect provided that at the same time the required majority still obtains.

    (d)   Subject to the provisions of Articles 5(2)(e), 9sexies(2), 12 and 13(2), the decisions of the Assembly shall require two-thirds of the votes cast.

    (e)   Abstentions shall not be considered as votes.

    (f)   A delegate may represent, and vote in the name of, one member of the Assembly only.

(4)   In addition to meeting in ordinary sessions and extraordinary sessions as provided for by the Madrid (Stockholm) Agreement, the Assembly shall meet in extraordinary session upon convocation by the Director General, at the request of one-fourth of the members of the Assembly having the right to vote on the matters proposed to be included in the agenda of the session. The agenda of such an extraordinary session shall be prepared by the Director General.

Article 11
International Bureau

(1)
International registration and related duties, as well as all other administrative tasks, under or concerning this Protocol, shall be performed by the International Bureau.

(2)

    (a)   The International Bureau shall, in accordance with the directions of the Assembly, make the preparations for the conferences of revision of this Protocol.

    (b)   The International Bureau may consult with intergovernmental and international non-governmental organizations concerning preparations for such conferences of revision.

    (c)   The Director General and persons designated by him shall take part, without the right to vote, in the discussions at such conferences of revision.

(3)   The International Bureau shall carry out any other tasks assigned to it in relation to this Protocol.

Article 12
Finances

As far as Contracting Parties are concerned, the finances of the Union shall be governed by the same provisions as those contained in Article 12 of the Madrid (Stockholm) Agreement, provided that any reference to Article 8 of the said Agreement shall be deemed to be a reference to Article 8 of this Protocol. Furthermore, for the purposes of Article 12(6)(b) of the said Agreement, Contracting Organizations shall, subject to a unanimous decision to the contrary by the Assembly, be considered to belong to contribution class I (one) under the Paris Convention for the Protection of Industrial Property.

Article 13
Amendment of Certain Articles of the Protocol

(1)   Proposals for the amendment of Articles 10, 11, 12, and the present Article,

may be initiated by any Contracting Party, or by the Director General. Such proposals shall be communicated by the Director General to the Contracting Parties at least six months in advance of their consideration by the Assembly.

(2)   Amendments to the Articles referred to in paragraph (1) shall be adopted by the Assembly. Adoption shall require three-fourths of the votes cast, provided that any amendment to Article 10, and to the present paragraph, shall require four-fifths of the votes cast.

(3)   Any amendment to the Articles referred to in paragraph (1) shall enter into force one month after written notifications of acceptance, effected in accordance with their respective constitutional processes, have been received by the Director General from three-fourths of those States and intergovernmental organizations which, at the time the amendment was adopted, were members of the Assembly and had the right to vote on the amendment. Any amendment to the said Articles thus accepted shall bind all the States and intergovernmental organizations which are Contracting Parties at the time the amendment enters into force, or which become Contracting Parties at a subsequent date.

Article 14
Becoming Party to the Protocol; Entry into Force
(1)
    (a)   Any State that is a party to the Paris Convention for the Protection of Industrial Property may become party to this Protocol.
    (b)   Furthermore, any intergovernmental organization may also become party to this Protocol where the following conditions are fulfilled:

        (i) at least one of the member States of that organization is a party to the Paris Convention for the Protection of Industrial Property;
        (ii) that organization has a regional Office for the purposes of registering marks with effect in the territory of the organization, provided that such Office is not the subject of a notification under Article 9quater.

(2)   Any State or organization referred to in paragraph (1) may sign this Protocol. Any such State or organization may, if it has signed this Protocol, deposit an instrument of ratification, acceptance or approval of this Protocol or, if it has not signed this Protocol, deposit an instrument of accession to this Protocol.

(3)   The instruments referred to in paragraph (2) shall be deposited with the Director General.

(4)

    (a)   This Protocol shall enter into force three months after four instruments of ratification, acceptance, approval or accession have been deposited, provided that at least one of those instruments has been deposited by a country party to the Madrid (Stockholm) Agreement and at least one other of those instruments has been deposited by a State not party to the Madrid (Stockholm) Agreement or by any of the organizations referred to in paragraph (1)(b).

(b)   With respect to any other State or organization referred to in paragraph (1), this Protocol shall enter into force three months after the date on which its ratification, acceptance, approval or accession has been notified by the Director General.

(5)   Any State or organization referred to in paragraph (1) may, when depositing its instrument of ratification, acceptance or approval of, or accession to, this Protocol, declare that the protection resulting from any international registration effected under this Protocol before the date of entry into force of this Protocol with respect to it cannot be extended to it.

Article 15
Denunciation
(1)   This Protocol shall remain in force without limitation as to time.

(2)   Any Contracting Party may denounce this Protocol by notification addressed to the Director General.

(3)   Denunciation shall take effect one year after the day on which the Director General has received the notification.

(4)   The right of denunciation provided for by this Article shall not be exercised by any Contracting Party before the expiry of five years from the date upon which this Protocol entered into force with respect to that Contracting Party.

(5)
(a)   Where a mark is the subject of an international registration having effect in the denouncing State or intergovernmental organization at the date on which the denunciation becomes effective, the holder of such registration may file an application for the registration of the same mark with the Office of the denouncing State or intergovernmental organization, which shall be treated as if it had been filed on the date of the international registration according to Article 3(4) or on the date of recordal of the territorial extension according to Article 3ter(2) and, if the international registration enjoyed priority, enjoy the same priority, provided that

(i)   such application is filed within two years from the date on which the denunciation became effective,
(ii)   the goods and services listed in the application are in fact covered by the list of goods and services contained in the international registration in respect of the denouncing State or intergovernmental organization, and
(iii)such application complies with all the requirements of the applicable law, including the requirements concerning fees.

(b)   The provisions of subparagraph (a) shall also apply in respect of any mark that is the subject of an international registration having effect in Contracting Parties other than the denouncing State or intergovernmental organization at the date on which denunciation becomes effective and whose holder, because of the denunciation, is no longer entitled to file international applications under Article 2(1).

Article 16
Signature; Languages; Depositary Functions
(1)

(a) This Protocol shall be signed in a single copy in the English, French and Spanish languages, and shall be deposited with the Director General when it ceases to be open for signature at Madrid. The texts in the three languages shall be equally authentic.

(b) Official texts of this Protocol shall be established by the Director General, after consultation with the interested governments and organizations, in the Arabic, Chinese, German, Italian, Japanese, Portuguese and Russian languages, and in such other languages as the Assembly may designate.

(2) This Protocol shall remain open for signature at Madrid until December 31, 1989.

(3) The Director General shall transmit two copies, certified by the Government of Spain, of the signed texts of this Protocol to all States and intergovernmental organizations that may become party to this Protocol.

(4) The Director General shall register this Protocol with the Secretariat of the United Nations.

(5) The Director General shall notify all States and international organizations that may become or are party to this Protocol of signatures, deposits of instruments of ratification, acceptance, approval or accession, the entry into force of this Protocol and any amendment thereto, any notification of denunciation and any declaration provided for in this Protocol.

Common Regulations under the Madrid Agreement Concerning the International Registration of Marks and the Protocol Relating to that Agreement

(as in force from January 1, 1998)

Source: International Bureau of WIPO.

LIST OF RULES

Chapter 1:   *General Provisions*

    Rule 1:   Abbreviated Expressions
    Rule 2:   Communications With the International Bureau; Signature
    Rule 3:   Representation Before the International Bureau
    Rule 4:   Calculation of Time Limits
    Rule 5:   Irregularities in Postal and Delivery Services
    Rule 6:   Languages
    Rule 7:   Notification of Certain Special Requirements

Chapter 2:   *International Applications*

    Rule 8:   Several Applicants
    Rule 9:   Requirements Concerning the International Application
    Rule 10:   Fees Concerning the International Application
    Rule 11:   Irregularities Other Than Those Concerning the Classification
            of Goods and Services or Their Indication

    Rule 12:   Irregularities With Respect to the Classification of Goods and

            Services
    Rule 13:   Irregularities With Respect to the Indication of Goods and
            Services

Chapter 3:   *International Registrations*

    Rule 14:   Registration of the Mark in the International Register
    Rule 15:   Date of the International Registration in Special Cases

Chapter 4:   *Facts In Contracting Parties Affecting International*
            Registrations

    Rule 16:   Time Limit for Refusal in Case of Opposition
    Rule 17:   Notification of Refusal
    Rule 18:   Irregular Refusals
    Rule 19:   Invalidations in Designated Contracting Parties
    Rule 20:   Restriction of the Holder's Right of Disposal
    Rule 21:   Replacement of a National or Regional Registration by an
            International Registration
    Rule 22:   Ceasing of Effect of the Basic Application, of the Registration
            Resulting Therefrom, or of the Basic Registration
    Rule 23:   Division of the Basic Application, of the Registration
            Resulting Therefrom, or of the Basic Registration

Chapter 5:   *Subsequent Designations; Changes*

Rule 24:   Designation Subsequent to the International Registration
Rule 25:   Request for Recordal of a Change; Request for Recordal of a Cancellation
Rule 26:   Irregularities in Requests for Recordal of a Change and for Recordal of a Cancellation
Rule 27:   Recordal and Notification of a Change or of a Cancellation; Declaration That a Change in Ownership Has No Effect
Rule 28:   Corrections in the International Register

Chapter 6:   *Renewals*

Rule 29:   Unofficial Notice of Expiry
Rule 30:   Details Concerning Renewal
Rule 31:   Recordal of the Renewal; Notification and Certificate

Chapter 7:   *Gazette And Data Base*

Rule 32:   Gazette
Rule 33:   Electronic Data Base

Chapter 8:   *Fees*

Rule 34:   Payment of Fees
Rule 35:   Currency of Payments
Rule 36:   Exemption From Fees
Rule 37:   Distribution of Supplementary Fees and Complementary Fees
Rule 38:   Crediting of Individual Fees to the Accounts of the Contracting Parties Concerned

Chapter 9:   *Miscellaneous*

Rule 39:   Continuation of Effects of International Registrations in Certain Successor States
Rule 40:   Entry into Force; Transitional Provisions

CHAPTER 1
General Provisions

Rule 1
Abbreviated Expressions

For the purposes of these Regulations,

    (i) 'Agreement' means the Madrid Agreement Concerning the International Registration of Marks of April 14, 1891, as revised at Stockholm on July 14, 1967, and amended on October 2, 1979;

    (ii) 'Protocol' means the Protocol Relating to the Madrid Agreement Concerning the International Registration of Marks, adopted at Madrid on June 27, 1989;

    (iii) 'Contracting Party' means any country party to the Agreement or any State or intergovernmental organization party to the Protocol;

    (iv) 'Contracting State' means a Contracting Party that is a State;

    (v) 'Contracting Organization' means a Contracting Party that is an inter-governmental organization;

    (vi) 'international registration' means the registration of a mark effected under the Agreement or the Protocol or both, as the case may be;

    (vii) 'international application' means an application for international registration filed under the Agreement or the Protocol or both, as the case may be;

    (viii) 'international application governed exclusively by the Agreement' means an international application whose Office of origin is the Office

        – of a State bound by the Agreement but not by the Protocol, or
        – of a State bound by both the Agreement and the Protocol where all the States designated in the international application are bound by the Agreement (whether or not those States are also bound by the Protocol);

    (ix) 'international application governed exclusively by the Protocol' means an international application whose Office of origin is the Office

        – of a State bound by the Protocol but not by the Agreement, or
        – of a Contracting Organization, or
        – of a State bound by both the Agreement and the Protocol where the international application does not contain the designation of any State bound by the Agreement;

    (x) 'international application governed by both the Agreement and the Protocol' means an international application whose Office of origin is the Office of a State bound by both the Agreement and the Protocol and which is based on a registration and contains the designations

    –   of at least one State bound by the Agreement (whether or not that State is also bound by the Protocol), and

    –   of at least one State bound by the Protocol but not by the Agreement or of at least one Contracting Organization;

    (xi) 'applicant' means the natural person or legal entity in whose name the international application is filed;

    (xii) 'legal entity' means a corporation, association or other group or organization which, under the law applicable to it, is capable of acquiring rights, assuming obligations and suing or being sued in a court of law;

    (xiii) 'basic application' means the application for the registration of a mark that has been filed with the Office of a Contracting Party and that constitutes the basis for the international application for the registration of that mark;

    (xiv) 'basic registration' means the registration of a mark that has been effected by the Office of a Contracting Party and that constitutes the basis for the international application for the registration of that mark;

    (xv) 'designation' means the request for extension of protection ('territorial extension') under Article 3*ter*(1) or (2) of the Agreement or under Article 3*ter*(1) or (2) of the Protocol, as the case may be; it also means such extension as recorded in the International Register;

    (xvi) 'designated Contracting Party' means a Contracting Party for which the extension of protection ('territorial extension') has been requested under Article 3*ter*(1) or (2) of the Agreement or under Article 3*ter*(1) or (2) of the Protocol, as the case may be, or in respect of which such extension has been recorded in the International Register;

    (xvii) 'Contracting Party designated under the Agreement' means a designated Contracting Party for which the extension of protection ('territorial extension') requested under Article 3*ter*(1) or (2) of the Agreement has been recorded in the International Register;

    (xviii) 'Contracting Party designated under the Protocol' means a designated Contracting Party for which the extension of protection ('territorial extension') requested under Article 3*ter*(1) or (2) of the Protocol has been recorded in the International Register;

    (xix) 'refusal' means a notification by the Office of a designated Contracting Party according to Article 5(1) of the Agreement or Article 5(1) of the Protocol that protection cannot be granted in the said Contracting Party;

    (xx) 'Gazette' means the periodical gazette referred to in Rule 32;

    (xxi) 'holder' means the natural person or legal entity in whose name the international registration is recorded in the International Register;

    (xxii) 'International Classification of Figurative Elements' means the Classification established by the Vienna Agreement Establishing an International Classification of the Figurative Elements of Marks of June 12, 1973;

    (xxiii) 'International Classification of Goods and Services' means the Classification established by the Nice Agreement Concerning the International Classification of Goods and Services for the Purposes of the Registration of Marks of June 15, 1957, as revised at Stockholm on July 14, 1967, and at Geneva on May 13, 1977;

(xxiv) 'International Register' means the official collection of data concerning international registrations maintained by the International Bureau, which data the Agreement, the Protocol or the Regulations require or permit to be recorded, irrespective of the medium in which such data are stored;

(xxv) 'Office' means the Office of a Contracting Party in charge of the registration of marks, or the common Office referred to in Article 9*quater* of the Agreement or Article 9*quater* of the Protocol, or both, as the case may be;

(xxvi) 'Office of origin' means the Office of the country of origin defined in Article 1(3) of the Agreement or the Office of origin defined in Article 2(2) of the Protocol, or both, as the case may be;

(xxvii) 'official form' means a form established by the International Bureau or any form having the same contents and format;

(xxviii) 'prescribed fee' means the applicable fee set out in the Schedule of Fees;

(xxix) 'Director General' means the Director General of the World Intellectual Property Organization;

(xxx) 'International Bureau' means the International Bureau of the World Intellectual Property Organization.

Rule 2
Communications With the International Bureau; Signature

(1)*[Communication in Writing; Several Documents in One Envelope]*

(a) Subject to paragraph (6), communications addressed to the International Bureau shall be effected in writing by typewriter or other machine and, except where the communication is by telex or telegram, shall be signed.

(b) If several documents are mailed in one envelope, they should be accompanied by a list identifying each of them.

(2)*[Signature]* A signature shall be handwritten, printed or stamped; it may be replaced by the affixing of a seal or, as regards the electronic communications referred to in paragraph (6), by a mode of identification agreed upon between the International Bureau and the Office concerned.

(3) *[Communications by Telefacsimile]* (a) Any communication may be addressed to the International Bureau by telefacsimile, provided that,

(i) where the communication must be presented on an official form, the official form is used for the purposes of the telefacsimile communication, and that,

(ii) where the communication consists of the international application, the original of the page of the official form bearing the reproduction or reproductions of the mark, signed by the Office of origin and containing sufficient indications to allow identification of the international application to which it relates, is sent to the International Bureau.

(b)   Where the original referred to in subparagraph (a)(ii) is received by the International Bureau within a period of one month from the day on which the communication by telefacsimile was received, that original shall be deemed to have been received by the International Bureau on the date on which the communication by telefacsimile was received.

(c)   Where an international application is addressed to the International Bureau by telefacsimile, examination by the International Bureau as to conformity of the international application with the applicable requirements shall start

(i)   upon receipt of the original referred to in subparagraph (a)(ii) if such original is received within a period of one month from the date on which the communication by telefacsimile was received, or

(ii)   upon expiry of the period of one month referred to in subparagraph (b) if the said original is not received by the International Bureau within that period.

(4)[Communications by Telex or Telegram]

(a)   Communications other than the international application or a designation made subsequent to the international registration may be addressed to the International Bureau by telex or telegram, provided that, where the use of an official form is prescribed, the official form, duly signed and corresponding in its contents to the contents of the telex or telegram, is received by the International Bureau within a period of one month from the day on which the communication by telex or telegram was received.

(b)   Where the requirements under subparagraph (a) are complied with, the official form shall be deemed to have been received by the International Bureau on the day on which the communication by telex or telegram was received. Where the requirements under subparagraph (a) are not complied with, the communication by telex or telegram shall be deemed not to have been made.

(5)[Acknowledgement and Date of Receipt of Telefacsimile by the International Bureau]

(a)   The International Bureau shall promptly and by telefacsimile inform the sender of a telefacsimile communication of the receipt of that communication, and, where the telefacsimile communication received is incomplete or illegible, of that fact also, provided that the sender can be identified and can be reached by telefacsimile.

(b)   Where a communication is transmitted by telefacsimile and, because of the time difference between the place from where the communication is transmitted and Geneva, the date on which the transmittal started is different from the date of receipt by the International Bureau of the complete communication, the earlier of the two dates shall be considered as the date of receipt by the International Bureau.

(6)[Electronic Communications; Acknowledgement and Date of Receipt of Electronic Transmission by the International Bureau]

(a) Where an Office so desires, communications between that Office and the International Bureau, including the presentation of the international application, shall be by electronic means in a way agreed upon between the International Bureau and the Office concerned.

(b) The International Bureau shall promptly and by electronic transmission inform the originator of an electronic transmission of the receipt of that transmission, and, where the electronic transmission received is incomplete or otherwise unusable, also of that fact, provided that the originator can be identified and can be reached.

(c) Where a communication is by electronic means and, because of the time difference between the place from where the communication is sent and Geneva, the date on which the sending started is different from the date of receipt by the International Bureau of the complete communication, the earlier of the two dates shall be considered as the date of receipt by the International Bureau.

Rule 3
Representation Before the International Bureau

(1)*[Representative; Address of Representative; Number of Representatives]*
(a) The applicant or the holder may have a representative before the International Bureau.
(b) The address of the representative shall be,
(i) in respect of an international application governed exclusively by the Agreement, in the territory of a Contracting Party bound by the Agreement;
(ii) in respect of an international application governed exclusively by the Protocol, in the territory of a Contracting Party bound by the Protocol;
(iii) in respect of an international application governed by both the Agreement and the Protocol, in the territory of a Contracting Party;
(iv) in respect of an international registration, in the territory of a Contracting Party.

(c) The applicant or the holder may have one representative only. Where the appointment indicates several representatives, only the one indicated first shall be considered to be a representative and be recorded as such.
(d) Where a partnership or firm composed of attorneys or patent or trademark agents has been indicated as representative to the International Bureau, it shall be regarded as one representative.

(2)*[Appointment of the Representative]*
(a) The appointment of a representative may be made in the international application, or in a subsequent designation or a request under Rule 25 if such subsequent designation or request is made through an Office.
(b) The appointment of a representative may also be made in a separate communication which may relate to one or more specified international applications or international registrations, or to all future international applications and international registrations, of the same applicant or holder. The said communica-

tion shall be presented to the International Bureau

      (i) by the applicant, the holder or the appointed representative,

     (ii) by the Office of origin, or

    (iii) by another interested Office if the applicant, the holder or the appointed representative asks for, and that Office admits, such presentation.

The communication shall be signed by the applicant or the holder, or by the Office through which it was presented.

(3)[Irregular Appointment]

      (a) Where the address of the purported representative is not in the territory relevant under paragraph (1)(b), the International Bureau shall treat the appointment as if it had not been made and shall inform accordingly the applicant or holder, the purported representative and, if the sender or transmitter is an Office, that Office.

      (b) Where the International Bureau considers that the appointment of a representative under paragraph (2) is irregular, it shall notify accordingly the applicant or holder, the purported representative and, if the sender or transmitter is an Office, that Office.

      (c) As long as the relevant requirements under paragraphs (1)(b) and (2) are not complied with, the International Bureau shall send all relevant communications to the applicant or holder himself.

(4)[Recordal and Notification of Appointment of a Representative; Effective Date of Appointment]

      (a) Where the International Bureau finds that the appointment of a representative complies with the applicable requirements, it shall record the fact that the applicant or holder has a representative, as well as the name and address of the representative, in the International Register. In such a case, the effective date of the appointment shall be the date on which the International Bureau received the international application, subsequent designation, request or separate communication in which the representative is appointed.

      (b) The International Bureau shall notify the recordal referred to in subparagraph (a) to both the applicant or holder and the representative. Where the appointment was made in a separate communication presented through an Office, the International Bureau shall also notify the recordal to that Office.

(5)[Effect of Appointment of a Representative]

      (a) Except where these Regulations expressly provide otherwise, the signature of a representative recorded under paragraph (4)(a) shall replace the signature of the applicant or holder.

      (b) Except where these Regulations expressly require that an invitation, notification or other communication be addressed to both the applicant or holder and the representative, the International Bureau shall address to the representative recorded under paragraph (4)(a) any invitation, notification or other communication which, in the absence of a representative, would have to be sent to the applicant or holder; any invitation, notification or other communication so addressed to the said representative shall have the same effect as if it had been addressed to the applicant or holder.

(c) Any communication addressed to the International Bureau by the representative recorded under paragraph (4)(a) shall have the same effect as if it had been addressed to the said Bureau by the applicant or holder.

(6)[Cancellation of Recordal; Effective Date of Cancellation]

(a) Any recordal under paragraph (4)(a) shall be cancelled where cancellation is requested in a communication signed by the applicant, holder or representative. The recordal shall be cancelled *ex officio* by the International Bureau where a new representative is appointed or, in case a change in ownership has been recorded, where no representative is appointed by the new holder of the international registration.

(b) Subject to subparagraph (c), the cancellation shall be effective from the date on which the International Bureau receives the corresponding communication.

(c) Where the cancellation is requested by the representative, it shall be effective from the earlier of the following:

(i) the date on which the International Bureau receives a communication appointing a new representative;

(ii) the date of the expiry of a period of two months counted from the receipt of the request of the representative that the recordal be cancelled.

Until the effective date of the cancellation, all communications referred to in paragraph (5)(b) shall be addressed by the International Bureau to both the applicant or holder and the representative.

(d) The International Bureau shall, upon receipt of a request for cancellation made by the representative, notify accordingly the applicant or holder, and add to the notification copies of all communications sent to the representative, or received by the International Bureau from the representative, during the six months preceding the date of the notification.

(e) The International Bureau shall, once the effective date of the cancellation is known, notify the cancellation and its effective date to the representative whose recordal has been cancelled, to the applicant or holder and, where the appointment of the representative had been presented through an Office, to that Office.

Rule 4
Calculation of Time Limits

(1)[Periods Expressed in Years] Any period expressed in years shall expire, in the relevant subsequent year, in the month having the same name and on the day hav-

ing the same number as the month and the day of the event from which the period starts to run, except that, where the event occurred on February 29 and in the relevant subsequent year February ends on the 28th, the period shall expire on February 28.

(2)*[Periods Expressed in Months]* Any period expressed in months shall expire, in the relevant subsequent month, on the day which has the same number as the day of the event from which the period starts to run, except that, where the relevant subsequent month has no day with the same number, the period shall expire on the last day of that month.

(3)*[Periods Expressed in Days]* The calculation of any period expressed in days shall start with the day following the day on which the relevant event occurred and shall expire accordingly.

(4)*[Expiry on a Day on Which the International Bureau or an Office Is Not Open to the Public]* If a period expires on a day on which the International Bureau or the Office concerned is not open to the public, the period shall, notwithstanding paragraphs (1) to (3), expire on the first subsequent day on which the International Bureau or the Office concerned is open to the public.

(5)*[Indication of the Date of Expiry]* The International Bureau shall, in all cases in which it communicates a time limit, indicate the date of the expiry, according to paragraphs (1) to (3), of the said time limit.

Rule 5
Irregularities in Postal and Delivery Services

(1)*[Communications Sent Through a Postal Service]* Failure by an interested party to meet a time limit for a communication addressed to the International Bureau and mailed through a postal service shall be excused if the interested party submits evidence showing, to the satisfaction of the International Bureau,

(i) that the communication was mailed at least five days prior to the expiry of the time limit, or, where the postal service was, on any of the ten days preceding the day of expiry of the time limit, interrupted on account of war, revolution, civil disorder, strike, natural calamity, or other like reason, that the communication was mailed not later than five days after postal service was resumed,

(ii) that the mailing of the communication was registered, or details of the mailing were recorded, by the postal service at the time of mailing, and

(iii) in cases where all classes of mail do not normally reach the International Bureau within two days of mailing, that the communication was mailed by a class of mail which normally reaches the International Bureau within two days of mailing or by airmail.

(2)*[Communications Sent Through a Delivery Service]* Failure by an interested party to meet a time limit for a communication addressed to the International Bureau and sent through a delivery service shall be excused if the interested party submits evidence showing, to the satisfaction of the International Bureau,

(i) that the communication was sent at least five days prior to the expiry of the time limit, or, where the delivery service was, on any of the ten days preceding the day of expiry of the time limit, interrupted on account of war, revolution, civil disorder, strike, natural calamity, or other like reason, that the communication was sent not later than five days after the delivery service was resumed, and

(ii) that details of the sending of the communication were recorded by the delivery service at the time of sending.

(3)*[Limitation on Excuse]* Failure to meet a time limit shall be excused under this Rule only if the evidence referred to in paragraph (1) or (2) and the communication or a duplicate thereof are received by the International Bureau not later than six months after the expiry of the time limit.

(4)*[International Application and Subsequent Designation]* Where the International Bureau receives an international application or a subsequent designation beyond the two-month period referred to in Article 3(4) of the Agreement, in Article 3(4) of the Protocol and in Rule 24(6)(b), and the Office concerned indicates that the late receipt resulted from circumstances referred to in paragraph (1) or (2), paragraph (1) or (2) and paragraph (3) shall apply.

Rule 6
Languages

(1)*[International Application]*
(a) Any international application governed exclusively by the Agreement shall be in French.
(b) Any international application governed exclusively by the Protocol or governed by both the Agreement and the Protocol shall be in English or French according to what is prescribed by the Office of origin, it being understood that the Office of origin may allow applicants to choose between English and French.
(2)*[Communications Other Than the International Application]*
(a) Any communication concerning an international application governed exclusively by the Agreement or the international registration resulting therefrom shall, subject to Rule 17(2)(v) and (3), be in French, except that, where the international registration resulting from an international application governed exclusively by the Agreement is or has been the subject of a subsequent designation under Rule 24(1)(b), the provisions of subparagraph (b) shall apply.
(b) Any communication concerning an international application governed exclusively by the Protocol or governed by both the Agreement and the Protocol, or the international registration resulting therefrom, shall, subject to Rule 17(2)(v) and (3), be
(i) in English or French where such communication is addressed to

1147

the International Bureau by the applicant or holder, or by an Office;

(ii) in the language applicable under Rule 7(2) where the communi-cation consists of the declaration of intention to use the mark annexed to the inter-national application under Rule 9(6)(d)(i) or to the subsequent designation under Rule 24(3)(b)(i);

(iii) in the language of the international application where the com-munication is a notification addressed by the International Bureau to an Office, unless that Office has notified the International Bureau that all such notifications are to be in English or that all such notifications are to be in French; where the notification addressed by the International Bureau concerns the recordal in the International Register of an international registration, the notification shall indicate the language in which the relevant international application was received by the International Bureau;

(iv) in the language of the international application where the com-munication is a notification addressed by the International Bureau to the applicant or holder, unless that applicant or holder has expressed the wish to receive such notifications in English although the language of the international application is French, or in French although the language of the international application is English.

(3)[Recordal and Publication]

(a) Where the international application is governed exclusively by the Agreement, the recordal in the International Register and the publication in the Gazette of the international registration resulting therefrom and of any data to be both recorded and published under these Regulations in respect of that international registration shall be in French.

(b) Where the international application is governed exclusively by the Protocol or is governed by both the Agreement and the Protocol, the recordal in the International Register and the publication in the Gazette of the international regis-tration resulting therefrom and of any data to be both recorded and published under these Regulations in respect of that international registration shall be in English and French. The recordal and publication of the international registration shall indicate the language in which the international application was received by the International Bureau.

(c) If a subsequent designation made under Rule 24(1)(b) is the first subsequent designation made under that Rule in respect of a given international registration, the International Bureau shall, together with the publication in the Gazette of that subsequent designation, publish the international registration in English and republish the international registration in French. Thereafter, that sub-sequent designation shall be recorded in the International Register in English and French. The recordal in the International Register and the publication in the Gazette of any data to be both recorded and published under these Regulations in respect of the international registration concerned shall be in English and French.

(4)[Translation]

(a The translations from English into French or from French into English needed for the notifications under paragraph (2)(b)(iii) and (iv), and recordals and publications under paragraph (3)(b) and (c), shall be made by the International Bureau. The applicant or the holder, as the case may be, may annex to the international application, or to a request for the recordal of a subsequent designation or of a change, a proposed translation of any text matter contained in the international application or the request. If the proposed translation is not considered by the International Bureau to be correct, it shall be corrected by the International Bureau after having invited the applicant or the holder to make, within one month from the invitation, observations on the proposed corrections.

(b) Notwithstanding subparagraph (a), the International Bureau shall not translate the mark. Where, in accordance with Rule 9(4)(b)(iii) or Rule 24(3)(c), the applicant or the holder gives a translation or translations of the mark, the International Bureau shall not check the correctness of any such translations.

Rule 7
Notification Of Certain Special Requirements

(1)*[Presentation of Subsequent Designations by the Office of Origin]* Where a Contracting Party requires that, where its Office is the Office of origin and the holder's address is in the territory of that Contracting Party, designations made subsequently to the international registration be presented to the International Bureau by the said Office, it shall notify that requirement to the Director General.

(2)*[Intention to Use the Mark]* Where a Contracting Party requires, as a Contracting Party designated under the Protocol, a declaration of intention to use the mark, it shall notify that requirement to the Director General. Where that Contracting Party requires the declaration to be signed by the applicant himself and to be made on a separate official form annexed to the international application, the notification shall contain a statement to that effect and shall specify the exact wording of the required declaration. Where the Contracting Party further requires the declaration to be in English even if the international application is in French, or to be in French even if the international application is in English, the notification shall specify the required language.

(3)*[Notification]*
(a) Any notification referred to in paragraph (1) or (2) may be made at the time of the deposit by the Contracting Party of its instrument of ratification, acceptance or approval of, or accession to, the Protocol, and the effective date of the notification shall be the same as the date of entry into force of the Protocol with respect to the Contracting Party having made the notification. The notification may also be made later, in which case the notification shall have effect three months after its receipt by the Director General, or at any later date indicated in the notification, in respect of any international registration whose date is the same as or is later than the effective date of the notification.

(b) Any notification made under paragraph (1) or (2) may be withdrawn at any time. The notice of withdrawal shall be addressed to the Director General. The withdrawal shall have effect upon receipt of the notice of withdrawal by the Director General or at any later date indicated in the notice.

Chapter 2
International Applications

Rule 8
Several Applicants

(1)*[Two or More Applicants Applying Exclusively Under the Agreement or Applying Under Both the Agreement and the Protocol]* Two or more applicants may jointly file an international application governed exclusively by the Agreement or governed by both the Agreement and the Protocol if the basic registration is jointly owned by them and if the country of origin, as defined in Article 1(3) of the Agreement, is the same for each of them.

(2)*[Two or More Applicants Applying Exclusively Under the Protocol]* Two or more applicants may jointly file an international application governed exclusively by the Protocol if the basic application was jointly filed by them or the basic registration is jointly owned by them, and if each of them qualifies, in relation to the Contracting Party whose Office is the Office of origin, for filing an international application under Article 2(1) of the Protocol.

Rule 9
Requirements Concerning
the International Application

(1)*[Presentation]* The international application shall be presented to the International Bureau by the Office of origin.

(2)*[Form and Signature]*
      (a) The international application shall be presented on the official form in one copy.
      (b) The international application shall be signed by the Office of origin and, where the Office of origin so requires, also by the applicant. Where the Office of origin does not require the applicant to sign the international application but allows that the applicant also sign it, the applicant may do so.

(3)*[Fees]* The prescribed fees applicable to the international application shall be paid as provided for in Rules 10, 34 and 35.

(4)*[Contents of All International Applications]* (a) Subject to paragraphs (5), (6) and (7), the international application shall contain or indicate

      (i) the name of the applicant; where the applicant is a natural person, the name to be indicated is the family or principal name and the given or secondary name(s) of the natural person; where the applicant is a legal entity, the name to be indicated is the full official designation of the legal entity; where the name of the applicant is in characters other than Latin characters, the indication of that name shall consist of a transliteration into Latin characters which shall follow the phonetics of the language of the international application; where the applicant is a legal entity, and its name is in characters other than Latin characters, the said transliteration may be replaced by a translation into the language of the international application,

    (ii) the address of the applicant; that address shall be given in such way as to satisfy the customary requirements for prompt postal delivery and shall consist, at least, of all the relevant administrative units up to, and including, the house number, if any; in addition, telephone and telefacsimile numbers as well as a different address for correspondence may be indicated; where there are two or more applicants with different addresses, one address for correspondence shall be indicated; where no such address is indicated, the address for correspondence shall be the address of the applicant named first in the international application,

    (iii) the name and address of the representative, if any; in addition, telephone and telefacsimile numbers may be indicated; where the name of the representative is in characters other than Latin characters, the indication of that name shall consist of a transliteration into Latin characters which shall follow the phonetics of the language of the international application; where the representative is a legal entity, and its name is in characters other than Latin characters, the said transliteration may be replaced by a translation into the language of the international application,

    (iv) where the applicant wishes, under the Paris Convention for the Protection of Industrial Property, to take advantage of the priority of an earlier filing, a declaration claiming the priority of that earlier filing, together with an indication of the name of the Office where such filing was made and of the date and, where available, the number of that filing, and, where the priority claim relates to less than all the goods and services listed in the international application, the indication of those goods and services to which the priority claim relates,

    (v) a reproduction of the mark that shall fit in the box provided on the official form; that reproduction shall be clear and shall, depending on whether the reproduction in the basic application or the basic registration is in black and white or in color, be in black and white or in color,

    (vi) where the applicant wishes that the mark be considered as a mark in standard characters, a declaration to that effect,

    (vii) where, according to Article 3(3) of the Agreement or Article 3(3) of the Protocol, the applicant claims color as a distinctive feature of the mark, an indication of that fact and an indication by words of the color or combination of colors claimed and, where the reproduction furnished under item (v) is in black and white, one reproduction of the mark in color,

    (viii) where the basic application or the basic registration relates to a three-dimensional mark, the indication 'three-dimensional mark,'

    (ix) where the basic application or the basic registration relates to a sound mark, the indication 'sound mark,'

(x) where the basic application or the basic registration relates to a collective mark or a certification mark or a guarantee mark, an indication to that effect,

(xi) where the basic application or the basic registration contains a description of the mark by words, the same description; where the said description is in a language other than the language of the international application, it shall be given in the language of the international application,

(xii) where the mark consists of or contains matter in characters other than Latin characters or numbers expressed in numerals other than Arabic or Roman numerals, a transliteration of that matter in Latin characters and Arabic numerals; the transliteration into Latin characters shall follow the phonetics of the language of the international application,

(xiii) the names of the goods and services for which the international registration of the mark is sought, grouped in the appropriate classes of the International Classification of Goods and Services, each group preceded by the number of the class and presented in the order of the classes of that Classification; the goods and services shall be indicated in precise terms, preferably using the words appearing in the Alphabetical List of the said Classification; the international application may contain limitations of the list of goods and services in respect of one or more designated Contracting Parties; the limitation in respect of each Contracting Party may be different, and

(xiv) the amount of the fees being paid and the method of payment, or instructions to debit the required amount of fees to an account opened with the International Bureau, and the identification of the party effecting the payment or giving the instructions.

(b) The international application may also contain,

(i) where the applicant is a natural person, an indication of the State of which the applicant is a national;

(ii) where the applicant is a legal entity, indications concerning the legal nature of that legal entity and the State, and, where applicable, the territorial unit within that State, under the law of which the said legal entity has been organized;

(iii) where the mark consists of or contains a word or words that can be translated, a translation of that word or those words into French if the international application is governed exclusively by the Agreement, or into English or French or both if the international application is governed exclusively by the Protocol or is governed by both the Agreement and the Protocol;

(iv) where the applicant claims color as a distinctive feature of the mark, an indication by words, in respect of each color, of the principal parts of the mark which are in that color.

(5)*[Additional Contents of an International Application Governed Exclusively by the Agreement]*
(a) In the case of an international application governed exclusively by the Agreement, the international application shall contain or indicate, in addition to the indications referred to in paragraph (4)(a),

(i) the Contracting State party to the Agreement in which the applicant has a real and effective industrial or commercial establishment; if there is no such Contracting State, the Contracting State party to the Agreement in which the applicant is domiciled; if there is no such Contracting State, the Contracting State party to the Agreement of which the applicant is a national,

(ii) where the address of the applicant given in accordance with paragraph (4)(a)(ii) is in a State other than the State whose Office is the Office of origin, the address of the establishment or the domicile, referred to in item (i),

(iii) the States that are designated under the Agreement,

(iv) the date and the number of the basic registration, and

(v)the declaration by the Office of origin as specified in subparagraph (b).

(b) The declaration referred to in subparagraph (a)(v) shall certify

(i) the date on which the Office of origin received or, as provided in Rule 11(1), is deemed to have received, the request by the applicant to present the international application to the International Bureau,

(ii) that the applicant named in the international application is the same as the holder of the basic registration,

(iii) that any indication referred to in paragraph (4)(a)(viii) to (xi) and appearing in the international application appears also in the basic registration,

(iv) that the mark that is the subject matter of the international application is the same as in the basic registration,

(v) that, if colors are claimed in the international application, the claim for color is the same as in the basic registration, and

(vi) that the goods and services indicated in the international application are covered by the list of goods and services appearing in the basic registration.

(c) Where the international application is based on two or more basic registrations of the same mark in the Office of origin, the declaration referred to in subparagraph (a)(v) shall be deemed to apply to all those basic registrations.

(6)*[Additional Contents of an International Application Governed Exclusively by the Protocol]*
(a) In the case of an international application governed exclusively by the Protocol, the international application shall contain or indicate, in addition to the indications referred to in paragraph (4)(a),

(i) where the basic application has been filed with, or where the basic registration has been made by, the Office of a Contracting State of which the applicant is a national or in which the applicant is domiciled or has a real and effective industrial or commercial establishment, that Contracting State,

(ii) where the address of the applicant given in accordance with paragraph (4)(a)(ii) is in a State other than the State whose Office is the Office of origin, the domicile or the address of the establishment, referred to in item (i),

(iii) where the basic application has been filed with the Office of a Contracting Organization or where the basic registration has been made by such an Office, that organization and the State member of that organization of which the applicant is a national, or a statement that the applicant is domiciled in the territory in which the constituting treaty of the said organization applies, or a statement that the applicant has a real and effective industrial or commercial establishment in that territory,

      (iv) where the address of the applicant given in accordance with paragraph (4)(a)(ii) is not in the territory in which the constituting treaty of the Contracting Organization whose Office is the Office of origin applies, the domicile or the address of the establishment, referred to in item (iii),

      (v) the Contracting Parties that are designated under the Protocol,

      (vi) the date and the number of the basic application, or the date and the number of the basic registration, as the case may be, and

      (vii) the declaration by the Office of origin as specified in subparagraph (b).

      (b) The declaration referred to in subparagraph (a)(vii) shall certify

      (i) the date on which the Office of origin received the request by the applicant to present the international application to the International Bureau,

      (ii) that the applicant named in the international application is the same as the applicant named in the basic application or the holder named in the basic registration, as the case may be,

      (iii) that any indication referred to in paragraph (4)(a)(viii) to (xi) and appearing in the international application appears also in the basic application or the basic registration, as the case may be,

      (iv) that the mark that is the subject matter of the international application is the same as in the basic application or the basic registration, as the case may be,

      (v) that, if colors are claimed in the international application, the claim for color is the same as in the basic application or the basic registration, as the case may be, and

      (vi) that the goods and services indicated in the international application are covered by the list of goods and services appearing in the basic application or basic registration, as the case may be.

      (c) Where the international application is based on two or more basic applications for or basic registrations of the same mark in the Office of origin, the declaration referred to in subparagraph (a)(vii) shall be deemed to apply to all those basic applications and basic registrations.

      (d) The international application shall also contain, where a designation concerns a Contracting Party that has made a notification under Rule 7(2), a declaration of intention to use the mark in the territory of that Contracting Party; the declaration shall be considered part of the designation of the Contracting Party requiring it and shall, as required by that Contracting Party,

      (i) be signed by the applicant himself and be made on a separate official form annexed to the international application, or

      (ii) be included in the international application.

(7)*[Contents of an International Application Governed by Both the Agreement and the Protocol]* In the case of an international application governed by both the Agreement and the Protocol, the international application shall contain or indicate, in addition to the indications referred to in paragraph (4)(a), the indications referred to in paragraphs (5) and (6), it being understood that only a basic registration, and not a basic application, may be indicated under paragraph (6)(a)(vi), and that that basic registration is the same basic registration as the one referred to in paragraph (5)(a)(iv).

Rule 10
Fees Concerning the International Application

(1)*[International Applications Governed Exclusively by the Agreement]* An international application governed exclusively by the Agreement shall be subject to the payment of the basic fee, the complementary fee and, where applicable, the supplementary fee, specified in item 1 of the Schedule of Fees. Those fees shall be paid in two instalments of ten years each. For the payment of the second instalment, Rule 30 shall apply.

(2)*[International Applications Governed Exclusively by the Protocol]* An international application governed exclusively by the Protocol shall be subject to the payment of the basic fee, the complementary fee and/or the individual fee and, where applicable, the supplementary fee, specified or referred to in item 2 of the Schedule of Fees. Those fees shall be paid for ten years.

(3)*[International Applications Governed by Both the Agreement and the Protocol]* An international application governed by both the Agreement and the Protocol shall be subject to the payment of the basic fee, the complementary fee and, where applicable, the individual fee and the supplementary fee, specified or referred to in item 3 of the Schedule of Fees. As far as the Contracting Parties designated under the Agreement are concerned, paragraph (1) shall apply. As far as the Contracting Parties designated under the Protocol are concerned, paragraph (2) shall apply.

Rule 11
Irregularities Other Than Those Concerning
the Classification of Goods and Services
or Their Indication

(1)*[Premature Request to the Office of Origin]*
      (a) Where the Office of origin received a request to present to the International Bureau an international application governed exclusively by the Agreement before the mark which is referred to in that request is registered in the register of the said Office, the said request shall be deemed to have been received by the Office of origin, for the purposes of Article 3(4) of the Agreement, on the date of the registration of the mark in the register of the said Office.
      (b) Subject to subparagraph (c), where the Office of origin receives a

request to present to the International Bureau an international application governed by both the Agreement and the Protocol before the mark which is referred to in that request is registered in the register of the said Office, the international application shall be treated as an international application governed exclusively by the Protocol, and the Office of origin shall delete the designation of any Contracting Party bound by the Agreement.

(c) Where the request referred to in subparagraph (b) is accompanied by an express request that the international application be treated as an international application governed by both the Agreement and the Protocol once the mark is registered in the register of the Office of origin, the said Office shall not delete the designation of any Contracting Party bound by the Agreement and the request to present the international application shall be deemed to have been received by the said Office, for the purposes of Article 3(4) of the Agreement and Article 3(4) of the Protocol, on the date of the registration of the mark in the register of the said Office.

(2) *[Irregularities to Be Remedied by the Applicant]*
(a) If the International Bureau considers that the international application contains irregularities other than those referred to in paragraphs (3), (4) and (6) and in Rules 12 and 13, it shall notify the applicant of the irregularity and at the same time inform the Office of origin.

(b) Such irregularities may be remedied by the applicant within three months from the date of the notification of the irregularity by the International Bureau. If an irregularity is not remedied within three months from the date of the notification of that irregularity by the International Bureau, the international application shall be considered abandoned and the International Bureau shall notify accordingly and at the same time the applicant and the Office of origin.

(3)*[Irregularity to Be Remedied by the Applicant or by the Office of Origin]*
(a) Notwithstanding paragraph (2), where the fees payable under Rule 10 have been paid to the International Bureau by the Office of origin and the International Bureau considers that the amount of the fees received is less than the amount required, it shall notify at the same time the Office of origin and the applicant. The notification shall specify the missing amount.

(b) The missing amount may be paid by the Office of origin or by the applicant within three months from the date of the notification by the International Bureau. If the missing amount is not paid within three months from the date of the notification of the irregularity by the International Bureau, the international application shall be considered abandoned and the International Bureau shall notify accordingly and at the same time the Office of origin and the applicant.

(4)*[Irregularities to Be Remedied by the Office of Origin]*
(a) If the International Bureau
(i) finds that the international application does not fulfill the requirements of Rule 2(1)(a) or was not presented on the official form prescribed under Rule 9(2)(a),
(ii) finds that the international application contains any of the irreg-

ularities referred to in Rule 15(1)(a),
   (iii) considers that the international application contains irregularities relating to the entitlement of the applicant to file an international application,
   (iv) considers that the international application contains irregularities relating to the declaration by the Office of origin referred to in Rule 9(5)(a)(v) or (6)(a)(vii),
   (v) finds that the original referred to in Rule 2(3)(a)(ii) has not been received within the one-month period referred to in Rule 2(3)(b), or

   (v.) finds that the international application is not signed by the Office of origin,

it shall notify the Office of origin and at the same time inform the applicant.

(b) Such irregularities may be remedied by the Office of origin within three months from the date of notification of the irregularity by the International Bureau. If an irregularity is not remedied within three months from the date of the notification of that irregularity by the International Bureau, the international application shall be considered abandoned and the International Bureau shall notify accordingly and at the same time the Office of origin and the applicant.

(5)*[Reimbursement of Fees]* Where, in accordance with paragraphs (2)(b), (3) or (4)(b), the international application is considered abandoned, the International Bureau shall refund any fees paid in respect of that application, after deduction of an amount corresponding to one-half of the basic fee referred to in items 1.1.1, 2.1.1 or 3.1.1 of the Schedule of Fees, to the party having paid those fees.

(6)*[Other Irregularity With Respect to the Designation of a Contracting Party Under the Protocol]*
   (a) Where, in accordance with Article 3(4) of the Protocol, an international application is received by the International Bureau within a period of two months from the date of receipt of that international application by the Office of origin and the International Bureau considers that a declaration of intention to use the mark is required according to Rule 9(6)(d)(i) or (7) but is missing or does not comply with the applicable requirements, the International Bureau shall promptly notify accordingly and at the same time the applicant and the Office of origin.
   (b) The declaration of intention to use the mark shall be deemed to have been received by the International Bureau together with the international application if the missing or corrected declaration is received by the International Bureau within the period of two months referred to in subparagraph (a).
   (c) The international application shall be deemed not to contain the designation of the Contracting Party for which a declaration of intention to use the mark is required if the missing or corrected declaration is received after the period of two months referred to in subparagraph (b). The International Bureau shall notify accordingly and at the same time the applicant and the Office of origin, reim-

burse any designation fee already paid in respect of that Contracting Party and indicate that the designation of the said Contracting Party may be effected as a subsequent designation under Rule 24, provided that such designation is accompanied by the required declaration.

(7)*[International Application Not Considered as Such]* If the international application is presented direct to the International Bureau by the applicant or does not comply with the requirement applicable under Rule 6(1), the international application shall not be considered as such and shall be returned to the sender.

Rule 12
Irregularities With Respect to the
Classification of Goods and Services

(1)*[Proposal for Classification]*

(a) If the International Bureau considers that the requirements of Rule 9(4)(a)(xiii) are not complied with, it shall make a proposal of its own for the classification and grouping and shall send a notification of its proposal to the Office of origin and at the same time inform the applicant.

(b) The notification of the proposal shall also state the amount, if any, of the fees due as a consequence of the proposed classification and grouping.

(2) *[Opinion Differing From the Proposal]* The Office of origin may communicate to the International Bureau an opinion on the proposed classification and grouping within three months from the date of the notification of the proposal.

(3) *[Reminder of the Proposal]* If, within two months from the date of the notification referred to in paragraph (1)(a), the Office of origin has not communicated an opinion on the proposed classification and grouping, the International Bureau shall send to the Office of origin and to the applicant a communication reiterating the proposal. The sending of such a communication shall not affect the three-month period referred to in paragraph (2).

(4)*[Withdrawal of Proposal]* If, in the light of the opinion communicated under paragraph (2), the International Bureau withdraws its proposal, it shall notify the Office of origin accordingly and at the same time inform the applicant.

(5)*[Modification of Proposal]* If, in the light of the opinion communicated under paragraph (2), the International Bureau modifies its proposal, it shall notify the Office of origin and at the same time inform the applicant of such modification and of any consequent changes in the amount indicated under paragraph (1)(b).

(6)*[Confirmation of Proposal]* If, notwithstanding the opinion referred to in paragraph (2), the International Bureau confirms its proposal, it shall notify the Office of origin accordingly and at the same time inform the applicant.

(7) *[Fees]*

(a) If no opinion has been communicated to the International Bureau under paragraph (2), the amount referred to in paragraph (1)(b) shall be payable within four months from the date of the notification referred to in paragraph (1)(a), failing which the international application shall be considered abandoned and the International Bureau shall notify the Office of origin accordingly and at the same time inform the applicant.

(b) If an opinion has been communicated to the International Bureau under paragraph (2), the amount referred to in paragraph (1)(b) or, where applicable, paragraph (5) shall be payable within three months from the date of the communication by the International Bureau of the modification or confirmation of its proposal under paragraph (5) or (6), as the case may be, failing which the international application shall be considered abandoned and the International Bureau shall notify the Office of origin accordingly and at the same time inform the applicant.

(c) If an opinion has been communicated to the International Bureau under paragraph (2) and if, in the light of that opinion, the International Bureau withdraws its proposal in accordance with paragraph (4), the amount referred to in paragraph (1)(b) shall not be due.

(8)*[Reimbursement of Fees]* Where, in accordance with paragraph (7), the international application is considered abandoned, the International Bureau shall refund any fees paid in respect of that application, after deduction of an amount corresponding to one-half of the basic fee referred to in items 1.1.1, 2.1.1 or 3.1.1 of the Schedule of Fees, to the party having paid those fees.

(9)*[Classification in the Registration]* Subject to the conformity of the international application with the other applicable requirements, the mark shall be registered with the classification and grouping that the International Bureau considers to be correct.

Rule 13
Irregularities With Respect to the
Indication of Goods and Services

(1)*[Communication of Irregularity by the International Bureau to the Office of Origin]* If the International Bureau considers that any of the goods and services is indicated in the international application by a term that is too vague for the purposes of classification or is incomprehensible or is linguistically incorrect, it shall notify the Office of origin accordingly and at the same time inform the applicant. In the same notification, the International Bureau may suggest a substitute term, or the deletion of the term.

(2)*[Time Allowed to Remedy Irregularity]*

(a) The Office of origin may make a proposal for remedying the irregularity within three months from the date of the notification referred to in paragraph (1).

(b) If no proposal acceptable to the International Bureau for remedying the irregularity is made within the period indicated in subparagraph (a), the International Bureau shall include in the international registration the term as appearing in the international application, provided that the Office of origin has specified the class in which such term should be classified; the international registration shall contain an indication to the effect that, in the opinion of the International Bureau, the specified term is too vague for the purposes of classification or is incomprehensible or is linguistically incorrect, as the case may be. Where no class has been specified by the Office of origin, the International Bureau shall delete the said term *ex officio* and shall notify the Office of origin accordingly and at the same time inform the applicant.

Chapter 3
International Registrations

Rule 14
Registration of the Mark in the International Register

(1)*[Registration of the Mark in the International Register]* Where the International Bureau finds that the international application conforms to the applicable requirements, it shall register the mark in the International Register, notify the Offices of the designated Contracting Parties of the international registration and inform the Office of origin accordingly, and send a certificate to the holder.

(2)*[Contents of the Registration]* The international registration shall contain
(i) all the data contained in the international application, except any priority claim under Rule 9(4)(a)(iv) where the date of the earlier filing is more than six months before the date of the international registration,
(ii) the date of the international registration,
(iii) the number of the international registration,
(iv) where the mark can be classified according to the International Classification of Figurative Elements, and unless the international application contains a declaration to the effect that the applicant wishes that the mark be considered as a mark in standard characters, the relevant classification symbols of the said Classification as determined by the International Bureau,
(v) an indication, with respect to each designated Contracting Party, as to whether it is a Contracting Party designated under the Agreement or a Contracting Party designated under the Protocol.

Rule 15
Date of the International Registration
in Special Cases

(1)*[Irregular International Application]*
(a) Where the international application received by the International

Bureau does not contain all of the following elements:

    (i)   indications allowing the identity of the applicant to be established and sufficient to contact the applicant or his representative, if any,

    (ii) indications permitting the conclusion that the applicant is entitled to file an international application,

    (iii) the Contracting Parties which are designated,

    (iv) the date and number of the basic application or basic registration, as the case may be,

    (v) the declaration of the Office of origin referred to in Rule 9(5)(a)(v) or Rule 9(6)(a)(vii),

    (vi) a reproduction of the mark,

    (vii) the indication of the goods and services for which registration of the mark is sought,

the international registration shall bear the date on which the last of the missing elements has reached the International Bureau, provided that, where the last of the missing elements reaches the International Bureau within the two-month time limit referred to in Article 3(4) of the Agreement and Article 3(4) of the Protocol, the international registration shall bear the date on which the defective international application has been received by the Office of origin.

    (b) Where the international application received by the International Bureau does not comply with any applicable requirement other than those which are referred to in subparagraph (a), but where all such irregularities have been remedied within three months following the date of the notification referred to in Rule 11(2)(a), (3)(a) or (4)(a), the international registration shall bear

    (i) the date on which the defective international application was received by the Office of origin, if the International Bureau has received the international application within the two-month time limit referred to in Article 3(4) of the Agreement and Article 3(4) of the Protocol;

    (ii) the date on which the defective international application was received by the International Bureau, if the International Bureau has received the international application after the expiry of the two-month time limit referred to in Article 3(4) of the Agreement and Article 3(4) of the Protocol.

(2)   *[Irregular Classification]* The date of the international registration shall not be affected by an irregularity in respect of the classification of goods and services if the amount referred to in Rule 12(1)(b) is paid to the International Bureau within whichever of the periods referred to in Rule 12(7)(a) and (b) is applicable.

Chapter 4
Facts in Contracting Parties
Affecting International Registrations

Rule 16
Time Limit for Refusal in Case of Opposition

(1)*[Information Relating to Possible Oppositions]*
    (a) Where a declaration has been made by a Contracting Party pursuant to Article 5(2)(b) and (c), first sentence, of the Protocol, the Office of that Contracting Party shall, where applicable, inform the International Bureau of the number, and the name of the holder, of the international registration in respect of which oppositions may be filed after the expiry of the 18-month time limit referred to in Article 5(2)(b) of the Protocol.
    (b) Where, at the time of the communication of the information referred to in subparagraph (a), the dates on which the opposition period begins and ends are known, those dates shall be indicated in the communication. If such dates are not yet known at that time, they shall be communicated to the International Bureau once they become known.
    (c) Where subparagraph (a) applies and the Office referred to in the said subparagraph has, before the expiry of the 18-month time limit referred to in the same subparagraph, informed the International Bureau of the fact that the time limit for filing oppositions will expire within the 30 days preceding the expiry of the 18-month time limit and of the possibility that oppositions may be filed during those 30 days, a refusal based on an opposition filed during the said 30 days may be notified to the International Bureau within one month from the date of filing of the opposition.

(2)*[Recordal and Transmittal of the Information]* The International Bureau shall record in the International Register the information received under paragraph (1), and shall transmit that information to the Office of origin, if that Office has informed the International Bureau that it wishes to receive such information, and, at the same time, to the holder.

Rule 17
Notification Of Refusal

(1)*[Notification of Refusal]* The notification of any refusal of protection under Article 5 of the Agreement and Article 5 of the Protocol shall relate to one international registration, shall be dated and shall be signed by the Office making the notification.

(2)*[Refusals Not Based on an Opposition]* Where the refusal of protection is not based on an opposition, the notification referred to in paragraph (1) shall contain or indicate
    (i) the Office making the notification,

(ii) the number of the international registration, preferably accompanied by other indications enabling the identity of the international registration to be confirmed, such as the verbal elements of the mark or the basic application or basic registration number,

(iii) [Deleted]

(iv) all the grounds on which the refusal is based together with a reference to the corresponding essential provisions of the law,

(v) where the grounds on which the refusal is based refer to a mark which has been the subject of an application or registration and with which the mark that is the subject of the international registration appears to be in conflict. the filing date and number, the priority date (if any), the registration date and number (if available), the name and address of the owner, and a reproduction, of the former mark, together with the list of all or the relevant goods and services in the application or registration of the former mark, it being understood that the said list may be in the language of the said application or registration,

(vi) if the refusal does not affect all the goods and services, those which are affected by the refusal or those which are not affected by the refusal,

(vii) whether the refusal may be subject to review or appeal and, if so, the time limit, reasonable under the circumstances, for any request for review of, or appeal against, the refusal and the authority to which such request for review or appeal shall lie, with the indication, where applicable, that the request for review or the appeal has to be filed through the intermediary of a representative whose address is within the territory of the Contracting Party whose Office has pronounced the refusal, and

(viii) the date on which the refusal was pronounced.

(3)*[Refusals Based on an Opposition]* Where the refusal of protection is based on an opposition or on an opposition and other grounds, the notification referred to in paragraph (1) shall, in addition to complying with the requirements referred to in paragraph (2), contain an indication of that fact and the name and address of the opponent; however, notwithstanding paragraph (2)(v), the Office communicating the refusal must, where the opposition is based on a mark which has been the subject of an application or registration, communicate the list of the goods and services on which the opposition is based and may, in addition, communicate the complete list of goods and services of that earlier application or registration, it being understood that the said lists may be in the language of the earlier application or registration.

(4)*[Recordal; Review or Appeal]*

(a) The International Bureau shall record the refusal in the International Register together with the data contained in the notification, with an indication of the date on which the notification of refusal was sent or is regarded under Rule 18(1)(c) as having been sent to the International Bureau.

(b) Where the notification of refusal under paragraphs (2) or (3) indicates that the refusal may be subject to review or appeal, the Office that communicated the refusal

(i) shall, where a request for review or an appeal has been lodged, or where the applicable time limit has expired without a request for review or an appeal having been lodged, and the said Office is aware thereof, inform the International Bureau of that fact in a way agreed upon between the International Bureau and that Office;

(ii) shall, where it has informed the International Bureau that a request for review or an appeal has been lodged or where a request for review or an appeal has been lodged without the International Bureau having been informed accordingly, notify the International Bureau as soon as possible of the final decision taken on the review or appeal or, where the request for review or the appeal has been withdrawn, inform as soon as possible the International Bureau of that withdrawal.

(c) The International Bureau shall record in the International Register the relevant facts and data referred to in subparagraph (b) of which it has been informed.

(5)*[Transmittal of Copies of Notifications]* The International Bureau shall transmit copies of notifications received under paragraphs (2) to (4) to the Office of origin, if that Office has informed the International Bureau that it wishes to receive such copies, and, at the same time, to the holder.

Rule 18
Irregular Refusals

(1)*[Contracting Party Designated Under the Agreement]*
(a) In the case of a refusal concerning the effect of the international registration in a Contracting Party designated under the Agreement, the notification of refusal shall not be regarded as such by the International Bureau

(i) if it does not indicate the number of the international registration concerned, unless other indications contained in the notification permit the said registration to be identified,

(ii) if it does not indicate any grounds for refusal, or

(iii) if it is sent too late to the International Bureau, that is, if it is sent after the expiry of one year from the date on which the recordal of the international registration or the recordal of the designation made subsequently to the international registration has been effected, it being understood that the said date is the same as the date of sending the notification of the international registration or of the designation made subsequently. In the case of a notification of refusal sent through a postal service, the date of dispatch shall be determined by the postmark. If the postmark is illegible or missing, the International Bureau shall treat such notification as if it was sent 20 days before the date of its receipt by the International Bureau. However, if the date of dispatch thus determined is earlier than the date on which the refusal was pronounced, the International Bureau shall treat such notification as if it had been sent on the latter date. In the case of a notification of refusal sent through a delivery service, the date of dispatch shall be determined by the indication given by such delivery service on the basis of the details of the mailing as recorded by it.

(b) Where subparagraph (a) applies, the International Bureau shall nevertheless transmit a copy of the notification to the holder, shall inform, at the same time, the holder and the Office that sent the notification that the notification of refusal is not regarded as such by the International Bureau, and shall indicate the reasons therefor.

(c) If the notification of refusal

(i)   is not signed on behalf of the Office which communicated the refusal, or does not otherwise comply with the requirements of Rule 2(1)(a) or with the requirement applicable under Rule 6(2),

(ii)   does not contain, where applicable, the details of the mark with which the mark that is the subject of the international registration appears to be in conflict (Rule 17(2)(v) and (3)),

(iii)   does not contain, where the refusal indicates that not all the goods and services are affected, the indication of those goods and services that are affected by the refusal or the indication of those goods and services that are not affected by the refusal (Rule 17(2)(vi)),

(iv)   does not contain, where applicable, the indication of the authority to which a request for review or an appeal lies and the applicable time limit, reasonable under the circumstances, for lodging such a request or appeal (Rule 17(2)(vii)),

(v)   does not contain the indication of the date on which the refusal was pronounced (Rule 17(2)(viii)), or

(vi)   does not contain, where applicable, the name and address of the opponent and the indication of the goods and services on which the opposition is based (Rule 17(3)),

the International Bureau shall invite the Office which communicated the refusal to rectify its notification within two months from the invitation and shall transmit to the holder copies of the irregular notification of refusal and of the invitation sent to the Office concerned. If the notification is so rectified, the rectified notification shall be regarded as having been sent to the International Bureau on the date on which the defective notification had been sent to it. The International Bureau shall transmit copies of the rectified notification to the Office of origin, if that Office has informed the International Bureau that it wishes to receive such copies, and to the holder. If the notification is not so rectified, it shall not be regarded as a notification of refusal. In the latter case, the International Bureau shall inform, at the same time, the holder and the Office that sent the notification that the notification of refusal is not regarded as such by the International Bureau, and shall indicate the reasons therefor.

(2)*[Contracting Party Designated Under the Protocol]*

(a)   Paragraph (1) shall also apply in the case of a refusal concerning the effect of the international registration in a Contracting Party designated under the Protocol, it being understood that the time limit referred to in paragraph (1)(a)(iii) shall be the time limit applicable under Article 5(2)(a), (b) or (c)(ii) of the Protocol.

(b) Paragraph (1)(a) shall apply to determine whether the time limit before the expiry of which the Office of the Contracting Party concerned must give the International Bureau the information referred to in Article 5(2)(c)(i) of the Protocol has been complied with. If such information is given after the expiry of that time limit, it shall be regarded as not having been given and the International Bureau shall inform the Office concerned accordingly.

(c) Where the notification of refusal is made under Article 5(2)(c)(ii) of the Protocol without the requirements of Article 5(2)(c)(i) of the Protocol having been complied with, it shall not be regarded as a notification of refusal. In such a case, the International Bureau shall nevertheless transmit a copy of the notification to the holder, shall inform, at the same time, the holder and the Office that sent the notification that the notification of refusal is not regarded as such by the International Bureau, and shall indicate the reasons therefor.

Rule 19
Invalidations In Designated Contracting Parties

(1)*[Contents of the Notification of Invalidation]* Where the effects of an international registration are invalidated in a designated Contracting Party under Article 5(6) of the Agreement or Article 5(6) of the Protocol and the invalidation is no longer subject to appeal, the Office of the Contracting Party whose competent authority has pronounced the invalidation shall notify the International Bureau accordingly. The notification shall contain or indicate

    (i) the authority which pronounced the invalidation,

    (ii) the fact that the invalidation is no longer subject to appeal,

    (iii) the number of the international registration,

    (iv) the name of the holder,

    (v) if the invalidation does not concern all the goods and services, those in respect of which the invalidation has been pronounced or those in respect of which the invalidation has not been pronounced, and

    (vi) the date on which the invalidation was pronounced and, where possible, its effective date.

(2)*[Recordal of the Invalidation and Information of the Office of Origin and the Holder]* The International Bureau shall record the invalidation in the International Register, together with the data contained in the notification of invalidation, and shall inform accordingly the Office of origin, if that Office has informed the International Bureau that it wishes to receive such information, and, at the same time, the holder.

Rule 20
Restriction of the Holder's Right of Disposal

(1)*[Communication of Information]* The Office of any designated Contracting Party may inform the International Bureau that the holder's right of disposal has been restricted in respect of the international registration in the territory of that Contracting Party. Such information, if given, shall consist of a summary statement of the main facts concerning the restriction.

(2)*[Partial or Total Removal of Restriction]* Where the International Bureau has been informed of a restriction of the holder's right of disposal in accordance with paragraph (1), the Office of the Contracting Party which communicated the information shall also inform the International Bureau of any partial or total removal of that restriction.

(3)*[Recordal]* The International Bureau shall record the information communicated under paragraphs (1) and (2) in the International Register and shall inform the holder accordingly.

(4)*[Licenses]* The present Rule shall not apply to licenses.

Rule 21
Replacement of a National or Regional Registration
by an International Registration

(1)*[Notification]* Where, in accordance with Article 4*bis*(2) of the Agreement or Article 4*bis*(2) of the Protocol, the Office of a designated Contracting Party has taken note in its Register, following a request made direct by the holder with that Office, that a national or a regional registration has been replaced by an international registration, that Office shall notify the International Bureau accordingly. Such notification shall indicate
      (i) the number of the international registration concerned,
      (ii) where the replacement concerns only one or some of the goods and services listed in the international registration, those goods and services, and
      (iii) the filing date and number, the registration date and number, and, if any, the priority date of the national or regional registration which has been replaced by the international registration.

(2)*[Recordal]* The International Bureau shall record the indications notified under paragraph (1) in the International Register and shall inform the holder accordingly.

Rule 22
Ceasing of Effect of the Basic Application,
of the Registration Resulting Therefrom,
or of the Basic Registration

(1)*[Notification Relating to Ceasing of Effect of the Basic Application, of the Registration Resulting Therefrom, or of the Basic Registration]*
      (a) Where Article 6(3) and (4) of the Agreement or Article 6(3) and (4) of the Protocol, or both, apply, the Office of origin shall notify the International

Bureau accordingly and shall indicate

      (i)   the number of the international registration,

      (ii)   the name of the holder,

      (iii)   the facts and decisions affecting the basic registration, or, where the international registration concerned is based on a basic application which has not resulted in a registration, the facts and decisions affecting the basic application, or, where the international registration is based on a basic application which has resulted in a registration, the facts and decisions affecting that registration, and the effective date of those facts and decisions, and

      (iv)   where the said facts and decisions affect the international registration only with respect to some of the goods and services, those goods and services which are affected by the facts and decisions or those which are not affected by the facts and decisions.

      (b)   Where a judicial action referred to in Article 6(4) of the Agreement, or a proceeding referred to in item (i), (ii) or (iii) of Article 6(3) of the Protocol, began before the expiry of the five-year period but has not, before the expiry of that period, resulted in the final decision referred to in Article 6(4) of the Agreement, or in the final decision referred to in the second sentence of Article 6(3) of the Protocol or in the withdrawal or renunciation referred to in the third sentence of Article 6(3) of the Protocol, the Office of origin shall, where it is aware thereof and as soon as possible after the expiry of the said period, notify the International Bureau accordingly.

      (c)   Once the judicial action or proceeding referred to in subparagraph (b) has resulted in the final decision referred to in Article 6(4) of the Agreement, in the final decision referred to in the second sentence of Article 6(3) of the Protocol or in the withdrawal or renunciation referred to in the third sentence of Article 6(3) of the Protocol, the Office of origin shall, where it is aware thereof, promptly notify the International Bureau accordingly and shall give the indications referred to in subparagraph (a)(i) to (iv).

(2)[Recordal and Transmittal of the Notification; Cancellation of the International Registration]

      (a)   The International Bureau shall record any notification referred to in paragraph (1) in the International Register and shall transmit a copy of the notification to the Offices of the designated Contracting Parties and to the holder.

      (b)   Where any notification referred to in paragraph (1)(a) or (c) requests cancellation of the international registration and complies with the requirements of that paragraph, the International Bureau shall cancel, to the extent applicable, the international registration in the International Register.

      (c)   Where the international registration has been cancelled in the International Register in accordance with subparagraph (b), the International Bureau shall notify the Offices of the designated Contracting Parties and the holder of the following:

      (i)   the date on which the international registration was cancelled in the International Register;

      (ii)   where the cancellation concerns all goods and services, that fact;

      (iii) where the cancellation concerns only some of the goods and services, the goods and services indicated under paragraph (1)(a)(iv).

Rule 23
Division of the Basic Application,
of the Registration Resulting Therefrom,
or of the Basic Registration

(1)*[Notification of the Division of the Basic Application]* Where, during the five-year period referred to in Article 6(3) of the Protocol, the basic application is divided into two or more applications, the Office of origin shall notify the International Bureau accordingly and shall indicate
      (i) the number of the international registration or, if the international registration has not yet been effected, the number of the basic application,
      (ii) the name of the holder or applicant,
      (iii) the number of each application.

(2)*[Recordal and Notification by the International Bureau]* The International Bureau shall record the notification referred to in paragraph (1) in the International Register and shall notify the Offices of the designated Contracting Parties and, at the same time, the holder.

(3)*[Division of the Registration Resulting From the Basic Application or of the Basic Registration]* Paragraphs (1) and (2) shall apply, *mutatis mutandis*, to the division of any registration which resulted from the basic application referred to in Article 6(3) of the Protocol and to the division of the basic registration referred to in Article 6(3) of the Agreement and in Article 6(3) of the Protocol.

Chapter 5
Subsequent Designations; Changes

Rule 24
Designation Subsequent to the
International Registration

(1)*[Entitlement]*
      (a) A Contracting Party may be the subject of a designation made subsequent to the international registration (hereinafter referred to as 'subsequent designation') where, at the time of that designation, the holder is entitled, under Articles 1(2) and 2 of the Agreement or Article 2 of the Protocol and subject to Article 9*sexies* of the Protocol, to designate such a Contracting Party.
      (b) The holder of an international registration resulting from an international application governed exclusively by the Agreement may designate Contracting Parties bound by the Protocol but not by the Agreement, provided that,

at the time of that designation, the Contracting Party whose Office is the Office of origin is bound by the Protocol, or, where a change in ownership has been recorded, the Contracting Party, or at least one of the Contracting Parties, in respect of which the new holder fulfills the conditions to be the holder of an international registration is bound by the Protocol.

(c) The holder of an international registration resulting from an international application governed exclusively by the Protocol may designate Contracting Parties bound by the Agreement, whether or not those Contracting Parties are bound also by the Protocol, provided that, at the time of that designation, the Contracting Party whose Office is the Office of origin is bound by the Agreement, or, where a change in ownership has been recorded, the Contracting Party, or at least one of the Contracting Parties, in respect of which the new holder fulfills the conditions to be the holder of an international registration, is bound by the Agreement, and provided that either the international registration is based on a basic registration, or, if it is based on a basic application, the said application resulted in a registration.

(2)[Presentation; Form and Signature]

(a) A subsequent designation shall be presented to the International Bureau by the holder, by the Office of origin, or by another interested Office if the holder asks for, and that Office admits, such presentation; however,

(i) where Rule 7(1) applies, it must be presented by the Office of origin;

(ii) where any of the Contracting Parties are designated under the Agreement, the subsequent designation must be presented by the Office of origin or another interested Office.

(b) The subsequent designation shall be presented on the official form in one copy. Where it is presented by the holder, it shall be signed by the holder. Where it is presented by an Office, it shall be signed by that Office and, where the Office so requires, also by the holder. Where it is presented by an Office and that Office, without requiring that the holder also sign it, allows that the holder also sign it, the holder may do so.

(3)[Contents]

(a) The subsequent designation shall contain or indicate

(i) the number of the international registration concerned,

(ii) the name and address of the holder,

(iii) the Contracting Party that is designated,

(iv) where the subsequent designation is for all the goods and services listed in the international registration concerned, that fact, or, where the subsequent designation is for only part of the goods and services listed in the international registration concerned, those goods and services,

(v) the amount of the fees being paid and the method of payment, or instructions to debit the required amount of fees to an account opened with the International Bureau, and the identification of the party effecting the payment or giving the instructions, and,

(vi) where the subsequent designation is presented by an Office, the date on which it was received by that Office.

(b) Where the subsequent designation concerns a Contracting Party that has made a notification under Rule 7(2), that subsequent designation shall also contain a declaration of intention to use the mark in the territory of that Contracting Party; the declaration shall, as required by the said Contracting Party,
(i) be signed by the holder himself and be made on a separate official form annexed to the subsequent designation, or
(ii) be included in the subsequent designation.

(c) The subsequent designation may also contain
(i) the indications and translation or translations, as the case may be, referred to in Rule 9(4)(b),
(ii) a request that the subsequent designation take effect after the recordal of a change or a cancellation in respect of the international registration concerned or after the renewal of the international registration.

(d) Where the international registration is based on a basic application, the subsequent designation shall be accompanied by a declaration, signed by the Office of origin, certifying that the said application has resulted in a registration and indicating the date and number of that registration, unless such a declaration has already been received by the International Bureau.

(4)*[Fees]* The subsequent designation shall be subject to the payment of the fees specified or referred to in item 5 of the Schedule of Fees.

(5)*[Irregularities]*
(a) If the subsequent designation does not comply with the applicable requirements, and subject to paragraph (9), the International Bureau shall notify that fact to the holder and, if the subsequent designation was presented by an Office, that Office.

(b) If the irregularity is not remedied within three months from the date of the notification of the irregularity by the International Bureau, the subsequent designation shall be considered abandoned, and the International Bureau shall notify accordingly and at the same time the holder and, if the subsequent designation was presented by an Office, that Office, and refund any fees paid, after deduction of an amount corresponding to one-half of the basic fee referred to in item 5.1 of the Schedule of Fees, to the party having paid those fees.

(c) Notwithstanding subparagraphs (a) and (b), if a subsequent designation is presented under paragraph (1)(b) or (c) and the requirements of paragraph (1)(b) or (c), as the case may be, are not complied with in respect of one or more of the designated Contracting Parties, the subsequent designation shall be deemed not to contain the designation of those Contracting Parties, and any complementary or individual fees already paid in respect of those Contracting Parties shall be reimbursed. If the requirements of paragraph (1)(b) or (c) are not complied with in respect of all the designated Contracting Parties, subparagraph (b) shall apply.

(6)*[Date of Subsequent Designation]*

    (a) A subsequent designation presented by the holder direct to the International Bureau shall, subject to subparagraph (c)(i), bear the date of its receipt by the International Bureau.

    (b) A subsequent designation presented to the International Bureau by an Office shall, subject to subparagraph (c)(i), bear the date on which it was received by that Office, provided that the said designation has been received by the International Bureau within a period of two months from that date. If the subsequent designation has not been received by the International Bureau within that period, it shall, subject to subparagraph (c)(i), bear the date of its receipt by the International Bureau.

    (c) Where the subsequent designation does not comply with the applicable requirements and the irregularity is remedied within three months from the date of the notification referred to in paragraph (5)(a),

        (i) the subsequent designation shall, where the irregularity concerns any of the requirements referred to in paragraph (3)(a)(i), (iii) and (iv) and (b)(i), bear the date on which that designation is put in order, unless the said designation was presented to the International Bureau by an Office and the irregularity is remedied within the period of two months referred to in subparagraph (b); in the latter case, the subsequent designation shall bear the date on which it was received by the said Office;

        (ii) the date applicable under subparagraph (a) or (b), as the case may be, shall not be affected by an irregularity concerning requirements other than those which are referred to in paragraph (3)(a)(i), (iii) and (iv) and (b)(i).

    (d) Notwithstanding subparagraphs (a), (b) and (c), where the subsequent designation contains a request made in accordance with paragraph (3)(c)(ii), it may bear a date which is later than that resulting from subparagraph (a), (b) or (c).

    (7) *[Recordal and Notification]* Where the International Bureau finds that the subsequent designation conforms to the applicable requirements, it shall record it in the International Register and shall notify accordingly the Office of the Contracting Party that has been designated in the subsequent designation and at the same time inform the holder and, if the subsequent designation was presented by an Office, that Office.

(8)*[Refusal]* Rules 16 to 18 shall apply *mutatis mutandis.*

(9)*[Subsequent Designation Not Considered as Such]* If the requirements of paragraph (2)(a) are not complied with, the subsequent designation shall not be considered as such and the International Bureau shall inform the sender accordingly.

Rule 25
Request for Recordal of a Change;
Request for Recordal of a Cancellation

(1)*[Presentation of the Request]*
    (a) A request for recordal shall be presented to the International Bureau on the relevant official form, in one copy, where the request relates to any of the following:
        (i) a change in the ownership of the international registration in respect of all or some of the goods and services and all or some of the designated Contracting Parties;
        (ii) a limitation of the list of goods and services in respect of all or some of the designated Contracting Parties;
        (iii) a renunciation in respect of some of the designated Contracting Parties for all the goods and services;
        (iv) a change in the name or address of the holder;
        (v) cancellation of the international registration in respect of all the designated Contracting Parties for all or some of the goods and services.

    (b) The request shall be presented by the holder or by the Office of origin or another interested Office, except that
        (i) the request for recordal of a change other than a change in the name or address of the holder or of the representative must be presented by the Office of origin or another interested Office where the change affects any Contracting Party designated under the Agreement, and
        (ii) the request for the recordal of a cancellation must be presented by the Office of origin or another interested Office where any of the designated Contracting Parties covered by the international registration to be cancelled had been designated under the Agreement.

    (c) Where the request is presented by the holder, it shall be signed by the holder. Where it is presented by an Office, it shall be signed by that Office and, where the Office so requires, also by the holder. Where it is presented by an Office and that Office, without requiring that the holder also sign it, allows that the holder also sign it, the holder may do so.

(2)*[Contents of the Request]*
    (a) The request for the recordal of a change or the request for the recordal of a cancellation shall, in addition to the requested change or cancellation, contain or indicate
        (i) the number of the international registration concerned,
        (ii) the name of the holder, unless the change relates to the name or address of the representative,
        (iii) in case of a change in the ownership of the international registration, the name and address, indicated in accordance with Rule 9(4)(a)(i) and (ii), of the natural person or legal entity mentioned in the request as the new holder of the international registration (hereinafter referred to as 'the transferee'),

(iv) in case of a change in the ownership of the international registration, the Contracting Party or Parties in respect of which the transferee fulfills the conditions, under Articles 1(2) and 2 of the Agreement or under Article 2(1) of the Protocol, to be the holder of an international registration,

(v) in case of a change in the ownership of the international registration, where the address of the transferee given in accordance with subparagraph (a)(iii) is not in the territory of the Contracting Party, or of one of the Contracting Parties, given in accordance with subparagraph (a)(iv), and unless the transferee has indicated that he is a national of a Contracting State or of a State member of a Contracting Organization, the address of the establishment, or the domicile, of the transferee in the Contracting Party, or in one of the Contracting Parties, in respect of which the transferee fulfills the conditions to be the holder of an international registration,

(vi) in case of a change in the ownership of the international registration that does not relate to all the goods and services and to all the designated Contracting Parties, the goods and services and the designated Contracting Parties to which the change in ownership relates, and

(vii) the amount of the fees being paid and the method of payment, or instructions to debit the required amount of fees to an account opened with the International Bureau, and the identification of the party effecting the payment or giving the instructions.

(b) The request for the recordal of a change in the ownership of the international registration may also contain,

(i) where the transferee is a natural person, an indication of the State of which the transferee is a national;

(ii) where the transferee is a legal entity, indications concerning the legal nature of that legal entity and the State, and, where applicable, the territorial unit within that State, under the law of which the said legal entity has been organized.

(c)The request for recordal of a change or a cancellation may also contain a request that it be recorded before, or after, the recordal of another change or cancellation or a subsequent designation in respect of the international registration concerned or after the renewal of the international registration.

(3)*[Request Not Admissible]* A change in the ownership of an international registration may not be recorded in respect of a given designated Contracting Party if that Contracting Party

(i) is bound by the Agreement but not by the Protocol, and the Contracting Party indicated under paragraph (2)(a)(iv) is not bound by the Agreement, or none of the Contracting Parties indicated under that paragraph is bound by the Agreement;

(ii) is bound by the Protocol but not by the Agreement, and the Contracting Party indicated under paragraph (2)(a)(iv) is not bound by the Protocol, or none of the Contracting Parties indicated under that paragraph is bound by the Protocol.

(4)[Several Transferees] Where the request for the recordal of a change in the ownership of the international registration mentions several transferees, that change may not be recorded in respect of a given designated Contracting Party if any of the transferees does not fulfill the conditions to be holder of the international registration in respect of that Contracting Party.

Rule 26
Irregularities in Requests for Recordal of a Change
and for Recordal of a Cancellation

(1)[Irregular Request] If the request for the recordal of a change, or the request for the recordal of a cancellation, referred to in Rule 25(1)(a) does not comply with the applicable requirements, and subject to paragraph (3), the International Bureau shall notify that fact to the holder and, if the request was made by an Office, to that Office.

(2)[Time Allowed to Remedy Irregularity] The irregularity may be remedied within three months from the date of the notification of the irregularity by the International Bureau. If the irregularity is not remedied within three months from the date of the notification of the irregularity by the International Bureau, the request shall be considered abandoned, and the International Bureau shall notify accordingly and at the same time the holder and, if the request for the recordal of a change or the request for the recordal of a cancellation was presented by an Office, that Office, and refund any fees paid, after deduction of an amount corresponding to one-half of the relevant fees referred to in item 7 of the Schedule of Fees, to the party having paid those fees.

(3)[Requests Not Considered as Such] If the requirements of Rule 25(1)(b) are not complied with, the request shall not be considered as such and the International Bureau shall inform the sender accordingly.

Rule 27
Recordal and Notification of a Change or of a Cancellation;
Declaration That a Change in Ownership Has No Effect

(1)[Recordal and Notification of a Change or of a Cancellation]
      (a) The International Bureau shall, provided that the request referred to in Rule 25(1)(a) is in order, promptly record the change or the cancellation in the International Register, shall notify accordingly the Offices of the designated Contracting Parties in which the change has effect or, in the case of a cancellation, the Offices of all the designated Contracting Parties, and shall inform at the same time the holder and, if the request was presented by an Office, that Office. Where the recordal relates to a change in ownership, the International Bureau shall also inform the former holder in the case of a total change in ownership and the holder of the part of the international registration which has been assigned or otherwise transferred in the case of a partial change in ownership. Where the request for the

1175

recordal of a cancellation was presented by the holder or an interested Office during the five-year period referred to in Article 6(3) of the Agreement and Article 6(3) of the Protocol, the International Bureau shall also inform the Office of origin.

(b) The change or the cancellation shall be recorded as of the date of receipt by the International Bureau of a request complying with the applicable requirements, except that, where a request has been made in accordance with Rule 25(2)(c), it may be recorded as of a later date.

(2) *[Recordal of Partial Change in Ownership]* Assignment or other transfer of the international registration in respect of some only of the goods and services or some only of the designated Contracting Parties shall be recorded in the International Register under the number of the international registration of which a part has been assigned or otherwise transferred; any assigned or otherwise transferred part shall be cancelled under the number of the said international registration and recorded as a separate international registration. The separate international registration shall bear the number of the registration of which a part has been assigned or otherwise transferred, together with a capital letter.

(3) *[Recordal of Merger of International Registrations]* Where the same natural person or legal entity has been recorded as the holder of two or more international registrations resulting from a partial change in ownership under paragraph (2), the registrations shall be merged at the request of the said person or entity, made either direct or through the Office of origin or another interested Office. The international registration resulting from the merger shall bear the number of the international registration of which a part had been assigned or otherwise transferred, together, where applicable, with a capital letter.

(4) *[Declaration That a Change in Ownership Has No Effect]*

(a) The Office of a designated Contracting Party which is notified, by the International Bureau, of a change in ownership affecting that Contracting Party may declare that the change in ownership has no effect in the said Contracting Party. The effect of such a declaration shall be that, with respect to the said Contracting Party, the international registration concerned shall remain in the name of the transferor.

(b) The declaration referred to in subparagraph (a) shall indicate
    (i) the reasons for which the change in ownership has no effect,
    (ii) the corresponding essential provisions of the law, and
    (iii) whether such declaration may be subject to review or appeal.

(c) The declaration referred to in subparagraph (a) shall be notified to the International Bureau which shall notify accordingly the party (holder or Office) that presented the request for the recordal of a change in ownership and the new holder.

(d) Any final decision relating to the declaration referred to in subparagraph (a) above shall be notified to the International Bureau which shall notify accordingly the party (holder or Office) that presented the request for the recordal of a change in ownership and the new holder.

(e) The International Bureau shall record in the International Register any declaration referred to in subparagraph (a) which is not subject to review or appeal or any final decision referred to in subparagraph (d), and, as the case may be, record as a separate international registration that part of the international registration which has been the subject of the said declaration or final decision. The separate international registration shall bear the number of the registration of which a part has been assigned or otherwise transferred, together with a capital letter.

Rule 28
Corrections in the International Register

(1)*[Correction]* Where the International Bureau, acting *ex officio* or at the request of the holder or of an Office, considers that there is an error concerning an international registration in the International Register, it shall modify the Register accordingly.

(2)*[Notification]* The International Bureau shall notify accordingly the holder and, at the same time, the Offices of the designated Contracting Parties in which the correction has effect.

(3)*[Refusal of Effects of Correction]* Any Office referred to in paragraph (2) shall have the right to declare in a notification to the International Bureau that it refuses to recognize the effects of the correction. Article 5 of the Agreement or Article 5 of the Protocol and Rules 16 to 18 shall apply *mutatis mutandis*, it being understood that the date of sending the notification of the correction shall be the date from which the time limit for pronouncing a refusal is counted.

Chapter 6
Renewals

Rule 29
Unofficial Notice of Expiry

The fact that the unofficial notice referred to in Article 7(4) of the Agreement and Article 7(3) of the Protocol is not received shall not constitute an excuse for failure to comply with any time limit under Rule 30.

Rule 30
Details Concerning Renewal

(1) *[Fees]*
(a) The international registration shall be renewed upon payment, at the latest on the date on which the renewal of the international registration is due, of
      (i) the basic fee,
      (ii) where applicable, the supplementary fee, and,

(iii) the complementary fee or individual fee, as the case may be, for each designated Contracting Party for which no refusal or invalidation is recorded in the International Register in respect of all the goods and services concerned,

as specified or referred to in item 6 of the Schedule of Fees. However, such payment may be made within six months from the date on which the renewal of the international registration is due, provided that the surcharge specified in item 6.5 of the Schedule of Fees is paid at the same time.

(b) If any payment made for the purposes of renewal is received by the International Bureau earlier than three months before the date on which the renewal of the international registration is due, it shall be considered as having been received three months before the date on which renewal is due.

(2)[Further Details]

(a) Where the holder does not wish to renew the international registration in respect of a designated Contracting Party for which no refusal is recorded in the International Register in respect of all the goods and services concerned, payment of the required fees shall be accompanied by a statement that the renewal of the international registration is not to be recorded in the International Register in respect of that Contracting Party.

(b) Where the holder wishes to renew the international registration in respect of a designated Contracting Party notwithstanding the fact that a refusal is recorded in the International Register for that Contracting Party in respect of all the goods and services concerned, payment of the required fees, including the complementary fee or individual fee, as the case may be, for that Contracting Party, shall be accompanied by a statement that the renewal of the international registration is to be recorded in the International Register in respect of that Contracting Party.

(c) The international registration may not be renewed in respect of any designated Contracting Party in respect of which an invalidation has been recorded for all goods and services under Rule 19(2) or in respect of which a renunciation has been recorded under Rule 27(1)(a). The international registration may not be renewed in respect of any designated Contracting Party for those goods and services in respect of which an invalidation of the effects of the international registration in that Contracting Party has been recorded under Rule 19(2) or in respect of which a limitation has been recorded under Rule 27(1)(a).

(d) The fact that the international registration is not renewed in respect of all of the designated Contracting Parties shall not be considered to constitute a change for the purposes of Article 7(2) of the Agreement or Article 7(2) of the Protocol.

(3)[Insufficient Fees]

(a) If the amount of the fees received is less than the amount of the fees required for renewal, the International Bureau shall promptly notify at the same time both the holder and the representative, if any, accordingly. The notification shall specify the missing amount.

(b) If the amount of the fees received is, on the expiry of the period of six months referred to in paragraph (1)(a), less than the amount required under paragraph (1), the International Bureau shall not, subject to subparagraph (c), record the renewal, and shall reimburse the amount received to the party having paid it and notify accordingly the holder and the representative, if any.

(c) If the notification referred to in subparagraph (a) was sent during the three months preceding the expiry of the period of six months referred to in paragraph (1)(a) and if the amount of the fees received is, on the expiry of that period, less than the amount required under paragraph (1) but is at least 70% of that amount, the International Bureau shall proceed as provided in Rule 31(1) and (3). If the amount required is not fully paid within three months from the said notification, the International Bureau shall cancel the renewal, notify accordingly the holder, the representative, if any, and the Offices which had been notified of the renewal, and reimburse the amount received to the party having paid it.

(4)*[Period for Which Renewal Fees Are Paid]* The fees required for each renewal shall be paid for ten years, irrespective of the fact that the international registration contains, in the list of designated Contracting Parties, only Contracting Parties designated under the Agreement, only Contracting Parties designated under the Protocol, or both Contracting Parties designated under the Agreement and Contracting Parties designated under the Protocol. As regards payments under the Agreement, the payment for ten years shall be considered to be a payment for an instalment of ten years.

Rule 31
Recordal of the Renewal; Notification and Certificate

(1)*[Recordal and Effective Date of the Renewal]* Renewal shall be recorded in the International Register with the date on which renewal was due, even if the fees required for renewal are paid within the period of grace referred to in Article 7(5) of the Agreement and in Article 7(4) of the Protocol.

(2)*[Renewal Date in the Case of Subsequent Designations]* The effective date of the renewal shall be the same for all designations contained in the international registration, irrespective of the date on which such designations were recorded in the International Register.

(3)*[Notification and Certificate]* The International Bureau shall notify the Offices of the designated Contracting Parties concerned of the renewal and shall send a certificate to the holder.

(4)*[Notification in Case of Non-Renewal]*

(a) Where an international registration is not renewed, the International Bureau shall notify accordingly the Offices of all of the Contracting Parties designated in that international registration.

(b) Where an international registration is not renewed in respect of a designated Contracting Party, the International Bureau shall notify the Office of that Contracting Party accordingly.

Chapter 7
Gazette And Data Base

Rule 32
Gazette

(1)*[Information Concerning International Registrations]*
    (a) The International Bureau shall publish in the Gazette relevant data concerning
        (i) international registrations effected under Rule 14;
        (ii) information communicated under Rule 16(1);
        (iii) refusals recorded under Rule 17(4), with an indication as to whether there is a possibility of review or appeal, but without the grounds for refusal;
        (iv) renewals recorded under Rule 31(1);
        (v) subsequent designations recorded under Rule 24(7);
        (vi) continuation of effects of international registrations under Rule 39;
        (vii) changes in ownership, limitations, renunciations and changes of name or address of the holder recorded under Rule 27;
        (viii) cancellations effected under Rule 22(2) or recorded under Rule 27(1);
        (ix) corrections effected under Rule 28;
        (x) invalidations recorded under Rule 19(2);
        (xi) information recorded under Rules 20, 21, 22(2)(a), 23, 27(4) and 40(3);
        (xii) international registrations which have not been renewed.
    (b) The reproduction of the mark shall be published as it appears in the international application. Where the applicant has made the declaration referred to in Rule 9(4)(a)(vi), the publication shall indicate that fact.

    (c) Where a color reproduction of the mark is furnished under Rule 9(4)(a)(v) or (vii), the Gazette shall contain both a reproduction of the mark in black and white and the reproduction in color.

(2)*[Information Concerning Particular Requirements and Certain Declarations of Contracting Parties, and Other General Information]* The International Bureau shall publish in the Gazette
        (i) any notification made under Rule 7;
        (ii) any declarations made under Article 5(2)(b) or Article 5(2)(b) and (c), first sentence, of the Protocol;
        (iii) any declarations made under Article 8(7) of the Protocol;
        (iv) any notification made under Rule 34(1)(b);

(v) a list of the days on which the International Bureau is not scheduled to be open to the public during the current and the following calendar year and such a list for each Office which has communicated it to the International Bureau.

(3)*[Yearly Index]* In respect of every year, the International Bureau shall publish an index indicating, in alphabetical order, the names of the holders of the international registrations concerning which one or more entries were published in the Gazette during that year. The name of the holder shall be accompanied by the number of the international registration, the page number of the Gazette issue in which the entry affecting the international registration was published and the indication of the nature of the entry, such as registration, renewal, refusal, invalidation, cancellation or change.

(4)*[Number of Copies for Offices of Contracting Parties]*
(a) The International Bureau shall send to the Office of each Contracting Party copies of the Gazette. Each Office shall be entitled, free of charge, to two copies and, where during a given calendar year the number of designations recorded with respect to the Contracting Party concerned has exceeded 2,000, in the following year one additional copy and further additional copies for every 1,000 designations in excess of 2,000. Each Contracting Party may purchase every year, at half of the subscription price, the same number of copies as that to which it is entitled free of charge.
(b) If the Gazette is available in more than one form, each Office may choose the form in which it wishes to receive any copy to which it is entitled.

Rule 33
Electronic Data Base

(1)*[Contents of Data Base]* The data which are both recorded in the International Register and published in the Gazette under Rule 32 shall be entered in an electronic data base.

(2)*[Data Concerning Pending International Applications and Subsequent Designations]* If an international application or a designation under Rule 24 is not recorded in the International Register within three working days following the receipt by the International Bureau of the international application or designation, the International Bureau shall enter in the electronic data base, notwithstanding any irregularities that may exist in the international application or designation as received, all the data contained in the international application or designation.

(3)*[Access to Electronic Data Base]* The electronic data base shall be made accessible to the Offices of the Contracting Parties and, against payment of the prescribed fee, if any, to the public, by on-line access and through other appropriate means determined by the International Bureau. The cost of accessing shall be borne by the user. Data entered under paragraph (2) shall be accompanied by a warning to the effect that the International Bureau has not yet made a decision on the international application or on the designation under Rule 24.

Chapter 8
Fees

Rule 34
Payment Of Fees

(1)*[Payments]*
    (a) The fees indicated in the Schedule of Fees may be paid to the International Bureau by the applicant or the holder, or, where the Office of origin or another interested Office accepts to collect and forward such fees, and the applicant or the holder so wishes, by that Office.

    (b) Any Contracting Party whose Office accepts to collect and forward fees shall notify that fact to the Director General.

(2)*[Modes of Payment]* The fees indicated in the Schedule of Fees may be paid to the International Bureau
    (i) by debit to a current account with the International Bureau,
    (ii) by payment into the Swiss postal cheque account or to any of the specified bank accounts of the International Bureau,
    (iii) by a banker's cheque,
    (iv) by payment in cash at the International Bureau.

(3)*[Indications Accompanying the Payment]* At the time of the payment of any fee to the International Bureau, an indication must be given,
    (i) before international registration, of the name of the applicant, the mark concerned and the purpose of the payment;
    (ii) after international registration, of the name of the holder, the number of the international registration concerned and the purpose of the payment.

(4)*[Date of Payment]*
    (a) Subject to Rule 30(1)(b) and to subparagraph (b), any fee shall be considered to have been paid to the International Bureau on the day on which the International Bureau receives the required amount.

    (b) Where the required amount is available in an account opened with the International Bureau and that Bureau has received instructions from the holder of the account to debit it, the fee shall be considered to have been paid to the International Bureau on the day on which the International Bureau receives an international application, a subsequent designation, a request for the recordal of a change, or an instruction to renew an international registration.

(5)*[Change in the Amount of the Fees]*
    (a) Where the amount of the fees payable in respect of the filing of an international application is changed between, on the one hand, the date on which the request to present the international application to the International Bureau is received, or is deemed to have been received under Rule 11(1)(a) or (c), by the Office of origin and, on the other hand, the date of the receipt of the international application by the International Bureau, the fee that was valid on the first date shall

be applicable.

(b) Where a designation under Rule 24 is presented by the Office of origin or by another interested Office and the amount of the fees payable in respect of that designation is changed between, on the one hand, the date of receipt, by the Office, of the request by the holder to present the said designation and, on the other hand, the date on which the designation is received by the International Bureau, the fee that was valid on the first date shall be applicable.

(c) Where the amount of the fees payable in respect of the renewal of an international registration is changed between the date of payment and the due date of the renewal, the fee that was valid on the date of payment, or on the date considered to be the date of payment under Rule 30(1)(b), shall be applicable. Where the payment is made after the due date, the fee that was valid on the due date shall be applicable.

(d) Where the amount of any fee other than the fees referred to in sub-paragraphs (a), (b) and (c) is changed, the amount valid on the date on which the fee was received by the International Bureau shall be applicable.

Rule 35
Currency Of Payments

(1)*[Obligation to Use Swiss Currency]* All payments due under these Regulations shall be made to the International Bureau in Swiss currency irrespective of the fact that, where the fees are paid by the Office of origin or by another interested Office, such Office may have collected those fees in another currency.

(2)*[Establishment of the Amount of Individual Fees in Swiss Currency]*

(a) Where a Contracting Party makes a declaration under Article 8(7)(a) of the Protocol that it wants to receive an individual fee, the amount of the individual fee indicated to the International Bureau shall be expressed in the currency used by its Office.

(b) Where the fee is indicated in the declaration referred to in subparagraph (a) in a currency other than Swiss currency, the Director General shall, after consultation with the Office of the Contracting Party concerned, establish the amount of the individual fee in Swiss currency on the basis of the official exchange rate of the United Nations.

(c) Where, for more than three consecutive months, the official exchange rate of the United Nations between the Swiss currency and the other currency in which the amount of an individual fee has been indicated by a Contracting Party is higher or lower by at least 5% than the last exchange rate applied to establish the amount of the individual fee in Swiss currency, the Office of that Contracting Party may ask the Director General to establish a new amount of the individual fee in Swiss currency according to the official exchange rate of the United Nations prevailing on the day preceding the day on which the request is made. The Director General shall proceed accordingly. The new amount shall be applicable as from a date which shall be fixed by the Director General, provided that such date is between one and two months after the date of the publication of the said amount in the Gazette.

(d) Where, for more than three consecutive months, the official exchange rate of the United Nations between the Swiss currency and the other currency in which the amount of an individual fee has been indicated by a Contracting Party is lower by at least 10% than the last exchange rate applied to establish the amount of the individual fee in Swiss currency, the Director General shall establish a new amount of the individual fee in Swiss currency according to the current official exchange rate of the United Nations. The new amount shall be applicable as from a date which shall be fixed by the Director General, provided that such date is between one and two months after the date of the publication of the said amount in the Gazette.

Rule 36
Exemption From Fees

Recordal of the following shall be exempt from fees:
(i) the appointment of a representative, any change concerning a representative and the cancellation of the recordal of a representative,
(ii) any change concerning the telephone and telefacsimile numbers of the holder,
(iii) the cancellation of the international registration,
(iv) any renunciation under Rule 25(1)(a)(iii),
(v) any limitation effected in the international application itself under Rule 9(4)(a)(xiii) or in a subsequent designation under Rule 24(3)(a)(iv),
(vi) any request by an Office under Article 6(4), first sentence, of the Agreement or Article 6(4), first sentence, of the Protocol,
(vii) the existence of a judicial proceeding or of a final decision affecting the basic application, or the registration resulting therefrom, or the basic registration,
(viii) any refusal under Rule 17, Rule 24(8) or Rule 28(3), any declaration under Rule 27(4), or any notification under Rule 17(4)(b),
(ix) the invalidation of the international registration,
(x) information communicated under Rule 20,
(xi) any notification under Rule 21 or Rule 23,
(xii) any correction in the International Register.

Rule 37
Distribution of Supplementary Fees
and Complementary Fees

(1) The coefficient referred to in Article 8(5) and (6) of the Agreement and Article 8(5) and (6) of the Protocol shall be as follows:

for Contracting Parties which examine only for absolute grounds of refusal ....

two

for Contracting Parties which also examine for prior
rights:

    (a) following opposition by third parties ....
three
    (b) *ex officio* ....
four

(2)Coefficient four shall also be applied to Contracting Parties which carry out *ex officio* searches for prior rights with an indication of the most significant prior rights.

Rule 38
Crediting of Individual Fees to the Accounts
of the Contracting Parties Concerned

Any individual fee paid to the International Bureau in respect of a Contracting Party having made a declaration under Article 8(7)(a) of the Protocol shall be credited to the account of that Contracting Party with the International Bureau within the month following the month in the course of which the recordal of the international registration, subsequent designation or renewal for which that fee has been paid was effected.

Chapter 9
Miscellaneous

Rule 39
Continuation of Effects of International Registrations
in Certain Successor States

(1)Where any State ('the successor State') whose territory was, before the independence of that State, part of the territory of a Contracting State ('the predecessor country') has deposited with the Director General a declaration of continuation the effect of which is that the Agreement is applied by the successor State, the effects in the successor State of any international registration with a territorial extension to the predecessor country which is effective from a date prior to the date fixed under paragraph (2) shall be subject to
    (i) the filing with the International Bureau, within six months from the date of a notice addressed for that purpose by the International Bureau to the holder of the international registration concerned, of a request that such international registration continue its effects in the successor State, and
    (ii) the payment to the International Bureau, within the same time limit, of a fee of 23 Swiss francs, which shall be transferred by the International Bureau

to the Office of the successor State, and of a fee of 41 Swiss francs for the benefit of the International Bureau.

(2)The date referred to in paragraph (1) shall be the date notified by the successor State to the International Bureau for the purposes of this Rule, provided that such date may not be earlier than the date of independence of the successor State.

(3)The International Bureau shall, upon receipt of the request and the fees referred to in paragraph (1), notify the Office of the successor State and make the corresponding recordal in the International Register.

(4)With respect to any international registration concerning which the Office of the successor State has received a notification under paragraph (3), that Office may only refuse protection if the time limit referred to in Article 5(2) of the Agreement has not expired with respect to the territorial extension to the predecessor country and if the notification of refusal is received by the International Bureau within that time limit.

(5)This Rule shall not apply to the Russian Federation.

Rule 40
Entry Into Force; Transitional Provisions

(1)*[Entry into Force]* These Regulations shall enter into force on April 1, 1996, and shall, as of that date, replace the Regulations under the Agreement as in force on March 31, 1996 (hereinafter referred to as 'the Regulations under the Agreement').

(2)*[General Transitional Provisions]*
    (a) Notwithstanding paragraph (1),
        (i) an international application the request for presentation to the International Bureau of which was received, or is deemed to have been received under Rule 11(1)(a) or (c), by the Office of origin before April 1, 1996, shall, to the extent that it conforms to the requirements of the Regulations under the Agreement, be deemed to conform to the applicable requirements for the purposes of Rule 14;
        (ii) a request for the recording of a change under Rule 20 of the Regulations under the Agreement sent by the Office of origin or by another interested Office to the International Bureau before April 1, 1996, or, where such date can be identified, whose date of receipt by the Office of origin or by another interested Office for presentation to the International Bureau is earlier than April 1, 1996, shall, to the extent that it conforms to the requirements of the Regulations under the Agreement, be deemed to conform to the applicable requirements for the purposes of Rule 24(7) or to be in order for the purposes of Rule 27;
        (iii) an international application, or a request for the recording of a change under Rule 20 of the Regulations under the Agreement, that, before April 1, 1996, has been the subject of any action by the International Bureau under Rules 11, 12, 13 or 21 of the Regulations under the Agreement, shall continue to be

processed by the International Bureau under the said Rules; the date of the resulting international registration or recordal in the International Register shall be governed by Rules 15 or 22 of the Regulations under the Agreement;

(iv) a notification of refusal or a notification of invalidation sent by the Office of a designated Contracting Party before April 1, 1996, shall, to the extent that it conforms to the requirements of the Regulations under the Agreement, be deemed to conform to the applicable requirements for the purposes of Rule 17(4) and (5) or of Rule 19(2).

(b) For the purposes of Rule 34(5), the fees valid at any date before April 1, 1996, shall be the fees prescribed by Rule 32 of the Regulations under the Agreement.

(c) Notwithstanding Rule 10(1), where, in accordance with Rule 34(5)(a), the fees paid in respect of the filing of an international application are the fees prescribed for 20 years by Rule 32 of the Regulations under the Agreement, no second instalment shall be due.

(d) Where, in accordance with Rule 34(5)(b), the fees paid in respect of a subsequent designation are the fees prescribed by Rule 32 of the Regulations under the Agreement, paragraph (3) shall not apply.

(3)*[Transitional Provisions Applicable to International Registrations for Which Fees Have Been Paid for 20 Years]*

(a) Where an international registration for which the required fees had been paid for 20 years is the subject of a subsequent designation under Rule 24 and where the current term of protection of that international registration expires more than ten years after the effective date of the subsequent designation as determined in accordance with Rule 24(6), the provisions of subparagraphs (b) and (c) shall apply.

(b) Six months before the expiry of the first period of ten years of the current term of protection of the international registration, the International Bureau shall send to the holder and his representative, if any, a notice indicating the exact date of expiry of the first period of ten years and the Contracting Parties which were the subject of subsequent designations referred to in subparagraph (a). Rule 29 shall apply *mutatis mutandis*.

(c) Payment of complementary and individual fees corresponding to the fees referred to in Rule 30(1)(iii) shall be required for the second period of ten years in respect of the subsequent designations referred to in subparagraph (a). Rule 30(1) and (3) shall apply *mutatis mutandis*.

(d) The International Bureau shall record in the International Register the fact that payment has been made to the International Bureau for the second period of ten years. The date of recordal shall be the date of expiry of the first period of ten years, even if the fees required are paid within the period of grace referred to in Article 7(5) of the Agreement and in Article 7(4) of the Protocol.

(e) The International Bureau shall notify the Offices of the designated Contracting Parties concerned of the fact that payment has or has not been made for the second period of ten years and shall at the same time inform the holder.

Appendix 7

Miscellaneous Registry material

GUIDE TO THE CROSS SEARCHING OF TRADE MARKS IN THE UNITED KINGDOM: JULY 1999 EDITION

(Trade Marks Registry)

The details set out in this document reflect changes made in the Registrar's cross searching practice. This revised cross search list came into force on the 1ˢᵗ of July 1999, and will be applied to all cases pending before the office.

Users should note that this updated guide to the cross searching of trade marks is not exhaustive, but reflects the extent to which the Registrar now considers it appropriate to search between classes (Section 37 of the Trade Marks Act refers). However, in the light of the decisions of the European Court in *SABEL v PUMA* and *CANON v MGM*. Examiners will, of course, have the discretion to restrict or expand their searches as appropriate.

CROSS SEARCH SUMMARY

Application Class	Search Classes
01	01*
02	02*
03	03 21
04	04 39
05	05 10 30 32
06	06 17 19 20
07	07 08 11 12 21
08	07 08
09	09 16 28 38 42
10	05 10
11	07 11 21
12	07 12 37
13	13*
14	14 21 37
15	15*
16	09 16 41 42

17	16 17 19
18	18 25 28
19	06 17 19
20	06 20 24 42
21	03 07 11 14 21
22	22*
23	23*
24	20 24 40
25	18 25 40 42
26	26*
27	27 37
28	09 18 28
29	29 30 31
30	05 29 30
31	29 31
32	05 32 33 42
33	32 33 42
34	34*
35	35 36 41
36	35 36 42
37	12 14 27 37 42
38	09 38 41 42
39	04 37 39 42
40	24 25 40 42
41	16 35 38 41 42
42	09 16 20 25 32 33 36 37 38 39 40 41 42

* Please note that there is no cross search for these classes.

CLASS 3
Household cleaning and polishing materials; dentrifices, toothpaste

21   Cleaning and polishing materials, toothbrushes and dental floss

CLASS 4
Fuels

39.02   Fuel distribution and delivery

CLASS 5
Plasters, materials for dressings; contraceptives; dietetic/infants/invalid foodstuffs and beverages

10   Elasticated bandages and elasticated socks, contraceptives

30   Confectionery; cereal foods (only search where Class 5 specification expressly includes dietetic/invalid/infants foods)

32   Non-alcoholic beverages and preparations for making into such beverages (only search where Class 5 specification expressly includes dietetic/invalid/infants beverages)

CLASS 6
Metal building materials; buildings of metal; ironmongery, small items of metal hardware; pipes and tubes of metal; signs and signboards of metal

17   Pipes and tubes
19   Non-metallic buildings; building materials and parts and fittings for buildings; signs and signboards
20   Non-metallic equivalents of Class 6 goods

CLASS 7
Powered hand tools; filters; parts and fittings for machine tools; boilers, heating and drying machines; dust removing and exhausting installations; motors and engines (except for land vehicles); machine coupling and transmission components (except for land vehicles); kitchen machines

8   Hand tools, sharpening stones
11   Boilers; heating and drying apparatus and installations; filters; dust removing and exhausting installations
        Fans for motors (other than land vehicle motors), (cite only marks filed before 1 October 1973)
12   Brake linings; brake segments; brake shoes; clutches; engines; gears; motors; silencers; wheels; bearings; couplings
        Fuel economisers; timing chains (cite only marks filed before 23 March 1971)
21   Non-electric kitchen machines

CLASS 8
Hand tools and implements

7   Powered hand tools; parts and fittings for machine tools

CLASS 9
Computer apparatus, computer software; electronic publications; electronic games and amusement apparatus; telecommunication apparatus; spectacles, contact lenses and accessories

16   Computer programmes in printed form (if specifically mentioned)

Publications, books, periodicals, newspapers (only to be searched where Class 9 specification expressly includes electronic publications or equivalent terms)

28	Electronic games and amusement apparatus
38.02	Telecommunications and rental of telecommunication equipment
42.08	Computer services
42.09	Optician services

CLASS 10
Elasticated bandages and socks

5	Medical and surgical plaster and non-elasticated bandages and non-elasticated socks for curative purposes; contraceptives

CLASS 11
Boilers, heating and drying apparatus and installations; filters; dust removing and exhausting installations; electrically heated cooking utensils

6	Boilers, heating and drying machines; filters (parts of machines); dust removing and exhausting installations
21	Cooking utensils

CLASS 12
Vehicles, engines and motors

7	Brake linings; brake segments; brake shoes; clutches; engines; gears; motors; silencers; wheels; bearings; couplings; belts; chains; timing chains
	Anti-pollution devices; automobile cylinders; belts for engines; fuel economisers; fan belts; crankcases; exhausts; mufflers; silencers; starters; fans for motors and engines; radiators (cooling)
	Connecting rods; transmission shafts (cite only marks filed before 1 January 1992)
37.03	Vehicle repair and servicing

CLASS 14
Household or kitchen utensils and containers made of or coated with precious metals; jewellery

22	Household or kitchen utensils and containers
37.04	Jewellery repair

CLASS 16
Computer programs; publications; photographs, albums

9   Computer programs (if specifically mentioned)
Electronic publications including newspapers, books etc (only to be cited where the Class 9 specification expressly includes the above or equivalent terms)

41.04   Publishing

42.12   Photography and photo montage

CLASS 17

Plastics materials for use in manufacture; sheets of plastic; insulating materials; pipes and tubes

6   Pipes and tubes

18   Plastics materials for use construction, plate glass for building

CLASS 18

Purses, handbags etc; holdalls

25   Articles of clothing for women and girls

28   Bags adapted to carry sporting articles (eg golf bags)

CLASS 19

Building materials (non-metallic); non-metallic buildings; pipes; signs and sign-boards (non-metallic); plastics materials for use in construction and plate glass for building

6   Buildings of metal; building materials and parts and fittings of buildings; signs and signboards of metal

17   Plastics materials for use in manufacturing; sheets of plastic; insulating materials

CLASS 20

Goods of wood, cork, reed, cane, wicker, horn, ivory, whalebone, shell amber, mother-of-pearl, meerschaum and substitutes for all these materials, or of plastics; plastic blinds; kitchen and bedroom furniture

6   Metallic equivalent of Class 20 goods

24   Textile blinds

42.03   Design of eg fitted kitchens and bedrooms

CLASS 21

Cleaning and polishing materials; toothbrushes, dental floss; non-electric kitchen machines; cooking utensils; household or kitchen utensils or containers

3	Household cleaning and polishing materials
7	Electric kitchen machines
11	Electrically heated cooking utensils
13	Household or kitchen utensils and containers made of, or coated with, precious metals

CLASS 24
Textile blinds, curtains, tapestries

20	Plastic blinds
40.01	Curtain making; tapestry weaving

CLASS 25
Clothing, footwear, headgear

18	Purses, handbags etc for women and girls (if specifically mentioned)
40.01	Tailoring, dressmaking
42.03	Design of clothing and footwear

CLASS 27
Carpets

37.02	Carpet laying

CLASS 28
Electronic games and amusement apparatus; bags adapted to carrying sporting articles

9	Electronic games and amusement apparatus for use with television receivers; coin-freed amusement apparatus
18	Holdalls

CLASS 29
Suet; jellies, jams; desserts, yoghurts; prepared meals, snack foods; sauces; preserved, dried and cooked fruits and vegetables and nuts; crustaceans, shellfish

30*	1. Pastry
	2. Honey, treacle, syrups
	3. Desserts, ices, non-medicated confectionery
	4. Prepared meals, snack foods
	5. Sauces

6. Pies, puddings
31   Fresh fruits and vegetables; live crustaceans, shellfish

* These items are to be cited against the corresponding number in Class 30

CLASS 30
Coffee, tea, cocoa, sugar, rice, tapioca, sago, artificial coffee; flour and preparations made from cereals, bread, pastry and confectionery, ices; honey, treacle; syrups; desserts; prepared meals, snack foods; pies, puddings; yeast, baking-powder; salt, mustard; vinegar, sauces (condiments); spices; ice

5   Dietetic/invalid/infant foodstuffs (cite only if expressly mentioned in Class 5 specification)
29*   1. Suet
         2. Jellies, jams
         3. Desserts, yoghurts
         4. Prepared meals, snack foods
         5. Sauces
         6. Snack foods

* These items are to be cited against the corresponding number in Class 29

CLASS 31
Fresh fruits, fresh vegetables and fresh nuts; live crustaceans and live shellfish

29   Preserved, dried or cooked fruits, vegetables and nuts; crustaceans, shell-fish

CLASS 32
Beers; non-alcoholic drinks; syrups and other preparations for making beverages

5   Beverages (only search where specification expressly includes dietetic/invalid/infant beverages
33   Alcoholic beverages
42.04   Inns, public houses (not restaurant services)

Explanatory note:
All beer (regardless of alcohol content) falls in Class 32; very low (1.2% or less alcohol by volume) or non-alcoholic wines, ciders or perries are proper to Class 32; wines, ciders or perries containing more than 1.2% alcohol by volume are proper to Class 33; therefore, low alcohol wine, cider or perry can be classified under either Class 33 or Class 32;

Alcoholic beverages at large in Class 33 are similar goods to beer in Class 32 but

NOT low or non-alcoholic beer;

Alcoholic beverages at large in Class 33 are similar goods to low or non-alcoholic wine, cider or perry in Class 32;

Wine, cider or perry in Class 33 are similar goods to their low or non-alcoholic equivalents in Class 32 and also to beer (but NOT similar to low or non-alcoholic beer);

Wine in Class 33 is similar to low or non-alcoholic wine in Class 32 and also to beer (but NOT similar to low or non-alcoholic beer or low or non-alcoholic cider or perry);

Cider in Class 33 is similar to low or non-alcoholic cider in Class 32 and also to beer (but NOT similar to low or non-alcoholic beer or low or non-alcoholic wine or perry);

Perry in Class 33 is similar to low or non-alcoholic perry in Class 32 and also to beer (bit NOT similar to low or non-alcoholic beer or low or non-alcoholic wine or cider);

Spirits and liqueurs in Class 33 are similar goods to beer in Class 32 (but NOT similar to low or non-alcoholic beer or low or non-alcoholic wine, cider or perry);

Shandies in Class 32 are NOT similar goods to any alcoholic beverages in Class 33;

CLASS 33
Alcoholic beverages (except beers)

32   Beer (cite against alcoholic beverages in Class 33);
42.05   Restaurants and wine bars (not inns and public houses)

Explanatory note:
Wine, cider or perry containing more than 1.2% alcohol by volume are proper to Class 33; very low (1.2% or less alcohol by volume) or non-alcoholic wines, ciders or perries are proper to Class 32; therefore, low alcohol wine, cider or perry can be classified under either Class 33 or Class 32. All beer (regardless of alcohol content) falls in Class 32;

Alcoholic beverages at large in Class 33 are similar goods to beer in Class 32 but NOT low or non-alcoholic beer;

Alcoholic beverages at large in Class 33 are similar goods to low or non-alcoholic wine, cider or perry in Class 32;
Wine, cider and perry in Class 33 are similar goods to their low or non-alcoholic

equivalents in Class 32 and also to beer (but NOT similar to low or non-alcoholic beer);

Wine in Class 33 is similar to low or non-alcoholic wine in Class 32 and also to beer (but NOT similar to low or non-alcoholic beer or low or non-alcoholic cider or perry);

Cider in Class 33 is similar to low or non-alcoholic cider in Class 32 and also to beer (but NOT similar to low or non-alcoholic beer or low or non-alcoholic wine or perry);

Perry in Class 33 is similar to low or non-alcoholic perry in Class 32 and also to beer (bit NOT similar to low or non-alcoholic beer or low or non-alcoholic wine or cider);

Spirits and liqueurs in Class 33 are similar goods to beer in Class 32 (but NOT similar to low or non-alcoholic beer or low or non-alcoholic wine, cider or perry);

Shandies in Class 32 are NOT similar goods to any alcoholic beverages in Class 33;

CLASS 35
Auctioneering, appraisals; business acquisition; auditing; business management, analysis, and research; organising and conducting of exhibitions relating to advertising and commerce; advisory, information and consultancy service; economic forecasting and analysis

35.01   Auctioneering, appraisals; business acquisitions
36.01   Real estate agency; valuations and appraisals
35.02   Auditing
36.02   Financial management; preparation of reports; advisory, information and consultancy services
35.03   Business management, analysis and research
36.02   Financial management; preparation of reports; advisory, information and consultancy services
35.04   Organising and conducting of exhibitions relating to advertising and commerce
41.03   Organising and conducting of educational or recreational exhibitions
35.05   Advisory, information and and consultancy service; economic forecasting and analysis
36.02   Financial management; preparation of reports; advisory, information and consultancy services

CLASS 36
Real estate agency; valuations and appraisals; financial management; preparation of reports; advisory, information and consultancy services; medical insurance

36.01   Real estate agency; valuations and appraisals
35.01   Auctioneering, appraisals; business acquisitions
42.02   Surveying (architectural)
36.02   Financial management; preparation of reports; advisory, information and consultancy services
35.02   Auditing
35.03   Business management, analysis and research
35.05   Advisory, information and consultancy services; economic forecasting and analysis
36.03   Medical insurance
42.06   Health care and dentistry

CLASS 37
Construction and real estate development; carpet laying; vehicle repair and servicing; jewellery repair; repair and maintenance of spectacles, frames, contact lenses, sunglasses

37.01   Construction and real estate development
42.02   Architecture and surveying
37.02   Carpet laying
27   Carpets
37.03   Vehicle repair and servicing
12   Vehicles and engines and motors
39.03   Rental and recovery of vehicles
37.04   Jewellery repair
14   Jewellery
37.05   Repair and maintenance of spectacles, frames, contact lenses, sunglasses
42.09   Optician services

CLASS 38
Broadcasting; telecommunications and rental of telecommunications equipment; providing access to the Internet

38.01   Broadcasting
41.01   Production of radio and TV programmes
38.02   Telecommunications and rental of telecommunications equipment
9   Telecommunications apparatus
38.04   Providing access to the Internet
42.07   Computer services

CLASS 39
Travel agency services; fuel distribution and delivery; rental and recovery of vehicles
39.01   Travel agency services

42.01   Booking of accommodation
39.02   Fuel distribution and delivery
4   Fuels
39.03   Rental and recovery of vehicles
37.03   Maintenance and repair of vehicles

CLASS 40
Curtain making; tapestry weaving; tailoring; waste recycling, destruction, incineration or shredding; tinting of lenses

40.01   Curtain making; tapestry weaving; tailoring
24   Curtains and tapestry
25   Tailored clothing, eg suits, skirts, coats, jackets
40.02   Waste recycling, destruction, incineration or shredding
42.11   Waste recycling, destruction, incineration or shredding (cite only marks
        filed before 1 January 1997)
        Sorting of waste and recyclable material
40.03   Tinting of lenses
42.09   Optician services

CLASS 41
Production of radio and television programmes; health club and leisure services;
organising and conducting educational or recreational exhibitions; publishing

41.01   Production of radio and television programmes
38.01   Broadcasting
41.02   Health club and leisure services
42.06   Saunas, massages, solariums
41.03   Organising and conducting educational or recreational exhibitions
35.04   Organising and conducting of exhibitions relating to advertising and commerce
41.04   Publishing
16   Publications (books, printed matter)

CLASS 42
Booking of accommodation; surveying; design of fitted kitchens and bedrooms;
clothing and footwear; inn; public house, restaurant and wine bar services; sauna.
massage, solarium services; health care and dentistry' computer services; opticians
services; fumigations, pest control, all for agricultural purposes; sorting of waste
and recyclable material; photography, photo montage

42.01   Booking of accommodation
39.01   Travel agency services
42.02   Architecture; surveying; architectural surveys; surveying of land; quantity

surveying

36.01	Real estate agency; valuations and appraisals
37.01	Construction and real estate development services
42.03	Design of eg fitted kitchens and bedrooms, clothing and footwear
20	Fitted kitchens and bedroom furniture etc
25	Clothing and footwear
42.04	Inns, public houses
32	Beer
42.05	Restaurants, wine bars
33	Wine
42.06	Saunas, massage, solariums
41.02	Health club and leisure services
42.07	Health care and dentistry
36.03	Medical insurance
42.08	Computer services
9	Computer hardware
38.03	Providing access to the Internet
42.08	Opticians services
9	Spectacles, frames, contact lenses, lenses, sunglasses, cases
37.05	Repair and maintenance of spectacles, frames, contact lenses, sunglasses
40.03	Tinting of lenses
42.10	Fumigation; infestation pest control; insecticide spraying; termite control; vermin exterminating, all for agricultural purposes
37	Fumigation; infestation pest control; insecticide spraying; termite control; vermin exterminating; all for agricultural purposes (cite only marks filed before 1 January 1992)
	No reverse search necessary
42.11	Sorting of waste and recyclable material
40.02	waste recycling, destruction; incineration or shredding
42.12	Photography; photo montage
16	Photographs, albums

Trade Marks Registry Forms

Contents

Form TM3	Application to register a trade mark
Form TM3A	Application for additional classes
Form TM5	Request to the Registrar for a statement of grounds of decision
Form TM7	Notice of opposition
Form TM8	Form for counterstatement
Form TM9	Request for an extension of time on an application
Form TM10	Payment of Registration fee for a Trade or Service Mark
Form TM11	Renewal of trade mark registration
Form TM12	Request to divide an application
Form TM16	Application to register a change of proprietor
Form TM17	Request to merge either applications or registrations
Form TM21	Request to change the details of an application or a registration
	Request to change the details of a designation under the Madrid Protocol
Form TM22	Notice to surrender a registration
Form TM23	Notice of a partial surrender of the specification of goods or services for which the mark is registered.....
Form TM24	Application to record or cancel a registrable transaction other than as assignment or licence
	Application to record or cancel a notifiable transaction for a designation under the Madrid Protocol
Form TM25	Request for alteration of a registered mark
Form TM26	Application for the revocation, invalidation, or rectification of a registration
	Application for the revocation or invalidation of a protected international trade mark (UK); rectification of the supplementary register
Form TM27	Application to intervene in proceedings for the revocation, invalidation or rectification of a registration
	Application to intervene in proceedings for the revocation or invalidation of a protected international trade mark (UK) or rectification of the supplementary register
Form TM28	Request for Recordal of concurrent registration
Form TM31C	Request for information about applications and registered marks
Form TM31R	Request for a Certified Copy
Form TM33	Request to appoint or change an agent or to enter or change an address for service
Form TM35	Filing of regulations governing the use of certification marks
Form TM50	Application to Register a Licensee
Form TM51	Application to remove or amend the recordal of a licence
Form EOT 1/4	Request for extension of time

Appendix 7

Form TM3

Official fee due

The
**Patent
Office**

Application to register a trade mark

The Patent Office
Trade Marks Registry
Cardiff Road, Newport
South Wales NP9 1RH

Please refer to notes for guidance on completing this form

1. Your reference	
2. Representation of the mark	
3. State "Yes" here if the mark is a word or words without any particular form of presentation	
4. If the mark is not a word or a picture, indicate here *(for example 3-dimensional)*	
5. If the application is for a series of marks, indicate how many marks in the series	
6. If this application claims priority, indicate the priority date(s) claimed, the country, and the number	Date Country Number
7. If this is a transformation application under the Madrid Protocol, state the transformation date and the international registration number	Date Registration number

(REV/2)

Form TM3

8. Specification of goods/services.

If the space provided for the specification of goods/services is insufficient then please continue on separate sheets. List the classes in consecutive numerical order and list alongside each class the goods or services appropriate to that class.

Class number	List of goods/services

Class number	

(REV/2)

Form TM3

1203

List the classes in consecutive numerical order and list alongside each class the goods or services appropriate to that class.

Class number	List of goods/services
Class number	

9. Indicate if this application is for :
     a) a trade mark
     b) a certification mark
   or c) a collective mark	

10. If colour is claimed, indicate here and state the colour(s)	
11. Indicate any limitations or disclaimers	
12. Full name, address and postcode of the applicant Trade Marks ADP number *(if you know it)* *If the applicant is a corporate body, give country and, if applicable, state of incorporation*	
13. Name of agent *(if appropriate)* Address for service in the United Kingdom to which all correspondence should be sent *(including postcode)* *[see note m]* Trade Marks ADP number *(if you know it)*	
The trade mark is being used by the applicant or with his or her consent, in relation to the goods or services stated, or there is a bona fide intention that it will be so used. Signature	
Name *(block capitals)*	
Date	
Name and daytime telephone number of person to contact	
State number of sheets attached to this form	

Appendix 7

Form TM3 A

Official fee due

The
Patent
Office

Application for additional classes

The Patent Office
Trade Marks Registry
Cardiff Road, Newport
South Wales NP9 1RH

Please refer to notes for guidance on completing this form

1. Application to which this request relates	Number	*(Lowest)* Class

2. Classes to be added to the original application

3. Specification of goods/services for the additional classes

List the classes in consecutive numerical order and list alongside each class the goods or services appropriate to that class.

Class number	List of goods/services

(REV/1)

Form TM3 A

4. Full name, address and postcode of the applicant	
Trade Marks ADP number *(if you know it)*	
5. Name of agent *(if appropriate)*	
'Address for service' in the United Kingdom to which all correspondence should be sent *(including postcode)* *[see note d]*	
Trade Marks ADP number *(if you know it)*	
Your reference	
Signature	
Name *(block capitals)*	
Date	
Name and daytime telephone number of person to contact	
State number of sheets attached to this form	

General notes

a) *Complete this form in capital letters or type it.*

b) *If there is not enough space for your answer to any section of this form, use separate sheets. Number each one and write on the form how many extra sheets you have used.*

c) *Once you have completed this form you must remember to sign and date it.*

d) *If your address for service is different from your agent, then please give us full details of both.*

e) *If you need help or have any questions, please contact the Trade Marks Registry on 0645 500505.*

Form TM3 A

Appendix 7

The
**Patent
Office**

Request to the Registrar for a statement
of grounds of decision

**The Patent Office
Trade Marks Registry**
Cardiff Road, Newport
South Wales NP9 1RH

Please refer to notes for guidance on completing this form

	Number	*(Lowest)* Class
1. Give details of the application or registration		
or		
the designation under the Madrid Protocol to which this request relates	Number	*(Lowest)* Class
2 Date of Registrar's decision	
3. Full name and address of applicant or agent making the request *(including postcode)*	
Trade Marks ADP number *(if you know it)*	
Your reference	
Signature	
Name *(block capitals)*	
Date	
Name and daytime telephone number of person to contact	
State number of sheets attached to this form	

Form TM5

Specific notes

a) *If your application for a trade mark is refused or protection of an international trade mark (UK) is refused you can ask the Registrar for a statement of grounds of the decision. This must be requested within one month of the date on which the decision was sent to you.*

General notes

b) *Complete the form in capital letters or type it.*

c) *If there is not enough space for your answer to any section of this form, use separate sheets. Number each one and write on the form how many extra sheets you have used.*

d) *Once you have completed the form you must remember to sign and date it.*

e) *If your address for service is different from your agent, then please give us full details of both.*

f) *If you need help or have any questions, please contact the Trade Marks Registry on 0645 500505.*

Form TM5

Form TM7

Official fee due

The
**Patent
Office**

Notice of opposition

The Patent Office
Trade Marks Registry
Cardiff Road, Newport
South Wales NP9 1RH

Please refer to notes for guidance on completing this form

	Number	*(lowest)* Class	Journal
1. Give details of the application or registration			
or			
the designation under the Madrid Protocol to which this opposition relates	Number	*(lowest)* Class	Journal
2. Full name of the applicant or registered proprietor			
3. Full name, address and postcode of opponent			
Trade Marks ADP number *(if you know it)*			
4. Name of agent *(if appropriate)*			
'Address for service' in the United Kingdom to which all correspondence should be sent *(including postcode)* *[see note i]*			
Trade Marks ADP number *(if you know it)*			
Your reference			
Signature			
Name *(block capitals)*			
Date			
Name and daytime telephone number of person to contact			
State the number of sheets attached to this form			

(REV/1)

Form TM7

Form TM7

Specific notes

a) *This form is used to notify the Registrar that you want to oppose any of the following:*

    1) an application
    2) an international trade mark (UK)
    3) re-classification from schedule 3 to 4
    4) an amendment of an application
    5) an amendment to a registered trade mark
    6) an amendment to the regulations relating to collective or certification marks

b) *This form must be filed within the period allowed for such action. For (1, 2, 3, 5 & 6) above, this period is three months from the date of publication in the Trade Marks Journal, for (4) the period is one month.*

c) *Please indicate each class you wish to oppose.*

d) *This form must be accompanied by a statement of the grounds of your opposition.*

e) *Guidance notes on opposition procedures are available on request from the Law Section of the Trade Marks Registry.*

General notes

f) *Complete this form in capital letters or type it.*

g) *If there is not enough space for your answer to any section of this form, use separate sheets. Number each one and write on the form how many extra sheets you have used.*

h) *Once you have completed the form you must remember to sign and date it.*

i) *If your address for service is different from your agent, then please give us full details of both.*

j) *If you need help or have any questions, please contact the Trade Marks Registry on 0645 500505.*

Form TM8

No official fee due

Form for counterstatement

The Patent Office
Trade Marks Registry
Cardiff Road, Newport
South Wales NP9 1RH

Please refer to the notes for guidance on completing this form

	Number	*(Lowest)* Class
1. Give details of the application or registration		
or		
the designation under the Madrid Protocol to which this counterstatement relates	Number	*(Lowest)* Class
2. Full name of applicant or registered proprietor		
3. Opposition or revocation number		
4. Name of agent *(if appropriate)*		
'Address for service' in the United Kingdom to which all correspondence should be sent *(including postcode)* *[see note g]*		
Trade Marks ADP number *(if you know it)*		
Your reference		
Signature		
Name *(block capitals)*		
Date		
Name and daytime telephone number of person to contact		
State the number of sheets attached to this form		

(REV/1)

Form TM8

Specific notes

a) *This form is used if you want to defend your application or international trade mark (UK) against a third party who has lodged **either** an opposition against your application **or** an application to revoke, rectify or invalidate your registration or protected international trade mark (UK). (Rules 13 and 31 of the Trade Marks Rules 1994 and Article 10 and 13 of the Trade Marks (International Registration) Order 1996 refer).*

b) *You must send us details of the grounds for this counterstatement on a separate sheet of paper.*

c) *Guidance notes on opposition and on revocation/rectification/invalidity procedures are available on request from the Law Section of the Trade Marks Registry.*

General notes

d) *Complete this form in capital letters or type it.*

e) *If there is not enough space for your answer to any section of this form, use separate sheets. Number each one and write on the form how many extra sheets you have used.*

f) *Once you have completed the form you must remember to sign and date it.*

g) *If your address for service is different from your agent, then please give us full details of both.*

h) *If you need help or have any questions, please contact the Trade Marks Registry on 0645 500505.*

Form TM9

Official fee due

The
Patent
Office

Request for an extension of time
on an application

The Patent Office
Trade Marks Registry
Cardiff Road, Newport
South Wales NP9 1RH

Please refer to notes for guidance on completing this form

1. Give details of the application	Number	*(Lowest)* Class
or		
the designation under the Madrid Protocol to which this request refers	Number	*(Lowest)* Class
2. Give the period of further time required in months		
3. Give the reasons for this request		
4. Full name of requestor		
5. Name of agent *(if appropriate)*		
'Address for service' in the United Kingdom to which all correspondence should be sent *(including postcode)* *[see note e]*		
Trade Marks ADP number *(if you know it)*		
Your reference		
Registry reference		
Signature		
Name *(block capitals)*		
Date		
Name and daytime telephone number of person to contact		
State number of sheets attached to this form		

FOR OFFICIAL USE ONLY
Dear Sir/Madam
Your request for an extension of time as detailed above has been granted.

Yours faithfully

(REV/1)

Form TM9

Specific notes

a) *You should use this form if you want an extension of time in the following instances:*

- *Any extension under Rule 13 (the filing of evidence); or*
- *Any extension under Rule 62 on an ex-parte hearing case which exceeds an initial three month period.*
- *Where this form is being used to request an extension of time in opposition, revocation, invalidity or rectification proceedings a copy of the request should be sent to every other person who at the time is a party to those proceedings.*

General notes

b) *Complete the form in capital letters or type it*

c) *If there is not enough space for your answer to any section of this form, use separate sheets. Number each one and write on the form how many extra sheets you have used.*

d) *Once you have completed the form you must remember to sign and date it.*

e) *If your address for service is different from your agent, then please give us full details of both.*

f) *If you need help or have any questions, please contact the Trade Marks Registry on 0645 500505.*

The Patent Office

Trade Marks
Form TM10

Payment of Registration fee
for a Trade or Service Mark

See note 1 | 1   Trade or Service Mark application number:

Class number:

See note 2 | 2.   Number of the journal in which this application was advertised:

See note 3 | 3   Address for service:

Patent Office ADP number *(if known)*:

Name:

Address:

Postcode:

Telephone contact: STD code   Telephone number:

See notes 4 and 5 | 4   **Declaration**

I/We declare that any written undertakings given to the Registrar to send notice of the advertisement of the application to other proprietors have been fulfilled. To the best of my/our knowledge and belief, either the period or extended period for filing opposition to the application has expired without any notice of opposition having been filed, or any oppositions filed have finally been determined in favour of the applicant.

Applicant's name:

Signature: Date: 19

Status:

Checklist

When you have filled in the form, tick the boxes below to show you have:

Fulfilled all the written undertakings described in the declaration at box 4

Enclosed the necessary fee   Signed at box 4

Prepared by the
Information Design Team

Form TM11

Official fee due

The
Patent
Office

Renewal of trade mark registration

Your trade mark renewal is due on the date shown below

The Patent Office
Trade Marks Registry
Cardiff Road, Newport
South Wales NP9 1RH

Please refer to notes for guidance on completing this form

1. Registration number

2. Classes

3. Full name and address of registered proprietor

    Trade Marks ADP number
    (if you know it)

4. Give the following details of the registration
    to be renewed

    Due date of renewal

    Specify which classes are to be renewed
    (if you are not renewing all of them)

    Amount of renewal fee

    Amount of additional renewal fee
    (if appropriate)

    Total amount paid

5. Full name, address and postcode of the person
    to whom the certificate should be sent

    Trade Marks ADP number
    (if you know it)

    Your reference

Signature	
Name *(block capitals)*	
Date	
Name and daytime telephone number of person to contact	

PLEASE DISREGARD THIS NOTICE IF YOU HAVE ALREADY SUBMITTED A TM11 AND RENEWAL FEE

An additional renewal fee of £50.00 will be incurred if your mark is renewed up to 6 months after the due date of renewal; thereafter the mark will be removed from the register.

(REV/1)

Form TM11

Specific notes

a) Please sign and return the TM11 with appropriate fee for renewal of your trade mark.

b) If you want to renew a multiclass registration you must send a fee for each class of goods or services. You may choose to renew only those classes which you retain an interest in.

c) The request for renewal must be made and the renewal fee paid before the expiry of the registration. Failing this if the request is made and the fee paid within 6 months then the mark may be renewed but an additional renewal fee will be payable. (Section 43 of the Trade Marks Act 1994 refers).

d) If you have not renewed the registration within the six month period immediately after expiry (see c above) you have a further six months in which to request the restoration of the registration on form TM13 and pay the appropriate fee. Applications for restoration will not be accepted if they are received by the Patent Office more than twelve months after the date of expiry. (Rule 30 of the Trade Marks Rules 1994 refers).

e) You must send a separate form for each trade mark number.

General notes

f) Complete the form in capital letters or type it.

g) If there is not enough space for your answer to any section of this form, use separate sheets. Number each one and write on the form how many extra sheets you have used.

h) Once you have completed the form you must remember to sign and date it.

i) If you need help or have any questions, please contact the Trade Marks Registry on 0645 500505.

Form TM12

Official fee due

The Patent Office

Request to divide an application

The Patent Office
Trade Marks Registry
Cardiff Road, Newport
South Wales NP9 1RH

Please refer to notes for guidance on completing this form

	Number	*(Lowest)* Class
1. Give details of the application to be divided		
2. Is this request to: a) divide the specification of goods or services? *or* b) divide a series of marks? *(indicate a) or b) as appropriate)* *[see note b]*		
3. If this request is to divide an application into more than two parts, write how many parts you want it divided into		
4. Full name, address and postcode of applicant Trade Marks ADP number *(if you know it)*		
5. Name of agent *(if appropriate)* 'Address for service' in the United Kingdom to which all correspondence should be sent *(including postcode)* *[see note b]* Trade Marks ADP number *(if you know it)* Your reference		
Signature		
Name *(block capitals)*		
Date		
Name and daytime telephone number of person to contact		
State number of sheets attached to this form		

Reminder:
List on a separate sheet (a) the goods or services (by class number) to be removed to a divisional application, or (b) representations of the marks to be divided

(REV/1)

Form TM12

1219

Specific notes

a) *You may use this form to divide a specification of goods or services, or on the basis of a geographical limitation or both, <u>or</u> to divide a series of marks. You cannot divide both a specification of goods or services and a series of marks on the same form.*

b) *Section 41 of the Trade Marks Act 1994 allows for the division of an application (Rule 19 also refers). This may apply, for example, where a multiclass application may not proceed because of objections arising against some of the goods or services covered by the application. In this case, the application could be divided, with part of the application proceeding to registration in respect of those goods or services which do not face objections, whilst the other part is held up until the objections are settled.*

c) *You cannot divide a registered trade mark.*

d) *If you are dividing a specification of goods or services then the only fee payable is the division fee.*
   If you are dividing a series of marks then the following fees are payable:
   - *one divisional fee;*
   - *a fresh application fee for each extra application created; and*
   - *any class fee if appropriate (see Rule 21(4)).*

General notes

e) *Complete the form in capital letters or type it.*

f) *If there is not enough space for your answer to any section of this form, use separate sheets. Number each one and write on the form how many extra sheets you have used.*

g) *Once you have completed the form you must remember to sign and date it.*

h) *If your address for service is different from your agent, then please give us full details of both.*

i) *If you need help or have any questions, please contact the Trade Marks Registry on 0645 500505.*

Form TM16

Official fee due

The
**Patent
Office**

Application to register a change of proprietor

The Patent Office
Trade Marks Registry
Cardiff Road, Newport
South Wales NP9 1RH

Please refer to notes for guidance on completing this form

	Number(s)	*(Lowest)* Class
1. Give details of the applications or registrations for which a change in ownership is to be recorded		
2. Full name of current applicant/registered proprietor		
3. Full name, address and postcode of new proprietor Trade Marks ADP number *(if you know it)*		
4. If the new proprietor is a corporate body give country and if applicable State of Incorporation *If the name of the new proprietor is the same as the old proprietor, then provide both the new and old company registration numbers:* old number new number		
5. Date new proprietor took over ownership		
6. If only part of the ownership has been transferred give the rights or goods or services transferred		

7. Indicate whether you wish to be:-
   a) Address for service
   b) Agent
   c) Both

   for

   d) This transaction only
   e) All transactions
   (indicate a) to e) as appropriate)
   [see note b]

   If you have indicated d) please note that
   original Agent and Address for Service will be
   re-entered into our records as soon as this
   transaction has been completed

   If you have completed this section please
   provide details and ADP Number

   Your reference

8. Please sign and confirm that Stamp Duty
   *has been paid/is not payable
   *(delete as appropriate)
   [see note c]

   Signature

9. Provide below an authorisation to change the
   record or send separate documentary evidence
   [see note a]

   Signature of the registered proprietor
   (or his or her representative)

   Status of Signatory

   Name *(block capitals)*

   Date

   Signature of the new proprietor
   (or his or her representative)

   Status of Signatory

   Name *(block capitals)*

   Date

   Name, signature and daytime telephone number
   (of person completing these forms)

   State number of sheets attached
   to this form

Form TM17

No official fee due

The
Patent
Office

Request to merge either applications or registrations

The Patent Office
Trade Marks Registry
Cardiff Road, Newport
South Wales NP9 1RH

Please refer to notes for guidance on completing this form

	Number(s)	*(Lowest)* Class
1. Give details of the applications or registrations to which this request relates		
2. Full name, address and postcode of the applicant or registered proprietor		
3. Give details of the merged specifications *[see note e]*		
4. Indicate whether you wish to be:- a) Address for service b) Agent c) Both *for* d) This transaction only e) All transactions *(indicate a) to e) as appropriate)* *[see note f]* If you have completed this section please provide details and ADP number *(if you know it)* Your reference		
Signature		
Name *(block capitals)*		
Date		
Name and daytime telephone number of person to contact		
State number of sheets attached to this form		

(REV/1)

Form TM17

Specific notes

a) Section 41 of the Trade Marks Act 1994 allows the merging of separate applications or registrations into a single application or registration (Rule 20 also refers). Applications cannot be merged with registrations.

b) Applications can be merged at any time before they are accepted for advertisement and must:
   - have the same <u>application date</u> (this is the date of filing, Section 40(3) of the Trade Marks Act 1994);
   - be for the same marks; and
   - be in the same ownership.

c) Registrations to be merged must:
   - be for the same marks; and
   - be in the same ownership.

   Registered marks can be merged even if the <u>registration dates</u> (this is the date of entry onto the register) are different, but the new merged registration will be given the latest filing date.
   The renewal date for the merged registration will be the one with the latest filing date. Renewal fees for all the classes covered by the merged registration will be due on this date.

d) You may want to use this procedure, for example, if an application has been divided or part of a registration was transferred legally to someone else but now returned to a single ownership.

e) You may wish to suggest an amended specification for all the merged applications or registrations. The Registry will consider the acceptability of the edited specification.

General notes

f) Complete the form in capital letters or type it.

g) If there is not enough space for your answer to any section of this form, use separate sheets. Number each one and write on the form how many extra sheets you have used.

h) Once you have completed the form you must remember to sign and date it.

i) If your address for service is different from your agent, then please give us full details of both.

j) If you need help or have any questions, please contact the Trade Marks Registry on 0645 500505.

Form TM21

No official fee due

The Patent Office

Request to change the details of an application or a registration

Request to change the details of a designation under the Madrid Protocol

Please refer to notes for guidance on completing this form

The Patent Office
Trade Marks Registry
Cardiff Road, Newport
South Wales NP9 1RH

1. Give details of the applications or registrations	Number(s)	*(Lowest)* Class	Licensee numbers *(if applicable)*
or			
the designations under the Madrid Protocol this will affect:	Number(s)	*(Lowest)* Class	Licensee numbers *(if applicable)*
Do you wish to change:			
a) All of the trade marks belonging to this proprietor			
or			
b) Only those listed			
(indicate a) or b) as appropriate)			
2. Full name, address and postcode of the proprietor or the licensee on the record			
Trade Marks ADP number *(if you know it)*			
3. Do you wish to record a change of:			
a) name of the proprietor *[for designations under the Madrid Protocol see note a]*			
b) name of the licensee(s)			
c) name of person having an interest in the mark			
d) address of the proprietor(s) *[for designations under the Madrid Protocol see note a]*			
e) address of the licensee(s)			
f) address of the person having an interest in the mark			
(indicate a) to f) as appropriate)			
For other changes please see Section 5			
4. New name or address and postcode to be entered on the Register or Supplementary Register			

(REV/1)

Form TM21

1225

5. Other amendments
 	
  a) give details of the changes
     (including, if appropriate, specifications)
 	
  b) give details if the change is because of
     a clerical error	

6. Name of agent *(if appropriate)* 'Address for service' in the United Kingdon to which all correspondence should be sent *(including postcode)* *[see note j]* Trade Marks ADP number *(if you know it)* Your reference	
Signature	**Declaration** *I declare that there has been no change in the actual proprietorship of the application(s) or registration(s).*
Name *(block capitals)*	
Date	
Name and daytime telephone number of person to contact	
State number of sheets attached to this form	

Form TM22

No official fee due

The
Patent
Office

Notice to surrender a registration

The Patent Office
Trade Marks Registry
Cardiff Road, Newport
South Wales NP9 1RH

Please refer to notes for guidance on completing this form

1. Give details of the registration to be surrendered	Registration Number *(Lowest)* Class
2. Full name, address and postcode of the registered proprietor	
3. Indicate whether you wish to be:- a) Address for Service b) Agent c) Both *(indicate a) to c) as appropriate)* If you have completed this section please provide details and ADP number *(if you know it)* Your reference	
4. Are there any licensees or does any one else have a registered interest in the registration? *(if yes write the details on a separate sheet)*	
5.	Declaration *I confirm that there are no parties having a registered interest in the mark* *or* *I confirm that those with a registered interest in the mark (see attached sheet), have been notified three months prior to this form being filed, or that they consent to the surrender.*
Signature	
Name *(block capitals)*	
Date	
Name and daytime telephone number of person to contact	
State number of sheets attached to this form	

(REV/1)

Form TM22

Specific notes

a) *The proprietor of a registered trade mark can surrender their legal rights to all or part of the goods or services for which it is registered. (Section 45 of the Trade Marks Act 1994 refers).*

b) *This form is used if you are giving up your legal rights to the whole trade mark registration, and you should use a separate form for each trade mark affected.*

c) *Do not use this form if you are giving up your legal rights to only some of the goods or services. Please use form TM23 instead.*

d) *A separate form is required for each registration to be surrendered.*

e) *You must tell the people that have an interest in your mark that you are going to give up your rights in the mark 3 months beforehand, or they should consent to this. You also need to attach a list of all the interested parties to this form. (Section 45 of the Trade Marks Act 1994 and Rule 26 of the Trade Marks Rules 1994 refer).*

General notes

f) *Complete the form in capital letters or type it.*

g) *If there is not enough space for your answer to any section of this form, use separate sheets. Number each one and write on the form how many extra sheets you have used.*

h) *Once you have completed the form you must remember to sign and date it.*

i) *If you need help or have any questions, please contact the Trade Marks Registry on 0645 500505.*

Form TM23

No official fee due

The
Patent
Office

Notice of a partial surrender of the specification of goods or services for which the mark is registered

Please refer to notes for guidance on completing this form

The Patent Office
Trade Marks Registry
Cardiff Road, Newport
South Wales NP9 1RH

1. Give details of the registration this applies to	Registration number *(Lowest)* Class
2. Full name, address and postcode of the registered proprietor	
3. Indicate whether you wish to be:- a) Address for Service b) Agent c) Both for d) This transaction only e) All transactions *(indicate a) to e) as appropriate)* *[see note j]* If you have completed this section please provide details and ADP Number *(if you know it)* Your reference	
4. Goods or services to be surrendered *[see note f]*	
5. Are there any licensees or does any one else have a registered interest in the registration? *(if yes write the details on an attached sheet)*	
Signature	**Declaration** *I confirm that there are no parties having a registered interest in the mark* *or* *I confirm that those with a registered interest in the mark (see attached sheet), have been notified three months prior to this form being filed, or that they consent to the surrender.*

(REV/1)

Form TM23

1229

Name *(block capitals)*	
Date	
Name and daytime telephone number of person to contact	
State number of sheets attached to this form	

Specific notes

a) *The proprietor of a registered trade mark can surrender their legal rights to all or part of the goods or services for which is registered. (Section 45 of the Trade Marks Act 1994 refers).*

b) *This form is used if you are giving up your legal rights to only some of the goods or services, and you should use an attached form for each trade mark affected.*

c) *Do not use this form if you are giving up your legal rights to the whole of the registration. Please use form TM22 instead.*

d) *Only one registration number is allowed on each form.*

e) *You must inform all of the people who have an interest in your mark that you are going to give up some of your rights in the mark 3 months beforehand, or they should consent to this. You also need to attach a list of all the interested parties to this form. (Section 45 of the Trade Marks Act 1994 and Rule 26 of the Trade Marks Rules 1994 refer).*

f) *If the goods or services to be surrendered fall in more than one class the they should be listed by class.*

General notes

g) *Complete the form in capital letters or type it.*

h) *If there is not enough space for your answer to any section of this form, use separate sheets. Number each one and write on the form how many extra sheets you have used.*

i) *Once you have completed the form you must remember to sign and date it.*

j) *If your address for service is different from your agent, then please give us full details of both.*

k) *If you need help or you have any questions, please contact the Trade Marks Registry on 0645 500505.*

Form TM23

Form TM24

No official fee due

The Patent Office

Application to record or cancel a registrable transaction other than an assignment or licence

Application to record or cancel a notifiable transaction for a designation under the Madrid Protocol

Please refer to notes for guidance on completing this form

The Patent Office
Trade Marks Registry
Cardiff Road, Newport
South Wales NP9 1RH

1. Give details of the registrations this will affect	Number(s) *(Lowest)* Class
or	
the designations under the Madrid Protocol this will affect	Number(s) *(Lowest)* Class
2. Full name, address and postcode of the grantor	
Trade Marks ADP number *(if you know it)*	
3. **FOR DOMESTIC TRADE MARKS:** Full name, address and postcode of the person recorded, or to be recorded, as having an interest in the registered trade marks shown above **FOR DESIGNATIONS UNDER THE MADRID PROTOCOL:** Full name, address and postcode of the licensee or person recorded, or to be recorded, as having an interest in the designations under the Madrid Protocol shown above	
4. Indicate whether you wish to be:- a) Address for service b) Agent c) Both *for* d) This transaction only e) All transactions *(indicate a) to e) as appropriate)* *[See note n]* If you have completed this section, please provide details and ADP number *(if you know it)* Your reference:-	

(REV/1)

Form TM24

5.　FOR DOMESTIC TRADE MARKS:	
Details of the registrable transaction to be recorded or cancelled including: (where appropriate)	
a)　the nature of the interest (whether fixed or floating)	
b)　the extent of the security and the right in or under the mark secured	
FOR DESIGNATIONS UNDER THE MADRID PROTOCOL:	
Details of the notifiable transaction to be recorded or cancelled as follows:-	
Where granting of any security interests:	
a)　the nature of the interest (whether fixed or floating)	
b)　the extent of the security and the right in or under the mark	
Where granting a licence:	
c)　date licence starts	
d)　date licence ends (if any)	
e)　is the licence to be exclusive?	
f)　is the licensee to be recorded for all the goods and services for which the international trade mark (UK) is protected?	
If not, state specific goods or services the licensee is to be recorded against in each case	
6.　Signature of the grantor *(or his or her representative)*	
Signature	
Name *(block capitals)*	
Date	
7.　Signature of the person shown at section 3 *(or his or her representative)*	
Signature	
Name *(block capitals)*	
Date	
Name and daytime telephone number *(of person completing this form)*	
State number of sheets attached to this form	

(REV/1)　　　　　　　　　　　　　　　　　　　　　　　　　　Form TM24

Form TM25

No official fee due

The
Patent
Office

Request for alteration of a
registered mark

The Patent Office
Trade Marks Registry
Cardiff Road, Newport
South Wales NP9 1RH

Please refer to notes for guidance on completing this form

1. Give details of the registrations this will affect	Number	*(Lowest)* Class

2. Full name, address and postcode of the registered proprietor

3. Details of the change to the mark

If the mark is pictorial then please attach a copy of the amended mark here

FOOTNOTE

The Trade Marks Act 1994, Section 44 states the Registrar may, at the request of the proprietor, allow the alteration of a registered trade mark where the mark includes the proprietor's name or address and the alteration is limited to alteration of that name or address and does not substantially affect the identity of the mark.

(REV/1)

Form TM25

Indicate whether you wish to be:- a) Address for Service b) Agent c) Both *for* d) This transaction only e) All transactions *(indicate a) to e) as appropriate)* *[see note d]* If you have completed this section please provide details and ADP number *(if you know it)* Your reference	
Signature	
Name *(block capitals)*	
Date	
Name and daytime telephone number of person to contact	
State number of sheets attached to this form	

:neral notes

Complete the form in capital letters or type it.

If there is not enough space for your answer to any section of this form, use separate sheets. Number each one and write on the form how many extra sheets you have used.

Once you have completed the form you must remember to sign and date it.

If your address for service is different from your agent, then please give us full details of both.

If you need help or have any questions, please contact the Trade Marks Registry on 0645 500505.

Form TM26

Official fee due

The
Patent
Office

Application for the revocation, invalidation, or rectification of a registration

Application for the revocation or invalidation of a protected international trade mark (UK); rectification of the supplementary register

The Patent Office
Trade Marks Registry
Cardiff Road, Newport
South Wales NP9 1EH

Please refer to notes for guidance on completing this form

1. Give details of the registration		Number	*(Lowest)* Class
or			
the designation under the Madrid Protocol for which revocation, rectification or invalidity is sought		Number	*(Lowest)* Class
2. Is this request for			
a) revocation			
or b) rectification			
or c) declaration of invalidity			
(indicate as appropriate. You may use this form for more than one category of request)			
3. Full name of registered proprietor			
4. Full name, address and postcode of applicant for revocation, rectification or invalidity			
5. Name of agent *(if appropriate)*			
'Address for service' in the United Kingdom to which all correspondence should be sent *(including postcode)* *[see note j]*			
Trade Marks ADP number *(if you know it)*			
Your reference			

(REV/1)

Form TM26

6.	Declaration
Signature	*I declare that to the best of my knowledge there is no action concerning the registration pending in the courts*
Name *(block capitals)*	
Date	
Name and daytime telephone number of person to contact	
State the number of sheets attached to this form	

Specific notes

a) *This form is used to request the revocation, invalidation or rectification of a registered trade mark,*

   or

b) *the revocation or invalidation of a protected international trade mark (UK); rectification of the supplementary register.*

c) *If proceedings concerning the trade mark are waiting to be dealt with in court, you must apply to the court.*

d) *The Registrar may refer an application for revocation, rectification or declaration of invalidity to the court at any stage.*

e) *This form must be accompanied by a statement of the grounds of your application.*

f) *Guidance notes on revocation/rectification/invalidity procedures are available on request from the Law Section of the Trade Marks Registry.*

General notes

g) *Complete the form in capital letters or type it.*

h) *If there is not enough space for your answer to any section of this form, use separate sheets. Number each one and write on the form how many extra sheets you have used.*

i) *Once you have completed the form you must remember to sign and date it.*

j) *If your address for service is different from your agent, then please give us full details of both.*

k) *If you need help or have any questions, please contact the Trade Marks Registry on 0645 500505.*

(REV/1)   **Form TM26**

Form TM27

No official fee due

**The
Patent
Office**

Application to intervene in proceedings for the revocation, invalidation or rectification of a registration

Application to intervene in proceedings for the revocation or invalidation of a protected international trade mark (UK) or rectification of the supplementary register

Please refer to notes for guidance on completing this form

The Patent Office
Trade Marks Registry
Cardiff Road, Newport
South Wales NP9 1RH

1. Give details of the registration this will affect	Number	*(Lowest)* Class	Revocation/invalidation number	
or				
the designation under the Madrid Protocol to which this request relates	Number	*(Lowest)* Class	Revocation/invalidation number	
2. Full name and address of registered proprietor				
3. Full name, address and postcode of applicant for intervention				
4. Name of agent *(if appropriate)*				
'Address for service' in the United Kingdom to which all correspondence should be sent for the intervenor *(including postcode)* *[see note g]*				
Trade Marks ADP number *(if you know it)*				
Your reference				

REMINDER

Have you attached the grounds of your application to intervene?

(REV/1)

Form TM27

Signature	
Name *(block capitals)*	
Date	
Name and daytime telephone number of person to contact	
State the number of sheets attached to this form	

Specific notes

a) *This form is used if you wish to intervene in proceedings for the revocation, rectification or declaration of invalidity of the registration of a trade mark,*

or

b) *to intervene in proceedings for the revocation or invalidation of a protected international trade mark (UK) or rectification of the supplementary register.*

c) *This form must be accompanied by a statement of the grounds of your application.*

General notes

d) *Complete the form in capital letters or type it.*

e) *If there is not enough space for your answer to any section of this form, use separate sheets. Number each one and write on the form how many extra sheets you have used.*

f) *Once you have completed the form you must remember to sign and date it.*

g) *If your address for service is different from your agent, then please give us full details of both.*

h) *If you need help or have any questions, please contact the Trade Marks Registry on 0645 500505.*

Form TM28

No official fee due

Request for Recordal of concurrent registration

The Patent Office
Trade Marks Registry
Cardiff Road, Newport
South Wales NP9 1RH

Please refer to notes for guidance on completing this form

	Number(s)	*(Lowest)* Class
1. Give details of the domestic registration(s) this will affect		
Give details of the designation(s) under the Madrid Protocol to which this request relates	Number(s)	*(Lowest)* Class
2. Full name, address of the holder of the protected international trade mark (UK)		
3. Name of agent *(if appropriate)* Address for service in the United Kingdom to which correspondence should be sent *[see note e]*		
Your Reference		
Signature		
Name *(block capitals)*		
Date		
Name and daytime telephone number of person to contact		
State the number of sheets attached to this form		

(REV/1)

Form TM28

Specific notes

a) *This form is used to request that the protected international registration (UK) is noted in the register against the registered trade mark.*

b) *The provisions of Article 21 apply only where:*

- *the registered trade mark is also a protected international trade mark (UK)*
- *the proprietor of the registered trade mark is the holder of the international trade mark (UK)*
- *all the goods or services in respect of which the trade mark is registered are protected under the protected international trade mark (UK)*
- *the date of registration of the registered trade mark is earlier than the date specified in relation to the international trade mark (UK).*

General notes

c) *Complete the form in capital letters or type it.*

d) *If there is not enough space for your answer to any section of this form, use separate sheets. Number each one and write on the form how many extra sheets you have used.*

e) *If your address for service is different from your agent, then please give us full details of both.*

f) *Once you have completed the form you must remember to sign and date it.*

g) *If you need help or have any questions please contact the Trade Marks Registry on 0645 500505.*

Form TM31C

Official fee due

The
**Patent
Office**

Request for information about
applications and registered marks

The Patent Office
Trade Marks Registry
Cardiff Road, Newport
South Wales NP9 1RH

Please refer to notes for guidance on completing this form

1. Give details of the application or registration to which this request relates	Number *(Lowest)* Class
2. Indicate for which category or categories of events you require notification *(A to H as detailed below)* *(A separate fee is payable for each category indicated)*	

Category   *You will be notified of:*

A   application published or withdrawn, refused or deemed abandoned before publication

B   current or future formal opposition filed against a new trade mark application

C   application registered or withdrawn, refused or abandoned after publication

D   unpaid renewal (registration in additional renewal fee period)

E   registration renewed or expired

F   full surrender or successful revocation resulting in the removal of a mark from the register

G   assignment application received

H   assignment in full or partial assignment

(REV/1)

Form TM31C

Form TM31C

3. If your request is for an event not listed in 2, give details here	
4. Full name, address and postcode to which notifications should be sent Trade Marks ADP number *(if you know it)* Your reference	
Signature	
Name *(block capitals)*	
Date	
Name and daytime telephone number of person to contact	
State number of sheets attached to this form	

Reminder

A fee is required for each category you have indicated.

Specific notes

a) *Since the Trade Marks Register is a public record, anyone can ask to be told about any action on any application or registration. The form lists the categories which you can be notified about. This form is not open to public inspection and information is disclosed only to the person filing the form.*

b) *A separate form should be used for each trade mark number.*

c) *A separate fee is payable for each category you want to be notified of.*

General notes

d) *Complete the form in capital letters or type it.*

e) *If there is not enough space for your answer to any section of this form, use separate sheets. Number each one and write on the form how many extra sheets you have used.*

f) *Once you have completed the form you must remember to sign and date it.*

g) *If you need help or have any questions, please contact the Trade Marks Registry on 0645 500505.*

Form TM31C

Form TM31R

Official fee due

The
Patent
Office

Request for a Certified Copy

The Patent Office
Trade Marks Registry
Cardiff Road, Newport
South Wales NP9 1RH

Please refer to notes for guidance on completing this form

1. Give details of the applications or registrations which the certificates are for	Number(s)	*(Lowest)* Class
or		
designation(s) under the Madrid Protocol for which a certificate is required	Number(s)	*(Lowest)* Class
2. State the number of certified copies required		
3. If certificates are for obtaining registration abroad list the countries		
4. State any special requirements needed: a) representation of the mark in colour *[see note c]* b) details as filed *[see note c]* c) for use in legal proceedings d) anything else, please specify *(indicate a) to d) as appropriate)*		
5. Full name, address and postcode to which the certificates should be sent Your Reference		
Signature		
Name *(block capitals)*		
Date		
Name and daytime telephone number of person to contact		
State the number of sheets attached to this form		

REMINDER   *A fee is required for each certificate requested*

(REV/1)

Form TM31R

1243

Specific notes

a) *This form is used to request a certificate from the Registrar concerning the details of a trade mark or a protected international trade mark (UK). You might need a certificate to prove you have made an application, or have a registration in the United Kingdom, or a protected international trade mark (UK), or in legal proceedings (Rule 37 of the Trade Marks Rules 1994 refers).*

b) *If you are going to use the certificate for obtaining registration abroad you must list the country or countries, so that the certificate is prepared in the correct way.*

c) *For domestic applications please provide a copy of the Form TM3 as originally filed if you require a certificate showing:*

    (i) *trade mark in colour; or*

    (ii) *TM3 as filed if the form TM3 has subsequently been amended during the course of the examination.*

General notes

d) *Complete the form in capital letters or type it.*

e) *If there is not enough space for your answer to any section of this form, use separate sheets. Number each one and write on the form how many extra sheets you have used.*

f) *Once you have completed the form you must remember to sign and date it.*

g) *If you need help or have any questions please contact the Trade Marks Registry on 0645 500505.*

Form TM33

No official fee due

The
Patent
Office

Request to appoint or change an agent or to enter or change an address for service

Please refer to notes for guidance on completing this form

The Patent Office
Trade Marks Registry
Cardiff Road, Newport
South Wales NP9 1RH

	Number(s)	*(Lowest)* Class	Licensee Numbers
1. Give details of the applications or registrations this will affect			
or			
the designation under the Madrid Protocol to which this request relates	Number(s)	*(Lowest)* Class	Licensee Numbers

2. Full name of
    (a) proprietor
    (b) opponent
    (c) licensee
(indicate a) to c) as appropriate)

3. On behalf of the proprietor, grantor, licensee or opponent we notify you that we are the authorised:
    a) agent and address for service
or b) address for service
or c) agent
(indicate a) to c) as appropriate)

4. Is the agent or address for service authorised for:
    a) all transactions
    or
    b) this transaction only
(indicate a) or b) and if b) provide details of transaction)

5. New address for service or agent's details to be recorded

Trade Marks ADP number
(if you know it)

Your reference

Signature	
Name *(block capitals)*	
Date	
Name and daytime telephone number of person to contact	
State number of sheets attached to this form	

(REV/1)

Form TM33

1245

Specific notes

a) *This form is used if you want to appoint an agent either for the first time or to replace an existing agent recorded against a trade mark application or registration or international trade mark (UK) or protected international trade mark (UK). You may also use it to enter or change an address for service. (Rules 10 and 38 of the Trade Marks Rules 1994 refer).*

b) *This form can be used for as many cases as you need. You should indicate at Section 1 the registration or application numbers of all the cases affected by these changes.*

General notes

c) *Complete the form in capital letters or type it.*

d) *If there is not enough space for your answer to any section of this form, use separate sheets. Number each one and write on the form how many extra sheets you have used.*

e) *Once you have completed the form you must remember to sign and date it.*

f) *If you need help or have any questions, please contact the Trade Marks Registry on 0645 500505.*

Form TM35

Official fee due

Filing of regulations governing the
use of certification or collective marks

The Patent Office
Trade Marks Registry
Cardiff Road, Newport
South Wales NP9 1RH

Please refer to notes for guidance on completing this form

	Number(s)	*(Lowest)* Class
1. Give details of the applications to which the regulations relate		
or		
the designation under the Madrid Protocol to which this request relates	Number(s)	*(Lowest)* Class
2. Does this request relate to: a) certification marks *or* b) collective marks *(indicate a) or b) as appropriate)*		
3. Full name of applicant		
4. Name of agent *(if appropriate)* 'Address for service' in the United Kingdom to which all correspondence should be sent *(including postcode)* *[see note f]* Trade Marks ADP number *(if you know it)* Your reference		
Signature		
Name *(block capitals)*		
Date		
Name and daytime telephone number of person to contact		
State number of sheets attached to this form		

(REV/1)

Form TM35

Specific notes

a) *This form is used to file the regulations for a certification or collective mark within nine months from the date of application (Schedule 2 Paragraph 6, and Schedule 1 Paragraph 5, of the Trade Marks Act 1994 refer).*

b) *You should say in Section 2 of the form if the regulations apply to certification or collective marks. The regulations can refer to a number of marks, but they cannot apply to a mixture of both certification and collective marks.*

General notes

c) *Complete the form in capital letters or type it.*

d) *If there is not enough space for your answer to any section of this form, use separate sheets. Number each one and write on the form how many extra sheets you have used.*

e) *Once you have completed the form you must remember to sign and date it.*

f) *If your address for service is different from your agent, then please give give us full details of both.*

g) *If you need help or have any questions, please contact the Trade Marks Registry on 0645 500505.*

Form TM50

No official fee due

**The
Patent
Office**

Application to Register a Licensee

**The Patent Office
Trade Marks Registry**
Cardiff Road, Newport
South Wales NP9 1RH

Please refer to notes for guidance on completing this form

1. Give details of the trade marks you want a licensee recorded against	Number(s)	*(Lowest)* Class
2. Full name, address and postcode of the proprietor		
3. Full name, address and postcode of the licensee		

4. a) Date licence starts
 	
   b) Date licence ends
      (if any)		

5. Is the licence to be exclusive		
6. Is the licensee to be recorded for all goods or services for which the mark is registered/ application applied for? If not, state which specific goods or services or limited geographical area the licensee is to be recorded against in each case		

(REV/1)

Form TM50

7. Name of agent *(if appropriate)*	
'Address for service' in the United Kingdom to which all correspondence should be sent *(including postcode)* *(see note f)*	
Trade Marks ADP number *(if you know it)*	
Your reference	
8. Signature of the registered proprietor or grantor *(or his or her representative)*	
Signature	
Name *(block capitals)*	
Date	
9. Signature of the new licensee *(or his or her representative)*	
Signature	
Name *(block capitals)*	
Date	
Name and daytime telephone number *(of person to contact)*	
State number of sheets attached to this form	

Form TM51

No official fee due

The
Patent
Office

Application to remove or amend the recordal of a licence

The Patent Office
Trade Marks Registry
Cardiff Road, Newport
South Wales NP9 1RH

Please refer to notes for guidance on completing this form

1. Give details of the trade marks affected	Number(s)	*(Lowest)* Class	Licensee numbers
or			
the designations under the Madrid Protocol this will affect	Number(s)	*(Lowest)* Class	Licensee numbers
2. Full name of the proprietor of the trade marks or designations under the Madrid Protocol shown above			
3. Full name of the licensee whose licence will be removed or amended			
4. Please indicate whether this request is for: a) removal b) amendment *(if b) please give details)*			
5. Name of agent *(if appropriate)* Address for service in the United Kingdom to which all correspondence should be sent *(including postcode)* *[see note g]* Your reference			

(REV/1)

Form TM51

6. Signature of grantor of licence *(or his or her representative)*	
Name *(block capitals)*	
Date	
Name and daytime telephone number of person to contact	
7. Name of person completing this form *(if different from 6 above)*	
State number of sheets attached to this form	

Specific notes

a) *This form is used if an existing record of a licence is to be removed or amended (Section 25 of the Trade Marks Act 1994 refers and Article 6 of the Trade Marks (International Registration) Order 1996).*

b) *If you are the licensee you must get either the registered proprietor or the grantor (or their representative) of either the domestic trade mark or protected international trade mark (UK) to sign the form .*

c) *This form must be signed by the grantor of the licence (or his or her representative). It is acceptable for this to be signed in the name of the firm or company. If you cannot do this, you may send us documentary evidence to support this transaction. Any documentary evidence submitted with this form will be open to public inspection.*

General notes

d) *Complete the form in capital letters or type it.*

e) *If there is not enough space for your answer to any section of this form, use separate sheets. Number each one and write on the form how many extra sheets you have used.*

f) *Once you have completed the form you must remember to sign and date it.*

g) *If your address for service is different from your agent, then please give us full details of both.*

g) *If you need help or have any questions please contact the Trade Marks Registry on 0645 500505.*

REQUEST FOR EXTENSION OF TIME

To:
The Registrar
Trade Marks Registry   DATE ....

APPLICATION NUMBER* ....   **CLASS*** ....

REGISTRY (UNIT) REF* ....   **AGENTS REF*** ....

Dear Sir

*An extension of time is requested for .... months from .... to ....
in respect of the above application in order to deal with outstanding matters. The reasons for
the request are as follows:

Yours faithfully

Agents details*	FOR OFFICIAL USE ONLY

APPLICATION NUMBER* ....   **CLASS*** ....

REGISTRY (UNIT) REF* ....   **AGENTS REF*** ....

APPLICANTS NAME* ....

Dear Sirs

Your request for an extension of time has been granted as shown above.

Yours faithfully

DDU/4210/04.98

1253

The International Classification of Goods and Services

CLASSES 1-3

Class 1
This class encompasses:

- chemicals used in industry, science, photography, agriculture, horticulture and forestry;
- unprocessed artificial resins and unprocessed plastics;
- manures;
- fire extinguishing compositions;
- tempering and soldering preparations;
- chemical substances for preserving foodstuffs;
- tanning substances;
- adhesives used in industry.

Explanatory note: This class includes mainly chemical products used in industry, science and agriculture, including those that go to the making of products belonging to other classes.

Class 2
This class encompasses:

- paints, varnishes and lacquers;
- preservatives against rust and against deterioration of wood;
- colorants;
- mordants;
- raw natural resins;
- metals in foil and powder form for painters, decorators, printers and artists.

Explanatory note: This class includes mainly paints, colorants and preparations used for protection against corrosion.

Class 3
This class encompasses:

- bleaching preparations and other substances for laundry use;
- cleaning, polishing, scouring and abrasive preparations;
- soaps;
- perfumery, essential oils, cosmetics and hair lotions;
- dentifrices.

Explanatory note: This class includes mainly cleaning preparations and toilet preparations.

Last updated 12 July 1999

CLASSES 4-6

Class 4
This class encompasses:

- industrial oils and greases;
- lubricants;
- dust absorbing, wetting and binding compositions;
- fuels (including motor spirit) and illuminants;
- candles and wicks.

Explanatory note: This class includes mainly industrial oils and greases, fuels and illuminants.

Class 5
This class encompasses:

- pharmaceutical, veterinary and sanitary preparations;
- dietetic substances adapted for medical use;
- food for babies;
- plasters and materials for dressings;
- material for stopping teeth and dental wax;
- disinfectants;
- preparations for destroying vermin;
- fungicides and herbicides.

Explanatory note: This class includes mainly pharmaceutical and other preparations for medical purposes.

Class 6
This class encompasses:

- common metals and their alloys;
- metal building materials;
- transportable buildings of metal;
- materials of metal for railway tracks;
- non-electric cables and wires of common metal;
- ironmongery and small items of metal hardware;
- pipes and tubes of metal;
- safes;
- goods of common metal not included in other classes;
- ores.

Explanatory note: This class includes mainly unwrought and partly wrought common metals as well as simple products made of them.

Last updated 12 July 1999

CLASSES 7-9

Class 7
This class encompasses:

- machines and machine tools;
- motors and engines (except for land vehicles);
- machine coupling and transmission components (except for land vehicles);
- agricultural implements;
- incubators for eggs.

Explanatory note: This class includes mainly machines, machine tools, motors and engines.

Class 8
This class encompasses:

- hand tools and implements (hand operated);
- cutlery;
- side arms;
- razors.

Explanatory note: This class includes mainly hand-operated implements used as tools in the respective professions.

Class 9
This class encompasses:

- scientific, nautical, surveying, electric, photographic, cinematographic, optical, signalling, checking (supervision), life-saving and teaching apparatus and instruments;
- apparatus for recording, transmission or reproduction of sound or images;
- magnetic data carriers and recording discs;
- automatic vending machines and mechanisms for coin-operated apparatus;
- cash registers, calculating machines, data-processing equipment and computers;
- fire-extinguishing apparatus.

Last updated 12 July 1999

CLASSES 10-13

Class 10
This class encompasses:

- surgical, medical, dental and veterinary apparatus and instruments;
- artificial limbs, eyes and teeth;
- orthopaedic articles;
- suture materials.

Explanatory note: This class includes mainly medical apparatus, instruments and articles.

Class 11
This class encompasses:

- apparatus for lighting, heating, steam generating, cooking, refrigerating, drying, ventilating, water supply and sanitary purposes.

Class 12
This class encompasses:

- vehicles;
- apparatus for locomotion by land, air or water.

Class 13
This class encompasses:

- firearms;
- ammunition and projectiles;
- explosives;
- fireworks.

Explanatory note: This class includes mainly firearms and pyrotechnical products

Last updated 12 July 1999

CLASSES 14-16

Class 14
This class encompasses:

- precious metals and their alloys and goods in precious metals or coated therewith, not included in other classes;
- jewellery and precious stones;
- horological and chronometric instruments.

Explanatory note: This class includes mainly precious metals, goods in precious metals and, in general, jewellery, clocks and watches.

Class 15

This class encompasses:

- musical instruments.

Class 16

This class encompasses:

- paper, cardboard and goods made from these materials, not included in other classes;
- printed matter;
- bookbinding material;
- photographs;
- stationery;
- adhesives for stationery or household purposes;
- artists' material;
- paintbrushes;
- typewriters and office requisites (except furniture);
- instructional and teaching material (except apparatus);
- plastic materials for packaging (not included in other classes);
- playing cards;
- printers' type;
- printing blocks.

Explanatory note: This class includes mainly paper, goods made from paper and office requisites.

Last updated 12 July 1999

CLASSES 17-19

Class 17

This class encompasses:

- rubber, gutta-percha, asbestos, mica and goods made from these materials, not included in other classes;
- plastics in extruded form for use in manufacture;
- packing, stopping and insulating materials;
- flexible pipes, not of metal.

Explanatory note: This class includes mainly electrical, thermal and acoustic insulating materials and plastics, being for use in manufacture in the form of sheets, blocks and rods.

Class 18
This class encompasses:

- leather and imitations of leather, and goods made of these materials and not included in other classes;
- animal skins, hides;
- trunks and travelling bags;
- umbrellas, parasols and walking sticks;
- whips, harnesses and saddlery.

Explanatory note: This class includes mainly leather, leather imitations and travel goods not included in other classes.

Class 19
This class encompasses:

- building materials (non-metallic);
- non-metallic rigid pipes for building;
- asphalt, pitch and bitumen;
- non-metallic transportable buildings;
- monuments, not of metal.

Explanatory note: This class includes mainly non-metallic building materials.

Last updated 12 July 1999

CLASSES 20-23

Class 20
This class encompasses:

- furniture, mirrors, and picture frames;
- goods (not included in other classes) of wood, cork, reed, cane, wicker, horn, bone, ivory, whalebone, shell, amber, mother of pearl, meerschaum and substitutes for all these materials, or of plastics.

Explanatory note: This class includes mainly furniture and its parts, and plastic goods not included in other classes.

Class 21
This class encompasses:

- household or kitchen utensils and containers (not of precious metal or coated therewith);
- combs and sponges;
- brushes (except paintbrushes);
- brush-making materials;
- articles for cleaning purposes;

- steel wool;
- unworked or semi-worked glass (except glass in building);
- glassware, porcelain and earthenware not included in other classes.

Explanatory note: This class includes mainly small, hand-operated utensils and apparatus for household and kitchen use as well as toilet utensils, glassware and articles in porcelain.

Class 22
This class encompasses:

- ropes, string, nets, tents, awning, tarpaulins, sails, sacks and bags (not included in other classes);
- padding and stuffing materials (except of rubber or plastics);
- raw fibrous textile materials.

Explanatory note: This class includes mainly rope and sail manufacture products, padding and stuffing materials and raw fibrous textile materials.

Class 23
This class encompasses:

- yarns and threads for textile use.

Last updated 12 July 1999

CLASSES 24-28

Class 24
This class encompasses:

- textiles and textile goods, not included in other classes;
- bed and table covers.

Explanatory note: This class includes mainly textiles (piece goods) and textile covers for household use.

Class 25
This class encompasses:

- clothing;
- footwear;
- headgear.

Class 26
This class encompasses:

- lace and embroidery;
- ribbons and braid;

- buttons, hooks and eyes, pins and needles;
- artificial flowers.

Explanatory note: This class includes mainly dressmakers' articles.

Class 27
This class encompasses:

- carpets, rugs, mats and matting;
- linoleum and other materials for covering existing floors;
- wall-hangings (non-textile).

Explanatory note: This class includes mainly products intended to be added as furnishings to previously constructed floors and walls.

Class 28
This class encompasses:

- games and playthings;
- gymnastic and sporting articles not included in other classes;
- decorations for Christmas trees.

Last updated 12 July 1999

CLASSES 29-31

Class 29
This class encompasses:

- meat, fish, poultry and game;
- meat extracts;
- preserved, dried and cooked fruits and vegetables;
- jellies, jams, and fruit sauces;
- eggs, milk and milk products;
- edible oils and fats.

Explanatory note: This class includes mainly foodstuffs of animal origin, as well as vegetables and other horticultural comestibles products that are prepared for consumption or conservation.

Class 30
This class encompasses:

- coffee, tea, cocoa, sugar, rice, tapioca, sago and artificial coffee;
- flour and preparations made from cereals, bread, pastry and confectionery, ices;
- honey and treacle;

- yeast and baking powder;
- salt and mustard;
- vinegar and sauces (condiments);
- spices;
- ice.

Explanatory note: This class includes mainly foodstuffs of plant origin prepared for consumption or conservation as well as auxiliaries intended for the improvement of the flavour of food.

Class 31
This class encompasses:
- agricultural, horticultural and forestry products and grains not included in other classes;
- live animals;
- fresh fruits and vegetables;
- seeds, natural plants and flowers;
- foodstuffs for animals;
- malt.

Explanatory note: This class includes mainly land products not having been subjected to any form of preparation for consumption, live animals and plants as well as foodstuffs for animals.

Last updated 12 July 1999

CLASSES 32-34

Class 32
This class encompasses:
- beers;
- mineral and aerated waters and other non-alcoholic drinks;
- fruit drinks and fruit juices;
- syrups and other preparations for making beverages.

Explanatory note: This class includes mainly non-alcoholic beverages, as well as beer.

Class 33
This class encompasses:
- alcoholic beverages (except beer).

Class 34
This class encompasses:

- tobacco;
- smokers' articles;
- matches.

Last updated 12 July 1999

CLASSES 35-37

Class 35
This class encompasses:

- advertising;
- business management;
- business administration;
- office functions.

Explanatory note: This class includes mainly services rendered by persons or organisations principally with the object of:
1. help in the working or management of a commercial undertaking; or
2. help in the management of the business affairs or commercial functions of an industrial or commercial enterprise,

as well as services rendered by advertising establishments primarily undertaking communications to the public, declarations or announcements by all means of diffusion and concerning all kinds of goods and services.

Class 36
This class encompasses:

- insurance;
- financial affairs;
- monetary affairs;
- real-estate affairs.

Explanatory note: This class includes mainly services rendered in financial and monetary affairs and services rendered in relation to insurance contracts of all kinds.

Class 37
This class encompasses:

- building construction;
- repair;
- installation services.

Explanatory note: This class includes mainly services rendered by contractors or sub-contractors in the construction or making of permanent buildings, as well as services rendered by persons or organisations engaged in the restoration of objects to their original condition or in their preservation without altering their physical or chemical properties.

Last updated 12 July 1999

CLASSES 38-40

Class 38
This class encompasses:

• telecommunications.

Explanatory note: This class includes mainly services allowing at least one person to communicate with another by sensory means. Such services include those that:
1. allow a person to talk to another;
2. transmit messages from one person to another;
3. place a person in oral or visual communication with another (radio and television).

Class 39
This class encompasses:

• transport;

• packaging and storage of goods;

• travel arrangement.

Explanatory note: This class includes mainly services rendered in transporting people or goods from one place to another (by rail, road, water, air or pipeline) and services necessarily connected with such transport, as well as services relating to the storing of goods in a warehouse or other building for their preservation or guarding.

Class 40
This class encompasses:

• treatment of materials.

Explanatory note: This class includes mainly services not included in other classes, rendered by the mechanical or chemical processing or transformation of objects or substances either inorganic or organic.

Last updated 12 July 1999

CLASSES 41-42

Class 41
This class encompasses:

- education;
- providing of training;
- entertainment;
- sporting and cultural activities.

Explanatory note: This class contains mainly services rendered by persons or institutions in the development of the mental faculties of persons or animals, as well as services intended to entertain or to engage the attention.

Class 42
This class encompasses:
- provision of food and drink;
- temporary accommodation;
- medical, hygienic and beauty care;
- veterinary and agricultural services;
- legal services;
- scientific and industrial research;
- computer programming;
- services that cannot be placed in other classes.

Explanatory note: This class contains all services that cannot be placed in other classes.

Last updated 12 July 1999

Index

Absolute grounds of refusal–*contd*
  acquired distinctiveness
    effect, **5.75**
    generally, **5.74**
    geographical origins, **5.86**
    incapable of distinguishing, **5.87–5.88**
    meaning, **5.76–5.85**
  arms or insignia, **5.115**
  bad faith, applications in, **5.118–5.121**
  basic grounds
    devoid of distinctiveness, **5.23–5.52**
    designating characteristics of goods or
      services, **5.33–5.68**
    examples of decisions, **5.70–5.72**
    generic signs, **5.69**
    introduction, **5.13–5.14**
    outside the definition of trade mark,
      5.15–5.22
    provisos, **5.73–5.92**
  colours, **5.22**
  Community collective marks, and, **30.4**
  Community trade marks, and, **24.9–24.16**
  contrary to law, marks being, **5.107**
  deceptive marks, **5.102–5.106**
  designate characteristics of goods or services,
      signs which
    foreign language words, **5.67**
    generally, **5.33–5.56**
    geographical names, **5.57–5.64**
    'Penguin', **5.68**
    surnames, **5.66**
    time of production or rendering of services,
      5.65
  devoid of distinctiveness, signs which are
    famous persons. names and pictures of,
      5.50–5.51
    forenames, **5.48**
    full names, **5.49**
    generally, **5.23–5.24**
    geographical names, **5.39**
    numerals, **5.37–5.38**

Absolute grounds of refusal–*contd*
    devoid of distinctiveness, signs which
      are–*contd*
      pictorial marks, **5.28–5.34**
      proviso to ground, **5.52**
      single letters, **5.36**
      stylised letters, **5.36**
      stylised words, **5.35**
      surnames, **5.40–5.47**
      words, **5.25–5.27**
  examples of decisions
    generally, **5.70–5.71**
    list, **5.72**
  famous persons, names and pictures of.
      5.50–5.51
  foreign language words, **5.67**
  foreign nations, emblems of
    flags, **5.112**
    generally, **5.111**
  forenames, **5.48**
  full names, **5.49**
  generic signs, **5.69**
  geographical names
    designate characteristics of goods or
      services, **5.57–5.64**
    devoid of distinctiveness, **5.39**
  geographical origins, **5.86**
  immoral marks, **5.102–5.106**
  international organisations, emblems of
    armorial bearings, **5.113–5.114**
    flags, **5.113–5.114**
    generally, **5.111**
    names, **5.113–5.114**
  introduction
    capable of distinguishing, **5.7**
    generally, **5.1–5.2**
    objections, **5.5–5.6**
    precedents, **5.4**
    saving provisions, **5.8–5.12**
    Work Manual, **5.3**
  invalidity, and, **7.25–7.26**
  letters, **5.36**

Absolute grounds of refusal–*contd*
  morality, marks contrary to, **5.102–5.106**
  numerals, **5.37–5.38**
  Olympic Symbol, **5.116–5.117**
  outside the definition of trade mark, signs
      which are
    colours, **5.22**
    generally, **5.15–5.21**
    smells, **5.22**
    sounds, **5.22**
  'Penguin' , **5.68**
  pictorial marks, **5.28–5.34**
  prior rights, **5.89–5.91**
  prohibited by law, marks being, **5.107**
  provisos
    acquired distinctiveness, **5.74–5.88**
    introduction, **5.73**
    prior rights, **5.89–5.91**
    restricting specification, **5.92**
  public policy, marks contrary to, **5.102–5.106**
  restricting specification, **5.92**
  Royal Family, **5.109**
  shape of goods
    case law, **5.96–5.101**
    generally, **5.93–5.95**
  single letters, **5.36**
  smells, **5.22**
  sounds, **5.22**
  specially protected emblems
    arms or insignia, **5.115**
    foreign nations, emblems of, **5.111–5.112**
    international organisations, emblems of,
        5.111–5.114
    introduction, **5.108**
    Olympic Symbol, **5.116–5.117**
    Royal Family, **5.109**
    UK flag, **5.110**
  stylised letters, **5.36**
  stylised words, **5.35**
  surnames
    designate characteristics of goods or
        services, **5.66**
    devoid of distinctiveness, **5.40–5.47**
  time of production or rendering of services,
      5.65
  UK flag, **5.110**
  words, **5.25–5.27**
  Work Manual
    designate characteristics of goods or
        services, **5.55–5.56**
    devoid of distinctiveness, **5.35–5.51**
    generally, **5.3**
    generic signs, **5.69**
    proviso, **5.73**
    public policy, marks contrary to, **5.103**
    shape of goods, **5.95**
    specially protected emblems, **5.108**

Acquiescence
  infringement, and
    Community trade marks, **24.35**
    generally, **12.58–12.59**
  international marks, and, **21.29**

Acquiescence–*contd*
  invalidity, and, **7.31–7.33**

Acquired distinctiveness
  effect, **5.75**
  generally, **5.74**
  geographical origins, **5.86**
  incapable of distinguishing, **5.87–5.88**
  meaning, **5.76–5.85**

Acquisition of rights
  TRIPS Agreement, and, **22.52**

Actionable statements
  introduction, **15.1**
  malicious falsehood
    defamation, and, **15.2–15.14**
    emergency legislation, **15.20–15.21**
    generally, **15.15–15.16**
    trade marks, and, **15.17–15.18**
  slander of title, **15.19**
  trade libel
    defamation, and, **15.2–15.14**

Actionable threats
  exclusions, **13.14–13.16**
  generally, **13.5–13.6**
  nature, **13.8–13.11**
  registered marks, **13.7**

Address for service
  generally, **3.8–3.9**
  purpose, **3.10**

Adverse assertions of rights
  threats, and, **13.20–13.23**

Advertising of goods with mark
  criminal offences, and, **20.41**

Aiding and abetting
  criminal offences, and, **20.47–20.55**

**Agreement on Trade-Related Aspects of
  Intellectual Property Rights**
  counterfeit goods, and, **17.5**

Alteration of registration
  Community trade marks, and, **27.3–27.4**
  generally, **9.12–9.13**

Amendment of applications
  Community trade marks, and
    generally, **26.12**
    publication, **26.13**
  generally, **8.15**

'Any sign'
  definition of trade mark, and, **4.3**

Appeals
  appointed person, to
    conduct of hearings, **16.32–16.33**

Appeals–*contd*
appointed person. to–*contd*
evidence, **16.28–16.31**
generally, **16.24–16.26**
security for costs, **16.34**
Boards of Appeal, to
generally, **29.1**
procedure, **29.3–29.15**
relevant decisions, **29.2**
European Court of Justice, to, **17.33, 29.16**
High Court, to, **16.22–16.23, 16.36**
prosecution of marks, and
appointed person, to, **16.24–16.34**
Court of Appeal, to, **16.57**
generally, **2.39–2.40, 8.12, 16.18**
High Court, to. **16.22–16.23**
judicial review, by, **16.19–16.21**
procedure, **2.41**

Appeals to appointed person
conduct of hearings, **16.32–16.33**
evidence
examination of witnesses, **16.29**
generally, **16.28**
reply, in, **16.31**
statutory declarations, **16.30**
generally, **16.24–16.26**
procedure
conduct of hearings, **16.32–16.33**
evidence, **16.28–16.31**
generally, **16.27**
security for costs, **16.34**

Appeals to Boards of Appeal
generally, **29.1**
procedure
decisions, **29.12–29.14**
examination, **29.10–29.11**
formalities, **29 3**
inadmissibility, **29.4–29.5**
interlocutory revision, **29.8**
joinder, **29.6**
questions of general interest, on, **29.9**
reimbursement of fees, **29.15**
remission, **29.7**
relevant decisions, **29.2**

Appeals to Court of Appeal
prosecution of marks, and, **16.57**

Appeals to European Court of Justice
Community trade marks, and, **17.33, 29.16**

Appeals to High Court
prosecution of marks, and, **16.22–16.23, 16.36**

Application of infringing mark to goods
generally, **20.35–20.36**
mistaken identity, **20.39**
packaging, **20.37–20.38**

Applications for action
contents, **19.48–19.56**

Applications for action–*contd*
determination
Consequential Provisions Regulations (UK),
19.95–19.104
Customs Regulations (UK), **19.85–19.94**
effects, **19.73–19.83**
generally, **19.70–19.72**
generally, **19.44–19.47**
fee, **19.57**
procedures
prospective, **19.68–19.69**
retrospective, **19.60–19.67**
submission, **19.58**

Applications for registration
amendment, **8.15**
appeals
appointed person, to, **16.24–16.34**
Court of Appeal, to, **16.57**
generally, **8.12, 16.18**
High Court, to, **16.22–16.23**
judicial review, by, **16.19–16.21**
Community trade marks, and
amendment, **26.12–26.13**
contents, **25.2–25.3**
examination, **17.8–17.11, 26.2–26.6**
evidence, **17.16**
filing, **17.5–17.7, 25.1**
form, **17.14–17.15**
generally, **17.14–17.21, 26.1**
hearings, **17.17**
language, **17.18**
observations, **26.14–26.15**
opposition, **17.22–17.23, 26.16–26.24**
publication, **17.12, 26.11**
registration, **17.13, 26.36**
restriction, **26.12**
search, **26.7–26.10**
time limits, **17.19**
withdrawal, **26.12**
contents, **8.1–8.2**
date, **16.6**
division, **8.16–8.17**
examination, **16.7**
filing date, **8.3**
generally, **16.4**
hearings, **8.11**
manner, **16.5**
merger, **8.18**
objections
Registrar, by, **16.8**
third parties, by, **16.9–16.15**
opposition
concurrent use, and, **16.14–16.15**
formal, **16.10–16.12**
generally, **16.9**
informal, **16.13**
pending at commencement, **8.21**
post-acceptance procedure
publication, **8.13–8.14**
restrictions of goods and services, **8.15**
withdrawal of application, **8.15**

Applications for registration–*contd*
priority
generally, **8.4**
information requirements, **8.7**
other countries, **8.6**
Paris Convention countries, **8.5**
transitional provisions, 8.8
procedure
examination, **16.7**
generally, **16.4**–**16.6**
objection, **8.10**, **16.8**
opposition, **16.9**–**16.13**
search, **8.9**
restrictions of goods and services, **8.15**
search, **8.9**, **16.7**
series of marks, **8.19**–**8.20**
withdrawal, **8.15**

Armorial bearings
international organisations, of, **5.113**–**5.114**

Arms or insignia
absolute grounds for refusal, and, **5.115**

Assignment
generally, **11.4**
Paris Convention, and, **22.13**
pre-31st October 1994 assignment, **11.5**

Attempts
criminal offences, and, **20.69**–**20.75**

Bad faith, applications in
absolute grounds for refusal, and, **5.118**–**5.121**

Basic grounds of refusal
designate characteristics of goods or services,
signs which
foreign language words, **5.67**
generally, **5.33**–**5.56**
geographical names, **5.57**–**5.64**
'Penguin' , **5.68**
surnames, **5.66**
time of production or rendering of services,
5.65
devoid of distinctiveness, signs which are
famous persons, names and pictures of,
5.50–**5.51**
forenames, **5.48**
full names, **5.49**
generally, **5.23**–**5.24**
geographical names, **5.39**
numerals, **5.37**–**5.38**
pictorial marks, **5.28**–**5.34**
proviso to ground, **5.52**
single letters, **5.36**
stylised letters, **5.36**
stylised words, **5.35**
surnames, **5.40**–**5.47**
words, **5.25**–**5.27**
examples of decisions
generally, **5.70**–**5.71**
list, **5.72**
generic signs, **5.69**

Basic grounds of refusal–*contd*
introduction, **5.13**–**5.14**
outside the definition of trade mark, signs
which are
colours, **5.22**
generally, **5.15**–**5.21**
smells, **5.22**
sounds, **5.22**
provisos
acquired distinctiveness, **5.74**–**5.88**
introduction, **5.73**
prior rights, **5.89**–**5.91**
restricting specification, **5.92**

Border controls
and see COUNTERFEIT GOODS
and see INFRINGING GOODS
and see SEIZURE OR DETENTION OF GOODS
domestic procedure
condemnation procedure, **18.6**–**18.72**
introduction, **18.1**–**18.5**
pre-condemnation procedure, **18.73**–**18.123**
EC procedure
pre-condemnation procedure, **19.1**–**19.161**
pre-condemnation procedure (EC)
applications for action, **19.45**–**19.69**
article 3 notices, **19.70**–**19.104**
article 6 notices, **19.105**–**19.124**
article 7 notices, **19.125**–**19.129**
Community Customs Code, **19.8**–**19.18**
conditions precedent, **19.19**–**19.43**
destruction of goods, **19.130**
liability for failure to detain goods,
19.131–**19.136**
introduction, **18.73**–**18.79**, **19.1**–**19.7**
miscellaneous provisions,**19.141**
notification of suspension, **19.105**–**19.124**
penal sanctions, **19.138**–**19.140**
travellers luggage, **19.137**
pre-condemnation procedure (UK)
defences, **18.111**–**18.119**
generally, **18.81**–**18.83**
interlocutory declarations, **18.1014**–**18.104**
introduction, **18.73**–**18.80**
notice of importation of infringing goods,
18.84–**18.88**
seizure of infringing goods, **18.91**–**18.110**
subsequent proceedings, **18.1206**–**18.123**
seizure or detention of goods
condemnation procedure, **18.11**–**18.72**
method, **18.6**–**18.10**
pre-condemnation procedure (EC),
19.1–**19.161**
pre-condemnation procedure (UK),
18.73–**18.123**
purpose, **18.1**–**18.5**

Brussels Convention 1968
infringement proceedings, and, **31.2**

Cancellation of marks
Community trade marks, and
appeals, **17.27**
generally, **17.25**

Cancellation of marks–*contd*
Community trade marks, and–*contd*
appeals, **17.27**
invalidity, **17.26**
revocation, **17.26**

Capable of distinguishing
definition of trade mark, and, **4.12–4.13**

Capable of graphic representation
colour marks, **4.6**
generally, **4.4–4 5**
smells, **4.10**
sounds, **4.9**
three-dimensional marks, **4.6**
word marks, **4.7–4.8**

Certification marks
background, **10.1–10.2**
definition
differences from ordinary marks, **10.4**
generally, **10.3**
generally, **4.2**
infringement, **10.9**
invalidity, **10.10**
pending applications, **10.8**
regulations as to use
amendment, **10.7**
examination, **10.6**
existing marks, **10.8**
generally, **10 5**
revocation, **10.10**

Charities
definition of trade mark, and, **4.13**

Civil Procedure Rules
generally, **16.53–16**

Civil proceedings
infringement of marks, for
High Court, **16.43–16.51**
introduction, **16.38**
introduction, **16.1**
passing off, for, **16.52**
prosecution of marks, for
appeals to appointed person, **16.24–16.34**
appeals to Court of Appeal, **16.57**
appeals to High Court, **16.22–16.23**
application, **16.4–16.6**
examination, **16.7**
introduction, **16.2–16.3**
judicial review, **16.18–16.21**
objections, **16.8**
opposition, **16.9–16.15**
Registration, **16.16–16.17**
validity of marks, for
High Court, **16.43–16.51**
introduction, **16.38**
Trade Marks Registry, **16.39–16.42**

Classification of goods and services
background, **2.5**
Community trade marks, and, **25.3**

Classification of goods and services–*contd*
generally, **2.6–2.7**
goods, **2.8**

Collective marks
definition
differences from ordinary marks, **10.12**
generally, **10.11**
generally, **4.2**
infringement, **10.16**
invalidity, **10.17**
Paris Convention, and, **22.26**
regulations as to use
amendment, **10.15**
examination, **10.14**
generally, **10.13**
revocation, **10.17**

Colour
graphic representation, and, **4.6**
absolute grounds for refusal, and, **5.22**

Common field of activity
misrepresentation, and, **14.32–14.34**

Community collective marks
absolute grounds for refusal, **30.4**
definition, **30.2–30.3**
infringement, **30.9**
introduction, **30.1**
invalidity, **30.11**
regulations as to use
amendment, **30.9**
examination, **30.8**
generally, **30.5–30.7**
revocation, **30.10**

Community Customs Code
generally, **19.8–19.9**
introduction, **19.5**
presentation, **19.16–19.18**
supervision, **19.13–19.15**
tariff system, **19.10–19.12**

Community trade marks
absolute grounds of refusal, **24.9–24.16**
administrative decisions, **17.24**
amendment
application, of, **26.12**
publication, in, **26.13**
appeals to Boards of Appeal
appealable decisions, **29.2**
decisions, **29.12–29.14**
examination, **29.10–29.11**
formalities, **29.3**
generally, **29.1**
inadmissibility, **29.4–29.5**
interlocutory revision, **29.8**
joinder, **29.6**
questions of general interest, on, **29.9**
reimbursement of fees, **29.15**
remission, **29.7**

Community trade marks–*contd*
appeals to ECJ, **17.33**, **29.16**
applications
  amendment, **26.12–26.13**
  contents, **25.2–25.3**
  examination, **17.8–17.11**, **26.2–26.6**
  evidence, **17.16**
  filing, **17.5–17.7**, **25.1**
  form, **17.14–17.15**
  generally, **17.14–17.21**, **26.1**
  hearings, **17.17**
  language, **17.18**
  observations, **26.14–26.15**
  opposition, **17.22–17.23**, **26.16–26.24**
  publication, **17.12**, **26.11**
  registration, **17.13**, **26.36**
  restriction, **26.12**
  search, **26.7–26.10**
  time limits, **17.19**
  withdrawal, **26.12**
cancellation
  appeals, **17.27**
  generally, **17.25**
  invalidity, **17.26**
  revocation, **17.26**
classification of goods and services, **25.3**
condemnation, **23.19–23.20**
conversion of CTM
  generally, **23.16**, **24.24–24.25**
  refusal, on, **26.35–26.36**
  revocation, on, **27.49**
costs, **17.21**, **28.34**
decisions
  administrative, **17.24**
  contents, **28.10**
  generally, **17.20**
definition, **24.2–24.4**
duration
  generally, **27.1**
  renewal, **27.2**
EC Decisions, **23.10**
EC Regulation
  appeals, **29.1–29.16**
  arrangement, **23.26–23.28**
  filing procedure, **25.1–25.16**
  general provisions, **24.1–24.59**
  implementation, **23.9**
  infringement proceedings, **31.1–31.33**
  interpretation, **23.24–23.25**
  introduction, **23.1**
  languages, **23.5–23.7**
  loss of rights, **27.1–27.49**
  miscellaneous procedures, **28.1–28.45**
  purpose, **23.2**
  registration procedure, **26.1–26.36**
  scheme, **23.3–23.4**
effects
  acquiescence, **24.35**
  conferred rights, **24.29–24.30**
  exhaustion of rights, **24.33–24.34**
  generally, **24.26**
  limitations, **24.31–24.32**
  use in dictionaries, **24.27–24.28**
evidence, **17.16**, **28.13**

Community trade marks–*contd*
examination
  absolute grounds of refusal, **17.11**,
    26.4–26.6
  generally, **26.2–26.3**
  OHIM's own motion, **28.11–28.12**
  other formalities, **17.9**
  preliminary, **17.8**
  relative grounds of refusal, **17.10**
exhibition priority
  effect, **25.16**
  generally, **25.12**
seniority of national mark, **25.13–25.15**
false representation, **23.21**
fees, **28.33**
filing of application
  communications, **17.7**
  date, **25.4**
  generally, **17.5**, **25.1**
  time limits, **17.6**
grounds for refusal
  absolute grounds, **24.9–24.16**
  generally, **24.8**
  relative grounds, **24.17–24.23**
hearings, **17.17**
information, provision of
  administrative co-operation, **28.40**
  electronic databank, **28.39**
  file inspection, **28.36–28.37**
  generally, **28.35**
  periodical publications, **28.38**
infringement
  acquiescence, **24.35**
  conferred rights, **24.29–24.30**
  exhaustion of rights, **24.33–24.34**
  generally, **17.28–17.29**
  jurisdiction of court, **17.30–17.32**
  generally, **24.26**
  limitations, **24.31–24.32**
  national law, and, **24.36**
  procedure, **31.1–31.33**
  proprietors of other rights, **24.37**
  use in dictionaries, **24.27–24.28**
infringement proceedings
  appeals, **31.21**
  applicable law, **31.17**
  counterclaims, **31.13–31.16**
  forum, **31.5–31.10**
  generally, **31.1–31.2**
  jurisdiction, **31.11**
  protective measures, **31.19**
  related actions, **31.22–31.33**
  relevant courts, **31.3–31.4**
  remedies, **31.18–31.20**
  validity of mark, **31.12**
inspection of files, **28.36–28.37**
interruption of proceedings, **28.7–28.9**
introduction, **17.1–17.2**
invalidity
  absolute grounds, **27.19–27.21**
  acquiescence, **27.25–27.27**
  appeals, **17.27**
  effects, **27.29–27.33**
  generally, **17.25–17.26**, **27.18**

Community trade marks–*contd*
  invalidity–*contd*
    procedure, **27.34–27.48, 31.1–31.33**
    relative grounds, **27.22–27.24**
    UK Regulations, **23.15**
  languages
    EC Regulation, **23.5–23.7**
    generally, **17.18, 28.45**
  loss of rights
    acquiescence, **27.25–27.27**
    generally, **27.9**
    invalidity, **27.18–27.48**
    revocation, **27.10–27.17, 27.25–27.48**
    surrender, **27.8–27.9**
    non-use, **24.38–24.43**
  notifications to OHIM
    advertisement, by, **28.24–28.25**
    deposit at Office, by, **28.22**
    electronic means, by, **28.23**
    fax, by, **28.23**
    form, **28.15, 28.44**
    generally, **28.14**
    hand, by, **28.21**
    irregularities, **28.26**
    post, by, **28.16–28.20**
    observations, **26.14–26.15**
  opposition
    admissibility, **26.25–26.26**
    examination, **26.27–26.33**
    generally, **17.22, 26.16**
    language, **26.23–26.24**
    multiple oppositions, **26.34**
    procedure, **17.23, 26.17–26.22**
  prior application, priority based on
    effect, **25.10–25.11**
    generally, **25.6–25.8**
    procedure, **25.9**
  priority
    exhibition priority, **25.12–25.15**
    generally, **25.5**
    prior application, priority based on,
      25.6–25.11
  professional privilege, **23.22**
  property rights
    bankruptcy proceedings, **24.56**
    effects, **24.59**
    generally, **24.44–24.49**
    in rem, **24.55**
    levy of execution, **24.55**
    licensing, **24.57–24.58**
    transfer, **24.50–24.54**
  proprietors, **24.5–24.7**
  publication, **17.12, 26.11**
  refunds, **28.33**
  refusal
    absolute grounds, **24.9–24.16**
    generally, **24.8**
    relative grounds, **24.17–24.23**
  register, amendment of
    CTM registration, **27.3–27.4**
    other details, **27.5–27.6**
  registration
    alteration, **27.3–27.4**
    generally, **17.13, 26.36**

Community trade marks–*contd*
  registration–*contd*
    seniority claims, **27.7**
    relative grounds of refusal, **24.17–24.23**
    representation, **28.41–28.43**
    restitutio in integrum, **27.28–27.31**
  restriction of application, **26.12**
  revocation
    appeals, **17.27**
    generic marks, **27.15**
    effects, **27.28–27.33**
    generally, **17.25–17.26, 27.10–27.11**
    misleading marks, **27.16**
    non-use, **24.38–24.43, 27.12–27.14**
    procedure, **27.34–27.48, 31.1–31.33**
    proprietor not qualified, **27.17**
    UK regulations, **23.15**
    search, **26.7–26.10**
    surrender, **27.8–27.9**
  threats, **23.18**
  time limits
    expiry, **28.5–28.6**
    extensions, **28.3–28.4**
    generally, **17.19, 28.2**
  UK Regulations
    background, **23.11–23.13**
    condemnation, **23.19–23.20**
    conversion of CTM, **23.16**
    false representation, **23.21**
    introduction, **23.14**
    invalidity, **23.15**
    professional privilege, **23.22**
    revocation, **23.15**
    threats, **23.18**
  use
    generally, **24.38–24.43**
    restrictions, **24.37**
  withdrawal of application, **26.12**

Community Trade Marks Courts
  designation, **23.17**
  generally, **17.28–17.29**
  jurisdiction, **17.30–17.32**

Comptroller-General
  generally, **2.1**
  liability, **2.2**
  prosecution of marks, and, **16.3**

Concurrent registration
  international marks, and, **21.36–21.37**

Condemnation
  claimant's notice
    failure to serve, **18.13**
    generally, **18.12**
    HMC&E response, **18.14–18.15**
  Community trade marks, and, **23.19–23.20**
  county court, in
    allocation, **18.34–18.36**
    commencement of proceedings,
      18.38–18.39
    costs, **18.43–18.44**
    disclosure, **18.40–18.42**

Condemnation–*contd*
county court, in–*contd*
financial limits, **18.31–18.33**
general procedure, **18.11–18.26**
jurisdiction, **18.30**
territorial jurisdiction, **18.37**
evidence
burden of proof, **18.24–18.25**
conduct of proceedings, **18.26**
generally, **18.18**
rebuttable presumptions, **18.19–18.23**
generally
claimant's notice, **18.12–18.14**
evidence, **18.18–18.26**
notice of liability to forfeiture, **18.11**
security for costs, 18.16–18.17
stay of proceedings, **18.15**
High Court, in
allocation, **18.34–18.36**
commencement of proceedings,
18.38–18.39
costs, **18.43–18.44**
disclosure, **18.40–18.42**
financial limits, **18.31–18.33**
general procedure, **18.11–18.26**
introduction, **18.27–18.29**
territorial jurisdiction, **18.37**
international marks, and
generally, **21.31**
offences, **21.32**
magistrates' court, in
amendment of complaint, **18.57–18.68**
commencement of proceedings,
18.51–18.53
costs, **18.69–18.72**
evidence, **18.54–18.56**
generally, **18.45**
jurisdiction, **18.46–18.50**
notice of liability to forfeiture
claimant's response, **18.12–18.14**
generally, **18.11**
security for costs, **18.16–18.17**
stay of proceedings, **18.15**

Confidentiality
Registry procedure, and, **2.23–2.24**

Conflict with rights
earlier rights
effect, **6.77**
examples of decisions, **6.78**
generally, **6.74–6.75**
infringement of copyright, **6.79**
scope, **6.76**
earlier trade marks
identical marks and identical goods or
services, **6.8–6.13**
identical marks but dissimilar goods or
services, **6.55–6.71**
introduction, **6.7**
meaning, **6.3–6.5**
no identical marks or goods but similar
goods or services, **6.14–6.54**
priority of use, **6.6**

Conflict with rights–*contd*
earlier trade marks–*contd*
well-known trade marks, **6.72–6.73**
honest concurrent use
effects, **6.82–6.83**
generally, **6.80**
scope, **6.81**
identical marks and identical goods or services
identity of goods or services, **6.13**
identity of marks, **6.9–6.12**
introduction, **6.8**
identical marks but dissimilar goods or
services
detriment, **6.61–6.71**
generally, **6.55–6.56**
likelihood of confusion, **6.57–6.58**
reputation, 6.59–6.60
unfair advantage, **6.61–6.71**
identity of marks
added matter, **6.12**
colours, **6.10–6.11**
generally, **6.9**
introduction
meaning, **6.1**
removal of Registrar's powers, **6.2**
likelihood of confusion
Cannon case, **6.41–6.45**
The European case, **6.46–6.49**
generally, **6.26–6.31**
meaning, **6.32**
recent decisions, **6.50–6.52**
Sabel decision, **6.38–6.40**
Wagamama decision, **6.33–6.37**
meaning, **6.1**
no identical marks or goods but similar goods
or services
examples of decisions, **6.17–6.19**
families of marks, **6.53–6.54**
generally, **6.14–6.16**
likelihood of confusion, **6.32–6.52**
separate consideration of marks and goods
or services, **6.26–6.31**
similarity between goods or services,
6.20–6.25
passing off, and, **6.74**
reputation, marks with, **6.59–6.60**
well-known trade marks, **6.72–6.73**

Consent
criminal offences, and
counterfeit goods, **20.30**
generally, **20.20–20.24**
parallel imports, **20.25–20.29**

Conspiracy
defraud, to, **20.85–20.90**
generally, **20.76–20.79**
sentencing, **20.80**
statutory conspiracy
actus reus, **20.82**
generally, **20.81**
mens rea, **20.83–20.84**

Contrary to law, marks being
absolute grounds for refusal, and, **5.107**

Conversion of marks–*contd*
Community trade marks, and
generally, **23.16**, **24.24–24.25**
refusal, on, **26.35–26.36**
revocation, on, **27.49**
international marks, and, **21.34–21.35**

Co-ownership
co-owner's rights, **11.3**
generally, **11.2**

Correction of irregularities
Registry procedure, and, **2.25**

Costs
Community trade marks, and, **17.21**, **28.34**
generally, **2.43**
security, **2.36–2.37**

Counselling
criminal offences, and, **20.56–20.57**

Counterfeit goods
condemnation, and
claimant's notice, **18.12–18.14**
county court, in, **18.27–18.447**
evidence, **18.18–18.26**
High Court, in, **18.27–18.44**
magistrate's court, in, **18.45–18.72**
notice of liability to forfeiture, **18.11**
security for costs, **18.16–18.17**
stay of proceedings, **18.15**
criminal proceedings, and
false representation of marks, **20.13**
introduction, **20.1–20.5**
legislative background, **20.6–20.12**
unauthorised use of marks, **20.14–20.129**
meaning, **18.73–18.76**
Paris Convention, and, **22.28–22.29**
seizure or detention, and
condemnation procedure, **18.11–18.72**
method, **18 6–18.10**
pre-condemnation procedure (EC),
19.1–19.161
pre-condemnation procedure (UK),
18.73–18.123
purpose, **18.1–18.5**

County courts
jurisdiction, **16.55–16.56**

Court's powers
appeal, on
generally, **2.39–2.40**
procedure, **2.41**
generally, **2.38**
Registrar's appearance, **2.42**

Criminal proceedings
false representation of marks, **20.13**
introduction, **20.1–20.5**
legislative background, **20.6–20.11**
Trade Marks Act 1994, under
generally, **20.13**

Criminal proceedings–*contd*
Trade Marks Act 1994, under
unauthorised use of marks, **20.14–20.129**
unauthorised use of marks
and see UNAUTHORISED USE
actus reus, **20.31–20.40**
advertising, **20.41**
defences, **20.95–20.106**
generally, **20.13–20.14**
inchoate offences, **20.45–20.90**
mens rea, **20.15–20.30**
other elements, **20.91–20.94**
procedure, **20.115–20.180**
sentencing, **20.107–20.114**
tools of deception, **20.42–20.44**

Cross-examination of witnesses–*contd*
Registry procedure, and, **2.34**

CTM Regulations
and see COMMUNITY TRADE MARKS
appeals, **29.1–29.16**
arrangement, **23.26–23.28**
filing procedure, **25.1–25.16**
general provisions, **24.1–24.59**
implementation, **23.9**
infringement proceedings, **31.1–31.33**
interpretation, **23.24–23.25**
introduction, **23.1**
languages, **23.5–23.7**
loss of rights, **27.1–27.49**
miscellaneous procedures, **28.1–28.45**
purpose, **23.2**
registration procedure, **26.1–26.36**
scheme, **23.3–23.4**

Customs procedures
and see COUNTERFEIT GOODS
and see INFRINGING GOODS
and see SEIZURE OR DETENTION OF GOODS
domestic procedure
condemnation procedure, **18.6–18.72**
introduction, **18.1–18.5**
pre-condemnation procedure, **18.73–18.123**
EC procedure
pre-condemnation procedure, **19.1–19.161**
pre-condemnation procedure (EC)
applications for action, **19.44–19.59**
article 3 notices, **19.68–19.72** conditions
precedent, **19.19–19.43**
destruction of goods, **19.130**
liability of customs officers, **19.131–19.136**
introduction, **18.73–18.79**
miscellaneous provisions, **19.141**
penal sanctions, **19.138–19.140** purpose,
19.1–19.3
retrospective procedure, **19.60–19.67**
scope, **19.4–19.7**
suspension of goods, **19.73–19.104**
travellers luggage, **19.137**
pre-condemnation procedure (UK)
defences, **18.111–18.119**
generally, **18.81–18.83**, **19.1–19.2**
interlocutory declarations, **18.101–18.104**

Customs procedures–*contd*
  pre-condemnation procedure (EC)–*contd*
    introduction, **18.73–18.80**
    notice of importation of infringing goods,
      18.84–18.88
    seizure of infringing goods, **18.91–18.110**
    subsequent proceedings, **18.120–18.123**
    seizure or detention of goods
    condemnation procedure, **18.11–18.72**
    method, **18.6–18.10**
    pre-condemnation procedure (EC),
      19.1–19.161
    pre-condemnation procedure (UK),
      18.73–18.123
    purpose, **18.1–18.5**

Damage
  passing off, and
    erosion of goodwill, **14.47–14.48**
    generally, **14.41–14.46**

Damages
  threats, and, **13.18–13.19**

Dealings with marks
  assignment
    generally, **11.4**
    pre-31st October 1994 assignment, **11.5**
  Community trade marks, and
    bankruptcy proceedings, **24.56**
    effects, **24.59**
    generally, **24.44–24.49**
    in rem, **24.55**
    levy of execution, **24.55**
    licensing, **24.57–24.58**
    transfer, **24.50–24.54**
  co-ownership
    co-owner's rights, **11.3**
    generally, **11.2**
  equities, **11.6**
  generally, **11.1**
  licensing
    exclusive licences, **11.10**, **11.12**
    general licences, **11.9**
    generally, **11.7–11.8**
    licensee's rights, **11.13–11.14**
    limited licences, **11.9**
    pre-31st October 1994 licences, **11.11**
  registration of transactions
    amendment of particulars, **11.22**
    applications, **11.17–11.20**
    consequences of delay or failure, **11.21**
    generally, **11.15**
    registrable transactions, **11.16**
  trusts, **11.6**

Deceptive marks
  absolute grounds for refusal, and, **5.102–5.106**

Decision-making
  generally, **2.35**
  security for costs, **2.36–2.37**

Declarations
  threats, and, **13.18**

Defences
  criminal offences, and
    exhaustion of rights, **20.103**
    generally, **20.95**
    reasonable belief that use not an infringing
      use, **20.96–20.99**
    use to identify goods, **20.104–20.106**

Definition of trade mark
  any sign, **4.3**
  capable of graphic representation
    colour marks, **4.6**
    generally, **4.4–4.5**
    smells, **4.10**
    sounds, **4.9**
    three-dimensional marks, **4.6**
    word marks, **4.7–4.8**
  generally, **4.1–4.2**

Descriptive marks
  passing off, and
    generally, **14.35–14.36**
    secondary meaning, **14.37**

**Designate characteristics of goods or services,
signs which**
  foreign language words, **5.67**
  generally, **5.33–5.56**
  geographical names, **5.57–5.64**
  'Penguin', **5.68**
  surnames, **5.66**
  time of production or rendering of services,
    5.65

Devoid of distinctiveness, signs which are
  famous persons, names and pictures of,
    5.50–5.51
  forenames, **5.48**
  full names, **5.49**
  generally, **5.23–5.24**
  geographical names, **5.39**
  numerals, **5.37–5.38**
  pictorial marks, **5.28–5.34**
  proviso to ground, **5.52**
  single letters, **5.36**
  stylised letters, **5.36**
  stylised words, **5.35**
  surnames, **5.40–5.47**
  words, **5.25–5.27**

Disclaimers
  Infringement, and, **12.49**
  International marks, and, **21.23**

Disclosure
  criminal offences, and
    compulsory, **20.174–20.175**
    continuing obligations, **20.178–20.180**
    generally, **20.160 20.164**
    primary, **20.172–20.173**
    privileged evidence, **20.165–20.171**
    voluntary, **20.176 20.177**

Discovery
Registry procedure, and, **2.30–2.33**

Disposal of goods with infringing mark
course of business, **20.33**
generally, **20.40**

Dispute resolution
TRIPS Agreement, and, **22.53–22.54**

Division of applications
applications for registration, and, **8.16–8.17**

Domestic procedure
infringement of marks, for
High Court, **16.43–16.51**
introduction, **16.38**
introduction, **16.1**
passing off, for, **16.52**
prosecution of marks, for
appeals to appointed person, **16.24–16.34**
appeals to Court of Appeal, **16.57**
appeals to High Court, **16.22–16.23**
application, **16.4–16.6**
examination, **16.7**
introduction, **16.2–16.3**
judicial review, **16.18–16.21**
objections, **16.8**
opposition, **16.9–16.15**
Registration, **16.16–16.17**
validity of marks, for
High Court, **16.43–16.51**
introduction, **16.38**
Trade Marks Registry, **16.39–16.42**

Duration of registration
Community trade marks, and
generally, **27.1**
renewal, **27.2**
generally, **9.8**
TRIPS Agreement, and, **22.47**

Earlier rights, conflict with
effect, **6.77**
examples of decisions, **6.78**
generally, **6.74–6.75**
infringement of copyright, **6.79**
scope, **6.76**

Earlier trade marks, conflict with
identical marks and identical goods or services
identity of goods or services, **6.13**
identity of marks, **6.9–6.12**
introduction, **6.8**
identical marks but dissimilar goods or
services
detriment, **6.61–6.71**
generally, **6.55–6.56**
likelihood of confusion, **6.57–6.58**
reputation, **6.59–6.60**
unfair advantage, **6.61–6.71**
identity of marks
added matter, **6.12**
colours, **6.10–6.11**

Earlier trade marks, conflict with–*contd*
identity of marks–*contd*
generally, **6.9**
infringement, and, **12.2**
introduction, **6.7**
likelihood of confusion
Cannon case, **6.41–6.45**
The European case, **6.46–6.49**
generally, **6.26–6.31**
meaning, **6.32**
recent decisions, **6.50–6.52**
Sabel decision, **6.38–6.40**
Wagamama decision, **6.33–6.37**
meaning, **6.3–6.5**
no identical marks or goods but similar goods
or services–*contd*
examples of decisions, **6.17–6.19**
families of marks, **6.53–6.54**
generally, **6.14–6.16**
likelihood of confusion, **6.32–6.52**
separate consideration of marks and goods
or services, **6.26–6.31**
similarity between goods or services,
6.20–6.25
priority of use, **6.6**
well-known trade marks, **6.72–6.73**

EC Directive 1989
generally, **1.1**
implementation, **1.18**
interpretation, **1.19–1.22**

EC Regulation 3295/94, procedure under
applications for action
contents, **19.48–19.56**
determination, **19.70–19.104**
generally, **19.44–19.47**
fee, **19.57**
procedures, **19.60–19.69**
submission, **19.58**
article 3 notices
Consequential Provisions Regulations (UK),
19.95–19.104
Customs Regulations (UK), **19.85–19.94**
effects, **19.73–19.83**
generally, **19.70–19.72**
article 6 notices
generally, **19.105**
recipients, **19.106–19.124**
article 7 notices
generally, **19.125–19.129**
other EC language texts, **19.153–19.161**
TRIPS, and, **19.142–19.152**
Community Customs Code
generally, **19.8–19.9**
introduction, **19.5**
presentation, **19.16–19.18**
supervision, **19.13–19.15**
tariff system, **19.10–19.12**
counterfeit goods
generally, **19.34–19.36**
test, **19.37–19.43**

EC Regulation 3295/94, procedure under
—contd
conditions precedent
counterfeit goods, **19.34–19.43**
customs supervision, **19.22–19.26**
free-zone placement, **19.31–19.33**
goods entered for specified purposes and
declared, **19.19–19.21**
introduction, **19.7**
re-exportation subject to notice, **19.32**
suspensive procedure, **19.27–19.30**
destruction of goods, **19.130**
liability for failure to detain goods
domestic law, and, **19.131–19.136**
generally, **19.131**
introduction, **18.73–18.79**
miscellaneous provisions, **19.141**
generally, **19.105**
recipients, **19.106–19.124**
parties, **19.6**
penal sanctions, **19.138–19.140**
procedures
applications for action, **19.45–19.69**
article 3 notices, **19.70–19.104**
article 6 notices, **19.105–19.124**
article 7 notices, **19.125–19.129**
destruction of goods, **19.130**
generally, **19.44**
notification of suspension, **19.105–19.124**
purpose, **19.1–19.3**
scope, **19.4–19.7**
travellers luggage, **19.137**

ECJ, references to
generally, **16.58**
procedure, **16.62–16.**
test, **16.59–16.61**

Emblems
foreign nations, of
flags, **5.112**
generally, **5.111**
international organisations, of
armorial bearings, **5.113–5.114**
flags, **5.113–5.114**
generally, **5.111**
names, **5.113–5.114**

Enforcement of rights
TRIPS Agreement, and, **22.50–22.51**

Equities
property rights, and, **11.6**

European procedure
appeals to CFI, **17.33**
cancellation of marks
appeals, **17.27**
generally, **17.25**
invalidity, **17.26**
revocation, **17.26**
infringement of marks
generally, **17.28–17.29**
jurisdiction of court, **17.30–17.32**
introduction, **17.1–17.2**

European procedure—*contd*
prosecution of marks
administrative decisions, **17.24**
appeals, **17.27**
examination, **17.8–17.11**
general procedure, **17.14–17.21**
filing of application, **17.5–17.7**
opposition, **17.22–17.23**
publication, **17.12**
registration, **17.13**

Evidence
appeals to appointed person
examination of witnesses, **16.29**
generally, **16.28**
reply, in, **16.31**
statutory declarations, **16.30**
applications
Community trade marks, **17.16, 28.13**
generally, **2.30–2.34**
condemnation procedure, and
burden of proof, **18.24–18.25**
conduct of proceedings, **18.26**
generally, **18.18**
rebuttable presumptions, **18.19–18.23**
criminal offences, and
business documents, **20.150–20.153**
disclosure, **20.160–20.180**
hearsay, **20.152**
introduction, **20.129**
registration of marks, **20.154–20.159**
Weights & Measures authorities, powers of,
20.129–20.149
witness statements, **20.15–20.153**
invalidity, **9.17**
magistrates' court, in, **18.54–18.56**
misrepresentation, **14.25–14.29**

Ex parte hearings
applications for registration, and, **8.11**

Examination
Community trade marks, and
absolute grounds of refusal, **17.11,
26.4–26.6**
generally, **26.2–26.3**
OHIM's own motion, **28.11–28.12**
other formalities, **17.9**
preliminary, **17.8**
relative grounds of refusal, **17.10**
generally, **16.7**
international marks, and, **21.16**

Exclusive licences
property rights, and, **11.10, 11.12**

Exhaustion of rights
EEA, within, **12.42–12.48**
generally, **12.34–12.36**
passing off, and, **14.53–14.57**
Silhouette decision, **12.37–12.40**
TRIPS Agreement, and, **22.44**
Zino Davidoff decision, **12.41**

Exhibition priority
effect, **25.16**
generally, **25.12**
seniority of national mark, **25.13–25.15**

Extension of time
generally, **2.27–2.28**
irregularities, **2.29**

False indications
Madrid Protocol, and, **21.33**
Paris Convention, and, **22.30**

False representation of marks
Community trade marks, and, **23.21**
generally, **20.13**
international marks, and, **21.33**

Famous persons, names and pictures of
absolute grounds for refusal, and, **5.50–5.51**

Filing date
Community trade marks, and, **25.4**
generally, **8.3**

Flags
foreign nations. of, **5.112**
international organisations, of, **5.113–5.114**
UK, of the, **5.110**

Foreign language words
absolute grounds for refusal, and, **5.67**

Foreign nations, emblems of
flags, **5.112**
generally, **5.111**

Forenames
absolute grounds for refusal, and, **5.48**

Formal opposition
generally, **16.10**
s 8 TMA 1994. **16.11–16.12**

Full names
absolute grounds for refusal, and, **5.49**

Function of trade mark
capable of distinguishing, **4.12–4.13**
generally, **4.11**
nature of trade or activity, **4.14–4.15**

Generic signs
absolute grounds for refusal, and, **5.69**
revocation, and, **7.18–7.19**

Geographical indications
TRIPS Agreement, and, **22.49**

Geographical names
designate characteristics of goods or services,
5.57–5.64
devoid of distinctiveness, **5.39**

Geographical origins–*contd*
absolute grounds for refusal, and, **5.86**

Goodwill
duration, **14.20**
generally, **14.12–14.14**
UK, in the, **14.15–14.19**

Goschen Committee recommendations, 1.10

High Court
appellate jurisdiction
generally, **16.36**
prosecution of marks, and, **16.22–16.23**
prosecution of marks, and,
Civil Procedure Rules, **16.53–16 54**
introduction, **16.35**
original jurisdiction
allocation, **16.49**
pplications, **16.44**
disclosure, **16.50–16.51**
generally, **16.43**
introduction, **16.38**
pleadings, **16.45–16.49**
passing off, and, **16.52**
supervisory jurisdiction
generally, **16.19, 16.37**
nature, **16.21**
procedure, **16.20**

Honest concurrent use
effects, **6.82–6.83**
generally, **6.80**
scope, **6.81**

Hours of business
Registry procedure, and, **2.16**

**Identical marks and identical goods or
services**
identity of goods or services, **6.13**
identity of marks
added matter, **6.12**
colours, **6.10–6.11**
generally, **6.9**
introduction, **6.8**

**Identical marks but dissimilar goods or
services**
detriment, **6.61–6.71**
generally, **6.55–6.56**
likelihood of confusion, **6.57–6.58**
reputation, **6.59–6.60**
unfair advantage, **6.61–6.71**

Immoral marks
absolute grounds for refusal, and, **5.102–5.106**

Informal opposition
prosecution of marks, and, **16.13**

Infringement
acquiescence, and
Community trade marks, and, **24.35**

Infringement–*contd*
  acquiescence, and–*contd*
    generally, **12.58–12.59**
  certification marks, and, **10.9**
  collective marks, and, **10.16**
  Community collective marks, and, **30.9**
  Community trade marks, and
    acquiescence, **24.35**
    conferred rights, **24.29–24.30**
    exhaustion of rights, **24.33–24.34**
    generally, **17.28–17.29**
    jurisdiction of court, **17.30–17.32**
    generally, **24.26**
    limitations, **24.31–24.32**
    national law, and, **24.36**
    procedure, **31.1–31.33**
    proprietors of other rights, **24.37**
    use in dictionaries, **24.27–24.28**
  conferred rights
    Community trade marks, and, **24.29–24.30**
    generally, **12.4**
    relevant proprietors, **12.5**
  definition
    conferred rights, **12.4–12.5**
    generally, **12.3**
    infringing acts, **12.6–12.15**
    limitations, **12.16–12.33**
  disclaimers, **12.49**
  earlier trade marks, and, **12.2**
  exhaustion of rights
    Community trade marks, and, **24.33–24.34**
    EEA, within, **12.42–12.48**
    generally, **12.34–12.36**
    Silhouette decision, **12.37–12.40**
    Zino Davidoff decision, **12.41**
  infringing acts
    generally, **12.6**
    in relation to goods and services,
      12.9–12.13
    principles, **12.14**
    use of a sign, **12.7–12.8**
  introduction, **12.1–12.3**
  labelling, **12.15**
  limitations
    Community trade marks, and, **24.31–24.32**
    descriptive matter, use of, **12.26–12.28**
    earlier right in particular locality, use of,
      12.31–12.33
    generally, **12.16**
    goods or services of proprietor, use on,
      12.17–12.21
    intended purpose of product, use necessary
      to, **12.29–12.30**
    own name, use of, **12.24–12.5**
    own registered mark, use of, **12.22–12.23**
  meaning
    course of trade, **12.10**
    generally, **12.6**
    in relation to goods and services,
      12.9–12.13
    use of a sign, **12.7–12.8**
  packaging materials, **12.15**
  procedure (OHIM)
    appeals, **31.21**

Infringement–*contd*
  procedure (OHIM)–*contd*
    applicable law, **31.17**
    counterclaims, **31.13–31.16**
    forum, **31.5–31.10**
    generally, **31.1–31.2**
    jurisdiction, **31.11**
    protective measures, **31.19**
    related actions, **31.22–31.33**
    relevant courts, **31.3–31.4**
    remedies, **31.18–31.20**
    validity of mark, **31.12**
  procedure (UK)
    allocation, **16.49**
    applications, **16.44**
    disclosure, **16.50–16.51**
    generally, **16.43**
    pleadings, **16.45–16.49**
    transitional provisions, **12.50–12.52**
  well-known marks, and
    generally, **12.53**
    likelihood of confusion, **12.57**
    meaning, **12.54–12.55**
    time of knowledge, **12.56**

Infringing goods
  condemnation, and
    claimant's notice, **18.12–18.14**
    county court, in, **18.27–18.447**
    evidence, **18.18–18.26**
    High Court, in, **18.27–18.44**
    magistrates' court, in, **18.45– 18.72**
    notice of liability to forfeiture, **18.11**
    security for costs, **18.16–18.17**
    stay of proceedings, **18.15**
  criminal proceedings, and
    false representation of marks, **20.13**
    introduction, **20.1–20.5**
    legislative background, **20.6–20.12**
    unauthorised use of marks, **20.14–20.129**
  international marks, and
    generally, **21.31**
    offences, **21.32**
  Paris Convention, and, **22.28–22.29**
  seizure or detention, and
    condemnation procedure, **18.11–18.72**
    method, **18.6–18.10**
    pre-condemnation procedure (UK),
      18.73–18.123
    purpose, **18.1–18.5**

Injunctions
  threats, and, **13.18**

Inspection
  confidentiality, **2.23–2.24**
  generally, **2.19–2.22**

International Bureau of WIPO
  international registration, and, **21.1**

**International Classification of Goods and
  Services**
  generally, **2.5**

International Classification of Goods and Services–*contd*
immoral marks, **5.102–5.106**

International conventions
and see under individual headings
generally, **1.1**
Madrid Agreement 1894
general provisions, **21.3–21.5**
introduction, **21.1–21.2**
purpose, **21.3**
Madrid Protocol 1989
general provisions, **21.14–21.39**
generally, **21.6–21.9**
implementation, **21.10–21.13**
introduction, **21.1–21.2**
miscellaneous provisions, **21.40–21.41**
Paris Convention 1883
background, **22.1**
general provisions, **22.5–22.37**
introduction, **22.3–22.4**
TRIP Agreement 1994
background, **22.2**
conclusions, **22.56**
final provisions, **22.55**
general provisions, **22.41–22.54**
introduction, **22.38–22.40**

International organisations, emblems of
armorial bearings, **5.113–5.114**
flags, **5.113–5.114**
generally, **5.111**
names, **5.113–5.114**
Olympic Symbol, **5.116–5.117**

International marks
acquiescence, **21.29**
basic registration, **21.38–21.39**
concurrent registration, **21.36–21.37**
condemnation
generally, **21.31**
offences, **21.32**
disclaimers, **21.23**
effect of international mark, **21.22**
false representation, **21.33**
infringing goods
generally, **21.31**
offences, **21.32**
introduction
application of rules, **21.12–21.13**
background, **21.1–21.2**
registration structure, **21.6–21.9**
statutory rules, **21.10–21.13**
invalidity
acquiescence, **21.29**
generally, **21.28**
procedure, **21.30**
licensing, **21-26**
miscellaneous provisions, **21.40–21.41**
procedure
date of protection, **21.19–21.21**
examination, **21.16**
generally, **21 14**
observations, **21.18**

International marks–*contd*
procedure–*contd*
opposition, **21.17**
priority, **21.15**
publication, **21.17**
property rights
generally, **21.25**
licensing, **21-26**
transaction notification, **21.27**
revocation
acquiescence, **21.29**
generally, **21.28**
procedure, **21.30**
threats, **21.24**
transaction notification, **21.27**
transformation to national application,
21.34–21.35

Interruption of use
discretion, and, **7.9**
effect, **7.16**
examples, **7.14–7.15**
generally, **7.5**
meaning
export packaging, **7.8**
generally, **7.6**
similar marks, **7.7**
partial cancellation
examples, **7.15**
generally, **7.13**
proper reasons, **7.10**
resumption of use, **7.11–7.12**
transitional provisions, **7.17**

Invalidity
acquiescence, **7.31–7.33**
certification marks, and, **10.10**
collective marks, and
Community marks, **30.11**
UK marks, **10.17**
Community collective marks, and, **30.11**
Community trade marks, and
absolute grounds, **27.19–27.21**
acquiescence, **27.25–27.27**
appeals, **17.27**
effects, **27.29–27.33**
generally, **17.25–17.26, 27.18**
procedure, **27.34–27.48, 31.1–31.33**
relative grounds, **27.22–27.24**
UK Regulations, **23.15**
effect, **7.29**
generally, **7.23–7.24**
grounds
absolute, **7.25–7.26**
relative, **7.27**
international marks, and
acquiescence, **21.29**
generally, **21.28**
procedure, **21.30**
invalid goods or services, **7.28**
procedure (OHIM)
appeals, **31.21**
applicable law, **31.17**
counterclaims, **31.13–31.16**

Invalidity–*contd*
  procedure (OHIM)–*contd*
    forum, **31.5–31.10**
    generally, **31.1–31.2**
    jurisdiction, **31.11**
    protective measures, **31.19**
    related actions, **31.22–31.33**
    relevant courts, **31.3–31.4**
    remedies, **31.18–31.20**
    validity of mark, **31.12**
  procedure (UK)
    application, **9.16**
    evidence, **9.17**
    generally, **9.15**
    intervention, **9.18**
    reference to court, **9.19–9.21**
  refusal of registration, and, **7.23**
  transitional provisions, **7.30**

Judicial review
  generally, **16.19**, **16.37**
  nature, **16.21**
  procedure, **16.20**

Labelling
  infringement, and, **12.15**

Languages
  Community trade marks, and
    EC Regulation, **23.5–23.7**
    generally, **17.18**, **28.45**

Letters
  absolute grounds for refusal, and, **5.36**

Licensing
  Community trade marks, and, **24.57–24.58**
  exclusive licences, **11.10**, **11.12**
  general licences, **11.9**
  generally, **11.7–11.8**
  international marks, and, **21.26**
  licensee's rights, **11.13–11.14**
  limited licences, **11.9**
  pre-31st October 1994 licences, **11.11**

Likelihood of confusion
  identical marks but dissimilar goods or
    services, and, **6.57–6.58**
  no identical marks or goods but similar goods
    or services, and
    Cannon case, **6.41–6.45**
    The European case, **6.46–6.49**
    generally, **6.26–6.31**
    meaning, **6.32**
    recent decisions, **6.50–6.52**
    Sabel decision, **6.38–6.40**
    Wagamama decision, **6.33–6.37**

Limited licences
  property rights, and, **11.9**

Loss of rights
  Community trade marks, and
    acquiescence, **27.25–27.27**

Loss of rights–*contd*
  Community trade marks, and–*contd*
    generally, **27.9**
    invalidity, **27.18–27.48**
    revocation, **27.10–27.17**, **27.25–27.48**
    surrender, **27.8–27.9**
  introduction, **7.1**
  invalidity
    acquiescence, **7.31–7.33**
    generally, **7.23–7.24**
    grounds, **7.25–7.30**
  rectification of the register
    generally, **7.34–7.36**
    Registrar's powers, **7.37–7.38**
  revocation
    discretion, **7.3–7.4**
    generally, **7.2**
    generic names, **7.18–7.19**
    misleading names, **7.20–7.22**
    non-use, **7.5–7.17**

Madrid Agreement 1894
  and see MADRID PROTOCOL 1989
  general provisions, **21.3–21.5**
  generally, **1.1**
  introduction, **21.1–21.2**
  purpose, **21.3**

Madrid Protocol 1989
  and see INTERNATIONAL REGISTRATIONS
  general provisions, **21.14–21.39**
  generally, **1.1**, **21.6–21.9**
  implementation, **21.10–21.13**
  introduction, **21.1–21.2**
  miscellaneous provisions, **21.40–21.41**

Malicious falsehood
  defamation, and, **15.2–15.14**
  emergency legislation, **15.20–15.21**
  generally, **15.15–15.16**
  trade marks, and, **15.17–15.18**

**Memorandum on the Creation of an EC
Trade Mark (EC Bulletin) 1976**
  function of marks, **1.12–1.15**

Merchandise Marks Act 1862
  generally, **1.8**

Merger of applications
  applications for registration, and, **8.18**

Misleading names
  revocation, and, **7.20–7.22**

Misrepresentation
  common field of activity, **14.32–14.34**
  confusion
    generally, **14.23–14.24**
    evidence, **14.25–14.29**
    nature, **14.30–14.31**
  descriptive marks
    generally, **14.35–14.36**
    secondary meaning, **14.37**
  generally, **14.21–14.22**

Misrepresentation–*contd*
inconsequential deception, **14.38–14.39**
momentary deception, **14.38–14.39**
taking advantage of developed market, **14.40**

Morality, marks contrary to
absolute grounds for refusal, and, **5.102–5.106**

National industrial property office
Paris Convention, and, **22.36–22.37**

National treatment
TRIPS Agreement, and, **22.43**

Nice Agreement 1957 (as revised)
generally, **2.5**
No identical marks or goods but similar
goods or services
examples of decisions, **6.17–6.19**
families of marks, **6.53–6.54**
generally, **6.14–6.16**
likelihood of confusion
Cannon case, **6.41–6.45**
The European case, **6.46–6.49**
generally, **6.26–6.31**
meaning, **6.32**
recent decisions, **6.50–6.52**
Sabel decision, **6.38–6.40**
Wagamama decision, **6.33–6.37**
separate consideration of marks and goods or
services, **6.26–6.31**
similarity between goods or services,
6.20–6.25

Non-use of marks
Community trade marks, and, **24.38–24.43**
discretion, and, **7.9**
effect, **7.16**
examples, **7.14–7.15**
generally, **7.5**
meaning
export packaging, **7.8**
generally, **7.6**
similar marks, **7.7**
partial cancellation
examples, **7.15**
generally, **7.13**
proper reasons, **7.10**
resumption of use, **7.11–7.12**
transitional provisions, **7.17**

Numerals
absolute grounds for refusal, and, **5.37–5.38**

Objections
international marks, and, **21.18**
Registrar, by, **16.8**
third parties, by
concurrent use, and, **16.14–16.15**
formal, **16.10–16.12**
generally, **16.9**
informal, **16.13**

Observations
Community trade marks, and, **26.14–26.15**
international marks, and, **21.18**

**Office for the Harmonisation of the Internal
Market (OHIM)**
administration, **23.4**
Community trade marks
and see COMMUNITY TRADE MARKS
administrative decisions, **17.24**
appeals, **17.33**
cancellation, **17.25–17.27**
introduction, **17.1–17.2**
prosecution, **17.5–17.23**
organisation, **23.8**
role, **17.3**
structure, **17.4**

Olympic Symbol
absolute grounds for refusal, and, **5.116–5.117**

Opposition to registration
Community trade marks, and
admissibility, **26.25–26.26**
examination, **26.27–26.33**
generally, **17.22, 26.16**
language, **26.23–26.24**
multiple oppositions, **26.34**
procedure, **17.23, 26.17–26.22**
concurrent use, and, **16.14–16.15**
formal opposition
generally, **16.10**
s 8 TMA 1994, **16.11–16.12**
generally, **16.9**
grounds
generally, **9.1**
proprietor of mark in Convention country,
9.2
informal opposition, **16.13**
international marks, and, **21.17**
procedure
evidence, **9.6**
generally, **9.3**
pre-31st October 1994 objections, **9.7**
timetable, **9.4–9.5**

**Outside the definition of trade mark, signs
which are**
colours, **5.22**
generally, **5.15–5.21**
smells, **5.22**
sounds, **5.22**

Packaging materials
infringement, and, **12.15**

Paris Convention 1883
background, **22.1**
general provisions
assignment, **22.13**
collective marks, **22.26**
counterfeit goods, **22.28–22.29**
effect in other countries, **22.14–22.22**
false indications, **22.30**

Paris Convention 1883–*contd*
  general provisions–*contd*
    filing, **22.11**
    generally, **22.5**
    national industrial property office,
      22.36–22.37
    nature of goods, **22.25**
    principles, **22.7**
    priority, **22.8**
    remedies, **22.34**
    scope, **22.6**
    service marks, **22.23**
    specially protected emblems, **22.12**
    temporary protection, **22.35**
    trade names, **22.27**
    unauthorised registration, **22.24**
    unfair competition, **22.31–22.33**
    user requirements, **22.9–22.10**
    well-known marks, **22.12**
  generally, **1.1**
  introduction, **22.3–22.4**
  rectification, and, **7.34**
  specially protected emblems, and, **5.111**
  unauthorised registration, and
    generally, **22.24**
    rectification, **7.34**
  well-known marks, and
    generally, **6.72–6.73**
    infringement, **12.1, 12.53–12.57**

Passing off
  background, **14.1–14.4**
  class-type actions
    defined class of goods, **14.67–14.70**
    differences from single trader actions, **14.66**
    generally, **14.64–14.65**
    misrepresentation, **14.71–14.73**
    parties, **14.74**
    representative proceedings, **14.75**
  confusion
    generally, **14.23–14.24**
    evidence, **14.25–14.29**
    nature, **14.30–14.31**
  damage
    erosion of goodwill, **14.47–14.48**
    generally, **14.41–14.46**
  descriptive marks
    generally, **14.35–14.36**
    secondary meaning, **14.37**
  elements
    damage, **14.41–14.48**
    generally, **14.5–14.11**
    goodwill, **14.12–14.20**
    misrepresentation, **14.21–14.22**
  exhaustion of rights, **14.53–14.57**
  goodwill
    duration, **14.20**
    generally, **14.12–14.14**
    UK, in the, **14.15–14.19**
  inconsequential deception, **14.38–14.39**
  instruments of deception
    common venture, **14.63**
    generally, **14.58–14.60**
    sale, **14.61**

Passing off–*contd*
  instruments of deception–*contd*
    supply, **14.62**
  meaning
    excluded situations, **14.8–14.9**
    factual issues, **14.10–14.11**
    generally, **14.5–14.7**
  misrepresentation
    common field of activity, **14.32–14.34**
    confusion, **14.23–14.24**
    descriptive marks, **14.35–14.37**
    evidence, **14.25–14.31**
    generally, **14.21–14.22**
    momentary deception, **14.38–14.39**
    taking advantage of developed market, **14.40**
  procedure, **16.52**
  relative grounds for refusal, and, **6.74**
  reverse form of, **14.49–14.52**

Patents, Designs and Trade Marks Act 1883
  generally, **1.9**

Patent Office
  classification of goods and services
    background, **2.5**
    generally, **2.6–2.7**
    goods, **2.8**
  Comptroller-General
    generally, **2.1**
    liability, **2.2**
  introduction
    classification of goods and services, **2.5–2.8**
    Comptroller-General, **2.1–2.2**
    register, **2.4**
    registry, **2.3**
    Rules, **2.10–2.12**
    Trade Marks Journal, **2.9**
  Trade Marks Registry
    and see TRADE MARKS REGISTRY
    correction, **2.25**
    costs, **2.43**
    court's powers, **2.38–2.42**
    decision-making, **2.35–2.37**
    evidence, **2.30–2.34**
    inspection, **2.19–2.24**
    introduction, **2.1–2.15**
    representation, **3.1–3.15**
    time, **2.26–2.29**
    transaction of business, **2.16–2.18**

Pending applications
  certification marks, and, **10.8**
  property rights, and, **11.1**

'Penguin'
  absolute grounds for refusal, and, **5.68**

Pictorial marks
  absolute grounds for refusal, and, **5.28–5.34**

Possession of goods with infringing mark
  course of business, **20.34**
  generally, **20.40**

Possession of tools to create infringing mark
generally, **20.42**
relevant tools, **20.43–20.44**

Post-acceptance procedures
invalidity proceedings
generally, **9.15–9.17**
intervention, **9.18**
reference to court, **9.19–9.21**
opposition to registration
grounds, **9.1–9.2**
procedure, **9.3–9.7**
publication, 8.13–8.14
rectification proceedings
generally, **9.15–9.17**
intervention, **9.18**
reference to court, **9.19–9.21**
restrictions of goods and services, **8.15**
revocation proceedings
generally, **9.15–9.17**
intervention, **9.18**
reference to court, **9.19–9.21**
withdrawal of application, **8.15**

Pre-condemnation procedure
and see below
EC Regulation 3295/94, under
applications for action, **19.45–19.69**
article 3 notices, **19.70–19.104**
article 6 notices, **19.105–19.124**
article 7 notices, **19.125–19.129**
Community Customs Code, **19.8–19.18**
conditions precedent, **19.19–19.43**
destruction of goods, **19.130**
liability for failure to detain goods,
19.131–19.136
introduction, **18.73–18.79**
miscellaneous provisions, **19.141**
notification of suspension, **19.105–19.124**
penal sanctions, **19.138–19.140**
travellers luggage, **19.137**
introduction, 18 73–18.79
TMA 1994, s.89, under
defences, 18.111–18.119
generally, **18.81–18.83**
interlocutory declarations,
18.101–18.104introduction, **18.73–18.80**
notice of importation of infringing goods,
18.84–18.88
seizure of infringing goods, **18.91–18.110**
subsequent proceedings,**18.120–18.123**

Pre-condemnation procedure (EC)
applications for action
contents, **19.48–19.56**
determination, **19.70–19.104**
generally, **19.44–19.47**
fee, **19.57**
procedures, **19.60–19.69**
submission, **19.58**
article 3 notices
Consequential Provisions Regulations (UK),
19.95–19.104
Customs Regulations (UK), **19.85–19.94**

Pre-condemnation procedure (EC)–*contd*
article 3 notices–*contd*
effects, **19.73–19.82**
generally, **19.70–19.72**
article 6 notices
generally, **19.105**
recipients, **19.106–19.124**
article 7 notices
generally, **119.125–19.129**
other EC language texts, **19.153–19.161**
TRIPS, and,**19.142–19.152**
Community Customs Code
generally, **19.8–19.9**
introduction, **19.5**
presentation, **19.16–19.18**
supervision, **19.13–19.15**
tariff system, **19.10–19.12**
counterfeit goods
generally, **19.34–19.36**
test, **19.37–19.43**
conditions precedent
counterfeit goods, **19.34–19.43**
customs supervision, **19.22–19.26**
free-zone placement, **19.31–19.33**
goods entered for specified purposes and
declared, **19.19–19.21**
introduction, **19.7**
re-exportation subject to notice, **19.32**
suspensive procedure, **19.27–19.30**
destruction of goods, **19.130**
liability for failure to detain goods
domestic law, and, **19.131–19.136**
generally, **19.131**
introduction, **18.73–18.79**
miscellaneous provisions, **19.141**
notification of suspension
generally, **19.105**
recipients, **19.106–19.124**
parties, **19.6**
penal sanctions,**19.138–19.140**
procedures
applications for action, **19.45–19.69**
article 3 notices, **19.70–19.104**
article 6 notices, **19.105–19.124**
article 7 notices, **19.125–19.129**
destruction of goods, **19.130**
generally, **19.44**
notification of suspension, **19.105–19.124**
purpose, **19.1–19.3**
scope, **19.4–19.7**
travellers luggage, **19.137**

Pre-condemnation procedure (UK)
defences, 18.111–18.119
generally, **18.81–18.83**
interlocutory declarations, **18.101–18.104**
introduction, **18.73–18.80**
notice of importation of infringing goods,
18.84–18.88
seizure of infringing goods, **18.91–18.110**
subsequent proceedings, **18.120–18.123**

Prior application, priority based on
effect, **25.10–25.11**

Prior application, priority based on–*contd*
generally, **25.6–25.8**
procedure, **25.9**

Prior rights
absolute grounds for refusal, and, **5.89–5.91**

Priority of applications
Community trade marks, and
exhibition priority, **25.12–25.15**
generally, **25.5**
prior application, priority based on,
25.6–25.11
generally, **8.4**
information requirements, **8.7**
international marks, and, **21.15**
other countries, **8.6**
Paris Convention, and
generally, **22.8**
relevant countries, **8.5**
transitional provisions, **8.8**

Professional privilege
common law, at, **3.12**
Community trade marks, and, **23.22**
statute, under, **3.13–3.15**

Prohibited by law, marks being
absolute grounds for refusal, and, **5.107**

Prohibited goods
and see COUNTERFEIT GOODS
and see INFRINGING GOODS
condemnation, and
claimant's notice, **18.12–18.14**
county court, in, **18.27–18.44**
evidence, **18.18–18.26**
High Court, in, **18.27–18.44**
magistrates' court, in, **18.45–18.72**
notice of liability to forfeiture, **18.11**
security for costs, **18.16–18.17**
stay of proceedings, **18.15**
criminal proceedings, and
false representation of marks, **20.13**
introduction, **20.1–20.5**
legislative background, **20.6–20.12**
unauthorised use of marks, **20.14–20.129**
meaning, **18.7–18.8**
Paris Convention, and, **22.28–22.29**
seizure or detention, and
condemnation procedure, **18.11–18.72**
method, **18.6–18.10**
pre-condemnation procedure (EC),
19.1–19.161
pre-condemnation procedure (UK),
18.73–18.123
purpose, **18.1–18.5**

Property rights
assignment
generally, **11.4**
pre-31st October 1994 assignment, **11.5**

Property rights–*contd*
professional privilege, **23.22**
Community trade marks, and
bankruptcy proceedings, **24.56**
effects, **24.59**
generally, **24.44–24.49**
in rem, **24.55**
levy of execution, **24.55**
licensing, **24.57–24.58**
transfer, **24.50–24.54**
generally, **11.2**
co-owner's rights, **11.3**
equities, **11.6**
generally, **11.1**
international marks, and
generally, **21.25**
licensing, **21-26**
transaction notification, **21.27**
licensing
exclusive licences, **11.10, 11.12**
general licences, **11.9**
generally, **11.7–11.8**
licensee's rights, **11.13–11.14**
limited licences, **11.9**
pre-31st October 1994 licences, **11.11**
registration of transactions
amendment of particulars, **11.22**
applications, **11.17–11.20**
consequences of delay or failure, **11.21**
generally, **11.15**
registrable transactions, **11.16**
trusts, **11.6**

Prosecution of marks
appeals
appointed person, to, **16.24–16.34**
Court of Appeal, to, **16.57**
generally, **16.18**
High Court, to, **16.22–16.23**
judicial review, by, **16.19–16.21**
appeals to appointed person
conduct of hearings, **16.32–16.33**
evidence, **16.28–16.31**
generally, **16.24–16.26**
security for costs, **16.34**
appeals to High Court, **16.22–16.23**
application
date, **16.6**
examination, **16.7**
generally, **16.4**
manner, **16.5**
objection, **16.8**
opposition, **16.9–16.13**
Community trade marks, and`
administrative decisions, **17.24**
appeals, **17.27**
examination, **17.8–17.11**
general procedure, **17.14–17.21**
filing, **17.5–17.7**
opposition, **17.22–17.23**
publication, **17.12**
registration, **17.13**
examination, **16.7**

Prosecution of marks–*contd*
formal opposition
generally, **16.10**
s 8 TMA 1994, **16.11–16.12**
generally, **16.2–16.3**
informal opposition, **16.13**
introduction, **16.1**
judicial review
generally, **16.19, 16.37**
nature, **16.21**
procedure, **16.20**
objections
Registrar, by, **16.8**
third parties, by, **16.9–16.15**
opposition
concurrent use, and, **16.14–16.15**
formal, **16.10–16.12**
generally, **16.9**
informal, **16.13**
reference to ECJ, **16.58–16. 66**
registration
date, **16.17**
generally, **16.16**
search, **16.7**

Public policy, marks contrary to
absolute grounds for refusal, and, **5.102–5.106**

Publication
applications for registration, and
generally, **8.13–8.14**
restrictions to goods and services, **8.15**
Community trade marks, and, **17.12, 26.11**
international marks, and, **21.17**

Qualification of Attorneys
exclusions, **3.5**
generally, **3.6–3.7**

Rectification of the register
generally, **7.35–7.36**
introduction, **7.34**
procedure
application, **9.16**
evidence, **9.17**
generally, **9.15**
intervention, **9.18**
reference to court, **9.19–9.21**
Registrar's powers, **7.37–7.38**

Reference to ECJ
generally, **16.58**
procedure, **16.62–16.66**
test, **16.59–16.61**

Refusal of registration
absolute grounds
bad faith, applications in, **5.118–5.121**
basic grounds, **5.13–5.92**
contrary to law, marks, **5.107**
deceptive marks, **5.102–5.106**
immoral marks, **5.102–5.106**
introduction, **5.1–5.12**
public policy, marks contrary to,
5.102–5.106

Refusal of registration–*contd*
absolute grounds,–*contd*
shape of goods, **5.93–5.101**
specially protected emblems, **5.108–5.117**
Community trade marks, and
absolute grounds, **24.9–24.16**
generally, **24.8**
relative grounds, **24.17–24.23**
absolute grounds, **7.25–7.26**
generally, **7.23**
relative grounds, **7.27**
relative grounds
earlier rights, **6.74–6.79**
earlier trade marks, **6.3–6.71**
honest concurrent use, **6.80–6.83**
introduction, **6.1–6.2**
well-known trade marks, **6.72–6.73**

Register of Trade Mark Attorneys
generally, **3.2–3.3**
partnerships, **3.4–3.5**
qualification
exclusions, **3.5**
generally, **3.6–3.7**

Register of Trade Marks
generally, **2.4**
rectification
generally, **7.34–7.36**
Registrar's powers, **7.37–7.38**

Registered marks
and see under individual headings
absolute grounds for refusal
bad faith, applications in, **5.118–5.121**
basic grounds, **5.13–5.92**
contrary to law, marks, **5.107**
deceptive marks, **5.102–5.106**
immoral marks, **5.102–5.106**
introduction, **5.1–5.12**
public policy, marks contrary to,
5.102–5.106
shape of goods, **5.93–5.101**
specially protected emblems, **5.108–5.117**
application for registration
appeals, **8.12**
contents, **8.1–8.2**
division, **8.16–8.17**
filing date, **8.3**
hearings, **8.11**
merger, **8.18**
pending at commencement, **8.21**
post-acceptance, **8.13–8.15**
priority, **8.4–8.8**
procedure, **8.9–8.10**
series of marks, **8.19–8.20**
definition
any sign, **4.3**
capable of graphic representation, **4.4–4.10**
generally, **4.1–4.2**
function
generally, **4.11–4.13**
nature of trade or activity, **4.14–4.15**

Registered marks–*contd*
  infringement
    acquiescence, **12.58–12.59**
    conferred rights, **12.4–12.5**
    disclaimers, **12.49**
    exclusions, **12.16–12.33**
    exhaustion of rights, **12.34–12.48**
    introduction, **12.1–12.3**
    meaning, **12.6–12.13**
    transitional provisions, **12.50–12.52**
    well-known marks, **12.53–12.57**
  loss of rights
    introduction, **7.1**
    invalidity, **7.23–7.33**
    rectification, **7.34–7.38**
    revocation, **7.2–7.22**
  property, as
    assignment, **11.4–11.5**
    co-ownership, **11.2–11.3**
    equities, **11.6**
    generally, **11.1**
    licensing, **11.7–11.14**
    registrable transactions, **11.15–11.22**
    trusts, **11.6**
  Registry
    and see TRADE MARKS REGISTRY
    correction, **2.25**
    costs, **2.43**
    court's powers, **2.38–2.42**
    decision-making, **2.35–2.37**
    evidence, **2.30–2.34**
    inspection, **2.19–2.24**
    introduction, **2.1–2.15**
    representation, **3.1–3.15**
    time, **2.26–2.29**
    transaction of business, **2.16–2.18**
  relative grounds for refusal
    earlier rights, **6.74–6.79**
    earlier trade marks, **6.3–6.71**
    honest concurrent use, **6.80–6.83**
    introduction, **6.1–6.2**
    well-known trade marks, **6.72–6.73**
  special types
    certification marks, **10.1–10.10**
    collective marks, **10.11–10.17**
  threats
    actionable threats, **13.5–13.11**
    adverse assertions, **13.20–13.23**
    aggrieved persons, **13.12–13.13**
    defences, **13.17**
    excluded threats, **13.14–13.16**
    generally, **13.1–13.3**
    remedies, **13.18–13.19**

Registrability
  absolute grounds
    bad faith, applications in, **5.118–5.121**
    basic grounds, **5.13–5.92**
    contrary to law, marks, **5.107**
    deceptive marks, **5.102–5.106**
    introduction, **5.1–5.12**
    public policy, marks contrary to,
      5.102–5.106
    shape of goods, **5.93–5.101**

Registrability–*contd*
  absolute grounds–*contd*
    specially protected emblems, **5.108–5.117**
  acquired distinctiveness
    effect, **5.75**
    generally, **5.74**
    geographical origins, **5.86**
    incapable of distinguishing, **5.87–5.88**
    meaning, **5.76–5.85**
  arms or insignia, **5.115**
  bad faith, applications in, **5.118–5.121**
  basic grounds
    devoid of distinctiveness, **5.23–5.52**
    designating characteristics of goods or
      services, **5.33–5.68**
    examples of decisions, **5.70–5.72**
    generic signs, **5.69**
    introduction, **5.13–5.14**
    outside the definition of trade mark,
      5.15–5.22
    provisos, **5.73–5.92**
  colours, **5.22**
  contrary to law, marks being, **5.107**
  deceptive marks, **5.102–5.106**
  designate characteristics of goods or services,
    signs which,
    foreign language words, **5.67**
    generally, **5.33–5.56**
    geographical names, **5.57–5.64**
    Penguin', **5.68**
    surnames, **5.66**
    time of production or rendering of services,
      5.65
  devoid of distinctiveness, signs which are
    famous persons, names and pictures of,
      5.50–5.51
    forenames, **5.48**
    full names, **5.49**
    generally, **5.23–5.24**
    geographical names, **5.39**
    numerals, **5.37–5.38**
    pictorial marks, **5.28–5.34**
    proviso to ground, **5.52**
    single letters, **5.36**
    stylised letters, **5.36**
    stylised words, **5.35**
    surnames, **5.40–5.47**
    words, **5.25–5.27**
  examples of decisions
    generally, **5.70–5.71**
    list, **5.72**
  famous persons, names and pictures of,
    5.50–5.51
  foreign language words, **5.67**
  foreign nations, emblems of
    flags, **5.112**
    generally, **5.111**
  forenames, **5.48**
  full names, **5.49**
  generic signs, **5.69**
  geographical names
    designate characteristics of goods or
      services, **5.57–5.64**
    devoid of distinctiveness, **5.39**

Registrability
geographical origins, **5.86**
immoral marks, **5.102–5.106**
international organisations, emblems of
armorial bearings, **5.113–5.114**
flags, **5.113–5.114**
generally, **5.111**
names, **5.113–5.114**
introduction
capable of distinguishing, **5.7**
generally, **5.1–5.2**
objections, **5.5–5.6**
precedents, **5.4**
saving provisions, **5.8–5.12**
Work Manual, **5.3**
letters, **5.36**
morality, marks contrary to, **5.102–5.106**
numerals, **5.37–5.38**
Olympic Symbol, **5.116–5.117**
outside the definition of trade mark, signs
which are
colours, **5.22**
generally, **5.15–5.21**
smells, **5.22**
sounds, **5.22**
'Penguin', **5.68**
pictorial marks, **5.28–5.34**
prior rights, **5.89–5.91**
prohibited by law, marks being, **5.107**
provisos
acquired distinctiveness, **5.74–5.88**
introduction, **5.73**
prior rights, **5.89–5.91**
restricting specification, **5.92**
public policy, marks contrary to, **5.102–5.106**
restricting specification, **5.92**
Royal Family, **5 109**
shape of goods
case law, **5.96–5.101**
generally, **5.93–5.95**
single letters, **5.36**
smells, **5.22**
sounds, **5.22**
specially protected emblems
arms or insignia, **5.115**
foreign nations, emblems of, **5.111–5.112**
international organisations, emblems of,
5.111–5.114
introduction, **5.108**
Olympic Symbol, **5.116–5.117**
Royal Family, **5.109**
UK flag, **5.110**
stylised letters, **5.36**
stylised words, **5.35**
surnames
designate characteristics of goods or
services, **5.66**
devoid of distinctiveness, **5.40–5.47**
time of production or rendering of services,
5.65
UK flag, **5.110**
words, **5.25–5.27**
Work Manual
designate characteristics of goods or
services, **5.55–5.56**

Registrability
Work Manual–*contd*
services, **5.55–5.56**
devoid of distinctiveness, **5.35–5.51**
generally, **5.3**
generic signs, **5.69**
proviso, **5.73**
public policy, marks contrary to, **5.103**
shape of goods, **5.95**
specially protected emblems, **5.108**

Registration
and see under individual headings
alteration, **9.12–9.13**
application for
appeals, **8.12**
contents, **8.1–8.2**
division, **8.16–8.17**
filing date, **8.3**
hearings, **8.11**
merger, **8.18**
pending at commencement, **8.21**
post-acceptance, **8.13–8.15**
priority, **8.4–8.8**
procedure, **8.9–8.10**
series of marks, **8.19–8.20**
Community trade marks, and
alteration, **27.3–27.4**
generally, **17.13, 26.36**
seniority claims, **27.7**
duration, **9.8**
invalidity
acquiescence, **7.31–7.33**
generally, **7.23–7.24**
grounds, **7.25–7.30**
opposition to
grounds, **9.1–9.2**
procedure, **9.3–9.7**
procedure
date, **16.17**
generally, **16.16**
renewal
failure to apply, **9.11**
generally, **9.9**
procedure, **9.10**
revocation
discretion, **7.3–7.4**
generally, **7.2**
generic names, **7.18–7.19**
misleading names, **7.20–7.22**
non-use, **7.5–7.17**
surrender, **9.14**

Registration of transactions
applications
generally, **11.17**
particulars, **11.18**
stamp duty, **11.19**
consequences of delay or failure, **11.21**
generally, **11.15**
multiple countries, covering marks in, **11.20**
particulars
amendment, **11.22**
generally, **11.18**

Registration of transactions–*contd*
registrable transactions, **11**.16
stamp duty, **11**.19

Regulations as to use of marks
certification marks, and
amendment, **10**.7
examination, **10**.6
existing marks, **10**.8
generally, **10**.5
collective marks, and
amendment, **10**.15
examination, **10**.14
generally, **10**.13
Community collective marks, and
amendment, **30**.9
examination, **30**.8
generally, **30**.5–**30**.7

Relative grounds for refusal
Community trade marks, and, **24**.17–**24**.23
earlier rights
effect, **6**.77
examples of decisions, **6**.78
generally, **6**.74–**6**.75
infringement of copyright, **6**.79
scope, **6**.76
earlier trade marks
identical marks and identical goods or
services, **6**.8–**6**.13
identical marks but dissimilar goods or
services, **6**.55–**6**.71
introduction, **6**.7
meaning, **6**.3–**6**.5
no identical marks or goods but similar
goods or services, **6**.14–**6**.54
priority of use, **6**.6
well-known trade marks, **6**.72–**6**.73
honest concurrent use
effects, **6**.82–**6**.83
generally, **6**.80
scope, **6**.81
identical marks and identical goods or services
identity of goods or services, **6**.13
identity of marks, **6**.9–**6**.12
introduction, **6**.8
identical marks but dissimilar goods or
services
detriment, **6**.61–**6**.71
generally, **6**.55–**6**.56
likelihood of confusion, **6**.57–**6**.58
reputation, **6**.59–**6**.60
unfair advantage, **6**.61–**6**.71
identity of marks
added matter, **6**.12
colours, **6**.10–**6**.11
generally, **6**.9
introduction
meaning, **6**.1
removal of Registrar's powers, **6**.2
invalidity, and, **7**.27
likelihood of confusion
Cannon case, **6**.41–**6**.45
The European case, **6**.46–**6**.49
generally, **6**.26–**6**.31

Relative grounds for refusal–*contd*
likelihood of confusion–*contd*
meaning, **6**.32
recent decisions, **6**.50–**6**.52
Sabel decision, **6**.38–**6**.40
Wagamama decision, **6**.33–**6**.37
meaning, **6**.1
no identical marks or goods but similar goods
or services
examples of decisions, **6**.17–**6**.19
families of marks, **6**.53–**6**.54
generally, **6**.14–**6**.16
likelihood of confusion, **6**.32–**6**.52
separate consideration of marks and goods
or services, **6**.26–**6**.31
similarity between goods or services,
6.20–**6**.25
passing off, and, **6**.74
reputation, marks with, **6**.59–**6**.60
well-known trade marks, **6**.72–**6**.73

Renewal of registration
failure to apply, **9**.11
generally, **9**.9
procedure, **9**.10

Representation
address for service, **3**.8–**3**.10
agents
Attorneys, **3**.2–**3**.7
generally, **3**.1
Attorneys, register of
enerally, **3**.2–**3**.5
qualification, **3**.6–**3**.7
use of term, **3**.11
Community trade marks, and, **28**.41–**28**.43
privilege, **3**.12–**3**.15

Reputation, marks with
relative grounds for refusal, and, **6**.59–**6**.60

Restitutio in integrum
Community trade marks, and, **27**.28–**27**.31

Restricting specification
Community trade marks, and, **26**.12
generally, **5**.92

Revocation of registration
certification marks, and, **10**.10
collective marks, and, **10**.17
Community collective marks, and, **30**.10
Community trade marks, and
appeals, **17**.27
generic marks, **27**.15
effects, **27**.28–**27**.33
generally, **17**.25–**17**.26, **27**.10–**27**.11
misleading marks, **27**.16
non-use, **24**.38–**24**.43, **27**.12–**27**.14
procedure, **27**.34–**27**.48, **31**.1–**31**.33
proprietor not qualified, **27**.17
UK regulations, **23**.15
discretion, and
decisions, **7**.4

Revocation of registration–*contd*
discretion, and–*contd*
generally, **7.3**
generally, **7.2**
generic names, **7.18–7.19**
international marks, and
acquiescence, **21.29**
generally, 21 28
procedure, 21.30
interruption of use
discretion, **7.9**
effect, **7.16**
examples, 7.14–7.15
generally, 7.5–7.8
partial cancellation, **7.13**
proper reasons, **7.10**
resumption of use, **7.11–7.12**
transitional provisions, **7.17**
misleading names, **7.20–7.22**
non-use
discretion, **7.9**
effect, **7.16**
examples, 7.14–7.15
generally, 7.5–7.8
partial cancellation, **7.13**
proper reasons, **7.10**
resumption of use, **7.11–7.12**
transitional provisions, **7.17**
procedure
application, **9.16**
evidence, **9.17**
generally, **9.15**
intervention, **9.18**
reference to court, **9.19–9.21**

Rights, loss of
Community trade marks, and
acquiescence, **27.25–27.27**
generally, 27 9
invalidity, **27.18–27.48**
revocation, **27.10–27.17, 27.25–27.48**
surrender, **27.8–27.9**
introduction, **7.1**
invalidity
acquiescence, **7.31–7.33**
generally, 7.23–7.24
grounds, **7.25–7.30**
rectification of the register
generally, 7.34–7.36
Registrar's powers, **7.37–7.38**
revocation
discretion, **7.3–7.4**
generally, **7.2**
generic names, **7.18–7.19**
misleading names, **7.20–7.22**
non-use, **7.5–7.17**

Royal Family, marks relating to
absolute grounds for refusal, and, **5.109**

Search
Community trade marks, and, **26.7–26.10**
generally, **8.9, 16.7**

s 89 TMA 1994 procedure
defences, **18.111–18.119**
generally, **18.81–18.83, 19.1–19.2**
interlocutory declarations, **18.101–18.104**
introduction, **18.73–18.80**
notice of importation of infringing goods,
18.84–18.88
seizure of infringing goods, **18.91–18.110**
subsequent proceedings, **18.120–18.123**

Security for costs
condemnation, and, **18.16–18.17**
generally, **2.36–2.37**

Seizure or detention of goods
condemnation procedure
and see CONDEMNATION
claimant's notice, **18.12–18.14**
county court, in, **18.27–18.44**
evidence, **18.18–18.26**
High Court, in, **18.27–18.44**
magistrates' court, in, **18.45–18.72**
notice of liability to forfeiture, **18.11**
security for costs, **18.16–18.17**
stay of proceedings, **18.15**
EC Regulation 3295/94 procedure
applications for action, **19.45–19.69**
article 3 notices, **19.70–19.104**
article 6 notices, **19.105–19.124**
article 7 notices, **19.125–19.129**
Community Customs Code, **19.8–19.18**
conditions precedent, **19.19–19.43**
destruction of goods, **19.130**
liability for failure to detain goods,
19.131–19.136
introduction, **18.73–18.79**
miscellaneous provisions, **19.141**
notification of suspension, **19.105–19.124**
penal sanctions, **19.138–19.140**
travellers luggage, **19.137**
introduction, **18.1–18.5**
meaning
generally, **18.6**
liable to forfeiture, **18.7–18.8**
prohibited goods, **18.7**
pre-condemnation procedure
EC Regulation 3295/94, under, **19.1–19.161**
introduction, **18.73–18.79**
Trade Marks Act 1994, s 89, under,
18.80–18.123
pre-condemnation procedure (EC)
applications for action, **19.45–19.69**
article 3 notices, **19.70–19.104**
article 6 notices, **19.105–19.124**
article 7 notices, **19.125–19.129**
Community Customs Code, **19.8–19.18**
conditions precedent, **19.19–19.43**
destruction of goods, **19.130**
liability for failure to detain goods,
19.131–19.136
introduction, **18.73–18.79**
miscellaneous provisions, **19.141**
notification of suspension, **19.105–19.124**
penal sanctions, **19.138–19.140**

Seizure or detention of goods–*contd*
pre-condemnation procedure–*contd*
travellers luggage, **19**.137
pre-condemnation procedure (UK)
defences, **18**.111–**18**.119
generally, **18**.81–**18**.83
interlocutory declarations, **18**.101–**18**.104
introduction, **18**.73–**18**.80
notice of importation of infringing goods,
18.84–**18**.88
seizure of infringing goods, **18**.91–**18**.110
subsequent proceedings, **18**.120–**18**.123
s 89 TMA 1994 procedure
defences, **18**.111–**18**.119
generally, **18**.81–**18**.83, **19**.1–**19**.2
interlocutory declarations, **18**.101–**118**.104
introduction, **18**.73–**18**.80
notice of importation of infringing goods,
18.84–**18**.88
seizure of infringing goods, **18**.91–**18**.110
subsequent proceedings, **18**.120–**18**.123

Series of marks
applications for registration, and, **8**.19–**8**.20

Service marks
generally, **4**.1
Paris Convention, and, **22**.23

Shape of goods
case law, **5**.96–**5**.101
generally, **5**.93–**5**.95

Single letters
absolute grounds for refusal, and, **5**.36

Slander of title
actionable statements, and, **15**.19

Smells
graphic representation, and, **4**.10
absolute grounds for refusal, and, **5**.22

Sounds
graphic representation, and, **4**.9
absolute grounds for refusal, and, **5**.22

Specially protected emblems
arms or insignia, **5**.115
foreign nations, emblems of
flags, **5**.112
generally, **5**.111
international organisations, emblems of
armorial bearings, **5**.113–**5**.114
flags, **5**.113–**5**.114
generally, **5**.111
names, **5**.113–**5**.114
introduction, **5**.108
Olympic Symbol, **5**.116–**5**.117
Paris Convention, and, **22**.12
Royal Family, **5**.109
UK flag, **5**.110

Standardisation marks
and see CERTIFICATION MARKS
generally, **10**.1

Statutory conspiracy
actus reus, **20**.82
generally, **20**.81
mens rea, **20**.83–**20**.84

Stylised letters
absolute grounds for refusal, and, **5**.36

Stylised words
absolute grounds for refusal, and, **5**.35

Surnames
absolute grounds for refusal, and
designate characteristics of goods or
services, **5**.66
devoid of distinctiveness, **5**.40–**5**.47
foreign nations, emblems of
flags, **5**.112
generally, **5**.111
international organisations, emblems of
armorial bearings, **5**.113–**5**.114
flags, **5**.113–**5**.114
generally, **5**.111
names, **5**.113–**5**.114

Surrender of registration
Community trade marks, and, **27**.8–**27**.9
generally, **9**.14

Temporary protection at exhibitions
Paris Convention, and, **22**.35

Test purchases
Weights & Measures authorities, powers of,
20.130

Threats jurisdiction
actionable threats
exclusions, **13**.14–**13**.16
generally, **13**.5–**13**.6
nature, **13**.8–**13**.11
registered marks, **13**.7
adverse assertions, **13**.20–**13**.23
aggrieved persons, **13**.12–**13**.13
Community trade marks, and, **23**.18
defences, **13**.17
excluded threats, **13**.14–**13**.16
international marks, and, **21**.24
introduction
nature, **13**.3–**13**.4
purpose, **13**.1–**13**.2
remedies
damages, **13**.18–**13**.19
declarations, **13**.18
injunctions, **13**.18

Three-dimensional marks
graphic representation, and, **4**.6

Time
Community trade marks, and
expiry, **28**.5–**28**.6
extensions, **28**.3–**28**.4
generally, **17**.19, **28**.2

Time–*contd*
  extension
    generally, **2.27–2.28**
    irregularities, **2.29**
  generally, **2.26**

Time of production or rendering of services
  absolute grounds for refusal, and, **5.65**

Trade libel
  actionable statements, and, **15.2–15.14**

Trade Mark Attorneys
  generally, **3.2–3.5**
  professional privilege
    common law, at, **3.12**
    statute, under **3.13–3.15**
  qualification
    exclusions, **3.5**
    generally, **3.6–3.7**
  register
    generally, **3.2–3.3**
    partnerships, **3.4–3.5**
    qualification, **3.6–3.7**
  use of term, **3.11**

Trade Marks Act 1905
  generally, **1.9**

Trade Marks Act 1919
  generally, **1.9**

Trade Marks Act 1938
  application, **1.10**
  generally, **1.1**

Trade Marks Act 1994
  application, **1.23–1.25**
  generally, **1.1**
  reforms, **1.10**

Trade Marks Journal
  generally, **2.9**
  publication, and, **8.13**

Trade Marks Register
  generally, **2.4**
  rectification
    generally, **7.34–7.36**
    Registrar's powers, **7.37–7.38**

Trade Marks Registrar
  and see COMPTROLLER-GENERAL
  generally, **2.1**
  liability, **2.2**
  prosecution of marks, and, **16.3**

Trade Marks Registration Act 1875
  application, **1.11**
  generally, **1.9**

Trade Marks Registry
  appeals
    generally, **2.39–2.40**

Trade Marks Registry–*contd*
  appeals–*contd*
    procedure, 2.41
  classification of goods and services
    background, **2.5**
    generally, **2.6–2.7**
    goods, **2.8**
  Comptroller-General
    generally, **2.1**
    liability, **2.2**
  confidentiality, **2.23–2.24**
  correction of irregularities, **2.25**
  costs
    generally, **2.43**
    security, **2.36–2.37**
  court's powers
    appeal, on, **2.39–2.41**
    generally, **2.38**
    Registrar's appearance, **2.42**
  cross-examination of witnesses, **2.34**
  decision-making
    generally, **2.35**
    security for costs, **2.36–2.37**
  discovery, **2.30–2.33**
  evidence
    cross-examination of witnesses, **2.34**
    discovery, **2.30–2.33**
  extension of time
    generally, **2.27–2.28**
    irregularities, **2.29**
  hours of business, **2.16**
  inspection
    confidentiality, **2.23–2.24**
    generally, **2.19–2.22**
  introduction, **2.3**
  prosecution of marks, and
    appeals to appointed person, **16.18–16.34**
    application, **16.4–16.6**
    examination, **16.7**
    introduction, **16.2–16.3**
    objections, **16.8**
    opposition, **16.9–16.15**
    registration, **16.16–16.17**
  representation
    address for service, **3.8–3.10**
    agents, **3.1–3.7**
    privilege, **3.12–3.15**
  Rules
    fees, **2.14**
    forms, **2.15**
    generally, **2.10–2.12**
    pre-31st October 1994, **2.13**
  security for costs, **2.36–2.37**
  time
    extension, **2.27–2.29**
    generally, **2.26**
  Trade Marks Journal, **2.9**
  transaction of business
    filing, **2.17**
    hours of business, **2.16**
    translation, **2.18**
  validity of marks, and
    applications, **16.40–16.42**
    generally, **16.39**

Trade Marks Registry–*contd*
  witnesses, cross-examination of, **2.34**

Trade Marks Rules 1994 (as amended)
  application
    fees, **2.14**
    forms, **2.15**
    generally, **2.10–2.12**, **23.23**
    pre-31st October 1994, **2.13**
  generally, **1.1**

Trade marks law
  EC Directive 1989
    generally, **1.1**
    implementation, **1.18**
    interpretation, **1.19–1.22**
  historical development
    EC Directive, **1.18–1.21**
    legislation, **1.8–1.11**
    modern role, **1.12–1.17**
    pre-registration, **1.6–1.7**
    Trade Marks Act 1994, **1.23–1.25**
  subject-matter, **1.1–1.5**

Trade names
  Paris Convention, and, **22.27**

Transaction of business
  filing, **2.17**
  hours of business, **2.16**
  translation, **2.18**

Transactions, registration of
  applications
    generally, **11.17**
    particulars, **11.18**
    stamp duty, **11.19**
  consequences of delay or failure, **11.21**
  generally, **11.15**
  international marks, and, **21.27**
  multiple countries, covering marks in, **11.20**
  particulars
    amendment, **11.22**
    generally, **11.18**
  registrable transactions, **11.16**
  stamp duty, **11.19**

TRIPS Agreement 1994
  background, **22.2**
  conclusions, **22.56**
  counterfeit goods, and, **17.5**
  final provisions, **22.55**
  general provisions
    acquisition of rights, **22.52**
    confirmation of obligations, **22.42**
    dispute resolution, **22.53–22.54**
    duration of rights, **22.47**
    enforcement of rights, **22.50–22.51**
    exhaustion of rights, **22.44**
    geographical indications, **22.49**
    limitations, **22.46**
    national treatment, **22.43**
    principles, **22.41**
    protectable goods, **22.45**

TRIPS Agreement 1994–*contd*
  general provisions–*contd*
    unjustified requirements, **22.48**
    generally, **1.1**
  introduction, **22.38–22.40**

Trusts
  property rights, and, **11.6**

UK flag
  absolute grounds for refusal, and, **5.110**

Unauthorised registration
  generally, **7.34**
  Paris Convention, and, **22.24**

Unauthorised use of marks
  actus reus
    advertising of goods, **20.41**
    application of mark, **20.35–20.39**
    disposal of goods, **20.40**
    generally, **20.31–20.34**
    possession of goods, **20.40**
    possession of tools, **20.42–20.44**
  aiding and abetting, **20.47–20.55**
  advertising of goods with mark, **20.41**
  application of mark to goods
    generally, **20.35–20.36**
    mistaken identity, **20.39**
    packaging, **20.37–20.38**
  attempts, **20.69–20.75**
  commencement of prosecution
    charge, by, **20.117**
    generally, **20.116**
    summons, by, **20.118–20.119**
  committal, **20.121**
  concealment after the event, **20.6–20.67**
  consent
    counterfeit goods, **20.30**
    generally, **20.20–20.24**
    parallel imports, **20.25–20.29**
  conspiracy
    defraud, to, **20.85–20.90**
    generally, **20.76–20.79**
    sentencing, **20.79**
    statutory conspiracy, **20.81–20.84**
  conspiracy to defraud, **20.85–20.90**
  counselling, **20.57**
  defences
    exhaustion of rights, **20.103**
    generally, **20.95**
    reasonable belief that use not an infringing
      use, **20.96–20.102**
    use to identify goods, **20.104–20.106**
  disclosure
    compulsory, **20.174–20.175**
    continuing obligations, **20.178–20.180**
    generally, **20.160–20.164**
    primary, **20.172–20.173**
    privileged evidence, **20.165–20.171**
    voluntary, **20.176–20.177**
  disposal of goods with mark
    course of business, **20.33**
    generally, **20.40**

Unauthorised use of marks–*contd*
elements of offence
  actus reus, **20.31–20.44**
  generally, **20.13–20.14**
  mens rea, **20.15–20.30**
  trade mark, goods subject to, **20.91–20.94**
evidence
  business documents, **20.150–20.153**
  disclosure, **20.160–20.180**
  hearsay, **20.152**
  introduction, **20.129**
  registration of marks, **20.154–20.159**
  Weights & Measures authorities, powers of,
    20.129–20.149
  witness statements, **20.150–20.153**
  first hearing, **20.120**
generally, **20.13–20.14**
inchoate offences
  aiding and abetting, **20.47–20.55**
  attempts, **20.69–20.75**
  concealment after the event, **20.65–20.67**
  conspiracy, **20.76–20.90**
  counselling, **20.56–20.57**
  generally, **20.45–20.46**,
  procuring, **20.58–20.64**
  mens rea
  consent, **20.20–20.30**
  intention, **20.15–20.19**
possession of goods with mark
  course of business, **20.34**
  generally , **20.40**
possession of tools to create mark
  generally, **20.42**
  relevant tools, **20.43–20.44**
procedure
  commencement of prosecution,
    20.116–20.119
  committal, **20.121**
  disclosure, **20.160–20.180**
  evidence, **20.129–20.180**
  first hearing, **20.120**
  generally, **20.115**
  trial, **20.122–20.128**
procuring, **20.58–20.64**
sentencing
  generally, **20.107–20.108**
  seriousness of offence, **20.109–20.114**
statutory conspiracy
  actus reus, **20.82**
  generally, **20.81**
  mens rea, **20.83–20.84**
  trial, **20.122–20.128**
  Weights & Measures authorities, powers of,
    20.129–149
  conclusion, **20.149**
  confidential information, **20.148**
  entry to premises, **20.144–20.147**
  generally, **20.129–20.131**
  permitted objective, **20.133–20.134**
  reasonable cause, **20.138–20.143**
  relevant officers, **20.135–20.136**
  search warrants, **20.132**
  test purchases, **20.130**

Unfair competition
Paris Convention, and, **22.31–22.33**

Validity of marks
High Court procedure
  allocation, **16.49**
  applications, **16.44**
  disclosure, **16.50–16.51**
  generally, **16.43**
  pleadings, **16.45–16.49**
  introduction, **16.38**
Trade Marks Registry procedure
  applications, **16.40–16.42**
  generally, **16.39**

Weights & Measures authorities, powers of
conclusion, **20.149**
confidential information, **20.148**
entry to premises, **20.144–20.147**
generally, **20.129–20.131**
permitted objective, **20.133–20.134**}
reasonable cause, **20.138–20.143**
relevant officers, **20.135–20.136**
search warrants, **20.132**
test purchases, **20.130**

Well-known trade marks
infringement, and
  generally, **12.53**
  likelihood of confusion, **12.57**
  meaning, **12.54–12.55**
  time of knowledge, **12.56**
Paris Convention, and, **22.12**
relative grounds for refusal, and, **6.72–6.73**

Withdrawal of application
Community trade marks, and, **26.12**
generally, **8.15**

Witnesses, cross-examination of
Registry procedure, and, **2.34**

Words
absolute grounds for refusal, and, **5.25–5.27**
graphic representation, and, **4.7–4.8**

Work Manual
designate characteristics of goods or services,
  5.55–5.56
devoid of distinctiveness, **5.35–5.51**
generally, **5.3**
generic signs, **5.69**
proviso, **5.73**
public policy, marks contrary to, **5.103**
shape of goods, **5.95**
specially protected emblems, **5.408**

BP D.C.S.
Group Trade Mark
Library

BP 316
Hongkong Trade Marks

Library